Complete

COMPUTERS
Are Your Future

12th
EDITION

Catherine LaBerta

Prentice Hall
Boston Columbus Indianapolis New York San Francisco Upper Saddle River
Amsterdam Cape Town Dubai London Madrid Milan Munich Paris Montréal Toronto
Delhi Mexico City São Paulo Sydney Hong Kong Seoul Singapore Taipei Tokyo

Editor in Chief: *Michael Payne*
Associate VP/Executive Acquisitions Editor,
   Print: *Stephanie Wall*
Product Development Manager: *Eileen Bien Calabro*
Editorial Project Managers: *Virginia Guariglia /*
   Meghan Bisi
Development Editor: *Linda Harrison*
Editorial Assistant: *Nicole Sam*
Director of Marketing: *Kate Valentine*
Marketing Manager: *Tori Olson Alves*
Marketing Coordinator: *Susan Osterlitz*
Marketing Assistant: *Darshika Vyas*
Senior Managing Editor: *Cynthia Zonneveld*
Associate Managing Editor: *Camille Trentacoste*
Senior Production Project Manager: *Rhonda*
   Aversa
Production Project Manager: *Ruth Ferrera-Kargov*
Operations Director: *Nick Sklitsis*
Senior Operations Specialist: *Natacha Moore*
Art Director: *Anthony Gemmellaro*

Text and Cover Designer: *Anthony Gemmellaro*
Cover Photo: *Shutterstock Images / Stian Iversen*
Photo Researcher: *David Tietz*
Rights and Permissions Manager:
   Hessa Albader
Text Permission Researcher: *Joanna Green*
Director of Digital Development: *Zara Wanlass*
Editor-Digital Learning & Assessment:
   Paul Gentile
Product Development Manager, Media:
   Cathi Profitko
Media Project Manager, Editorial: *Alana Coles*
Media Project Manager, Production: *John Cassar*
Supplements Editor: *Lori Damanti*
Full-Service Project Management:
   MPS Content Services
Composition: *MPS Limited, a Macmillan Company*
Printer/Binder: *Courier Kendallville*
Cover Printer: *Lehigh-Phoenix Color / Hagerstown*
Text Font: *New Century Schlbk, 9.5 / 11.5*

Credits and acknowledgments borrowed from other sources and reproduced, with permission, in this textbook appear on appropriate page within text (or on pages 640–641).

Microsoft® and Windows® are registered trademarks of the Microsoft Corporation in the U.S.A. and other countries. Screen shots and icons reprinted with permission from the Microsoft Corporation. This book is not sponsored or endorsed by or affiliated with the Microsoft Corporation.

Many of the designations by manufacturers and seller to distinguish their products are claimed as trademarks. Where those designations appear in this book, and the publisher was aware of a trademark claim, the designations have been printed in initial caps or all caps.

Library of Congress Cataloging-in-Publication Data

LaBerta, Catherine.
   Computers are your future. Complete / Catherine LaBerta. — 12th ed.
       p. cm.
   Includes bibliographical references and index.
   ISBN 0-13-254494-6 (alk. paper)
   1. Microcomputers. I. Title.
   QA76.5.C669 2010c
   004.16—dc22

                                        2010045386

Prentice Hall
is an imprint of

www.pearsonhighered.com

10 9 8 7 6 5 4 3 2
ISBN-10:   0-13-254494-6
ISBN-13: 978-0-13-254494-8

With **love**

to my parents, Chester and Eleanore, for their unending support; to my son, Michael, for years of laughter, challenges, and insight; to my brother, sister, and brother-in-law for help during the tough times; and to Stephanie Wall for providing me with an exceptional opportunity, one I truly enjoyed.

Acknowledgments

Thanks to the many professionals at Prentice Hall who made this book possible and assisted with questions and feedback during the writing process. Special thanks to Stephanie Wall, Executive Editor, for providing me with this wonderful opportunity, and to my project managers, Virginia Guariglia and Meghan Bisi, for keeping me on schedule and connected to the process. Thanks also to Linda Harrison, my developmental editor, for her input, guidance, patience, and incredible eye for detail throughout the development cycle, and to Amanda Roscoe for using her insight and skill to convert storyboards into the exceptional videos included in this edition. I am grateful for the friends and colleagues who, through the years, have encouraged my professional growth and energy. Finally, thanks to my family and friends, but especially my parents, Chester and Eleanore, for encouraging me when I was young, and to my son, Michael, for keeping me on my toes, providing me with input when asked, and being patient when I was writing and could not join him on the golf course. I am sure I forgot to mention someone, but in my heart I have forgotten no one. Thank you all!

Brief Contents

Contents

Preface

A Reference Tool for Today's Students

Today, students are not as "wowed" by technology as they used to be; it is part of their everyday lives. This book has been written to match what they already know with what instructors have told us they should know.

Computers Are Your Future serves as a reference tool without being overwhelming or intimidating. Today's students want a practical "what it is" and "how it works" approach to computers, with less explanation of "why." This new edition has been written with this in mind. For example, the new Spotlight about cloud computing highlights the many newer Web-based tools available that many students aren't necessarily aware of.

Computers Are Your Future, 12/e, will help you with the challenge of teaching even the most diverse class—without sacrificing quality, integrity, or choice.

The 12th edition includes the following new items:

- NEW! Videos that illustrate key concepts in each chapter are included on a CD that accompanies the book.
- NEW! You will find a Facebook page for the text with updated content.
- NEW! Fast Forward boxes in each chapter keep students up to date on emerging technologies.
- NEW! A How-to element was added in each chapter, providing students with a hands-on activity utilizing information covered in the chapter.
- New Spotlight on cloud computing covers this emerging technology.
- All new end-of-chapter assignments are included in all chapters.
- Updated statistics and screen captures are incorporated.
- In Spotlight sections, we added Key Terms, Multiple Choice questions, and 50%+ new projects.
- Added focus on collaboration, a key concept in today's world, is covered.
- Coverage of social networking has been expanded.
- Enhanced coverage of Web-based applications is included.
- The application software chapter has been revised to cover Microsoft Office 2010.
- Updated hardware coverage includes the iPad, iPhone 4, and Droid, as well as additional content on netbooks.
- The chapter on the Internet and the World Wide Web has been completely reorganized.
- Content on viruses and virus protection as well as programming has been heavily revised.
- Some topics students found challenging in previous editions, including storage, operating system functions, and the use of cache memory, have been clarified.

ABOUT THIS BOOK

Spotlight sections are essentially mini-chapters that cover the practical, as well as the innovative, in various subject areas. For example, Ethics, File Management, and Buying and Upgrading Your Home Computer System focus on the practical, whereas Web 2.0, Cloud Computing, and Digital Life cover innovation in software, hardware, and technology for the future. We've added reinforcing exercises at the end of each Spotlight, and most of them are new in this edition.

Teamwork exercises are included as an end-of-chapter activity to reinforce chapter concepts by requiring students to work in teams to conduct research and interviews and to create group papers and presentations.

Green Tech Tips provide eco-friendly solutions to living and working with technology. These range from actions students can apply on their own to those that are initiated by companies in an effort to preserve the environment.

Ethics boxes offer an ethical perspective on decisions and situations that involve computers and technology. They raise "what if"-type questions in a "What would you do format?" to prompt thoughtful discussion and debate on complicated issues.

New **Fast Forward** boxes address emerging technologies relevant to each chapter. Adding these boxes enabled us to eliminate the Spotlight on Emerging Technologies found in previous editions, and allows for more coverage of these topics throughout the book.

The new **How-to** feature provides students with hands-on opportunities to use the information covered in the chapter.

INSTRUCTOR'S RESOURCE CENTER CD-ROM

The Pearson Prentice Hall Instructor's Resource Center on CD-ROM includes the tools you expect from a Prentice Hall Computer Concepts text, such as these:

- Teaching Notes
- Solutions to all questions and exercises from the book and Web site
- Customizable PowerPoint slide presentations for each chapter
- Sample syllabus
- Assignments

- Discussion questions
- Internet exercises
- Web resources
- Key terms
- An image library of all of the figures from the text
- Test bank

TESTGEN SOFTWARE

TestGen is a test generator that lets you view and easily edit test bank questions, transfer them to tests, and print the tests in a variety of formats best suited to your teaching situation. Powerful search and sort functions enable you to easily locate questions and arrange them in the order you prefer.

TOOLS FOR ONLINE LEARNING

myitlab *Computers Are Your Future* content is now included in my**it**lab's Content Library. This enables instructors to make learning tools such as PowerPoint presentations and end-of-chapter quizzes available to students, as well as to deliver performance-based testing on Microsoft Office applications and objective testing on both computer concepts and office applications.

Companion Web Site This text is accompanied by a companion Web site at **www.pearsonhighered.com/cayf**. This site offers an interactive study guide, downloadable supplements, additional Internet exercises, Web resource links such as Careers in IT and crossword puzzles.

CourseCompass CourseCompass, available at **www.coursecompass.com**, is a dynamic, interactive online course-management tool powered exclusively for Pearson Education by Blackboard. This exciting product allows you to teach market-leading Pearson Education content in an easy-to-use, customizable format.

Blackboard Prentice Hall's abundant online content, combined with Blackboard's popular tools and interface, results in robust Web-based courses that are easy to implement, manage, and use—taking your courses to new heights in student interaction and learning.

WebCT Course-management tools within WebCT, available at **www.pearsonhighered.com/webct**, include page tracking, progress tracking, class and student management, a grade book, communication tools, a calendar, reporting tools, and more.

About the Author

Catherine LaBerta is currently an adjunct professor with SUNY at Buffalo and Canisius College, an independent contractor that provides application and technical training for the Western New York Work Force Development Institute, and a former Professor of Computer Science/Mathematics at Erie Community College in Buffalo, NY. She teaches courses that range from an introduction to computers to programming in C++ and Web development. Originally a math major, LaBerta took additional courses in computers and programming and found another field that clicked for her. She enjoys the constant changes in the computer and related fields because they force her to keep up and constantly learn. Not a total bookworm, LaBerta loves skiing (with Purgatory, CO, being a favorite spot) and boating (especially schooner trips off the coast of Maine) and will always be working on that golf game.

Spotlight sections highlight important ideas about computer-related topics and provide in-depth, useful information to take your learning to the next level.

USB DEVICES AND CONFIDENTIAL DATA

USB flash drives are incredibly popular, but many experts worry that they pose a great security risk. Some companies are so concerned about corporate espionage that they disable USB ports to prevent the unauthorized copying of data. Even so, many people carry a lot of critical or personal data on their USB flash drives. What are the implications if the device is lost? Should USB drive manufacturers be required to provide a means of securing these devices or some type of registration process? With such processes in place, a lost device could be returned to the manufacturer and matched to the owner. What actions should individuals take to safeguard their data? Is hooking a USB flash drive to your backpack or keychain a very good idea? If you found a USB flash drive and did not know who it belonged to, what would you do? What should you do?

More than 700 million inkjet and laser toner cartridges are sold every year. What happens when they are empty? Although many organizations and retail stores have recycling programs, every second nearly eight used cartridges are thrown away in the United States—approximately 875 million pounds of environmental waste each year! So what can you do? Take advantage of your local recycling program. Some programs even pay you for your old cartridges because they can be recycled and sold again. Keeping them out of the waste stream reduces toxicity levels and saves landfill space. Besides, half a gallon of oil is saved for every toner cartridge you recycle! ●

COURTROOMS OF THE FUTURE

Are you familiar with the sayings: "Seeing is believing," and "A picture is worth a thousand words"? If these words of wisdom are placed in the content of a courtroom, they gain even more strength. Now, add the ability to use technology to magnify voices, provide testimony from a witness confined to a hospital bed via webcam, obtain a translator through videoconferencing, and reproduce the scene and figures to provide a reenactment of the event digitally. Yes, it sounds like an episode from your favorite crime investigation show. But this is no television episode. With jurors traditionally having information organized for them in bulleted lists, slide shows, and presented in visual images.

Ethics Boxes highlight ethical issues for students to think about.

Green Tech Tips share ways to be aware of the effects of technology on our earth.

Fast Forward boxes address emerging technologies relevant to each chapter.

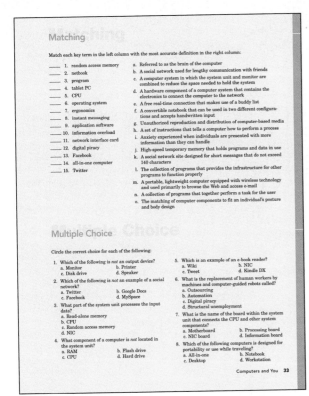

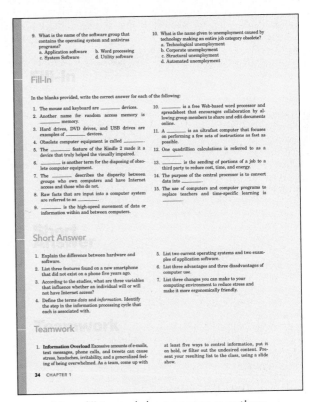

End-of-Chapter Material includes updated multiple-choice, matching, fill-in, and short-answer questions, identification, teamwork, as well as Web research projects so students can prepare for tests.

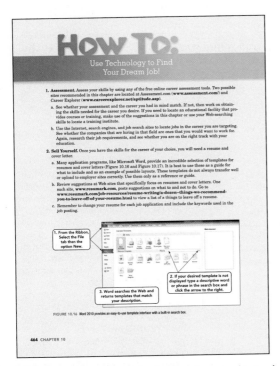

The **How To** activity in each chapter has students do some sort of hands-on exercise (such as creating something or choosing the appropriate technology) in which they apply what they learned in the chapter and demonstrate understanding.

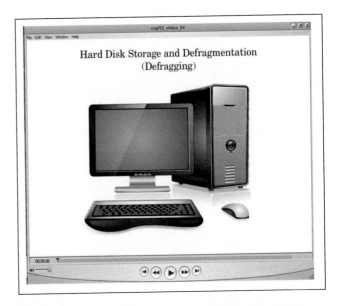

NEW videos accompany the text, illustrating a key concept covered in each chapter.

Complete

COMPUTERS
Are Your Future

12th
EDITION

1

Computers and You

Chapter Objectives

So you have a cell phone in your hand and an iPod in your pocket and consider yourself a technologically savvy individual. But have you taken the time to look back and understand how the developments in technology have affected your family, friends, and way of life? Likewise, do you daydream of a future where you and your family members use communication devices with embedded translation capabilities, visit virtual reality vacation centers, and use solar- and wind-powered phone chargers?

The more you work with computers, the deeper and richer your understanding of computers and technology will become; eventually you will grow to be confident in your abilities. As your confidence and knowledge expand, you will become more adept in your use of computers and better prepared for the changes computer technology brings. No one is insulated from the impact that computers have or will continue to have on daily life.

This text provides information and insight into technology—its uses, assets, and drawbacks—related careers, and the knowledge and skill set required to make informed decisions about technology in all areas of your life. When you understand these concepts, you'll be better able to

- Decide whether to purchase new equipment or upgrade specific components.
- Judge the likely impact of computer innovations on your personal and business activities.
- Be aware of the different types of computing systems, their capabilities, and the businesses that they best compliment.
- Select the best applications for the information that you are processing or presenting.
- Keep abreast with and maintain a balance between the increase in mobile and portable computing and your privacy.
- Make career choices that use the technology skills you have acquired.
- Sort through the difficult ethical, moral, and societal challenges that computer use brings. ■

Check out **f** Facebook for our latest updates

www.facebook.com

Computers: Yesterday, Today, and Tomorrow

Computers have become so integral to our daily lives that it's difficult to think of a time without them. There are millions of individuals that wake up and turn on their computer every day in hundreds of cities across all nations. This increase in computer popularity has also caused an increase in its diversity of applications. Think about it, how many technology based applications or devices do you use in one day? How many of these applications or devices did not exist 10 years ago? How many will be extinct 10 years from now? Look over the list of computer applications and devices below; how many have you used or encountered?

- Word-processor—an application that automatically checks spelling and grammar in a document
- Internet—a connected system of computers that enables users to obtain information quicker than from a library and perform such communication activities as video conferencing
- Online Banking—the ability to use the Internet to open a new account, transfer your own money from one account to another, or pay a mortgage, all from the comfort of your own home
- Online classes—classes offered using applications such as Blackboard and Angel via the Internet that enable students and teachers to communicate outside of the physical classroom
- GPS systems—computing devices that are either portable or embedded within the dashboard of many vehicles and provide driving directions from your current location to the entered destination as well as help you locate restaurants, gas stations, and fast food chains, even the phone number for your favorite pizza place
- ATM machines—devices that can connect to the database of banking institutions to allow a customer to withdraw and deposit funds without entering the brick and mortar structure of the bank itself
- Mobile phones—the telecommunication favorites of most individuals today, replacing landline twisted pair technology and offering additional features such as calculators, calendars, and even Internet connectivity
- Weather prediction—the use of supercomputers and satellite connections to determine weather patterns and predict the location and strength of a weather event

I am sure that you can add a few additional devices and applications to this list that you use personally on a daily basis. But you get the point.

Computers are used at home, at work, and in school; they're embedded into our cars, phones, and cameras. You use them daily to perform the tasks listed above; but your future isn't about just performing single, unrelated tasks. The real power of the use of computers comes when you begin to relate the tasks, understand the technology used to perform them, use that technology to collect information, share that information with others locally and globally, and then singularly or collectively use the information to make decisions. Let's look back at the events that led up to our current technology state and then forward to the preparation you will need in order to capitalize on future technological advancements.

> " The real power of the use of computers . . . **relate** the tasks, **understand** the technology used to perform them, use that technology to **collect** information, **share** that information with others locally and globally, and then singularly or collectively **use** the information to make decisions. "

A Brief Look Back

A look at the past can help clarify the present and direct the future. Think about the changes that have occurred as a result of technological innovation during the past several decades. When nations were

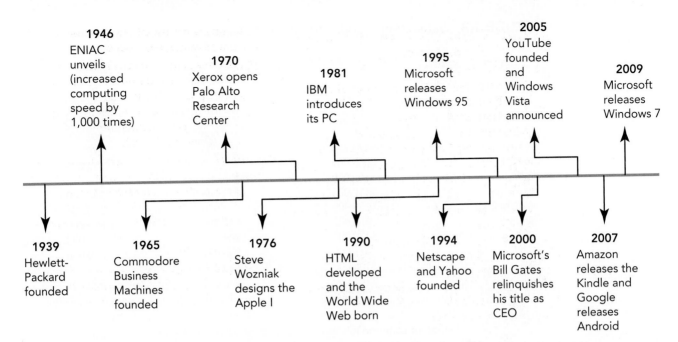

1946 ENIAC unveils (increased computing speed by 1,000 times)

1970 Xerox opens Palo Alto Research Center

1981 IBM introduces its PC

1995 Microsoft releases Windows 95

2005 YouTube founded and Windows Vista announced

2009 Microsoft releases Windows 7

1939 Hewlett-Packard founded

1965 Commodore Business Machines founded

1976 Steve Wozniak designs the Apple I

1990 HTML developed and the World Wide Web born

1994 Netscape and Yahoo founded

2000 Microsoft's Bill Gates relinquishes his title as CEO

2007 Amazon releases the Kindle and Google releases Android

FIGURE 1.1 This timeline focuses on a few of the critical events that occurred in the computer development lifecycle and provided the foundation for the devices that we use today.

attempting something as complex as sending a person to the moon, there were no telephone answering machines, no cell phones, no handheld calculators, and no personal computers. People wrote letters by hand or with a typewriter, kept track of numbers and data in ledgers, and communicated in person or over the telephone. Those telephones were physically connected: Cordless handsets didn't come onto the market until the late 1970s, and cell phones followed in the 1980s.

In the 1980s only the U.S. government, colleges, and universities were able to access the Internet (including e-mail); cell phones were just coming into use; and fax machines were the fastest way for most businesses to share documents across distances. The World Wide Web would not become viable until 1993. Today millions of people use the Internet daily in both their professional and personal lives. Cell phones and personal digital assistants seem to be a necessary part of everyday life; GPS units guide travelers to their destinations; and retail e-commerce, which didn't begin until 1995 and had sales of $ 32.0 billion in the third quarter of 2009, is projected to grow to $203 billion by 2013.

For a look back in time, view Figure 1.1, a compressed computer history timeline, or go to **www.computerhope.com/history/** for a year-by-year breakdown of computer developments and advances. For those interested in the development of the Apple, you can view a timeline at **http://en.wikipedia.org/wiki/History_of_Apple** that displays the progress of Apple from 1976 to the present.

FIGURE 1.2 Computers were once considered tools for programmers and technical developers. Today they, and the devices they are embedded within, are part of most jobs and our daily life.

A Glance at the Present

Today it's becoming difficult to find an activity that doesn't involve computers, technology, and sharing information (Figure 1.2). It would be advantageous to learn all you can about computers and become comfortable with application programs, the Internet, and the World Wide Web. You'll need computer and Internet skills to succeed in almost any occupational area. Studies consistently show that workers with such skills are in demand and earn salaries significantly above the median personal

FIGURE 1.3   Salaries of Workers in Computer and Computer-Related Jobs

Categories	Salary Ranges		
	High ($/yr.)	Low ($/yr.)	Average ($/yr.)
Computer operations	$220,000	$23,000	$59,000
Database systems	$120,000	$30,000	$67,000
E-commerce/Internet	$175,000	$37,000	$79,000
Executive level	$250,000	$69,000	$118,000
Hardware	$100,000	$30,000	$56,000
Help desk	$110,000	$23,000	$44,000
Networking	$333,000	$22,000	$69,000
New media	$65,000	$32,000	$43,000
Project management	$130,000	$34,000	$83,000
Technical writing	$77,000	$45,000	$59,000
UNIX	$108,000	$50,000	$79,000
Windows development	$101,000	$40,000	$69,000
Wireless systems	$95,000	$46,000	$66,000

This is a selection of common job types; the original survey had 2,145 positions listed. Average salary of all positions in the original survey: $70,000 per year.

income level of approximately $30,000 (Figure 1.3). Check out **www.cis.udel. edu/jobs/market** for information about the future of the computer science job market and links to related sites. Another site, **www.ticker.computerjobs. com/content/ticker.aspx**, lists computer-related jobs and their average salaries.

An Insight into the Future

Isolated skills won't be enough to keep you connected or job-ready in the future. To be a fully functioning member of the computerized world of tomorrow, you need to understand the concepts that underlie computer and Internet technologies, such as the distinction between hardware and software, and how to manage the excessive amount of files that are created each day, insure the privacy of data as it makes its way across a variety of new technologies, and perform a continual evaluation of your skills to determine the need for re-education and fine tuning.

As computers and the Internet play an increasingly direct and noticeable role in our personal lives, understanding the difference between their appropriate and inappropriate use becomes increasingly difficult. Should you shop on the Internet on company or school time? Are the photos you share with friends on social networking sites like Facebook or MySpace

going to turn up when you least expect or cause an employer to disqualify your application because of your Web content? Is your credit card information, Social Security number, or personal communication safe from intrusion or misuse? In the past the only way to shop during work or school was to leave the premises; employers had to call a reference to find personal information about an applicant; and the only time you needed to worry about losing your personal information was if your wallet or mail had been stolen!

You also need to know enough to the correct types of technology to use in your personal and professional lives (Figure 1.4). Use the questions below as a starting point to evaluate your technology needs.

- How much power and speed do you need for everyday tasks?
- What will a more powerful and faster computer, smartphone, or iPad enable you to do better?
- What types of technology tools do you need (as opposed to want)?
- Will you need advanced training?

The more you understand about computers and become familiar with how they work, the less mysterious they seem and the easier they are to use. Like driving a car or riding a bike, the more you practice and use the equipment, the more comfortable you will be and the better able you will be to adjust to future models and variations. Let's start by describing the machine that's at the center of what you need to know.

Computer Fundamentals

Learning computer and Internet concepts is partly about learning new terms and the connection between them. So let's start with the most basic terms.

Understanding the Computer: Basic Definitions

A **computer** is an electronic device that performs four basic operations: input, processing, output, and storage (Figure 1.5). Together these four operations are called the **information processing cycle**.

- **Input** is the action of receiving data—raw facts like a user's login ID number.
- **Processing** is the manipulation done on the input by a program (instructions), to convert the input (data) into information (data converted into a meaningful form). An example of processing could be aligning a letter's return address in a Word document, averaging a column of grades by following a formula that has been entered in an Excel worksheet, or searching a database to confirm a login ID number.
- **Output** is the actual displaying of the information, the processed data. This would be displaying the shifted return address in the Word document, placing the average below the column of grades in the Excel worksheet, or confirming the entry of a valid ID.
- **Storage** is saving the information for later use.

Because these operations depend on one another, the information processing cycle (sometimes abbreviated as the IPOS cycle) is always performed in this sequence.

You'll often hear the term *computer system,* which is normally shortened to *system*. This term is more inclusive than *computer*. A **computer system** is a collection of related components that have been designed to work together to meet

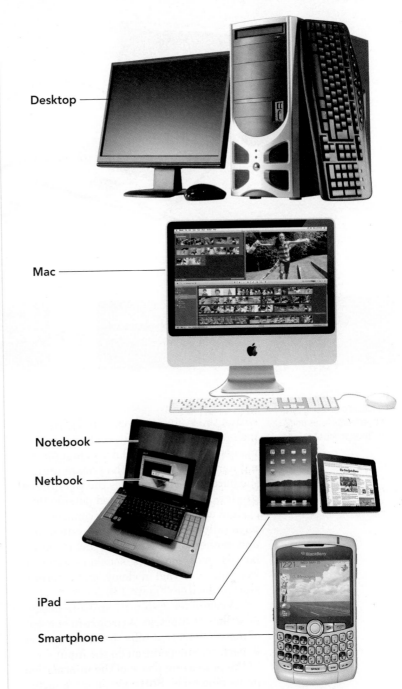

Desktop

Mac

Notebook

Netbook

iPad

Smartphone

FIGURE 1.4 Being familiar with the latest technology tools will help you become more confident in your abilities to select the correct technology based on need and usability, not advertising hype.

the needs of the user. These components can be placed in two major categories: hardware and software. A computer system's **hardware** includes all the physical components of the computer and its related devices. The components include the **system unit**: the base unit of the computer made up of the plastic or metal enclosure, the motherboard, and the integrated peripherals. The **motherboard** is the circuit board that connects the central processing unit(s) anchored on the board and other system components. **Integrated peripherals** are the devices embedded

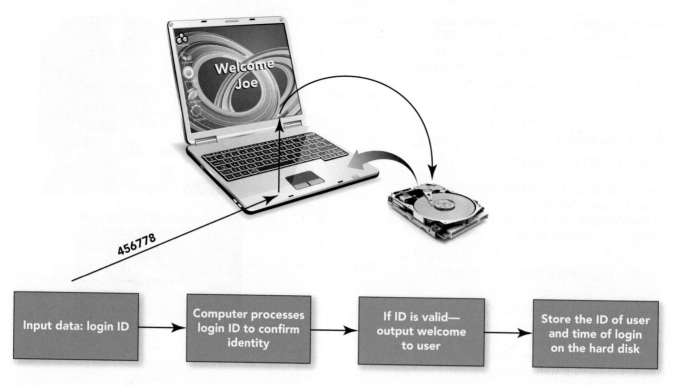

| Input data: login ID | → | Computer processes login ID to confirm identity | → | If ID is valid— output welcome to user | → | Store the ID of user and time of login on the hard disk |

456778

FIGURE 1.5 The information processing cycle is the path data takes from input through output.

within the system unit case and generally include the power supply, cooling fans, memory, CD drive, DVD drive, and internal hard drive. Besides the system unit, the hardware also includes the **peripheral devices**: components located outside the system unit housing that are connected physically or wirelessly to the system unit and motherboard. Examples include keyboards, mice, monitors, speakers, external webcams, external modems, and external storage devices (Figure 1.6).

A computer system's hardware needs programs to function. A **program** is a set of instructions that tells the hardware how to perform an operation on the input data in the processing phase of the information processing cycle. **Software**, a more inclusive term, is the collection of programs, and the associated documentation, that directs the operation of the computer to complete a desired end result. Software can be divided into two categories: system software and application software.

System software is the collection of programs written and configured to provide the infrastructure, basic services, and hardware control that let other programs function properly. The most important and well-recognized type of system software is the computer's **operating system (OS)**, which integrates and controls the computer's internal functions and provides the connectivity for the user to interact with

the computer's hardware. Common operating systems include Microsoft Windows 7, Microsoft Vista, Microsoft Windows XP, Linux, and Mac OS X Snow Leopard. Consumers may get frustrated with the frequency with which new versions of operating systems are released, but operating systems are actually updated to improve performance and accommodate new hardware devices. The most current operating systems are Windows 7, released by Microsoft in July 2009, and Mac OS X Snow Leopard, released by Apple in August 2009. Besides operating systems, other examples of system software include system utility programs that aid in system maintenance, such as backup programs, cleanup tools, and antivirus software.

Application software can be thought of as sitting on top of the operating system. The programs that are integrated to create application software provide instructions that direct the computer's hardware to perform a task for the user. For example the programs to spell check, grammar check, locate synonyms, and insert a header or footer are combined with many other such programs to create a word processing application. Typical examples of application software include word processing, spreadsheet, database, presentation, e-mail, Web browser, and communication software.

Webcam

Monitor

Keyboard

Mouse

System unit

CD or DVD drive

Media card reader

USB ports

Speakers

Sound connections

Cable or DSL modem

Network interface card

Printer

Headset with microphone

To better understand how computer system components are interrelated, you might compare a computer system to an aquarium. The computer hardware is like the fish tank, the operating system is like the water, and the software applications are like the fish (Figure 1.7). You wouldn't put fish in an empty aquarium. Fish can't survive without water, just as software applications can't function without an operating system to support them. And without the water and fish, an aquarium is an empty box—just as computer hardware isn't much use without an operating system and applications.

Now that we know the basic terms, let's take a closer look at the operations in the information processing cycle (input, processing, output, and storage) and at the hardware devices involved in each step.

Input: Getting Data into the Computer

During input, the computer receives data. The term **data** refers to raw facts, which can be made up of words, numbers, images, sounds, or a combination of these.

Input devices enable you to enter data into the computer for processing. The most common input devices are the keyboard and mouse (Figure 1.8). Microphones, scanners, and devices such as digital cameras and camcorders offer other ways of getting different types of data into the computer.

FIGURE 1.7 A computer system can be compared to an aquarium.

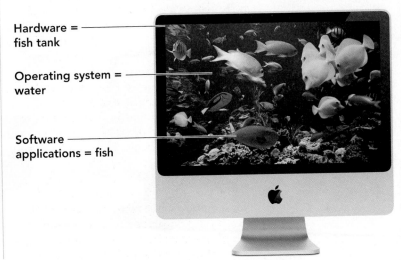

Hardware = fish tank

Operating system = water

Software applications = fish

Processing: Transforming Data into Information

Processing transforms data into information. **Information** is data that has been consolidated and organized in a way that people can use. During processing, the computer's processing circuitry (Figure 1.9), called the **central processing unit (CPU)** or **microprocessor** (or just **processor** for short), is directed by the software in use to per-

form operations on the input data. The CPU is located within the system unit and is a component on the motherboard.

Even though the CPU is often referred to as the "brain" of the computer, computers don't really think. They are capable of performing only repetitive processing actions organized into an **algorithm**—a series of steps that results in the solution to a problem. After an algorithm is tested for accuracy, it is coded into a language that the computer hardware understands and becomes the program or software that the system uses to solve that problem.

Because the CPU needs to juggle multiple input and output requests at the same time, it uses high-speed memory chips to store program instructions and data so it can move between requests quickly. Memory is essential to the smooth operation of the CPU. A typical computer contains several types of

FIGURE 1.9 The CPU (microprocessor or processor) is the component on the motherboard that performs operations on the data to convert it to information.

memory on the motherboard; the most important of these is **random access memory (RAM)**, which temporarily stores the programs and data with which the CPU is interacting. RAM is also referred to as primary memory or temporary memory. The second name comes from the fact that it does not retain any content when power is interrupted or turned off.

Output: Displaying Information

Output commonly is dispensed through **output devices**, like monitors, printers, and speakers that enable people to see, hear, and—with some newer inventions—feel the results of processing operations (Figure 1.10).

Storage: Holding Programs and Data for Future Use

The storage operation makes use of **storage devices**, hardware that retains the programs and data even when power is disrupted or turned off. Storage devices, also referred to as **secondary storage**, can be both integrated and external peripherals (see Figure 1.11), depending on whether the information being stored is to remain within the current system or must be portable and transferable to another system, notebook, or computing device. The internal hard disk holds all the programs, system and application

FIGURE 1.10 Most users view the output of computer-related work either on the monitor screen or hard copy that has been printed.

Internal hard drive   External hard drive

FIGURE 1.11 Hard drives can store very large quantities of data, making them the media of choice for activities that generate large files like movies, pictures, and backups.

software, and data that are intended to remain within that computer system. This storage device is usually an integrated peripheral that is mounted inside the system unit's enclosure and not visible to the user. However, for individuals who require a lot of graphic and multimedia data to be portable, or those that want to back up critical data, hard disks can also be purchased as nonintegrated peripherals and connected to the system unit through USB cables. These external storage devices can be colorful, fit into an average sized eyeglass case, and are economical, costing approximately $100 for 500GB of storage. For some, data portability is necessary. Due to smaller file sizes, an external hard drive may not always be needed. For this type of convenience, individuals usually make use of CDs, DVDs, media cards, or USB flash drives (Figure 1.12).

These portable devices have replaced the floppy disk drive and zip drive that might be found in some older systems. Devices like these, now obsolete, are often referred to as **legacy technology**. The popular **USB flash drive** is the average user's choice of portable storage today. It is about the size of an adult's thumb; can hold up to 64 GB of data (approximately 180 CDs), although a larger 256 GB one is available only in the United Kingdom and Europe; uses solid-state technology; conveniently plugs into a computer's USB port; and is easy to use, rewritable, and inexpensive. If you have never used a flash drive, go to **http://usb-flash-drive-review.toptenreviews.com/usb-flash-drive-c180-video-1.html** and view the very brief and easy-to-understand video. Visit **www1.pacific.edu/comp25/reading/1-InfoProcessing Cycle.html** to find out more about the information processing cycle.

Communications: Moving Data

Communications, the high-speed movement of data or information within and between computers, has become more important due to our increasingly global and mobile society. Such needs as getting data from your computer to the server hosting your Web site or from a school computer to the one at your house have taken communications technology from the back office and communications department at work to your own desk at home. To communicate, computers have to be connected to a network by a **communications device**, which is a hardware component that moves data into and out of a computer. Two or more connected computers are called a **network**. The primary reason to create a network is to share data, information, input/output devices, and other resources. If sharing is easy, individuals will collaborate more, distribute information more freely, increase their knowledge,

FIGURE 1.12 Popular external inexpensive storage devices include CD and DVD drives, media card readers that are used with flash memory cards, and flash drives that connect though a USB port.

CD & DVD drives   Media card reader   Flash drive

expand their scope of reasoning, become more global, and make better individual and group decisions.

Most computers are equipped with a **modem** (short for modulator/demodulator), a communications device that converts data from one form into another. It enables the computer, a digital device, to access data through nondigital media, such as telephone lines, cable, satellite, and cellular connections. Many computers have internal modems that can be used for dial-up Internet access over a standard telephone line. External modems are used for high-speed access to the Internet via cable, DSL, or satellite.

Another important component, a **network interface card (NIC)**, is a hardware element located in the system unit that houses the electronic components used to connect a computer to a network. Many computers already have a NIC integrated into the motherboard, but external NICs can be plugged into a USB port or inserted into a specially designed slot. NICs can connect to wired or wireless networks.

Now that you have had a brief introduction to hardware and software and know their purpose and location in a typical computer system, let's look at an example of how the computer uses the basic functions of input, processing, output, and storage.

The Information Processing Cycle in Action

Even if you haven't wondered what goes on behind the scenes when you use a computer, the following example illustrates your role and the computer's role in each step of the information-processing cycle (Figure 1.13):

- *Input:* You're writing a research paper for a class. You know it has misspellings and grammatical errors, but you keep typing because you can run your word processing program's spell-checker at any time to help correct the errors. In this example, your entire word-processed document is the input.

- *Processing:* A spell checker is a program that uses the computer's ability to quickly perform simple processing operations to construct a list of all of the words in your document. It then compares yours words against a huge list of correctly spelled words. If you've used a word that isn't in this internal dictionary, the program puts that word into a list of apparent misspellings.

  Note that the computer isn't really "checking spelling" when it performs this operation. The computer can't check your spelling because it doesn't possess the intelligence to do so. All it can do is tell you which words you've used do not appear in the dictionary

FIGURE 1.13 The Information Processing Cycle in Action

Your role:	Your role:	Computer's role:	Your role:
Enter word-processed document.	Start spell-checker program.	Display list of misspelled words.	Save corrected document.

Computer's role:	Computer's role:	Your role:	Computer's role:
Receive document.	Spell-checker program compares words in document to built-in dictionary.	Accept or reject suggested misspelled words.	Store final document to disk or drive.

Input → Processing → Output → Storage

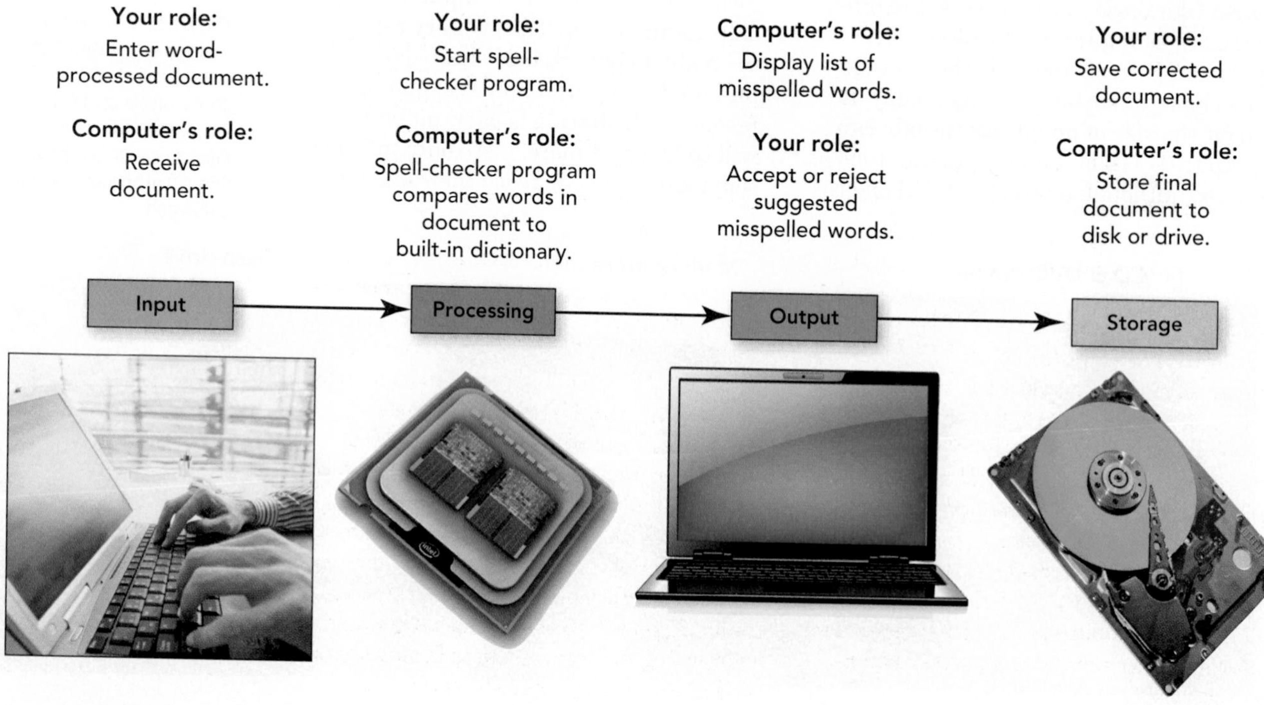

list. Ultimately, only you can decide whether a given word is misspelled.

- *Output:* The result of the processing operation is a list of apparent misspellings. The word *apparent* is important here because the program doesn't actually know whether a word is misspelled. It can tell you only that a word isn't in its massive, built-in dictionary. But many correctly spelled words, such as proper nouns and technical terms, aren't likely to be found in the computer's dictionary. For this reason, the program won't make any changes without asking you to confirm them.

- *Storage:* After you've corrected the spelling in your document, you save or store the revised document to the integrated hard disk or an external portable storage device.

In summary, computers transform data (here a document full of misspellings) into information (a document that is free of misspellings).

Up to this point, we've been talking about computers in a general sense. Let's be more specific and examine the various types of computers, their components, and the tasks that they are built to perform.

Types of Computers

Computers come in all sizes, from large to small. For discussion, it is convenient to divide them into two categories: computers for individuals and computers for organizations. Computers for individuals are designed for one user at a time. They process and store smaller amounts of data and programs, such as a research paper, household budget, or a personal Web page. In contrast, computers for organizations are designed to meet the needs of many people concurrently. They process and store large amounts of data and more complex programs, such as the database of all students on campus or a school's entire Web site. Computers are further subcategorized by power (their processing speed) and purpose (the tasks they perform).

> " Computers for **individuals** are designed for one **user** at a time . . . . computers for **organizations** are design to meet the needs of **many** people concurrently. "

Computers for Individuals

A **personal computer (PC)**, also called a **microcomputer**, is designed to meet the computing needs of an individual or, when connected to a network, can be used by a contributor in a collaborative project. The two most commonly used types of personal computers are Apple's Macintosh (Mac) systems and the more numerous IBM-compatible systems, which are made by manufacturers such as Dell, Gateway, Sony, Hewlett-Packard (HP), and many others. These PCs are called *IBM-compatible* because the first such computer was made by IBM. The acronym *PC*, although originally used to refer to all personal computers, has become more closely aligned with IBM-compatible personal computers, while Apple has coined the term *Mac*. Although PC sales have exceeded those of the Mac, the Mac has a loyal following and has been increasing in popularity. Statistics on the use of the Safari browser, used primarily on Apple systems, indicate a continuous increase in its use from 2007 to 2009. Apple advocates point to this statistic as an indication of an increase in Apple system sales. Go to **www.w3schools.com/ browsers/browsers_stats.asp** and decide for yourself.

Personal computers are subcategorized by size, power, and function. They include the larger units like the **desktop** and **all-in-one computer** systems down to the more portable styles like the **notebook**, **subnotebook**, and **tablet PC**. The table in Figure 1.14 displays such features as size, use, and price of these popular categories of computers used by individuals.

With the trend to smaller size, wireless connectivity, and a greater focus on communication, many individuals are finding a less powerful, less expensive device is meeting their needs. These devices include **netbooks**, **handheld computers**, **personal digital assistants (PDAs)**, **smartphones**, the **iPad**, and dedicated devices like the **Kindle DX**, an **e-book reader**. For the consumer, it is becoming harder to make choices because every manufacturer offers new features or applications. Figure 1.15 categorizes handheld computing devices, outlines their features, and gives an approximate price range.

FIGURE 1.14 Computers for Individual Use

Category	Size	Application	Cost	Image
Desktop Manufacturers: Dell, Gateway, Sony, Hewlett-Packard, Apple	Consists of a system unit approximately the size of a printer with an independent monitor and keyboard.	Home or office environment	$300 to $5,000 depending on customized features	
All-in-one Manufacturers: Apple iMac (trend leader), Lenovo, Hewlett-Packard, Dell, Sony	Combines the system unit and monitor into one.	Home or office environment, good for small cubicles or apartments	$300 to $5,000 depending on customized features	
Notebook (laptop) Manufacturers: Dell, Sony, Gateway	The size of a spiral bound notebook. Fits into a briefcase or backpack.	Designed for portability, popular with students and business people that travel.	$300 to $5,000	
Subnotebook Manufacturers: Apple, Dell, Sony, and Asus	Omits components as CDs or DVDs, weigh 3 pounds or less, approximately 1 inch thick but still runs a full operating system	Used by individuals that like full application features but not all the peripherals devices.	$200 to $500	
Tablet PC (convertible notebook) Manufacturers: Hewlett-Packard, Fujitsu, Lenovo, Dell	The size of a notebook with a screen that swivels and lies flat over the keyboard. A stylus can be used to handwrite input that is then converted to digital text by handwriting recognition software.	Designed for portability, and ease of note taking. Used by sales persons and others that need to input data quickly.	$300 to $5,000	

FIGURE 1.15 Handheld Computers for Individual Use

Category	Size	Application	Cost	Image
Netbook Manufacturer: Acer, Asus, Dell, HP, and Lenovo	Between 5 and 15 inches in size and weighs 2 to 3 pounds	Primary use is Web browsing and e-mail. Because netbooks usually do not have large hard drives, they are great for cloud computing, an online service that provides applications and document storage remotely instead of on the user's hard drive.	$150 to $400	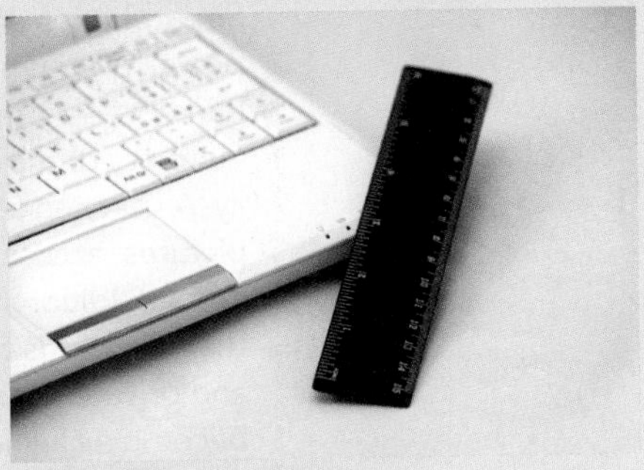
iPad Manufacturer: Apple	Dimensions are 7.47 inches wide by 9.56 inches high and a depth of 0.5 inches, weight is 1.5 to 1.6 pounds	The iPad can download and read e-books; surf the Internet; play movies, TV shows, and other media; make calls; send instant messages/texts; take still photos or video; edit photos and videos; run off battery power for a full day; connect to a TV and play media; and sync its media with a computer.	$500	
Handheld computers or personal digital assistants Manufacturers: Asus, Dell, HP, Palm, and Sony	Fits in the palm of your hand or the pocket of your jeans	Designed for portability, these devices usually use a stylus or virtual keyboard, one that appears on the touch screen, to manage contacts, use e-mail, and schedule appointments.	$200 to $400	
Smartphone Manufacturers: Apple iPhone, BlackBerry Curve, HP iPAQ, Motorola Droid, Palm Pre, and Treo Pro	Fits in the palm of your hand or the pocket of your jeans	Designed to use as a mobile phone with Web access. With the added features and downloadable applications, the line between the smartphone and handheld computers has become blurred.	$100 to $300	
Dedicated Devices Example: Kindle DX Reader by Amazon, the Nook by Barnes and Noble, and the Sony Reader	Dimensions are approximately 7.2 inches wide by 10.4 inches high, depth of 0.4 inches, and weight of 1.1 pounds	Dedicated to a specific activity. The Kindle DX Reader is an e-book reader (electronic book reader) designed to download, display, and read books obtained through an e-bookstore (an electronic book store accessed via the Internet where books are purchased online and downloaded to a Kindle reader, smartphone, iPad, netbook or other connected device for the purchaser to read).	$299 to $400	

Smartphones are becoming popular and powerful communication tools, containing more information than just the phone numbers of the owner's friends and family. A user can send text messages, take pictures, access e-mail, and surf the Web. Additionally it is possible to store the passwords to access bank accounts and private networks. Yes, a phone has become a lifeline of connectivity.

Have you ever found a cell phone that someone had misplaced or left at the checkout of the grocery store? If you ever did find one, what would you do? With the price of a cell phone between $100 and $300, would you surrender it to the store manager? If the phone does not have a lockout code or pad sequence, would you try to call a number in the contact list and try to locate the user? Is even looking in the contact list a violation of the owner's privacy? Would you take it to the provider in hopes that they return it to the owner?

There is really no actual set of rules for this event. However consider the disruption your life would suffer if your smartphone was suddenly missing in action. How helpless would you feel after you misplaced it? How grateful would you be to the individual who returned it?

Computers for Organizations

Organizations or corporations usually need computing systems that are capable of performing transactions faster than those done on a computer designed for individual or small business use. Additionally, these larger entities need more storage capacity for databases and files that contain customer and employee information.

Professional workstations (Figure 1.16) are high-end desktop computers with system units designed for technical or scientific applications, requiring exceptionally powerful processing and output capabilities. Used by engineers, architects, circuit designers, financial analysts, game developers, and other professionals, they are often connected to a network and are equipped with more powerful CPUs, extra RAM, additional graphics power, and multitasking capabilities. For these reasons they are more expensive than desktop PCs. Manufacturers include HP, Dell, and Lenovo.

Servers (Figure 1.17) are computers that range in size from a personal computer to a four-drawer file cabinet.

FIGURE 1.17 Servers contain software that enables them to provide services to users connected to the server through a network. Depending on the configuration, they can range in cost from a couple of thousand to tens of thousands of dollars.

They are equipped with the hardware and software to make programs and data available to people who are connected via a network. They are not designed for individual use and are typically centralized or operated from one location. Users connect to a network on **clients**, which can be desktops, notebooks, workstations, or **terminals** (primarily input/output devices consisting of keyboards and video displays, used as an inexpensive means to connect to a server). A **fat client** accesses the server but does most data processing in its own system; a **thin client** relies on the server for its processing ability. This use of client computers and a centralized server is called a **client/server network**. Servers play an important role in today's businesses and can be as small as a personal computer or as large as a computer that runs a banking institution with millions of clients. These larger units are typically housed in a secure, temperature-regulated environment to protect them from deliberate or accidental damage. The top three server manufacturers are HP, Dell, and IBM.

FIGURE 1.16
Workstations can be mistaken for a desktop due to their similar size; however, the engineering and mathematical applications that they are designed to handle require high-end components that usually place it in the $2,000 to several thousand dollar price range.

FIGURE 1.18 Minicomputers or midrange servers like the IBM AS/400 (iSeries) and HP 300 Alpha family have a wide price range. Although units start as low as $25,000, they can easily exceed $500,000.

Minicomputers or **midrange servers** (Figure 1.18) are midsized servers approximately the size of one or several four-drawer file cabinets with the hardware and software to handle the computing needs of 4 to approximately 200 client computers in a smaller cor-poration or organization. In size and capability, minicomputers fall between workstations and mainframes; but as these markets have evolved and work-stations have become more powerful and mainframes less expensive, the demand for minicomputers has decreased. Minicomputers are manufactured by IBM and HP.

Mainframes or **enterprise servers** (Figure 1.19) are powerful servers that are part of a networked system designed to handle hundreds of thousands of clients at the same time. They are usually used in large corporations or government agencies that handle a high volume of data and can fill an entire wall of an average room. For example, an airline might use a

mainframe to handle airline reservations, or a bank might manage customer accounts on such a system. Mainframes are usually stored in special secure rooms that have a controlled climate. They are manufactured by firms such as IBM, Fujitsu, and Amdahl.

Supercomputers (Figure 1.20) are ultrafast systems that process large amounts of scientific data, often to search for underlying patterns. A supercomputer can be a single computer or a series of computers working in parallel as a single computer. Like mainframes, they are stored in special, secure rooms that have a controlled climate. The main difference between a supercomputer and a mainframe is that a supercomputer focuses on performing a few sets of instruction as fast as possible, whereas a mainframe executes many instructions concurrently.

FIGURE 1.20
Supercomputers can perform mathematical calculations at lightning speed and are used in such fields as weather prediction and space travel. The price of these room-sized systems usually runs several million dollars.

The TOP500 list (**www.top500.org**) tracks the most powerful computer systems worldwide. As of November 2009, ORNL's Jaguar, located at the Department of Energy's Oak Ridge Leadership Computing Facility, recorded a 1.75 petaflops per second performance speed. Jaguar surpassed the prior leader, IBM Roadrunner, located at the Department of Energy's Los Alamos National Laboratory, which recorded a 1.04 petaflops per second performance speed. One **petaflop** is the equivalent of one quadrillion calculations per second. In a more understandable comparison, that is the same as 150,000 calculations for every human being on the planet per second.

Visit **www.unm.edu/~tbeach/ terms/types.html** to learn more about the various types of computers. Now that you know about the variety of computers available, let's look at how their use affects you as an individual and society in general.

FIGURE 1.19 Mainframes or enterprise servers connect thousands of clients concurrently, are used by large organizations and government agencies, and can cost from several thousand to millions of dollars.

Computers, Society, and You

Computers help us be more productive and creative, reducing the amount of time spent on tedious tasks. A good example of this is using a word processing program to create a term paper. The program being used provides spelling and grammar assistance, often automatically, as well as formatting suggestions and easy options to include graphics. Without a computer, the student would need dictionaries and encyclopedias, not to mention style guides and other special resources, along with extra time to gather and go through all of these sources.

Computers let us collect, organize, evaluate, and communicate information. Although computers are merely tools, requiring humans to write the programs and set up the data, we can use them for a variety of common activities to ease our daily lives. Rather than going to the mall to buy the latest movie on DVD, you can now purchase it or even view it online. To organize your music or movie collection before computers, you would have had to physically sort through and arrange it on your shelf. A computer makes it possible to organize your entire collection and sort it in a variety of ways, including by title, artist, release date, or genre, making it simple to reorganize and update your collection. And there's no need to wait for movie reviews to come out in the newspaper—just go online to find the latest reviews from critics and other moviegoers, or watch the trailer yourself. You can select your favorite movie, use your smartphone to locate a nearby theater, make dinner reservations before the show, and even display driving directions. To invite or inform family and friends of your plans, simply use a digital method of social networking and post the information to your Facebook page, blog, Web page, or send out a tweet. The amount of time we save during a day by using computers or computer-related devices is phenomenal.

A computer, with the appropriate software, can perform various tasks on all types of data. That is a major reason for the remarkable penetration of computers into almost every occupational area and into 80 percent of U.S. households in 2008 (a significant increase from 49 percent in 2001 and 2002). So, four out of every five households in the United States have a computer. Although computers seem to be everywhere, computers and the Internet aren't readily accessible in some segments of society. Computers and the Internet possess the ability to cut across all educational, racial, and economic boundaries; but there are still inequities.

The Digital Divide

The more educated you are and the more income you make, the more likely you are to own a computer and have Internet access. Figure 1.21 displays the results of the Nielsen report comparing income and home Internet access though the third quarter of 2008. The chart clearly highlights the income discrepancy with respect to Internet connectivity. This same report also identified the East South Central region (Alabama, Mississippi, Tennessee, and Kentucky) of the United States as the geographic region with the highest number of households (26%) having no Internet access. Further, a study by Pew Internet and American Life Project in December 2008 showed that approximately one-third of people in the United States have a bachelor's degree, and 95 percent of college-educated individuals use the Internet; but only 53 percent of people with a high school education do.

FIGURE 1.21 The digital divide is often thought of as the difference in computer and Internet use between the have and have-not nations. This Nelson report actually highlights the digital divide that exists over Internet use within the United States.

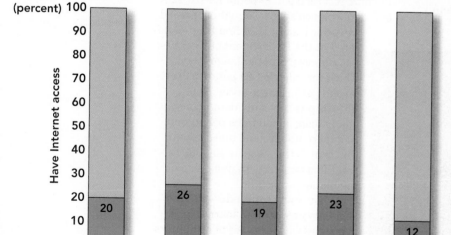

U.S. Internet access by household income

Age, race, and income are also factors in U.S. computer use. The December 2009 Pew Internet and American Life Project indicated that only 38 percent of adults 65 and older use the Internet, compared with 70 percent of 50- to 64-year-olds, 81 percent of 30- to 49-year-olds, and 93 percent of 18- to 29-year-olds. Another Pew report in the same year substantiated that 80 percent of whites, 72 percent of African Americans, and only 61 percent of the Hispanics have Internet use. This disparity in computer ownership and Internet access, known as the **digital divide**, isn't limited to the United States. Similar statistics exist for other countries, indicating that this is a global problem. Studies of the expansion or reduction of the digital divide are contradictory; however, government and educational programs are working to bridge this gap by attempting to provide computer access for all (Figure 1.22).

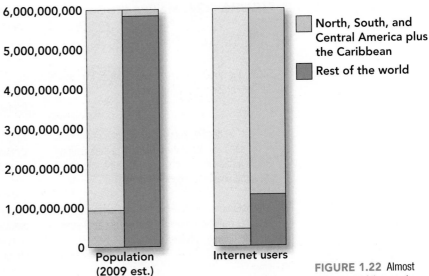

Source of data: Internet World Stats

FIGURE 1.22 Almost 50 percent of the populations of North America, South America, Central America, and the Caribbean have Internet connectivity, while only 20 percent of the rest of the world enjoys that technology.

Social Networking

Some of the uses of computers, such as social networking, seem to be more for communication or entertainment than for information or learning. It would be a mistake to dismiss these types of sites or applications as child's play. Results from statistics provided by a Forrester Research Report can be seen in Figure 1.23 These summarizations substantiate that the contact between adults on these sites and the amount of information being shared daily is real, on the rise, and reaching a population demographic that is staggering. One of the most basic forms of this interaction is **instant messaging (IM)**, a free, real-time connection between two or more parties that uses a buddy list to identify and restrict the contacts a person wishes to communicate with.

The use of online **social network sites** such as Facebook, MySpace, LinkedIn, and Twitter is increasing rapidly. These are sites that individuals are invited or allowed to join and support such tools as instant messaging and e-mail among members. **Facebook**, the largest of

FIGURE 1.23 The Use of Social Network Sites by Adults

Statistics	Related Sites
A third of adults post at least once a week to a social site.	A social site can be Facebook, MySpace, Twitter, as well as eHarmony, Match.com, and Yahoo singles.
A quarter of adults publish a blog and upload video/audio they created.	The most recognized video broadcasting site is YouTube. Blogs created by individuals contain entries that resemble journal entries.
Nearly 60% of adults maintain a profile on a social networking site.	The most popular social networking sites are Facebook and Twitter.
Approximately 70% read blogs, tweets, and watch UGC (user-generated content) videos.	Blogs can be located on almost any Web page and on any topic. Radio and TV stations as well as political sites are popular for hosting blogs to collect opinions. UGC videos can be posted on individually created Web pages or, for viewing by a larger audience, YouTube.

FIGURE 1.24 Making the Social Network Work for Businesses

Action	Purpose
Encourage supervisors and colleagues to investigate the Web presence of competitors.	To size up the competition, their manner of presentation on a social network site, the type of offers and interaction they provide for the customer.
Sharpen leadership knowledge of some of the high profile sites and learn the language of their users. Create a page in Facebook or become a follower of a favorite coach or actor on Twitter.	To get the feel of the social environment and learn its language, and interface. Being comfortable is a prerequisite for launching a business site.
Poll customers and analyze their responses. Use a variety of options to connect with target audiences or promote different product lines.	To determine the type of customer involved in the social networking world. This will determine the tone the business decides to project on its page and the type of offers that are posted.
Once the decision is made to create a Web presence for the business, assign the task of maintaining it to an individual that understands the technology. Old or inaccurate information will have a negative effect on business.	To maintain consistency and currency of layout, design, and content in order make the customer comfortable.

such social networking sites, allows anyone over the age of 13 with a valid e-mail account, residing in a country where it has not been banned, to become a Facebook user. Often users will join groups set up by region, job, interest, or school and communicate with group members. Adult Internet users who have profiles on online social network sites have more than quadrupled in the past four years—from 8 percent in 2005 to 35 percent in 2008, according to the Pew Internet and American Life Project December 2008 report. Mark Brooks, a social network and online dating analyst, suggests that these sites are locations where individuals are looking for friends. Sites dedicated to matchmaking offer more anonymity, but social networking sites offer an environment that allows someone to look at a friend's postings, follow their social interaction with others, and allow for a more insightful view of a members personality and behavior.

Twitter, the newest phenomenon, is a free, real-time social messaging utility that allows postings of up to 140 characters. The exchanges are short and usually in a question-and-answer mode. People need merely look up the Twitter accounts of their friends and indicate that they want to become a follower and view their Twitter posts, which are called **tweets**.

From a business point of view, using these social networking sites can enable a business to reach individuals standard advertising media might miss and provide much more exposure than any commercial or single Web site posting. Most organizations and companies are looking to increase their Web presence. What better way than to use a social networking site? The suggestions in Figure 1.24 offer a starting point to evaluate the Web presence of a business and the target population it is trying to reach. It also provides suggestions on making necessary adjustments. For many businesses, it might be time to make the jump to a more dynamic Web presence that includes social networking sites. When each Twitter account holder has an average following of 126 users, the amount of information that is dispersed in seconds through this portal alone is phenomenal. Think about how quickly a happy customer can spread the word.

Collaborative Work

Computers also help us work, teach, and learn together. Computers facilitate collaboration with others to solve problems. For instance, computers are increasingly part of law enforcement activities. They facilitate quick and efficient communication between jurisdictions, enable law enforcement officials to browse criminal databases like the Automated Fingerprint Identification System (AFIS) (Figure 1.25), and allow pertinent data to be shared nationally and globally. Additionally, as cybercrime becomes a bigger concern, police are using the Internet and **computer forensics**, a branch of forensic science that deals with legal evidence found on computers, to find and apprehend these criminals.

Collaboration software, the collection of programs that help people share ideas, create documents, and conduct meetings, regardless of location or time zone, are making their move into the academic and business worlds. Whether you're an employee of a multinational firm developing a new product with a group of colleagues located halfway around the globe or a student enrolled in a distance learning course, computers and their facilitation of collaboration play a big part in making these tasks possible.

The need to stay connected to complete group projects and research has caused a rise in the use of online applications that advance collaboration. **Google Docs**, a free Web-based word processor and spreadsheet, allows project members to share and edit documents online. A **wiki** is a collection of Web pages designed to let anyone with access contribute or modify content. Wikis are often used to create collaborative or community Web sites. The collaborative encyclopedia Wikipedia is one of the best-known wikis. **Google Groups** is a free service provided by Google to help users connect, share information, and communicate effectively over the Internet. Its current version allows group members to collaborate on shared Web pages; set group pictures, colors, and styles; upload and share individually created work; and learn more about other members in the group. After the project is finalized, you can use your own computer to print, store, and present the finished product.

Even though computers offer us many advantages and communication options, the responsible computer user should also be aware of the disadvantages of computer use.

Advantages and Disadvantages of Using Computers

It seems that for every positive effect an invention provides there is a negative effect.

FIGURE 1.25 The ability to convert a fingerprint into a digital image and send it over the Internet to other law enforcement agencies enables comparisons to be made quicker and a suspect apprehended faster.

That is also true for computers. A computer system provides certain advantages to its users, such as speed, memory for work in progress, storage for access later, hardware reliability, and accuracy. However, with these advantages come some disadvantages (Figure 1.26), including information overload, the expense of computer equipment, data inaccuracy, and an increasing dependence on unreliable software.

Speed is one of the greatest advantages of a computer. It can perform, in a minute, calculations or tasks that would take a human days. In fact, people are generating so much information via computers today that they often succumb to **information overload**: a feeling of anxiety and incapacity experienced when people are presented with more information than they can handle. According to research from the firm Basex, which chose information overload as its 2008 problem of the year, constant e-mail messages, phone calls, text messages, and tweets across the U.S. workforce resulted in $650 billion of lost productivity in a single year. That is an estimate of up to eight hours a week per worker. Some see this connectivity as an annoyance. However, young people do not seem as irritated at the multitasking demands of technology. They listen to music while reading, IM friends while typing a paper, tweet constantly, and do not seem annoyed. It remains to be seen whether this ability to handle information overload will produce a future workforce that is better able to handle an overfilled Inbox.

FIGURE 1.26 Advantages and Disadvantages of Computer Use

Advantages	Disadvantages
Speed	Information overload
Memory	Cost
Storage	Data inaccuracy
Hardware reliability and accuracy	Software unreliability

Cost is another drawback that must be weighed against computer performance. A computer's performance is enhanced by the amount of random access memory the system possesses. Random access memory (RAM) is high-speed, temporary memory that holds all programs and data currently in use; in other words, it holds our work in progress. The processor accesses programs and data in RAM quickly. The faster the processor receives the data, the faster it returns results. Once we are done with it, the information in RAM must be placed on a storage device so we can retrieve it later. Depending on the quantity of data you process and the number of files you save, you may need to purchase additional RAM and storage devices.

Purchasing more RAM or additional storage can be costly. Most computers are equipped with just enough RAM and storage to hold an average amount of programs and data. If you use many high-end applications, you may experience a slowdown when moving between graphics, see a pause in a long video, or receive a message that one of your storage units is full. If that happens, you need to investigate the reason for the slowdown and may need to purchase more RAM or storage. High-end users or intense gamers may also find that when new applications are installed on an older machine, the computer might not have enough CPU power to keep up with the new software speed and graphics. This might require upgrading the CPU or purchasing a new system. Investigate the benefits and drawbacks of either decision on a case-by-case basis.

Hardware reliability and accuracy are two more advantages of computers. Computers show up at school or work every day and almost always respond when turned on. If given a calculation to do several times, they consistently output the same result. A computer can transcribe your speech with an accuracy of 95 percent or more, which is better than most people's typing accuracy. In fact, almost all "computer errors" are actually caused by flaws in software or errors in the data supplied by people. Some more interactive programs allow the user to correct an error and save the correction. This enables the program to automatically fix future occurrences of that error.

Along with computers' strengths and weaknesses, consider some additional points in your quest to become a respon-sible user.

Become Comfortable with Hardware

Some people feel threatened by computers because they fear that computers are too complicated. But without humans, computers have no intelligence at all. They process simple repetitive operations. Remember, without a person and a program to tell it what to do, the computer is no more frightening—or useful—than an empty fish tank.

One way to get comfortable with your computer is to learn how to care for it. Read any instructions that accompany your purchase and remember that dust, moisture, static electricity, and magnetic interference may affect your system's performance. Additionally, keeping cords and devices in places that do not interfere with the traffic pattern of the room will avoid unnecessary accidents and make your work environment safe and comfortable. Does your work area look like the one in Figure 1.27?

To maintain a safe working environment for you and your hardware, heed the following advice:

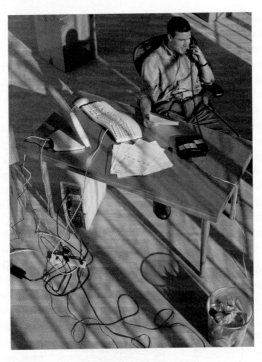

FIGURE 1.27 A messy computer environment is an unsafe and unproductive one.

- Use a surge protector and avoid plugging too many devices into the same electrical outlet.
- Place computer equipment in a secure position so it won't fall or cause accidents.
- Leave plenty of space around computer equipment for sufficient air circulation to prevent overheating.
- Make sure computer cables, cords, and wires are fastened securely and not strung haphazardly or left lying where you could trip over them or where they could cause a fire.
- Keep the computer area free of food and liquids, as one spill can cause the loss of weeks of work.

Now that you know how to create a safe computing environment, it is equally important to understand how to avoid eye, back, and wrist strain that can occur from long periods of use. Healthy computing habits combined with ergonomic devices and proper positioning and arrangement of equipment and lighting can make all the difference in your computing environment and physical health.

Ergonomics is the field of study that is concerned with the fit between people, their equipment, and their work. It takes into account worker limitations and capabilities in attempting to ensure that the tasks, equipment, and overall environment

suit each worker (Figure 1.28). The most common injuries related to prolonged computer use occur to the wrist and back. Prolonged keyboard use can cause **carpal tunnel syndrome** (also known as cumulative trauma disorder or repetitive strain injury), which is caused by repeated motions that damage sensitive nerves in the hands, wrists, and arms. Sometimes these injuries are so serious that they require surgery. To help prevent these problems, ergonomic keyboards, such as the Microsoft Natural Keyboard, have been designed to keep your wrists flat, reducing (but not eliminating) your chance of an injury (Figure 1.29). Because of the back strain sitting at a computer causes, many hotel chains try to attract business travelers by promoting their ergonomic desk chairs

FIGURE 1.28 Keys to an Ergonomically Correct Work Station

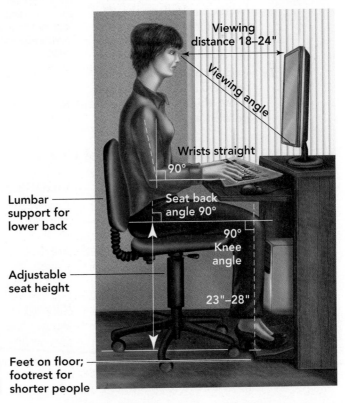

Viewing distance 18–24"

Viewing angle

Wrists straight

90°

Lumbar support for lower back

Seat back angle 90°

90° Knee angle

Adjustable seat height

23"–28"

Feet on floor; footrest for shorter people

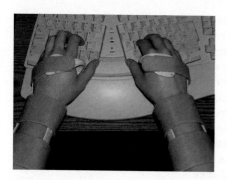

FIGURE 1.29 A typist using an ergonomic keyboard is taking an extra precaution and also using wrist guards designed to reduce the damage to nerves in the wrist, arms, and hands.

(Figure 1.30) along with high-speed Internet access. Go to **http://ergo.human. cornell.edu** to view a list of links that include videos and worksheets that provide information to help you make healthy ergonomic decisions.

In addition to using properly designed equipment, you can promote a safe and comfortable computer environment by following the tips below.

- Position the top of your monitor at eye level.
- Tilt the monitor back 10 to 20 degrees and keep it no closer than 20 inches from your eyes.
- Try to keep your wrists flat; use a wrist rest if necessary.
- Rest your eyes frequently by focusing on an object 20 or more feet away.
- Stand and stretch periodically.

If you purchase devices that fit your body, treat the physical components of your computer with respect, and monitor your work health habits, you will get the most return for your money and promote a healthy work and life style. For guidance, a workspace planner is provided at **www.ergotron. com/tabid/305/language/en-US/ default.aspx**.

Recognize the Risks of Using Flawed Software

Computer hardware can be amazingly reliable, but software is another matter. Most programs contain some errors or **bugs**, as they are called. Many programs contain millions of lines of code (Figure 1.31). In general, each line of program code tells the computer to perform an action, such as adding two numbers or comparing them.

FIGURE 1.30 The multi-positioning chair, made from breathable fabric, and a well-positioned head rest should help alleviate neck and lower back stress.

Consider this: The program that allows you to withdraw cash from an ATM contains only 90,000 lines of code. But when you file your taxes, the Internal Revenue Service (IRS) program that calculates your refund contains 1,000 times that—100 million lines of code!

With so many lines of code, bugs are inevitable—and they are almost impossible to eradicate completely. On average, commercial programs contain between 1 and 7 errors for every 1,000 lines of code. This means that an ATM is likely to have approximately 360 errors in its code, and the IRS program code might have over 400 hundred thousand errors. Fortunately, most errors simply cause programs to run slowly or to perform unnecessary tasks; but some errors cause miscalculations or other inconveniences, such as your computer becoming nonresponsive. According to IBM's annual X-Force and Trend Risk Report for 2009, the overall number of bugs in software decreased, but bugs in document readers and multimedia applications saw a 50 percent increase.

These are ample reasons why it's not a good idea to put off writing a paper, especially if you plan to embed a multimedia component, until the night before your assignment is due. Bugs in a word processing program aren't usually life threatening, but computers are increasingly being used in mission-critical and safety-critical systems. Mission-critical systems are essential to

FIGURE 1.31 Code Length for Key Programs

Program	Lines of Programming Code
Bank ATM	90,000
Air traffic control	900,000
Microsoft Windows 2000	35 million
Microsoft Windows Vista	50 million
Microsoft Office XP	35 million (estimated)
Internal Revenue Service (IRS)	100 million (all programs)

an organization's viability, such as a company's computerized cash register system. If the system goes down, the organization can't function—and the result is often an expensive fiasco. A safety-critical system is one on which human lives depend, such as an air traffic control system or a computerized signaling system used by high-speed commuter trains (Figure 1.32). When these systems fail, human lives are at stake. Safety-critical systems are designed to much higher quality standards and have backup systems that kick in if the main computer goes down. For a specific case, do an Internet search on "F-22 software problems."

FIGURE 1.32 Subway and train systems, like the Intercity Express (ICE) in Cologne, Germany, along with air traffic control, defense, and security systems are run by safety-critical software. Code for such systems must be of the highest standards and bug-free.

Take Ethics Seriously

One disturbing thing about computers is what some people do with them. *Ethics* is the behavior associated with your moral beliefs. You have learned what is right and wrong from your parents, teachers, and spiritual leaders. By this stage of your life, you should know which behaviors fall into which category. However, people's use of computers and the Internet has created ethical situations that we might not have otherwise encountered. **Computer ethics**, a branch of philosophy that continues to evolve, deals with computer-related moral dilemmas and defines ethical principles for computer use.

How many people do you know who have "borrowed" software, downloaded movies from the Web, shared music files with friends, or illegally burned copies of music CDs? If you ask around, you'll find that you're surrounded by people who don't think it's wrong to steal digital data. They view **digital piracy**, the unauthorized reproduction and distribution of computer-based media, differently from photocopying a book or taking a DVD from a store without paying. In reality, these forms of theft are similar. Current statistics show that global losses due to digital piracy amount to more than $40 billion annually, with a 30 percent decrease in sales in the music industry alone from 2004 to 2009. This is not just a loss of products, but jobs, retail business, and collected tax dollars. The Business Software Alliance reports that reducing U.S. piracy rates by just 10 percent over the next four years could create more than 32,000 new jobs, generate $6.7 billion in tax revenues, and result in $40 billion in economic growth. The Anti-Counterfeiting Trade Agreement is an international assault on software piracy and trademark violations. The chief players in this agreement include the United States, South Korea, Japan, Australia, Canada, and members of the European Union. With the Internet rapidly becoming the leader in dispersing all forms of media, governments cannot ignore piracy.

Responsible computing requires that you understand the advantages and disadvantages of using a computer as well as the potential harm from computer misuse. There are daily reports about the misuse of computerized data. Names and e-mail addresses are distributed freely without permission or regard for privacy. Viruses are launched against unsuspecting victims. Credit card information is stolen and fraudulently used. Children and women are stalked. Pornography abounds. Illegitimate copies of software are installed every day. Research papers are bought and sold over the Internet. Homework assignments are copied and then modified to look like original work. The Internet is a hotbed of illicit and sometimes illegal content. Computers are very powerful tools. They can magnify many positive aspects of our lives but can also highlight negative aspects, including unethical behavior.

Societal Impacts of Computer Use

Computers and the Internet are here to stay, and they have improved the quality of our lives and society as a whole. Almost everyone has been affected by computers and the Internet. Although most people are able-bodied, consider the effect of technologies that support and provide opportunities to the disabled and the disadvantaged (Figure 1.33).

With the integration of individuals with special needs into the regular classrooms and workforce environments, schools and employers must provide computer access and the devices needed to facilitate that access for special needs students and employees. Here are just some of the developments to provide adaptive technologies.

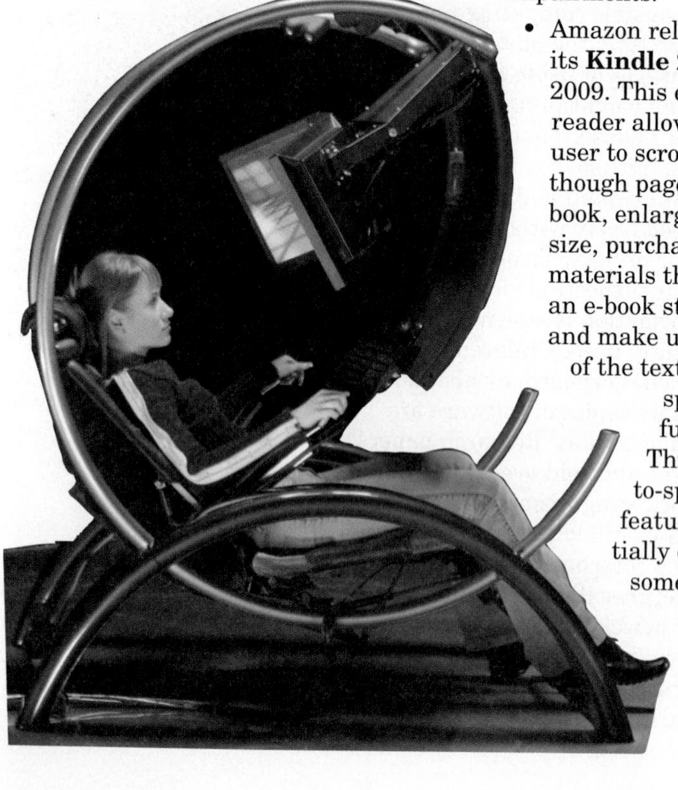

FIGURE 1.33
Continued innovation in computers, software, and related technologies help individuals with myriad disabilities. Shown here, the Alternative Computer Control System (ACCS) manufactured by Gravitonus is designed to provide computer access for severely motor-impaired individuals.

- Your school must, in order to meet the requirements of the Americans with Disabilities Act of 1990, provide computer access to people with disabilities. Special speech recognition software is needed to help people with vision impairments use computers. Input and output devices designed for the physically disabled can be installed, or existing devices can be modified, to accommodate users with hearing or motor impairments.

- Amazon released its **Kindle 2** in 2009. This e-book reader allows the user to scroll though pages of a book, enlarge text size, purchase materials through an e-book store, and make use of the text-to-speech function. This text-to-speech feature initially caused some copyright issues as books that are read usually receive additional royalties. Amazon tried to recall the Kindle 2, but protests from individuals and agencies that represent the disabled were effective and royalty agreements were worked out.

- Other computer controlled devices that help those with physical disabilities lead more independent lives include treadmills, muscle stimulators, and video game therapy.

- The blue-sky research division of the Defense Advance Projects Research Agency (DARPA) is developing a "neurally" controlled artificial limb that will restore full motor and sensory capability to people who have had their arms amputated. This prosthesis will be controlled, feel, look, and perform like a natural arm.

Students can use computers to take advantage of inexpensive training and learning opportunities.

- **E-learning** is the use of computers and computer programs to replace teachers and the time–place specificity of learning.

- Libraries have improved their computer-related resources, and most have Internet connectivity.

- Online classes make use of specially developed software to provide an interface for students to interact with the instructor in a secure and private environment from the comfort of their own homes.

- Internet cafés and workforce agencies provide access to the Internet for social purposes or to enable access to research and employment sites.

- You can find online training, templates for all types of documents, and instruction on how to do just about anything.

The Effect of Computers on Employment

Although computers are creating new job opportunities, they're also shifting labor demand toward skilled workers—particularly those who are computer proficient. As a result, these skilled workers are in greater demand and earn higher wages.

Computer skills have never been more important to a person's future. A recent ad from an IT (information technology) staffing firm in Providence, Rhode Island, announced that the company would host its first Rhode Island Young Information Technology Happy Hour. Free food would be provided during the event and free drink tickets given to individuals who signed up to attend before the event. Anyone signing up to attend on the Web site and completing a short survey would also be entered for a chance to win a free Asus Eee mini-laptop computer; registrants had to be present at the event to win. This ad shows the extremes that staffing agencies will go to in hopes of attracting IT and computer-knowledgeable professionals.

As we've pointed out, computers help people complete their work; however, advanced technology can also free people from occupations with hazardous working conditions and ones with repetitive tasks, making workflow safer and more efficient—and increasing productivity. The result is that fewer workers may be required to perform a task, and certain jobs may be eradicated. **Automation**, the replacement of human workers by machines and computer-guided robots, is taking over many manufacturing jobs that people once held (Figure 1.34).

Robots might play a more important role in the future. The robot named ASIMO (Advance Step in Innovative Mobility) is the result of more than two decades of experimentation by Honda engineers (Figure 1.35). It has human-like flexibility and endless possibilities. Visitors to the Disneyland park in Anaheim, California, can see ASIMO in action at the Honda ASIMO theater in the Innoventions attractions. ASIMO is still a work in progress.

On a larger scale, more than 1 million robots are in use worldwide, mostly in Japan, although the United States ranks

second. Contrary to popular opinion, fewer than half of the robots used in the United States are found in automotive plants. The rest are used in industries such as health care and in locations such as warehouses, laboratories, and energy plants.

FIGURE 1.34 Computer-guided robots are taking over many manufacturing jobs that people once held.

The government of South Korea has promised to invest 1 trillion won (about $750 million) in that country's robotics industry in an attempt to accelerate its growth. The goal is to help the global robotics market grow to more than $30 billion by 2013 and to help Korean companies take as much as 10 percent of that market, according to the Director General for Emerging Technologies. This will make Korea one of the top three producers of robotic products by 2013 and the leading producer by 2018.

Globalization of jobs is another effect of technology on employment. No longer is a product made and sold in the same country. More often, pieces of a product are produced in several countries, assembled into subunits, and shipped to another location where the subunits are pulled together into the finished product. The term **outsourcing**, the subcontracting of portions of a job to a third party to reduce cost, time, and energy, has become closely related to globalization. Outsourcing is blamed for eliminating as many as 12,000 to 15,000 jobs monthly, with the total amount of lost outsourced jobs predicted to reach

FIGURE 1.35 Asimo is a humanoid robot that stands 4 feet 3 inches and weighs 114 pounds. It can walk and run on two feet at rates of up to 4.3 miles per hour.

3.3 million by 2015. Some studies argue that increased productivity is an associate cause of job loss. Increasing U.S. productivity by as little as 1 percent can eliminate up to 1.3 million jobs a year. **Structural unemployment** results when advancing technology makes an entire job category obsolete. Structural unemployment differs from the normal economic cycles of layoffs and rehires. People who lose jobs because of structural unemployment are not going to get them back. Their only option is to retrain themselves to work in other careers.

Consider this: Half of all the jobs that will be available in 10 years don't exist today. So, who will survive—and flourish—in a computer-driven economy? The answer is simple: The survivors will be people who understand technology, know that education is a lifelong process, and adapt quickly to change.

Being a Responsible Computer User

You use a computer and the Internet; have a smartphone; and send e-mail, text messages, and tweets throughout the day. All of this seems okay within your own personal space; but how does your usage affect others in your school, office, family, community, and the environment? For starters, don't hog public computer resources. If you are using a computer and Internet connection at a library or in a wireless hot spot, don't download or upload large files; be considerate of others who might be sharing the connection. Recycle paper and printer cartridges to help protect the environment. Don't talk on your phone or text message while driving; many states have enacted laws against using handheld devices while operating a vehicle and impose stringent fines. Be aware of the people near you in the theater; they paid for tickets to watch the show—not to hear your phone or conversation or see your screen light up with a text message.

Another concern is how to dispose of obsolete computer equipment, also called **e-waste**. More than 100 million computers, monitors, and TVs become obsolete each year, and these numbers keep growing. In the first quarter of 2008, 294.3 million mobile phone units were sold, a 13.6 percent increase over the first quarter of 2007. Because monitors, batteries, and other

electronic components contain hazardous materials, they can't just be thrown in the trash. Unfortunately, only 12.5 percent of this e-waste is properly recycled. At least 24 states either have passed or are considering laws regarding e-waste disposal (Figure 1.36). Responsible users look for computer and electronics equipment disposal and recycling companies in their area or check state and federal Web sites, such as the Environmental Protection Agency site (**www.epa.gov**), for tips on computer disposal.

Private companies are stepping up recycling services. Dell has initiated a program that will recycle anyone's PC, regardless of manufacturer. HP will recycle any manufacturer's computer hardware or printer cartridges and has also set up battery recycling programs in many computer stores. Gateway gives you cash for your old technology; if your product has zero value, Gateway will pay for shipping it and will recycle it free of charge. For more information, go to **www.gateway. com/about/corp_responsibility/ env_options.php**.

Another way to solve the disposal problem and give back to your community is by donating old computer equipment to

FIGURE 1.36
Responsible computer users and manufacturers recycle old computers, printers, monitors, batteries, and other types of e-waste.

local charities that could refurbish it to help new users learn the basics. Perhaps you might consider donating a little of your time to help too.

Being a responsible technology user also means being aware of how computers and Internet use can affect your own well-being and personal relationships. Researchers at Carnegie Mellon University were surprised to find that people who spent even a few hours a week on the Internet experienced higher levels of depression and loneliness than those who did not. These people interacted with other Internet users online, but this interaction seems to have been much shallower than time spent with friends and family. The result? According to the researchers, Internet use leads to unhealthy social isolation and is a deadened, mechanized experience that is lacking in human emotion. Interestingly, other studies show just the opposite; these studies demonstrate that there is no difference in socialization between those who use the Internet and those who do not. Who is right? It will take years of research to know. But for now, keep in mind that computer and Internet overuse may promote unhealthy behaviors.

Staying Informed About Changing Technology

It is important to stay informed about software and hardware advances in technology. Upgrading the application software on your computer helps you enjoy the most current features the software manufacturer offers. Upgrading your antivirus application helps prevent the latest computer viruses from infecting and harming your system. (A *virus* is a malicious program that enters your computer with or without your permission.) Some viruses are harmless; others slow down performance; and still others delete programs and files. Viruses wreak havoc on computers every day. By knowing all you can about the latest viruses and how they're spread, you can keep your computer from getting infected.

The steady advance of computer hardware has created faster processors, cheaper storage devices, and lighter, thinner, vision-friendly monitors. For the user, this means that next month's computer will be more powerful than this month's computer and will probably cost less. You can stay informed about the latest technology by reading periodicals, visiting Web sites such as CNET (**www.cnet.com**), subscribing to print and online newsletters and publications, and reading technology columns in your local newspaper. Learning about computers and technology will help you be a better consumer, a more productive student and employee, and, in general, a more responsible computer user.

Choose between a Mac and a PC?

Mac and PC users have been battling it out for years. Each side is entrenched in its beliefs and loyalty. As a potential buyer, it it critical to investigate all possibilities before making a purchase and not let habit or marketing sway your decision. The logical comparison of components, intended use, the opinion of current users, and cost should weigh in on your final evaluation. Each user has to determine his or her budget and purpose, review the features of each type of computer, and make an educated decision. Use the following chart to help you make the decision about whether you would prefer a Mac or a PC.

▶ PC					
COST	**SETUP**	**HARDWARE**	**OPERATING SYSTEM**	**SECURITY AND STABILITY**	**APPLICATIONS**
Usually **less expensive** initially, but might require more hardware to run advanced programs.	Usually requires **some configuration** with external devices.	Intel processor.	Vista and Windows 7 both have **over 5 versions** from which to choose, each with different options. The key here is **familiarity**. A lot of individuals have used previous versions of a PC operating system and feel more comfortable with it.	PCs are **subject to viruses** and will require the purchase of additional antivirus software.	Most (95%) of the world uses PCs. So to share files in the **business world,** a PC is the better choice. A PC is **better suited for gaming**, but a special gaming machine is probably better for the serious gamer.
▶ MAC					
More expensive out of the box, but comes with more hardware and rarely needs any upgrades.	Little to **no set up** required.	Intel processor.	The Mac OS has only **one version** and an extremely appealing and graphic interface.	The Mac is **more stable** and has seldom been compromised by a virus.	Mac is more used in the **graphics community**. Microsoft makes applications for the Mac but does not upgrade them as frequently as they do for the PC. Mac is **better suited for working with graphics**, photo editing, and video creating.

Chapter Summary

Computers and You

- A computer system is a collection of related components that have been designed to perform the information processing cycle: input, processing, output, and storage.

- A system includes both hardware—the physical components such as the system unit, keyboard, monitor, and speakers—and software—the programs that run on it.

- In a typical computer system, a keyboard and a mouse provide input capabilities. Processing is done by the microprocessor (CPU) on programs and data held in RAM (random access memory). You see the results (output) on a monitor or printer, and a hard disk is typically used for long-term storage.

- A computer is an electronic device that performs four operations; input, processing output, and storage. These four operations, performed in sequential order, are called the information processing cycle.

- There are two major categories of computers: computers for individuals and those for organizations. Types of computers for individuals include personal computers (PCs), desktop computers, all-in-one computers, notebooks, subnotebooks, tablet PCs, and handheld computers (such as PDAs and smartphones). Types of computers for organizations include professional workstations, servers, minicomputers, mainframes, and supercomputers.

- Computers have advantages and disadvantages. Some advantages include speed, memory, storage, hardware reliability, accuracy, and assistance to those with disabilities. Disadvantages include information overload, expense, data inaccuracy, unreliable software, viruses, software piracy, identity theft, loss of jobs to automation, and health problems due to improperly fitting equipment and poorly arranged work environments.

- The use of social networking sites such as Facebook, MySpace, LinkedIn, and Twitter is growing daily. Such sites provide a method of connectivity that is inexpensive (most often free), available 24/7, and globally accessible. Businesses have realized the power of such sites and have become users to analyze their customers and keep an eye on competitors.

- Computers are creating new job opportunities, shifting labor demand toward skilled workers, helping people complete their work; freeing workers from occupations with hazardous working conditions, making workflow safer and more efficient, and increasing productivity.

- Being a responsible computer user means respecting others when using technology, recycling computer hardware, sharing public computing resources, being aware of computer and Internet overuse, and staying informed about changing technology and its effect on the environment.

Key Terms and Concepts

Identification

Label each device as input, output, processing, or storage.

1. _____

2. _____

3. _____

4. _____

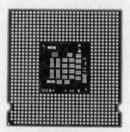

5. _____

6. _____

7. _____

8. _____

Matching

Match each key term in the left column with the most accurate definition in the right column:

_____ 1. random access memory

_____ 2. netbook

_____ 3. program

_____ 4. tablet PC

_____ 5. CPU

_____ 6. operating system

_____ 7. ergonomics

_____ 8. instant messaging

_____ 9. application software

_____ 10. information overload

_____ 11. network interface card

_____ 12. digital piracy

_____ 13. Facebook

_____ 14. all-in-one computer

_____ 15. Twitter

a. Referred to as the brain of the computer

b. A social network used for lengthy communication with friends

c. A computer system in which the system unit and monitor are combined to reduce the space needed to hold the system

d. A hardware component of a computer system that contains the electronics to connect the computer to the network

e. A free real-time connection that makes use of a buddy list

f. A convertible notebook that can be used in two different configurations and accepts handwritten input

g. Unauthorized reproduction and distribution of computer-based media

h. A set of instructions that tells a computer how to perform a process

i. Anxiety experienced when individuals are presented with more information than they can handle

j. High-speed temporary memory that holds programs and data in use

k. A social network site designed for short messages that do not exceed 140 characters

l. The collection of programs that provides the infrastructure for other programs to function properly

m. A portable, lightweight computer equipped with wireless technology and used primarily to browse the Web and access e-mail

n. A collection of programs that together perform a task for the user

o. The matching of computer components to fit an individual's posture and body design

Multiple Choice

Circle the correct choice for each of the following:

1. Which of the following is *not* an output device?
   a. Monitor
   b. Printer
   c. Disk drive
   d. Speaker

2. Which of the following is *not* an example of a social network?
   a. Twitter
   b. Google Docs
   c. Facebook
   d. MySpace

3. What part of the system unit processes the input data?
   a. Read-alone memory
   b. CPU
   c. Random access memory
   d. NIC

4. What component of a computer is *not* located in the system unit?
   a. RAM
   b. Flash drive
   c. CPU
   d. Hard drive

5. Which is an example of an e-book reader?
   a. Wiki
   b. NIC
   c. Tweet
   d. Kindle DX

6. What is the replacement of human workers by machines and computer-guided robots called?
   a. Outsourcing
   b. Automation
   c. Digital piracy
   d. Structural unemployment

7. What is the name of the board within the system unit that connects the CPU and other system components?
   a. Motherboard
   b. Processing board
   c. NIC board
   d. Information board

8. Which of the following computers is designed for portability or use while traveling?
   a. All-in-one
   b. Notebook
   c. Desktop
   d. Workstation

9. What is the name of the software group that contains the operating system and antivirus programs?
   a. Application software   b. Word processing
   c. System Software   d. Utility software

10. What is the name given to unemployment caused by technology making an entire job category obsolete?
   a. Technological unemployment
   b. Corporate unemployment
   c. Structural unemployment
   d. Automated unemployment

Fill-In

In the blanks provided, write the correct answer for each of the following:

1. The mouse and keyboard are _____ devices.

2. Another name for random access memory is _____ memory.

3. Hard drives, DVD drives, and USB drives are examples of _____ devices.

4. Obsolete computer equipment is called _____.

5. The _____ feature of the Kindle 2 made it a device that truly helped the visually impaired.

6. _____ is another term for the disposing of obsolete computer equipment.

7. The _____ describes the disparity between groups who own computers and have Internet access and those who do not.

8. Raw facts that are input into a computer system are referred to as _____.

9. _____ is the high-speed movement of data or information within and between computers.

10. _____ is a free Web-based word processor and spreadsheet that encourages collaboration by allowing group members to share and edit documents online.

11. A _____ is an ultrafast computer that focuses on performing a few sets of instructions as fast as possible.

12. One quadrillion calculations is referred to as a _____.

13. _____ is the sending of portions of a job to a third party to reduce cost, time, and energy.

14. The purpose of the central processor is to convert data into _____.

15. The use of computers and computer programs to replace teachers and time-specific learning is _____.

Short Answer

1. Explain the difference between hardware and software.

2. List three features found on a new smartphone that did not exist on a phone five years ago.

3. According to the studies, what are three variables that influence whether an individual will or will not have Internet access?

4. Define the terms *data* and *information*. Identify the step in the information processing cycle that each is associated with.

5. List two current operating systems and two examples of application software.

6. List three advantages and three disadvantages of computer use.

7. List three changes you can make to your computing environment to reduce stress and make it more ergonomically friendly.

Teamwork

1. **Information Overload** Excessive amounts of e-mails, text messages, phone calls, and tweets can cause stress, headaches, irritability, and a generalized feeling of being overwhelmed. As a team, come up with at least five ways to control information, put it on hold, or filter out the undesired content. Present your resulting list to the class, using a slide show.

2. **"I am a Mac, and I am a PC"** As a team, use a search engine to locate and review at least three of the "I am a Mac, and I am a PC" commercials. These are 30-second commercials that praise the features of the Mac while mocking the PC. Cite the commercials viewed. Create a new 30-second commercial that will reverse the ad: Have the commercial support the PC while mocking the Mac. Your team will have to research both systems to find a PC asset that the Mac lacks. Rehearse your commercial and present it to the class.

3. **Netbook or iPad—You Decide** As a team, determine whether you would purchase a netbook or an iPad. Use the Internet or contact a local vendor and compare the prices for similarly equipped units. Based on your needs and finances, prepare a report to present to the class explaining which device you would buy and give reasons that support your decision.

4. **Ergonomics** As a team, use a search engine and locate at least three Web sites that contain information about the ergonomics of setting up computer stations.

Prepare a report that covers the following items. First, define the term *ergonomics,* and then list at least five items that should be ergonomically designed in a computer station for the user's health and comfort. For at least three of these five items, find two retailers that sell such ergonomic products. Describe the products, explain how they will ergonomically correct or prevent a problem, and note how much the devices cost. Be sure to cite your resources.

5. **Social Networks** As a team create a survey of at least 10 questions on social networking. Your questions should try to find out the social networking site to which each respondent belongs, the number of times in a week the individual visits that site, and the number of friends or followers the individual has for starters. Additionally, the age and gender of the individual might give you some more insight into trends. Give the survey to 30 people from a variety of backgrounds. Regroup and, using a spreadsheet, summarize your survey data, citing any trends that your collected data exposed.

On the Web

1. **Green Computers** Go to **www.worldchanging. com/archives/004350.html** and use Google (**www. google.com**) or another search engine to locate sources of information about green computers. List at least three green computer features and their components. Then use the Internet to locate three manufacturers of green computers. State the name of each computer, its price, and the green features that each system possesses. Present this information in a one- or two-page, double-spaced report. Be sure to cite your references.

2. **Trends in Education** Using either your school or another in your community, collect information from the online course catalog on the number of classes that are traditional or seated classes, how many are hybrids (a combination of seated and online meetings), and how many are purely online. Interview a few students and ask about the type of classes they have taken and their opinion of the three different class structures. Then interview several instructors and get their opinions. Collect all of your course data, state the percentage of courses that fall into each category, and summarize your student and instructor replies. Present your results in a slide presentation.

3. **Input Hardware Trends** Use your favorite search engine to locate information on the Luxeed dynamic Pixel LED keyboard, virtual laser keyboards, and the new touch screen on the iPad. In a one–page, double-spaced paper summarize your findings. Include the

new or unusual features of each device, a summary of any online reviews that you could locate, and your opinion of each input device.

4. **Ethics** Use your favorite search engine and locate the "Ten Commandments of Computer Ethics" published by the Computer Ethics Institute. Read each one, and in a one-page paper indicate at least three commandments with which you agree and three with which you disagree. Give logical and historical reasons for your statement. You might want to reference the Bill of Rights or other historical documents to support your stance. Cite your references and present your reasons in a one- or two-page, double-spaced paper.

5. **Employment** Use your favorite search engine to locate computer-related jobs in your area. Make a list of the positions, the type of required computer skill required, and, if possible, the level of education needed for the position and the salary range. Using a word processor, make a table of your results. Determine whether there is an employment trend in your region. Do you or any of you family members qualify for any of the jobs located? Does your school offer the courses or degrees to meet the demands of your local job market? Submit your table and summary comments in a one-page, double-spaced word processed report.

Spotlight

Ethics

What's the difference between ethical and unethical behavior? Is it possible for an action to be unethical but still legal? You might not realize it, but in some way you probably face this question daily, especially when you use computers and, more specifically, the Internet. Have you downloaded any music recently, ripped any CDs lately, or copied music from a friend? Did you pay for that music? Have you watched a DVD movie or played a video game this weekend? Was the DVD or game a legally purchased copy? Perhaps you've posted a nasty comment about someone on a discussion board or sent an anonymous nasty e-mail that caused someone undo stress. These are some of the behaviors at school, home, or on the job to consider in the scope of ethical behavior.

Ethics is often described as knowing the difference between right and wrong, based on approved standards of social and professional behavior, and choosing to do what is right. In other words, we *choose* to behave in an ethical way so we can live with our conscience. Ethics is not about whether we'll get caught but more about our ability to live with the decision we make.

This spotlight examines some of the most common issues in computer ethics, including ethical dilemmas, in which the difference between right and wrong is not so easy to discern. We look at ethical principles that can serve as guides for making decisions that might be difficult or in an unfamiliar area. Additionally, we consider the significance of a code of conduct. Ethical standards are provided to act as guides for computer users, professionals, and organizations. Finally we look at unethical behavior that is also illegal.

Ethical choices are often personal and are made with great consideration and thought by the individual making the choice. Hopefully, some of the insights in this chapter will help serve as a basic steering guide or reference points to alleviate some of the uncertainty surrounding making ethical decisions even when they are difficult.

Computer Ethics for Computer Users

It isn't always easy to determine the right thing to do. Even when you know what's right, it isn't always easy to act on it. Peer pressure is a tremendous force. Why should you be the one to do the right thing when you believe everyone else is getting away with using copied software and music files?

Computers cause new ethical dilemmas by pushing people into making decisions in unprecedented situations (Figure 1A). **Computer ethics** is the use of basic ethical principles to help you make the right decisions in your daily computer use. Ethical principles help you think through your options.

FIGURE 1A Computers present new ethical dilemmas where individuals must choose among paths they are unfamiliar with.

ETHICAL PRINCIPLES

An **ethical principle** defines the standards that promote trust, fairness, good behavior, and kindness. These principles are used as justification for considering an act or a rule to be morally right or wrong. Over the centuries, philosophers have come up with many ethical principles. For many people, it's disconcerting to find that these principles sometimes conflict. An ethical principle is only a tool that you can use to think through a difficult situation. In the end, you must make your choice and live with the consequences.

The Belmont Report from the U.S. Department of Health, Education, and Welfare shows three of the most useful ethical principles:

- *An act is ethical if, were everyone to act the same way, society as a whole would benefit.*

- *An act is ethical if it treats people as an end in themselves rather than as a means to an end.*

- *An act is ethical if impartial observers would judge that it is fair to all parties concerned.*

If you still find yourself in an ethical dilemma related to computer use even after careful consideration of these ethical principles, talk to people you trust. They might be able to provide insight into the dilemma that you face, pointing out factors that you might have not considered, helping you to make the correct ethical decision. Make sure you have all the facts. Think through alternative courses of action based on the different principles. Would you be proud if your parents knew what you had done? What if your actions were mentioned in an article on the front page of your local newspaper? Can you live with your conscience? Remember, always strive to find a solution you can be proud of and live with.

FOLLOWING YOUR SCHOOL'S CODE OF CONDUCT

When you use a computer, one of the things you will have to determine is who owns the data, programs, and Internet access you enjoy. If you own your computer system and its software, the work you create is clearly yours, and you are solely responsible for it. However, when you use a computer at school or at work, it is possible that the work you create there might be considered the property of the school or business. In short, you have greater responsibility and less control over content ownership when you use somebody else's system than when you use your own.

Sometimes this question isn't just an ethical one but a legal one as well. How companies and schools enforce computer usage rules tends to vary. So where can you, the college computer user, find guidance when dealing with ethical and legal dilemmas? Your college or place of employment probably has its own code of conduct or **acceptable use policy** for computer users. You can usually find this policy on your organization's Web site (Figure 1B), in a college or employee handbook, or included in an employment contract that you have been asked to sign. You might call the help desk at your computing center and ask for the Web site address of the policy or request a physical copy of it. Read the policy carefully and follow the rules.

Common to most acceptable-use policies are such guidelines as these:

- **Respect yourself.** If you obtain an account and password to use the campus computer system, don't give your password to others. They could do something that gets you in trouble. In addition, don't say or do anything on the Internet that could reflect

Information Technology Policies

University at Buffalo The State University of New York

Computer and Network Use Policy
(Updated 3.26.2007)

I. Introduction

Access to modern information technology is essential to the state university mission of providing the students, faculty and staff of the State University of New York with educational services of the highest quality. The pursuit and achievement of the SUNY mission of education, research, and public service require that the privilege of the use of computing systems and software, internal and external data networks, as well as access to the World Wide Web, be made available to all members of the SUNY community. The preservation of that privilege for the full community requires that each faculty member, staff member, student, and other authorized user comply with institutional and external standards for appropriate use.

To assist and ensure such compliance, the University at Buffalo establishes the following policy, which supplements all applicable SUNY policies, including sexual harassment, patent and copyright, and student and employee disciplinary policies, as well as applicable federal and state laws.

II. General Principles

1. Authorized use of computing and network resources owned or operated by the University at Buffalo shall be consistent with the education, research and public service mission of the State University of New York, and consistent with this policy.
2. Authorized users of University at Buffalo computing and network resources include faculty, staff, students, and other affiliated individuals or organizations authorized by the Provost or his designee. Use by non-affiliated institutions and organizations shall be in accordance with SUNY Administrative Procedures: Use of Computer Equipment or Services by Non-affiliated Institutions and Organizations.
3. This policy applies to all University at Buffalo computing and network resources, including host computer systems, University at Buffalo-sponsored computers and workstations, software, data sets, and communications networks controlled, administered, or accessed directly or indirectly by University at Buffalo computer resources or services, employees, or students.

Related Links

» Digital Millenium Copyright Act (DMCA)

» DMCA Summary

» ACEI Background Discussion of Copyright Law and Potential Liability for Students Engaging in P2P File Sharing on University Networks

FIGURE 1B Many organizations and schools publish their computer and network use (or acceptable use) policy on their Web site.

poorly on you, even if you think no one will ever find out. Internet content has a way of resurfacing.

- **Respect others.** Obviously, you shouldn't use a computer to threaten or harass anyone. You should also avoid using more than your share of computing resources, such as disk space. If you publish a Web page on your college's computers, remember that your page's content affects the college's public image.

- **Respect academic integrity.** Always give credit for text you've copied from the Internet. Obtain permission before you copy pictures. Don't copy or distribute software unless the license specifically states you have permission to do so.

Classroom computer etiquette is increasingly becoming an academic issue. Within their course syllabi, instructors are providing clear guidelines for the use of computers and portable devices, such as cell phones, in a classroom. Such statements may look like the excerpt below and even tie improper use to a grade reduction.

Appropriate Classroom Laptop Use . . . Although having a laptop [or other portable device] in class opens up new learning possibilities for students, sometimes students utilize it in ways that are inappropriate. Please refrain from instant messaging, e-mailing, surfing the Internet, playing games, writing papers, doing homework, etc., during class time. Acceptable uses include taking notes, following along with the instructor on PowerPoint, with demonstrations, and other whole-class activities, as well as working on assigned in-class activities, projects, and discussions that require laptop use. It is easy for your laptop

[or portable device] to become a distraction to you and to those around you. Inappropriate uses will be noted and may affect your final grade.

TEN COMMANDMENTS FOR COMPUTER ETHICS

The Computer Ethics Institute of the Brookings Institution, located in Washington, DC, has developed the following "Ten Commandments for Computer Ethics" for computer users, programmers, and system designers. Many businesses, academic institutions, and organizations post or refer to these principles:

1. Thou shalt not use a computer to harm other people.
2. Thou shalt not interfere with other people's computer work.
3. Thou shalt not snoop around in other people's computer files.
4. Thou shalt not use a computer to steal.
5. Thou shalt not use a computer to bear false witness.
6. Thou shalt not copy or use proprietary software for which you have not paid.
7. Thou shalt not use other people's computer resources without authorization or proper compensation.
8. Thou shalt not appropriate other people's intellectual output.
9. Thou shalt think about the social consequences of the program you are writing or the system you are designing.
10. Thou shalt always use a computer in ways that ensure consideration and respect for your fellow humans.

NETIQUETTE

General principles such as the "Ten Commandments for Computer Ethics" are useful for overall guidance, but they don't provide specific help for the special situations you'll run into online—such as how to behave properly in chat rooms or while playing an online game (Figure 1C). As a result, computer and Internet users have developed a lengthy series of specific behavior guidelines called **netiquette** for the various Internet services available

FIGURE 1C Netiquette refers to guidelines for behaving properly in online interactions.

SPOTLIGHT 1

(such as e-mail, mailing lists, social networking sites, discussion forums, and online role-playing games) that provide specific pointers on how to show respect for others—and for yourself—while you're online. A document posted by the Responsible Use of the Network Working Group (RUN) of the Internet Engineering Task Force at **www.dtcc.edu/cs/rfc1855.html** provides detailed netiquette guides for online activities that effect one-to-one and one-to-many communications.

A consolidation of rules from the site above and **www.albion.com/netiquette** as well as other Internet sources are categorized and summarized below.

- **Discussion forums.** Before posting to a discussion forum, review the forum and various topics to see what kinds of questions are welcomed and how to participate meaningfully. If the forum has a FAQ (frequently asked questions) document posted on the Web, be sure to read it before posting to the forum; your question may already have been answered in the FAQ. Post your message under the appropriate topic or start a new topic if necessary. Your post should be helpful or ask a legitimate question. Bear in mind that some people using the discussion forum may not speak English as their native language, so don't belittle people for spelling errors. Don't post inflammatory messages; never post in anger. If you agree with something, don't post a message that says "Me too"—you're just wasting everyone's time. Posting ads for your own business or soliciting answers to obvious homework questions is usually frowned on.

- **E-mail.** Check your e-mail daily and respond promptly to the messages you've been sent. Download or delete messages after you've read them so that you don't exceed your disk-usage quota. Remember that e-mail isn't private; you should never send a message that contains anything you wouldn't want others to read. Always speak of others professionally and courteously; e-mail is easily forwarded, and the person you're describing may eventually see the message. Check your computer frequently for viruses that can propagate via e-mail messages. Keep your messages short and to the point; focus on one subject per message. Don't type in all capital letters; this comes across as SHOUTING. Spell check your e-mail as you would any other written correspondence, especially in professional settings. Watch out for sarcasm and humor in e-mail; it often fails to come across as a joke. Requesting a return receipt may be an acceptable academic policy to verify the submission of an assignment, but in some situations it might be considered an invasion of privacy.

- **Instant messages (IM) and text messages.** IM and text messages are ideal for brief conversa-

tions; but complex or lengthy discussions may be better handled in person, by e-mail, or by phone. IM can be easily misinterpreted because tone is difficult to convey. Never share bad news or a major announcement in a text message or send an IM while you are angry or upset. Don't assume that everyone knows what IM acronyms such as BRB (be right back) and LOL (laughing out loud) mean. Be mindful that some smartphone plans still charge for text messages. Also, remember to set away messages and use other status messages wisely.

- **Chat rooms.** Only visit chat rooms that are appropriate for your age and follow the rules and regulations of the chat. If you are unsure of the protocols, contact the administrator or host of the chat room. Say hello when you enter the room, and take some time to review the conversation currently taking place before jumping in. Avoid entering personal information, and respect other chatters. Foul language may get you expelled or permanently banned from the room. Some rooms allow you to put a chatter on ignore status if you are being bothered by that person. This type of behavior should be immediately reported to the administrator or chat room host.

"*Remember that e-mail isn't private; you should never send a message that contains anything you wouldn't want others to read*"

Netiquette is important in the classroom. According to an article published in *The Journal of Higher Education*, several colleges have offered guidelines and suggestions for curbing misuse of computers in class and have set netiquette standards, like turning off the computer's volume before class begins.

In addition to respectful use of Internet services, playing computer games is another area in which you might face ethical dilemmas.

COMPUTER GAMES: TOO MUCH VIOLENCE?

Computer gaming isn't universally admired, but statistics support that it is universally on the increase. Sixty-five percent of households in the United States have at least one member who plays video games. Seventeen billion hours have been logged on Xbox Live by some 20 million players; this is roughly two hours for every person on the planet. To further support this growth, recent statistics estimate online gaming revenue at $15 billion. How is this related to ethics? Approximately 94 percent of the video games fall into the fantasy category and include such titles as *Halo*, *World of Warcraft*, and *Call of Duty: Modern Warfare*. These games emphasize strategy development and team play, but they also emphasize violent behaviors. Parents and politicians are concerned that children who play these games may be learning aggressive behaviors that will prove dysfunctional in real life.

Fears concerning the impact of violent computer games were heightened by the Columbine High School tragedy in 1999, in which two Littleton, Colorado, teenagers opened fire on teachers and fellow students before committing suicide. Subsequently, investigators learned that the boys had been great fans of splatter games such as *Doom* and *Quake* and may have patterned their massacre after their gaming experiences. In 2009, there was a school shooting in Germany that left 15 dead. A neighbor and childhood friend of the shooter was quoted as saying, "He [the shooter] was fascinated by video games; he used to play a shooting game called *Tactical Ops* and he used to watch horror films like *Alien* and *Predator*."

Still, psychologists disagree on the effect of violent computer games. Some point out that they're little more than an extension of the World War II "combat" games children used to play on street corners before television—and the computer—came along. Others claim that violent video games provide an outlet for aggression that might otherwise materialize in homes and schools.

One thing is for certain: Computer games are becoming more violent. In the past few years, the video game industry has released a slew of new titles that offer a more streamlined gaming experience, particularly when a player is connected to the Internet in multiplayer mode—and of course, much more realistic portrayals of violent acts (Figure 1D).

So who is responsible? Is it the software manufacturers who create the programs? Is it the consumers who purchase and use the programs? More importantly, is there anything you can do about it? Refer back to the "Ten Commandments for Computer Ethics," especially numbers 9 and 10. Think about the personality of the person you are purchasing a game for or inviting to play a game. If the content of the game seems to be inappropriate, select a different game or activity. With regard to minors, parents certainly have a responsibility over what their children do, but what about you—do you make "good" decisions when it comes to your own exposure to violence?

Now that you know about the ethical issues individuals face, let's take a look at how organizations deal with computer ethics.

Computer Ethics for Organizations

Every day, newspapers carry stories about people getting into trouble by using their computers to conduct personal business while they're at work. In many cases, the offenders use company computers to browse the Web, make personal travel plans, send personal e-mail on company time, or to commit crimes such as cyberstalking or distributing pornography. The use of a company computer for non-business-related tasks is generally prohibited. Such policies are typically included in the company's acceptable use policy.

However, those are rules set by the company to control individuals' behavior while at work. What ethical responsibilities do the companies themselves have to their employees, customers, and the general public? A business or organization needs to protect its data from loss, damage, error, and misuse. Each business entity needs to have business continuity and disaster recovery plans in place to prevent and respond to security breaches or other malfunctions that occur.

Protecting data from loss or change is often simply a matter of following proper backup procedures. **Backup procedures** involve making copies of data files to protect against data loss, change, or damage from natural or other disasters. Without backup procedures, an organization may place its customers' information at risk. Moreover, it is unethical not to keep regular backups, because the loss of the company's data could negatively impact the stakeholders in the business (Figure 1E). What would happen to a bank, for example, if it lost all of its data and didn't have any backups? As our dependency on information increases, our tolerance for lost data is decreasing. It is this dependency that

FIGURE 1D Some computer games are both engrossing and violent.

has led to the use of **continuous backups**, programs that automatically create a backup when a change in a system or a data file occurs.

Data errors can and do occur. It is the ethical responsibility of any organization that deals with data to ensure that its data is as correct as possible. Data that hasn't been properly maintained can have serious effects on the individual or associated organization.

Data misuse occurs when an employee or company fails to keep data confidential. A breach of confidentiality occurs when an employee looks up data about a person in a database and uses that information for something other than what was intended. For example, U.S. government workers accessed the passport files for 2008 presidential candidates John McCain, Barack Obama, and Hillary Clinton, in addition to more than 100 celebrities. Such actions are grounds for termination.

Companies may punish employees for looking up customer data, but many of them think nothing of

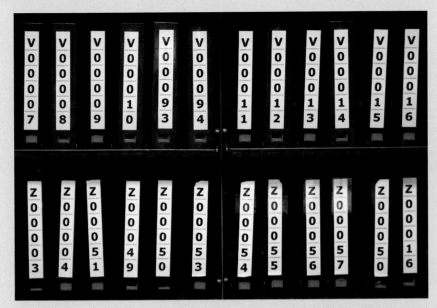

FIGURE 1E A backup system can help protect a business's information assets and enable the business to continue to operate as usual. A computer tape library is one way to store backed-up files.

considered the most innovative and far reaching. According to the ACM general moral imperatives, a computing professional

1. Contributes to society and human well-being
2. Avoids harm to others
3. Is honest and trustworthy
4. Is fair and takes action not to discriminate on the basis of race, sex, religion, age, disability, or national origin
5. Honors property rights, including copyrights and patents
6. Gives proper credit when using the intellectual property of others
7. Respects the right of other individuals to privacy
8. Honors confidentiality.

Like other codes of conduct, the ACM code places public safety and well-being at the top of the list.

CODE OF CONDUCT FOR THE INSTITUTE FOR CERTIFICATION OF COMPUTING PROFESSIONALS

Other organizations also have codes of conduct or define elements of good practice for professionals. The Institute for Certification of Computing Professionals is one such organization. It prides itself on the establishment of professional standards for those who work with computers. According to the organization, the essential elements related to conduct that identify a professional activity are as follows:

- A high standard of skill and knowledge
- A confidential relationship with people served
- Public reliance upon the standards of conduct and established practice
- The observance of an ethical code

SAFETY FIRST

Computer professionals create products that affect many people and may even expose them to risk of personal injury or death. Increasingly, computers and computer programs figure prominently in safety-critical systems, including transportation monitoring (such as with air traffic control) and patient monitoring in hospitals (Figure 1F).

Consider the following situation. An airplane pilot flying in poor visibility uses a computer, called an autopilot, to guide the plane. The air traffic control system also relies on computers. The plane crashes. The investigation discloses minor bugs in both computer programs. If the plane's computer had been dealing with a person in the tower rather than a computer or if the air

selling it to third parties. A mail-order company, for example, can gain needed revenue by selling customer lists to firms marketing related products. Privacy advocates believe that it's unethical to divulge customer data without first asking the customer's permission. These advocates are working to pass tougher privacy laws so the matter would become a legal concern, not an ethical one.

As an employee, what can you do to stop companies from misusing data or to protect your customers' privacy? Often, there's no clear-cut solution. If you believe that the way a company is conducting business poses a danger to the public or appears to be illegal, you can report the company to regulatory agencies or the press, an action called whistle-blowing. But what if your whistle-blowing causes your company to shut down, putting not only you but also all of your coworkers out of work? As this example illustrates, codes of ethics don't solve every ethical problem, and innocent individuals may suffer as a result of an ethical action; however, ethical principles at least provide solid guidance for most situations.

Computer Ethics for Computer Professionals

No profession can stay in business for long without a rigorous (and enforced) code of professional ethics. That's why many different types of professionals subscribe to ethical **codes of conduct**. These codes are developed by professional associations, such as the Association for Computing Machinery (ACM).

THE ACM CODE OF CONDUCT

Of all the computing associations' codes of conduct, the one developed by the ACM (**www.acm.org**) is

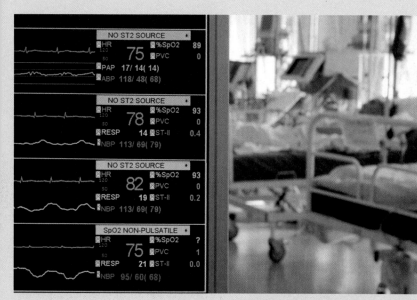

NO ST2 SOURCE	
HR 120 50	%SpO2 89
75	PVC 0
PAP 17/ 14(14)	
ABP 118/ 48(68)	

NO ST2 SOURCE	
HR 120 50	%SpO2 93
78	PVC 0
RESP 14	ST-II 0.4
NBP 113/ 69(79)	

NO ST2 SOURCE	
HR 120 50	%SpO2 93
82	PVC 0
RESP 19	ST-II 0.2
NBP 113/ 69(79)	

SpO2 NON-PULSATILE	
HR 120 50	%SpO2 ?
75	PVC 1
RESP 21	ST-II 0.0
NBP 95/ 60(68)	

FIGURE 1F Patient monitoring in hospitals helps to create a safer environment, with audio warnings and information automatically transmitted to a central, monitoring station.

traffic control program had been interacting with a human pilot, the crash would not have occurred. Where does the liability lie for the loss of life and property?

Experienced programmers know that programs of any size have bugs. Most complex programs have so many possible combinations of conditions that it isn't feasible to test for every combination. In some cases, the tests would take years; in other cases, no one could think of all the possible conditions. Because bugs are inevitable and programmers can't predict all the different ways programs interact with their environment, most computer experts believe that it's wrong to single out programmers for blame.

Software companies are at fault if they fail to test and document their products. In addition, the organization that buys the software may share part of the blame if it fails to train personnel to use the system properly.

At the center of every computer code of ethics is the underlying intention of computer professionals to develop, maintain, upgrade, and evaluate programs and devices to preserve and protect human life and to avoid harm or injury. If the public is to trust computer professionals, those professionals must have the ethics needed to protect our safety and welfare—even if doing so means that the professional or the company he or she works for suffers financially.

Unlike the ethical dilemmas we've discussed up to now, right and wrong are more easily defined when it comes to matters of the law.

It's Not Just Unethical, It's Illegal Too

Some unethical actions are also illegal and have serious consequences. Let's start with something that gets many college students into serious trouble: plagiarism.

PLAGIARISM

Imagine the following scenario. It's 4 AM, and you have a paper due for your 9 AM class. While searching for sources on the Internet, you find a Web site with an essay on your topic. What's wrong with downloading the text, reworking it a bit, and handing it in? Plenty.

The use of someone else's intellectual property (their ideas or written work) is called **plagiarism**. Plagiarism predates computers; in fact, it has been practiced for thousands of years. But, computers—and especially the Internet—make the temptation and ease of plagiarizing even greater. It's not only very easy to copy and paste from the Internet but some sites are actually set up specifically to sell college-level papers to the lazy or desperate. The sites selling the papers aren't guilty of plagiarism, but you are if you turn in the work as your own.

Plagiarism is a serious offense. How serious? At some colleges, even a first offense can get you thrown out of school. You might think it's rare for plagiarizers to be caught, but the truth is that college instructors are often able to detect plagiarism in students' papers without much effort. The tip-off can be a change in the sophistication of phraseology, writing that is a little too polished, or errors in spelling and grammar that are identical in two or more papers. Software programs such as Turnitin are available that can scan text and then compare it against a library of known phrases (Figure 1G). If a paper has one or more recognizable phrases, it is marked for closer inspection. Furthermore, even if your actions are not discovered now, someone could find out later, and the evidence could void your degree and even damage your career.

The more well-known you are, the more you're at risk of your plagiarism being uncovered. Take noted historian and Pulitzer Prize–winning author Doris Kearns Goodwin, for example. In 2002, she was accused of plagiarizing part of her best-selling 1987 book, *The Fitzgeralds and the Kennedys*. Although she claimed her plagiarizing was inadvertent and due to inadequate research methods, she suffered a significant decline in credibility and even felt obligated to leave her position at the PBS news program *NewsHour with Jim Lehrer*. It took 15 years for Goodwin's plagiarism to come to light.

Plagiarism is both unethical and illegal: The unethical part is the dishonesty of passing someone else's work off as your own. The illegal part is taking the material without permission. Plagiarizing copyrighted material is called **copyright infringement**, and you can be sued and may have to pay damages in addition to compensating your victim for any financial losses due to your theft of the material. Trademarks, products, and patented processes are also protected. If you're tempted to copy anything from the Web, bear

FIGURE 1G Turnitin is one of the popular software packages used by professors at colleges and universities to identify instances of plagiarism.

in mind that the United States is a signatory to international copyright regulations, which specify that an original author does not need to include an explicit copyright notice to be protected under the law.

Does this mean you can't use the Internet source you found? No, you can use or refer to your source, but you must follow certain citation guidelines. In academic writing, you can make use of someone else's effort if you use your own words and give credit where credit is due. If you use a phrase or a few sentences from the source, use quotation marks. Attach a bibliography and list the source. For Internet sources, you should list the Web site's address (or Uniform Resource Locator [URL]), the date the article was published (if available), the date and time you accessed the site, the name of the article, and the author's name. You can usually find a link at the bottom of a Web site's home page that outlines the owner's copyright policy. If not, there is usually a "contact us" link that you can use to contact the owner. You cannot assume that it is legal to copy content from a Web site just because you cannot find a disclaimer. Starting with Microsoft Office 2007, adding citations to a research paper became even easier. One of the features of the software is a tool to help you organize and input the correct reference information in a variety of different referencing styles.

You'll often hear people use the term **fair use** to justify illegal copying. The fair use doctrine justifies *limited* uses of copyrighted material without payment to or permission from the copyright holder. This means that a *brief* selection from a copyrighted work may be excerpted for the purposes of commentary, parody, news reporting, research, and education. Such excerpts are short—generally, no more than 5 percent of the original work—and they shouldn't compromise the commercial value of the work. Of course, you must still cite the

source. In general, the reproduction of an entire work is rarely justifiable by means of the fair use doctrine.

As a responsible computer user, you should be concerned not only about wrongly using someone else's words but also about the correctness of the content you create yourself. The written word carries a lot of power. Publishing words that are untrue about a business or individual could be crossing into dangerous, and illegal, territory.

LIBEL

The power of computers, with their ease of uploading, publishing, and reaching a huge group of viewers in seconds, has also caused an increase in cases of libel. In the United States, **libel** is the publication, in written or faxed form, of a false statement that injures someone's business or personal reputation. A plaintiff who sues for libel must prove that a false statement caused injury and demonstrate some type of resulting damage. This could include being shunned by friends and associates or the inability to obtain work because potential employers believed the false accusations. Some states allow a jury to assess damages based generally on harm to the person's reputation. It is in your best interest to ensure that any electronic publication statement you make about an individual or a corporation is truthful.

SOFTWARE PIRACY

Here's another common situation. You need to have Microsoft Office 2007 for your computer class. A friend gives you a copy that she got from her mom's office. You've just installed that copy on your computer. Have you done something wrong? Yes, of course you have! In fact, so has your friend. It is illegal for her to have a copy of the software from her mom's office in the first place.

Just like written works, most computer software (including computer games) is copyrighted, which means that you can't make copies for other people without infringing on the software's copyright. Such infringements are called **software piracy** and are a federal offense in the United States (Figure 1H).

How serious is software piracy? The information technology industry loses billions of dollars a year because of piracy. If you're caught pirating software, you may be charged with a felony. If you're convicted of a felony, you could spend time in jail, lose the right to vote, and ruin your chances for a successful career.

When you purchase commercial software, you're really purchasing a **software license**, which generally grants you the right to make backups of the program disks and install the software. You need to read the license agreement to determine how many machines you can install the software on. You are not allowed to provide the program to others or modify the program's function. A blank sample of a software license can be

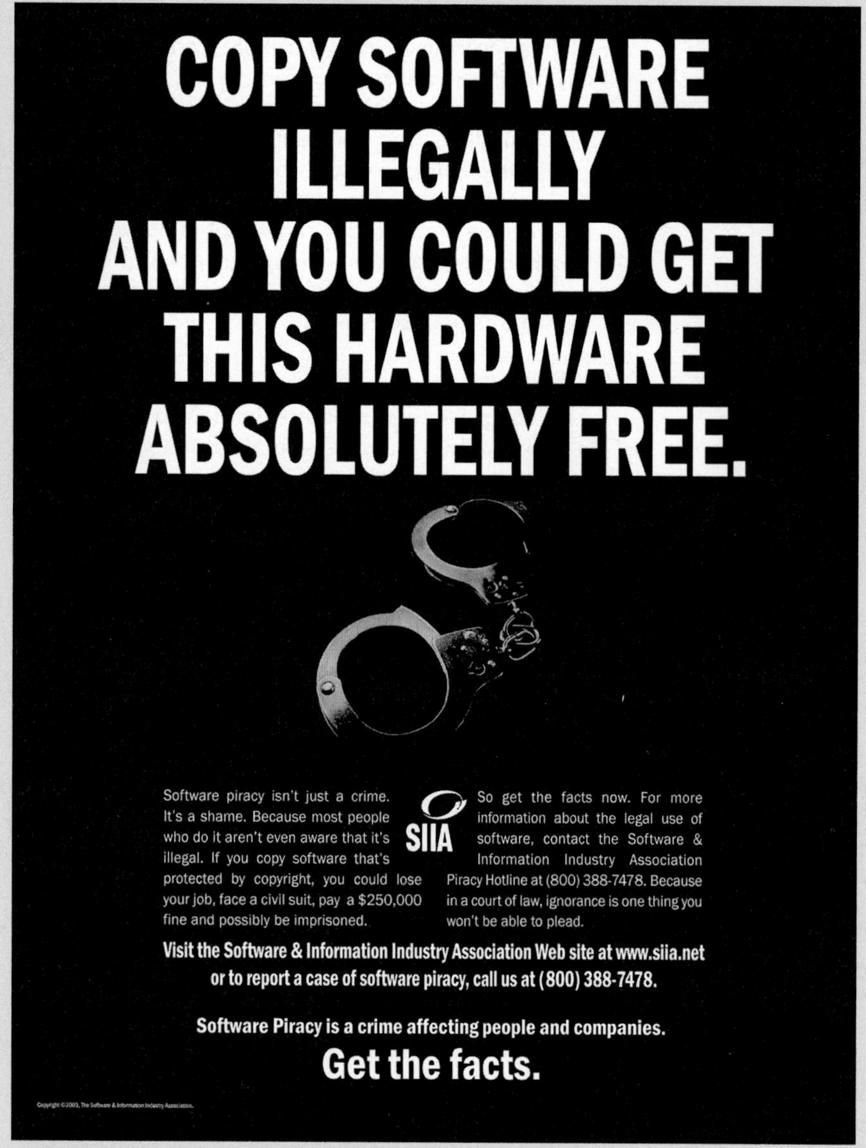

FIGURE 1H The Software & Information Industry Association (SIIA) is trying to raise consciousness about software piracy.

found at **www.lawsmart.com/documents/ software_license.shtml.** Note that this is a sample, and reading it is *not* a substitute for examining the software license for each program you purchase.

Free programs that users can copy or modify without restriction are called **public domain software**. However, don't assume that a program is public domain unless you see a note (often in the form of a Read Me text file) that explicitly identifies the file as being copyright free.

Unlike public domain software, you can't copy or modify **shareware** programs without permission from the owner. You can usually find the owner and licensing information by accessing the Help menu or by locating and reading a Read Me file that is usually placed in the same directory as the program. You may, however, freely copy trial or evaluation versions of shareware programs. When the evaluation period expires, you must pay a **registration fee** or delete the software from your computer.

Other programs qualify under the provisions of the Free Software Foundation's **General Public License (GPL)**, which specifies that anyone may freely copy, use, and modify the software, but no one can sell it for profit.

Organizations with many computers (including colleges) also have to be concerned about software piracy. A **site license** is a contract with the software publisher that allows an organization to use multiple copies of the software at a reduced price per unit. Taking copies outside the organization usually violates the contract. However, check the license agreement. Some organizations negotiate the agreement to allow employees to load the software on their home computers as well, as long as only one copy is in use at any one time and the programs are used for academic and noncommercial tasks.

Software manufacturers are working very hard to develop **copyright protection schemes** to thwart the illegal use of their programs. Increasingly, software is becoming **machine dependent**. This means that the program captures a machine ID during the installation process and writes that ID back to the software company's server during a mandatory online registration process. If you attempt to install the program on another machine, the code will be checked and the installation will terminate unless your license allows multiple installations. Microsoft checks your computer for a valid copy of its software before it will permit you to make updates, access templates, or download other add-ons.

How can you tell whether you're guilty of software piracy? All of the following actions are illegal:

- *Continuing to use a shareware program past the evaluation version's expiration date without paying the registration fee.*
- *Violating the terms of a software license, even if you've paid for the program. For example, if you have copies of the same program on your desktop and notebook computers but the license allows only one installation, you are in violation of the license.*
- *Making copies of site-licensed programs that you use at work or school and installing them on your home computer (unless expressly allowed through the license).*

- *Giving or selling copies of commercial software to others.*
- *Incorporating all or part of a GPL program in a commercial program that you offer for sale.*

Do you have pirated programs on your computer? The police aren't likely to storm into your home or dorm room and take you away kicking and screaming. Most software piracy prosecutions target individuals who are trying to distribute or sell infringing copies, or companies that have illegally made multiple copies for their employees. If you have any pirated software, you should remove those programs from your computer right away. In the future, consider whether your actions constitute software piracy before the software is installed on your computer. If you still don't see the need to delete pirated software from your computer, consider this: It's very, very wise to become accustomed to a zero-tolerance approach to pirated software. If you're caught with an infringing program at work, you could lose your job. A company can't risk retaining employees who expose the firm to prosecution. There are software auditing applications that a school or company can purchase to monitor software usage.

Some software sold on auction sites and installed on systems created by build-it-yourself computer vendors may be unlicensed (and therefore illegal) software. Ask for the product registration key and the original CDs or DVDs for any products purchased online or pre-installed on a system. A **product registration key** is a unique alphanumeric code specific to that particular copy of the program. It is necessary to enter this key after installation in order to validate its authenticity and activate the program. The key may be necessary later to download upgrades, patches, or templates.

The Business Software Alliance (BSA) helps combat software piracy by educating the public and businesses about the legal and safety issues regarding commercial software use. You can even fill out a confidential form on their Web site at **https://reporting.bsa.org/usa** to report incidences of piracy. By doing so, you could be eligible for a $1 million reward.

FILE SHARING: MUSIC, MOVIES, AND MORE

You may have heard that it's okay to download a copyrighted MP3 file as long as you keep it for no longer than 24 hours, but that's false. If you upload music copied from a CD you've paid for, you are violating the law. You can't justify spreading a band's copyrighted music around by saying it's "free advertising;" if the group wants advertising, they'll arrange it themselves (Figure 1I). Moreover, don't fall into the trap of thinking that sharing MP3s is legal as long as you don't charge any money for them. Anytime you're taking royalties away from copyright holders, it's illegal.

Several years ago eschoolnews.com reported that more than 400 students were slated to be

sued for allegedly using Internet2, a network of academic, business, government, and not-for-profit organizations, for music and movie piracy. The situation has not improved significantly. A 2008 survey found that the average digital music player contains 842 illegally copied songs. Although many people seem to believe that illegal file sharing is okay because so many others are doing it, the entertainment industry is fighting back. Ohio State University recently led the nation in music piracy—its students received more than 2,300 warning letters about pirated music in just one school year. A report by the Institution for Policy Innovation (IPI) indicates that not only is the copyright holder of the pirated digital product injured, but so are all citizens and taxpayers. As a result of global and U.S. piracy, the report states:

- The U.S. economy losses $12.5 billion annually.
- Approximately 71,000 jobs are lost in the United States in both the recording industry and related fields.
- U.S. workers lose $2.7 billion in annual earnings.
- U.S. federal, state, and local governments lose $422 million in annual tax revenue.

More recently, a 2009 report estimated 9 million pirated e-book copies were downloaded, representing nearly $3 billion in lost revenue. However, in April 2010, the U.S. Government Accountability Office issued a report on the economic effects of counterfeit and pirated goods. This statement concluded that after reviewing data from both government and outside sources, it was "difficult, if not impossible, to quantify economy-wide impacts." The reason for this statement is cited as being the inability to accurately detect and account for pirated activity due to the illegal and undetectable nature of piracy itself, and that prior statistics assumed that the obtaining of a pirated copy implied

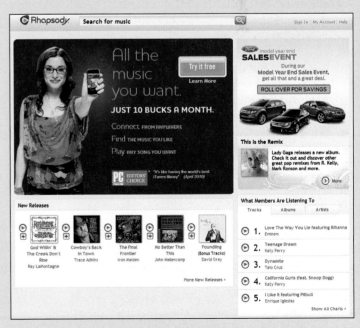

FIGURE 1I Sites such as Rhapsody offer fans the opportunity to play music, not download it, by connecting to their Web site for a price of $10 a month.

the loss of sale of a legitimate copy, again an assumption that is unsubstantiated. Statistics can always be argued and slanted to support one's favored opinion. However, any illegal or counterfeit copy of any product is a source of lost income in any economy. The size of the loss can be debated—but not the loss itself.

Students can face fines or even jail time for copyright infringement, but schools may also be penalized. Some colleges are taking steps to reduce their liability, such as limiting bandwidth and providing students with free, legal download service.

Key Terms and Concepts

Multiple Choice

1. Which action is *not* behavior that illustrates academic integrity?
   a. Citing the reference to a source of information that you copied from the Internet or a printed source
   b. Sharing licensed software without permission
   c. Obtaining permission before using an image obtained from the Internet or other source
   d. Using only your allotted share of computer resources

2. In which Internet interaction should the participant check the frequently asked questions document (FAQ) prior to posting his or her own question?
   a. E-mail
   b. Chat room
   c. Discussion forum
   d. Instant messaging

3. _____ is/are basic ethical principles or guidelines that can be used to help you make the right decisions in your daily computer use.
   a. Computer ethics
   b. Netiquette
   c. Code of conduct
   d. Acceptable use policy

4. What term refers to the act of using someone else's intellectual property as if it were your own?
   a. Acceptable use policy
   b. Piracy
   c. Libel
   d. Plagiarism

5. What defines the standards that promote trust, fairness, good behavior, and kindness, and is used as justification for considering an act or a rule to be morally right or wrong?
   a. Code of conduct
   b. Acceptable use policy
   c. Netiquette
   d. Ethical principle

6. Which is a true statement about ethics?
   a. Ethics is concerned about getting caught.
   b. Some unethical actions are legal.
   c. Ethical actions are evaluated by the consequences they produce, not their innate value of right or wrong.
   d. Peer pressure is not a factor in ethical behavior.

7. What is the term for publishing of a false statement that injures someone's business or personal reputation?
   a. Piracy
   b. Libel
   c. Plagiarism
   d. Whistle-blowing

8. Which action is considered illegal?
   a. Uploading music from a CD that you paid for
   b. Downloading a copyrighted MP3 file and listening to it for only 24 hours, then deleting it
   c. Sharing MP3s with others as long as you do not charge a fee for the music
   d. All of the above

9. What is the lengthy series of specific behavior guidelines developed for computer and Internet users in general?
   a. Netiquette
   b. "Ten Commandments for Computer Ethics"
   c. Code of conduct
   d. Acceptable use policy

10. The use of no more than 5 percent of a copyrighted document, without payment or permission, is called _____.
    a. Piracy
    b. Copyright infringement
    c. Fair use
    d. Plagiarism

Spotlight Exercises

1. Obtain the acceptable use policy provided by your school. Have you ever seen this policy without actively searching for it? If so, where did you see it for the first time? In a one-page, double-spaced report created in a word processing program, summarize the policy. Cite the statements that you think are the most aggressive and those that you believe are overkill or unnecessary. Overall, do you feel that the statement is being upheld by the student body, or is there a need for more enforcement?

2. Go to **www.ibackup.com** and view the demonstration located on the home page. In a PowerPoint presentation of at least five slides, provide a brief description of the various backup services that this site offers. Identify the services that are suitable for your home system and which ones might be suitable for the servers at your school. From what you discovered about this online company, would you make use of this service? Provide justification for your decision.

3. The disagreement between online auctions and software companies over who is responsible for the sale of pirated software is a constant debate. Using the Internet and your favorite browser, locate at least three policy statements regarding liability from online auction or other Web sites that sell software. Do these statements state who is responsible for the sale of a pirated product? Is any advice given to help the buyer determine whether a product is authentic? Do these statements indicate that you can obtain a refund or offer to act as an arbitrator between you and the seller if the product you receive cannot be authenticated? Present your statements of liability and answer to the questions above in a one-page, double-spaced report created in a word processing program.

4. Create a survey consisting of descriptions of several scenarios that could occur in an academic situation that requires the involved individual to make an ethical decision. For example, a student leaves the computer lab and forgets to logoff: If you were the next individual to sit at that computer, what action would you perform? Present at least five scenarios in your survey and administer it to 25 students at your school. Summarize the survey results and determine whether in these five situations the surveyed individuals responded more often in an ethical or an unethical manner. In a three- to five-minute presentation, describe your scenarios to the class and summarize the survey results.

5. With technology becoming more portable, popular, and embedded into social settings, computer ethics becomes even more important. Develop a list of five additional commandments for computer ethics that can be applied specifically to portable computing devices. Present your five commandments and the reasons for your choices in a one-page, double-spaced report created with a word processing program.

6. You downloaded the beta version of a software program over three months ago. The beta was good for a 90-day period that has now expired. You continue to get e-mails stating that your trial period has expired for this product and that you can purchase the final release version by going to a specified Web site. You ignore the e-mails and continue to use the expired beta version. Now every time you try to open the program, you are presented with several pop-ups warning you that you are using an expired and unauthenticated copy. You also notice that it is taking longer to load the program and that after 10 minutes of use the program automatically closes. Analyze the ethical issue of using an expired copy of a program. Do you feel it is right to continue using the program when the trial period has expired? Would you be more inclined to purchase the program if the trial program self-destructed on the expiration date instead of slowly deteriorating? Is it ethical for the manufacturer to slowly undermine your work with this gradual product degeneration? Present your opinions on the ethical issues concerning software offered for trial periods in a one-page, double-spaced report created in a word processing program.

2

Inside the System Unit

Chapter Objectives

You feel empowered, full of technological information and ready to make that big new computer purchase. You go online, browse a few popular manufacturer sites, and quickly recognize that there is a gap in what you thought was your flawless knowledge. Questions start to come to mind. How much RAM is enough? What is cache? Do I need a separate video card? How many USB ports should my system have? What type of processor do I need? You finally ask yourself the most important question: Do I really know enough to make this purchase?

No one wants to make you nervous about your purchase; but when the price of a new computer ranges from $300 to $1,000, you might want to take a closer look at the details. There is a difference in talking about computers with your friends over lunch and having a conversation with a salesperson or someone with more expertise. With your friends, the conversation centers on the visible and most used components of a computer, the monitor, keyboard, USB ports, and network capability. You don't need to be a technology whiz to purchase a computer, but more information on the internal components will shed light on the ability of the system to meet your price and performance needs.

In this chapter we provide insight into the hardware components of a computer system and the way they work including:

- How computers represent data
- How the components inside the system unit process data to create information
- How to make intelligent decisions when buying a computer system, upgrading a system, or just talking about technology ∎

Check out **f Facebook**
for our latest updates

www.facebook.com

How Computers Represent Data

Computers need data to work with, but that data must be represented in a specific way for the computer's hardware to accept and understand it. When you type on a keyboard and the information appears on the monitor, the information passes from the input device to the output device in a manner that is probably not what you expect. The letter Z is not passed inside your system looking anything like a Z; it is represented by units of information called bits. A **bit** is a single circuit that either contains a current or does not. The **binary digits** of 0 and 1 are used as a means of representing the off/on state of a computer switch, or bit. In the Off state, current is not flowing through the switch and is represented by the digit 0. In the On state, current is flowing through the switch and is represented by the digit 1. The bit is the smallest piece of data a computer can process. Remember that the use of 1 and 0 are for human representation; it is the current that is actually flowing through the circuitry of the computer that the system understands (Figure 2.1).

FIGURE 2.1 A bit has two states: Current (On represented by 1) and No Current (Off represented by 0).

Binary Digit	0	1
Bit (circuitry)	○ no current	● current
Status	Off	On

Representing Data as Bits and Bytes

You are familiar with the decimal system of numbers, which consist of 10 digits (0, 1, 2, 3, 4, 5, 6, 7, 8, 9). Computers do not use the decimal system to represent numbers or characters. Rather, computers use a series of circuits whose pattern of off/on current is converted into strings of binary digits called **binary numbers** (Figure 2.2).

To grasp this idea, it might help to think of a bit as acting like a light switch. Both a light switch and a bit have the same two states, off and on. If a computer system used one bit (or one switch) to transfer data, your keyboard would have only two keys: a key with the number 0 and a key with the number 1. If the switch were off, that would represent the fact

FIGURE 2.2 Common Keyboard Characters and Their Equivalent Binary Number Representation

Keyboard Character	Binary Number Representation
R	01010010
S	01010011
T	01010100
L	01001100
N	01001110
E	01000101

that you pressed 0; if the switch were on, it would represent you pressing the 1 key. If your system had two light switches, you would have four possibilities and thus a keyboard with four keys representing the four options: both switches on, both switches off, the first switch on and the second switch off, or the first switch off and the second switch on. Three switches allow eight possibilities, and so on. The number of possible combinations of on/off patterns is calculated by the formula 2^n, where n is the number of switches. So, how many switches (bits) are needed to represent an entire keyboard, which can contain from 128 to 256 different characters, including all the letters of the alphabet (both uppercase and lowercase), the numbers 0 through 9, and punctuation marks? The answer is somewhere between 7 and 8 because $2^7 = 128$ and $2^8 = 256$ (Figure 2.3).

FIGURE 2.3 Number of Bits versus Number of Possibilities

Number of Bits	Number of Possibilities
1	$2^1 = 2$
2	$2^2 = 4$
3	$2^3 = 8$
4	$2^4 = 16$
5	$2^5 = 32$
6	$2^6 = 64$
7	$2^7 = 128$
8	$2^8 = 256$

A **byte** is a group of eight bits and is the method of representing one character of data, such as the essential numbers (0–9), the basic letters of the alphabet like the character Z (uppercase and lowercase), and the most common punctuation symbols. For this reason, you can use the byte as a baseline unit to express the amount of information a computer's storage device can hold. Because it takes eight bits (on/off switches) to make a byte, and eight bits result in 256 possible on/off combinations, you'll see the number 8 and multiples of 8 appearing behind the scenes in many computer functions, applications, and references to storage capacity. For example, a typical college essay contains 250 words per page, and each word contains (on average) 5.5 characters. Therefore, the page contains approximately 1,375 characters. In other words, you need about 1,375 bytes of storage to save one page of a college paper.

For clarity, the terms *bit* and *byte* are used to present different types of information. Whereas bytes are used to express storage capacity, bits (1s and 0s) are commonly used for measuring the data transfer rate of computer communications devices such as modems. To describe rapid data transfer rates, the measurement units **kilobits per second (Kbps)**, **megabits per second (Mbps)**, and **gigabits per second (Gbps)** are used. These respectively correspond (roughly) to 1 thousand, 1 million, and 1 billion bits per second. Remember that these terms refer to *bits* per second, not *bytes* per second (Figure 2.4).

Bytes are commonly used to measure data storage. The measurements—**kilobyte (KB)** for one thousand bytes, **megabyte (MB)** for one million bytes, **gigabyte (GB)** for one billion bytes, and **terabyte (TB)** for one trillion bytes—describe the amount of data a computer is managing either in RAM memory or in longer-term storage (hard disk, CD, DVD, or USB drive). Figure 2.5 shows these units and the *approximate* value of text data for each. For these units the equivalents of a thousand, a million, and so on, are not exact; rounding numbers has become acceptable. For example, a kilobyte is actually 1,024 bytes.

As the uses of computers escalate and the amount of information we use and save increases, storage devices have had to expand their capacity. Originally, storage units held kilobytes and megabytes of data. Today most devices express their capacity in gigabytes and terabytes. In anticipation of a continued increase in data use and storage, terms already exist for representing even

FIGURE 2.4 Units of Data Transfer Rates

Unit	Abbreviation	Transfer Rate	Text Equivalent
Kilobits per second	Kbps	1 thousand bits per second	125 characters
Megabits per second	Mbps	1 million bits per second	125 pages
Gigabits per second	Gbps	1 billion bits per second	125,000 pages

FIGURE 2.5 Current Units of Data Storage

Unit	Abbreviation	Storage Amount	Text Equivalent
Byte	B	8 bits	1 character
Kilobyte	KB	1 thousand bytes	1 page
Megabyte	MB	1 million bytes	1,000 pages
Gigabyte	GB	1 billion bytes	1,000 books
Terabyte	TB	1 trillion bytes	1 million books

larger units. A **petabyte** is 1 quadrillion bytes; an **exabyte** is 1 quintillion bytes; a **zettabyte** is 1 sextillion bytes; and a **yottabyte** is 1 septillion bytes (Figure 2.6).

FIGURE 2.6 Larger Units of Data Storage

Unit	Abbreviation	Storage Amount	Text Equivalent
Petabyte	PB	1 quadrillion bytes	1 billion books
Exabyte	EB	1 quintillion bytes	7,500 libraries the size of the Library of Congress
Zettabyte	ZB	1 sextillion bytes	Not able to estimate
Yottabyte	YB	1 septillion bytes	Not able to estimate

Hexadecimal: An Alternate Representation for Binary Numbers

Binary numbers are difficult to work with because many digits are required to represent even a small number. For example, when you enter the decimal number 14 into your computer, the binary number representation uses four bits or switches, and 14 is represented as 1110.

When computer programmers need to look at the data that is passing through a

FIGURE 2.7 Decimal, Binary, and Hexadecimal Numbers

Decimal Number	0	1	2	3	4	5	6	7	8	9	10	11	12	13	14	15
Binary Number	0000	0001	0010	0011	0100	0101	0110	0111	1000	1001	1010	1011	1100	1101	1110	1111
Hexadecimal Number	0	1	2	3	4	5	6	7	8	9	A	B	C	D	E	F

computer system, often to locate an error in a program, they frequently convert the binary numbers the system displays into **hexadecimal numbers** (**hex** for short). The hexadecimal number system uses the numbers 0 through 9 and the letters A through F to represent a binary string. These digits and letters are referred to as the *base 16 characters*. For example, the decimal number 100 is represented as the lengthy binary number 01100100 and then quickly translated to 64 in hex notation. Each single hex digit represents four binary digits, making it a shorter, faster, and more compact representation of a binary number (Figure 2.7). You can convert among decimal, binary, and hex by using the converter at **http://easycalculation.com/decimal-converter.php**. To learn the procedure to convert between decimal, binary, and hexadecimal through manual arithmetic go to **www.mindspring.com/~jimvb/binary.htm**.

Representing Very Large and Very Small Numbers

To represent and process numbers with fractional parts (such as 1.25) or numbers that are extremely large (in the billions and trillions), computers use **floating point standard**. The term *floating point* suggests how this notation system works: There is no fixed number of digits before or after the decimal point (thus the word *float*), so the computer can work with very large and very small numbers. Floating point standard, set by the Institute of Electrical and Electronics Engineers (IEEE), requires special processing circuitry, which is generally provided by the floating-point unit (FPU). Modern computers integrate one or more FPUs with the CPU (processor or microprocessor), but in older computers the FPU was sometimes a separate chip called the *math coprocessor*.

So, how does floating point standard convert very small or very large numbers into binary representation? The IEEE single precision floating point standard representation requires the use of 32 bits, which may be represented as numbers from 0 to 31, left to right. The first bit is the sign bit, S; the next eight bits are the exponent bits, E; and the final 23 bits are the fraction, F. So what does the decimal number +6.5 look like in floating point standard? For the answer and an explanation, refer to Figure 2.8. The

FIGURE 2.8 Bit Layout for Floating Point Standard and the Number +6.5

Sign	Exponent	Fraction
S	EEEEEEEE	FFFFFFFFFFFFFFFFFFFFFFF
IEEE Single Precision Floating Point Standard Bit Layout		
0	1 8	9 31
+6.5 Represented in Single Precision Floating Point Standard		
0	10000001	10100000000000000000000
An **Off** bit stands for a **positive** number.	This binary number is decimal 129. However, the exponent for the base number of 2 is calculated by taking this number, 129, and subtracting 127, for an actual exponent of 2.	This last component is actually the binary number 1.101, which in decimal form is 1.625.
+1	2^2	1.625
So, the actual conversion calculation is $+1 * 2^2 * 1.625 = +1 * 4 * 1.625 = +6.5$		

purpose of this example is not to make you a binary converter expert but rather to demonstrate the complexity of the conversions that take place inside the system unit.

We know that computers process not only numeric data but also character data. Because we communicate with spoken and written text, let's look next at the processing of the character data that composes our daily interactions.

Representing Characters: Character Code

Character code uses an algorithm as a bridge between the computer's bit patterns and the letters, numbers, and symbols on our keyboards called **characters** that we're accustomed to using. Depending on your system, the conversion from computer code to actual keyboard characters is accomplished by using one of three different character coding formats: ASCII, EBCDIC, or Unicode.

The most widely used character code is **ASCII** (pronounced "ask-ee"), the **American Standard Code for Information Interchange**, which is used in minicomputers, personal computers, and computers that make information available over the Internet. ASCII uses seven bits and can thus represent 128 ($2^7 = 128$) different characters (see Figure 2.9). A variation of ASCII code, called **Extended ASCII** (see Figure 2.10), uses eight bits and allows 128 additional characters, like the fractions ½; and ¼; and logical symbols such as ≥, for a total of 256 ($2^8 = 256$). In

both systems the first 128 codes represent the same characters. The code order for ASCII starts with the lowest codes representing punctuation marks and numbers, followed by more punctuation marks, uppercase letters, more punctuation marks, and finally lowercase letters. Go to **www.asciitable.com** to view the complete ASCII and Extended ASCII listings.

IBM mainframe computers and some midrange systems use a different eight-bit code system, **EBCDIC** (pronounced "ebb-see-dic"), **Extended Binary Coded Decimal Interchange Code**. EBCDIC code is ordered using a low-to-high sequence starting with punctuation, lowercase letters, uppercase letters, and then numbers.

Although ASCII and EBCDIC provide enough bits to represent all characters used in the English language and some foreign language symbols, neither has enough binary combinations for some Eastern languages and historic symbols that exceed 256 characters. Because computers make international communication and business transactions possible, a new coding system—**Unicode**—is becoming popular. Unicode uses 16 bits, can represent over 65,000 characters, and can symbolize all the world's written languages. The first 128 codes in the Unicode system represent the same characters as the first 128 in the ASCII system.

When discussing numbers and alphabetical characters, it is important to remember that all data being transmitted through a computer system is represented by bits or circuit notation. A fingerprint, picture, or company logo is also converted

FIGURE 2.9 Sample of a Section of ASCII Code

Character	ASCII Code	Character	ASCII Code	Character	ASCII Code
!	00100001	E	01000101	e	01100101
#	00100011	P	01010000	p	01110000
$	00100100	A	01000001	a	01100001
space	00100000	Y	01011001	y	01111001

FIGURE 2.10 Pay $6.50! Written in Extended ASCII Code

P	a	y	space	$	6.50	!
01010000	01100001	01111001	00100000	00100100	0 10000001 10100000000000000000000	00100001

by appropriate programs into patterns of binary digits (Figure 2.11).

Now that you understand bits, bytes, and how computers represent data, it is important to understand their connection to the rest of the system. Let's take a closer look at the system unit, its components, and how these concepts will come into play.

FIGURE 2.11 The Automated fingerprint identification system (AFIS) smoothes and converts fingerprints to binary code.

Introducing the System Unit

The **system unit** is a boxlike case that comes in a variety of shapes and sizes, and houses the computer's main hardware components (Figure 2.12). The system unit is actually more than just a case: It provides a sturdy frame for mounting internal components, including storage devices, a power supply, a fan, and connectors for input and output devices; it protects those components from physical damage; and it keeps them cool. A good case also provides room for system upgrades, such as additional disk drives.

System units come in a variety of styles. In some desktop computing systems, the system unit is a separate metal or plastic box. Originally, these cases were horizontal and were positioned on top of a desk, often with a monitor sitting on top—thus the name "desktop." To minimize the space it occupied, the case needed a small **footprint**, which is the amount of space used by the device. However, a small case didn't allow enough room for add-on components. The **tower case**, a system unit case designed to sit on the floor next to a desk, provided the solution. The tower case has a vertical configuration, being tall and deep. A smaller version of the tower that has less internal room for components is called a **minitower case**.

In a notebook computer or a personal digital assistant (PDA), the system unit contains all the computer's components, including input components, such as a keyboard, and output components, such as the display. Some desktop computers, such as Apple's iMac, contain the display within the system unit, making them all-in-one systems. To ensure access identification and security, biometric authentication devices like fingerprint readers, retina scanners,

FIGURE 2.12 Every kind of computer has a system unit: all-in-one, notebook, smartphone, and desktop.

All-in-one system unit

Notebook system unit

Desktop system unit

Smartphone system unit

FIGURE 2.13 This fingerprint reader is one of several devices that provide biometric authentication.

and face recognition systems are embedded into some individual system units (Figure 2.13).

System units also vary in their form factor. A **form factor** is a specification for how internal components, such as the motherboard, are mounted inside the system unit. Let's take a look!

Inside the System Unit

Most computer users don't need to and don't want to open their system units; they receive their computers in ready-to-use packages. However, if you ever need to open your system unit, remember that the computer's components are sensitive to static electricity. If you touch certain components while you're charged with static electricity, you could damage them.

To avoid this disaster, always disconnect the power cord before opening your computer's case, and discharge your personal static electricity by touching something that's well grounded or by wearing a grounding bracelet. A **grounding bracelet** is a bracelet that has a cord attached to a grounded object. If it's one of those low-humidity days when you're getting shocked every time you touch a doorknob, don't work on your computer's internal components.

The basic components you would see if you were to open a system unit include such items as the motherboard, power supply, cooling fan, internal speakers, internal drive bays, external drive bays, and various expansion cards, regardless of the manufacturer or type of computer (see Figures 2.14 and 2.15).

An overview of these basic components will help you to identify and clarify the purpose of each.

- *Motherboard:* The motherboard is the large circuit board located within your system unit to which all other components are connected. It specifically contains a chip referred to as the computer's central processing unit (CPU). You'll learn more about the motherboard and the CPU later in this chapter; for now remember that the CPU, referred to as the "brain" of the computer, is the central component of the computer; all other components (such as disk drives, monitors, and printers) exist only to bridge the gap between the user and the CPU.

FIGURE 2.14 The Location of the Components of the System Unit on a Tower

Power supply

Cooling fan
Memory cards

Expansion card
Expansion slot
Motherboard

External drive bay

Internal drive bay

Internal speaker (not present)

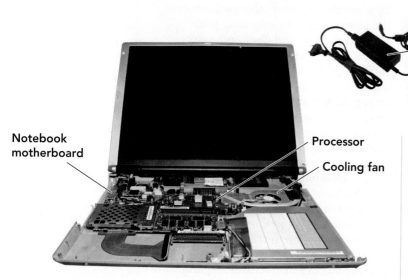

Power supply

Notebook motherboard

Processor

Cooling fan

FIGURE 2.15 The Location of the Components of the System Unit in a Notebook

- *Power supply:* A computer's power supply transforms the alternating current (AC) from standard wall outlets into the direct current (DC) needed for the computer's operation. It also steps the voltage down to the low level required by the motherboard. Power supplies are rated according to their peak output in watts. A 350-watt power supply is adequate for most desktop systems, but 500 watts provide sufficient voltage if you plan to add many additional components. If it is ever necessary to replace a power supply on a desktop computer, seek the help of a professional. You can replace your own power supply on a notebook because it is usually outside of the box and part of the component that plugs into the wall. However, be sure to replace the power supply with an identical component, preferably from the same manufacturer. This assures that the amperage and voltage are within your system limitations and eliminates the possibility of damaging the battery or other components.

- *Cooling fan:* The computer's components can be damaged if heat accumulates within the system unit. A **cooling fan** keeps the system unit cool. The fan often is part of the power supply, although many systems include auxiliary fans to provide additional cooling.

- *Internal speaker:* The computer's **internal speaker** is useful only for the beeps you hear when the computer starts up or encounters an error. Current computers include sound cards and external speakers for better-quality sound.

- *Drive bays:* **Drive bays** accommodate the computer's disk drives, such as the hard disk drive, CD or DVD drive, and portable drives. Internal drive bays are used for hard disks that are permanently contained in the system unit; therefore, they do not enable outside access. External drive bays mount drives that are accessible from the outside (a necessity if you need to insert and remove a CD from the drive). External drive bays vary in size to accommodate different media devices. Current systems offer 5.25-inch external drive bays to accommodate CD or DVD drives.

- *Expansion slots:* The system unit also contains **expansion slots**, which are receptacles that accept additional circuit boards or expansion cards. **Expansion cards**, also referred to as **expansion boards**, **adapter cards**, or **adapters**, contain the circuitry for peripherals that are not normally included as standard equipment. Examples of expansion cards are additional memory modules, enhanced sound cards, modem cards, network interface cards (NICs), video cards, and on some systems' wireless network cards (Figure 2.16).

Now that you have an overview of the internal components of the system unit, let's look more closely at the most important component: the computer's motherboard.

What's on the Motherboard?

The **motherboard** is a large flat piece of plastic or fiberglass that contains thousands of electrical circuits etched onto the board's surface. The circuits connect numerous plug-in receptacles that accommodate the computer's most important components (such as the CPU and RAM). The motherboard provides the centralized physical and electrical connectivity to

Memory module (RAM)

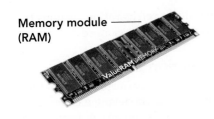

Modem card

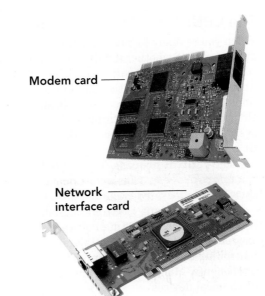

Network interface card

Sound card

Video card

enable communication among these critical components. Most of the components on the motherboard are integrated circuits. An **integrated circuit (IC)**, also called a **chip**, carries an electric current and contains millions of transistors. To view a short video about how chips are created, go to **www97.intel. com/en/TheJourneyInside/ ExploreTheCurriculum/EC_ Microprocessors/MPLesson4**.

A **transistor** is an electronic switch (or gate) that controls the flow of electrical signals through the circuit. Transistors are made out of layers of special material, called a **semiconductor**, that either conducts electrical current or blocks its passage through the circuit. Semiconductor material, like silicone, produces the off and on impulses that enable the binary representation of characters within the system unit. A computer uses such electronic switches to route data in different ways, according to the software's instructions. Encased in black plastic blocks or enclosures, most integrated circuits or chips fit specially designed receptacles or slots on the motherboard's surface. What do these chips do? Let's look at some of the most important components you'll see on the motherboard: the CPU (or microprocessor), the system clock, the chipset, input/output buses, and memory (Figure 2.17).

FIGURE 2.16 Expansion cards enable you to enhance and customize your system to meet your own personal needs.

Heat sink and fan

Memory (RAM)

CPU

Power supply

Video card

Expansion slots

Motherboard

DVD burner

Hard drive

FIGURE 2.17 This typical PC motherboard shows the system unit's main components and where they would be located or connected on the motherboard.

The CPU: The Microprocessor

When you're ready to buy a computer and determine whether it will meet your computing needs, you will need to understand the capabilities and limitations of current microprocessors. No single element of a computer determines its overall performance as much as the CPU.

The **central processing unit (CPU)** is a **microprocessor** (or **processor** for short)—an integrated circuit chip that is capable of processing electronic signals. It interprets and carries out software instructions by processing data and controlling the rest of the computer's components. Many electronic and mechanical devices we use daily, such as smartphones, calculators, automobile engines, and industrial and medical equipment, contain **embedded processors**. These processors are designed and programmed to perform only the tasks intended to be done by that device.

CPUs (microprocessors) that are within a computer system unit are incredibly complex devices. They must be able to perform many different functions, depending on the program running at the time.

Processor Slots and Sockets

An integrated circuit of incredible complexity, a CPU plugs into a motherboard in much the same way that other integrated circuits do—through a series of pins that extend out from the bottom of the chip. However, only special slots and sockets can accommodate CPUs. Part of the reason for this is that CPUs are larger and have more pins than most other chips. In addition, CPUs generate so much heat that they could destroy themselves or other system components. The CPU is generally covered by a **heat sink**, a heat-dissipating component that drains heat from the chip. To accomplish this, the heat sink may contain a small auxiliary cooling fan. The latest high-end CPUs include

> " No **single element** of a **computer** determines its **overall performance as much as** the CPU. "

their own built-in refrigeration systems to keep these speedy processors cool.

The Instruction Set

Every processor can perform a fixed set of operations, such as retrieving a character from the computer's memory or comparing two numbers to see which is larger. Each of these operations has a unique number, called an *instruction*. A processor's list of instructions is called its **instruction set**. Because each type of processor has a unique instruction set, programs devised for one type of CPU won't necessarily run on another. For example, a program written for an Intel chip may not run on a Motorola chip. A program that can run on a given computer is said to be compatible with that computer's processor. If a program is compatible, it's said to be a **native application** for a given processor design.

The Machine Cycle

A CPU contains two subcomponents: the control unit and the arithmetic logic unit. Both components play a part in the four-step process called the **processing** or **machine cycle**. The **control unit**, under the direction of an embedded program, switches from one stage to the next and performs the action of that stage. The four steps of the machine cycle are:

- *Fetch:* Retrieves the next program instruction from the computer's RAM or cache memory.
- *Decode:* Takes the fetched instruction and translates it into a form that the control unit understands.
- *Execute:* Performs the requested instruction using the **arithmetic logic unit (ALU)** to perform **arithmetic operations**, which include addition, subtraction, multiplication, and division, and **logical operations**, which involve the comparison of two or more data items. Arithmetic operations return a numeric value, whereas logical operations return a value of true or false.

- *Store:* Stores the results in an internal register (a location on the CPU) or in RAM.

Registers are temporary storage areas located within the microprocessor. Even though the word *store* is used when describing their function, they are not considered as part of memory and act more as digital scratch pads. There are different types of registers, depending on their function. Some accept, hold, and transfer instructions or data, and others perform arithmetic or logical comparisons at high speed. The importance of registers lies in the fact that they work extremely fast, actually at the same speed as the CPU they are embedded within.

These four steps of the machine cycle, or processing cycle, are grouped into two phases: the **instruction cycle** (fetch and decode) and the **execution cycle** (execute and store). Today's microprocessors can go through this entire four-step process billions of times per second (Figure 2.18).

Microprocessor Performance

The number of transistors available has a huge effect on the performance of a processor. The more transistors and the closer they are in proximity to each other, the faster the processing speed. The data bus width and word size, clock speed, operations per microprocessor cycle, use of parallel processing, and type of chip are also factors that contribute to microprocessor performance.

Data Bus Width and Word Size The **data bus** is a set of parallel wires that acts as an electronic highway on which data travels between computer components. It is the medium by which the entire system communicates with the CPU. More technically, the bus is a pathway for the electronic impulses that form bytes. The more lanes this highway has, the faster data can travel. Data bus width is measured in bits (8, 16, 32, or 64).

The width of a CPU's data bus partly determines its **word size**, or the maximum number of bits the CPU can process at once. Data bus width also affects the CPU's overall speed: A CPU with a 32-bit data bus can shuffle data twice as fast as a CPU with a 16-bit data bus. The terms *8-bit CPU*, *16-bit CPU*, *32-bit CPU*, and *64-bit CPU* indicate the maximum number of bits a CPU can handle at a time.

A CPU's word size is important because it determines which operating systems the CPU can use and which software it can run.

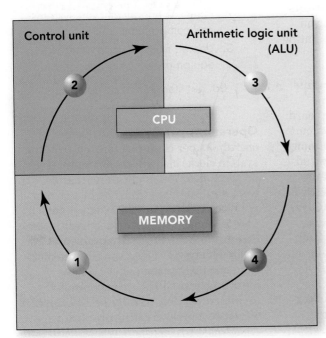

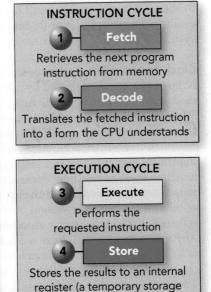

FIGURE 2.18 The four steps of the machine cycle are the same in all systems, from personal computers to mainframes. What differs is the speed at which the cycle is performed.

FIGURE 2.19 Word Size Capacity (in Bits) of Popular Operating Systems

Operating System	Word Size	When Used
Windows 95/98/NT/2000/XP	32	Past (but still used)
Windows Vista (all editions except Starter)	64	Current
Windows 7	64	Current
Linux	64	Current
Mac OS X Snow Leopard (with Velocity Engine chip)	64	Current

Figure 2.19 lists the word size requirements of current operating systems.

Today's PC market consists of older 32-bit CPUs that run 32-bit operating systems and the more commonplace 64-bit CPUs that run 64-bit operating systems. Intel's 64-bit Itanium processor, introduced in 2001, brought 64-bit computing to the PC market for the first time. Linux was the first OS to use the 64-bit technology in 2001. In 2003 Apple released a 64-bit version of Mac OS X, and in 2005 Microsoft released Windows XP Professional ×64. The current Windows operating systems, Windows Vista and Windows 7, are available in both 32-bit and 64-bit versions, while the Mac OS X Snow Leopard comes in one version that runs both 32-bit and 64-bit applications.

Visit **http://windows.microsoft.com/en-US/windows7/32-bit-and-64-bit-Windows-frequently-asked-questions** to obtain information that will help you decide whether a 32-bit or 64-bit operating system is adequate for your needs.

Clock Speed Within a computer, events happen at a pace controlled by a tiny electronic "drummer" on the motherboard: The **system clock** is an electronic circuit that generates rapid pulses to synchronize the computer's internal activities, including the movement from one stage of the machine cycle to another. These electrical pulses are measured in **gigahertz (GHz)**, or billions of cycles per second, and are referred to as a processor's **clock speed**. Any new computer will have a clock speed of 3 GHz or higher; a 3-GHz processor is capable of processing 3 billion cycles in 1 second. In general, the higher the clock speed of the processor, the faster the computer. For editorial reviews of the latest products, such as the fastest processors, memory, graphics chips, and more, go to **www.geek.com/articles/chips**.

GREEN tech tips

The Climate Savers Computing Initiative, whose members include Intel and Google along with more than 30 other organizations, is working to save energy and reduce greenhouse gas emissions. Their mission is to "slow climate change one computer at a time." Visit them at **www.climatesaverscomputing.org**. You can join the movement, read the informational blogs, browse through catalogs of energy-efficient equipment, and use the interactive toolkit to determine the financial and electrical savings that can be achieved by managing the power of your computer. Their goal is to reach a 50 percent reduction in computer power consumption by the end of 2010.

Did you know that the United States is responsible for 22 percent of the world's greenhouse gas emissions yet has only 4 percent of the world's population? How can you get started and do your share? Climate Savers recommends three basic steps to go green:

1. Use the power management feature on your computer.
2. Purchase energy efficient systems and components.
3. Unplug from power sources when equipment is not in use.

So, get started and do your share! ●

Green Tech Tips

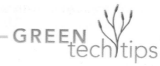

Operations per Cycle The number of *operations* per clock tick (one pulse of the system clock) also affects microprocessor performance. You might think that a CPU can't perform more than one instruction per clock tick (Figure 2.20), but thanks to new technologies, that's no longer the case. **Superscalar architecture** refers to the design of any CPU that can execute more than one instruction per clock cycle; today's fastest CPUs use superscalar architectures. Superscalar architectures often use a process called **pipelining**, a technique that feeds a new instruction into the CPU at every step of the processing cycle so that four or more instructions are worked on simultaneously.

Processing cycle without pipelining

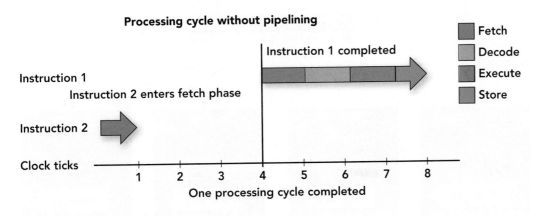

FIGURE 2.20 In a processor that does not have the ability to pipeline, one instruction goes through the fetch–decode–execute–store cycle before another one is fetched and begins the processing cycle.

Pipelining resembles an auto assembly line in which more than one car is being worked on at once. Before the first instruction is finished, the next one is started (Figure 2.21). If the CPU needs the results of a completed instruction to process the next one, that condition is called **data dependency**. It can cause a pipeline stall in which the assembly line is held up until the results are known. To cope with this problem, advanced CPUs use a technique called **speculative execution**, in which the processor executes and temporarily stores the next instruction in case it proves useful. CPUs also use a technique called **branch prediction**, in which the processor tries to predict what will happen (with a surprisingly high degree of accuracy).

Parallel Processing Another way to improve CPU performance is by using **parallel processing**, a technique that uses more than one processor to execute a program. It usually is found on systems that run programs that perform a lot of computations, such as simulations or graphic processing software. These processors can be located within one system, on the same motherboard, or on independent systems networked with sophisticated distributed processing software (Figure 2.22). The idea is to speed up the execution of a program by dividing the program into multiple fragments that can execute simultaneously, each on its own processor. In theory, a program should execute faster in a system making use of parallel processing. In reality, it is difficult to divide a program into segments in a way that one segment does not interfere or need to wait for the result generated by another. Parallel processing should not be confused with **multitasking**, a process by which the CPU gives the user the illusion of performing instructions from multiple programs at once when in reality the CPU is rapidly switching between the programs and instructions. Most computers have one CPU, but some have several. Today multicore processors are becoming the norm.

Multi-Core Processing The newest computers being sold are equipped with dual-core and quad-core processors. These

STUDENT VIDEO

Processing cycle with pipelining

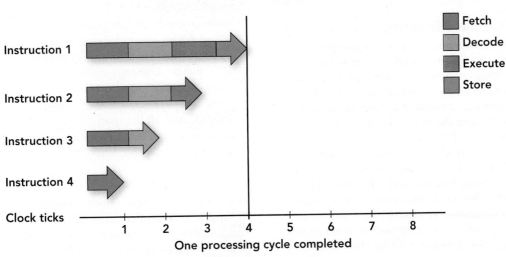

FIGURE 2.21 In a processor that does have pipelining, when an instruction moves from one phase of the processing cycle to the next, another instruction moves into the vacated phase. With four different instructions being in the cycle at one time, it takes less time to process instructions.

FIGURE 2.22 Because the processor is the most expensive system unit component, a system with more than one processor, capable of parallel processing, is costly.

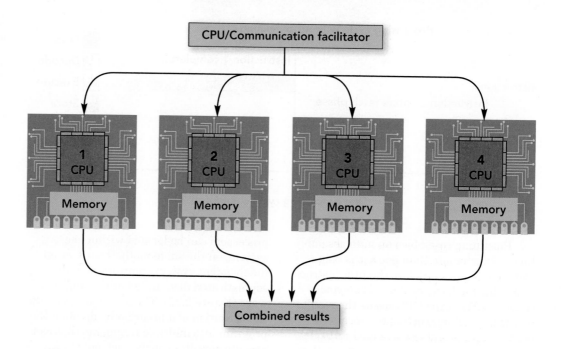

processors attempt to correct the slowdown that occurs in the processing cycle when the CPU needs to access instructions and data from RAM or a hard disk. In dual-core and quad-core processors, access time is reduced and overall processing time improved because each core handles incoming streams of data or instructions at the same time. This behavior reinforces the concept that two hands are better than one. AMD and Intel offer multi-core 64-bit processors. For a dual-core or quad-core processor to be used to full capacity, your system must use a compatible operating system and specifically designed application software. When the operating system and application software are not designed to make use of the multiple cores of the processor, only one core will be recognized, and the processor will never work to its full potential.

Popular Microprocessors

The most commonly used microprocessors are those found in IBM-compatible computers and Macs. Most PCs are powered by chips produced by Intel and AMD. Figure 2.23 shows how popular microprocessors for PCs have improved since the days of the first PC.

In 2010 Intel released the Core i7 Extreme Edition microprocessor with a clock speed of 3.30 GHz (Figure 2.24). Since 2003 Intel has been concentrating on producing processors that are suited to certain computing needs—such as the Centrino processor for mobile computing

GREEN tech tips

Did you know that keeping computers turned on all the time drains the community power supply, stresses the computers' internal components, and wastes energy? The Environmental Protection Agency (EPA), technology manufacturers, and nonprofit organizations are working on ways to keep you connected 24/7 with reduced environmental consequences. If you purchase a computer with the EPA's Energy Star Logo, it can go to sleep during intervals of inactivity, thus boosting its energy efficiency.

Are you and your friends aware of the fact that U.S. college students could save over 2.3 billion kilowatt hours of electricity per year by enabling power-saving features on their desktop PCs? That is a saving of over $200 million in energy costs and a 1.8 million–ton reduction in CO_2 emissions—an equivalent of taking 350,000 cars off the road. So, power down when not using your electrical devices, and do your share! ●

and the Core Extreme family of processors for multimedia and gaming. Intel now rates its processors not only by cycles per second, but also by features such as

Green Tech Tips

FIGURE 2.23 The Evolution of Intel Microprocessors

Year	Chip	Bus Width	Clock Speed	Transistors
1971	4004	4 bits	108 KHz	2,300
1993	Pentium	32 bits	Up to 66 MHz	3.1 million
2000	Pentium 4	32 bits	Up to 2 GHz	42 million
2006	Core Duo	32 bits	Up to 2 GHz	151 million
2007	Core 2 Quad	64 bits	Up to 2.4 GHz	582 million
2008	Core 2 Extreme, Quad Processor	64 bits	3.2 GHz	820 million
2010	Core i7 Extreme Edition	64 bits	3.3 GHz	732 Million

architecture, cache, and bus type. The rating, then, represents the power and usefulness of the processor—not just the clock speed. Visit **http://download. intel.com/pressroom/kits/ IntelProcessorHistory.pdf** to view a detailed timeline of the history of Intel processors.

Normally faster is better; however, the cost of microprocessor speed can keep it out of reach. When deciding on a processor, list the activities you plan to use your system for over the next few years. Then match the processor capabilities to those activities. For example, the Intel Celeron is a processor geared to users who perform basic tasks such as word processing, Web surfing, and listening to and buying music. The Intel Pentium Core 2 and Core i7 family of processors are geared toward advanced applications such as gaming, video editing, and advanced digital photography. The Intel Atom is specifically designed for handheld and mobile Internet devices.

After you match your needs with the processors that can manage them, you can address the processor's speed. For most users an increase of 0.4 GHz in speed would not perceptibly change performance, but it would make a noticeable difference in cost. For articles, videos, forums, and charts that provide detailed information about a large variety of processors and other hardware elements, go to **www. tomshardware.com/cpu**.

For years Motorola Corporation and IBM made the chips for Apple computers, producing the 68000 series and the PowerPC series. Apple gave its own name to the PowerPC chips: Motorola's 750 was the same chip as Apple's G3, Motorola's 7400 was the G4, and the 64-bit IBM chip was the G5. In January 2006, Apple began transitioning to Intel processors for the Mac, with all new Macs using Intel processors by August of that year.

FIGURE 2.24 New multi-core processors, like the Intel Core i7, require software written to use all of the cores for them to function at their peak.

The Chipset and the Input/Output Bus

Another important motherboard component is the **chipset**, which is a collection of chips that work together to provide the switching circuitry needed by the microprocessor to move data throughout the computer. One of the jobs handled by the chipset is linking the microprocessor's system bus with the computer's input/output buses.

An **input/output (I/O) bus** refers specifically to the pathway that extends beyond the microprocessor to communicate with input and output devices. Typically, an I/O bus contains expansion slots to accommodate plug-in expansion cards.

Today's PCs use the **PCI (peripheral component interconnect) bus,** a slower bus that connects devices like hard drives and sound cards to the faster microprocessor system bus. Many motherboards still contain an industry standard architecture (ISA) bus and have one or two ISA slots available. The accelerated graphics port (AGP) is a bus designed for video and graphics display.

The microprocessor is just one of several chips on the computer's motherboard. Among the others are those that provide the computer with various types of memory.

Memory

Memory refers to the chips, located on the motherboard or within the CPU, that retain instructions and data to be accessed by the CPU. As a program is running, the instructions and data are loaded from a permanent storage device, such as a hard drive, into these memory chips. Once transferred, the other components of the system access this information only from its memory location and not the permanent storage device. The main reason for what appears as a double set of information is that the access time from memory is significantly less than the access time from a storage device like a hard drive. Access from memory improves overall system performance. As you'll see in this section, the computer's motherboard contains several different types of memory, each optimized for its intended use.

RAM

The large, rectangular memory modules housed on the computer's motherboard contain the computer's **random access memory (RAM)**. RAM is volatile memory, which means it is not permanent and its contents are erased when the computer's power is switched off. The purpose of RAM is to

- Receive and hold program instructions and data while being used by the system.
- Provide those instructions and data to the CPU when needed.
- Hold the results of the CPU's processing until an instruction is received to

transfer it to a printer or permanent storage device.

Why is it called *random access memory*? RAM is called *random access* because any storage location can be accessed directly without having to go from the first location to the last in sequential order. Perhaps it should have been called *nonsequential memory*, because RAM access is hardly random. RAM is organized and controlled in a way that can be compared to post office boxes (Figure 2.25). Each location has a **memory address** (in binary form) that enables the location to be found and the content within to be accessed directly. IBM preferred the term *direct access storage*. Note that other forms of storage such as the hard disk and CD-ROM are also accessed directly or randomly (meaning out of sequential order), but the term *random access* is never applied to these forms of storage.

Of the various types of RAM available, today's newest and fastest PCs contain either DDR2-SDRAM (double-data-rate two synchronous dynamic RAM) or DDR3-SDRAM. RAM appears today in the form of **memory modules** or **memory cards**. A memory module is actually a small circuit board that holds several RAM chips and fits into special slots on the motherboard. Today RAM modules are usually **dual inline memory modules (DIMM)** that have a 168-pin connector and a 64-bit data transfer rate. Their predecessor, **single inline memory modules (SIMM)**, used a 72-pin connector and a 32-bit data transfer rate. Remember that any type of RAM must have a constant power supply or it loses its contents. RAM is not permanent storage!

How much RAM does a computer need? In general, the more memory a system has,

the better. Windows Vista and Mac OS X theoretically require only 512 MB of RAM, but neither system functions well with so little. For today's Microsoft Windows, Linux, and Macintosh operating systems, 1 GB of RAM is a practical working minimum.

Windows 7 touts a new reduced **memory footprint**, the amount of RAM the program uses while it operates. In the past, each successive Windows OS required larger amounts of system resources like RAM. The fact that Windows 7 is bucking that trend is giving people hope that OS RAM requirements might stabilize.

Operating systems frequently use **virtual memory** in addition to RAM. With virtual memory, the computer looks at RAM to identify data that has not been used recently and copies this data onto the hard disk. This frees up space in RAM to load a new application or increase the space needed by a program currently in use. The computer uses virtual memory when RAM gets full (which can easily happen if you run several programs at once). Accessing data on a disk drive is much slower than using RAM, so when virtual memory kicks in, the computer may seem to slow to a crawl. To avoid using virtual memory, choose a system with at least 2 GB of RAM. Many new systems are being advertised with 3 to 4 GB of RAM. If you have a system and need to increase the amount of RAM, visit **www.crucial.com.** This Web site provides you with a three-step advisor to guide you to the correct memory purchase:

- *Step 1:* Select a manufacturer.
- *Step 2:* Select a product line.
- *Step 3:* Select a model.

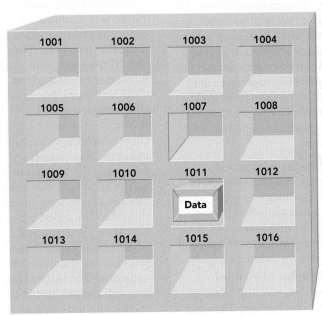

FIGURE 2.25 The addressing scheme used to identify RAM locations makes storage and retrieval fast and easy.

If you are unsure of any of the requested information, you can allow the Web site to scan your system and, within its ability, determine the appropriate type of RAM you should add.

Cache Memory

RAM is fast, but it isn't fast enough to support the processing speeds of today's superfast microprocessors, such as the Intel Core i7 Extreme Edition or the AMD Phenom X4. These microprocessors use cache memory to function at maximum speed. **Cache memory** is a small unit of ultrafast memory built into or near the processor that stores frequently or recently accessed program instructions and data. Cache (pronounced "cash") memory is much faster than RAM, but it's also more expensive. Although the amount of cache that comes on a system is relatively small compared with RAM, 2GB to 4 GB, cache memory greatly improves the computer system's overall performance because the CPU retrieves data more quickly from cache than from RAM.

Cache is identified by its location relative to the CPU. There can be three levels of cache in a system.

- **Level 1 (L1) cache**, also called **primary cache**, is a unit of 4 KB to 16 KB of ultrafast memory included in the microprocessor chip that runs at approximately 10 **nanoseconds**. A nanosecond is one-billionth of a second. Primary cache is the fastest memory.
- **Level 2 (L2) cache**, also called **secondary cache**, is a unit of up to 512 KB of ultrafast memory that can be located within the microprocessor, but further from the registers than Level 1 cache, or on a separate cache chip located on the motherboard very close to the microprocessor. It runs at 20 to 30 nanoseconds.
- **Level 3 (L3) cache**, is found on some systems with newer microprocessors, like Intel's Xeon processor, that are located in some servers and workstations. It is located outside of the processor on a separate cache chip on the motherboard very close to the microprocessor.

Keeping the Level 2 and Level 3 cache as close as possible to the microprocessor improves overall system performance (Figure 2.26).

Now that you know the different levels of cache and where they can be located, how is the information in them accessed? There is a sequence that the CPU (microprocessor) follows when looking for an instruction or data. The sequence goes like this: If the next instruction or data to be fetched is not already in a register, the CPU (microprocessor) attempts to locate that instruction in Level 1 cache. If it is not located in Level 1 cache, the CPU checks Level 2 cache; and if the instruction is not in Level 2 cache, then it checks Level 3 cache, if any Level 3 cache exists on the system. If the command is not already loaded into one of the cache chips, then the CPU must make the longer and slower trip and check RAM.

Because cache is part of the microprocessor or the motherboard, it cannot be upgraded. For this reason, it is important to check the amount of the various levels of cache on a system when you purchase a computer.

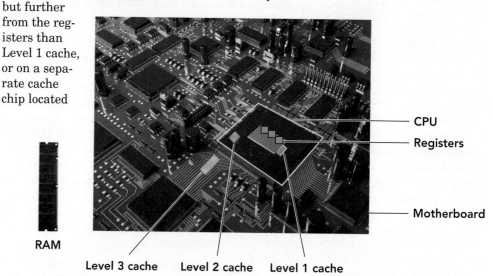

RAM

Level 3 cache   Level 2 cache   Level 1 cache

CPU
Registers
Motherboard

FIGURE 2.26 The close proximity of cache to the CPU is one reason why accessing information from cache is quicker than from RAM.

ROM and Other Types of Memory on the Motherboard

If everything in RAM is erased when the power is turned off, how does the computer start up again? The answer is **read-only memory (ROM)**, a type of nonvolatile memory in which instructions are prerecorded and not erased when the system is shut down. Listed here are some of the programs stored in ROM:

- **BIOS,** the **basic input/output system**—the first code run when a system is powered on. It checks and initializes such devices as the keyboard, display screens, and disk drives. Many modern systems have flash BIOS, which means that the BIOS is stored on flash memory chips and can be updated if needed.
- **Bootstrap Loader**—a program that locates and loads the operating system into RAM.
- **CMOS** or **complementary metal-oxide semiconductor**—controls a variety of actions including starting the power-on self test and verifying that other components of the system are functioning correctly. Many settings can be altered in the CMOS configuration screen, available by pressing certain keys during the boot process. This screen contains information about the components of the system, for example, the hard drive type and size, and should only be altered by an experienced user. CMOS is often mistaken for the BIOS.
- **POST,** also called the **power-on self test**—a program that is run when the system is started. It checks the circuitry and RAM, marking any locations that are defective so that they do not get used.

ROM has evolved over the decades from read-only memory that cannot be changed to variations that can be programmed and re-programmed.

- **PROM**—programmable read-only memory that can be written on only once, but requires a special writing device. It cannot be erased and reused. It is used to hold startup programs that are bug free and are never meant to be changed.
- **EPROM**—electrically programmable read-only memory is erasable PROM that can be reused many times. Erasure is accomplished using a UV (ultraviolet) light source that shines

through a quartz erasing window in the EPROM package. It is used primarily by programmers in the development process of programs so that errors can be corrected.

- **EEPROM**—electrically erasable programmable read-only memory that can be rewritten many times while the chip is in the computer. EEPROM is erased one byte at a time, using an electric field instead of an UV light source, eliminating the need for an erasing window. It is used in the development process to allow for the quick correction or editing of programs being tested.

- **Flash EPROM**—similar to an EEPROM except that flash EPROMs are erased in blocks, whereas regular EEPROMs erase one byte at a time. This is the type of chip that currently holds the BIOS so that it can be altered by the user during the boot process by holding down certain keys. Again, changes should be made with care only by an experienced user.

The following sections explore what can be found on the outside of the system unit of a typical desktop computer.

What's on the Outside of the Box?

You'll find the following features on the outside of a typical desktop computer's system unit:

- The front panel with various buttons and lights
- The power switch

FIGURE 2.28 The connectors on the outside of a system unit enable you to connect peripherals such as a printer, keyboard, or mouse.

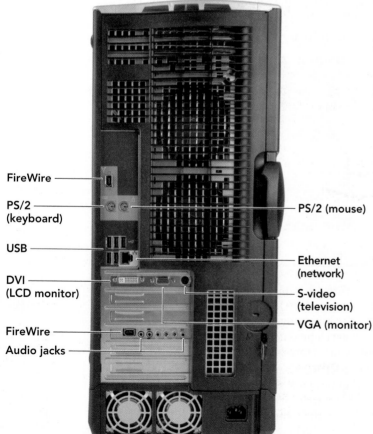

FireWire

PS/2 (keyboard)

USB

DVI (LCD monitor)

FireWire

Audio jacks

PS/2 (mouse)

Ethernet (network)

S-video (television)

VGA (monitor)

- Connectors and ports for plugging in keyboards, mice, monitors, and other peripheral devices

On the front panel of some system units, you'll find a **drive activity light**, which indicates your hard disk is accessing data, and a **power-on light**, which indicates whether the power is on.

The power switch is usually on the front of the system unit. In earlier days it was placed on the back of the unit because of fears that users would accidentally press it and inadvertently shut down their systems. Computers don't handle sudden power losses well. For example, a power outage could scramble the data on your hard drive, corrupting files and making them inaccessible the next time you try to use them. Likewise, just turning off your computer instead of shutting it down properly can leave the system unstable and possibly unable to restart. You should always follow the appropriate shutdown procedure to shut off your computer.

If your computer freezes or won't respond to any key or mouse commands, first try pressing the Ctrl, Alt, and Del keys simultaneously to activate the Windows Task Manager. The dialog box the Task Manager opens allows the user to force the closing of a nonresponsive program. Using this should be a last resort because using the Ctrl, Alt, Del action will cause any unsaved work to be lost.

Connectors and Ports

A **connector** is a physical receptacle located on the system unit or an expansion card that is visible on the outside of the unit. Each connector is designed for a specific type of plug. Plugs are sometimes secured by **thumbscrews**—small screws that are usually attached to the plug and are used to secure the plug to the system unit or expansion card extender to prevent an accidental disconnect. Expansion cards are plug-in adapters that fit into slots on the motherboard and connect the computer with various peripherals. The connectors on these cards are located on extender pieces that are visible through slots on the outside of the system and are described as being *male* (those with external pins) or *female* (those with receptacles for external pins).

Figure 2.28 summarizes the connectors you may find on the computer's case. Most of these connectors are on the back of the case, but on notebook computers (Figure 2.29) it's now common to find several on the front or

Right side (15-inch and 17-inch)

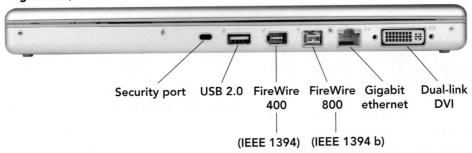

Security port USB 2.0 FireWire 400 FireWire 800 Gigabit ethernet Dual-link DVI

(IEEE 1394)   (IEEE 1394 b)

Left side (15-inch)

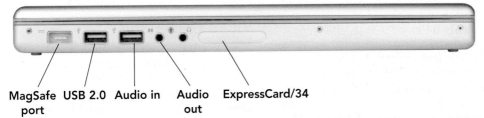

MagSafe port USB 2.0 Audio in Audio out ExpressCard/34

FIGURE 2.29 The location of connectors on a notebook may vary. Many are located on the sides, and some might even appear on the front.

side, providing easier access for many different peripheral devices.

It's important to remember that a connector isn't the same thing as a port. A **port** is an electronically defined pathway or interface for getting information into and out of the computer. A connector is a physical device—a plug-in. A port is an interface—the matching of input and output flows. A port almost always uses a connector, but a connector isn't always a port. For example, a telephone jack is just a connector—not a port. To function, a port must be linked to a specific receptacle. This linking is done by the computer system's start-up and configuration software located in ROM memory. For more information about connectors and ports, their location on the system unit, and the devices that connect to each, go to **www.howstuffworks.com** and type "**connectors and ports**" in the search box located near the top of the screen.

The following section uses *port* as if it were synonymous with *connector*, in line with everyday usage; however, keep the distinction in mind. Let's look next at the types of ports found on the exterior of a typical computer system's case.

USB Ports

USB (universal serial bus) ports can connect a variety of devices, including keyboards, mice, printers, and digital cameras, and were designed to replace older parallel and serial ports. A single USB port can connect up to 127 peripheral devices, eliminating the need for special ports that work only with specific devices (Figure 2.30).

Although introduced in 1995, USB ports didn't become widespread until the 1998 release of the best-selling iMac. The current standard, USB 2.0 (high-speed USB), replaced USB 1.1 and was released in April 2000. USB 2.0 is fully compatible with USB 1.1 products, cables, and connectors.

USB 2.0 ports use an external bus standard that supports data transfer rates of 480 Mbps (480 million bits per second) between the computer and its peripheral devices; they do not transfer data between devices within the system. Some advantages include hot swapping and support for plug-and-play. **Hot swapping** is the ability to connect and disconnect devices without shutting down your computer. This is convenient when you're using portable devices that you want to disconnect often, such as a digital camera. **Plug-and-play (PnP)** refers to a set of standards, jointly developed by Intel Corporation and Microsoft, which enable a computer to automatically detect the brand, model, and characteristics of a device when you plug it in and configure the system accordingly.

Computer manufacturers have been installing increasing numbers of USB ports because of their convenience and versatility; many systems now have six or more. Ports on the back of a computer are typically used for peripherals that won't be

FIGURE 2.30 USB ports and connectors will be the standard for years to come. Because of their universal connectivity, they are replacing expansion boards for some devices.

FIGURE 2.31 If your computer needs more USB ports, a USB hub can expand your options.

removed often, like a printer or keyboard, whereas front ports are ideal for syncing a handheld device or MP3 player. If your computer doesn't have enough USB ports, it is possible to obtain a **USB hub**—a device that plugs into an existing USB port and contains four or more additional ports (Figure 2.31).

Up next on the horizon is USB 3.0, known as *SuperSpeed USB*. USB 3.0 is expected to use a fiber optic link to attain a data transfer rate of 4.8 Gbps—up to 10 times faster than USB 2.0. Additionally, USB 3.0 will be compatible with older versions, providing the same benefits while consuming less power.

1394 Ports (FireWire)

In 1995 Apple introduced **FireWire**, an interface Apple created and standardized as the IEEE 1394 High Performance Serial Bus specification. It is also known as Sony i.Link or IEEE 1394, the official name for the standard. FireWire is similar to USB in that it offers a high-speed connection for dozens of peripheral devices (up to 63 of them). It is especially well suited for transmitting digital video and audio data (Figure 2.32).

On non-Apple systems a FireWire port is called a **1394 port**, after the international standard that defines it. Like USB, FireWire enables hot swapping and PnP. However, it is more expensive than USB and is used only for certain high-speed peripherals, such as digital video cameras,

FIGURE 2.32 FireWire cables are used with FireWire ports to transmit digital video or audio files at high rates of speed.

that need greater throughput (data transfer capacity) than USB provides.

FireWire 400 has a data transfer rate of 400 Mbps; FireWire 800 offers 800 Mbps. The next generation, FireWire S3200, is expected to transfer data at 3.2 Gbps. Although some experts consider FireWire technologically superior to USB, the popularity and affordability of USB 2.0, coupled with the promise of an even faster USB interface in the future, lead most to believe that the 1394 FireWire standard may fade away.

Video Connectors

Most computers use a video adapter (also called a video card) to generate the output that is displayed on the computer's screen or monitor. On the back of the adapter you'll find a standard **VGA (video graphics array) connector**, a 15-pin male connector that works with standard monitor cables. VGA connectors transmit analog video signals and are used for legacy technology cathode ray tube (CRT) monitors.

Many liquid crystal display (LCD) monitors can receive analog or digital video signals. A **DVI (digital visual interface) port** lets LCD monitors use digital signals. However, unless you have a keen eye or are doing professional video editing, the difference between analog and digital signals may not be noticeable.

On some computers the video circuitry is built into the motherboard. This type of video circuitry is called **onboard video**. On such systems the video connector is on the back of the system unit case.

Additional Ports and Connectors

You may find the following additional ports and connectors on the exterior of a computer's case or on one of the computer's expansion cards:

- *Telephone connector:* The typical modem interface, a telephone connector (called RJ-11), is a standard modular telephone jack that will work with an ordinary telephone cord.

- *Network connector:* Provided with networking adapters, the network connector (called an RJ-45 or Ethernet port) looks like a standard telephone jack but is bigger and capable of much faster data transfer.

- *PC card slots:* Notebook computers provide one or more PC card slots for plugging in PC cards or ExpressCards.

Like USB devices, these cards can be inserted or removed while the computer is running.

- *Sound card connectors:* PCs equipped with sound cards (adapters that provide stereo sound and sound synthesis), as well as Macs with built-in sound, offer two or more sound connectors. These connectors, also called jacks, accept the same stereo miniplug used by portable CD players. Most sound cards provide four connectors: Mic (microphone input), Line In (accepts input from other audio devices), Line Out (sends output to other audio devices), and Speaker (sends output to external speakers).
- *Game card:* Game cards provide connectors for high-speed access to the CPU and RAM for graphics-intensive interaction.
- *TV/sound capture board connectors:* If your computer is equipped with TV and video capabilities, you'll see additional connectors that look like those found on a television monitor. These include a connector for a coaxial cable, which can be connected to a video camera or cable TV system.
- *ExpressCard:* This is the newest standard for the PC card, originally known as the PCMCIA card (short for Personal Computer Memory Card International Association). Mostly designed for and used in notebook computers, the ExpressCard can also be found in desktops. The **ExpressCard** is a credit card–sized adapter that fits into a designated slot to provide expanded capabilities such as wireless communication, additional memory, multimedia, or security features.

Some legacy ports are being replaced by technologies like **SATA (serial advance technology attachment)**. The Serial ATA International Organization (SATA IO) is responsible for developing, managing, and pushing the adoption of the serial ATA specifications. Users of the SATA interface benefit from greater speed, simpler upgradable storage devices, and easier configuration. The interface greatly increases the data transfer rate between the motherboard and storage devices like hard drives and optical drives.

Legacy Technology

Legacy technology is an older technology, device, or application that is being phased out in favor of new advances in technology. Although legacy technology may still work, it may not be available on newer computer systems. The following types of ports are all considered legacy technology (Figure 2.33).

Legacy Technologies	
Connector	Use
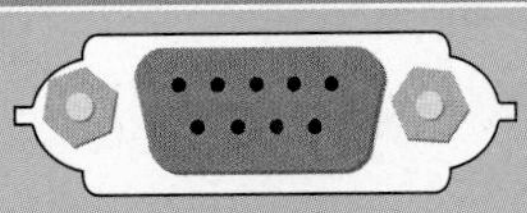 Serial	Dial-up modems, mice, scanners, or printers
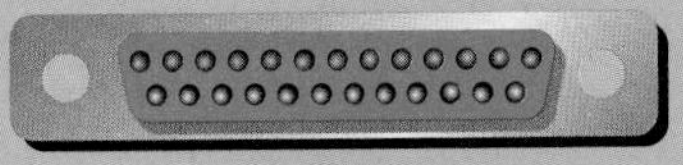 Parallel	Printers, external storage devices, or scanners
 PS/2	Mice and keyboards
 SCSI	Scanners, zip drives, and external hard drives

FIGURE 2.33 Legacy Technologies

- **Serial ports** were one of the earliest types of ports and were often used with dial-up modems to achieve two-way communication. Although they are still in use on servers, many new computers no longer include serial ports, opting to use USB ports instead.
- **Parallel ports** were commonly used to connect a PC to a printer but have been replaced by USB ports and Ethernet ports.
- **PS/2 ports** were typically used for mice and keyboards, but were not interchangeable. Today most mice and keyboards connect via USB connectors.
- **SCSIs** (pronounced "scuzzy"; short for **small computer system interface ports**) were a type of parallel interface that enabled users to connect up to 15 SCSI-compatible devices, such as printers, scanners, and digital cameras, in a daisy-chain series.

These legacy ports are becoming obsolete because newer ports, such as USB, FireWire, and SATA, provide greater flexibility and faster data transfer rates.

Select System Unit Components for a New Computer System

▶ **Use this checklist of components within the system unit to keep your purchase in line with your needs.**

1. Uses

   a. What will you use your system for? ☐ Work ☐ Personal ☐ Gaming

   b. What is more important to you? ☐ Speed ☐ Memory

2. Portability

   a. Do you need to take your system with you? ☐ Yes ☐ No

   b. Do you need to have Internet access? ☐ Yes ☐ No

   c. If you answer yes to part b, indicate whether you will you need an ☐ Ethernet connector network interface card or ☐ wireless network interface card

3. Processor Speed

   a. What is the processor speed of your current system? _____

   b. Do you need a system with a processor that runs faster? ☐ Yes ☐ No

   If yes, why? _____

4. Processor Type

   a. What is the processor type of your current system? _____

   b. Do you need a dual- or quad-core processor? ☐ Yes ☐ No

   If yes, why? _____

5. Memory Usage

   a. What is the amount of RAM in your current system? _____

   b. Do you need a system with more RAM? ☐ Yes ☐ No

   If yes, why? _____

6. Cache Types and Amount

   a. What types of cache is in your current system? ☐ L1 ☐ L2 ☐ L3

   b. Do you need a system with more cache? ☐ Yes ☐ No

   If yes, why? _____

Chapter Summary

Inside the System Unit

- The basic unit of information in a computer is the bit—a single circuit whose electrical state is represented by the binary digits—0 or 1. A sequence of eight bits, called a *byte*, is sufficient to represent the basic letters, numbers, and punctuation marks of most languages.

- Bits are used to describe data transfer rates, whereas bytes describe storage capacity. Common transfer rates are kilobits per second (Kbps) megabits per second (Mbps), and gigabits per second (Gbps). These respectively correspond (roughly) to 1 thousand, 1 million, and 1 billion bits per second. Common storage units are kilobyte (KB), megabyte (MB), gigabyte (GB), and terabyte (TB). The respective sizes of these units are 1 thousand, 1 million, 1 billion, and 1 trillion characters.

- The system unit contains the motherboard, memory, circuits, power supply, cooling fan(s), internal speakers, drive bays for storage devices, and expansion cards.

- The computer's motherboard contains the microprocessor, the system clock, the chipset, memory modules, and expansion slots.

- The computer's central processing unit (CPU) processes data in a four-step machine cycle using two components: the control unit and the arithmetic logic unit (ALU). The control unit follows a program's instructions and manages four basic operations: fetch, decode, execute, and store. The ALU performs arithmetic and logical operations.

- The performance of the microprocessor is determined by number of transistors, their proximity to each other, processing speed, the data bus width and word size, clock speed, operations performed per microprocessing cycle, the use of parallel processing, and the type of chip.

- The computer's main memory, random access memory (RAM), holds programs, data, and instructions currently in use for quick access by the processor. Level 1, Level 2, and Level 3 cache, physically positioned within or close to the CPU, operate at speeds faster than RAM and keep frequently accessed data available to the processor. Read-only memory (ROM) holds prerecorded start-up operating instructions.

- A variety of ports and connectors enable peripheral devices, such as USB drives, external hard drives, digital cameras, and iPods, to function effectively.

Key Terms and Concepts

Identification

Label each hardware component.

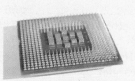

1. _____

3. _____

2. _____

4. _____

5. _____

7. _____

6. _____

8. _____

Matching

Match each key term in the left column with the most accurate definition in the right column:

_____ 1. ASCII

_____ 2. gigabyte

_____ 3. ROM

_____ 4. register

_____ 5. multitasking

_____ 6. virtual memory

_____ 7. parallel processing

_____ 8. RAM

_____ 9. megabyte

_____ 10. Extended ASCII

_____ 11. pipelining

_____ 12. memory footprint

_____ 13. terabyte

_____ 14. Unicode

_____ 15. cache

a. A character coding system that uses eight bits and can represent 256 characters.

b. Temporary storage, located on the motherboard, used to hold programs and data currently in use

c. A small unit of very high-speed memory that works closely with the microprocessor and is either located in the microprocessor or in close proximity

d. A unit of storage capacity that refers to 1 million characters

e. Memory that is not volatile and contains start-up instructions

f. A character coding system that uses seven bits and can represent 128 characters

g. The amount of memory that a program uses while running

h. A unit of storage capacity that refers to 1 trillion characters

i. A technique that feeds a new instruction into the CPU at every step of the processing cycle

j. A character coding system that uses 16 bits and can represent 65,000 characters.

k. A unit of storage capacity that refers to 1 billion characters

l. The use of more than one processor to execute program instructions

m. The rapid switching between programs and instructions in use

n. A high-speed temporary storage location that runs at the same speed as the central processing unit it is embedded within

o. Temporary use of the hard drive to hold programs and data in use

Multiple Choice

Circle the correct choice for each of the following:

1. What is the term used to refer to the ability to connect and disconnect devices without shutting down a system?
   a. Hot swapping   b. Memory footprint
   c. PnP   d. Parallel processing

2. What is the smallest unit of information a computer can work with?
   a. Megabyte   b. Kilobyte
   c. Byte   d. Bit

3. Which of the following is listed in order from largest to smallest?
   a. MB, GB, TB, KB   b. GB, MB, TB, KB
   c. TB, GB, MB, KB   d. KB, MB, GB, TB

4. Which of the following can be added by an expansion card?
   a. Cache   b. RAM
   c. Registers   d. ROM

5. Which step of the machine cycle retrieves the next program instruction from memory?
   a. Fetch   b. Decode
   c. Execute   d. Store

6. Which of the following is an example of a binary number?
   a. AF   b. 0002
   c. 0101   d. 08A

7. Which number describes a computer's word size?
   a. 30   b. 64
   c. 60   d. 4

8. What is plug-and-play (PnP)?
   a. A multifunctional port that allows the connection of various peripherals
   b. A feature that automatically detects new compatible peripherals connected to a system
   c. Hard drive storage that is used as RAM when RAM is filled
   d. The name of a new CPU for systems used by gamers

9. Which component of the CPU is responsible for performing addition, subtraction, multiplication, and division?
   a. L1 cache   b. L2 cache
   c. ALU   d. Control unit

10. What is the freeway of parallel connections that allows internal and external components of the system unit to communicate?
    a. CPU   b. Port
    c. Connector   d. Bus

Fill-In

In the blanks provided, write the correct answer for each of the following:

1. If your computer freezes and won't respond, press the three keys _____ simultaneously to access the Windows Task Manager.

2. A(n) _____ processor is placed within a device and is designed and programmed to perform only the tasks done by that device.

3. Current is converted from alternating (AC) to direct (DC) by the _____ located within the system unit.

4. _____ is a situation in which the CPU needs the results of a previous instruction to process another one.

5. The _____ step of the machine cycle translates an instruction into a form that the processor can understand.

6. The two subcomponents of the CPU are the _____ and the _____.

7. _____ is the maximum number of bits a CPU can process at once.

8. Video circuitry built into the motherboard is called _____.

9. The network connector called RJ-45 that looks like a standard phone jack but is bigger and capable of faster data transfer is also called a(n) _____ port.

10. The execution portion of the machine cycle contains the _____ and _____ steps.

11. The _____ numbering system uses the digits 0 through 9 and the characters A through F.

12. _____ is a type of ROM that is erased in blocks and currently holds a system's BIOS.

13. The number _____ is the binary representation for a circuit that contains current.

14. The instruction portion of the machine cycle contains the _____ and _____ steps.

15. The two types of operations performed by the ALU are _____ and _____ operations.

Short Answer

1. List the four operations of the processing cycle and provide a brief description of their function.

2. What are the differences between pipelining, multitasking, and parallel processing?

3. Place the following hardware in order from the one with the fastest access speed to the one with the slowest access speed: Level 2 cache, Level 1 cache, RAM, registers, hard disk. Indicate the reason for the differences in their access speeds.

4. What is the difference between Level 1, Level 2, and Level 3 cache? Why is it important to have some amount of cache on a system today?

5. List the two subcomponents of the CPU and explain the function of each.

Teamwork

1. **Dream Machine** For this exercise your team will use the information in this chapter and your computing needs and desires to come up with the technical specs and price for your dream computer. Include the name and details of the processor you select, the amount of RAM, the type and amount of cache, and the type of video and sound card you want installed. Additionally, cite the purposes for which your team members intend to use the system. Use an Excel spreadsheet to display each component, its technical specs, and its associated price. Provide a total for the dream system. Below the technical specs, include the list of purposes that the team proposed in ranked order from the use that most members cited to the one that was cited the least.

2. **Design a New Computer Lab** As a team, use a word processing program to create a questionnaire with options for possible computer systems to be placed in a hypothetical new computer lab on campus. Use the hardware and system information in this chapter to help create the checklist on the questionnaire. Distribute the questionnaire to at least 30 students on campus. Collect the data and, using prices from local vendors or Internet retail sites, generate a spreadsheet. The spreadsheet should list the most popular components chosen by the survey participants and their cost from at least two different vendors. Use the cost of the least expensive units to estimate the cost for 20 units. If time allows, add to the spreadsheet the cost of 20 desks and 20 chairs for a more comprehensive lab cost estimate. Turn in the questionnaire distributed, the responses to the questionnaire, the spreadsheet with the cost comparisons of at least two vendors, and your final lab estimate.

3. **Step into the Game** Your team is to research three of the newest and most popular gaming systems. Research the components within each system. Your team members will probably be surprised to find out that the internal components of these systems are similar to a desktop or notebook computer. Make a comparison chart of the three units in an Excel spreadsheet. Include the type of central processor (CPU), the type of gaming processor (GPU), the amount of RAM, the type of audio processors, and the number of controller ports. Come up with a list of the games that your team would use on each system. Then, as a team, rank the units as 1, 2, or 3, with 1 being the unit most desired and 3 being the unit least desired. State the reasons for your ranking.

4. **Let Your Imagination Soar** As a team, make a list of the features that you would want in a desktop, notebook, or netbook of the future. Include such features as processor speed, monitor size or shape, input devices, output devices, the size and shape of the system unit, and any green features that you want it to include. You might search the Internet for some creative ideas. After all ideas have been discussed, as a team, select the best five to eight ideas and present them to the class in a PowerPoint slide show. If you used the Internet, identify your source and include a picture, if one is available. If any members can draw an image of your own future idea or concept, include those images also.

5. **Buy New or Upgrade?** Whether to buy a new computer or upgrade is a question that every computer owner faces at some time. Your team members should locate several references on this topic. Make a list of some of the behaviors that a computer can exhibit that might indicate that the system is old or malfunctioning. In a one-page, double-spaced report, use your list of behaviors to support a decision to buy a new system or to simply upgrade a current one. Remember to cite your references.

On the Web

1. **All Aboard the Motherboard** Go to **http://videos.howstuffworks.com/howstuffworks/23-computer-tour-video.htm** and watch the video about the components found on the motherboard. In a one-page, double-spaced report, describe the seven components on the motherboard that the video reviews. In addition, detail five additional pieces of information that the video covers that are not discussed in this chapter.

2. **Let the Games Begin!** Computer gaming has created a use for computer systems that demands more speed and graphic capabilities than are available from most systems in a business environment. Go to **www.cyberpowerpc.com**. On the menu across the top of the page, select the Intel desktop and AMD desktop options. From each of these two choices, additional choices appear. Select an option under each that contains the word *gamer*. After reviewing several gaming systems, pick two from Intel and two from AMD. In a spreadsheet or table, list the following information: name of each system, price, CPU name and speed, amount of RAM, name and number of video cards, size of hard drive, and any additional fans or cooling systems. When you have researched all four systems, indicate the one you favor and the reasons for your choice.

3. **Code Converter** Use your favorite search engine to locate a Web site that displays the "ASCII code binary table." Use that table to code the message here into binary form. Once it's converted, use the converter calculator in the chapter, or any other such calculator located on the Web, to convert the binary code into hexadecimal.

   Message to convert: Less is more!

4. **The Base of Mobility** In mobile devices, the brain or processor is one of the most important components. Use your favorite search engine to locate information about processors for mobile devices. Locate several Web sites that either give you information about the new AMD processors or direct you to articles about this topic. In a one-page, double-spaced report, provide information about the competition in this mobile market. Who are the key players? Which devices use which processors? What are the capabilities of competing processors? Remember to cite your Web references.

5. **Recycle, Recycle, Recycle** With the emphasis today on reusability, recycling, and a greener environment, it should not surprise you that the disposal of computing devices has become a great concern. Using the Internet and your favorite Web browser, research the recycling and disposal options available to a user when getting rid of an aging computing device. Indicate the cost of recycling, if any, and whether the owner of the device, the manufacturer, or the recycling source pays the cost. Present your options in a PowerPoint slide show. Remember to include the reasons for recycling, the cost and who pays it, and the possible recycling options.

chapter 3

Input/Output and Storage

Chapter Objectives

You've selected a system unit from your favorite manufacturer and decided on a processor and the amount of RAM you want. Do you think all your choices are made? Think again. Today, you can choose just about all of the remaining system components. Have you considered a wireless or flexible keyboard? What about an ergonomic mouse and mouse pad? How many USB ports to do you need to connect your iPod, digital camera, and other portable devices? How about an OLED monitor instead of an LCD? At this point, you must be wondering, how many additional devices are there to consider?

Input, output, and storage devices are components of a system that you physically interact with every time you use your computer, regardless of whether it's a desktop, notebook, netbook, iPad, or smartphone. Often the selection of these components is taken lightly, and the effect they have on us physically and in terms of productivity is ignored. This chapter will help facilitate your input, output, and storage decisions by

- Describing a variety of of input and pointing device options, such as a mouse, keyboard, joystick, and touch pad.
- Explaining the different monitor types, sizes, and resolutions and how they work.
- Clarifying the operation of hard drive storage and its importance to your overall system performance.
- Evaluating the various portable storage options, such as USB flash drives, CDs, and DVDs. ∎

Check out **f** Facebook
for our latest updates

www.facebook.com

Input Devices: Giving Commands

Input refers to providing data and instructions into the computer for processing. This section discusses **input devices**, the hardware components that make it possible for you to get data and instructions into RAM, or temporary memory, where it is held while in use (Figure 3.1).

Keyboards

Despite all of the high-tech input devices on the market, the keyboard is still the most common. A **keyboard** is an input device that uses switches and circuits to translate keystrokes into a signal a computer understands. With a keyboard, a user can enter a document, access menus, use keyboard shortcuts, control game settings and characters, and perform many other actions, depending on the application being run. The 80 keys (or keycaps) on most keyboards are the same and include letters of the alphabet, numbers, punctuation marks, control keys, and function keys, whose purpose usually change with the program in use. **Enhanced keyboards** contain

FIGURE 3.1 Input devices today can vary depending on the type of computing device, user preference, and application in use.

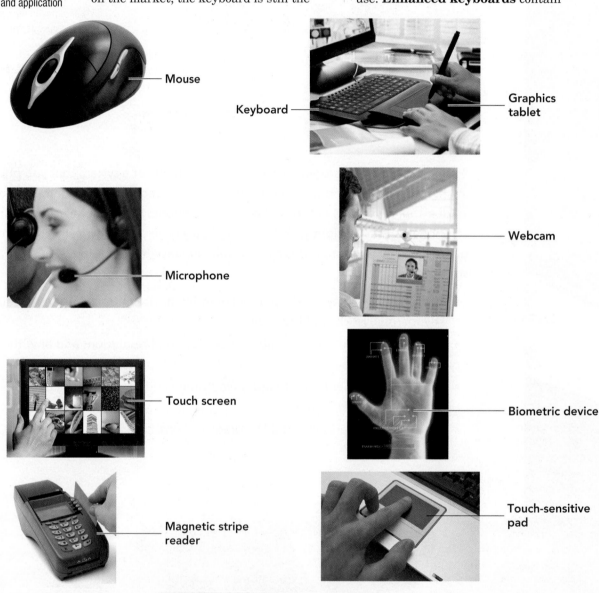

Mouse

Keyboard

Graphics tablet

Microphone

Webcam

Touch screen

Biometric device

Magnetic stripe reader

Touch-sensitive pad

Magnetic ink character recognition

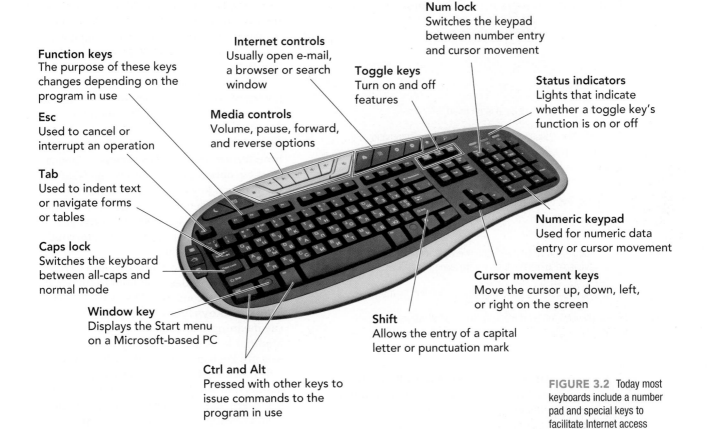

Function keys
The purpose of these keys changes depending on the program in use

Esc
Used to cancel or interrupt an operation

Tab
Used to indent text or navigate forms or tables

Caps lock
Switches the keyboard between all-caps and normal mode

Window key
Displays the Start menu on a Microsoft-based PC

Ctrl and Alt
Pressed with other keys to issue commands to the program in use

Internet controls
Usually open e-mail, a browser or search window

Media controls
Volume, pause, forward, and reverse options

Toggle keys
Turn on and off features

Num lock
Switches the keypad between number entry and cursor movement

Status indicators
Lights that indicate whether a toggle key's function is on or off

Numeric keypad
Used for numeric data entry or cursor movement

Cursor movement keys
Move the cursor up, down, left, or right on the screen

Shift
Allows the entry of a capital letter or punctuation mark

FIGURE 3.2 Today most keyboards include a number pad and special keys to facilitate Internet access and control media.

additional keys, such as media control buttons that adjust speaker volume and access the optical disc drive, and Internet controls that open e-mail, a browser, or a search window with a single keystroke (Figure 3.2). The value of using these enhanced keyboards depends on the operating system, applications you use, and whether you have a desktop or notebook unit.

How Do Keyboards Work? There is a **key matrix**, a grid of circuits, located under the keys. When you press a key, it presses a switch, completing the circuit and allowing a tiny amount of current to flow. When the processor finds a circuit that is complete, also referred to as closed, it compares the location of that circuit on the key matrix to the character map located in its read-only memory (ROM) on the motherboard. A **character map** is a comparison chart or lookup table that tells the processor what key is being pressed. For example, the character map lets the processor know that pressing the z key by itself corresponds to a small letter z, but the Shift and z keys pressed together correspond to a capital Z.

The character then appears onscreen at the location of the **cursor** (also called

the **insertion point**). The cursor indicates where text will appear when you type and may take the shape of a blinking vertical line, a blinking underscore, or a high-lighted box.

How do the impulses get from the keyboard to the monitor? Today, many keyboards are connected to the computer through a cable with a USB (Universal Serial Bus) connector. Notebooks, in which the keyboard is part of the system unit, use internal connectors. Regardless of the type of connector, the cable must carry power into the keyboard and signals from the keyboard out to the computer.

Wireless keyboards are increas-ing in popularity. They connect to the computer through infrared (IR), radio frequency (RF), or Bluetooth connections instead of physical cables. IR and RF connections are similar to what you'd find in a television remote control. Regardless of which sort of signal they use, wireless keyboards require either a built-in receiver or one that is plugged into the USB port to communicate with the computer. Because they aren't physically connected to the computer or any direct power supply, wireless keyboards are battery powered.

FIGURE 3.3 Special Keys on a PC Keyboard

Key Name	Typical Function
Alt	In combination with another key, enters a command (example: Alt + F displays the File tab options in Office 2010).
Caps Lock	Toggles Caps Lock mode on or off.
Ctrl	In combination with another key, enters a command (example: Ctrl + S executes the instruction to save the current file).
End	Moves the cursor to the end of the current line.
F1	Displays on-screen help.
Home	Moves the cursor to the beginning of the current line.
Insert	Toggles between insert and overwrite mode, if these modes are available in the program you're using.
Print Screen	Captures the screen image and places it in memory.
Windows key	Displays the Start menu in Microsoft Windows.

Using Special Keyboard Keys In addition to numeric and alphanumeric characters, a computer keyboard has several special keys that facilitate scrolling and cursor movement and thus increase productivity (Figure 3.3).

To reposition the cursor, you use the mouse or the appropriate **cursor-movement keys** (also called **arrow keys**). These are a set of four keys clustered together to the left of the number pad that move the cursor up, down, left, or right.

A **toggle key** is a key named after a type of electrical switch that has only two positions: on and off. For example, the Caps Lock key functions as a toggle key. When the Caps Lock mode is engaged, or on, you don't have to press the Shift key to enter uppercase letters, and all letters you type are capitalized.

FIGURE 3.4 Common PC Keystroke Shortcuts

File Management		Text Editing	
Ctrl + N	Opens a new blank document	Ctrl + C	Copies selected text
Ctrl + S	Saves the active document	Ctrl + X	Cuts the selected text
Ctrl + O	Opens the Open File dialog box	Ctrl + V	Pastes text that was copied or cut
Ctrl + P	Opens the Print dialog box	Ctrl + H	Locates and replaces text

To turn off the Caps Lock mode, just press the Caps Lock key again. When Caps Lock is off, letters typed without holding down the Shift key are entered as lowercase letters.

Above the letters and numbers on the keyboard, you'll find function keys (labeled F1 through F12 or F15). The action a **function key** performs depends on the program in use; however, the F1 key has been termed the *help key* because it opens the help option in most programs. Near the function keys, you'll also notice the Esc (short for Escape) key. The Esc key's function also depends on which program you're using, but it's generally used to interrupt or cancel an operation.

Some keys, like Shift, Alt, and Ctrl, have no effect unless you hold them down and press a second key. These are called **modifier keys** because they modify the meaning of the next key you press. Modifier keys are frequently used to execute keyboard shortcuts, which provide quick keyboard access to menu commands and window controls. For example, if you are using a Microsoft Office application, pressing Ctrl + S (the + notation means to hold down the Ctrl key while pressing the S key) saves an active document, and Windows + L locks the screen quickly. Frequently used keystroke shortcuts are listed in Figure 3.4. Visit **www.microsoft.com/enable/products/keyboard.aspx** for a detailed list of shortcut keys for many of Microsoft's products. If you are a Mac user, **http://support.apple.com/kb/HT1343** displays a list of Mac shortcut keys and unique control, command, and option keys (that do not appear on a PC keyboard).

Keyboards in a Notebook or Netbook Unit Because of their smaller size, some notebooks and netbooks have more compact keyboards. All of the same functionality is provided through the use of an additional Function key labeled as *Fn* in combination with other keys. One noticeably missing element of these keyboards is a numeric keypad. Instead the keys labeled 7, 8, 9, U, I, O, J, K, L, and M are often used to act as a number pad when they are struck while the Fn function key is held down (Figure 3.5).

Keyboards for Mobile Devices A **soft keyboard**, **virtual keyboard**, or **on-screen keyboard**, is a keyboard that appears on a touch-sensitive screen. With such keyboards, a full set of keys is displayed, and tapping the key on the screen with a stylus or finger is the same as pressing a key on a traditional keyboard. The iPhone has taken the idea of the onscreen keyboard and added software that makes it appear to be an **intelligent keyboard** by providing the user with such features as these:

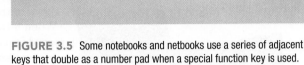

FIGURE 3.5 Some notebooks and netbooks use a series of adjacent keys that double as a number pad when a special function key is used.

- Suggestions for misspelled words and corrections for grammar mistakes, such as inserting of apostrophes and periods, and capitalizing the first letter of a sentence
- Magnifying the on-screen text being entered or modified
- Displaying an enlarged image of each key on the screen as you type, providing visual confirmation of the keystroke for the user
- Allowing the use of editing features such as cut, copy, and paste with a simple touch of the screen

Whether we consider this on-screen keyboard intelligent or not, these features do make texting and using the phone to create short documents while on the go an easier and more intuitive experience.

A **mini-keyboard** is an option available on many smartphones and portable devices. This is a keyboard that has a key for each letter of the alphabet. It is usually hidden when the phone is held in a vertical position, but slides out when the phone is turned horizontally. A **keypad** is a smaller and more compact keyboard, also popular on smartphones. On this device, each key represents multiple letters. The user needs to strike a key one to four times to get the desired character entered as input. Figure 3.6 illustrates the keyboard options on smartphones. With a 107 percent increase in text messaging from 2008 to 2009, and 2.5 billion text messages being sent daily in the U.S. alone, it is no surprise that the type of keyboard a smartphone has might be an important factor in a purchase decision.

A **virtual laser keyboard**, designed to work with portable devices like PDAs and smartphones, generates an image of a full-sized keyboard onto almost any surface. The device itself is about the size of a small cellular phone and works by monitoring the motion of the user's finger movements to determine the key that was struck. It even generates the clicking produced on a regular keyboard. Because the virtual keyboard is an

On-screen intelligent keyboard

Mini-keyboard

Keypad

FIGURE 3.6 Today, mobile devices come equipped with several keyboard options.

image projected by light, it disappears completely when not in use. Virtual laser keyboards are currently not very common and are still a bit trendy; however, they are another alternative to enhance productivity when using portable devices (Figure 3.7).

Using Alternative Keyboards There are many substitutes available if a conventional keyboard just doesn't work for you. A flexible keyboard is a very adaptable foldable keyboard that weighs just 250 grams. The size and layout are the same as a standard PC keyboard. The keyboard is completely sealed, so it is spill and dust resistant, making it the perfect choice for use in factories, wet areas, and retail environments. The characters on the keys will not rub off; they are printed under the protective flexible membrane (Figure 3.8).

FIGURE 3.7 A virtual laser keyboard projects a full-sized keyboard onto almost any surface.

The Ergodex DX1 is a recently developed input system that is available with 25 to 50 keys and an 11-inch × 9.3-inch pad you connect to your computer through a high-speed USB connector. Through its Manager application, you can manipulate the location of the keys to create a unique key arrangement that conforms to the shape of your hand and assign a macro or sequence of functions to execute by pressing a single key. This is rapidly becoming the keyboard of choice for gamers and task-oriented professionals. Other proponents of this input system are developers of applications for young children and physically impaired individuals. Both of these groups find that this system removes the barriers of tedious typing, spelling, and hand span limitations (Figure 3.9).

In most cases, traditional keyboards have keys in the same places. When a traditional keyboard is used for an extended length of time, users can suffer from repetitive strain injuries (RSI) of wrists and hands. Using an ergonomically designed keyboard—one engineered for comfort, ease of use, and injury avoidance—can prevent such injuries (Figure 3.10).

Media center PCs are becoming more and more popular. These all-in-one entertainment devices provide easy access to photos, TV, movies, and the latest in online media—all from the comfort of the couch, by using a remote control. These additional features and placement of the units in family rooms have generated the need for a remote keyboard that is stylish and unobtrusive. The small, wireless keyboards that accompany media center PCs combine a cursor control pad with a miniature keyboard to allow you to manage your unit and

FIGURE 3.8 A flexible keyboard is perfect for travel. It is lightweight, can be purchased with 85 or 109 keys, costs around $25.00, and can be rolled or flexed to fit any suitcase space.

FIGURE 3.9 The Ergodex DX1 is revolutionizing input systems by allowing individuals to customize the location and function of input keys.

FIGURE 3.10 Ergonomic keyboards usually have a raised surface, a wrist rest, and a key display split down the middle.

entertainment viewing experience with your fingertips (Figure 3.11).

Now that we've discussed the basics of using keyboards, let's move on to another piece of equipment commonly used for input: pointing devices.

FIGURE 3.11 Keyboards for PC home entertainment systems, such as the Logitech DiNovo Mini, are compact and allow users to control various media components by keyboard or touchpad.

The Mouse and Other Pointing Devices

A **pointing device** (see Figure 3.12) is an input device that allows you to control the movements of the on-screen pointer. The **pointer** is an on-screen symbol, usually an arrow, that shows the current location of on-the-screen activity. The shape of the on-screen symbol also signifies the type of command, input, or response a user gives. If the pointer is an arrow with the head pointing to the upper-left corner of the screen, the mouse is set to accept the item clicked on as input, or the user's choice. If the arrowhead is pointing to the upper

Mouse
Trackball
Pointing stick
Touchpad
Joystick
Touch screen
Stylus

right, the mouse is a text selection tool and will highlight a portion of text. Some applications allow the user to substitute other shapes for the familiar arrow; however, most users keep the arrow, as it is the most familiar. The behavior of a pointing device is related to the software program used. The most common actions performed by these devices—clicking, double-clicking, selecting, and dragging—are actually means of giving commands and responses to the program. Pointing devices are also used to provide input. For example, they're used in graphics

FIGURE 3.12 Pointing devices come in many shapes and styles and are located in a variety of devices.

programs to draw and paint on the screen, just as if they were a pencil or brush.

The most widely used pointing device is the mouse. A standard piece of equipment on most computer systems, a **mouse** is a palm-sized device designed to move about on a clean, flat surface. The direction and speed of the mouse is mirrored by the on-screen pointer, and other actions are initiated by using the mouse buttons located on the top or on the side of the mouse. Although older roller-ball mice needed a mouse pad for traction, newer mice require less maintenance and only need a mouse pad if the surface that supports them is reflective or the wrong texture. Commonly used mouse devices include the following:

- An **optical mouse** makes use of an LED (light-emitting diode) light on the underside of the mouse and a small camera that takes continuous images of the changes in the surface under the mouse as it is moved. The differences are compared. The direction and speed of the mouse movement are recognized and the on-screen pointer shifted accordingly (Figure 3.13).
- Notebook users may like the **travel mouse**, a pointing device half the size of a normal mouse, but with all the same capabilities.
- The **wheel mouse**, developed by Microsoft, includes a rotating wheel that is used to scroll text vertically within a document or on a Web page.
- The **wireless mouse** (also called a **cordless mouse**), transmits infrared or radio signals (RF) to a base station receiver on the computer. Wireless

mice eliminate the cord tangling associated with the corded variety. The infrared mouse requires line of sight to the receiver, whereas the RF variety uses radio waves that transmit in a wider pattern, eliminating the line of site requirement and allowing the mouse to be positioned further from the system unit.

- An air mouse is a motion-sensing device that recognizes the typical forward, back, left, and right motions made by a mouse. The difference in this device is that it does not need to rest on a surface to function. Instead, it works as it moves through the air. This allows for other directions of motion, like that of up and down, to be programmed to control such media elements as volume and fast forward. The air mouse application 1.5 for the iPhone actually converts your iPhone into an air mouse. Check out **http://cnettv.cnet.com/air-mouse-1-5-iphone/9742-1_53-50005123.html** to view a brief video.

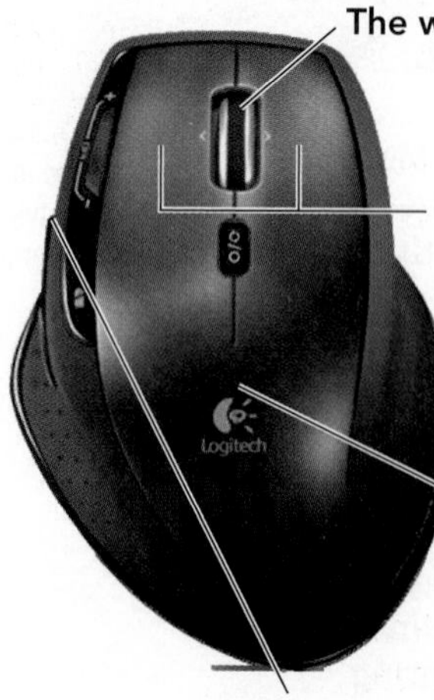

Mouse Alternatives Although the mouse is by far the most popular pointing device, there are some alternatives such as trackballs, pointing sticks, or touch pads. These alternatives work well when desktop space is limited or nonexistent (as is often the case when using a notebook or netbook computer). Other devices, such as joysticks, touch screens, and styluses, are popular for playing games, using ATMs, and managing handheld devices. Let's look at each of these input alternatives.

- A **trackball** is a stationary pointing device that contains a movable ball held in a cradle. The on-screen cursor is moved by rotating the ball with one's fingers or palm. From one to three keys can be located in various positions, depending on the unit, to perform the equivalent of mouse actions like a click and right-click. Today, smartphones and some keyboards make use of a trackball.
- A **pointing stick** is a pointing device that looks like a pencil eraser between the G, H, and B keys. It is pressure sensitive and is pressed and moved in various directions with the forefinger. IBM popularized this device by introducing the TrackPoint on its ThinkPad notebooks.

FIGURE 3.13 An optical mouse can be equipped with several thumb buttons that allow you to move between Web pages, zoom in on photos, or even reassign actions to them that meet your current needs.

The wheel provides quick scrolling.

Finger buttons activate commands.

An optical sensor reads mouse movement.

Reprogrammable thumb buttons allow you to perform specific actions.

- A **touchpad** (also called a **trackpad**) is a small, stationary, pressure-sensitive, flat surface located on the notebook. An area is set aside along the right and bottom edges of the pad to accommodate vertical or horizontal scroll operations. The user slides a finger in these areas to move the cursor, using the same movements as you would with a mouse. Apple's Scrolling TrackPad has added additional flexibility to the use of this device by allowing users to use two fingers instead of one and removing the restricted areas of the right and bottom edges for input. You create the scrolling action by moving both fingers across the pad's surface in the direction you wish to scroll. Current MacBooks, MacBook Pros, and MacBook Airs have a Scrolling Multi-Touch pad.

- A variation of the touchpad is the popular **click wheel**, a pad that looks like a circle and uses a circular motion to move through song lists, movie lists, or photos. The click wheel is the method of navigation on the iPod and the iTouch. You issue commands through one of the touchpad keys located near the edge of the pad or by tapping on the pad's surface.

- A **joystick** is a pointing device used to move objects easily in any direction on-screen. It employs a vertical rod mounted on a base with one or two buttons. Although you can use joysticks as pointing devices, they're most often used to control the motion of an on-screen object in computer games, training simulators, or CAD (computer-aided design) systems.

- A **stylus**, which looks like an ordinary pen except that the tip is dry and semi-blunt, is commonly used as an alternative to fingers on touch-screen devices such as smartphones and with pressure-sensitive graphics tablets used for sketching complex images, for example, buildings and robots in CAD and other graphics applications. You may have also used a stylus to create your digital signature when you use your credit card or accept a package from a delivery person.

- A **touch screen** is a display screen that is sensitive to the touch of a finger or stylus. Used on ATM machines, airport kiosks, retail point-of-sale terminals, car navigation systems, medical monitors, and industrial control panels, the touch screen became wildly popular on handhelds after Apple introduced the iPhone with its improved user-friendly interface in 2007. The primary advantage of a touch screen is the unlimited ways the user display can be designed for input compared to a fixed set of physical keys or buttons. If there is no hardware keyboard on the unit, a soft keyboard can be displayed on screen. Touch screens also accept handwriting, graphics, and finger movements. Figure 3.14 displays several uses of touch-screen applications.

The latest in touch-screen technology, Microsoft's Surface Display, uses a table top as its high-resolution display. The prototype, designed for restaurant use, displays the menu items on the table's surface, allowing the customer to order by simply dragging choices into a center ordering ring. When dining is complete, the bill can be split among individuals in your party by dragging the ordered items into separate payment rings on the display, which includes a slider bar to automatically apply a gratuity. Additional features like videos on the wine you chose and items you previously ordered can appear on the display (Figure 3.15). The idea is to have the display embedded into items like desks, countertops, and coffee tables. Its use for collaborative possibilities in education and business are endless. To see the surface in action, go to **www.seattlepi.com/business/317737_msftdevice30.html#vids** and watch the demonstration video.

Airport check-in

Self-check-out center

Automated banking site

GPS device

Smartphone

FIGURE 3.14 Touch-screen technology is often used to display special-purpose programs. There are usually fewer choices on a screen and larger on-screen buttons to accommodate individual touch.

FIGURE 3.15 The Surface Display, developed by Microsoft, could revolutionize the order and payment process for the service industry.

Alternative Input Devices

Although keyboards and pointing devices are most commonly used to input data, specialized input devices are also available. This section introduces some of these alternative input devices and their uses.

Speech recognition, also called **voice recognition**, is the conversion of spoken words into computer text. The spoken word is first digitized and then matched against a dictionary of coded voice waves. The matches are converted into text as if the words were typed on the keyboard. This method of input is favored by individuals for whom traditional input devices are not an option (for example, those with limited hand movement) and by those who want to significantly limit their use of the mouse and keyboard while maintaining or increasing their overall productivity (for example, writers). To accept speech, a computer must have a microphone, an input device that converts sound waves into electrical signals that the computer is able to process. Speaker-dependent recognition systems require that users speak sample words into the system in order to adjust it to their individual voices. Speaker-independent

FAST FORWARD ▶▶

The next generation of touch-screen input is being jointly developed by Carnegie Mellon University and Microsoft. Known as *Skinput*, the technology uses your body as the touch interface for computer and portable media input (Figure 3.16). Not what you expected, is it? The driving idea behind the development of Skinput is the fact that computers and computer embedded devices are becoming smaller and smaller, yet the input devices, such as keyboards, and output devices, such as monitors, have not gotten much smaller. Through the use of acoustic and impact-sensing software along with a *pico projector*, a very small projection system attached to an armband, images are projected onto your skin, making your wrist and hand the equivalent of a touch screen. No electronics are attached to the skin; instead, you wear a sensing array. When you tap your body with a finger, bone densities, soft tissues, and joint proximity change, resulting in a sound pattern made by the motion. The software recognizes these different acoustic patterns and interprets them as function commands, with accuracies as high as 95.5 percent. Imagine, you will be able to answer your phone by pressing a location on your own wrist, text message on a keypad displayed on your arm, and play video games with your fingers. For a live demonstration, go to **www.gizmag.com/skinput-body-touch-screen-keypad/14408/** to view the video of the prototype.

FIGURE 3.16 A small pico projector will display choices on your skin. The selection you make is detected by a device that senses the sound generated by touching skin, muscle, or bone.

systems do not require tuning and can recognize limited vocabularies such as numeric digits and a handful of words. It is the speaker-independent system that replaces human operators for telephone services.

There are three types of voice recognition systems:

- Command systems recognize only a few hundred words and eliminate using the mouse or keyboard for repetitive commands like open file or close file. This is the least taxing on the computer.
- Discrete voice recognition systems are used for dictation but require a pause between each word. You might have used this technology in a customer-service routing system, where the voice prompts you to answer a question with a one-word reply like yes or no.
- Continuous voice recognition understands natural speech without pauses and is the most process intensive.

Dragon NaturallySpeaking is a speech-recognition software package developed by Dragon Systems. It was among the first programs to make speech recognition practical on a PC. NaturallySpeaking uses a simple visual interface. Dictated words appear in a floating tooltip as they are spoken; when the speaker pauses, the program writes the words in the active window at the location of the cursor. Like other speech recognition software, early versions of the software had to be trained to recognize the user's voice, a process that took approximately 10 minutes. With the release of version 9, training the software is no longer necessary.

A speech recognition system that works with Microsoft's mainstream applications is included in the Microsoft Vista and Windows 7 operating systems. It is a speaker-independent continuous system that allows the user to dictate documents and e-mails, use voice commands to start and switch between applications, control the operating system, fill out forms on the Web, and dictate content into compatible applications (Figure 3.17). Go to **www.youtube.com/watch?v=N3VZnyKViC4** to view a simple demonstration. The system is easy to set up. Follow the steps below to set up the system, and then begin

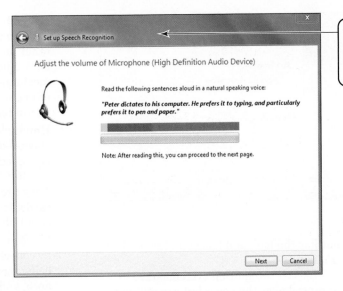

The microphone user interface shows speech status and provides additional information.

to speak the commands you normally type or use a mouse to activate.

1. Click the Start button.
2. Click *Control Panel*.
3. Click *Ease of Use* if your Control Panel is set to view by Category, and then click *Speech Recognition*. If your Control Panel is set to view icons, select *Speech Recognition*.
4. Click *Take Speech Tutorial* from the options presented.

If you plan to use a speech recognition tool, you should invest in a decent microphone to avoid static interference, and take the tutorial to help you understand the types of commands the system has been programmed to accept.

Windows 7 has improved speech recognition by extending it to additional Windows applications. When using this feature with a program that Microsoft considers incompatible, the spoken text is placed into a text box rather than directly into the document. After finishing a sentence or paragraph, the user clicks the Insert or Cancel button. If inserted, the text is placed in the document at the location of the cursor. This feature does not work with all applications, so be sure to confirm its compatibility before you try to use it.

The Apple speech recognition program, MacSpeech Dictate 1.5, is up to 20 percent more accurate than previous versions, comes in versions for medical and legal users, recognizes 13 English dialect variations, and is optimized for performance with key Macintosh productivity applications. It uses the same recognition technology as Dragon NaturallySpeaking

FIGURE 3.17 Speech recognition technology, available in Windows 7 and used in applications like Word 2010, makes opening and closing documents, as well as dictating content, easier.

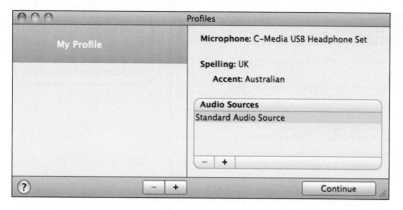

but has the look and feel of a Mac product (Figure 3.18).

Speech recognition systems have improved over the years but are still not perfect. Read about some of the weaknesses and flaws of these systems at **http://electronics.howstuffworks.com/gadgets/high-tech-gadgets/speech-recognition3.htm**.

Input devices are constantly being developed to automate and reduce data entry time. A **scanner** copies anything that's printed on a sheet of paper, including artwork, handwriting, and typed or printed text, and converts the input into a graphics image for the computer. The scanner does not recognize or differentiate the type of material it is scanning. Everything is converted into a graphic **bitmapped image**, a representation of an image as a matrix of dots called picture elements (pixels). All images acquired by digital cameras and camcorders, scanners, and screen capture programs are bitmapped images. Most scanners use **optical character recognition (OCR)** software to automatically convert scanned text into a text file instead of a bitmapped image. Even though this technology has greatly improved, foreign characters and poor quality of the original document will increase the number of errors in the final file.

There are several types of scanners (see Figure 3.19):

- Flatbed scanners copy items placed on a stationary glass surface. They are

good for books or other bulky objects and are also useful for photos and other documents that shouldn't be bent. Sheet-fed scanners use a roller mechanism to draw in multiple sheets of paper, one sheet at a time, and are useful for high-volume scanning.

- Handheld scanners are similar to sheet-fed scanners in that the item to be copied must pass through the scanner, but they are smaller and portable. They are often used to copy business cards, receipts, magazine articles, small photos, or business documents.

- 3D scanners analyze real-world input by collecting information on the item being scanned, including shape, appearance, and color. A three-dimensional model of the image is generated by the scanner. Some current users are in the entertainment and movie industry, video game design, production quality control, and industrial design.

Other examples of input devices include these:

- A handheld or desktop-mounted **bar code reader** can scan an item's Universal Product Code (UPC). The UPC is a pattern of bars printed on merchandise that the store's computer system uses to retrieve information about an item and its price. Today, bar codes are used to update inventory and ensure correct pricing. For example, FedEx uses a bar code system to identify and track packages.

- A special scanning device called an **optical mark reader (OMR)** scans your grid-like Scantron test form and senses the magnetized marks from your no. 2 pencil. It compares your answer against a Scantron form with the correct answers submitted by the instructor. Almost any type of questionnaire can be designed for OMR devices, making it helpful to researchers who need to tabulate responses to large surveys.

Flatbed scanner   Handheld scanner   3D scanner   3D scanner image

- Radio frequency identification technology uses an **RFID reader** to detect radio signals being emitted from a tag placed on an item. What makes these readers so practical? The signal emitted by the tag can be picked up by

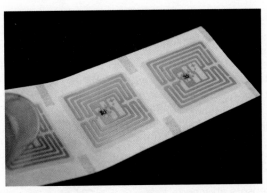

FIGURE 3.20 New RFID tags can be embedded in packaging and allow merchandise to be scanned as the user walks through the checkout, without removing individual items.

RFID readers mounted on a wall and do not have to be scanned by a hand-held scanning device. Today the tags are inexpensive and capable of being embedded within the packaging of the product (Figure 3.20). This makes the tags invisible to the human eye and impossible to remove. Retailers see RFID readers as a means to deter theft and automatically update inventory.

- Magnetic-ink character recognition employs a **MICR reader** to scan and input characters printed with special ink. This ink is used on the bottom of your checks and some billing statements. When the check or statement is returned to the creator, the numbers are scanned by a MICR reader and inputted into the company's data system. No human entry is needed and thus no human error occurs.

- A **magnetic stripe card reader** can detect and read information stored on magnetic strips that are usually located on the back of credit cards, gift cards, and other cards of similar use.

- A **biometric input device** uses physical or chemical features of an individual's body to provide a unique method of identification. The device analyzes the features, for example, fingerprints, hand shape and size, retinal patterns, and voice patterns,

to identify the owner as a legitimate user (Figure 3.21). Many notebooks today are equipped with biometric fingerprint input devices to serve as a means of identification and authentication, thus making unauthorized access to the computer more difficult.

- Devices like a **digital camera** and **digital video camera** can input images and video into your sytem directly through a USB or FireWire port.
- A **webcam**, an inexpensive camera attached to the computer, can be used to hold live chat sessions and make video phone calls. In most newer systems, a webcam is standard equipment.

If you have a Smartphone, you might realize that input into your phone can be made easier by downloading an application from the Internet. There is an app that inserts a photo taken with your phone into an Internet search, avoiding the keying in of a book title or ISBN number. Another app inserts the content of a photo of a business card taken with your phone into the contact list on both your phone and computer, if they are synchronized, again avoiding manual typing. As input becomes more automated and portable, data will become quicker to input and retrieve, and will be less prone to errors, allowing individuals to be more productive and have more time for leisure.

Output Devices: Engaging Our Senses

Output devices enable people to see, hear, and even feel the results of processing operations. The most widely used output devices are monitors and printers.

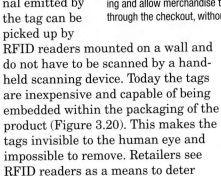

Retina scan

Fingerprint reader

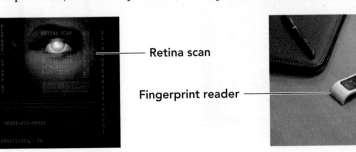

FIGURE 3.21 Biometric input devices use retinal scans to match the shape and pattern of an individual's eye and fingerprint readers to detect the shape, curve, and unique pattern of lines on a finger.

With the population of the world aging and placing increased demands on an already taxed medical system, new methods of taking care of this aging generation are being developed. Japan leads the way in bio-signal telemetry, with the HRS-I, or human recorder, system. What exactly is *bio-signal telemetry*? It is a method of using sensors attached to a human chest to receive bio-medical information on the individual (Figure 3.22). This health-related information is then transferred wirelessly to a phone or computer. The system can call physicians to review data on an individual whose bio-input indicates a deviation from the norm, allowing treatment to be started immediately. This automated form of medical information may reduce the need for some office visits, and home health-care providers may be able to reduce the number of visits they make to the elderly to take their blood pressure, heart rate, and other such vital statistics.

FIGURE 3.22 Biometric monitoring devices will generate constant output and require either human or computerized observation.

Monitors

Monitors (also called **displays**) are screens that display data and processed information called **output**. It's important to remember that the screen display isn't a permanent record. To drive home this point, screen output is sometimes called **soft copy**, as opposed to **hard copy** (printed output). To make permanent copies of your work, you should save it to a storage device or print it.

There are two basic types of monitors: the big cathode-ray tube (CRT) monitors that are very bulky and are usually connected to older desktop computers, and the thin, popular liquid crystal display (LCD) monitors like those that accompany new desktops and all-in-one units, and are incorporated into notebooks, handheld computers, and smartphones (Figure 3.23).

Liquid crystal displays (LCDs), or **flat-panel displays**, have largely replaced CRT monitors. An LCD screen is a grid of pixels. A florescent panel at the back of the system generates light waves to make the images and colors. These waves pass through a layer of crystal solution. The electric current moves the crystals and either blocks the light or lets it through, thus creating the images and colors viewable on the display

FIGURE 3.23 LCD monitors are lightweight and thin, making them ideal for small portable devices.

 — Notebook

Personal digital assistant

 — Smartphone

(Figure 3.24). The least expensive LCDs are called **passive-matrix** LCDs (also called **dual scans**). In these units, the electrical current drives the display by charging groups of pixels, either in a row or column, at once. The screen brightens and fades as the current moves from group to group. Appliances, toys, remote controls, and home medical products use this type of display. Passive-matrix LCD displays are usually not as sharp as active-matrix displays, have less of a viewing angle, and are too slow for full-motion video. **Active-matrix**, or **thin film transistor (TFT)**, technology drives the display by charging each pixel individually as needed. As the price of active-matrix displays drops, passive-matrix displays may become obsolete.

Other flat-panel display technologies include field-emission displays (FEDs), which look and operate in much the same way as an LCD monitor, except that tiny stationary carbon nanotubes illuminate each on-screen pixel. Although FEDs are considered more rugged and are better for harsh environments, they have not seen any mass-market adoption.

Screen Size The size of a monitor is determined by measuring it diagonally. This is fairly straightforward for LCD monitors. Typical desktop PC monitors range from 17 to 21 inches, whereas notebook computers measure 12 to 17 inches. Larger monitors are popular with gamers, graphic designers, and others who have to display two documents side by side. In fact, a recent study commissioned by Apple looked at the productivity impact of using a 30-inch monitor as compared to a 20-inch or 17-inch monitor. The results indicated that a user on a 30-inch monitor would save about 1.3 hours per week over a person using a 17-inch monitor. The report is based on what they consider to be normal usage. Depending on your work, the savings in productivity could vary.

Resolution The term **resolution** generally refers to the sharpness of an image and is controlled by the number of pixels on the screen. The higher the resolution, the sharper the image. Units of resolution are written, for example, as 1024 × 786. This notation means the display has 1,024 distinct dots on each of 768 lines. Figure 3.25 lists common PC monitor resolutions.

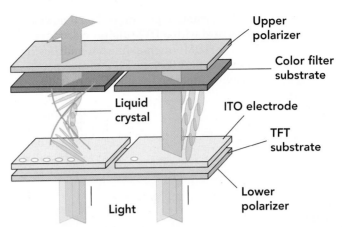

FIGURE 3.24 LCD technology allows the display to be an inch or less in thickness, making it usable in small work areas and with portable devices.

For color graphics displays, **Video Graphics Array (VGA)** is the lowest resolution standard (640 × 480). Most of today's monitors can be adjusted to resolutions up to **Extended Graphics Array (XGA**, 1024 × 768). The newest models sport Super and Ultra Extended Graphics Array video adapters—allowing for an amazing 1600 pixels per line and 1200 lines of pixels per screen!

Televisions as Monitors The resolution on older TVs was much lower than PCs, so the viewing results were less than optimal. However, newer **high-definition televisions (HDTVs)** have higher resolutions, typically 1920 × 1080 or better, making this less a problem. To the casual observer, there doesn't seem to be much difference between an LCD monitor and an LCD TV, so why not hook up your PC to your TV for an even bigger computer screen? HDTV, a digital television standard that provides extremely high-quality video and audio, makes this a possibility. HDTV displays include direct-view, plasma, rear screen, and front screen projection. These units require an HDTV tuner to view

FIGURE 3.25 Common PC Monitor Resolutions

Size	Standard	Acronym
640 × 480	Video Graphics Array	VGA
800 × 600	Super Video Graphics Array	SVGA
1024 × 768	Extended Graphics Array	XGA
1280 × 1024	Super Extended Graphics Array	SXGA
1600 × 1200	Ultra Extended Graphics Array	UXGA

HDTV-formatted programs. You'll need a video card with a DVI (digital video interface) or HDMI (high-definition multimedia interface) port on your PC and the corresponding input on the TV (Figure 3.26).

If you'd rather watch live TV on your PC, you can do that too. Install a TV tuner card in your PC, and get ready to watch or record your favorite shows.

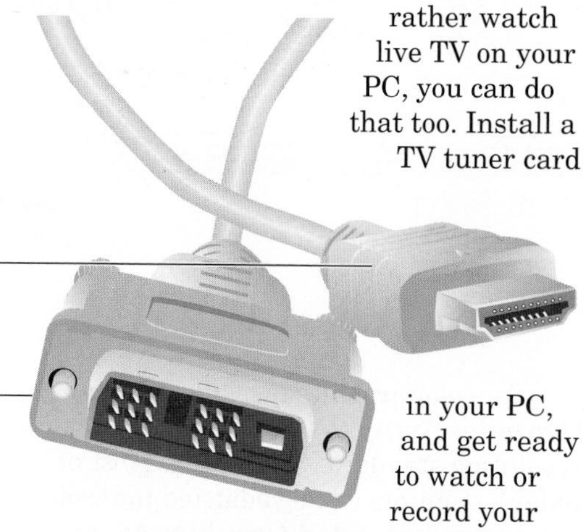

FIGURE 3.26 If your PC doesn't have an HDMI port, an HDMI-DVI cable can be used to connect the PC to the TV.

The HDMI end of the cable plugs into the TV.

The DVI end of the cable plugs into the PC.

You might be surprised to find that LCD display is not your only option. **OLED (organic light emitting diode) displays** are becoming popular. Unlike LCDs, which require backlighting, OLED displays are emissive devices, meaning they emit light rather than modulate transmitted or reflected light. The light is produced when electric current passes through carbon-based material that is sandwiched between two conductors (an anode and cathode) that are pressed together between two plates of glass called the seal and substrate (Figure 3.27). These displays are extremely thin and lightweight, and produce outstanding color, contrast, brightness, and viewing angles. Sales for OLED displays hit 1billion in 2009 and are predicted to exceed 7 billion by 2016.

FIGURE 3.27 OLED displays consume less energy and are extremely thin.

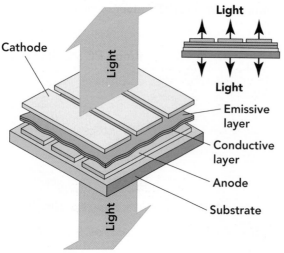

Light

Light

Light

Light

Cathode

Emissive layer

Conductive layer

Anode

Substrate

Flexible OLED displays (FOLED) will revolutionize the advertising and motion picture industries and increase the ease and portability of output (Figure 3.28). FOLED displays can be paper-thin and appear as posters on walls. In addition, these displays can be made so small and flexible that they can be worn on your wrist and used to watch a movie or surf the Web. If you think that the possibilities for entertainment are endless, just imagine the military and security applications that will develop from this technology.

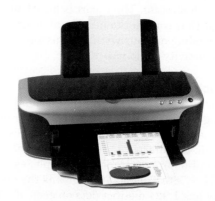

FIGURE 3.28 This flexible OLED communication device is worn on the wrist and was developed in conjunction with the U.S. Department of Defense.

Now that we've discussed monitors and soft copy, let's move on to devices that produce hard-copy output: printers.

Printers

Printers produce a permanent version, or hard copy, of the output on the computer's display screen. Some of the most popular printers are inkjet printers and laser printers.

Inkjet printers are relatively inexpensive nonimpact printers that produce excellent color output, making them popular choices for home users (Figure 3.29). They spray ionized ink from a series of

FIGURE 3.29 Inkjet printers produce high-quality color output.

small jets onto a sheet of paper, creating the desired character shapes. Today, inkjet printers are capable of producing high-quality print approaching that produced by laser printers. A typical inkjet printer provides a resolution of 300 dots per inch, although some newer models offer higher resolutions. One drawback of an inkjet printer is that it is relatively slow compared with its laser competitor.

A **laser printer** is a high-resolution nonimpact printer that uses an electrostatic reproductive technology similar to that used by copiers (Figure 3.30). Under the printer's computerized control, a laser beam creates electrical charges on a rotating print drum. These charges attract toner, which is transferred to the paper and fused to its surface by a heat process. Laser printers print faster than inkjets; some laser printers can crank out 60 or more pages per minute. Black-and-white laser printers are becoming more affordable and generally have a lower per-page print cost than inkjet printers; however, color laser printers are still more expensive to buy and maintain.

FIGURE 3.30 Black-and-white laser printers provide quick output at affordable prices.

Dot-matrix printers (also known as **impact printers**) were once the most popular type of printer but are declining in use. Such printers create characters by striking pins against an ink ribbon. Each pin makes a dot, and combinations of dots form characters and illustrations. Although they are capable of printing 3,000 lines per minute, their print quality is lower than other printers and they are noisy. Dot-matrix printers are used for printing backup copies and, because they physically strike the paper, for printing multipart forms such as invoices or purchase orders.

Thermal-transfer printers use a heat process to transfer an impression onto paper. There are two types of thermal printers. Thermal-wax transfer printers adhere a wax-based ink onto paper, whereas direct thermal printers burn dots onto coated paper when the paper passes over a line of heating elements. The best thermal-wax transfer printers are called **dye sublimation printers**. These printers are slow and expensive, but they produce results that are difficult to distinguish from high-quality color photographs. Thermal printers are becoming popular for mobile and portable printing. These are the printers used by car rental agencies to generate an instant receipt or by a traffic officer to print out a traffic ticket (Figure 3.31).

FIGURE 3.31 Thermal printers are small and portable, making them useful for issuing tickets or receipts.

Photo printers are either inkjet or laser printers and use special inks and good-quality photo paper to produce pictures that are as good as those generated by commercial photo processors. Many allow you to bypass your computer to print directly from a digital camera or memory card.

A **plotter** is a printer that produces high-quality images by physically moving ink pens over the surface of the paper. A continuous-curve plotter draws maps from stored data (Figure 3.32). Computer-generated maps, such as those used by cartographers and weather analysts, can

GREEN tech tips

More than 700 million inkjet and laser toner cartridges are sold every year. What happens when they are empty? Although many organizations and retail stores have recycling programs, every second nearly eight used cartridges are thrown away in the United States—approximately 875 million pounds of environmental waste each year! So what can you do? Take advantage of your local recycling program. Some programs even pay you for your old cartridges because they can be recycled and sold again. Keeping them out of the waste stream reduces toxicity levels and saves landfill space. Besides, half a gallon of oil is saved for every toner cartridge you recycle! ●

FIGURE 3.32 Plotters are useful for printing over-sized output such as maps, charts, and blueprints.

FIGURE 3.33 Projection systems and colored hand-outs make lecture material and discussion more dynamic and visually stimulating.

be retrieved and plotted or used to show changes over time.

Additional Output Devices

All systems include basic built-in speakers to transmit the beeps normally made during processing. These speakers, however, are not designed for playing CDs. You'll have to purchase speakers to listen to computer-generated sound, such as music and synthesized speech, unless higher-end speakers were included with your system. Like microphones, speakers require a sound card to function. Sound cards play the contents of digitized recordings, such as music recorded in WAV (short for waveform) and MP3 sound file formats. Some sound cards do this job better than others. Quality is most noticeably a consideration when the sound card reproduces MIDI (musical instrument digital interface) files. MIDI is the language used to communicate between musical instruments and the computer that controls them during performances. MIDI files do not actually record the sound of the instruments; instead, they provide instruction on how to create those sounds. MIDI files play over synthesizers, electronic devices that produce music by generating musical tones. Sound cards have built-in synthesizers. Better sound cards use wavetable synthesis, whereby the sound card generates sounds using ROM-based recordings of actual musical instruments. The latest sound cards may include surround sound (systems set up so that they surround you with sound as in a theatre) and subwoofer (speakers that produce only low bass sounds) effects.

Data projectors display a computer's video output on a screen for an audience to view. They range from small, lightweight devices used for business or class presentations and home theaters, to larger, more expensive models suitable for use in auditoriums or stadiums. Individuals and businesses often use LCD or DLP projectors. In an **LCD projector**, an image is formed by light passing through three colored panels—red, green, and blue. LCD projectors produce sharp, accurate color images; however, they are subject to pixilation and have less contrast than a DLP projector. **DLP (digital light-processing) projectors** (Figure 3.33) project light onto a chip made up of millions of microscopic mirrors. DLP projectors are often smaller and lighter than LCD projectors and have better contrast; but in some models, the reflected light can create a rainbow effect that causes eyestrain for some people.

Computers equipped with a fax modem and fax software can receive incoming faxes. The incoming document is displayed on the screen, and it can be printed or saved.

Computers also send faxes as output. To send a fax using your computer, you must save your document, using a special format that is compatible with the fax program. The fax program then sends the document through the telephone system to a traditional distant fax machine. This output function is helpful because you don't have to print the document to send it as a fax.

Multifunction devices combine inkjet or laser printers with a scanner, a fax machine, and a copier, enabling home office users to obtain all of these devices without spending a great deal of money (Figure 3.34).

FIGURE 3.34 Multifunction devices are common in home office environments.

Now that you've learned about a variety of output devices, let's look at how you can store data for later use.

Storage: Holding Data for Future Use

Storage (also called **mass storage**, **auxiliary storage**, or **secondary storage**) refers to the ways a computer system retains software and data for future use. Storage relies on hardware components, collectively called **storage devices**, such as hard disks, flash memory, USB drives, CDs, and DVDs, on which data is held (Figure 3.35). For photos and descriptions of current storage devices, go to **www.worldstart.com/tips/tips.php/3769**. Organizations increasingly turn to computer storage systems that can include one or several of these mediums, to store all of their computer software, data, and information. The reason? Storing information on paper is expensive and offers no opportunity for electronic manipulation and sharing. A simple storage device can store the amount of information that would cost $10,000 to store on paper for less than $10 per gigabyte (1 billion characters). In fact, storage devices are increasing in capacity to the point that they can hold an entire library's worth of information. Read on to learn why storage is necessary, what kinds of storage devices and media are out there, and which best fit your computing needs.

Memory versus Storage

To understand the distinction between memory and storage, think of the last time you worked at your desk. In your file drawer, you store all your personal items and papers, such as your checking account statements. The file drawer is good for long-term storage. When you decide to work on one or more of these items, you take it out of storage and put it on your desk. The desktop is a good place to keep the items you're working with (work in progress); they're close at hand and available for use right away. Your desktop can be thought of as memory—the place where you temporarily put things that you are using or working on.

Computers work the same way. When you want to work with the contents of a file, the computer transfers the file to a temporary workplace: the computer's memory—technically called RAM (random access memory) or primary memory. This memory is a form of storage—a holding area for items in use—but it is temporary. Why don't computers just use RAM to hold all of a user's files, regardless of whether or not they are in use? Here are some reasons:

- **Recording media retain data when the current is switched off.** The computer's RAM is volatile. This means that when you switch off the computer's power, all of the information in RAM is irretrievably lost. So, if your work in progress has not been saved onto a recording medium (e.g., CD, DVD, etc.) by a storage device, it

Hard drive with enclosure opened

Flash memory card in reader

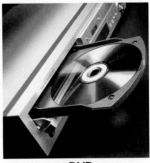

USB drive

DVD

is no longer retrievable unless the application you were running has an autosave feature for emergency rescue. In contrast, recording media are nonvolatile; they will not lose data when the power goes off or when they are removed from the system.

- **Storage devices are cheaper than memory.** RAM operates very quickly to keep up with the computer's CPU. For this reason, RAM is expensive—much more expensive than storage. In fact, most computers are equipped with just enough RAM to accommodate all of the programs a user wants to run at once. In contrast, a computer system's storage devices hold much more data and software than the computer's memory (Figure 3.36). Today, you can buy a storage device capable of storing more than 300 GB of software and data for about the same amount you would pay for 2 GB of RAM.

FIGURE 3.35 Many types of recording media are common on most portable and nonportable systems.

FIGURE 3.36 Memory versus Storage

		Access Speed	Cost per MB	Storage Capacity
Memory	Cache memory	Fastest	Highest	2 MB
	RAM	Fast	High	4 GB
Storage	Hard disk	Medium	Medium	1 TB
	CD-R disc	Slow	Low	700 MB

- **Storage devices play an essential role in system startup operations.** When you start your computer, the operating system appears on the monitor. Actually, a copy of the operating system software is transferred from the hard disk, where it is permanently stored, into the computer's RAM—making it available and ready for use.
- **Storage devices are needed for output.** When you've finished working, you use the computer's storage system as an output device to save a file. When you save a file, the computer transfers your work from the computer's RAM to recording media via a storage device. If you forget to save your work, it will be lost when you switch off the computer's power. Remember, the computer's RAM is volatile!

For all of these reasons, demand for storage capacity is soaring. Storage capacity is measured in bytes (KB, MB, GB, TB, and PB). A report presented in January 2009 by Coughlin Associates at the Storage Visions Conference cites a 12-fold increase in required storage media (what we have termed recording media here) between 2008 and 2014 and, for the same time span, a total increase in revenue related to storage media from $387 M to $807 M. Now that you understand the importance of storage, let's look at the devices and media used to hold data.

Hard Disk Drives

On almost all computers, the hard disk drive is by far the most important storage device. A **hard disk drive** (or simply **hard drive**) is a high-capacity, high-speed storage device, usually housed in the system unit, that consists of several rapidly rotating disks called **platters** on which programs, data, and processed results are stored. To communicate with the CPU, hard disks require a hard disk controller. A **hard disk controller** is an electronic circuit board that provides an interface between the CPU and the hard disk's electronics. The controller may be located on the computer's motherboard, on an expansion card, or within the hard disk.

The computer's hard disk, also referred to as **secondary storage** or **fixed storage**, can also be categorized as both random access and magnetic storage. A **random access storage device** can go directly to the requested data without having to go through a linear search sequence. **Magnetic storage devices** use disks that are coated with magnetically sensitive material.

Magnetic storage devices use an electromagnet called a **read/write head** that moves across the surface of a disk and records information by transforming electrical impulses into a varying magnetic field. As the magnetic materials pass beneath the read/write head, this varying field forces the particles to be rearranged in a meaningful pattern of positive and negative magnetic indicators that represent the data. This operation is called *writing*. When *reading*, the read/write head senses the recorded pattern and transforms this pattern into electrical impulses that are decoded into text characters. A hard disk contains two or more vertically stacked platters, each with two read/write heads (one for each side of the disk). The platters spin so rapidly that the read/write head floats on a thin cushion of air at a distance 1/300th the width of a human hair. To protect the platter's surface, hard disks are enclosed in a sealed container.

How does the read/write head know where to look for data in order to access it randomly? To answer this question, you need to know a little about how stored data is organized on a disk. Disks are formatted, physically laid out, in circular bands called **tracks**. Each track is divided into pie-shaped wedges called **sectors**. Two or more sectors combine to form a **cluster** (Figure 3.37).

FIGURE 3.37 Disks are configured into tracks and sectors, similar to a street name and house number, in order to provide an addressing scheme and quick access to information.

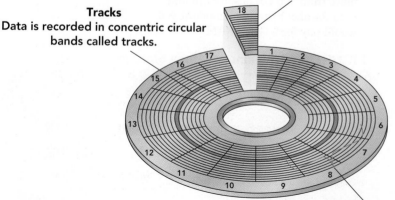

Sector
Each track is divided into pie-shaped wedges called sectors.

Tracks
Data is recorded in concentric circular bands called tracks.

Clusters
Two or more sectors form a cluster.

FIGURE 3.38 NTFS File System

Filename	Track	Sector
letter.docx	4	3
sales.xlsx	14	8
memo.doc	10	9
Forcast.pptx	deleted	
Logo.gif	6	11
Agenda.docx	13	2

To keep track of where specific files are located, the computer's operating system records a table of information on the disk. This table contains the name of each file and the file's exact location on the disk (Figure 3.38). The current system for Windows NT, 2000, XP, Vista, and Windows 7 is known as **NTFS (new technology file system)**. Its improved security and encryption ability provide another layer of protection for stored data. Hard disks can be divided into partitions. A **partition** is a section of a hard disk set aside as if it were a physically separate disk. Partitions are required if a system is going to give the user an option of running more than one operating system. The average user won't need to partition the hard disk, but some individuals like to create one partition for Linux and another for Microsoft Windows. In this way, they work with programs developed for either operating system.

Factors Affecting Hard Disk

Performance If a hard disk develops a defect or a read/write head encounters an obstacle, such as a dust or smoke particle, the head bounces on the disk surface, preventing the computer from reading or writing data to one or more sectors of the disk. Hard disks absorb minor jostling without suffering damage, but a major jolt—such as one caused by dropping the computer while the drive is running—could cause a head crash to occur. Head crashes are one of the causes of **bad sectors**, areas of the disk that have become damaged and can no longer reliably hold data. If you see an on-screen message indicating that a disk has a bad sector, try to copy the data off the disk and don't use it to store new data.

A hard drive's most important performance characteristic is the speed at which it retrieves desired data. The amount of time it takes a device from the request for the information to the delivery of that information is its **access time**. Access time includes the **seek time**, the time it takes the read/write head to locate the data before reading begins. **Positioning performance** refers to the time that elapses from the initiation of drive activity until the hard disk has positioned the read/write head so that it can begin transferring data.

Transfer performance refers to how quickly the read/write head transfers data from the disk to random access memory. One way disk manufacturers improve transfer performance is to increase the speed at which the disk spins, which makes data available more quickly to the read/write heads. Another way is to improve the spacing of data on the disk so that the heads can retrieve several blocks of data on each revolution.

Hard disk performance can also be improved with a type of cache memory called disk cache. **Disk cache**, a type of RAM, is usually incorporated on the circuit board within the hard drive case. When the CPU needs to get information, it looks in the disk cache first. If it doesn't find the information it needs, it retrieves the information from the hard disk (Figure 3.39).

There are two types of disk cache:

- Read cache allows the hard drive to read information or instructions related to the ones currently in use. The idea is to have them available in advance so the user doesn't have to wait for the hard disk to read the data when it is requested. Instead, the hard disk gets the data immediately from the cache.
- Write cache allows the disk to write content to cache and immediately frees

FIGURE 3.39 Disk cache is included on all hard drives today. It is one way to reduce the time it takes to access an instruction.

Hard disk drive

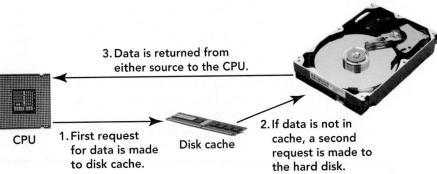

3. Data is returned from either source to the CPU.

CPU

1. First request for data is made to disk cache.

Disk cache

2. If data is not in cache, a second request is made to the hard disk.

the disk up to read other instructions from the disk that the user is requesting. The process of writing to the disk from cache can be completed later.

Although disk cache improves overall system performance, write cache can cause trouble if your system crashes before the cache content is written to the hard disk. For this reason, write cache is not enabled on personal computers or notebooks, or when running database management systems.

Network Attached Storage (NAS) As demands for data storage have increased, **network attached storage (NAS)** devices are becoming more popular. NAS devices are comprised primarily of hard drives or other media used for data storage and are attached directly to a network. The network connection permits each computer on the network to access the NAS to save or retrieve data.

Some external hard drives sold for the home market can function as NAS devices. The advantage is that one device can be used to coordinate and store backup files for all PCs connected to the home network.

Remote Storage A storage space on a server that is accessible from the Internet is called **remote storage** and is sometimes referred to as an **Internet hard drive**. In most cases, a computer user subscribes to the storage service and agrees to rent a block of storage space for a specific period of time. Instead of sending e-mail attachments to share with family and friends, you might simply post the files to the remote storage site and then allow them to be viewed or retrieved by others. You might save backup copies of critical files or all the data on your hard disk to your Internet hard drive.

The key advantage of this type of remote storage is the ability to access data from multiple locations. You can access your files from any device that connects with the Internet, so everything you store on the site is available to you at any time. The concerns about using remote storage center on such issues as data security, data corruption, and the possibility that the company offering the Internet storage may go out of business.

Flash Drives and Storage

Although hard disks are currently the most important storage media, the devices explored in this section are examples of portable storage, which means that you can remove one from one computer and insert it into another. A **flash drive** is a type of storage device that uses solid-state circuitry and has no moving parts (Figure 3.40). Flash drives are also known as **solid-state drives (SSDs)** and use flash memory, which is nonvolatile, electronic memory. **Flash memory** stores data electronically on a chip in sections known as **blocks**. Rather than erasing data byte by byte, flash memory uses an electrical charge to delete all of the data on the chip or just the data contained in a specific block, which is a much quicker method than other types of storage use. Flash memory

FIGURE 3.40 Flash drives provide a durable, lightweight alternative to hard disks.

is limited to 100,000 write cycles. This means information can be written and erased 100,000 times to each block, which could conceivably take years to occur. Because of their lack of moving parts, lower power consumption, and lighter weight, flash drives are becoming an alternative to hard drives, especially in notebook computing. Flash drives are also found in some MP3 players, smartphones, and digital cameras. Although flash drives are more expensive and have less storage capacity than hard drives, these differences are expected to erode over time. Additionally, some hard drives are incorporating flash technology, creating **hybrid hard drives (HHDs)** that use flash memory to speed up the boot process.

Another form of flash storage is the USB flash drive. **USB flash drives**, also known as **memory sticks, thumb drives**, or **jump drives**, are popular **portable storage (removable storage)** devices. Because of their small size and universal ease of use, they have supplanted floppy disks and Zip disks as the removable storage medium of choice. Both floppy disks and Zip disks are now considered legacy technologies. USB flash drives work with both the PC and the Mac. No device driver is required—just plug it

Because your USB drive has no moving parts, it can be difficult to tell when it is working. Usually, if the contents of a USB drive are being accessed, a small LED light on the drive flashes. It is very important not to disconnect the flash drive when a file is being saved or accessed, because this can corrupt the data. Make sure any files on your USB drive are closed, then look for the Safely Remove Hardware icon in the system tray on the bottom right side of the screen. Double-click the icon to open the dialog box, then select USB Mass Storage Device, and click the Stop button. Another box may appear with a list of USB devices—if it does, click the device name that matches the USB flash drive, then click OK. Unplug the flash drive when the message appears indicating that it is safe to do so.

CD and DVD Technologies

Software, music, and movies used to be distributed primarily on CDs and DVDs; however, today direct downloads from the Internet have caused some manufacturers to make these drives an optional component of the system unit. If a unit does not come with a CD or DVD drive, you can purchase an external unit and connect it via the USB port. **CD-ROM** (short for **compact disc read-only memory**) and **DVD-ROM (digital video [or versatile] disc read-only memory**) are the most popular and least expensive types of optical disc standards and are referred to as optical storage devices. These discs are read-only discs, which means that the data recorded on them can be read many times, but it cannot be changed or erased. Notice that when the storage medium is optical, the correct spelling is *disc*. Magnetic storage media are spelled with a *k—disk*.

A **CD drive** and a **DVD drive** (Figure 3.42)

into a USB port and it's ready to read and write. USB flash drives are made of plastic and are shockproof, moisture proof, and magnetization proof. Many USB flash drives include security and encryption software to help protect your data in case you lose it. Some devices have a retractable USB connector, eliminating the need for a protective cap, which is often misplaced. Others are available in different colors and novelty shapes (Figure 3.41). One interesting characteristic is that the drives get their power supply from the device they are plugged into. Capacities range from 1 GB to 64 GB, and they are able to read and write at speeds up to 30 Mbps. Watch for capacities to go up and prices to come down.

FIGURE 3.41 The look of USB flash drives varies from the ordinary to ones disguised as key chains and pens, to still others that are the caricatures of favorite TV or sport personalities.

are read-only disk drives that read data encoded on CDs and DVDs and transfer this data to a computer. These drives are referred to as optical storage devices. **Optical storage devices** use tightly

STUDENT
VIDEO

focused laser beams to read microscopic patterns of data encoded on the surface of plastic discs (Figure 3.43). The format of a CD or DVD includes microscopic indentations called **pits** that scatter the laser's light in certain areas. The drive's light-sensing device receives no light from these areas, so it sends a signal to the computer that corresponds to a 0 in the computer's binary numbering system. Flat reflective areas called **lands** bounce the light back to a light-sensing device, which sends a signal equivalent to a binary 1.

CD-ROMs can store up to 700 MB of data. They are a different format than the audio CDs, from which they evolved, in that some space is used for an additional level of error detecting and correcting code. This is necessary because data CDs cannot tolerate the loss of a handful of bits now and then, the way audio CDs can. DVD-ROMs store up to 17 GB of data—enough for an entire digitized movie. Whereas CD drives transfer data at speeds of up to 150 Kbps, DVD drives transfer data at even higher speeds (up to 12 Mbps; comparable to the data transfer rates of

hard drives). DVD drives read CD-ROMs as well as DVD-ROMs.

CD-R, CD-RW, DVD-R, and DVD+RW Discs and Recorders Several types of optical read/write media and devices are available. Many PCs now include a combination drive that reads and writes CDs and DVDs. For this reason, these read/write discs are a popular, cost-effective alternative medium for archival and storage purposes.

CD-R (short for **compact disc–recordable**) is a "write-once" technology. After you've saved data to the disc, you can't erase or write over it. An advantage of CD-Rs is that they are relatively inexpensive. **CD-RW** (short for **compact disc–rewritable**), which is more expensive than CD-R, allows data that has been saved to be erased and rewritten. **CD-RW drives**, also known as **burners** or **CD burners**, provide full read/write capabilities.

DVDs come in two standards. The first (newer) format is the DVD+ (DVD plus) standard. This standard employs two types of discs, DVD+R and the DVD+RW. **DVD+R** is a recordable format that enables the disc to be written to one time and read many times. The **DVD+RW** is a recordable format that enables the disc to be rewritten to many times.

The second format, which is older and more compatible, is the DVD– (DVD dash) standard. **DVD-R** operates the same way as CD-R; you can write to the disc once and read from it many times. With **DVD-RW**, you can write to, erase, and read from the disc many times.

One of the newest forms of optical storage, Blu-ray, also known as Blu-ray Disc, is the name of a next-generation optical disc format jointly developed by the Blu-ray Disc Association (BDA, a group of the world's leading consumer electronics, personal computer, and media manufacturers, including Apple, Dell, Hitachi, HP, JVC, LG, Mitsubishi, Panasonic, Pioneer, Philips, Samsung, Sharp, Sony, TDK, and Thomson). The name is derived from the blue-violet laser beams (blue rays) used to read and write data. The **Blu-ray Disc (BD)** format was developed to enable recording, rewriting, and playing back of high-definition video (HD), as well as storing large amounts of data. The format offers more than five times the storage capacity of traditional DVDs and can hold up to 25 GB on a single-layer disc

FIGURE 3.42 CD and DVD drives use popular and inexpensive optical discs.

FIGURE 3.43 In optical storage devices such as CD and DVD drives, a tightly focused laser beam reads data encoded on the disc's surface. Some optical devices write data as well as read it.

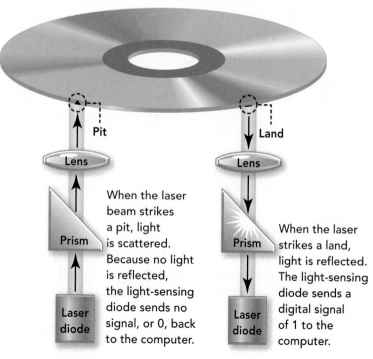

Pit

Land

Lens

Lens

When the laser beam strikes a pit, light is scattered. Because no light is reflected, the light-sensing diode sends no signal, or 0, back to the computer.

Prism

Prism

When the laser strikes a land, light is reflected. The light-sensing diode sends a digital signal of 1 to the computer.

Laser diode

Laser diode

and 50 GB on a dual-layer disc—the equivalent of 9 hours of high-definition video or 23 hours of standard definition (SD) video. This extra capacity combined with the use of advanced video and audio features offers consumers an unprecedented HD experience.

Multilayer discs capable of even more storage are under development. **BD-ROM** discs are a read-only format used for video or data distribution. **BD-R** is a recordable disc useful for HD video or PC data storage, and **BD-RE** is the rewritable format, allowing data or video to be recorded and erased as needed. Currently, a dedicated Blu-ray player or recorder is required to use this new technology; however, there are plans to create a hybrid Blu-ray Disc/DVD that can be used in Blu-ray or DVD players. It is expected that Blu-ray will eventually replace DVDs, especially when HDTVs become more commonplace.

FIGURE 3.44 ExpressCards are about the size of a credit card and fit into ExpressCard slots, which are standard in most notebooks.

Protecting the Data on Your Discs As with magnetic disks, it's important that you handle CDs and DVDs carefully. The following are a few things to remember when caring for discs:

- Do not expose discs to excessive heat or sunlight.
- Do not touch the underside of discs. Hold them by their edges.
- Do not write on the label side of discs with a hard instrument, such as a ballpoint pen.
- To avoid scratches, do not stack discs.
- Store discs in jewel boxes (plastic protective cases) or paper-like sleeves when not being used.

Solid-State Storage Devices

A **solid-state storage device** consists of nonvolatile memory chips, which retain the data stored in them even if the chips are disconnected from a computer or power source. The term *solid state* indicates that these devices have no moving parts; they consist only of semiconductors. Solid-state storage devices have important advantages over mechanical storage devices such as hard drives: They

are small, lightweight, highly reliable, and portable. In addition to the flash drives discussed earlier, some solid-state storage devices in common use are ExpressCards, flash memory cards, and smart cards.

An **ExpressCard** is a credit card–sized accessory typically used with notebook computers (Figure 3.44). Previous versions were known as **PC cards** or **PCMCIA cards**. ExpressCards can serve a variety of functions. For example, some ExpressCards are modems, others are network adapters, and still others provide additional memory or storage capacity.

When used as storage devices, ExpressCards are most commonly used to transfer data from one computer to another. (However, each computer must have an ExpressCard slot.) For example, a notebook computer user can store documents created on a business trip on a solid-state memory card and then transfer the documents to a desktop computer.

ExpressCards follow standards set by the Personal Computer Memory Card International Association (PCMCIA), a consortium of industry vendors. As a result, a notebook computer equipped with an ExpressCard slot can use ExpressCards from any ExpressCard vendor.

Flash memory cards (Figure 3.45), which use nonvolatile flash memory chips, are becoming increasingly popular. **Flash memory cards** are wafer-thin, highly portable solid-state storage systems that are capable of storing as much as 64 GB of data. They are also used with smartphones, MP3 players, digital video cameras, and other portable digital devices. To use a flash memory card, the device must have a

FIGURE 3.45 Flash memory cards are thin, portable solid-state storage systems.

FIGURE 3.46 A flash memory reader can be used to transfer the contents of a memory card to your PC.

compatible **flash memory reader**— a slot or compartment into which the flash memory card is inserted (Figure 3.46).

The SmartMedia flash memory card was one of the first examples of this technology. Many others, in various sizes and storage capacities, soon followed, including CompactFlash, Secure Digital, Memory Stick, miniSD, and microSD. It is important to know what type of memory card a specific device requires, because they are not interchangeable.

A **smart card**, also known as a **chip card** or an **integrated circuit card (ICC)**, is a credit card–sized device that combines flash memory with a tiny microprocessor, enabling the card to process as well as store information. It is viewed as a replacement for magnetic stripe cards, from which data is eventually lost. Smart cards, not being magnetic, provide an additional longevity and may include a hologram to help prevent counterfeiting. Smart cards also promote quicker transactions with little need for personal interaction. If you've ever waved your card at the gas pump to pay for your gas or used a specially encoded student ID card to pay for your meal in the dining hall or unlock your dorm room, you may have used a smart card (Figure 3.47).

More smart card applications exist or are on the way. For example, **digital cash systems**, which are widespread in Europe and Asia, enable users to purchase a prepaid amount of electronically stored money to pay the small amounts required for parking, bridge tolls, transport fares, museum entrance fees, and similar charges.

Storage Horizons

In response to the explosive demand for more storage capacity, designers are creating storage media and devices that store larger amounts of data and retrieve it more quickly. Exemplifying these trends are holographic storage and wireless flash memory cards.

FIGURE 3.47 Smart cards can be used for quick transactions, to identify the user, or to access electronically controlled doors.

Holographic Storage **Holographic storage** uses two laser beams to create a pattern on photosensitive media, resulting in a three-dimensional image similar to the holograms you can buy in a novelty shop. It is anticipated that this 3D approach will enable much higher-density storage capacities, and it is being promoted for its archiving capabilities. Although still under development, experts predict that holographic storage may enable us to store terabytes of data in a space no thicker than the width of several CDs. Or to put it another way, imagine storing 50,000 music files on an object the size of a postage stamp!

Wireless Memory Cards The Eye-Fi **wireless memory card** takes all the storage features of a regular flash memory card and combines them with wireless circuitry, so it can connect with your PC via a wireless network or send pictures directly from your digital camera to your favorite online photo site. The Eye-Fi card can store up to 2 GB of pictures and works like a traditional memory card if you are out of wireless range. Digital photography is the only application this wireless memory card is currently marketed for, but new uses are being explored.

Racetrack Memory Flash memory and hard drives are the main storage devices in today's computing devices. But the designers of storage devices constantly face these challenges: making data storage more cost effective, reducing the size of storage devices, and decreasing the power consumption of storage devices. These issues are extremely critical for mobile devices. Hard drives and flash memory may eventually be replaced by a new technology called "racetrack" memory, which is under development by Stuart Parkin and his colleagues at IBM's Almaden Research Center.

Racetrack memory uses the spin of electrons to store information. This allows the memory to operate at much higher speeds than today's storage media, which is a boon for transferring and retrieving data. In addition, it is anticipated that racetrack memory will consume much less power and that mobile devices may be able to run for as long as several weeks on a single charge. After the memory is rolled out for the mass market, it should be even cheaper to produce than flash memory.

A current limitation of flash memory is that it can only be written to (store data) several thousand times before it wears out. Racetrack memory will not suffer from this limitation and will have no moving parts, making it much less susceptible to breakage than conventional hard drives. The capacity of racetrack memory could allow iPods to store 500,000 songs instead of the 40,000 that the largest units can handle today.

Secondary Storage Devices Data on any secondary storage device, like a USB drive or a hard drive, will at some point get damaged or "lost" and be irretrievable. A wise computer user has a backup strategy in place and uses it. A **backup** is a copy of programs, data, and information created in one secondary storage medium that is duplicated to another. The following questions will help you determine the best backup strategy:

- How much data do you have to back up?
- Do you need to back up every program and all data files at every backup or just those data files that were recently modified?
- How large are the files? Is there enough room on the backup media for all of the files?
- Should you use a remote service?

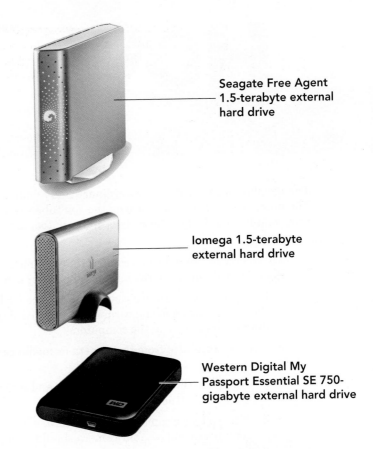

Seagate Free Agent 1.5-terabyte external hard drive

Iomega 1.5-terabyte external hard drive

Western Digital My Passport Essential SE 750-gigabyte external hard drive

FIGURE 3.48 External hard drives, which can be purchased in sizes ranging from gigabytes to terabytes, are the frequent choice of backup medium.

- How frequently will you perform a backup?
- What is the capacity of the backup storage media (Figure 3.48)?
- Will you back up manually by using the Copy and Paste commands or purchase a backup program that can be set up to automatically back up certain folders at certain intervals?
- Have you located a secure remote location to keep your backup copies?

Do not take backing up your data lightly. If you don't backup on a regular schedule, you could permanently lose critical data and information, resulting in frustration, time wasted on recreating the data, and loss of revenue.

How To:

Take a Home Video and Upload It to YouTube

The popular site YouTube allows ordinary individuals to share homemade digital videos with the world. The process of getting your video on the YouTube site might seem overwhelming; but the procedure is not that complicated. Follow these steps and you, too, can share moments of surprise, sincerity, or just plain craziness.

1. Learn how to use the video camera that you purchased and take a video. Transfer the video from your digital video camera to the hard drive on your computer.

   a. Connect the camera to a computer with the USB or FireWire cable provided with the camera. If the camera has a media card, remove the card from the camera and insert it into the corresponding media reader in the computer.

   b. Transfer the video from the camera or media card to your computer. This can be done in several ways.

      i. If your camera came with software and it is installed, access the program and follow the transfer instructions.

      ii. If no software came with the camera, click on the computer icon on your desktop to open the computer window. Your camera should appear in the same location as other removable devices. Copy the video from the camera to the hard drive.

2. Locate the video and test its audio and video qualities from the hard drive by double-clicking the video file and watching it run from your own computer system. The video you upload to YouTube must be in .aiv, .mov, .wmv, or .mrg format, be less than 10 minutes long, and be 2 GB or smaller in size.

   a. You might want to rename the video file, on your hard drive, as your camera usually assigns meaningless titles that make your video difficult to locate later. Also remember that you will be uploading this file to the YouTube server so, for security purposes, use a naming convention that does not include your name or personal data.

   b. You can either keep the video on your camera or media card or delete it to free up space for additional recordings.

   c. After you have successfully transferred the video to your computer, disconnect the digital video camera by using the Safely Remove Hardware icon on the system tray (Figure 3.49).

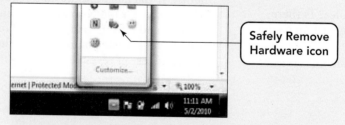

FIGURE 3.49 Using the Safely Remove Hardware icon, located in the system tray or in the hidden icons box (as shown here), to eject devices like USB flash drives, digital cameras, and video cameras assure that no data is lost or damaged when removing the device.

3. Log into YouTube.

    a. Open a Web browser and navigate to **www.youtube.com** The YouTube Broadcast Yourself Web page will appear.

    b. You will need to log in. If you do not have an account you can create one by clicking the Sign up for YouTube! link and following the instructions.

4. Upload your video from your hard drive to the YouTube site.

    a. Once you are logged in, click the *Upload* button to display the Video File Upload Web page.

    b. Click the *Upload Video* button to display the Select File dialog box.

    c. Locate the video that you transferred to your hard drive in step 2.

    d. Fill in the relevant data. To help others locate your video, enter a description and tags, and select a Category from the drop-down list.

    e. You can make the video private by clicking the Private button. This makes the video viewable only by you and 25 other people.

    f. Click the *Save Changes* button.

5. View the Video

    a. On the File Upload Page mouse over your user name and select *My Videos*.

    b. Click the *Play* button to preview the video.

    c. Sign out of YouTube.

Chapter Summary

Input/Output and Storage

- The computer's main input devices are the keyboard and mouse. Other pointing devices include trackballs, pointing sticks, touchpads, joysticks, touch screens, and styluses. Additional input devices include speech recognition; optical character, bar code, optical mark, RFID, magnetic ink, and magnetic stripe readers; biometric input devices; digital cameras and digital video cameras; and webcams.

- Monitors display data and processed information. There are two basic types of monitors; CRT and LCD. CRT monitors, considered legacy technology, are bulky and usually found on older systems. LCD monitors are thin, lightweight and come standard on most systems and portable devices. The new OLED monitors that are even thinner than LCD monitors and have outstanding color, contrast, brightness, and viewing angles are gaining in popularity. Resolution, the sharpness of an image on a monitor, is controlled by the number of pixels on the screen. The higher the resolution, the sharper the image.

- Printers are output devices that produce hard copy. The most popular printers use inkjet or laser technology. Inkjet printers produce excellent-quality text and images for a reasonable price. However, they are slow and ink cartridges may be expensive. Laser printers are faster and produce excellent-quality text and graphics, but color models are expensive.

- Memory is a form of storage; however, it is temporary. Storage devices save programs, data, and information on nonvolatile storage media. These types of media retain information even when the power is switched off.

- Storage media and devices can be categorized as read only or read/write; random access; magnetic, flash, or optical; and secondary (online or fixed), external, or portable (removable).

- The main method of storage on most systems is an internal hard drive on which the operating system and application programs are stored. Hard disk behavior is evaluated by its access time, positioning performance, and transfer performance. Disk cache is sometimes added to the circuit board of a hard drive to further improve performance.

- Flash drives, a form of portable storage, are considered solid-state circuitry and have no moving parts. Within their plastic housing, data is stored on a chip electronically in sections referred to as blocks. Due to their lack of moving parts, quick storage capability, low power consumption, and light-weight design, flash drives are becoming the preferred method of portable storage.

- CD-ROMs and DVD-ROMs are the most popular and least expensive types of optical disc storage media. They use lasers to burn patterns of pits and lands to encode data. A CD-ROM can hold up to 700 MB of data, while a DVD-ROM can hold up to 17 GB. These discs are read-only and cannot be written on by the user. Other variations of optical storage include CD-R, CD-RW, DVD-R, and DVD+RW Discs. These variations allow data to be written to as well as read from the discs. A CD-R, DVD+R, and DVD-R are all write-once technologies. After you've saved data to the disc, you can't erase or write over it. CD-RW, DVD+RW, and DVD-RW can be erased and rewritten on repeatedly. The use of the + and − symbols in the DVD notation indicates the two types of DVD standards, with the DVD− being the older and more compatible.

- A solid-state storage device consists of nonvolatile memory chips, which retain the data stored in them even if the chips are disconnected from a computer or power source. These devices have no moving parts; they consist only of semiconductors. They are small, lightweight, highly reliable, and portable. In addition to the flash drives, other examples of solid state devices are ExpressCards, flash memory cards, and smart cards.

Key Terms and Concepts

Identification

Label each as an input, output, or storage device.

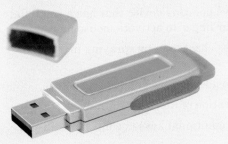

1. _____

2. _____

3. _____

6. _____

4. _____

7. _____

5. _____

8. _____

Matching

Match each key term in the left column with the most accurate definition in the right column.

_____ 1. NTFS

_____ 2. MICR Reader

_____ 3. hybrid hard drive

_____ 4. scanner

_____ 5. laser printer

_____ 6. soft keyboard

_____ 7. plotter

_____ 8. touchpad

_____ 9. soft copy

a. Output viewable on a monitor or through speakers

b. A printer that produces high-quality output by moving pens over the surface of paper

c. A stationary, pressure-sensitive pointing device that has a small flat surface on which you slide your finger to activate mouse movement

d. A nonimpact printer that forms characters by spraying ink from a series of small nozzles

e. Output that is printed and considered permanent

f. A method used to track the location of files on a hard drive

g. An input device that contains additional keys to control media and Internet devices

h. Uses a physical or chemical feature of an individual's body as input

i. An input device that changes all input, including text, into a graphic

_____ 10. LCD

_____ 11. touch screen

_____ 12. hard copy

_____ 13. inkjet printer

_____ 14. enhanced keyboard

_____ 15. biometric input device

j. A device used to automate input by recognizing characters printed with magnetic ink

k. An input device that appears as a keyboard on a touch-sensitive screen

l. A nonimpact printer that uses the electrostatic reproduction technology of copying machines

m. A display that creates images using a back light and the movement of crystals suspended in liquid

n. An input device sensitive to the touch of a finger or stylus used at ATM machines and airport kiosks

o. A magnetic storage device that uses flash memory to improve the time it takes to boot up

Multiple Choice

Circle the correct choice for each of the following:

1. Which keyboard is *not* used on portable devices like smartphones?
   a. Keypad
   b. Soft keyboard
   c. Mini-keyboard
   d. Enhanced keyboard

2. Which of the following is an input device?
   a. Speaker
   b. Blu-ray Disc
   c. FOLED
   d. Webcam

3. A flash drive is an example of _____ storage.
   a. optical
   b. magnetic
   c. solid-state
   d. cache

4. Which is a portable input device that converts printed items like business cards into an image, enabling them to be stored on a computer?
   a. Flatbed scanner
   b. 3D scanner
   c. Handheld scanner
   d. RFID reader

5. Keys that change the meaning of the next key pressed, for example, Alt and Ctrl, are called _____ keys.
   a. modifier
   b. function
   c. alias
   d. media

6. Which term describes what you create in order to compartmentalize a hard drive so that it is capable of storing two operating systems and allowing you to select one at startup?
   a. Sector
   b. Tag
   c. Cluster
   d. Partition

7. Which statement is true about RFID technology?
   a. It must be read with a handheld device.
   b. It is becoming obsolete.
   c. It makes use of magnetic characters.
   d. It can be detected by readers located several feet away.

8. Hard drive performance is improved with the use of _____ located on the circuit board within the hard drive case.
   a. RAM
   b. Disk cache
   c. Holographic memory
   d. NTFS

9. Which is *not* an output device?
   a. DLP projector
   b. NTFS
   c. Scanner
   d. Touch screen

10. Which of the following statements about flash storage is true?
    a. Flash storage is not portable.
    b. Flash storage does not require an installed device driver.
    c. The largest flash storage device is 8 gigabytes.
    d. Flash storage is also called Internet storage.

Fill-In

In the blanks provided, write the correct answer for each of the following:

1. A USB drive is properly removed from a system by using the Remove Hardware icon located in the _____.

2. Flash drives store data in units referred to as _____.

3. _____ memory uses the spin of electrons to store information.

4. Flash, jump, or thumb drives connect to a computer system through _____ ports.

5. A(n) _____ is an input device that looks like a circle, is used to move through lists on portable devices, and is activated by circular finger motion.

6. _____ is the conversion of spoken words to computer text.

7. On some smaller notebook and netbook keyboards, the _____ key, when used with other keys, allows this smaller keyboard to perform all of the functions of a normal-sized keyboard.

8. CDs and DVDs are a form of _____ storage media.

9. A(n) _____ is a duplicate copy of data and programs saved on a different storage device.

10. _____ storage uses laser beams to create three-dimensional storage images.

11. A hard disk drive consists of several rotating disks called _____.

12. A(n) _____ is a portable printer used to print receipts and tickets.

13. Trackballs, joysticks, and scanners are all examples of _____ devices.

14. Hard drive storage is physically laid out in circular bands called _____.

15. The keys located at the top of the keyboard and labeled F1 through F12 are called _____ keys.

Short Answer

1. Give a brief description of the three types of keyboards found on portable devices or smartphones today.

2. What is the difference between an optical mouse, wireless mouse, and an air mouse?

3. What is the difference between an LCD display and an OLED display?

4. Name the two most common types of printers and briefly explain how they operate.

5. Give two examples of optical storage and provide a brief explanation of how it works.

Teamwork

1. **Input Device Usage** Have all team members make a log of the input devices they use every day for one week. Indicate the type of input device, the location or transaction it was used for, and the time of day. (For example: GPS in the car, 8:00 AM., touch screen at the bank, 1:00 PM.) At the end of the week, combine your logs into one and see which devices, uses, or times of day seem to be most popular. Present the combined list and any conclusions in a report no longer than two double-spaced pages.

2. **Finding the Solution** You have just purchased a new enhanced ergonomic keyboard with media and Internet controls. You rush home and plug it into a USB port on your system unit. The keys work, but the media and Internet controls do not. As a team, research the possible causes of the malfunctioning keyboard. You can interview professors in the IT department, talk to your technical support staff, inquire at a local computer retail store, and search the Web. Create a list of possible reasons for the malfunction and the steps needed to correct it. Use a PowerPoint presentation to describe each of the possible causes and solutions in the order you would attempt to use them to solve this dilemma.

3. **Who Is Watching You?** As a team, come up with a list of at least 10 places that information about you is being gathered, stored, and inputted into a database without your consent. Remember to consider tollbooths, ATMs, and other places where a picture or video of you or a possession of yours, like your car or parking permit, is being taken without you knowing or approving. Security officials believe that such input is valuable security data and helps deter individuals from breaking the law. As a team, debate the ethical pros and cons of such surveillance. Create a PowerPoint presentation listing the 10 places and devices the team agreed gathered and stored information without consent, and additional slides with supporting and opposing arguments for the ethical issues surrounding such input.

4. **The Relationship between Applications and Storage** Your IT team has been given $5,000 to add input, output, and additional storage to a computer system for the Director of Marketing. Currently the system has an Intel i7 processor, with 4 GB of RAM and a 170-GB hard drive. It also has an enhanced keyboard, ergonomic mouse, and a 19-inch CRT monitor. Research the type of software

that someone in that position would use and the amount of storage space it would occupy on the hard drive. Estimate the additional amount of storage space needed for all of the programs and data and list any additional input and output devices someone in that position would need in order to be productive. You might also want to consider upgrading equipment or devices that do not follow new energy efficiency policies for equipment established by the company. Then go shopping. In an Excel spreadsheet, list the input, output, and storage devices you would purchase, as well as the software applications you would purchase. Using your favorite search engine and the Internet, research the products and determine an average price for each and add the price to the spreadsheet. Sum the column of costs and see whether your team stayed within budget. If you were over budget, justify the added expense.

5. **Portable Memory Choices** As a team, research portable memory devices. Include memory sticks, memory cards (used in digital cameras), and USB flash drives. As a group, list each device in a table with its current manufacturer, and compare each device's cost per megabyte and maximum storage capacity. Include a picture of each device, if possible. Come to a group consensus as to which portable device the team prefers. Present the table, your conclusion, and the reasons for your decision in a one-page, double-spaced report.

On the Web

1. **Adaptive Technologies** Visit **www.indiana.edu/ ~iuadapts/technology/index.html** and **www. maltron.com/** to begin research on alternative software and hardware devices to aid individuals with disabilities. Using these sites and at least two other Web sites, find four hardware devices (input, output, or storage) and/or software programs that can be used to assist individuals with special needs. In a one- to two-page, double-spaced report, describe each device or program, list the manufacturer, describe the population it would service, list the cost, provide a picture of the device or a screen capture of the program, and cite your references.

2. **Apps, Apps, and More Apps?** A smartphone has the ability to input data through several types of input devices and even act as a portable storage device for your digital data. Using the Web and observing other smartphone users, create an Excel spreadsheet listing the input and storage options such phones offer. Then investigate the applications you can download to enhance your phone's ability. Add a section to the spreadsheet listing the name of these apps, their cost, and the additional input or feature they enable. For example, I can download a coin toss app that enables a flipping motion with my phone, causing the coin on the screen to behave as if it were flipped in the air. Lastly, at the bottom of the spreadsheet list models of smartphones that are capable of becoming a storage device for data on a notebook or desktop and the amount of storage space they provide. Submit the Excel spreadsheet; remember to cite your references.

3. **Engaging the Sense of Smell** Computers commonly produce results for a user in visual or audio form. We either see the results of our computing efforts on a display or in printable form, or we can hear it in synthesized speech. Investigate the most recent sense to become computer generated, the sense of smell. That's right. Use your favorite browser and the Internet to investigate the technology behind making your kitchen smell like a coffee shop or fresh-baked apple pie when neither is in near proximity. Research the types of devices that are available, their manufacturers, cost, and how they are being used. Present your research plus any additional uses that you see for this output in a one- to two-page, double-spaced paper.

4. **Talk, Talk, Talk** One of the features of Windows 7 and Microsoft Vista is the embedded speech recognition feature. Go to your favorite search engine and type in the keywords **Windows 7 Speech Recognition** and **Vista Speech Recognition** to learn about this method of entering input. Go to the Microsoft site (**www.microsoft.com**) and enter the same keywords in the search box there. On the basis of your research, describe the commands to set up and activate speech recognition in Windows 7. What three actions can speech recognition help users perform? What types of users will benefit from this technology? What are two suggestions for minimizing speech recognition errors? Cite your references and present your findings in a one-page, double-spaced paper.

5. **Visual Output from Voicemail** In many types of exchange e-mail programs, Exchange Unified Messaging (UM) makes it easy to manage voice messages by placing them in your Inbox. Investigate the output options for voice messages offered by Exchange Unified Messaging 2010. Describe some of the benefits of these output options and provide examples of where they might be used. Do you see this as a feature you would use? Present your findings in a one-page, double-spaced paper.

Spotlight

File Management

You've just finished your term paper—where should you save it? You never know when you may need a writing sample for a graduate school or job application, so you'll want to keep it someplace safe. The secret to finding what you're looking for in the future is good file management now. Managing computer files is an essential skill for any computer user. Are your skills honed? Do you understand how to save and back up your files effectively?

Once you learn the basics, file management is intuitive. You can think of managing computer files as being similar to the way you organize and store paper files and folders in a file cabinet (Figure 2A). You start with a storage device (the filing cabinet), divide it into definable sections (folders), and then fill the sections with specific items (documents) that fit the defined sections. Most people tend to organize the things in their lives, and the organizational principles used are the same ones used when managing computer files.

The Big Picture: Files, Folders, and Paths

A **file** is a named unit of related data stored in a computer system. The data and the programs installed on your computer are stored in files. Files store Word documents, music, photo images, Excel spreadsheets, applications, and a variety of other digital compilations.

Every file that is stored has certain properties. A **property** is a setting that provides information such as the file's date of creation, its size, and the date it was last modified.

You use **folders** (also called **directories**) to organize groups of files that have something in common. Many folders have **subfolders**—folders within folders—that enable you to organize your files even further. For example, you might create a folder called "Classes," and then create subfolders for each school course and then subfolders within each course for each assignment.

All of the files and folders you create must reside on a storage device called a **drive**. The primary storage devices on desktop computers are the hard drive, the CD and DVD drives, the external hard drives, and USB flash drives. Older computers may also have a floppy disk drive. On PCs, these storage devices are designated by drive letters. A **drive letter** is simply a letter of the alphabet followed by a colon and a backslash character. If your computer has a floppy disk drive, it is typically referred to as A:\. The hard drive is generally referred to as C:\. The CD or DVD drive might be labeled drive D (D:\), and other drives are often labeled sequentially, so a USB flash drive might be labeled drive E (E:\). On the Mac, drives are not labeled with letters. You'll see them as icons appearing on your screen.

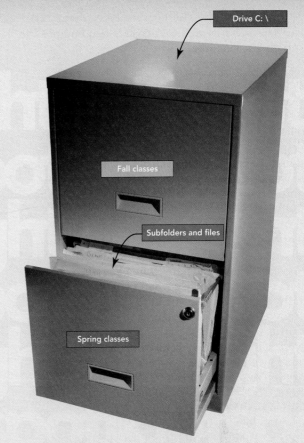

FIGURE 2A   You can organize files on your computer the same way you would organize documents in a filing cabinet.

For the computer to access a particular file, it needs to know the path it should take to get to the file. A **path** is the sequence of directories that the computer must follow to locate a file. A typical path might look like this:

C:\Classes\ Expository Writing 201\Homework #1\ Homework#1_draft1.docx

In Figure 2B, the C:\ in the path indicates that the file is located on the C:\ drive. The **top-level folder**, "Classes," contains, as the name indicates, things that have to do with classes. The subfolder named "Expository Writing 201" is the subfolder for your writing class and contains two subfolders, one for each homework assignment. The file at the end of the path, "Homework#1_draft1.docx," is the first draft of your first homework assignment. The .docx extension indicates that the file is a Microsoft Word 2007 or 2010 document. We'll

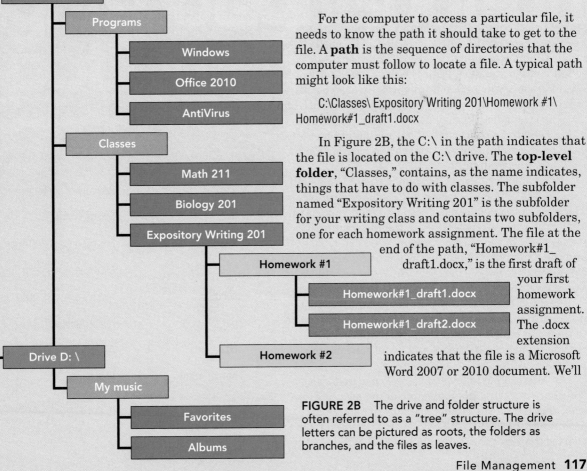

FIGURE 2B   The drive and folder structure is often referred to as a "tree" structure. The drive letters can be pictured as roots, the folders as branches, and the files as leaves.

discuss file names in greater depth shortly. Figure 2B illustrates what a hierarchical drive, folder, and file structure might look like.

FILE-NAMING CONVENTIONS

To save a file, you need to know where you're going to store it—in other words, on which storage device and in which folder. In addition, each file needs a specific file name. The **file name** is the name that the storage device uses to identify each unique file, so the name must differ from all other file names used within the same folder or directory. You may use the same name for different files, but they must exist on different drives or in different folders. Be careful to include enough detail in naming a file so that you will be able to recognize the file name when you need the file later. The name you use when you create a file is usually very obvious to you at the time—but the name may elude you when you try to remember it in the future.

Every file name on a PC has two parts that are separated by a period (read as "dot"). The first part, the part you're probably most familiar with, is called the **name**. The second part is called the **extension**, an addition to the file name, typically three to five characters in length. In a file called "Homework#1_draft1.docx," Homework#1_draft1 is the name and .docx is the extension; together they make up the file name.

Typically, an extension is used to identify the type of data that the file contains (or the format it is stored in). Sometimes it indicates the application used to create the file. In Microsoft Office, each application automatically assigns an extension to a file when you save it for the first time. For example, Microsoft Word 2010 automatically assigns the .docx extension. Workbooks created in Microsoft Excel 2010 use the .xlsx extension. When naming files, you never need to be concerned about typing in an extension, because all programs attach their extension to the file name by default.

Program files, also called application files, usually use the .exe extension, which stands for executable. The term *executable* is used because when you use an application, you execute, or run, the file. Figure 2C lists several of the most commonly used extensions and their file types. Note that when using Mac OS, extensions are not needed because Macintosh files contain a code representing the name of the application that created the file. However, it is generally recommended that Mac users add the appropriate extension to their file names so that they can more easily exchange them with PC users and avoid conversion problems.

In Microsoft Windows 7, you can use up to 260 characters in a file name, including spaces. However, this length restriction includes the entire file path name; therefore, file names actually need to be shorter than 260 characters to be valid. Windows file names cannot include any of the following characters: forward slash (/), backslash (\), greater than sign (>), less than sign (<), asterisk (*), question mark (?), quotation mark ("), pipe symbol (|), colon (:), or semicolon (;). In Mac OS and Windows XP, you can use up to 255 characters in a filename, including spaces, and all characters except the colon. Although you can use a large number of characters to create a file name, it is still best to keep file names concise and meaningful. Longer file names may be subject to automatic truncation (shortening), which can create file management difficulties.

Now that you understand the basics of paths, folders, and file naming conventions, let's turn our attention to the business of managing files.

Managing Files

Files can be managed in two ways: (1) with a file management utility such as Windows Explorer or (2) from within the programs that create them. In the following sections, we'll explore both methods.

FILE MANAGEMENT UTILITIES

Microsoft Windows uses the Windows Explorer program for file management. There are a number of ways that you can launch this program. The Start, All Programs, Accessories menu sequence is one method. Another method is to click Start and select one of the options shown on the top right side of the Start menu to view the contents of a specific folder

FIGURE 2C Commonly Used File Name Extensions

Extension	File Type
.exe	Program or application
.docx	Microsoft Word 2007 and 2010
.xlsx	Microsoft Excel 2007 and 2010
.pptx	Microsoft PowerPoint 2007 and 2010
.accdb	Microsoft Access 2007 and 2010
.pdf	Adobe Acrobat
.txt	ASCII text
.htm or .html	Web pages
.rtf	Files in rich text format
.jpeg or .jpg	Picture or image format

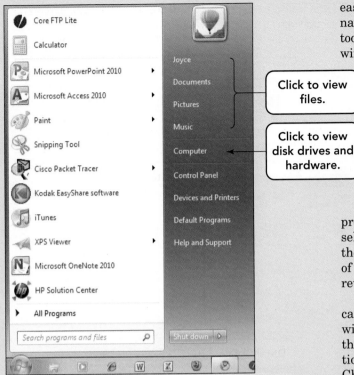

Click to view files.

Click to view disk drives and hardware.

FIGURE 2D The Start menu provides various options for viewing commonly accessed files and programs.

easier and more versatile. Windows Explorer provides navigation buttons, an address bar, a search box, and a toolbar at the top of the window. The main body of the window is split into two panes—a navigation pane and a content pane—and a detail pane is often displayed at the bottom of the window (Figure 2F). The **navigation pane** on the left allows you to navigate directly to specific folders listed in the Favorites area or access a prior search that you have saved by clicking on a desired folder. You can also add a shortcut to a frequently used folder by dragging the folder into the Favorite Links area of the navigation pane.

The **details pane** at the bottom of the window provides a thumbnail view and information about the selected file or folder. The details vary depending on the object that has been selected. Users can edit many of these items. Just click the item you wish to change, revise it, and press the Save button.

The right pane, or **content pane**, sometimes called a **file list**, displays subfolders and files located within the selected folder. You can view the contents of the right pane in several ways. Eight different view options are accessible from the View menu or from the Change your view button on the Standard toolbar. You can click the Change your view button to cycle through the choices or click the dropdown arrow next to the button to make a selection. The Tiles view and various icon views are particularly helpful if you're searching through pictures and photographs, because they show you a small copy of the images you have in the folder—before you open them. The List view simply lists the names of the files, whereas the Details view offers you information regarding file size, file type, and the

(Figure 2D). The Start menu can also be used to access the Computer folder, which lets you view the disk drives and other hardware connected to your computer (Figure 2E).

The Windows Explorer program in Windows 7 has a number of features that make file management

FIGURE 2E The Computer window provides quick access to information about the disk drives and other hardware that are connected to your computer.

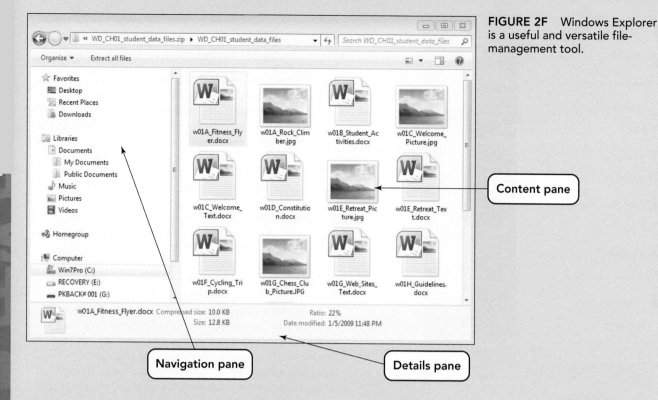

FIGURE 2F Windows Explorer is a useful and versatile file-management tool.

Content pane

Navigation pane

Details pane

date a file was last modified. There are additional optional headings available to further customize the Details view.

The column headings at the top of the file list can be used to change how the files are organized—if you use the Details view. New column headings can be added by right-clicking a heading and selecting one or more options from the shortcut menu. You can also delete column headings by selecting the heading that is checked to remove the checkmark. As in previous versions of Windows Explorer, it is possible to sort the contents of a folder, but users can now also group, stack, and filter the items displayed in the right pane.

To sort, simply click a column heading; click the column heading a second time to reverse the sort order. A sorted column displays a small triangle in the column heading; the direction of the triangle indicates whether the column has been sorted in ascending or descending order. If a folder contains subfolders and files, the subfolders are sorted separately from the files.

To access the group options, click the dropdown arrow beside the column heading to reveal the submenu. The group option arranges files and folders within specified groups, depending on the column heading you've selected. You can select how you want to group files and folders (Figure 2G). It is possible to

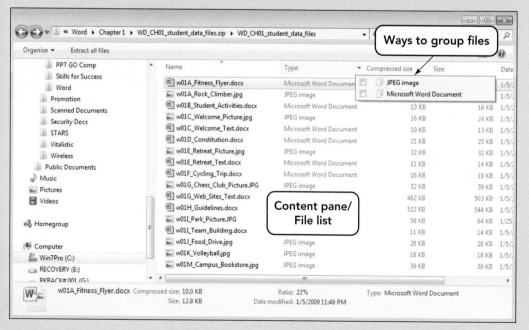

Ways to group files

Content pane/ File list

FIGURE 2G The dropdown list on the Type heading provides a way to group files by type.

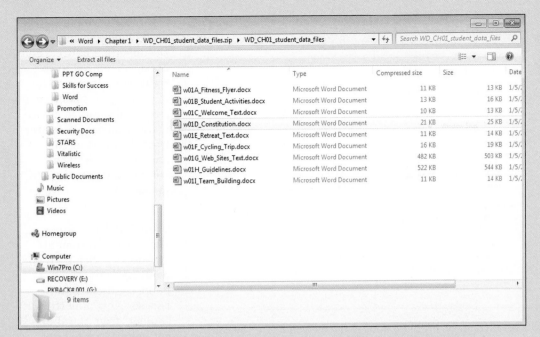

FIGURE 2H The Select by type option shows only files created with that specific type, Microsoft Word in this example.

display only the files created by a specific application (Figure 2H).

The **address bar (breadcrumb bar)** has also been updated. It is now possible to use it for breadcrumb navigation. The address bar displays the route you've taken to get to the current location. It may or may not correspond with a file's path name. To view the actual path name, click the folder icon on the left side of the address bar. The breadcrumbs can be used to easily move from one location to another—simply click the dropdown arrow to reveal a list of destinations (Figure 2I).

Locating Files and Folders Despite your best efforts, it's possible to forget where you've saved a

file. The **Search box** in Windows Explorer can make locating a lost file less painful. Select one of the four default Libraries, such as Documents and begin typing a search term in the box. As you type, Windows Explorer searches the contents of the selected folder and subfolders, immediately filtering the view to display any files that match the search term. Windows Explorer searches file names, file properties, and file contents for the search term. If the search returns too many results, or you need to create a more complex search, the Advanced Search feature can help.

If you can't locate the file or folder by using Search, you can customize your search in the Search Documents window by adding a filter

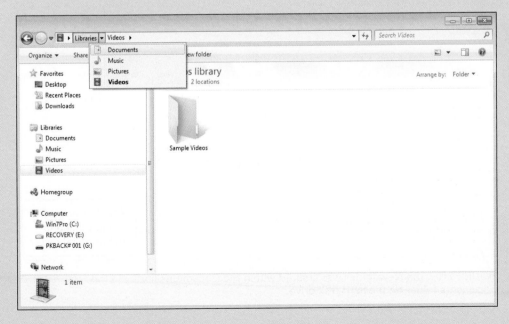

FIGURE 2I The address bar lets users navigate by breadcrumbs. Click the dropdown arrow to reveal a list of possible destinations.

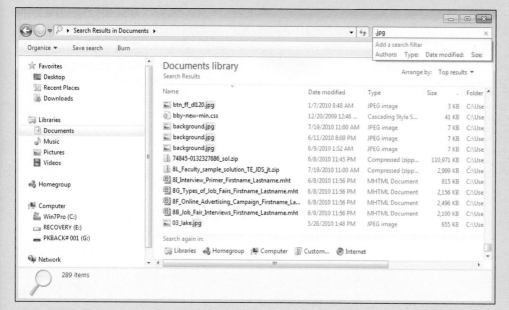

FIGURE 2J   You can add a search filter or, if you do not see the file you need, you can search other locations.

a number of commonly used folders, such as Documents, Pictures, and Music, displayed in the right pane. If you prefer to create your folder on a removable storage device, instead choose Computer from the Start menu and double-click the storage device you wish to use.

Step 2. Select a folder, such as My Documents, and double-click it. While pointing to the right pane, right-click and choose "New" and then "Folder" from the short-cut menus to create a folder within the selected folder. In other words, if you have selected the Documents library, the new folder will be placed at the top level. See Figure 2K for an example of a new folder that has been created within the Documents library.

You can repeat this process as many times as is necessary to create your desired folder structure. For example, if you're taking three classes, you might want to create three separate subfolders with the appropriate class names under a top-level folder called "Classes." That way, you'll know exactly where to save a file each time you create one, and you'll

(Figure 2J). If you find that you are often searching for the same files, click the Save Search button on the toolbar. Assign a name for your search and, by default, the results will be stored in the Searches folder. Searches are **dynamic**, which means that the next time you open a saved search, the results are automatically refreshed—new files are added and files that no longer meet the search criteria are not included.

Creating Folders   Another way to manage your files effectively is to create a **folder structure** or **directory structure** (the terms *folder* and *directory* are synonymous) —an organized set of folders in which to save your files. The process of creating a folder structure is accomplished in two steps:

Step 1. Decide on which drive, such as a USB flash drive, hard drive, or CD drive, you will create your folder. To create a folder on your computer's hard disk drive, click the Start menu and select your personal folder—typically, this folder will use your name and will appear at the top of the Start menu. Windows Explorer will open with

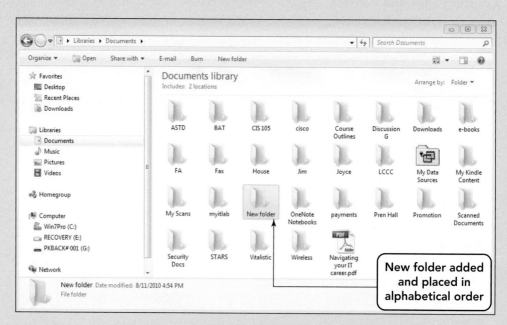

FIGURE 2K   The New folder was created within the Documents library in the Documents folder on the hard disk drive.

avoid having a cluttered and disorganized storage space.

Of course, creating a well-organized folder structure requires that you add, rename, and move folders as your needs change. For example, if you add a class to your schedule, you'll want to create a new subfolder in your top-level "Classes" folder. Next term, you'll create new subfolders for each of your classes.

One Windows method that is effective for managing, modifying, and creating folders, subfolders, and files is the use of the right-click mouse action. Right-clicking within the right pane of Windows Explorer, in a blank space, will cause a pop-up context-sensitive menu to appear. Right-clicking on a folder or file will provide a menu with different choices.

Right-clicking a file invokes a context-sensitive menu that enables you to choose among many common tasks, such as copying, deleting, and renaming files and creating shortcuts (Figure 2L). You may also use the toolbar to accomplish these and other file management tasks.

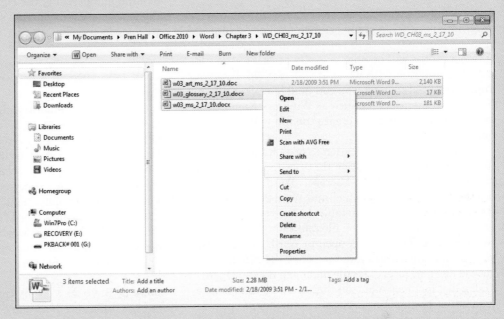

FIGURE 2L The context menu that appears when you right-click provides you with a shortcut to common tasks.

Transferring Files When you've created a useful folder structure, you're ready to transfer files and folders that already exist. Whether you're working with files or folders, the same rules apply. Files and folders can be transferred in two ways: You can copy them or you can move them. The easiest way to accomplish these tasks is to *right-drag* the files you want to transfer to the new location. Press the right mouse button and drag to new location. When you release the right mouse button, a context-sensitive menu appears, allowing you to choose the result of your right-drag. The choices on this menu are Copy Here, Move Here, Create Shortcuts Here, and Cancel.

- Copying creates a duplicate file at the new location and leaves the existing file as is.
- Moving is similar to cutting and pasting; the file is moved from its original location to the new location.
- Creating a shortcut leaves the original file in place and creates a pointer that will take you to the file for which you've created the shortcut. This action is handy for files that you access often.

If you *left-drag* a file *within the same drive*, the file is automatically moved to the new location on the drive. Left-dragging by pressing the left mouse button and dragging the file *between drives* creates a copy of the file in the new location.

Backing Up You can create a backup copy of your files in several ways. The first, and easiest, way is to create intermediate copies as you work. You can do this by saving your original file, and then using the Save As sequence to save the original file with changes every 15 or 20 minutes. Name your intermediate copies by appending a number or letter to the file name. For example, "Writing121_homework.docx" would become "Writing121_homework1.docx," then "Writing121_homework2.docx," and so forth. After saving, close the new intermediate file and reopen the original file you saved to continue working.

Additionally, you can use the Windows Explorer program to drag a copy of your file to a USB flash drive or CD/DVD drive. Backing up files to the same drive that the original copy is on risks losing both copies in a disk failure or other disaster, so you should always use a remote or portable medium for your backups.

A third way to be sure that you don't lose your work is to use backup software that is specifically designed to back up files.

Getting Help If you need help when working within the Windows Explorer program, click the Get help button on the right side of the toolbar and then type "managing files" into the Search box of the Windows

Help and Support dialog box. This will bring up a variety of links to topics that will help you to further understand file management practices.

MANAGING FILES FROM WITHIN PROGRAMS

As mentioned earlier, all software applications use program-specific file name extensions. The advantage of using a default file extension is that both you and your computer will be able to easily associate the file with the program with which it was created. By using appropriate extensions, you can double-click a file in a file management utility such as Windows Explorer and the program used to create the file will be launched.

You can use an application to open a file or use a file to launch the application that created it. Let's say you create a document in Microsoft Word. You give the file the name "Letter_Home," and Word 2010 assigns the extension ".docx" by default. Later, you use Windows Explorer to locate the file and then double-click the file name. The file will open in Word. Alternately, you could launch Word and then click the *File* tab and choose *Open* to locate the file and open it. The Open dialog box includes a button that allows you to decide which files to display—there are a number of options to choose from. Selecting *All Files* from the dropdown list will display all files in the current location, no matter what the file type might be. Choosing *All Word Documents* displays files created in any version of Microsoft Word along with macros and templates, whereas selecting Word Documents will show only Word 2007 and 2010 files.

Choosing the *File, Open* menu sequence in many programs, or clicking the *File* tab and then choosing *Open* in Microsoft Office 2007 and 2010 applications, also enables you to manage files. There are icons for creating new folders and for changing the current view, and there is an icon called Organize that enables you to copy, rename, and create shortcuts to files. Pointing to a file and pressing the right mouse button within the Open menu also invokes a file management menu with various tasks.

SAVING FILES

Saving refers to the process of transferring a file from the computer's temporary memory, or RAM, to a permanent storage device, such as a hard disk. In Microsoft Office, documents are saved by default to a folder called Documents unless you specify another folder from within the *Organize this folder's contents* button and then selecting *Properties*, and then the *Location* tab. For Office 2010 applications, you can do this from within the program's Word *Options* menu, which can be found by clicking the *File* tab (Figure 2M). A critical decision you'll make when managing files is whether to use the Save or Save As command to save files.

Save or Save As? Many computer users never figure out the difference between Save and Save As. It is actually quite simple. When you choose the Save command under the File tab, the program takes what you've created or modified in memory and writes over, or replaces, it to the same storage device and folder, with the same file name that it had when it was opened in the application. When you first save a file, the initial Save menu sequence always invokes the

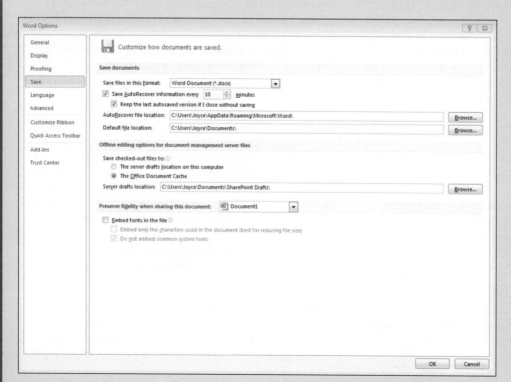

FIGURE 2M To change the default location for saved files in Microsoft Office 2010, click the File tab, then click Options, and then click Save to access the dialog box.

Save As dialog box, because the drive, path, and file name must be designated the first time a file is saved. You can select any folder by using the navigate pane. However, when you're working with a previously saved file, you need to be more careful. The Save command doesn't allow you to designate a different drive, folder, or file name; it simply replaces what is stored with the contents of memory.

The Save As command, however, brings up a dialog box that offers all of the choices you had when you first saved a file. You may choose a different drive or a different folder or a different file name. Modifying the file name is a good way to save various versions of your work, just in case something happens to what is in memory and you need to go back to a previous version.

Once you've successfully saved a file, you can always save another copy elsewhere by using the Save As command, which enables you to save the file using a new location, a new file name, or both. You might also use the Save As command to save a copy of your finished work on a USB flash drive, CD, or DVD or in an alternate folder as backup, just in case something happens to your original work. Once you use Save As, all subsequent saves of that file will now be saved in that location.

Managing E-mail

Many e-mail users quickly become overwhelmed by the number of messages they receive. It's not unusual to get dozens, or even hundreds, of messages every day. You can handle the deluge by organizing your messages into folders.

Most e-mail programs enable you to create your own mail folders. For example, you could create folders for each of the classes you're taking. In each folder, you can store mail from the teacher as well as from other students in the same class. You could create another folder to store mail from your family. In many e-mail programs you can create a rule to send e-mail to a specific folder or send an auto reply.

If you're trying to find a message in a lengthy message list, remember that you can sort the mail in different ways. By default, your e-mail program probably sorts mail in the order the messages were received. You can also sort by sender or recipient; some programs give you more ways to sort. With Microsoft Outlook you can quickly sort messages by clicking one of the buttons at the top of the message list. For example, to sort messages by date, click the Received button. Click it again to sort the list in the opposite order.

Still can't find a message or your e-mail program does not allow you to sort messages? Most e-mail programs provide a Find or Search command, which enables you to search for information in the message header. The best programs enable you to search for text in the message body as well. To search for a message within Outlook, enter a search term in the Search box. Results begin to display as soon as you begin typing.

A Few Last Reminders

Good file management is the hallmark of a competent computer user. File management should not be an intimidating or frustrating task. Computers are tremendously complex and powerful devices, but the principles of managing your work are simple. Plan and construct folder structures that make sense to you. Name your files in such a way that you can easily find them. Always begin at the beginning. If something doesn't work, go back to when it did. Read the manual. Follow directions carefully. Make backup copies of your work. And if all else fails, don't be afraid to ask for help.

Key Terms

Multiple Choice

Circle the correct choice for each of the following:

1. The default extension for Microsoft Word 2010 is:
   a. .pptx.
   b. .xlsx.
   c. .accdb.
   d. .docx.

2. A file name has two parts, the name and the
   _____.
   a. extension
   b. directory
   c. path
   d. letter

3. Another name for folder is _____.
   a. director
   b. directory
   c. file
   d. link

4. In Microsoft Windows 7, you can use up to _____ characters in a file name.
   a. unlimited
   b. 260
   c. 255
   d. 525

5. The file management utility that comes with Microsoft Windows 7 is called:
   a. Windows Internet.
   b. Internet Explorer.
   c. Windows Explorer.
   d. Windows Folders.

6. To locate a file or folder you can use the _____.
   a. Search box
   b. Where is it box
   c. Dynamic search
   d. Main folder

7. To invoke a context sensitive menu, you _____.
   a. right-click
   b. double-click
   c. left-click
   d. roll over the item

8. The Navigation pane on the left allows you to _____.
   a. navigate to the search box
   b. navigate directly to specific folder
   c. navigate directly to specific files
   d. navigate to the Internet

9. There are _____ different view options from the Change your view button.
   a. six
   b. seven
   c. eight
   d. nine

10. Which of the following does not leave a file in its original location.
    a. Copying
    b. Moving
    c. Saving As
    d. Creating a Shortcut

Spotlight Exercises

1. Launch Windows Explorer. Select a folder from the navigation pane. Sort the contents in the content pane, using the column headings. Sort it several different ways. Add or remove a few columns from the content pane. Write a brief paper that answers the following questions. Why is sorting beneficial? Which sort would you use most often? Why? List the sorts you tried and how you would use them. Why are some columns more beneficial than others? Which columns did you find more useful?

2. In this exercise, you will use the Windows Explorer program to use the group, stack, and filter options. Select a folder from the navigation pane. Using the dropdown arrow next to the sorted column, choose one of the options. Experiment with how it works and how it can be used. Repeat for the other options available. Write a one-page paper on the different options and how they can be used to help you in your courses.

3. Being able to locate your files and folders is very important. To locate files and folders we create a folder (directory) structure. In this exercise, you will use the Windows Explorer program to build a folder structure within the Documents folder. Create a top-level folder named with your name that contains three subfolders and then right-drag two or more files from some other source into one of the three subfolders (make sure you copy these files and do not move them). Click the new folder that has your name and then double-click on the subfolder that contains the files. Note the extensions on the files or the file names. Click in the Search Documents box and type in either the extension or file name. Once the list appears, press the *Print Screen* key that is at the top of the right side of your keyboard. Open a Microsoft Word document and press *Ctrl+v*. Type your name below the picture on your screen and follow your instructor's instructions to send it to him or her. When you are finished with all your exercises, you may want to delete the new folder structure you created if it is not on your personal computer.

4. Open your e-mail program. Create a new folder using the File, New, Folder menu sequence (in Outlook—other mail readers will have a similar method but may call folders something different, for example Gmail calls them labels). For the folder or label name, use the name and year of the term you are in now, such as Fall_2012. Open your new folder and create a folder/label for each of your classes. Now practice dragging messages back and forth between your Inbox folder and your new folders. Feel free to delete these folders/labels when you are through; make sure any e-mails in the folders can be deleted, or drag them back to their original locations. Write a paragraph describing your experience.

5. It is a very frustrating day when you go to open the term paper you spent hours creating and either it is not there or the content is incorrect. One way to help prevent this situation is to make backups of your files. Open Microsoft Word and create a short document stating why you should do backups. Save the file with the name "backup1.docx." You can use the folder structure you created earlier. After the file has been saved, make some changes to the document. Use Save As to save the document with the name "backup2.docx." Reopen backup1.docx. Make a few more changes to the document, explaining what you did. Save the document one more time as "backup3.docx." Be prepared to hand in your work.

6. Create a simple folder structure on your hard drive that consists of three folders named "draft_1," "draft_2," and "draft_3." Using the documents from Exercise 5 or others you may have on your computer, practice moving and copying the files to different folders. Use a flash drive to copy and move files. Write a short paper on the benefits of moving and copying files. When and why would you move a file? When and why would you copy a file?

chapter 4

System Software

Chapter Objectives

1 List the two major components of system software. (p. 129)

2 List the five basic functions of an operating system. (p. 130)

3 Explain why a computer needs an operating system. (p. 130)

4 Explain what happens when you turn on a computer. (p. 130)

5 List the three major types of user interfaces. (p. 138)

6 List the three categories of operating systems. (p. 141)

7 Discuss the strengths and weaknesses of the most popular operating systems. (p. 141)

8 List the system utilities that are considered to be essential. (p. 151)

9 Discuss data backup procedures. (p. 152)

10 Understand troubleshooting techniques and determine probable solutions to any operating system problems you may encounter. (p. 157)

Whatever happened to simple? When it comes to operating systems it seems that the names are as confusing as the products: Windows 95, Windows 98, Windows XP, Windows Vista, Windows 7—and don't forget Tiger, Leopard, and Snow Leopard. A little confused? Well, you're not alone. Besides wondering what the numbers and names stand for, you may have several other questions about operating systems. Which one is on my home computer, notebook, and smartphone? If different, are they all compatible? When is it necessary to upgrade an operating system, and how do I do it? How many more versions will there be? What is the difference between operating system software and application software?

This chapter will reveal answers to these questions while providing insight into the power and purpose of operating systems in use today.

Without software—the set of instructions that tells the computer what to do—a computer is just an expensive collection of wires and components. **System software** includes all the programs that provide the infrastructure and hardware control needed for a computer, its peripheral devices, and other programs to function smoothly. Although some system software works behind the scenes, some requires your guidance and control.

System software is often confused with application software—programs that assist user productivity such as writing a college essay or creating a presentation. System software has two major components: (1) the operating system and (2) system utilities that provide various maintenance functions. This chapter explains

- The difference between the operating system and system utilities, along with the functions each are responsible for

- Different operating systems, their newest versions, and their identifying features

- Utilities that every user should be familiar with, how to access them, and some of the settings that might help facilitate their use

- Some basic troubleshooting techniques in case of system software malfunction

Learning how to use an operating system and system utilities is the first step you should take toward mastering any computer system and ensuring a safe and enjoyable computing experience. ■

Check out **f Facebook** for our latest updates

www.facebook.com

The Operating System

The **operating system (OS)** is a set of programs designed to manage the resources of a computer. Its primary functions include

- Starting the computer and transferring files from the storage device to RAM memory
- Managing programs that are active and on the desktop and taskbar or running in the background
- Managing memory (RAM) to optimize its use
- Coordinating tasks including the communication between input and output devices and programs
- Providing a user interface to allow for easy and seamless communication with the user

The primary reason that a computer needs an operating system is to coordinate the interactions of its hardware components with each other as well as to coordinate their interaction with application software. The OS is most often located on a hard disk, although it can be stored and loaded from a USB drive, CD, or DVD. On some small handheld computers and smartphones, it is held on a memory chip within the system unit.

You can think of the OS as a traffic officer standing at a busy intersection (Figure 4.1). Imagine the traffic at a downtown New York City intersection at rush hour, and you'll have a good idea of what it's like inside a computer. Bits of information are whizzing around at incredible speeds, sent this way and that by the OS, the electronic equivalent of a harried traffic officer. Impatient peripherals and programs are honking electronic "horns," trying to get the officer's attention. As if the scene weren't chaotic enough, the "mayor" (the user) wants to come through right now. Just like a traffic officer, the computer's OS, standing at the intersection of the computer's hardware, application programs, and user, keeps traffic running smoothly.

Now that you have a visual of the importance and amount of control that the operating system has on your computer, notebook, or smartphone, let's examine the five functions of an OS more closely.

Starting the Computer

The first function of the operating system is to start the computer. When you start a computer, it loads the OS into the computer's RAM (remote access memory). To **load**

FIGURE 4.1 The operating system works at the intersection of application software, the user, and the computer's hardware.

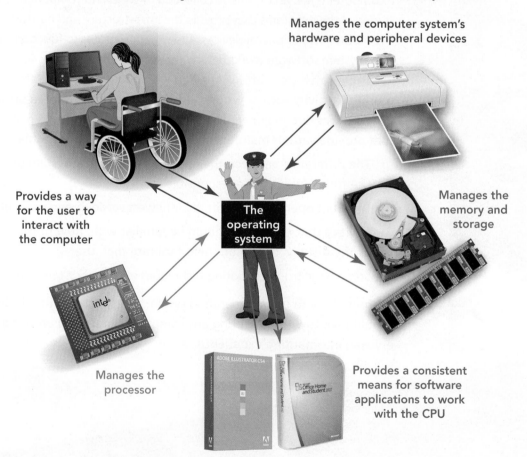

Manages the computer system's hardware and peripheral devices

Provides a way for the user to interact with the computer

The operating system

Manages the memory and storage

Manages the processor

Provides a consistent means for software applications to work with the CPU

means to transfer something from a storage device, such as the hard disk, to memory. RAM is a form of volatile memory. **Volatile memory** is storage that is very fast but that is erased when the power goes off. RAM is located on the motherboard and holds all programs in use and all documents in progress. The process of loading the OS to memory is called **booting**. This term has been used in computing circles since the very early days. It comes from an old saying that people can pull themselves up by their boot straps or, in other words, get started on their own. With a **cold boot**, you start a computer that has not yet been turned on. With a **warm boot**, you restart a computer that is already on. Warm boots, or **restarts** as they are currently called, are often necessary after installing new software or after an application crashes or stops working. In a PC you can restart a computer running a Windows OS by following these steps (Figure 4.2):

1. Click the Start button in Windows Vista and Windows 7.
2. Click on the right arrow located to the right of the lock button in Vista and to the right of the Shut down button in Windows 7.
3. Select Restart.

On a Mac press the Control + Command + Eject keys to restart the computer with the option to save changes in open documents. Use Control + Command + Power button to restart without the option to save changes in open documents. On either system, when the unit refuses to respond, attempt a warm boot or restart before using the Power off button on the system unit.

With both types of booting, the computer copies the kernel along with other essential portions of the OS from the hard disk into the computer's memory, where it remains while the computer is powered on and functioning. The **kernel** is the central part of the OS that consists of the instructions that control the actions the OS uses most frequently, for example,

starting applications and managing hardware devices and memory. The kernel resides in RAM at all times, so it must be kept as small as possible. Less frequently used portions of the OS are stored on the hard disk and retrieved as needed. Such portions are called *nonresident* because they do not reside in memory.

The booting of a system, whether it is a cold or warm boot, is a step-by-step process (Figure 4.3):

1. Activate the basic input/output system (BIOS)
2. Perform the power-on-self-test (POST)
3. Load the operating system into RAM
4. Configure and customize settings
5. Load needed system utilities
6. Authenticate the user

The following sections discuss each of these boot-up steps in detail.

Step 1: Activate the BIOS and Setup Program When you first turn on or reset a PC, electricity flows from the power supply through the system. When the CPU receives the signal that the power level is sufficient for the system to run, the CPU will

FIGURE 4.2 In a newer OS like Windows 7, using the Restart option from the Start button is the preferred way of restarting a nonresponsive system.

Getting Started
Magnifier
Remote Desktop Connection
Snagit 9
Notepad
Windows Media Center
Calculator
Snagit 9 Editor
Microsoft PowerPoint 2010 (Beta)
Sticky Notes
Microsoft Outlook 2010 (Beta)
Paint
Microsoft Word 2010 (Beta)
Solitaire
All Programs

Documents
Pictures
Music
Games
Computer
Control Panel
Devices and Printers
Default Programs
Help and Support

Switch user
Log off
Lock
Restart
Sleep
Hibernate

3. Restart

1. Start button

2. Right arrow

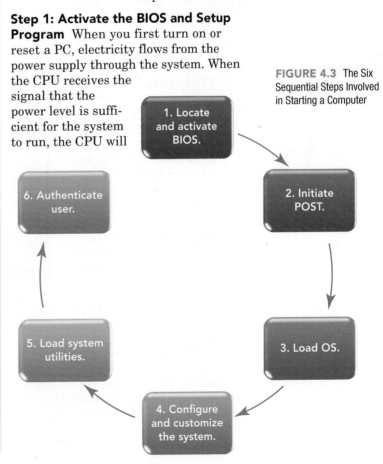

FIGURE 4.3 The Six Sequential Steps Involved in Starting a Computer

1. Locate and activate BIOS.
2. Initiate POST.
3. Load OS.
4. Configure and customize the system.
5. Load system utilities.
6. Authenticate user.

System Software **131**

Leaving a computer running when it's not in use is wasteful. By default, a computer running Windows Vista and Windows 7 will go into Sleep mode after a period of inactivity, saving its owner $70 or more in annual energy costs. There are three energy settings you can adjust in Windows 7 to help conserve energy.

- Use **Sleep mode** to transfer the current state of your computer to RAM, turn off all unneeded functions, and place the system in a low-power state. Returning from Sleep mode is faster than returning from Hibernate due to the state of the computer being held in memory.

- Choose **Hibernate mode** to save battery power. Used primarily in notebooks, this mode puts your open documents and programs on your hard disk and then actually turns off your computer. When you restart your system, it is returned to the state prior to hibernation. All windows and programs that were open are restored automatically.

- If you are using a desktop, **Hybrid sleep** may be the option for you. This mode is a combination of sleep and Hibernate mode and puts open documents and programs in both RAM and on your hard disk, and then places the system in a low-power state so you can quickly resume your work. If power is suddenly terminated, the Hibernate portion of this mode guarantees that your work can be restored. Hybrid sleep is usually turned on by default on most desktops.

To access the settings for Sleep and Hibernate modes in either Windows 7 or Windows Vista, click the Start button and select the Control Panel option from the menu on the far right. Then find the power options, which are located in the System and Security category in Windows 7 and the System and Maintenance category in Windows Vista (Figure 4.4).

FIGURE 4.4 The On battery options should be 5 minutes or less to conserve battery life on a notebook computer.

In Windows 7, to place your system in Sleep or Hibernate mode, click the Start button and from the arrow to the right of the Shut down button select either Sleep or Hibernate (Figure 4.5). You can also put your computer into Sleep mode from the Start button by clicking the icon of the Power button. To wake your system, press the Power button on your system unit.

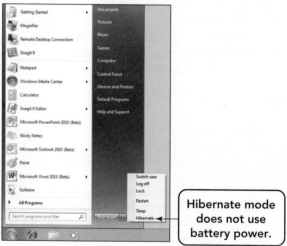

Hibernate mode does not use battery power.

FIGURE 4.5 In Windows 7, Hibernate and Sleep are easily activated from the Start menu.

If you are purchasing a new system, go one step further and purchase an Energy Star–qualified computer and monitor. New efficiency specifications mean that these products save energy while in use, not just while in Sleep mode. ●

start executing. The CPU can be said to have amnesia at this time; it has absolutely nothing at all in memory to execute or work on. So the processor makers have written programs, activated during this stage of start-up, to direct the CPU to the same place in the system, the BIOS ROM, for the start of the system's BIOS boot program. The **BIOS (basic input/output system)** is the part of the system software that provides the computer with the descriptions of the equipment that your system contains, typically the CPU, hard disk, RAM, and video component—equipment not usually replaced by the user. The operating system then uses the BIOS data to control those devices. Other external devices, such as jump drives and speakers, which are frequently replaced by a user, are not run by BIOS, but are controlled and accessed by the operating system. The BIOS is encoded, or permanently written, in the computer's ROM. **ROM**, or **read-only memory**, is **nonvolatile memory**—memory that is not easily edited and keeps its content even when the system powers off. It's these features that guarantee the reliability and reusability of the programs stored there. After the BIOS is located, you may briefly see the BIOS screen, a text-only screen that provides information about BIOS-controlled devices (Figure 4.6).

While the BIOS information is visible, you can access the computer's setup program by pressing a special key, such as Del or F8. (During the boot process, you'll see an on-screen message indicating which key to press to access the setup program.) If your system displays a logo instead of the BIOS access information, press the Esc or Tab key while the logo is showing to enter the setup program. The **setup program** includes settings that control the computer's hardware. Entering this program is not easy and you should *not* alter or change *any* of these settings without understanding the purpose of each setting and the problems that can arise from incorrect entries. Making an incorrect change to a BIOS device will cause the system not to boot.

Step 2: Initiate the Power-On Self-Test

After the BIOS instructions are loaded into memory, a series of tests are conducted to make sure that the computer and associated peripherals are operating correctly.

Collectively, these tests are known as the **power-on self-test (POST)**. Among the components tested are the computer's main memory (RAM), the keyboard, mouse, disk drives, and the hard disk. If any of the power-on self-tests fail, you'll hear a beep, see an on-screen error message, and the computer will stop. You often can correct such problems by making sure that components, such as keyboards, are plugged in securely.

However, some failures are so serious that the computer cannot display an error message; instead, it sounds a certain number of beeps. If this happens, it's time to call for technical support. To help the technician repair the computer, write down any error messages you see and try to remember how many beeps you heard.

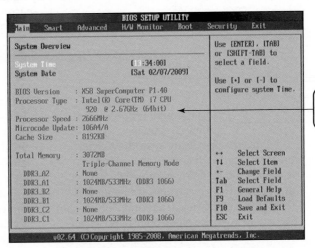

CPU manufacturer, type, and speed

FIGURE 4.6 This BIOS screen is for a system with an Intel Core i7 CPU running at 2666 MHz.

Step 3: Load the Operating System

Once the power-on self-test is successfully completed, the BIOS initiates a search for the operating system. Options (or settings) in the setup program determine where the BIOS looks for the OS. If multiple possible locations exist (such as an optical drive, a floppy drive, or a hard disk), the settings also specify the search order. If no OS is found in the first location, the BIOS moves on to the next location.

On most PCs, the BIOS first looks for the OS on the computer's hard disk. When the BIOS finds the OS, it loads the OS's kernel into memory. At that point, the OS takes control of the computer and begins loading system configuration information.

Step 4: Configure the System

In Microsoft Windows, configuration information about installed peripherals and software is stored in a database called the **registry**. The registry also contains information about your system configuration choices, such as

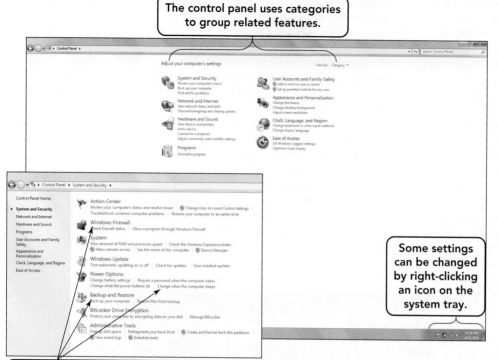

The control panel uses categories to group related features.

Some settings can be changed by right-clicking an icon on the system tray.

Key system settings can be set from the System and Security category.

FIGURE 4.7 Many options for managing and customizing your computer system can be found on the Control Panel under one of the eight main categories.

background graphics and mouse settings.

Once the operating system's kernel has been loaded, it checks the system's configuration to determine which drivers and other utility programs are needed. A **driver** is a utility program that contains instructions to make a peripheral device addressable or usable by an OS. If a peripheral device that is already installed on the system requires a driver to operate, that peripheral's driver will be installed and loaded automatically. If the driver is missing or has become corrupted, you may be prompted to insert a CD or download the needed driver from the manufacturer's Web site.

Windows and Mac operating systems are equipped with **plug-and-play (PnP)** capabilities, which automatically detect new PnP-compatible peripherals that you might have installed while the power was switched off, load the necessary drivers, and check for conflicts with other devices. Peripheral devices equipped with PnP features identify themselves to the OS and require no action on the part of the user.

Step 5: Load System Utilities After the operating system has detected and configured all of the system's hardware, it loads system utilities such as speaker volume control, antivirus software, and power management options. In Microsoft Windows, you can view available custom configuration choices by right-clicking the

icon of the feature you want to reconfigure located in the system tray (located on the right side of the Windows taskbar) or through the Control Panel located on the Start menu (Figure 4.7).

Step 6: Authenticate a User When the operating system finishes loading, you may see a request for a user name and password. Through this process, called **authentication** (or **login**), you verify that you are indeed the person who is authorized to use the computer.

Today, most consumer-oriented operating systems, such as Microsoft Windows and Mac OS, require or highly recommend that you supply a user name and password to use the computer. A **profile**, a record of a specific user's preferences for the desktop theme, icons, and menu styles, is associated with a user name. If you set up a profile for yourself, your preferences will appear on the screen after you log on. You can enable other users to create profiles that are associated with their user names and passwords so that when they log in they'll see their preferences without disturbing yours. It is always wise to create an Administrator account to manage installing and uninstalling software, operating system devices, and resetting forgotten passwords. The Administrator account should be password protected with only one or two trusted users having access.

On multiuser computer systems such as in a university lab or a corporate office environment, you must have an account to access a computer. Your **account** consists of your user name, password, and storage space, which is called a *user folder* or *user directory*. The account is usually created by a server/computer administrator, who is a person responsible for managing the accounts.

Now that the OS is loaded and running, let's look at another important task that the OS handles: managing applications.

Managing Applications

The operating system function that most dramatically affects overall quality of the system is the ability to run and manage applications. When you start an application, the CPU loads the application from storage into RAM. In the early days of personal computing, **single-tasking operating systems** could run only one application at a time, which was often inconvenient. To switch between applications, you had to quit one application before you could start the second.

Today, multitasking operating systems are the norm. **Multitasking operating systems** enable more than one application to run at the same time. With multitasking operating systems, the computer may not actually run two applications at once, but switches between them as needed. For example, a user might be running two applications, such as Word and Excel, simultaneously. From the user's perspective, one application (the **foreground application**) is active, whereas the other (the **background application**) appears inactive, as indicated by its appearance on the desktop (Figure 4.8).

A clear measure of the operating system's stability is the technique it uses to handle multitasking. If one of the running applications invades another's memory space, one or both of the applications will become unstable or, at the extreme, crash.

Most current operating systems use a more recent, improved type of multitasking called **preemptive multitasking**, an environment in which programs do not run from start to finish but are interrupted or suspended in order to start or continue to run another task. In this system each task receives a recurring slice of time from the CPU. Depending on the operating system, the time slice may be the same for all programs or it may be adjustable to meet a program's hardware and user demands. When one task uses its time slice or is interrupted by a task of higher priority, the task is suspended and the other started. This method of multitasking ensures that all applications have fair access to the CPU and prevents one program from monopolizing it at the expense of the others. Even if one program becomes unstable or stops working, the OS and other applications will continue to run. Although you may lose unsaved work in the application that fails to respond, chances are good that everything else will be fine.

Now that you understand how the OS manages individual and multiple applications, let's take a look at how it manages RAM, its primary memory.

Managing Memory

If the operating system had to constantly access program instructions from their storage location on your computer's hard disk, programs would run very slowly. A **buffer**, an area that temporarily holds data and instructions, is needed to make the processing of instructions more fluid. Computers use RAM, a temporary storage medium, to function as this buffer. The computer's OS is responsible for managing this memory. The OS gives each running program and some devices their own portion of RAM and attempts to keep the

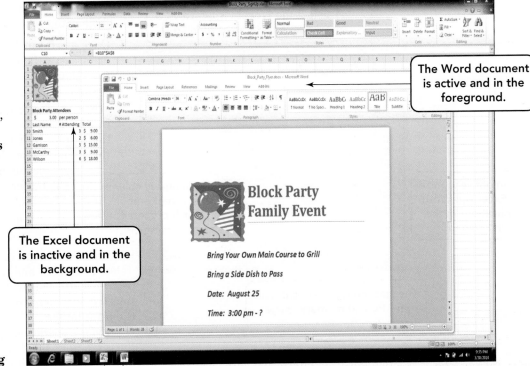

The Word document is active and in the foreground.

The Excel document is inactive and in the background.

An icon appears on the taskbar for each open application.

FIGURE 4.8 Today multitasking operating systems are the norm, and most users keep more than one application open at a time. The taskbar displays an icon for each open program.

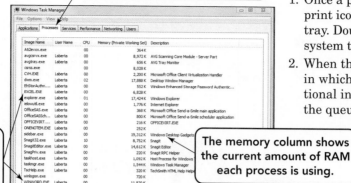

Select the Processes tab to view a list of processes running.

You might recognize the Excel and Word applications in the first column.

The memory column shows the current amount of RAM each process is using.

The status bar provides details on CPU and memory usage.

FIGURE 4.9 Access the Windows Task Manager by pressing Ctrl + Alt + Del and selecting the Start Task Manager option. Details on all processes running are displayed along with total CPU usage.

FIGURE 4.10 The print icon on the system tray provides fast access to the print queue. If the printer is on a network, you might need administrator rights to access and delete documents in the queue.

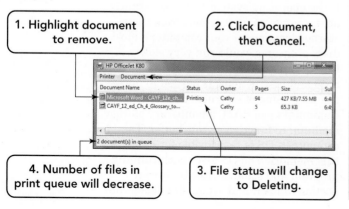

1. Highlight document to remove.

2. Click Document, then Cancel.

3. File status will change to Deleting.

4. Number of files in print queue will decrease.

programs from interfering with each other's use of memory (Figure 4.9).

A print buffer is a good example. Have you ever given the command to print three documents of reasonable length, one right after another? While the printer is printing the first document, the second and third documents are being held in the print buffer. The documents wait in the buffer until the spooling program, a program that monitors the print jobs in the buffer and the busy state of the printer, indicates that the printer is available. The second document will then move from the buffer to the printer. This process continues until the print buffer is empty. Have you ever wondered why turning off the printer to stop the printing of a document doesn't work? Well, stopping the printer does not erase the print buffer. When you turn the printer on again, the documents in the print buffer continue to print. So, how do you stop

documents in the print buffer from printing? Follow the steps listed below:

1. Once a print instruction is given, a print icon will appear on the system tray. Double-click the print icon on the system tray.

2. When the dialog box opens, a window in which the user can supply additional information, you will see the queue, a list of names of the documents in the print buffer.

3. Select the document you want to erase from the queue.

From the menu in this dialog box, select Document and then Cancel (Figure 4.10). This will remove the selected document from the queue and the print buffer.

Today's operating systems can make the computer's RAM seem larger than it really is. This trick is accomplished by means of **virtual memory**, a method of using a portion of the computer's hard disk as an extension of RAM. In virtual memory, program instructions and data are divided into units of fixed size called **pages**. If memory is full, the OS starts storing copies of pages in a hard disk file called the **swap file**. This file is not an application but a temporary storage space for bits and bytes that the OS will access as you do your work. When the pages are needed, they are copied back into RAM (Figure 4.11). The transferring of files from the hard disk to RAM and back is called **paging**.

Although virtual memory enables users to work with more memory than the amount of RAM installed on the computer, excessive paging is called **thrashing** and slows down the system. Accessing data from a hard disk is much slower than accessing it from RAM. For this reason, adding more RAM to your computer is often the best way to improve its performance. With sufficient RAM, the OS makes minimal use of virtual memory.

Instead of using the hard drive for virtual memory, Windows Vista and Windows 7 come with Windows ReadyBoost, a feature that allows for the allocation of space on removable memory devices that can be used to increase the size of RAM memory. ReadyBoost performance is better than hard disk virtual memory because accessing files on flash memory (USB flash drives and secure digital SD memory cards) is quicker than accessing

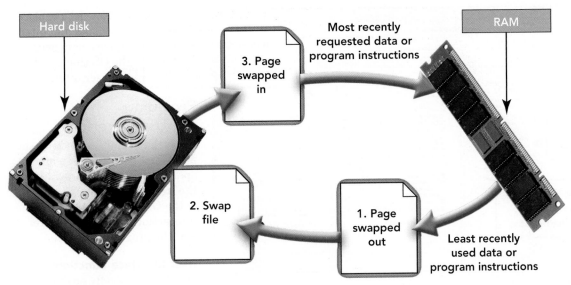

Hard disk

3. Page swapped in

Most recently requested data or program instructions

RAM

2. Swap file

1. Page swapped out

Least recently used data or program instructions

information on a hard drive. To allocate flash memory, follow these steps (Figure 4.12):

1. Insert a flash device into your system. The operating system checks to see whether the device can perform fast enough to work with Windows Ready-Boost. If it can, an additional option, Speed up my system, will appear at the bottom of the AutoPlay menu.

2. From the AutoPlay menu, select Speed up my system (usually the last option).

3. If your device is ReadyBoost-compatible, the next dialog box should open with the ReadyBoost tab active. Select the radio button option to Use this device and set the amount of space you want to allocate for memory use. In Windows 7 there is no upper limit on the amount that can be allocated. If your flash media does not have the option to make use of ReadyBoost, the ReadyBoost tab will indicate that the device is not compatible.

4. Click Apply and then click OK.

Once the computer's OS is running and managing applications and memory, its next responsibility is to be able to coordinate activities from accepting data and commands to representing the results of processing operations.

Coordinating Tasks

How does your computer "know" that you want it to do something? How does it

show you the results of its work? Another operating system function is coordinating tasks involving input and output devices, as well as enabling communication with these devices and the programs in use.

Most operating systems come with drivers for popular input and output devices. Device drivers are programs that contain specific instructions to allow a particular brand and model of input or output device to function properly. The driver enables communication between the OS and the input and output devices connected to a computer system. Printers, scanners, monitors, speakers, and the mouse all have drivers (Figure 4.13). Hardware manufacturers usually update their drivers when they develop a new operating system. You can also obtain updated drivers yourself from the manufacturer's Web site if they are not already included with the OS. When you change devices, the Windows operating system provides a feature called Windows Update that can automatically detect new hardware and install the required driver in less than one minute. Windows Update also

FIGURE 4.11 Only a portion of RAM is allocated to virtual memory. A user can increase this amount; however, a better solution would be to purchase more RAM.

FIGURE 4.12 It is fairly easy to set up ReadyBoost to enhance your virtual memory.

1. From the AutoPlay menu, select Speed up my system.

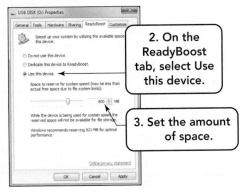

2. On the ReadyBoost tab, select Use this device.

3. Set the amount of space.

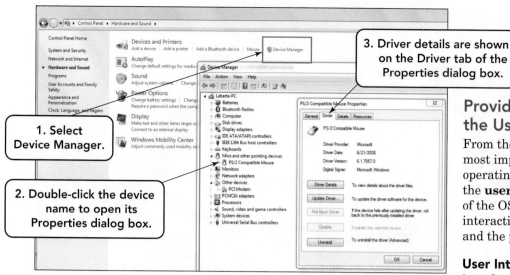

1. Select Device Manager.

2. Double-click the device name to open its Properties dialog box.

3. Driver details are shown on the Driver tab of the Properties dialog box.

FIGURE 4.13 The Device Manager is accessible from the Hardware and Sound option in the Control Panel and provides information on the devices connected to your computer and the drivers they are using.

handles the retrieval and installation of new drivers as they are needed. But new drivers aren't always needed. If your device is working properly, you may not need to upgrade the driver. A good rule of thumb is: If it's not broken, don't fix it.

Hardware, such as input and output devices, as well as software can generate **interrupts**, signals that inform the OS that an event has occurred and is in need of immediate attention. For hardware, this can be the user pressing a key, the mouse moving to a new position, or a notice that a document is waiting to print. A software event that generates an interrupt would be an attempt to divide by zero. This operation is undefined and throws the system into an interrupt to prevent the processor from attempting something that cannot be done. Software interrupts are handled mostly by the processor, whereas hardware interrupts are handled by the OS. Our discussion will focus on hardware interrupts.

The OS provides **interrupt handlers**, also called **interrupt service routines**, which are miniprograms that immediately respond when an interrupt occurs. The type of response or action the handler initiates depends on the type and source of the interrupt. On a busy system, multiple interrupts can occur at the same time. Remember the traffic officer analogy at the beginning of this chapter. In the case of multiple interrupts, the responses are held in RAM in an **interrupt vector table** and are processed, by the operating system, starting with the one having the highest priority rating to the one with the lowest. The actual interrupting of an event by an interrupt signal is called an **interrupt request (IRQ)**.

Now let's explore the visual and interactive components of the OS that create the user interface.

Providing the User Interface

From the user's perspective, the most important function of an operating system is providing the **user interface**, the part of the OS that facilitates your interaction with the computer and the programs you use.

User Interface Functions User interfaces typically enable you to do the following:

- Start (launch) application programs.
- Manage storage devices, such as hard disks, optical drives, and USB drives, and organize files. The interface provides options to copy files from one storage device to another, rename files, and delete files.
- Shut down the computer safely by following an orderly shutdown procedure.

Types of User Interfaces The three types of user interfaces are graphical, menu driven, and command-line interfaces (Figure 4.14).

By far the most popular user interface, a **graphical user interface** (**GUI**; pronounced "goo-ee"), uses graphics and the point-and-click technology of the mouse to make the operating system and programs easier to use. On most of today's computers, GUIs are used to engage the user through the **desktop**, the screen image that appears after the OS finishes loading into memory (RAM). A typical desktop on most personal computers can be divided into three regions (Figure 4.15):

- The left side of the desktop is where the Start button and icons appear. **Icons** are small images that represent computer resources such as programs, data files, and network connections.
- The right side of the desktop is where an invisible 1-inch vertical strip called the **sidebar** is positioned. In the sidebar the user can place and arrange **gadgets**, applications that appear as active icons that are

Graphical interface

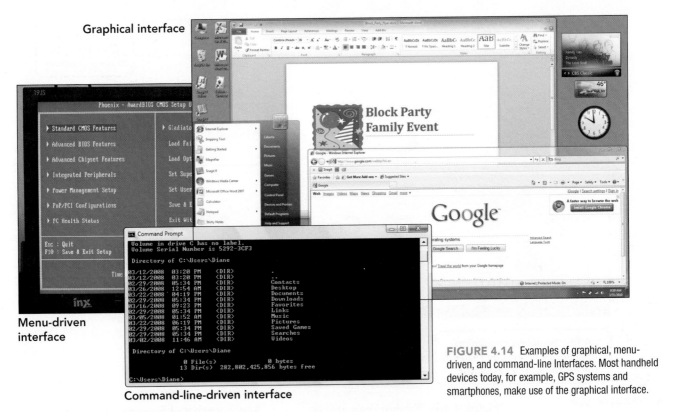

Menu-driven
interface

Command-line-driven interface

FIGURE 4.14 Examples of graphical, menu-driven, and command-line Interfaces. Most handheld devices today, for example, GPS systems and smartphones, make use of the graphical interface.

constantly running to keep you updated on weather changes, stock prices, and current events, to name a few. This feature was not available in operating systems prior to Vista.

- The center of the desktop is where the programs you open will appear in a window structure. Windows can be resized and rearranged so that multiple ones can be cascaded or tiled and viewed on the screen at the same time

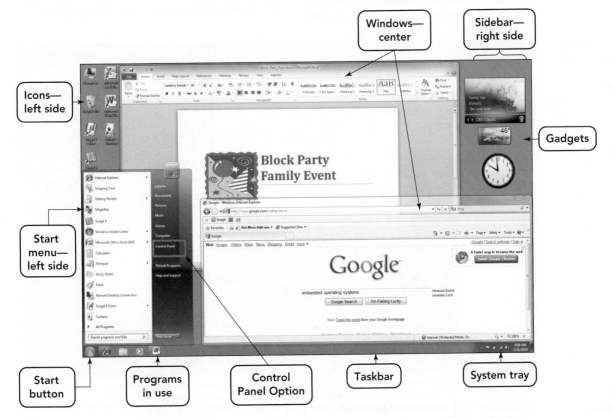

FIGURE 4.15 Remember that the desktop has a left, center, and right region, with certain icons appearing in each region.

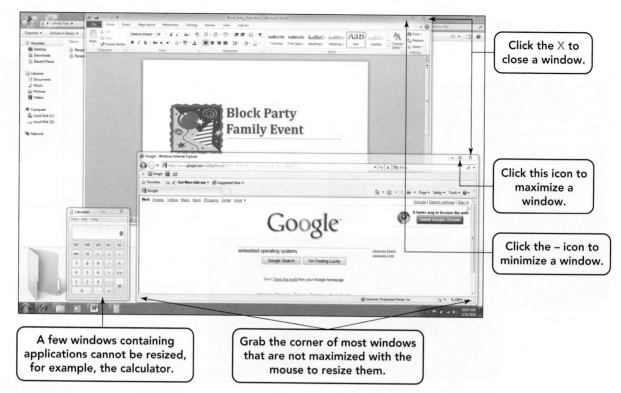

Click the X to close a window.

Click this icon to maximize a window.

Click the − icon to minimize a window.

A few windows containing applications cannot be resized, for example, the calculator.

Grab the corner of most windows that are not maximized with the mouse to resize them.

FIGURE 4.16 Most users have a preference for the arrangement of open windows and use the maximize, minimize, and resize features of a window to create a unique layout.

(Figure 4.16). Windows can also be maximized to take up the entire desktop. In maximized form they will cover your icons and gadgets.

The desktop image can change with the OS or OS version, and certain components of it can be customized by the user to create a personal look. The use of the Appearance and Personalization option located in the Control Panel is one way for a user to make changes in the desktop appearance, while other features, such as gadgets, can be added and deleted by right-clicking in the sidebar (Figure 4.17).

Menu-driven user interfaces enable you to avoid memorizing key words

FIGURE 4.17 You can set desktop options from the Control Panel or by right-clicking the sidebar.

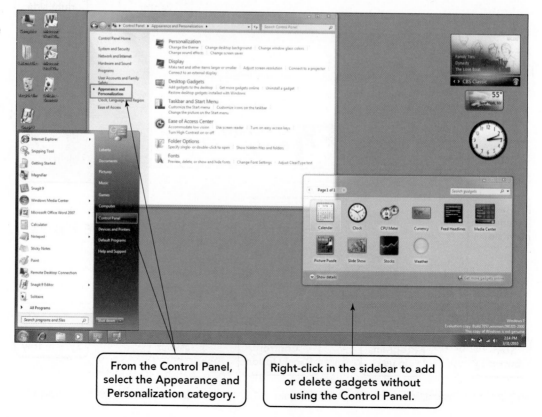

From the Control Panel, select the Appearance and Personalization category.

Right-click in the sidebar to add or delete gadgets without using the Control Panel.

(such as *copy* and *paste*) and syntax (a set of rules for entering commands). On-screen, text-based menus show all the options available at a given point. With most systems, you select an option with the arrow keys and then press Enter, click the desired option with the mouse, or strike a designated keyboard letter.

So what type of interface is used in Windows 7 and Vista? Are they systems that use a GUI or menu-driven user interface? If you have used one or both of these operating systems, then you know that they are actually a combination of both. It is very difficult to place an icon for every option somewhere on the main window of any program. Often the icons for the most frequently used options are visible on the Ribbon or toolbar. The less frequently used features can be accessed though menus or dialog boxes that were opened by selecting a menu option or clicking an icon.

Command-line user interfaces require you to type commands using keywords that tell the OS what to do (such as *Format* or *Copy*) one line at a time. You must observe complicated rules of syntax that specify exactly what you can type in a given place. For example, the following command copies a file from the hard disk drive C to a removable USB drive identified as drive F:

```
copy C:\myfile.txt F:\myfile.txt
```

Command-line user interfaces aren't popular with most users because they require memorization, and it's easy to make a typing mistake. Although the commands are usually very simple, such as *Copy* and *Paste*, others are more cryptic. However, some experienced users actually prefer command-line interfaces because they can operate the computer quickly after memorizing the keywords and syntax.

Now that you've seen how the OS makes itself available to you, let's explore the most popular OSs in depth.

Exploring Popular Operating Systems

We will look at the three categories of operating systems: **stand-alone operating systems** that are used by single users, **server operating systems** used in client/server network environments, and **embedded operating systems** that are

FIGURE 4.18 Operating Systems by Category

Category	Name
Stand-alone	DOS—developed for original IBM PC Windows 3.X, Windows 95, Windows 98, Windows 2000 Professional, Windows ME, Windows XP, Windows Vista, Windows 7 MAC OS X UNIX Linux
Server	Windows NT Server, Windows 2000 Server, Windows Server 2003, Windows Server 2008 UNIX Linux Novell Netware Solaris Red Hat Enterprise Server
Embedded	Windows CE (variations are Windows Mobile, Pocket PC) iPhone OS Palm OS BlackBerry OS Embedded Linux Google Android Symbian OS

found on ROM chips in the portable or dedicated devices we use today (Figure 4.18). Although your choice of operating system might be limited by the computing device you own and the network you are using, you should know how the various systems have evolved and their strengths and weaknesses.

Stand-Alone Operating Systems

A stand-alone operating system works on a desktop computer, notebook, or any portable computing device. The name *stand-alone* comes from the fact that it does not need to be connected to any other system or computer in order to run. Almost all of the operating systems in this class (category) have been enhanced with enough networking capabilities and connectivity options to allow them to manage a home or small business network. The keyword here is *small*.

Microsoft Windows Microsoft **Windows** is by far the most popular group of operating systems. Over the years, it has gone through several iterations and is now considered *the* operating system of

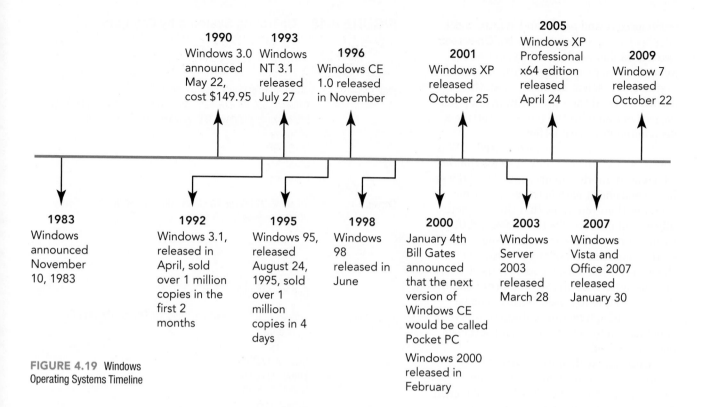

1983
Windows announced November 10, 1983

1990
Windows 3.0 announced May 22, cost $149.95

1992
Windows 3.1, released in April, sold over 1 million copies in the first 2 months

1993
Windows NT 3.1 released July 27

1995
Windows 95, released August 24, 1995, sold over 1 million copies in 4 days

1996
Windows CE 1.0 released in November

1998
Windows 98 released in June

2000
January 4th Bill Gates announced that the next version of Windows CE would be called Pocket PC

Windows 2000 released in February

2001
Windows XP released October 25

2003
Windows Server 2003 released March 28

2005
Windows XP Professional x64 edition released April 24

2007
Windows Vista and Office 2007 released January 30

2009
Window 7 released October 22

FIGURE 4.19 Windows Operating Systems Timeline

PCs worldwide. Figure 4.19 is a compressed timeline highlighting some key developments in the Windows OS over the years. A very detailed timeline is available at **www.computerhope.com/history/windows.htm**. When you purchase a computer, it usually comes with an OS already installed. Microsoft has agreements with the major computer manufacturers to provide Windows on almost all of the personal computers that are made today. Some manufacturers offer a choice of operating systems, but Windows is expected to remain the standard for years to come.

Microsoft Windows 7, the latest version of the Microsoft Windows operating system, was released in late 2009 and is available in six different versions: Starter, Home Basic, Home Premium, Professional, Enterprise, and Ultimate (Figure 4.20). All versions of Windows 7 promise to be more efficient than its predecessor, performing equally or better on the same hardware, and claim to have resolved the compatibility issues that existed between applications.

Windows 7 includes several new features to make using a PC notebook easier. See Figure 4.21 for an overview of four of these features. Test them out and decide for yourself whether they make your notebook computing experience more enjoyable and somewhat faster.

Released to the general public in January 2007, **Microsoft Windows Vista** replaced the popular Windows XP operating system and is designed for home and professional use. Vista is available in five different versions—Basic, Home Premium, Business, Ultimate, and Enterprise. Vista introduced features such as translucent windows, three-dimensional animation, and live taskbar thumbnails—just hover the mouse over a button on the taskbar to get a preview of its contents. Vista also addressed the growing popularity of mobile computing. Previously, tablet PCs required the Windows XP Tablet PC Edition OS, but Vista supported tablet PCs and other mobile devices through the Windows Mobility Center. This OS differentiated itself from previous Windows releases by its improved search features and networking tools, integrated speech recognition capabilities, and new multimedia tools such as gadgets.

MAC OS

The original Macintosh operating system, called **Mac OS**, released in 1984, was the first OS to bring the GUI to the world. Although Apple eventually lost market share to Microsoft, it has a diehard fan base. Many prefer the Mac OS for its stability and ease of use, although the

FIGURE 4.20 Windows 7 Editions

Edition	Features
Windows 7 Starter	Designed for small notebook computers, this edition was originally known as "the one that would not let you run more than three applications at a time." The decision on the limit of three was reversed, and the final version can run just about any Windows task. When multitasking, it is recommended that you avoid high-resource tasks like watching a DVD. This edition must be preinstalled on notebooks and is not available for individual purchase.
Windows 7 Home Basic	This is the other "nonpremium" edition available only in emerging markets (not in the United States, Canada, Europe, and other developed nations). It is more graphically interesting than Starter but lacks premium features like Windows Media Center.
Windows 7 Home Premium	This is the entry-level edition for most average consumers. It has the full Aero interface (translucent design, subtle animation, and additional colors) and Windows Media Center.
Windows 7 Professional	This is the preferred edition for businesses and advanced home users. It builds on Home Premium and runs a remote desktop server, encrypts files, and makes network folders available offline.
Windows 7 Enterprise	Enterprise and Ultimate editions have most of the same features, but the Enterprise edition is geared to enterprise users and is available through volume licensing.
Windows 7 Ultimate	The Ultimate edition is for the high-end user, gamer, and multimedia professionals. It includes BitLocker disk encryption, which now works on USB flash drives.

interfaces of Macs and PCs are becoming very similar (Figure 4.22). Operating systems for the MAC were numbered as Mac OS 8, Mac OS 9, and Mac OS X (X for the Roman numeral 10). Newer versions of Mac OS X have, in addition to their numeric identification, been given names associated with large cats. Mac OS v10.0 is called Cheetah and Mac OS v10.6 is labeled Snow Leopard.

FIGURE 4.21 Windows 7 Features That Make Using a Notebook PC Simple

Feature	Description
Jump list	A list activated by right-clicking an icon on the taskbar or the Start menu. The options in the list are specific to the icon clicked. By selecting an option in the jump list, the user instantly gets the result.
Pin	A method of attaching your favorite program anywhere on the taskbar by dragging it from the desktop to the taskbar. Removing it from the taskbar is done by dragging it off the taskbar.
Snap	A quick (and fun) new way to resize open windows by dragging them to the edges of your screen.
Windows Search	A feature activated by simply typing a description of what you want to locate in the search box located at the bottom of the Start menu. The results will be a list of relevant documents, pictures, music, and e-mail that match your entered description. Because most users store data on several devices, Windows 7 is designed to search external hard drives, networked PCs, and libraries (a Windows 7 feature that groups related files together regardless of their storage location).

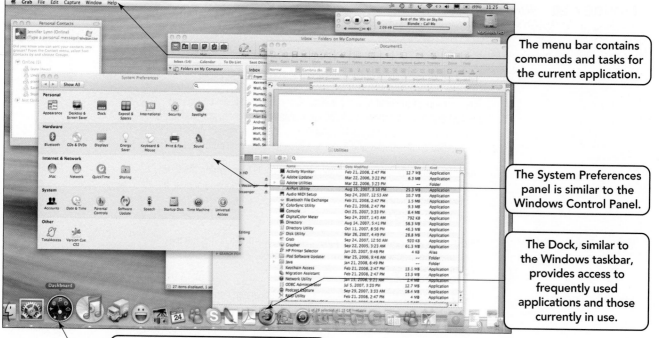

The menu bar contains commands and tasks for the current application.

The System Preferences panel is similar to the Windows Control Panel.

The Dock, similar to the Windows taskbar, provides access to frequently used applications and those currently in use.

The dashboard icon is used to access widgets, similar to the gadgets stored on the sidebar in Windows 7.

FIGURE 4.22 Today the Mac OS X interface and Windows 7 are very similar.

For a detailed explanation on what Mac OS X is, go to **www.apple.com/ macosx/what-is-macosx/**.

Mac OS X Snow Leopard, the current version of Mac OS X released in August 2009, has a smaller memory footprint (taking up to 50 percent less RAM than the previous version). It includes a more responsive and snappier Finder, a Put Back option to return deleted items to their original location, more reliable ejection of external drives, faster shut down and wake up, four new fonts, 80 percent faster Time Machine backup, increased Airport signal strength for wireless networks, and built-in support for Microsoft Exchange Server 2007. For a detailed review of the features incorporated into Snow Leopard, visit **www.apple.com/ macosx/refinements/enhancements- refinements.html**.

UNIX

Developed at AT&T's Bell Laboratories in 1969, UNIX is a pioneering operating system that continues to define what an OS should do and how it should work. **UNIX** (pronounced "you-nix") was the first OS written in the C language. It is a free OS installed primarily on workstations and features preemptive multitasking.

If UNIX is so great, why didn't it take over the computer world? One reason is the lack of compatibility among the many different versions of UNIX. Another reason is that it's difficult to use. UNIX defaults to a command-line user interface, which is challenging for new computer users. An online tutorial on UNIX is available at **www.ee.surrey.ac.uk/Teaching/Unix**.

In the past few years, a number of GUI interfaces have been developed for UNIX, improving its usability (Figure 4.23). Did you know that the Mac OS X is based on UNIX?

Linux

In 1991, Finnish university student Linus Torvalds introduced **Linux**, his new freeware operating system for personal computers (Figure 4.24). He hoped Linux would offer users a free alternative to UNIX. Linux has since been further developed by thousands of programmers, who have willingly donated their time to make sure that Linux is a very good version of UNIX. The community approach to Linux has made it a marvel of the computer world and has made Torvalds a folk legend.

Linux is **open source software**, meaning that its source code (the code of the program itself) is available for all to see and use. Unlike most other commercial software, which hide the program's code and prohibit users from analyzing it to see how the program was written, users of open source software are invited to scrutinize the source code for errors and to share their discoveries with the software's publisher. Experience shows that this approach is often a very effective measure against software defects.

What makes Linux so attractive? Two things: It's powerful and it's free. Linux brings many features similar to those found in commercial versions of UNIX, including multitasking, virtual memory, Internet support, and a GUI, to the PC.

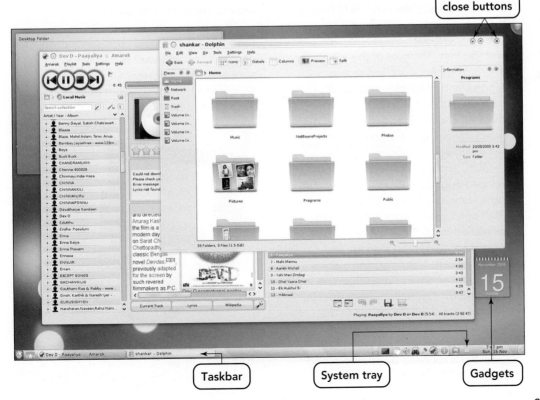

Minimize and close buttons

Taskbar

System tray

Gadgets

FIGURE 4.24 Ubuntu version 9.10, also referred to as Karmic Koala, is a popular version of Linux that features a Windows-like GUI interface and includes programs such as a media player, image editor, and the Firefox Web browser.

Although Linux is powerful and free, there are some versions that are proprietary or are available for a fee. Because Linux isn't a commercial product with a single stable company behind it, many corporate chief information officers shy away from its adoption. When someone needs technical support, they have to find a Web site such as **www.redhat.com** or someone who knows more about Linux than they do—this is not the same as calling technical support when your Mac OS X or Windows 7 operating system ceases to operate. Linux is gaining acceptance, especially for use with Web servers. One main drawback to using Linux was its inability to run Microsoft Office applications. Recently, through the development of proprietary software as VMWare and WINE, this is becoming less of a problem.

The beauty of Linux, and its development model, is that it doesn't run on any particular type of computer: It runs on them all. Linux has been translated to run on systems as small as iPods and as large as homegrown supercomputers. For the latest in Linux news and developments, visit Linux Today at **www.linuxtoday. com**. Linux beginners can get assistance at **www.justlinux.com** and at **www. linux.org**.

ETHICS

The inequity in computer equipment and computer-related knowledge between developed, developing, and underdeveloped nations always brings economic, educational, and ethical issues to the foreground. Whose responsibility is it to bridge this gap? The One Laptop per Child (OLPC) initiative is trying to bring equity in access to computers to these diverse populations by focusing on the child. The idea was founded by Nicholas Negroponte and others associated with MIT Media Lab in conjunction with several corporate partners, such as Google, AMD, and Red Hat. The goal of the initiative is to provide low-cost, low-power, rugged, and connected notebook computers to the world's poorest children. The aim is to encourage self-discovery, collaboration, and self-empowered learning.

OLPC and Red Hat have jointly developed Sugar, the OLPC Linux operating system, which is based on Red Hat's open source operating system called Fedora (actually named for the type of hat that is the logo for Red Hat products). This operating system focuses on activities rather than the applications. Figure 4.25 illustrates the first image a child will see when the system boots. It is symbolic of a man (represented by an O on top of the letter X) surrounded by other symbols that stand for home, friends, and community.

Although support is strong, there are still some obstacles, for example, getting Internet to some of the remote and poorer regions. Those who don't support the project say that without Internet accessibility in the poorest regions, the computers given to the children won't close the digital divide. Instead, they will increase the toxic waste from discarded computers that either don't work or are in need of repairs.

What do you think? Is the initiative something that should continue despite the problems? Is it truly the answer to the problem? Or do the dangers to the environment outweigh the potential benefits?

FIGURE 4.25 The Notebook Provided to Children through the One Laptop per Child Initiative

PC Versus Mac Versus Linux

Traditionally, computer users have had two major platforms to choose from. A **platform** is determined by the combination of microprocessor chip and operating system used by a distinct type of computer, such as a Mac or a PC. Previously, Macs used a Motorola or IBM chip and the Mac OS, and PCs have used an Intel or AMD chip and the Windows OS. Macs have since switched to Intel chips, which has blurred the platform lines a bit because they can now run the Windows OS too. Depending on which OS is loaded on a computer, it is simply referred to as a Mac or a PC. As the Linux OS becomes more popular, some people may want to consider a third alternative.

The debate over which platform is best has raged for years, and if market power is anything, PCs are winning by a landslide. But Apple hangs in there with its slew of adherents who choose to "think different." What's the difference between the platforms? Although you'd never know from listening to people who love or hate Macs, there's really not much difference, at least not in terms of power. Still, the debate goes on.

On the one side, Mac lovers say their machines are easier to set up and use. Macs come with everything you need built right in— simply plug them in and you're on your way. Mac lovers also point out that Apple has developed some incredibly advanced technology. (Even PC users will agree to that.)

It's not just the system and the software Mac users love. Most Macophiles love their one-button mice as well as their many shortcut keys. In addition, certain professions, especially creative fields such as graphic design, rely almost exclusively on Macs.

Linux offers another option. Linux can be installed on a Mac or a PC, and because it is open source software, cost isn't an issue. Security is another benefit. Few types of malware are targeted at Linux machines. Experts disagree on whether this is due to the security of the Linux OS or the fact that there are so few systems that hackers can't create the chain reaction they can easily muster using Windows. The casual user cites the lack of structured computer support and the level of computer knowledge required to set up a Linux system as the main deterrent.

However, PCs still dominate, and the race isn't even close. PCs claim the largest chunk of the marketplace and are the choice of corporate America. They tend to be cheaper in terms of both their hardware and software, with a much larger selection of software products to choose from than their Mac or Linux counterparts. In recent years, Apple, through its humorous "I am a Mac, I am a PC" commercials, has tried to woo PC users by playing on the idea that Macs are easier to use. However, software products developed for Windows greatly outnumber those written for Macs, one reason PCs have led the marketplace. But now that Mac OS X can run Windows, Mac users are able to run existing Windows software. Unfortunately, as Apple moves into the PC market with its recent innovations, it may make itself more vulnerable to the viruses that have been, until now, mostly a PC headache. In any case, both Macs and Linux have a long way to go to catch PCs—and few experts see that happening any time soon. It is only fair to mention that, although slow to catch on in the PC market, the growth of Linux in the area of server installations has been exponential.

For a look at a humorous spin on the familiar "I am a Mac, I am a PC" commercial that includes the arrival of Linux, watch the clip at **www.youtube.com/watch?v=cldeHjFig_c**. Figure 4.26 illustrates differences in the use of the big three as of March 2010.

The cost of software and frequent upgrades is a source of concern for all users, regardless of the platform they are using. Open source software seems to be a viable solution for this problem; however, some warning is needed. Arguments can be presented to support the fact that although the software is free, you pay for quality support or the courses to learn to support the OS yourself.

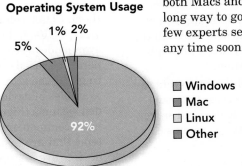

Operating System Usage

1% 2%
5%
92%

☐ Windows
☐ Mac
☐ Linux
☐ Other

FIGURE 4.26 Windows operating systems dominate the market, with Mac OS X and Linux quite a distance behind.

Server Operating Systems

Server operating systems are designed for network use. Normally they are complete operating systems with a file and task manager. Additional features like a Web server, directory services, and a messaging system may also be included.

Microsoft Windows Server 2008 An upgrade to Microsoft Windows Server 2003, **Microsoft Windows Server 2008** is a sophisticated operating system specifically designed to support client/server computing systems in a corporate environment. Servers are special computers used to manage various resources on a network, including printers and other devices, file storage, and Web sites. Windows Server 2008 shares many similarities in architecture and functionality with Windows Vista because the underlying code is closely related. Benefits include the following:

- **Security.** New technologies help prevent unauthorized access to corporate networks, data, and user accounts.
- **Web server.** Enhanced capabilities are available for developing and hosting Web applications and services.
- **Administration.** All configuration and maintenance is done through the command-line interface or through remote administration.
- **Virtualization.** Multiple servers can be consolidated as separate virtual machines on a single physical server, and multiple operating systems can run in parallel.

Other Server Operating Systems Other server operating systems that you might hear mentioned are listed below:

- UNIX and Linux are also categorized in the stand-alone section. They are actually referred to as multipurpose operating systems because they fall into both categories.
- Netware by Novell is a client/server system that manages concurrent requests from clients and provides the security needed in a multiuser environment.
- Solaris, a version of UNIX developed by Sun Microsystems, is designed for networks using e-commerce applications. It is known for its scalability—ability to expand, an essential feature when handling e-commerce apps.
- Mac OS X Server, by Apple, can be used with an unlimited number of users and is suitable for big companies and IT departments as well as small businesses and retail stores.

Embedded Operating Systems

Embedded operating systems are specialized operating systems designed for specific applications. They are usually very compact and efficient. They also eliminate many features that nonembedded computer operating systems provide because the specialized application has no need for them. PDAs, cell phones, point-of-sale devices, VCRs, industrial robot controls, and even modern toasters that control the temperature based on bread type and the settings for the attached egg poacher, are examples of devices that contain embedded systems (Figure 4.27). Some of the more common embedded operating systems that are installed on our handheld devices are Microsoft Windows Mobile, Windows CE, Palm OS, Symbian OS, Android, and iPhone OS.

Microsoft Windows Mobile Designed for smartphones and PDAs, **Microsoft Windows Mobile** provides a user interface

FIGURE 4.27
Embedded operating systems can be found in devices that we use every day. How many more devices can you come up with?

Automobiles that display the fuel and energy use   All smartphones   Programmable thermostats

THE BIONIC EYE

Researchers at Bionic Vision Australia (BVA) have produced a prototype of a bionic eye implant that could bring limited vision to the blind by 2013. With the Australian government contributing $40 million to the research, the timeframe and continual improvements on the prototype look promising. Here's how the system works:

- A camera is mounted on top of a pair of glasses.
- The images are sent to a small processor housed in a unit about the size of a cell phone and carried by the individual.
- The processor, with the help of an embedded operating system, sends a condensed image to the chip directly implanted onto the retina.

- The chip stimulates the visual neurons that, in turn, send rough images to the brain for processing.

The challenge in the bionic eye is not to get the signals to the brain—that has been accomplished—but to improve the resolution and detail of that signal (Figure 4.28). The implication for visually impaired individuals is beyond anything ever hoped for. What are some of the possible applications for those of us with sight? Think about having text magnified without a magnifying glass, shading your eyes from bright light without having to wear sunglasses, and mom actually having eyes in the back of her head. Although the immediate excitement is site for the blind, who can't help but take that glimpse into the future!

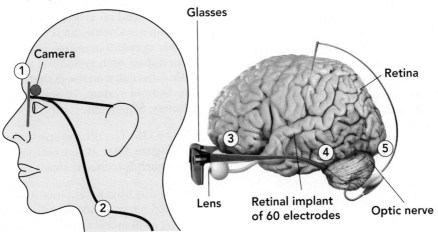

1. Camera on glasses views image.
2. Signals are sent to handheld device.
3. Processed information is sent back to glasses and wirelessly. transmitted to receiver under surface of eye.
4. Receiver sends information to electrodes in retinal implant.
5. Electrodes stimulate retina to send information to brain.

FIGURE 4.28 This is only one of several variations of a bionic eye implant currently under development.

---

for simplified versions of Windows programs, such as Microsoft's own Office applications. Users can create documents on the go and then transfer them to a desktop computer for further processing and printing. Personal information management tools, such as a calendar and address book, along with an e-mail client and a Web browser are also included (Figure 4.29). Windows Mobile supports handwriting recognition and voice recording. Users can

quickly synchronize their mobile devices with corresponding programs on their desktop computers.

Windows CE One of the early embedded operating systems, **Windows CE** was first introduced in 1996, with a significant upgrade made available in 1997. It consists of a low overhead device driver and built-in power manager. Windows CE is used by consumer electronic devices like handheld PCs, video game players, and digital cameras, and by industrial products like barcode readers.

Palm OS The **Palm OS** was initially developed by Palm Inc. for personal digital assistants (PDAs) in 1996. It was designed for use with a touch screen using graphical user interfaces and comes with a suite of personal information management applications. The most current versions power smartphones like the Palm Pixi that runs on the Palm webOS platform and responds to a multitouch screen and natural gestures (Figure 4.30).

Symbian OS An open industry standard operating system for data-enabled mobile phones, **Symbian OS** continues to power devices at the lower end of the smartphone price spectrum because of its reasonable cost, ample suppliers of add-on devices, and the operating system's reduced demand on the processor and memory. The open industry standard guarantees that the OS must be freely and publicly available (e.g., from a stable Web site) under royalty-free terms at reasonable cost.

Android Google released the latest version of its operating system for mobile devices, **Android** 1.6 in late 2009. The updated OS adds support for CDMA (Code

FIGURE 4.29 Although Windows Mobile can look slightly different depending upon the phone vendor, it still brings Windows functionality to mobile devices.

Division Multiple Access) and more screen resolutions. Supporting CDMA will allow operators, such as Verizon, to add Android phones to their portfolios. Android phones use a touch-screen scroll system that allows you to scroll to the left and right, creating the same three divisions (left, center, and right) on your portable device that you have on a computer monitor. The marketplace is filled with applications from a simple coin toss to games that were played on the Sega systems of 17 years ago. The view and On-screen Keyboard changes from vertical to horizontal automatically when the phone changes position. Some interesting statistics from January 2010 indicate that iPhone and Android users, between the ages of 25 and 34, spend an average of 79 minutes a day on apps, while an iPod Touch user spends over 100 minutes. The average cost of an app on both systems is around $8. A little different statistic is that more males use Android system, 73 percent, than iPhones, 57 percent.

iPhone OS The iPhone sports the **iPhone OS** (Figure 4.31). Its current version 3.1 offers such features as these:

- Genius Mixes—automatically generated music mixes based on what types of music are already in your library
- Genius Recommendations—suggestions for apps based on the apps you have already downloaded
- Saving video from mail and MMS (multimedia message service) directly into Camera Roll
- Save as New Clip option—allows you to keep your original video and save the new version when trimming a video on the iPhone 3Gs.

Open Source Software

The open source model is revolutionizing the software world. Because the basic code is free, you can find pieces of it running iPods, supercomputers, smartphones, and many other computer systems. Need Linux in Hungarian, Thai, or Zulu? Don't

FIGURE 4.30 The Palm webOS, used on mobile devices like the Palm Pixi, offers quick access icons for e-mail and contacts along with a full set of menus to set preferences and access photos and text messages.

worry: Volunteers have translated versions of Linux into dozens of languages, giving computer users of all types—individuals, government organizations, and research groups—a free alternative to buying traditional operating systems. You can even download free open source programs for applications such as word processing and database management.

Although Linux remains free, adapting it to the needs of corporations and other large-scale users has become big business. For example, IBM will customize Linux for corporate customers; Red Hat offers a Linux version, as well as consulting, development, and training services to Linux users. With assistance and

FIGURE 4.31 The MMS in the iPhone allows for images, videos, and contact information to be included in the message.

customization so readily available (for a fee), it's not surprising that Linux's popularity with large-scale users is growing.

Linux has always been more popular in the server market than in the desktop market. There are, however, signs that this may be changing. France's police force, the National Gendarmerie, has switched 70,000 desktop computers from Windows to Linux and low-cost computers like the OLPC XO, Everex CloudBook, Classmate PC, and the Asus Eee PC are being offered with the choice of Linux OS. Linux is also making inroads in mobile computing, with Motorola expecting to offer Linux on 60 percent of their phones within the next few years. Other devices, such as TiVo and Amazon Kindle, also use Linux-based operating systems.

No matter what operating system you or your company are running, you need to work with associated programs, called utilities, that help maintain the smooth operability of your system.

System Utilities: Housekeeping Tools

Providing a necessary addition to an operating system, **system utilities** (also called **utility programs**) are programs that work in tandem with the operating system and perform services that keep the computer system running smoothly. Sometimes these programs are included in the OS; sometimes you must purchase them from other software vendors. System utility programs are considered essential to the effective management of a computer system. They include programs that perform such tasks as these:

- Backing up system and application files
- Providing antivirus protection
- Searching for and managing files
- Scanning and defragmenting disks and files
- Compressing files so that they take up less space on storage media

FIGURE 4.32 Some utilities run only when selected; others can be programmed to run on a regular schedule.

- Providing additional accessibility utilities to meet the needs of individuals with special needs

You can access these utilities by opening the Start menu, selecting All Programs, then selecting Accessories, and from the Accessories submenu selecting System Tools (Figure 4.32).

Backup Software

An essential part of safe, efficient computer usage, **backup software** copies data from the computer's hard disk to backup devices, such as flash drives, CDs, DVDs, an external hard drive, or an online storage location. Should the hard disk fail, you can recover your data from the backup disk (Figure 4.33).

Backup software can run a **full backup**, which includes all files and data on the entire hard disk, or an incremental backup. In an **incremental backup**, the backup software copies only those files that have been created or changed since the last backup occurred. In this way, the backup disk always contains an up-to-date copy of all data. Full backups should be made at least once each month. Incremental backups should also be made on a regular basis. In a business environment, that can be as frequently as one or more times a day.

Drive imaging software creates a mirror image of the entire hard disk—including the OS and applications, as well as all files and data. In the event of a hard disk or computer system failure, the drive image can be used to restore the system. This avoids the individual reinstallation of each program and can save an incredible amount of time.

Even if you don't have backup software, you can still make backup copies of your important files: Just copy them to an alternative storage device. Don't ever rely on a hard disk to keep the only copies of your work. Backups should be stored away from the computer system, usually in a different building that can withstand natural disasters and is located in a geologically stable region so that in the event of a fire or flood, they don't suffer the system's fate.

Windows 7 includes a backup utility that you can access from the System and Security category of the Control Panel by clicking Backup and Restore Center. The Complete PC Backup option will create an exact image of your computer—backing up all files and data, plus the OS and applications. Basic Backup is available on all versions of Windows 7, but the option to back up to a home or network drive is only available on the Professional, Enterprise, and Ultimate editions. Although many people know that backing up their files is important, most forget. Relying on the Automatic Backup option solves that problem with

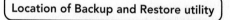

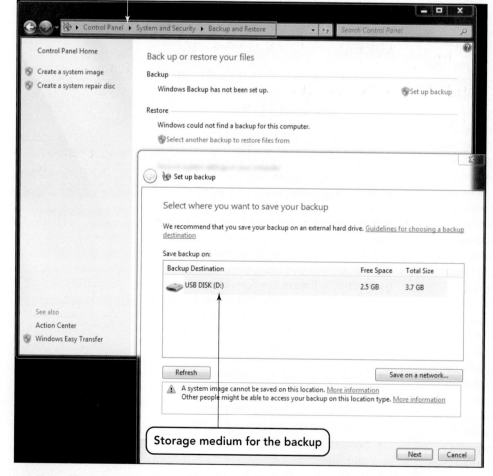

FIGURE 4.33 Backing up applications and data is an important part of maintaining a viable system. Using the automatic backup feature in Windows 7 will guarantee that backups are performed on a regular schedule.

the inclusion of the File Backup Scheduling Wizard. Choose the time and backup location you prefer and Windows 7 will do the rest! You can also obtain stand-alone backup or imaging software from local or online retailers, or check for user reviews and find free utility programs on sites like Download.com (**www.download.com**).

Antivirus Software

Antivirus software protects a computer from computer viruses. Such software uses a pattern-matching technique that examines all of the files on a disk, looking for telltale virus code "signatures." One limitation of such programs is that they can detect only those viruses whose signatures are in their databases, and there are plenty of those. As of this writing, one antivirus program, Webroot, scans for nearly 2 million viruses and adds more each day. Most antivirus programs enable you to automatically update the software. However, new viruses appear every day. If your system becomes infected by a virus that's not in the system's database, it may not be detected. Because of this shortcoming, many antivirus programs now include programs that monitor system functions to detect abnormal behavior and stop the destructive activities of unknown viruses before they start.

An antivirus software review conducted in 2009 by TopTenREVIEWS, an independent evaluation company, ranked these as the top five preferred antivirus programs:

1. BitDefender Antivirus
2. Kaspersky Anti-virus
3. Webroot AntiVirus with SpySweeper
4. Norton AntiVirus
5. ESET Nod32 Antivirus

All five programs provide users with frequent updates for the term of a license. Licenses are typically issued for a year. Additionally, many ISPs now offer free antivirus protection and other security tools to help keep their customers safe online.

Some viruses do their damage immediately, whereas others hide on your hard disk waiting for a trigger before doing their work. Regardless of when they do their damage, viruses spread quickly and can affect thousands, even millions, of users in a short time if the malware can locate targeted hosts. Some argue that the resistance to viruses is more a function of market share and concentration than security advances. This might be true; however, it takes only one nasty virus to cause you a lot of grief. So, install and use antivirus software to avoid hours of aggravation and data loss.

Searching for and Managing Files

Another important system utility is the **file manager**, a program that helps you organize and manage the data stored on your disk. The file manager enables you to perform various operations on the files and folders created on your computer's storage devices. You can use file managers to make copies of your files, manage how and where they are stored, and delete unwanted files. Windows 7 and Vista use Explorer, Mac OS X uses Finder, and Linux has various file management utilities. Explorer has been enhanced considerably in the latest Window operating systems and includes many new features (Figure 4.34).

On a large hard disk with thousands of files, the task of finding a needed file can be time-consuming and frustrating

FIGURE 4.34 A file manager, such as Windows Explorer, enables you to organize your files and folders.

Content of the current folder appears on the right side of the screen.

Breadcrumbs in the Address bar show the path to your current location.

Content can be sorted or filtered by using the column headings.

The Navigation pane, on the left side of the window, displays folders and drives.

The Details pane displays specifics on the selected file.

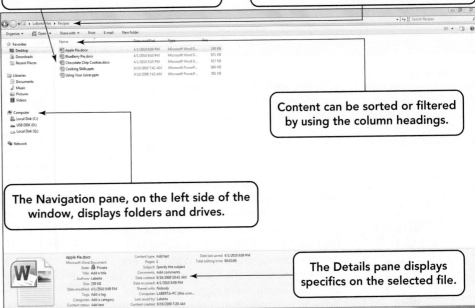

if you try to do it manually. For this reason, most operating systems include a **search utility**, which enables you to search an entire hard disk or any indexed network storage device for a file. In Microsoft Windows, Instant Search is integrated into every Explorer window, and you can query for files in a number

dialog box to access the utilities. The Mac OS X scanning utility is called Disk Utility. You can find commercial products that perform this function, but the one that comes with your operating system is usually adequate and best suited for managing your hard disk.

A physical problem that a scanning program might detect involves an irregularity on the disk's surface that results in a **bad sector**, a portion of the disk that is unable to store data reliably. The scanning program can fix the problem by locking out the bad sector so that it's no longer used.

Logical problems are usually caused by a power outage that occurs before the

Enter the description of your search into the Search box located at the bottom of the Start menu.

The Save Search tool can save frequently used searches.

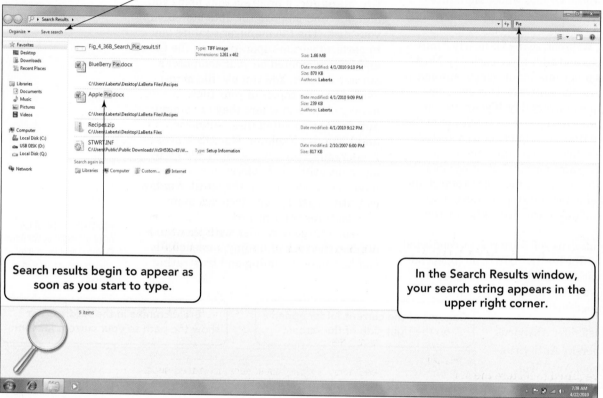

Search results begin to appear as soon as you start to type.

In the Search Results window, your search string appears in the upper right corner.

5 items

FIGURE 4.35
Windows Instant Search tool is part of the Explorer window. It searches file names, file properties, and text within files, using the search terms you provide.

STUDENT VIDEO

of ways, including by name, date, and size (Figure 4.35). The Spotlight utility in the Mac OS performs similar tasks.

Scanning and Defragmenting Disks

A **disk scanning program**, or error checking program, can detect and resolve a number of physical and logical problems that may occur when your computer stores files on a disk. The error-checking and defragmenting utilities in Windows are found by clicking the Computer option in the Start menu, then right-clicking the drive to be checked and choosing Properties. Select the Tools tab in the Properties

computer is able to finish writing data to the disk. In this situation, the system is unable to place an end of file marker (eof), and there is some confusion as to where the file actually terminates. Logical errors are more complex to correct than physical ones.

A **disk cleanup utility** differs from a disk scanning program in that it doesn't rectify any problems. Instead, it improves system performance and increases storage space by removing files that you no longer need. Without your knowledge, some programs create temporary files on the hard drive to perform actions that improve their performance. These files are automatically removed when the program is properly

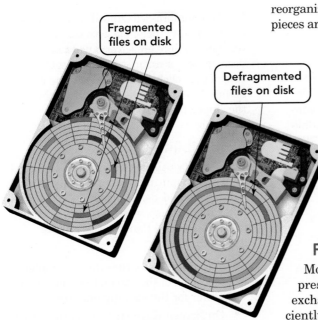

Fragmented files on disk

Defragmented files on disk

reorganize data on the disk so that file pieces are reassembled as one chunk of disk space (decreasing disk search time), storage is made more efficient (by clustering files into structures more efficiently searched), and the time needed to access files decreased (Figure 4.36). Scanning and defragmentation utilities should be run anywhere from once every three or four months for the light computer user to as much as once every three to four weeks for the power user.

FIGURE 4.36 The defragmentation process repositions the sectors of a file into adjacent locations.

closed. A power outage can cause these files to remain on your hard drive and waste valuable storage space. A disk cleanup utility will search for and delete these unusable files along with any files in the Recycle Bin.

As you use a computer, it creates and erases files on the hard disk. The result is that the disk soon becomes a patchwork of files, with portions of files scattered here and there. This slows disk access because the system must look in several locations to find all of a file's segments. A disk with data scattered around in this way is referred to as being **fragmented**. A fragmented disk isn't dangerous—the locations of all the data are known, thanks to the operating system's tracking mechanisms—but periodic maintenance is required to restore the disk's performance. **Disk defragmentation programs** are utility programs used to

File Compression Utilities

Most downloadable software is compressed. A **file compression utility** exchanges programs and data efficiently by reducing the size of a file by as much as 80 percent without harming the data (Figure 4.37). Most file compression utilities work by searching the file for frequently repeated but lengthy data patterns and then substituting short codes for these patterns. Compression enables faster downloads, but you must decompress a file after downloading it. When the file is decompressed, the utility restores the lengthier pattern where each short code is encountered. Both compressed and decompressed files can be saved and opened on a computer system, but a file needs to be decompressed prior to use if changes that are made to that file are to be saved.

Most compression utilities also can create archives. An **archive** is a single file that contains two or more files stored in a compressed format. Archives are handy for storage as well as file-exchange purposes because as many as several hundred separate files can be stored in a single, easily handled unit. The most basic archiving

FIGURE 4.37
A compressed file is saved to the same folder as the original file, but with a different icon and file type.

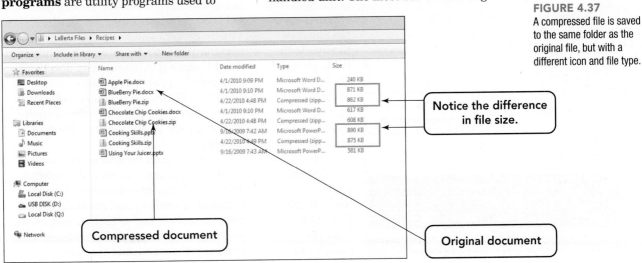

Notice the difference in file size.

Compressed document

Original document

FIGURE 4.38 The On-Screen Keyboard, along with other accessibility utilities, makes computer use easier for many individuals.

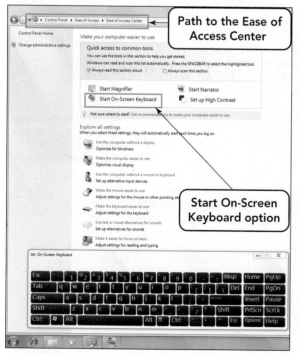

programs sequentially attach or pack files into the archive, including some additional information about each file, for example, the name and lengths of each original file, so that proper reconstruction or unpacking is possible. To edit and save the changes to any file in the archived packet, the packet must first be restored to its original format.

To compress, or zip, a file in Windows 7 or Vista, right-click it and choose Send To Compressed (zipped) Folder. This creates a new zipped file with the same file name. There are several ways to decompress, or unzip, a zipped file. One way is to double-click the file and use the Extract all files button. Another way is to right-click the zipped file and choose Extract All.

Accessibility Utilities

Accessibility utilities are utilities designed to make computing easier for individuals with special needs. Windows 7 includes the following utilities, which are accessible from the Control Panel in the Ease of Access category:

- Magnifier—A feature that magnifies a portion of the screen to make reading easier for the visually impaired
- On-Screen Keyboard—A feature used by clicking or hovering over the keys on the screen with a pointing device (Figure 4.38)
- Speech Recognition—A program that allows you to use your voice to control your system and dictate documents
- Narrator—A very basic speech program that reads everything on the screen.

Additional features can be activated through the Ease of Access category in the Control Panel.

System Update

Because the world of computers is rapidly changing, Microsoft provides an operating system update service called **Windows Update** that is meant to keep your operating system up to date with fixes (service patches) or protections against external environment changes. If you are using Windows 7, you can ensure that your OS is current by opening the Control Panel's System and Security category, clicking Windows Update, and setting Windows Update to automatically download and install updates at a time of your choosing (Figure 4.39). You can also get more information at Microsoft's Security at Home page (**www.microsoft.com/protect**).

Updates may include service packs, version upgrades, and security updates. They are designed to maintain your computer's security and reliability and to help protect against malicious software and exploits. Mac users have access to a similar software update service.

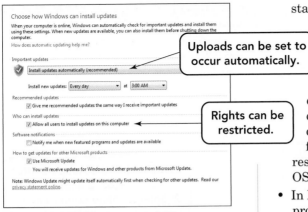

Choose how Windows can install updates

When your computer is online, Windows can automatically check for important updates and install them using these settings. When new updates are available, you can also install them before shutting down the computer.

How does automatic updating help me?

Uploads can be set to occur automatically.

Important updates

Install updates automatically (recommended)

Install new updates: Every day at 3:00 AM

Recommended updates

☑ Give me recommended updates the same way I receive important updates

Who can install updates

☑ Allow all users to install updates on this computer

Rights can be restricted.

Software notifications

☐ Notify me when new featured programs and updates are available

How to get updates for other Microsoft products

☑ Use Microsoft Update

You will receive updates for Windows and other products from Microsoft Update.

Note: Windows Update might update itself automatically first when checking for other updates. Read our privacy statement online.

FIGURE 4.39 Setting the appropriate Windows Update options ensures your system will receive the latest software patches and antivirus protection and that it is optimized for the best performance.

Besides system utilities, there are additional ways to safeguard your data or take care of operating problems.

Troubleshooting

Almost every user of a computer system experiences trouble from time to time. The trouble can stem from an error in the boot cycle, the failure of a command to work in a running program, or the addition of hardware or software. Before you panic, review the problems and possible causes below for some practical tips that might help get you through the crisis.

- If your computer fails to start normally, you may be able to get it running by inserting a **boot disk** (also called an **emergency disk**). The boot disk is a storage device, like a USB drive, CD, DVD, or network device, that in case of an emergency or boot failure can load a reduced version of the OS that can be used for troubleshooting purposes. Sometimes the boot disk comes with a new computer, but often you need to create it yourself. Consult the documentation that came with your computer or choose Help and Support from the Windows Start menu to learn about this process.

- Improperly shutting down your system may cause trouble on restarting. When you've finished using the computer, be sure to shut it down properly. Don't just switch off the power without going through the full shutdown procedure. In Microsoft Windows 7, click Start and then click the Shut Down button. In Windows Vista, click

start, then click the arrow to the right of the Lock button, and click Shut Down. In Mac OS, choose Shut Down from the Apple menu. If you switch the power off without shutting down, the operating system may fail to write certain system files to the hard disk. File fragments that result from improper shutdown could result in permanent damage to the OS or to personal files.

- In Microsoft Windows, configuration problems, issues with new equipment communicating with other devices, can occur after adding a new peripheral device such as an external hard drive or new printer to your system. Some of these additions may cause conflicts that could interfere in the boot cycle. Conflicts can often be resolved by starting the computer in Windows **Safe Mode**, an operating mode in which Windows loads a minimal set of drivers that are known to function correctly. Within safe mode, you can use the Control Panel to determine which devices are causing the problem. You access safe mode by pressing the F8 key repeatedly during the start-up process (before the Windows splash screen with the logo appears). Safe Mode will reset or report any conflicting programs or device drivers. Once the reset is complete, shut down the system, boot up normally, and then correct any conflicts that were not reset in safe mode (Figure 4.40).

FIGURE 4.40 An error during the boot process may cause your system to open in Safe mode, where some settings may be adjusted. To exit Safe Mode, shut down your computer and then restart the system.

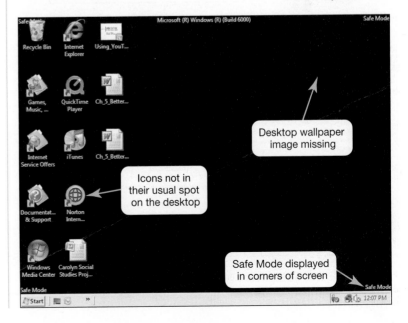

Desktop wallpaper image missing

Icons not in their usual spot on the desktop

Safe Mode displayed in corners of screen

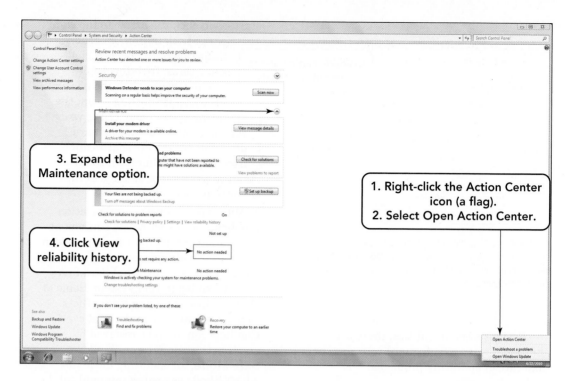

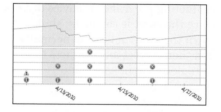

3. Expand the Maintenance option.

1. Right-click the Action Center icon (a flag).
2. Select Open Action Center.

4. Click View reliability history.

FIGURE 4.41 The Action Center icon is a flag located on the system tray.

- System slowdown can sometimes occur because something has changed gradually over time to cause performance to degrade or there has been an addition made in hardware or software to the system. The Windows operating system has a tool to help diagnose these problems—the

FIGURE 4.42 Each different symbol on the graph represents a different type of activity. An *x* represents an improper shut down, whereas an *i* indicates that a system update occurred.

Reliability and Performance Monitor. With this feature you can check to see when your system's performance began to degrade and get details about individual events that might have caused the problem. The best way to ensure that your system runs optimally is never to change more than one thing at a time. That way, if the system has problems, you can undo your last action or installation and see whether the problem goes away. Follow these steps to access this tool in Windows 7.

1. Right-click the *Action Center* icon in the system tray (the icon is a flag) (Figure 4.41).
2. From the window that opens choose *Open Action Center*.
3. Expand the Maintenance category by clicking the arrow to its right.
4. Click the *View reliability history* option.
5. Windows 7 will display the stability of your system in graphical form (Figure 4.42).

   - Help and Support, just a click away on your own computer, is sometimes the best place to look for troubleshooting guidance. Microsoft Windows includes a Help and Support utility. You can explore its contents by clicking the *Start* button and then clicking *Help and Support*. The

Windows Help and Support Center includes several ways to manage and maintain your computer.

- Additional troubleshooting help is available for both PCs and Macs on the Web. Some offer free advice and user forums, whereas others, such as Ask Dr. Tech, offer support packages for a price. Type **troubleshooting** into your favorite search engine or visit sites such as **www.macfixit.com** or **www.askdrtech.com** to find out more.

How To:

Adjust the Settings for Sleep, Hibernate, and Hybrid Power Modes

Be careful when you increase the amount of time your computer waits before activating any of these power-saving modes on a battery-powered PC. A loss of data may occur if you make the delay time too long and the battery goes dead. The purpose of changing these settings is to optimize your power usage, keeping in mind your work habits and battery strength.

1. Open the Start menu and select the *Control Panel*. From the Control Panel options, select *System and Security* and then select *Power Options* (Figure 4.43).

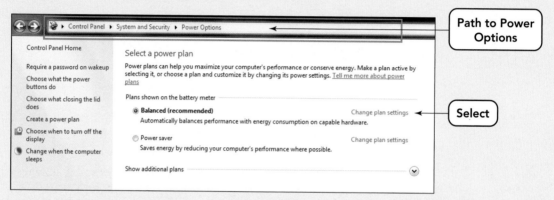

FIGURE 4.43 Changes to power settings are done through the System and Security option of the Control Panel.

2. Under Select a power plan, to the left of the Balanced (Recommended) option, select *Change plan settings*. If you do not see the word *Balanced*, your manufacturer may have edited this option and replaced it with a more identifying phrase, such as *HP Recommended*.

3. In the Change settings for the plan screen, select *Change advanced power settings* (Figure 4.44).

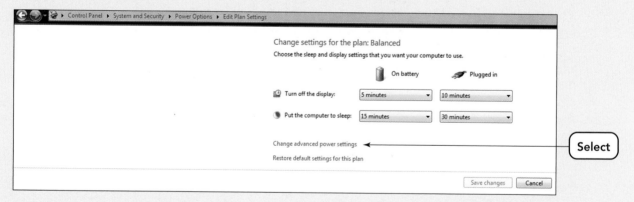

FIGURE 4.44 The advanced power settings make it possible to change settings for specific behaviors such as Sleep and Hibernate.

4. In the Power Options dialog box, there are three settings:

- **Expand the Sleep and Sleep after options.** Set the time for On battery and Plugged in settings based on whether you are using a notebook or desktop system and the time length of inactivity that would trigger the system to enter Sleep mode (Figure 4.45). The interval of inactivity for a notebook (On battery) should be less than 15 minutes to conserve battery power. On a plugged in

FIGURE 4.45 Each option in the dialog box can be expanded, and additional features set by the user.

system, like a desktop, usually 30 minutes is tops, but that is up to the individual. Entering Sleep or Hibernate mode too frequently can be very annoying and frustrating. Monitor your habits and set the interval accordingly.

- **Expand the Hibernate after option.** Set the time for On battery and Plugged in settings again based on whether you are using a notebook or desktop system and the length of inactivity that would trigger the system to enter Hibernate mode. Remember that Hibernate mode saves your open programs and data on the hard disk and totally powers down your system. If you are very energy conscientious, then you might choose this setting over Sleep. However, due to the total power down, returning from Hibernate mode takes longer than returning from Sleep mode.

- **Expand the Allow hybrid sleep option.** The settings for Sleep and Hibernate should be set before this step because Hybrid will activate sleep first, and then, if no activity occurs, it moves your system into Hibernate. Here your only choices are On or Off for both On battery and Plugged in settings.

5. Click *OK* to save changes. Close the Control Panel.

6. Test your system and make sure that the delays work.

Chapter Summary

System Software

- System software has two major components: (1) the operating system (OS) and (2) system utilities. The OS coordinates the various functions of the computer's hardware and provides support for running application software. System utilities provide such features as backup, defragmenting, and file compression.

- An operating system acts as an interface between the user and the computer's hardware. Its five basic functions are starting the computer, managing applications, managing memory, coordinating tasks, and providing a means of communicating with the user.

- A computer needs an operating system to coordinate the interaction of hardware components with each other as well as with application software.

- When you start or restart a computer, it reloads the operating system into the computer's memory. A computer goes through six steps at start-up: loading the BIOS, performing the power-on self-test, loading the OS, configuring the system, loading system utilities, and authenticating users.

- The three major types of user interfaces are graphical user interfaces (GUIs), menu-driven user interfaces, and command-line user interfaces. Most users prefer to use graphical user interfaces, which makes use of small images called icons to identfy linked programs. The next most popular type of interface is the menu-driven interface, in which you open programs and selecte options by clicking on a selection in an on-screen menu. Command-line interfaces are hardly ever used anymore because they require the memorization of key-words and punctuation that must be typed on a text line. Such commands are executed when you press the Enter key.

- Operating systems can be placed in three categories: stand-alone, server, and embedded. A stand-alone system does not need to be connected to any other system or computer in order to run.

- A server system, on the other hand, is designed to work in a network with other units and peripherals. Embedded operating systems are not designed for general purposes but for the specific conditions and actions of the device that they are embedded within.

- The major strength of Windows is that it has dominated the market for more than 15 years and is installed and maintained on more than 90 percent of the personal computers in the world. The major strength of OS X is that it has been modified and upgraded for more than 20 years and is the most stable graphical OS. The biggest weakness of Windows is that Microsoft continues to bring new versions to market before all of the bugs and security holes have been resolved. The main disadvantage of OS X is that it is used on only approximately 8 percent of the computers in the world and thus does not support as many applications as Windows does.

- Essential system utilities include backup software, antivirus software, a file manager, search tools, file compression utilities, disk scanning programs, disk defragmentation programs, and access utilities for those with special needs. Additionally, features like Windows Update keep your OS up to date with fixes (service patches) or protections against external environment changes. These features are also available for a Mac in the Mac OS X Toolbox (or Utilities folder).

- An incremental backup creates a duplicate copy of files that have changed or have been created since the last backup. A full backup duplicates all of the files and data on a hard disk. Each individual or business needs to set a schedule for the time and tye of backup to be performed. This can be automated through such utilities as Windows Update.

- Be aware of problems with your system and attempt to troubleshoot them at the onset. Make use of such features as Help and Support, Safe Mode, and the Action Center to help correct the problem.

Key Terms and Concepts

Identification

Label each interface item with its name.

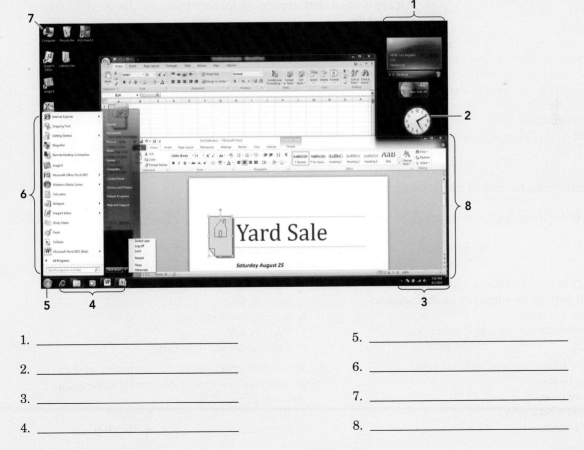

1. _____

2. _____

3. _____

4. _____

5. _____

6. _____

7. _____

8. _____

Matching

Match each key term in the left column with the most accurate definition in the right column.

_____ 1. cold boot

_____ 2. load

_____ 3. warm boot

_____ 4. menu driven

_____ 5. graphical user interface (GUI)

_____ 6. interrupt

_____ 7. thrashing

_____ 8. sidebar

_____ 9. page

_____ 10. icon

_____ 11. kernel

_____ 12. platform

_____ 13. gadget *or widget*

_____ 14. command-line

_____ 15. profile

a. A term used to describe excessive paging

b. A method of interacting with a program or OS by selecting choices from on-screen, text-based options

c. A record of a specific user's preferences for the desktop theme, icons, and menu styles

d. A method of interacting with a program or OS by typing instructions one line at a time, using correct syntax

e. The central part of the operating system that resides in RAM

f. The process of transferring a file from storage to memory

g. A small image that represents a computer resource

h. Starting a computer that is not already on

i. The combination of the processor and operating system

j. A fixed size unit of data used to swap content between RAM and virtual memory

k. Starting a computer that is already on

l. The far right side of the screen in Windows 7, in which gadgets can be positioned

m. The use of small images to activate choices, making a program or OS easier to use

n. A signal from a device to the operating system to inform it that an event has occurred

o. An application that appears as an active icon on the far right side of the desktop

Multiple Choice

Circle the correct choice for each of the following:

1. Which OS is *not* designed for smartphones and PDAs?
   a. Android
   b. Symbian
   c. Mac OS X
   d. Windows Mobile

2. What utility program reduces a file size by as much as 80 percent by substituting short codes for lengthy data patterns?
   a. Defragmentation
   b. Compression
   c. Interrupt
   d. Cleanup

3. Which of the following is an OS function?
   a. Creating letters
   b. Managing memory
   c. Defragmenting a disk
   d. Writing e-mail

4. Windows ReadyBoost allows a _____ to be used for virtual memory.
   a. hard disk
   b. CD
   c. flash drive
   d. DVD

5. Virtual memory is used when:
   a. booting fails.
   b. an IRQ conflict occurs.
   c. RAM is full.
   d. a power-on self-test fails.

6. Which test makes sure the computer and its peripherals are working correctly during the start-up process?
   a. BIOS
   b. POST
   c. Upgrade
   d. ReadyBoost

7. Which device is *not* managed by BIOS?
   a. Hard drive
   b. CPU
   c. Jump drive
   d. RAM

8. Which system utility creates duplicates of the files and programs on a system?
   a. Compression
   b. Defragmentation
   c. Backup
   d. Driver

9. Utilities that make computer use easier, especially for individuals with special needs are categorized as
   a. encryption utilities.
   b. supplemental utilities.
   c. accessibility utilities.
   d. system software.

10. Which power-saving mode places a copy of your system's state on the hard drive and shuts off the system?
    a. Sleep   b. Hibernate
    c. Power down   d. Screen saver

Fill-In

In the blanks provided, write the correct answer for each of the following:

1. _____ automatically installs fixes and upgrades service patches to maintain a computer's security and reliability.

2. When troubleshooting a system, one strategy is to boot your system in _____, an operating mode in which only a minimum number of drivers that are known to function correctly are loaded.

3. The _____ is a utility program that repositions file sectors in adjacent locations on a hard disk.

4. Linux makes its source code available for everyone to see and use. This is an example of _____ software.

5. A device _____ is a program that enables communication between the operating system and a peripheral device.

6. A disk with data scattered and empty locations where files have been deleted is said to be _____.

7. A copy of all the files and data on an entire hard disk is called a(n) _____.

8. The _____, or login, process verifies that the user is authorized to use the computer.

9. BIOS information is stored in nonvolatile memory called _____.

10. An area of RAM used to temporarily hold information when printing multiple files is a print _____.

11. _____ is the name of the most current Windows operating system for a PC.

12. Windows Explorer and Mac Finder are both examples of a(n) _____ utility.

13. _____ is the name of the most current Mac operating system.

14. _____ is a feature that allows compatible devices to be automatically detected.

15. _____ is the feature in Windows 7 and Vista that allows the user to use a flash device as virtual memory.

Short Answer

1. Briefly describe the three types of user interfaces. Indicate which are in use today, and provide an example.

2. Explain the Sleep, Hibernate, and Hybrid power options and the type of computer user they best suit.

3. What is virtual memory and how does it improve system performance?

4. Explain which devices in a system are controlled by the BIOS and which are controlled by the operating system.

5. Identify three of the accessibility utilities included with Windows 7. State the purpose of each and how it improves computing for those with special needs.

Teamwork

1. **Operating Systems** Your team is to research three of the operating systems presented in this chapter. In a table created in Microsoft Word or Excel, compare the basic functions performed by each. What future improvements in each OS can you envision or do you see as essential? If you have used several versions of the same OS, what improvements have been incorporated into new versions? Present your comparison table and answers to the questions above in a one-page, double-spaced paper.

2. **Find a Solution** You turn on your computer and enter your user name and password. The system indicates that the password is invalid. You try again and receive the same error message. As a team, come up with at least three possible explanations for the invalid password message and how they might be resolved. Present your troubleshooting results and suggestions for fixes in a slide show of at least five slides.

3. **Windows vs. Mac OS X vs. Linux with Some Added Humor** Review the humorous spin on the familiar "I am a Mac, I am a PC" commercial that includes the arrival of Linux at **www.youtube.com/watch?v=cldeHjFig_c**. As a team, research the difference between these three systems. Create a short commercial, under 90 seconds, that actually provides some information (and humor) to the viewer on the strengths, differences, or shortcomings of each. Cite your references in a Word document.

4. **Using System Tools** As a team, research some of the system tools found in the System Tools folder located in the Accessories option of the Start menu. Split into groups of two or three. Each group should select two tools that were not covered in detail in this chapter. Investigate the purpose of the tool and any options that will need to be set for it to work correctly. What will be the effect of using this tool on your system? Then try to use the tool yourself and evaluate its performance and results. Regroup and, as a team, combine your information into a one- to two-page, double-spaced report.

5. **Buying a Smartphone** You and your teammates are to consider the purchase of a smartphone. Split into groups and visit local mobile device stores. What companies manufacture smartphones? What operating system and applications are installed on the phones that you are researching? Obtain literature and try out several models. Specifically, try out the operating system. What OS and version of that OS does each use? How does this OS compare with those on desktop and notebook computers? How does it differ? With regard to the OS, what phone would you recommend and why? Collate your findings and present a summary in a one-page, double-spaced paper.

On the Web

1. **Examine Deep Freeze** Many educational institutions and lab settings are installing a program on their computers called Deep Freeze. Research this product and in a one-page, double-spaced paper, explain how this program produces a safer computer experience for individuals that have to work in a multiuser environment. What does this program do to protect the operating system and system utilities from change?

2. **Antivirus Programs** In this exercise, use your favorite browser to obtain information on the five top antivirus software programs listed in this chapter. In a Word document, make a list of at least 10 features that all five have in common. Below this list make another list that identifies one feature unique to each one. Then locate the home page of two of the popular antivirus applications. In your Word document include the following additional information:

   - The name of the program and URL of each home page
   - The operating systems each antivirus program works with.
   - List the current versions and suggested retail prices of each.
   - Locate free or evaluation versions, if any exist.

   From your research, would you purchase one of these products? Explain why or why not.

3. **Windows 7 versus Mac OS X Snow Leopard** Using the Internet and a search engine of your choice, research the features of each of the two top operating systems, Windows 7 and Mac OS X Snow

Leopard. In a Word table or Excel spreadsheet, list the features and make a chart that clearly displays which features each OS supports. Indicate the various versions of each system and the cost of each.

4. **Smartphone Accessibility Utilities** In this chapter the accessibility utilities of Windows 7 were reviewed. Smartphones service a very large and general population and contain embedded operating systems that have limitations that single-user operating systems don't have to worry about. Use the Internet and research the accessibility utilities available on smartphones and other mobile devices. Come up with at least five utilities that make using a device easier and less frustrating. Indicate the device and operating system each utility is associated with. Can you come up with any suggestions for additional utilities that would make using a smartphone and its features easier? Use Word and present your research and suggestions in a one-page, double-spaced paper.

5. **Oh Where, Oh Where Can Linux Be?** In the ethics section of this chapter, we discuss the One Laptop Per Child initiative. The laptops for this movement run an operating system called Sugar, a derivative of Linux. Use the Internet and locate at least 10 other devices that are running the Linux operating system, or a variation of Linux. List the devices and any additional information on the Linux system it is running in a Word document.

Spotlight

Buying and Upgrading Your Computer System

You are in the market to purchase a computer. There are several questions that should be going through your head before running off to the local retail store or online site. What will the system be used for? Will it need to run applications or just access the Internet? Will an internal CD or DVD player be required? How much RAM and processing power is necessary? What operating system will best suit your needs and demands? Is portability essential? How much are you willing to spend?

By having your own PC, you can type term papers, create slide presentations, and in many cases use the high-speed wireless network all over campus. Many schools encourage students to purchase a computer before they arrive on campus. Even though schools still provide computer labs, with your own computer you can work when you want and, in the case of notebooks and netbooks, where you want. Buying a computer doesn't have to be intimidating! This spotlight will guide you step by step through the process of buying your own computer. Read on to learn how to choose the equipment you'll need, at the best prices on today's market.

Getting Started the Right Way

There's a right way and a wrong way to select a computer system. The right way involves understanding the terminology and the relative value of computer system components. You then determine your software needs and choose the computer that runs this software in the most robust way. What's the wrong way? Buying a computer system based only on price, being influenced by sales hype, or purchasing a system you know nothing about. First, we'll discuss how to select the best type of computer for your needs.

Notebook, Netbook, or Desktop?

Deciding whether to buy a notebook (also referred to as a laptop), a netbook, or a desktop computer is often one of the hardest decisions you'll have to make when considering which computer to buy (Figure 3A). Today's notebook computers rival the power of desktop machines. The best of them are truly awesome machines, with big (17-inch or larger) displays, fast processors, plenty of memory, and lots of hard drive space. An average notebook with a 17-inch monitor has the dimensions 16.38″ (W) × 10.83″ (D) × 1.25″ (H) and weighs 7.5 lbs. Netbooks are lighter and smaller than notebooks; with a screen size of up to 11 inches and a weight less than half the weight of a 17-inch laptop, a netbook is easier to carry. Netbooks have a substantially longer battery life than a notebook. They also have lower power consumption due to absence of an optical drive and a smaller screen. A netbook with 2 GB of RAM and a 250 GB hard drive is 10.55 inches (L) × 6.9 inches (D) × 0.9–1.11 inches (H) and weights 2.7 lbs.

The main advantages of a notebook computer are portability and size. Because notebooks are portable, you can take them to class in a specially designed

FIGURE 3B Notebook computer bags come in a variety of sizes and styles designed to protect your computer and hold your work.

carrying case (Figure 3B). In class, a notebook fits easily on your desk so you can type notes. As you're probably well aware, campus housing or shared rental units often have a limited amount of desk space, which makes notebooks even more appealing. Although desktops are not as portable as notebooks and netbooks, they can have more processing speed and more RAM. This makes them quite powerful. They can also have a larger internal hard drive.

On the downside, notebook computers cost more than comparable desktop models. You should also consider that notebooks are easily lost or stolen. Moreover, if your notebook goes missing, your precious data will go along with it. For that reason alone, it is crucial to

FIGURE 3A   Which one is right for you? Notebook? Netbook? Desktop?

backup your data at least every week. Here are some interesting facts on notebook theft:

- The FBI reported that over 1.5 million notebooks were stolen in the United States alone in 2009.
- Every second of the day 2.85 notebooks are stolen in the United States.
- Notebook theft doubled over the past year.
- Over 85 percent of notebook theft is an insider job.
- Notebook theft is one of the top three computer crimes, along with virus creation and hacking.
- Approximately 81 percent of U.S. firms lost notebooks with sensitive data in the past year.

Thieves also target college campuses, making safety another important factor when considering a notebook.

Netbooks are even smaller, making them easier to carry with you. The downside to them is they do not have internal CD/DVD drives, and they have smaller hard drives, less processing power, and memory. Still, if you want something very portable to take to class, a netbook might be the answer. If you want to listen to music, view a DVD, or install software, you will need an external device or to be connected to a network.

A desktop computer tends to be less expensive than a notebook computer of similar specification. Desktop computers are easier to upgrade and have internal slots for expansion cards and additional hard drives. Faulty accessories and components, such as a monitor or keyboard, are easier to replace on a desktop system.

In the end, the decision most often hinges on convenience versus expense. It's a good idea to speak with friends, family, and instructors about their experiences with different computers. Additionally, many computer sites like **www.pcmag.com** or **www.cnet.com** regularly review and rate products from many different manufacturers. Besides choosing a notebook or desktop model, another decision you'll need to make is which platform you want to work on: Mac or PC?

MAC or PC?

There are two main computer system platforms: Windows (PC) and Mac (Figure 3C). If you ask around, you'll find that some users prefer the Mac, whereas others prefer Windows. Each thinks their platform is the best, and rarely do they cross platforms. How do you know which platform is best for you?

Today's top-of-the-line Macs and PCs are virtually indistinguishable in terms of features and performance. In January 2010, the market share for Macs was only about 10.9 percent. Apple's relative share of the market grew by 29.4 percent in 2009, while Windows lost 3.8 percent. This has been attributed to Macs now using Intel processors and being capable of running the Microsoft Windows operating system and Windows-based software. So how do you decide? First, you need to know some of the differences between Macs and PCs that can become major issues for some people.

One difference between Macs and PCs is software availability. More than 87 percent of the computers in use today are PCs, and developers are more inclined to develop software for the broadest market. The most noticeable gap is within the gaming software industry, which is primarily Windows based. With the advent of VM (virtual machine) software, which is an application in the host operating system that synthesizes or virtualizes a hardware environment for the guest OS, you can create a virtual Windows PC on your MAC and run Windows based-software. Some examples of VM for the Mac are Parallels, Parallels Desktop, Virtual Machine, Virtualbox, VMware, VMware Fusion, and Windows on Mac OS X. Although game play is possible, performance will not be the same as running the application with the Windows operating system because the resources are being shared.

Some software publishers have discontinued some of their Mac products altogether. For example, Autodesk, publisher of the top-selling computer-aided design (CAD) program Auto-CAD, dropped its sluggish-selling Mac version to focus on its Windows products, but it still produces other applications for Macs. Even software publishers that continue to support the Mac typically bring out the Mac versions later and may not include as many features. However, many of the most popular software packages, including Microsoft Office, are available for Macs as well as PCs. For

FIGURE 3C PCs are most frequently found on the desktops of engineers and businesspeople. Macs have a strong niche market in artistic fields, such as music, graphic design, and illustration.

PC

Mac

example, Microsoft Office 2010 was released in Spring 2010, Microsoft Office for Mac 2011, based on the Office 2010 release, is scheduled for release in late fall 2010. Microsoft Office file formats are compatible between the Mac and the PC. You can also choose to run Windows on your Mac using VM software. If you do, you will be able to use Windows-based software too. This, however, adds to the cost of the system because you have to purchase VM software.

In the past, file compatibility between Macs and PCs was a problem, but that's no longer true. Not only can users easily share files between Macs and PCs, they can attach both types of computers to a network and share printers, Internet access, and other resources.

So does software availability really make a difference? If you're planning to use your computer only for basic applications, such as word processing, spreadsheets, databases, presentation graphics, e-mail, and Web browsing, the Mac-versus-PC issue really isn't important. Because many of the formats are compatible (particularly if you use Microsoft Office or Google Docs), you can often move files from the PC to the Mac and back again using a flash drive. Excellent software for all of these important applications is available for both platforms. Look down the road. What if you declare a major a couple of years from now, only to find that your professors want you to use special-purpose programs that run on the platform that you don't have?

Thus, when deciding whether to buy a PC or a Mac, it's important that you anticipate your future software needs. Find out which programs students in your major field of study are using, as well as which programs are used by graduates working in the career you're planning to pursue. To find out what type of computer is preferred by people working in your chosen career, interview appropriate professionals. PCs figure prominently on the desktops of engineers and businesspeople. The classic stereotype is that the successful artist has a Mac, but her accountant uses a PC. However, like all stereotypes, this is not always the case. For example, you might think that scientists would use PCs, but that's not necessarily true. In the "wet" sciences (chemistry and biology), Macs have many adherents, because these sciences involve visual representation, an area in which Macs excel.

If you're on a budget, consider cost too. Although the price gap is narrowing, Macs and Mac peripherals and software are somewhat more expensive than comparable PC equipment. Macs used to be easier to set up and use, but thanks to improvements in Microsoft Windows, Macs and PCs are now about even. To assist you with your decision, try out different computers, keyboards, and monitors at a store location. With the introduction of Apple stores, you have the opportunity to see and work with a Mac before you purchase it.

Now that you've determined whether your computer will be a Mac or a PC, we'll discuss how to select the right hardware.

Choosing the Right Hardware

You'll need to understand and evaluate the following hardware components when buying your computer:

- Processors
- Memory
- Hard disks
- Internal and external drives
- Monitors and video cards
- Printers
- Speakers and sound cards
- Modems and network cards
- Keyboards and mice
- Uninterruptible power supplies
- Notebook cooling pads

The following sections examine each of these components.

PROCESSORS

One of the most important choices you'll make when buying a computer is the microprocessor (also known as the processor or CPU). This decision may seem overwhelming. Not only do you have to compare brands—Intel versus AMD—and each brand's models, you also have to consider features such as clock speed, number of cores, and power consumption. With the advent of multicore processing, a processor's performance isn't defined solely by its clock speed (typically measured in GHz). In most modern applications, a dual-core CPU can outperform a single-core CPU, even if the single-core has a higher clock speed. Using this reasoning, you might think that a quad-core CPU would be even better, but many applications are unable to take advantage of the quad-core's power. Using a quad-core processor for ordinary computer tasks such as word processing and surfing the Internet is a bit like taking a Formula One racecar around the block to the minimarket! Visit the Intel (**www.intel.com**) and AMD (**www.amd.com**) sites to compare the different types of processors each company manufactures. Many sites, such as PassMark Software (**www.cpubenchmark.net**), rigorously test processors. Known as benchmarking, these tests provide a good way to compare overall processor performance results (Figure 3D). Keep these results in mind as

> " . . . when **deciding** whether to **buy** a PC or Mac, it's **important** that you **anticipate** your future software needs. "

Intel Core i7 930 @ 2.80 GHz

Average CPU mark

Description: Intel® Core™ i7-930 processor (8M cache, 2.80 GHz, 4.80 GT/s Intel® QPI)

5825

CPU first benchmarked: 2010-02-19
CPUmark/$Price: 20.09   **Overall rank:** 25
Last price change: $289.99 USD (2010-08-26)

Samples: 1508

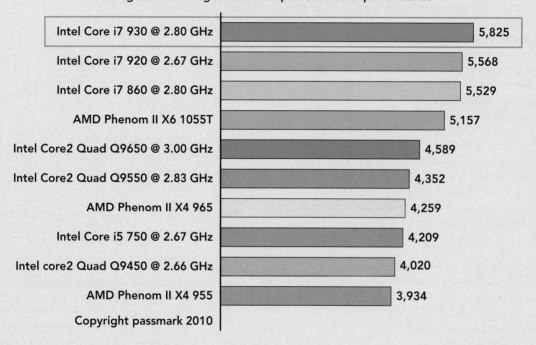

CPU mark relative to top 10 common CPUs
29/August/2010 - Higher results represent better performance

Intel Core i7 930 @ 2.80 GHz	5,825
Intel Core i7 920 @ 2.67 GHz	5,568
Intel Core i7 860 @ 2.80 GHz	5,529
AMD Phenom II X6 1055T	5,157
Intel Core2 Quad Q9650 @ 3.00 GHz	4,589
Intel Core2 Quad Q9550 @ 2.83 GHz	4,352
AMD Phenom II X4 965	4,259
Intel Core i5 750 @ 2.67 GHz	4,209
Intel core2 Quad Q9450 @ 2.66 GHz	4,020
AMD Phenom II X4 955	3,934
Copyright passmark 2010	

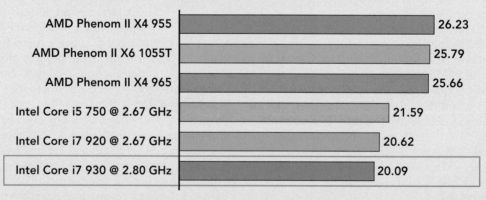

CPU value (CPU mark/$Price)
29/August/2010 - Higher results represent better value

CPU	value
AMD Phenom II X4 955	26.23
AMD Phenom II X6 1055T	25.79
AMD Phenom II X4 965	25.66
Intel Core i5 750 @ 2.67 GHz	21.59
Intel Core i7 920 @ 2.67 GHz	20.62
Intel Core i7 930 @ 2.80 GHz	20.09

FIGURE 3D   PassMark Software (**www.cpubenchmark.net**) provides benchmark test results for more than 300 CPU models and updates its results daily. The first graph shows the relative performance of the CPU compared to the 10 other common CPUs in terms of PassMark CPUmark. The second graph shows the value for money, in terms of the CPUmark per dollar.

you compare computer systems. Each system will have its strengths and weaknesses; however, the processor is the brain of the machine and often dictates the robustness of the rest of the components. It's important that the processor be a good match for the rest of the system. You don't want to put a high-performance processor on a low-end machine or use an underperforming processor on a high-end system.

When researching different processors, keep in mind that you'll pay a premium if you buy the newest, most powerful processor available. One approach is to buy the second-best processor on the market. That way you'll get plenty of processing power without paying a premium for being the first to have the most. You only need enough processing power to handle the work or play you intend to accomplish. If you're a heavy game user, you may need a lot of processing power, but if you plan to use your computer only to surf the Web, play audio files, access social networking sites, and communicate using e-mail and instant messaging, a mid-speed processor should suit your needs just fine.

MEMORY

The next item to consider when buying a computer is how much memory you need. Two important issues are the amount of RAM (random access memory) and whether the system has cache memory.

RAM To maximize your computer's performance, you should seriously consider purchasing as much RAM as you can. You need to check the operating system's requirements and any applications you will be running. If you are purchasing a new computer and a new operating system is being released, you will want to make sure your computer's RAM can handle the requirements or, better yet, the recommendation for RAM, especially if you plan to use a virtual environment or play games. The operating system and applications use RAM for temporary storage. Increasing the amount of available memory allows the CPU to process more instructions and permits more applications to be run simultaneously. Computers with sufficient amounts of RAM are quicker and more responsive than computers with inadequate amounts.

When purchasing a new computer, ask whether the memory can be upgraded and what the maximum amount of memory is for the system. You never know what your future use will demand. You may find that you already own a perfectly good system that just needs more memory to be effective and efficient.

Secondary Cache When researching cache memory, keep in mind that systems with cache memory tend to be faster than systems without it. **Secondary cache**, also known as L2 cache, provides an additional location for memory storage that can be quickly accessed by the processor. It may be located on the processor's architecture or very close to it. If a CPU already includes L2 cache, another level, known as L3 cache, may be located close to the processor on the motherboard.

HARD DISKS

A common mistake made by first-time buyers is underestimating the amount of disk storage they'll need. Today, a 500 GB hard drive may sound like quite a lot, but you won't believe how easy it is to fill it up. (For example, 500 high-resolution photos take up approximately 1 GB of storage.) A good rule of thumb is never to use more than 75 percent of available disk space. Many entry-level systems on the market today come with a hard drive that store anywhere from 160 GB to more than 1 TB. Yes, that's correct—1 trillion bytes! Storage has become very inexpensive, so purchase as much as you can.

INTERNAL AND EXTERNAL DRIVES

A **drive** is a connected storage device. Drives can be internal (installed within the system unit) or external (attached to the system unit by a cable connected to a port). For instance, to install new software from a DVD or CD, you'll need a drive that is capable of reading these discs. Although it is possible to have individual DVD and CD drives installed internally or attached as stand-alone devices, most new computers include a combination DVD±RW/CD-RW drive (Figure 3E) that is capable of reading

FIGURE 3E   DVD drives are used for recording and playing high-definition video and storing large quantities of data.

and writing both DVDs and CDs. Not only will you be able to read CDs, you'll also be able to view movies on DVDs and save files to either storage medium.

The latest optical disc format is Blu-ray Disc (BD), which was developed to enable recording and viewing of high-definition video. Blu-ray also enables you to store large amounts of data. Up to 25 GB of data can be stored on a single-layer disc, and up to 50 GB can be stored on a dual-layer disc. BD drives are now affordable for PCs. Blu-ray has become more popular as high-definition material becomes more prevalent.

Flash drives, also known as thumb drives or USB drives, are an excellent supplement to your hard drive. They come in many different sizes from 512 MB to 64 GB and higher. You can also purchase external hard drives that can be as big as 2 TB. These drives are great for backing up your system or storing your digital photos and videos—and, of course, for your classwork.

MONITORS AND VIDEO CARDS

Monitors are categorized by the technology used to generate images, the colors they display, their screen size, and additional performance characteristics.

In the past few years, as LCD (liquid crystal display) monitor pricing has dropped, CRT (cathode ray tube) monitors have become obsolete and are now considered legacy technology. LCD monitors have become popular because they consume less electricity, have a slimmer design, and weigh less than older CRT monitors weigh. LCD monitors are sometimes referred to as flat-screen or flat-panel monitors because they are very thin, usually no more than 2 inches deep, and they are getting thinner. The flat screen also causes less distortion, resulting in decreased eyestrain—which is critical for people who spend long stretches of time working on a computer.

The quality and resolution of the display you see on your monitor is determined by the computer's **video card**. Display standards vary depending on whether you have a standard monitor with a 4:3 aspect ratio or a widescreen monitor with a 16:10 aspect ratio. **Aspect ratios** are determined by dividing a monitor's width by its height. Standard 17- and 19-inch monitors typically use **Super Extended Graphics Array (SXGA)** with a resolution of 1280 × 1024. Widescreen standards include **Widescreen Extended Graphics Array plus (WXGA+)** for 19-inch monitors with a 1440 × 900 resolution, **Widescreen Super Extended Graphics Array plus (WSXGA+)** for 20-inch monitors with a 1680 × 1050 resolution, and **Widescreen Ultra Extended Graphics Array (WUXGA)** for 24-inch monitors with a 1920 × 1200 resolution. The

higher the resolution, the more memory required. Generally, video cards made before 2006 are unable to support widescreen monitors and standard monitors larger than 19 inches.

To increase performance speed, video data is transferred directly from the video graphics card to the motherboard. The interface used by the graphics card is determined by the motherboard. Older systems used the **Accelerated Graphics Port (AGP)** interface; however, AGP is being phased out in favor of the faster **PCI Express** (Peripheral Component Interconnect Express) and **PCI Express Base 2.1** interface (which is the most current as of this writing). PCI Express 2.1 supports a large proportion of the management, support, and troubleshooting systems. However, the speed is the same as PCI Express 2.0. The data and transfer rate improve with each version. Most current video cards from manufacturers like ATI and NVIDIA use PCI Express (Figure 3F).

Monitors are available in different sizes. You can purchase anything from a 17-inch to a 29-inch monitor. Some monitors are over 30 inches, but the larger the monitor, the higher the cost. The industry standard for desktop monitors ranges from 19 to 22 inches, and the typical notebook computer screen measures 15.4 to 17 inches. If you plan to do any desktop publishing or CAD work, you may want to upgrade to a 24-inch monitor.

The monitor's dot pitch is also an important factor. **Dot pitch** (also called **aperture grill**) is the distance between the dots (pixels) on a CRT monitor. The lower the dot pitch, the closer the dots are to each other—and the sharper the image produced. Don't buy a monitor with a dot pitch larger than 0.28 mm—the smaller the dot pitch, the better your display. Many computer systems can now use your LCD or plasma TV as a monitor.

FIGURE 3F Current video graphics cards use PCI Express Base 2.1 technology for improved performance.

PRINTERS

Printers fall into four basic categories: color inkjet printers, monochrome laser printers, color laser printers, and multifunction devices that fax and scan as well as print. The difference in print quality between inkjets and laser printers is virtually indistinguishable. Color inkjets and monochrome laser printers are popular and affordable choices for college students. However, the pricing for color lasers and multifunction devices is becoming more competitive, making these viable options too. There are still impact printers that are used for multipart forms.

You should also consider the cost of supplies such as ink or toner for your printer. Toner for laser printers is often more expensive than the ink used by inkjet printers, but it also lasts longer. When shopping for a new printer, be sure to research a printer's cost per page, not just the purchase price.

Speed matters, too. The slowest laser printers are faster than the fastest inkjet printers, and the slowest inkjet printers operate at a glacial pace. High-end monochrome laser printers can print as many as 200 ppm (pages per minute). Still, the best inkjet printers for home use churn out black-and-white pages at a peppy pace—as many as 35 ppm. High-end inkjet printers can print 120 ppm. If you go the inkjet route, look for a printer that can print at least 15 ppm. In addition, look for the ability to print on both sides of the paper (duplexing). You too can help save our environment.

If you have a notebook, you may not want to be encumbered by wires. One option is a wireless printer. It can be across the room from you and still print. The speed of wireless printers is about the same as for their wired relatives. You also have the option of choosing a laserjet, inkjet, or multifunction printer.

Stay with a major brand name, and you'll be served well. It's always a good idea to purchase an extra print cartridge and stash it away with 30 or 40 sheets of paper. This way, Murphy's Law won't catch you at 2 AM trying to finish an assignment without ink or paper.

SPEAKERS AND SOUND CARDS

To take full advantage of the Internet's multimedia capabilities, you will need speakers and a sound card. The sound card is built into the motherboard; however, you'll need external speakers to hear high-quality stereo sound. For the richest sound, equip your system with a subwoofer, which realistically reproduces bass notes.

Be aware that many computers, especially the lowest-priced systems, come with low-end speakers. If sound matters a lot to you—and it does to many college students—consider upgrading to a higher-quality, name-brand speaker system.

If you are taking your notebook to class or have a roommate, be considerate and purchase a good set of headphones.

NETWORK CARDS

If you plan to log on to the campus network, you'll need a **network interface card (NIC)**, consider wired or wireless or both. A NIC is a hardware device that handles the interface to a computer network and allows a network-capable device to access that network. Check with your campus computer center to find out how to connect to your school's system and what kind of network card you need. Most colleges run 100-Mbps (100Base-T) Ethernet networks, but some require you to get a 1000-Mbps (1000Base-T) network card.

Macs and PCs have built-in support for Ethernet networks. If you have purchased a computer without a wireless NIC, you can buy one and install it in your PC, or you can purchase a USB wireless NIC.

KEYBOARDS AND MICE

Most computers come with standard keyboards. If you use your computer keyboard a lot and you're worried about carpal tunnel syndrome, consider upgrading to an ergonomic keyboard, such as the Microsoft Natural Keyboard.

Most systems also come with a basic mouse, but you can ask for an upgrade. With Windows PCs, there's good reason to do so, thanks to the improved mouse support built into the Windows operating system. Any mouse that supports Microsoft's IntelliMouse standard includes a wheel that enables you to scroll through documents with ease. Wheel mice also include programmable buttons to tailor your mouse usage to the software application you're using (Figure 3G).

FIGURE 3G   An ergonomic keyboard (left) may be for you if you have pain when typing on a standard keyboard. A wheel mouse (right) includes a scrolling wheel and programmable buttons.

There is also an option for using a wireless mouse and keyboard with your desktop system. Many of the new notebooks use Bluetooth for the mouse and external keyboards.

To choose a good keyboard and mouse, go to a local store that sells computers and try some out. The button placement and action vary from model to model. You'll be using these input devices a lot, so be sure to make an informed decision.

UNINTERRUPTIBLE POWER SUPPLIES

"I'm sorry I don't have my paper. I finished it, and then a power outage wiped out my work." If this excuse sounds familiar, you may want to purchase an **uninterruptible power supply (UPS)**, a device that provides power to a computer system for a short time if electrical power is lost (Figure 3H). With the comparatively low price of today's UPSs—you can get one with surge protection for less than $200—consider buying one for your campus computer, especially if you experience frequent power outages where you live or work. A UPS gives you enough time to save your work and shut down your computer properly until the power is back on. Many UPS devices act as surge protectors to help against power spikes and may have multiple outlets so you can protect more than one piece of computer equipment.

FIGURE 3H   A UPS device can easily justify its purchase price by saving your data in an unexpected power outage.

NOTEBOOK COOLING PADS

Due to the amount of processing and memory in today's notebooks, they run very hot. To safeguard your notebook, it is wise to purchase a cooling pad (Figure 3I). The prices vary depending on the features you select. Some are adjustable to variable heights, some have extra USB ports, some have multiple fans, some are plastic, and some are aluminum. It doesn't matter which one you get, but it is strongly recommended that you get one. They are lightweight and can add years to the life of your notebook. Check to see whether your notebook has vents on the bottom. If it does, a cooling pad will be beneficial. Even though notebooks are often called laptops, do not place notebooks with vents on the bottom on your lap. It will block the cooling ability of the internal fan.

A few other items you might consider are a backup system and locks for your desktop and notebook. Now that you know what to look for when choosing hardware for your computer system, let's examine the

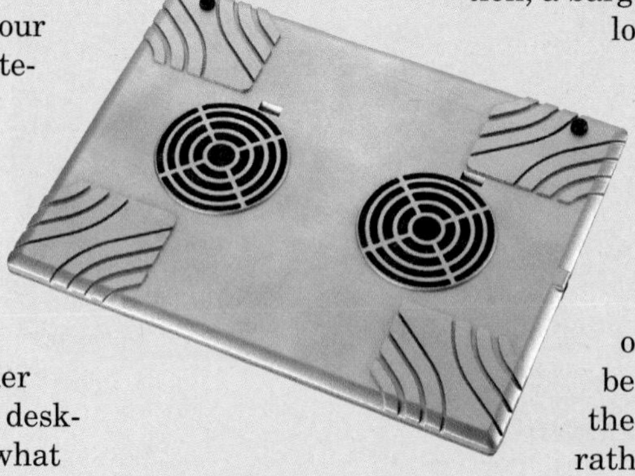

FIGURE 3I   A Cooling Pad for Notebooks

decisions you need to make about what model you want and where you want to buy it.

Shopping Wisely

When you buy a computer, it's important to shop wisely. Should you buy a top-of-the-line model or a bargain-bin special? Is it better to buy at a local store or through a mail-order company? What about refurbished or used computers or a name brand versus a generic PC? Let's take a look at some of these issues.

TOP-OF-THE-LINE MODELS VERSUS BARGAIN-BIN SPECIALS

A good argument for getting the best system you can afford is that you don't want it to become obsolete before you graduate. Inexpensive systems often cut corners by using less powerful CPUs, providing the bare minimum of RAM, and including an operating system with fewer features and capabilities. For example, if the word *home* is part of the name of your operating system, it may not be as robust as what you might need for your studies; however, it will be great for writing papers and sending e-mail. In your senior year, do you want to spend time upgrading your hardware and software when you should be focusing on your studies? In addition, every time you open the computer's cover and change something, you risk damaging one of the internal components.

The most important consideration is the type of software you plan to run. If you'll be using basic applications such as word processing, you don't need the most powerful computer available. In this situation, a bargain-bin special may be okay, as long as you exercise caution when making such a purchase. But what if you decide to declare a major in mechanical engineering? You might want to run a CAD package, which demands a fast system with lots of memory. In that case, you'd be better off paying extra to get the memory you need up front, rather than settling for a bargain-bin special that may end up being inadequate later.

LOCAL STORES VERSUS MAIL-ORDER AND ONLINE COMPANIES

Whether you're looking for a Windows PC or a Mac, you need to consider whether to purchase your system locally or from a mail-order or online company. If you buy locally, you can resolve problems quickly by going back to the store (Figure 3J). With a system from a mail-order or online company, you'll have to call the company's technical support line.

If you are considering ordering through the mail or online, look for companies that have been in business a long time—particularly those that offer a no-questions-asked return policy for the first 30 days. Without such a policy, you could be stuck with a lemon that even the manufacturer won't be able to repair. Be aware that the lowest price isn't always the best deal—particularly if the item isn't in stock and will take weeks to reach you. Also, don't forget about shipping and handling charges, which could add considerably to the price of a system purchased online or through the mail.

In addition, make sure you're not comparing apples and oranges. Some quoted prices include accessories such as monitors and keyboards; others do not. To establish a level playing field for comparison, use the shopping comparison worksheet in Figure 3K. For the system's actual price, get a quote that includes all of the accessories you want, such as a printer, a monitor, and a UPS.

You should also consider warranties and service agreements. Most computers come with a one-year warranty for parts and service. Some companies offer service agreements for varying lengths of time that will cover anything that goes wrong with your system—for a price. In the vast majority of cases, a computer will fail within the first few weeks or months. You should feel comfortable with the amount of coverage you have during the first year. Be aware, though, that extra warranty coverage and service contracts can add significantly to the cost of your system. You may also want to check to see where repairs need to be completed. Do you have to take the system back to where you purchased it? Do you have to mail it back to the manufacturer? Will a service technician come to your house or dorm? What happens if a component goes bad? Do you have to replace it yourself or take it into a shop? These are all things to consider when purchasing a computer and extended warranty.

BUYING USED OR REFURBISHED

What about buying a used system? It's risky. If you're buying from an individual, chances are the system is priced too high. People just can't believe how quickly computers lose their value. They think their systems are worth a lot more than they actually are. Try finding some ads for used computers in your local newspaper and then see how much it would cost to buy the same system new, right now, if it's still on the market. Chances are the new system is cheaper than the used one.

A number of computer manufacturers and reputable businesses refurbish and upgrade systems for resale. National chains such as TigerDirect.com or Newegg.com have standards to ensure that their systems are "as good as new" when you make a purchase. As always, check out the storefront and stay away from establishments that don't look or feel right. In addition, and most important, your refurbished machine should come with a warranty and should include software that has a valid license.

FIGURE 3J   If you buy a computer at a local retail store, you can evaluate different models and speak with a salesperson to obtain additional information.

NAME-BRAND VERSUS GENERIC PCS

Name-brand PC manufacturers, such as HP (Hewlett-Packard), Dell, and Acer, offer high-quality systems at competitive prices. You can buy some of these systems from retail or mail-order stores, but some systems are available only by directly contacting the vendor.

If you're buying extended warranty protection that includes on-site service, make sure the on-site service really is available where you live; you may find out that the service is available only in major metropolitan areas. Make sure you get 24-hour technical support; sometimes your problems don't occur between 8 AM and 5 PM.

If something breaks down, you might have only one repair option: Go back to the manufacturer. After the warranty has expired, you may end up paying a premium price for parts and repairs. Fortunately, this is becoming less of an issue. Almost all of today's name-brand computers run well right out of the box, and in-service failure rates are declining.

What about generic PCs? In most cities, you'll find local computer stores that assemble their own systems using off-the-shelf components. These systems are

Shopping Comparison Worksheet

VENDOR _____ Date _____

    Brand Name _____

    Model _____

    Real Price _____ (including selected components)

PROCESSOR

    Brand _____

    Model _____

    Speed _____ MHz

RAM

    Type _____

    Amount _____ MB

HARD DRIVE

    Capacity _____ GB   Seek time _____ ns

    Speed _____rpm   Interface _____

MONITOR

    Size _____ x _____ pixels   Dot pitch _____mm

VIDEO CARD

    Memory _____ MB   Max. resolution _____ x _____ pixels

    Accelerated? .... ☐ yes ☐ no

REMOVABLE DRIVE

    Type _____

    Location ....☐ internal ☐ external

DVD DRIVE

    Speed _____

DVD BURNER

    Included? .... ☐ yes ☐ no

BLU-RAY DISC DRIVE

    Included? .... ☐ yes ☐ no

SPEAKERS

    Included? .... ☐ yes ☐ no

    Upgraded? .... ☐ yes ☐ no

SUBWOOFER

    Included? .... ☐ yes ☐ no

NETWORK CARD

    Included? .... ☐ yes ☐ no

    Wireless? .... ☐ yes ☐ no

    Speed (100/1000)_____

KEYBOARD

    Upgraded? .... ☐ yes ☐ no

    External for notebook? .... ☐ yes ☐ no

    Wireless? .... ☐ yes ☐ no

    Model _____

MOUSE

    Included? .... ☐ yes ☐ no

    Wireless? .... ☐ yes ☐ no

    Upgraded? .... ☐ yes ☐ no

UPS

    Included? .... ☐ yes ☐ no

SOFTWARE

_____

_____

WARRANTY _____

    Service location _____

    Typical service turnaround time _____

FIGURE 3K Shopping Comparison Worksheet

often just as fast (and just as reliable) as name-brand systems. You save because you don't pay for the name-brand company's marketing and distribution costs. Because of their smaller client base, the staff at local computer stores has a better chance of knowing their customers personally and thus may provide more personalized service. Their phones are not nearly as busy, and if something goes wrong with your computer, you won't have to ship it halfway across the country. Ask the technician about his or her training background and experience. Another thing to consider is that the industry's profit margin is razor thin; if the local company goes bankrupt, your warranty may not mean much.

What if you don't need an entire new computer system, but just want to improve your current system's performance? That's when you should consider upgrading.

Upgrading Your System

You may want to upgrade your system for a variety of reasons. You may have purchased new software that requires more memory to run properly. You may decide to add a game controller. You could decide that a new monitor and printer will enhance your computing experience. Many computer owners improve their system's performance and utility by adding new hardware, such as RAM, sound cards, and additional memory. This section discusses the two most common hardware upgrades: adding expansion boards and adding memory.

Some upgrades, such as upgrading the hard drive, can be accomplished by using an external device. Some thumb drives or flash drives can be used to supplement the RAM on your computer. However, many enhancements require more invasive actions. Before you decide to upgrade your computer on your own, be aware that doing so may violate your computer's warranty. Read the warranty to find out. You may need to take your computer to an authorized service center to get an upgrade. Although it can be relatively simple to install new components, it can be risky. If you have a notebook or a netbook, you may want to take your computer to a trained technician. Upgrading a notebook is more expensive than upgrading a desktop and is not an easy task. It is not recommended that you attempt this yourself. If you aren't absolutely certain of what you're doing—don't do it! If you have some knowledge, it may be more feasible for you to add, remove, or change components. But proceed with care! Also, before you start any upgrade, consider whether it may

be more cost-effective to purchase a new computer than to upgrade your existing one.

REMOVING THE COVER

If you have a desktop computer, begin upgrading your computer by unplugging the power cord and removing all the cables attached to the back of the system unit. Make a note of which cable went where so that you can plug the cables back in correctly. With most systems, you can remove the cover by removing the screws on the back of the case. If you don't know how to remove the cover, consult your computer manual. Keep the screws in a cup or bowl so they'll be handy when you reassemble the computer.

ADDING EXPANSION BOARDS

To add an expansion board to your system, identify the correct type of expansion slot (PCI [Peripheral Component Interconnect], PCI Express, or AGP [Accelerated Graphics Port]) and unscrew the metal insert that blocks the slot's access hole. Save the screw, but discard the insert. Gently but firmly press the board into the slot. Don't try to force it, though, and stop pressing if the motherboard flexes. If the motherboard flexes, it is not properly supported, and you should take your computer to the dealer to have it inspected. When you've pressed the new expansion board fully into place, screw it down using the screw you removed from the metal insert. Before replacing the cover, carefully check that the board is fully inserted.

UPGRADING MEMORY

Many users find that their systems run faster when they add more memory. With additional memory, it's less likely that the operating system will need to use virtual memory, which slows the computer down. To successfully upgrade your computer's memory, visit a leading memory site like Kingston (**www.kingston.com**) or Crucial (**www.crucial.com**). There are several different kinds of memory, but only one type will work with your computer. Both of these sites include tools to help you determine what type of memory your computer requires. Crucial also includes a system scanner that will tell you how much memory is currently installed in your computer. Both sites will tell you the maximum amount of memory your system can use, what type of memory is compatible with your system, and whether you need to buy the memory modules singly or in pairs. You can purchase the specified memory directly from the site or use this information to check pricing and shop around. Following are some of the types of memory that your computer might use: Apple, DDR

> " Before you decide to upgrade your computer on your own, be aware that doing so may violate your computer's warranty. Read the warranty to find out. "

FIGURE 3L SDRAM Chip Showing Both Sides

RAM, DDR-Dual Channel, DDR-Laptop , Memory, DDR2 RAM, DDR2-Dual Channel, DDR2-Laptop Memory, DDR3 RAM, DDR3 Tri-Channel, ECC Memory, and SDRAM (Figure 3L).

When you purchase memory modules, a knowledgeable salesperson might help you determine which type of module you need and how much memory you can install. In many cases, the salesperson doesn't know any more about installing memory than you do. Before you install memory modules, be aware that memory chips are easily destroyed by static electricity. Do not attempt to install memory chips without grounding yourself. You can do this by wearing a **grounding strap**, a wrist-attached device that grounds your body so that you can't zap the chips. Remember, don't try to force the memory modules into their receptacles; they're supposed to snap in gently. If they won't go in, you don't have the module aligned correctly or you may have the wrong type of module.

REPLACING THE COVER

When you have checked your work and you're satisfied that the new hardware is correctly installed, replace the cover and screw it down firmly. Replace the cables and then restart your system. If you added PnP (Plug and Play) devices, you'll see on-screen instructions that will help you configure your computer to use your new hardware.

If you're thinking about upgrading your system or if you want to understand what a particular component does, the Internet is a great resource. Sites like CNET (**www.cnet.com**) and PCMag.com (**www.pcmag.com**) can be used to learn about the newest products and read expert reviews. Other sites like HowStuffWorks (**www.howstuffworks.com**) can provide details and explanations for various components. Using a search engine for specific questions can also turn up valuable information.

Whether your computer system is brand new or merely upgraded, you need to know how to properly maintain your system's components.

Caring for Your Computer System

After your computer is running smoothly, chances are it will run flawlessly for years if you take a few precautions:

- Equip your system with a surge protector, a device that will protect all system components from power surges caused by lightning or other power irregularities (Figure 3M). Remember a power strip is not necessarily a surge protector. Most surge protectors come with a guarantee. APC, one of the largest makers of UPSs and surge protectors, has a lifetime Equipment Protection Policy on most of its equipment.

FIGURE 3M Surge protectors prevent costly damage to delicate circuitry and components.

- Consider purchasing a UPS. These devices protect your system if the computer loses power by providing time to save your work and shut down your computer properly before you lose power.
- Don't plug your dorm refrigerator into the same outlet as your computer. A refrigerator can cause fluctuations in power, and a consistent power supply is critical to the performance and longevity of your computer.
- There should be sufficient air circulation around the components. Don't block air intake grilles by pushing them flush against walls or other barriers. Heat and humidity can harm your equipment. Your computer should not be in direct sunlight or too close to a source of moisture.
- Before connecting or disconnecting any cables, make sure your computer is turned off.
- Cables shouldn't be stretched or mashed by furniture. If your cables become damaged, your peripherals and computer might not communicate effectively.

- Clean your computer and printer with a damp, soft, lint-free cloth.
- To clean your monitor, use a soft, lint-free cloth and gently wipe the surface clean. If the monitor is very dirty, unplug it—and wipe it with a cloth slightly dampened with distilled water. Never apply any liquids directly to the surface, and don't apply too much pressure.
- Avoid eating or drinking near your computer. Crumbs can gum up your mouse or keyboard, and spilled liquids (even small amounts) can ruin an entire system.
- To clean your keyboard, disconnect it from the system unit, turn it upside down, and gently shake out any dust or crumbs. You can also use cans of compressed air to clear dust or crumbs from underneath the keys. Vacuums specially designed for keyboards also are on the market. Never use a regular vacuum cleaner on your keyboard. The suction is too strong and may damage the keys.
- To keep your hard disk running smoothly, run a disk defragmentation program regularly. This program ensures that related data is stored as a unit, increasing retrieval speed.
- Get antivirus and antispyware software and run it frequently. Don't install and run any software or open any file that you receive from anyone until you check it for viruses and spyware. Be sure to update your antivirus and antispyware software. They won't be beneficial to you if you do not keep them updated.

Some Final Advice

Conducting research before you buy a computer is fairly painless and very powerful. To prepare for buying a computer, peruse newspaper and magazine ads listing computer systems for sale. Another great source is the Web, which makes side-by-side comparison easy. For instance, typing **"PC comparison shopping"** (without the quotes) into the Google search engine returns close to 772,000 links, and the Bing search engine returns 12 million links. It's also a good idea to visit a comparison site, such as CNET, PCMag.com, Yahoo!, AOL, or PCWorld. To research particular computer manufacturers (such as Apple, Dell, Sony, Toshiba, Lenovo, Gateway, and so on), simply type the manufacturer's name in the address bar of your Web browser and add the .com extension or use your favorite search engine. Use as many resources as you can when you shop for a computer, and then remember that no matter how happy or unhappy you are with your end purchase, you'll most likely be doing it all again within three to five years.

Key Terms and Concepts

Multiple Choice

1. The device that will allow you to save your data if the power goes out is called a(n) _____.
   a. UPS
   b. surge protector
   c. memory card
   d. expansion card

2. Processor speed is measured in _____.
   a. megabits
   b. bytes
   c. hertzbytes
   d. gigahertz

3. Which of the following is a major consideration when purchasing a computer?
   a. Software to be used
   b. Sound system
   c. Monitor size
   d. Color

4. The hard drive size should:
   a. be just enough for your application installations.
   b. not even be considered.
   c. be larger than anticipated.
   d. be the lowest priority.

5. In order to avoid loss of data, you should do all of the following *except* _____.
   a. get a UPS
   b. backup your data
   c. protect your computer from theft
   d. leave your computer unattended

6. Blu-ray discs can store _____ GB of data on a dual-layer disc.
   a. 50
   b. 100
   c. 150
   d. 200

7. A printer that can scan, fax, and print is called a(n) _____ printer.
   a. inkjet
   b. laser
   c. impact
   d. multifunction

8. If you own a Mac and need to run Windows-based software you can do this by installing software that will create a(n) _____.
   a. imaginary PC
   b. virtual machine
   c. image of a PC
   d. terminal machine

9. _____ is *not* an interface that is used for video cards.
   a. AGP
   b. TSA
   c. PCI
   d. PCI Express

10. To take care of the monitor, you want to keep it clean by _____.
    a. using a damp cloth to clean it
    b. spraying cleaner on it and then wiping it down
    c. putting it in the sink to clean it
    d. making sure it is on when you clean it

Spotlight Exercises

1. Have you considered purchasing a used or refurbished computer? You can purchase a computer from a company or from an individual. What are some of the advantages and disadvantages of purchasing a used or refurbished computer from a company or individual? Visit **www.tigerdirect.com** or **www.newegg.com** and search for refurbished computers. Select a specific notebook computer. Identify the computer, its specifications, and its cost. Where would you search to buy a used notebook computer from an individual? Write a short paper on where you would purchase the computer and its specifications. The paper should show that you understand at least six terms from the Spotlight as they apply to purchasing a used computer.

2. You need to upgrade your computer because the new computer game you just purchased needs more RAM than you have in your system. Go to **www.crucial.com** or **www.kingston.com** and see how much RAM your computer has and how much more you can add. Once you determine how much RAM you need to add to max out your system, go shopping for that specific configuration on three Web sites, including the one you used to obtain the information. Use your word processor or spreadsheet program to create a table of the costs. Remember to add the shipping cost if that is not included in the purchase price.

3. Write a one- to two-page paper on the proper care and maintenance of a computer. Explain why each of the items is important.

4. Create a comparison chart on the differences, advantages, and disadvantages of desktop, netbook, and notebook computers. Explain in a one-page paper which computer you would purchase and why.

5. Go to a computer retailer or manufacturer's Web site where you can select the components you want in a computer. Build the computer and price it. Make sure to include any tax and shipping charges. Take those specifications, go into a local store that sells computers, and see if you can match the components. What is the price of the computer in the store? Don't forget to include tax. Do a comparison of the two systems.

6. It is important to know what is in your computer if you plan to upgrade or purchase a new computer. Windows provides a utility to check your computer. System Information is the utility that shows the hardware that is in your system, regardless of whether it is a notebook or desktop. Use the *Start, All Programs, Accessories, System Tools* menu sequence to access the System Information utility. If you use Control Panel in the classic view and select *System,* you will get an experience rating and suggestions of how to improve performance by selecting the *Windows Experience Index*. Write a short paper that includes a table with the values for the following components: the operating system, processor, total physical memory, available physical memory, total virtual memory, and available virtual memory. Using what you learned in the sections on processing, memory, and RAM, is your system current with today's standards? Should you upgrade your computer? Why or why not?

chapter 5

Application Software: Tools for Productivity

Chapter Objectives

You have a resume to write, a graph displaying annual expenses to create, and a slide show highlighting the goals of a new committee to develop. Where do you start? Every task has an application (app for short) that best suits its purpose. How many apps are on your desktop, notebook, or smartphone? Do you know how to use each one? How many of the apps are for school or work, and how many are for entertainment? Although most users say that they can't live without their computer or smartphone, don't they really mean they can't live without their applications?

Application software refers to all of the programs that enable you to use your desktop computer, notebook, or smartphone to perform tasks that assist in accomplishing work or facilitating play. In this sense, application software differs from system software, the programs that provide the infrastructure and hardware control so other programs can function properly. Recall our aquarium analogy. In that analogy, applications are the fish that swim in the water (the operating system). In more technical terms, the operating system provides the environment in which the applications run. In this chapter you'll learn more about the world of apps, including the following:

- Categories of applications
- Hints and directions on proper installation of apps
- Guidance on default settings
- Details of some of the newly released software ■

Check out **f** Facebook for our latest updates

www.facebook.com

General-Purpose Applications

General-purpose applications are programs used by many people to accomplish frequently performed tasks. These tasks include writing documents (word processing), working with numbers (spreadsheets), keeping track of information (databases), developing multimedia and graphic content, facilitating Internet usage, and a variety of other tasks handled by home and educational programs. These applications were once found only on home and business computers, but today they are on mobile devices and media-specific technology such as iPods. We'll cover these applications within the categories that they fit. Figure 5.1 lists the various types of general-purpose application software, including some applications that work through and run from the Internet.

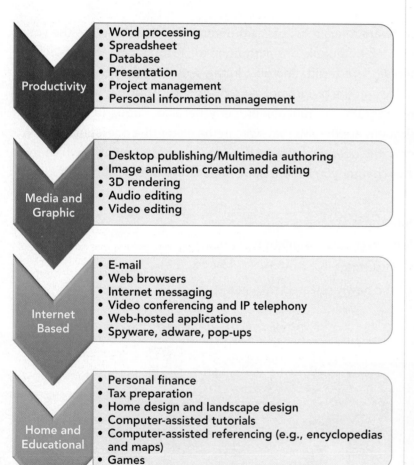

- Productivity
  - Word processing
  - Spreadsheet
  - Database
  - Presentation
  - Project management
  - Personal information management

- Media and Graphic
  - Desktop publishing/Multimedia authoring
  - Image animation creation and editing
  - 3D rendering
  - Audio editing
  - Video editing

- Internet Based
  - E-mail
  - Web browsers
  - Internet messaging
  - Video conferencing and IP telephony
  - Web-hosted applications
  - Spyware, adware, pop-ups

- Home and Educational
  - Personal finance
  - Tax preparation
  - Home design and landscape design
  - Computer-assisted tutorials
  - Computer-assisted referencing (e.g., encyclopedias and maps)
  - Games

FIGURE 5.1 Application software can be categorized based on use. Each product provides an interface to perform a variety of tasks without having to understand the intricacies of how it works.

Productivity Programs

The most popular general-purpose applications are **productivity programs**, which, as the name implies, help individuals work more efficiently and effectively on both personal and business-related documents. Productivity software includes word processors, spreadsheets, databases, presentation, project management, and personal information management programs (Figure 5.2). Their value is that they perform their functions regardless of the subject matter. For instance, a word processor is equally valuable for typing a term paper for your history class, writing a letter to mom, or creating the agenda for the Board of Directors meeting.

Using the appropriate application for the appropriate purpose further facilitates tasks. Excel can be used for a presentation, but it is much better to use Power-Point as the presentation program and import Excel spreadsheets and charts into it. In Word, you can use tables to add numbers together, but Excel is much better suited for this task. One maxim you may have heard is, "You can drive a screw with a hammer—but a hammer is best used for driving nails and a screw should be set with a screwdriver." The same rule applies to using the right productivity program for the right task. You can increase your productivity by choosing an application such as Excel to manage numbers, Word to manage text, Access to manage your customer database, PowerPoint to present a slide show, Project to allocate resources among jobs in progress, and Outlook to keep reminders and appointments.

There are several companies that create programs for home and business productivity. Figure 5.3 lists these applications by type, along with some of the more popular manufacturers. However, because Microsoft Office is the group of productivity applications chosen most often by home and business users, we'll review some of the features of its most current version, Office 2010.

An Overview of Microsoft Office 2010

With the release of Office 2010, Microsoft has included changes to meet the demands of its users. Some of these new 2010 features are listed here:

- The change of the Office Button to a tab on the Ribbon labeled "File" and an improved File menu interface.

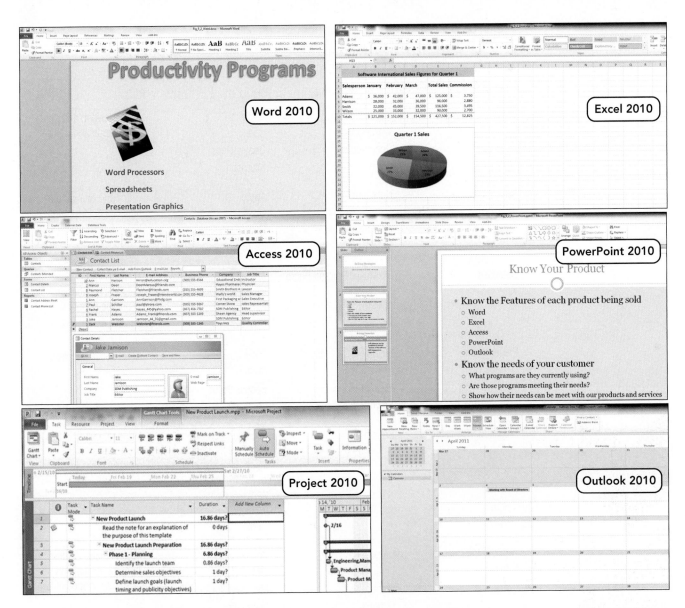

FIGURE 5.2 Productivity programs include Microsoft Word (word processing), Microsoft Excel (spreadsheet), Microsoft Access (database), Microsoft PowerPoint (presentation graphics), Microsoft Project (project management), and Microsoft Outlook (personal information management).

- The ability to customize the Ribbon, allowing the user to create a custom workspace.
- Live preview for the paste clipboard.
- The option to capture and insert screen shots.
- Enhanced multimedia editing in PowerPoint, including the ability to do video cutting, remove backgrounds, and record a slide show as a video.
- The introduction of Office Web applications, a direct attempt to counter the popularity of Google Docs and Zoho (free Web-based office apps). Web Office provides free online companions to Word, Excel, PowerPoint, and OneNote (an electronic notebook), allowing documents made with these programs to be accessed through Internet Explorer, Firefox, or Safari browsers. It is designed to provide a convenient method of retreiving and editing documents for those individuals who need their data constantly available or who work in teams. These Web applications display a real-time buddy list that identifies the individual who is currently editing a document and allows changes made by that person to be viewed by others.

- Stronger security settings that include "Restrict Editing" and "Block Author" modes, both added to enable or restrict users working on a collaborative project.

These are just some of the upgrades included in Office 2010 productivity programs. One feature that has not changed is the familiar interface and tools that all

FIGURE 5.3 Productivity Applications

Productivity Category	Example Programs	Manufacturer	Uses
Word Processing	Pages WordPerfect Documents Word	Apple Corel Google Docs Microsoft	Write, format, and print documents and reports
Spreadsheet	Numbers Quatro Pro Spreadsheets Excel	Apple Corel Google Docs Microsoft	Enter and manipulate financial data through the use of formulas
Database	FileMaker Pro and Bento Paradox Access	Apple (actually FileMaker, Inc., a subsidiary of Apple) Corel Microsoft	Manage and connect data between related tables to produce queries, reports, and forms
Presentation	Keynote Presentation Presentations PowerPoint	Apple Corel Google Docs Microsoft	Create slide shows
Project Management	Project Tenrox	Microsoft (runs on Windows XP, Windows Vista, Windows 7) Tenrox (runs on Windows XP, Windows Vista, Windows 7), Mac OS, Linux)	Manage and schedule resources among multiple projects
Personal Information Manager	Calendar Lotus Organizer Entourage Outlook Desktop	Google IBM Microsoft (for the Mac OS) Microsoft Palm (Free)	Keep e-mails, contact lists, schedules, and calendars of appointments

of the Office applications possess. Before looking at individual programs, let's first identify and review these shared features.

The Shared Office Interface Office applications use many interfaces that are similar to those of Microsoft's Windows operating systems. When an application is opened, you'll see some or all of the following features within the **application window**, the area that encloses and displays the application (Figure 5.4).

- The **application workspace**—the area that displays the document you are currently working on.
- The **document**—any type of product you create with the computer, including typewritten work, an electronic spreadsheet, or a graphic.
- The **title bar**—the top bar of each program interface that includes the program icon, the name of the application, and the name of the file you are working on. If you haven't yet saved the file, you'll see a generic file name, such as Untitled, Document1, Book 1, or another such name.
- The three **window control buttons**—located on the right side of the title bar, they enable the user to minimize, maximize, restore, or close the application's window. The left button enables you to **minimize** the window so that it is cleared from the

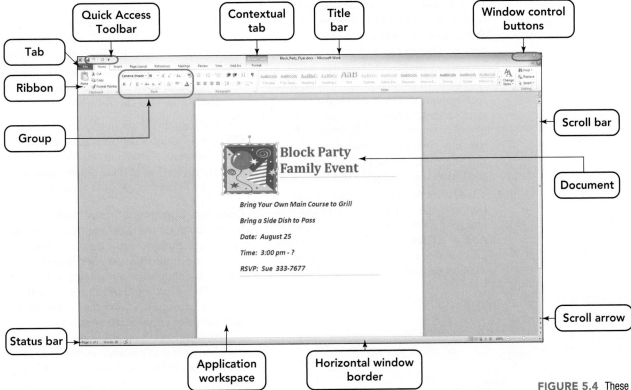

The following labels appear around the figure:

- Tab
- Quick Access Toolbar
- Contextual tab
- Title bar
- Window control buttons
- Ribbon
- Group
- Scroll bar
- Document
- Status bar
- Application workspace
- Horizontal window border
- Scroll arrow

Block Party Family Event

Bring Your Own Main Course to Grill

Bring a Side Dish to Pass

Date: August 25

Time: 3:00 pm - ?

RSVP: Sue 333-7677

FIGURE 5.4 These shared components are found in most Microsoft Office 2010 applications.

screen and reduced down to a button on the task bar. Simply click the task bar button to retrieve the document. The right button is used to close the window once you finish with the document. The middle button toggles between two functions, depending on whether the program is occupying the entire screen (known as full screen) or is a smaller size. If the window is full screen, the button is in the **restore down** mode, which means clicking it will cause the window to revert to a smaller size. If the window is not full screen, clicking this button enables you to **maximize**, or enlarge, the window so that it fills the whole screen.

- The **window border**—a thick line that encloses the window. In Microsoft applications, you can change the size of a window by dragging on its border. If you click and drag a window corner, you can resize the window both horizontally and vertically at the same time. Note that this process will work only if a window is not maximized.

- The **status bar**—located at the bottom of the application interface, it displays information about the application and the document, such as the current page number and the total number of pages.

- The **scroll bars**—located at the right and bottom of a document, they allow you to see different parts of a document by using a mouse and dragging the rectangular button that is located on the bar. The section of the document displayed on the screen depends on the direction in which the rectangle is dragged.

- The **scroll arrows**—appear on the scroll bar and can be clicked to scroll the document line by line.

- The **Ribbon**—a band located across the top of the application window and below the title bar. It consists of tabs with icons assembled into groups based on their function. Each application has a Ribbon with tab options that match the activities performed by that application.

- A **tab**—a segment of the Ribbon that contains category titles of tasks you can accomplish within an application. Several advanced tabs, such as Add-Ins and Developer, which are not visible by default, can be turned on by clicking the File tab and then the Options choice from the menu that appears, and then selecting Customize Ribbon.

- A **contextual tab**—a tab, or tabs, that appears on the right side of the Ribbon, but only when specific objects are selected. The editing options for the selected object are located in its contextual tab(s). For example, in Word, when a table is selected, a contextual Design tab and a Layout tab become available on the Ribbon.

- A **group**—a collection of icons on a tab that appear within a rectangular region on the Ribbon. The items in a group perform related functions. For instance, you might choose the Home tab and then, in the Font group, select the button for changing the font color.
- The **Quick Access Toolbar**—a bar that appears on the left side of the window just above the Ribbon. The Quick Access Toolbar displays a series of buttons used to perform common tasks such as saving a document and undoing

or redoing the last action. The Quick Access Toolbar is customizable and remains available at all times, no matter which tab on the Ribbon is selected.

- Additional tabs applied by third-party programs, such as Adobe Acrobat, may also appear on the Ribbon.

Not only do the programs in Microsoft Office 2010 share a common interface, but they also share a common sequence to frequently performed actions. These sequences will be explained in the next section.

Common Command Sequences

Instructions such as opening an application, saving a document, closing a document, and closing the application are performed in a similar manner among most applications today. The steps listed in Figure 5.5 will help you accomplish these four common tasks in most Office 2010 programs.

Now that we have reviewed the common features and common commands of most Office 2010 programs, let's look briefly at the individual programs and their features that make your home and business activities easier and more professional.

FIGURE 5.5 Sequences for Common Application Commands

Command	Steps
Opening a program	Click the Start button. From the Start menu, select *All Programs*. From the list of programs or categories, select the correct one. If you selected a category, then, from the category list, select the program. The program will open.
Opening a document	Within the application window, click the *File* tab. From the *File* menu select *Open*. A dialog box will open, allowing you to select the storage location and specific file.
Saving a document (for the first time)	Within the application window, click the *File* tab. From the File menu, select *Save As*. In the Save As dialog box, select the correct storage device and folder. Give the file an appropriate name. Leave the *Save as type* option alone, unless you want the file to be saved in a previous version or a type that can be opened by another program. Click *Save*. Verify that the name on the title bar is the name you just entered in the Save As dialog box
Closing a document	Within the application window, click the *File* tab. From the File menu select *Close*.
Closing the program	Within the application window, click the *File* tab. From the File menu select *Exit*. (This action can also be accomplished by clicking on the window control button labeled with an X.)

Microsoft Word 2010

Microsoft Word is a very powerful word processing program. As with other Office applications, it uses the shared office interface and the common command sequences. The opening screen is basically a blank sheet of paper on which you can create your documents.

Using Word at its most basic level to create short letters, memos, and faxes is extraordinarily simple; you just type text into the Word document, click the File tab, and click Print from the menu to send your document to the printer or Save As to save the document for future use. Word includes features such as these:

- Automatic text wrapping
- A Find and Replace utility
- The ability to cut, copy, and paste items like text, images, and screen captures both within the document and between documents or other programs
- Editing and formatting tools to insert headers and footers, page breaks, page numbers, and dates
- The ability to embed pictures, graphics, charts, tables, footnotes, and endnotes, as well as import other

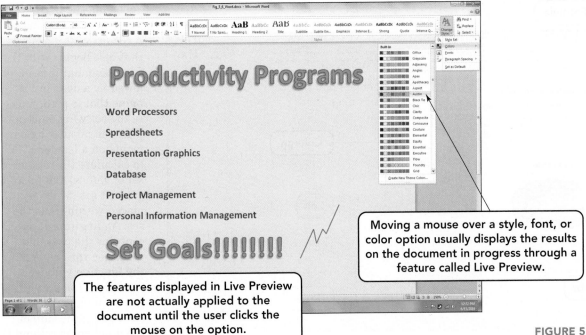

Productivity Programs

Word Processors

Spreadsheets

Presentation Graphics

Database

Project Management

Personal Information Management

Set Goals!!!!!!!!!

The features displayed in Live Preview are not actually applied to the document until the user clicks the mouse on the option.

Moving a mouse over a style, font, or color option usually displays the results on the document in progress through a feature called Live Preview.

FIGURE 5.6 Live Preview reduces use of the undo feature because you can see the results of a selection before you actually make it on the document.

documents to enhance your work in progress

- Tables, columns, tabs, and bulleted or numbered lists to align text and display information other than in paragraph form
- A theme feature, for those less artistic among us, that provides precreated color schemes and font selections to give your documents a more pleasing appearance
- A Live Preview option that displays the formatting options you mouse over in the actual document without actually selecting it (Figure 5.6)
- Portrait (vertical) or landscape (horizontal) orientation print options

This is just a partial list of the features available in Word. As you probably can see from the above list, just about anything you can imagine, you can do in Word. To learn more about these and other features consult the online help and demonstrations at **www.microsoft.com** or use the Word Help feature accessed by pressing the F1 function key.

If you're using a PC, the files that you create in Word 2010 include the .docx extension by default. Word can also save your documents as plain text (.txt), HTML (.htm), Rich Text Format (.rtf), or formats that can be read by previous versions of Word or competing products, such as WordPerfect.

Now that you have a basic understanding of what Word can do for you,

you're ready to move on to other Office applications. The following section will introduce you to Excel.

Microsoft Excel 2010

Microsoft Excel is the leading spreadsheet program for business and personal use. The primary function of a spreadsheet program is to store and manipulate numbers. You use a spreadsheet either to record things that have actually happened or to predict things that might happen, through a method called **modeling** or **what-if analysis**.

Excel uses the shared office interface and the common command sequences. In Excel, each file is called a **workbook**. A workbook is made up of **worksheets**. Each worksheet is composed of **columns** (vertical lines of data), and **rows** (horizontal lines of data), and the intersections of rows and columns, which are called **cells** (Figure 5.7).

A cell is identified by its column letter and its row number—known as the **cell address**. The columns in a spreadsheet are identified by the letters of the alphabet; rows are represented by numbers. For example, A1 represents an individual cell in column A, row 1; and AC342 represents a cell located in column AC, row 342.

A **range** of cells consists of two or more adjacent cells selected at the same time and identified by the addresses of the top-left and bottom-right cells, separated by a

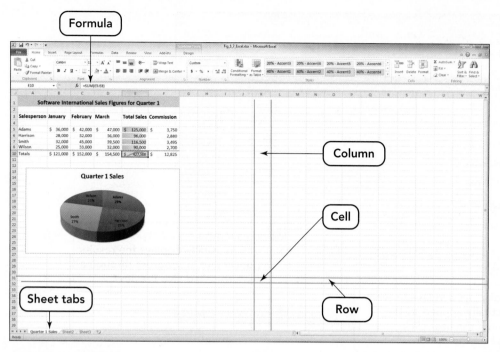

Formula

Column

Cell

Row

Sheet tabs

FIGURE 5.7 By default,
an Excel 2010 workbook
includes three worksheets.
Each worksheet is made up
of 16,000 columns and
1 million rows.

colon. For example, the range from cell A1
to cell D5 would be represented as A1:D5.

Spreadsheets contain several different
types of entries and features:

- Text entries, commonly referred to as
  labels, are identifying phrases used
  to explain numeric entries and the
  results of formulas.

- Numbers are the values on which
  mathematical operations can be
  performed.

- A **formula** is a combination of numeric constants, cell references, arithmetic operators, and functions that is
  used to calculate a result. Excel interprets a cell entry as a formula if the
  entry starts with an equal sign (=).
  There are two types of formulas:

  - In a **mathematical formula**, the
    user actually writes the formula
    using the mathematical order of
    operations, where values in paren-
    theses are acted on first, followed by
    exponentiation, multiplication and
    division, and then addition and sub-
    traction. (Perhaps you remember
    this order of operations through the
    mnemonic Please Excuse My Dear
    Aunt Sally, or PEMDAS.) For exam-
    ple, the formula = 6 * (4 − 2)/3 + 2
    is equal to 6, because the equa-
    tion in parentheses is done first,
    so 4 minus 2 is 2; then 6 times 2
    is 12; 12 divided by 3 is 4; and
    lastly 4 plus 2 is 6. Note the expla-
    nation and answer is the result of

following the PEMDAS
sequence.

  - A **function** is a formula
    that also begins with the
    equal sign but is then fol-
    lowed by a descriptive
    name that is predefined
    in the software (such as
    PMT for calculating pay-
    ments on a loan or SUM
    to calculate the total of a
    set of values) and an ar-
    gument set, which is
    placed within parenthe-
    ses. An **argument set**
    contains the passable
    values or variables that
    the function will need
    to produce the answer.
    For example, when
    calculating the sum of
    the numbers in column B
    from B4 through B7
    the function =SUM(B4:B7) would do
    the job, with the range B4:B7 being
    the argument for the SUM function.

- Excel **charts** are graphical represen-
  tations of data that are based on data
  ranges and the labels that identify
  the ranges. There are 11 different categories of charts in Excel, and each
  category includes several different
  chart styles.

- The use of **sparklines**, tiny charts embedded into the background of a cell,
  helps users visualize their data and
  more easily detect trends.

- Pivot tables and pivot charts are used
  to pivot data about one field of interest.

- Additional data analysis tools, such as
  sorts and subtotals, are available to
  assist in extracting information from
  your data set.

The files that you create and save in
Excel 2010 use the .xlsx extension by default. Excel can also save your documents as
plain text (.txt), HTML (.htm), eXtensible
Markup Language (.xml), or in formats that
can be read by previous versions of Excel.

This is just an overview of some of the
new and frequently used features of Excel
2010. To learn more about creating charts
and reports in Excel, consult the online help
and demonstrations at **www.microsoft.
com** or use the Excel Help feature accessed
by pressing the F1 function key.

Next, we'll take a look at the Office
application for managing databases.

Microsoft Access 2010

Microsoft Access is a database management system (DBMS), a software application designed to store related data in tables, create relationships between the multiple tables, and then generate forms, queries, and reports to present this data in a more informative and pleasing manner. The opening Access interface offers choices for opening an existing database, using a template to create a new database, or beginning a new blank database from scratch. Access does not offer a default blank database screen like the blank document in Word or the blank worksheet in Excel. In Access, you must always work on an existing database or on a new database that you've named and saved to disk before doing any data entry. The main reason for this is that Access has a feature that automatically saves changes or new entries into a database table immediately when the user leaves the record, a row of data in a database table. The program has to know where to save the new entries or updates. The purpose of this feature is to minimize the amount of information in a database that can be lost if a system refuses to respond.

Access uses tables, forms, filters, queries, and reports to manage and present data (Figure 5.8).

- A **table** is a series of columns (fields) and rows (records) that compose the **data set**, the contents of a table. Data can be imported from another program, such as Excel or entered directly into a table by the user.

- A **form** is a template with blank fields in which users input data one record at a time. You have filled out physical and electronic forms many times in your life. Forms should be organized so that the person who is typing in the data can easily move from one field to the next in a logical order.

- The use of filters and queries provides a way to process the data in tables based on specified criteria and displays only the records that match that criteria. A **filter** is less complicated and displays all the fields of matching records. A **query**, however, can specify more criteria, limit the fields to be displayed, and be saved for re-use.

- The **report** feature displays information from tables, queries, or a combination of both in a professionally styled manner.

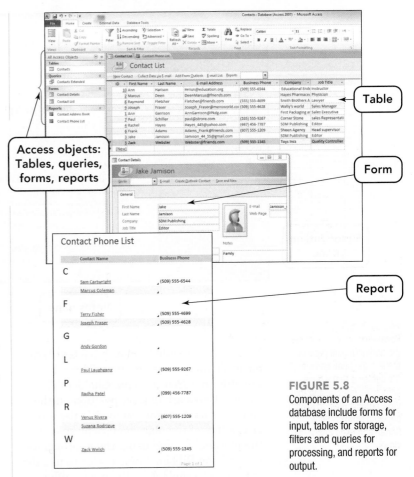

Access objects: Tables, queries, forms, reports

Table

Form

Report

FIGURE 5.8
Components of an Access database include forms for input, tables for storage, filters and queries for processing, and reports for output.

Access 2010, which uses the .accdb file extension by default, has added more wizards to help users create tables, queries, forms, and reports with ease. Access has long been seen as a program that is difficult to use, but the new and upgraded wizards are a giant step forward.

To learn more about how to use Access, visit the online help provided at **www.microsoft.com** or use the Access Help feature by pressing the F1 function key.

Let's now look at a program that's a favorite among many college students: PowerPoint.

Microsoft Powerpoint 2010

Microsoft PowerPoint is a popular program used to create and deliver presentations. When you open PowerPoint, you are presented with a blank slide. A **slide** is the canvas on which you organize text boxes and graphics to present your ideas or points. PowerPoint offers nine slide layouts. All layouts, with the exception of the

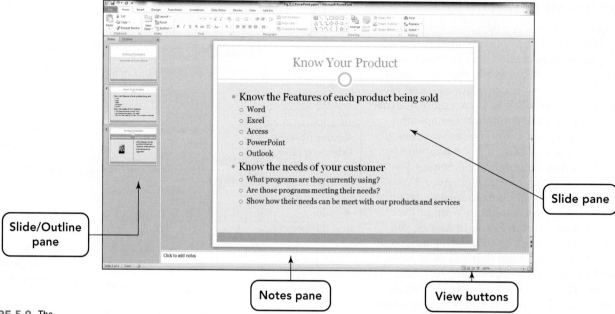

Slide/Outline pane

Slide pane

Notes pane

View buttons

FIGURE 5.9 The PowerPoint screen features the Slides/Outline pane on the left, the Slide pane in the center, a Notes pane across the bottom, and the View buttons used to switch between Normal, Slide Sorter, and Slide Show views.

Blank Layout slide format, have text boxes for inserting text or graphics. These boxes are often referred to as placeholders. The various boxes are in a set position on the slide canvas, but you can modify the size or position of the placeholders by selecting the placeholder and using the appropriate tools on the Ribbon. Some prefer to use the mouse and simply drag the placeholder to a new location or drag on the resize arrows that appear on the placeholder's border to alter its size.

PowerPoint (Figure 5.9) provides the user with a lot of bells and whistles to jazz up a presentation:

- Professionally created **design templates** that apply a coordinated background color, font type, and bullet style
- A variety of slide **transitions** that create the visual movement and effects that appear as one slide exits the presentation and another enters
- Placeholder and image **animation** options that determine how each placeholder for an object makes its appearance on the slide
- An animation painter that permits the copying of animation from one slide to another
- An option to directly insert a video into a presentation
- A converter that will transform your presentation into a WMV video file

It's very easy to get caught up with all of the animation and transition effects.

A good PowerPoint slideshow should serve as a backdrop and enhancement to your presentation; it shouldn't be the main feature.

PowerPoint 2010 applies the .pptx extension by default. PowerPoint can also save your documents as a .pdf or in formats that can be read by previous versions of PowerPoint. To learn more about how to use PowerPoint, visit the online help provided at **www.microsoft.com** or access the Help feature by pressing the F1 function key.

Next let's take a look at a program that is not as popular as Word, Excel, or PowerPoint, but for the business graduate, it is quickly becoming a necessity: Project 2010.

Microsoft Project 2010

Microsoft Project is a productivity program that has more utility for the business user than the home user. It provides an environment for the overall management of one or more projects that can vary in complexity. This program offers such features as these:

- A visually enhanced timeline that emphasizes due dates and deadlines
- A team-planning capability that, by simply dragging and dropping, allows for the easy creation of a team with the right individuals and resources
- A portfolio manager that monitors the allocation of scarce resources and current project costs

In Project 2010 the emphasis was on improving the ease of use and fitting its functionality within the familiar interface. Much of the project content can be viewed in several ways, from bulleted lists to a view that represents the Outlook calendar layout (Figure 5.10).

Project, like Access, has often been thought of as one of the more difficult productivity programs to use. Microsoft is hoping that, with the new features and enhanced interface, this perception will change.

Let's now move on to a productivity program that will help you communicate with others and manage your busy schedule: Microsoft Outlook.

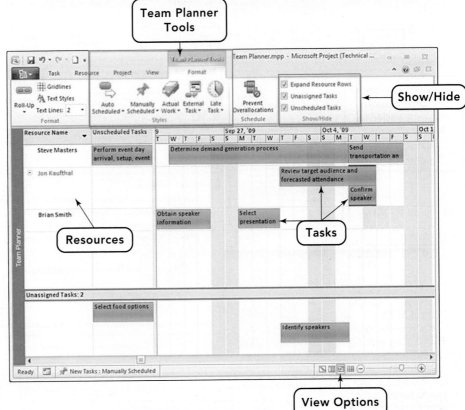

FIGURE 5.10 The new Team Planner Tools feature in Project 2010 displays resources (including people) and tasks in a view similar to an Outlook calendar.

Microsoft Outlook 2010

Microsoft Outlook is a personal information management system that brings all the tools you need to manage your time and work effectively into one program. Included are these features:

- E-mail—a feature that does everything from auto completing a previously used e-mail address to prompting you to add new e-mail addresses to your contacts. Additionally, users can create their own e-mail folders to sort their mail in a way that suits their organization's or their individual needs.
- Conversation grouping—a new 2010 addition that intelligently groups e-mails or conversations by sender and subject. A conversation is a group of e-mails that contain the same subject. When a new e-mail arrives, the entire conversation that it is a part of moves to the top of the message list. This makes it easy to follow a sequence of e-mails from different sources on the same subject.
- Ignoring conversations—another new 2010 feature that enables a user to tag a conversation he or she wants to ignore. Just a warning: Doing this will cause any incoming conversations on the same topic or from the same source to automatically be redirected to your Trash folder.
- Think before you send—a feature that will warn you that a mailing mistake, like sending an e-mail to too many users, is being made. This will help avoid the embarassment of using the "Reply to All" option when simply "Reply" should have been used.
- The calendar—an easy-to-use tool that is very helpful in managing all of the activities associated with school, work, and socializing. It includes alarms to alert you to upcoming events, a recurrence feature that allows you to enter regularly scheduled events efficiently, and tags to set priorities for messages.

In today's busy world, it is the combination of all of these features that have made personal information managers like Outlook indispensible in both the office and home (Figure 5.11).

The best way to learn how to use Outlook is to experiment with it. Also remember that you can use the Help program to learn how to use the various features Outlook includes. You'll be surprised at just how easy it is to manage your life with Outlook.

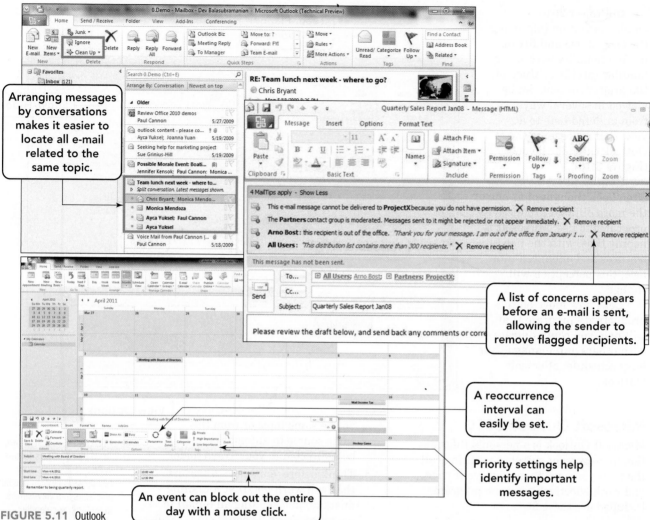

Arranging messages by conversations makes it easier to locate all e-mail related to the same topic.

A list of concerns appears before an e-mail is sent, allowing the sender to remove flagged recipients.

A reoccurrence interval can easily be set.

Priority settings help identify important messages.

An event can block out the entire day with a mouse click.

FIGURE 5.11 Outlook can improve personal productivity with features that facilitate e-mail organization and add calendar entries.

Media and Graphic Software

When discussing applications, **media** refers to the technology used to present information. This technology encompasses pictures, sound, and video. Most media and graphic software today are referred to as **multimedia** programs because they enable the user to incorporate more than one of these technologies. By this definition, items such as PowerPoint presentations, TV shows, and movies are multimedia experiences because they use audio, video, and graphic components. Computer applications use multimedia features where text alone would not be effective. Graphics, sounds, animations, and video can often do a better job of involving the user, conveying information, and keeping the viewer's attention than text alone. These features, which once were considered entertainment or amusement, have become standard components of business and educational programs (Figure 5.12).

Some multimedia applications offer another exciting characteristic: interactivity. For example, in an interactive multimedia presentation, users can choose their own path through the presentation. This creates different outcomes for each viewer, depending on the choices made. The use of interactivity in education and business enables the learner to view the possible outcomes of decisions and the associated consequences, thus creating a simulated environment and a great learning tool.

Interactivity is a big factor in the popularity of the Web. In fact, the Web could be viewed as a gigantic interactive multimedia presentation. Most Web pages include graphics along with the text, and many also offer animations, videos, and sounds. On some Web pages, you can click parts of a graphic or a link to access different pages, videos, pop-ups, or other sections of the same page.

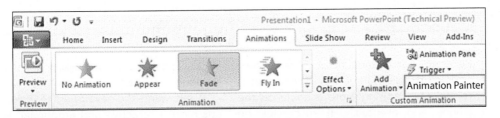

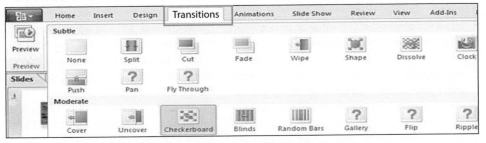

FIGURE 5.12 Creating professional multimedia presentations in PowerPoint 2010 will be less complicated with the addition of the animation painter, 3D transitions, and insert video options.

Multimedia and graphics software includes desktop publishing programs (such as QuarkXPress and Publisher) and multimedia authoring programs; paint, drawing, and animation programs; image-editing programs (such as Photoshop); three-dimensional (3D) rendering programs (such as computer-aided design [CAD] programs); audio software; and video-editing programs.

A multimedia presentation typically involves some or all of the following: bitmapped graphics, vector graphics, edited photographs, rendered 3D images, edited videos, and synthesized sound. In the following sections, we'll discuss each of these and look briefly at some of the software used to create multimedia productions. For information, articles, and tutorials on multimedia products and current industry trends visit **http://graphicssoft.about.com**.

Compression and Decompression

Computers can work with art, photographs, videos, and sounds only when these multimedia resources are stored in digitized files, which require huge amounts of storage space. To use the space on your hard disk more efficiently and improve file transfer speeds over the Internet, most multimedia software programs reduce file size by using

codecs, the technical name for compression/decompression or code/decode algorithms.

Codecs use two different approaches to compression: lossless compression and lossy compression. With **lossless compression**, the original file is compressed so that it can be completely restored, without flaw, when it is decompressed. With **lossy compression**, the original file is processed so that some information is permanently removed from the file. Lossy compression techniques eliminate information that isn't perceived when people see pictures or hear sounds, such as frames from a video that are above the number needed to eliminate the flicker effect and very high musical notes that are outside of the frequency range for most users. Both techniques have been blended into a hybrid technique used in the area of medical imaging for CTs and MRIs. The dilemma in this field is to keep high image quality in the region of interest (ROI). Therefore, a very lossy compression scheme is suitable in non-ROI regions to provide a global picture to the user, whereas in the ROI a lossless compression scheme is necessary.

Why do we need codecs? Without the use of codecs downloads would take three to five times longer than they do now because the files would be significantly larger. How many codecs are there?

Recently, Apple announced, iAds, a new addition to its iPhone OS4. The concept is to make advertising more suitable on the iPhone and eventually, if successful, on mobile devices in general. Apple used its observations about the difference between desktop and mobile device users as the basis for adding iAds to this mobile operating system. According to Apple, desktop users are most familiar with using search engines and working in multiple browser windows; so, most ads appear with the results of a search and, when clicked on, usually open in a new browser window. For the mobile device and smartphone user, however, it's all about not having their apps interrupted or closed when the user clicks on or views an ad. Using multiple windows on a smartphone provides a very different experience from what users might experience with a desktop or notebook.

So, how does this new iAd accommodate the mobile device user? Currently, when an iPhone user clicks an ad, it takes the user out of the application and opens the Web page for that advertisement. Apple sees the action of ending the application as the cause of fewer mobile users willing to click on ads. With an iAd, the content of the ad will run with the mobile application

in use. The app will not close, it will just be suspended while the ad runs.

Apple wants the developers to make the ads more interactive and emotional. With over 85 million iPhones and iPods sold, these devices are the advertising media of the future. Apple will sell and host the ads, with 60 percent of the income going to the developers (Figure 5.13). The ads will be rendered in standard HTML5.

Annual ad revenue for Google is approximately $23 billion and for Facebook, approximately $300 million. As Apple jumps into the ad business, only time will tell whether iPhone, iPod, and iPad users will accept it or become irritated with the insertion of ads into their apps. As always, it will be the revenue generated by iAds that will be used to measure its true success or failure in the future.

FIGURE 5.13 iAds, still in their infancy, could change the look and interactivity of advertising on mobile devices forever.

Unfortunately, there are hundreds of codecs; some are for audio and video compression, whereas others reduce the size of streaming media over the Internet. If you download frequently, you probably use 5 to 10 different codecs on a regular basis. Common codecs you might recognize include MP3, WMA, RealVideo, DivX, and XviD.

Audio Video Interleave (AVI) is often mistaken for a codec, but it is not. It is a Microsoft-created specification for packaging audio and video data into a file. AVI makes no guarantee on the content of the package or the codec used to compress it.

How do you know which codec decodes which files? Right-click the file

and select *Properties*; in the Properties dialog box, the Details tab will indicate the file type and thus the codec (Figure 5.14). If your system cannot open the file, record this code and then use a search engine to locate a download.

Desktop Publishing Programs

These programs are used to create newsletters, product catalogs, advertising brochures, and other documents that require unusual design and layout that a normal word processor doesn't provide. Documents from such programs can be printed or saved in formats that allow them to be sent to a professional printer. Microsoft Publisher is an entry-level desktop publishing program that has the familiar interface of other Microsoft products, whereas QuarkXPress by Quark is more complicated and is viewed as a product for the professional.

Paint Programs

Paint programs are used to create **bitmapped graphics** (also called **raster graphics**), which are composed of tiny dots, each corresponding to one pixel on the computer's display. Microsoft-based operating systems include a fundamental program called Paint to work with this type of graphic (Figure 5.15). This rudimentary program is great for beginners and provides a tools panel with features that allow an image to be cropped, colors altered, and areas erased. If you are looking for more advanced features and are willing to spend more money, you can purchase a professional paint program such as Corel Painter

Tool panel

In most graphic programs an image can be cropped to keep only the desired section.

FIGURE 5.15 Although it is not a full-featured professional paint program, Paint provides a tool panel with the basic image-editing features and is a great way to start to create your own bitmapped graphics or edit existing images.

to create a wider scope of effects through a more enhanced tool panel. Although paint programs enable artists to create pictures easily, the resulting bitmapped image is difficult to edit. To do so, you must zoom the picture so that you can edit the individual pixels, and any attempt to enlarge the image usually produces an unattractive distortion called the *jaggies* (Figure 5.16).

It is possible, in some graphic applications, to convert a graphic in bitmapped graphic format (.bmp) to JPEG format through the Save As option. Once the Save As dialog box appears, select *.jpeg* in the Save As type input box.

Paint programs can save your work to the following standard formats:

- **Graphics Interchange Format (GIF;** pronounced "jiff" or "giff"). GIF is a 256-color file format that uses lossless compression to reduce file size. It's best for simple images with large areas of solid color. Because this file format is a Web standard, it's often used for Web pages.

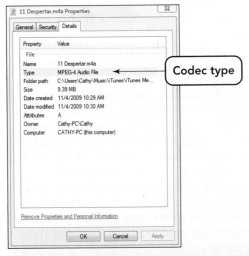

Codec type

FIGURE 5.14 Locate the codes in the Properties dialog box. If the codec is not already downloaded to your system, obtain it from a Web site like **www.fourcc.org/fcccodec.htm**.

www.**FOURCC**.org — Video codec and pixel format definitions

Intro YUV Formats	MP4V	Eval download	Media Excel	MPEG-4 Video. LEAD's MCMP codec also supports this format.
RGB Formats Video Codecs	MPEG	MPEG	?	MPEG video - presumably MPEG I ?
Graphics Chips Sample Code	MPG4	MPEG-4 (automatic WMP download)	Microsoft	MPEG-4 Video High Speed Compressor. Downloadable here, I am told. This codec was shipped with some versions of the Microsoft Netshow encoder (probably 3.0). This codec was based on early drafts of the MPEG-4 spec.
Registration Links	MPGI	MPEG	Sigma Designs	Editable MPEG codec
Help Me Out	MR16	?	?	?
Site Credits	MRCA	Mrcodec	FAST Multimedia	And I thought it stood for "Multi Role Combat Aircraft".
	MRLE	Microsoft RLE	Microsoft	Run length encoded RGB format from Microsoft. Basically the same as the BI_RLE formats but Michael Knapp clarifies: "MRLE is just "nearly" the same compression as the existing 4 and 8bit RLE formats but the 'copy bytes-chunk' always has an even byte-length. That means that an empty byte is added if the 'copy chunk' contains an odd

you create inde-pendent lines and shapes; you can then add colors and textures to these shapes. Because the resulting image has no inherent resolu-tion, it can be any size you want. The picture will be printed using the output device's highest resolution. See Figure 5.18 for a comparison of the enlarge-ment of a vector image versus a bitmapped image.

Professional drawing pro-grams, such as CorelDRAW Graph-ics Suite and Adobe Illustrator, save files by outputting instructions in Post-Script, which is one of several automated page-description languages (PDL). PDLs consist of commands given by the com-puter and carried out by the printer to pre-cisely re-create the image on a printed page. Modern PDLs describe page ele-ments as geometric objects such as lines and arcs. The descriptions are not for a specific printer and result in the same image regardless of the printer in use. PostScript graphic files are saved to the Encapsulated PostScript (EPS) format, which combines the original PostScript document in a file that also contains a bitmapped thumbnail image of the en-closed graphic. (The thumbnail image en-ables you to see the graphic on the screen.)

Drawing programs have been optimized to create art for the Web and mobile devices. Adobe Illustrator is tightly integrated with Adobe Flash, a program commonly used to create animated Web graphics.

A standard tool for diagramming in business, project management,

- **Joint Photo-graphic Experts Group** (**JPEG**; pronounced "jay-peg"). JPEG files can store up to 16.7 million colors and are best for complex images such as photographs. This image format is also a Web standard. The JPEG file format uses lossy compression to re-duce file size.

- **Portable Network Graphics** (**PNG**; pronounced "ping"). A patent-free alternative to GIF, PNG produces images that use lossless compression and are best suited to Web use only.

- **Windows Bitmap (BMP).** BMP is a standard bitmapped graphics format developed for Microsoft Windows. Compression is optional, so BMP files tend to be very large.

- **Tag Image File Format (TIFF).** A TIFF file can be identified as a file with a ".tiff" or ".tif" file name suffix. This format, used in publishing, allows very specific instructions to be attached to an image and captures as much detail as possible. In fact, most of the images in this book were sub-mitted in TIFF file format.

Drawing Programs

Drawing programs are used to cre-ate **vector graphics**, images gener-ated by the use of points, lines, curves, polygons, and basically any shape that can be generated by a mathematical descrip-tion or equation (Figure 5.17). What this means, in practice, is that the final prod-uct in a vector graphic can be independ-ently edited and resized, by a change in an equation, without introducing edge distor-tion, the curse of bitmapped graphics. To compose an image with a drawing program,

FIGURE 5.17 The elephant is a vector image generated by points, lines, and curves.

and communication is Microsoft's Visio. This drawing program, which makes use of predesigned images, has gained popularity as a method of documenting processes for business, industrial, and recreation events. It can be used to create a visual map of the process to file a complaint, create a seating chart for a conference, or produce a diagram of the assembly order of a product. Like the rest of the Office programs, Visio 2010 has been overhauled and includes these features:

- The integration of real-time data—enabling the linking of Visio diagrams to Excel, Access, SQL Server, Share-Point Services, or any Open Database Connectivity (ODC) data source by using the new data selector and link wizards.
- Better management of complex diagrams—allowing the creation of containers to group sections of a diagram related to a single task (Figure 5.19).
- Breaking larger tasks into sub-processes—allowing the subprocess to be individually edited and then linked back into the larger diagram.
- Addition of new templates—enabling change of background colors, shapes, borders, and themes and the use of live preview.

Visio is an uncomplicated and user-friendly way to move a business into representing its processes in a more visual way, and one that makes editing and reorganizing those processes more hands-on and less frustrating than editing text.

Vector

Bitmap

Three-Dimensional Rendering Programs

A 3D rendering program adds three-dimensional effects to graphic objects. The results are strikingly realistic. Objects can be rotated in any direction to achieve just the result the artist is looking for.

In the past, rendering software required a high-powered engineering workstation, but today's top desktop computers are up to the task. One rendering

FIGURE 5.18 The enlargement of the image demonstrates the difference between enlarging a bitmap and vector image.

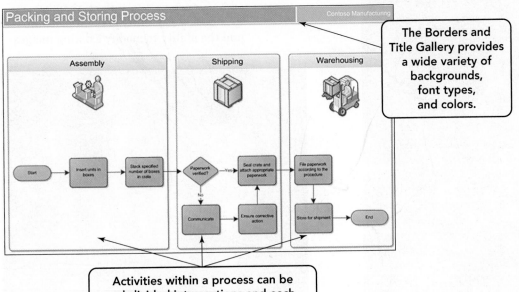

The Borders and Title Gallery provides a wide variety of backgrounds, font types, and colors.

Activities within a process can be subdivided into sections and each section diagramed in its own container.

FIGURE 5.19 The use of the border and title gallery and container features make Visio diagrams of business processes easy to understand, visually appealing, and an improvement over paragraphs of explanatory text.

FIGURE 5.20 Ray tracing is a technique that uses color and color intensity to create the illusion of light and makes drawn images appear more realistic.

technique, **ray tracing**, adds amazing realism to a simulated three-dimensional object by manipulating variations in color intensity that would be produced by light falling on the object from multiple directions, which is the norm in the real world (Figure 5.20). Detailed steps to create night lighting using ray tracing can be found at **www.cgdigest.com/index. php/night-rendering-tutorial-vray/**.

Computer Aided Design (CAD) Programs

FIGURE 5.21 CAD diagrams vary in complexity and purpose but provide detail and depth that other drawing programs lack.

Such programs are sophisticated 3D rendering programs used frequently by engineers to design entire structures and by scientists to display cell structure. These diagrams (Figure 5.21) can range from

something as simple as the design of a new nut or bolt, to the design of a bridge, security system, shopping complex, or visual representation of DNA molecules. These are more complicated drawing programs and usually require some practice to become proficient.

For a list of available programs, issues, and general information on 3D graphics, go to **www.google.com/Top/ Computers/Software/Graphics/3D/ Rendering_and_Modelling**. To view a brief video on the capabilities of AutoCAD, a three-dimensional rendering program, check out **http://download.autodesk. com/us/autocad/interactiveoverview/ autodesk.htm**. Click on *Explore*, then select *Watch Video*.

Image editors are sophisticated versions of paint programs that are used to edit and transform—but not create—complex bitmapped images, such as photographs. Free programs like Picasa and GIMP, designed for personal and home use, incorporate automated image-processing algorithms to add a variety of special effects, remove blemishes, crop portions, and adjust coloring to photographic images. In the hands of a skilled user, such programs can doctor photographs in ways that leave few traces behind (Figure 5.22). Recent versions of these programs are being praised as providing professional quality tools similar to those found in programs that cost hundreds of dollars. After using image editors to improve your photos, you can share them with friends and family at Web sites such as **www.Flickr.com**.

Professional design studios use image editors, such as Adobe Photoshop, which include the capability of paint software and the ability to modify existing images

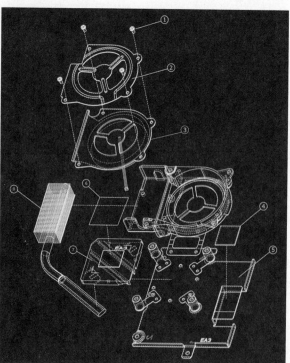

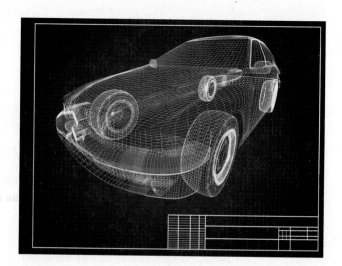

FIGURE 5.22 A photo can be edited with GIMP.

and photos. Adobe's new release of Photoshop CS5 has once again improved the program's editing and enhancement capabilities. Such features as the Content Aware Fill tool that blends the pixels with absolute precision after an image has been removed from a picture, and high dynamic range (HDR) imaging that provides 14 preset tones, from the cartoonish to realistic, can be applied to any photo. Because seeing is believing, go to **www. youtube.com/watch?v=NH0aEp1oDOI &feature= player_embedded** and watch the video on this new product release. Trick photography just reached a new high! (Figure 5.23).

For years programs like Adobe Photoshop were limited to use by professionals, but today image editors have captured a wider market because of the popularity of digital cameras. This has forced the

development of easier to use and more intuitive editors such as Adobe's Photoshop Elements. These types of programs are designed to perform the most common image-enhancement tasks quickly and easily and then print their pictures on a color printer. The programs can be used to remove red-eye from flash snapshots; adjust a picture's overall color cast; and rotate, frame, shadow, and title an image, giving your finished product a professional and unique appearance (Figure 5.24).

It is difficult to keep up with the new applications and the new versions of current applications on the market, especially in the graphics industry. Figure 5.25 is a short list of some of the current applications for drawing, image editing, and photo editing.

Animation Programs

When you see a movie at a theater, you're actually looking at still images shown at a frame rate (images per second) that is sufficiently high to trick the eye into seeing continuous motion. Like a movie, computer animation consists of the same thing: images that appear to move. Computer animators create each of the still images separately in its own frame with the help of computer programs that contain tools to facilitate the image creation as well as animation.

It's relatively easy to create a simple animation, banner, or

FIGURE 5.24 Adobe Photoshop Elements 8 is an affordable image editor with a lot of power. The Recompose tool, used here, allows for the intelligent removal of part of an image.

The Recompose tool highlights the area to be removed in red and the areas to keep in green.

The program then removes red sections and recomposes the image.

FIGURE 5.23 Current releases of applications that edit and create images are including additional capabilities of 3D and animation.

FIGURE 5.25 Drawing, Image Editing, and Photo Editing Applications

Category	Example Program	Manufacturer	Use
Desktop publishing	Publisher	Microsoft	Home/educational
	QuarkXPress	Quark	Professional
Paint/image editor	Painter	Corel	Professional
	Paint	Microsoft	Home/educational
Drawing/design	Illustrator	Adobe	Professional
	AutoCAD	Autodesk	Professional
	CorelDraw Graphics	Corel	Professional
	Visio	Microsoft	Professional
Photo/image editing	PhotoShop	Adobe	Professional
	PhotoShop Elements	Adobe	Home/educational
	PaintShop Photo Pro	Corel	Home/educational
	Picassa	Google	Home/educational
	GIMP	Open Source	Home/educational

button using a GIF animator, a program that enables the storage of more than one image in a GIF file (Figure 5.26). The file also stores a brief script that tells the application to play the images in a certain sequence and to display each image for a set time. Because Web browsers can read GIF files and play the animations, GIF animations are common on the Web.

Professional animation programs, like Flash, provide more sophisticated tools for creating and controlling animations,

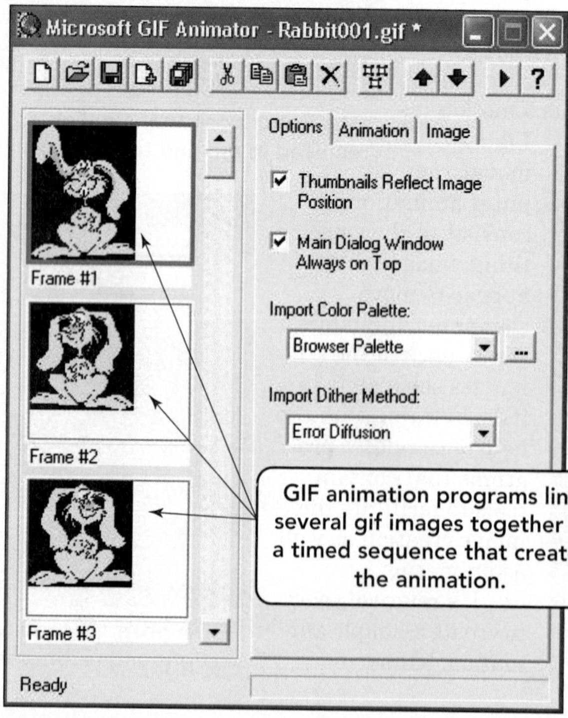

FIGURE 5.26 Advanced GIF Animator by Microsoft (**www.gif-animator.com**) is an example of Web animation software.

GIF animation programs link several gif images together in a timed sequence that creates the animation.

including a panel to create and animate layers, an extended Tools panel, a timeline to set the frame that an image appears in and disappears from, a motion editor to tweak the motion from frame to frame, and a Properties panel to display and edit the features of a selected item (Figure 5.27). The main restricting feature of this program is that it creates a **proprietary file**, a file whose format is patented or copyright protected and controlled by a single company. The extent of restriction depends on the company and its policies. To view these files on the Web, you need a special free plug-in program. Common plug-ins include Shockwave Player and Flash Player from Adobe.

Audio Editing Software

A variety of programs are available for capturing and processing sound for multimedia presentations, including sound mixers, compression software, bass enhancers, synthesized stereo, and even on-screen music composition programs. Most programs include options to create unique music mixes, record podcasts and streaming audio, convert between file formats, filter out background noises and static, and edit content through cut, copy, and paste features. Recent reviews at **http:/audio-editing-software-review. toptenreviews.com/dexster-audio- editor-review.html** have favored Dexter Audio Editor, Music Maker, and WavePad for the novice or less experienced editor and GoldWave for the more experienced.

Tools panel

Layers

FIGURE 5.27 Applications today provide user-friendly interfaces and incorporate layers and a panel of tools that provide options to increase image complexity and add animation.

Sound files contain digitized data in the form of digital audio waveforms (recorded live sounds or music), which are saved in one of several standardized sound formats. These formats specify how sounds should be digitally represented and generally include some type of data compression that reduces the size of the file:

- *MP3*. MP3 is a patented audio sound file format that enables you to compress CD-quality digital audio by a ratio of 12:1 using lossy compression format. The compression greatly reduces the file size with no perceptible loss in sound quality (Figure 5.28).
- *Windows Media Audio (WMA)*. WMA is a Microsoft proprietary data compression file format that is similar to the MP3 format. This proprietary

format produces files smaller in size that require less processing power than the MP3 format but still maintain the same audio quality. WMA is one of the most popular audio file formats and currently has four variations: Windows Media Audio, Windows Media Audio Professional, Windows Media Audio

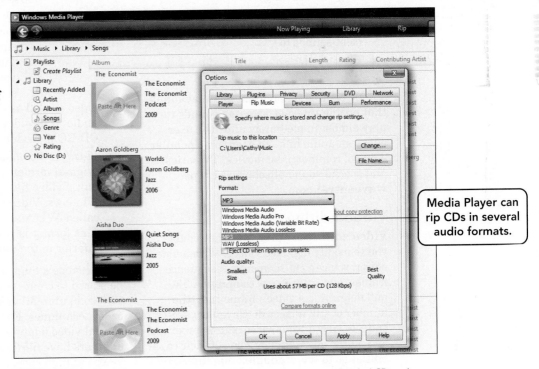

Media Player can rip CDs in several audio formats.

FIGURE 5.28 The Windows Media Player is handy for ripping (also known as burning) CDs and for creating MP3 files.

Lossless, and Windows Media Audio Voice.

- *WAV.* The default Microsoft Windows sound file format uses the .wav extension (short for "Wave Sounds"). It can be saved with a variety of quality levels, from low-fidelity mono to CD-quality stereo. WAV sounds usually aren't compressed, so they tend to take up a lot of disk space.

- *Ogg Vorbis.* An open source format that is an even faster format than MP3, Ogg files are also about 20 percent smaller than MP3 files. You can fit more of them on your hard disk or MP3 player. See **www.vorbis.com**.

- *Musical Instrument Digital Interface (MIDI).* MIDI is actually a language that enables the creation of an electronic instrument sound out of an acoustical instrument. MIDI files, generally small in size, contain a text-based description that tells a synthesizer when and how to play individual musical notes. MIDI sound samples of an instrument can be added to a MIDI song file, allowing overlapping and stacking of instrument sounds to create a flawless track.

> "**Streaming audio formats** are **available** that enable Internet-accessed sounds to **play almost immediately** after the **user clicks** and audio link. "

Streaming audio formats are available that enable Internet-accessed sounds to play almost immediately after the user clicks an audio link. To hear some popular snips of commercials, movies, TV series, and special sound effects visit **http://wavcentral.com**.

Video Editing

Video editors are programs that enable you to modify digitized videos. With a video editor, you can cut segments, resequence frames, add transitions, compress a file, and determine a video's frame rate (the number of still images displayed per second). To view a list of video editing programs and a brief description of some of their capabilities go to **www.google.com/Top/Arts/Video/Video_Editing/Equipment_and_Software/Professional**. Recent reviews

of some of the top 10 products, along with comparison charts to help distinguish between the features each offers, are at **http://video-editing-software-review.toptenreviews.com/**. Among the preferred home/educational programs are Video Studio Pro, Premier Elements, and Creator. Professional editing programs can be expensive, but they permit you to produce professional-looking video clips without having to purchase costly, high-end video equipment.

Video editors also enable you to save video files to some or all of the following video file formats:

- *Moving Picture Experts Group (MPEG).* A family of video file formats and lossy compression standards for full-motion video, MPEG includes MPEG-2, the video format used by DVD-ROMs. MPEG-2 videos offer CD- and DVD-quality audio. MPEG-4 absorbs many of the features of MPEG-1 and MPEG-2 and other related standards but includes new features as (extended) virtual reality modeling language (VRML) support for 3D rendering, object-oriented composite files (including audio, video, and VRML objects), and it supports various types of interactivity.

- *QuickTime.* A video file format developed by Apple Computer, Quick-Time 7 Pro is the latest version. It plays full-screen, broadcast-quality video as well as CD- and DVD-quality audio. It is widely used in multimedia CD-ROM productions.

- *Video for Windows.* The native (or original format a program uses internally) video file format for Microsoft Windows, Video for Windows is often called AVI (Audio Video Interleave). This format is still widely used but is inferior to the new MPEG-4 standard.

Because a huge amount of data must be stored to create realistic-looking video on a computer, all video file formats use codec techniques. For the best playback, special video adapters are required. These adapters have hardware that decodes videos at high speed.

To make video available on the Internet, streaming video formats have been developed. These formats enable the video picture to start playing almost immediately after the user clicks the video link. (With nonstreaming video, users have to wait for the entire file to be transferred to their computer before it begins to play.) Streaming video formats rely on compression, low frame rates, and small image size to deliver video over the Internet, which does not have sufficient bandwidth (signal-carrying capacity) to disseminate broadcast-quality video. Other, competing streaming video formats are available; the most popular is RealNetwork's RealVideo format.

Multimedia Authoring Systems

Authoring tools are used to create multimedia presentations. These tools enable you to specify which multimedia objects to use (such as text, pictures, videos, or animations), how to display them in relation to each other, how long to display them, and how to enable the user to interact with the presentation (Figure 5.29). To take full advantage of an authoring tool's capabilities, it's often necessary to learn a scripting language (a simple programming language). Leading authoring packages for home or educational purposes include iMovie by Apple and Windows Live Movie Maker; at the professional level, Adobe Director is state of the art.

Many commercial authoring tools, such as Adobe Director, save output in proprietary file formats. To view Adobe presentations on a Web site, it's necessary to download and install a plug-in program (software that extends another program's capabilities). Some users do not like to download plug-ins, so the organization that sets Web standards, the World Wide Web Consortium (W3C), recently approved **Synchronized Multimedia Integration Language (SMIL)**, a simple multimedia scripting language designed for Web pages. SMIL enables Internet users to view multimedia without having to download plug-ins. However, multimedia that use plug-ins (like Shockwave) are still more widely used.

One thing to keep in mind is that multimedia authoring programs tend to use lots of disk space and often require extra memory to run efficiently. Additionally, due to the intensive computational processes needed, it is advisable not to run other applications while rendering video. Be sure to read the program's system requirements and usage recommendations, which are usually listed on the packaging or in the documentation. Realize that the

Windows Live Movie Maker

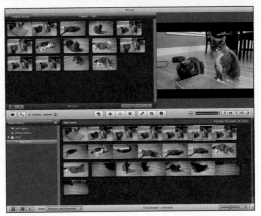

iMovie

FIGURE 5.29 iMovie and Windows Live Movie Maker allow the user to convert photos, video, and music into a movie, add transitions and titles, and upload the movie to YouTube to share with family and friends.

hardware requirements stated are truly minimum requirements.

Web Page Authoring Programs

The Adobe Creative Suite media development kit is a powerful combination of programs used to develop multimedia Internet applications. Productivity programs like Word and Excel have options to save your work as a Web page. These are fine for the beginner, but high-end features that you see in some of the professional Web sites are created with development tools that have greater scope. Adobe Creative Suite contains several programs, but the three at the core of Web page development are these:

- *Dreamweaver*—an environment in which the user develops Web pages visually or directly in code and provides the connectivity to other languages used in Web interactivity and design.
- *Flash*—a platform that contains the tools to create animation and interactivity that can be added to Web pages.
- *Fireworks*—a program that allows for the creation of highly optimized images that can be edited in both vector and bitmap modes.

FIGURE 5.30 Animation, Sound, Video, and Multimedia Applications

Category	Example Program	Manufacturer	Use
Animation	Flash	Adobe	Professional
	GIF Animator	Microsoft	Home/educational
Sound editing	Soundbooth	Adobe	Professional
	Music Maker	MAGIX	Home/educational
	Media Player	Microsoft	Home/educational
	Dexster Audio Editor	Softdiv Software	Home/educational
Video editing	Premier Elements	Adobe	Home/educational
	Premier Pro	Adobe	Professional
	Final Cut Pro	Apple	Home/educational
	Studio Pro	Corel	Home/educational
Multimedia authoring	Director	Adobe	Professional
	iMovie	Apple	Home/educational
	Video Studio	Corel	Home/educational
	Windows Live Movie Maker	Microsoft	Home/educational
Web authoring	Dreamweaver	Adobe	Professional
	Fireworks	Adobe	Professional
	Flash	Adobe	Professional

If you are a Mac user, you might be interested in visiting **www.apple.com/ilife** to learn about Apple's multimedia iLife suite. With the iLife package, you can create music with GarageBand; integrate and organize your music, photos, and home videos with iTunes, iPhoto, and iMovie; and share your creations over the Internet on a Web site created with iWeb.

Again, programs of this type are constantly being upgraded and new ones are always entering the playing field. The lines between many are blurred because video editors now can edit sound and vice versa. Figure 5.30 provides a list of some of the products available in this advanced media authoring and editing group.

Applications that Work through and Run from the Internet

There are a many types of Internet applications. Some work through the Internet, using it as the transport medium. Others actually run from the Internet, using programs that reside there.

Applications that Work through the Internet

A variety of applications work through the Internet, meaning that they use the Internet as their transport medium. Such applications include e-mail clients, instant messaging programs, Web browsers, and videoconferencing software, which will be discussed in detail elsewhere in this book. For now, simply note that they are general-purpose applications because they help us to communicate, learn, and interact.

Applications that Run from the Internet: Web-Hosted Technology

The new wave in office suites is **Web-hosted technology**, which for application software means the capability to upload files to an online site so they can be viewed and edited from another location. Using this technology, sharing your files and collaboration are easier. Windows Office Live (**http://workspace.officelive.com**) and Google Docs (**http://docs.google.com**) are two examples of sites that offer these capabilities. Most of these services are free to use, but you do need to create an account and sign in.

If you haven't heard, there is a battle in the media world. That battle is between Apple and Adobe (Figure 5.31) over the use of the Adobe Flash Player to create apps for the iPhone and iPad. Such headlines as "The Apple-Adobe War Escalates" are not un-common. Apple delib-erately left off or banned Flash from the iPad and instead promoted HTML5. In direct response to Adobe creation of a Flash-to-iPhone converter, which would have allowed developers to create apps in Flash and port them over to the iPhone, Apple rewrote the IPhone OS rules for de-velopers. The new guidelines ban cross-compilers and insist that an app must be written in Apple preapproved languages— C, C++, and Objective-C—or it will be de-nied access to Apple apps stores. This seems like a private battle between two

Apple vs Adobe

FIGURE 5.31 Apple versus Adobe: Who is really getting hurt in the crossfire?

companies, but innocent developers are scratching the apps they created in Flash and restarting their efforts.

Is it ethical for Apple to specify the tools that can be used to create an app for the iPhone or iPad? Does any other industry make these specifications? I did not tell my contractor to use only a tool made by a cer-tain company when remodeling my kitchen. It was the outcome I was concerned with, not the tool used to create the outcome.

Anyone in media development knows that Flash is a great animation develop-ment tool that does not require in-depth technical knowledge of the Apple develop-ment languages, such as C, C++, and Objective-C. Is Apple's decision to limit the tools a developer can use also reducing the pool of creativity by eliminating those developers unfamiliar with Apple's ap-proved languages? Is it ethical for Apple to limit the tools a developer uses to create an application? With the developers caught in the crossfire, this is not a private war!

Office Live provides storage space for your files and enables you to create sepa-rate areas called workspaces, some of which have themes and include sample files (Figure 5.32). You can share an indi-vidual document, an entire workspace, or even the screen you're currently working on by sending an e-mail invitation to one or more people. You can also set a person's access level by assign-ing viewing or editing rights. With the new Office Web applica-tions (Word, Excel, PowerPoint, and OneNote), not only will you be able to access and view all files on-line, but you'll also be able to edit them. The newest versions of these Web-hosted programs allow two or more people who have the appropriate permissions on a file to be able to edit the file at any point, regard-less of who is already

making edits. The only step you need to take to enable collaboration is to grant the proper permissions on the file to those you want to be able to edit the content.

Google Docs also provides file storage space and enables you to share your files with others and open and edit files directly within your Web browser. In 2009, 20 percent of Google Docs users said that

FIGURE 5.32 Web-hosted software suites like Microsoft's Office Live are popular with individuals who travel and work on collaborative projects.

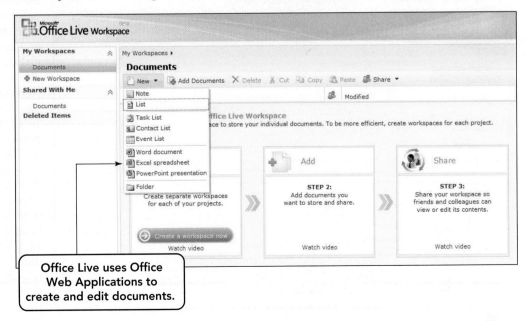

Office Live uses Office Web Applications to create and edit documents.

Google Docs was widely used in their companies, with projections increasing that number to 27 percent in 2010. With statistics like that, it is no wonder that Microsoft added the Office Web apps to its 2010 upgrade.

Web-hosted technology can help avoid file incompatibility problems that may arise when using traditional file-sharing methods. Proprietary file formats can limit file usage to a specific vendor's software or computer model. For instance, if Microsoft Word is not installed on your system, you can't view a Word file unless you use a conversion program or a free display/reader program, which you can download from the Internet. Such problems can also arise when software publishers introduce new file formats in new versions to support new features. The ability to save a file to a Web-hosted software suite can eliminate file conversion costs, because the file can be read and edited by anyone with a Web browser. A word of caution: Due to this global accessibility, passwords should be complex in design and carefully guarded when using these sites.

Undesirable Internet Software: Spyware, Adware, and Pop-Ups

Right now, your hard drive probably holds some programs that you don't know about, didn't mean to install, and don't really want—and they're not viruses. **Spyware** is Internet software that is installed on your computer without your knowledge or consent. It may monitor your computer or online activity, relay information about you to the spyware's source, or allow others to take control of your computer. Spyware usually enters your system through the Internet, sometimes when you open seemingly innocent e-mails and sometimes when you download software—especially shareware and freeware. Some types of spyware, known as keyloggers, can record every keystroke you type and every Internet address you visit. It can capture your login name and password, your credit card numbers, and anything else you input while the spyware is active. Other spyware programs look only at your Web browsing habits so they can arrange for ads keyed to your interests.

If you've ever downloaded software and then seen a banner or **pop-up**, a small window, that suddenly appears ("pops up") in the foreground of the current window, you've downloaded a form of adware. **Adware** is like spyware, only it's created specifically by an advertising agency to collect information about your Internet habits, or encourage you to purchase a product. Although the practice is ethically questionable, shareware and freeware creators sometimes allow advertisers to tag along invisibly by bundling adware with their software.

No matter how they get into your system, spyware and adware invade your privacy and present a serious security threat.

FIGURE 5.33 Programs such as Spyware Doctor help protect your system from spyware.

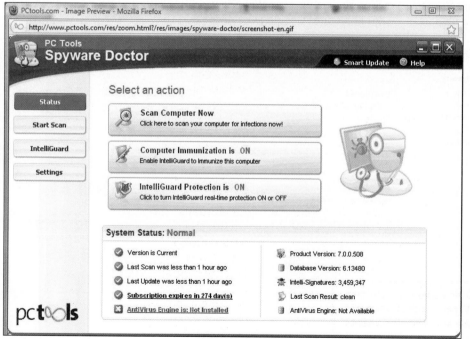

How can you get rid of them? First, find out whether your ISP can help. Many ISPs provide built-in clean-up utilities that find and remove spyware and adware. Second, look into utilities from antivirus companies such as Symantec's Norton (**www.symantec.com**) and spyware specialists such as PC Tools Spyware Doctor (**www.pctools.com**), Spybot Search and Destroy (**www.safer-networking.org**), and Webroot (**www.webroot.com**). These utilities scan your computer's memory, registry, and hard drive for known spyware and then safely eliminate these sneaky programs (Figure 5.33). Because new spyware is created all the time, remember to scan your system frequently (experts recommend at least once a week) so you can root out hidden programs.

Home and Educational Programs

General-purpose software also includes **home and educational programs**, such as personal finance and tax preparation software, home design and landscaping software, computerized reference information (such as encyclopedias, street maps, and computer-assisted tutorials), and games.

Hot sellers in the reference CD/DVD-ROM market include multimedia versions of dictionaries (which include recordings that tell you how to pronounce difficult words), encyclopedias (complete with sound and video clips from famous moments in history), and how-to guides (which use multimedia to show you how to do just about anything around the home; Figure 5.34).

Computer Games

By any standard, computer games are big business. The worldwide video game industry has predicted that the video game boom will continue, with total sales soaring

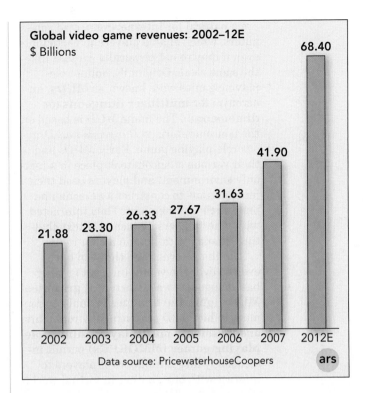

Global video game revenues: 2002–12E
$ Billions

68.40

41.90

31.63

27.67

26.33

23.30

21.88

2002 2003 2004 2005 2006 2007 2012E

Data source: PricewaterhouseCoopers **ars**

to $68.4 billion by 2012 (Figure 5.35). This highly profitable industry got its start in the 1970s, when the earliest computer video games (such as Pong) appeared in bars and gaming arcades. Video games then entered the living room with the advent of Atari, Nintendo, and Sega console game players, which are special-purpose computers designed to display their output on a TV screen. Games soon migrated to personal computers—and from there, to the Internet.

Multiplayer online gaming enables players to interact with characters who are controlled by other players rather than by the computer. Combining a rich graphical virtual environment with multiplayer thrills, these types of games are attracting increasing numbers of users. Role-playing games

FIGURE 5.35 The video gaming industry pattern of continual growth is displayed in this chart of industry revenue, along with estimated revenues for 2012.

Final view

Glass House view

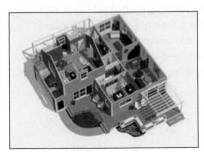
Doll House view

Cross-Section view

FIGURE 5.34 Home Designer software changes the average person into an amateur architect, allowing him or her to create a variety of structures and analyze them through several different views.

are a natural for Internet-connected computers, which enable players to participate even if they're not physically present in the same room. Originally, online role-playing games were known as **MUDs**, an acronym for **multiuser dungeons** (or **dimensions**). The name *MUD* is based on the noncomputerized *Dungeons and Dragons* role-playing game. Early MUDs and their various offshoots took place in a text-only environment, and players used their imaginations to construct a persona and build their environment. They interacted with other players by means of text chatting, similar to talking in a chat room.

As the Internet and the Web have evolved over the years, Internet gaming has changed as well. Currently, **graphical MUDS (gMUDs)** bring the virtual environment to life in 3D graphical environments, and **massively multiplayer online role-playing games (MMORPGs)** permit increasingly larger numbers of players to interact with one another in virtual worlds (Figure 5.36). These virtual worlds are often hosted and maintained by the software publisher, unlike other environments that end when the game is over. MMORPGs also encourage teambuilding: To progress to higher levels, it is frequently necessary to band with others whose skills and abilities complement those of your character.

Some MMORPGs are directly accessible online and do not require any special equipment other than a Web browser, whereas others require a locally installed game package to speed up processing. Examples of such games include *EverQuest* and *World of WarCraft*. Players purchase the locally installed software and pay a monthly fee for online access.

Recent statistics on gaming popularity, sales, age group usage, and international

FIGURE 5.36
MMORPGs bring the virtual world to life with 3D graphical environments.

ETHICS

Does the video gaming industry have an ethical obligation to produce games that have less violent and addictive content? Gaming has become a method of entertainment, with at least half of the individuals that you meet having tried to play one at least once. But is it really entertainment? Entertainment is an act that should relax people and take their mind off their troubles. Serious gamers, the ones that play for hours on end, don't seem to be getting entertainment, in the traditional sense of the word, from the game. Watching some of them, you can see signs of frustration and irritation.

Often the games have activities that are not legal in the real world, for example, stealing or abuse of another individual. Is the difference between the ethics in the real world and gaming world one of the problems with serious gaming? It is possible for the individual to have a subconscious conflict between right and wrong? Is it possible for an individual to transfer the rules of the gaming world into the real world and begin to exhibit these unethical behaviors in his or her real life? Is it possible to become addicted to the gaming world environment and stay there for longer and longer periods of time? When is it enough? How should the games be rated so that parents can distinguish violent games from ones that are truly entertainment? Can the gaming industry change its strategy and develop games that encourage a healthier mind set—one that promotes the ethics of a nonviolent society? Should the government get involved and set development guidelines and mandate a rating system? Just who is responsible when the behavior of a game is transferred to the real world and some innocent bystander is injured?

comparisons have revealed some interesting trends:

- A gamer spends an average of 18 hours a week playing video games.
- Two out of every five gamers are female.

SOFT WALLS

After September 11, 2001, programmers went to work on creating a program that would prevent aircraft from being used as weapons. The concept of *Soft Walls* was developed at the University of Berkeley under Professor Edward A. Lee. A Soft Wall would behave like a virtual bubble around forbidden air space. The software consists of a database of forbidden zones. The plane's computer would check the GPS against the database. If the plane were approaching a forbidden zone, the pilot would be notified and given the opportunity to change course. If the pilot did not cooperate, the plane would meet with resistance, similar to a forceful wind, causing the plane to change paths (Figure 5.37). Soft Walls are independent of ground controls, but that does not make the system less vulnerable to tampering. There are still many safety and security issues to iron out, but in the future individuals attempting to use planes as weapons might come up against this invisible shield of defense.

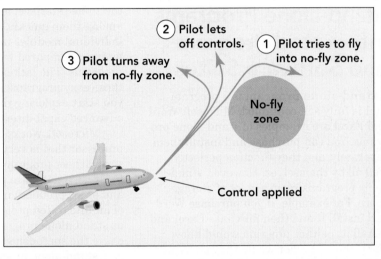

FIGURE 5.37 Soft Wall software creates the equivalent of a virtual shield around the forbidden zone and guides the plane in another direction.

- Members of 65 percent of U.S. households play video games.
- The age of the average gamer is 32.

Go to **www.onlineeducation.net/videogame/** for more revealing gaming statistics.

If you can't find general-purpose applications to meet your computing needs, you might consider tailor-made applications.

Tailor-Made Applications

Tailor-made applications are designed for specialized fields or the business market. Examples of such areas include military projects, billing needs of medical offices, restaurant management systems, and occupational injury tracking software.

Tailor-made applications designed for professional and business use often cost much more than general-purpose applications. In fact, some of these programs cost $10,000 or more. The high price is due to the costs of developing the programs and the small size of most markets.

If the right application isn't available, programmers can create custom software to meet your specific needs.

Custom Versus Packaged Software

In the world of application software, a distinction can be made between custom software and packaged software. **Custom software** is developed by programmers and software engineers to meet the specific needs of an organization. Custom software can be quite expensive, but sometimes an organization's needs are so specialized that no alternative exists. An example of a custom software package might be the grade-tracking software that has been programmed to meet the needs of your college registrar's office. Custom software is almost always a tailor-made application.

Packaged software, in contrast, is aimed at a mass market that includes both home and business users. Although packaged software can be customized, it is designed to be immediately useful in a wide variety of contexts. An example of packaged software is the presentation software program your instructor may use to create class presentations. The payoff comes with the price: Packaged software is much cheaper than custom software.

In addition to the choices of custom or packaged software, users have three other options when purchasing software: stand-alone programs, integrated programs, and software suites.

Stand-alone Programs, Integrated Programs, and Software Suites

A **stand-alone program** is a program that is fully self-contained. Microsoft Word and Excel are examples of stand-alone programs. You can purchase and install them separately, and they function perfectly well all by themselves. However, stand-alone programs require a lot of storage space. For example, if you purchase Word and install it and then purchase Excel and install it, neither program would know about the other, nor would they share any resources such as menus, drivers, graphics libraries, or tools. Obviously, this is a very inefficient way to install and use software

when the programs have so many resources they could share.

An **integrated program** is a single program that manages an entire business or set of related tasks. It combines the most commonly used functions of many productivity software programs, like word processing, database management, spreadsheet, accounting, and customer service, into one single application. Integrated programs such as Microsoft Works offer easy-to-learn and easy-to-use versions of basic productivity software (Figure 5.38). All of the functions, called **modules**, share the same interface, and you can switch among them quickly. In some cases, the individual modules may be short on features compared with stand-alone programs. The lack of features may make these easy programs seem deficient when you start exploring the program's more advanced capabilities.

Microsoft Works contains a word processor that is very similar to Word, a spreadsheet program that is very similar to Excel, a database program, a calendar, and other productivity tools. The modules of an integrated program are not available as stand-alone programs—you cannot purchase the spreadsheet program in Works as a stand-alone product.

A **software suite** (sometimes called an **office suite**) is a collection of individual, full-featured, stand-alone programs, usually possessing a similar interface and a common command structure, that are bundled and sold together. The cost of purchasing a suite is usually less than buying each program individually. Today, most personal productivity software is sold in office suites, such as Corel WordPerfect Office, IBM Lotus SmartSuite, and the market leader, Microsoft Office. The advantage of a software suite is that the individual applications in the suite share common program code, interface tools, drivers, and graphics libraries. For instance, if you purchased stand-alone

FIGURE 5.38 Microsoft Works modules provide basic productivity tools that are helpful for new users.

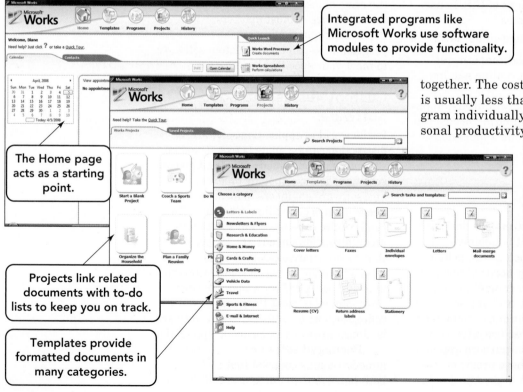

Integrated programs like Microsoft Works use software modules to provide functionality.

The Home page acts as a starting point.

Projects link related documents with to-do lists to keep you on track.

Templates provide formatted documents in many categories.

applications, each would require you to install a printer. Each would have its own dictionary, thesaurus, toolbars, and graphics library. When you use Word and Excel as a part of Microsoft Office, all of these features are shared.

Office suites typically include a full-featured version of leading word processing, spreadsheet, presentation graphics, database, and personal information management programs.

- **Word processing programs** enable you to create, edit, and print your written work. They also offer commands that enable you to format your documents so that they have an attractive appearance.
- **Spreadsheet programs** present users with a grid of rows and columns, the computer equivalent of an accountant's worksheet. By embedding formulas within the cells, you can create "live" worksheets, in which changing one of the values forces the entire spreadsheet to be recalculated.
- **Presentation graphics programs** enable you to create transparencies, slides, and handouts for presentations.
- **Database programs** give you the tools to store data in an organized form and retrieve the data in such a way that it can be meaningfully summarized and displayed.
- **Personal information managers (PIMs)** provide calendars, contact managers, task reminders, and e-mail capabilities.

To learn more about other office suites that offer Web integration, visit **www.wordperfect.com**, **www.openoffice.org**, and **www.sun.com/software/star/staroffice**.

System Requirements and Software Versions

When you buy software, your computer system will need to meet the program's **system requirements**, the minimal level of equipment that a program needs in order to run. For example, a given program may be designed to run on a PC with an Intel Core i3 processor, a CD or DVD drive, at least 1 GB of RAM, and 50 GB of free hard disk space. If you're shopping for software, you'll find the system requirements printed somewhere on the outside of the box or online through a link that is usually

GREEN tech tips

A recent survey by Pricewaterhouse-Coopers revealed that 60 percent of technology manufacturers are developing green products and services, using recycled or recyclable materials, and creating packaging that meets or exceeds global environmental standards. For instance, Microsoft has eliminated the use of PVC in their packaging, and McAfee encourages users to download their software, thereby eliminating the need for packaging. Want to do your part? If you have old copies of software on CD, stacks of obsolete floppy disks, or other unwanted computer accessories, GreenDisk (**www.greendisk.com**) will safely and responsibly dispose of them for you for a small fee. ●

called "system requirements." Although a program will run on a system that meets the minimum requirements, it's better if your system exceeds them, especially when it comes to memory and disk space.

You've no doubt noticed that most program names include a number, such as 6.0, or a year, such as 2010. Software publishers often bring out new versions of their programs, and these numbers help you determine whether you have the latest version. In a version number, the whole number (such as 6 in 6.0) indicates a major program revision. A decimal number indicates a **maintenance release** (a minor revision that corrects bugs or adds minor features). The year 2010 would indicate the year that the software was published; however, it does not indicate how many versions of the software there were previously. For example, Office 2003 is technically Office 11, Office 2007 is Office 12, and Office 2010 is Office 14. Some say that Office 13 was skipped based on the superstition of the number; others say that it was actually Office 2008 for the Mac.

Software publishers sometimes offer **time-limited trial versions** of commercial programs on the Internet, which expire or stop working when a set trial period (such as 60 or 90 days) ends. You can download, install, and use these programs for free, but after the time limit is up, you can no longer use them.

Beta versions of forthcoming programs are sometimes available for free. A **beta version** is a preliminary version of a program in the final phases of testing. Beta software is known to contain bugs (errors); it should be installed and used with caution. Users try out these preliminary versions and tell the publisher about any major bugs so they can be fixed before the applications are officially released. Beta testers like trying out new applications for several reasons.

> " . . . you should **occasionally visit** the **software manufacturer's** Web site to **see** whether there are **any** services releases or **patches.** "

- Many testers are power users who are extremely involved with a certain program and interested in seeing (and influencing) how it evolves.
- Some testers want their voices to be heard when they give the publisher feedback about bugs, features, and functionality.
- Others enjoy being on the cutting edge, among the first people to try new versions.
- Often, if an error was detected or a suggestion is used, the tester may get the software for free or at a discount.

Software Upgrades

Software upgrading describes the process of keeping your version of an application current with the marketplace. Some upgrades are small changes called *patches*; sometimes they are major fixes called *service releases* or *service packs*. Service releases keep the current version up to date. The ultimate upgrade is when you purchase and install the next version or release of a program. For instance, you might have recently upgraded from Microsoft Office 2007 to Microsoft Office 2010.

So, how do you know whether you should purchase the next version of a software application or whether there is a patch or fix available that will make your current version perform better? Well, when it comes to upgrading you should look at two things: datedness and features. Is your current version so out of date that you are having compatibility or security problems? Or, has the

manufacturer stopped providing patches, thus affecting the security of the application? Are there features in the newer version that you find attractive? Consider the fact that newer versions provide more compatibility options and include security built to withstand the vulnerabilities of the Internet. As for patches, you should occasionally visit the software manufacturer's Web site to see whether there are any service releases or patches. Microsoft software has a built-in capability to automatically check with Microsoft's Web site to determine whether updates are available.

Distribution and Documentation

Before the Internet came along, most software was available only in shrink-wrapped packages that included floppy disks or CD-ROMs containing the program installation files. Now, many software publishers use the Internet to distribute programs and program updates. Doing so, rather than physically delivering a program in a box, is much cheaper for the company and often more convenient for the consumer.

If you buy software in a shrink-wrapped package, you typically get at least some printed documentation in the form of a brief tutorial to help you get started. Downloaded software contains Read Me files and Help files. A Read Me file is a plain-text document that is readable by any text-reading program. It contains information the software manufacturer thinks you'll find helpful. Many programs also have Help screens that enable you to consult all or part of the documentation on screen (Figure 5.39). At a software publisher's Web site you may also find additional information and possibly the actual manual itself in PDF file format. Collectively, these items are considered **documentation**.

Now that you've chosen the right application software version, considered upgrades, and looked over the documentation, let's look at some other considerations you might have when using application software.

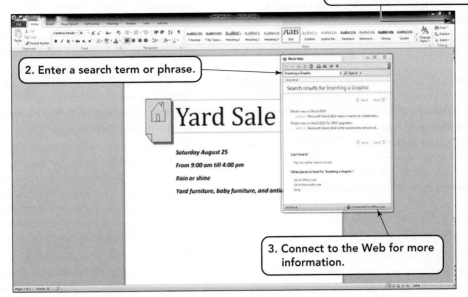

1. Click the Question mark button to access the help dialog box.

2. Enter a search term or phrase.

3. Connect to the Web for more information.

FIGURE 5.39 Instead of looking up information in a printed user's manual, you can use a program's Help feature to read documentation right on the computer.

Software Licenses and Registration

A **software license** is a contract distributed with a program that gives you the right to install and use the program on one computer (Figure 5.40). Typically, to install a program on more than one computer, you must purchase additional licenses. However, some programs allow home users to install software on one or two additional computers. Always read the license to be sure.

Organizations such as colleges and universities often purchase **site licenses**, which are contracts with a software publisher that enable an organization to install copies of a program on a specified number of computers. Site licenses offer large organizations multiple software licenses at a slightly reduced cost.

In addition, when you own an original and legitimate copy of a program, you're entitled to certain warranties and guarantees. With regard to warranties, most software publishers will be happy to replace a defective CD or DVD, but that's it. The software license expressly denies any liability on the publisher's part for any damages or losses suffered through the use of the software. If you buy a program that has bugs and if these bugs wipe out your data, it's your problem. At least that's what software companies would like you to believe. In the past, these licenses haven't stood up in court; judges and juries have agreed that

the products were sold with an implied warranty of fitness for a particular use. Some unethical publishers may bundle spyware with their programs and actually include this information in their license. If you accept the license, they may claim you have no right to complain about the spyware! You should always carefully read any licensing agreement before installing software.

Every day, customers worldwide are victims of counterfeit programs, especially Windows and Office applications. Often a user does not realize the program is an unofficial or invalid copy until he or she attempts to upgrade from a valid site or invoke a warranty. When you purchase a

FIGURE 5.40 A software license gives you the right to install and use a program on a specified number of computers. If you want to install the program on additional computers, you must purchase additional licenses.

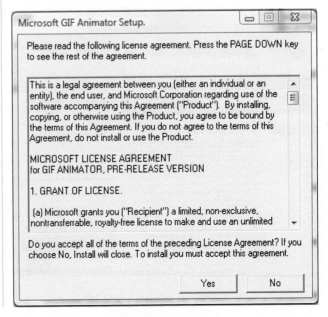

program, you may need to **validate** your software by providing a special code or product key before you can use it. Validation proves that you are using a legal copy, not a pirated version. You may also be asked to register your software. Doing so may provide you with product news or notifications about software upgrades. You may get the chance to upgrade to new versions at a lower price than the one offered to the general public. Registration may also qualify you for technical assistance or other forms of support. To learn more about software validation, visit the Genuine Microsoft Software site at **www.microsoft.com/genuine**.

Commercial Software, Shareware, Freeware, and Public Domain Software

The three types of copyrighted software are commercial software, shareware, and freeware.

- Software that must be purchased is **commercial software**. The current trend is to make these programs available as an online download or initially as shareware, to give the potential customer a trial period. Once the trial period is over, the user can pay for the program directly on the Web site and download an official copy. Microsoft Office, Adobe Acrobat, and Mac OS X are examples of commercial software.

- **Shareware** is more of a marketing method than a type of software. It permits a user to have a set period of time in which to "try before buying" the program (Figure 5.41). If you like

the program after using it for a specified trial period, you must pay a registration fee or you violate the copyright. What makes noncommercial shareware different from commercial software that uses shareware marketing strategies? Noncommercial shareware purchasers usually receive product support that exceeds that of commercial products, often including the opportunity to speak directly to the actual developer of the product.

- Software given away for free is referred to as **freeware**, you can't turn around and sell it for profit. Included in the freeware category are programs distributed under the Free Software Foundation's General Public License (GPL).

- There is one type of software that is not copyrighted. **Public domain software** is expressly free from copyright, and you can do anything you want with it, including modify it or sell it to others. Some popular sources of such software include **www.freewarefiles.com/** and **www.cleansoftware.org/**.

When a program includes some mechanism to ensure that you don't make or run unauthorized copies of it, it is called **copy-protected software**. Examples of such software include the Microsoft Windows operating system and some CDs and DVDs. Copy-protected software isn't popular with users because it often requires extra steps to install and usually requires a call to technical support if any program files become corrupted. Perhaps the loudest objection to copy-protected software, though, is that the copy-protection schemes are beginning to work. It is becoming difficult to "share" a copy of major software programs with friends and family.

Copyright or not, you're always better off owning a legitimate copy of the software you're using. It's the right thing to do, and it offers you the greatest opportunity to derive benefits from the software. You're entitled to full customer support services should anything go wrong and to add-ons or enhancements the company offers. You should also be sure that any shareware or freeware is from a reliable source.

FIGURE 5.41
Shareware is a marketing method for copyrighted and commercial software that you can use on a "try before you buy" basis. Tucows (**www.tucows.com**) is renowned for its large library of shareware.

Now that you know what to look for when you purchase application software, let's look at what to do with that software once you have it.

Installing and Managing Application Software

To use your computer successfully, you'll find it useful to understand the essential concepts and acquire the skills of using application software, including installing applications, launching and exiting applications, and choosing options. The following sections briefly outline these concepts and skills.

Installing Applications

Before you can use an application, you must install it on your computer. After you've purchased software, read the directions both before and during installation. When you purchase the right to use a software program, you are usually provided with CDs or DVDs that contain the program and an installation or setup utility. If you purchase software online as a download, it is a good practice to make a CD or DVD of the loaded software for backup purposes. **Installing** an application involves more than transferring the software to your computer's hard disk. The program must also be configured properly to run on your system. Installation software makes sure that this configuration is performed properly.

To install an application on a computer running the Windows operating system, you insert the disk into the appropriate drive. The operating system automatically senses the insertion and attempts to locate and run an install or start-up file. You are then prompted for any necessary input as the program installs.

Should inserting the disk not invoke the installation program, you will need to click the Windows Start button and then type the drive letter designation for the drive (such as E:\) in the Start Search box. A list of the files on the disk will appear in the Start pane. Click the installation or start-up file to begin the installation.

If the software was obtained from the Internet, you may first have to decompress it, although some decompression occurs automatically when opened. Most programs are installed using a wizard. The installation wizard is a step-by-step process that installs the program in the correct location and may also provide some customization options. After the program has been installed, you will see its name in menus or on the desktop, and you can start using it.

You should know where the program is being installed, how to access it, and whether shortcuts have been created on the desktop. Shortcuts usually carry the name of the program and use the company logo for an icon. If you don't want these shortcuts on your desktop, delete them by right-clicking the icons and choosing Delete. This doesn't affect the program in any way, because a shortcut is just a pointer to a program or file. The program

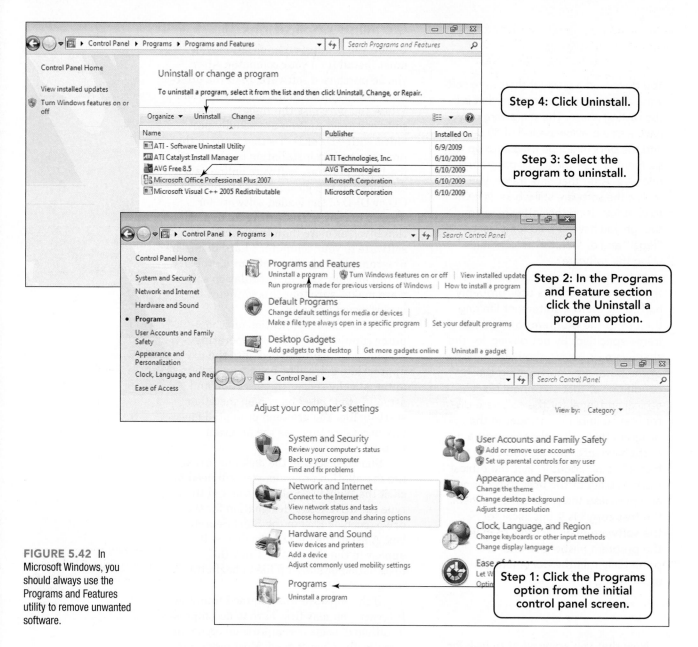

FIGURE 5.42 In Microsoft Windows, you should always use the Programs and Features utility to remove unwanted software.

will still be available via the Start, Programs menu sequence.

If you later decide that you don't want to use an application, you shouldn't just delete it from your hard disk. The proper way to remove, or uninstall, a program from your computer is to use the Windows Programs and Features utility located on the Control Panel, which is listed on the Start menu (Figure 5.42). **Uninstalling** removes the application's files from your hard disk. Choose the program that you wish to uninstall from the list of installed programs and then provide any input the uninstaller asks you for. Because most programs create library files and ancillary files in various directories, all of the files will not be removed if you simply delete the program icon or delete the program

files from within the file management utility. If you don't remove all of the program files correctly, the operating system may not run efficiently. Always use the Programs and Features utility to remove unwanted programs.

Launching Applications

After you have installed an application, you can launch it. **Launching** an application transfers the program code from your computer's hard disk to memory, and the application then appears on the screen. Programs can be launched in a number of ways. The two most reliable ways in Microsoft Windows are to click the Start menu, point to All Programs, and choose the application you want to launch or to type the program name in the Start Search text box (Figure 5.43). In Mac OS, you locate the application's folder and double-click the application's icon. Application icons are also often available on the desktop, in the System Tray on the taskbar, or on the Quick Launch toolbar.

Choosing Options

Applications typically enable you to choose **options** that specify how you want the program to operate. Your choices can change the program's **defaults**, which are the settings that are in effect unless you deliberately override them. For example, in Microsoft Word you can choose an option for displaying formatting marks on the screen—such as tabs, paragraph marks, and object anchors.

When you start working with a newly installed application, check the options menu for a setting—usually called **AutoSave** or **AutoRecover**—that automatically saves your work at a specified interval (Figure 5.44). With this option enabled, you'll ensure that you won't lose more than a few minutes' worth of work should the program fail for some reason.

Exiting Applications

When you've finished using an application, don't just switch off the computer. **Exiting** an application refers to quitting, or closing down, the program. You exit an application by choosing the Exit command from the File menu or by clicking the X icon in the upper-right-most corner of the application window. By doing so, you ensure that the application will warn you if you've failed to save some of your work. In addition, you'll save any options you set while using the program.

FIGURE 5.44 Most Microsoft applications enable you to choose options for program defaults by clicking the File tab at the top left corner of the Ribbon.

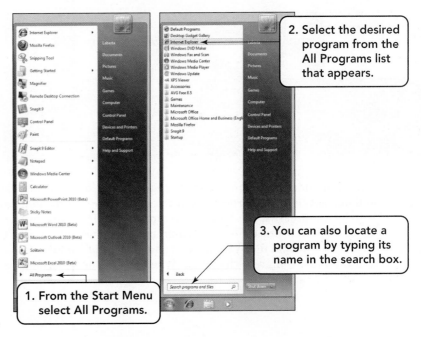

2. Select the desired program from the All Programs list that appears.

3. You can also locate a program by typing its name in the search box.

1. From the Start Menu select All Programs.

FIGURE 5.43 You may have an icon on the desktop to open some programs, but every installed program appears in the Start menu under the All Programs option.

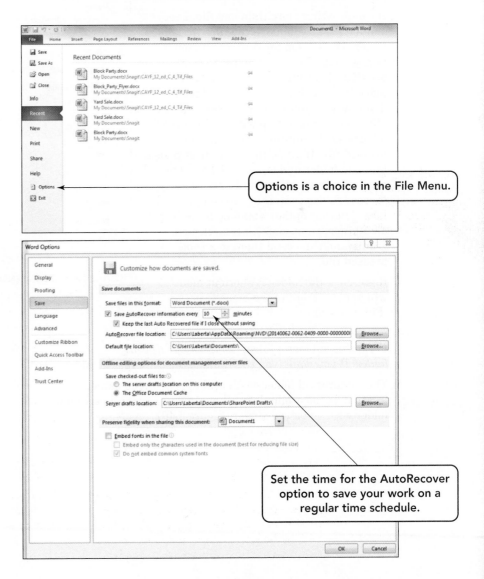

Options is a choice in the File Menu.

Set the time for the AutoRecover option to save your work on a regular time schedule.

How To:

Zip (Compress) and Decompress a File or Folder

Files and folders are compressed to reduce their size. A compressed file is better to attach to e-mails and deposit in digital drop boxes located in online course management systems. If more than one file is to be compressed, the Windows compression algorithm will combine them into one compressed file. When the compressed file is decompressed, the individual files will reappear. If you are uncomfortable with this multiple file system, you can place all of the files you want to compress into a single folder and then just compress the folder. When the folder is decompressed, the individual files you placed inside will appear.

Compression

1. Save and close all files to be compressed.

2. If compressing more than one file, I recommend that you move the files into one folder. The reason for this recommendation is that when a single file is compressed, the compression program will place that file into a compressed folder. So if you were compressing 10 files individually, you would end up with 10 compressed folders, each containing a single compressed file. If all 10 files were first placed into one folder and then the folder compressed, the result would be one compressed folder containing 10 compressed files. Another option would be to highlight all 10 files, right-click on the selected group, and then send them to a compressed file.

3. Right-click the folder. A shortcut menu will appear. Point to the Send To option (Figure 5.45).

4. An additional submenu will be displayed. From this submenu select *Compressed (zipped) folder*. If you want, you can rename the compressed folder.

5. The compressed folder or file will appear in the same location as the original, but the icon will appear as a yellow folder with a vertical zipper (Figure 5.46).

Shortcut menu

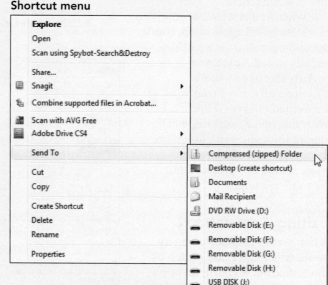

FIGURE 5.45 The compression option is located in the shortcut menu.

FIGURE 5.46
A compressed item is identified by a yellow folder icon containing an image of a zipper.

Decompression

1. Locate the compressed file or folder.

2. Right-click the compressed item. A shortcut menu will appear (Figure 5.47). Select the *Extract All* option.

FIGURE 5.47 The decompression option is located in the shortcut menu.

3. A dialog box will appear and allow you to select the destination where the decompressed folder or file will be placed (Figure 5.48).

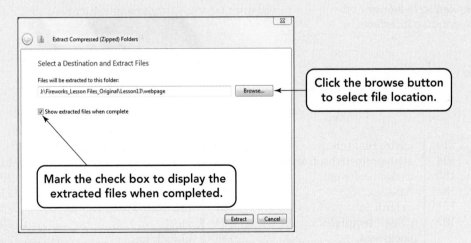

FIGURE 5.48 A default file location can be changed by clicking the Browse button and selecting a new location.

4. You can check the option to show extracted files when completed. Selecting this option will cause a window to open automatically after the decompression is complete. The files display the destination location you set in the step above.

5. Click *Extract*.

Chapter Summary

Application Software: Tools for Productivity

- System software provides the environment in which application software performs tasks. Application software enables users to create, communicate, and be entertained.

- The most popular general-purpose applications are productivity programs (word processors, spreadsheets, database programs, presentation software, project management applications, and personal information managers), multimedia and graphics software, Internet programs, and home and educational programs.

- Web-hosted technology is the new wave for office suites. For application software, such technologies enable users to upload files to an online site so they can be viewed and edited from another location. This technology makes file sharing and collaboration easier. Windows Office Live and Google Docs are two examples of online services that offer these capabilities.

- A stand-alone program provides the software tools that you need, but it is often nearly as expensive as a complete office suite. Integrated programs are aimed at beginning users and may not include features that some users will want as they become more comfortable with the software. Most people who need personal productivity software purchase an office suite because they can save money and use programs that share a common interface.

- Publishers often bring out new or updated versions of their software. In a version number, the whole number (such as 6 in 6.0) indicates a major program revision. A decimal number indicates a maintenance release. Software upgrades enable you to keep your version of an application current with the marketplace by downloading and installing small changes called *patches* or major fixes called *service releases* or *service packs*.

- Commercial software, like Microsoft Office, is copyrighted software that must be purchased. The current trend is to make software available as an online download or initially as shareware, to give the potential customer a trial period. Once the trial period is over, the user can pay for the program directly on the Web site and download their official copy. Shareware is copyrighted but distributed on a "try before you buy" basis. You may use the program for a specified trial period without paying. Freeware is copyrighted but available for free, as long as you don't turn around and sell it. Public domain software is not copyrighted. You can do anything you want with it, including modify it or sell it to others.

- Most application software shares some general practices when it comes to such routine tasks as installation, management, setting options, launching, and exiting. Paying attention to the way one application works should provide insight into the processes that will work for other similar applications.

Key Terms and Concepts

Identification

Identify each labeled item.

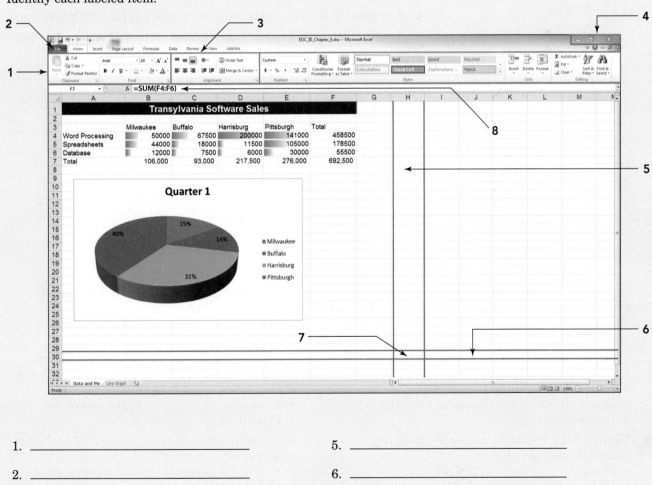

1. _____
2. _____
3. _____
4. _____

5. _____
6. _____
7. _____
8. _____

Matching

Match each key term in the left column with the most accurate definition in the right column.

_____ 1. slide

_____ 2. group

_____ 3. video editor

_____ 4. codec

_____ 5. Quick Access Toolbar

_____ 6. sparkline

_____ 7. form

_____ 8. lossless

_____ 9. range

_____ 10. SMIL

_____ 11. installing

_____ 12. launching

_____ 13. image editor

_____ 14. uninstalling

_____ 15. lossy

a. A compression technique that allows a file to be completely restored without any flaws

b. Two or more adjacent cells in a worksheet

c. A template with blank locations designed to receive information from the user; usually used to facilitate the entry of data into a database

d. A collection of related icons that appears in a rectangular region on the Ribbon

e. A canvas on which transitions can be applied and placeholders repositioned and animated

f. A compression technique that permanently removes some data from the file

g. The transferring of software to a computer's hard drive

h. The transfer of program code from hard disk to memory

i. The removal of a program from the hard disk

j. A type of software used to cut segments, sequence frames, add transitions, compress files, and determine frame rate

k. A program that edits and transforms images but does not create them

l. A multimedia scripting language for Web pages approved by the W3C

m. A tiny chart embedded into the background of an Excel cell

n. A compression/decompression algorithm

o. Appears above the Ribbon in Microsoft applications, is customizable, and contains icons for the most common application tasks

Multiple Choice

Circle the correct choice for each of the following.

1. _____ is a preliminary version of a software program in the final testing phase.
   a. Alpha
   b. Beta
   c. Bitmap
   d. PDF

2. What type of programs are Picasa and Gimp ?
   a. 3D rendering programs
   b. Animation programs
   c. Sound capturing and processing programs
   d. Image editors

3. Which is *not* a format for saving an image created in a paint program?
   a. JPEG
   b. PNG
   c. WAV
   d. BMP

4. _____ is a small or minor software update.
   a. Service pack
   b. Patch
   c. Codec
   d. License

5. Which of the following is *not* a Web authoring application?
   a. Visio
   b. Dreamweaver
   c. Flash
   d. Fireworks

6. Apple and Adobe are in disagreement about the use of _____ to create apps for the iPhone and iPad.
   a. Fireworks
   b. Dreamweaver
   c. Photoshop
   d. Flash

7. Which of the following is an example of productivity software?
   a. Personal information management programs
   b. Web browsers
   c. graphical MUD
   d. Flash

8. Which program is a MMORPG?
   a. MUD
   b. Illustrator
   c. World of WarCraft
   d. TurboTax

9. The minimum level of equipment that a program needs to run is referred to as _____.
   a. system requirements
   b. system update
   c. beta value
   d. default value

10. _____ software is software that is expressly free from copyright.
    a. Shareware
    b. Commercial
    c. Public Domain
    d. Freeware

Fill-In

In the blanks provided, write the correct answer for each of the following:

1. The _____ image type can be resized without edge distortion.

2. Settings that are created when a program is installed and remain until they are deliberately changed are referred to as _____ settings.

3. A(n) _____ application is any application that involves two or more types of media, such as audio, video, or graphics.

4. _____ is more of a marketing method than a type of software that you can use on a "try before you buy" basis.

5. A(n) _____ allows an organization to install copies of a program on a specified number of computers.

6. _____ is Internet software created by an advertising agency to promote a product and collect information on your Internet habits.

7. _____ is the technique that adds realism to an image by what appears to be the addition of natural light.

8. _____ is an undesirable program written by an advertising agency to collect information on your Internet habits and installed, without your permission over the Internet.

9. A(n) _____ is a minor software revision that corrects bugs or adds insignificant features.

10. A(n) _____ is a file whose format is patented or copyright protected and controlled by a single company.

11. Bitmapped graphics are also called _____ graphics.

12. Adobe Director and iLife are examples of _____ software.

13. Read Me files are an example of _____.

14. Microsoft Works is an example of a(n) _____ program.

15. _____ is software given away for free that can't be sold for profit.

Short Answer

1. Explain five of the shared interface features of productivity applications in the Office 2010 suite.

2. What is a codec? Why are they used?

3. Explain the difference between bitmap and vector graphics and list an application program that works with each.

4. Explain the difference between spyware and adware.

5. Define the acronyms MUD and MMORPGS as they relate to gaming applications. Provide an example of a popular game that falls into each category.

Teamwork

1. **Apps for Mobile Media** As a team, create a survey of 7 to 10 questions on the use of mobile devices and mobile apps. Include such questions as the type of mobile devices an individual uses on a daily basis (smartphone, iPad, Kindle, and so on), the types of apps they use, the amount they pay for an app, and the time they spend using their apps. Include any other questions that might shed light on app usage. Give the survey to at least 15 individuals. Use an Excel spreadsheet and graphs to summarize your

results. Look up the national statistics on app usage and see how your sample group compares to the national average on time and money spent on apps for portable media. Enter your findings on at the bottom of your Excel report. Remember to cite the references from which the national statistics were obtained.

2. **Applications for a Web Developer** This chapter has given a overview of applications that are used for personal and professional tasks. As a team, interview faculty in the computer and graphic art departments of your school and create a list of courses and applications that an individual interested in developing Web pages or becoming a Web developer should take. Using a table in Word, list each course, any prerequisites, the software used in the course (if any), and the number of credit hours assigned to the course. Use your local newspapers or online job sites, and include at least five jobs in the area of Web development, the employer, and the required skills in your table. How do the real world criteria match up with the academic recommendations? Present your findings at the bottom of the Word table.

3. **Use a Photo Editor** Download the current version of the Picasa photo editor. Using a digital camera, take a series of photos or use a team member's photos and experiment with some of Picasa's photo editing features. After making a change to a photo, save it under a new name so that the original is unaltered in order to compare the before and after versions. Select at least 10 photos and record the changes made to the each photo, the Picasa feature

you used, the level of usage difficulty your team assigned to that feature, and what your team thought of the finished image. Attempt to make a least one collage, and learn how to create an album. Insert your before and after pictures, a summary of the features you used, and their level of difficulty in a PowerPoint slide show. Conclude the show with the features your team thought produced the best results.

4. **There Is a Game for Everyone** As a team, develop a survey to determine the gaming behavior of individuals. Make a list of the popular computer games that exist today. Include Internet-based games like *Halo* and *World of WarCraft* along with games designed for specific game platforms like Wii, Xbox, and PlayStation. Have the survey respondents select the game or games they play most frequently. Ask respondents how many hours a week they spend gaming. Are they members of a gaming club (either local or online)? Do other members of their family game? Give the survey to at least 15 individuals. Collect the data and present your results in a table, slide show, or one-page, double-spaced summary report.

5. **It Takes More Than the Application** As a team, research the qualities of a good business presentation. From the ones located, select eight that the team believes would have the greatest effect on the overall quality of a business presentation. Use your findings to create, as a team, a high-quality PowerPoint presentation demonstrating your eight features. Remember to cite your references.

On the Web

1. **A Look Back in Time** It is easy to take the programs that we use today for granted and complain about all of the features that they lack. Visit **http://royal.pingdom.com/2009/06/17/first-version-of-todays-most-popular-applications-a-visual-tour/**, and review the 1.0 versions of today's popular programs. Select five programs you are familiar with from this site and, in a table or spreadsheet, list each program and the features of each that are still in use today. In the same table list the features that have changed or been added to make the programs suitable for today's users. Finally, get creative and make a wish list of the features that you would like to see each application include in future versions. Explain how your suggested features would improve the overall objective of the application. Appropriately title your report, and submit your table or spreadsheet with your insights and assessments.

2. **Spyware versus Adware** Anyone whose computer seemed to slow down for no reason or whose work was interrupted by a banner or pop-up ad knows how disruptive spyware and adware software can be. Using your favorite search engine, locate five programs that remove spyware and/or adware. Locate at least one that is freeware. In a table in Word, list the names of the programs, the cost of each (if not freeware), manufacturer, and what types of undesirable software it targets for removal. Do you notice any major difference between the products? Look up user comments and see whether one seems to stand out above the rest. Try to download the free program and run it. The program will conclude with a report that provides statistics on the number of spyware or adware programs it removed from your system. Provide a summary of the statistics displayed after the table in your Word document.

3. **Free Personal Information Managers** Do you want some free or inexpensive software? The Internet is frequently used to distribute shareware and freeware applications. Go to **www.yahoo.com** and type **freeware** in the Search box at the top of the window. Browse some of the more than 242 million sites returned by your search. Perform a more limited search to zero in on free personal information management programs. Download two programs. Use both and critically compare their interfaces, e-mail, contacts, and calendars. Include the product names, the URLs from which you downloaded the product, the file size, comparisons of the interfaces, and your assessment of functionality in a one-page, double-spaced summary report.

4. **Uninstall or Delete?** Using your favorite search engine, locate information on uninstalling software. Why is it important to use the uninstall process to remove applications, as opposed to simply deleting the program file? What is the process to uninstall a program in Windows 7? What is the process to uninstall a program in Snow Leopard on a Mac? Using the Web, research at least three uninstall programs. For each program, list its features, cost (unless freeware), and approval ratings (if provided). Present your findings in a one-page, double-spaced report.

5. **Comparing Competitive Products** Use your favorite search engine to locate information on iMovie and Windows Live Movie Maker. In a PowerPoint slide show of 10 or more slides, state the similarities and differences between both products. Your presentation should cite your references and make use of text, images, and animation. Remember to include price and any online reviews that might give insight into the products ease of use and compatibility with media editing programs.

Web 2.0

When was the last time you called a friend or spoke f2f (face-to-face) to ask a question or to tell your friend what you were doing, and when did you send your last e-mail? Today, there are so many ways to keep everyone informed. One of the top choices is using the technologies that have been described in this book and Web 2.0, which has a language all its own. "OMG GTG BRB ur gr8 roflol" is a little shorter than "Oh my gosh, got to go, be right back, you are great, rolling on the floor, laughing out loud." So, what exactly is Web 2.0?

What Is Web 2.0?

No one recognized the Web as Web 1.0 until after Web 2.0 was named, which makes sense because Web 1.0 was the precursor to the type of Web experience we now are able to create. **Web 1.0** consisted of static Web pages with no interactivity other than hyperlinks. The links allowed a user to move around a Web site from page to page or item to item. There was no other interaction of the type that would come with Web 2.0.

WEB 1.0

Web 1.0 has the following characteristics:

- **Web 1.0 sites are static.** They contain information that might be useful, but there's no reason for a visitor to return to the site later. An example might be a personal Web page that gives information about the site's owner, but never changes. A Web 2.0 version might be a blog or MySpace account that owners can frequently update.

- **Web 1.0 sites aren't interactive.** Visitors can only visit these sites; they can't impact or contribute to the sites. Most organizations have profile pages that visitors can look at but not impact or alter, whereas a wiki allows anyone to visit and make changes.

- **Web 1.0 applications are proprietary.** Under the Web 1.0 philosophy, companies develop software applications that users can download, but they can't see how the application works or change it. A Web 2.0 application is an open source program, which means the source code for the program is freely available. Users can see how the application works and make modifications or even build new applications based on earlier programs. For example, Netscape Navigator was a proprietary Web browser of the Web 1.0 era. Firefox follows the Web 2.0 philosophy and provides developers with all the tools they need to create new Firefox applications.

WEB 2.0

There are so many definitions of Web 2.0; it could make your head spin. **Web 2.0** is a set of techniques that collectively provide an upgraded presentation and usefulness for the World Wide Web.

The term *Web 2.0* was coined by Tim O'Reilly. His philosophy of Web 2.0 included these ideas:

- Using the Web as an applications platform
- Democratizing the Web
- Employing new methods to distribute information

Because Web 2.0 has so many meanings, many people refer to it by the particular facet they are using, for example, social networking. The Web 2.0 toolbox includes such applications as:

- Blogs and vlogs
- Wikis
- Podcasts and vodcasts
- Social networking
- Photosharing
- Communication
- Collaboration
- Content sharing

Let's take a look at how we use those Web 2.0 technologies.

Blogs and Vlogs

Many of us were taught to keep journals. At one point, they were very private. Some of us even kept them under lock and key hidden somewhere in our rooms. Today, many people want to share the thoughts they write. To share with the most readers at any time, the media of choice is the World Wide Web.

WHY BLOG?

The journals people create on the Web are called **blogs** (short for **Web log**). The Merriam-Webster dictionary defines a *blog* "as a Web site that contains an online personal journal with reflections, comments, and often hyperlinks provided by the writer." If you want to create a blog, you can access many free sites that provide helpful instructions and tutorials to guide you as you set up your blog. One of the most popular is **www.blogger.com** (Figure 4A). Another is iGoogle (**http://googleblog.blogspot.com/**). If you don't like one of these, just search for free blogging sites and you'll find over 270,000,000 possibilities. Hopefully, there will be one that works for you.

FIGURE 4A   Blogger is one of the more popular blogging Web sites.

Today we are all concerned about identity theft and privacy. We'll discuss the issues related to Web 2.0 and security more throughout this spotlight. The Web 2.0 tools can be safe if you take the necessary precautions. With regard to blogs, you may want to share your thoughts with friends, but not strangers. If so, you can restrict who has access to your blog by protecting it with a password and privacy settings.

If you don't want to blog, but want to see what others have written, you can locate a blog on just about any subject in any language. Google has a blog search engine. Visit **http://blogsearch.google.com** and you can search for a blog by subject. If you go to the advanced search on blogsearch, you can search by author and date. While using blogsearch and the advanced search capability, select the *Filter using safe search* option, and you can screen for sites that contain explicit sexual content and delete them from your search results. If you are taking this course online or have access to your school's Learning Management System, there may be a blog component that will permit you to create a blog for your classmates.

WHY VLOG?

When written blogs are just not enough, some journalers turn to video logs. A **vlog** (short for **video log**) is a series of personal reflective videos that are usually created simply by talking to a webcam and uploading the video. Many vloggers post their vlogs on YouTube, even though the video postings can only be 10 minutes long and up to 2GB in size. The stoutest vloggers update their vlogs daily. If you are reporting from a conference or are a personality, you might update your vlog on a regular basis.

There aren't as many sites for posting your vlog as there are blogging sites. The one that turns up at the top of this list is **www.freevlog.org/**. Depending on the site you use to post your vlog, you can password protect it, which is really a good idea. Just remember that what you post is out there for the world to view. If you only want to view vlogs, use the same Google blog search to search for vlogs.

Wikis

Wiki, which means "quick" in Hawaiian, was created by Ward Cunningham in 1995. A **wiki** is an online information source that allows anyone to edit, delete, or modify content that has been added to the Web site. Wikis are said to be self-correcting—if you add content that is incorrect, someone will correct it for you. Although wikis are a good source for information, they should not be a primary source for research or academic assignments because they are not always created by content experts and there may be errors in the text. They can, however, be used for confirmation of other sources.

There are many sites that have wikis. Wikipedia is one of the popular Web sites for information. It lists itself as the free encyclopedia. You can visit the site (**www.wikipedia.com**) and search on terms to gain insight into a variety of different topics. Even though it is a free site, it is important to cite your source if you use information you find on Wikipedia. If you'd like to participate in the community that keeps Wikipedia updated, you have to create an account. Once you have an account, you can correct the entries you find.

To create your own wiki, **www.wikispaces.com** has different levels of space for business, higher education, nonprofit organizations, and K–12 education. You can create an account, then start working on your wiki. PBworks.com is another popular wiki site. You can make your wiki private or public by assigning who can see or edit it.

You can edit a wiki in several different ways. You can use plain text editing, which we are all familiar with, or simple markup language, which is a variation of hypertext markup language. Figure 4B is an example of input and output using markup language.

FIGURE 4B   Editing a Wiki Using HTML

HTML Text	Rendered Output

`<p>"Take some more`
`<a href="/wiki/Tea"`
`title="Tea">tea</a>,"`
`the March Hare said`
`to Alice, very`
`earnestly.</p>`
	"Take some more tea," the March Hare said to Alice, very earnestly.

`<p>"I've had nothing`
`yet," Alice replied`
`in an offended tone:`
`"so I can't take`
`more."</p>`
	"I've had nothing yet," Alice replied in an offended tone: "so I can't take more."

`<p>"You mean you`
`can't take`
`<i>less</i>," said`
`the Hatter: "it's`
`very easy to take`
`<i>more</i> than`
`nothing."</p>`
	"You mean you can't take *less*," said the Hatter: "it's very easy to take *more* than nothing."

CoffeeCup (Figure 4C) is an HTML wiki software. This software gives you a sophisticated way to do HTML editing using a graphic user interface (GUI). You can preview the text before it is posted. Of course, you don't *have* to edit a wiki; you can just read it. Many wikis are private to small groups, such as a class.

FIGURE 4C   CoffeeCup is a free software download.

can see the available podcasts, **www.podcastdirectory. com** and **www.podcastalley. com** are two sites where you can get a directory of podcasts on a variety of subjects.

To create your own podcast you can use software such as Audacity, which is available as a free download at **http://audacity. sourceforge.net/ download**. You will also need a microphone that will work with your computer to record the podcast. Once completed, you can save and upload your own podcasts to the podcast directory sites, but you must be a registered user to do so.

Podcasts and Vodcasts

Do you like to listen to lectures while working out? Do you want to watch the world's funniest commercials on your time schedule, not when they are scheduled on TV? If so, consider a podcast or a vodcast.

PODCASTS

A **podcast** is a blend of the words *iPod* and *broadcast*. It has come to mean a program (music or talk) that is made available in digital format for automatic download over the Internet. Although, podcasts were originally for Apple's iPod, you can listen to them on other media players. You can also download podcasts to a computer and upload them to a handheld device such as an iPod or MP3 player.

There are many sources for podcasts in many different subjects. One of the premier sources of podcasts is iTunes. Most podcasts are free; others have nominal charges. Want to listen to a book? Try **www.openculture.com/ 2006/10/audio_book_podc.html** or **http://librivox.org** (Figure 4D). In additon to iTunes (**www.itunes.com**), which you have to download before you

VODCASTS

A **vodcast** or **video podcast** is a term used for the on-line delivery of a video clip on demand. Over the past few years, creating such videos has become very popular.

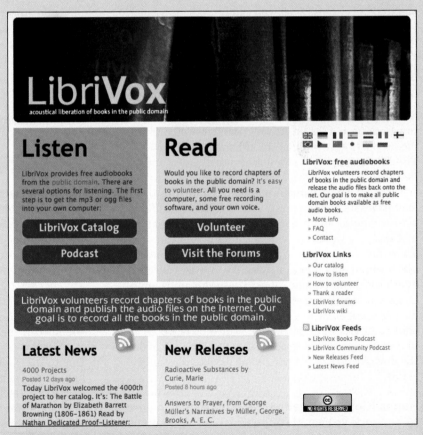

FIGURE 4D   LibriVox Home Page

YouTube YouTube (www.youtube.com) is a popular video-sharing Web site at which users can upload vodcasts and vlogs. As previously mentioned, you are limited to the size and length of the video or vlog you can upload, and you must be registered to upload videos, but anybody can watch them. The site warns users that they must have permission before they can upload any material that has been copyrighted. An excellent video on YouTube, created by mwesch and entitled *Information R/evolution,* explores the changes in the way we find, store, create, critique, and share information (www.youtube.com/watch?v=-4CV05HyAbM). This video was created as a conversation starter. Watch it and see what you think!

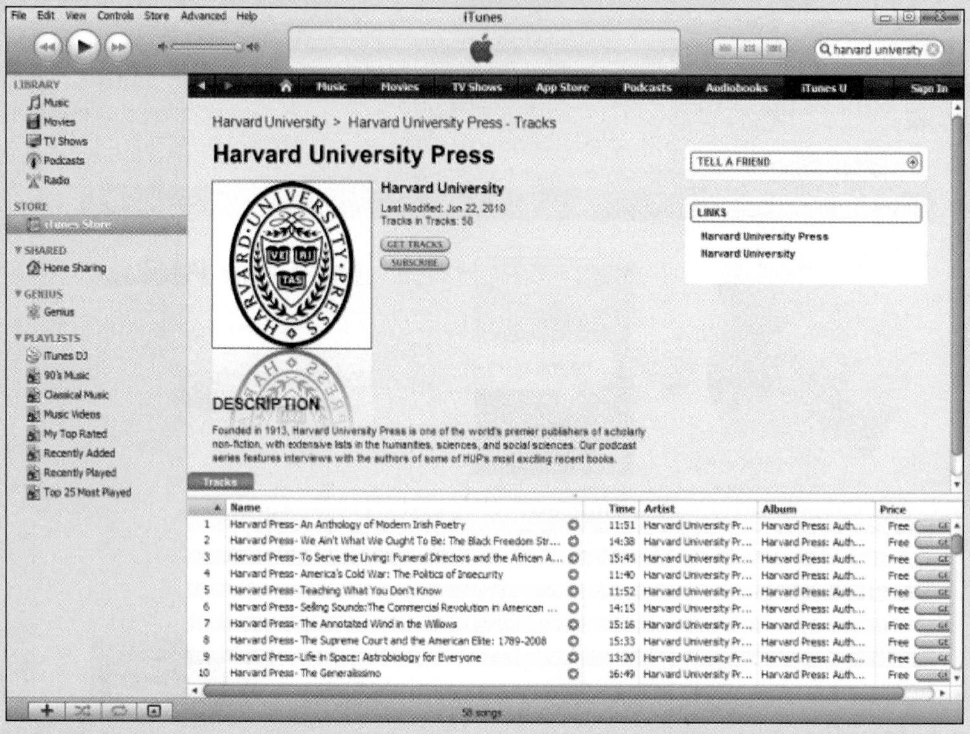

You can locate short videos on a multitude of topics on YouTube. Do you like to watch mints explode in carbonated beverages? If so, you can find about 27,000 videos on the site. YouTube is also being used by colleges and universities as a recruiting tool.

iTunes iTunes is another source of short videos. Yes, iTunes is a proprietary digital media player application used for playing and organizing digital music and video files, but it is also an interface you can use to manage the files on Apple's popular iPod digital media players as well as the iPhone and iTouch. The iTunes application must be downloaded and installed.

In addition to using iTunes on your devices to download podcasts and vodcasts, you can also install it on your computer and use it to manage your playlist. Or just listen or watch the videos through your computer. There are versions for Windows and Macs. iTunes will allow you to play music, movies, TV shows, podcasts, audio books, and applications. These can all be purchased at the iTunes store. There is a nominal charge for most, but some are free. You can create a playlist on your computer and upload it to your iPod or MP3 player. You just need to be aware of which type of device the downloads will play on. Some devices play only MP3s.

iTunes Higher Education Need to relisten to a lecture to pick up something you missed? Many professors also use iTunes as a place to post lecture supplements and other pertinent information for

FIGURE 4E Harvard University is one of many colleges that post podcasts or coursework on iTunes.

their courses. Similarly, some colleges and universities have set up a virtual campus in iTunes. These include some of the Ivy League schools (Figure 4E). Such campuswide storehouses of course content were very popular in 2008. Many schools have set up in-house access through their own Learning Management Systems and have not updated their virtual iTunes campus in years. Others colleges, however, are still actively using iTunes as their primary site. There may be a page on your school's Web site that provides access to a number of podcasts.

Social Networking

Social networking is a group of individuals creating a community. Social networking sites include Facebook, MySpace, LinkedIn, Twitter, Ning, and Digg, to name a few. Social networking provides a way for you to share pictures, what you are doing, and some of your thoughts with friends and family. And, it is relatively easy to share your common interests with people around the world. Rather than call or e-mail each person, all you have to do is post once, and all your friends can see what you wrote.

However, social networking is not without risks. Due to the popularity of social networking sites, there have been breaches in security. In June 2010, a threat called Clickjacking occurred. The attack allowed malicious Web site publishers to control the links that visitors can click on Facebook. Identity theft is also an issue with respect to safety on social networking sites because of the amount of information available at these sites. Features that invite user participation—messages, invitations, photos, open platform applications, and so on—are often the avenues less scrupulous individuals use to gain access to private information. This is especially true in the case of Facebook because of its popularity and the amount of information some people include. The problems plaguing social network security and privacy issues, for now, can only be resolved if users take a more careful approach to what and how much they share. Facebook has been in the news about changing privacy settings. It is important that, as a user, you constantly check to make sure the settings are where you set them.

Network World Panorama, a group from *Network World* magazine that interviews industry experts, presented a podcast on how social networks can help recruiters in their search for quality employees. The podcast references how companies can benefit by looking at sites like Facebook and Twitter in order to find the best possible employee. It stresses that potential employees should use their social networking sites and skills to find out more about companies to help them land jobs. The following sections list several of the most popular social networking sites.

SECOND LIFE

Second Life defines itself as a free online virtual world imagined and created by its residents. From the moment you enter Second Life, you'll discover a fast-growing digital world filled with people, entertainment, experiences, and opportunity. Philip Rosedale founded Linden Lab in 1999. He created a revolutionary new form of shared

experience (Figure 4F). It provides a venue where individuals jointly inhabit a 3D landscape and build the world around them. The monetary unit is called Linden dollars. You can use these dollars in the virtual world in the same way that you use "real" dollars in the "real world," to purchase goods and services. Many businesses

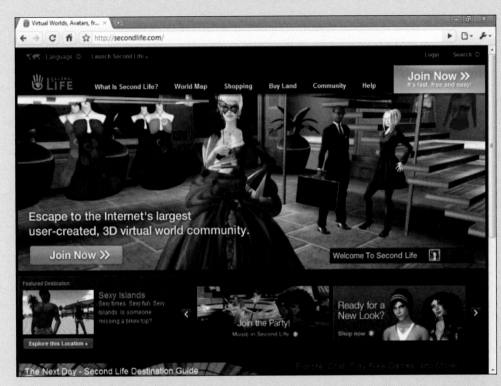

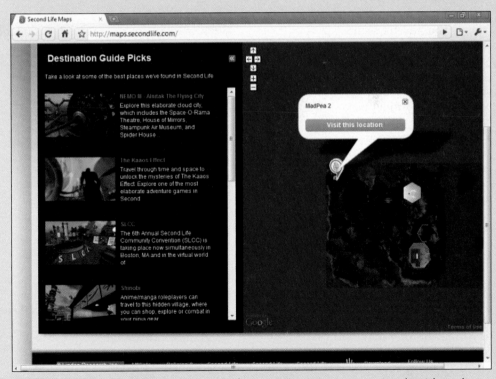

FIGURE 4F   The possibilities in Second Life are endless. Get set to enjoy the ride and meet some interesting people (avatars) along the way.

and schools have purchased land and built a virtual complex where you can learn about their products or attend classes. If you are studying Edgar Allen Poe, you can go and visit his house. Second Life has its own blog and wiki. Second Life was featured on an episode of CSI: NY in Season 4, Episode 5: "Down the Rabbit Hole."

To get started, go to **http://secondlife.com/** and download the software to build your avatar. An **avatar** is a virtual representation of the player in a game, in this case, Second Life. Creating a basic avatar is free. If you don't like the standard choices, however, you can purchase hair and clothes using Linden dollars. Don't have any Linden dollars? You can use your credit card to buy some. Once you have chosen your name and are logged in, there is an excellent tutorial to get you flying. Then visit the virtual world.

FACEBOOK

The Facebook mission is "Giving people the power to share and make the world more open and connected." There are over 500 million people signed up on Facebook—you, movie stars, rock groups, the President, and me, just to name a few. President Barack Obama embraced Facebook during his run for office. He uses it now for town hall meetings. You can visit the White House page to join discussions. People are using Facebook (**www.facebook.com**) to stay updated on what's happening around them and share with the people in their lives.

Facebook has limitless possibilities. You can join groups, start groups, become a fan, start a fan club, get updates, send updates, and connect with friends you haven't seen in a while or those you see every day. You can upload photos, share your position or political thoughts, or let folks know just how you feel at the moment. You can play games and share the score, or play games against your friends, or find your horoscope, or what kind of sandwich you are in a Facebook quiz.

Remember, however, on this social networking site and others, be sure to protect your personal information. Don't post those party pictures or anything else that may present you in a less than favorable light. Some potential employers are looking at these social networking sites. And, in any instance, keep in mind that the more information you post, the more help you give to identity thieves.

TWITTER

Twitter (**www.twitter.com**) is a service for friends, family, and coworkers to communicate and stay connected through the exchange of quick, frequent answers to one simple question: What are you doing? With Twitter, you can stay hyperconnected to your friends and always know what they're doing. On the other hand, you can stop following them any time. You can even set quiet times on Twitter so you're not interrupted. Twitter puts you in control and becomes a modern antidote to information overload. Well, that is how it was; now Twitter is just one more information source to manage. You can follow your favorite person or movie star. Among the notables listed you can follow are Oprah, Tony Hawk, and the latest movie or album. Check **http://celebwitter.com** for a more complete listing. There have been unofficial contests about who can get the most followers. Ashton Kutcher challenged CNN to a Twitter popularity contest—and won. The potential is staggering. You can tweet from your mobile device or your computer. Staying connected is what it's all about (Figure 4G).

FLICKR

Flickr (**www.flickr.com**) is an online service that allows users to store and share photos. It is a way to get

FIGURE 4G Sign up for Twitter. It doesn't cost anything and will keep you connected.

your photos and videos to the people who matter to you. You can:

- Upload from your desktop, send by e-mail, or use your camera phone.
- Edit to get rid of red eye, crop a photo, or get creative with fonts and effects!
- Organize your photos by setting up collections, sets, and tags.
- Share photos and videos using group and privacy controls.
- Map where your photos and videos were taken.
- See photos and videos taken near you.
- Make stuff such as cards, photo books, framed prints, DVDs, and so on.
- Send photos to a vendor for printing and pickup
- Keep in touch by getting updates from family and friends.

MYSPACE

MySpace (**www.myspace.com**) permits users to view profiles, connect with others, blog, rank music, and much more! MySpace is the application that started the big push to social networking. When you set up your page, you can change the wallpaper, layout, and add music. Many sites specialize in writing the scripts you can use to change your background or make other design-related changes. Just search on "MySpace backgrounds" in any search engine. Use MySpace to find friends and classmates, meet new people, listen to free music and build playlists, share photos, and watch videos (Figure 4H). You can also blog and join forums. MySpace is not as popular as it once was and is losing marketshare. In 2010, there were only 18 million members. As previously mentioned, one big advantage to MySpace is the ability to customize.

LINKEDIN

Professionals use LinkedIn (**www.linkedin.com**) as a social networking site to exchange information, ideas, and opportunities. According to the LinkedIn Public Relations Office, as of August 2010, LinkedIn had more than 75 million registered users, spanning more than 200 countries and territories worldwide. On this site, your network consists of your connections, your connections' connections, and the people those connections know, linking you to a vast number of qualified professionals and experts. Through your network you can:

- Manage the information that's publicly available about you as a professional.
- Find and be introduced to potential clients, service providers, and subject experts who come recommended.
- Create and collaborate on projects, gather data, share files, and solve problems.
- Find potential business partners with whom to collaborate.
- Be invited by others to become involved in a business venture.
- Gain new insights from discussions with like-minded professionals in private group settings.
- Discover inside connections that can help you land jobs and close deals.
- Post and distribute job listings to find the best talent for your company.
- Start discussions and dialogues on topics of interest or questions you have.

Many employers are using this site to help screen potential employees. It is a way to interface in a professional manner.

NING

Ning (**www.ning.com**) allows you to create and join new social networks related to your interests and passions. This is a paid subscription. You can try it

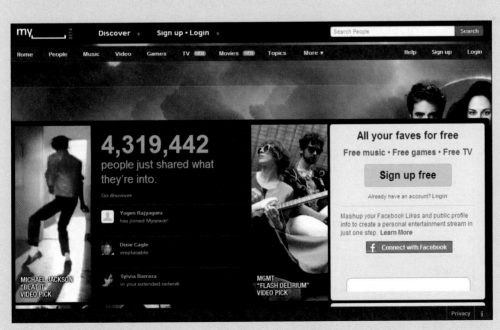

FIGURE 4H Find your friends on MySpace.

for a 30-day risk-free trial. If Facebook and MySpace are not enough for you, you can have your own social network. With over 2 million social networks created and more than 43 million registered members, millions of people everyday are coming together across Ning Networks to explore and express their interests, discover new passions, and meet new people around shared pursuits.

Ning also enables artists, brands, and organizations to simplify and control their online presence with their own unique social network that beautifully integrates with other social media services while providing the most direct, unique, and lucrative relationship with fans, consumers, and members.

DIGG

Digg is a place for people to discover and share content from anywhere on the Web. A disclosure on the Digg site (**www.digg.com**) states, "The person who associated a work with this document has dedicated this work to the Commons by waiving all of his or her rights to the work under copyright law and all related or neighboring legal rights he or she had in the work, to the extent allowable by law." This means that you no longer have ownership to what you post here. It can be copied and used anywhere without your permission. As with most social networking sites, you can link Digg with Facebook and Twitter.

RSS FEEDS

In the good old days, when you needed updates on information, you looked it up. Today, it looks you up. **RSS (Really Simple Syndication** or **Rich Site Summary**) will publish information to you and let you know when Web content has been updated or news events are taking place. Does this symbol look familiar to you? You have seen it on numerous Web sites. You click on this icon to select the feed you want. Once you request a feed, it can be sent to your computer, personal digital assistant (PDA), or any mobile device that has Web access. Want to find out what RSS feeds are available to you? Go to your favorite search engine and search for "RSS feed directory." In a recent search, over 100,000,000 were listed (Figure 4I).

As with any Web 2.0 application, security can be an

issue with RSS. There are two principal approaches for hackers to take advantage of RSS. In the first situation, the feed owner is malicious and injects malicious code into the feed directly. That's not the most popular way RSS feeds are hacked. The more common approach is for a hacker to inject an attack into an RSS feed instead of defacing a Web site. In such a scenario, the attacker would then "own" all of the site's subscribers. So, before you sign up for an RSS feed, make sure you know where your feeds are coming from. Check source Web sites for authenticity. Request RSS feeds only from Web sites with which you are familiar. Check the copyright information or learn more about the company to see whether they are who they say they are.

Instant Messaging

Instant messaging (IM) is a quick way of chatting with your buddies. There are several popular IM software packages you can download. AOL Instant Messenger (AIM) **www.aim.com**, Microsoft's Live Messenger **www.download.live.com/messenger**, and Yahoo! **http://messenger.yahoo.com/** are just a few. If you are mobile, most IMs have Web versions or mobile versions. Using IM, you never have to be too far from your buddies. The problem is that not all your friends may be on the same IM network, and individual IM networks don't play well together. If you have friends on different IM networks, there are a few programs that allow you to aggregate your buddies into one list. To use them, you also need to be a member of that platform. Two examples are Trillian (**www.trillian.com**) and Gaim (**www.gaim.com**). Many social networking sites have their own chat features. For example, you can have a live chat with your

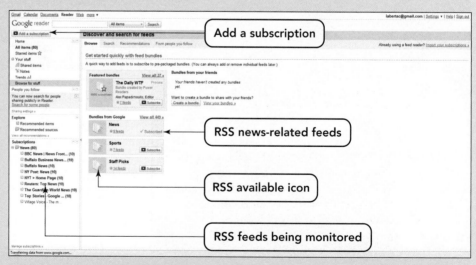

FIGURE 4I RSS feeds from several sites can be combined into one viewable location by aggregators like Google Reader.

FIGURE 4J   Chatting online.

friends on Facebook or while you're playing an online game.

Instant messaging has become so popular that many colleges and universities have IM for various departments: Admissions, Registration, and even Counseling. Some businesses and software applications have live help (chat) to assist you rather than making you look up a response or send an e-mail to explain a problem. It's a great way to provide customer service in the digital world.

When you are chatting with someone, you have to do a lot of typing. So, maybe you'd like to chat by voice. Add a webcam, microphone, and speakers to your system along with a service such as Skype (**www. skype.com**), and you can talk your way through a conversation (Figure 4J). Chatting is a **synchronous communication** activity, where you and your buddy are both online at the time and have a coherent conversation. Texting, however, is **asynchronous communication**—you are not necessarily both online at the same time. And only one of you can send a message at a time.

Texting

Court reporters have a language all their own. Gregg shorthand is a language all its own. Well, so is texting. Usually accomplished using a mobile phone, **texting** provides quick communication. Texting has been extended to include messages containing image, video, and sound content. Messages are referred to as *text messages* or *texts*.

Most texts are person-to-person, but many schools have automated systems for alerts or weather closings. Advertisers and service providers may use texting for promotions. Internet Service Providers (ISPs) have plans for texting or charge a fee for each text message you send or receive.

Because texting is usually done on a small keyboard and because they are short messages, typing full words is not efficient. Instead, text messages have their own language. Having trouble translating? Try the Lingo2word Web site (**www.lingo2word.com/ translate.php**). This Web site allows you to translate Lingo to plain English or from plain English to lingo.

Figure 4K is a short list of some of the favorite text abbreviations:

FIGURE 4K   Favorite Text Abbreviations

Lingo Expression	English Translation
@TEOTD	at the end of the day
ur gr8	you are great
Adip	another day in paradise
ILU	I love you
JAS	just a second
TTFN	ta-ta for now
np	no problem
BFF	best friend forever

You can locate a full list if you search the Web.

SEXTING

Sexting is a combination of sex and texting—the sending of sexually explicit messages or photos electronically, primarily between cell phones. In 2009, *ABC News* did a story about the consequences of sexting. Several students who thought the sexually explicit message was just for each other were shocked when they discovered the message had been shared. A 17-year-old was arrested for child pornography after he uploaded pictures of his 16-year-old girlfriend online. Reuter's News Service published an article in 2009 entitled "Safe 'Sexting? No Such Thing, Teens Warned." The article states, "In the United States, a survey last fall (2008) found one in five teenagers said they had sent or posted online nude or semi-nude pictures of themselves and 39 percent said they had sent or posted sexually suggestive messages, according to the National Campaign to Prevent Teen and Unplanned Pregnancy."

Several states have proposed legislation to prevent sexting. The legislation is designed to help young Internet users avoid sex predators, bullies, stalkers, and other dangerous contacts while interacting with friends through electronic devices. Sexting and related behaviors are also receiving attention at the federal level. The Web site for The National Conference of State Legislatures (**www.ncsl.org/**) shows legislation that has been passed by several states.

Once compromising photos are transmitted, they will never go away. Once something has been put into cyberspace, it is there forever. Just because it has been deleted from your phone doesn't mean it has been deleted from your service provider's servers or their backups. Those photos can (and sometimes do) come back to haunt those whose pictures were taken and those who transmitted them. So, stay away from questionable practices and practice safe texting.

SAFE TEXTING

WiredSafety (**www.wiredsafety.org/**), the world's largest Internet safety, help, and education resource, is a great source for information and resources on protecting yourself and others online. It provides guidance on creating a safe online presence, protecting yourself against cybercrime, and understanding cyberlaw.

Texting while driving is an international issue, and according to an article in the TimesOnline, it is more dangerous than driving under the influence of alcohol or drugs (Figure 4L). The reaction times for texters deteriorated by 35 percent, whereas the performance of those who drank alcohol at the legal limit decreased by only 12 percent. These statistics are not presented to suggest that you drink and drive. Rather, they suggest that you pay attention to the road. Avoid texting when you are:

- In motion: walking, running, jogging, riding a bike, skateboarding, skiing
- Sitting alone in a remote public place (where you could be surprised, robbed, or attacked by someone coming up behind you.
- Walking in crowds (where someone could come up behind you and either attack you or grab your purse or wallet)
- Driving

FIGURE 4L Texting and driving are a dangerous combination. Don't mix them!

Here are three more ways to make sure texting doesn't send you to the hospital:

- Always put your phone in an easily accessible place.
- If you need to text right away, stop what you're doing or pull off the road.
- Turn off your phone when you're doing something that requires your full attention.

Texting safely is not just avoiding texting while you are moving; it also includes protecting yourself. To guard yourself, don't send text messages to people you don't know. If you receive a text from a stranger, don't even open it. Delete it immediately. In addition, don't give out any personal information in a text message. Following these guidelines will start you on the road to safe texting.

Tagging

A **tag** is any user-generated word or phrase that helps organize Web content and label it in a more human way. You use tags when you want someone to find your Web page or blog. In Web development, they are called *metatags*. Using tags can bring your Web site to the top of the list when people are searching for specific content. For example, if you want someone to locate your blog on the latest way to fold napkins, you might use the tags: napkins, folding, napkin folding, and napkin folding techniques. This will help insure that your blog will show up on the list. In another meaning of the word, you may have been tagged in a photo posted on Facebook. Someone picks a photo and assigns names to the people or objects in the photo. Sometimes it is a real photo of your group and sometimes, for the novelty, it is a gag photo. You might see a lamppost tagged with the name of a friend. To tag a photo on Facebook, click on a person's face in the photo and then select their name in the box that pops up. If their name is not already in the box, you can provide it. Repeat this process for everyone in the photo. If you need to tag yourself, select "me."

A note about tagging: When you tag a friend in a photo, that photo will appear in their profile. If they don't want the photo in their profile, they can simply click "remove" next to their name. There are many Web sites where you can find group pictures and photos you can use for this purpose. Just remember turnabout is fair play.

Collaboration Tools

Web 2.0 has opened up a new world for online collaboration. **Collaboration tools** help you work in partnership with team members online. Working on a project is hard enough, but what happens when you need to share a document or idea? These tools provide a way to work together without having to physically meet. Virtual worlds are everywhere. There are many different types of collaboration tools. Some are free and some have a cost associated with them. Some are for a specific type of application such as project management, and some are a suite of applications.

One of the first of its kind is Google Apps, a suite that combines Gmail, Google Docs, Google Calendar, and other Web applications. Google hosts it all, providing space on its servers for you to save documents and collaborate. You can edit your documents from any device in the world as long as it has Internet access and can access Google Apps. Many companies and colleges are switching or have switched to these applications. For personal use, Google Apps includes:

- Gmail—Send and receive fast, searchable e-mail with less spam.
- Google Talk—IM and call your friends through your computer.
- Google Calendar—Organize your schedule and share events with friends.
- Google Docs—Share online documents, presentations, and spreadsheets.
- Google Sites—Create websites and secure group wikis.

Google Docs is a free, Web-based word processor, spreadsheet, presentation, and form application offered by Google (**http://docs.google.com**). This URL for Google Docs has information and a tour you can take to see how these applications can help you collaborate. Google Docs allows users to create and edit documents online while collaborating in real time with other users. You can create, edit, and upload the documents quickly. One handy feature is that you can import your existing documents, spreadsheets, and presentations, or create new ones from scratch. Many of the popular document extensions are accepted. With this software, you can access and edit your files from anywhere; all you need is a Web browser. Your documents, spreadsheets, and presentations are stored securely online. The collaboration feature is that you can share changes in real-time and invite people to view your documents and make changes together, at the same time.

> " Web 2.0 has opened up a new world for online collaboration. Collaboration tools help you work in partnership with team members online. "

Microsoft Office Web Apps are available on Sky Drive through Windows Live. You can get started for free at **http://office.microsoft.com/en-us/web-apps/**. If you have a Windows Live password you can log right in; if not, you can create an account. Office Apps online provides all the applications with which you are familiar: Word, Excel, PowerPoint, Hotmail, and MSN, to name a few. In addition to One Note, there is also a Bing search tool. Microsoft Office 2010 has what it calls the Backstage area. Clicking on it brings up all the controls for saving, sharing, printing, and so on.

Web 2.0 in the Classroom

Web 2.0 has many uses in the classroom. Forums and discussion boards are very, very useful. There has been some debate about the differences between these tools, but the commonality wins. They differ from a blog or a wiki in that forums and discussion boards are threaded discussions in which someone asks a question or expresses an idea and others can add their thoughts or answers. Discussion boards are common on Learning Management Systems such as ANGEL or Blackboard, where the class meets in a virtual classroom instead of face-to-face. Some are formal discussions started by the professor; some are informal and are started by a classmate.

Forums and discussion boards can be monitored or unmonitored. When you post a comment to an article on a Web site, you may not see it posted until it has been cleared for content. If you have a hobby, you will probably be able to find a forum on that topic. Having a problem with something, such as your car not starting? You can find a forum on that. You name it, and there is most likely a forum on that topic. To locate a forum or discussion board directory, use your favorite search engine. If you were working on a team project and you sent an e-mail to each member, you would receive individual responses. Then you would have to take the time to put it all together. If you had taken advantage of a discussion board, all the responses would be in one place, where each of the team members can immediately read and respond to what the other members had to say.

Collaboration is very important in courses that have you doing team projects. You can use many tools for this. Podcasts on iTunes, videos on YouTube, and Web searches are all very relevant to today's classroom. To locate podcasts that can be used in the classroom, check the section on podcasts. And don't forget blogs and wikis. Some professors are even exploring using Twitter in the classroom. They believe it has made the student and the classroom more productive; some disagree and have banned all computer and mobile access in the classroom.

The use of digital devices in the classroom is something that will be debated for years. Remember netiquette is applicable in the classroom. It is rude to have someone clicking keys while a serious discussion is going on, as is the sound you hear when you receive an IM. If you need to listen to something that is on your computer, be courteous and use headphones. Web 2.0 can enhance a classroom or subject, but be careful not to make it the only way you communicate in the classroom.

When the search engines online are not enough, along comes Rollyo. Do you have a group of Web sites that are your favorites? Or a set of online resources that you use frequently to answer homework or reference questions? Well, Rollyo (**www.rollyo.com**) may be the tool for you. Rollyo allows you to create your own search tool for the just the Web sites you know and trust. It is a perfect application to help with your research papers.

Web 2.0 in Business

An article in *PC World* magazine states that more and more employers are checking social networking sites of potential employees. Careerbuilder.com has researched this and noted that although 24 percent of employers had hired a staff member based on his or her social-networking profile, 33 percent had also decided *not* to make a job offer after reviewing the content on a profile. Use of drugs or drinking and the posting of photographs deemed inappropriate or provocative were identified as the most popular reasons why employers eliminated a candidate after viewing his or her social networking profile. So, be careful what you post on your social networking sites. Having a proper profile on Facebook or MySpace can be beneficial in your job search, as can having a professional LinkedIn page.

Similarly, many businesses are embracing Web 2.0 technologies for their Web sites. Consider Amazon.com. When you visit a book page on Amazon.com, a list of prices for that book on other sites pops up. This shows you, the buyer, other options.

Did you ever wonder who is looking at where you are traveling on the Internet? Those top five lists you do on Facebook—who really reads them? According to *Network World* magazine, LivingSocial, the company behind the application that lets you create the lists, is selling your Top 5 data to major entertainment outfits. When asked what LivingSocial does with all the data they collect from the Top 5 applications on Facebook, the CEO of LivingSocial said, "We go to marketers and say, 'Here are a couple million people into music, and here are a couple million into movies.' We're working with *American Idol,* Green Day, TNT, a lot of large brands." So not only are you sharing your Top 5 movies and books with your friends, you are potentially sharing that data with producers, rock bands, TV stations, and who knows what else. Businesses love this stuff and use the information in formulating marketing strategies.

Safety and Privacy

Here are some tips for safe social networking to help you have a good experience. After all, participating in online social networking sites leaves a trail of personal information that can make stealing your identity a whole lot easier.

" . . . although **24 percent** of **employers** had hired a staff member **based on** his or her **social-networking-profile**, 33 percent had also decided *not* to make a **job offer** after reviewing the **content** on a **profile**. "

- Beware of giving out too much information. You never want to share your Social Security number (including just the last four digits), your birth date, home address, or phone number. Protect all your passwords, PINs, bank account numbers, and credit card information.

- Use the privacy options. Don't let people who you do not know see your information.

- Don't trust, just verify. Verify the page belongs to who it says it does. For URLs and domain names, you can do this by going to **www.whois.com** and doing a WHOIS lookup. That will tell you who owns a domain name.

- Control comments. You can set comments so they can't be left anonymously. However, this will not stop people from using false names. Therefore, you may not want comments to post until you approve them.

- Avoid sharing personal details accidentally. Be careful about what information you list.

- Search yourself. It is a good idea to search your name on several search engines and to check your profile as others see it on the social networking sites.

- Don't violate your school or company's social networking policies. Be aware of the acceptable use policies (AUP) of your school or company, and follow them.

- Learn how Web sites can use your information. Read the privacy statement.

- Don't play the popularity content. There is no race to see who has the most friends. Do not invite strangers into your networks.

- Create smaller social networks. You may be better served by creating a smaller, more personal network using Ning.

Web 2.0 is an exciting concept. Use it, but be careful about abusing it. Protect yourself from fraud and you will be able to enjoy the benefits. So, what's next?

Web 3.0?

Some experts believe the next generation of the Web, **Web 3.0**, will make tasks like your search for movies and food faster and easier. Many of these experts believe that the Web 3.0 browser will act like a personal assistant, learning what you are interested in as you browse. The more you use the Web, the more your browser learns about you and the less specific you'll need to be with your questions. You'll be able to sit back and let the Internet do all the work for you.

Some experts insist that the trend that could help the development of Web 3.0 is the **mashup**, which combines two or more applications into a single application. As an example, programs that allow users to review restaurants and at the same time locate them with Google Maps are mashups. Some Internet experts believe that in Web 3.0, creating mashups will be so easy anyone should be able to do it.

Smartphones provide many of these search functions. Just use the movie app and you can discover movies and showtimes at the local theater. The Web is with us all the time through our smartphones. Now more than ever, we are keeping in touch with friends and family. Many of us have added them to our social networks. Just remember, when you post that you are going to the Bahamas for Spring Break, everyone on your social network knows. Who knows who might say something to someone whom you would rather not know that you are away and where you are.

Key Terms and Concepts

Multiple Choice

Circle the correct choice for each of the following.

1. The information in a wiki can _____.
   a. be accepted as the truth
   b. be updated by anyone
   c. be updated only by experts
   d. never be updated

2. Instant messaging is _____.
   a. synchronous communication
   b. asynchronous communication
   c. always secure
   d. only available on computers

3. Which of the following is *not* an example of a Web 2.0 application?
   a. Netscape Navigator   b. YouTube
   c. Facebook   d. Blogger

4. If a blog has a high amount of traffic, which of the following statements is true?
   a. The blog earns a lot of revenue.
   b. The blog has a lot of readers.
   c. The blog's author posts multiple blog entries on a daily basis.
   d. The blog contains a number of links to other sites.

5. Which of the following can be used to notify you when a blog or Web site has posted new content?
   a. blog
   b. wiki
   c. SRS feed
   d. RSS feed

6. It is dangerous to text your friends while _____.
   a. you are sitting in your room
   b. you are driving a car
   c. you are a passenger in a car
   d. you are in class

7. Which of the following is an example of a social network designed for professionals?
   a. LinkedIn
   b. MySpace
   c. Twitter
   d. Facebook

8. Which of the following sites can be used to create your own social network?
   a. Facebook
   b. YouTube
   c. LinkedIn
   d. Ning

9. Podcasts that contain videos are sometimes referred to as _____.
   a. video casts
   b. vodcasts
   c. audio casts
   d. broadcasts

10. The term Web 2.0 can best be defined as
    a. a set of techniques that collectively provide an upgraded presentation and usefulness for the World Wide Web.
    b. the term used to describe the new programming language used to create content for the Web.
    c. the term that venture capitalists use to describe the World Wide Web.
    d. an expression that describes technology used to promote and create dotcom businesses.

Spotlight Exercises

1. With your instructor's permission, set up a classroom discussion board. Use it to discuss Web 3.0 and how you believe it can be used in the business world. Send the link to your instructor so he or she can follow the discussion. Write a one-page paper on the advantages and disadvantages of discussion boards.

2. In small groups of three or four, create a Google Site page for your group. Each person in the classroom should set up an ID. Everyone should be invited to join each group. Take time to post to the page and share ideas. Add an event, chat with a classmate. Write a one-page paper on how you could use Google Sites in all your classes. How did you like the opportunity to set up your own social network?

3. To gain experience in setting up a community, create a blog on one of the blogging sites about the impact smartphones are having and share the address with the class. If you created a Google Sites page, use it to share the address. Write a one-page paper detailing your blogging experience. What did you like and/or dislike? Be sure to comment on two of your classmates' blogs.

4. Set up a Windows Live account. Then access Microsoft Office Web Apps. Create a simple document about the advantages to using an online application to create documents. Share it with your classmates and your instructor.

5. If you do not have an account on Second Life, set one up. Go through the tutorial on how to use Second Life. Communicate with one of your classmates through the chat. Write a one- to two-page paper on your experience. Did you like the site? Did you find it easy to manipulate your avatar? Will you go back and do some more exploring. What are some of the benefits and drawbacks of Second Life? Include a screen capture of your avatar in your paper.

6. With RSS feeds becoming more popular, create and share your feeds. Create a free online Bloglines account (**www.bloglines.com**) for yourself and subscribe to at least 10 newsfeeds to your reader using Bloglines tutorial steps 1 through 3 for instructions. You can search for the tutorial on Google videos. Once you have created your account, subscribe to several of your classmates' feeds. This is as easy as typing the blog URL into the subscribe field in Bloglines. Try it—it's easy! Then try adding a few other types of news feeds from news sources.

chapter 6

The Internet and the World Wide Web

Chapter Objectives

It seems that being connected 24/7 has become a necessity in our world and that the Internet is no longer just for fun, but for work, social contact, education, and everyday information. You know how to use the Internet, but do you know how to use it effectively? How would you rate your search skills? How do you know whether the information from a Web source is reputable? Are you a potential victim of cybercrime? Is the site you are about to provide with your credit card number a secure site?

The Internet has created a shift in communication methods by providing a medium that allows interactivity. With the Internet, individuals can create information as well as consume it. Perhaps that is its real appeal, the ability to speak and be heard around the world, which is propelling its use to regions and populations isolated from media in the past.

The Internet offers many benefits and is ripe with pitfalls for those who don't understand it and the responsibilities that go along with Internet usage. This chapter is your guide to understanding the Internet and using it safely for personal, educational, and business purposes. Key concepts include those listed here:

- How the Internet works and how you connect to it
- The difference between the Web and Internet
- An overview of the different browsers
- The parts of a Web address
- Tools and strategies to streamline your Internet searches
- Key Internet services such as e-mail, chats, instant messaging, social networking, online discussions, and electronic mailing lists
- Different types of e-commerce
- Good online behavior and safe surfing techniques ■

Check out **f** Facebook for our latest updates

www.facebook.com

What Is the Internet and How Does It Work?

The **Internet**, also called the **Net**, is a global computer network made up of thousands of privately and publicly owned computers and networks that grew and interlinked, over time, into one giant network. In short, the Internet is a network of networks.

This idea of connecting computers of different designs and over distant locations started in the 1960s with the U.S. Department of Defense and project called ARPANET (Advanced Research Projects Agency Network). The purpose of the project was to create a form of secure communication for military and scientific purposes and to create a method for transferring such communications between computers. The outcome of the project was a network that consisted of four computers located at The University of California at Los Angeles, the University of California at Santa Barbara, the University of Utah, and Stanford Research Institute. In turn, each of these four nodes connected hundreds of other computers to the network. The Internet is the offspring of the ARPANET project. To learn more about the history of the Internet, go to **www.isoc.org/internet/history/brief. shtml**, a page posted by The Internet Society, an organization for professionals who are interested in supporting the technical development of the Internet.

Today, the Internet is composed of more than 750 million hosts. A **host** is a computer that has two-way access to other computers; it can receive requests and reply to those requests. These hosts are interconnected and geographically spread out over the world. Figure 6.1 provides a simplified image of a single network that is set up to provide its users with access to the Internet and any of its hosts. A study done by the Internet Systems Consortium substantiates the astronomical growth of the Internet by citing an increase of over 208 million hosts between 2008 and 2010.

The Internet has come a long way since its inception as a communication and file-exchange network for government agencies; scientific research; and, later, academic institutions. Today it has become a medium for discovering and exploring information, marketing products, shopping, taking classes, and socializing (Figure 6.2). Through a combination of surveys done by comScore, Inc., a global leader in measuring the digital world, the global Internet audience (defined as users ages 15 and older) as of December 2009, using home and work computers, was approaching 2 billion unique visitors. With these numbers constantly on the rise, the leap to three billion users is expected to come quickly.

But technology is not equally distributed, and Internet access and usage is no different. Countries or regions in which over 70 percent of the population has Internet access include the United States, Canada, Japan, United Kingdom, South Korea, and Spain. Countries in which less than 40 percent of the populate has Internet access include China, India, Brazil, Mexico, and the Philippines. The bar graph in Figure 6.3 makes this inequity even more apparent.

Now that you know what the Internet is and a little about how it started, let's explore how it works and how it is used.

How the Internet Works

The unique feature about the Internet is that nobody owns it. It is best thought of as the granddaddy of networks in which

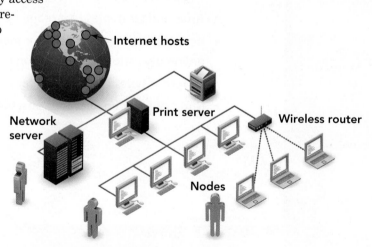

FIGURE 6.1 Both wired and wireless technologies are used to connect to the Internet.

every connected computer can exchange data with any other computer on the network. The term **cyberspace** is often used when talking about the Internet. It's an appropriate term because it captures the concept of the intangible, nonphysical territory that the Internet encompasses. The networks that make up the Internet are not maintained by one company or organization. Instead, the Internet is maintained by a conglomerate of volunteers across the world. Some governing bodies restrict control and/or provide equipment. But the majority of network servers and connectivity equipment are provided by universities, telecommunications companies, businesses, corporations, and services that sell Internet access. It really is amazing that it all works!

Architecture

The **Internet backbone**, the main high-speed routes through which data travels, are maintained by **network service providers (NSPs)** such as AT&T, NCI, Sprint, BBN, and UUNET. The equipment of these providers is linked at **network access points (NAPs)** so that data may, for example, begin its journey on a segment maintained by AT&T but cross over to a Sprint segment in order to reach its destination. Between your computer or business network and the Internet backbone are **routers**, specialized devices that connect networks, locate the best path of transmission, and ensure that your data reaches its destination (Figure 6.4). Visit **www.internet2.edu/about/** for information on a nonprofit consortium of universities, government agencies, and computer and telecommunication companies in over 50 countries that develop and deploy advanced networking applications and technologies.

Interoperability

The Internet does more than merely allow the free exchange of data among millions of computers; it provides the ability for computers to exchange data

Social network
www.facebook.com

Entertainment
www.apple.com/itunes/store

FIGURE 6.2 The Internet, with applications in education, entertainment, marketing, and social networking, is the fastest and most universal form of mass media ever developed.

Source: www.internetworldstats.com/stats.htm

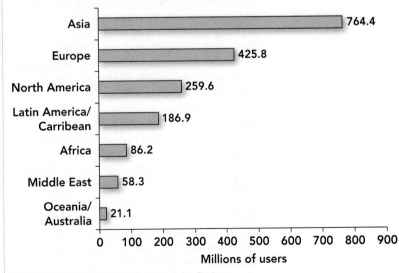

FIGURE 6.3 Internet Users by Geographic Region

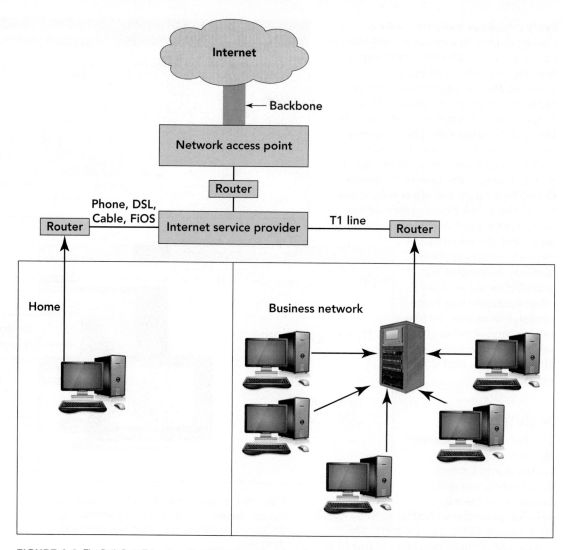

FIGURE 6.4 The Path Data Takes from Your Computer to the Internet

regardless of the brand, model, or operating system the computers are running. This feature is called **interoperability**. This remarkable characteristic of the Internet comes into play every time you use the network. When you access the Internet using a Mac, for example, you contact a variety of machines that may include other Macs, Windows PCs, UNIX machines, and even mainframe computers. You don't know what type of computer you're accessing and it doesn't make any difference.

The Internet's interoperability helps explain the network's popularity. No network could match the Internet's success if it forced people to use just one or two types of computers. The **TCP/IP (Transmission Control Protocol/ Internet Protocol)** suite of protocols, which supply the standard methods of

packaging and transmitting information on the Internet are responsible for enabling interoperability (see Figure 6.5). When you obtain direct access to the Internet, usually through an Internet access provider, your computer is provided with a copy of the TCP/IP programs just as is every other computer that is connected to the Internet. The TCP/IP suite employs a two-layer communication design. The TCP layer, **Transmission Control Protocol**, manages the assembling of a message or file into smaller packets that are transmitted over the Internet and then received by a TCP layer on the destination computer that reassembles the packets into the original message. The lower layer, the **Internet Protocol (IP)**, handles the address part of each packet so that it gets to the right destination.

Now that you've learned about how the Internet works, the next section explores how you go about getting online.

Accessing the Internet: Going Online

When you access the Internet, it is referred to as *going online.* You usually do not connect directly to the Internet backbone. Instead, you usually connect to an Internet access provider that in turn connects you to the backbone via some type of wired or wireless connection.

Internet Access Providers

Internet access providers are companies or businesses that provide access to via Internet free, for a fixed monthly charge, or for an itemized per use fee.

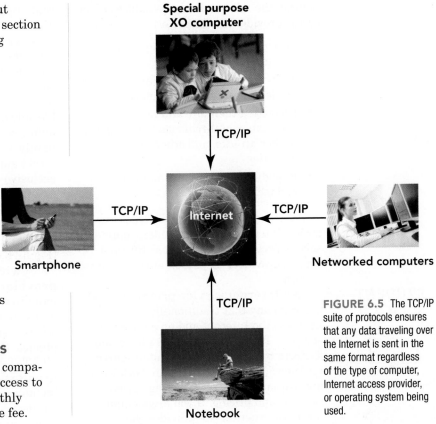

FIGURE 6.5 The TCP/IP suite of protocols ensures that any data traveling over the Internet is sent in the same format regardless of the type of computer, Internet access provider, or operating system being used.

GREEN tech tips

It is easy to think of the Internet as just something out there, an intangible, having no effect on our physical world. In reality, 2009 estimates indicate that Internet data centers worldwide consumed 2 percent of global electricity production. Most of the energy was to power forced-air cooling systems in the data centers. One data center operator compared the heat emitted from a rack of servers in a data center to the amount of heat emitted by a 7-foot stack of toaster ovens. The energy to cool such centers undoubtedly did not come from green sources and cost $30 billion (U.S.).

Another way to cool the data centers is under development, with a working model named Aquasar expected to be completed in 2010. This new idea is to use water, not air, to cool the computing environment. Water cooled to 60–70°C (158°F), cool enough to keep the processing chips below their maximum heat of 85°C (185°F), will be pumped through tiny channels in the computer systems of the data centers and will absorb heat from the metal along the way. The working model, developed by IBM Zurich and the Swiss Federal Institute of Technology Zurich (ETH), will be located on the ETH campus. In this prototype, the water used to absorb the heat from the computer systems will release that heat into the building and then recirculate to cool the computer system. It is estimated that this system will reduce the carbon footprint of the ETH campus by 85 percent and save up to 30 tons of carbon emissions a year. For more information, go to **www.youtube.com/watch?v=FbGyAXsLzIc** to view a video on this new cooling concept. ●

Some of the roles and responsibilities of an access provider are listed here:

- Providing and maintaining a connection to the Internet
- Supporting the hardware and software needed to service that connection
- Protecting their site and network from external threats such as viruses, hacker attacks, and other illegal activities
- Providing 24-hour customer service and technical support

Access providers fall into three categories: Internet service providers, online service providers, and wireless Internet service providers. Let's look at the features of each.

STUDENT VIDEO

An **Internet service provider (ISP)** is a company that traditionally provided access to the Internet and no additional services. Today these providers have added features to make them a one-stop source for Internet services. There are both local and national ISPs, each having varied services and pricing. If you are looking for an Internet service provider, you might want to start with "The List" (**www.thelist.com**). This is a buyer's guide to ISPs and can be searched by area or country.

An **online service provider (OSP)** is a for-profit firm that provides a proprietary network and offers special services

that are available only to subscribers. Members may participate in instant messaging, chat rooms, and discussions, and take advantage of fee-based content, such as magazines and newspapers. When they began, online services provided a large amount of content that was accessible only by those who subscribed to that online service, whereas ISPs predominantly served to provide access to the Internet and generally provided little, if any, exclusive content of their own. The distinction between these two services has become less defined as OSPs today offer Internet access and ISPs offer more user services. Popular OSPs are MSN and AOL (Figure 6.6).

A **wireless Internet service provider** can be a local or national company that provides wireless Internet access to computers and other mobile devices, such as notebooks and smartphones. Some familiar providers are AT&T, T-Mobile, and Verizon Wireless. Requirements for a wireless connection include a portable device, an internal wireless adapter or a USB port for connecting an external adapter, and a wireless Internet access plan from a provider. Wireless connectivity for portable devices in your home or office is usually provided through a wireless router located in close proximity and connected to your provider. A **hot spot** is usually a public location like an airport, college campus, or coffee shop that provides Internet access for devices fitted with the wireless technology listed above. Some hot spots allow free access; others charge a nominal fee. When using a connection at a hotspot, always turn on your system's firewall and avoid accessing private information because transmissions at these locations are usually not encrypted and are susceptible to detection by others. For a list of free Internet access locations by state go to **www.wififreespot .com**.

To access the Internet backbone, access providers distribute software that runs on users' computers to enable the connection. Essentially, the provider acts

Access to e-mail and messenger require a sign-in.

Links to news events, careers, and finance.

FIGURE 6.6 Internet access providers, such as MSN, AT&T, and Comcast, provide Internet access and extra features to meet the needs of both individual and business subscribers.

as an access ramp to an expressway; in this case, the expressway is the Internet backbone. These various providers usually charge a monthly fee for Internet access, again like the fee you pay to use some expressways, but you can sometimes obtain free trial accounts for a certain number of days or hours.

Now that the difference between access providers has been covered, let's move on to the various types of physical connections that can be used to gain entry to the Internet.

Connection Options

In addition to obtaining an Internet account, you have to decide how you will access the Internet (Figure 6.7). Be aware that the speed of access advertised by an access provider is often a maximum. Few users actually find their usage reaching these advertised numbers. Your access choices typically include the following options:

- **Dial-up access.** If you are searching for an affordable connection solution and speed is not a high priority, then a dial-up provider will likely meet your needs. A dial-up connection does not require any special hardware; it uses your existing phone jack and dial-up modem configurations.

The downside of this type of access is the speed; it is the slowest of all Internet services. Many people use a dial-up connection as a backup for their existing broadband service.

- **Digital subscriber line (DSL).** A DSL connection offers faster access speeds than dial-up, while making use of ordinary phone lines with the addition of a special external modem. One drawback of DSL is that service doesn't extend more than a few miles from a telephone switching station or central office (CO). Although this distance is being extended, DSL service may be unavailable in some rural areas.
- **Cable access.** Many cable TV companies provide permanent online connections and offer high-speed Internet access, comparable to—and sometimes surpassing—DSL speeds. No phone line is needed, but a cable modem is required.
- **Satellite access.** If your geographical area has been overlooked by DSL and cable providers, go outside. If you have a clear view of the sky, then you can most likely get high-speed satellite Internet service! The connection to your high-speed satellite service is comprised of both indoor and outdoor equipment. Outside,

FIGURE 6.7 Types of Internet Access

Type	Price Range per Month	Speed of Access (receiving data)	Advantages	Disadvantages
Dial-up	$5 to $20	Slow: 56 kilobits per second (Kbps)	Availability Low user cost	Slow speed
DSL	$10 to $30	Average: 1.5 megabits per second (Mbps) Maximum: 7+ Mbps	Speed Reliability	Availability High user cost
Cable	$30 to $60	Average: 3 Mbps Maximum: 30+ Mbps	Speed Reliability	Availability High user cost
Satellite	$60 to $100	Average: 700 Kbps Maximum: 1.5 Mbps	Availability Speed	High user cost Reliability
Fiber-optic service	$40 to $140	Average: 15 Mbps Maximum: 50+ Mbps	Speed	Availability High user cost

there is an antenna and electronics to transmit and receive data, along with a connection to a small, unobtrusive dish. This equipment connects to an indoor receive unit (IRU) and indoor transmit unit (ITU) that connect to your computer through a simple USB connector. Satellite is more costly than cable or DSL, but if you live in a rural area, it might be a viable alternative to dial-up.

- **Fiber-optic service.** Fiber-optic lines running directly to the home provide users with an incredibly fast Internet connection, easily surpassing other methods. With more than 1.5 million customers (with a goal of 3 to 4 million by 2010) in at least 16 states, **fiber-optic service** is rapidly becoming a challenger to DSL and cable providers, especially in the suburbs. However, this service is still unavailable in many cities and rural areas and is usually offered by a limited number of providers. No modem is needed, but fiber-optic cable may have to be run to and within your home.

If you don't need a constant, daily Internet connection, some businesses offer special leased lines for companies, educational institutions, and large organizations. Internet access is attained through the organization's network and is usually free to the users because the company or institution pays the bill.

Now that you understand the various ways to connect to the Internet, let's differentiate the Internet from its most popular entity, the World Wide Web.

FIGURE 6.8 The Internet provides the infrastructure used to transport the ideas, queries, and information available on the World Wide Web to and from users.

The Internet and the Web: What's the Difference?

What's the difference between saying, "I'm on the Internet" versus "I'm on the Web"? Although many people talk as if the Internet and the Web were the same thing, they are not. Recall, the Internet is a network of hardware (computers, cables, and routers) through which any computer can directly access other computers and exchange data. The **World Wide Web** (or **Web** or **WWW**) is a portion of the Internet that contains billions of documents. So, the Internet is the physical connection of millions of networks, like an interstate, whereas the Web *uses* the Internet as its transport mechanism to distribute its collection of documents, called Web pages. The Web uses the Internet architecture in the same way cars and trucks use an interstate—to move goods and people (Figure 6.8).

Who owns or controls the Web? As with the Internet, no one owns the Web. Both involve thousands of publicly and privately owned computers and networks, all of which agree to follow certain standards and guidelines and share resources on the network. Standards and guidelines related to all aspects of the Web are published by the World Wide Web Consortium (W3C), an international organization based in Cambridge, Massachusetts. Visit **www.w3.org** to review the mission of the W3C, a list of its 332 members, and various Internet standards (Figure 6.9).

Besides the W3C, many other organizations contribute to the development of different aspects of the Internet and Web. Figure 6.10 provides a list of some of the more established and recognized organizations and a brief description of their missions.

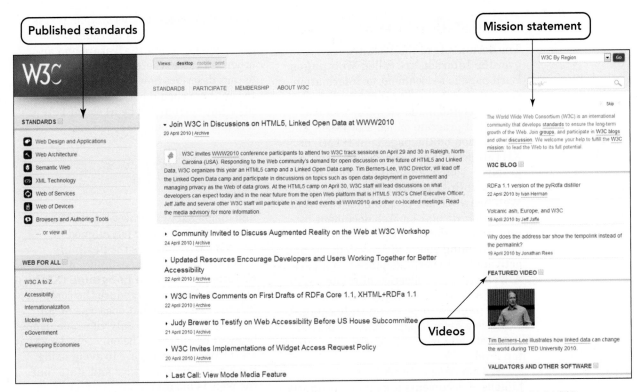

Published standards

Mission statement

Videos

FIGURE 6.9 The W3C has members from all over the world that participate in the development of vendor-neutral standards for the Web.

FIGURE 6.10   Internet and Web Management Organizations

Name	Purpose
ICANN—Internet Corporation for Assigned Names and Numbers **www.icann.org**	Nonprofit, international organization responsible for coordinating the Internet's Domain Name System and assigning IP addresses.
IETF—Internet Engineering Task Force **www.ietf.org**	International community of information technology (IT) professionals, including network designers, operators, vendors, and researchers, responsible for developing Internet standards, best current practices, and informational documents.
ISOC—Internet Society **www.isoc.org**	Nonprofit, international association consisting of over 80 organizations and 28,000 individual members, formed to provide leadership in Internet-related standards, education, and policy for the benefit of people throughout the world.
IAB—Internet Architecture Board **www.iab.org**	Advisory body to the ISOC, this international committee of the IETF is comprised of 13 volunteers from the IT community who oversee the development of Internet architecture, protocols, procedures, and standards.
IRTF—Internet Research Task Force **www.irtf.org**	A task force of individual contributors from the research community working together in small, long-term research groups that report to the IAB and explore important topics related to the evolution of the Internet.
Network Solutions **www.networksolutions.com**	Organization responsible for managing the central domain name database.

Content on the Web

The documents of the Web, transported over the Internet, are called **Web pages**. Each page is a document or information resource created using the established standards and made viewable to a user through a program called a browser. The information on the page is in HTML or XHTML format and can include text, graphics, sound, animation, video, and hypertext links to other Web pages. A **Web browser** is a program on your computer that displays a Web document by interpreting the HTML or XHTML format, enabling you to view Web pages and activate the hyperlinks placed on a page. A **Web site** is a collection of related Web pages. A Web site typically contains a **home page** (also called an **index page**), which is a default page that's displayed automatically when you enter a site at its top level.

It's amazing to think that the Web's billions of documents are almost instantly accessible by means of the computer sitting on your desk. Tens of thousands of new Web pages appear every day. The Web has increased appeal due to its graphical richness, made possible by the integration of text and images.

In the following section, you'll learn how all of these pieces work together to make a Web page, starting with the concept of hypertext.

The Hypertext Concept

Hypertext is a system in which objects (text, pictures, music, programs, and so on) can be creatively linked to each other. It works by means of **hyperlinks** (also called **links**), elements in an electronic document that act as the connector to another place in the same document or to an entirely different document. Typically, you click on the hyperlink to bring another object into view. Hyperlinks are an important ingredient of the World Wide Web (Figure 6.11).

This system of hypertext is created by a special code called **Hypertext Markup Language (HTML)** or **Extensible Hypertext Markup Language (XHTML)**. HTML is a language that uses a tag system of code to create Web pages. In this system, text is surrounded by a pair of markers called *tags*. One tag starts the feature and another indicates where it is to stop. This pair of tags describes how the text located between them should be displayed. For example a line surrounded by h1 (level 1 heading) tags would be coded as:

```
<h1>Welcome to Computers Are
   Your Future</h1>
```

and displayed by a browser as boldfaced, a larger font size, and left aligned.

XHTML combines the flexibility of HTML with the extensibility of **Extensible Markup Language (XML)**, a language designed to reduce the complexity of HTML. But what does this mean? Some HTML tags are only viewable in one browser or another. The only solutions that an HTML writer has are to avoid using those tags, use those tags and state that the page is meant for one browser or another, or write multiple pages and direct readers to the appropriate pages. With XHTML, however, if you need to define a tag for clarity across different browsers or create a new markup tag, you simply define the tag in an XHTML module and use it in your page as you would any other HTML tag. The browser interpreting the page reads the definition of the tag and presents it as defined. This feature makes a page truly compatible with all browsers.

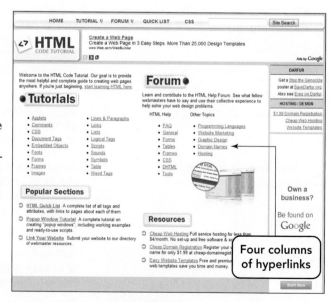

FIGURE 6.11 Hyperlinks, often displayed in blue characters and underlined, are perfect for tutorial Web sites. The user just clicks a hyperlink to view a Web page on a specific topic.

As stated earlier, the agency responsible for standardizing HTML and XHTML is the World Wide Web Consortium (W3C).

In addition to being a global hypertext system, the Web is a distributed hypermedia system. A **distributed hypermedia system** is a network-based content development system that uses multimedia resources, such as sound, video, and text, as a means of navigation or illustration. In this system, the responsibility for creating content is distributed among many people. The current generation of the Web, known as **Web 2.0**, takes this concept further by providing even more opportunities for individuals to collaborate, interact with one another, and create new content by using applications such as blogs, wikis, and podcasts. The more people who create content, the easier information creation and dissemination will become. For example, if you are researching the White House, you might link to **www.whitehouse.gov** for an overview of the current events taking place. From there you can click one of several hyperlinks (links) that will take you to additional Web pages, like Photo and Videos, Briefing Room, and Issues, which zero in on the details of that topic. Notice in Figure 6.12 that the arrows go in both directions. This is because the Web pages included in a Web site usually provide links to related pages, links that return you to the previous page, and almost always a link back to the home page. These crosslinks provide easy navigation and reduce backtracking.

The Web's distribution of content does have some drawbacks:

- Not all links work. There's no guarantee that the Web page's author will keep the page updated or active. The author can delete it or move it at any time without notice. For this reason, **dead links** (also called **broken links**), which are links to documents that have disappeared, are common on the Web.
- No individual or organization validates information posted on the Web. When

FIGURE 6.12 In hypertext documents, links can take you further into a site for more information or take you back to revisit a Web page you have already viewed.

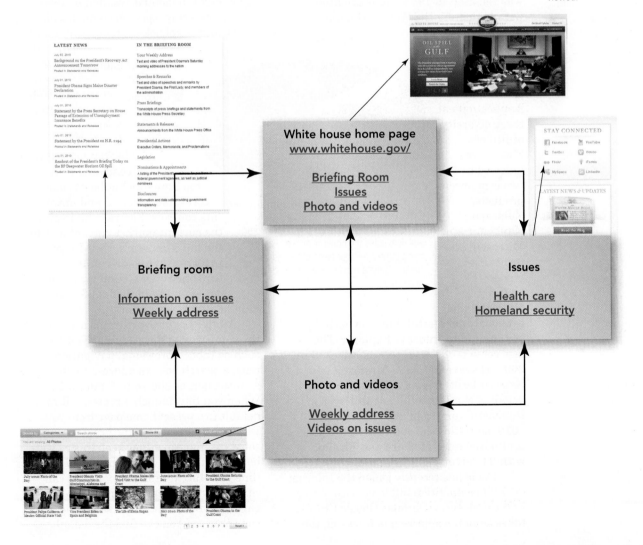

you create a hyperlink to a Web site you didn't create, investigate the credentials of the source and the accuracy of the content. This is critical to the integrity of your own Web site or Web page.

- Basic Web pages are not expensive to create or host. This has lead to the proliferation of Web content or information overload. This overload works both ways: The presenter can supply too much data, more than what is necessary to substantiate a point; and the researcher can get caught up in the search, becoming saturated with content and sidebars and losing focus.

Now that you understand hypertext and its use in providing a quick jump to Web content, let's discuss Web browsers and Web servers, items that enable us to view Web pages and make use of hyperlinks.

Viewing Content: Web Browsers

The first graphical Web browser, Mosaic, was released in 1993 and is credited with launching the Web on the road to popularity. Developed by the National Center for Supercomputing Applications at the University of Illinois, Mosaic was followed by two commercial products, Netscape Navigator and Microsoft Internet Explorer (IE). Initially, Netscape was extremely successful, but it eventually lost ground to Internet Explorer. The last version of Netscape was released in 2008. However, Mozilla Firefox, a new browser built using the Netscape model, began to challenge the popularity of Internet Explorer in 2004. As of April 2010, statistics showed IE with 54 percent of the market share and Firefox with 33 percent.

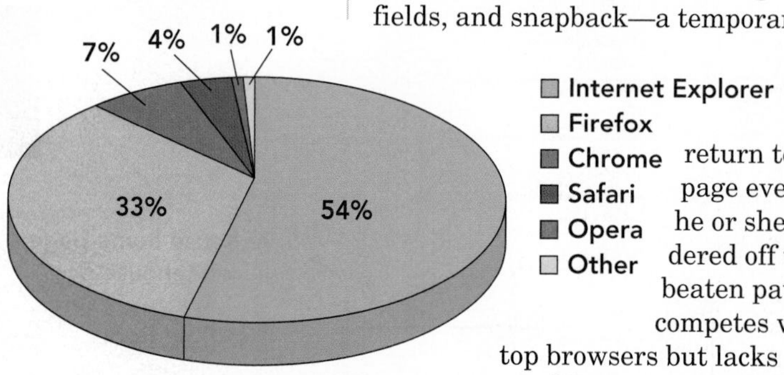

Google has recently joined the Internet browser competition full force with a very impressive entry, Chrome. Google Chrome takes a unique approach to browsing the Web by making complex features easy to use. In Google Chrome, every time you open a new tab, you'll see a visual sampling of your most visited sites, most used search engines, recently bookmarked pages, and closed tabs. You can drag tabs out of the browser to create new windows, gather multiple tabs into one window, or re-arrange them. Every tab you use is run independently in the browser; so if one application crashes, it won't take anything else down. Even bookmarking is easy: Just click the star icon at the left edge of the address bar and you're done.

Another browser, Opera, originated as a research project in 1994. Within a year, it branched out into an independent company named Opera Software ASA. Today Opera is a high-quality product for navigating the Internet that is compatible with a wide range of operating systems.

Previously available exclusively for Mac users, Safari is now available for PCs as well. Safari provides the Mac look and feel in the Internet environment. It is lightweight, nonobtrusive, and enables tabbed browsing, spell checking for all fields, and snapback—a temporary marker that allows a user to return to a Web page even after he or she has wandered off the beaten path. Safari competes with the top browsers but lacks some features like parental and antiphishing controls. Figure 6.13 displays the current market percentages for the top 5 browsers. Visit **http://internet-browser-review.toptenreviews.com/** for more detail on the individual features each browser offers.

All five browser programs are opened the same way and use similar features, such as tabbed browsing, navigation buttons, a search box, an address toolbar, and a status bar, as shown in Figure 6.14. When you first launch a browser, it may default to a preset home page from your ISP or the publisher of the browser software. You can either keep this as your home page, which will be displayed each time you start your browser, or you can change the browser's default home page, also referred to as customizing your browser. You can find the default

7% 4% 1% 1%

33% 54%

Source: http://gs.statcounter.com/

- ☐ Internet Explorer
- ☐ Firefox
- ☐ Chrome
- ☐ Safari
- ☐ Opera
- ☐ Other

FIGURE 6.13 Although Internet Explorer still dominates the browser market, Firefox has captured a larger piece of the pie, and Google Chrome has made a good showing in its infancy.

home page settings in Internet Explorer under the Tools, Internet Options menu (Figure 6.15).

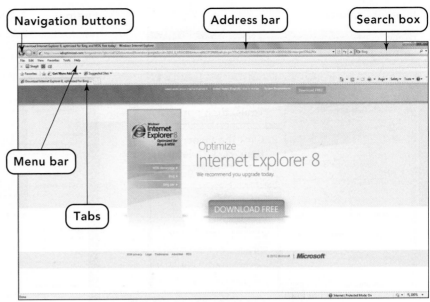

Navigation buttons
Address bar
Search box
Menu bar
Tabs

It is the browser that interprets and displays the content of a Web page and makes hyperlinks active. In short, browsers are meant to work with Web pages. Sometimes you need to upgrade your browser to the latest version so that you can fully enjoy the features of a Web site.

New Web page creation software is being developed all the time, and eventually older browsers don't have the capability of displaying the newest features or animations. Browsers use **plug-ins**, which are additional software programs, located on the user's computer, that extend the ability of the browser, usually to enable multimedia features. If a Web site requires a plug-in to function or be viewed properly, a pop-up message will appear in newer browsers, indicating which plug-in is needed, with an option to install the plug-in or cancel the installation. There are many kinds of plug-ins, but most Web surfers are probably familiar with one or more of those listed here:

- Acrobat Reader—allows pdf files to be read, navigated, and printed within a browser window.
- Adobe Flash Player—provides the interface to view Flash scripts, which create animation and sound and are embedded with a Web page, through a browser window.
- Adobe Shockwave Player—is used for interactive games, multimedia, graphics, and streaming audio and video.
- Apple QuickTime—enables movies, animation, music, and virtual reality worlds to be viewed within a browser window.
- Real Player—is used for streaming audio, video, movies, and live video broadcasts.
- Windows Media Player—enables MP3 and WAV files, movies, live audio, and live video broadcasts.

Another feature that browsers share is the ability to cache, or store, Web page files and graphics on a computer's hard drive. When you browse a Web page for the first time, the page is actually stored on your hard drive in a storage space referred to as **browser**

FIGURE 6.14 The major browsers have similar features.

cache. If the user attempts to retrieve the page again, the browser does not head back out on the Internet, but instead retrieves the page from the browser's cache. This eliminates excessive roundtrips to the server, brings the page up more quickly on the user's system, and greatly reduces Internet traffic. However, if you are visiting a news provider's Web site that is constantly updating current stories, browser cache might not seem like such a good idea. You really don't want to view old news. This problem has been solved by including HTTP directives, called freshness indicators, at the beginning of Web pages, images, and included scripts, that specify how long the page or item is considered fresh. If you retrieve the page within the allotted time, the page is retrieved from the browser's cache; otherwise the roundtrip is made back to the originating server and a new page is returned to the user. Because a browser's cache is not

FIGURE 6.15 You can change your default home page in your browser.

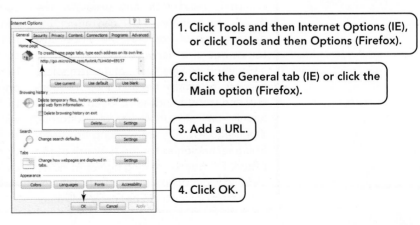

1. Click Tools and then Internet Options (IE), or click Tools and then Options (Firefox).

2. Click the General tab (IE) or click the Main option (Firefox).

3. Add a URL.

4. Click OK.

Internet Explorer

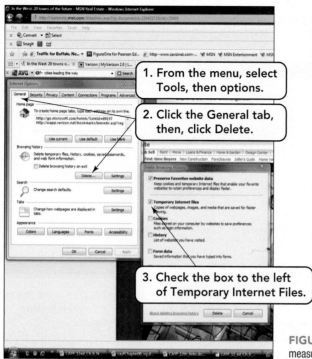

1. From the menu, select Tools, then options.

2. Click the General tab, then, click Delete.

3. Check the box to the left of Temporary Internet Files.

Firefox

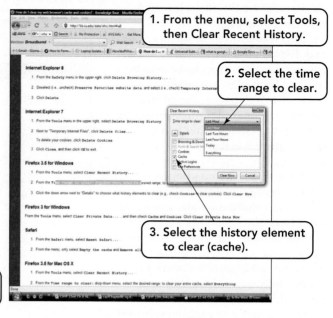

1. From the menu, select Tools, then Clear Recent History.

2. Select the time range to clear.

3. Select the history element to clear (cache).

FIGURE 6.16 Clearing cache on a shared system can provide a small measure of privacy.

deleted when a user logs off or a system is shut down, it is a good idea to clear the cache after every browser session, especially on shared systems. Figure 6.16 provides the steps to clear the cache in the Internet Explorer and Firefox browsers.

Storing Content: Web Servers

Web sites and their associated images and scripts are housed on **Web servers**, a computer running special software that enables it to respond to requests for information or accept inputted information.

FAST FORWARD ▶▶

Video-on-demand (VOD), being delivered wirelessly over the Internet, is creating network slowdowns and congestion. There was a 63 percent increase in VOD users in the fourth quarter of 2009. Due to the increased demand for this service, its large swings in bandwidth, and excessive demands on a server, VOD can affect the performance of not only the video customer but also network applications. To accommodate this form of transmission, wireless networks need higher frequencies and wider bandwidth. Electrical engineers from the University of California, San Diego (UCSD), are working on developing technologies for the network of the future. The key to creating higher frequencies and wider bandwidth is advances in silicon-based circuits that operate at millimeter

and microwave frequencies. Research at the university is focused on advanced radio-frequency CMOS chips, planar antennas, and system-level design that will increase data transfer 10 to 100 times, yet maintain the same energy consumption. Lawrence Larson, who leads the Radio Frequency Integrated Circuit (RFIC) group, captures the potential of the new technology by comparing the current connection and transport ability between your smartphone and tower to a straw. He claims that this technology under development will be the equivalent of replacing the straw with a fire hose. This analogy provides a good visual for the projected increased bandwidths and speed that research promises.

Millions of Web servers are located all over the world. When you click a hyperlink on a Web page, you either request information from a server (a list of sweatshirts available in size medium) or ask the server to accept your information (your order for three size medium sweatshirts in blue). Your browser sends a message to a Web server, asking the server to retrieve or accept the information. The server either sends the requested information or a confirmation that the sent information was received back to the initiating browser through the Internet. If the file isn't found, the server sends an error message.

Finding Information on the Web

With the millions of Web pages that make up the World Wide Web, how do you locate the ones that contain the information you want? Moving around the Web can feel like walking though a room with no lights; you're not sure where you are going and hope to bump into something you recognize. Although this method might lead you to the information you are looking for, there are more efficient and less frustrating methods to locate content on the Web. Let's look at of few of these techniques.

Web Addresses

To locate a resource on the Web, you have to know how to find the Web server on which it resides. Every host, computer, server, device, and application that communicates over the Internet is assigned an **Internet Protocol address (IP address)**, a numerical identification and logical address that is assigned to devices participating in a computer network. The IP address consists of four groups of numbers, separated by periods. The value in each group ranges from 0 to 255. As an example, 64.12.245.203 is the IP address for the AOL Web site.

IP addresses are either static or dynamic. A static IP address never changes. It's the type used by most major Web sites. A dynamic IP address is automatically assigned to a computer when you log on to a network. Internet service providers (ISPs) are assigned dynamic IP addresses that they, in turn, dispense to their customers. Although this numeric system works well

for computers, it doesn't work as well for people. You could type the numeric address into your browser, but most of us find that it's much easier to use a URL. A **URL (Uniform Resource Locator)** is a string of characters that precisely identifies an Internet resource's type and location. It is much easier to access the AOL Web site by typing the URL, **www.aol.com**, than it is to remember 64.12.245.203.

At times, keying in a URL can seem tedious. A complete URL actually has four distinct parts: protocol, domain name, path, and resource/filename. Each component provides a piece of data needed to locate the site (Figure 6.17).

Protocol The first part of a complete URL specifies the **Hypertext Transfer Protocol (HTTP)**, the Internet standard that supports the exchange of information on the Web. The protocol name is followed

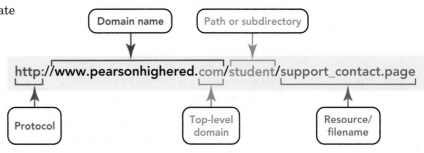

by a colon and two forward slash marks (//). You can generally omit the http:// protocol designation when you're typing the URL of a Web page, because the browser assumes that you are browsing an unsecured hypertext Web page. For example, you can access **http://www.pearsonhighered.com/cayf** by typing **www.pearsonhighered.com/cayf**. Most browsers can also access information using other protocols such as FTP (File Transfer Protocol), used to transfer files from one computer on the Internet to another; POP (Post Office Protocol), used to receive e-mail; and HTTPS (Hypertext Transfer Protocol Secure), used when the content being transferred requires encryption and a secure identification of the server (as is required for financial transactions).

Domain Name The second part of a complete URL specifies the Web site's **domain name**, which correlates to the Web server's IP address. The domain name has two parts: a host name and a top-level domain name. Some domain names also include a

FIGURE 6.17 A complete URL has four parts: protocol, domain name, path, and resource/filename. This is the URL for the Pearson student support and contact page.

prefix, the most common of which is "www." The **host name** is usually the name of the group or institution hosting the site. The **top-level domain (TLD) name** is the extension (such as .com or .edu) following the host name and indicates the type of group or institution to which the site belongs. This two-part identifier is referred to as the **Domain Name System (DNS)**. It links domain names with their corresponding numerical IP addresses, functioning like a phone book for the Internet. The Domain Name System enables users to type an address that includes letters as well as numbers, for example *pearsonhighered.com* instead of 165.193.140.24, its IP numerical address. Through a process called **domain name registration**, individuals and organizations register a *unique* domain name with a service organization, such as InterNIC, and are assigned a *unique* Internet address (IP address) that will be associated with that domain name. You can use your favorite search engine to search for domain name registrars to find other sites that provide this service.

Domain names can tell you a great deal about where a computer is located. For Web sites hosted in the United States, top-level domain names (the *last* part of the domain name) indicate the type of organization to which the Web site belongs (Figure 6.18). Outside the United States, the top-level domain indicates the name of the country from which the Web site is published or of which the owner is a citizen, such as .ca (Canada), .uk (United Kingdom), and .jp (Japan). For more information on domain names visit the Internet Corporation for Assigned Names and Numbers (ICANN) at **www.icann.org**.

Path The third part of a complete URL specifies the location of the document on the server. It contains the document's location on the computer, including the names of subfolders (if any). In the example in Figure 6.17, the path to the student contact page on the Web server at **www.pearsonhighered. com** is "student."

Resource/Filename The last part of a complete URL gives the file name of the resource you're accessing. A resource is a file, such as an HTML file, a sound file, a video file, or a graphics file. The resource's extension (the part of the file name after the period) indicates the type of resource it is. For example, HTML documents have the .html or .htm extension.

Many URLs don't include a resource name because they reference the server's default home page. If no resource name is specified, the browser looks for a file named *default* or *index*—a default page that's displayed automatically when you enter the site at its top level. If it finds such a file, it loads it automatically. For example, **www.microsoft.com/windows** displays the default Microsoft Windows home page. Other URLs omit both the path name and the resource name. These URLs reference the Web site's home page. For example, although entering **www.microsoft.com** into a browser's address bar displays Microsoft's home page, its actual URL is **http://www.microsoft. com/en/us/default.aspx**.

Surfing the Web

Once you've subscribed and connected to an Internet service provider and downloaded and opened a browser, you are ready to surf the Web. To access a Web page, you can do any of the following, as illustrated in Figure 6.19:

- **Type a URL in the Address bar.** You don't need to type http://. Watch for spelling errors, and don't insert spaces.

- **Click a tab in the browser window.** Both major browsers, IE and Firefox, offer **tabbed browsing**, which enables a user to have several Web pages open at once and switch quickly between them. You can customize your home page by adding tabs for sites that you frequently access. The tabs are not visible in Figure 6.19 because the History list is extended.

- **Click a hyperlink.** Hyperlinks are usually underlined, but sometimes they're embedded in graphics or highlighted in other ways, such as with shading or colors. Most browsers indicate the presence of a hyperlink by changing the on-screen pointer to a hand shape when it is over a hyperlink.

FIGURE 6.18 Common Top-Level Domain Names

Top-Level Domain Name	Used By
.biz	Businesses
.com	Commercial sites
.edu	Educational institutions
.gov	Government agencies
.info	Information
.mil	Military
.name	Individuals
.net	Network organizations (such as ISPs)
.org	Nonprofit organizations

- **Use the History list.** The **History list** is a list of previously visited Web pages. It is accessed in Internet Explorer by clicking the arrow to the right of the address bar and in Firefox by selecting the History option on the menu bar. Both browsers then display a drop-down list from which the user can select a Web page.
- **Make use of the Favorites or Bookmarks feature.** This feature, called Favorites in IE and Bookmarks in Firefox, is located on the menu bar. When selected, you can mark a Web page that you visit frequently. To return to that page later, simply click the Favorite or Bookmarks option and select the Web page name from the drop-down list. Favorites can be grouped into categories.

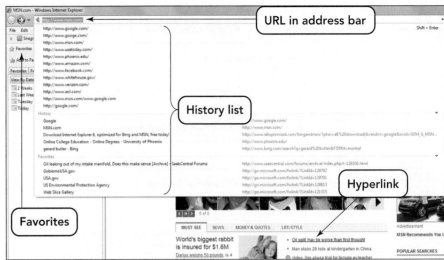

Uploading and Downloading After you have browsed the Web and accessed various Web pages, you may want to try downloading or uploading data. With **downloading**, a document or file is transferred from another computer to your computer, as in downloading music from iTunes. Your computer is the destination; the other computer is the source. With **uploading**, you transfer files from your computer to another computer, as you do when you upload a video you created to Youtube. In uploading, your computer is the source and the other computer is the destination. Most students download and upload files when using a Web-based course management system, such as Blackboard, Angel, or MyITLab. These teaching systems allow an instructor and student to interact in classes delivered entirely online or to complement a face-to-face teaching situation. Students download course notes or application files to their own computers. When a student completes an assignment, he or she uploads the completed assignment to a drop box for the instructor to grade.

No matter how familiar you are with the source, you should exercise caution when downloading files of unknown origin from the Web. If you download software from a site that doesn't inspect files using up-to-date antivirus software, you could infect your computer with a virus. Most Internet users believe that it's safe to download software from Web sites maintained by software companies or files

created with popular software. However, be aware that some viruses are spread in the data files of popular programs, such as Microsoft Word or Excel. Be sure to use an antivirus program to check any software or data files that you download. Now that you understand the basics of the Internet and Web, let's examine how to conduct research on the Web.

Sharing Information

Sometimes the best way to get information online is from an individual or agency that is also online and communicating or contributing through an online feed, conversation, or Web posting.

Really Simple Syndication One of the current ways to keep abreast of updates on news, weather, and sports in our fast-moving and informative world is through the use of **Really Simple Syndication (RSS)**. Once a user sets up a connection to a Web site that has an RSS feed, he or she will receive constant updates over the Internet from that site without any further involvement. The URL or Web page that allows its up-to-date information to be published on another Web site is said to have an RSS feed or is referred to as being *syndicated*.

So how does RSS work? A Web page that displays constantly changing data maintains a list of RSS feeds. Individuals interested in getting updated information from locations on the list can, through an RSS file, select sources from the list and receive the updated information on their own Web page. There are hundreds of Web sites that provide RSS feeds, for example, the *New York Times*, the BBC, Reuters, and many blogs. If your site will be updating several feeds, you can use an RSS aggregator. An **aggregator**

FIGURE 6.19 There are many ways to access a typical Web page.

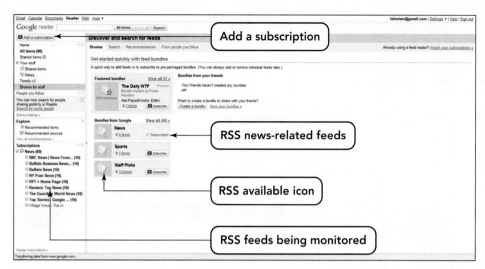

Add a subscription

RSS news-related feeds

RSS available icon

RSS feeds being monitored

FIGURE 6.20 Google Reader is a free aggregator that can be set up by going to **www.google.com/reader/view/**.

is a program that remembers your subscription list, checks each site on a regular basis, alerts you if new information has been published, and organizes the results for you. Many RSS aggregators are available through your browser. Some are even integrated into your e-mail, and others are stand-alone applications (Figure 6.20).

Wikis Want to share information fast through the Web, for either personal or professional reasons? A wiki, a blog, or a podcast might be just what you need. A **wiki** (short for *wiki-wiki*, the Hawaiian word for "fast") is a simple Web page on which any visitor can post text or images, read previous posts, change posted information, and track earlier changes. No elaborate coding needed—just click to post, click to refresh the page, and you're done. If a visitor changes what you've posted and you don't like the change, just click to revert to an earlier version. Information referenced from a wiki should be verified through another source because wiki entries can be made by anyone and the content is not always verified. Next time you're online, surf over to **www. wikimusicguide.com**, an open-content music guide. Fans can create new pages, share information about their favorite songs or artists, and edit the entries others have created.

Wikis can be public or restricted to specific members. In addition to their use in the entertainment industry, this information-sharing option is being used by business and educational institutions to reduce e-mail and increase collaboration.

Blogs Another way to share information online is via a **blog** (short for Weblog). A blog is the Internet equivalent of a journal or diary. Bloggers post their thoughts and opinions, along with photos or links to interesting Web sites, for the entire world to see. Over 1 million blogs are posted on the Web. Some are meant for family and friends; some offer running commentary on politics and other timely topics; and others are written by employees about their jobs, interview hints, and various other subjects. Many Microsoft blogs have loyal followings because of their insightful observations and technical know-how. If you are interested in finding out about the Microsoft interview process check out **http://microsoftjobsblog.com/blog/**. Here blogs are posted from individuals that have been interviewed and include everything from sample categories of questions to advice on how to dress (Figure 6.21). Visit **www.blogsearchengine.com** to search for blogs by subject and for FAQs about blogging. If you are interested in creating a blog, **www.blogger.com/start** is a great place to get started.

Podcasts If you'd rather get your information in an audio or video format, podcasts may be just what you need! Despite the name, and its link to music, **podcasts** have evolved from containing just sound

FIGURE 6.21 Blogs like this one from individuals who have gone through the Microsoft job interview process can provide valuable hints and advice.

to including any kind of audio as well as images and video. Podcasts files are released periodically by means of Web syndication, a delivery method that makes use of **podcatchers** (applications such as Apple Inc.'s iTunes or Nullsoft's Winamp) that can automatically identify and retrieve new files in a given series and make them available through a centrally maintained Web site.

You can listen to podcasts on your computer or on an MP3 player. You can go to sites that provide podcasts or sign up for one using an RSS feed. Imagine taking a physics class at Massachusetts Institute of Technology or catching the radio interview with your favorite musician that you missed last week. Podcasts can make it happen. Check the Podcast Directory at **http://podcast.com** and hear what's new!

Through the simplicity of wikis, blogs, and podcasts, the Web has been expanded into a means of interactive communication.

Using Hyperlinks to Surf the Web

Although browsing or surfing the Web is easy and fun, it falls short as a means of information research. When you are looking for specific and reliable data, you need to employ more targeted methods.

Using hyperlinks on a reliable Web page could be a start. The URL of the link might provide you with some of the desired data. In general, starting this way usually has the user clicking link after link, searching for information that they never find.

Some Web sites offer a **subject guide**, a list of subject-related categories such as

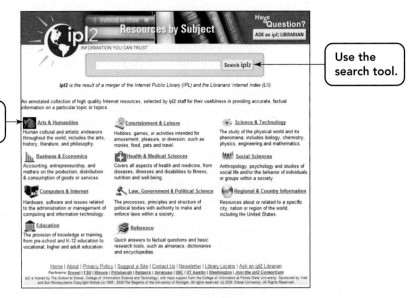

business, news, or trends that, when selected, displays a page of more related links (Figure 6.22). These guides don't try to include every Web page on the World Wide Web, but they offer a selection of high-quality pages that represent some of the more useful Web pages in a given category. If you're just beginning your search for information, a subject guide is an excellent place to start.

A **portal** is a Web page that acts as a gateway to a lot of diverse sources and presents those sources in an organized way. It enables a user to locate fast-breaking news, local weather, stock quotes, sports scores, and e-mail with the click of a mouse. Portal sites usually use indexes and lists of links to provide a jumping-off point for your search. Sites such as MSNBC, AOL, iGoogle, and Yahoo! are examples of portals (Figure 6.23).

FIGURE 6.22 Subject guides can help you find the information you seek quickly.

FIGURE 6.23 Portals usually make use of RSS to provide the viewer with the most update news and sporting events.

A side effect of your search method is the clickstream you leave in your wake. A **clickstream** is the trail of Web links you have followed to get to a particular site. Internet merchants are quite interested in analyzing clickstream activity so that they can do a better job of targeting advertisements and tailoring Web pages to potential customers.

If you can't find the information you're looking for using any of the methods above, try using a search engine. You've no doubt heard of Google, Yahoo!, Bing, and Ask. Although these and other Web search tools are far from perfect, knowing how to use them effectively (and knowing their limitations) can greatly increase your chances of finding the information you want.

Search engine returns can be extensive and broad in scope. A user has to be familiar with techniques that can be used to zero in on specific search content. Let's look at these techniques and strategies in more detail.

Using Search Engines

Using search engines is more complex than using the other methods of locating information on the Web. **Search engines** make use of databases of the Web pages they've indexed. To add pages to their databases, search engines make use of computer programs, referred to as **spiders**, to roam the World Wide Web via the Internet, visit sites and databases, and keep the search engine's database of Web pages up to date. Also known as *crawlers, knowledge bots,* or *knowbots*, they obtain new pages, update known pages, and delete obsolete ones. Most large

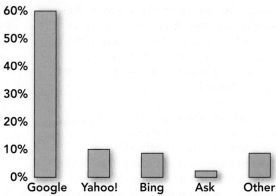

Source: www.seoconsultants.com/search-engines/

FIGURE 6.24 Google gets approximately 76 billion searches a month of the 113 billion searches completed on all search engines.

search engines operate several spiders all the time. Even so, the Web is so enormous that it can take six months to cover the content, resulting in a certain degree of "outdatedness." This outdatedness results in **link rot**, hyperlinks that no longer work and Web pages that have been removed or restructured. Such links can make a Web search frustrating and tedious.

Internet users seem to have their favorite search engine; however, Google is definitely at the top of the list. Figure 6.24 displays April 2010 statistics on the four core search engines. As the chart illustrates, Google use far exceeded any of the others, with Yahoo! a distant second.

Feel like you're stuck in a rut? Not all search engines use the same strategy to locate Web content. Try using a different search engine. Visit sites like Mahalo (**www.mahalo.com**), Dogpile (**www.dogpile.com**), FindSounds (**www.findsounds.com**), SurfWax (**www.surfwax.com**), or BlogPulse (**www.blogpulse.com**) and see what you find (Figure 6.25)!

To use a search engine, type one or more words that describe the subject

FIGURE 6.25 Search Engine Comparisons

Web Search Engine	Strategy Used to Obtain Results
Mahalo	Serves as a human-powered search engine and knowledge-sharing service.
Dogpile	Accumulates search results from leading search engines to present the best results in one easy-to-find place
FindSounds	Focuses on locating sound effects and musical instrument samples
SurfWax	Makes use of a patent pending spiraling matrix design to search, sort, and extract information in a simple natural interface
BlogPulse	Uses machine learning and natural language to provide a search engine that focuses on blogs

you're looking for into the search text box and click *Search* (or press *Enter*). Generally, it's a good idea to type several words (four or five) rather than just one or two. If you use only one or two words, the Web search will produce far more results than you can use.

Why do search engines sometimes produce unsatisfactory results? The problem lies in the ambiguity of the English language. Suppose you're searching for information on the Great Wall of China. You'll find some information on the ancient Chinese defensive installation, but you may also get the menu of the Great Wall of China, a Chinese restaurant; information on the Great Wall hotel in Beijing; and the lyrics of "Great Wall of China," a song by Billy Joel.

Specialized Search Engines Full Web search engines generally don't index specialized information such as names and addresses, job advertisements, quotations, or newspaper articles. To find such information, you need to use **specialized search engines**. Examples of such specialized search engines include Indeed, a database of more than 1 million jobs, and Infoplease, which contains the full text of an encyclopedia and an almanac (Figure 6.26).

You can save the results of your searches—the Web pages you visit by following the results links of a search engine—to your hard drive by using your browser's File, Save As menu sequence. If you don't want or need the entire Web page, you can right-click the various elements of the page and choose from a variety of options (Save Target As, Save Picture As, Print Target, Print Picture, E-mail Picture). You can also use your mouse and cursor to highlight and then copy text on a Web page for pasting into a word-processing file or other document. The benefit of saving a Web page offline, to your own storage device, is that you can view that page later without connecting to the Internet. This is easily accomplished by opening your browser and then choosing the File, Open menu sequence. Simply browse through your folders and files to locate the Web page file and then open it.

Some Web sites have their own site search engines. You will often find this feature on the site's home page. It is usually a clearly marked box into which you type the keywords you are looking for. Some home pages will have a Search icon or button that will take you to the site's search page.

For the socially conscious Web searcher, there are search sites that will make donations to your favorite charity. Check out **www.goodsearch.com** and begin to donate to the charity of your choice.

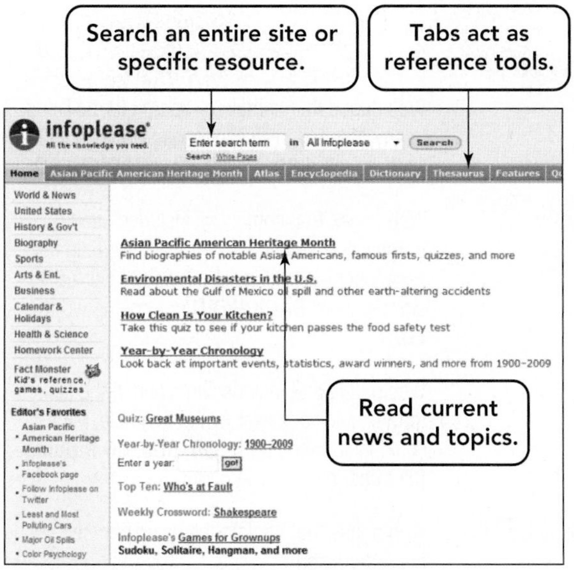

Search Basics

By learning a few search techniques, you can greatly increase the accuracy of your Web searches. **Search operators**, which are symbols or words used for advanced searches, can be helpful. Most search engines include a link for advanced searches or provide search tips to explain which search operators you can use. Although specific methods may vary, some or all of the following techniques will work with most search engines.

Wildcards Many search engines enable you to use wildcards. **Wildcards** are symbols such as * and ? that take the place of zero or more characters in the position in which they are used. The use of wildcards, also called **truncation symbols**, to search for various word endings and spellings simultaneously is a technique called **truncation**.

Wildcards help you improve the accuracy of your searches and are

Search an entire site or specific resource.

Tabs act as reference tools.

Read current news and topics.

FIGURE 6.26 Specialized search engines, like Infoplease, provide access to selected reference tools and resources.

useful if you are unsure of the exact spelling of a word. Wildcards may be handled differently, depending upon the search engine used. So the search term *bank** might return *bank*, *banks*, *banking*, *bankruptcy*, *bank account*, and so forth.

Phrase Searches Another way to improve the accuracy of your searches is through **phrase searching**, which is generally performed by typing a phrase within quotation marks. This tells the search engine to retrieve only those documents that contain the exact phrase (rather than some or all of the words anywhere in the document).

Inclusion and Exclusion Operators With many search engines, you can improve search performance by specifying an **inclusion operator**, which is generally a plus (+) sign. This operator states that you only want a page retrieved if it contains the specified word. By listing several key terms with this search operator, you can zero in on pages that only contain one or more of the essential terms. If the list of retrieved documents contains many items that you don't want, you can use the **exclusion operator**, which is generally a minus (−) sign. You can exclude the undesired term by prefacing it with the exclusion operator (Figure 6.27).

GREEN tech tips

Green Tech Tips

Environmental concerns generate a lot of interest. Now there's even a "green" search engine—Green Maven (**www.greenmaven.com**). Use it to find environmentally conscious Web sites and news.

You can also find a variety of ecologically and socially conscious search engines that donate to various causes based on the searches people run. Two such engines are Ecosearch (**www.ecosearch.org**) powered by Google and GoodSearch (**www.goodsearch.com**) powered by Yahoo. There are, however, plenty of other such sites. Use them as you would your normal search engine, and you'll get great results. Don't just click to donate. Without attempting a legitimate search, you'll jeopardize the relationships that enable such sites to fund their initiatives. ●

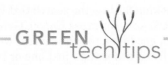

Boolean Searches

Some search engines enable you to perform Boolean searches. **Boolean searches** use logical operators (AND, OR, and NOT) to link the words you're

FIGURE 6.27 Improving Your Search Results with Search Operators

Operator/Symbol	Example	Result
Inclusion/Plus sign (+)	CD+Radiohead	Web pages that contain all search terms listed, in any order. In this case, pages would include *both* the word **CD** *and* the word **RADIOHEAD**.
Exclusion/Minus sign (−)	CD+Radiohead − eBay	Web pages that contain all included search terms listed, but not the excluded term. In this case, pages would include *both* the word **CD** *and* the word **RADIOHEAD** but *not* the word **EBAY**.
Wildcards (*)	CD*	Web pages that include variations of the search term or additional words. For example, pages could include the terms **CD**, **CDs**, **CD Ripping**, **CD Files**, etc.
Quotation Marks (" ")	"Radiohead Just Push Play CD"	Web pages that contain the exact phrase in the order listed.

FIGURE 6.28 Using Boolean Search Terms to Fine-Tune Your Search

Terms	Examples	Result
AND	CD **AND** Radiohead	Returns the same result as using the plus sign (+)
OR	CD **OR** Radiohead	Web pages that include either or both of the search terms listed, usually providing a large number of hits. For this example, results would include *either* the word **CD** *or* the word **RADIOHEAD** or *both*.
NOT	CD **AND** Radiohead **NOT** eBay	Returns the same results as using the minus sign (−)
Parenthesis ( )	(CD **OR** MP3 **OR** Record) **AND** Radiohead	Search terms in parenthesis are located first, using the search operator provided. In this case, results would include pages that included any combination of **CD**, **MP3**, or **RECORD** *and* the word **RADIOHEAD**

searching for (Figure 6.28). By using Boolean operators, you can gain more precise control over your searches. Let's look at a few examples.

The AND, OR, and NOT Operators
When used to link two search words, the AND operator tells the search engine to return only those documents that contain both words (just as the plus sign does). You can use the AND operator to narrow your search so that it retrieves fewer documents.

If your search retrieves too few documents, try the OR operator. This may be helpful when a topic has several common synonyms, such as car, auto, automobile, and vehicle. Using the OR operator usually retrieves a larger quantity of documents.

To exclude unwanted documents, use the NOT operator. This operator tells the search engine to omit any documents containing the word preceded by NOT (just as the minus sign does).

Using Parentheses Many search engines that support Boolean operators allow you to use parentheses, a process called **nesting**. When you nest an expression, the search engine evaluates the expression from left to right and searches for the content within the parentheses first. Such expressions enable you to conduct a search

with unmatched accuracy. To learn more about search engines, their specialized capabilities, and specific examples go to **www.internettutorials.net/**.

Using Information from the Web

After you've found information on the Web, you'll need to evaluate it critically. Anyone can publish information on the Web; many Web pages are not subject to the fact-checking standards of newspapers or magazines, let alone the peer-review process that safeguards the quality of scholarly and scientific publications. Although you can find excellent and reliable information on the Web, you can also find pages that are biased or blatantly incorrect.

Critically Evaluating Web Pages
As you're evaluating a Web page for possible use or reference, read with a critical eye and consider the issues raised here:

- Who is the *author* of this page? Is the author affiliated with a recognized institution, such as a university or a well-known company? Is there any evidence that the author is qualified and possesses credentials with respect to this topic?

- Does the author *reference* his or her sources? If so, do they appear to be from recognized and respected publications?
- Who is the Web page *affiliated* with? Who pays for this page? The association between the page server, sponsor, and author should be above board. The hosting organization should not be able to exert influence over the information on the site.
- Is the language *objective* and dispassionate, or is it strident and argumentative? Is it written in a form and level that suits the target population?
- What is the *purpose* of this page? Is the author trying to sell something or promote a biased idea? Who would profit if this page's information were accepted as true? Does the site include links to external information, or does it reference only itself?
- Does the information appear to be *accurate*? Is the page free of sweeping generalizations or other signs of shoddy thinking? Do you see many misspellings or grammatical errors that would indicate a poor educational background?
- Is this page *current*? The information should be up to date.

In the next section, you will explore the practical applications of Web research to both the work and school environments.

Using the Web for Schoolwork

Finding information on the Web can help you as a consumer. But how can it help you as a student? The following sections provide some helpful hints.

Authoritative Online Sources Many respected magazines and journals have established Web sites where you can search back issues, giving you the best of both worlds—the power and convenience of the Internet, plus material that is more reliable than the average Web page.

Locating Material in Published Works
Remember that the Web is only one of several sources you can and should use

for research. Many high-level research tools can be found in your institution's library. Additionally, librarians are trained research professionals who are there to assist you. As institutions have begun to offer distance-learning courses, student access to library materials has become a critical issue. To meet the needs of distance-learning students, many college libraries now provide online access to their services. You can almost certainly access and search your library's inventory of books and can often order them online. The library's search engine will allow you to search books (and sometimes articles) by author, title, or key term. Your library may also provide access to valuable search tools such as EBSCOhost, LexisNexis, and other professional databases. Sometimes you can access these online materials from off campus as well as on campus. Materials may be accessible only to faculty and students, or they may also be available to the general public. Check your library's home page to find out what Internet services are available.

ETHICS

The Internet and Web have produced an environment that makes accessing information from the comfort of your home or favorite coffee shop effortless. Locating the information is simple—and so is borrowing it and embedding it into your own work. By simply using copy and paste or right-clicking and selecting the *Save Image As* option, information, pictures, and data found on Web pages can be lifted from their source and inserted into another document or Web page under development. Copyright violations and infringements often occur with material that is available online, especially when it is re-used without permission. Make sure you understand your rights and responsibilities. Visit the Electronic Frontier Foundation (**www.eff.org**), a civil liberties group that defends your rights in the digital world, or the U.S. Copyright Office (**www.copyright.gov**) for more information on the ethical use of material you find on the Internet.

FIGURE 6.29 Google Scholar uses the power of Google to search scholarly literature and provide high-quality results for academic research.

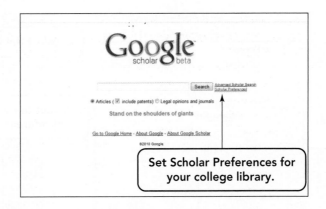

Set Scholar Preferences for your college library.

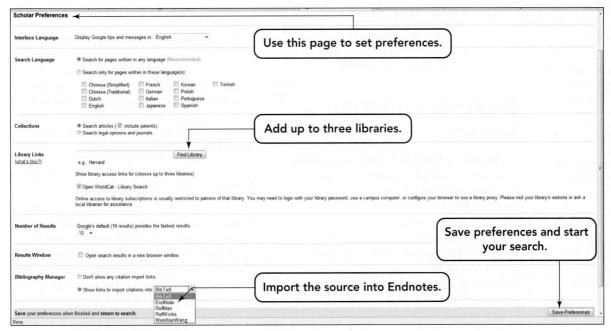

Use this page to set preferences.

Add up to three libraries.

Save preferences and start your search.

Import the source into Endnotes.

Also, visit Google Scholar (**http://scholar.google.com**) to search for scholarly literature from many academic disciplines. You can use the advanced search methods covered in this chapter and even personalize your searches to have Google Scholar indicate when materials are held by your local library. Google Scholar can help you locate peer-reviewed papers, theses, books, abstracts, and articles from academic publishers and professional sources (Figure 6.29).

Citing Online and Offline References

Including citations in your work is an important way to honor copyright and avoid accusations of plagiarism. Because citing Internet-based sources is not the same as citing traditional references, visit University of California Berkeley's General Guides site at **www.lib.berkeley.edu/**

Help/guides.html to learn how to properly cite online and electronic resources. You should know how to cite Web sites, e-mail messages, and online databases. When citing electronic resources, it is important to include the date the site was last accessed. Even more than the written and published sites, electronic sites are time sensitive.

Application developers like Microsoft have begun to include reference options within their current word processing programs. Such features prompt the user to input the necessary information into a template that the application then formats into the style the user selects, usually APA or MLA for college papers (Figure 6.30)

Now that you're familiar with how to evaluate information on the Web, let's look at some of the Internet's most useful services.

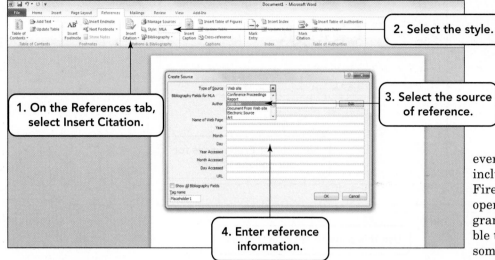

2. Select the style.

1. On the References tab, select Insert Citation.

3. Select the source of reference.

4. Enter reference information.

FIGURE 6.30 Microsoft Word 2010 includes a References tab on the Ribbon where a user can add new citations, footnotes, endnotes, or bibliography references, with all of the appropriate formatting required by the selected style.

Exploring Internet Services

An **Internet service** is best understood as a set of standards (protocols) that define how two types of programs—a client, such as a Web browser that runs on the user's computer, and a server—can communicate with each other through the Internet. By using the service's protocols, the client requests information from a server program that is located on some other computer on the Internet.

At one time, some browsers, such as Netscape Navigator and the Mozilla Suite, were distributed as software suites that included client programs to handle e-mail, newsgroups, and chat services, as well as browsing. However, most current browsers, including Internet Explorer, Firefox, and Safari (for Macs), operate as stand-alone programs. Although it's still possible to obtain client software for some of these services, many of them are Web based and don't require any special software to use, but you may need to install an appropriate plug-in to ensure full functionality. Figure 6.31 lists a selection of commonly used Internet services.

E-Mail: Staying in Touch

The most popular Internet service is e-mail. **E-mail** (short for **electronic mail**) is a software application that enables you to send and receive messages via networks. E-mail has become an indispensable tool for businesses and individuals due to its speed, convenience, and its ability to be saved and

FIGURE 6.31 Commonly Used Internet Services

Service	Client	Web-Based	Comments
E-mail			
AOL Mail	X	X	Available with AOL Desktop installation or as Web-based service
Google Mail		X	
Microsoft Outlook	X		Part of the Microsoft Office suite
Instant Message			
AOL AIM	X	X	Available with AOL Desktop installation or as a Web-based service
Google Talk	X	X	Available for download or as Web-based service
Yahoo! Messenger		X	
Windows Live Messenger		X	Formerly MSN Messenger

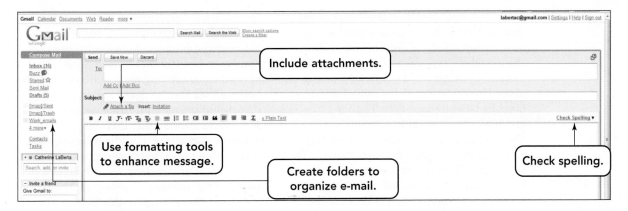

Include attachments.

Use formatting tools to enhance message.

Create folders to organize e-mail.

Check spelling.

retrieved. However, for immediacy, text messaging is preferred. Both of these communications tools have become media of choice for interpersonal written communication, far outpacing the postal system.

When you receive an e-mail, you can reply to the message, forward it to someone else, store it for later action, or delete it. In addition to writing the text message, you can format the text, check spelling, organize your e-mail into folders, and include an e-mail attachment (Figure 6.32). An **e-mail attachment** can be any type of computer file—document, photo, audio, or video—that is included

with an e-mail message. If you receive an e-mail message containing an attachment, your e-mail program displays a distinctive icon, such as a paper clip, to notify you. E-mail usually arrives at the destination server in a few seconds. It is then stored on the server until the recipient logs on to the server and downloads the message.

To send an e-mail, you need to know the recipient's e-mail address. An **e-mail address** is a unique cyberspace identity for a particular recipient that follows the form myname@somedomain.com. The components of an e-mail address are the user

FIGURE 6.32 E-mail can be saved and used to provide a record of past communications.

GREEN tech tips

The use of electronic communication methods can help us reduce the environmental effect of keeping in touch. Let's start with some facts:

- The average worker uses 10,000 sheets of copy paper a year. A large financial service company reported that they could save $700,000 a year if all copies were double-sided.

- The United States, which has less than 5 percent of the world's population, consumes 30 percent of the world's paper.

- Just under 50 percent of wood pulp goes to the production of paper. Reducing paper production would help reduce greenhouse gases. As an example, the greenhouse emission to create 40 reams of paper is equivalent to 1.5 acres of pine forest absorbing carbon for a year.

- It takes more than 1.5 cups of water to make one sheet of paper.

So in short, less is better. What can an average user do to help this environmental movement? Start by thinking before you print or copy. Ask yourself whether you really need a paper copy. If you do, how many do you need? Use the Print preview option of your application before printing. This eliminates printing a version with errors and having to reprint it. Change the setting on your printer to print double-sided by default (if it has that capability). Fit more on one page by changing margin and font size. And remember to recycle discarded paper.

These options may seem like small steps, but if individuals all over the world incorporate them into a daily practice, these small actions can spread and create a lasting environmental effect. ●

name or other identifier, the name of the domain that is hosting the e-mail service, and the top-level domain that identifies the provider's type of institution. For instance, you can send mail to the president of the United States at the e-mail address president@whitehouse.gov. In this instance, the user name is "president," the domain is "whitehouse," and the top-level domain is ".gov" (for government). You can often tell quite a bit about someone just by seeing his or her e-mail address!

If you normally send e-mails to the same group of individuals frequently, you might consider creating a distribution list. A distribution list is a grouping of individuals in your contacts that you want to receive the same e-mails. Instead of listing each recipient individually in the "To" section of a new e-mail you select the precreated distribution list. Everyone in that list will receive the e-mail.

E-mail has many benefits:

- It is inexpensive, fast, and easy to access.
- It enables collaboration.
- It creates an electronic paper trail.
- It saves paper.

The benefits of e-mail are tempered by some potential problems that you should be aware of. Sometimes e-mail systems fail to properly send or receive mail.

Attachments may not be delivered or they may be blocked by e-mail system administrators as potentially unsafe. Messages can become corrupted and may not display properly. Sometimes, if you don't regularly check your mail, your Inbox may overflow, which causes messages received past the overflow point to be bounced out of the box and never delivered.

Perhaps the worst thing that can happen with e-mail is that you hastily send a message that you later wished you hadn't, or you use the Reply All or Forward feature to send inappropriate or irrelevant messages that can embarrass you or that inconvenience the receiver.

Spam: Can It Be Stopped?

Many e-mail users receive unsolicited e-mail advertising called **spam**. In fact, according to a report released in May 2009

" **Attachments** may **not** be **delivered** or they may be **blocked** by **e-mail system administrators** as potentially **unsafe.** "

from the security vendor Symantec, 90.4 percent of all e-mail (1 out of every 1.1 e-mails) is spam. This mail is sent by spammers, businesses or individuals that specialize in sending such mail. Spammers believe that they're doing only what direct-marketing mail firms do: sending legitimate advertising. But they don't acknowledge a crucial difference between unsolicited postal advertising and spam. With postal advertising, the advertiser pays for the postage. With spam, the recipient pays the postage in the form of lost time and productivity for individuals and businesses. A 2009 study estimated that the total cost of combined consumer and corporate spam in the United States was $108.8 billion annually. Some $92.2 billion of that cost comes from lost productivity and the balance from the cost of administering and purchasing preventative services and programs.

Most Internet users detest spam but feel helpless to prevent it. For businesses, spam is a costly nuisance. It's not unusual for a massive amount of spam messages to overwhelm mail servers, resulting in impaired service for legitimate, paying customers.

In most cases, little or nothing of worth is being peddled: pornographic Web sites, get-rich-quick scams, bogus stock deals, rip-off work-at-home schemes, health and diet scams, and merchandise of questionable quality. Some spam can contain **malware**, malicious software, that places a computer in the spammer's control. This type of software can wreak havoc on a user's system by deleting files and directory entries; it can also act as **spyware**, gathering data from a user's system without the user knowing it. This can include anything from the Web pages a user visits to personal information, such as credit card numbers.

Can you filter out spam? You can try. It's often possible to set up a spam or bulk mail folder in your e-mail account. Check your mail options for how to enable this service (Figure 6.33). A word of caution on using such filters: Sometimes filters can misroute messages. Check your trash and spam folders periodically to be sure

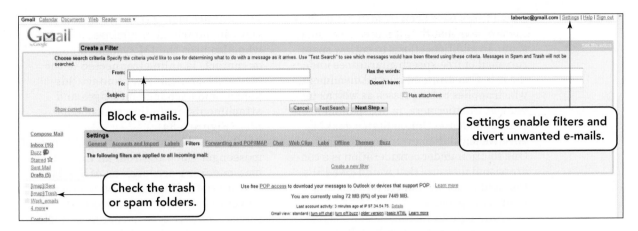

Block e-mails.

Check the trash or spam folders.

Settings enable filters and divert unwanted e-mails.

FIGURE 6.33 Check your e-mail account's mail settings to set spam filters.

FIGURE 6.33 Check your e-mail account's mail settings to set spam filters.

important messages haven't been directed to the wrong folders.

Spam can originate from a new account, which is almost immediately closed down after the service provider receives hundreds of thousands of outraged complaints. The spammer just moves on to a new account. A more modern way to send spam is through a **botnet**, a set of computers infected with a malicious program that places the computers under the control of a **bot herder**. Vulnerable systems are ones without current security patches or antispam protection. Once infected, a machine becomes one of many zombies in a botnet and responds to commands given by the bot herder.

Some of the steps you can take to prevent spam include the following:

- Avoid posting your e-mail address in any public place.
- Don't open e-mail from a source that you do not recognize.
- Deactivate the preview option in your e-mail. The preview option automatically triggers the opening of the e-mail.
- Don't reply to spam or request to be removed from a spammer's mailing list.
- Modify your e-mail account to disable graphics.
- Get involved in reporting incidents of spam to help others and stop the source of the problem.
- Make sure that security patches on your system are current.

Increasingly, state and federal legislatures are attempting to pass laws against spam. Bills have been introduced in Congress, and the Senate's CAN-SPAM Act of 2003 is aimed at deceptive e-mails,

unsolicited pornography, and marketing. The Direct Marketing Association (DMA), an advocacy group for both online and offline direct marketers, counters that the appropriate solution is an opt-out system, in which spam recipients request that the sender of spam remove their names from the mailing list—but that's just what

ETHICS

With the widespread use of electronic communication, most offices today are equipped with Internet access. Many employers make new employees sign Internet usage clauses that limit the use of the company Internet connection to business-related tasks. How does the employer know whether an employee used the Internet to conduct personal business? One simple method is for the employer to check the browser's history feature. A second might be to review security cameras that have your monitor screen in the range of view. A third is by purchasing a program that allows eavesdropping on Internet use that can be used by a network administrator from a remote location to drop in on an Internet session of an employee.

By signing the Internet usage clause, the employee does agree to the company's policy of Internet use, but does that give the employer the right to use any methods of surveillance without notifying the employee? Some of these methods monitor more than Internet use. At what point are the rights of the individual violated for the good of the company?

e-mail users have been trained not to do because of fear that they'll receive even more spam. In addition, efforts to outlaw spam run afoul of free-speech guarantees under the U.S. Constitution's First Amendment, which applies to businesses as well as individuals. Furthermore, many spammers operate outside the United States, making effective legislation even more difficult. One solution under consideration is a congressional measure that would give ISPs the right to sue spammers for violating their spam policies.

Although it's no fun, most of us have learned to live with spam by following the simple rule: If you don't know who sent it—don't open it! For more information and tips on how to avoid spam, recent

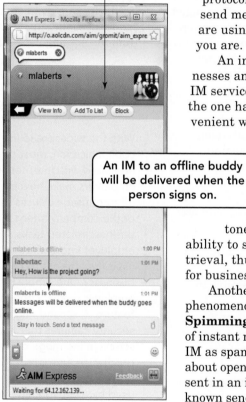

Buddies displays contacts available to chat.

Offline Buddies are not currently available.

Once a buddy is selected, the message window opens.

An IM to an offline buddy will be delivered when the person signs on.

FIGURE 6.34 Instant messaging is a popular way for Internet users to exchange near real-time messages.

law enforcement actions against deceptive commercial e-mail and spammers, and a location to file a complaint, check out the Federal Trade Commission's spam site at **www.ftc.gov/spam**.

Instant Messaging: E-Mail Made Faster

What's faster than e-mail and more convenient than picking up the phone?

Instant messaging (IM) systems alert you when a friend or business associate who also uses the IM system (a buddy or contact) is online (connected to the Internet). You can then contact this person and exchange messages and attachments, including multimedia files (Figure 6.34).

To use IM, you need to install instant messenger software from an instant messenger service, such as AOL's AIM or Microsoft's Windows Live Messenger, on your computer. You can use IM systems on any type of computer, including handhelds. Many IM services also give you access to information such as daily news, stock prices, sports scores, and the weather, and you can keep track of your appointments. There is no standard IM protocol, which means that you can send messages only to people who are using the same IM service that you are.

An increasing number of businesses and institutions are trying out IM services, with mixed results. On the one hand, IM is a novel and convenient way to communicate. On the other hand, voice communication is faster and richer. Other drawbacks to instant messaging include the misinterpretation of the tone of the message and the inability to save an IM for later retrieval, thus posing some legal issues for businesses and corporations.

Another threat to the use of IM is a phenomenon known as spimming. **Spimming** is spam that targets users of instant messaging. Spimming is to IM as spam is to e-mail. Be very careful about opening files or clicking on a link sent in an instant message by an unknown sender.

Internet Relay Chat: Text Chatting in Real Time

Internet relay chat (IRC) is an Internet service that enables you to join chat groups, called **channels**, and participate in real-time, text-based conversations. Popular in the early days of the Internet, IRC has been replaced by tools like IM. Today it is mostly the province of specialized communities, such as gamers or programmers.

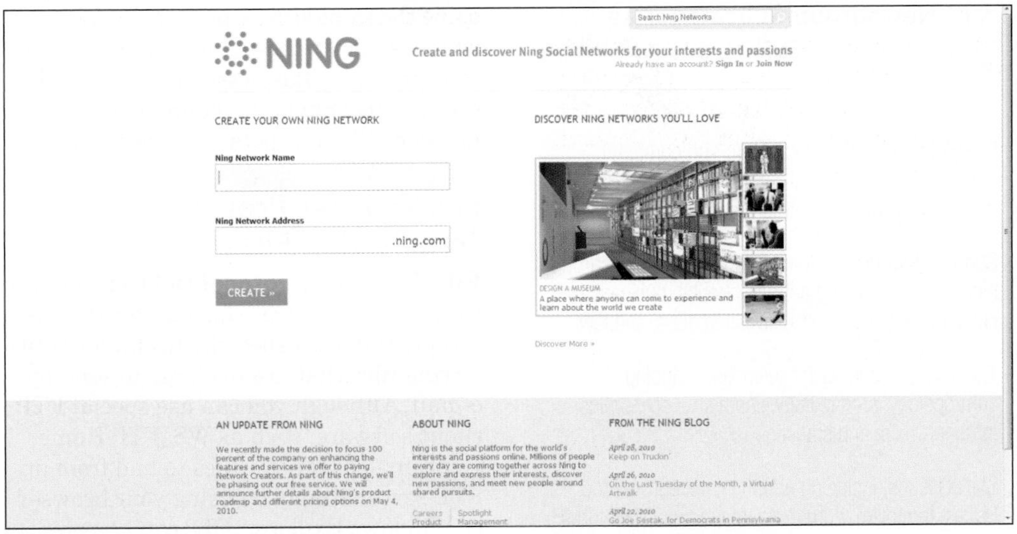

FIGURE 6.35 Social networking sites, like Ning.com, that allow users to create their own social network communities are becoming popular with political candidates and business entrepreneurs.

Social Networking: Helping People Connect

Social networking is a way to build expanding online communities. On a social networking site like Facebook or MySpace, you can create an online profile, invite friends and acquaintances to join your network, and invite their friends to join too. Some sites, like LinkedIn, are used by business professionals to expand their network of business contacts. Tired of Facebook or MySpace? Why not start your own social network? Ning (**www.ning.com**) is a site that encourages people to start their own social networking community (Figure 6.35). Artists, hobbyists, educators, athletes—the list continues to grow. Find a community to join or start your own!

Many privacy and security concerns surround the use and access of social networking sites. Statistics from a Pew Internet 2008 report support this concern, citing that 73 percent of American teens who participated in the survey indicated that they use social networking Web sites. This is a significant increase over statistics from 2007 and fuels the concern over security and the need to educate teens on the use and possible repercussion of postings placed on such sites. Once posted, pictures and content are easily shared and distributed to others, sometimes with detrimental effects. Users should give thought to the information they publicly display and consider the possible consequences. If you are searching for employment, make sure that your social networking site is not offensive. Employers are researching candidates' Facebook or MySpace sites to gain insight into a potential employee's personality and behavior.

Usenet: Joining Online Discussions

Usenet is a worldwide computer-based discussion system accessible through the Internet. It consists of thousands of topically named **newsgroups**, which are discussion groups devoted to a single topic. A newsgroup typically requires participants to use a program called a news reader. Each newsgroup contains articles that users have posted for all to see. Users can respond to specific articles by posting follow-up articles. Over time, a discussion thread develops as people reply to the replies. A **thread** is a series of articles that offer a continuing commentary on the same specific subject.

Usenet newsgroups are organized into the following main categories:

- **Standard newsgroups.** You're most likely to find rewarding, high-quality discussions in the standard newsgroups (also called world newsgroups). Figure 6.36 lists the standard newsgroup subcategories.
- **Alt newsgroups.** The alt category is much more freewheeling. Anyone can create an alt newsgroup (which explains why so many of them have silly or offensive names).
- **Biz newsgroups.** These newsgroups are devoted to the commercial uses of the Internet.

The easiest way to access Usenet is through Google Groups (**http://groups.google.com**).

You can read and post messages, but be careful what you post on Usenet. When you post an article, you're publishing in the public domain. Sometimes articles are stored for long periods in Web-accessible archives.

FIGURE 6.36 Standard Newsgroup Subcategories

Subcategory Name	Description of Topics Covered
Comp	Everything related to computers and computer networks, including applications, compression, databases, multimedia, and programming
Misc	Subjects that do not fit in other standard newsgroup hierarchies, including activism, books, business, consumer issues, health, investing, jobs, and law
Sci	The sciences and social sciences, including anthropology, archaeology, chemistry, economics, math, physics, and statistics
Soc	Social issues, including adoption, college-related issues, feminism, human rights, and world cultures
Talk	Debate on controversial subjects, including abortion, atheism, euthanasia, gun control, and religion
News	Usenet itself, including announcements and materials for new users
Rec	All aspects of recreation, including aviation, backcountry sports, bicycles, boats, gardening, and scouting

A **message board** is similar to a newsgroup, but it is easier to use and does not require a newsreader. Many colleges and universities have switched to message boards for this reason.

Electronic Mailing Lists

Electronic mailing lists of e-mail addresses are similar in many ways to newsgroups and forums, but they automatically broadcast messages to all individuals on a mailing list. Because the messages are transmitted as e-mail, only individuals who are subscribers to the mailing list receive and view the messages. Some colleges and universities host electronic mailing lists. Eric Thomas developed the first electronic mailing list program, Listserv, in 1986 for BITNET. The most common freeware version of an electronic mailing list manager program is Majordomo.

VoIP

VoIP (Voice over Internet Protocol) allows a user to speak to others over a broadband Internet connection instead of traditional analog phone line. What do you need to use VoIP? This form of communication requires a broadband Internet connection, a VoIP service provider, and a normal telephone with a VoIP adapter or a computer with supporting software. Calls to others using the same service are usually free, whereas calls to those using other services can vary. Many businesses are using VoIP services, like Skype, to reduce their communication bills and operating expenses.

File Transfer Protocol: Transferring Files

File Transfer Protocol (FTP) is one way that files can be transferred over the Internet, and it is especially useful for transferring files that are too large to send by e-mail. Although you can use special FTP client software, such as WS_FTP Home, you can also transfer files to and from an FTP server simply by using your browser or Windows Explorer. FTP can transfer two types of files: ASCII (text files) and binary (program files, graphics, or documents saved in proprietary file formats).

In most cases, you need a user name and a password to access an FTP server. However, with **anonymous FTP**, files are publicly available for downloading. A word of warning: Due to the lack of security on an anonymous FTP site, do not use it to send sensitive information such as financial account numbers and passwords. FTP sites are structured hierarchically—that is, they use a folder and file structure similar to that used on your own computer. Depending on how you access the site, downloadable files may appear as hyperlinks. Just click the link to download the file. If you access the site using Windows Explorer, you can use the same file management techniques you use to organize your own files.

FTP is also used to upload Web pages from your computer to the ISP or hosting service's Web server, making your Web site available to other Internet users.

E-Commerce

A large portion of Internet traffic and Web sites are associated with e-commerce. **Commerce** is the selling of goods or services with the expectation of making a reasonable profit. **E-commerce (electronic commerce)** is the use of networks or the Internet to carry out business of any type. Many **e-tailers** (Web-based retailers) hope that while you are surfing the Web, you will stop and make a purchase. Online merchants sell books, CDs, clothes, and just about anything else you might want to buy. If you've ever made a purchase online, you're one of millions engaging in e-commerce.

E-commerce supports many types of traditional business transactions, including buying, selling, renting, borrowing, and lending. E-commerce isn't new; companies have used networks to do business with suppliers for years. What is new is that, thanks to the Internet and inexpensive PCs, e-commerce has become accessible to anyone with an Internet connection and a Web browser.

The U.S. Census Bureau reported that total retail e-commerce sales for the fourth quarter of 2009 was $42.0 billion, an increase of 34.1 percent from the third quarter of 2009. For the fourth quarter of 2009, e-commerce sales accounted for 4.3 percent of total sales (Figure 6.37). There are three types of e-commerce: business-to-business (B2B), consumer-to-consumer (C2C), and business-to-consumer (B2C).

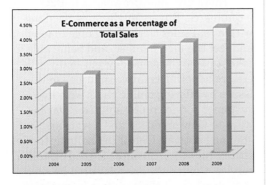

FIGURE 6.37 Statistics from the U.S. Census Bureau substantiate that e-commerce has been on the rise.

Business-to-Business E-Commerce (B2B)

When a business uses the Internet to provide another business with the materials, services, and/or supplies it needs to conduct its operations, they are engaging in **business-to-business (B2B) e-commerce**. Even though you might not personally engage in B2B, you'll probably recognize many of the industries and companies that do, for example, companies in the health care, aerospace and defense, real estate, automotive, and construction industries, and familiar computer and software companies such as Dell, IBM, and Microsoft.

In addition, many traditional and online retailers have special B2B units. For instance, the popular office supplies chain Staples has a B2B division that operates the Web site **www.staplesadvantage.com** for mid-size and Fortune 1000 companies. The Staples Contract division has experienced double-digit growth for the last seven years and launched the office supply industry's first online B2B catalog in 2007.

Unlike B2B, you may have engaged in the next type of e-commerce: consumer-to-consumer.

Consumer-to-Consumer E-Commerce (C2C)

The online exchange or trade of goods, services, or information between individual consumers is **consumer-to-consumer (C2C) e-commerce**. Often C2C e-commerce involves the use of an intermediate site, such as the popular online auction destination eBay. eBay has more than 89.5 million active users. The value of goods sold through eBay's online marketplaces, excluding autos, rose 24 percent in the fourth quarter of 2009 to $13.37 billion from $10.80 billion in the same quarter of 2008, with 58 percent of marketplace revenue from outside the U.S. (Figure 6.38). Other C2C sites include craigslist and Amazon Marketplace.

Business-to-Consumer E-Commerce (B2C)

When a business uses the Internet to supply consumers with services, information, or products, they are engaging in **business-to-consumer (B2C) e-commerce**. B2C is essentially the same as shopping at a physical store—you have a need or want, and the online marketplace offers products and solutions. The primary difference is that

FIGURE 6.38 eBay is the most well-known C2C trading site. However, its competitors like Craig's List and Amazon Marketplace are also popular.

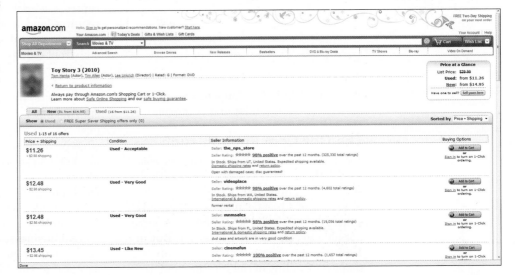

B2C e-commerce is not place or time specific, which means that you don't have to be in any particular place at any particular time to participate. This freedom of time and place enables you to shop whenever you wish and to choose from more products and services than could ever be assembled in any one physical location.

Online Shopping

The trend is for more Web users to purchase merchandise online. In addition, many more people use the Web to research purchases from brick-and-mortar stores.

Getting Good Deals Online Have you ever tried to comparison shop on the Web? After surfing at 10 different sites (or more!), it can be daunting to keep track of where you saw the best price on that new digital camera you want. You might want to turn to shopping portals such as PriceGrabber.com, Shopzilla, NexTag, and others. These sites help you conduct price and product comparisons. They also offer reviews on just about any product you can imagine (Figure 6.39). You can search and sort by brand, price range, or product rating. To save even more, you can also

FIGURE 6.39 Shopping comparison sites can help users locate items, compare prices, view consumer feedback, and buy products.

check sites that offer coupons and rebates, such as The Bargainist and eCoupons.

The Dot-Com Phenomenon

Much e-commerce occurs in the *dot-com world,* the universe of Web sites with the suffix *.com* appended to their names. This unique world has been in existence only since 1995. Before 1995, companies were not able to sell over the Internet. But in 1995, the government eliminated all taxpayer funding of the Internet and

opened it up to commercial development. The period between 1995 and 2000 is referred to as the *dot-com boom*. As the dot-com crash of 2000 made painfully clear, not every online business is able to succeed.

Amazon.com is a dot-com company that has held its ground and become profitable. Amazon quickly discovered that books are a commodity well suited for online trade, but it didn't stop there. Its offerings have grown to include music, videos, groceries, tools, jewelry, and clothing. Amazon entices buyers to access, shop, and complete their sales online by offering professional and peer product reviews; author, artist, and subject matching; and book excerpts and music samples. Shoppers can choose from a variety of shipping options and track their purchases.

There are some drawbacks to B2C e-commerce. Buyers might miss speaking with a real sales clerk, being able to touch and feel the merchandise, and being able to take it home the same day, but many sellers are adopting creative solutions to these issues by offering online chats with live customer service representatives, various ways to view products, and a wide array of shipping options. One of the hallmarks of a successful online business is good customer service. Customers are reassured by sites that clearly post their contact information, offer pages of frequently asked questions, and respond quickly to customer inquiries.

Building Your Own Online Business

One of the tremendous advantages of B2C e-commerce is the low capital investment needed to start an online business. For less than $50, a person can open a Web storefront and start selling products online. In contrast, a brick-and-mortar business requires land, a building, utilities, display shelving, and salespeople. A Web-based storefront requires only an ISP, a Web site, and the ability to ship goods or services to customers.

The first thing you need to do when starting any business is to develop a business plan (Figure 6.40). You must decide what products to offer, determine your target market, and select how many items you plan to sell and at what price. Who will pay for shipping? Will there be service provided after the sale? Who are your competitors? What profit margin do you expect to achieve?

All businesses need to have a name, and an online business is no different, except that the online business's name is almost always the same as its Web site or domain name. So, after you've completed your business plan, you will need to shop for a domain name and a Web hosting service. Many Web hosting companies, such as 1&1 (**www.1and1.com**), offer domain name search and registration services as part of their package. You will most likely want a name with a .com extension. Try to pick a name that will be easy for your customers to remember.

You may also wish to employ an electronic shopping cart. This feature is much like the physical shopping cart you'd use at a grocery store. It remembers your customer's order items and provides the results to the summary order page. Your Web site should project a professional image and be structured to meet your customers' needs to encourage their confidence in your product or service. Go to GoodPractices (**www.goodpractices.com**) for some Web site development guidelines.

You will also need to make arrangements for Web hosting, if you haven't already done so. Web hosting services provide server space, make your site available to the public, and offer site management utilities such as preprogrammed shopping cart services. There are thousands of Web hosting companies. Many Web hosting services offer templates and other tools to make it simple to build a professional-looking site. Sites such as 1&1, GoDaddy, and Yahoo! offer a variety of pricing plans for personal and commercial sites. Expect to pay a start-up fee as well as a monthly amount that is usually based on a one-year contract.

You can ensure that your site gets listed with search engines by visiting each engine's Web site (**www.google.com**, **www.yahoo.com**, **www.msn.com**, and so on) and searching for "submitting my site."

FIGURE 6.40 Sites such as Bplans.com can help get your small business plan off to a good start.

Provide the information requested, and then when someone searches for keywords that match your site, it will be one of the sites that are provided in the search results answer screen.

To operate a business, you need a way to receive payments. Just like in a traditional retail business, perhaps the best option may be to take credit cards. You should be aware that there are many costs involved with setting up and maintaining a credit card acceptance account—but the benefits may well outweigh the costs. Customers are comfortable using their credit cards online, and many feel more secure knowing that the credit card company is there in case of a dispute or fraudulent use (Figure 6.41).

One common method to accept credit cards is to use a PayPal merchant account. PayPal also acts as a secure intermediary, offering users the ability to make payments from their bank account, credit card, or PayPal account without revealing their personal financial

FIGURE 6.41 For online purchases, merchants prefer if customers use an electronic alternative like PayPal but customers may feel more secure using a credit card that provides dispute mediation and protection from fraud.

FIGURE 6.42 Sites such as Travelocity (www.travelocity.com) are popular because they help travelers find the cheapest fares and reservations available.

information to the seller. PayPal manages more than 40 million accounts worldwide. Transaction fees range from 2 to 3 percent, and there is a per-transaction fee of about 30 cents per transaction.

Other Areas of E-Commerce Growth

Making travel reservations is an area of e-commerce experiencing rapid growth. Sites such as Travelocity, Expedia, and CheapTickets enable leisure travelers to book flights, hotels, and car rentals online, as well as find the cheapest fares based on their trip parameters (Figure 6.42). Most travel sites provide e-tickets so that you can quickly check in at airport terminals by using small self-service kiosks.

Another rapidly growing online activity is banking. Access to your banking accounts enables you to use a Web browser to check account balances, balance your checkbook, transfer funds, and even pay bills online (Figure 6.43). In fact, 40 million Americans used online banking services by the end of 2005. The use of online banking is expected to grow by 55 percent by the end of 2011. By that time, some 76 percent of Americans (72 million households) will be using online banking services. Currently, banks that offer online banking gain a competitive advantage over those that do not because most customers now consider it a necessary and expected service, like ATMs. What else is in it for banks? Plenty. Online banking helps banks cut down on the expenses of maintaining bank branches and paying tellers and also allows them to provide advanced levels of electronic customer service.

The sale of stock through the Internet has only been possible since 1996; however, online stock trading now accounts for one out of every six stock trades, easily making it the fastest-growing application in B2C e-commerce. Offering secure connections through the customer's Web browser, online stock trading sites enable investors to buy and sell stocks online without the aid of a broker.

The attraction of online stock trading can be summed up in one word: cost. Fees paid to traditional, full-service brokerages can add up. But the most aggressive e-traders have cut the charges to $10 per trade or less. E-traders, such as E*TRADE and Ameritrade, can offer such low prices because the trading is automatic—no human broker is involved.

Nonretail online services have spiked in activity in the last few years. These activities include dating services; credit reports; health and medical advice; news, weather, and sports information; real estate listings (for homes and apartments); and insurance products. These sites offer various levels of access and services for members and nonmembers. Some services, such as insurance quotes, up-to-the-minute news reports, and severe weather alerts, are free. You can also post dating profiles or receive diet and other health-related profiles as well as trial passes for sports subscriptions.

FIGURE 6.43 Online banking enables customers to access their accounts, balance checkbooks, and even pay bills online.

Rules of Netiquette

Along with the privilege of using the Internet comes the responsibility of using it correctly and not causing harm to others. Courtesy is as important in the online world as it is in reality.

Netiquette, short for Internet etiquette, is the code for acceptable behavior and manners while on the Internet. The basic rule is this: Talk to others the same way you would want them to talk to you. Some more specific, useful rules of netiquette for e-mail, chat rooms, instant messaging, and message boards include the following:

- Keep the message short.
- Avoid sarcasm or the use of phrases or words that could offend the reader.
- Read the message before sending or posting it, correcting spelling and grammar mistakes.
- Do not type in all capital letters as it means that you are yelling.
- Avoid sending a **flame**. Such messages express an opinion without holding back any emotion and are frequently seen as being confrontational and argumentative.

When you follow the rules of netiquette, you put your best foot forward and make a good impression. The other side of using the Internet is protecting yourself from those that are out to deceive or harm you. Let's look at some safe surfing suggestions to protect you from this dark side of technology.

Safe Surfing

Safe surfing seems to be a constant topic of discussion. Just as many hazards exist online as there are in the real world. The added online element is that individuals are difficult to recognize due to the anonymity the Internet provides.

Safe Surfing Guidelines

By taking some simple precautions you can make your Internet experience an enjoyable and safe activity.

- Never give out identifying information.
- Never respond to suggestive messages.
- Never open e-mail from an unknown source.
- Never allow a child to make arrangements for a face-to-face meeting alone, for any reason, without being accompanied by an adult.
- Remember individuals online may not be who they seem.
- Set reasonable rules and guidelines for computer use by children.
- Make using the computer a family activity.

Additional online hazards to avoid include malware; identity theft; threats to you and your family; and unscrupulous vendors.

Avoiding Malware

Malware refers to software programs designed and written to damage a computer system. Examples of malware events range from deleting files on a hard drive or removing directory information to gathering data from a user's system that can include Web sites the user visited and account numbers or passwords that were keyed in. It is unfortunate that there are individuals out there with malicious intent, but there are—and you must be prepared. You can keep your system free of malware by installing antivirus and antispyware utilities on your computer. These utility programs will seek and destroy the malware programs they find on your computer.

> "More than **half a million** people find themselves **victims** of identity theft each year. . . . And, **nothing** is more **difficult** than restoring your credit after an **identity theft** has **destroyed** your credit rating."

Protecting Your Identity

More than half a million people find themselves victims of identity theft each year. Nothing is more frustrating than having to spend the time and energy to clean up the mess created by a loss of identification. And, nothing is more difficult than restoring your credit after an identity theft has destroyed your credit rating.

There are steps you can take to greatly reduce the risk of having your identity stolen or a portion of it pilfered. Try to avoid shoulder-surfers; these are individuals who stand close enough to see PIN numbers keyed in by users at ATMs and phone booths. When shopping with an e-merchant for the first time, look for the secure Web site features before entering any personal or credit card information. These features usually include one or several of the items in the following list:

- *https://* in the address of the site instead of the usual *http://*. The added "s" stands for "secure site" and means that the data is encrypted all the way from your computer to the computer that receives it. No other computer will be able to read your input as it passes along the Internet.
- A site seal provided by a security vendor, such as VeriSign, GeoTrust, or SSL.com
- A locked padlock symbol somewhere on the Web site that, when double-clicked, displays details of the site's security (make sure that the logo is not just an image and a fake)
- The logo from other site-security entities, such as Verified by Visa
- A message box that notifies you when you are leaving (or entering) a secure site

In addition to these visible identifiers, check out any feedback provided by previous purchasers or any comments by the Better Business Bureau. Shop only on Web sites that enable you to view their privacy policy. Make it a habit to print out privacy policies, warranties, price guarantees, and other important information. Most importantly, *never* include any financial account numbers or passwords in an e-mail or respond in any way to spam. And be sure to change the passwords on your accounts frequently.

Simply being watchful and careful with your personal information, completing transactions only on validated Web sites, and knowing the signs of a secure site will help you use the Web to its full potential safely.

"**[Never]** include any **financial account numbers** or passwords in an **e-mail** or **respond** in any way to spam."

Protecting Children in Cyberspace

With statistics supporting the use of social networks, chat rooms, and other forms of anonymous communication by minors, there have been some creative protective responses to insulate youth from cyberstalkers, cyberbullies, and other online predators. A couple in Fanwood, New Jersey, contacted CyberAngels (**www.cyberangels.org**), a volunteer organization of thousands of Internet users worldwide, after their computer-addicted 13-year-old daughter ran away from home. The group's purpose: to protect children in cyberspace.

CyberAngels was founded in 1995 by Curtis Sliwa, who also started the Guardian Angels (the volunteer organization whose members wear red berets as they patrol inner-city streets). Today, CyberAngels volunteers scour the Internet for online predators, cyberstalkers, and child pornographers, and they've been responsible for a number of arrests. Their Web site and newsletter provide many useful articles about practical safety measures to keep you and your loved ones safe and has brought their Children's Internet Safety Program to thousands of school-children across the United States. So, what about the New Jersey couple? Their daughter is home and safe thanks to the CyberAngels, who successfully used their network to identify the child's online contact.

The Internet can be a dangerous place for young children and older ones too! **Cyberbullying** occurs when one individual targets another for some form of torment or abuse through digital tools. The term used to apply to children acting against other children. However, the recent suicide death of a teen in Missouri due to cyberbullying by a parent who masqueraded as another youth has shed light on the intensity of this problem. Online stalkers and sexual predators haunt social networking sites. **Cyberstalkers** use e-mail, instant messaging, chat rooms, pagers, cell phones, or other forms of information technology to make repeated, credible threats of violence against another individual or family member of an individual. To learn more about how to protect yourself or the children in your household, visit Stop Cyberbullying (**www.stopcyberbullying.org**), SocialSafety.org (**www.socialsafety.org**), and the Family Online Safety Institute (**http://fosi.org/icra/**).

Speaking with children about Internet safety practices, being aware of where and when they surf, and knowing who their cyberfriends are should be a top priority. Concerned parents can implement the parental controls that are provided by their ISPs or included in safety and security software. Web site blocking and content-filtering software and monitoring programs like Net Nanny (**www.netnanny.com**), and bsecure (**www.bsecure.com**) can add another level of security (Figure 6.44).

After covering the personal uses for the Internet and addressing its benefits and drawbacks, let's change the focus to the Internet user conducting business.

Avoiding E-Commerce Hazards

Although there are many benefits to engaging in e-commerce, it also entails risks. These risks include identity theft, personal information exposure, money loss, and being ripped off by unscrupulous charlatans. To protect yourself, carefully create user names and passwords, particularly at sites where you must pay for goods or services. It is also wise to avoid e-commerce with little-known companies, at least until you've taken the opportunity to check their legitimacy. Checking shopping portals or other review sites to locate feedback from other users or conducting an online search combining the company's name with keywords such as *problem*, *fraud*, or *scam* can help you be better informed.

Even though you are most likely protected from monetary losses by your credit card company, you should always be careful when giving out your credit card information—and do so only on secure sites. Never share credit card numbers, account numbers, user name, or password information with others, even if you receive an e-mail requesting that information from what seems to be a legitimate source.

Sometimes you will find that the seller is a person just like you—that the seller doesn't have the ability to take credit cards and that he or she has set up an account with an online transaction processing system such as PayPal. It is the seller who decides which vendor to use for the payment. For instance, if you see the PayPal logo on an eBay auction item site, it means that you can use PayPal as a payment option. In fact, sometimes this is the only option available. The PayPal Web site even offers a tool to help you manage your buying experience. The PayPal AuctionFinder searches eBay for items you've recently won and prefills your payment form with details taken straight from the item listing. With AuctionFinder, you can eliminate errors and pay for your items instantly. Always use extra care and caution whenever you conduct financial transactions on the Internet.

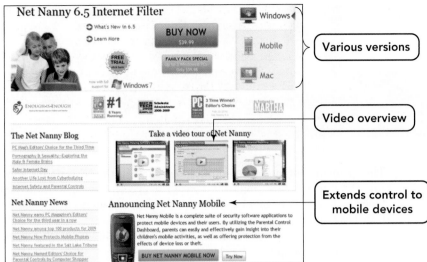

Various versions

Video overview

Extends control to mobile devices

FIGURE 6.44 Content-filtering software like Net Nanny are extending parental control from notebooks and desktop system to mobile devices.

How To:

Use the Favorites Feature of the Internet Explorer (IE) Browser

The Favorites menu located on the menu bar in the IE browser window allows you to insert a Web page into the Favorites list, making it easier to access later by not having to retype the URL in the address bar. Once you make a page a Favorite, all you have to do is click the name and the Web page will display in the browser window.

In this section, we cover how to perform two actions with respect to managing your Favorites:

- Adding a Web page to the Favorites list
- Organizing your Favorite list into folders

To add a Web page to the Favorites list:

1. Enter the URL of the page you want to access in the browser's address bar.

   After the page appears, click *Favorites* on the menu bar.

2. From the drop-down menu that appears, select *Add to Favorites* (Figure 6.45).

3. In the Add a Favorite dialog box you can do these things:

   a. Name the page you are inserting into the Favorites list or use the default.

   b. Create a new folder and place the current page into that folder.

   c. Place the page into a folder that already exists by clicking the arrow to the right of the *Create in* option.

4. After selecting your option, click *Add*. The current page is now an entry in your Favorites list.

You can organize your Favorites list into folders while you are adding the page as described above or after pages have been placed in the Favorites list.

To organize your Favorites list after Web pages have been added:

1. Click *Favorites* on the menu bar.

2. Select the *Organize Favorites* option.

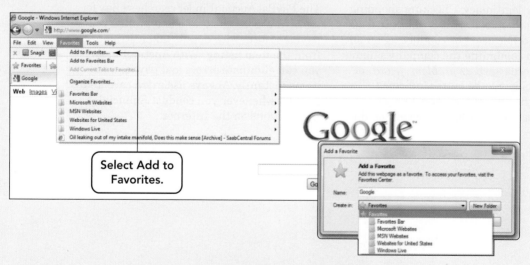

FIGURE 6.45 Select the *Add to Favorites* option to open the Add a Favorite dialog box.

3. In the Organize Favorites dialog box that appears, you have four choices: New Folder, Move, Rename, or Delete (Figure 6.46).

- Select *New Folder* to create and name a new folder.

- Highlight a Favorites entry and then select *Move*. A dialog box will open and ask you to select the location to which you want to move the entry.

- Select *Rename*, with an entry highlighted, and rename that entry in the top section of the dialog box.

- Select *Delete*, with an entry highlighted, to remove the entry from the Favorites list.

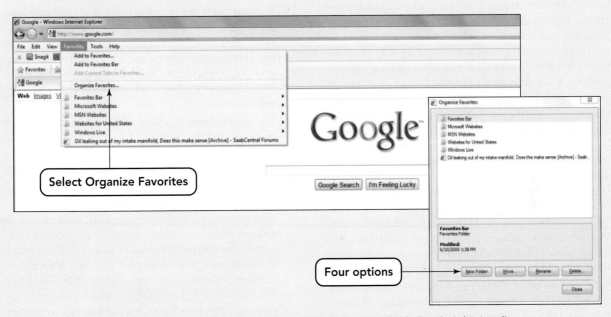

FIGURE 6.46 Your Favorites list can get very long. Adding folders will organize the list and make it easier to locate a site.

Chapter Summary

The Internet and the World Wide Web

- The Internet is the network of networks that, because of its interoperability, allows connected computers to exchange data regardless of model, brand, or operating system. Interoperability is made possible by the use of TCP/IP (Transmission Control Protocol/Internet Protocol) suite of protocols, the standard methods of packaging and transmitting information on the Internet.

- Users access the Internet by way of an Internet access provider. Access providers fall into three categories: Internet service provider (ISP), online service provider, and a wireless Internet service provider. A user connects to the access provider by way of a telephone modem, a digital service line (DSL), a cable modem, a satellite, or a fiber-optic cable.

- Whereas the Internet is a global computer network that connects millions of smaller networks, the World Wide Web is a global system of billions of hypertext documents, called Web pages. These documents use hyperlinks to connect to each other and the Internet as a transport mechanism. Web pages are displayed though a combination of elements, including hyperlinks to jump from one Web page to another, a browser to interpret the HTML tags and display the Web document, including enabling of hyperlinks, and a Web server that stores the Web pages and retrieves them when a request is made by a browser.

- Information on the Web can be located by entering the URL (Web address) in the address bar of the browser, general surfing, using searches with search operators to get more specific results, and using sites and technology that allow the sharing of information with other Web users, such as RSS feeds, blogs, and wikis. Search expressions can include search operators (+, −, *) or Boolean search terms (AND, OR, NOT) to narrow down the list of results.

- Features of a reliable Web source include an author with credentials, the affiliation of the Web site with the host, the objectivity of the material presented, the overall purpose of the site, and the accuracy and currency of the information.

- Popular Internet services include e-mail and instant messaging (IM) for sending messages, Internet relay chat (IRC) for text chatting, chat rooms, social networking sites for online communities, discussion groups, newsgroups, VoIP, message boards, and File Transfer Protocol (FTP) for file exchange, and e-commerce.

- There are three types of e-commerce, business-to-business (B2B), consumer-to-consumer (C2C), and business-to-consumer (B2C).

- When using the Web, be courteous and respect the rules of netiquette.

- Follow safe surfing guidelines, avoid malware, change your passwords frequently, never enter your account number unless you are on a secured site, watch the computer usage of your children, and install software to protect your children from cyberstalkers, cyberbullies, and undesirable Web sites. When conducting online business, be aware of security indicators on Web sites conducting e-commerce, and perform transactions only with secured sites.

Key Terms and Concepts

Identification

Label each item.

1. _____   3. _____   5. _____

2. _____   4. _____   6. _____

Matching

Match each key term in the left column with the most accurate definition in the right column.

_____ 1. hot spot

_____ 2. uploading

_____ 3. interoperability

_____ 4. portal

_____ 5. hyperlink

_____ 6. router

_____ 7. home page

_____ 8. clickstream

_____ 9. downloading

_____ 10. dead link

_____ 11. RSS

_____ 12. subject guide

_____ 13. browser

_____ 14. plug-in

_____ 15. link rot

a. Transferring a document or file from another computer to your computer

b. An element in an electronic document that acts as the connector to another place in the same document or to an entirely different document

c. The set of Web links that indicates the trail a user followed to reach a Web page

d. A method of providing constant information updates over the Internet without any user involvement

e. A public location, like an airport, college campus, or coffee shop, that provides Internet access for devices fitted with wireless technology

f. A list of subject-related categories that, when selected, displays a page of more related links

g. Additional software programs that extend the multimedia ability of a browser

h. Links to documents on the Web that have disappeared

i. Transferring a document or file from your computer to another computer

j. A program on the user's computer that interprets HTML or XHTML forms, enabling the user to view Web pages

k. A Web page that acts as a gateway to diverse sources presented in an organized way

l. Outdatedness due to the delay in accumulating data and updating a search engine's database

m. Specialized devices that connect networks, locate the best path of transmission, and ensure that your data reaches its destination

n. The default page that is automatically displayed when you enter a site at its top level

o. Describes the Internet's ability to work with computers and applications of different brands and models, through the use of a common protocol

Multiple Choice

Circle the correct choice for each of the following:

1. Which of the following is *not* a search operator?
   a. –
   b. +
   c. !
   d. *

2. Which of the following is an example of a valid IP address?
   a. 12.256.56.78
   b. 38.155.400.56
   c. 45.254.77.125
   d. 266.54.77.89

3. Which of the following is *not* a top-level domain name?
   a. .edu
   b. .car
   c. .net
   d. .gov

4. RSS feeds can be grouped together through the use of a(n) _____ program.
   a. browser
   b. aggregator
   c. syndication
   d. plug-in

5. Which Internet service is plagued by spam?
   a. Instant messaging
   b. E-mail
   c. VoIP
   d. Chat rooms

6. What does the appearance of a VeriSign logo on a Web site indicate?
   a. The site is a commercial site.
   b. The site has been recently updated.
   c. The site is hosted in the United States.
   d. The site is secure.

7. What term refers to the act of abusing or tormenting an individual through digital methods?
   a. Cyberbullying
   b. Cyberstalking
   c. E-tailing
   d. Flaming

8. Which is *not* a method of e-commerce?
   a. B2B   b. C2C
   c. C2B   d. B2C

9. What is the name of spam that targets users of instant messaging?
   a. Spimming
   b. Botnet
   c. Spyware
   d. Beacon

10. A(n) _____ is a Web page on which any visitor can post text or images, read previous posts, change earlier posts, and track changes.
    a. blog
    b. wiki
    c. newsgroup
    d. electronic mailing list

Fill-In

In the blanks provided, write the correct answer for each of the following.

1. _____ is a search technique that makes use of wildcards to locate words with various endings.

2. _____ is the next generation of the Web that provides increased opportunities for collaboration.

3. _____ is a unique numerical identifier for each computer or device connected to the Internet.

4. A(n) _____ is the equivalent of an Internet diary or journal.

5. A(n) _____ is a program that travels the Web and populates the database of a search engine.

6. _____ is unsolicited e-mail.

7. A(n) _____ provides individuals and businesses with access to the Internet via phone, DSL, cable, satellite, or fiber-optic lines, for a fee.

8. A(n) _____ is a series of articles that offer a continuing commentary on the same subject.

9. _____ is a worldwide computer-based discussion system accessible through the Internet.

10. E-bay is an example of a(n) _____ e-commerce site.

11. A(n) _____ is an angry or critical response to a violation of netiquette.

12. _____ is a type of spam that collects data from a user's system without his or her knowledge.

13. _____ is the online exchange or trade of goods, services, or information between two businesses.

14. A _____ is a method of sharing information over the Internet in audio, image, or video format.

15. A(n) _____ is a Web-based retailer.

Short Answer

1. Explain the difference between the Internet and the Web.

2. List the three types of access providers and give a brief description of each.

3. List three drawbacks of distributing content over the Web.

4. What is Real Simple Syndication (RSS)?

5. List the characteristics that help to evaluate the credibility of content on Web pages.

Teamwork

1. **Security Vendors** As a team, research at least three security certificate vendors. Provide a brief description of each and describe the logo that each is identified by. Then locate at least 10 Web sites that display one of the logos that you described. Present your vendor's descriptions, logos, and the 10 associated Web sites in a PowerPoint presentation. Remember to cite your references and include the full URL of your Web site examples.

2. **Evaluating Web content** Break into groups of two or three. Each group should locate a Web site with information on a topic being covered in class or another topic approved by the instructor. Evaluate the site based on the criteria listed in this chapter. Using your word processor, create a table to display your findings. List the criteria in column 1 and your evaluation in column 2. Using the reference feature of your word processor, create end notes and reference the Web sites used. Present your evaluations in a one- to two-page word processing document.

3. **Using a Search Engine** As a team, evaluate each of the search statements below and describe the result that each will achieve. Use **www.internettutorials.net** for help with symbols you might not understand. Then create the search string to meet the specified change. Take a screen capture of the results from each search. Complete the table that follows and turn in the completed table and the screen capture from each one of the five searches.

   To create a screen capture, first press *PrtScrn* on the keyboard while the search result is on the screen. Open the Word file you plan to submit for this question. Position the cursor in the location where you want the capture to appear, and from the contextual menu in the Word window select *Edit*, then select *Paste*. The PrintScrn image captured earlier will appear in the Word document. Then save and print the document.

4. **Web-Based Course Management Systems** Most colleges and universities use some sort of Web-based course management system to provide online classes or an additional resource for face-to-face classes. Evaluate the effectiveness of the course management system at your school by breaking into two groups. Have one group create a survey and distribute it to students that are using the system. Have the other group create a survey and distribute it to faculty that are using the system. The survey should contain 8 to 10 questions and focus on the type of materials that are posted on the system, the amount of time respondents use or access the system on a weekly basis, their opinion of the effectiveness of this media for learning, and the integrity of the learning that takes place in this environment. Distribute the survey to at least 10 students and 10 faculty members. As a team, collect and summarize the results. Present your summary and analysis of the data in a PowerPoint presentation.

5. **Digital Communication** As a team, create a survey to evaluate the digital communication preferences of students at your school. Include questions on the type of devices they use (smartphones, notebooks, desktops), the type of media they use (blogs, wikis, e-mail, text messaging, course management system), the amount they pay for the service (if they pay), the frequency of use, and some general questions like the gender and class level (freshman, sophomore, junior, or senior). Distribute the survey to at least 20 students on campus. Collect and analyze the responses. As a team, draw usage conclusions from the data collected. Use a PowerPoint presentation to present a summary of your results and the conclusions your team drew from the data.

Search String	Purpose	Change to Be Made	Search String with Change
Sports + Hockey		exclude the Sabres	
"Absence makes the heart grow fonder"		include Shakespeare	
logo sports		include baseball	
clothing + LLBean + women		remove women and add men	
Go Green + US		remove US and add clothing	

1. **Blogging for Beginners** Go to **www.blogger.com/start** and create a blog that you will add content to daily for a week. The blog content is to be about your experience in using a blogging site, the features of the site that you like or don't like, and an evaluation of the whole experience. Invite some of your classmates to participate in the blog. Your blog will be your report, so make it detailed and professional. Provide your instructor with the blog address so he/she can follow the postings. Remember the blog and its content will be considered as your submitted assignment.

2. **Using an Aggregator** Use a search engine to locate free aggregators. Review a few aggregators and select one to use in this exercise. Aggregator sites usually have categories like news and sports that contain several Web sites having RSS feeds. Select a category and then view the individual subscriptions that are available. Use the *Add* option to subscribe to a feed, and include a few of your own preferred Web sites (ESPN, USA Today) with RSS feeds in the subscription list. When they appear, locate the manage subscription option and organize the ones you added by placing them into existing categories or by creating a new separate category. Delete a few of the ones that are in the category you chose. Check out some of the other features of the aggregator. There is usually an option to return to a home page, some way to track your reading trends, and even a way to share your reader with others. After using the program for a while, review your experience. In a one-page, double-spaced paper, describe the aggregator site you chose and explain why you chose that site. Also discuss how easy (or difficult) the site was to use, the amount of feeds you received, and whether or not you would use such a program. Include any other observations and bits of advice for another user. Remember to cite your references.

3. **Plug-ins: Are They Cool or Irritating** Go to **www.coolhomepages.com/** or **www.ebizmba.com/articles/best-flash-sites** to view Web sites that make use of Flash animation. Select and view three sites. Did you have to download a plug-in, or did you already have the necessary one on your system? Are the displayed graphics of high quality and does the animation enhance the site? How long was the load time? If the site had a Flash introduction, would you like the opportunity to skip the intro?

Evaluate the three sites you viewed. Answer the previously listed questions and provide any other thoughts about your Flash experience in a one-page, double-spaced paper. Remember to cite the URL of each site.

4. **Internet Ethics** The one area of Internet use that seems to cause more controversy than others is downloading music. For some reason, the consensus is not as clear-cut on the legality of this behavior. Users compare downloading music to lending a CD to a friend. Producers and artists consider it theft. Using a search engine, identify at least two Web sites that facilitate music downloads. Review their policy, legal statements, and agreements. Who is liable if the sharing done on their site is found to be illegal? Are there any fees to subscribe to or use the site? In what country is the site being hosted? Attempt to locate statistics on the number of music downloads and the loss of revenue to the music and related industries related to downloading music files. In a PowerPoint presentation, review your findings for these and other related issues that you come across in your research. Suggest any viable solutions that you see as a compromise to this ongoing controversy. Remember to cite your references.

5. **Create Your Own Avatar** With all of the methods of animation that appear on the Internet, let's try one that is relatively new, an avatar. These talking images can be embedded within e-mails, Facebook pages, blogs, and Web sites. Using a search engine, locate a reputable Web site that allows you to create and publish you own avatar for free (**www.voki.com** is just one suggestion). Some sites offer avatars of comic book characters, television personalities, and individuals from history. Locate a site and create and customize your avatar. Most sites allow you to choose an image and then change the features of that image. Once you have your avatar's appearance completed, you will need to add the words that you want the avatar to say. This can be done by recording the words yourself with a microphone, typing them into a text box, or uploading an audio file. If you are not using your own voice, you can select the voice to speak your content. Make the content of your recording focus on your experience with this method of communication. When your avatar is complete, publish it and send an e-mail to your instructor that includes the avatar.

Spotlight

Cloud Computing

Are you tired of storing your data on external hard drives, flash drives, and DVDs? Do you check these portable devices before you leave for school or work to make sure that they contain the information you need for the day? Are you frustrated with renaming versions of a file so that you know which file on which storage device is the most recent? Do you travel and need your files to be accessible from any location at any time of the day? If you answered yes to any of these questions, then cloud computing may be the solution you have been waiting for.

A few years ago cloud computing was a new buzzword and IT concept that was surrounded by confusion and uncertainty. Most individuals weren't sure exactly what cloud computing was. They didn't understand how it was going to affect IT departments, the academic environment, the business world, and enterprise planning for future technology resources. Today, *cloud computing* is a common term in IT circles, and articles about it, containing both positive and negative content, appear daily on RSS news feeds. It seems that it has gone from a buzzword to a reality while we were sleeping. No longer can it be ignored by individuals who use technology for work, education, or even entertainment. Cloud computing is here, and such companies as salesforce.com and Workday are trying to persuade the world that it is here to stay. This spotlight clarifies what cloud computing is, focusing on its essential characteristics, service categories, and deployment models, and pointing out both its positive and negative features. We'll also look at statistics that support cloud computing's predicted continuing growth.

What Is Cloud Computing?

The cloud has been a familiar image or symbol for the Internet for sometime; however, connecting it with the word *computing* has caused some confusion and created a blurry image. **Cloud computing**, according to the Computer Security Division of the National Institute of Standards and Technology, "is a model for enabling convenient, on-demand network access to a shared pool of configurable computing resources that can be rapidly provisioned and released with minimal management effort or service provider interaction. This cloud model promotes availability and is composed of five general characteristics: on-demand self-service, broad network access, resource pooling, rapid elasticity, and measured service" (Figure 5A).

That is quite a comprehensive definition. Let's start to break it down by first examining each of the listed general characteristics.

- **On-demand self-service.** The customer or subscriber, without the need to contact or interact with a human from the cloud provider (self-service), can increase or decrease computing requirements as needed (on-demand). Computing requirements can include such necessities as server use, network storage, and software applications.

- **Broad network access.** This is the most significant component of cloud computing. The services offered by a provider must be accessible over a network, from any location, and on any standardized platform, including mobile phones and PDAs. This means that the hardware and software that you use to perform tasks on your local computer are actually on someone else's system, the provider's. You access them through a network—for a fee. The Internet, the only network that provides this scope of capability, is the core of cloud computing and is associated with the cloud image that is a part of every cloud computing illustration.

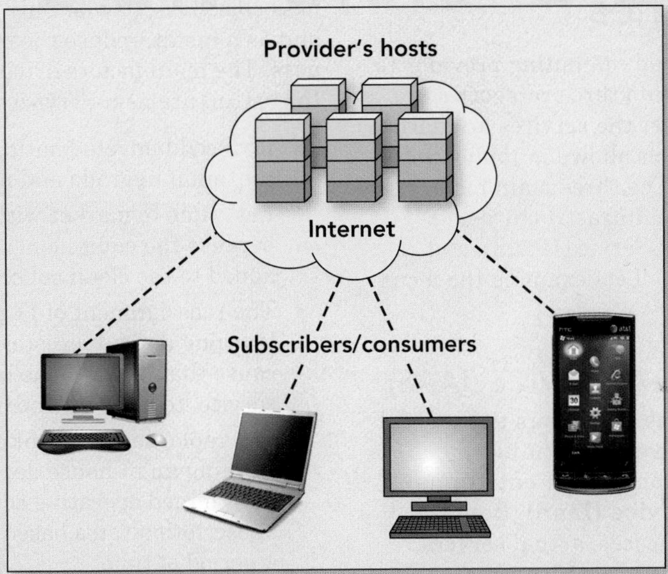

- **Resource pooling.** This characteristic refers to the provider's ability to pool services to accommodate their use by multiple subscribers at the same time. These resources are assigned when a subscriber signs on and are dynamically reassigned as demands by other subscribers occur. The subscriber (user or client) is unaware of the location of the resources he or she is using or any reassignment taking place. In cloud computing, the user gets the programs and hardware support that he or she needs, and the provider (cloud owner) gets paid. In a cloud computing environment, the burden of work is on the cloud provider to maintain, upgrade, and administer the hosts (servers) that constitute their cloud.

- **Rapid elasticity.** This term refers to the ability of a subscriber to increase computing resources in spike or peak times without having to worry about overloading a system or having to purchase additional hardware for a minimal amount of high-performance need. The size and capacity of a cloud provider allow the subscriber to scale up or down as needed and pay for only the time and amount of services used.

- **Measured service.** The cloud provider must meter usage to use this information for billing, but more importantly, to analyze usage and respond appropriately. Predictions for changes and upgrades for a cloud provider are developed primarily from the data obtained from its usage meters. If it intends to keep subscribers, it must expand, reallocate, and change in a manner that meets its subscribers' needs.

FIGURE 5A The main component of cloud computing is the Internet, the broad network that acts as a delivery vehicle used to transport services from a provider to a subscriber.

In general, hosting computers (servers) and subscribers (clients) are the main components of cloud computing—just as they are in a traditional client/server network. So what distinguishes cloud computing from a traditional client/server network? There are three major differences:

- In cloud computing, the delivery of the services from the provider to a subscriber must be over the Internet.

- The services provided over the cloud by a provider are scalable; they can be increased or decreased as the needs of an individual subscriber or company change. Services are typically offered and billed by the minute or hour.

- The services provided are managed completely by the cloud provider, the owner or manager of the host. The client or subscriber of the service does not have to worry about having a specific computer or operating system, or a certain processor or amount of RAM, and does not need to purchase software upgrades or download service patches. The subscribed services are not on the individual's computer or system. They are on the provider's hosts and are maintained by that provider and simply accessed by the subscriber.

Now that the main characteristics of cloud computing have been covered, let's investigate the three primary categories into which all cloud computing can be divided.

Cloud Computing Service Categories

The features offered by a cloud computing provider to a subscriber can be divided into three categories or models, depending on whether the services are hardware based, software based, or allow for application and interface development. The three main models of cloud computing services are: Infrastructure-as-a-Service (IaaS), Platform-as-a-Service (PaaS), and Software-as-a-Service (SaaS). Lets examine the focus of each.

INFRASTRUCTURE-AS-A-SERVICE (IAAS)

The category of cloud services that refers to the outsourcing of hardware, the equipment used to sustain the operations of a company or enterprise, is **Infrastructure-as-a-Service (IaaS)**. Because IaaS encompasses storage devices, actual servers, and network components it is also referred to as **Hardware-as-a-Service (HaaS)**. Providers of IaaS, such as Cloud.com, VMware, and Citrix, offer subscribers an offsite virtual datacenter as part of their information technology (IT) environment. This movement of the IT infrastructure from in-house to off premises aligns itself with the view that owning and operating a datacenter is no longer cost-effective (Figure 5B).

Through the use of virtualization and grids, IaaS is able to provide the hardware structure and scalability needed for both small business and enterprise functions. In **virtualization**, the application and infrastructure are independent. This means that one physical machine can run several virtual machines. A **virtual machine** is not an actual physical machine, but a software-created segment of a hard drive that contains its own operating system and applications, which makes it behave as a separate physical machine in the eyes of the user. For a brief, humorous (yet informative) video on virtualization and cloud computing in plain English, go to **www.youtube.com/watch?v=XdBd14rjcs0&feature=player_embedded#!**

A **grid** is a combination of several computers or virtual machines that are connected over a network to make them appear and function as one single computer (Figure 5C). The use of both virtualization and grids has made it possible for Infrastructure- as-a-Service to provide virtual datacenters and enable companies to eliminate the high cost of equipment and personnel to manage such a facility; focus more on their core business objectives; pay for only the equipment they use; and as a result, reduce the overall cost of doing business. The main factors driving enterprises to use Infrastructure-as-a-Service are as follows:

- Reduced budgeted outlay for equipment and its continual upgrade and maintenance
- Fast time to market with programs and ideas because the equipment needed to run them can be added to the cloud subscription
- The reassignment of IT personnel from a focus on learning and administering new equipment, because that is now done by the provider of the service, to more business-related tasks
- The replacement of unknown costs associated with running an in-house datacenter with known, predetermined operating costs provided through set subscription rates based on the services used over a period of time

PLATFORM-AS-A-SERVICE (PAAS)

The category of cloud services that permits subscribers to have remote access to application development, interface development, database development, storage, and testing is **Platform-as-a-Service**. This is the feature that enables the creation and testing of subscriber-developed programs and interfaces, using a cloud provider's hardware and development environment. For the subscriber, this is a huge savings because the equipment

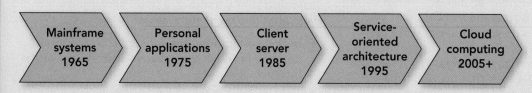

FIGURE 5B The development of IT infrastructure over time.

Mainframe systems 1965 → Personal applications 1975 → Client server 1985 → Service-oriented architecture 1995 → Cloud computing 2005+

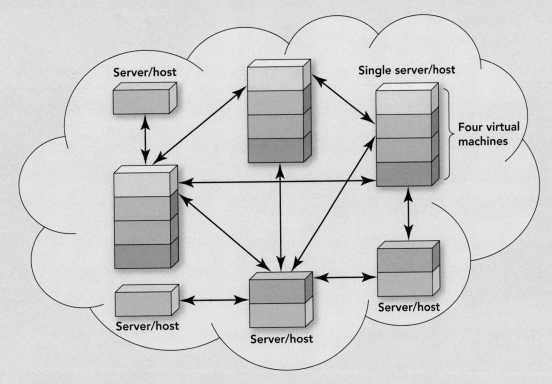

FIGURE 5C Virtualization and computer grids enable a cloud provider to create a network of widely dispersed computers and make it appear to run as a traditional centralized datacenter.

and software do not have to be purchased to test a possible application or interface and the fear of crashing a system during testing is alleviated by using the provider's secure test environment. Platform-as-a-Service providers include Google App Engine, Force.com, and Oracle SaaS.

SOFTWARE-AS-A-SERVICE (SAAS)

The most widely used and widely known form of cloud computing is **Software-as-a-Service (SaaS)**. The SaaS model of cloud computing enables software to be deployed from a cloud provider, delivered over the Internet, and accessed by a subscriber through a browser. Statistics from a recent survey of SaaS users by Datamation and THINKstrategies indicate that approximately 85 percent of subscribers are satisfied with the service, 80 percent would renew their subscriptions, and 61 percent would expand services. The primary reasons to subscribe to SaaS include these:

- Limited risk
- Rapid deployment
- Fewer upfront costs, such as the expense of purchasing a server
- Increased reliability as seen in reduced downtime caused by service disruptions
- Standardized backup procedures

- Lower total cost of ownership (TCO) through reduced hardware costs, software purchases, license agreements, and personnel to run and administer the systems

There are two major categories of SaaS: consumer services and business services. **Consumer-oriented services**, like those supplied by Google Apps and Google Docs, are offered to the public either on a subscription basis or, if supported by advertisement, for no cost (Figure 5D). **Business services** are sold to enterprise and business organizations of all sizes, usually on a subscription basis. This category of SaaS services

FIGURE 5D Google Docs offers SaaS with a limited amount of storage to individual users, free of charge.

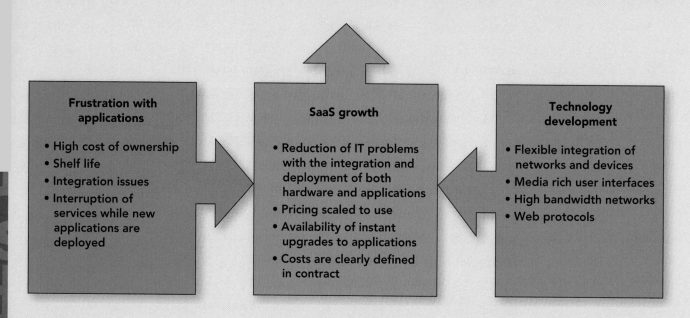

FIGURE 5E   Key Factors in the High Success Rate of Software-as-a-Service

focuses on facilitating business practices, for example financial services and customer relationship management (CRM). Two of the main incentives for the success of Software-as-a-Service are the user's frustration with his or her installed applications and the maturity of technology that enables the sharing of an application by multiple users over a reliable, flexible, high-bandwidth network. Figure 5E provides a more detailed list of factors behind the success of SaaS. Providers of Software-as-a-Service include Salesforce, Oracle on demand, and Google Apps.

The categories of cloud computing help to departmentalize cloud services, but how these services are deployed adds to their security and accessibility. Let's take a closer look at the main models of cloud deployment.

Cloud Deployment Methods

The way cloud services are accessed, owned, used, and physically located determines the deployment of the cloud service (Figure 5F). There are three basic types of deployment models:

- **Private cloud. A private cloud** is operated for a single organization and its authorized users. The infrastructure can exist on-site or off-site and is controlled by either the organization or a contracted third party. A **community cloud** is an extension of a private cloud in which organizations with similar missions share the infrastructure to reduce cost. This variation of the private cloud disperses cost while providing a high level of

FIGURE 5F   Features of Cloud Deployment Methods

Cloud Deployment	Managed by	Infrastructure Ownership	Infrastructure Location	Accessible by
Private cloud	Organization	Organization or third party	On premises or off premises	Trusted users
Public cloud	Third-party provider	Third-party provider	Off premises	Untrusted users
Hybrid cloud	Both the organization and third-party provider	Both the organization and third-party provider	Both on premises and off premises	Both trusted and untrusted users

Modified from **www.rationalsurvivability.com/blog/?p=743**

FIGURE 5G The type of cloud deployment chosen by an enterprise may be directly related to security issues.

conformity and security by allowing access only to trusted users. Google's Gov Cloud is an example of a community cloud.

- **Public cloud.** Available to the general public, large organizations, or a group of organizations, the **public cloud** offers the most risk because it is accessed by users that have not been authenticated or established as trusted. Its infrastructure is owned and operated by a cloud provider and is located off site.

- **Hybrid cloud.** The **hybrid cloud** deployment method is a combination of two or more clouds (private, community, or public) that are unique but are connected by common, standard technology that enables the sharing of applications and data. Its infrastructure can be located both on-site and off the premises, and it can be managed by both the organization and a cloud provider. Users can be trusted and untrusted.

A big difference between cloud deployment models is the concern over security. A careful needs assessment and examination of security requirements are key to making the right choices for cloud computing.

As you can see in Figure 5G, a private network operates in what can be viewed as its own private disconnected cloud. The only users are those authorized and approved by the organization that owns and manages the cloud. The entire private cloud, its services, and users are behind a firewall, a security device that is actually a combination of software and hardware that stops data from exiting a network or private cloud and filters data attempting to enter a network from the Internet or public cloud. While logged into a private network and accessing its resources, the right to use the Internet or public network may be denied.

A public cloud is the least secure deployment method because its infrastructure and resources are subscribed to from a cloud provider that operates outside of the firewall. The provider of public cloud services is responsible for the security of the data and resources that it stores and provides to subscribers. This loss of control over security is a concern of some and a relief for other public cloud users.

A hybrid cloud is a combination of both types of deployment. In a hybrid cloud model, a portion of the cloud is private and behind the firewall, whereas another portion is public and outside of the firewall. Hybrids can be used to ease the transition from a private cloud to a public cloud or to secure portions of enterprise data in the private segment while still enabling access to the wide scope of services offered by public segment.

Any attempt to implement cloud computing will include a hard look at both the pros and cons of such a decision. Let's examine that area next.

Pros and Cons of Cloud Computing

Remember that technology is always changing, so the pros and cons of cloud computing will change with new developments. Additionally, something viewed as a negative feature by one enterprise or individual can be seen as an asset by another. A closer look at the current pros and cons of cloud computing might provide some insight into the features to consider if a move to the cloud is in your future (Figure 5H).

THE PROS OF CLOUD COMPUTING

The cloud seems to present a delicate balance between benefits and risks. If subscribers are willing to manage some of the risks themselves and not rely completely on the provider, then the downside of cloud computing is less of a gamble. Let's first review the positive

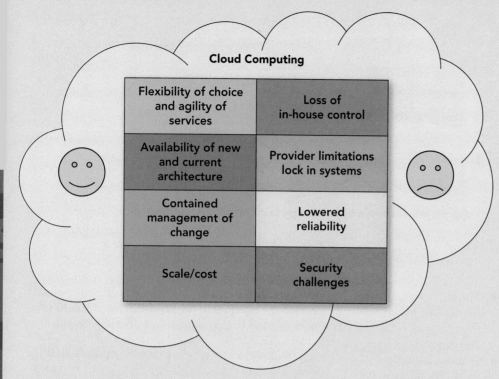

Cloud Computing

Flexibility of choice and agility of services	Loss of in-house control
Availability of new and current architecture	Provider limitations lock in systems
Contained management of change	Lowered reliability
Scale/cost	Security challenges

FIGURE 5H The Main Advantages (+) and Disadvantages (−) of Cloud Computing

features of cloud computing in the light of today's technology.

Scale and Cost A big factor in transitioning to cloud computing for many organizations is the ability to meet increasing IT demands without having to absorb the high cost of equipment. This means that offerings can be expanded on a trial basis and analyzed to determine the business assets of such an implementation without accruing the "high cost of doing business." The organization or enterprise does not have to purchase equipment, license software, and hire personnel. If the innovation were not successful, the business's losses would be confined to the increase in the cloud subscription for the hardware, software, and management activities used for the period that the services were engaged. This is the beauty of cloud computing. Services can be scaled up or back depending on need. The only cost to the organization or enterprise is a change in their subscription rate that reflects the costs for only those services used.

Encapsulated Change Management The maintenance, upgrade, or even a total change to the infrastructure of an enterprise is no longer a huge concern because cloud providers make use of a cloud operating system and virtualization. A **cloud operating system**, like Windows Azure, is specially designed to run a cloud provider's datacenter and is delivered to subscribers over the Internet or other network. Recall that virtualization is used by cloud

providers to wrap an operating system and application in a self-contained segment of a hard drive, making it appear as if it were an independent stand-alone machine. Through the use of virtualization and a cloud operating system, hardware and associated technology can be maintained, redistributed, and redirected to accommodate a subscriber's request without major reconfiguration.

Choice and Agility Without having to make costly commitments to hardware purchases and software licensing, cloud computing enables a subscriber to deploy solutions that best suit current needs and trends. It also allows flexibility to alter those solutions if the market or corporate financial situation changes. With this ability to amend solutions to match market demands comes the additional flexibility to choose among vendors. This freedom of choice is referred to as **interoperability**, the ability of a service from one provider to work with the services of another, without any subscriber interaction. What enables interoperability is **middleware**, a broad term for software that enables interoperability by assisting the passing of data among applications. Middleware provides a smooth and safe interface between network nodes and servers (Figure 5I). The results are an improvement in overall performance and flexibility because a subscriber is not tied to one provider, an essential factor if a provider goes out of business or one of its datacenters goes down. Middleware is essential for scalability as well as interoperability in the cloud.

Next-Generation Architectures The cloud enables innovation and creativity by allowing the testing and piloting of new database structures, languages, and framework through PaaS providers. Using this service provides a safe development environment, without the developer having to purchase expensive hardware and software or worrying that the deployment of the new application might interfere or crash their in-house system. Through cloud computing, innovation and foresight in IT areas are not a threat to the bottom line or current operations. Instead, they are viewed as futuristic and inventive.

Shifting from the positive to the negative, let's examine some of the shortcomings of cloud computing.

THE CONS OF CLOUD COMPUTING

Lock-in Not all cloud providers offer interoperability or the agility of choice, so "buyer beware." If you foresee your needs changing or the need for a future application that one provider supplies and another does not, make sure that you are not locked in to your provider and can switch providers without losing your ability to access or read your data. Total interoperability within the cloud is one of the long-term goals of the "Open Cloud" movement.

Reliability There is a possibility that the cloud provider will lose power, run into trouble, burn down, or simply go out of business. If any of these actions did occur and your provider did not have interoperable services, you might lose all of your data. If you believe that this could never happen, you are wrong. In mid-2009, within one week, there were power outages at several datacenters that host high-profile sites like the video site Daily motion, the credit card authorization service Authorize.net, and Microsoft's Bing Travel. Additionally, with the economy the way it is, it is not impossible that a cloud provider might have to go out of business for financial reasons. If this happens, how would you access your files? Once again "buyer beware." Read the subscription conditions carefully and look for the features that give you reliability, agility, and choice.

Lack of Control Some enterprise IT staff might be uncomfortable surrendering control over resources to someone else. Not only does cloud computing surrender control to a perfect stranger, but that stranger is someone somewhere in the cloud that in-house staff will probably never meet. Scheduled maintenance, upgrades, and backups are no longer done on the premises by employees but by the provider. Administrative tasks like adding users, deleting users, and altering access rights may be done either by the subscriber's IT staff or the provider. Letting go of the daily maintenance of your infrastructure can be a difficult concession to make to receive the benefits that the cloud offers.

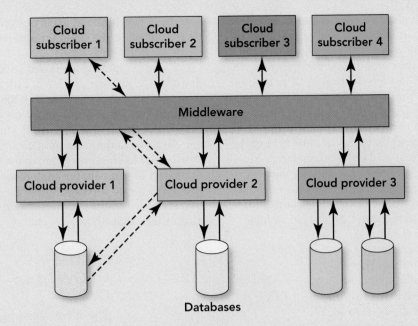

FIGURE 5I Middleware is the reason that a change in provider, indicated by the dotted line, can appear seamless to a subscriber.

Security There are hundreds, maybe thousands, of articles on the security, or lack of security, in the cloud. Many of the security concerns are centered on the data being stored on servers owned and controlled by the cloud provider not the subscriber. The main issues are over who actually owns the data, the secure storage of Social Security numbers and credit card numbers, and compliance with **Sarbanes-Oxley (SOX)**—an act administered by the Securities and Exchange Commission (SEC) that specifies the type of records that need to be stored and how long they must be kept, but leaves the method of storage up to the business.

This concern of ownership and security is heightened when a cloud provider, sometimes called the primary cloud, makes use of composite clouds. A **composite cloud** evolves when a primary cloud provider offers services that are distributed through another cloud provider. Such services can include storage, computing power, or application hosting. This nesting of cloud services can have serious reliability and security issues. In addition to ownership and compliance issues, there is also a loss of control over security when a service is deployed to a cloud provider.

With cloud computing **risk management**, the process of analyzing exposure to risk and determining how to best handle it within the tolerance level set by the enterprise, is transferred to the cloud provider. Chief security officers (CSOs) have the problem of defining the risk tolerance of the enterprise and then matching it with the risk tolerance of a cloud provider, a task that is not easily done. Choosing a private or hybrid cloud deployment is often based on security issues, with hybrid deployment often viewed as a transition or test of the services, including security, in the public cloud. An August 2009 survey of 200 information technology (IT) professionals reported that 43 percent felt that cloud computing was less secure than performing such services in house.

Another issue that CSOs have to deal with is that moving services to a cloud provider is often viewed by IT staff members as a threat to their positions. These individuals have the power to create havoc with corporate information and operations. In the same August 2009 report, 47 percent of the 200 IT professionals felt that a shift to cloud services was perceived as a prelude to a reduction in IT personnel. This is supported by the IBM claim that a business could see up to a 50 percent reduction in IT labor costs as the result of a shift to cloud computing.

So, in the end, it usually comes to some type of compromise between cost and risk management. For those shopping for a cloud provider, I guess the best advice is to realize that not all cloud providers are created equal. Conducting due diligence is essential when transferring services to the cloud. As the old saying goes, "All that glitters is not gold." For all of the positive arguments supporting cloud computing, those that oppose the technology can list an equal number of negative arguments. However, projections seem to indicate that even with its negative features, the future is in the cloud. A look at some of the current statistics and future projections might surprise you.

The Future of Cloud Computing

Every new and emerging technology sparks articles, arguments, and documentation from supporters and opponents. Cloud computing is no different. Statistics from an IDC report published in mid-2010 support the continued growth of cloud computing, despite the concerns over security. The report cited some interesting projections:

- In 2009, cloud services were centered in the western hemisphere, with the United States receiving 70.2 percent of the revenue. However, the report predicts that by 2014, that figure will decline to 51.4 percent, with Western Europe and the Asia/Pacific regions making up the difference.
- Worldwide revenue from public IT cloud computing was $16 billion in 2009. The report projects 2014 revenue to exceed $55.5 billion.
- Cloud computing is growing at a rate that is five times greater than any traditional IT product.
- Cloud applications (Software-as-a-Service) were the main service in 2009. The 2014 projection of revenue redistribution leans toward a decrease in the importance of this service (SaaS) and an increase in Infrastructure-as-a-Service (IaaS) and Platform-as-a-Service (PaaS).

Another survey completed in 2010 by the PEW Internet & American Life Project and Elon University's Imagining the Internet Center, using a nonrandom sample of 895 Internet experts, supports the projection on migration to the cloud for applications and online storage.

Cloud computing is viewed as a means to test and distribute a new generation of killer apps, a method to penetrate global markets, and a means for smaller or medium-sized businesses to compete in the global market, because of decreased IT start-up costs.

As more and more organizations and individuals subscribed to cloud services, more and more providers appeared to compete for customers. This growth in providers led to the need for some guiding principles to provide a strategy for new cloud providers and realign those that already exist.

> " Conducting **due diligence** is **essential** when transferring **services** to **the cloud.** "

GUIDELINES FOR THE GROWTH OF AN OPEN CLOUD

The current and predicted growth of cloud computing indicate that the number of cloud providers will also increase. In March 2009, the **Open Cloud Manifesto** was published. This document provided some guides and business practices for cloud providers in an attempt to guarantee subscribers the freedom of choice, flexibility, and openness they need in order to take full advantage of the benefits of cloud computing. Some of the key principles stressed include the following:

- Cloud providers must work together and collaborate to see that the vulnerabilities and assets of the cloud are addressed.
- A provider should not lock subscribers into its platform, thus removing their freedom of choice.
- Providers should reduce repetition of standards by using those in existence and create new ones that do not repeat or reinvent those that already exist.
- Any changes to the standards should be driven by subscribers, not the needs of the provider.

Since its publication, the manifesto has over 375 supporters and is still growing. You can view the complete document at **http://opencloudmanifesto.org/**

The Effect of Cloud Computing on the Enterprise

Cloud computing affects not only the workings of the information technology divisions of an enterprise but also the way the entire enterprise views and uses its cloud computing capability. Some of the effects that will result from shifting to the cloud for infrastructure, platform, and software include the following:

- IT costs will be more directly related to value. If the IT department can utilize the cloud to maximize capacity on demand and meet the fluctuating needs of its customers, the result of decreased computing costs will result in a decrease in the cost of goods sold—and thus an increase in overall market value of the enterprise.
- IT departments will be more agile. The ability of an enterprise to select or change providers as their needs change and the "open cloud" concept solidifies will make the corporate IT infrastructure more elastic, agile, and amenable to change.

- Creating and testing new innovations with a greatly reduced capital outlay will encourage businesses to promote creativity, resulting in more changes taking place in less time.
- The need to stay current with business and customer demands and requests is pushing the cloud toward real-time switching among cloud resources. Real-time switching is the seamless moving of cloud computing workloads between private clouds and public clouds to maximize the best value available at the time.

It appears that the sky is the limit and that the future is in the clouds!

Key Terms and Concepts

Multiple Choice

1. Which is *not* one of the three main categories of cloud computing services?
   a. Infrastructure-as-a-Service (IaaS)
   b. Platform-as-a-Service (PaaS)
   c. Communication-as-a-Service (CaaS)
   d. Software-as-a-Service (SaaS)

2. Which model of cloud computing services provides the servers, storage devices, and networks for a subscriber?
   a. Infrastructure-as-a-Service (IaaS)
   b. Platform-as-a-Service (PaaS)
   c. Communication-as-a-Service (CaaS)
   d. Software-as-a-Service (SaaS)

3. Which cloud deployment model is operated solely for a single organization and its authorized users?
   a. Community cloud   b. Hybrid cloud
   c. Public cloud   d. Private cloud

4. Which cloud characteristic refers to the ability of a subscriber to increase or decrease its computing requirements as needed without having to contact a human representative of the cloud provider?
   a. Rapid elasticity
   b. On-demand self service
   c. Broad network access
   d. Resource pooling

5. Which cloud deployment model is managed by a cloud provider, has an infrastructure that is off site, and is accessible to the general public?
   a. Community cloud
   b. Hybrid cloud
   c. Public cloud
   d. Private cloud

6. In which category of SaaS services does customer relationship management (CRM) software fall?
   a. Consumer services
   b. Communication services
   c. Infrastructure services
   d. Business services

7. Which statistic correctly represents cloud computing?
   a. In 2009, Western Europe received a majority of cloud computing revenue.
   b. Global cloud computing revenue for 2009 exceeded $16 million.
   c. Cloud computing growth is five times greater than any traditional IT product
   d. In 2009, the main cloud computing service was PaaS.

8. Which is considered the most widely used cloud computing service?
   a. Infrastructure-as-a-Service (IaaS)
   b. Platform-as-a-Service (PaaS)
   c. Communication-as-a-Service (CaaS)
   d. Software-as-a-Service (SaaS)

9. Interoperability is enabled by _____.
   a. a cloud operating system
   b. middleware
   c. a community cloud
   d. a composite cloud

10. Which refers to the practice of a primary cloud provider offering services that are distributed through another cloud provider?
    a. Hybrid cloud
    b. Composite cloud
    c. Virtualization
    d. Grid computing

Spotlight Exercises

1. View the video on cloud computing at **http://commoncraft.com/cloud-computing-video**. This is a very simple and easy to understand explanation of cloud computing. Using this video as a model, develop a simple PowerPoint presentation that explains how Software-as-a-Service can be beneficial for colleges and for students. Use a common cloud provider of SaaS, for example Google Docs, to make your presentation more specific and relative. Present the slide show to the class. Follow up the presentation with a discussion on how the cloud might be a viable option for your classmates as students or future employees.

2. Interview the chief information officer (CIO) at your school or the director of information technology (IT). Inquire about the possibility of the school moving to cloud computing. Ask if such considerations were included in the long-term plan and what the financial benefit for such a move would be to the school and the students. Come up with a few of your own questions to determine the direction that the administrators of your school are considering. Using a word processor, summarize your findings in a one-page, double-spaced report.

3. Create a free account in Google Docs, a Software-as-a-Service (SaaS) provider. Try the document, spreadsheet, and presentation applications for a few days. Transfer files from your portable storage device or hard disk drive to the cloud storage provided by Google Docs. Access the files in Google Docs' cloud storage from another location. See whether a file made in any of the applications on this site can be opened by any of the comparable Microsoft office applications. After a few days, using a word processor, summarize your experience in a one-page, double-spaced report.

4. A direct result of any new IT development is an abundance of new terms, acronyms, and organizations. Cloud computing is no different. Several cloud-related terms have surfaced: intercloud, cloud broker, and mashup. Additionally, several cloud-related organizations have emerged: Open Cloud Consortium, The Cloud Security Alliance, and The Global Inter-Cloud Technology Forum. Research each term and organization. For each term, provide a clear definition. Describe the mission of each organization. Compile your information into a one-page, double-spaced document. Remember to cite your sources.

5. This spotlight highlighted the three main categories of cloud services: IaaS, PaaS, and SaaS. Many providers provide additional services like MaaS, CaaS, and SaaS. In a PowerPoint presentation, using one or more slides for each service, define and provide details of at least five services not covered in this chapter. If possible, include the names of several cloud providers that offer each service. Remember to cite your references.

6. Using the Internet, locate five cloud providers. Using a table in a word processing document or a spreadsheet, list the five providers, their associated Web sites, and the services and resources that each offers.

chapter

7

Networks: Communicating and Sharing Resources

Chapter Objectives

Being connected with people all over the world without hesitation or assistance of a third party is a reality today. Do you take for granted the ease with which you can communicate with others and the devices that enable it? Can you even imagine spending a day without your iPhone, Blackberry, Kindle, or GPS unit? You would probably go into disconnect trauma. You use the devices, but do you understand the technology behind your instant phone calls, text messages, e-book downloads, and the directions spoken by your GPS unit? Will you be able to adjust to the communication technology of tomorrow if you are not comfortable with the technology of today?

Computer networking is essential to both business and home users. As an informed and literate computer user, you need to know enough about networking to understand the benefits and possibilities of connecting computers. Organizations spend billions of dollars on networking equipment each year that enables them to create centralized pools of information and connect international offices. These organizations are looking to employ workers who understand basic networking concepts and know how to utilize this technology.

Computer networking is here to stay. Traditional methods of communication have been replaced with e-mail, blogs, tweets, and Facebook—methods that make use of a network. Did you know that 247 billion e-mails are sent each day—that is, one every 0.00000035 seconds? This figure might seem staggering; yet, it is only representative of one method of communication over a network in use today. The goal of this chapter is to introduce you to networking concepts and help you understand the basics by covering such topics as these:

- The hardware needed to connect communication devices
- The difference between basic types of networks like a LAN and a WAN
- The devices and topologies that can compose a network
- An overview of the design of both a wireless and a wired network
- A discussion on the design of a home network
- The use of Internet Protocol and packet switching on a WAN
- The advantages and disadvantages of being networked ■

Check out **f Facebook** for our latest updates

www.facebook.com

Network Fundamentals

A **network** is a group of two or more computer systems linked together to exchange data and share resources, including expensive peripherals such as high-performance laser printers. Through the use of networked computers, people and businesses are able to communicate and collaborate in ways that were not possible before.

Computer networks for business and organizations had two original classifications: local area networks and wide area networks. These categories are based on the size of the geographical region that a network spans. Over the years, additional categories have evolved.

A **local area network (LAN)** uses cables, radio waves, or infrared signals to link computers or peripherals, such as printers, within a small geographic area, such as a building or a group of buildings. LANs are typically owned and managed by a single person or organization. A **wide area network (WAN)** uses long-distance transmission media to link computers separated by a few miles or even thousands of miles. A WAN is a geographically dispersed collection of LANs. The Internet is the largest WAN; it connects millions of LANs all over the globe. Unlike a LAN, a WAN is not owned by a single organization. Instead, it has a collective ownership or management, like the Internet (Figure 7.1).

Over the years, additional definitions of various types of networks that fall between those of a LAN and a WAN have emerged. A **metropolitan area network (MAN)** is a network designed for a city or town. It is usually larger than a LAN but smaller than a WAN. Typically, a MAN is owned by a single government or organization. Some more essential examples of a MAN include a network used to connect firehouses across a region or county and the network that supports a site like 511NY (**www.511ny.org/traffic.aspx**), which informs travelers of statewide traffic conditions. A **campus area network (CAN)** includes several LANs that are housed in various locations on a college or business campus. Usually smaller than a WAN, CANs use devices such as switches, hubs, and routers to interconnect (Figure 7.2).

One of the more recent classifications is that of a **personal area network (PAN)**. This is a network created among an individual's own personal devices, usually within a range of 32 feet. Such networks involve wireless technology (Figure 7.3).

Any network requires communications devices to convert data into signals that can travel over a physical (wired) or wireless medium. **Communication devices** include computers, modems, routers, switches, hubs, wireless access points, and network interface cards. These devices transform data from analog to digital signals and back again, determine efficient data-transfer pathways, boost signal strength, and facilitate digital communication (Figure 7.4).

Any device connected to a network is referred to as a **node**. A node can be any computer, peripheral (such as a printer or scanner), or communication device (such as a modem). Each node on the network has a unique **logical address**, or name, assigned by the software in use, as well as a unique numeric or **physical address**, called the data link control address, data link control/connection identifier (DLCI), or media access control (MAC) address, which is built into the hardware. Depending on the format of the network, the DLCI, MAC address, or logical address can be used to identify the node.

A computer must have a network interface card to make a physical connection to a network. A **network interface card (NIC)** is an expansion board that fits into an expansion slot, or adaptor, that is built into the computer's motherboard (Figure 7.4). It provides the electronic components to make the connection between a computer and a network. Today's desktop computers usually include NICs. Portable devices, such as a notebook or netbook, may come with a network

> " Through the use of **networked computers, people** and businesses are able to **communicate** and **collaborate** in ways that **were not possible** before. "

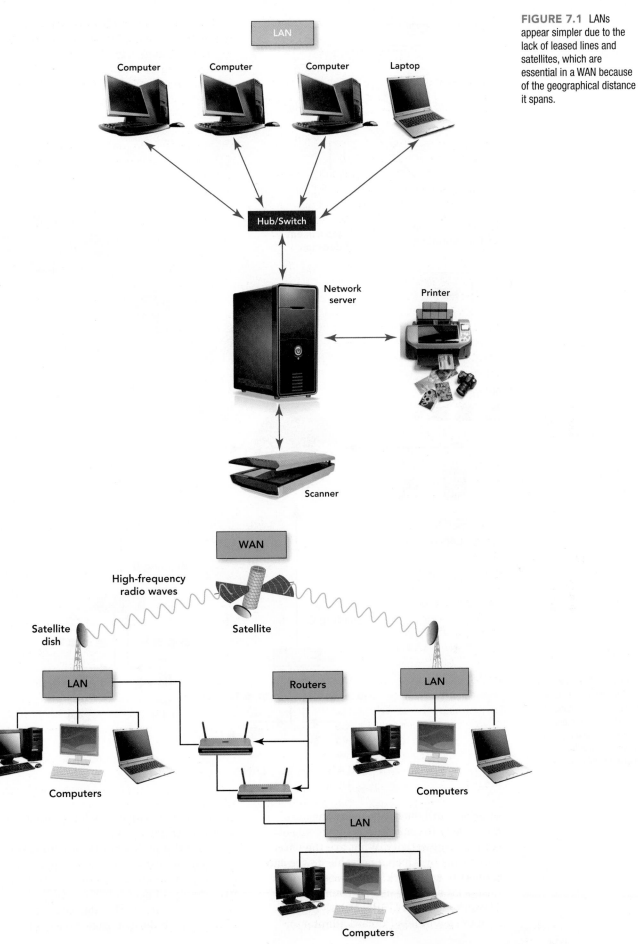

FIGURE 7.1 LANs appear simpler due to the lack of leased lines and satellites, which are essential in a WAN because of the geographical distance it spans.

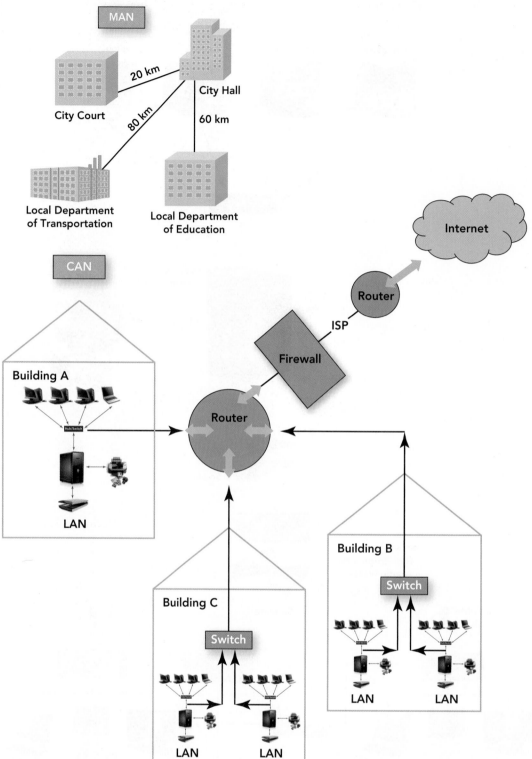

FIGURE 7.2 A MAN and a CAN each use various devices and methods of transmission to create the connections among their devices across their geographical distance.

interface card; however, today they are more likely to come with some means of wireless connectivity. What are the wireless means by which a portable device can connect to a network? The three common means for a mobile user to connect to a network include a USB wireless network adapter, a wireless PC card adapter, or

native wireless capability built into a processor (Figure 7.5).

A **USB wireless network adapter** is a communication device that plugs into a USB port and usually provides an intuitive graphical user interface (GUI) for easy configuration. This device is the same size as a USB data storage device, roughly

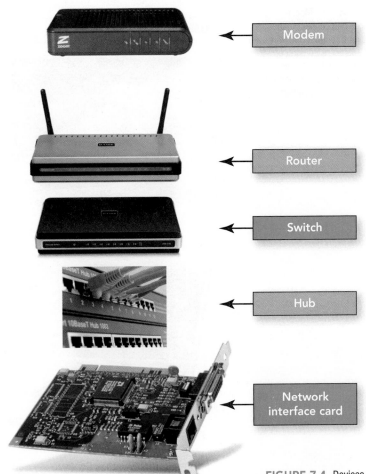

FIGURE 7.3 Do you have a PAN set up to connect your devices?

Notebook   Notebook

Smartphone

Modem

Router

Switch

Hub

Network interface card

FIGURE 7.4 Devices used to facilitate communication include computers, modems, routers, switches, hubs, and network interface cards.

3 inches long, three-quarters of an inch wide, and one-quarter of an inch thick. It supports data encryption for secure wireless communication and is perfect for the traveler and notebook user. These devices are also referred to as USB dongles. A **USB dongle** is a device that is inserted into a USB port and adds additional features to the base system, such as enabling network connectivity, increasing RAM memory, and permitting Bluetooth communication. A camera that connects through a USB port to a system would *not* be considered a USB dongle because it does not provide additional functionality to the system; it is only a method to transfer images.

A **wireless PC card adapter**, approximately the size of a credit card, is inserted into a slot on the side of most notebooks and netbooks. The card adapter has a built-in WiFi antenna that provides wireless capability and LED lights that indicate whether the computer is connected.

If you are purchasing a new notebook, you might want to look for one in which the wireless technology is built into the processor (CPU). Intel's Centrino 2 processor and Centrino 2 with vPro technology provide fast wireless connectivity without the hassle of having to insert an external peripheral. Go to **www.intel.com/products/centrino/** for more information on these processors.

In addition to your data passing through a NIC card or wireless adapter to get to and from a network, there is a high probability it has also passed through such devices as routers, switches, hubs, and wireless access points on its network journey from source to destination. A **hub** is a simple, inexpensive device that joins multiple computers together in a single network but does not manage the traffic between the connections, which usually results in frequent collisions. **Switches** are more intelligent than hubs. Instead of just passing data packets along the network, a switch contains software that inspects the source and target of a data package and attempts to deliver it to that destination. By doing this, a switch condenses bandwidth and has better performance than a hub. Switches and hubs only move data between nodes within a single network. A **router** is a more complex device, or in some cases more complex software, that is used to connect two or more networks. Routers also have the capability to inspect the source and target of a data package and determine the best path to route data or locate alternative pathways so that the data reaches its destination. A **wireless access point**, also known as an **AP** or **WAP**, is a node on a network that acts as a receiver and transmitter of wireless radio signals between other nodes on a network. A WAP can also act as a joint or bridge

FIGURE 7.5 Mobile devices can connect to the Internet through a USB wireless adapter, a PC card, or through the wireless capability provided by the newer processors being embedded into portable devices.

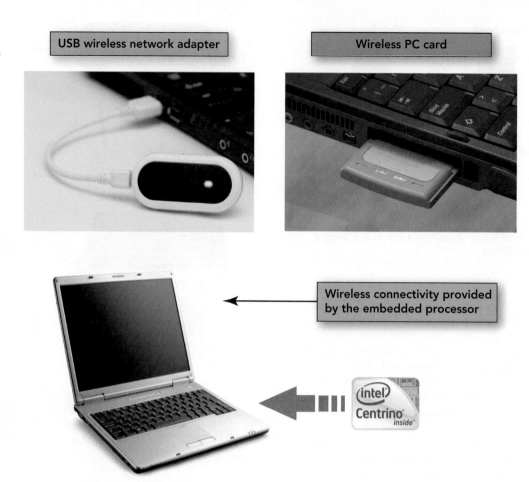

USB wireless network adapter

Wireless PC card

Wireless connectivity provided by the embedded processor

FIGURE 7.6 A wireless access point saves the time, hassle, and expense of running cable to connect devices in a hard-to-wire home or office.

connecting wireless nodes to a wired network (Figure 7.6).

Each computer on the network must also be equipped with additional system software that enables the computer to connect to the network and exchange data with other computers. Most operating systems, including UNIX, Linux, Windows, and Mac OS, now include such software in their standard installations.

Most business networks also typically include one or more **servers**, a computer or device with software that manages network resources

like files, e-mails, printers, and databases. The most common type of server is the **file server**, a high-capacity, high-speed computer with a large hard disk. A file server is set aside (dedicated) to make program and data files available to users on a network who have been granted access permission. The file server also contains the **network operating system (NOS)**, an operating system designed to enable data transfer and application usage among computers and other devices connected to a local area network. A network operating system, such as Novell SUSE or Microsoft Windows Server 2008, is a complex program that requires skilled technicians to install and manage it. A network operating system provides the following:

- File directories that make it easy to locate files and resources on the LAN

- Automated distribution of software updates to the desktop computers on the LAN

- Support for Internet services such as access to the World Wide Web and e-mail
- Protection of services and data located on the network
- Access to connected hardware by authorized network users

In addition to a network's special hardware and software, people are also necessary for the proper functioning of a network. **Network administrators** (sometimes called *network engineers*) install, maintain, and support computer networks (Figure 7.7). They interact with users, handle security, and troubleshoot problems.

A network administrator's most important task is granting access to the network. In most cases, a network user logs into a network by providing a user name and a password. When logged in, the user has access to his or her folders that reside on the server and possibly other people's folders and files. The user may also have the right to access peripheral devices on the network, such as printers, and the Internet. The network administrator sets permissions for which files, folders, and network devices a user has the right to access, based on such items as the division of the organization where the user is employed, the level of security clearance the user holds, and the confidentiality of the data itself.

As you read through this chapter, note that some of the concepts discussed apply to local networking, in which all of the computers and peripherals are locally connected, whereas others apply to networks that are made up of computers and peripherals that may be tens or hundreds of miles apart. For some additional information on LANs, WANs, and networks in general, visit **http://compnetworking.about.com/cs/basicnetworking/f/whatsnetworking.htm**.

What's the point of having a computer network instead of many stand-alone computers and peripherals? Let's look at some of the benefits as well as the risks of networking.

FIGURE 7.7 Network administrators have to understand both the hardware and software to manage a network efficiently.

GREEN tech tips

Cisco Systems has taken a broader approach to energy management with its control architecture called *Cisco Energy-Wise*. The EnergyWise system allows network administrators and other IT leaders to measure, monitor, and control the power consumption of all devices connected to the corporate network. With corporate partners and intelligent middleware software, Cisco has expanded its EnergyWise system to manage power consumption for the entire building. This includes such systems as lighting, elevators, heat, and air-conditioning. EnergyWise was rolled out in three phases:

- Phase 1 (February 2009): The network control portion of the program was released. This phase managed the energy consumption of such IP devices as phones, surveillance cameras, and wireless access points.
- Phase 2 (summer 2009): IT control was expanded to include such devices as personal computers, notebooks, and printers.
- Final phase (early 2010): Building control was added and extended control over lighting, heating, air-conditioning, elevators, employee badge access systems, fire systems, and security systems.

Cisco's claims that its network technology can support a low-carbon economy, reduce energy use, and play a major role in the way the world manages its environment and energy needs. For more information visit **http://newsroom.cisco.com/dlls/2009/prod_012709.html**. ●

Advantages and Disadvantages of Networking

When you connect two or more computers, you see gains in every aspect of computing, especially with regard to efficiency and costs:

- **Reduced hardware costs.** Networks reduce costs because users can share expensive equipment. For example, dozens of users on a network can share a high-capacity printer, storage devices, and a common connection to the Internet.

- **Application sharing.** Networks enable users to share software. Network versions of applications installed on a file server can be used by more than one user at a time. For example, companies that have implemented server-based order-tracking programs that enable their sales representatives to upload orders from their notebook computers have found that the salespeople gained up to 20 percent more time to focus on their customers' needs.

- **Sharing information resources.** Organizations can use networks to create common pools of data that employees can access. At publisher Pearson Education, for example, book designers can use the network to access a vast archive of illustrations, greatly reducing the amount of time spent tracking down appropriate photographs for textbooks and other publishing projects.

- **Centralized data management.** Data stored on a network can be accessed by multiple users. Organizations can ensure the security and integrity of the data on the network with security software and password protection. Centralized storage also makes it easier to maintain consistent backup procedures and develop disaster recovery strategies.

- **Connecting people.** Networks create powerful new ways for people to work together. For example, workers can use groupware applications to create a shared calendar for scheduling purposes. Team members can instantly see who's available at a given day and time. What's more, these people don't have to work in the same building. They can be located at various places around the world and still function effectively as a team.

The advantages of networks are offset by some disadvantages:

- **Loss of autonomy.** When you become a part of a network, you become a part of a community of users. Sometimes this means that you have to give up personal freedoms for the good of the group. For example, a network administrator may impose restrictions on what software you can load onto network computers.

- **Lack of privacy.** Network membership can threaten your privacy. Network administrators can access your files and may monitor your network and Internet activities.

- **Security threats.** Because some personal and corporate information is inevitably stored on network servers, it is possible that others may gain unauthorized access to files, user names, and even passwords.

- **Loss of productivity.** As powerful as networks are, they can still fail. Access to resources is sometimes restricted or unavailable because of viruses, hacking, sabotage, or a simple breakdown. Data loss can be minimized by good backup practices, but waiting for your data to be restored is an inconvenience or, worse yet, a direct threat to your ability to produce work on time.

Now that you know the benefits and risks of using networks, let's look at the specific types of networks.

> "**Networks** create **powerful** new ways for people to work together."

Local Area Networks

Have you ever walked into your dorm, your school's computer lab, or your office at work and wondered how all of the separate computers in each room or office are able to work at the same time and communicate with each other? The answer is through a local area network. A home network is also an example of a LAN. Remember, a LAN is made up of two or more computers, in a close geographical setting, connected together to facilitate communication with each other and with peripheral devices such as a printer or cable modem (Figure 7.8).

LANs transform individual hardware devices into what appears to be one gigantic computer system. From any computer on the LAN, you can access any data, software, or peripherals (such as fax machines, printers, or scanners) that are on the network.

With a **wireless LAN**, users access and connect to other nodes on the network through radio waves instead of wires. Wireless LANs come in handy when users need to move around in or near a building. In hospitals, for example, wireless LANs help personnel track the distribution of controlled substances, a job that's both time-consuming and prone to error without a computer's help. Nurses use bedside computers that are connected to the network through wireless signals to track the administration and dosage of these controlled substances. This form of data sharing on the network protects the patient from receiving an unauthorized drug or an unsuitable quantity of an authorized drug. Most colleges have installed wireless LANs to serve students seamlessly as they move around the campus. These campus networks enable students to receive e-mail and access the Internet while having lunch or lounging in the common room of a dorm. A student does not have to be at a desk in his or her own room to have use of these features.

Many wireless LANs ensure security with a radio transmission technique that spreads signals over a seemingly random series of frequencies. Only the receiving device knows the series, so it isn't easy to eavesdrop on the signals. A conscientious user should still look into using encryption software to guarantee a higher level of protection. Wireless LAN signals have an effective inside range of between 125 and 300 feet but can be shorter if the building construction interferes with the signal.

Whether wired or wireless, LANs can be differentiated by the networking model they use: peer-to-peer or client/server.

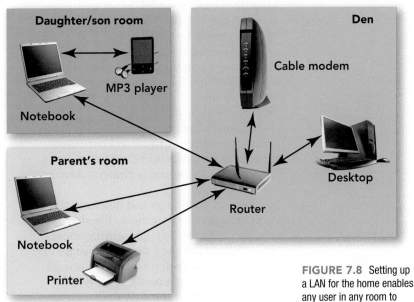

FIGURE 7.8 Setting up a LAN for the home enables any user in any room to access the connected devices located anywhere in the house.

Peer-to-Peer Networks

In a **peer-to-peer (P2P) network**, all of the computers on the network are equals, or peers—that's where the term *peer-to-peer* comes from. So, on a P2P network there's no file server, but each computer user decides which, if any, files will be accessible to other users on the network. Users also may choose to share entire directories, entire disks, and even peripherals, such as printers and scanners.

P2P networks are easy to set up; people who aren't networking experts do it all the time, generally to share an expensive laser printer or to provide Internet access to all of the computers on the LAN (Figure 7.9). P2P networks are often used for home networks or small businesses.

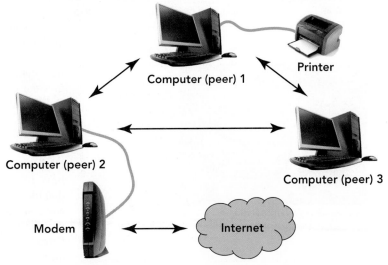

FIGURE 7.9 Peer-to-peer networks have no servers. Users share resources equally.

They do not require a NOS (network operating system) and can be set up with most operating systems in use today. They tend to slow down as the number of users increases, and keeping track of all of the shared files and peripherals can quickly become confusing. Most importantly, security is not strong due to the lack of hierarchy among the participants. For this reason, peer-to-peer LANs are best used for simple networks connecting no more than 10 computers and peripheral devices, such as printers.

P2P networking gained notoriety when Napster, a peer-to-peer music file-sharing site, was sued for copyright infringement. Since then, other sites, like Kazaa and LimeWire, which claim their P2P network is just like sharing a music or movie CD with a friend, have also lost similar battles with the entertainment industry. Current proposed legislation is seeking to hold colleges and universities responsible for monitoring students' download activity. Additionally, ISPs are in contention with Web sites like BitTorrent, a P2P site that consumes large amounts of bandwidth by sharing videos, thus causing other users to experience access delays.

However, not everybody wants to stop P2P music swapping. Some artists offer free downloads in hopes that fans will share the files with friends and buy more songs. Some companies are even sponsoring music downloads that link their products with promising new groups and build goodwill as the music of the new group moves from computer to computer. P2P networks are good for sharing more than music. Legitimate companies such as Skype (**www.skype.com**) use the power of P2P technology to provide voice over IP (VoIP) phone service and streaming television content to their users (Figure 7.10).

If you decide to join a P2P network, give some thought to privacy and security. You might have to disable some security features on your

system in order to make use of some of the offered features. Unless you read all the fine print before you download free versions of programs such as Kazaa, you may not realize that you're also downloading other files, for example, adware and spyware. Be sure to keep your antivirus software up to date to avoid getting a nasty surprise in the form of infected files from another computer on the P2P network.

Client/Server Networks

The typical corporate or university LAN is a **client/server network**, which includes one or more servers as well as clients (Figure 7.11). Some common servers on a client/server network include those that provide e-mail, file storage, and database

FIGURE 7.10 Sites like Skype use P2P technology to distribute high-bandwidth video content to their subscribers legally.

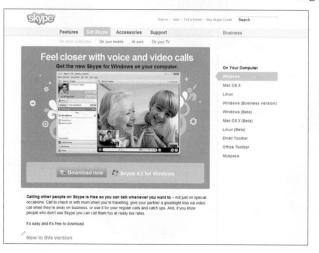

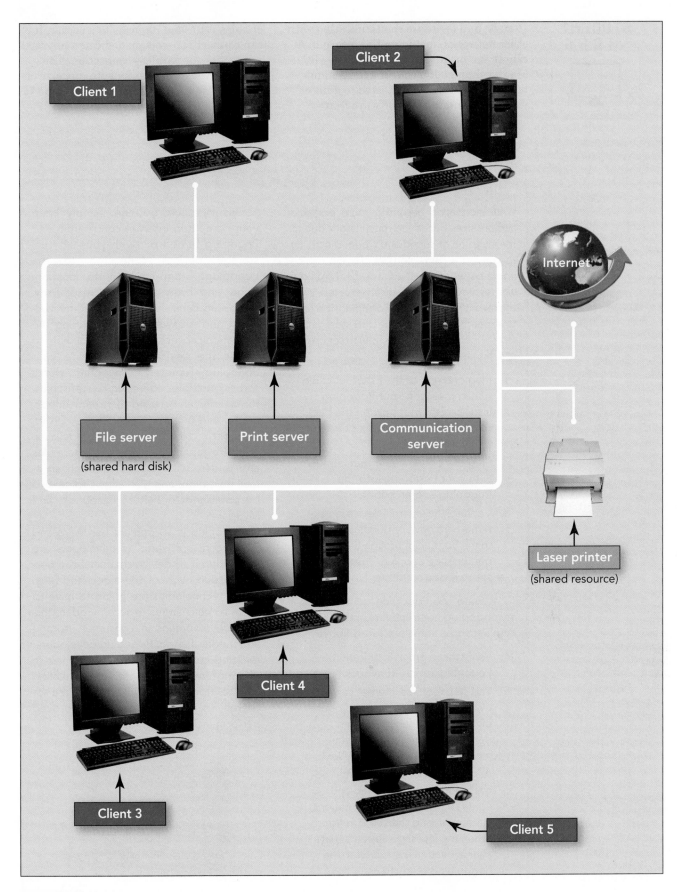

Client 1

Client 2

Internet

File server

(shared hard disk)

Print server

Communication server

Laser printer

(shared resource)

Client 4

Client 3

Client 5

FIGURE 7.11   A client/server network includes one or more servers as well as other nodes on the network.

storage, and facilitate communication with other networks, including the Internet. A **client** can be any type of computer—PC, Mac, desktop, notebook, or even a hand-held device—that is connected to a network and contains the software that enables it to send requests to a server. It can connect via modem, dedicated physical connection, or wireless connection. The client/server model works with any size or physical layout of LAN and doesn't tend to slow down with heavy use.

FAST FORWARD ▶▶

With information becoming more portable and file sizes becoming much larger due to the inclusion of sound and video, the ability to convert a portable USB storage device into a network attached storage (NAS) device, or file server, is a logical next step. With the recent release of the Pogoplug, it is easy to expand the role of your USB storage devices (Figure 7.12). Here is how to set up and use this new technology.

1. Plug one end of the Ethernet cable that comes with your Pogoplug into the Ethernet port on the back of the Pogoplug and the other end into your router.

2. Plug the power cable that comes with your Pogoplug into the Pogoplug and an outlet.

3. Connect the external device, an external hard drive or USB flash drive, to the Pogoplug through the USB port on the Pogoplug. The physical set up is now complete.

To activate the Pogoplug go to **https://my.pogoplug.com/activate/index.html**. The first three steps are listed above.

4. Verify that a green light is on the Pogoplug device. Then click *Next*.

5. This step requires Internet connectivity. It will autolocate your Pogoplug device. When it has been detected, a congratulatory statement will appear. Then click *Next*.

6. Assign the Pogoplug an e-mail address and password. Read and agree to the terms and conditions statement, and then click *Finish*. When the message appears that your activation is successful, the Pogoplug is ready to use.

Pogoplug connects your external devices to the Internet so you have full access wherever you go. Simply keep your computer, Internet connection, and Pogoplug turned on, with your external storage devices connected to the Pogoplug. From any remote location, using any browser, go to **https://my.pogoplug.com/**, log in with the e-mail account and password entered during the activation process, and you will be able to access the devices connected to your Pogoplug remotely. Pogoplug works across multiple operating system platforms and can be used to stream videos, music, and pictures to an iPhone, Droid, Blackberry, or other mobile devices. Using Pogoplug enables you to share files and folders with anyone, through an e-mail invitation, and also allows folders to be published to Twitter, Facebook, and MySpace.

Pogoplug is 10 percent hardware and 90 percent software. Its developers are promoting it as device that acts as a personal cloud, without the associated fees. Other technologies are going to have to make some changes to accommodate this new development in consumer storage and media sharing. Pogoplug developers, realizing current limitations, are smart in offering free updates for life, enabling you to upgrade your software free of charge, to match changes and improved performance features.

FIGURE 7.12 Pogoplug converts a local USB storage device into a network attached storage device.

Virtual Private Network (VPN)

Many businesses today have extended their network structure from an **intranet**, a password-protected network controlled by the company and accessed only by employees, to a **virtual private network (VPN)**. A VPN operates as a private network over a public network, usually the Internet, making data accessible to authorized users in remote locations through the use of secure, encrypted connections and special software (Figure 7.13).

Now that you've learned about the different types of LANs, let's look at their various physical layouts.

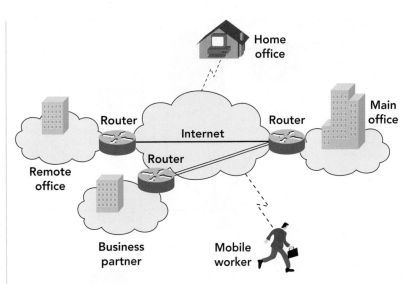

FIGURE 7.13 In a virtual private network, local and private businesses make use of the Internet to transmit data between locations and remote mobile employees.

LAN Topologies

Consider the typical college dorm or corporate office. Each separate room, office, or cubicle contains a computer. How does data travel across the network when you are in your dorm room working on your computer at the same time as your neighbor across the hall and your neighbor next door? How can you all use the same Internet connection and the printer in the common area down the hall at the same time? It all depends on the type of network topology in place. The physical layout of a LAN is called its **network topology**. A topology isn't just the arrangement of computers in a particular space; a topology provides a solution to the problem of **contention**, which occurs when two computers try to access the LAN at the same time. Contention sometimes results in **collisions**, the corruption of network data caused when two computers transmit simultaneously.

With a **bus topology**, every node, whether it is a computer or peripheral device, is attached to a common cable or pathway referred to as the bus (Figure 7.14). At the ends of the bus, special connectors called **terminators** signify the end of the circuit. With a bus topology, only one node can transmit at a time. If more than one node tries to send data at the same time, each node waits a small, random amount of time and then attempts to retransmit the data. Other limitations of a bus topology include length restrictions because of the loss of signal strength and practical limits as to the number of nodes attached because of increases in contention caused by each added node. On the plus side, bus networks are simple, reliable, and

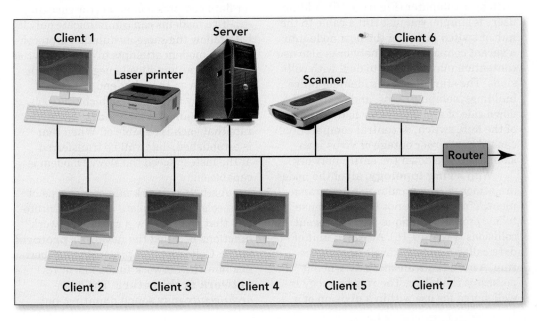

FIGURE 7.14 The network cable forms a single bus to which every computer or peripheral device is attached.

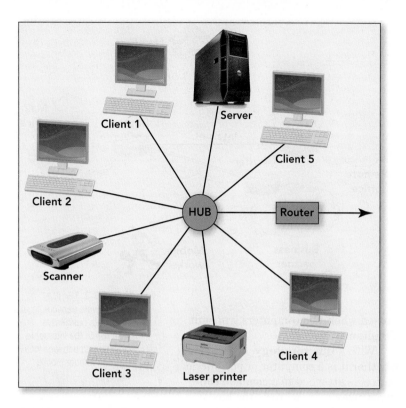

FIGURE 7.15 A central wiring design makes it easy to connect a new node in a star topology.

easy to expand. The bus topology is practical in a relatively small environment such as a home or small office.

To resolve the contention problem, bus networks use some type of **contention management**, a technique that specifies what happens when a collision occurs. A common contention-management technique is to abandon any data that could have been corrupted by a collision.

A **star topology** solves the expansion problems of the bus topology with a central wiring device, which can be a hub, switch, or computer (Figure 7.15). Adding users is simple; you just run a cable to the hub or switch and plug the new node into a vacant connector. Star networks also use contention management to deal with collisions. The star topology is ideal for office buildings, computer labs, and WANs. The down side of a star topology is that the loss of the hub, switch, or central computer, caused by a power outage or virus invasion, can bring down the entire network.

With a **ring topology**, all of the nodes are attached in a circular wiring arrangement. This topology, not in common use today, provides a unique way to prevent collisions (Figure 7.16). A special unit of data called a **token** travels around the ring. A node can transmit only when it possesses the token. The ring topology is well suited for use within a division of a company or on one floor of a multi-floor office building.

LAN Protocols

In addition to the physical or wireless transmission media that carry the network's signals, a network also uses **protocols** (standards or rules) that enable network-connected devices to communicate with each other. Protocols may be implemented by hardware, software, or a combination of the two.

Protocols can be compared to the manners you were taught when you were a child. When you were growing up, you were taught to use appropriate comments, such as "It's nice to meet you," when you met someone in a social situation. The other person was taught to reply, "It's nice to meet you too." Such exchanges serve to get communication going. Network protocols are similar. They are fixed, formalized exchanges that specify how two dissimilar network components can establish a communication.

All of the communications devices in a network conform to different protocols. Take modems, for example. To establish communications, modems must conform to standards called **modulation protocols**, which ensure that your modem can communicate with another modem even if the second modem was made by a different manufacturer.

Several modulation protocols are in common use. Each protocol specifies all of the necessary details of communication, including the data transfer rate, or the rate at which two modems can exchange data. The protocol also includes standards for data compression and error checking.

Two modems can communicate only if both follow the same modulation protocol. When a modem attempts to establish a connection, it automatically negotiates with the modem on the other end. The two modems try to establish which protocols they share and the fastest data transfer rate that each is capable of. When that is established, data will be transferred at the fastest speed the slower modem is capable of.

A single network may use dozens of protocols. The complete package of protocols that specify how a specific network functions is called the network's **protocol suite**. Collectively, a protocol suite specifies how the network functions, or its **network architecture**. The term *architecture* may sound daunting, but in the next section you'll learn that the basic idea isn't much more complicated than the stacking of a layer cake.

Network Layers Because they're complex systems, networks use a network architecture that is divided into separate **network layers**. Each network layer has a function that can be isolated and treated separately from other layers. Because each layer's protocol precisely defines how each layer passes data to another layer, it's possible to make changes within a layer without having to rebuild the entire network.

How do layers work? To understand the layer concept, it's helpful to remember that protocols are like manners, which enable people to get communication going. Let's look at an example.

Suppose you're sending an e-mail message. Now imagine that each protocol is a person, and each person has an office on a separate floor of a multistory office building. You're on the top floor, and the network connection is in the basement. When you send your message, your e-mail client software calls the person on the next floor down: "Excuse me, but would you please translate this message into a form the server can process?" The person on the floor below replies, "Sure, no problem." That person then calls the person on the next floor down: "If it isn't too much trouble, would you please put this translated message in an envelope and address it to such-and-such computer?" And so it goes, until the message finally reaches the physical transmission medium, the hardware layer, which connects the computers in the network.

At the receiving computer, precisely the opposite happens. The message is received by the hardware in the basement and is sent up. It's taken out of its envelope, translated, and handed up to the top floor, where it's acted on.

To summarize, a network message starts at the top of a stack of layers and moves down through the various layers until it reaches the bottom (the physical medium). Because the layers are arranged vertically like the floors in an

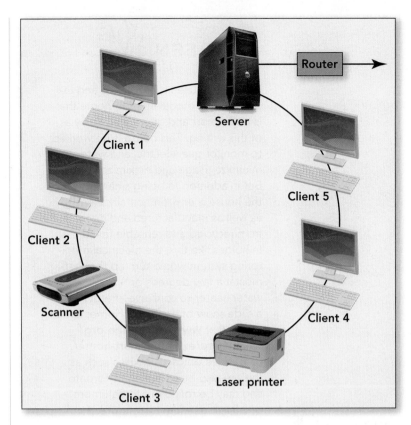

office building, and because each is governed by its own protocols, the layers are called a **protocol stack**. On the receiving end, the process is reversed: The received message goes up the protocol stack. First, the network's data envelope is opened, and the data is translated until it can be used by the receiving application. Figure 7.17 illustrates this concept.

FIGURE 7.16 All nodes are attached in a circular wiring arrangement in a ring topology.

FIGURE 7.17 Open system interconnection (OSI) model defines a networking framework for implementing protocols in seven layers.

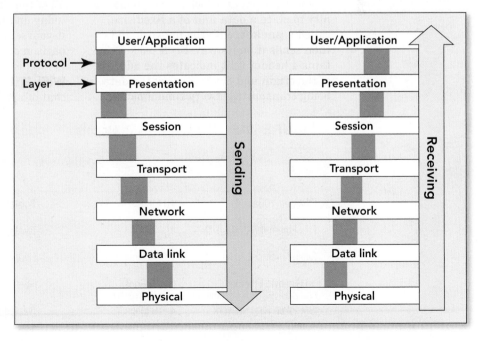

LAN Technologies By far the most popu-
lar LAN standard for large and small
businesses is **Ethernet**. According to
International Data Corporation (IDC),
approximately 85 percent of all installed
networks use various versions of Ethernet.

Ethernet uses a protocol called carrier sense multiple access/collision detection, or CSMA/CD. Using the CSMA/CD
protocol, a computer looks for an opportunity to place a data unit of a fixed size,
called a **packet**, onto the network and
then sends it on its way. Each packet contains a header that indicates the address
of the origin and destination of the data
being transmitted. Every time a packet
reaches its destination, the sender gets
confirmation, and the computer waits for
a gap to open to shoot off another packet.
Devices such as routers read the address
of a passing packet and direct the packet
along to the next device, routing it toward
its destination. Occasionally, two devices
send a packet into the same gap at the
same time, resulting in a collision and the
loss of both packets, but only for the
moment. When packets collide, the computers that sent them are instantly notified, and each chooses a random interval
to wait before it resends the packet. This
approach helps prevent network gridlock.

Although early versions of Ethernet
(called 10Base2 and 10Base5) used coaxial
cable in bus networks, the most popular
versions today are Ethernet star networks
that use switches and twisted-pair wire.
Currently, three versions of Ethernet are in
use: 10Base-T (10 Mbps), Fast Ethernet
(100 Mbps, also called 100Base-T), and
Gigabit Ethernet. The hardware needed to
create a 10Base-T Ethernet for five PCs can
cost as little as $200 but can be more if each
PC needs an Ethernet card. The newest version, 10 Gigabit Ethernet, is making possible next-generation applications such as
cloud computing, server virtualization, network convergence, and multicasting.

These superfast connections are often
used to create large metropolitan and regional networks because they prevent data
bottlenecks. To learn more about Ethernet,
check out Charles Spurgeon's Ethernet
Web site at **www.ethermanage.com/
ethernet/ethernet.html**. The site covers
all of the Ethernet technologies in use
today and includes a practical guide for do-
it-yourselfers. Figure 7.18 provides a comparison of several popular LAN protocols.

WiFi WiFi is a wireless LAN standard
that offers Ethernet speeds through the

FIGURE 7.18 Popular LAN Protocols

Protocol Name	Data Transfer Rate	Physical Media	Topology
Ethernet (10Base-T)	10 Mbps	Twisted-pair cable	Star
Fast Ethernet (100Base-T)	100 Mbps	Twisted-pair or fiber-optic cable	Star
Gigabit Ethernet	1,000 Mbps	Fiber-optic cable	Star
10 Gigabyte Ethernet	6.375 Gbps	Fiber-optic cable	Star
IBM Token Ring Network	4–16 Mbps	Twisted-pair cable	Ring

FIGURE 7.19 Global Wireless Networking Standards

Standard	Frequency	Transmission Speed	Description
802.11g	2.4 GHz	Up to 54 Mbps	The most commonly used standard, 802.11g is fast and backward compatible with 802.11b.
802.11n	2.4 GHz and/ or 5 GHz	Up to 540 Mbps	This recently approved standard improves speed and range and operates on both frequencies, as well as being backward compatible with 802.11a/b/g standards.
802.11r	2.4 GHz and/ or 5 GHz	Up to 540 Mbps	An amendment to the 802.11 standard that governs the way roaming mobile clients communicate with access points, this standard will speed up the handoff of data between access points or cells in a wireless LAN to less than 50 ms (milliseconds), greatly improving VoIP or Internet-based telephony.
802.15	2.4 GHz	Up to 50 Mbps	Used for Bluetooth technology, this standard has a very short range (up to 32 feet).
802.16	2–11 GHz	Up to 70 Mbps	Mobile WiMax provides high-speed wireless Internet access over long distances (more than 30 miles).
802.20	3.5 GHz	Up to 80 Mbps	A multi-megabyte mobile data and voice system, this standard can be used in vehicles moving at up to 250 km/hr.

use of radio waves instead of wires. WiFi networks, even though wireless, still need a central server, or access point. In other words, with WiFi technology computers can communicate with each other, but to access the Internet or to communicate across distances, a central access point is required. Wireless routers sold for home use contain a wireless access point inside the router. The router also has an omnidirectional antenna to receive the data transmitted by wireless transceivers. External WiFi transceivers connect to desktop computers through USB wireless adapters or PC adapter cards, whereas most notebooks are equipped with built-in wireless network adapters or processors with wireless capability.

WiFi uses the IEEE 802.11 wireless networking standard (Figure 7.19) and transmits on the 2.4-GHz or 5-GHz radio frequency band. There are currently three popular IEEE 802.11 standards. The 802.11g standard is the most common, with 802.11n and 802.11r being the newest standards. IEEE 802.16e and IEEE 802.16 are becoming two promising technologies for broadband wireless access systems. Figure 7.20 provides a visual of the standards and the network they are best suited to serve.

Although WiFi is convenient, there are some security risks. Wired networks require a computer or other device to be physically connected, but wireless networks broadcast radio waves that can be picked up by anyone using the correct configuration. These signals can extend beyond the walls of your home or office, so it is important to properly secure your network and data. To safeguard your network do the following:

- Always use a firewall and updated antivirus and antispyware software.
- Change the router's default network name, also known as an SSID, and the default password.

FIGURE 7.20
Transmission standards are constantly being upgraded and new standards proposed by the IEEE in order to stay in step with current technology.

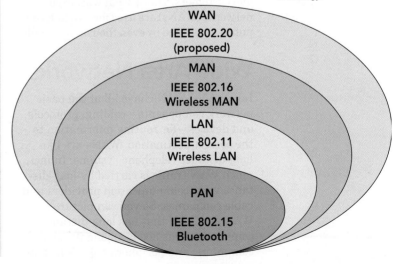

WAN
IEEE 802.20
(proposed)

MAN
IEEE 802.16
Wireless MAN

LAN
IEEE 802.11
Wireless LAN

PAN
IEEE 802.15
Bluetooth

- If possible, turn off SSID broadcasting to avoid detection by hackers.
- Ensure your router's software has been upgraded to the most recent version.
- Turn on WPA (WiFi Protected Access) to enable encryption.
- Turn on MAC (media access control) address filtering so only authorized devices can obtain access.

Similarly, when using a public wireless access location, known as a **hot spot**, you should take the following precautions:

- Be aware of your surroundings—ensure no one is watching over your shoulder for logon and password information.
- Be sure to log on to the correct wireless network, not a look-alike or so-called evil twin network.
- Disable file and printer sharing.
- Don't transmit confidential data—if you must, be sure to use encryption.
- Turn off your wireless access when it is not in use.

Whether wired or wireless, LANs enable an organization to share computing resources in a single building or across a group of buildings. However, a LAN's geographic limitations pose a problem. Today, many organizations need to share computing resources with distant branch offices, employees who are traveling, and even people outside the organization, including suppliers and customers. This is what wide area networks (WANs) are used for—to link computers separated by even thousands of miles.

Wide Area Networks

Like LANs, WANs have all of the basic network components—cabling, protocols, and devices—for routing information to the correct destination. WANs are like long-distance telephone systems. In fact, much WAN traffic is carried by long-distance voice communication providers and cable companies. So you can picture a WAN as a LAN that has long-distance communications needs among its servers, computers, and peripherals. Let's look at

the special components of WANs that differentiate them from LANs: a point of presence and backbones.

Point of Presence

To carry computer data over the long haul, a WAN must be locally accessible. Like long-distance phone carriers or Internet access providers, WANs have what amounts to a local access number, called a point of presence. A **point of presence (POP)** is a wired or wireless WAN network connection point that enables users to access the WAN. To provide availability to it users, WANs have a POP in as many towns and cities as needed. However, in many rural areas, POPs may still not be available, reducing a potential subscriber's choices and ability to connect.

> "WANs are like long-distance telephone systems. In fact, much WAN traffic is carried by long-distance voice communication providers and cable companies."

Backbones

The LANs and WANs that make up the Internet are connected to the Internet backbone. **Backbones** are the high-capacity transmission lines that carry WAN traffic. A variety of physical media are used for backbone services, including microwave relays, satellites, and dedicated telephone lines. Some backbones are regional, connecting towns and cities in a region such as Southern California or New England. Others are continental, or even transcontinental, in scope (Figure 7.21).

A **gigaPOP (gigabits per second point of presence)** is a POP that provides access to a backbone service capable of data transfer rates exceeding 1 Gbps (1 billion bits per second). These network connection points link to high-speed networks that have been developed by federal agencies. Whatever their scope, backbones are designed to carry huge amounts of data traffic. Cross-country Internet backbones, for example, can handle up to 13 Gbps, and much higher speeds are on the way.

To understand how data travels over a WAN, it helps to understand how data travels over the largest WAN, the Internet. This journey can be compared to an interstate car trip. When you connect to

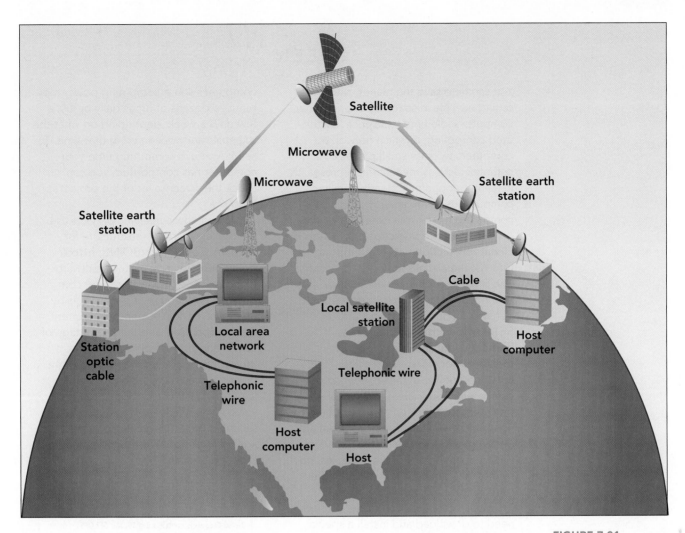

Satellite

Microwave

Microwave

Satellite earth station

Satellite earth station

Cable

Local satellite station

Host computer

Station optic cable

Local area network

Telephonic wire

Telephonic wire

Host computer

Host

FIGURE 7.21
Backbones can connect local regions and continents, and even expand in scope to connect transcontinental destinations.

the Internet and request access to a Web page, your request travels by local connections—the city streets—to your Internet access provider's local POP. From there, your Internet access provider relays your request to the regional backbone—a highway. Your request then goes to a network access point—a highway on-ramp—where regional backbones connect with national backbone networks. And from there, the message gets on the national backbone network—the interstate. When your request nears its destination, your message gets off the national backbone network and travels regional and local networks until it reaches its destination.

Some argue that the highway analogy to the Internet is no longer valid because the cause of backups has changed. Initially the backups on the Internet occurred on the backbone. Today, the improved backbone structure and maintenance can handle the traffic with no problem; the bottlenecks occur at the network access points. Oversubscribed providers with limited shared

bandwidth are the current problem. No matter what the argument, the highway analogy accurately provides the image of a very busy WAN backbone (interstate) with network access points (on-ramps) that provide access to that backbone.

WAN Protocols

Like any computer network, WANs use protocols. For example, the Internet uses more than 100 protocols that specify every aspect of Internet usage, such as how to retrieve documents through the Web or send e-mail to a distant computer. Internet data can travel over any type of WAN because of Internet protocols.

The Internet Protocols The Internet Protocols, collectively called **TCP/IP**, are open protocols that define how the Internet works. TCP/IP is an abbreviation for Transmission Control Protocol (TCP)/Internet Protocol (IP). However, more than 100 protocols make up the entire Internet Protocol suite.

You can help save the planet, save lives, or find new life in space by offering your computer's idle time to science. Distributed computing, in which networked computers work on small pieces of large complex tasks, is revolutionizing research in a number of areas. Nearly 5 million computer users are already lending their computing power to a variety of diverse projects. Climateprediction.net (**http://climateprediction.net**) is attempting to forecast the climate for the 21st century. The Folding@home project (**http://folding.stanford.edu**) studies the behavior of human proteins, and SETI@home (**http://setiathome.berkeley.edu**) analyzes radio signals in the search for extraterrestrial life. The combined power of these networked computers is equivalent to years of supercomputer time—an enormous help to nonprofits with limited resources but ambitious goals. If you volunteer your computing power to any of these causes, be sure to take the necessary security precautions to safeguard your system.

To volunteer your computer, you will need to download and install a special screensaver program. If this software detects that your computer is on and not busy with something else, it uses your Internet connection to reach the research center's server, downloads numbers to crunch or data to sift, and then submits the results to the server. At the other end, the research center's computer assembles all of these bite-size answers to complete one task and then parcels out pieces of the next task. Your computer's spare computing power may be used dozens of times daily or just a few days a week, depending on what the scientists are working on at that time. To see how much computing time your computer has contributed, you can check the screensaver or the project's Web site.

Many of these research projects use the Berkeley Open Infrastructure for Network Computing (BOINC; **http://boinc.berkeley.edu**) as their software platform, which means that your computer can work on multiple projects by using just a single screensaver. Current statistics on users and the percentage of computing power being donated to a project are displayed in the upper-right corner of the Web site's home page (Figure 7.22). If you decide to get involved, you will need to update your security program regularly to protect against hackers. Is distributed computing in your future? ●

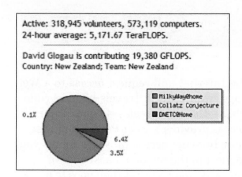

FIGURE 7.22 Statistics on distribution of the computing power donated by the top 100 volunteers are continuously updated and displayed on the BOINC home page.

Of all of the Internet protocols, the most fundamental one is the **Internet Protocol (IP)** because it defines the Internet's addressing scheme, which enables any Internet-connected computer to be uniquely identified. IP is a connectionless protocol. This means that with IP, two computers don't have to be online at the same time to exchange data. The sending computer just keeps trying until the message gets through.

Because IP enables direct and immediate contact with any other computer on the network, the Internet bears some similarity to the telephone system (although the Internet works on different principles). Every computer on the Internet has an **Internet address**, or **IP address** (similar to a phone number). A computer can exchange data with any other Internet-connected computer by "dialing" the other computer's address. An IP address has four parts, which are separated by periods (such as 128.254.108.7).

The **Transmission Control Protocol (TCP)** defines how one

Internet-connected computer can contact another to exchange control and confirmation messages. You can see TCP in action when you use the Web; just watch your browser's status bar. You'll see messages such as "Contacting server," "Receiving data," and "Closing connection."

Circuit and Packet Switching WAN protocols are based on either circuit- or packet-switching network technology, but most use packet switching. The Internet uses packet switching, whereas the public switched telephone network (PSTN) uses circuit switching. Still, the Internet does for computers what the telephone system does for phones: It enables any Internet-connected computer to connect almost instantly and effortlessly with any other Internet-connected computer anywhere in the world.

With **circuit switching**, the method used in the public switched telephone system, there is a direct connection between the communicating devices. Data is sent over a physical end-to-end circuit between the sending and receiving computers. Circuit switching works best when avoiding delivery delays is essential. In a circuit-switching network, high-speed electronic switches handle the job of establishing and maintaining the connection.

With **packet switching**, the method used for computer communication, no effort is made to create a single direct connection between the two communicating devices. The sending computer's outgoing message is divided into packets (Figure 7.23). Each packet is numbered and addressed to the destination computer. The packets then travel to a router, which examines each packet it detects. After reading the packet's address, the router consults a table of possible pathways that the packet can take to get to its destination. If more than one path exists, the router sends the packet along the path with the least congestion. The packets may not all take the same path or arrive in the order they were sent, but that's not a problem. On the receiving computer, protocols put the packets in the correct order and decode the message they contain. If any packets are missing, the receiving computer sends a message requesting retransmission of the missing packet.

So which type of switching is best? Compared with circuit switching, packet switching has many advantages. It's more efficient and less expensive than circuit switching. What's more, packet-switching networks are more reliable. A packet-switching network can function even if portions of the network aren't working.

However, packet switching does have some drawbacks. When a router examines a packet, it delays the packet's progress by a tiny fraction of a second. In a huge packet-switching network—such as the Internet—a given packet may be examined by many routers, which introduces a noticeable delay called **latency**. If the

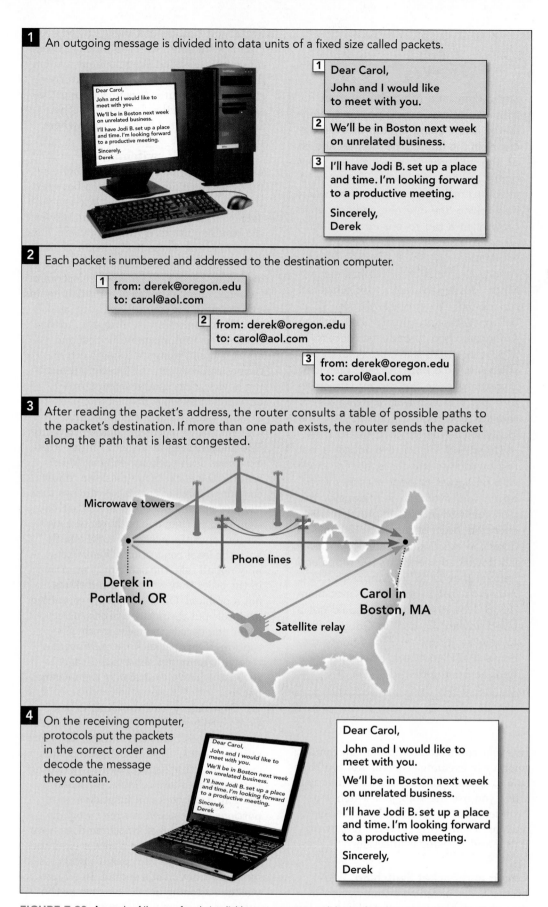

1 An outgoing message is divided into data units of a fixed size called packets.

1 Dear Carol,

John and I would like to meet with you.

2 We'll be in Boston next week on unrelated business.

3 I'll have Jodi B. set up a place and time. I'm looking forward to a productive meeting.

Sincerely,
Derek

2 Each packet is numbered and addressed to the destination computer.

1 from: derek@oregon.edu
to: carol@aol.com

2 from: derek@oregon.edu
to: carol@aol.com

3 from: derek@oregon.edu
to: carol@aol.com

3 After reading the packet's address, the router consults a table of possible paths to the packet's destination. If more than one path exists, the router sends the packet along the path that is least congested.

Microwave towers

Phone lines

Derek in Portland, OR

Carol in Boston, MA

Satellite relay

4 On the receiving computer, protocols put the packets in the correct order and decode the message they contain.

Dear Carol,

John and I would like to meet with you.

We'll be in Boston next week on unrelated business.

I'll have Jodi B. set up a place and time. I'm looking forward to a productive meeting.

Sincerely,
Derek

FIGURE 7.23 A sample of the use of packet switching on a message as it is sent from its source to its destination.

network experiences **congestion** (overloading), some of the packets may be further delayed, and the message can't be decoded until all of its packets are received. For these reasons, packet switching is not well suited to the delivery of real-time voice and video.

The oldest packet-switching protocol for WAN usage, **X.25**, is optimized for dial-up connections over noisy telephone lines and is still in widespread use. Local connections generally offer speeds of 9.6 to 64 Kbps. X.25 is best used to create a point-to-point connection with a single computer. A point-to-point connection is a single line that connects one communications device to one computer. It is widely used with ATMs and credit card authorization devices. New protocols designed for 100 percent digital lines, such as switched multimegabit data service (SMDS) and asynchronous transfer mode (ATM), enable much faster data transfer rates (up to 155 Mbps).

To learn more about WAN protocols, visit Cisco's WAN documentation site at **www.cisco.com/en/US/docs/internetworking/technology/handbook/Intro-to-WAN.html**.

Now that you understand how WANs work, let's explore how they are used.

WAN Applications

WANs enable companies to use many of the same applications that you use, such as e-mail and conferencing, document exchange, and remote database access. Some WANs are created to serve the public, such as those maintained by online service providers such as AOL and MSN. Other WANs are created and maintained for the sole purpose of meeting an organization's internal needs.

LAN-to-LAN Connections
In corporations and universities, WANs are often used to connect LANs at two or more geographically separate locations. This use of WANs overcomes the major limitation of a LAN—its inability to link computers separated by more than a few thousand feet. Companies can connect their LANs over their Internet access provider connection, which often provides bandwidth that far exceeds capabilities of internal networks. With these connections, users get the impression that they're using one huge LAN that connects the entire company and all of its branch offices.

Transaction Acquisition
When you make a purchase at a point-of-sale (POS) terminal, information about your transaction is instantly relayed to the company's central computers through its WAN (Figure 7.24). The acquired data is collected for accounting purposes and analyzed to see whether sales patterns have changed.

As you've seen, networking is a powerful tool, allowing users to communicate, share resources, and exchange data.

FIGURE 7.24 Information gathered through POS terminals monitors consumer purchases and patterns.

Home Networks

When people hear the word *network*, they often think, "Oh, that's too technical for me." Although networks require hardware and software technology, you should simply think of a network as a way to share computing power and resources. Setting up a home network may not be as difficult as you think, and the advantages are well worth the effort. Today the software that enables networking capabilities is integrated within all modern operating systems. Additionally portable devices, like notebooks and netbooks, come with the hardware already embedded within the system unit to enable network connectivity. For these reasons, it is easy to share data among computers, portable media devices, and, of course, connect to the world's biggest network—the Internet. Approximately 80 percent of all U.S. households own a computer. Market research indicates that

FIGURE 7.25 Today it is not unusual to have several family members with media devices. A home network makes it possible to share data, music, other content, and devices like printers.

By the end of 2012, it is estimated that there will be more than 160 million home networks in place worldwide, and as many as 70 percent of them will be using wireless technology. A **home network**, also referred to as a **home area network** or **HAN**, is a personal and specific use of network technology that provides connectivity between users and devices located in or near one residence. It enables users who reside at that location to quickly and conveniently share files and resources by using network connections between computers and peripheral devices. Home networks can accommodate both wired and wireless communications. Wired home networks typically use Cat-5 or Cat-6 Ethernet cable or a home's electrical wiring. Wireless home networks rely on WiFi radio signals. Let's first look at wired networks.

multicomputer households are becoming more common because people who already own PCs are still buying new ones. It is not unusual for each parent and one or more children in a household to have his or her own computer or mobile device, such as a smartphone (Figure 7.25). Why is this important? People in multicomputer households want to share scanners, printers, data, music, movies, and games among multiple family members using different computers. In addition, they want every member of the household to share a single Internet connection. The computers in a single household may be of different makes and models (such as a mix of Macs and PCs). How can these computers share information and resources? The answer is a home network.

Wired Home Networks

A wired network is the network of choice for online gamers and those that transfer large files where speed is a priority. Today wired home networks are not as popular due to the hassle of physically pulling wire to each device on the network and the inexpensive cost of a wireless network setup. Still, learning to set a network up and understanding how it works can be helpful, as most home networks are a **hybrid network**, a combination of both wired and wireless technology (Figure 7.26).

Ethernet has become the standard of choice for home networks that are still

FIGURE 7.26 The home network of today usually include a wired network router and a wireless access point.

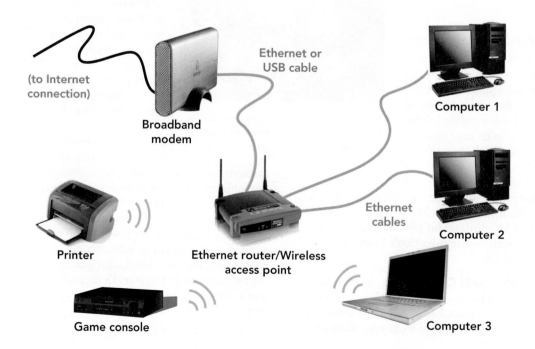

FIGURE 7.27 A home network uses a RJ-45 Ethernet connector.

using a wired system. Ethernet standards detail the types of wires that must be used and how fast data can travel across the network.

Home Ethernet Network Ethernet is a communications standard that uses packets to send data between physically connected computers in a network. The most popular type of Ethernet wiring is twisted-pair wire. Home networks use either the Cat-5 or Cat-6 version of twisted-pair wire. These wires are then connected by RJ-45 connectors (Figure 7.27), which look like large telephone jacks. Cat-5 wire transfers data at speeds of up to 100 Mbps; Cat-6 transfers data at speeds of up to 1,000 Mbps (1 Gbps).

The simplest form of Ethernet network links different computers with a connecting switch or router. Devices connected by a switch can communicate only with other devices on the same network, whereas devices connected by a router can access other networks, including the Internet. See Figure 7.28 for an example of a simple Ethernet network. In this example, the computer can send a message to the notebook or the printer by way of the router. Routers and switches are available in many configurations. Most have 4 to 12 ports. The majority of home networks use a 100Base-TX router that is capable of a transfer rate of 100 Mbps (100 million bits per second). If you

have the money, you can upgrade to a 1000Base-T router with a transfer rate of 1 Gbps. Also known as gigabit Ethernet, 1000Base-T is useful when transferring large amounts of data, such as digital multimedia.

With an Ethernet network, each networked computer must have an Ethernet network adapter, also called a network interface card (NIC). Most newer computers already include a NIC, but a NIC can also be installed as an expansion card on an older system.

Wireless Home Networks

Although several wireless network standards are currently available, WiFi is the wireless standard used for home networking. Wireless network standards have been developed to ensure that companies that build wireless connecting devices do so in compliance with strict definitions and

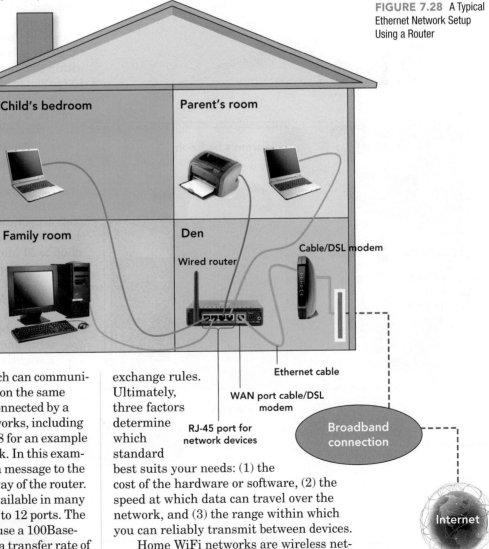

FIGURE 7.28 A Typical Ethernet Network Setup Using a Router

exchange rules. Ultimately, three factors determine which standard best suits your needs: (1) the cost of the hardware or software, (2) the speed at which data can travel over the network, and (3) the range within which you can reliably transmit between devices.

Home WiFi networks are wireless networks in which each computer on the

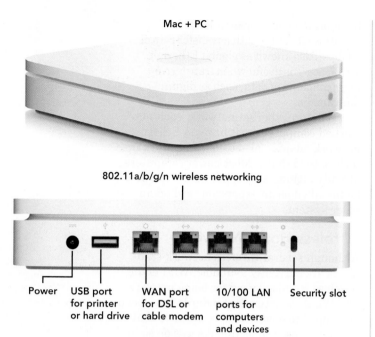

Mac + PC

802.11a/b/g/n wireless networking

Power | USB port for printer or hard drive | WAN port for DSL or cable modem | 10/100 LAN ports for computers and devices | Security slot

FIGURE 7.29 Apple's AirPort Extreme is a wireless router that is compatible with Macs and PCs.

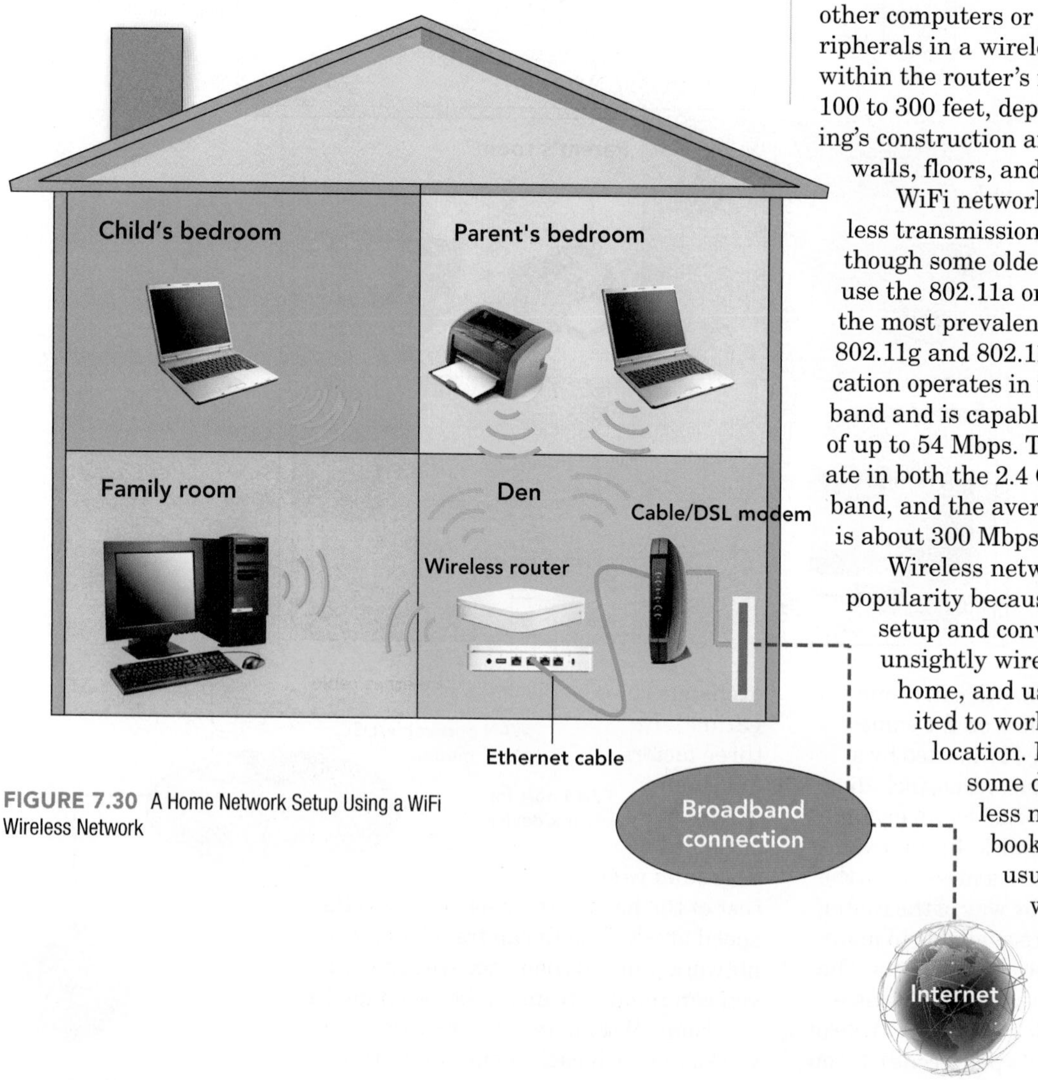

Child's bedroom

Parent's bedroom

Family room

Den

Cable/DSL modem

Wireless router

Ethernet cable

Broadband connection

Internet

FIGURE 7.30 A Home Network Setup Using a WiFi Wireless Network

network broadcasts its information to another using radio signals. WiFi networks use communications devices called network access points, also referred to as wireless access points, to send and receive data between computers that have wireless adapters. In a home network, in addition to enabling communication between networked devices and other networks, wireless routers also act as network access points. Network access points enable you to move a notebook with a wireless adapter from room to room or to place computers in different locations throughout a house (Figure 7.29).

A peer-to-peer relationship exists among all of the computers in a wireless network (Figure 7.30). This means that all the computers are equals, or peers, with no particular computer acting as the server. However, some home wireless networks can also be of the client/server type. In a client/server home network, each computer communicates with the server, and the server then communicates with other computers or peripherals. All peripherals in a wireless network must be within the router's range, which is usually 100 to 300 feet, depending on the building's construction and thickness of the walls, floors, and ceilings.

WiFi networks use the 802.11 wireless transmission specifications. Although some older systems may still use the 802.11a or 802.11b standards, the most prevalent standards are 802.11g and 802.11n. The 802.11g specification operates in the 2.4 GHz radio band and is capable of data transfer rates of up to 54 Mbps. The 802.11n can operate in both the 2.4 GHz and 5 GHz radio band, and the average data transfer rate is about 300 Mbps.

Wireless networks are gaining in popularity because of their ease of setup and convenience. There are no unsightly wires to run through the home, and users are no longer limited to working in just one location. However, there are some disadvantages to wireless networks. Newer notebook computers are usually equipped for wireless access, but older notebooks may require the addition of a wireless adapter card, which plugs into a slot on the notebook. A USB adapter can be connected to the USB port of a notebook or desktop PC. Another alternative is to install a wireless adapter expansion card in a desktop PC (Figure 7.31). Wireless networks may be affected by interference from other devices such as microwave ovens and cordless phones. And some users may find that reception can be a problem if the radio waves are unable to pass through interior walls. Conversely, because radio waves are able to pass through walls, it is important to take appropriate measures to safeguard your privacy from passersby outside your home.

Now that we've examined the various types of home networks, let's look at the steps involved in setting one up.

Setting up a Home Network

Setting up any network, including one for your home, goes much more smoothly if you can follow a series of steps. The steps presented in this section correspond roughly to those followed by computer professionals who develop large-scale networks. Don't let that intimidate you though! You don't have to be a computer professional to set up a home network successfully.

Planning As with any type of project, you must first come up with a plan based on your specific home networking needs. Ask yourself realistic questions: What are you trying to accomplish with your network? Is it for a small business or just for personal use? Is it only for your computer and peripherals or will it support multiple family members? Will the hardware be concentrated in one room (such as an office or den) or be spread throughout many rooms? Based on your answers to these questions and the type of home network you choose, you should develop a needs, or requirements, checklist. You can determine your specific requirements by visiting your local home electronics store or by reading recommendations you find on the Web. Go to **http://compnetworking. about.com/od/homenetworking/a/ homeadvisor.htm** and launch the Home Network Interactive Advisor. This interactive questionnaire will ask you relevant

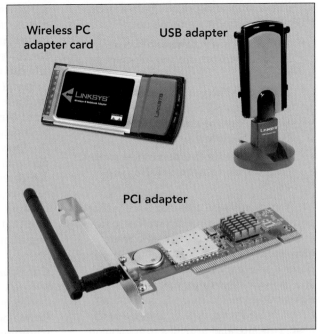

Wireless PC adapter card

USB adapter

PCI adapter

FIGURE 7.31 A wireless adaptor card can be installed in a notebook's PC card slot. A USB adapter can be used for notebooks or desktop PCs, and a PCI adapter can be used to enable wireless access for a desktop PC.

networking questions and, based on your answers, make network recommendations that will meet your needs.

When planning a home network, you will need to do two things. First, you will have to decide which network technology to use and then, based on your first choice, you will need to purchase the appropriate hardware. You may want to visit a home electronics store for advice, but many manufacturers such as Linksys and Netgear, as well as retailers such as Best Buy and Circuit City, provide tutorials on their Web sites to help you determine what type of network would best suit your needs and what equipment you will require. You may already have a NIC and a modem but will probably need a router (wired or wireless) and possibly a wireless adapter.

ETHICS

Not everyone takes the steps necessary to secure their wireless network. Do you know how to tell which wireless network you're using? Have you ever used a neighbor's unsecured network to access the Internet? In most areas, this is considered theft of services. How do you feel about that? Would you warn your neighbor about your ability—and the ability of other people—to access their unsecured network?

These sites also provide help and advice about setting up a home network:

- Microsoft (**www.microsoft.com/athome/moredone/wirelesssetup.mspx**)
- About.com (**http://compnetworking.about.com/od/homenetworking/Home_Networking_Setting_Up_a_Home_Network.htm**)
- CNET Reviews (**http://reviews.cnet.com/wireless-network-buying-guide**)

You should also consider purchasing and installing personal firewall software to keep your home network safe from viruses and hackers. Visit the U.S. Computer Emergency Readiness Team Web site (**www.us-cert.gov/cas/tips/ST04-004.html**) to find out more about firewalls and what type of firewall is the best. This site also provides hints on configuration settings (Figure 7.32).

A wired Ethernet network is best installed during home construction if you want to conceal the wires. When installing this type of network in an existing home, it is possible to route the cables through the walls by use of either attic or basement access, but it will take a lot of work. If you decide to use Ethernet, you will need to determine whether you are going to do the job yourself or whether you are going to hire someone to do it. In either case, the installer must carefully plan the routing of the cables through walls and across floors. You can find tutorials on the Web that will help you lay out the appropriate locations to drill into your walls. Search for "home network wiring" in your favorite search engine to find guides to wiring your home network.

Once you have purchased the appropriate hardware and software, you must configure the network so that all of the components function together. When your network is properly configured, you will find that a home network improves your home-computing experience.

Configuring a Wired Network Computer networks for homes and small businesses can be built using either wired or wireless technology. Wired Ethernet has been the traditional choice in homes. Every computer on the network needs a network interface that bundles data into chunks to travel across the network, as well as a connection point, or port, for the special wiring that connects all the PCs. The port is either built into the computer or provided as an add-in NIC. The NIC sends data to the network and receives data sent from other computers on the network. Wired LANs generally also require central

FIGURE 7.32 The US-CERT Web site provides security suggestions to keep your data safe and intruders out.

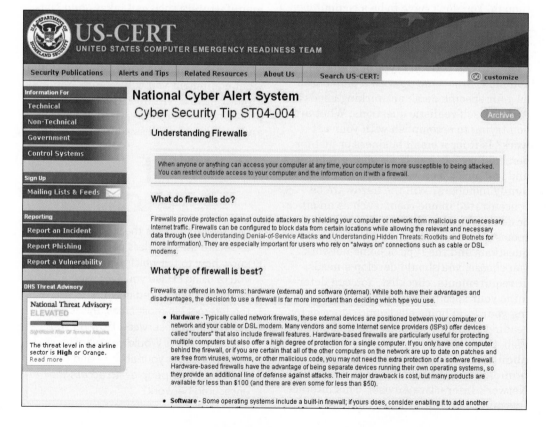

devices like hubs, switches, or routers to accommodate more computers.

The next step is to configure the central hub, most frequently a router. In a wired network, a wire runs from the back of each computer to the router, which serves as a communications point to connect the signal to the appropriate cable that goes to the intended destination. Printers, scanners, and other peripherals are usually plugged into one of the networked computers and then shared with the others. However, many new peripherals come with network interfaces that allow them to be plugged directly into the router. The router must be placed in a convenient location so that you can string individual cables from the router to each port in each room in which you want to use the network. Wired cables, hubs, switches, and routers are relatively inexpensive and provide superior performance and high reliability.

Configuring a Wireless Network As with a wired network, a wireless network also requires equipment. To create a wireless network, you will need a wireless router, which will act as a hub of the service. The wireless router changes the signals coming across your Internet connection into a wireless broadcast, sort of like a cordless phone base station. Today, 802.11g wireless broadband routers are usually recommended because they offer excellent performance and are compatible with almost any device. Each node that is to be connected to the wireless network will need a wireless adapter that will connect and communicate to the wireless router. Newer computers and devices may already have them embedded within the system unit. For older equipment, you will have to purchase an adapter and connect it through a USB port. To make your setup easier, choose network adapters made by the same vendor that made your wireless router. Finally, connect your DSL or cable modem to your wireless router.

Wireless networks have some performance issues usually associated with interference from devices like microwave ovens. Careful positioning of the router and nodes is required in the planning stage. Wireless equipment can cost more than the equipment needed for a wired network. This cost, however, is often offset by the savings provided by the inclusion of security software in wireless routers. Security for wired systems requires the purchase of additional software.

The final step in configuring a wired or wireless network is to access the operating systems control panel and locate the network configuration option. Windows 7 has a Network Setup Wizard that can be accessed from the Control Panel by choosing the Network and Sharing Center, and selecting Set up a new connection or network (Figure 7.33). You can also search for "network" from the Start menu to access the Network and Sharing Center. Setup information may also be available from the store where you purchased your networking supplies or from Web searches on home networks.

Maintenance and Support

Computer and network problems can be extremely frustrating. You should set up a regular maintenance schedule for both your computer and your network. The good news is that there isn't much to maintain

FIGURE 7.33 The Network and Sharing option from the Control Panel will guide you through the steps to connect to a wired or wireless network.

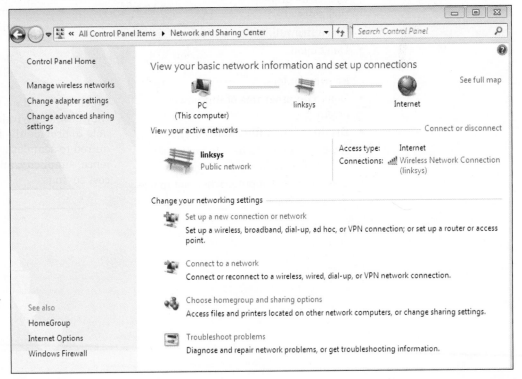

with today's home networking solutions. You may need to blow off dust and lint that accumulates on your router, wireless adapter, or modem. You may also need to use your operating system's network utilities to refresh your network's settings.

When something goes wrong, you should try to think of what might have caused the problem. Sometimes the solution is as simple as restarting your computer and/or unplugging your router and other peripherals from the power source and then plugging them back in. You may also need to restart each computer that is connected to your system. If these actions do not solve the problem, you have several other options. If the problem produces an error message, type the subject of the error message into the search box on your favorite search engine site. You can also search manufacturers' Web sites. For instance, if you have a Linksys router, you could go to **www.linksys.com** to see whether downloads are available to update your network device.

Most disasters can be avoided by following some guidelines:

- Use virus protection software.
- Use a firewall.
- Don't open e-mails from unknown senders.
- Don't run programs of unknown origin.
- Disable hidden file name extensions.
- Keep all applications and your operating system updated.
- Turn off your computer when not in use.

- Disable Java, JavaScript, and ActiveX, if possible.
- Disable scripting features in e-mail programs.
- Make regular backups.
- Make a boot disk in case your system becomes damaged or compromised.

The Future of Home Networking

Convergence will be the future of home networking systems. You may be skeptical, but someday you may be able to use home networks to control household appliances, prepare food, or maintain a home's appearance. Networked home security systems already help protect us from intrusion or damage from natural events.

In the near future, new houses will have a central control unit that is capable of managing home network events as well as communication, entertainment, temperature regulation, lighting, and household appliances. It is very possible that someday your refrigerator may send you an e-mail informing you of the state of its cooling coils, including a request that you vacuum out the lint that is blocking good air circulation.

In the future, home network systems will almost certainly be wireless and have the capability to adapt to new technologies as they develop. Wireless technology will be able to provide the flexibility that is required to seamlessly integrate convenience, simplicity, and, hopefully, long-term cost savings.

" ...someday you may be able to use home networks to control household appliances, prepare food, or maintain a home's appearance. "

Setup a Hybrid Home PC Network

Most home networks are a combination of wired and wireless technology and thus create a hybrid network. This how-to section will assume that you want to keep one desktop wired and set up another desktop and/or a notebook for wireless access in another location in the house.

1. Select an Internet access provider and purchase the correct hardware:
   a. If you do not have an Internet access provider, your first step will be finding one. Research the possibilities in your region and compare price and performance.
   b. Your selected provider will supply you with a modem that will permit you to use their WAN to access the Internet. Most regions have cable and DSL access; others might have fiber optic.
   c. The desktop that will be wired to the network will need a network interface card.
   d. The desktop that will be connected wirelessly will need a PCI card.
   e. The notebook that will be connected wirelessly will need a USB wireless adapter or a PC card.
   f. In addition to the modem provided by your Internet access provider, you will need to purchase a wireless router.

2. Connect your wireless router (Figure 7.34):
   a. Turn off all devices, including your cable modem.
   b. Plug one end of an Ethernet cable into the Ethernet LAN port located on the network interface card in the desktop unit to be physically wired to the network. Plug the other end of this same cable into one of the Ethernet LAN ports on the back of the router.
   c. Using a second Ethernet cable, plug one end into the WAN port of the router and the other end into the WAN port on the modem.

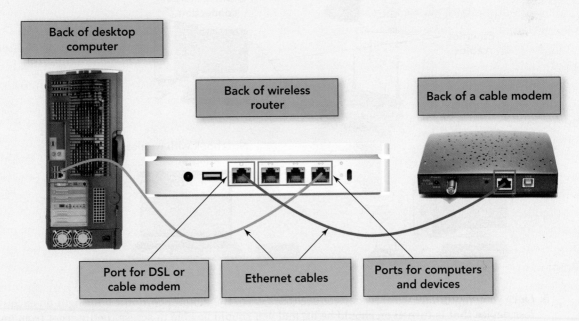

FIGURE 7.34 Proper cable connection is important for the modem, router, and desktop to communicate.

d. Once both Ethernet cables are connected:

   i. Turn on the modem and wait till the lights indicate power is on.

   ii. Plug in the router; wait for status lights to blink and diagnostics to finish.

   iii. Boot up the wired desktop computer.

3. Configure the router:

   a. Locate your router's printed start-up guide. Launch your Web browser and enter the address indicated in the guide.

   b. The onscreen setup wizard should guide you through the process step by step.

   c. Enable your router's security functions. You have two options: WEP and WPA. WEP enables wireless encryption and WPA enables WiFi protected access. Depending on the router, you might have to go to advanced settings to complete this step.

      i. Change the default administrator's password. This is important because hackers might know the default name.

      ii. Change the SSID, the name you give your network, from the default name. Again, hackers might know the default.

4. Connect your other computers to the wireless network (Figure 7.35):

   a. On your notebook computer, insert a PC card into an empty PC slot or a USB wireless adapter into a USB port.

   b. On the desktop unit to be connected wirelessly, install a PCI card or use a wireless USB adapter.

   c. The operating system will automatically detect the new adapter and prompt you to insert the CD that came with the adapter. The onscreen instructions should guide you through the configuration process.

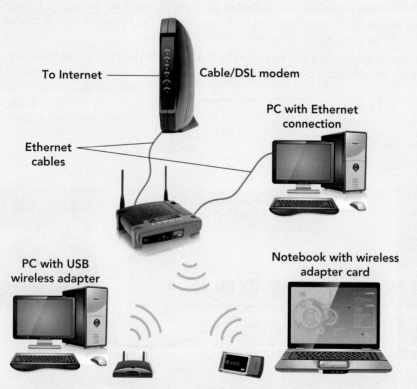

FIGURE 7.35 Your final configuration should look similar to this diagram.

To Internet — Cable/DSL modem

PC with Ethernet connection

Ethernet cables

PC with USB wireless adapter

Notebook with wireless adapter card

5. Once your router and wireless devices are configured, the adapter card indicator light on each wireless device that is turned on should be lit, and you should be able to access the Internet from any connected device.

Chapter Summary

Networks: Communicating and Sharing Resources

- Computer networks link two or more computers so that they can exchange data and share resources, such as high-performance laser printers, enabling communication and collaboration between individuals and businesses. Networks are often labeled by the geographic distance they span.

- Local area networks (LANs), serve a building or an equivalent region. Wide area networks (WANs) span multiple buildings, states, and nations; actually, a WAN can be viewed as a geographically dispersed collection of LANs. Metropolitan area networks (MAN) service a city or town, whereas campus area networks (CAN) are designed for college campuses and business parks. On a more individual level, home area networks (HAN) are used to provide connectivity between users and devices located in or near a single residence, and personal area networks (PAN) connect an individual's communication devices located within 32 feet of each other.

- Computer networks can be advantageous by reducing hardware costs, enabling application and data sharing, and fostering teamwork and collaboration. Disadvantages of computer networks include loss of autonomy, threats to security and privacy, and potential productivity losses due to network outages.

- A peer-to-peer LAN doesn't use a file server. It is most appropriate for small networks of fewer than 10 computers. Client/server networks include one or more file servers as well as clients such as desktops, notebooks, and handheld devices. The client/server model works with any size or physical layout of LAN and doesn't slow down with heavy use. A home network can be set up as either type of network. A VPN operates as a private network over a public network, usually the Internet, making data accessible to authorized users in remote locations through the use of secure, encrypted connections and special software.

- The physical layout of a LAN is called its network topology. The three different LAN topologies are bus (single connections to a central line), star (all connections to a central switch), and ring (tokens carry messages around a ring).

- Protocols are the rules that define how network devices can communicate with each other. Messages move through the layers of the protocol stack. When a computer sends a message over the network, the application hands the message down the protocol stack. At the receiving end, the message goes up a similar stack in reverse order.

- The most widely used LAN protocol for wired networks is Ethernet. Popular versions include Ethernet (10Base-t), Fast Ethernet (100Base-T), Gigabyte Ethernet, and 10 Gigabyte Ethernet. The most commonly used wireless protocol is 802.11g. Additional wireless protocols are 802.11n, 80211r, 802.15, 802.16, and the new 802.20.

- WANs and LANs have all the same basic components—cabling, protocols, and routing devices. But a WAN is different in that it has a backbone, high-capacity transmission lines, and points of presence, connection points that enable users to access the network.

- WAN protocols include circuit switching and packet switching. Circuit switching creates a permanent end-to-end circuit that is optimal for voice and real-time data. Circuit switching is not as efficient or reliable as packet switching; it is also more expensive. Packet switching does not require a permanent switched circuit. A packet-switched network can funnel more data through a medium with a given data transfer capacity. However, packet switching introduces slight delays that make the technology less than optimal for voice or real-time data.

- Home networks can be wired, wireless, or a hybrid and have a peer-to-peer or client/server relation. The steps in setting up a home network include the planning phase, configuration of the system, and maintenance.

Key Terms and Concepts

Identification

Label each item.

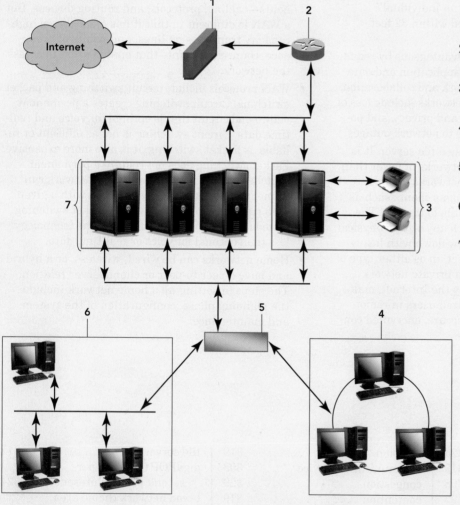

1. _____

2. _____

3. _____

4. _____

5. _____

6. _____

7. _____

Matching

Match each key term in the left column with the most accurate definition in the right column.

_____ 1. router

_____ 2. node

_____ 3. ring

_____ 4. hub

_____ 5. star

_____ 6. backbone

_____ 7. latency

_____ 8. switch

_____ 9. bus

_____ 10. protocol

_____ 11. logical address

_____ 12. physical address

_____ 13. topology

_____ 14. contention

_____ 15. congestion

a. A communications device that inspects the source and target of a data package and attempts to deliver it to its destination on the same network

b. A delay in packet delivery due to repeated examination by routers

c. A network layout that consists of a central wiring device to which all other network devices are connected

d. The physical arrangement of network devices

e. The rules that define how network devices can communicate with each other

f. A name assigned by the network software to a node

g. A complex communications device, used to connect two or more networks, capable of inspecting the source and target of a data package and determining the best path to send the data

h. A performance interruption that is caused by a segment of a network experiencing an overload

i. A network layout in which all of the devices are attached in a circular wiring arrangement

j. A situation caused when two or more computers try to access a network at the same time

k. The numeric identifier assigned to a network node

l. A simple, inexpensive communications device that joins multiple computers together in a single network and does not have the ability to inspect the source and target of the data packet

m. A network layout in which every node is attached to a single cable or pathway

n. High-capacity transmission lines that carry WAN traffic

o. Any device connected to a network

Multiple Choice

Circle the correct choice for each of the following:

1. Which is an advantage of networking?
   a. Increased hardware costs
   b. Increased autonomy
   c. Centralized data management
   d. Increased privacy of network members

2. What is the acronym for a computer network within a single residence?
   a. WAN   b. PAN
   c. HAN   d. CAN

3. Which is a type of network topology?
   a. client/server
   b. Star
   c. P2P
   d. WAN

4. A _____ is necessary to make the connection between a local area network and the Internet.
   a. hub
   b. switch
   c. router
   d. POP

5. Which of the following statements about peer-to-peer networks is true?
   a. They require at least one router.
   b. They require at least one server.
   c. They require a network operating system.
   d. They perform best when connecting 10 or fewer computers.

6. Encryption on a wireless network is activated by enabling _____.
   - a. WPA
   - b. NOS
   - c. WEP
   - d. NIC

7. Which is *not* a hardware device used to attach a device to a wireless network?
   - a. PC card
   - b. NIC
   - c. USB adapter
   - d. PCI card

8. Which of the following is a common contention management technique?
   - a. Abandoning data corrupted by a collision
   - b. Adding terminators to minimize signal loss
   - c. Generating a new token
   - d. Retransmitting unreceived packets

9. Which is a feature of packet switching?
   - a. There is a direct connection between the communicating devices.
   - b. All packets of a message are sent and received in order.
   - c. Packets of a message are split up and reassembled at the destination device.
   - d. All packets travel on the same path to the destination.

10. A(n) _____ is a network device with software that manages network resources like files, e-mails, printers, and databases.
   - a. client
   - b. server
   - c. firewall
   - d. switch

Fill-In

In the blanks provided, write the correct answer for each of the following:

1. A(n) _____ is assigned to every computer on the Internet to facilitate the exchange of data.

2. A(n) _____ is a wired or wireless WAN network connection point that enables users to access the WAN.

3. A network model that does not require a network operating system is called a _____ network.

4. A(n) _____ is a computer professional that installs, maintains, and supports computer networks.

5. A wireless LAN uses _____ instead of wires to transmit data.

6. A(n) _____ is node on a network that acts as a receiver and transmitter of wireless radio signals between other nodes on a network.

7. A(n) _____ operates as a private network that runs over a public network, usually the Internet.

8. The _____ is the largest WAN.

9. A public wireless access location as known as a(n) _____.

10. Data in a ring topology is referred to as a(n) _____.

11. _____ is the communication method used in the public telephone system, where a direct connection exists between communicating devices.

12. A(n) _____ is a computer network that is limited to a college campus or business park.

13. A(n) _____ is a password-protected network controlled by the company and accessed only by employees.

14. The _____ network topology makes use of a token.

15. _____ is the collection of open protocols that define how the Internet works.

Short Answer

1. List at least two benefits of a wired network and two benefits of a wireless network.

2. How do LANs, WANs, MANs, CANs, and HANs differ?

3. What is the difference between circuit switching and packet switching?

4. Name three types of LAN topologies and describe how each works.

5. List four precautions you can take to protect a home network from failure or infection by malware.

Teamwork

1. **Your Campus Area Network** As a team, or in subgroups, interview the IT staff at your college and inquire about the physical layout of your campus network (CAN). How many local area networks (LANs) are connected? What is the topology of each LAN? Are all LANs wired, or are some wireless? How are the students in the dorm connected to the network? How many routers/switches/hubs compose the CAN? What network operating system is running the CAN? Ask these and any additional questions that help you zero in on the configuration of your school's network. Using Microsoft's Visio or any other drawing program, create a diagram of the CAN. Submit the diagram and a one-page, double-spaced paper that combines the questions asked and the answers received that led to your network diagram.

2. **Develop an Analogy** Several articles have been written indicating that the highway analogy to the Internet and its access providers is no longer applicable due to the change in where the bottlenecks occur today. As a team, come up with another analogy for the Internet. Make sure the analogy you develop clearly identifies the backbone, network access points, and the Internet access provider. In a one-page, double-spaced paper, explain why you chose to describe the Internet in this manner, and list the components of the Internet and its corresponding elements in your analogy.

3. **Popular Network Systems** As a team, develop a survey on the type of network individuals have in their homes or dorms. Include questions on whether the network is wired, wireless, or a hybrid; the type of modem and Internet access provider that are used; the number of computers and other peripheral devices that are connected to the network; the average amount of time spent on the network on a daily basis; and any other questions that the team considers relevant. Distribute the survey to at least 25 individuals and compile the replies. Using an Excel spreadsheet, summarize your responses. As a team, come up with a diagram of the network system used by most respondents. Submit your diagram and the Excel spreadsheet containing your summary data.

4. **Creating Your Own Business** Assume the members of your team are going to create a small business selling items on e-Bay for individuals that are not computer confident. Come up with a company name, statement of policy, services that you will provide, and fees that you will charge. Initially, there will be three individuals in this small business: a secretary, an individual that is very familiar with e-Bay, and a photographer that will take images of the products and post them on e-Bay. As a team, decide whether a wired, wireless, or hybrid network would best suit this company and its three employees. Use any drawing program that the team members are familiar with to create a diagram of your dream office suite. Include the number of rooms needed, the computer equipment needed by each individual, and a schematic of the ideal network. Make sure the diagram is detailed and clearly labeled. Using a word processor, organize all of this information into a two-page, double-spaced report. Submit both your diagram and report.

5. **The Network Behind a GPS** As a team, research the network used by a Global Positioning System (GPS). This system involves the use of satellites and has the ability to communicate with moving devices. Describe the hardware that makes up a GPS and the wireless network that makes its communication possible. As a team, create a sketch of a GPS network in action. Submit your sketch and present your research in a PowerPoint presentation of at least five slides.

On the Web

1. **Solve the Problem** You recently subscribed to an Internet service for your home network. After performing several tests, you realize that your access speed is significantly slower than what your provider advertised. Using the Internet or any other reliable reference sources, determine at least three possible causes for the slowdown. Present your findings in a one-page, double-spaced report. Remember to cite your references.

2. **Going, Going, Green** With the emphasis on reducing our carbon footprint, many companies and research groups are attempting to develop technologies that will reduce the amount of energy used by networks. One such idea is presented in this chapter. Using a search engine, locate at least two other research projects that are attempting to reduce the amount of energy consumed by computer networks. Cite the source of your research, specify

the name of the company developing the technology or the name of the research project, and describe the method(s) the group is trying to implement to create the reduction or control of energy use, the target date for completion, and the estimated amount of reduced energy consumption attributed to the project. Present your findings in a one-page, double-spaced paper or a PowerPoint presentation of at least eight slides.

3. **Network Administrators** Especially essential to the efficient management of a network is the network administrator. Interview the network administrator at your school and use job postings on the Web to obtain the education and/or certifications required, the level or years of experience needed, and a range of possible salaries for this type of position. Compile your information in a word processing document and create an advertisement for a network administrator. Remember to cite your references.

4. **Using a Hot Spot** The dangers of accessing the Internet from hot spots like a coffee shop, shopping mall, library, or airport were touched on in this chapter. Investigate the possible problems that can occur through the use of such sites, and explain how a hacker gains access to your system through such sites. Come up with a user's guide to hot spot use that includes such topics as safe surfing tips, information on how to validate the site in use, and the software you should have on your system to provide protection. Use a word processor and present your guide to hot spot use in the form of a flyer.

5. **Hiring a Hacker** Although the practice has been going on for some time, the subject of whether a former hacker should be hired as a security consultant always seems to be a touchy issue. There are strong opinions on both sides. Using the Internet and any other reliable sources of research, investigate both sides of this debate. Present the pros and cons in a one-page, double-spaced paper.

chapter 8

Wired and Wireless Communication

Chapter Objectives

1. Differentiate between *bandwidth* and *throughput*, and discuss the bandwidth needs of typical users. (p. 348)

2. Discuss how modems transform digital computer signals into analog signals and analog into digital. (p. 350)

3. List various physical and wireless transmission media and explain several transmission methods. (p. 351)

4. Explain the limitations of the public switched telephone network (PSTN) for sending and receiving computer data. (p. 358)

5. Describe digital telephony and multiplexing, including their impact on line usage. (p. 358)

6. Discuss last-mile technologies that connect users with their communication providers. (p. 359)

7. Provide examples of how digitization and convergence are blurring the boundaries that distinguish popular communications devices, including phones and computers. (p. 363)

8. Discuss various wired and wireless applications. (p. 369)

You are leaving the house for the day and grab your smartphone, Kindle 2, and notebook and walk out the door. You place your key in the cup holder and press a button on the dashboard to start your car. As your engine comes to life, the GPS system appears on the monitor embedded in the dash and your smartphone automatically connects to the Bluetooth device. This is not a sci-fi episode; it describes the connected life of a typical person today. How many of these devices do you or family members use? With wireless connectivity, are you even aware of the activity behind the scene that is enabling the communication you take for granted? Could you ever go back to using an atlas for directions, read a printed book, or rely solely on a landline phone?

Today everyone wants, or needs, to be connected. From the minute we get up to the minute we go to bed, notebooks and phones ding to notify us of incoming e-mails and text messages, we rely on automatic notices to update a program, and Global Positioning Systems to direct us to our destinations. **Connectivity**, defined broadly, refers to the ability to link various media and devices. In this chapter, we'll examine the various technologies, both wired (connected by a physical medium) and wireless (connected through the air or space), involved in creating the connectivity that enables communication. Some of the concepts covered include:

- The difference between analog and digital signals and how the conversion between them is essential to make the connection between various devices in use today
- The meaning of such terms associated with transmission as *bandwidth* and *throughput*
- The type of modems available and the associated transfer rates
- How the public switched telephone network connects global users and how last-mile technologies bring those signals to your door
- Web-enabled technologies such as VoIP, videoconferencing, faxing, and webcams
- Hints on the safe use of communication devices ■

Check out **f Facebook** for our latest updates

www.facebook.com

Moving Data: Bandwidth and Modems

Communications (data communications or telecommunications) is the process of electronically sending and receiving messages between two or more computers or devices regardless of the distance between those devices. The **sending device** initiates the transmission while the **receiving device** accepts the transmission and responds. Communications can be split into two parts: the message (data, information, or an instruction) and the **communications channel** (also referred to as the **link**), the transmission media on which the message is sent from one location to the next.

Signals in the real world, like sound and light, are **analog signals**, or continuous waves that vary in strength and quality. Before these real-world signals can be used by digital equipment, like a computer, the signal passes through an analog-to-digital converter. An **analog-to-digital converter (ADC)** is simply a microchip that contains the circuitry to convert an analog signal into a digital signal. A **digital signal** is one that includes discontinuous pulses in which the presence or absence of electronic pulses is represented by 1s and 0s. In reverse, when a computer signal has to be sent out to the real world, for example as sound, the digital signal must pass through a digital-to-analog converter. A **digital-to-analog converter (DAC)** is a microchip that contains the circuitry to convert a digital signal to analog (Figure 8.1).

In communications, both analog and digital signals move data over communications channels. The conversion from analog to digital or digital to analog is normally not something a user can detect or has to be concerned with. However, if you have ever scanned an image, recorded your voice or used VoIP on your computer, or talked on a phone, you used an analog-to-digital converter. Likewise, if you have ever listened on the phone or played back a CD, you made use of a digital-to-analog converter.

A codec, short for code-decode algorithm, is responsible for the conversion between analog and digital signals. Codecs accomplish the conversion by sampling the analog signal several thousand times per second. A common audio codec, the G.711 codec, samples the audio 64,000 times a second. It then converts each sample onto digitized data and compresses it for transmission. When the samples are reassembled, the missing pieces between the samples go undetected by the human ear. The most common codec for VoIP samples the analog signal 8,000 times a second. Because a digital signal is discrete, composed of 0s and 1s that are sampled from an analog signal, the data arrives in a much clearer format. The receiving end knows exactly how to reconstruct the data back into its original form (Figure 8.2). Digital signals also transfer much more data than analog and at much greater speeds. For instance, digital TV systems can now deliver more than 500 stations across digital cable, which allows not only more stations than analog cable, but also more features such as being able to view news stories related to a certain program.

Let's look at two features to consider when sending a message over communications channels: bandwidth and modems.

Bandwidth: How Much do You Need?

Bandwidth refers to the theoretical maximum amount of data that can be transmitted through a given communications channel at one time (usually per second). Two factors affect bandwidth: the physical characteristics of the transmission medium and the method used to represent and transmit the data. For analog signals, bandwidth is expressed in cycles per second, or hertz (Hz). For digital signals, bandwidth is expressed in bits per second

STUDENT VIDEO

FIGURE 8.1 The transmission of real-world sounds through digital communication devices requires the conversion of analog signals to digital signals for transmission and then back to analog in order to be heard by the receiving party.

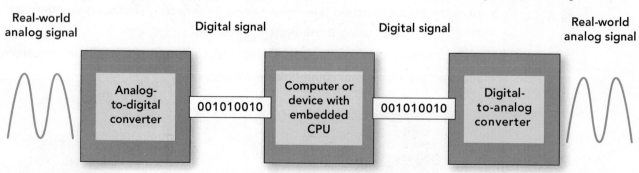

| Real-world analog signal | Digital signal | | Digital signal | Real-world analog signal |

Analog-to-digital converter — 001010010 — Computer or device with embedded CPU — 001010010 — Digital-to-analog converter

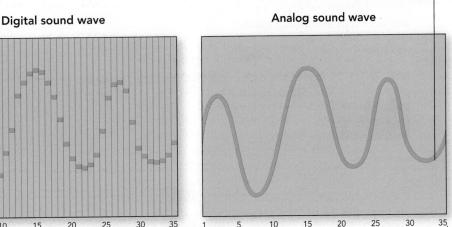

Digital sound wave

Analog sound wave

Digital signal reassembled
into an analog signal

Samples
of analog
signal

TIME

TIME

FIGURE 8.2 Digital signals are composed by sampling an analog wave at discrete points in time. The analog wave is then approximated by these discrete measurements.

(bps). **Throughput**, often used incorrectly as a synonym for bandwidth, is the *actual* amount of data that is transmitted. It is almost always lower than bandwidth, especially with wireless communications.

Broadband refers to any transmission medium that carries several channels at once and thus transports high volumes of data at high speeds, typically greater than 1 Mbps (megabits per second, or million bits per second). Cable TV uses broadband transmission. So how much bandwidth do you need? Conventional dial-up connections to the Internet use a relatively low bandwidth of 56 Kbps (kilobits per second, or thousand bits per second) or less. Most users find this painfully slow when searching the Web. But dial-up connections are still cheaper than broadband connections, so some people sacrifice

speed for low price. Through the practical comparisons provided in Figure 8.3, you should get an idea of what increased bandwidth can do for such Internet activities as streaming music or video. **Streaming** is the ability to hear or see content while it is being downloaded from a Web site instead of waiting till the download is complete.

If you are still confused, use the suggestions below as a guide:

- For normal use, from most providers, 1 Mbps offers the best balance between cost and performance.
- For e-mail and viewing Web pages but not streaming audio or video, then 256 Kbps to 512 Kbps should do.
- For gaming, a 2 Mbps connection or faster is necessary.

FIGURE 8.3   Basic Wired Internet Speeds and Abilities

Internet Connection Speed	Time to Download a 100 KB Web Page	Time to Download a 5 Minute Song in MP3 Format	Streaming Ability
56 Kbps dial-up modem	14 seconds	12 minutes 30 seconds	None
256 Kbps broadband	3 seconds	3 minutes	Low quality
512 Kbps broadband	1.6 seconds	1 minute 30 seconds	
1 Mbps broadband	0.8 seconds	41 seconds	
2 Mbps broadband	0.4 seconds	20 seconds	Medium quality
4 Mbps broadband	0.1 seconds	5 seconds	
6 Mbps broadband	instantaneous	3.5 seconds	
8 Mbps broadband or higher	instantaneous	2.5 seconds	TV quality

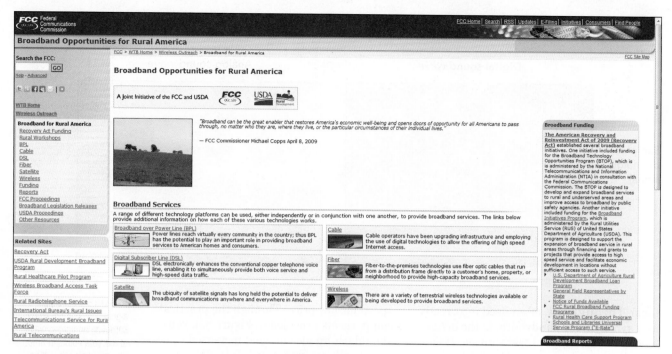

FIGURE 8.4 The options for broadband Internet services to rural locations in the United States are presented here in a cooperative effort between the Federal Communications Commission (FCC) and the Department of Agriculture (USDA) rural development.

- To share a connection between two or more computers, a minimum of a 4 Mbps connection is necessary to take advantage of music or video on demand or digital broadband Internet TV.

Broadband digital connections are now widely available in the United States. The major cable and telephone (DSL) companies added 5.4 million new subscribers in 2008, bringing the total of broadband users to 68 million. Numbers continued to rise in 2009, with broadband penetration in rural markets of 10,000 people or less up by 13 percentage points in a single year. A comparison of broadband speeds internationally in early 2010 found South Korea having the fastest home Internet service, with download speeds of 34.14 Mbps (megabits per second). The United States was ranked 26th with an average download time of 10.16 Mbps. In February of 2010, Google announced that it will test a direct-to-home fiber-optic connection with the capability of up to 1 gigabit per second. If this test becomes a reality, it will revolutionize the way we connect to the Internet and make cloud computing and other Internet-based services more appealing. Fueling the motivation to expand broadband usage is the commencement of the National Broadband Plan (**www.broadband.gov/**) developed by Congress and the Federal Communications Commission, to increase Internet access to rural America (Figure 8.4). Considering the extension of broadband services to rural communities, the increased use of wireless devices for Internet access, and the expansion of fiber-optic services, suppliers of Internet services are facing serious challenges.

Modems: Transform Signals

The term **modem** comes from combining the words **mod**ulate and **dem**odulate. It is an appropriate compressed term because a modem is a communication device used to send and receive data from one transmission system to another. On the sending end, a modem uses a process called *modulation* to transform the computer's digital signals into signals appropriate for the transmission system bring used. On the receiving end, the process used is *demodulation,* whereby the receiving modem transforms the signal from the transmission system back into digital form that a computer can understand. For systems that use telephone lines as a transmission medium, the modulator converts the computer's digital signals into analog tones that can be conveyed through the telephone system. The demodulator receives the analog signals and converts them to digital form (Figure 8.5).

Modems are available as internal or external units. An internal modem, the most common in computer systems today, is not visible. Instead, it is located within the system unit and is powered by the system unit's power supply. An external modem, located outside of the system unit, has its

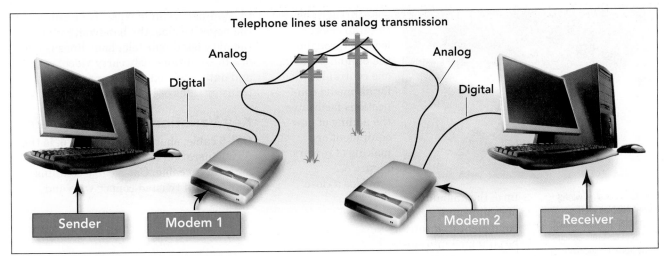

Telephone lines use analog transmission

Analog · Analog

Digital · Digital

Sender · **Modem 1** · **Modem 2** · **Receiver**

own case and power supply. For this reason, external modems are slightly more expensive. The types of modems available include analog, digital subscriber line (DSL), cable, and Integrated Services Digital Network (ISDN). Analog modems are used for dial-up connections. DSL and cable are high-speed broadband connections. ISDN modems transfer information in channels of 64 kilobits per second (Kpbs), which can be combined for higher speeds. We'll discuss integrated services digital networks in more detail later in this chapter.

The **data transfer rate**, the rate at which two modems can exchange data, is measured in bits per second and is referred to as the **bps rate**. Analog modems communicate at a maximum rate of 56 Kbps. (In practice, modems rarely achieve speeds higher than 42 Kbps.) A modem that can transfer 56 Kbps is transferring only about 7,000 bytes per second, or about five pages of text. Baud is often used incorrectly as a substitute for bps, the unit of data transfer rate. **Baud** is actually the number of signaling elements per second. At slower rates, bauds and bps may be equal, but on higher speed transmissions, more than one bit can be encoded in each signaling element. Thus a 4,800 baud rate may have a transmission rate of 9,600 bps.

Often, a single message travels over several different wired and wireless transmission media, including telephone lines, coaxial cable, fiber-optic cable, radio waves, microwaves, and satellite, before it arrives at its destination. We'll look at each of these types of wired and wireless transmission media in more detail.

Wired Transmission Media

Wired transmission media for data travel is still widely used today. Most new buildings incorporate a **wiring closet**, a central location that extends though all floors of the building in which the appropriate wiring is housed to support most types of data transfer that the individuals or companies that occupy the building might want to access (Figure 8.6). Cabling

FIGURE 8.5 A modem transforms the computer's digital signals into analog signals that can be transmitted through the telephone system. Once the transmission reaches its destination, the receiving modem converts the analog signal back to a digital signal.

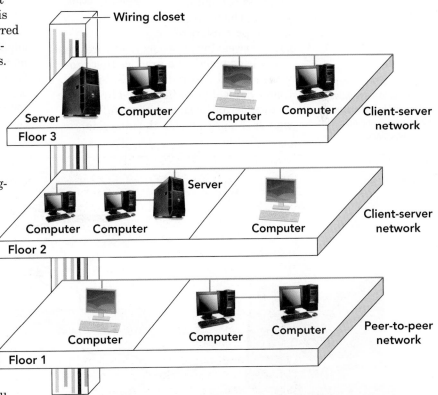

Wiring closet

Server · Computer · Computer · Computer · Client-server network
Floor 3

Server · Computer · Computer · Computer · Client-server network
Floor 2

Computer · Computer · Computer · Peer-to-peer network
Floor 1

FIGURE 8.6 A wiring closet consists of cables and a location for switches and routers. It provides a central location to facilitate access for maintenance and reconfiguration.

FIGURE 8.7 A wiring closet enables an IT technician to make adjustments to several connections from one location regardless of where the devices are located.

goes through the closet to devices located throughout the building. Having one central location for all media connections facilitates the adding of new equipment or making of repairs. Figure 8.7 provides a close up of the amount of cabling and equipment that can be crammed into single wiring closet. Now that you know where the cabling is located in a building, let's look more closely at the various forms of wired media that are essential to connect devices.

Twisted-Pair

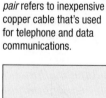

FIGURE 8.8 *Twisted-pair* refers to inexpensive copper cable that's used for telephone and data communications.

Twisted-pair wire is a copper cable used for telephone and data communications. The term *twisted-pair* refers to the interweaving of two pairs of wires that are twisted together, a practice that provides a shield that reduces interference from electrical fields generated by electric motors, power lines, and powerful radio signals (Figure 8.8). On the plus side,

twisted-pair is an inexpensive medium. On the negative side, the bandwidth of traditional twisted-pair telephone lines is too low to simultaneously carry video, voice, and data. Twisted-pair carries data at transfer rates of less than 1 Kbps.

Key Variations of Twisted-Pair

Cat-5 cable, short for **Category 5**, is the fifth generation of twisted-pair data communication cable. Cat-5 cable contains four pairs of twisted-copper wire and

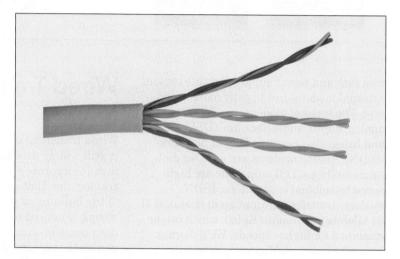

FIGURE 8.9 Cat-5e cable uses all four pairs of twisted wire and transmits data at 1,000 Mbps (1 Gbps).

supports speeds up to 100 Mbps over a maximum distance of 100 m (328 feet). However, only two of the four pairs of wires are actually used for most fast network communications. A newer variation of the Cat-5 cable, **Cat-5e**, short for **Category 5 enhanced**, uses all four wire pairs, enabling speeds up to 1,000 Mbps (1 Gbps) over a short distance. This enhanced medium is backward compatible with ordinary Cat-5 (Figure 8.9).

Cat-6, short for **Category 6**, is the sixth generation of twisted-pair cable and is backward compatible with Cat-5 and Cat-5e. It contains four pairs of copper wire like the previous

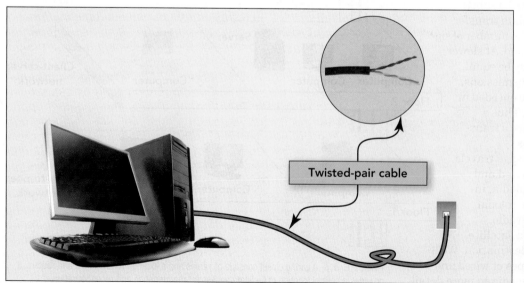

Twisted-pair cable

generation, utilizes all four pairs, supports speeds up to 1 gigabit per second (Gbps), expands available bandwidth from 100 MHz for Cat-5e to 200 MHz, and has superior immunity from external noise. Polls predict that 80 to 90 percent of new network installations will be cabled with Cat-6.

Coaxial Cable

Coaxial cable, familiar to cable TV users (Figure 8.10), consists of a center

FIGURE 8.10 In coaxial cable, data travels through the center copper wire core. The cable is connected to a coaxial wall jack.

copper wire surrounded by insulation, which is then surrounded by a layer of braided wire. Data travels through the center wire, and the braided wire provides a shield against electrical interference (Figure 8.11). Coaxial cable carries data at transfer rates of 10 Mbps. In contrast to twisted-pair, coaxial cable allows for broadband data communications. Your home is probably already wired with coaxial cable if you subscribe to a cable TV service.

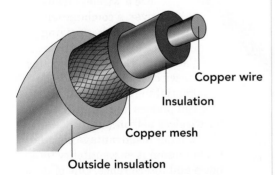

Copper wire

Insulation

Copper mesh

Outside insulation

FIGURE 8.11 The copper core of a coaxial cable is shielded from interference by a braided wire shield and an external layer of rubber that provides additional insulation.

Fiber-Optic Cable

Fiber-optic cable, another broadband transmission medium, consists of thin strands of glass or plastic about the diameter of a human hair. This medium is arranged in bundles called optical cables that carry data by means of pulses of light. Fiber-optic cable (Figure 8.12) provides

FIGURE 8.12 Fiber-optic cable consists of a bundle of fiber-optic strands.

transfer rates of 10 Gbps (gigabits per second) or more. A single fiber-optic strand is composed of three parts: the core, the cladding, and the buffer coat (Figure 8.13). The core is the thin glass or plastic center through which the light travels. The cladding is the optical material surrounding the core that reflects the light back into the core. The plastic coating that protects the fiber from moisture and damage is the buffer coat. Besides increased speed, additional benefits of fiber-optic cable include these:

- Light pulses are not affected by random radiation in the environment.
- Fiber-optic lines have a significantly lower error rate.
- Fiber optics can span longer distances before needing expensive repeaters to boost the signal.

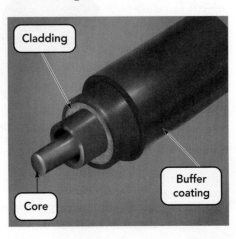

Cladding

Core

Buffer coating

FIGURE 8.13 Each fiber-optic strand has three parts.

- Security breaches in a fiber-optic line can be easily detected.
- Installation is simplified due to reduction in weight and size of fiber-optic cable as compared to coaxial cable.

Wireless Transmission Media

Unlike communications using wired transmission media such as twisted-pair, coaxial, and fiber-optic cables, wireless media don't use solid substances to transmit data. Rather, wireless media send data through air or space using infrared, radio, or microwave signals. Why would you want to use wireless media instead of cables? One instance would be in situations where cables can't be installed or the costs to do so are prohibitive. The popularity of portable computing devices has led most colleges, airports, hotels, shopping malls, and coffee shops to offer wireless access to customers. This option is usually cheaper than running wires through existing buildings. Let's investigate the wireless options of data transfer and their features.

Infrared

If you use a remote control to change television channels, you're already familiar with infrared signaling. **Infrared** is a wireless transmission medium that carries data via beams of light through the air. No wires are required, but the transmitting and receiving devices must be in line of sight or the signal is lost. When the path between the transmitting and the receiving devices is not obstructed by trees, hills, mountains, buildings, or other structures, infrared signals can work within a maximum of about 100 feet.

To use infrared technology with your computer system, you need an **IrDA port** (Figure 8.14). You may encounter an IrDA (infrared data association) port on a mobile computing device or wireless peripheral such as a PDA, digital camera, notebook, mouse,

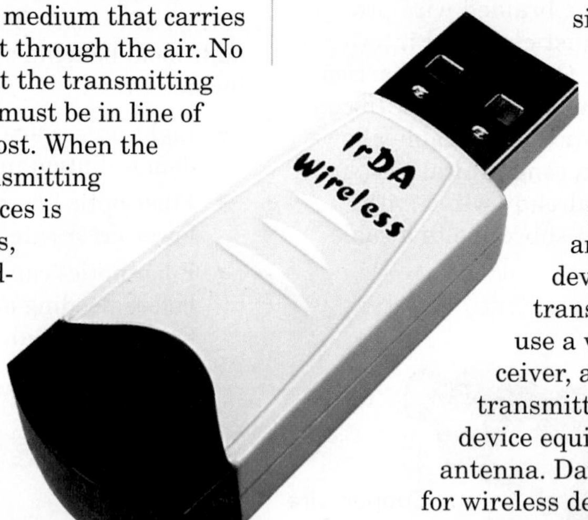

FIGURE 8.14 An IrDA port allows for wireless management of external devices such as a mouse, keyboard, phone, or PDA.

printer, or keyboard. The most common use of the IrDA port is to transfer data from your PDA to your desktop or notebook computer or another PDA. To enable data transfer, the IrDA port on the transmitting device must be in line of sight (usually within a few feet) of the port on the receiving device. IrDA ports offer data transfer rates of 4 Mbps. With these restrictions of distance and speed, why would you want to use infrared? If you had a situation where hooking devices together with cables wasn't an option, such as with a wireless keyboard or mouse, infrared would be a good choice. On modern networks, however, IrDA is too slow to be of practical use for transferring large amounts of data.

Radio

Radio transmissions offer an alternative to infrared transmissions. You probably have experienced one type of radio transmission by listening to your favorite radio station. But you may not realize the impact that radio waves have on your daily life or on society in general. All kinds of gadgets—from cell and cordless phones to baby monitors—communicate via radio waves. Although humans cannot see or otherwise detect them, radio waves are everywhere.

With **radio transmission**, data in a variety of forms (music, voice conversations, and photos) travels through the air as radio frequency (RF) signals or radio waves via a transmitting device and a receiving device. Instead of separate transmitting and receiving devices, radio transmissions can also use a wireless transceiver, a combination transmitting–receiving device equipped with an antenna. Data transfer rates for wireless devices have the potential to reach up to 3 Mbps for cell phones and up to 250 Mbps for wireless networks.

A major disadvantage of radio transmission is susceptibility to noise and interference. One of radio's advantages is that radio signals are effective at both long range (between cities, regions, and countries) and short range (within a home or office).

WiFi WiFi is a popular wireless network technology that uses radio waves to provide high-speed Internet and network connections for home systems, notebooks, video game consoles, and other enabled wireless devices. WiFi can be based on any of the IEEE 802.11 standards and communicates through radio frequency technology, with ranges reaching 300 to 500 feet. The cornerstone of a WiFi system, like other wireless systems, is the access point that broadcasts a signal that devices equipped with wireless network adapters detect.

Bluetooth Bluetooth is a short-range radio transmission technology that has become very popular in recent years. Named after the 10th-century Danish Viking and king Harald Blatand ("Bluetooth" in English) who united Denmark and Norway, Bluetooth was first conceived by Swedish cell phone giant Ericsson (Figure 8.15). Bluetooth technology relies on a network called a piconet or a PAN (personal area network) that enables all kinds of devices—desktop computers, mobile phones, printers, pagers, PDAs, and more—within 30 feet of each other to communicate automatically and wirelessly.

How exactly does Bluetooth work? Bluetooth-enabled devices, once setup, identify each other using identification numbers that are unique to each device. When these devices are within 30 feet of each other, they automatically "find" and link to one another. You don't have to worry about being connected to Bluetooth devices that you don't want to connect to: The device requires that you confirm a connection before making it final. Up to eight Bluetooth-enabled devices can be connected in a piconet at any one time.

Unlike infrared technologies, Bluetooth doesn't require a direct line of sight to connect devices. Because the frequency used by Bluetooth devices changes often, Bluetooth devices never use the same frequency at the same time and don't interfere with each other. The new Bluetooth 3.0 standard can accommodate data transfer rates of up to 24 Mbps, up from 3 Mbps. At Bluetooth's maximum transfer capacity, you would be able to move a document easily within just a few seconds. A testimony to the popularity of the connectivity provided by Bluetooth technology is verified by industry statistics

FIGURE 8.15 Bluetooth-enabled devices make tasks, such as synchronizing your phone calendar with your computer calendar or keeping your hands free while talking on the phone, easier.

that point to the 2 billion devices that have been shipped with Bluetooth installed.

Applications using Bluetooth technology and the devices that support the technology are on the rise. In August of 2009, Bag-Claim.com, a company of RBD Consulting International, introduced a new application called Bag-Claim. This application is designed for airport and travel use. It connects a Bluetooth-enabled wireless speaker that is placed inside a suitcase. The speaker alerts the owner, through an iPhone, when the suitcase is approaching. A comparison of WiFi and Bluetooth features are listed in Figure 8.16. For more information on Bluetooth technology and a brief video on the differences between Bluetooth and WiFi, visit **www.bluetooth.com/ Bluetooth.**

Microwaves

Microwaves are electromagnetic radio waves with short frequencies that travel at speeds of 1 to 10 Mbps and are used to transmit data from a source to a receiving site. Using relay stations similar to satellite dishes (including an antenna,

FIGURE 8.16 Bluetooth versus WiFi

	Bluetooth	WiFi
Hardware requirements	A Bluetooth adapter is required on all devices connecting with each other.	A wireless adapter is required on all devices in the network. Other needs include a wireless router and/or a wireless access point.
Year of development	1994	1991
Specifications	Bluetooth SIG	IEEE 802.11
Ease of use	Simple to use, can connect up to seven devices at a time, easy to switch between devices and connect new ones	Requires the configuration of hardware and software
Primary devices	Mobile phones, mouse, and keyboards	Notebooks, desktop computers, and servers
Range	30 feet	300–500 feet
Security	More secure than WiFi because it covers a smaller radius and requires two passwords	Has same security risks as all other networks
Power consumption	Low	High

ETHICS

The use of Bluetooth signals to collect statistics on how long individuals wait in airport security lines seems to be the start of a method of collecting data that is effortless, automatic, and undetected. Two Bluetooth wireless detectors with a range of 32 feet were placed in Indianapolis International Airport in 2009. Data collected validated that 6 percent of the travelers had a Bluetooth-enabled phone, MP3 player, PDA, or other detectable device that broadcast a unique hardware number. The units were used to monitor wait times in security checkpoints on several weekends, including the weekend of the Indianapolis 500. The analysis of the data proved that the average wait time during peak travel days and times was 20 minutes and that when security was prepared for an event, the wait time was shorter.

Statistics like this can prove to be valuable when trying to improve airport security. The use of detectable devices for other types of monitoring in the future can provide enormous amounts of data and improve service. Knowing when to book a flight or which gate has the least amount of traffic when trying to enter a sporting event could be beneficial. The detectors can pick up the Bluetooth signal and monitor it, but they cannot identify the individual owner of the device or communicate with him or her.

How ethical is collecting information on the whereabouts of an individual without them knowing it? Should signs be posted indicating that the detectors are active and scanning for Bluetooth signals? Do you know how to deactivate the Bluetooth feature of a mobile device that you own? Consider the pros and cons of the data collected by such detection devices, and then consider the ethical issue of violation of privacy and nonconsensual participation. What is your ethical stance?

transceiver, and so on), microwave signals are sent from one relay station to the next. Because microwaves get weaker as they get farther away from their source, must

travel in a straight line, and cannot be obstructed by buildings, hills, and mountains, relay stations are positioned approximately every 30 miles (the line-of-sight distance to the horizon), or closer if the terrain blocks transmission. To avoid obstacles, microwave relay stations are often situated on the tops of buildings or mountains (Figure 8.17). Microwaves are used in weather monitoring, air traffic control, speed limit enforcement, and missile guidance systems.

FIGURE 8.17 Any information that can travel over a telephone or coaxial cable can be transmitted via microwave.

The advantages of microwave transmission include the elimination of a wired infrastructure, enabling cellular telephone networks and connectivity in areas where the use of physical wires is impractical or impossible, and providing security through encrypting data as it is transmitted. Disadvantages include the 30-mile line-of-sight restriction, sensitivity to electrical or magnetic interference, and costs of maintaining the multitude of relay stations it takes to transfer messages across long distances.

Satellites

Essentially microwave relay stations in space, communications satellites are positioned in geosynchronous orbit, which matches the satellite's speed to that of the Earth's rotation, and are, therefore, permanently positioned with respect to the ground below. **Satellites** transmit data by sending and receiving microwave signals to and from Earth-based stations (Figure 8.18). Devices such as handheld computers and Global Positioning System (GPS) receivers can also function as Earth-based stations.

Direct broadcast satellite (DBS) is a consumer satellite technology that uses an 18- or 21-inch reception dish to receive digital TV signals at microwave frequencies directly from geostationary satellites

broadcast at a bandwidth of 12 Mbps. Increasingly, DBS operators offer Internet access as well as digital TV service, but at much lower bandwidth. A good overview of a DBS can be found at **http:// electronics.howstuffworks.com/ satellite-tv.htm**, where a video demonstrates the progression of an image from its initial capture by a camera to its reception and viewing on a home TV.

Currently, DIRECTV, a DBS operator, offers DirecWay 1-way and DirecWay 2-way Internet satellite systems. DirecWay 1-way offers high-speed broadband download via satellite link, with uploads requiring a telephone and modem. This is the inexpensive option for most broadband Internet users because downloading is used more frequently than uploading. No professional installation is required because you only receive the high-speed signal and don't transmit. DirecWay 2-way uses a high-speed satellite link both for uploading and downloading. The drawback of the 2-way system is its increased cost and the FCC's requirement that satellite dishes that both transmit and receive signals be installed professionally.

Broadband access is still not available in many rural or other low-population areas, thus many of these areas are prime candidates for DBS. If it is the only option available, something is better than nothing!

To use these various wireless transmission media, a computer system must also use a special communications device called a **network access point**, which sends and receives data between computers that contain wireless adapters. Access points are usually built into wireless routers.

So, what is it about wireless connectivity that is so interesting? Well, one answer is that wireless technology removes place-specific restrictions, that is, the need to be in a certain place to receive a service. Some forms of wireless technology allow you to be wherever you choose and still have the ability to be connected.

Now that you know more about wired and wireless media, the next section will explore the most common wired communication system: the public switched telephone network.

FIGURE 8.18
Communication satellites in space work by receiving information from one microwave station and sending it back to another at a different location on earth.

Wired Communication Via the Public Switched Telephone Network

Although many components of the conventional phone system have been enhanced, until all devices have been replaced with digital equivalents, limitations still exist.

The **public switched telephone network (PSTN)** is the global telephone system, a massive network used for data as well as voice communications, comprising various transmission media ranging from twisted-pair wire to fiber-optic cable. Some computer users derisively (and somewhat unfairly) refer to the PSTN as plain old telephone service (POTS). The derision comes from most analog telephone lines being based on standards that date back more than a century. Although a few parts of the PSTN remain based on analog communications, many sections of the system have been switched over to digital communications.

Those still using analog devices today include many homes and small business. These telephones are linked to subscriber loop carriers by means of twisted-pair wires. A **subscriber loop carrier (SLC)** is a small, waist-high curbside installation that connects as many as 96 subscribers; you've probably seen one in your neighborhood. The area served by an SLC is called the **local loop**. When the analog signal reaches the SLC, it is converted to digital form and remains that way throughout the PSTN network.

From the SLC, the digital signals are routed via high-capacity fiber-optic cables to the **local exchange switch**, a digital device capable of handling thousands of calls located in the local telephone company's central office (CO). From the local phone company's CO, the call can go anywhere in the world. It can continue on the digital portion of the PSTN's fiber-optic cables or be converted to radio waves and sent out over cellular networks (Figure 8.19).

Although analog connections still exist, **digital telephony**, a system in which the telephones and transmissions are digital, is the trend. Compared with analog devices, which are prone to noise and interference, digital phones offer noise-free transmission and high-quality audio. You might have used a digital phone at work or on campus. Typically companies and universities install their own internal digital telephone systems, called private branch exchanges (PBXs). Calls to the outside, however, must be translated into analog signals to connect to the PSTN.

Because long-distance lines must handle thousands of calls simultaneously (32 calls per second, 24 hours a day, 7 days a week in the United States), a technique called **multiplexing** is used to send more than one call over a single line. The electrical and physical characteristics of copper wire impose a limit of 24 multiplexed calls per line, whereas fiber-optic cables can carry as many as 48,384 digital voice channels simultaneously. In contrast to the analog local loop, most long-distance carriers use digital signals so that they can pack the

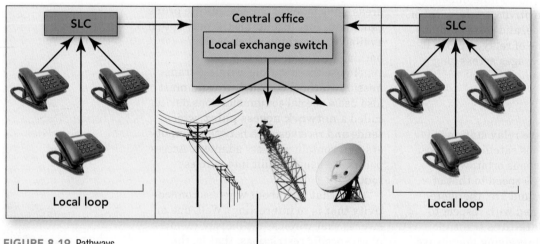

FIGURE 8.19 Pathways on the PSTN. In order for the signal to reach its final destination, it may travel across several different transmission medium, including a cellular network.

greatest number of calls into a single circuit.

The inability of homes or businesses to access the PSTN's high-speed fiber-optic cables, along with the bottleneck of data on the last mile of twisted-pair phone lines connecting homes and businesses, are often referred to as the **last-mile problem**. Here's why. In most areas of the United States, only the local loop is still using analog technology, because nearly all existing buildings were originally constructed with built-in twisted-pair wiring. These analog lines are vulnerable to noise and can't surpass a theoretical limit of 56 Kbps. But things are starting to change. Telephone companies are getting into other businesses (such as providing Internet connectivity) and need to deliver higher bandwidth to homes. Therefore, telephone companies are now replacing analog local loop technology with digital technology (such as FiOS). The last-mile problem might soon be solved in your neighborhood!

Last-Mile Technologies

Local loops are in the process of being upgraded, but until the upgrade is complete, phone companies and other providers offer a number of interim digital telephony technologies to bridge the gap from the Internet to a residence. This last section of the circuit is referred to as the last mile. Technologies that help bridge that gap, **last-mile technologies**, include digital telephone standards (such as ISDN and DSL) that use twisted-pair wiring, as well as high-speed wired services (such as coaxial cable and cable modems). To learn more about telephone technology from wiring a system to video conferencing and VoIP check out **http://telecom.hellodirect. com/docs/ Tutorials/ default.asp.**

Integrated Services Digital Network A standard for digital telephone and data service, **ISDN (integrated services digital network)**, offers connections ranging from 56 to 128 Kbps (basic rate ISDN) or 1.5 Mbps (primary rate ISDN), using

ordinary twisted-pair telephone lines. The cost of an ISDN line is often two to three times that of an analog phone line, but there's a payoff. With a 128-Kbps ISDN service, you get two telephone numbers with one ISDN account; you can use one for computer data and the other for voice or fax. When you're using the connection for computer data only, the system automatically uses both data channels to give you the maximum data transfer rate; if a phone call comes in, the connection automatically drops back to 64 Kbps to accommodate the incoming call. What's more, connection is nearly instantaneous. Unlike analog connections with a modem, there's no lengthy dial-in procedure and connection delay.

To connect computers to ISDN lines, you need an **ISDN adapter** (also called a **digital modem**, although it isn't actually a modem; Figure 8.20). Although ISDN has been largely supplanted by faster technologies (such as DSL and fiber optics), ISDN may be the only broadband solution in many rural areas. Keep in mind that ISDN requires that special wiring be installed from the subscriber loop carrier (SLC) to your home.

Digital Subscriber Line Another method of Internet access available in the United States is **DSL (digital subscriber line)**, also called **xDSL**. This term refers to a group of related technologies, including **ADSL (asymmetric digital subscriber line), SDSL (symmetrical digital subscriber line), HDSL (high bit-rate digital subscriber line)**, and **VDSL (very high bit-rate digital subscriber line)**, all forms of Internet access. DSL technologies, in general, can deliver data transfer rates of 1.54 Mbps or higher and are akin to ISDN in that they use existing

FIGURE 8.20 Various types of modems facilitate the connection between your computer and last-mile technologies.

FIGURE 8.21 The Details behind DSL Technologies

Name	Actual Name	Bandwidth	Users
ADSL	Asymmetrical digital subscriber line	Uploads at speeds of up to 640 Kbps, downloads at speeds of up to 8.1 Mbps	Frequently used with residential users in the United States.
SDSL	Symmetrical digital subscriber line	Supports data exchange rates each way, up to 3 Mbps	Popular with residents in Europe.
HDSL	High bit-rate digital subscriber line	1.544 Mbps of bandwidth each way	PBX network connections, digital loop carrier systems, interexchange point of presence (POPs), Internet servers, and private data networks.
VDSL	Very high bit-rate digital subscriber line	Uploads at speeds of up to 16 Mbps, downloads at speeds of up to 52 Mbps	VDSL is available worldwide in specific regions. Its use is growing all the time, though it's not easily found in the United States.

twisted-pair wiring. But because DSL is always on, requires no call set up time, and achieves much higher throughput than ISDN, it quickly became more popular. An overview of the technology features of each type of DSL should provide some clarification.

- **ADSL.** An ADSL modem separates an ordinary copper telephone line into three separate data channels with different capacities and speeds. The lowest capacity transmits analog voice for telephones; the second, medium capacity, uploads data to the network; and the third, highest capacity, downloads data from the network. This means that uploads are slower than downloads on an ADSL connection.

- **SDSL.** A SDSL modem splits the copper telephone line channels into three channels: telephone, upload, and download; but it does this so that the distributed bandwidth for each channel is equal. On SDSL connections, uploads and downloads occur at the same rate.

- **HDSL.** HDSL is the most mature DSL technology. It is a form of SDSL that provides T1 connections over two or three twisted-pair copper lines. Unlike most other forms of DSL, HDSL is not a typical consumer service, but it is often used for private data networks.

- **VDSL.** VDSL is the next generation DSL with super-accelerated rates of 52 Mbps for downloads and 12 Mbps for uploads. It will provide services like HDTV and Video-on-Demand along with Internet access.

For more information on the four DSL technologies, refer to Figure 8.21.

To use DSL, you need a DSL phone line and a DSL service subscription. Unlike conventional telephone service, which is available to almost any home, DSL service is limited by the distance from the CO, or telephone switching station, to your home. You also need a **DSL modem**, which is similar to a traditional telephone modem in that it modulates and demodulates analog and digital signals for transmission over communications channels. However, DSL modems use signaling methods based on broadband technology for much higher transfer speeds. DSL service is now standardized so that almost any DSL modem should work with the wiring your telephone provider uses. However, it is best to buy a DSL modem that your provider recommends. Check with your provider for a list of approved modems before purchasing one. Although DSL service is more expensive than dial-up, it is usually cheaper than other broadband access options, such as cable or fiber optics (Figure 8.22)

Cable-Based Broadband Aside from telephone companies, the leading provider of

> **"DSL service** is now **standardized** so that almost any **DSL modem should work** with the wiring **your telephone provider** uses. **"**

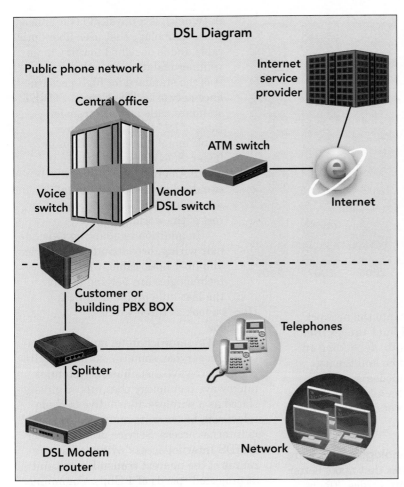

DSL Diagram

Public phone network

Central office

Internet service provider

ATM switch

Voice switch

Vendor DSL switch

Internet

Customer or building PBX BOX

Splitter

Telephones

DSL Modem router

Network

FIGURE 8.22 The Path of Data from an Internet Service Provider to a DSL Subscriber's Residence

broadband is your local cable TV company. Approximately 120 million homes in the United States had access to high-speed cable Internet service as of 2008 (Figure 8.23). Actual customers for this service reached 41.8 million in 2009 (Figure 8.24)

When cable and the cabling equipment were originally installed in homes, signals were designed to run in only one direction: to the home. When the Internet became popular, the cable companies invested tremendous amounts of money in equipment and cable to enable two-way communication to capture the Internet market.

For computer users, these services offer data transfer rates that exceed the speed of DSL. **Cable modems**, devices that enable computers to access the Internet by means of a cable TV connection, now deliver data at bandwidths of 1.5 to 6 Mbps or more, depending on how many subscribers are connected to a local cable segment. Bandwidth across a cable connection is shared among subscribers who are connected to the cable company in local groups. If you are lucky enough to

have subscribers in your group who don't use much bandwidth, you can experience impressive speed, up to 20 Mbps, while using the Internet. To help you decide which last-mile technology might be right for you, check out the "Cable or DSL" tutorial at **http://telecom. hellodirect. com/docs/ Tutorials/ CableVsDSL.1. 030801.asp.**

Leased Lines A **leased line**, sometimes called a dedicated line, is a connection set up by a telecommunication carrier and is usually a permanent fiber-optic or telephone connection that enables continuous, end-to-end communication between two points. Larger organizations, such as ISPs, corporations, and universities, connect using leased **T1 lines**, which are fiber-optic (or specially conditioned copper) cables that can handle 24 digitized voice channels or carry computer data at a rate of up to 1.544 Mbps. If the T1 line is being used for telephone conversations, it plugs into the users' phone system. If it is

FIGURE 8.23 In five years, high-speed Internet cable has been made accessible to an additional 30 million Americans.

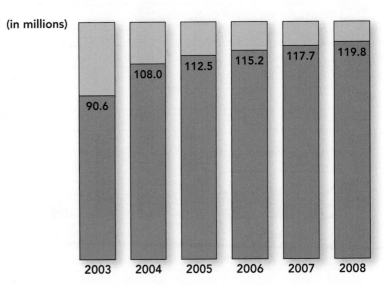

(in millions)

2003	2004	2005	2006	2007	2008
90.6	108.0	112.5	115.2	117.7	119.8

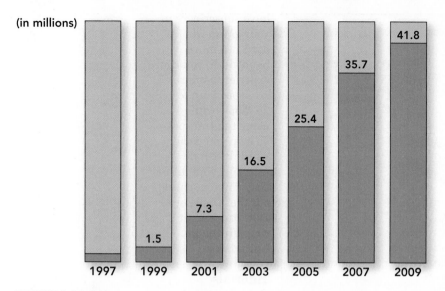

(in millions)

	1.5	7.3	16.5	25.4	35.7	41.8
1997	1999	2001	2003	2005	2007	2009

FIGURE 8.24 Cable subscribers have been on a steady increase due to its increased availability in some rural areas and more competitive pricing.

carrying data, it plugs into the network's router. The price of T1 lines ranges from $1,000 to $1,500 a month, depending on the provider, the location, and the use. Leased lines may use modems, cable modems, or other communications devices to manage the transfer of data into and out of the organization.

Other Last-Mile Technologies There are also interim technologies that make better use of existing fiber-optic cables. Fiber-optic **T2** and **T3 lines** can handle up to 44.7 Mbps of computer data. Although T3 lines can cost approximately $3,000 per month, Internet service providers, financial institutions, and large corporations that move a large amount of data find these lines critical to their operations. One T3 line is equivalent to having 28 T1 lines. Another technology, **SONET (synchronous optical**

network), is a physical layer of network technology that uses fiber-optic cable and is designed to carry large volumes of data over long distances. It is the standard for high-performance networks. The slowest SONET standard calls for data transfer rates of 52 Mbps; some higher levels enable rates of 20 Gbps or faster. SONET is widely used in North America, and a similar standard, synchronous digital hierarchy (SDH), is used in the rest of the world.

In addition to adapting twisted-pair wiring, broadband coaxial cable, and fiber-optic cable, wireless technologies are helping to solve the last-mile problem as well. Here's a look at three wireless solutions.

MMDS (multichannel multipoint distribution service, sometimes called multipoint microwave distribution system) is microwave technology that was originally slated as a wireless alternative to cable television, but now its main application is Internet access. Service providers offer MMDS Internet access within a 35-mile radius of the nearest transmission point at projected speeds of 1 Gbps. Communication with the network is through a roof-mounted disk connected with coaxial cable. The average cost is $50 per month for 2 Mbps of download speed. It is an affordable and viable option in areas where cable and DSL are not available.

MMDS will most likely be supplanted by WiMAX. **WiMAX (worldwide interoperability for microwave access)** is a wireless up-and-coming digital communication system designed to deliver high-speed access over long distances, either point to point (both sender and receiver are stationary) or through mobile access (sender or receiver is moving). WiMAX is effective for up to 30 miles for point-to-point access and 3 to 10 miles for mobile access. In mountainous areas or other places where there are obstructions, MMDS and WiMAX face challenges because they are susceptible to interference. To view a brief video on the technology behind WiMAX and an explanation of how it works, visit **www. wimax.com/education**. A general comparison of Internet connection speeds over common communication channels is displayed in Figure 8.25.

FIGURE 8.25 Often speed, price, and availability determine which method of Internet connection a user selects.

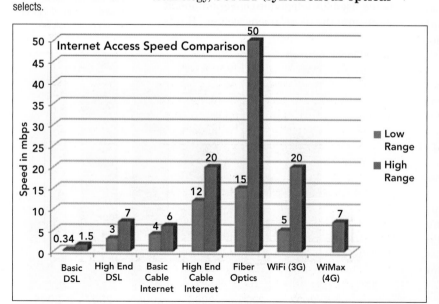

In the next section, we will explore the phenomenon of the coming together of these communications technologies.

Convergence: Is It a Phone or a Computer?

We've been examining technologies that carry computer data over voice lines as well as through the air. At the core of this process is **digitization**, the transformation of data such as voice, text, graphics, audio, and video into digital form. Digitization enables convergence. **Convergence** refers to the merging of disparate objects or ideas (and even people) into new combinations and efficiencies. Within the IT industry, convergence means two things: (1) the combination of various industries (computers, consumer electronics, and telecommunications) and (2) the coming together of products such as PCs and telephones.

Wireless devices are proliferating at a tremendous pace. Today, it is not unusual for your phone to double as a PDA or talk to your computer, or for your computer to be controlled by a wireless mouse or keyboard. Convergence has culminated in the transmission of data. With the advent of Internet telephony (the use of the Internet to transmit real-time voice data), all forms of information (voice, data, and video) now travel over the same network, the Internet (Figure 8.26).

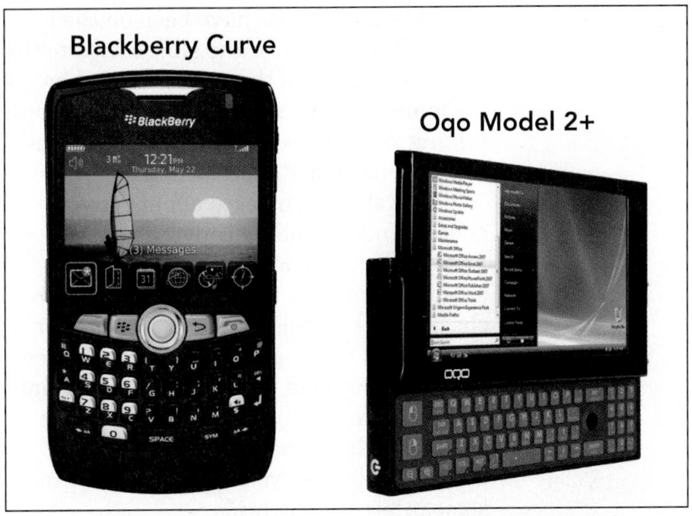

Digitization also enables media convergence. Media convergence is the unification of all forms of media (including newspapers, TV, and radio). The Internet is already a major source of breaking news, rivaling such traditional sources as newspapers and television. Many telephone calls are now transmitted across the Internet using a technology known as Voice over IP (VoIP). This trend could be signaling the end of the traditional public switched telephone network.

Another threat to the PSTN is the November 2003 legislation on telephone number portability. Under this rule, people can keep their existing phone number when changing providers, whether from traditional land-based or cellular phone service. Despite the ongoing challenges of cell phones (battery life, spotty connectivity, dropped calls), more and more U.S. households are opting to disconnect their conventional landline telephones and rely solely on cellular service. As of early 2010, 25 percent of U.S. households had only cell phones, and 15 percent of those with both landline and cell phones received most of their calls on their cell. Industry professionals expect this migration away from land-based telephones to continue as the need for portability and other cell phone features, such as text messaging, become more in demand. In support of this statistic, sales of smartphones like the iPhone, Droid, and BlackBerry, which can surf the Web and

Blackberry Curve

Oqo Model 2+

FIGURE 8.26
Convergence means smaller devices do more. The BlackBerry Curve 8350i is a PDA, phone, and Internet access device all rolled into one. The OQO model 2+ is one of the world's smallest computers at 5.6 × 3.3 inches, making it easy to take your computer with you.

provide e-mail access have been on the increase. The reason for the shift seems to the growing interest in the apps provided by the manufacturer and supported by the operating system not just the phone's operation or consistency of performance.

Why should you care about convergence? Understanding convergence will help you make more informed decisions about current and future technology purchases. This section explores some of the dimensions of computer-telephony convergence, a process of technological morphing in which previously distinct devices lose their sharply defined boundaries and blend together. As you'll see, it's creating some interesting hybrids.

Cellular Telephones

Cellular telephones are computing devices. Although cell phones started out as analog devices (**1G**, for first generation), the current generation of wireless cell phones (**4G**, for fourth generation) are all digital systems that provide high-speed access to transmit voice, text, images, and video data. Although 4G can be considered the current generation, most cell phones are still **3G** (third-generation) devices. For more information, dates, and features of each cell phone technology generation, refer to Figure 8.27.

In 1971, AT&T built a network of transmitters that automatically repeat signals. This network of transmitters, which are called **cell sites**, broadcasts signals throughout specific, but limited, geographic areas called **cells**. When callers move from cell to cell, each new cell site automatically takes over the signal to maintain signal strength. But who or what monitors your cell phone's signal strength so that you have the best reception? That's the job of the **mobile switching center (MSC)**, and each cellular network contains several MSCs that handle communications within a group of cells (Figure 8.28). Each cell tower reports signal strength to the MSC, which then switches your signal to whatever cell tower will provide the clearest connection for your conversation.

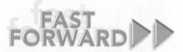

FIGURE 8.27 Cell Phone Generations

Wireless Technologies	Year	Feature
1G	1981	Analog mobile phone service allowed callers to make their own calls without operator assistance and move seamlessly from cell to cell.
2G	1991	Digital signaling decreased interference, improved reception, and provided better protection from eavesdropping. This generation also increased security features designed to discourage cell phone fraud.
3G	2001	These technologies enabled faster data transmission, greater network capacity, more advanced network services, and allowed transmission of voice, text, images, and video data.
4G (beyond 3G)	2010–2015 (estimated release)	This generation promises even higher data rates as well as real-time (streamed) formatting for voice, data, and high-quality multimedia. 4G is not currently available in all areas.

FAST FORWARD

Convergence is moving into another arena, with Microsoft signing an agreement with Australia's leading pay TV provider, Foxtel, to stream over 30 channels to Xbox 360 consoles through Xbox LIVE. Xbox 360 owners in Australia will use their units to access Foxtel channels instead of using a set-top box with an expensive installation fee. A user will need an Xbox 360 console, Xbox LIVE gold subscription, a broadband connection with high download limits, and a Foxtel by Xbox LIVE subscription. The plan will allow access to such channels as FOX Sports, Discovery, and Nickelodeon and will provide video on demand and online chat. It should appeal to users in areas that Foxtel does not currently service and those that move frequently and want to avoid all of the reconnect fees. Microsoft has similar agreements already in Europe, France, and the United Kingdom. There is currently no comparable service in the United States. Microsoft's convergence of game consoles and pay TV is another attempt to unite features and devices to provide better services for the consumer. How long will it be until one device controls our home media needs and returning set-top boxes and paying installation charges are events of the past?

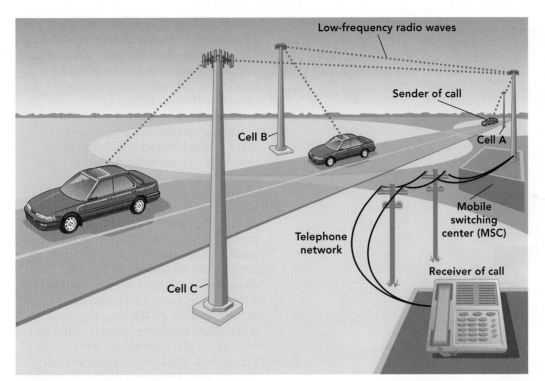

MSCs route calls to the gateway mobile switching center (GMSC), which in turn sends calls to their final destination. If the call is headed for a land-based phone, the GMSC sends the call to the PSTN. Otherwise, it forwards the call directly to another cellular network.

Terrain, weather, antenna position, and battery strength can all interfere and affect signal strength. However, there may be times when you've extended your antenna, recharged your battery, have clear weather, and are standing at the top of a hill—and still cannot achieve a good signal. Cell coverage is not perfect, and cellular networks have *holes* (areas in which you can't send or receive calls).

MSCs are also key players in another widely used cellular service, SMS (short messaging service), better known as text messaging and MMS (multimedia messaging service), commonly called picture messaging. As of December 2009, over 152.7 billion text messages were sent every month compared to just 18 billion in December 2006. That number has grown by 200 percent or more for each year for the last two years (Figure 8.29). Teens are the largest users of messaging. Subscribers between the ages of 13 and 17 sent and received 1,742 text messages a month in the second quarter of 2008. How do text and multimedia messaging work? The MSC forwards the message to a messaging center for storage and then locates the other cell phone that will receive the message.

FIGURE 8.29 In 2009, an average of 152.7 billion text messages were sent per month, with a majority by users between the ages of 13 and 44.

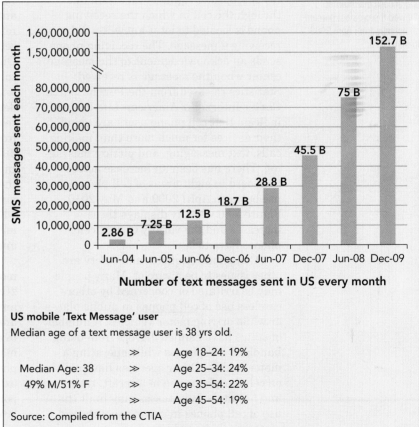

Number of text messages sent in US every month

US mobile 'Text Message' user
Median age of a text message user is 38 yrs old.

	≫	Age 18–24: 19%
Median Age: 38	≫	Age 25–34: 24%
49% M/51% F	≫	Age 35–54: 22%
	≫	Age 45–54: 19%

Source: Compiled from the CTIA

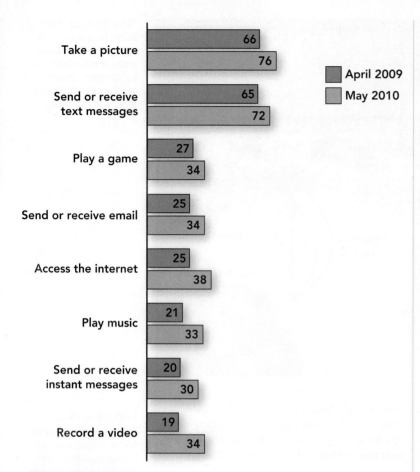

Take a picture
66
76

Send or receive text messages
65
72

Play a game
27
34

Send or receive email
25
34

Access the internet
25
38

Play music
21
33

Send or receive instant messages
20
30

Record a video
19
34

■ April 2009
■ May 2010

FIGURE 8.30 Using a cell phone to take videos and access the Internet showed the greatest percent of increase from April 2009 to May 2010.

An appropriate signal is then sent out through the cell in which the receiving phone is located to let it know it will be receiving a message. The receiving phone sends an acknowledgment to the message center when the message is received. Statistics released from the Pew Research Center Internet & American Life Project indicate that cell phone users are using their devices for much more than making calls, text messaging, and picture messaging. There has been an increase across the board in eight areas of cell phone use between April 2009 and May 2010. Figure 8.30 visually displays these increases and the variety of uses cell phones have today.

Cell phone etiquette and safety are other issues to be aware of. Many people may be irritated or concerned by others' careless use of cell phones in public places or while driving motor vehicles. A number of states have banned drivers from using handheld cell phones while operating a motor vehicle. Other agencies have policies on cellular phone use in aircraft, trains, and hospitals. Businesses may limit the use of cell phones in movie theaters and restaurants. In addition, your college or university may restrict the use of cell phones in classrooms. For a list of the top 10 cell phone etiquette rules people break go to **www.bspcn.com/2008/08/14/top-10-cell-phone-etiquette-rules-people-still-break**.

Besides cell phone etiquette and safety, burgeoning cell phone use has another societal impact. Just as with old computer equipment, you need to think about the proper disposal of your cell phone when you upgrade or damage it beyond repair. The average life of a cell phone is 18 months. Discarded cell phones produce toxic waste. When they end up in landfills, they threaten the environment through the release of arsenic, lead, cadmium, and other heavy metals that can creep into the water supply and cause cancer or birth defects. AT&T, Cingular, and many other providers, as well as indirect retailers, will accept old phones. Figure 8.31 displays the parts of a cell phone and indicates whether each component is recyclable, reusable, or hazardous. The bottom line: Recycling your old cell phone is good for the environment.

Personal Communication Service A group of related digital cellular technologies called **PCS (personal communication service)** quickly replaced most analog cellular services. PCS is also referred to as **2G**, for second-generation cellular technology, or dual-band service. Digital 2G phones made strides toward solving many of the problems that plagued analog phones. Improvements included decreasing signal interference, increasing reception, providing better protection from eavesdropping, and increasing the difficulty of committing cell phone fraud. In short, 2G design specifications enabled the manufacturers to use convergence to make the **smartphones** we enjoy today, which are handheld devices that integrate mobile phone capability, computing power, and Web access.

For millions of people, 2G made mobile computing a reality. Because 2G technology is digital, it's much more amenable to data communications than analog cellular services. It made it possible to access the Internet by means of a modem connected to an analog cellular phone, but data transfer rates were extremely low because of line noise and poor connections. Throughput of up to 384 Kbps for downloads was enabled by 2G standards.

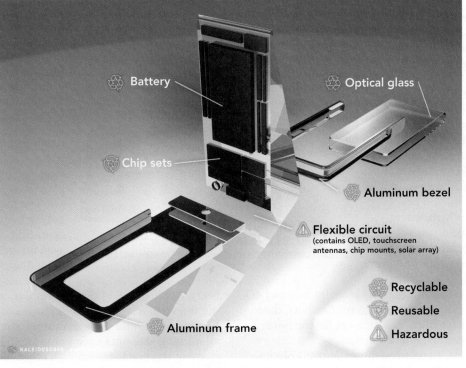

FIGURE 8.31 Over 130 million cell phones are disposed of annually in the United States, with only 10 percent of that number being recycled. Globally, only 3 percent of all cell phones are recycled.

GREEN tech tips

Simply throwing away a cell phone is hazardous to the environment. How you dispose of your old phone is left up to you. However, with cell phones made of mostly recyclable material (Figure 8.32) using a recycle drop off or donating it to an organization that gives them to those in need seems like the best and most environmentally sound decision. So, where can you dispose of your phone responsibly? Check out **www. nokia.com/environment/we-recycle**.

Nokia's We Recycle program will recycle your phone for no cost. With 5,000 recycle centers in 85 countries, Nokia is demonstrating corporate responsibility not only for its own product, but also for its competitors' products. Similarly, Verizon's HopeLine refurbishes or recycles old phones and uses the proceeds to help prevent domestic violence. Through this program, more than 1 million phones and more than 170,000 batteries have been disposed of properly.

Visit the Shelter Alliance (Fund Raising with Accountability) Web site at **www.shelteralliance.net/index.cfm** to learn about several cell phone recycling programs offered through this organization and its nonprofit partners. ●

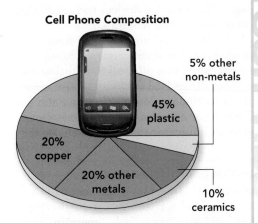

FIGURE 8.32 The materials in your mobile phone can be used to make musical instruments, jewelry, and park benches.

Technology has marched on with the introduction of 3G technology (Figure 8.33) and the recent introduction of 4G (fourth generation) cell phones. The main benefit of 3G is that it supports much higher numbers of data and voice customers and provides higher data transfer rates (greater than 384 Kbps while walking and up to 2 Mbps while stationary). The recently released 4G offers improvements in connectivity, data transfer rates, and support for the next generation of multimedia.

So, should you dump your 2G phone and opt for a 3G? If your phone is providing you with good-quality service and the feature set is sufficient for your needs, you should probably keep it. However, if you need to regularly access the Internet, you may wish to consider upgrading to a 3G phone to take advantage of the higher data transfer rates.

FIGURE 8.33 The Nokia E90 Communicator boasts high-speed 3G mobile broadband connections for Internet browsing and file transfer.

Web-Enabled Devices

A **Web-enabled device** is any device that can connect to the Internet and display and respond to the codes in markup languages, such as HTML (Hypertext Markup Language) or XML (Extensible Markup Language), typically used to build Web pages. Web-enabled devices include PDAs, smartphones, and notebook PCs.

PDAs are fast disappearing from the market because of convergence. Many smartphones now offer all the functionality that PDAs used to offer and also act as phones. Windows Mobile and the Palm OS are popular operating systems for smartphones that were originally developed for PDAs. BlackBerry devices (which use their own operating system called RIM) continue to be a popular choice for managing enterprise business life (which includes checking e-mail, making phone calls, and accessing the Internet). BlackBerry devices actually lead the smartphone revolution as one of the first truly convergent devices.

The market for mobile operating systems has heated up, with RIM BlackBerry, Apple iPhone OS and Symbian leading the way. Windows Mobile (based on Windows CE), and Google Android are all making attempts to compete for their share of the market. Although other mobile operating systems are gaining in popularity, a study completed in February of 2009 concluded that the most secure mobile platform for business use is the BlackBerry RIM. Refer to Figure 8.34 to view the criteria used to arrive at this assessment. If you are trying to decide on which smartphone to purchase, go to **http://cellphones.about.com/od/buyersguides/qt/best_cell_phone.htm** and answer approximately 15 questions on your cell needs and wants. When you complete all questions, the site will display a list of several devices that match your needs. You probably have heard the saying that when you are opening a business it's location, location, and location that counts. With all the facts considered, when buying a cell phone it might be coverage, coverage, and coverage that are the final factors in your choice. You might have to limit your phone selection from those offered by the carrier that provides service in your region.

To work over wireless networks, Web-enabled devices require **WAP (Wireless Application Protocol)**. WAP is a standard that specifies how users can access the Web securely using pagers, smartphones, PDAs, and other wireless handheld devices. It doesn't matter which operating system your device uses because WAP is supported by all of them. However, WAP-enabled devices do require a **microbrowser**, a special

FIGURE 8.34 An assessment of operating systems, based on five areas of focus, indicate that the BlackBerry RIM OS surpasses the iPhone OS and Windows Mobile OS.

Comparative Evaluation of Mobile OS Components

Features	BlackBerry OS	iPhone OS	Win Mobile OS
Authentication	3	1	2
Data Vaulting	3	-1	2
Reliability	3	3	2
Tamper Resistant	2	1	1
Meeting Security Validations	3	-2	1

Ranges of rankings go from a low of –2 to a high of 3.

Web browser that has all of the features of computer-based browsers but is simplified to meet handheld device limitations. These limitations include smaller screen size, smaller file sizes (due to the low memory capacities of WAP-enabled devices), and wireless networks with low bandwidth.

Now that you understand how convergence is blurring the boundaries between phone and computer devices, let's take a look at some wired and wireless applications used with these devices.

Wired and Wireless Applications

The world of wired and wireless applications is receiving more attention every day. You can't open a magazine, surf the Web, or watch TV without seeing ads for the latest wireless solutions. More and more businesses and home users are implementing these various applications to help them communicate, collaborate, and share text, graphics, audio, and video. You can sit in a classroom today and receive instant messages, e-mail, and stock quotes and even browse the Web—all from your smartphone! And it is happening at increasingly faster speeds, higher data transfer rates, and lower costs.

Internet Telephony: Real-Time Voice and Video

Internet telephony Using the Internet for real-time voice communication is commonly known as **VoIP (Voice over Internet Protocol)** or **Internet**

telephony. You can place calls via the Internet in a variety of ways, but first you'll need a computer equipped with a microphone, speakers or headphones, an Internet connection, and a telephony-enabled program such as Skype (**www.skype.com**). With Skype, you can make free calls to other similarly equipped Skype users. Stay posted as this might start to change. In May 2010 Skype announced its new iPhone app, which makes calls over the 3G network. Skype-to-Skype calls over the WiFi networks will remain free, but the company says that they will begin to charge for Skype-to-Skype calls over the 3G network by the end of 2010. Even though revenue may not be the best measure of success, a look at the graph in Figure 8.35 shows an unmistakably constant increase in Skype revenue over six consecutive quarters. The technology appears to be doing well.

What about placing a call to an ordinary telephone or cell phone? In most situations, you can't do it for free. However, VoIP service providers such as Vonage are stepping into the act by offering computer-to-phone and phone-to-phone services that use the Internet for long- distance transmission (Figure 8.36). The system is pretty

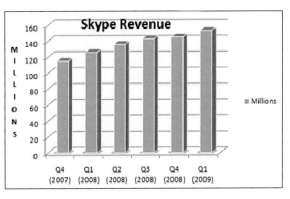

FIGURE 8.35 Between Quarter 3 and Quarter 4 of 2008, Skype revenue seemed to level out. This could be due to the economy or the fact that most users were making Skype-to-Skype free calls.

FIGURE 8.36 VoIP installation is relatively easy. The system can be configured by a novice computer user.

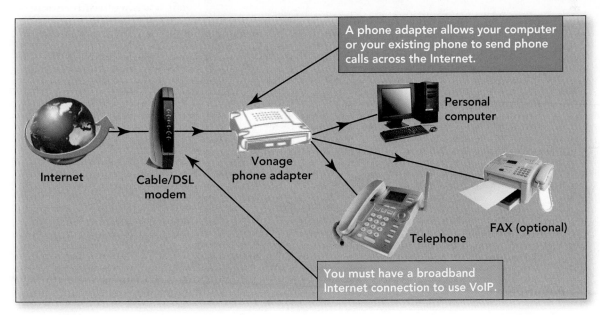

A phone adapter allows your computer or your existing phone to send phone calls across the Internet.

Internet — Cable/DSL modem — Vonage phone adapter — Personal computer — Telephone — FAX (optional)

You must have a broadband Internet connection to use VoIP.

simple to set up, rates are cheaper than conventional landline phones, and the quality is very good. The hottest markets for VoIP are Japan, China, and the United States.

The basic idea of Internet telephony has an enormous advantage: Because the Internet doesn't rely on switches to route messages, like the PSTN does, it's cheaper to operate. Providers can route dozens, hundreds, or even thousands of calls over the same circuit. Many conventional phone companies already send voice calls over the Internet. You may have actually experienced VoIP without even knowing it. You can try Internet telephony by using Skype (the incumbent leader), GizmoProject, PeerMe, or Jajah. Each offers free service to another computer user who has the same software installed, but most charge for connecting to a house or wireless cell phone.

Times are always changing in the world of technology. As of March 2010, Verizon and Skype have teamed up to provide free Skype-to-Skype phone calls over the Verizon voice network. With the 91 million Verizon wireless users and 600 million Skype users worldwide, that is a lot of talk. IM messages to other Skype users will also be free. Skype-to-Skype calls and IMs will not be charged against the Verizon data plan; however, a data plan is required to activate the service. Skype

mobile will only work on the Verizon's cellular voice network and not on WiFi networks in general, In addition, a Black-Berry or Android phone is needed. Video is not available as of yet, due to the limits of the devices and network. If you meet the criteria, you can simply text SKYPE to 2255 for a download link or visit **http://phones.verizonwireless.com/skypemobile.**

If you and the person you're calling have a digital video camera, you can converse through real-time videoconferencing as well. **Videoconferencing**, also called **Web conferencing**, is the use of digital video technology to transmit sound and video images to facilitate online, virtual meetings through which two or more people can have a face-to-face meeting even though they're geographically separated (Figure 8.37). Such meetings are practical, quick, and cost-effective. The many notebook computers sold today come with built-in video cameras (webcams) and Skype software to support video conferencing. However, you won't always have perfect quality; you'll hear echoes and delays in the audio, and the picture will be small, grainy, jerky, and susceptible to delays. But there are no long-distance charges (using Skype). Several vendors offer, for a price, software and packages to facilitate this online communication and improve the quality and interaction among participants. All attendees need to do is download the application to their computers or access a Web site or URL to join the group offering the meeting or presentation. To review an independent ranking of such services visit **www.webconferencing-test.com/en/webconference_home.html.**

In addition to Internet voice and video calls, Internet telephony products support real-time conferencing with such features as a shared whiteboard, file-exchange capabilities, and text chatting. A **whiteboard**, generally shown as a separate area of the videoconferencing screen, enables participants to create a shared workspace. Participants can write or draw in this space as if they were using a physical whiteboard in a meeting. Combine this with live video

FIGURE 8.37 In a videoconference or Web conference, participants still feel personally connected to other participants, but the electronic conference eliminates the frustration, time, and cost of travel.

Webcam

and audio and it's like being in a conference room with your group.

A **webcam** (Figure 8.38) is an inexpensive, low-resolution analog or digital video camera that is integrated into a notebook computer or designed to sit on top of a computer monitor. Sometimes an individual, company, or organization places a webcam in a public location, such as a street corner, a railway station, or a museum (Figure 8.39). Often, the camera is set up to take a snapshot of the scene every 15 minutes or so. The image is then displayed on a Web page. Some sites offer streaming cams, also called live cams, which provide more frequently updated images. Many resorts and ski areas have set up live cams so potential visitors can see weather conditions and tourist lines. Keep in mind that live cams cannot be set up to watch or spy without obtaining the proper legal documents. The consequences of posting a live cam on a social network site may come back to haunt you. To learn more about webcams and their use, and to obtain a few helpful hints, visit (**www.microsoft.com/canada/home/styleandhome/2.3.35_webcambasicshowdoesonework.aspx**).

If you want only to transmit voice over the Internet, and not video, you can use a dial-up modem and connection with transfer speeds of 56 Kbps. But for any high-bandwidth Internet application, such as streaming video, you need a broadband connection with transfer speeds of at least 1.5 Mbps. Network-based delivery of high-quality videoconferencing requires a bandwidth of at least 10 Mbps. Videoconferencing will be a much smoother experience for all participants with broadband's faster upload speeds.

Streaming video wasn't practical for home viewing before broadband and cheap, powerful computers became available for the home market. Now, streaming video sites such as YouTube are some of the most visited sites on the Internet. As popular as YouTube is for viewing videos,

FIGURE 8.38 If your computer lacks a webcam, you can buy one that is designed to be freestanding or placed on top of a monitor (or notebook).

Webcam

it has a video length limit of 10 minutes. This means that watching a 30-minute television program will require viewing three segments. **Internet TV** refers to the ability to view television shows, videos, and movies over the Internet, for no additional cost, via download or streaming video. The benefit of this type of viewing over YouTube is that the content is provided by the original source, so copyright is not an issue, there is no limit on length, the user has a variety of selections from which to choose, and there is no time restriction on when the video has to be watched. Powerful, inexpensive computers and increased bandwidth offered by ISPs have made Internet telephony and videoconferencing affordable and practical for small businesses. And millions of Internet users watch Internet TV and employ webcams and programs such as Skype to stay in touch with friends and family—often for free (at least for now)!

FIGURE 8.39 Web cams, like those provided by the National Parks Service, provide live satellite links to many popular locations.

Faxing: Document Exchange

Facsimile transmission—or **fax** as it's popularly known—enables you to send an image of a document over a telephone line or the Internet (Figure 8.40). The sending fax machine makes a digital image of the document. Using a built-in modem, the sending fax machine converts the image into an analog representation so that it can be transmitted through the analog telephone system. The receiving fax machine converts the analog signals to digital signals, converts the digital signals to an image of the document, and then prints the image.

Some computer users use fax modems instead of fax machines. A **fax modem** is a computerized version of a stand-alone fax machine. This device and software allow your computer to do everything a fax machine can: send and receive documents, print documents, and store documents. The big difference between using a regular

fax machine and using your computer as a fax machine is that the fax modem does everything in a digitized way. So, you may need a scanner to put a document into a digital format if you want to fax something that's printed or sketched on paper.

Traditional fax machines are quickly becoming obsolete. Some companies have chosen to use a spare computer as a fax server to handle incoming and outgoing faxes. Desktop software can convert e-mails to faxes and vice versa. This is referred to as fax-to-mail or mail-to-fax technology and reduces costs significantly because there is no need for a fax machine or an additional phone line. In addition, there is no extra charge for using your Internet connection to send a fax.

Faxes received in this way are usually converted to a digital file format, for example a PDF file, and attached to an e-mail, or they may be sent to a cell phone. Similarly, sent faxes are also converted to

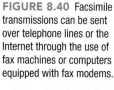

FIGURE 8.40 Facsimile transmissions can be sent over telephone lines or the Internet through the use of fax machines or computers equipped with fax modems.

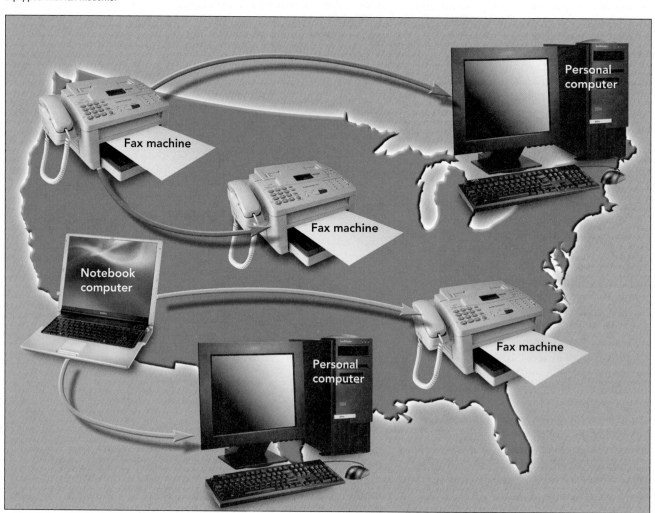

digital format before being sent over the Internet to their destinations. If the receiving fax machine is a conventional machine attached to a phone line, the fax is forwarded to the PSTN for delivery.

Because computers can send and receive faxes, it is not a far stretch of the imagination to see that sending and receiving documents will soon be accomplished by network-enabled cell phones or Web-enabled devices. One limiting feature of using this new medium for faxing is the inability to include a hard signature on the document. Although digital signatures, or soft signatures, can be embedded within an electronic document, they are not enough for some transactions especially those requiring legal signatures.

Satellite Radio, GPS, and More

Many applications use satellite technology, including air navigation, TV and radio broadcasting, paging, and videoconferencing. **Satellite radio** broadcasts radio signals to satellites orbiting more than 22,000 miles above the Earth. The satellites then transmit the signals back to a radio receiver. Unlike ground-based radio signal transmitters, satellite radio is not affected by location, distance, or obstructions. Because of their great height, satellites can transmit signals to a radio receiver wherever it might be located.

Satellite radio is a boon for folks living in areas with limited local radio stations or where regular AM/FM reception is hampered by terrain. Sirius XM Radio Inc. is one of the largest satellite radio subscriptions companies. Satellite radio can mimic your local radio broadcasting station's style, including commercials. It can provide you with more than 100 channels offering different genres, including continuous music, sports, news, and talk programs. In contrast to music programs that are offered by some cable or satellite in-home providers, satellite radio uses portable receivers that plug into your home or car stereo, so it is totally mobile and transportable to wherever you happen to want to listen. SIRIUS now offers Backseat TV, which streams live TV broadcasts to subscribers who have video receivers in their vehicles.

Total revenue for Sirius XM Radio Inc. grew by 1 percent, year over year, to $608 million, while total subscribers, currently estimated at 19 million, continued to decline, also by 1 percent, for the second quarter of 2009. The decline in subscribers is attributed to the economy and decline in auto sales, while the boost in revenue is due to an increase in monthly charges and a decrease in operating costs.

Sirius XM is battling for subscribers. Its iPhone application has been a hit with existing users of the service, but it has failed to bring in new subscribers due to its higher cost and reduced radio content. Competition from other sources like Internet radio services, for example, Pandora, which can stream music into smartphones and wireless-enabled cars such as certain Ford models, will continue to heat up as the auto industry and economy rebound.

> **"Most [GPS] systems** are accurate to **within 109 yards**; some systems boast a **164-yard range."**

GPS Another interesting application of satellite technology is GPS. **GPS (Global Positioning System)** is a cluster of 27 Earth-orbiting satellites (24 in operation and 3 extras in case one fails). Each of these 3,000- to 4,000-pound solar-powered satellites circles the globe at an altitude of 12,000 miles, making two complete rotations every day. The orbits are arranged so that at anytime, anywhere on Earth, at least four satellites are "visible" in the sky. A GPS receiver's job is to locate four or more of these satellites, figure out the distance to each, and use this information to deduce its own location. Most systems are accurate to within 109 yards; some systems boast a 164-yard range (Figure 8.41).

A GPS receiver can be either handheld or installed in a vehicle. Navigation systems in rental cars are a typical application of GPS. OnStar is a multifaceted GPS communications system that enables drivers to talk to a service representative to obtain driving directions and information on hotels, food venues, and the like. Drivers can also use OnStar to notify the police, fire department, or ambulance

4 of 24 possible satellites

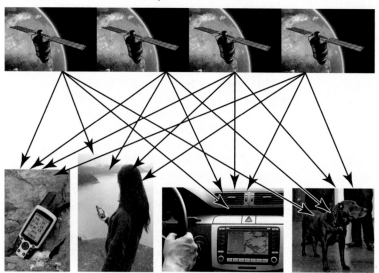

Locking into three satellites determines location in latitude and longitude.

Locking into a fourth satellite provides altitude and 3D positioning.

GPS receivers

FIGURE 8.41 GPS units lock in the signal from four satellites and use a mathematical principle called triangulation to determine the position of the receiving device in three dimensions.

service in case of an emergency. Through in-vehicle sensors, it can even detect when a car has been involved in an accident. Finally, OnStar can also aid a driver experiencing minor inconveniences, for example, by unlocking car doors should a driver accidentally lock car keys inside (Figure 8.42).

GPS units for cars have become more mobile. Many different models can be easily attached to a dashboard and moved from one vehicle to another. Some units can even convert maps from road maps to walking maps that list house numbers and specific points of interest. You can update the maps on many GPS units via the Internet. Higher priced units allow you to swap media cards to provide foreign travel maps or convert your unit into a marine GPS unit.

Other Satellite Applications Echelon is a satellite-based system operated on behalf of the five members of the UK–USA Security Agreement (Australia, Canada, New Zealand, United Kingdom, and the United States). Its mission is to intercept and process international communications passed via satellites. The system uses ground-based listening devices and up to 120 satellites to intercept messages (Figure 8.43). It combs through the huge volume of intercepted messages, looking for words and phrases such as "bomb" and "terrorist" and other information of interest to intelligence agencies.

Satellites also bring Internet access to areas that don't have a communications infrastructure. The Navajo Nation, which straddles the borders of Arizona, New Mexico, and Utah and covers a 26,000-square-mile area, faces special challenges for connecting its residents to the Internet. Approximately half the households

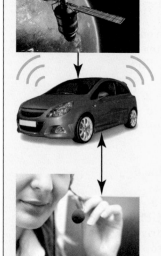

1. A GPS receiver in the vehicle connects to a satellite, establishes the location of the vehicle, and stores that location.

2. When an emergency feature of OnStar is activated, the unit places a call to the OnStar center and transmits the vehicle ID and GPS location.

3. The cellular call is routed to the landline phone system.

4. The call is picked up by a trained OnStar advisor.

FIGURE 8.42 OnStar makes use of a built-in GPS and cell phone system to provide assistance to drivers.

FIGURE 8.43 An Echelon Base Located in Germany

Text, Picture, and Video Messaging and More

The statistics on cell phone ownership and usage are staggering. Almost 9 out of 10 (87%) U.S. residents say they own a cell phone, and 16 percent own a PDA (personal digital assistant). An estimated 4 out of 5 teens (17 million) carry a wireless device, an increase of approximately 40 percent since 2004. Cell phones give teens (and a growing number of preteens) a sense of not only community but also freedom. Cell phone ownership is being compared with the freedom and individuality of having a driver's license.

Text, picture, and video messaging are the hot applications for mobile devices that e-mail and IM once were for computers. **Text messaging**, also called **SMS** (short message service), is similar to using your phone for instant messaging or as a receiver and transmitter for brief e-mail messages (Figure 8.45). Teens spend approximately the same amount of time texting as they do talking and no longer consider texting as an option but a necessity. In fact, 42 percent of them say that they can text blindfolded.

don't even have phone service, and those that do, find the quality of that service sometimes lacking. For data communications, the maximum reliable data speed is often limited to 28.8 Kbps. In addition, Internet access through a private service provider is virtually always a long-distance call.

Navajo Nation school administrators purchased a system called HughesNet, which uses a small 18-inch satellite dish to receive information from the Internet and regular telephone or data lines to send information (Figure 8.44). Because Internet use in an educational environment involves massive amounts of downloaded information, the satellite solution was ideal.

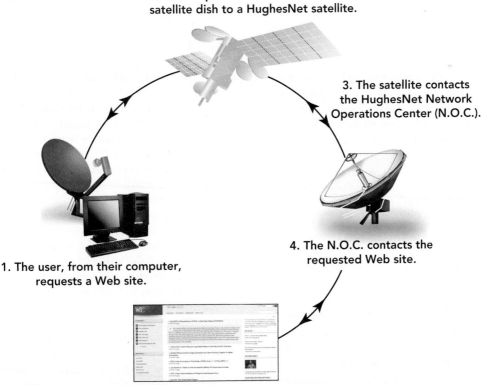

2. The request is sent from the user's satellite dish to a HughesNet satellite.

3. The satellite contacts the HughesNet Network Operations Center (N.O.C.).

1. The user, from their computer, requests a Web site.

4. The N.O.C. contacts the requested Web site.

5. The Web site forwards the information back to the user through the same path.

FIGURE 8.44
HughesNet, also used in Alaska, uses orbiting satellites to retrieve and relay information, delivering Internet access to remote locations.

FIGURE 8.45 Text messaging enables users to converse without bothering those nearby.

Picture and video messaging are mobile services that will transform the way we electronically interact with each other. People have sent pictures by way of FTP or as e-mail attachments for more than 10 years, but the use of the telephone for such services has exploded in recent years. Today, **picture messaging**, also referred to as **MMS** (multimedia messaging system) allows you to send full-color pictures, backgrounds, and even picture caller IDs on your cell phone. With picture messaging, your phone performs as a camera so that you can send pictures from your vacation or capture spontaneous moments and share them with others.

ETHICS

GPS devices can be extremely useful to individuals who are lost, trying to navigate through an unfamiliar neighborhood, or looking to avoid a traffic jam. But this same technology can also be viewed as an invasion of privacy. Taxi cab drivers in New York City are protesting against the installation of GPS units in all cabs citing the fear of constant surveillance. Large trucking firms are using units to keep track of drivers and inform them of alternate shorter routes or possible delays while in route. Some see the use of GPS units as a technological advance in providing knowledge and safety while reducing time and energy. Others view their use as an invasion of privacy. Do the benefits of GPS units outweigh the risk of reducing privacy?

Many people want to use their phones to take pictures instead of carrying a digital camera. In order to have your phone replace your digital camera, you have to consider the resolution of the cell phone camera, which is measured in megapixels. A megapixel is 1 million pixels, or points of light, that make up an image. For pictures that will be printed out in large format (8×10 inches or larger), you need a camera with a resolution of at least 4 megapixels. Otherwise, the picture will not be sharp.

Images you capture with your phone can be sent by way of e-mail attachments or as a single picture when calling or talking to someone. Note that the user on the other end needs to have a picture-enabled phone as well and that there is a charge for sending pictures or video.

One cell phone application that is more popular with parents than kids is **location awareness** (or **position awareness**). This technology uses GPS-enabled chips to pinpoint the location of a cell phone (and its user). Teens may find location awareness to be a downside of owning a cell phone because their parents can monitor their location. Teens often complain about such surveillance with statements such as "You're intruding on my privacy," "You're treading on my independence," and "I feel as though I'm always being watched." From the parents' perspective, however, they are simply keeping watch over their children in an effort to help them make better decisions.

Location awareness also has consumer and safety applications. The location-awareness feature enables your cell phone to quickly provide the location of the nearest restaurants and entertainment venues. It also can also be activated to provide your location to a police station or other emergency service if needed. Law enforcement and government officials with the right credentials can access a cell provider information on the location of a cell phone by the signal it repeatedly sends out to cell towers in its vicinity when the location feature is activated. The location feature and how it functions is dependent on the phone, provider, and service. Visit **www.ulocate.com** to learn more about location-awareness technology.

Along with all of its benefits, wireless technology also has its dark side that requires the user to be aware of evils lurking around the corner. As in the real world, predators exist and the user needs to keep a sharp eye for technology invasions.

Surfing Safely at Public Wireless Hot Spots

A wireless hot spot is easy to locate today. McDonald's, Starbucks, and many other merchants offer Internet connectivity to lure customers. But when using public hot spots, especially free ones, you need to take some extra precautions to keep you and your data safe. Here are a few issues to keep in mind at these sites: Wireless security is often not implemented on public hot spots; your shared files and directories might be accessible to others using the same wireless network; and you might be logging into a malicious network. A **malicious network** is a network set up by a hacker within the operating area of a legitimate hot spot. The hacker hopes to lure the user into the bogus network, referred to as an "evil twin," and gather sensitive information as passwords and credit card numbers.

Sounds scary, doesn't it? Well, you can't deny yourself the use of technology any more than you can deny yourself a trip to the mall for fear that something negative will happen. Here are a few precautions that you can follow to protect yourself while surfing on a public hot spot.

- Use firewalls and antivirus software.
- Ask an employee for the name of the legitimate network, to prevent connecting to an evil twin.
- Do not engage in sensitive financial transactions while connected to an unsecured hot spot.
- Select the appropriate operating system option to limit sharing of resources and discovery of your computer while connected to a public hot spot (Figure 8.46).

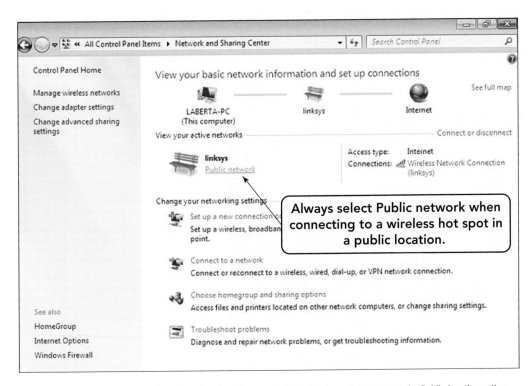

FIGURE 8.46 The screen displays the network settings available in Windows 7. Always use the Public location option when using a public wireless hot spot.

Set up and Access Skype VoIP

Make sure that you have a microphone, speakers, and headphones that are in working order and are compatible with your PC or Mac computer system. Additionally, you need an Internet connection and, if you want video calls, a webcam. This is the only equipment you will need for Skype-to-Skype VoIP, which allows communication from one computer using Skype software to another computer using Skype for no charge.

1. Download the Skype software from **www.skype.com.**

   a. Click the option to *Get Skype*.

   b. In the next window select your device type. You can select Get Skype for Windows or Get Skype on your mobile. Select *GetSkype for Windows*. This option selection will display a list of links for Windows, Mac Os X, Linux and several other operating systems (Figure 8.47).

   c. Select the Windows-based operating system for the unit on which you are installing the Skype software. Then click *Download Now*.

   d. The Skypesetup.exe file will be downloaded to the default download location on your system.

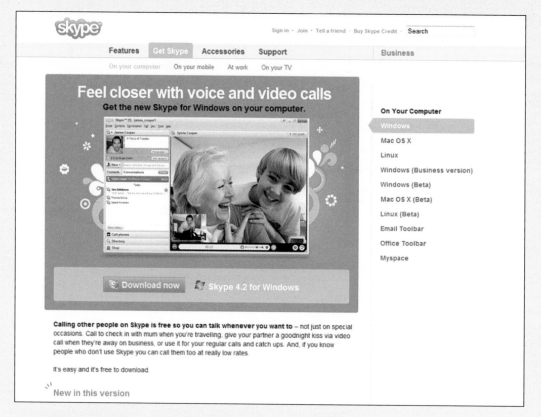

FIGURE 8.47 The Skype software download is available for most operating systems.

2. Locate the *Skypesetup.exe* file and double-click it to start the installation.

   a. Read the Warning dialog box and click *OK*.

   b. Select the language you want, and then click *Next*.

   c. Review and accept the licensing agreement. Click *Next,* and the installation will begin.

3. When the installation is complete, you can select the option to open Skype every time you start your computer. When you are done configuring your software as you would like it to appear, click *Finish* to start Skype.

4. The Skype window will open. If it doesn't, click the icon on the task tray to the left of the clock on the taskbar. If you have not used Skype before, you should click on *Don't have a Skype Name* to create your Skype name (this is the name your friends will see in their contact list) and a Personal Profile. Your Skype Personal Profile can be seen by other Skype users who will be able to search for you using this information.

5. Once you have created your Skype name and signed in, your Skype window, which includes a toolbar, will open. Skype is divided into several tabs. The main ones, the Contacts tab, Dial tab and History tab are always visible. The search option is also always available (Figure 8.48).

6. Conduct a sound test, also known as an echo test. Skype provides this facility through of the testing robot, Echo123. Simply enter **echo123** in the address bar at the bottom of Skype or add it to your contacts. When called, an automated voice recording will ask you to record a message and then play it back. If you hear your own voice clearly, Skype has been configured correctly.

7. You are now set to make Skype-to-Skype calls. Good Luck!

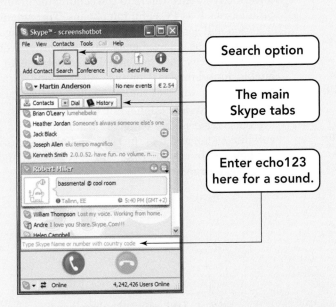

FIGURE 8.48 The Search option on the Skype toolbar will attempt to locate a Skype user's number if your know that user's Skype name. If it is able to find the user, it will insert that individual into your contact list.

Chapter Summary

Wired and Wireless Communication

- Bandwidth refers to the maximum data transfer capacity of a communications channel and is measured in Hertz (Hz) and bits per second (bps). To transmit text, you can get by with low bandwidth (such as a 56 Kbps connection). But for viewing multimedia on the Internet, a broadband connection of at least 1.5 Mbps is preferable. Throughput is the actual rate of data transfer. It is lower than bandwidth.

- To transmit digital data over dial-up phone lines, it's necessary to use a modem. On the sending end, the modem modulates the signal (transforms it into analog form). On the receiving end, the modem demodulates the signal (transforms it back into digital form).

- Communications require physical media, like twisted-pair wire, coaxial cable, and fiber-optic cable, or wireless media like infrared, radio, microwaves, and satellite. Additionally, WiMAX and MMDS are wireless technologies used to transmit signals over large geographic areas.

- The public switched telephone network (PSTN) is the global telephone system used for both data and voice. This system usually sends transmissons across various media ranging from twisted-pair to fiber-optic cable and makes use of a modem to convert between analog and digital signals. It is its use of analog devices that makes it prone to noise and interference and creates a bottleneck at the local loop portion of the system, reducing overall transmission time.

- Digital telephony offers noise-free transmission and high-quality audio. Many companies and universities have internal digital telephone systems; however, calls to the outside must be translated into analog signals to connect to the PSTN. Often such calls use multiplexing, in which multiple calls are carried on a single line, allowing more calls to travel over fewer lines.

- Last-mile technologies refers to the technologies, like ISDN, DSL, cable, leased lines, SONET, and WiMax, that bring data into your home or business. These technologies often rely on the services of a local broadband provider or the public switched telephone network (PSTN).

- Digitization is the transformation of data such as voice, text, graphics, audio, and video into digital form. Convergence refers to the coming together of products such as PCs and telephones. Through digitization and convergence the boundaries among such devices as smartphones, PCs, and other Web-enabled devices have become blurred because all enable digital information (voice, video, and data) to travel over wireless communication systems.

- Wired and wireless applications like VoIP; GPS systems; videoconferencing; fax transmissions; satellite radio; and text, picture, and video messaging help communicate, collaborate, entertain, and share text, graphics, audio, and video.

Key Terms and Concepts

Identification

Identify each of the following images as they apply to this chapter.

1. _____

2. _____

3. _____

4. _____

5. _____

6. _____

Matching

Match each key term in the left column with the most accurate definition in the right column.

_____ 1. whiteboard

_____ 2. sending device

_____ 3. streaming

_____ 4. WiFi

_____ 5. webcam

_____ 6. data transfer rate

_____ 7. WiMAX

_____ 8. baud

_____ 9. bandwidth

_____ 10. infrared

_____ 11. receiving device

_____ 12. convergence

_____ 13. leased line

_____ 14. throughput

_____ 15. communications

a. The actual amount of data that is sent though a specific transmission medium at one time

b. A specially conditioned telephone line that enables continuous end-to-end communication between two points

c. The maximum amount of data that can be sent though a specific transmission medium at one time

d. The rate at which two modems can exchange data

e. Accepts a transmission and responds

f. The number of signaling elements per second

g. Used to create a shared workspace for participants in a videoconference

h. The blending of industries and products

i. Initiates a transmission

j. A popular wireless network technology that uses radio waves to provide high-speed Internet and network connections

k. The process of electronically sending and receiving messages between two or more computers or devices regardless of the distance between those devices

l. A wireless transmission medium, which works within a maximum of about 100 feet, and carries data via beams of light through the air

m. A digital camera integrated into a notebook or connected to a desktop computer

n. An up-and-coming wireless digital communication system designed to deliver high-speed access over long distances

o. The ability to listen to or view content while it is being downloaded from a Web site

Multiple Choice

Circle the correct choice for each of the following:

1. What is the technology that facilitates meetings that provide voice and video of individuals in different geographical locations?
   a. Videoconferencing
   b. Piconet
   c. PAN
   d. Piggybacking

2. What communication medium must have a direct line of site between communicating devices and works within a maximum of 100 feet?
   a. WiMax
   b. Bluetooth
   c. WiFi
   d. Infrared

3. Which wireless technology makes use of short-range radio transmission to connect devices within 30 feet of each other?
   a. WiMAX
   b. Bluetooth
   c. DSL
   d. WiFi

4. GPS systems track locations by using which of the following technologies?
   a. PSTN
   b. Infrared
   c. Satellite
   d. PAN

5. Which is *not* a wired method of communication?
   a. WiFi
   b. Fiber optics
   c. Twisted-pair
   d. Cable

6. Which is an example of convergence?
   a. A smartphone
   b. The installation of fiber optics for last-mile connectivity
   c. A Global Positioning System (GPS)
   d. Converting a document to PDF format in order to be read by anyone.

7. Which communication medium uses light to transmit data?
   a. Twisted-pair
   b. Fiber optics
   c. Cable
   d. Microwave

8. Which of the following is true of VoIP (Internet telephony)?
   a. It is not quite perfected and provides poor quality.
   b. It is often cheaper than conventional phone service.
   c. It is too expensive for home use and is used primarily for business.
   d. It requires a cable modem.

9. Which is *not* an example of a wireless transmission media?
   a. Infrared   b. Microwave
   c. Satellite   d. Cable

10. When someone makes a cellular phone call to another cellular phone, which of the following eventually handles the call?
    a. Public switched telephone network (PSTN)
    b. Global Positioning System (GPS).
    c. Mobile switching center (MSC)
    d. Personal communication service (PCS)

Fill-In

In the blanks provided, write the correct answer for each of the following.

1. _____ is the transformation of data such as voice, text, graphics, audio, and video into digital form.

2. _____ is a broad term that describes the ability to link various media and devices to enhance communications and improve access to information.

3. A(n) _____ is the area serviced by a subscriber loop carrier (SLC).

4. _____ is the type of signal produced by human voice.

5. The region of coverage provided by a wireless phone network is called a(n) _____.

6. Accessing a network without permission is called _____.

7. _____ is the technique used to send more than one call over a single line.

8. On a wireless phone network, the _____ monitors the cell phone's signal strength to assure the best reception.

9. _____ is the set of standards that specifies how current wireless devices, through special Web browsers, can securely access the Web.

10. The bottleneck that occurs when data leaves high-speed cable transmission to unite with twisted-pair phone lines to connect homes and businesses is called the _____.

11. _____ uses the Internet for real-time voice communication.

12. _____ is the sending of an image of a document over a telephone line or the Internet.

13. Computers using wireless adapters use a special wireless communication device known as a(n) _____ to send and receive data.

14. A(n) _____ is a Web browser designed to meet the limitations of handheld portable devices.

15. A network set up by a hacker within the operating area of a legitimate hot spot is referred to as a(n) _____ network.

Short Answer

1. Define modem and explain the purpose of this device in the communication process.

2. List and describe three types of wired transmission media and three types of wireless transmission media.

3. Explain the difference between microwave and satellite transmissions and how the two depend on each other.

4. List three operating systems for mobile devices and provide an example of a device in which each is installed.

5. What is the difference between bandwidth and throughput?

6. Explain the last-mile problem. List the current technology being used to minimize this problem.

Teamwork

1. **Investigate the Quad Play** As a team, research the grouping of services like cell phone, TV, Internet, and landline phones into packages by local providers to offer reduced rates. The *Quad Play* is the name Verizon has given to its combination of such services. Investigate different local providers. Compare the difference between purchasing individual services versus the price of a package deal. After you complete your research, use an Excel spreadsheet to list each provider, the services it offers, and the prices of both the individual and package deals. As a team, decide whether the package deals are really a deal, and determine which provider offers the best rates. Indicate your decisions at the bottom of the spreadsheet.

2. **Cell Phone Use** As a team, using Word, develop a survey on the uses of a cell phone. Include the number of calls made in a day and the number of text and/or picture messages sent and received in a day. Inquire whether respondents are on an individual plan or a family plan, ask for an estimate of their monthly bill and whether they have Internet connectivity. Collect other general data that might shed light on your findings, such as age and gender of the user. Distribute the survey to approximately 30 individuals. Accumulate your findings in a Word table. As a team, analyze the collected data and look for patterns and trends. Include these findings in your Word document after your table. The entire report should be approximately one to two pages, double-spaced.

3. **Cell Phone Etiquette** As a team, come up with a list of 10 to 15 cell phone behaviors that a user should practice. Then rank them in order, with the first one being the practice that the group considers the most important. Present your list in a PowerPoint presentation, using one slide for each behavior, and include the reason the team placed them in that ranked position.

4. **Toys to Tools** As a team, investigate the use of cell phones in the area of education. Use your own school as an example. Inquire about courses and instructors that use cell phones or other digital technology in their classrooms. Investigate how they incorporate it into the subject matter. Use online references for additional examples and ideas. As a group, come up with a list of five ways in which cell phones (including text and picture messaging) can be helpful in learning. Present your best five in a PowerPoint presentation and indicate whether the team felt the idea was workable and how it would help or hinder learning. Remember to cite your references.

5. **Solve the Problem** You are on vacation and the house you rented has wireless network—or so it advertised. You brought your notebook, which is equipped with a wireless adaptor and connects to your wireless network at home with no problem. After you boot up, you try to access the Internet, but you receive the message that the connection is unsuccessful. Using the Internet or any other reliable reference sources, determine at least three possible causes for the problem. Present your findings in a one-page, double-spaced report. Remember to cite your references.

On the Web

1. **Green Cell Phones** Investigate the movement to control damage to the environment by reducing the toxic waste from cell phone disposal through the development of portable devices that are more environmentally friendly. Using your favorite browser, search the Internet for companies that are creating green cell phones and research the methods they are using to create them. List the companies that are leading the way, and explain exactly how they are making this change. Present your findings in a one-page, double-spaced report. Remember to cite your references.

2. **Investigate HBO to GO** The convergence of TV and computers just got a boost with the addition of HBO being enabled for viewing on desktop and notebook computers. You need a television and Internet account with your local provider. And, of course, you need to be an HBO subscriber. Investigate this new level of convergence. Use online references to see how many local providers are offering

this feature, and ask other class participants whether they would make use of viewing full-length movies on their notebooks or other portable devices. Present your findings in a one-page, double-spaced report. Remember to cite your references.

3. **What Is 4G Technology?** Sprint is already advertising the benefits of its 4G network, the next generation of mobile communications devices. Using the Internet, investigate the expected data transmission rates for 4G and answer the following questions: What will 4G offer over the current 3G network? When will 4G devices be widely available? What providers are leading the way? Investigate why some feel 4G networks might bridge the digital divide. Present your findings in a one-page, double-spaced report. Remember to cite your references.

4. **Technology and Your Responsibility** GPS units have been instrumental in locating and leading to the rescue of an experienced hiker lost in the Australian desert in January 2009. On the flip side, a female lost in Death Valley National Park in California in August 2009 is blaming a GPS unit for providing her with faulty directions that led her and her son to a desolate and extremely remote region of the park. After several days, she and her son depleted their water supply. Her 11-year-old son died. She places blame on the GPS provider. Using the Internet and other reliable forms of information, research cases in which technology helped people and cases in which it has malfunctioned and caused someone to be injured or something to be damaged. When is the incident the fault of the provider and when is it the fault of the human operator? What are the limits of technology and whose responsibility is it to know those limits? What can the technology provider do to disclaim responsibility? What can the user do to validate reliability of, in the case of the Death Valley hiker, navigational instructions? Present your findings and opinions in a one-page, double-spaced report. Remember to cite your references.

5. **Location Aware Devices: Safety versus Privacy** Using the Internet and your favorite search engine, search for articles on the use of OnStar for the collection of evidence in police investigations and national security issues. Explain how the device is configured in order to listen in on car conversations that can produce incriminating evidence. Locate any court decision on whether such configuring with the OnStar device is legal and within the rights of law enforcement and federal agencies. Additionally, locate references on the benefits and drawbacks of such location-aware devices. Present your findings, court decisions, and a list of the pros and cons of such devices in a one-page, double-spaced paper. Remember to cite your references.

Spotlight

Digital Life

Can you remember when you left for the day and did not take a cell phone, notebook, or e-book reader with you? When did you last take off on a trip without the aid of some type of global positioning system (GPS)? Can you recall how you felt having to go all day without these digital devices and the communication or information they provide? For most of us, carrying our digital devices is just as important as wearing our shoes. We simply feel incomplete without them.

Multimedia is one of the reasons the Web is so popular. Simply put, **multimedia** can be defined as multisensory stimulators that stimulate our senses of sight, sound, touch, smell, or taste. For our purposes, we'll consider multimedia that stimulates the senses of sight, sound, and touch. Just a few years ago, most personal computers needed additional equipment to run multimedia applications. Today, such equipment—sound cards, CD or DVD drives, and speakers—is standard issue. However, for advanced multimedia applications, you may still need additional equipment, such as a pen-based graphics tablet, a stereo microphone, a digital camera, or a video adapter. If you enjoy playing games, you'll want a 3D video accelerator—add-on video adapter that works with your current video card. For surround sound, you'll need a sound card capable of producing the surround effect. And you'll probably want to pick up a few extra speakers and a subwoofer. If you are a movie watcher, you'll want to add a Blu-ray disk drive.

Multimedia is an integral part of computer games of all kinds, but it is also being used more and more in computer-based education (CBE), distance learning, and computer-based training (CBT). Businesses use it in multimedia presentations that are created with software programs such as PowerPoint. It's also finding its way into **information kiosks**, which are automated presentation systems used to provide information to the public or for employee training (Figure 6A).

FIGURE 6A   Service kiosks that use touch-screen technology can be found in many locations.

What if you want your multimedia files to travel with you? Today, a number of portable multimedia devices are available, from MP3 players and digital cameras to Web-enabled devices such as smartphones, PDAs, e-books, and portable televisions. In this spotlight, you'll learn about a variety of multimedia devices, both mobile ones and those used with desktop computers.

Audio: MP3 Players and Voice Recorders

Unlike previous forms of push technology (products marketed by industries to consumers), such as cassette tapes and CDs, the MP3 movement has been largely fueled by music lovers' use of the Internet to compile and share libraries of digitized music files. Files are created and shared by the users—without industry involvement. An MP3 file is a compressed audio format that is usually used for music files. The term MP3 is derived from the acronym MPEG, which stands for the Motion Picture Experts Group; the 3 refers to audio layer 3.

Without losing any noticeable sound quality, the MPEG3 format reduces the size of sound files by eliminating frequencies and sounds the human ear cannot hear. A song on a typical music CD takes up approximately 32 MB. The same song in MP3 format takes only 3 MB.

MP3 works like this: A CD has a sample rate of 44,100 times per second. Each sample is two bytes in size, and separate samples are taken for the left and right speakers. Thus, the sample rate in bits per second is $44,100 \times 8$ bits per byte $\times 2$ bytes $\times 2$ channels, which is 1,411,200 bits per second. This equals a sample rate of 176,400 bytes per second $\times 180$ seconds in an average song, or roughly 32 MB per song. MPEG3 compresses the sound file by a factor of 10 to 14 by applying a compression algorithm.

You can record, store, and play MP3 files on your computer. You can legally create MP3 music files from CDs that you own, or you can purchase files from Web sites such as **www.apple.com/itunes**, **www.zune.net**, and **www.mp3.com** (Figure 6B). Windows-based PCs come with the Windows Media Player already

FIGURE 6B   You can use iTunes to copy, record, and play audio files and download them to a portable MP3 player.

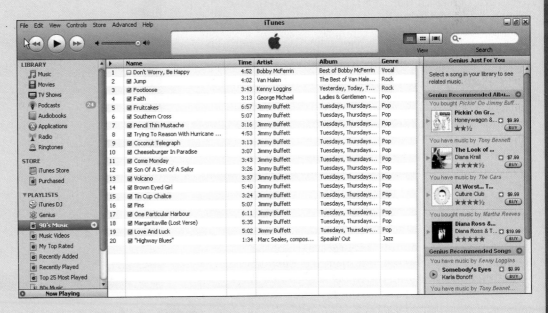

installed. Other systems may have a different default player or you may need to download one, such as Winamp (**www.winamp.com**), from the Internet. You can find a list of the various MP3 players that are available at **www.superwarehouse.com/**.

MP3 files also can be stored on portable players. Portable players come in many shapes and sizes (Figure 6C). When purchasing an MP3 player, make sure to consider the battery life and storage capacity of the device. ZDnet.com estimates that over 286 million MP3 players will have been purchased by 2010.

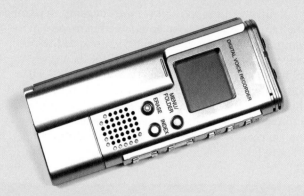

FIGURE 6D   A digital voice recorder is portable and has many uses.

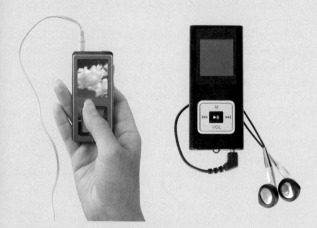

FIGURE 6C   You can use a portable MP3 player to take your music with you.

MP3 players have several components: a data port that is used to upload files, memory, a processor, a display screen, playback controls, an audio port for output, an amplifier, and a power supply. When you select a file to listen to on your MP3 player, the device's processor pulls the file from storage and decompresses the MP3 encoding. The decompressed bytes are converted from digital to analog, amplified, and then sent to the audio port for your enjoyment. MP3 players plug into your computer by way of a USB or FireWire port. Most players have solid-state memory, but some use a microdrive (a tiny hard drive) to store files. MP3 players are usually very small, portable, and battery powered. They range in price from less than $100 to $399 for the Apple iPod Touch with 64 GB of storage designed especially for video viewing.

You can use a digital voice recorder (Figure 6D) to record voice and sound that can later be retrieved from the device or downloaded to your computer. The device captures sound through a built-in microphone and then stores it on a memory chip. Several companies make these devices. Two things to consider when purchasing a digital voice recorder are the amount of storage offered and the price. Some of the newer phones, including the Apple iPhone and HTC Droid, also have the capability of recording voice messages, which can be stored and/or shared as an e-mail.

Visual: E-Books, Digital Cameras, and Camcorders

E-books have the potential to provide a richness that is not possible in a printed book. An **e-book** is a book that has been digitized and distributed by means of a digital storage medium (such as flash memory or a CD disc). An **e-book reader** is a device that displays e-books. E-book readers may be devices that are built solely for reading e-books or they may be PDAs, handheld devices, or other computing devices that have a processor and display screen (Figure 6E). The newest e-book readers are available in a larger size, increasing

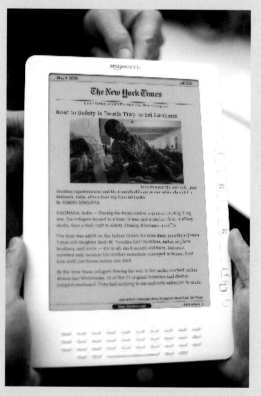

FIGURE 6E   E-book readers share the market with PDAs and other computing devices.

the ease of reading. Some even boast an auto-rotating screen with a text-to-speech mode.

There are many companies that have e-book readers. There is an e-reader designed for children called the V.Reader by VTech (**www.vtechkids.com**). Six of the most popular e-readers are Amazon.com's Kindle 2 and Kindle DX, Sony's Daily Edition, Barnes & Noble's Nook, Plastic Logic's Que proReader, and of course Apple's iPad (Figure 6F). It is estimated that 12-month sales of the iPad will reach 7 million units, based on sales since its release in April 2010. iphonelife.com describes the iPad as a sleek tablet that looks like a cross between an iPhone and the LCD case of the MacBook Air. It measures 7.5 × 9.6 inches and is only half an inch thick. It weighs a pound and a half, has a 9.7-inch multitouch screen with 1024 × 768 resolution, and WiFi and 3G network access. The iPad has the functionality of a large iPhone without the phone.

FIGURE 6F   The versatile iPad has a touch screen for easy navigating.

Someday you may read an e-book that provides background music for each page or scenario. You may find hot links on the page that will take you to pictures that support the scene. Better yet, you may find a link to a video of the scene. All of this extra material can be easily stored on a flash memory card along with the text of the story. If you don't want to purchase an e-book reader, you can download software to use your smartphone as an e-book reader! We also see schools using e-books, especially at the elementary level, when students need to carry more books than their book bag or little arms can handle. Many colleges and universities use e-books to help students defray the cost of books for their students.

DIGITAL CAMERAS

It seems as though it was just yesterday that computer technology was so difficult to use that only computer scientists were able to use it. However, today's digital technology is so easy to use that you can even digitize your family photo album!

One of the hottest products on today's consumer market is the digital camera (Figure 6G). A **digital camera** uses digital technology to store and display images instead of recording them on film. When you take a photo with a digital camera, the shot is stored in the camera until it is transferred to a computer for long-term storage or printing.

FIGURE 6G   Digital cameras are among today's hottest products.

Like traditional cameras, digital cameras have a lens, a shutter, and an optical viewfinder. What sets digital cameras apart from traditional cameras is their inner workings—specifically, how an image is saved. With digital cameras, the captured image's light falls on a **charge-coupled device (CCD)**, a photosensitive computer chip that transforms light patterns into pixels (individual dots). A CCD consists of a grid made up of light-sensitive elements. Each element converts the incoming light into a voltage that is proportional to the light's brightness. The digital camera's picture quality is determined by how many elements the CCD has. Each CCD element corresponds to one pixel, or dot, on a computer display or printout; the more elements, the sharper the picture.

A 1-megapixel digital camera has a CCD consisting of at least 1 million elements; such a camera can produce a reasonably sharp snapshot-size image. With at least 2 million elements, 2-megapixel cameras can take higher-resolution pictures; you can expect to get near-photographic-quality prints at sizes of up to 5 × 7 inches with such a camera. Three- and 4-megapixel cameras can produce images that can print at sizes of 8 × 10 inches or even 11 × 14 inches. Today's 5- to 18-megapixel cameras produce high-quality photographs that can be greatly enlarged without loss of quality.

Because digital cameras do not have film, any photos you take are stored in the camera until you transfer them to a computer for long-term storage or printing. Two popular methods of storing images in the camera are **CompactFlash** and **xD Picture Cards** (Figure 6H). Both use flash memory technologies to store anywhere from 64 MB to 32 GB of image data.

About 12 MB of flash memory is the equivalent of a standard 12-exposure film roll. However, most cameras enable you to select from a variety of resolutions, so the number of shots you get will vary depending on the resolution you choose. If you need more "film," you need only carry more flash memory cards. Digital cameras enable you to preview the shots you've taken on a small LCD screen, so you can create more room on the flash memory cards by erasing pictures that you don't like.

FIGURE 6I   A photo printer allows you to print your pictures at your convenience in a variety of sizes directly from your camera.

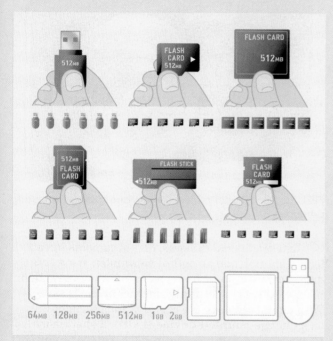

FIGURE 6H   Various types of flash memory card are available in capacities of 16 MB up to 32 GB.

In most cases, you'll need to download the image data to a computer for safekeeping and printing. Most cameras are designed to connect to a computer by means of a serial or USB cable. Others can transfer data into your computer by means of an infrared port. If you're using a digital camera that stores images on flash memory cards, you can obtain a PC card that contains a flash memory card reader. This type of PC card enables the computer to read the images from the flash memory card as if it were a disk drive. Also available are stand-alone flash memory readers, which serve the same purpose. Once you've transferred the images to the computer for safekeeping and printing, you can erase the flash memory card and reuse it, just as if you had purchased a fresh roll of film.

Once the images are transferred to the computer, you can use a **photo-editing program** to enhance, edit, crop, or resize the images. Photo-editing programs also can be used to print the images to a color printer. Some specially designed printers called **photo printers** have flash memory card readers that enable you to bypass the computer completely (Figure 6I).

How good are digital cameras? With the exception of a few expensive high-end digital cameras, most digital cameras are the equivalent of the point-and-shoot 35-mm cameras that have dominated the traditional (film-based) camera market. They take pictures that are good enough for family photo albums, Web publishing, and business use (such as a real estate agent's snapshots of homes for sale); however, they are not good enough for professional photography. Some professional photographers are moving to the high-end digital cameras and are pleased with the results: flexibility, ease of use, easy-to-view photos, and cost savings.

A color printer or a photo printer can make prints from digital camera images that closely resemble the snapshots you used to get from the drugstore, but only if you choose the highest print resolution and use glossy photo paper. Getting good printout results takes time—most consumer-oriented printers will require several minutes to print an image at the printer's highest possible resolution—and can be costly when you consider the printer, ink, and special photo paper.

However, printing is only one of the distribution options that are open to you when you use a digital camera—and that's exactly why so many people love digital photography. In addition to printing snapshots for the family album, you can copy the images onto CDs or DVDs, send them to friends and family via e-mail, and even display them on the Internet using Facebook or one of the many online photo sites such as Snapfish (**www.snapfish.com**).

Point-and-shoot digital cameras are designed so that anyone can take good pictures (Figure 6J). Their features typically include automatic focus, automatic exposure, built-in automatic electronic flash with red-eye reduction, and optical zoom lenses with digital enhancement. Point-and-shoot cameras come with a built-in LCD viewfinder, so you can preview the shot to make sure it comes out right.

Single-lens reflex (SLR) digital cameras are much more expensive than point-and-shoot cameras,

FIGURE 6J Point-and-shoot cameras are designed for portability and for grabbing quick shots.

but they offer the features that professional photographers demand, such as interchangeable lenses, through-the-lens image previewing, and the ability to override the automatic focus and exposure settings (Figure 6K).

FIGURE 6K Leading camera makers feature SLR digital cameras with 15 or more megapixels.

For reviews, comparisons, and price information for digital cameras, see the Digital Camera Buyer's Guide: **www.digitalcamerareview.com/**.

DIGITAL CAMCORDERS

Just as digital cameras are revolutionizing still photography, there are indications that digital video cameras are poised to do the same for full-motion images—animations, videos, and movies.

In the past, most full-motion images were captured and stored by means of analog techniques. A video-capture board (also called a video-capture card) is a device that inputs analog video into a computer and transforms the analog video into its digital counterpart. Because a digital video file for even a short video requires a great deal of storage space, most video-capture boards are equipped to perform on-the-fly data compression to reduce file size using one of several

codecs (compression/decompression standards), such as MPEG, Apple's QuickTime, or Microsoft's AVI. Three-dimensional games have driven computer video card manufacturers to new feats of technical innovation; today's 3D video cards offer sophisticated, ultra-fast graphics processing that only a few years ago would have required a supercomputer.

Video-capture boards enable computers to display and process full-motion video—a "movie" that gives the illusion of smooth, continuous action. Like actual movies, digitized video consists of a series of still photographs called **frames** that are flashed on the screen at a rapid rate. The frame-flashing speed—the **frame rate**—indicates how successfully a given video can create the illusion of smooth, unbroken movement. A rate of at least 24 frames per second (fps) is needed to produce an illusion of smooth, continuous action. What can you "capture" with a video-capture board? You can use just about any video source, including TV broadcasts, taped video, or live video from video cameras.

With the advent of the popular Internet site YouTube, **digital video cameras** (also known as **camcorders**) have become even more popular. A digital video camera (Figure 6L) uses digital rather than analog technologies to store recorded video images. Like digital cameras, digital video cameras can connect to a computer, often by means of a USB port. Because the signal produced by a digital video camera conforms to the computer's digital method of representing data, a video-capture board is not necessary. Most digital video cameras can take still images as well as movies. Like most technologies over the years, digital video cameras have increased capabilities at a reduced price. Today, many smartphones and cell phones can take digital pictures and videos. Some mobile devices have 8 megapixel cameras and can use 32 GB memory cards.

FIGURE 6L Small, but powerful, pocket-sized camcorders provide portability, allowing you to capture HD video anytime, anywhere.

Communication and Entertainment Devices

Multimedia devices continue to transform ordinary devices and expand their capabilities. A phone is no longer just a device used to speak with another person. Many are sophisticated, wireless devices that enable you to surf the Web, send text messages, take photos, and listen to music—and you can still call your friends too!

The most notable of these is the new Apple iPhone 4. The 4 stands for the fourth generation of mobile technology, which provides enhanced capability allowing the transfer of both voice and nonvoice data, including full-motion video, high-speed Internet access, and videoconferencing.

The original iPhone was first sold in July 2007, and later that year it was named *Time* magazine's invention of the year. The iPhone 4 combines four products in one—a phone with voice control, a widescreen iPod, a camera, and an Internet device with HTML e-mail and Web browser capability. It is a small device (4.5 × 2.31 × 0.37 inches, and weighing only 4.8 ounces) yet has a 3.5-inch display screen with a screen resolution of 960 × 640 pixels. To function as a phone, it requires a broadband connection with AT&T. Additionally, it has 802.11 b/g/n and Bluetooth 2.1 wireless compatibilities. As with an iPod player, you can scroll through songs, artists, albums, and playlists; browse the music library by album artwork; and view song lyrics that have been added to the library in iTunes. The video feature enables you to watch TV shows and movies from the iTunes Store. When you connect your iPhone to your computer, you can use iTunes to synchronize the audio and video files from your computer's iTunes library to your iPhone. The iPhone 4 has a 5-megapixel autofocus camera with flash and a battery that will support up to 7 hours on the 3G network. It also has a Micro SIM rather than a Standard SIM. And Apple continues to make improvements. The iPhone 5 is expected to be released in Spring 2011.

There are several contenders to the iPhone's popularity; these include the Palm Pre, introduced on June 6, 2009, and the first to use the new Linux-based Palm operating system. This multimedia smartphone, designed and marketed by Palm, Inc., has a touch screen with an enhanced keyboard. The touch screen enables it to function as a camera phone, a portable media player, a GPS navigator, and an Internet client. It also allows the user to text message, e-mail, browse the Web, and connect to local WiFi hot spots. Having just won recognition as CNET's Best in Show, the Pre appears to be a viable competitor as of the iPhone. There are many smartphones (Figure 6M) on the market. Other contenders to the iPhone as of the summer of 2010 are the Droid, EVO 4G, and Samsung Galaxy X. The Into-Mobile website (**www.intomobile.com**) lists the specs, as well as the good and bad qualities of each.

The Samsung Intercept is another smartphone. It works with fast 3G cellular networks, but it does not support WiFi. It contains GPS technology and is controlled by a multitouch interface. The Intercept is a phone, an audio and video player, and an Internet device with e-mail capability and a Web browser. It is a small device (4.4 × 2.2 × 0.6 inches, and weighing only 4.9 ounces) yet has a 3.0-inch display screen with a screen resolution of 400 × 240 pixels. To function as a phone, it requires a broadband connection with Sprint. You can get streaming media from more than 30 channels—music, videos, sporting news—streamed to your phone. The Intercept is Sprint TV enabled, which allows you to watch live TV and video-on-demand with full-motion video and sound. As with Apple's iTunes store, you can use Sprint's Music Store to download stereo-quality tracks to your wireless phone or PC. One of the newest smartphones on the market is the Droid from Motorola. It has a 3.7-inch touch-screen LCD. The slider measures 4.58 × 2.38 × 0.54 inches and weighs 6 ounces. It has an 854 × 480 resolution and uses the Android operating system. Some additional features of

FIGURE 6M A smartphone is a phone designed to make your life easier with enhanced, new capabilities featuring touch screens.

> "A **phone** is **no longer** just a device **used to speak** with **another person**. Many are **sophisticated, wireless devices** that **enable** you to surf the Web, **send text messages, take photos**, and listen to music—and **you** can **still call** your friends too!"

the Droid include the 1Ghz Snapdragon CPU, an 8-megapixel camera with dual-LED flash, 512 MB RAM, 1 GB ROM, 3G and 4G data connectivity, WiFi (b/g), GPS, microSD, an HDMI-out port, a 3.5-mm headphone jack, a front-facing camera for video calls, and a mobile hot spot feature.

DIGITAL VIDEO RECORDERS

Digital video recorders (DVRs) are similar to VCRs, but instead of using tape to store video, they use a hard disk. Hard disk storage is digital, thus the user can quickly move through video data, fast-forwarding through commercials. You can use a DVR just like a VCR or you can subscribe to a DVR-management service. One service provider, TiVo, can record up to 180 hours of your favorite shows automatically to a DVR every time they're on (Figure 6N). This way, all of your entertainment is ready for you to watch whenever you are. Just buy a DVR, activate the TiVo service, and you can enjoy television viewing your way. TiVo's competitors include UltimateTV, DirecTV, Dish Network, Arris Moxi, AT&T U-Verse, and others. Most cable and satellite companies will lease you a DVR.

FIGURE 6N   You can use a DVR and a service such as TiVo to capture your favorite shows and watch them at your convenience.

COMPUTER GAMING DEVICES

Computer game consoles such as Sony's PlayStation 3 (PS3), Nintendo's Wii, and Microsoft's Xbox 360 are popular multimedia devices. You can use these devices to load and play interactive games, using a television or computer screen as the display device. You also can go online and play games against a diverse population of players. Gaming accessories are available, such as game consoles, specialized backpacks, wireless support, and cable accessory packs.

Game consoles are similar to computers. A game console has a processor, a graphics driver, an audio driver, memory, and an operating system. It reads input from a storage device, such as a CD or memory card, processes that input into sounds and animation, and then stores user input for further processing as the game progresses.

Gamers can use portable handheld game consoles such as Nintendo's DS/DSi/DSi XL to take their games with them. When Nintendo entered the home market with the introduction of the Nintendo Wii, it captivated its audience. This popular gaming device features many games for the entire family that are activity based. The Wii Fit is especially popular for the all members of the family as it combines yoga, balance, strength training, and aerobics (Figure 6O).

FIGURE 6O   The Nintendo Wii brings a new level of interactivity to computer games.

According to *PC Magazine*, Microsoft was the first to enter the current console-gaming generation with its original Xbox 360, a hulk of a system that beat both Nintendo and Sony to the punch. The Xbox 360 gets more powerful every year; it is now slimmed down and souped up and has a 250-GB hard drive. Sony released the popular PlayStation Portable product line in fall 2009. Called PSP-Go, the device is touted as the smallest and mightiest of the handheld game systems. It features access to games, video, movies, and the Internet through the PlayStation Network. In 2010, Sony released its PlayStation 4 (PS4). This is in direct competition with the DSi series of handheld gaming consoles.

HEADSETS

Perhaps the ultimate multimedia device is the headset. A **headset** (also called a **head-mounted display**) is a wearable device that includes twin LCD panels. When used with special applications that generate stereo output, headsets can create the illusion that an individual is walking through a 3D environment (Figure 6P).

Gaming enthusiasts can use the **Cave Automated Virtual Environment (CAVE)** to dispense with the headsets in favor of 3D glasses. In the CAVE, the walls, ceiling, and

FIGURE 6P   Headsets are essential to many computer gaming experiences.

floor display projected 3D images. More than 50 CAVEs exist. Researchers use CAVEs to study topics as diverse as the human heart and the next generation of sports cars. The CAVE is a $10 \times 10 \times 9$ foot theater made up of three rear projection screens for walls and a down projection screen for the floor.

Smart Home

Homeowners continue to embrace technology with small, clever, interesting digital devices that help the performance of the home in general while making it more eco-friendly. During spring 2009, the Museum of Science and Industry in Chicago opened an exhibit that features a smart home that is both green and wired (Figure 6Q). The exhibit portrays an environmentally responsible, modular home full of technology. Of course, the home's climate, lighting, and entertainment are controlled by touch-screen panels throughout the home. Some other interesting features are that the lights, television, and music turn off when no one is in the room; the home greets the owners when they arrive home, telling them what's been going on with the house while they were gone; the baby's room can be broadcast via cribcast on video screens in the master bedroom and on the first floor; and the home has a hibernation mode that lowers shades and turns down heat/air when residents are leaving for a day or longer—and adjustments can be made remotely via a cell phone. Many of these features may be incorporated into homes in the future.

FIGURE 6Q   Interest in smart home technologies has increased, as evidenced by the latest Museum of Science and Industry exhibit.

Although many of the items mentioned are representative of features coming in the future, there are many smart features already in our homes today. The digital photo frame is one example. It displays JPEG pictures as a slide show from a screen often measuring from 7 to 15 inches in size. Newer varieties also may display

MPEG video files and play MP3 audio files from the camera's memory card or a USB drive (Figure 6R).

FIGURE 6R   A digital photo picture frame that also projects video and audio can be used to display family pictures.

Another home digital device is the Slingbox produced by Sling Media of San Mateo, California (Figure 6S). This device is for TV streaming, allowing users to view their home's cable or satellite TV remotely from an Internet-enabled computer with a broadband Internet connection, which could be a cell phone, your iPhone, or a Droid. Hulu (**www.hulu.com**) is a Web site and app that offers streaming video of TV shows and movies. Not only can you watch these shows on your computer, you can also watch them on most smartphones.

Technology has even advanced to help pet owners know what Fido is doing while they are gone. Dogs or cats wear a specially designed digital pet camera around their necks (Figure 6T). The owner may set the camera to take pictures at various intervals, from 1 to

FIGURE 6S   A Slingbox will allow you to view video from your home cable system while you are away from home, using a remote connection, which could be supplied by your cell phone if it has broadband Internet access.

FIGURE 6T Pets wear this device around their neck so that worried owners can view what they are doing throughout the day.

15 minutes. The photos can be uploaded to a computer via a USB cable for viewing.

Homeowners continue to be more aware of conserving energy in their homes. Almost every computer sold today comes with some type of a power management utility. Ideally, computers should have the designation of ENERGY STAR (Figure 6U). This rating means the computer meets the federal standards for energy consumption as determined by the EPA (Environmental Protection Agency) and the U.S. Department of Energy. ENERGY STAR notebooks utilize about 15 watts of electricity compared to a desktop, which uses from 200–400 watts. Solar-powered computers and/or battery packs are beginning to arrive in our markets. Ideally, however, we want to move to zero waste with eco-friendly, biodegradable digital components.

FIGURE 6U Computers with the designated ENERGY STAR label indicate that the computer is built to be energy efficient.

Key Terms and Concepts

Multiple Choice

1. Multisensory stimulators are known as _____.
   a. multiaccess
   b. multimedia
   c. multitasking
   d. multidata

2. Which of the following devices will *not* store music?
   a. CD
   b. MP3 player
   c. Smartphone
   d. DVC

3. Apple's Web site for downloading music and movies is called _____.
   a. iPad
   b. iPod
   c. iTouch
   d. iTunes

4. Which device will not display an e-book?
   a. E-book reader   b. Smartphone
   c. Computer   d. Camcorder

5. The Web site that enables you to download movies is named _____.
   a. Hala
   b. Halo
   c. Hulu
   d. Hola

6. Smart home technology allows your home to _____.
   a. help you do your homework
   b. monitor your lights and power consumption
   c. use the most power for tasks
   d. have parties without your parents finding out

7. A Slingbox is a device that permits you to _____.
   a. stream TV shows
   b. shoot an object into the air
   c. safeguard your arm after you hurt it
   d. upload your homework

8. An Energy Star rating means _____.
   a. the computer meets the federal standards for energy consumption
   b. the computer can be used in outer space
   c. the computer uses a lot of energy
   d. the computer meets the standards to receive a star rating

9. Game consoles are similar to computers. Which of the following is not a game console?
   a. Wii
   b. PS4
   c. DSi XL
   d. PS7

10. Digitized video consists of a series of still photographs called _____.
   a. codecs
   b. frames
   c. frame rate
   d. pixels

Spotlight Exercises

1. You want to buy an MP3 player for your music collection. Research which device would be best for you. Compare four different devices. Make sure you include at least one Apple device and one smartphone. Write a one- to two-page, double-spaced paper describing the devices, which one you would choose, and why you chose that one.

2. Visit the Museum of Science and Industry at **www.msichicago.org/whats-here/exhibits/smart-home/** Investigate the smart home and its many features. Write a short paper describing five features that, in your opinion, have merit and will be incorporated into our homes within the next few years. Also, select three features of the home that may not be embraced by the home consumer. Describe them and explain why you don't feel they will be popular.

3. Use your favorite search engine and the World Wide Web to research digital cameras. How many pixels will suffice for your picture-taking needs? What is the price range for such cameras? What is the difference between optical zoom and digital zoom? How much optical zoom would be acceptable for your personal use? What is the storage medium of your chosen camera? How many pictures can you store on a 16-MB disk? How much storage capacity will you buy? What will it cost? Write a brief paper describing what you've learned.

4. Video recording has become even more popular recently due to the advent of YouTube. Many people use small, inexpensive video recorders to record and then upload their files to YouTube or another site. However, there are other reasons people want video recorders, for example, family events, business presentations, and so on. Investigate the types of digital video recorders that are available today. Choose three different recorders at three different price points. Write a short paper describing each, including the manufacturer, price, functionality, warranty, peripheral items needed, and intended audience for each.

5. Did you miss your favorite TV show because you were in class? Do you want to watch that game again? Write a one-page paper on the advantages and disadvantages of Hulu (**www.hulu.com**). Include some information on some of the classic movies and TV shows that are available to watch.

6. Create a comparison chart of the different types of e-book readers. Include a conclusion on which one you would purchase if you were to buy one or why you would not purchase an e-reader. Don't forget to include size, resolution, weight, price, and other such comparisons.

Privacy, Crime, and Security

Today, *deter*, *detect*, and *defend* are the three words associated with protecting your privacy, preventing computer related crimes, and avoiding security breaches. The first of these three, *deter*, is something all individuals can focus on and take responsibility for. How often do you change your passwords for your school login and bank account? Is your password a "strong" password? Have you altered your privacy settings and profiles on your social network site to limit what viewers can see? When you surf at public hot spots, are you aware of potential shoulder surfers? What could you do to reduce the need for detect and defend strategies?

The extensive and public nature of the Internet raises privacy issues as greater numbers of corporations and private citizens increasingly rely on the Internet as a business medium. With the recent arrival of cloud computing and its use of remote servers to hold information and data for many users, the concern for security and privacy has increased. Just as brick-and-mortar businesses in your neighborhood lock their doors at night to protect merchandise and equipment, electronic businesses employ a variety of security measures to protect their interests and your privacy from cybercriminals. In this chapter, you will explore how online connectivity can threaten your privacy, personal safety, and computer system, and you will learn how to protect yourself from online threats. Topics covered include:

- The collection of information without consent
- Ubiquitous computing and how the use of multiple devices through an omnipresent network affects security issues
- Differentiating between computer crime and cybercrime
- Some of the causes of security risks and how to protect your personal and business data
- The use of encryption to protect transmitted data
- The collection of evidence and its use to prosecute cybercriminals ■

Check out **f** **Facebook**
for our latest updates

www.facebook.com

399

Privacy in Cyberspace

Of all the social and ethical issues raised by the use of widely available Internet linked computers, threats to privacy and anonymity are among the most contentious. Government-sponsored sites, like the Identity Theft site hosted by the Federal Trade Commission (Figure 9.1) and private sites, like the Privacy Rights Clearinghouse, a nonprofit consumer information and advocacy organization (Figure 9.2), are emerging to offer practical consumer advice, display privacy alerts, and cover hot privacy issues.

Defined by U.S. Supreme Court Justice Louis Brandeis in 1928 as "the right to be left alone," **privacy** refers to an individual's ability to restrict or eliminate the collection, use, and sale of confidential personal information. Some people say that privacy isn't a concern unless you have something to hide. However, this view ignores the fact that privacy means something different to every individual, government, and corporation, and it is not just the collecting of private information that is cause for concern, but the use of this information in ways that may harm people unnecessarily. With the distinction between what is private and what is public becoming more and more blurred, some privacy advocates, like the Electronic Frontier Foundation (EFF), have developed a "Bill of Rights for Social Network Users." The principles in this bill can be applied to any individual that posts information on a server owned by someone else. The rights that the EFF proposes include the following:

- *The right to informed decision making*—Web sites should provide a clear interface that allows users to make choices about who sees their data and how it is used.
- *The right to control*—The user maintains control over the use and disclosure of his or her data. Any changes to the original agreement must be, by default, "opt-in" acceptance, as opposed to "opt-out." That distinction means that a user's data cannot be shared unless a user makes an informed decision to share it.

FIGURE 9.1 This Identity Theft site provides a link to file a complaint with the FTC and an online quiz to test your knowledge about identity theft.

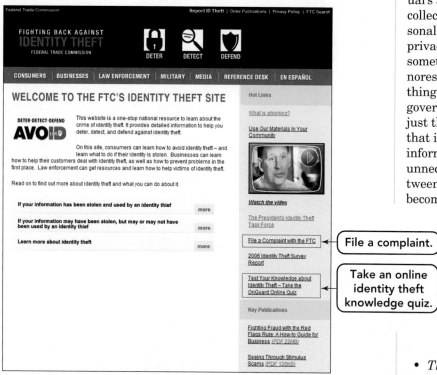

FIGURE 9.2 The Privacy Rights Clearinghouse (**www.privacyrights.org/index.htm**) acts as a source of information on privacy issues to consumers, the media, and policymakers.

- *The right to leave*—The user should have the right to delete, not disable, all data or the entire account from the database. Additionally there should be data portability, that is the right of the user to transfer his/her data to another site in a usable format.

With the early 2010 security breaches in Facebook and Google Buzz, the compromise of users' data has become more public, resulting in congressional support for more security features and guarantees of privacy for users.

The Problem: Collection of Information Without Consent

Many people are willing to divulge information when asked for their consent and when they see a need for doing so. When you apply for a loan, for example, the bank can reasonably ask you to list your other creditors to determine whether you'll be able to repay your loan.

Much information is collected from public agencies, many of which are under a legal obligation to make their records available to the public upon request (public institutions of higher education, departments of motor vehicles, county clerks, tax assessors, and so on). This information finds its way into computerized databases—thousands of them—that track virtually every conceivable type of information about individuals. You are probably aware of credit reporting databases that track your credit history (Figure 9.3). Other databases include information such as your current and former addresses and employers, other names you've used (like your previous name, if you're married and use a different name now), current and former spouses, bankruptcies, lawsuits, property ownership, driver's license information, criminal records, purchasing habits, and medical prescriptions.

Most of the companies that maintain databases today claim that they sell information only to bona fide customers such as lending institutions, prospective employers, marketing firms, and licensed private

investigators. They maintain that their databases don't pose a threat to the privacy of individuals because they are highly ethical firms, have security measures in place, and would not release this information to the general public. However, no matter how secure data appears, there are always people seeking to violate that security. On January 17, 2007, TJX, a $16 billion retail conglomerate that operates 2,500 stores around the world, including T.J. Maxx, Marshall's, Home Goods, Bob's Stores, A.J. Wright, Winners, and Homesense stores, reported a security breach in its customer transaction database system. The system that was

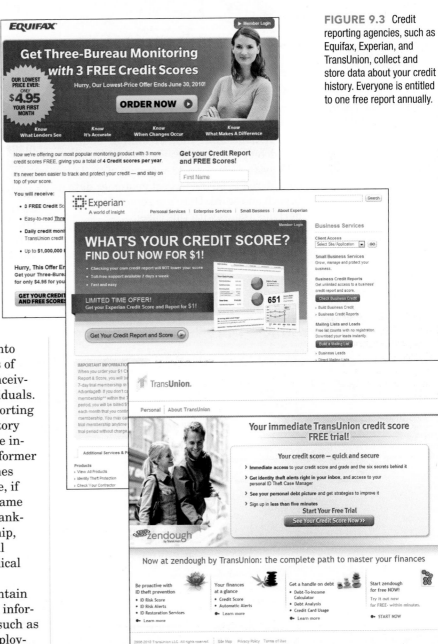

FIGURE 9.3 Credit reporting agencies, such as Equifax, Experian, and TransUnion, collect and store data about your credit history. Everyone is entitled to one free report annually.

FIGURE 9.4 PCI was founded by several financial organizations, including American Express, MasterCard Worldwide, Discover Financial Services, JCB International, and Visa Inc., to develop methods to secure account data.

compromised handled customer credit card, debit card, check, and merchandise return transactions. More than 45 million credit and debit card numbers were stolen from TJX systems over an 18-month period. It's considered to be the largest customer data breach on record. Here are some of the underlying issues with this case:

- The intruders had possession of the company's encryption key and could decode account numbers and create counterfeit credit and debit cards.

- Some of the credit card information went back to 2003, which indicated that TJX had been out of compliance with PCI standards for years. PCI (**www.pcisecuritystandards.org/index.shtml**) is a global forum for the ongoing development and implementation of security standards for account data protection (Figure 9.4).

- TJX had difficulty determining what data had been compromised and when.

With security measures in place and encryption used to guarantee privacy, the TJX case seems to indicate that no system is truly secure from modern cyberthieves.

According to privacy activists, the problem occurs after the information is compromised or sold. Before the TJX breach was even discovered, the thieves were able to steal $8 million in merchandise from Wal-Mart stores in Florida with counterfeit credit cards. The Internet has made it much easier and much cheaper for ordinary individuals to gain access to sensitive personal information, and at the same time made it easier and cheaper to distribute compromised data faster. A simple Web search for "Social Security numbers" results in a wide array of Web sites run by private investigators who offer to find someone's Social Security number for a small fee. A Google search can provide much useful information, but the personal information it can uncover can easily be misused (Figure 9.5).

Technology and Anonymity

Marketing firms, snoops, and government officials can use computers and the Internet to collect information in ways that are hidden from users. The same technology also makes it increasingly difficult for citizens to engage in anonymous speech. **Anonymity** refers to the ability to convey a message without disclosing your name or identity.

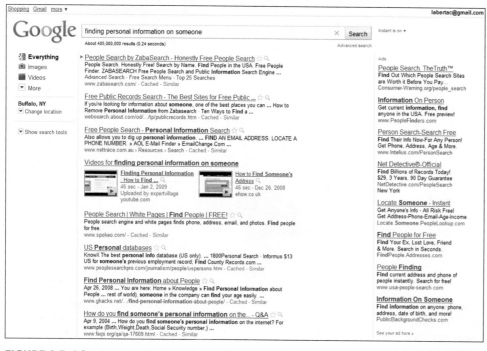

FIGURE 9.5 A Google search will return numerous Web sites that sell personal information to anyone they please. In the United States, you have little legal recourse against those who collect and sell sensitive personal information.

Anonymity is both a curse and a blessing. On one hand, it can be seen as an abuse because it frees people from accountability. On the other hand, as supported by the U.S. Supreme Court—it must be preserved in a democracy, to ensure that citizens have access to the full range of possible ideas to make decisions for themselves. Freeing authors from accountability for anonymous works, the Court argued, raises the potential that false or misleading ideas will be brought before the public, but this risk is necessary to maintain a free society.

Anonymity with respect to Internet use is necessary to protect whistleblowers. However, the right to anonymity is being challenged on an individual case basis. Recently, the Honorable Mr. Justice Eady ruled that bloggers have no right to privacy in what is essentially the public act of publishing. Eady, a high court judge in

England and Wales, overturned an injunction that had prevented *The Times* from revealing the identity of Richard Norton, the detective behind the controversial NightJack blog. Additionally, a few years earlier, a judge handed a Florida sheriff a victory in his mission to suppress what he says were inflammatory postings to an Internet message board used by law enforcement. Examples of technologies that threaten online anonymity include cookies, global unique identifiers, ubiquitous computing, and radio frequency identification.

Cookies Generally downloaded into folders that hold temporary Internet files, **cookies** are small text files that are written to your computer's hard disk by many of the Web sites you visit (Figure 9.6). Cookies can be located easily by searching for the word *cookie* from the start menu. Each cookie contains a unique ID, which is assigned by the Web site on the first visit, for each user. On return visits to that Web site, the ID is used to record the visit in the Web site's database. Several cookie-related terms that a user should be familiar with are listed here:

- Temporary cookies or sessions are cookies removed from your system after you close Internet Explorer.

FIGURE 9.6 Cookies can be helpful to a user by remembering login information and passwords; but, they can also act as an informant, providing the parent site with information on the habits and purchasing tendencies of the user without the user's permission.

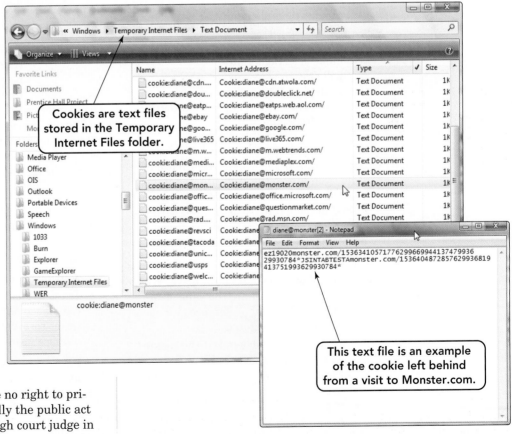

They are used to hold nonpermanent information like the contents of a shopping cart.

- Persistent cookies remain on your system after Internet Explorer is closed and hold reusable information like your login and password.
- First-party cookies come from the site you are visiting and can be temporary or persistent.
- Third-party cookies come from another Web sites' advertisements (such as pop-up or banner ads) on the Web site that you're viewing and might track your Web use for marketing purposes.

Often perceived as malicious, cookies are actually used for many useful and legitimate tasks.

- Cookies enable the Web site to obtain an actual count on the number of new and return visitors.
- They can store site preferences set by the user. When the user returns to the site, the preferences are automatically applied.
- Online retail sites use cookies to implement "shopping carts," which enable you to make selections that will stay in your cart so that you can return to the online store for more browsing and shopping.

Cookies, located on your hard disk, actually contain very little information. When you are on the Web site, the items you buy or the pages you are viewing are stored in the database associated with the Web page. Some users point to several problems with cookies, including these:

- Only one cookie from a Web site can be placed on a system's hard drive. When multiple users share the same computer, individual preferences for each user cannot be stored.
- Cookies can be deleted. If the cookie was holding your login ID and password, you might not remember them to log in again.
- If you use several computers, each computer will receive a new cookie

from the Web site with a different ID. As a result, the Web site will count you as a different user.

What troubles privacy advocates is the use of tracking cookies to gather data on Web users' browsing and shopping habits—without their consent. Several Internet ad networks, such as DoubleClick, use cookies to track users' browsing actions across thousands of the most popular Internet sites. When you visit a Web site that has contracted with one of these ad networks, a cookie containing a unique identification number is deposited on your computer's hard drive. This cookie tracks your browsing habits and preferences as you move among the hundreds of sites that contract with the ad network. When you visit another site, the cookie is detected, read, and matched with a profile of your previous browsing activity. On this basis, the ad network selects and displays a **banner ad** targeted to match the topic or type of products you were browsing through. A banner ad is not actually part of the Web page. Instead, it is an ad supplied separately by an ad network. The banner ad may appear at the top, side, or bottom of the page.

In response to concerns that their tracking violates Internet users' privacy, ad network companies claim that they do not link the collected information with users' names and addresses. However, current technology would enable these firms to do so—and privacy advocates fear that some of them already have. Internet ad networks such as DoubleClick can collect the following:

- Your e-mail address
- Your full name
- Your mailing address (street, city, state, and zip code)
- Your phone number
- Transactional data (names of products purchased online, details of plane ticket reservations, and search phrases used with search engines)

Internet marketing firms explain that by collecting such information, they can provide a "richer" marketing experience, one that's more closely tailored to an individual's interests. Privacy advocates reply that once

> "What troubles **piracy** advocates is the use of tracking **cookies** to gather data on Web **users'** browsing and shopping habits— **without** their consent."

collected, this information could become valuable to others. These kinds of debates ensure that cookies and the information they collect will remain on the forefront of the privacy controversy for years to come.

As a user, do you have any control over cookies? Current browsers have a setting that prevents any cookie from being placed on your hard drive. On the surface, this sounds appealing; but many Web sites will not let you browse if the cookie option is not enabled. You can also accept the cookie but set an option in your browser so that the browser informs you every time a site sends values into the cookie on your hard drive. This option allows you to accept or deny the values. The means by which you set these options differs from one browser to another. Use the help feature in your browser to locate these settings. If you are still confused about how cookies work, refer to Figure 9.7 or go to **http://computer.howstuffworks . com/cookie.htm**.

Globally Unique Identifiers A **globally unique identifier (GUID)** is an identification number that is generated by a hardware component or a program. Privacy advocates discovered GUIDs in several popular computer components and programs, such as Intel's Pentium III chip and Microsoft's Word 97 and Excel 97. The GUIDs can be read by Web servers or embedded in various documents, identifying the computer and inadvertently making it more difficult to use the Internet anonymously. Although the use of GUIDs does not seem to be as prevalent as it was earlier this decade, a similar concept has been discovered in color laser printers. The Electronic Frontier Foundation (**www.eff.org**), a civil liberties group that defends your rights in the digital world, has reported that many color laser printers embed printer tracking dots—nearly invisible yellow dots— on every page that is printed, at the urging of the U.S. government. These dots can identify the serial number and manufacturing code of the printer, as well as the time and date the document was printed. Officially, the tracking dots are designed to track counterfeiters, but privacy advocates are concerned because there is no law to prevent this information

from being used by U.S. government agencies, foreign governments, or individuals to identify materials printed and distributed by private citizens.

Companies that introduce GUIDs into their products generally conceal this information from the public. When forced to admit to using GUIDs, the firms typically remove the GUID-implanting code or enable users to opt out of their data collection systems. Advocates of online anonymity insist that these companies are missing the basic point: Users, not corporations, should determine when and how personal information is divulged to third parties.

Ubiquitous Computing The term **ubiquitous computing** was coined by Mark Weiser in 1988, during his tenure as Chief Technologist of the Xerox Palo Alto Research Center (PARC). It refers to a trend in which individuals no longer interact with one computer at a time but instead with multiple devices connected through an omnipresent network, enabling technology to become virtually embedded and invisible in our lives. The concept is to make technology implicit, built into the things we use. The proponents of this technology hold that this type of computing will be a more natural tool and envision a system where billions of miniature, ubiquitous intercommunication devices will be spread worldwide. An example of the use of ubiquitous computing would be the automatic adjustment of an environmental

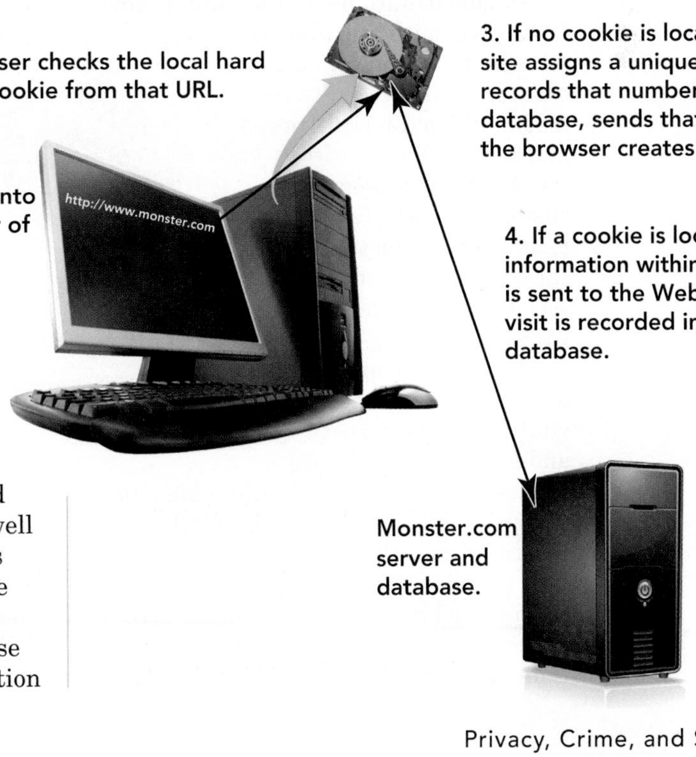

FIGURE 9.7 How a Cookie Works

2. The browser checks the local hard drive for a cookie from that URL.

3. If no cookie is located, the Web site assigns a unique ID number, records that number in its database, sends that ID back, and the browser creates the cookie.

1. Enter a URL into the address bar of a browser.

4. If a cookie is located, the information within the cookie is sent to the Web site and the visit is recorded in the site's database.

http://www.monster.com

Monster.com server and database.

setting, like heat or light, in your office or home based on the signals sent to these environmental devices by monitors built into the clothing of individuals in the setting.

Imagine your movements being tracked by an **active badge**, a small device worn by an individual that transmits a unique infrared signal every 5 to 10 seconds. Networked sensors detect these transmissions and the location of the badge and, hence, the location of its wearer, allowing e-mail, phone calls, or messages to be forwarded to wherever you are. Also imagine "electronic trails" left by you or others as they pass through the neighborhood, office, or conference. You already accept the idea of receiving e-mail anywhere; after all, that is already a feature of portable communication devices, the early ubiquitous computing tools. However, the concept of electronic trails probably made you a little uncomfortable. Proponents of ubiquitous computing say that a user can dissent and not wear a badge. Some experts argue that not being tracked, or not wearing a badge, should be the default. How do you feel about being tracked, having your movements monitored and recorded as you move about your daily routine?

Today, the closest devices to ubiquitous computing tools are digital music players, smartphones, and PCs that act as a media center for your entire home. These devices transmit data about us; they also search for data via Internet connections. Privacy can be compromised when smaller devices are lost or stolen. Most devices maintain some form of log, such as a playlist, records of incoming or outgoing calls, or a list of recently viewed media, which can be retrieved and exploited.

As users become accustomed to using such technology, privacy advocates are concerned that society has become more willing to tolerate lower levels of privacy in favor of convenience. A recent study by Pew Internet and American Life Project has found that young adults are more likely to take control of their digital identities than their older counterparts. This includes the changing of privacy settings and passwords, restricting access to their data, and removing their names from tagged photographs. However the study also found that users across all age levels were paying more attention to privacy-protecting activities than they did in a similar study in 2006.

ETHICS

Technology has provided a means of surveillance that is invisible and ever present. Even devices that are installed for protection can be manipulated and become mechanisms of surveillance. Recently the FBI served OnStar with a court order to give the agency access to the passive listening feature embedded within OnStar devices. Such access would enable the FBI to record conversations held in a vehicle. OnStar filed a suit and won, after a two-year court battle. The ruling in OnStar's favor, however, was not on the grounds of invasion of privacy. Instead, the court ruled that the fact that the use of the passive listening feature would disable the emergency calling feature and thus constitute a breach of the consumers' contract. How do you feel about the use of such devices for surveillance? When do such actions become a violation of privacy? How private are your private conversations?

Radio Frequency Identification The use of radio waves to track a chip or tag placed in or on an object is referred to as **radio frequency identification (RFID).** RFID tags (Figure 9.8) are often used, as an alternative to bar codes, for inventory control in the retail environment. RFID does not require direct contact or line-of-sight scanning. Instead, an antenna using radio frequency waves transmits a signal that activates the transponder, or tag. When activated, the tag transmits data back to the antenna. However, if the tag is not deactivated, the object's movements can continue to be tracked indefinitely. This technology is also used when microchips are inserted in pets and other livestock, and has even been used for people. The RFID chip can include contact information and health records for the individual or animal, or other personal details.

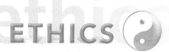

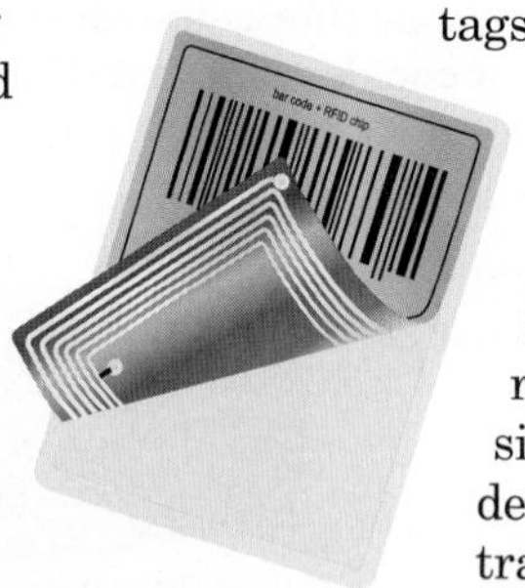

FIGURE 9.8 RFID tags are often used as antitheft devices or to track merchandise.

Privacy advocates have been concerned about the use of encrypted, passive RFID

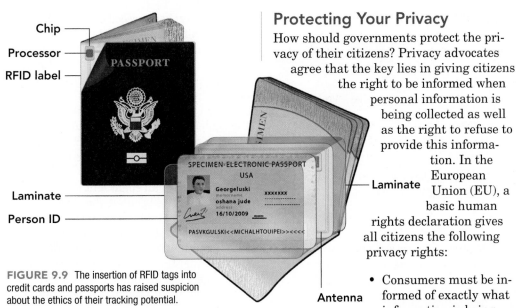

Chip
Processor
RFID label
PASSPORT
Laminate
Person ID

SPECIMEN-ELECTRONIC-PASSPORT
USA
Georgeluski
memo/name
oshana jude
address
16/10/2009
XXXXXXX
PASVKGULSKI<<MICHALHTOUIPEI>><<<<

Laminate

Antenna

FIGURE 9.9 The insertion of RFID tags into credit cards and passports has raised suspicion about the ethics of their tracking potential.

Protecting Your Privacy

How should governments protect the privacy of their citizens? Privacy advocates agree that the key lies in giving citizens the right to be informed when personal information is being collected as well as the right to refuse to provide this information. In the European Union (EU), a basic human rights declaration gives all citizens the following privacy rights:

- Consumers must be informed of exactly what information is being collected and how it will be used.
- Consumers must be allowed to choose whether they want to divulge the requested information and how collected information will be used.
- Consumers must be allowed to request that information about themselves be removed from marketing and other databases.

tags in U.S. passports for several years (Figure 9.9). The tag contains the same information included on the actual passport—name, nationality, gender, date of birth, and place of birth of the passport holder, as well as a digitized signature and photograph of that person. The government asserts that the RFID tag does not broadcast a signal and can only be read within close proximity of special scanning devices. However, a new passport card approved in 2008 as part of the Western Hemisphere Travel Initiative for travel to Mexico, Canada, Bermuda, and the Caribbean will use an unencrypted chip that can be read from up to 30 feet away, raising serious concerns that a passport holder's identity could easily be stolen or their location tracked without their consent or awareness.

About 100 million credit cards are now embedded with this technology, replacing the familiar magnetic strip. The new cards seem to make it so much easier that some folks are reading your credit cards before you even take them out of your wallet. These identity thieves use RFID readers to pick the data off your RFID chip as you walk by. Technology has made identity theft quite literally a stroll in the park. Where credit card skimming used to require the thief to have possession of your card, acquiring your personal data is now as easy as passing you on the street. Companies like Identity Stronghold (**www.idstronghold.com/**) offer a line of RFID blocking products like wallets and cell phone cases.

Now that you've read about some of the privacy threats posed by the Internet, let's discuss how you can protect your privacy.

Protecting the privacy rights of U.S. citizens has been a controversial area for years. Most of us agree that our rights should be protected, but our definition of acceptable levels of protection varies widely. Some of the legislation currently in place includes the Fair Credit Reporting Act, which provides limited privacy protection for credit information; the Health Insurance Portability and Privacy Act (HIPAA), which establishes standards for the transmission of electronic health care data and the security and privacy of this information; and the Family Educational Rights and Privacy Act (FERPA), which protects the privacy of student education records. However, there is no comprehensive federal law governing the overall privacy rights of U.S. citizens. Instead, privacy is protected by a patchwork of limited federal and state laws and regulations. Most of these laws regulate what government agencies can do. Except in limited areas covered by these laws, little exists to stop people and companies from acquiring and selling your personal information (Figure 9.10).

Marketing industry spokespeople and lobbyists argue that the U.S. government should not impose laws or regulations to

FIGURE 9.10 Summary of Major U.S. Laws Concerning Privacy Issues

Year	Legislation	Objective
2003	CAN-SPAM Act	Provides the tools to combat Internet spammers
2001	Children's Internet Protection Act (CIPA)	Addresses concerns about access to offensive content over the Internet on school and library computers
1996	Health Insurance Portability and Accountability Act (HIPAA)	Establishes standards for privacy and electronic transmission of health care data
1974	Family Education Rights and Privacy Act (FERPA)	Protects the privacy of student education records
1970	Fair Credit Reporting Act (FCRA)	Provides limited privacy protection for credit information.

protect consumers' privacy. They argue that the industry should regulate itself. Privacy advocates counter that technology has outpaced the industry's capability to regulate itself, as evidenced by the widespread availability of highly personal information on the Internet.

The Direct Marketing Association (DMA) claims to enforce a basic code of ethics among its member organizations. The organization takes steps to ensure that confidential information doesn't fall into the wrong hands and that consumers can opt out of marketing campaigns if they wish. For more information, visit the DMA Web site at **www. the-dma.org/ index.php**.

Be aware that many of the most aggressive Internet-based marketing firms have no ties to or previous experience with the DMA, and several opt-out systems on the Internet are already used for fraudulent purposes. For example, e-mail spammers typically claim that recipients can opt out of mass e-mail marketing campaigns. But recipients who respond

to such messages succeed only in validating their e-mail addresses, and the result is often a major increase in the volume of unsolicited e-mail. A report from the TRACE-labs team at M86 Security for the week ending June 6, 2010, revealed that India and the United States (Figure 9.11) were the leaders in relaying **spam**, unsolicited messages sent in bulk over electronic mailing systems, and that messages touting pharmaceutical products accounted for 84.03 percent of all spam sent (Figure 9.12).

In the United States, the CAN-SPAM Act of 2003 provided the tools to combat spammers. The Federal Trade Commission (FTC) and the Department of Justice have primary jurisdiction over spammers, but other agencies, including states and ISPs, can also prosecute them. The legislation has been criticized because it prevents states from enacting tougher laws, prevents individuals from suing spammers, and does not require e-mailers to request permission before sending messages. Additionally, it may be ineffective against foreign spammers who are outside U.S. jurisdiction. Although many contend that the act is just a drop in the bucket, the monetary threat the CAN-SPAM Act poses can't hurt. In 2008, MySpace successfully sued the so-called "Spam King" Sanford Wallace and a business partner for violations of the CAN-SPAM Act. A federal judge awarded MySpace close to $230 million, although it is doubtful the money will ever be collected. At one time, a National Do Not

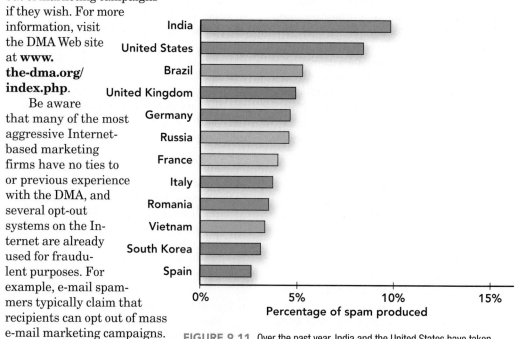

FIGURE 9.11 Over the past year, India and the United States have taken turns occupying the No. 1 position as the weekly leader in relaying spam.

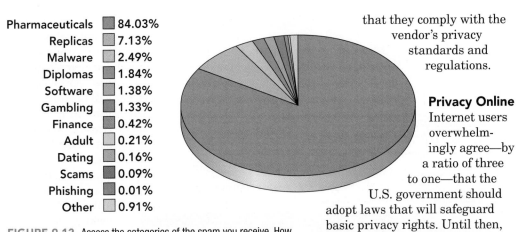

Pharmaceuticals	84.03%
Replicas	7.13%
Malware	2.49%
Diplomas	1.84%
Software	1.38%
Gambling	1.33%
Finance	0.42%
Adult	0.21%
Dating	0.16%
Scams	0.09%
Phishing	0.01%
Other	0.91%

FIGURE 9.12 Assess the categories of the spam you receive. How does your spam compare with the percentages presented in this chart?

Email Registry (similar to the National Do Not Call list to combat telemarketers) was considered but discarded because of the potential for misuse and the inability to provide effective enforcement. States are also enacting their own laws, within the parameters of the CAN-SPAM Act, and other types of legislation, such as the Anti-Phishing Consumer Protection Act of 2008. Such laws are being debated across the country. Private lawsuits have not been effective yet, but they may be a bright spot on the horizon. The threat of monetary penalties may be the only thing that can thwart the growth of the spam industry.

Although some individuals may be discouraged from participating in e-commerce activities because of privacy concerns and fears regarding the use of information collected by Web sites, the Internet retail sector continues to thrive. The Census Bureau records show that, despite economic issues, the estimate of U.S. retail e-commerce sales for the first quarter of 2010 was $38.7 billion, an increase of 1.5 percent from the fourth quarter of 2009.

According to a 2008 survey by the Pew Internet and American Life Project, 66 percent of Americans who use the Internet have made purchases online, despite the fact that 75 percent of online users are concerned about providing personal and financial information online. The survey results also indicate that if privacy concerns were addressed, Internet sales would increase by at least 7 percent. Most popular commercial Web sites have attempted to allay these fears by creating "privacy policy" pages that explain how they collect and use personal information about site visitors. Many also display privacy seals from third-party vendors such as TRUSTe, WebTrust, or the Better Business Bureau as a sign

that they comply with the vendor's privacy standards and regulations.

Privacy Online
Internet users overwhelmingly agree—by a ratio of three to one—that the U.S. government should adopt laws that will safeguard basic privacy rights. Until then, it's up to you to safeguard your privacy on the Internet. To do so, follow these suggestions:

- Surf the Web anonymously by using software products such as Anonymizer's Anonymous Surfing (**www.anonymizer.com**) or devices such as the IronKey Secure USB flash drive (**www.ironkey.com**), which includes special security software to protect your data and encrypt your online communications (Figure 9.13).

- Use a "throwaway" e-mail address from a free Web-based service such as Google's Gmail (www.google.com) for the e-mail address you place on Web pages, mailing lists, chat rooms, or other public Internet spaces that are scanned by e-mail spammers.

- Tell children not to divulge any personal information online without first asking a parent or teacher for permission. Although they seem computer savvy, many children are unaware of the evils that lurk on the Internet. The Children's Internet

FIGURE 9.13 Devices like the IronKey Secure USB flash drive include special security software to allow you to surf the Web privately and securely while protecting your identity and data.

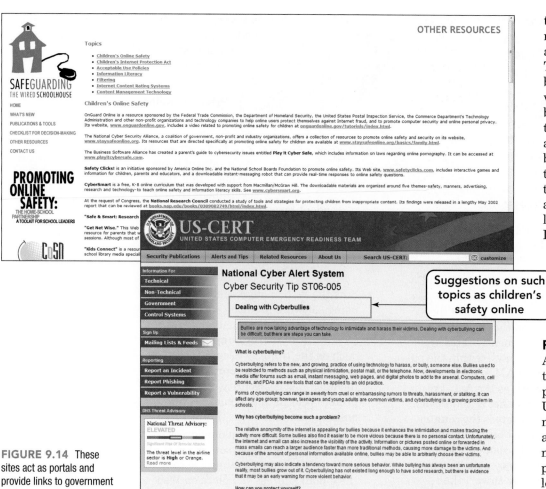

FIGURE 9.14 These sites act as portals and provide links to government and private sites that are related to Internet security and privacy.

third-party to monitor the activity of a site. Turning off the browser's cookies will prevent Web beacons from tracking the user's activity. A Web beacon can be detected by viewing the source code of a Web page and looking for an IMG tag that downloads from a different server than the rest of the page.

Privacy at Home

Are you aware that all new cell phones in the United States must have GPS awareness? This means that your phone can be located, usually within 30 feet, by law enforcement and emergency services personnel when you dial 911. Some services, such as Where (formerly known as uLocate) and BrickHouse child locator, provide the exact location of a cell phone. This can come in handy when a parent is trying to keep track of a child, but it can be intrusive when an employer uses it to track an employee using a company cell phone.

Some software is so powerful that it will send a notification to the home unit whenever the cell phone leaves a designated geographic area. MIT students recently developed programs using GPS capabilities for the Android mobile OS by Google. One program lets you change your phone's settings as your location changes, so it will be silent in a movie theater or classroom but will ring when you're outdoors. Another program will remind you that you need to pick up milk as you pass by the store! This location-aware tracking software is already in use by the criminal justice system to keep track of offenders who are sentenced to home detention. The subject is fitted with an ankle or wrist bracelet,

Protection Act (CIPA) of 2001 protects minors from inappropriate content when using computers in schools and libraries. Sites like **www.safewiredschools.org/other.html** and **www.us-cert.gov** provide links to Web pages that contain information on keeping kids safe while on the Web as well as information on Internet privacy and issues of digital security (Figure 9.14).

- Don't fill out site registration forms unless you see a privacy policy statement indicating that the information you supply won't be sold to third parties.
- Turn off cookies in order to prevent the activity of **Web beacons**, transparent graphic images, usually no larger than 1 pixel × 1 pixel, that are placed on a Web site or in an e-mail and used to monitor the behavior of the user visiting the Web site or sending the e-mail. Web beacons are typically used by a

and then the software is set to trigger an alarm if the wearer strays from the designated area. These bracelets also are being used to keep track of Alzheimer's patients.

As it has evolved, home computing is subject to a decrease in security caused by sharing computing devices and using portable devices in public. A lot of credit card fraud and unauthorized banking access can be traced back to Internet and e-mail use. Some of the security measures you can use on home and portable devices to deter unauthorized access to your accounts include these:

- Create strong logins and passwords for each individual who uses a system. This provides each user with a section to store documents that no other user can see or utilize when logged in. A **strong password** should
  - Be difficult to guess.
  - Be at least 14 characters or more in length.
  - Include uppercase letters, lowercase letters, numbers, and special characters.
  - Not be a recognizable word or phrase.
  - Not be the name of anything or anyone close to you, for example a family member or the name of the family pet.
  - Not be a recognizable string of numbers such as a Social Security number or birth date.

The longer the user login and password, the more time it takes for someone, or some program, to guess it (Figure 9.15). Use online strength testers to evaluate your passwords. The Password Meter at **www.passwordmeter.com** provides guidelines and indicates how including symbols and numbers can improve your score. Microsoft also provides an evaluation site at **www.microsoft.com/ protect/yourself/password/ checker.mspx.**

Using a strong password is a great start toward secure computer use, but there are some additional steps that users can follow to facilitate the privacy and security of their strong password.

- Do not save account numbers or passwords for access to secured sites such as bank accounts and personal e-mail on a shared system.

FIGURE 9.15 Password Length Versus Guess Time

Length of Password Using Mixed Letters, Numerals, and Symbols	Time to Guess (@10,000 Passwords per Second)
2	Instant
4	2.25 hours
6	2.5 years
8	22,875 years

- Do not leave a secured account active on the monitor and walk away. A passerby can easily brush a key and enter a transaction that could be critical.
- Do not leave devices like cell phones and PDAs on tables at restaurants and college facilities. Information left on the screen can easily be read, remembered, and reused. There are many free apps available today for portable devices that automatically lock the system after a brief period without use and require a special password or finger sequence on the touch screen to reopen.
- Turn off services that are not in use, especially Bluetooth.
- Ensure that devices are configured securely and, if necessary, require authentication.

Statistics from the Internet Crime Complaint Center (IC3), a partnership between the FBI, National White Color Crime Center, and the Bureau of Justice Assistance, substantiate that complaints registered on their Web site, **www.ic3. gov**, for Web-related crimes have increased significantly between 2008 and 2009 (Figure 9.16). Financial losses for

FIGURE 9.16
Complaints of Web crimes have been on a constant rise, with a 22.3 percent increase occurring between 2008 and 2009.

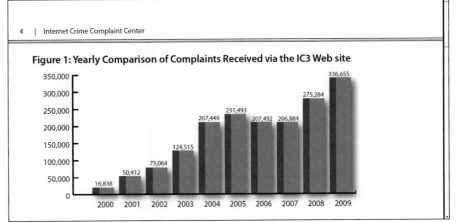

4 | Internet Crime Complaint Center

Figure 1: Yearly Comparison of Complaints Received via the IC3 Web site

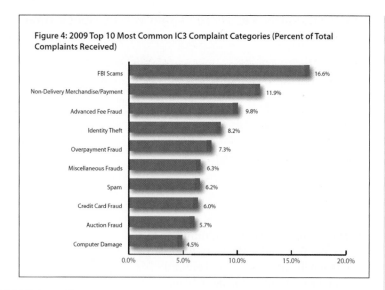

Figure 4: 2009 Top 10 Most Common IC3 Complaint Categories (Percent of Total Complaints Received)

FBI Scams — 16.6%
Non-Delivery Merchandise/Payment — 11.9%
Advanced Fee Fraud — 9.8%
Identity Theft — 8.2%
Overpayment Fraud — 7.3%
Miscellaneous Frauds — 6.3%
Spam — 6.2%
Credit Card Fraud — 6.0%
Auction Fraud — 5.7%
Computer Damage — 4.5%

0.0%   5.0%   10.0%   15.0%   20.0%

FIGURE 9.17 The main category of complaints to the IC3 was FBI scams.

complaints in 2009 reached an all-time high of $559.7 million, with a median dollar loss of $575. Complaints were received in many different categories of Internet activity, including scams that used the FBI's name (FBI scams), auction fraud, nondelivery of merchandise, credit card fraud, computer intrusion, spam/unsolicited e-mail, and child pornography (Figure 9.17).

Privacy at Work In the United States, more than three-quarters of large employers routinely engage in **employee monitoring**, observing employees' phone calls, e-mails, Web browsing habits, and computer files. One program, Spector, provides employers with a report of everything employees do online by taking hundreds of screen snapshots per hour (Figure 9.18).

About one company in four has fired an employee based on what it has found.

Such monitoring is direct and invasive, but it will continue until laws are passed against it. Why do companies monitor their employees? Companies are concerned about employees who may offer trade secrets to competitors in hopes of landing an attractive job offer. Another concern is sexual harassment lawsuits. Employees who access pornographic Web sites or circulate offensive jokes via e-mail may be creating a hostile environment for other employees—and that could result in a huge lawsuit against the company.

To protect your privacy at work, remember the following rules:

- Unless you have specific permission, don't use your employer's telephone system for personal calls. Make all such calls from a pay phone or from your personal cell phone.

- Never use your e-mail account at work for personal purposes. Send and receive all personal mail from your home computer.

- Be aware of **shoulder surfing**, the attempt by an individual to obtain information from your computer screen by looking over your shoulder.

- When entering a secured area that requires authorized access, be aware of anyone that is attempting to enter with you to avoid using the appropriate check-in or authorization procedure. This act is referred to as **tailgating**. Tailgating was once associated only with the physical entry

FIGURE 9.18 Employers can use Spector, an employee-monitoring program from SpectorSoft, to track everything employees do online.

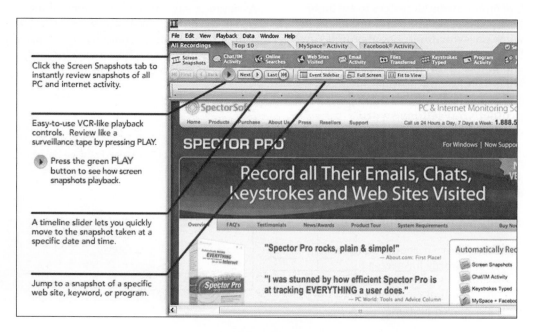

Click the Screen Snapshots tab to instantly review snapshots of all PC and internet activity.

Easy-to-use VCR-like playback controls. Review like a surveillance tape by pressing PLAY.

Press the green PLAY button to see how screen snapshots playback.

A timeline slider lets you quickly move to the snapshot taken at a specific date and time.

Jump to a snapshot of a specific web site, keyword, or program.

into a restricted zone, but it can also be extended to electronic entry and occurs when a user does not log out of a system and another user sits down and begins to work under the guise of the authorized user instead of logging out and re-logging in as themselves.

- Assume that everything you do while you're at work—whether it's talking on the phone, using your computer, taking a break, or chatting with coworkers—may be monitored and recorded.

Now that you've learned about some important privacy issues, let's take a look at some intentional invasions of your privacy—computer crime.

Computer Crime and Cybercrime

Privacy issues, such as collecting personal information and employee monitoring, should be distinguished from **computer crimes**, computer-based activities that violate state, federal, or international laws. **Cybercrime** describes crimes carried out by means of the Internet. A new legal field—**cyberlaw**—is emerging to track and combat computer-related crime.

In 2006, the United States ratified the Convention on Cybercrime. Developed by the Council of Europe, this is the first international treaty to address the issues and concerns surrounding cybercrime. Its goal is to provide guidelines for consistent cybercrime legislation that is compatible with other member countries and to encourage international cooperation in these areas. Many government agencies, such as the Department of Justice (**www.cybercrime.gov**) and the FBI (**www.fbi.gov/cyberinvest/cyberhome.htm**) have set up special sites to provide information and assistance to help combat cybercrime. The FTC's OnGuard Online site (**http://onguardonline.gov**) has collaborated with government agencies and technology organizations to provide tutorials and activities to educate consumers about the threats and risks posed by cybercriminals (Figure 9.19).

Types of Computer Crime

Anyone who wants to invade or harm a computer system can use a variety of tools and tricks. Pay close attention; you'll learn several facts that could help you avoid becoming a victim.

Identity Theft The phone rings and it's a collection agency demanding immediate payment for a bill for a $5,000 stereo system that's past due. You can't believe what you're hearing—you always pay your bills on time, and you haven't purchased any stereo equipment lately. What's going on?

It's identity theft, one of the fastest growing crimes in the United States and Canada. With **identity theft**, a criminal obtains enough personal information to impersonate you. With a few key pieces of information, such as your address and Social Security number, and possibly a credit card or bank account number, an identity thief can open a credit account, access your bank account, open accounts for utilities or cell phones, or apply for a loan or mortgage—all in your name! Although some laws may limit your liability for fraudulent charges, victims of identity theft have found themselves saddled with years of agony. The bad marks on their credit reports can prevent them from buying homes, obtaining telephone service, and even getting jobs. Although some reports show a slight decline in identity theft in the United States, according to a Javelin Strategy and Research report in 2009, there were 10 million victims of identity theft in 2008 in the United States.

FIGURE 9.19 The FTC's OnGuard Online site provides many resources to help educate the public about various types of cybercrime. Visitors can view tutorials, explore topics, or file a complaint if they've been victims.

Consider the following interesting identity theft statistics:

- Approximately 1.6 million households had their bank accounts or debit cards compromised.
- It can take up to 5,840 hours (the equivalent of working a full-time job for two years) to correct the damage from identity theft, depending on the severity of the case.
- Businesses across the world lose $221 billion a year due to identity theft.
- On average, victims lose between $851 and $1,378 out of pocket trying to resolve identity theft.
- Approximately 70 percent of victims have difficulty removing negative information that resulted from identity theft from their credit reports.
- About 43 percent of victims know the perpetrator.
- In cases of child identity theft, the most common perpetrator is the child's parent.

How do criminals get this information? Most identity theft doesn't even involve computers. Disgruntled employees may physically steal information from their company, thieves may steal your mail or wallet, or they may go through your trash or a company's trash, an act referred to as **dumpster diving**. However, information can also be electronically stolen by criminals if computer data is not properly secured, if you respond to spam or phishing attacks, or if you have malware on your computer. And unfortunately, many Web sites and spammers sell such data to others.

In a **phishing** attack, a "phisher" poses as a legitimate company in an e-mail or on a Web site in an attempt to obtain personal information such as your Social Security number, user name, password, and account numbers. For example, you might receive an e-mail that appears to come from XYZ Company asking you to confirm your e-identity (user name and password). Because the communication looks legitimate, you comply. The phisher can now gain access to your accounts.

Spear phishing, which is similar to phishing, also uses fake e-mails and social engineering to trick recipients into providing personal information to enable identity theft. But rather than being sent randomly, spear phishing attempts are targeted to specific people, such as senior executives or members of a particular organization.

Malware The term **malware** is short for *malicious software* and describes software designed to damage or infiltrate a computer system without the owner's consent or knowledge. Malware is used to commit fraud, send spam, and steal your personal data. It includes spyware and computer viruses, as well as other rogue programs like worms and Trojan horses. A study released by McAfee in early 2010 predicted the following computer-related threats to be key in the coming years:

- Threats to social networking sites such as Facebook will increase.
- E-mail-borne malware will become more sophisticated and will target journalists and corporations, in addition to individual users.
- Popular applications will continue to be the primary targets for cybercriminals.
- Cloud computing will provide a new arena for malware developers to exploit.

The National Cyber Security Alliance (**http://staysafeonline.org**) indicates that fewer than one in four Americans is fully protected against malware. This Web site offers a list tips to keep you safe online.

- Know who you're dealing with online.
- Keep your Web browsers and operating system up to date.
- Back up important files.
- Protect your children online.
- Use security software tools as your first line of defense, and keep them up to date.
- Use strong passwords or strong authentication technology to help protect your personal information.
- Learn what to do if something goes wrong.

> "**Threats** to **social networking** sites such as Facebook will **increase**. . . . Popular **applications** will continue to be the primary targets for **cybercriminals**."

Malware takes many different forms, the most common of which are discussed in this chapter. Although the United States was the biggest source of malware activity in 2009 (Figure 9.20), the exploits of those in other countries can have equally devastating consequences. Malware, by its nature, has no boundaries.

Spyware is software that collects your personal information, monitors your Web surfing habits, and distributes this information to a third party, often leading to identity theft. Some spyware, such as **adware**, generates pop-up ads and targeted banner ads, and is usually considered a nuisance rather than malicious. However, **keyloggers**, which can record all the keystrokes you type—such as passwords, account numbers, or conversations—and relay them to others, pose a more dangerous security threat.

Spyware is often distributed when you download free software or infected files. File-sharing sites are notorious for this. However, clicking on a pop-up ad can also install spyware, and visiting an infected Web site can trigger a "drive-by" download.

Most spyware is not designed to disable your computer, but you might find that your computer seems sluggish or crashes more frequently. Other signs of infection include an increase in pop-up ads, unauthorized changes to your home or search pages, and the appearance of new browser toolbars.

Your best defense is to do the following:

- Install and use antispyware software and update it frequently. Many experts recommend using at least two products, because one may catch something the other missed.
- Use a firewall, a program or device that allows users to access the Internet but strictly limits the ability of outside users to access local corporate or personal data.
- Avoiding visiting questionable Web sites.
- Never click on pop-up ads.
- Download software only from reputable sources.

Today Internet Explorer (IE) and Mozilla Firefox include pop-up blocking features. Although some pop-ups may be able to evade the browsers, most are blocked and a yellow information bar will appear at the top of the browser

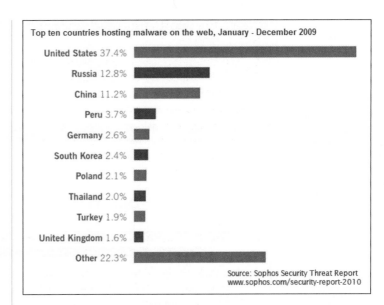

FIGURE 9.20 Sources of malware span the globe.

(Figure 9.21). It's important to read the message on the information bar. It usually gives you options about how to handle the incident it is reporting. Both browsers also offer built-in antiphishing features to help protect you from a list of known phishing sites that is updated regularly. Firefox will display a warning dialog box when you attempt to access a phishing site, and IE uses a color-coded Security Status bar. IE uses the familiar stoplight color code—green indicates a site that is using a new High Assurance identity verification certificate; yellow indicates a site that may be suspicious; and red is used for known phishing sites or sites whose identification does not match their encryption certificate. A white status bar simply means that no identity information is available. However, the lack of a warning color or dialog box does not guarantee that a site is safe. No matter how efficient these built-in browser features are, it is still important to practice safe surfing methods. Most Internet service providers, for an additional monthly fee, include antivirus software that blocks viruses and worms from infecting your computer.

A **computer virus** is hidden code that attaches itself to a program, file, or e-mail message referred to as a host. Viruses that are attached to program files, like an Excel spreadsheet, are called **file infectors** and spread to other programs or files on the user's hard disk when the file is opened. E-mail viruses travel as attachments to an e-mail message and are spread when the attachment is opened. Some viruses are designed as a prank or to sabotage and damage or destroy the infected file. The dangerous actions the virus performs are referred to as its **payload**. A computer

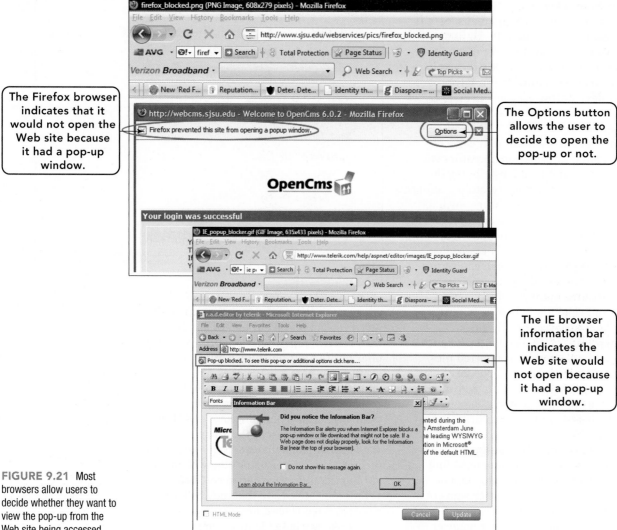

The Firefox browser indicates that it would not open the Web site because it had a pop-up window.

The Options button allows the user to decide to open the pop-up or not.

The IE browser information bar indicates the Web site would not open because it had a pop-up window.

FIGURE 9.21 Most browsers allow users to decide whether they want to view the pop-up from the Web site being accessed.

virus is similar to a human virus in that it requires a host (such as a program, file, or e-mail message) and is designed to duplicate and spread.

The number of viruses sent by e-mail increased by almost 300 percent in July 2009 and was at its highest level of the year, with approximately 12 viruses per customer per hour. The leading sources of these viruses are India (5.2%), Korea (6.2%), Brazil (14.11%), and the United States (16.59%). A virus can be spread on a system by simply opening an infected file or program, but how does a virus spread to another network or system? All a user has to do is simply copy an infected file or program to a USB drive, CD, or DVD and give it to someone. When the storage media with the infected program or file is inserted into the uninfected system, and the infected file is opened, the infection spreads to this system (Figure 9.22).

Many computer viruses are spread by e-mail attachments. When you open an e-mail, you may see a dialog box asking whether you want to open an attachment. Don't open it unless you're sure the attachment is safe.

Consider the following scenario. A professor with a large lecture section of 100 students receives an e-mail from a former student with an attachment named "Spring Break" that apparently contains a picture from the student's spring break. The professor opens the attachment, which appears to do nothing, and the professor moves on to the next e-mail. The attachment, however, is doing something. It is sending a copy of itself to everyone in the professor's e-mail address box—including each of the 100 students in the class. As students open the attachment, the virus will continue to propagate to the addresses in each of their contact lists. The attachment is received by parents, friends, other professors, and fellow students. Many open the attachment, and the process accelerates very rapidly.

Here are a few simple guidelines for not responding to or not opening an attachment to a message that might contains a virus:

- Never open an e-mail from an unknown sender.
- Never open an attachment unless you first pass it through a virus-checking program.
- Never open an attachment with the file extension of .pif.
- Never trust an e-mail with two "RE" entries in the subject line.

Executable file attachments pose the most serious risk. You can tell an executable file by its extension. In Microsoft Windows, the extension is .exe, but executable files also can be named .vbs, .com, .bin, .scr, or .bat. To make protecting yourself just a little more difficult, these files can be hidden within compressed files that have the extension of .zip. However, you can't be sure that a file is executable by its extension alone. You should also be wary of opening Microsoft Office documents, such as Word, Excel, and Access files. These files can contain **macros**, short segments of executable code, programmed by users, and used to automatically perform repeated tasks. Macros are performed, when needed, with a single command or keyboard stroke. A **macro virus**, takes advantage of the automatic execution. When the infected macro is called into use, the virus activates. The data file that contains the macro is contaminated, and the active virus is able to spread to other files. When these files are shared, the virus is spread and infects other systems. By default, macros are disabled in newer versions of Microsoft Office, but users can adjust security settings to enable them. The best policy is to check any attached file with an antivirus program before opening—no matter who sent the attachment.

Although some viruses are best categorized as nuisances or pranks, others can corrupt or erase data or completely disable a computer. All of them consume system memory and slow the computer's processing speed. In the prank category is the Wazzu macro virus, which randomly relocates a word in a Microsoft Word document and sometimes inserts "wazzu" into the text.

A far more serious type of virus is a boot sector virus. A **boot sector virus** also propagates by an infected program, but it installs itself on the beginning tracks of a hard drive where code is stored that

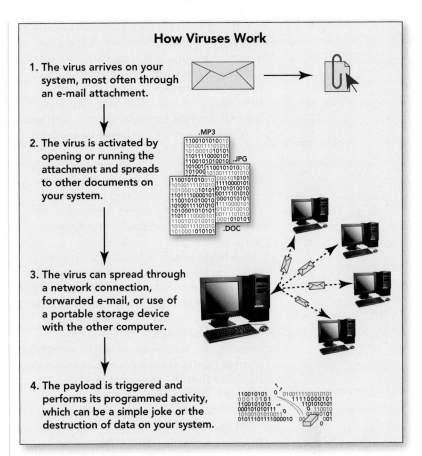

How Viruses Work

1. The virus arrives on your system, most often through an e-mail attachment.

2. The virus is activated by opening or running the attachment and spreads to other documents on your system.

3. The virus can spread through a network connection, forwarded e-mail, or use of a portable storage device with the other computer.

4. The payload is triggered and performs its programmed activity, which can be a simple joke or the destruction of data on your system.

FIGURE 9.22 Once activated, by opening an e-mail or infected file, a computer virus can be passed automatically from one computer to another by network connections or through portable media such as USB drives, CDs, and DVDs.

automatically executes every time you start the computer. Unlike file infectors, boot sector viruses don't require you to start a specific program to infect your computer; starting your system is sufficient. Boot sector viruses can be very malicious; one called Disk Killer will actually wipe out all of the data on a hard drive.

Malware has spread beyond computers. During the 2007 holiday season, many shoppers found that their new digital photo frames came from the factory with a preinstalled virus. Fortunately, it was an old virus and consumers using up-to-date antivirus software were protected. However, other devices, such as GPS units and digital music players, have had similar experiences. Mobile devices are also at risk.

A spam text message that is sent via a cell phone or Instant messaging service is known as **spim**. In March 2008, a spim message was sent to more than 200 million mobile phone users in China during just one day. Luckily, the spim did not include any malicious code, but it's a very real possibility. And contrary to popular belief, Mac and Linux computers are also vulnerable. Although not as prevalent, malware designed for these systems can also infect them, with the same negative results.

Computer virus authors are trying to "improve" their programs. Some new viruses are self-modifying; each new copy, known as a **variant**, is slightly different from the previous one, making it difficult to protect your computer. Sites such as Snopes.com and Vmyths.com can help you determine whether the latest news about a virus is real or a hoax.

Rogue Programs Spyware and viruses aren't the only types of rogue programs. Other destructive programs include time bombs, worms, zombies, Trojan horses, and botnets.

A **logic bomb** is hidden computer code that sits dormant on a system until a certain event or set of circumstances triggers it into action. That action, or payload, is usually malicious and devastating to the individual or company under attack. An example of a trigger could be the removal of an employee from a database, an action implying that the employee has been terminated. Logic bombs do not try to replicate themselves as a virus does and are often associated with the disgruntled employee syndrome. The reason for this association is that in order to set the trigger, an individual has to have access to the system and thus be an employee.

A **time bomb** is a hidden piece of computer code set to go off on some date and time in the future usually causing a malicious act to occur to the system. Time bombs are less sophisticated than logic bombs, because they are not programmed to be activated by a specific trigger. For

example, before leaving a Texas firm, a fired programmer planted a time bomb program that ran two days after he was fired and wiped out 168,000 critical financial records. The only way to prevent permanent loss of data is to perform regular backups on the system.

A **worm** is a program that resembles a computer virus in that it can spread from one computer to another. Unlike a virus, however, a worm can propagate over a computer network and doesn't require an unsuspecting user to execute a program or macro file. It takes control of affected computers and uses their resources to attack other network-connected systems. Some worms, such as Sasser and Slammer, exploit vulnerabilities found in Microsoft Windows and quickly propagate. Newer worms have begun infecting social networking sites such as MySpace and Facebook, retrieving user information and passwords, and directing users to phishing sites. Although patches are usually released quickly, if your computer isn't updated, it remains vulnerable. Even if you don't think your personal information is worth protecting, worms compromise the security of a computer, making it accessible to cybercriminals who can then use it for their own purposes.

Another type of threat is a denial of service attack. With a **denial of service (DoS) attack**, a form of network vandalism, an attacker attempts to make a service unavailable to other users, generally by bombarding the service with meaningless data. Because network administrators can easily block data from specific IP addresses, hackers must commandeer as many computers as possible to launch their attack. When multiple computer systems are involved, it becomes a **distributed denial of service (DDoS) attack**. The commandeered computers form a **botnet** (short for robot network). A **bot** (short for robot), an automated program, connects the individual computers to the controller, usually a server with some type of real time activity like Internet Relay Chat, that is under the power of a botnet controller. These individual computers are called **zombies**, and a group of zombies is called a zombie army. The term is appropriate as the computers do only what the controller tells them to do (Figure 9.23). Criminals also use botnets

FIGURE 9.23 Current botnet attacks are being directed at portable devices like smartphones and GPS units.

1. Bot programs use the Internet to turn ordinary computers into zombies.

2. Bots connect zombies to controllers.

3. Control servers are under the direction of botnet controllers.

4. Commands are sent to the zombies.

5. The zombies execute the commands, and a DDoS attack is launched or mass spam sent.

to send spam, host phishing attacks, and spread viruses and other malware. **Syn flooding** is a form of denial of service attack in which a hostile client repeatedly sends SYN (synchronization) packets to every port on the server, using fake IP addresses, which uses up all the available network connections and locks them up until they time out. This results in a denial of service for legitimate users.

According to a quarterly report from antivirus firm McAfee, botnet criminals took control of almost 12 million new IP addresses between January and May 2009. The number of zombie machines represented a 50 percent increase over 2008, with the largest concentration of botnet-controlled machines in the United States. No one seems safe. In February 2010, the NY Daily News reported that 75,000 computers worldwide, including those of 10 U.S. government agencies, were infected by a virus dubbed the Kneber botnet. The virus, the brainchild of an eastern European group likely selling the information on the black market, compromised 68,000

logins and credentials, several online banking sites, Yahoo, Hotmail, and social networking sites like Facebook.

A **rootkit** is a malicious program that is disguised as a useful program; however, it enables the attacker to gain administrator level access to a computer or network. The primary purpose of a rootkit is to allow an attacker repeated and undetected access to a compromised system. Creating a method to bypass authentication or replacing one or more of the files that run the normal connection processes can help meet this objective. Rootkits often facilitate the creation of a botnet.

A **Trojan horse** is a rogue program disguised as a useful program, but it contains hidden instructions to perform a malicious task instead. Sometimes a Trojan horse is disguised as a game or a utility program that users will find appealing. Then, when users begin running the game, they discover that they have loaded another program entirely. A Trojan horse may erase the data on your hard disk or cause other irreparable damage. More

FAST FORWARD

David versus Goliath—the fight to watch. Four students from New York University's Courant Institute are looking to take on social networking giant Facebook with their software called Diaspora—a distributed, open source social network. The idea is to address the privacy concerns that have recently put Facebook under fire by giving users complete control of their content and who they share it with. How will this be accomplished?

Diaspora will work as a peer-to-peer network in which individual computers will connect with each other instead of a central hub. The software is referred to as the Diaspora "seed" because each computer is considered to be a seed (a node on the Diaspora network) that is owned and hosted by the user. The information posted is stored on the user's computer, and the user can control who is allowed to view the information. Encryption will be used to guarantee the security of information shared over the Diaspora network. If you choose to use Diaspora, the software

will automatically aggregate content from Facebook, Twitter, and Flickr, so you won't miss a single minute of social interaction.

Diaspora founders state that their intention with its development is to avoid storing personal data on a server owned by someone else, which is the way that Facebook and other social networking Web sites operate. Having control of your own data on your own computer allows you to avoid the issues of who accesses or purchases your data and limits possible virus and botnet takeovers. Diaspora seeks to securely share information, pictures, video, and more by making each computer a personal Web server with the Diaspora seed software. Contributions to this venture currently exceed $100,000, allowing the four students to work through the summer of 2010. Their goal is to release the software by the end of the year. Go to **www.joindiaspora.com/project.html** for more information and to view a video introducing the founders.

frequently, Trojan horses are used to install malware or to open a port for easy access by hackers. The Storm Trojan, which is frequently delivered via holiday-themed or weather-related e-mails, has more than 50,000 variants and has infected millions of computers. These infected computers then send out more Storm-infected spam in an endless cycle. At one point, it was responsible for one in every six e-mails that were sent.

Fraud, Theft, and Piracy When computer intruders make off with sensitive personal information, the potential for fraud multiplies. For example, the Hannaford supermarket chain experienced a data breach that exposed credit and debit card numbers for more than 4 million customers, resulting in more than 2,000 cases of fraud.

Physical theft of computer equipment is a growing problem as well (Figure 9.24). An estimated 85 percent of computer thefts are inside jobs, leaving no signs of forced physical entry. In addition, it's difficult to trace components after they've been taken out of a computer and reassembled. Particularly valuable are the microprocessor chips that drive computers. **Memory shaving**, in which knowledgeable thieves remove some of a computer's RAM chips but leave enough to start the computer, is harder to detect. Such a crime might go unnoticed for weeks.

Software piracy is the unauthorized copying or distribution of copyrighted software. This can be done by copying, downloading, sharing, selling, or installing

FIGURE 9.24 To prevent theft, users should lock their doors and turn off their computers. In some cases, it may be wise to secure hardware to desks.

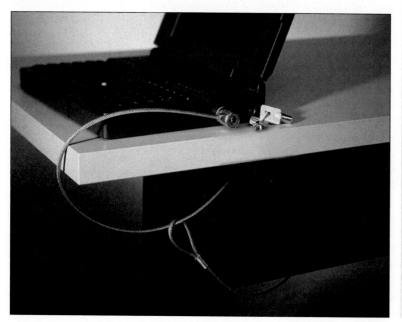

multiple copies onto personal or work computers. What a lot of people don't realize—or don't think about—is that when you purchase software, you are actually purchasing a license to use it, not the actual software. That license is what tells you how many times you can install the software, so be sure you read it. If you make more copies of the software than the license permits, you are pirating software.

Piracy can be intentional or unintentional. Regardless of intention, the Business Software Alliance (BSA), an antipiracy industry group, and the International Data Corporation (IDC), a market research firm, stated that the worldwide piracy rate rose in 2009 by 2 percent over 2008 figures. That means that for every $100 of legitimate software that was sold, $75 of unlicensed software made its way into the market. In dollars, that means that software theft exceeded $51 billion in commercial value in 2009.

Software piracy affects much more than just the global software industry. In the same 2009 study, the IDC predicted that reducing PC software piracy by 10 percent over four years would create as many as 500,000 additional jobs worldwide resulting in the infusion of $140 billion into ailing economies.

Software piracy also increases the risk of cybercrime and security problems. For example, the global spread of the Conficker virus has been attributed in part to the lack of automatic security updates for unlicensed software. An additional side effect of software piracy is that it *lowers tax revenues* at a time of increased fiscal pressures on governments worldwide.

Much software piracy takes place on file-sharing sites like LimeWire or BitTorrent or on online auction sites. It's difficult, but not impossible, to trace the actions of individuals. And when software pirates are found, it is becoming more likely that they will be prosecuted. In fact, the first criminal lawsuit against a member of a piracy group has resulted in a guilty verdict in federal court. Barry Gitarts hosted and maintained a server for the Apocalypse Production Crew that traded hundreds of thousands of pirated copies of movies, music, games, and software. He is facing up to five years in prison for conspiracy to commit criminal copyright infringement, a $250,000 fine, and three years of supervised release—and he must make full restitution. Gitarts may be the first person to go to jail for illegally uploading files to the Internet.

New legislation is being debated that would make piracy penalties even tougher. If passed, the Prioritizing Resources and Organization for Intellectual Property (Pro-IP) Act will strengthen civil and criminal penalties for copyright and trademark infringement, substantially increasing fines and allowing officials to confiscate equipment. What about sharing programs without money changing hands? That's illegal too—and subject to similar penalties: Under the No Electronic Theft (NET) Act, profit does not have to be a motive in cases of criminal copyright infringement.

Cybergaming Crime A large portion of the population today plays some sort of computer-based game. Some choose *Tetris,* others choose *Counter Strike,* and many choose the more virtual and global world of MMORPGs (Massive Multiplayer Online Role Playing Games). In these global battlefields, players can meet other players, become friends, engage in battle, fight shoulder to shoulder against evil, find their virtual destiny—and play, play, play. However, for as much as online virtual gaming is a method of entertainment, virtual evil can become greedy reality. Online games are played by real people,

including thieves and con artists who make real money by stealing other people's "virtual" property. The stolen items are put up for auction (on sites such as ebay.com and other forums), and can be sold to others for virtual or real money. Cybergaming criminals have been known to demand a ransom for the stolen items. Malicious game users can really rake in the money.

FIGURE 9.25 Techniques Used to Obtain Passwords

Password Guessing	Computer users too often choose a password that is easily guessed, such as "password." Other popular passwords are "qwerty" (the first six letters of the keyboard), obscene words, personal names, birthdays, celebrity names, movie characters such as Frodo or Gandalf, and cartoon characters such as Garfield.
Shoulder Surfing	In a crowded computer lab, it's easy to peek over someone's shoulder, look at the keyboard, and obtain his or her password. Watch out for shoulder surfing when using an ATM machine too.
Packet Sniffing	A program called a packet sniffer examines all of the traffic on a section of a network and looks for passwords, credit card numbers, and other valuable information.
Dumpster Diving	Intruders go through an organization's trash hoping to find documents that contain lists of user IDs and even passwords. It's wise to use a shredder!
Social Engineering	This is a form of deception to get people to divulge sensitive information. You might get a call or an e-mail from a person who claims, "We have a problem and need your password right now to save your e-mail." If you comply, you might give an intruder entry to a secure system.
Superuser Status	This enables system administrators to access and modify virtually any file on a network. If intruders gain superuser status, perhaps by using a rootkit, they would then have access to the passwords of everyone using the system.

Tricks for Obtaining Passwords The most publicized computer crimes involve unauthorized access, in which an intruder gains entry to a supposedly secure computer system. Typically, computer systems use some type of authentication technique—usually plaintext passwords—to protect the system from uninvited guests. Many techniques are used to guess or obtain a password (Figure 9.25). Another widely used technique involves exploiting well-known holes in obsolete e-mail programs, which can be manipulated to disclose a user's password.

Salami Shaving and Data Diddling
With **salami shaving**, a programmer alters a program to subtract a very small amount of money from an account—say, two cents—and diverts the funds to the embezzler's account. Ideally, the sum is so small that it's never noticed. In a business that handles thousands of accounts, an insider could skim tens of thousands of dollars per year using this method.

With **data diddling**, insiders modify data by altering accounts or database records so that it's difficult or impossible to tell that they've stolen funds or equipment. A Colorado supermarket chain recently discovered it was the victim of data diddling when it found nearly $2 million in unaccounted losses.

Forgery Knowledgeable users can make Internet data appear to come from one place when it's really coming from another. This action is referred to as **forgery**; third-party remailer sites and programs remove the sender's tracking data from a message and then resend the message.

Forged messages and Web pages can cause embarrassment and worse. A university professor in Texas was attacked with thousands of e-mail messages and Usenet postings after someone forged a racist Usenet article in his name. In Beijing, a student almost lost an $18,000 scholarship when a jealous rival forged an e-mail message to the University of Michigan turning down the scholarship. Fortunately, the forgery was discovered and the scholarship was reinstated, but only after a lengthy delay.

Internet Scams Internet auction sites such as eBay attract online versions of the same scams long perpetrated at live auctions. A **shill** is a secret operative who bids on another seller's item to drive up the price. In a recent case, an online jewelry store was charged with illegally bidding on its own merchandise. The store allegedly

FIGURE 9.26   Internet Scams

Scam	Definition	Example
Rip and tear	The action of accepting payment for goods that you have no intention of delivering.	A Seattle man posted ads for Barbie dolls and other goods on eBay, collected more than $32,000 in orders, and never delivered any goods. The swindlers moved to a new state once their activities were uncovered. The perpetrators believed that law enforcement wouldn't be concerned with the relatively small amounts involved in each transaction.
Pumping and dumping	The use of Internet stock trading sites, chat rooms, and e-mail to sing false praises of worthless companies in which an individual holds stock. Once the false hype drives up the share prices, that individual dumps the stocks and makes a hefty profit.	In 2001, Enron participated in an elaborate pump-and-dump scheme by falsely reporting profits and inflating their stock price, then covering the real numbers with questionable accounting practices. More than $1 billion was sold in overvalued stocks.
Bogus goods	The deliberate selling of goods that do not perform the advertised function.	Two Miami residents were indicted on charges of mail and wire fraud after selling hundreds of "Go-boxes," which reportedly turned red traffic lights to green. The boxes, which were actually nothing more than strobe lights, sold for between $69 and $150.

made more than 200,000 bids totaling more than $5 million and drove up auction prices by as much as 20 percent. In a settlement with the New York attorney general's office, the jeweler has agreed to pay $400,000 in restitution and is banned from online auctions for four years. For other types of cons that use the Internet to advertise or hype their scam, refer to Figure 9.26.

Meet the Attackers

A surprising variety of people can cause security problems, ranging from pranksters to hardened criminals. Motives vary too. Some attackers are out for ego gratification and don't intend any harm. Others are out for money or are on a misguided crusade; some are just plain malicious.

Hackers, Crackers, Cybergangs, and Virus Authors   To the general public, a hacker is a criminal who illegally accesses computer systems. Within the computing community, several terms are used to describe various types of hacking. However, it is important to note that accessing someone's computer without authorization is illegal, no matter what the motivation might be. The most celebrated intruders are computer hobbyists and computer experts for whom unauthorized access is something of an irresistible intellectual game. **Hackers** are computer hobbyists who enjoy pushing computer systems (and themselves) to their limits. They experiment with programs to try to discover capabilities that aren't mentioned in the software manuals. They modify systems to obtain the maximum possible performance. And sometimes they try to track down all of the weaknesses and loopholes in a system's security with the goal of improving security and closing the gaps. When hackers attempt unauthorized access, they rarely damage data or steal assets. Hackers generally subscribe to an unwritten code of conduct, called the **hacker ethic**, which forbids the destruction of data. **Cybergangs** are groups of hackers or crackers working together to coordinate attacks, post online graffiti, or engage in other malicious conduct. **IP spoofing**, one activity usually associated with hackers, is done by sending a message with an IP address disguised as an incoming message from a trusted source to a computer. The hacker must first locate and modify the message packet headers of a trusted source (called a port) and then manipulate the hacker's own communication so that it appears to come from the trusted port. IP spoofing deceives the message recipient into believing that the sender is a trusted source, and lures that person into responding to a false Web site.

Hacking goes beyond public sites. A few years ago, a 23-year-old hacker known as "RaFa" downloaded about 43 MB of data from a top-security NASA server, including a 15-slide PowerPoint presentation of a future shuttle design. He then sent the plans to a *Computerworld* reporter as proof that the NASA system was not secure. Although NASA didn't experience any direct financial loss from RaFa's activities, many companies do lose money because of hacker attacks—as much as $1 million can be lost from a single security incident.

However, a lot more is at stake than just money. What if terrorists or foreign agents could hack the U.S. government's computers and read, change, or steal sensitive documents? What if hackers could disrupt the networks that support vital national infrastructures such as finance, energy, and transportation? Recognizing the danger, the federal government, through The United States Computer Emergency Readiness Team (US-CERT), has emergency-response teams ready to fend off attacks on critical systems. Internationally, a group of security specialists is using **honeypots**—computers baited with fake data and purposely left vulnerable—to study how intruders operate in order to prepare stronger defenses (Figure 9.27).

Crackers (also called **black hats**) are hackers who become obsessed (often uncontrollably) with gaining entry to highly secure computer systems. Their intent, however, is to destroy data, steal information, or perform other malicious acts. The frequency and sophistication of their attacks can cause major headaches for system administrators. Many U.S. government sites are constant targets for crackers and hackers, but they are usually able to divert them. However, in June 2007, Chinese crackers were able to breach an unclassified e-mail system in the Department of Defense, affecting more than 1,500 users and shutting down the network for more than a week. An attack on the Epilepsy Foundation's forums caused actual headaches, and much worse, for their viewers. Crackers posted hundreds of pictures and links to flashing animations that caused severe migraines and seizures in some visitors.

Like hackers, crackers are often obsessed with their reputations in the hacking and cracking communities. To document their feats, they often leave calling cards, such as a prank message, on the systems they penetrate. Sometimes these traces enable law enforcement personnel to track them down.

Keep in mind that anyone who tries to gain unauthorized access to a computer system is probably breaking one or more laws. However, more than a few hackers and crackers have turned pro, offering their services to companies hoping to use hacker expertise to shore up their computer systems' defenses. Those who undertake this type of hacking are called **ethical hackers**, or **white hats**.

Computer virus authors create viruses and other types of malware to vandalize computer systems. Originally, authors were usually teenage boys, interested in pushing the boundaries of antivirus software and seeking to prove their authoring skills over those of their competitors. These days, virus authoring has become big business, and many authors are involved with organized crime. If caught and convicted, virus authors face prison and heavy fines. David L. Smith, the 33-year-old programmer who created the Melissa virus, was sentenced to 20 months in jail and a $5,000 fine in 2002, and in 2004 a 19-year-old female cracker known as Gigabyte faced up to three years in jail and almost $200,000 in fines. More recently, Li Jun, the 25-year-old creator of the Fujacks, or Panda, worm, was sentenced by a Chinese court to four years in prison. Hackers and other cyber-criminals can no longer be stereotyped—

FIGURE 9.27 US-CERT provides defense support against cyberattacks and disseminates cybersecurity information to the public.

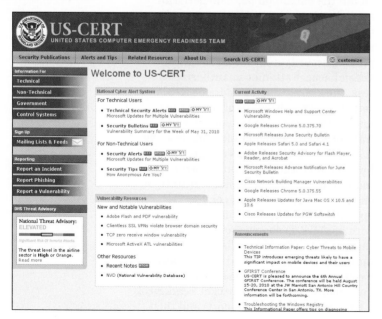

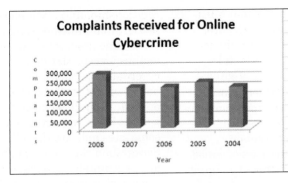

their members include all ages, both sexes, and many nationalities. With a 26.8 percent increase in infected computers around the world, and based on a total of 327,598,028 hacking attempts in the first quarter of 2010, knowing all you can about the current infections and how to prevent them seems essential. For more information on hackers, crackers, current threats, types of vulnerabilities that provide access, and what motivates these individuals, check out Kaspersky Lab's Securelist site at **www.securelist. com/en/**.

Swindlers **Swindlers** typically perpetuate bogus work-at-home opportunities, illegal pyramid schemes, chain letters, risky business opportunities, bogus franchises, phony goods that won't be delivered, overpriced scholarship searches, and get-rich-quick scams. Today, the distribution media of choice include e-mail, Internet chat rooms, and Web sites.

Estimates of the scope of the problem vary, especially because many cases of fraud are never reported. According to the 2008 Internet Crime Report, consumers reported losses of more than $265 million on a variety of Internet scams, that is 25 million more than in 2007 —and the figure is growing by leaps and bounds (Figure 9.28).

Cyberstalkers, Sexual Predators, and Cyberbullying One of the newest and fastest growing of all crimes is **cyberstalking**, or using the Internet, social networking sites, e-mail, or other electronic communications to repeatedly harass or threaten a person. Cyberstalking, like real-world stalking, is a repeated, unwanted, and disruptive break into the life-world of the victim.

For example, one San Diego university student terrorized five female classmates for more than a year, sending them hundreds of violent and threatening e-mail messages. In another situation, Kathy Sierra was a well-known technology blogger and author who began receiving offensive comments on her blog, Creating Passionate Users. These comments included disturbingly edited images of Sierra and violent, sexual threats that finally escalated to death threats from several sources. The posts also appeared on other blogs. Because of their seriousness, Sierra cancelled plans to make a presentation at a technology conference, claiming she feared for her life, and she eventually suspended her blog. Although several people were linked to the comments, no one was ever prosecuted.

Cyberstalking has one thing in common with traditional stalking: Most perpetrators are men, and most victims are women, particularly women in college. One in every 12 women and one in every 45 men will be stalked, including being watched, phoned, written, or e-mailed in obsessive and frightening ways, during their lifetime.

Concerns about online sexual predators and the risk they pose to children have continued to grow. The Crimes Against Children Research Center (CCRC) reports:

- Approximately 14 percent of 10- to 17-year-olds received some sort of sexual solicitation over the Internet.
- Just over one-third have been exposed to unwanted visually explicit sexual material.

FIGURE 9.28
Complaints concerning online crime in 2008 increased by 33.1 percent over 2007.

- Four percent received a sexual solicitation in which they were asked to meet an individual or where the individual called them on the telephone or sent them money or gifts.
- Of the youth who encountered unwanted sexual material, approximately 1 out of 4 told a parent or guardian, and 4 out of 10 told a parent or guardian if the encounter was defined as distressing or made them feel upset or afraid.

Some online predators may pose as children, but the CCRC reports that many predators admit that they are older and manipulate their victims by appealing to them in other ways. They attempt to develop friendships and often flatter or seduce their victims. Although there have been situations that have ended in kidnapping or murder, violence has occurred in only 5 percent of reported cases. In the majority of cases, the victims have gone with the predator willingly, expected to have a sexual relationship, and often met with the predator on multiple occasions.

Online predators also look for new victims on cyberdating sites. Most cyberdating sites use profiling to match potential mates. The downside is that it is difficult to check someone's cyberidentity against his or her actual identity. Although some sites indicate that they perform background checks, it's doubtful that they are as comprehensive as necessary. Most are based on user-provided information—usually a credit card and birth date. An effective background check would require more detailed information, such as a Social Security number, home address, and possibly fingerprints. And this information would apply only to paying customers—it would not apply to free social networking sites (Figure 9.29).

Cyberbullying involves situations in which one or more individuals harass or threaten another individual less capable of defending himself or herself, using the Internet or other forms of digital technology. Cyberbullying can include sending threatening e-mail or text messages or assuming someone else's online identity for the purpose of humiliating or misrepresenting him or her. In a weird twist of fate, the woman who created a fake MySpace profile of a 16-year-old boy to start an Internet relationship with Megan Meier, the Missouri teen who hung herself after receiving hurtful messages, is now believed to be the victim of a cyberbullying impersonator herself. The online harassment laws that were passed after Meier's death last year now may be used to help the middle-aged woman, who many believe was responsible for the 13-year-old girl's suicide. This isn't an isolated example. The Cyberbullying Research Center noted that 20 percent of the students they surveyed experienced cyberbullying in their lifetime (Figure 9.30).

Preventing cyberbullying can be just as difficult as preventing real-time bullying. In cases that involve school-age children, both the parents and schools need to make students aware of the dangers and provide them with the knowledge and confidence they need to stand up to bullies.

Now that you understand the types of perpetrators who pose a risk to your online privacy and safety, let's look more closely at the growing risks to equipment and data security.

FIGURE 9.29 To protect site users from unscrupulous predators, True.com conducts criminal and marital status checks on its communicating members and requires all site users to agree to a member code of ethics.

Safer Dating

Safer Dating Guidelines

At TRUE, we work to provide a safer dating environment for singles.

Email TRUE about this information

WE SCREEN FOR FELONS.

TRUE is committed to safer dating. We can't guarantee that felons, sex offenders and married people won't get on our site, but we can guarantee that they'll be sorry they did.

WE'RE SERIOUS ABOUT YOUR DATING SAFETY
TRUE SCREENS MEMBERS AGAINST A U.S. CRIMINAL DATABASE BEFORE THEY ARE ALLOWED TO COMMUNICATE WITH OTHER MEMBERS.

Before a member is allowed to communicate with other TRUE members, we screen for U.S. felony and sexual offense convictions — using one of the largest criminal records databases on the Internet. Anyone with a felony or sexual offense conviction recorded in these databases is prevented from communicating with TRUE members. Review the current list of covered jurisdictions.

We require that members provide their legal first and last name, as well as their date of birth (they must also certify that the information they provide is correct). We also resubmit a member for screening if he or she attempts to communicate with another member and it has been more than 90 days since the last screening.

We turn away tens of thousands of felons, sex offenders and marrieds who, despite our warnings, try to communicate with our TRUE members. At TRUE, we take our members' safety seriously. We don't want felons , sex offenders or marrieds on our website, period.

Remember, though: No system of dating is totally safe, including our online relationship site; YOU HAVE THE FINAL RESPONSIBILITY FOR YOUR OWN SAFETY!

Criminal background screenings are not foolproof:

- They may give members a false sense of security.
- They are not a perfect safety solution.
- Criminals may circumvent even the most sophisticated search technology.
- Not all criminal records are public in all states and not all databases are up to date.
- Only publicly available convictions are included in the screening.
- The screenings do not cover other types of convictions or arrests or any convictions from foreign countries.

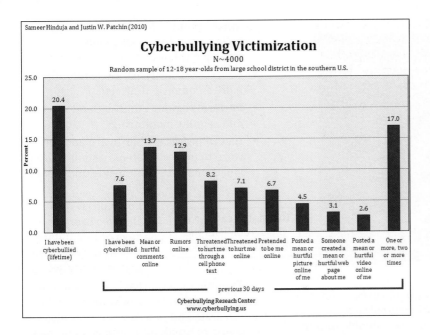

Sameer Hinduja and Justin W. Patchin (2010)

Cyberbullying Victimization
N~4000
Random sample of 12-18 year-olds from large school district in the southern U.S.

Cyberbullying Research Center
www.cyberbullying.us

FIGURE 9.30 This survey used a random sample of approximately 4,000 youth between the ages of 12 and 18 from a district in the southern United States. Data was collected in February of 2010 from 41 different schools.

Security

As our entire economy and infrastructure move to networked computer systems, breaches of computer security can be costly. Even when no actual harm has occurred, fixing the breach and checking to ensure that no damage has occurred require time, resources, and money. It's no wonder that security currently accounts for an estimated 10 to 20 percent of all corporate expenditures on computer systems.

Security Risks

Not all of the dangers posed to computer systems are caused by malicious, conscious intent. A **computer security risk** is any event, action, or situation—intentional or not—that could lead to the loss or destruction of computer systems or the data they contain. Some research indicates that security breaches may cost individuals and industry billions of dollars per year because of their impact on customer service, worker productivity, and so on.

Wireless Networks Wireless LANs pose challenges to security, especially hotspots that are designed for open access. Unlike wired networks, which send traffic over private dedicated lines, wireless LANs send their traffic across shared space—airwaves. Because no one owns the space that airwaves travel across, the opportunity for interference from other traffic is great, and the need for additional security is paramount.

To break into a wireless network, you must be within the proximity limits of the wireless signal. In a process called **wardriving**, an individual drives around with a wireless device, such as a notebook computer or smartphone, to look for wireless networks. Some people do this as a hobby and map out different wireless networks, whereas hackers look for wireless networks to break into. It is fairly easy to break into an unsecured wireless network and obtain confidential information (Figure 9.31).

Security methods for wireless networks include **WEP (Wired Equivalent Privacy)**, **WPA (WiFi Protected Access)**, and **WPA2**. WEP was the earliest of the three and has several well-known weaknesses, but it may be the only option for some devices or older equipment. WPA was developed to provide a stronger level of security, and WPA2 improves on WPA's abilities. WPA2 provides confidentiality and data integrity and is far superior to WEP because it uses AES (Advanced Encryption Standard) to provide government-grade security. The need for wireless security is great, and more powerful security systems continue to be developed. Wireless network owners should implement the security that is currently available so their systems are at least protected from the casual hacker.

The newest trend in Internet fraud is **vacation hacking**. Travelers are being targeting by cybercriminals who create phony WiFi hot spots, called **evil twins**, whose names make users believe they are legitimately connected to the airport, hotel, or airline. Users believe that they are using a valid WiFi access point; instead, they're signing onto a fraudulent network. The information being entered is not reaching the desired destination, but is being captured by criminals.

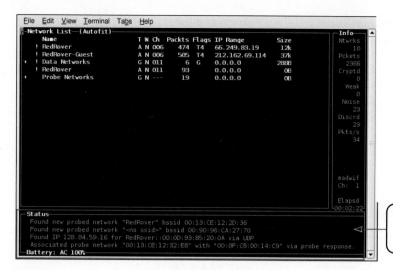

File Edit View Terminal Tabs Help
┌─Network List──(Autofit)──────────────────────────────┐┌─Info──┐
│ Name   T W Ch Packts Flags IP Range   Size ││Ntwrks │
│ ! RedRover   A N 006 474 T4 66.249.83.19   12k   ││   10 │
│ ! RedRover-Guest   A N 006 505 T4 212.162.69.114 37k   ││Pckets │
│+! Data Networks   G N 011   6 G   0.0.0.0   288B ││ 2366 │
│ ! RedRover   A N 011   93   0.0.0.0   0B ││Cryptd │
│+ Probe Networks   G N ---   19   0.0.0.0   0B ││   0 │
│   ││Weak   │
│   ││   0 │
│   ││Noise │
│   ││   23 │
│   ││Discrd │
│   ││   23 │
│   ││Pkts/s │
│   ││   34 │
│   ││   │
│   ││   │
│   ││madwif │
│   ││Ch: 6 │
│   ││   │
│   ││Elapsd │
│   ││00:02:22│
├─Status───┤└───────┘
│ Found new probed network "RedRover" bssid 00:13:CE:12:2D:36   │
│ Found new probed network "<no ssid>" bssid 00:90:96:CA:27:70   │
│ Found IP 128.84.59.16 for RedRover::00:6D:93:85:20:0A via UDP   │
│ Associated probe network "00:13:CE:12:32:E8" with "00:0F:C8:00:14:C9" via probe response. │
├─Battery: AC 100%─────────────────────────────────────┘

The status section of the screen lists the detected networks.

FIGURE 9.31 Wireless network detectors, sniffers, and intrusion detection systems like Kismet will work with any wireless card.

- Make employees aware of security policies and the consequences of violating them.
- Reassess security policies annually or more frequently if needed.
- Perform regular auditing, and random and regular monitoring.
- Install necessary hardware and software to protect systems and data from violations both from inside and outside sources.
- Force password changes every five days or less if data within the organization is highly secure.

Corporate Espionage Corporate computer systems contain a great deal of information that could be valuable to competitors, including product development plans and specifications, customer contact lists, manufacturing process knowledge, cost data, and strategic plans. According to computer security experts, **corporate espionage**, the unauthorized access of corporate information, usually to the benefit of a competitor, is on the rise—so sharply that it may soon eclipse all other sources of unauthorized access. The perpetrators are often ex-employees who have been hired by a competing firm precisely because of their knowledge of the computer system at their previous place of employment.

According to one estimate, 80 percent of all data loss is caused by company insiders. Unlike intruders, employees have many opportunities to sabotage a company's computer system, often in ways that are difficult to trace. Although incoming e-mail is routinely scanned for threats, outgoing mail is often overlooked, allowing employees to easily transfer data. Similarly, employees can use USB drives, iPods, or other removable storage media to create an unauthorized copy of confidential data, an activity known as **pod slurping**. They may discover or deliberately create security holes called **trap doors** that they can exploit after leaving the firm. They can then divulge the former employer's trade secrets to a competitor or destroy crucial data.

Companies can take a variety of steps to hinder corporate espionage:

- Identify and label sensitive information.
- Protect against data deletion and loss by write- and password-protecting documents and by creating regular backups.

The espionage threat goes beyond national borders. Nations bent on acquiring trade secrets and new technologies also are trying to break into corporate, municipal, state, and federal computer systems. According to a recent estimate, the governments of more than 125 countries are actively involved in industrial espionage. Several notable cases include these:

- A disgruntled former employee gained unauthorized access to the voice mail system of Standard Duplicating Machines Corporation (SDMC). The individual in question was found guilty of criminal charges in 1997 and received two years of probation. Through a civil suit, SDMC was awarded $1 million.
- In the mid-1990s a retired Eastman Kodak employee attempted to sell data extracted from confidential documents he had access to while employed. Those approached to buy this information notified the FBI, and the retired employee went to jail for 15 months and paid a $30,000 fine. Kodak additionally sued him in civil court.
- In June of 1997, two naturalized U.S. citizens, on behalf of their employer, the Yuen Foong Paper Manufacturing Co. of Taiwan, attempted to steal the formula for the cancer drug Taxol patented by Bristol-Myers Squibb (BMS). In July of 1997, both were indicted on 11 counts, including the theft of trade secrets.

Congress has attempted to help companies protect themselves with the Economic Espionage Act of 1996. The Act permits legal action regarding "financial, business, scientific, engineering, technical and economic information," if a company can demonstrate it has attempted to keep this information classified and protected. But many companies don't take advantage of the Act except as a last resort. They feel that news of the theft may damage the company's reputation. To view a segment of an award-winning video on industrial espionage titled "The Red Balloon" go to **www.tscmvideo.com/**.

Information Warfare The use of information technologies to corrupt or destroy an enemy's information and industrial infrastructure is called **information warfare**. A concerted enemy attack would include electronic warfare (using electronic devices to destroy or damage computer systems), network warfare (hacker-like attacks on a nation's network infrastructure, including the electronic banking system), and structural sabotage (attacks on computer systems that support transportation, finance, energy, and telecommunications). However, we shouldn't overlook old-fashioned explosives directed at computer centers. According to one expert, a well-coordinated bombing of only 100 key computer installations could bring the U.S. economy to a grinding halt.

According to experts, defenses against such attacks are sorely lacking. In April 2009, the Pentagon issued a statement placing the cost of cyberdefense over a period of six months at $100 million. This figure included the cost of cleanup after several attacks and fixing internal errors. Those advocating an increase in this portion of the budget argue that the emphasis should be on positioning defenses before an attack rather than repairing the system after an attack. A program named "Perfect Citizen" is being launched by the federal government to detect cyberattacks on private and government agencies. The focus of this program will be agencies that control the electrical grid and nuclear power plants that control the country's infrastructure.

A lesson on the damage that a cyberattack can create was made apparent by cyberattacks targeting Estonia in the spring of 2007. Estonia is a small country, but it is on the leading edge of technology, with most of its population relying on the Internet for news, communication, and

> " In April 2009, the **Pentagon** issued a statement placing the cost of **cyberdefense** over a period of six months at $100 million. "

finance. When a Soviet-era war monument was relocated, against the wishes of the Russian government, several days of civil unrest ensued. Once the rioting ended, the cyberattacks began. Estonian sites, including government agencies, ISPs, financial networks, and media outlets, suffered massive DoS attacks originating from botnets controlling nearly 1 million computers. Incoming Internet traffic, primarily from Russia but also from other countries, rose to thousands of times above normal, disrupting commerce and communications for several weeks. Although allegations were made against the Russian government, nothing was ever proven. Many believe the attacks were conducted by activist hackers rather than by a specific government agency. Many also fear that the attack against Estonia was just a test—a way of demonstrating the power of those who control the botnets and a warning to other countries.

In January 2010, Google announced it will no longer censor search results in China. The Chinese government threatened to block the Web site if Google continued to censor the search results. What provoked this action? In mid-December 2009, Google discovered it had a security breach. Quickly it was determined that the hack involved more than just a few workstations. As the investigation progressed, investigators discovered that at least 20 other large companies from a wide range of businesses, including the Internet, finance, technology, media, and chemical sectors, had been similarly targeted. The source of the attack was China. Due to the targeted companies, the fact that the attack focused on Gmail accounts of Chinese human rights activists, and the central location of the source, Google and others believe that the attack was sponsored by Beijing. Google investigated the incident thoroughly for three weeks before coming to its decision to no longer censor search results in China. The U.S. Secretary of State has asked the Chinese government to explain itself.

The U.S. Department of Homeland Security (DHS) reports that in 2007 there was an 81 percent increase in hacking attacks on banks. The U.S. Computer Emergency Readiness Team (US-CERT) is a national cyberwatch and warning center that coordinates activities with the private sector and handled more than 37,000 incidents in 2007. It also oversees EINSTEIN, an early-warning system that looks for malicious or irregular activity on the Internet. Once every two years, the DHS and US-CERT coordinate a national simulation known as Cyber Storm to assess the ability of the United States to identify and respond to a critical cyberattack. Cyber Storm II, held in March 2008, involved 18 government agencies, 5 countries, 9 states, 40 companies, and 10 information-sharing and analysis centers. The exercise simulated an attack on telecommunication centers, the Internet, and control systems. Preliminary results emphasize the need for improved communications between the public and the private sectors before, during, and after an attack (Figure 9.32).

Even if no enemy nation mounts an all-out information war on the United States, information terrorism is increasingly likely. Thanks to the worldwide distribution of powerful but inexpensive microprocessors, virtually anyone can construct electronic warfare weapons from widely available materials. These weapons include high-energy radio frequency (HERF) guns and electromagnetic pulse transformer (EMPT) bombs, which can damage or destroy computer systems up to a quarter mile away.

If this scenario sounds frightening, remember that information technology is a double-edged sword. Information technology gives despots a potent weapon of war, but it also undermines their power by giving citizens a way to organize democratic resistance. In Russia, for example, e-mail and fax machines played a major role in the failure of the 1989 military coup. In the United States, we have learned more about the importance of redundant data backup systems and the resiliency of the U.S. monetary system since the September 11 attacks, but we're still vulnerable and must develop ways to protect our computer systems and infrastructure.

Security Loophole Detection Programs

Intruders can use a variety of programs that automatically search for unprotected or poorly protected computer systems and notify them when a target is found. Such programs include Nessus, a security loophole detection program used by system administrators. In the wrong hands, the program can help an intruder figure out how to get into a poorly secured system.

Public Safety Perhaps the greatest threat posed by security breaches is the threat to human life; computers are increasingly part of safety-critical systems, such as air-traffic control. By paralyzing transportation and power infrastructures, attackers could completely disrupt the distribution of electricity, food, water, and medical supplies.

This threat nearly became a reality when a 14-year-old hacker knocked out phone and radio service to a regional airport's communications tower. Although the hacker didn't realize he had accessed an airport computer and meant no harm, his actions paralyzed the airport's computer system and forced air-traffic controllers to rely on cellular phones and battery-powered radios to direct airplanes until the system was back up and running.

Terrorism Perhaps the brightest spot in the war on terror is the identification of persons of interest by using special security software programs. One program that attempts to find such people is IBM's Real-Time Collaborative Criminal Investigation and Analysis tool. It quickly analyzes data to discover similarities and links among individuals to determine whether they are connected with unsavory characters. The SOMA Terror Organization Portal (STOP) permits analysts to network with other analysts to pool their knowledge and resources about the behavior of terrorist organizations and to forecast potential terrorist behavior. The downside of these

FIGURE 9.32 Cyber Storm II was the second in a series of congressionally mandated exercises that examined the nation's cybersecurity preparedness and response capabilities.

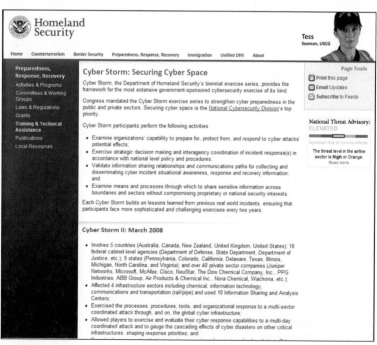

methods is the potential for violating individual privacy rights and mistakenly targeting innocent people.

Protecting Your Computer System

Several measures can safeguard computer systems, but none of them can make a computer system 100 percent secure. A trade-off exists between security and usability: The more restrictions imposed by security tools, the less useful the system becomes.

Power-Related Problems

Power surges, which are often caused by lightning storms or fluctuations in electrical currents, and power outages can destroy sensitive electronic components and carry the threat of data loss. To safeguard your equipment and data, you should always use a surge protector. Additionally, some applications offer an autosave feature that backs up your work at a specified interval (such as every 10 minutes). You can also equip your system with an **uninterruptible power supply (UPS)**, a battery-powered device that provides power to your computer for a limited time when it detects an outage or critical voltage drop (Figure 9.33). Many companies have electric generators to run large-scale computer systems when the power fails.

Controlling Access
Because many security problems originate with purloined passwords, password authentication is crucial to controlling authorized access to computer systems. Typically, users select their own passwords—and that is the source of a serious computer security risk. The use of strong passwords is essential as a first step in preventing an intruder from gaining access to your system and causing problems that appear to have been performed by you.

FIGURE 9.33 A UPS is a battery-powered device that provides power to your computer for a limited time during a power outage.

In addition to password authentication, **know-and-have authentication** requires using tokens, which are handheld electronic devices that generate a logon code. Increasingly popular are smart cards, devices the size of a credit card with their own internal memories. In tandem with a supplied personal identification number (PIN), a smart card can reliably establish that the person trying to gain access has the authorization to do so.

However, when used with digital cash systems, smart cards pose a significant threat to personal privacy. Because every smart card transaction is recorded, regardless of how small a transaction it is, a person's purchases can be assembled and scrutinized. An investigator could put together a list of the magazines and newspapers you purchase and read, where and when you paid bridge tolls and subway fares, and what you had for lunch.

The most secure authentication approach is **biometric authentication**, the use of a physical trait or behavioral characteristic to identify an individual (Figure 9.34). For example, Gateway now offers a built-in biometric fingerprint sensor on its latest notebook that locks access to the computer unless the correct fingerprint is matched. In an experiment in Barcelona, Spain, a soccer club used a database of ticket barcodes matched with

FIGURE 9.34 Biometric authentication devices such as retinal scanners, hand-geometry readers, and fingerprint scanners are often used to provide access to restricted locations.

Retinal scanner **Hand geometry reader** **Fingerprint scanner**

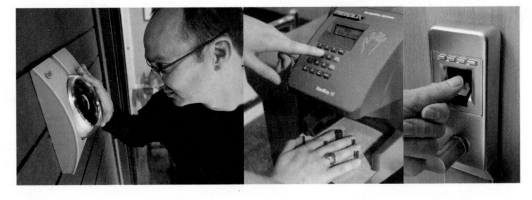

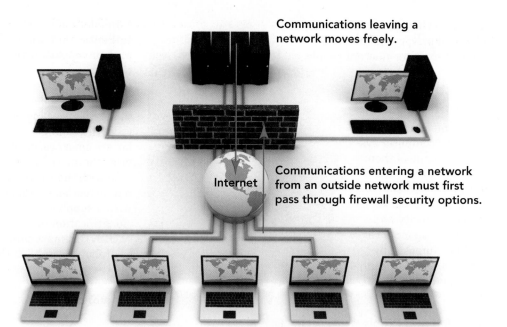

Communications leaving a network moves freely.

Internet

Communications entering a network from an outside network must first pass through firewall security options.

FIGURE 9.35 A firewall permits an organization's internal computer users to access the Internet but limits the ability of outsiders to access internal data.

fans' photographs to verify the tickets of more than 100,000 ticket holders as they entered the stadium. If the ticket holder's face did not match the face in the database, the person was not admitted to the stadium.

Firewalls A **firewall** is a computer program or device that permits an organization's internal computer users to access the external Internet but severely limits the ability of outsiders to access internal data (Figure 9.35). A firewall can be implemented through software, hardware, or a combination of both. Firewalls are a necessity, but they provide no protection against insider pilferage. Home users opting for "always on" broadband connections, such as those offered by cable modems or DSL, face a number of computer security risks. Personal firewalls are programs or devices, like routers, that protect home computers from unauthorized access. For information and additional diagrams on how a firewall works or how to choose a firewall for your system, visit **http:// computer.howstuffworks.com/ firewall.htm** or **www.microsoft.com/ security/firewalls/choosing.aspx**. To find out whether your firewall is configured properly, use the free ShieldsUP! service found at **www.grc.com**.

Protecting Yourself

In addition to protecting your system from intrusion or attack, it has become increasingly important to protect your personal data from theft and yourself from a

cyberattack. Following the old clichés of the real world, such as "User beware"; "Don't talk to strangers"; and "If something sounds too good to be true, it usually is," will keep you out of trouble in the cyberworld.

Avoiding Scams To avoid being scammed on the Internet, follow these tips:

- Do business with established companies that you know and trust.
- Read the fine print. If you're ordering something, make sure it's in stock and that the company promises to deliver within 30 days.
- Don't provide financial or other personal information or passwords to anyone, even if the request sounds legitimate.
- Be skeptical when somebody in an Internet chat room tells you about a great new company or stock.

Preventing Cyberstalking To protect yourself against cyberstalking, follow these tips:

- Don't share any personal information, such as your real name, in chat rooms. Use a name that is gender- and age-neutral. Do not post a user profile.
- Be extremely cautious about meeting anyone you've contacted online. If you do, meet in a public place and bring friends along.
- If a situation you've encountered online makes you uncomfortable or afraid, contact the police immediately. Save all the communications you've received.

Now that you've learned some ways to protect your security, let's discuss one of the major security measures used to keep information safe on the Internet: encryption.

The Encryption Debate

Cryptography is the study of transforming information into an encoded or scrambled format. Individuals who practice in this field are known as **cryptographers**. **Encryption** refers to a coding or scrambling process that renders a message unreadable by anyone except the intended recipient. Until recently, encryption was used only by intelligence services, banks, and the military.

E-commerce requires strong, unbreakable encryption; otherwise, money could not be safely exchanged over the Internet. But now, powerful encryption software is available to the public, and U.S. law enforcement officials and defense agencies aren't happy about it. Criminals, including drug dealers and terrorists, can use encryption to hide their activities. In the aftermath of the September 11 terrorist attacks, U.S. officials revealed that the terrorist network had used encrypted e-mail to keep their plans and activities secret.

Encryption Basics

To understand encryption, try this simple exercise: Consider a short message such as "I love you." Before it is encrypted, a readable message such as this one is in **plaintext**. To encrypt the message, for each character substitute the letter that is 13 positions to the right in the 26-letter alphabet. (When you reach the end of the alphabet, start counting from the beginning.) This is an example of an **encryption key**, a formula that makes a plaintext message unreadable. After applying the key, you get the coded message, which is now in **ciphertext**. The ciphertext version of the original message looks like this:

```
V YBIR LBH
```

It looks like gibberish, doesn't it? That's the idea. No one who intercepts this message will know what it means. Your intended recipient, however, can tell what the message means if you give him or her the decoding key: in this case, counting 13 characters down (Figure 9.36). When your recipient gets the message and decrypts it, your message reappears:

```
I LOVE YOU
```

With **symmetric key encryption**, the same key is used for encryption and decryption. Some of the keys used by banks and military agencies are so complex that the world's most powerful computer would have to analyze the ciphertext for several hundred years to discover the key. However, there is one way to defeat symmetric key encryption: stealing the key, or **key interception**. Banks deliver decryption keys using trusted courier services; the military uses trusted personnel or agents. These methods provide opportunities for key theft.

Public Key Encryption

Public key encryption is considered one of the greatest (and most troubling) scientific achievements of the 20th century. In brief, **public key encryption (asymmetric key encryption)** is a computer security process in which two different keys—an encryption key (the **public key**) and a decryption key (the **private key**)—are used. The use of two different keys safeguards data and thus provides confidentiality. Additionally it allows a digital signature to be decoded or verified only by individuals that a have access to the sender's public key, thereby proving that the sender is authentic and has access to the private key. The way it works is that people who want to receive secret messages publish their public key, for example, by placing it on a Web page or sending it to those with whom they wish to communicate. When the public key is used to encrypt a message, the message becomes unreadable. The message becomes readable only when the recipient applies his or her private key, which nobody else knows, guaranteeing confidentiality (Figure 9.37).

Public key encryption is essential for e-commerce. When you visit a secure site on the Web, for example, your Web browser provides your public key to the Web server; in turn, the Web server provides the site's public key to your Web browser. Once a secure communication channel has been created, your browser displays a distinctive icon, such as a lock in the address bar, or the address bar may turn green. You can now supply confidential information, such as your credit card number, with a

FIGURE 9.36
Decoding Key for "I Love You"

A	1
B	2
C	3
D	4
E	5
F	6
G	7
H	8
I	9
J	10
K	11
L	12
M	13
N	14
O	15
P	16
Q	17
R	18
S	19
T	20
U	21
V	22
W	23
X	24
Y	25
Z	26

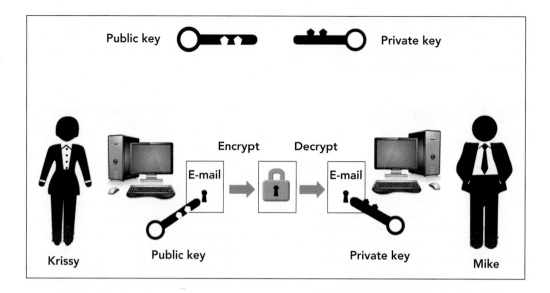

FIGURE 9.37 Krissy uses the public key, provided to her by Mike, to send an encrypted message to Mike. Mike uses his private key to decipher the message. The message would be unreadable to anyone intercepting it.

reasonable degree of confidence that this information will not be intercepted while it is traveling across the Internet.

Digital Signatures and Certificates

Public key encryption can be used to implement **digital signatures**, a technique that guarantees a message has not been tampered with. Digital signatures are important to e-commerce because they enable computers to determine whether a received message or document is authentic and in its original form. A digital signature can be compared to the sealing of an envelope with a personal wax seal. Anyone can open the envelope, but the seal authenticates the sender. So, a digital signature would provide an assurance that an order was authentic and not the result of a hacker who was trying to disrupt a business transaction.

Public key encryption also enables **digital certificates**, a method of validating a user, server, or Web site. For a user, a digital certificate validates identity in a manner similar to showing a driver's license when you cash a check. For example, to protect both merchants and customers from online credit card fraud, Visa, MasterCard, and American Express collaborated to create an online shopping security standard for merchants and customers called **secure electronic transaction (SET)** that uses digital certificates. They enable parties engaged in Internet-mediated transactions to confirm each other's identity. For a server or Web site, a digital certificate validates that the Web server or Web site is authentic, and the user can feel secure that his or her interaction with the Web site has no

eavesdroppers and that the Web site is who it claims to be. This security is important for electronic commerce sites, especially ones that accept credit cards as a form of payment.

Toward a Public Key Infrastructure A **public key infrastructure (PKI)** is a uniform set of encryption standards that specify how public key encryption, digital signatures, and digital certificates should be implemented in computer systems and on the Internet. Although there are numerous contenders, no dominant PKI has emerged.

One reason for the slow development of a PKI involves the fear, shared by many private citizens and businesses alike, that a single, dominant firm will monopolize the PKI and impose unreasonable fees on the public. This was a concern when Microsoft introduced their Windows Live ID system, which implements a Microsoft-developed PKI (Figure 9.38). Originally devised as a single sign-on service for e-commerce sites, consumers and businesses feared it might be used to drive Microsoft's competitors out of business and impose artificially high costs on e-commerce, but Live ID has failed to gain popular acceptance in the marketplace and those fears have proved unfounded. Another concern involving the implementation of a PKI is that governments may step in to regulate public key encryption—or at the extreme, outlaw its use entirely.

Encryption and Public Security Issues

Just one year before the September 11 terrorist attacks on the World Trade Center

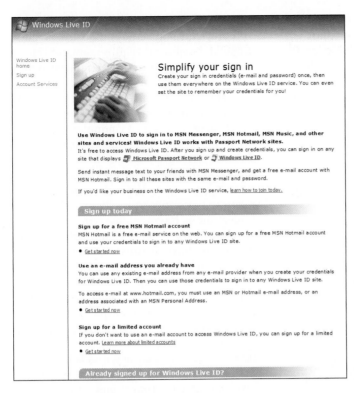

FIGURE 9.38 Windows Live ID, an identity and authentication system that permits a single sign-on for multiple sites, hasn't caught on as anticipated, and initial concerns have diminished.

of four random-number generators, one of which was included at the request of the National Security Agency (NSA). Upon examination, it was discovered that the NSA's random-number generator included a **backdoor**, a method of bypassing normal authentication to secure access to a computer, a vulnerability that could enable someone to crack the code, compromising the security of this encryption tool. Experts are still debating the ramifications of this discovery. In another instance, Sebastian Boucher was arrested on December 17, 2006, at the U.S.–Canada border when his notebook computer was found to contain child pornography. When authorities tried to examine his computer several days later, they found his data was encrypted by PGP and they

and Pentagon, FBI Director Louis Freeh told the U.S. Congress that "the widespread use of robust unbreakable encryption ultimately will devastate our ability to fight crime and prevent terrorism. Unbreakable encryption will allow drug lords, spies, terrorists, and even violent gangs to communicate about their crimes and their conspiracies with impunity." In light of the terrorists' use of public key encryption—specifically, Pretty Good Privacy (PGP)—Freeh's warning now seems prophetic. Soon after the attacks, there were calls in the U.S. Congress to outlaw public key encryption.

However, recognizing that public key encryption is vital to the electronic economy, U.S. law enforcement and security agencies have not recommended that public key encryption be outlawed entirely. Instead, they advise that the U.S. Congress pass laws requiring a public key algorithm or a PKI that would enable investigators to eavesdrop on encrypted communications. U.S. government agencies have proposed some possibilities.

The government's need to know often conflicts with the public's right to privacy. Recently, the government released a new random-number standard, a critical component of encryption methods. It consisted

were unable to access it without the password. The government has tried to force Boucher to reveal the password, but his attorneys successfully argued that this was in violation of his Fifth Amendment rights, which protect him against self-incrimination. On January 22, 2010, Boucher was sentenced to three years in prison and five years of supervised release for the possession of one count of child pornography transported in interstate or foreign commerce. Although Boucher eventually agreed to surrender the password, it was with the stipulation that what was found on the computer could not be used against him for sentencing. Detectives located 2,000 still images and 118 video files depicting sexual assaults on prepubescent children by adults. According to a computer forensics analyst for the Vermont Department of Corrections, the source of the images could not be located, and Boucher's computer had not been used in the production or distribution of the images.

The government doesn't dispute the importance of encrypting data. The theft of a government employee's notebook computer containing the names and Social Security numbers of more than 26.5 million veterans and military personnel resulted in the federal Data at Rest Encryption program, which is mandatory for all military agencies and optional for civilian agencies. The software is available for all notebooks and other portable or handheld devices. It's obvious that there is a fine line between security and privacy, and the debate is far from resolved.

Prosecuting Violators

How is evidence obtained in cases of electronic fraud, cyberstalking, cyberbullying, phishing, or hacking? Likewise, how is data collected electronically in a noncomputer-related crime like hit-and-run or murder? There are two relatively recent areas of study that address these questions: e-discovery and computer forensics.

E-Discovery

E-discovery, an abbreviated term for **electronic discovery**, is the obligation of parties to a lawsuit to exchange documents that exist only in electronic form, including e-mails, voicemails, instant messages, e-calendars, audio files, data on handheld devices, animation, metadata, graphics, photographs, spreadsheets, Web sites, drawings, and other types of digital data. Advances in technology have created an ever-expanding universe of such documents, making e-discovery more expensive, time-consuming, and burdensome than ever before. Consider this: The world sends over 60 billion e-mails daily, and 90 percent of all documents generated today are electronic. A single hard drive can store the equivalent of 40 million pages.

E-discovery is a $2 billion industry, and qualified professionals are in demand. E-discovery professionals use technology to discovery and manage electronic data. The e-discovery professional's knowledge of information technology and legal processes is invaluable to technology-challenged attorneys and clients. E-discovery professionals help identify, collect, process, review, and produce the electronic evidence in court cases.

Computer Forensics

Computer forensics, a complex branch of forensic science, pertains to legal evidence found in computers and digital storage media. It is a field that requires careful preparation and procedural strictness. Because of the scope and technical requirements of this field, there are many subsections such as firewall forensics and mobile device forensics. However, all have the same purposes: to analyze computer systems related to court cases, evaluate a computer after a break in, recover lost data, gather evidence against an employee by an employer, and reverse engineer. Taking the correct actions—in the right order—and recording evidence properly are often as important as having underlying knowledge of the issue being examined. Software developers have fortunately created several forensic tool kits to help in the logical and procedural components of this field (Figure 9.39). These kits spell out proper procedure and contain forms to correctly document every action and event involving a piece of digital evidence, guaranteeing its authenticity, accuracy, and thus its reliability as evidence. This is a current and growing industry that is going to require individuals with organized and logical minds, sharp perception skills, and a strong math and science focus.

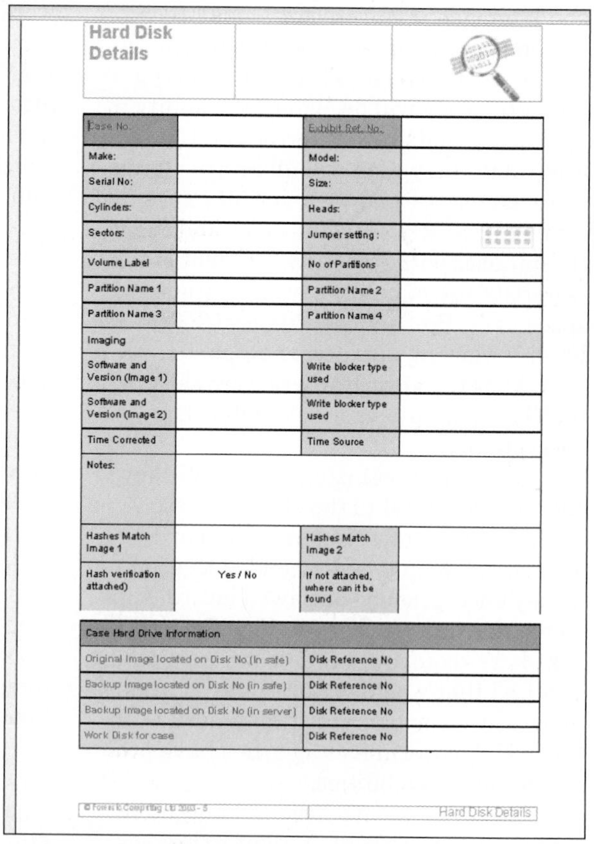
Hard Disk Details

Case No.		Exhibit Ref. No.	
Make:		Model:	
Serial No:		Size:	
Cylinders:		Heads:	
Sectors:		Jumper setting:	
Volume Label		No of Partitions	
Partition Name 1		Partition Name 2	
Partition Name 3		Partition Name 4	
Imaging			
Software and Version (Image 1)		Write blocker type used	
Software and Version (Image 2)		Write blocker type used	
Time Corrected		Time Source	
Notes:			
Hashes Match Image 1		Hashes Match Image 2	
Hash verification attached)	Yes / No	If not attached, where can it be found	

Case Hard Drive Information		
Original Image located on Disk No (In safe)	Disk Reference No	
Backup Image located on Disk No (in safe)	Disk Reference No	
Backup Image located on Disk No (in server)	Disk Reference No	
Work Disk for case	Disk Reference No	

Hard Disk Details

FIGURE 9.39 There are many forms in the Computer Forensics Toolkit designed to record actions and observations made on a digital client. This form helps investigators assess hard disk drives.

Users can set some controls over the general level of security at which their system operates and even list specific Web sites from which to either accept or reject cookies.

To set a general level of security:

1. Open Internet Explorer
2. From the menu, select *Tools* and then click *Internet Options*.
3. In the Internet Options dialog box that is displayed, select the *Privacy* tab.
4. In the settings section of the Privacy screen, move the slider bar, located on the left, to the security level you want. For each level, an explanation will appear to its right (Figure 9.40).
5. Click *Apply* and then click *OK*.

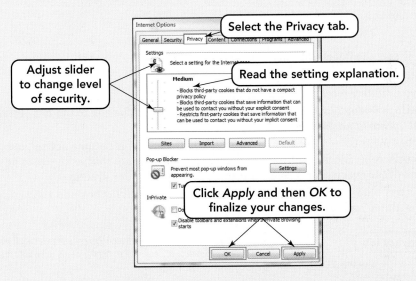

FIGURE 9.40 Security settings are located on the Privacy tab of the Internet Options dialog box.

To specifically list individual Web sites from which to accept or reject cookies:

1. Open Internet Explorer
2. From the menu select *Tools* and then click *Internet Options*.
3. In the Internet Options dialog box that appears, select the *Privacy* tab.
4. In the settings section of the Privacy screen, click the *Sites* button.
5. The Per Site Privacy Actions dialog box will open (Figure 9.41).
6. In this area, you can enter the URL of the Web sites from which you want to block cookies and the URL of the Web sites that you want to allow to leave cookies.
7. Repeat step 6 for each Web site you want to allow or block. Then Click *OK*.
8. The Internet Options dialog will still be on the screen to allow you to readjust the slider for your desired level of security. Click *OK* in the Internet Options dialog box.

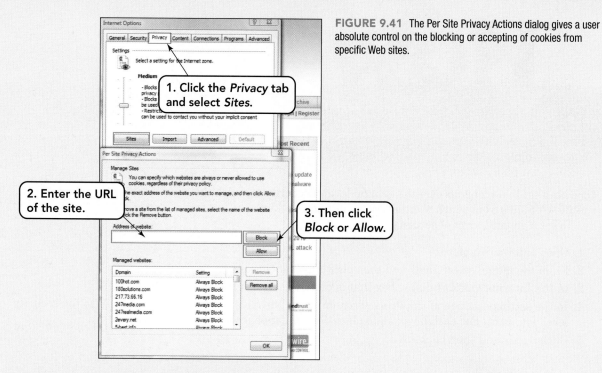

FIGURE 9.41 The Per Site Privacy Actions dialog gives a user absolute control on the blocking or accepting of cookies from specific Web sites.

1. Click the *Privacy* tab and select *Sites*.

2. Enter the URL of the site.

3. Then click *Block* or *Allow*.

To adjust control over first and third party cookies:

1. Open Internet Explorer
2. From the menu select *Tools* and then click *Internet Options*.
3. In the Internet Options dialog box that appears, select the *Privacy* tab.
4. In the settings section of the Privacy screen, click the *Advanced* button.
5. The Advanced Privacy Settings dialog box will appear (Figure 9.42). Check the box to the left of the option: *Override automatic cookie handling*.
6. The columns of options below *First-party Cookies* and *Third-party Cookies* will become active, and you can select the options to Accept, Block, or Prompt. Prompt causes a pop-up that asks you to accept or reject the cookie to appear every time a cookie attempts to write to your system.
7. Once your options are selected, click *OK* in the Advanced Privacy Settings dialog box and then click *OK* in the Internet Options dialog box.

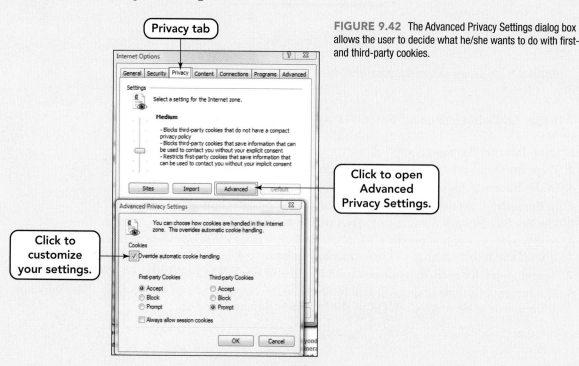

Privacy tab

Click to open Advanced Privacy Settings.

Click to customize your settings.

FIGURE 9.42 The Advanced Privacy Settings dialog box allows the user to decide what he/she wants to do with first- and third-party cookies.

Chapter Summary

Privacy, Crime, and Security

- Sensitive personal information such as Social Security numbers and browsing habits can be collected today without informing the owner. Public agencies have always had the ability to collect this data, but today Web pages and online merchants use computerized databases to track information about individuals while cookies and globally unique identifiers (GUIDs) embedded within hardware components and programs are used to track online browsing and shopping habits.

- Examples of computer crime and cybercrime include identity theft; malware, including spyware and viruses; other rogue programs such as time bombs, logic bombs, worms, botnets, zombies, and Trojan horses; fraud and theft; password theft; salami shaving and data diddling; forgery; blackmail; cyberstalking and cyberbullying; and Internet crimes like shilling, rip and tear, pump and dump, and bogus goods.

- These actions are performed by computer criminals that include hackers, crackers, cybergangs, virus authors, swindlers, shills, cyberstalkers, cyberbullies, and sexual predators.

- A computer security risk is any event, action, or situation—intentional or not—that could lead to the loss or destruction of computer systems or the data they contain.

- No computer system is totally secure, but you can do several things to cut down on security risks.

- Safe surfing guides should always be followed in addition to utilizing some software and hardware deterrents, including an uninterruptible power supply (UPS), strong passwords, know-and-have authentication, biometric authentication, encryption of sensitive data, and an installed firewall.

- Encryption, essential for e-commerce and online banking, makes use of encryption keys to encode and decode information traveling over a network. This process guarantees that a message is unreadable by anyone except the intended recipient, who possesses the key to decode the encoded message.

- The U.S. government continues to look for ways to balance the government's need to know with the public's right to privacy. The government recently released a new random-number standard, a critical component of encryption methods. However, a backdoor was discovered that could enable someone to crack the code, compromising the security of this encryption and obtaining confidential information. The U.S. government understands the importance of encryption and the need to collect information, but within the limits of retaining the privacy of its citizens.

- Electronic discovery is the exchange of electronic documents. Computer forensics, a branch of forensic science, examines hardware and software to detect cybercrime. Both facilitate the detection, apprehension, and conviction of cybercriminals.

Key Terms and Concepts

Identification

Identify each of the following types of security risks and electronic inconveniences.

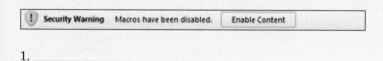

1. _____

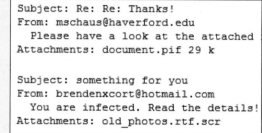

3. _____

2. _____

4. _____

5. _____

6. _____

Matching

Match each key term in the left column with the most accurate definition in the right column.

_____ 1. cybercrime

_____ 2. banner ad

_____ 3. Web beacon

_____ 4. dumpster diving

_____ 5. RFID

_____ 6. botnet

_____ 7. payload

_____ 8. spim

_____ 9. active badge

_____ 10. cookie

_____ 11. rootkit

_____ 12. shoulder surfing

_____ 13. computer crime

_____ 14. honeypot

_____ 15. salami shaving

a. A group of computers that have been unwillingly commandeered and are under the direction of a controller

b. Uses radio waves to identify lost pets; most recently embedded within passports and driver's licenses

c. Attempting to see private information by strategically positioning yourself to view of the computer screen of an unsuspecting user

d. A device that transmits a unique infrared signal every 5 to 10 seconds, creating an electronic trail of the user's location

e. Activities done on a computer that violate state, federal, or international laws

f. An embezzling technique in which small amounts of money are diverted into another account repeatedly over time, usually by altering a program

g. A text file deposited by a Web site on a Web user's computer system, without consent, that is used to gather data on browsing and shopping habits

h. Illegal activity carried out over the Internet

i. Advertising that appears on a Web page but is not actually part of that page

j. A spam text message

k. The attempt to obtain private information by going through discarded mail and trash

l. A computer baited with fake data and purposely left vulnerable in order to study how intruders operate and to prepare stronger defenses based on results

m. A disguised program that provides unauthorized administrative access to a system

n. The dangerous actions a malicious program performs

o. A transparent graphic image embedded within a Web site or e-mail for the purpose of monitoring the user

Multiple Choice

Circle the correct choice for each of the following:

1. Which is a characteristic of a strong password?
   a. A length of less than 5 characters
   b. A familiar word or the name of a family member or pet
   c. The use of characters, both upper and lower case, numbers, and special characters
   d. The use of an important date like a birth date or anniversary date

2. Which is *not* a benefit of cookies?
   a. They are used by online shopping carts to hold items prior to checkout.
   b. They can hold information like login and password, thus making it easier for individuals to login.
   c. They do not take up much disk space.
   d. They can be used to track a user's browser activity.

3. In public key encryption, which item is kept by the owner of the key?
   a. Public key
   b. Private key
   c. Digital key
   d. Rootkit

4. Who is an individual that deliberately attempts to obtain unauthorized access to a computer or network system with the intent to do harm?
   a. Zombie
   b. Bot
   c. Hacker
   d. Cracker

5. What is the process of observing the behavior of employees, including phone calls, e-mails, and Web browsing habits, with or without the aid of computers?
   a. Phishing
   b. Employee monitoring
   c. Computer forensics
   d. Backdoor

6. Which of the following is an example of malware?
   a. Employee monitoring programs
   b. Globally unique identifiers
   c. Time bombs
   d. Active badges

7. What is a type of software program that records all the keystrokes a user enters—such as passwords, account numbers, or conversations—and relays them to others?
   a. Keylogger
   b. Data diddler
   c. Macro
   d. Time bomb

8. Which is a form of malware that installs itself on the beginning tracks of a hard drive, where stored code is automatically executed every time you start the computer, and spreads the infection by simply starting the system?
   a. Macro virus   b. Rootkit
   c. Boot sector virus   d. Botnet

9. What is the name given to commandeered computers that are often used by botnets to distribute spam and malware?
   a. Zombies
   b. Backdoor
   c. Rootkits
   d. Time bombs

10. Which is an online shopping and security standard for merchants and customers?
    a. 802.11n
    a. WPA
    a. GUID
    a. SET

Fill-In

In the blanks provided, write the correct answer for each of the following:

1. _____ computing is a term used to describe the trend in which individuals interact with multiple devices through an omnipresent network.

2. _____ is a validation method that uses a variety of human features, such as voice recognition, retinal scans, and fingerprints to authenticate a user.

3. _____ is an auction behavior in which an accomplice of the seller drives the price up by bidding for an item he or she has no intention of buying.

4. _____ refers to the ability to send a message without revealing your name or identity.

5. A(n) _____ is an individual who attempts to access computers or network systems without permission, for the purpose of pointing out loopholes and security breaks, but who has no intention of performing any malicious acts on the system.

6. A(n) _____ attack is the flooding of a service with meaningless data in an attempt to make a service unavailable to other users.

7. _____ makes use of fake e-mails and social engineering to trick specific people, such as senior executives or members of a particular organization, into providing personal information, to enable identity theft.

8. A(n) _____ is an identification number that is generated by a hardware component or a program that can be read by Web servers or embedded in various documents, making anonymity difficult.

9. _____ is one of the earliest wireless security standards and may be the only option for older devices, despite known weaknesses.

10. _____ is a condensed term that describes software that is designed to damage and infiltrate a computer system without the owner's consent.

11. A(n) _____ is a method of computer access setup to permit the bypassing of normal authentication procedures.

12. _____ refers to a coding or scrambling process that renders a message unreadable by anyone except the intended recipient.

13. _____ is an activity, usually associated with hackers, which is done by sending an incoming message with a false address in an attempt to fool the receiver into believing that he or she is replying to a valid address.

14. A(n) _____ is a program that permits an organization's computers to use the Internet but places severe limits on the ability of outsiders to access internal data.

15. _____ makes use of both encryption and decryption keys.

Short Answer

1. List three of the rights stated in the "Bill of Rights for Social Network Users" issued by the Electronic Frontier Foundation (EFF).

2. Explain the difference between hackers and crackers.

3. Name and explain three of the laws that protect individual privacy.

4. List the five actions an organization can take to deter corporate espionage.

5. List three techniques used to obtain user passwords without their consent.

Teamwork

1. **Database Security** As a team, develop a list of all the databases members use within a week. Ask each team member to rank his or her login name and password for each database as strong, mild, or weak based on the content of this chapter. Additionally ask when each team member last changed his or her passwords. Collect this information and summarize it in a Word table or Excel spreadsheet. Below your table of data, summarize your findings on the use of databases, strength of passwords, and frequency of password changes. Do you think your findings are representative of your age group and region as a whole?

2. **Electronic Monitoring** Traffic congestion in Hong Kong is a matter of great concern to commuters, environmentalists concerned over air-borne pollution, and the government's Transport Department. Certain areas of the city that draw tourists get extremely congested at peak times during the day. It has been suggested that owners of private cars should be charged for driving in these tourist zones during peak times. The intention is to discourage locals from increasing the congestion and pollution and enable tourists a less harried view of the city. All registered car owners will have to display a scannable chip in the windshield of their car. The chip will be scanned when a vehicle enters a restricted zone, and the individual will be billed. Extensive use of these roads could also result in additional charges for overuse. As a team, consider both the plus side and minus side of this system. Discuss how this system might invade the privacy of a driver. Identify any barriers that might deter this plan. Report your team's stand on the plan in a one-page, double-spaced report.

3. **Clean, Quarantine, or Delete?** As a team, investigate these three choices, which are usually options to apply to infected files when detected by antivirus programs. Investigate at least three antivirus programs, state the options each provides, and explain what each option actually does to the infected file. Determine the type of malware each option is best suited to contain. Present your collective research in a PowerPoint presentation of 5 to 10 slides. Remember to cite your references.

4. **Are Privacy and Social Networking Incompatible?** As a team, investigate the current security issues of Google Buzz and Facebook. Describe the security breaches that occurred and how long it took to identify them. Find statistics on the amount of information that was compromised and the response that the manager of each site issued. As a team, come to a consensus on the initial statement in this question: Are privacy and social networking incompatible? In a one-page, double-spaced paper, respond to the question and cite your references.

5. **Solve the Problem** You are using an antivirus program on your home computer, and a pop-up appears indicating that an infected file has been detected on your system. Your attempt to move the file to quarantine fails. As a team, determine some of the some possible reasons for the quarantine failure. What steps would you need to take?

On the Web

1. **Phishing versus Pharming** Using a search engine and the content of this chapter, explain the difference between phishing and pharming. Locate at least two examples of each. Present your descriptions and examples in a one-page, double-spaced report. Remember to cite your references.

2. **Guilty by Digital Data** Today, an individual can be found guilty of a crime even though no witnesses

were present to verify that that individual actually did the act in question. Digital data and computer forensics are both becoming powerful tools in the courtroom, along with the use of re-enactment software to provide the jury with a virtual crime scene. What used to be circumstantial evidence is now becoming more solid and is not so easily dismissed in court. Cell phone records, GPS tracking, and Web browsing histories are all acceptable evidence in court proceedings and can establish an individual's whereabouts and intent. Using your favorite browser, locate and investigate three instances in which an individual was convicted of a crime when no actual witness could identify him/her, but the digital data proved them guilty. In a one-page, double-spaced paper, present each case, describe the circumstances, and explain how the digital data was used to prove guilt. Remember to cite your references.

3. **Red Flags Rules** Using the Internet and a search engine, locate information on the "Red Flags Rules," which require financial institutions and creditors to develop and implement identity theft programs. Explain the rules, who must comply, and any flexibility that there might be in this policy. Present your findings and cite your references in a one-page, double-spaced report.

4. **Logic Bombs** Using the Internet and your favorite browser, research logic bombs in more detail. The trigger that activates the logic bomb can be a positive trigger or a negative trigger. In a one-page, double-spaced paper, define each type of trigger, and describe two examples in which each type of trigger was used and the payload that each set off.

5. **President's Task Force on Identity** Using the Internet and your favorite browser, identify the year that the President's Task Force on Identity was created. What was the mission of this organization? Who are the members? What has the task force accomplished since its inception? Present your findings in a one-page, double-spaced report, and remember to cite your references.

chapter 10

Careers and Certification

Being a computer science major is cool again! Yes, it's hard to believe, but it is true. There will always be the traditional professions: doctors, dentists, lawyers, and teachers, but make room for the computer professional. Statistics from the U.S. Department of Labor have projected a 34 percent increase in computer software engineers by the year 2018. The idea must be catching on. The number of students enrolled as computer science majors increased by 8.1 percent in 2008, the first increase since 2000. Could this be a career field for you? Do you want to understand the workings of social networks or the latest iPhone? Do you see yourself as a problem solver, able to think out of the box, a good listener, and a creative thinker? These are just a few of the skills that any information technology (IT) or computer professional needs. What do you think? Is a challenging career in the computer field a possibility for you?

Today, almost all companies, regardless of their size, use computers and information technology (IT). But just because they use IT doesn't make them part of the IT industry. The **IT industry** is made up of organizations that are focused on the development and implementation of technology and applications. This includes well-known companies such as Microsoft, Dell, Apple, Cisco, Oracle, and Intel as well as companies from the telecommunications sector such as Verizon, resellers such as Best Buy, vendors like AMD, and suppliers of parts like TigerDirect.com.

This chapter will focus on the following topics:

- The importance of computer literacy in the general job market
- Jobs associated with information technology, their responsibilities, and required education
- Traditional and nontraditional paths to IT careers
- The difference between computer science and management information system curricula
- New jobs and their use of Web technology
- The positive and negative side of certifications
- How to use technology to get that IT dream job ■

Check out **f Facebook** for our latest updates

www.facebook.com

The Importance of Computer Literacy

Even employers that are not part of the IT industry are demanding higher levels of computer literacy than ever before. It does not matter whether your future career is in health care, retail, finance, agriculture, or any other industry. Such fields use computers to access medical records and perform procedures, ring up sales using POS terminals, research stock market or other financial information, analyze the environmental effects of vertical farming, and so on. According to a recent study, employers described **computer literacy**, the ability to understand how to use a computer effectively, as "important" or "very important" in their hiring decisions. Another survey of employers ranked computer literacy third, right below communication skills and analytical ability. According to the survey, the following computer literacy skills are particularly attractive to employers:

- The ability to create, format, save, open, and print computer documents created in such word processing programs as Microsoft Word
- Familiarity with e-mail programs, including attaching documents and setting priority levels
- Knowing enough about spreadsheet entries to keep track of petty cash or logs of phone calls and associated charges
- Understanding the use of databases, like Microsoft Access, and the basics of a table, query, report, and form
- Familiarity with presentation software and the use of simple animation to increase its appeal
- Possession of Web searching and drill-down techniques to get to the desired information
- Basic photo-editing skills
- Ability to create or edit a basic Web page

" [The] **demand** by employers for **current computer skills** makes computer **knowledge** a component of **lifelong learning** and a skill that will require **constant updating** and **retraining** as technology progresses. "

This demand by employers for current computer skills makes computer knowledge a component of lifelong learning and a skill that will require constant updating and retraining as technology progresses.

Computer Literacy in the Job Search

Not only are computer literacy skills both important in most jobs today and near the top of the list of employment requirements, but they are also essential in the job search itself. The traditional methods of locating, applying, and researching a job are being replaced by more technical and computer-based options, including these:

- Web sites that contain advice on creating resumes and cover letters along with helpful interview techniques
- Career assessments to help you zero in on a career that suits your personality and skills
- Salary surveys, obtained through Web searches, to help establish a salary range for positions you are considering
- Job postings on Web sites designed for such advertisements or on a company's own Web site
- Sending resumes or other requested documents using e-mail instead of snail mail (regular post office mail)

You can see that in order to use these options to search for a job, the hopeful applicant will need most of the computer literacy skills listed in the previous section. So, not only are literacy skills essential in a job, but they are also essential in finding one!

The Internet in the Job Search

How can you investigate careers or jobs that are available and make your resume accessible to potential employers? You can accomplish this very easily by using your computer literacy skills and locating Web sites that not only list available positions but also allow you to post your resume on the World Wide Web for potential employers to view. Job search sites can be global in scope and provide job categories in all areas (Figure 10.1), or they can be specific and list positions only in a targeted category or field (Figure 10.2). Perhaps the most widely known site for IT careers is Dice.com (www.dice.com). The Dice.com database is searchable by keyword, industry, company, or geographic location. The site lists hundreds of thousands of jobs as well as company information with hyperlinks to corporate Web sites. Companies that have joined Dice.com can place recruitment ads, post company profiles, and gain access to a database of resumes that grows in number daily.

FIGURE 10.1 Popular Job Search Sites

Web Sites for General Job Searches	URL
CareerBuilder.com	www.careerbuilder.com
Indeed	www.indeed.com
Monster	www.monster.com
Yahoo! HotJobs	http://hotjobs.yahoo.com
Federal Job Search Sites Studentjobs.gov	www.studentjobs.gov
USAJOBS	www.usajobs.gov

Besides using the Internet to locate and research possible employment opportunities, many companies want resumes and cover letters that they can scan, and in many cases they prefer such documents to be sent via e-mail. Using e-mail can actually be a method of testing a candidate's computer literacy skills and act as a first level of screening. You might have heard the term *keyword resume* being passed around. This type of resume requires the inclusion of **keywords**, descriptive words matching the qualifications that an employer posted somewhere in the resume. A potential employer will be looking for these keywords to match your skills with the posted required skills when your resume is reviewed. This basically means that job seekers might have to customize their resumes for every position for which they are applying.

FIGURE 10.2 Popular IT Job Search Sites

Web Sites for IT Job Searches	URL
CareerBuilder.com—IT Jobs	http://information-technology.careerbuilder.com
code-jobs.com	www.code-jobs.com
ComputerJobs.com	www.computerjobs.com
ComputerWork.com	www.computerwork.com
Dev Bistro	www.devbistro.com
Dice	www.dice.com
JustTechJobs.com	www.justtechjobs.com
Quintessential Careers	www.quintcareers.com/computer_jobs.html
Tech-centric.net	www.tech-centric.net
Tech-Engine	www.techengine.com

What does a keyword resume have to do with computers? One reason for the keyword emphasis is that many large companies cannot possibly go through all resumes that they receive so they pass them through an **application tracking system (ATS)**. An ATS is actually a computer program that scans the resumes and is set to

ETHICS

Some ingenious individuals who do not want to rewrite their resumes and adjust their layouts for each position they apply for have come up with a technique to circumvent the ATS system, called white formatting. **White formatting** is typing keywords in the footer or margin of a resume and then changing the font color to white. What is the purpose of this? To the human eye, the keywords are not visible; but, the ATS will detect them, not reject the resume, and will successfully move the resume to the next level of screening. How do you think a perspective employer will react to reading a resume that does not, to the human eye, seem to have the keywords that match the job requirements? Would you ever try this?

locate keywords. If a certain percentage of keywords in the resume match the pre-set scanned list of keywords, the application makes it to the next level. This system acts as a screening method and eliminates individuals that do not possess the minimum skills for the advertised position.

While job seekers use the Internet to search for jobs and e-mail to send resumes, companies are beginning to use the Internet to screen job candidates that are from outside their local region. These employers are switching from using the traditional phone interview as a pre-screening technique to conducting a Web interview. A **Web interview** is an interview conducted through the use of a webcam and the Internet. The interviewer and potential job candidate are able to have live interaction, or a virtual interview can be conducted in which the candidate sees the questions on the computer screen and replies. In the virtual interview, the webcam session is taped and the corporate recruiters can review it at their convenience. The benefits of a Web interview include these:

- Savings in time and money spent in arranging for a personal onsite interview

- The ability to tape the interview and make it available to other screeners in the same office or in offices located in other geographical areas

- The ability to accommodate the candidate's different time zone or accessibility through the use of a virtual interview

Some companies even contract with third-party affiliates like HireVue, which provides the Web cams and support for the Web interview.

This chapter looks at the traditional educational path to an IT career, alternative IT career paths, and IT careers of the future. Before reading further, see whether a career in information technology is a fit for your skills, abilities, and personality. Try one of the free online career assessment tools from Assessment.com (**www.assessment.com**) or Career Explorer (**www.careerexplorer.net/aptitude.asp**). These sites will ask for personal information to formulate an assessment. They take approximately 15 minutes or more and might offer additional services for a fee.

Traditional Information Technology Career Paths

In the world of technology, nobody knows what the future will bring. That can be a little troubling for future job seekers attempting to acquire today the skills they'll apply tomorrow. Will the job of your dreams be around when you're ready for employment? Does it even exist yet? How do you prepare for an uncertain career landscape?

Learning about computers and getting a bachelor's degree is a step in the right direction, as is keeping up with emerging technologies. Nobody wants to head down a path toward an occupation that won't exist in five years. Staying abreast of job trends is an excellent way to ensure you're heading in the right direction. Where do you find such information? The *Occupational Outlook Handbook* for 2010–2011, found on the U.S. Department of Labor's Bureau of Labor Statistics site (**www.bls.gov/oco/home.htm**), is a good place to start (Figure 10.3).

As we look to the year 2018, reports from the Bureau of Labor Statistics indicate that information technology (IT) professionals will continue to be in high demand. These reports foresee employment in professional, scientific, and technical services growing by

FIGURE 10.3 The Bureau of Labor Statistics Web site contains useful information about a wide array of IT-related occupations.

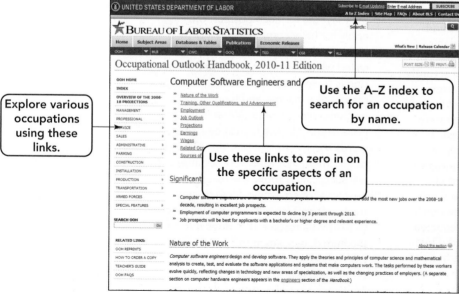

34 percent and adding 2.7 million new jobs by 2018. Employment in computer engineering is also predicted to grow by 34 percent, while the need for network system and data communication analysts will see a 53 percent increase. The information sector is expected to increase by 4 percent, adding 118,000 jobs by 2018. Software publishing will increase by 30 percent as organizations seek to adopt the newest products. Telecommunications is projected to decrease by 9 percent due to more reliable networks and organization consolidation. Figure 10.4 displays the top 10 occupations with the greatest predicted rate of growth.

Information technology (IT) professionals work with information technology in all its various forms (hardware, software, networks) and functions (management, development, maintenance). Both small and large companies will need computer specialists and administrators who can keep up with the fast-changing technologies that keep them growing and competitive. This is especially important when integrating emerging sophisticated technologies.

In the coming years, companies will need many more skilled IT professionals than they're likely to find. In the past, not enough students were graduating from U.S. colleges and universities with degrees in computer science, systems engineering, or management information systems to meet the forecasted employment needs. However, as of 2008, enrollment figures in the area of computer science had started to increase. Students are becoming more interested in the technology and portable media they are using, are majoring in the more technical curriculums, and will be in high demand when they enter the job market. Previous declines in these and other IT-related fields were attributed to two reasons. The first was **outsourcing**, the act of one company contracting to have services, that could be performed by in-house employees, performed by another company. The company being contracted to perform the outsourced services might be only a few blocks away or in another state, but within the same country. Examples include such activities as shipping, e-mail services, and payroll. The second reason cited was **labor dumping**, the flooding of a labor market with foreign workers. Both employment options will continue, but the jobs that are predicted to show the most growth are going to be in the areas of

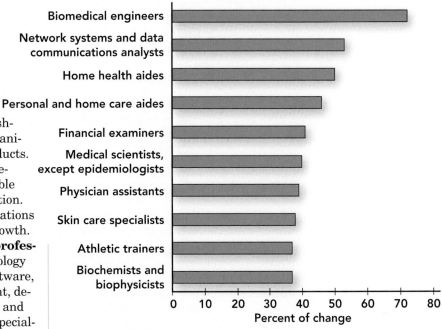

Ten top growth occupations—predictions of growth for 2018

FIGURE 10.4 Jobs for IT professionals are expected to grow at a faster rate than most other career tracks.

software engineering, network systems, and data communication analysis. These jobs involve the design and configuration of the programs and systems put into use, not the actual coding or implementation. Jobs in these categories will require degrees, and the associated salaries will be above the median average income. What this means for you is opportunity. If you have the right background, skills, and motivation, you can pursue an education in an IT field of demand and find a job as a technology professional.

Ten years ago, most people got into IT careers by obtaining a computer-related bachelor's degree and landing a job with a corporate **information systems (IS) department**, the functional area within companies or universities responsible for managing information technology and systems (Figure 10.5), or a software development firm (Figure 10.6), also called a **vendor**. The four-year college degree was, and still is, listed as the desired degree for most programming positions. A survey done a few years ago corroborated this statement with statistics confirming that 50 percent of surveyed computer programmers had a bachelor's degree, and 20 percent had a graduate degree.

Of course, as with any career, computer-related jobs aren't for everyone. Change, not continuity, is the norm in IT careers. Jobs are changed or eliminated and new ones created as technology forces a continuous shifting and updating of

FIGURE 10.5 Typical Job Titles and Responsibilities in a Corporate IS Department

Job Title	Responsibilities	Salary Range	Preferred Educational Level
Chief Information Officer (CIO)	*Senior-level management position* Defines the IS department's mission, objectives, and budgets and creates a strategic plan for the company's information systems	$149,000 to $329,000	Master's, Ph.D.
Director of Network Services	*Middle management position* Ensures overall network reliability	$70,000 to $148,000	Master's
Network Engineer	Installs, maintains, and supports computer networks; interacts with users; and troubleshoots problems	$45,000 to $117,000	Master's
Systems Administrator	Installs, maintains, and supports the operating system	$60,000 to $122,000	Bachelor's, Master's
Systems Analyst	Interacts with users and application developers to design information systems	$46,000 to $130,000	Bachelor's, Master's
Programmer	Writes code according to specifications	$60,000 to $100,000	Bachelor's, Master's

FIGURE 10.6 Typical Job Titles and Responsibilities in a Software Development Firm

Job Title	Responsibilities	Salary Range	Preferred Educational Level
Director of Research and Development	*Senior-level management position* Takes charge of all product development activities	$122,000 to $278,000	Master's, Ph.D.
Software Architect	Creates new, cutting-edge technologies	$116,000 to $235,000	Master's, Ph.D.
Software Engineer	Manages the details of software development projects	$50,000 to $144,000	Bachelor's, Master's
Systems Engineer	Assists the sales staff by working with current and prospective customers; gives technical presentations and supports products on-site	$55,000 to $100,000	Bachelor's, Master's
Software Developer	Develops new programs under the direction of the software architect	$50,000 to $114,000	Bachelor's, Master's
Customer Support Technician	Provides assistance to customers who need help with products	$39,000 to $76,000	Bachelor's

priorities and skills. Flexibility is essential because individuals must be comfortable adapting to change and willing to learn new skills and update existing ones frequently. And today's job market offers no such thing as job security. In a computer-related field, you'll probably work at as many as eight or nine different jobs before you retire. This trend is due, in part, to today's global environment in which most IT work is based.

Offshoring is the transfer of labor from workers in one country to workers in other countries. Two examples of job

GREEN tech tips

Hybrid cars may be helping the environment, but some people don't think that's enough. Many people are taking a second look at their job or the company they work for and wishing it were more environmentally conscious. If you're one of these people, try using a "green" job search site like GreenBiz.com (**www.greenbiz.com**) or Green Dream Jobs (**www.sustainablebusiness.com**) to find a company or position that can help you improve the environment and put your IT skills to good use. In addition to providing job listings, both sites offer news, networking opportunities, and a variety of green resources. So, take a look. Even if you are happy with your current job, you may find some ways to help your company be more environmentally conscious. •

FIGURE 10.7 Best Outsourcing Countries

Country	Ranking
India	1
Malaysia	2
Philippines	3
Indonesia	4
Jordan	5
Thailand	6
Egypt	7
Pakistan	8
China	9
Bulgaria	10

FAST FORWARD ▶▶

In the future, the most sought after corporate IT workers will be those with a technology background who possess communication skills, are adept at public speaking, and possess a sound business sense. Their skills, besides technological know-how, will include the ability to design and architect IT products, work with a team, manage projects, understand application development, and carry out IT plans that will not only add business value but will also cultivate relationships both within and outside of the company. The nuts-and-bolts jobs of programming and documentation will be outsourced. The new IT employee has been called the "versatilist." For individuals that possess these skills, the future looks bright. Three research groups agree that this change in the IT professional is being created by corporate mergers, outsourcing, the fast growth of mobile devices, and the increase in stored data. The IT professional will need to communicate better, be more outward focused, and become aware of the corporate realities of cost effectiveness when analyzing, designing, and producing a product.

categories that have seen work transferred from the United States to other countries, such as India, China, and the Philippines, are call center work and computer programming. Some companies are learning, though, that the transfer of labor has its costs—particularly in the case of call center workers who don't always meet customer expectations. Forrester Research has predicted that 3.3 million service jobs and $136 billion in wages will move overseas between 2000 and 2015. What is not clear is the total economic and social benefit to U.S. companies. Some companies are finding the price of offshore services is not as cost-effective as anticipated because of the rising labor costs in some countries and the additional cost of training. Implicit personnel costs may be overlooked and can create misleading figures, as companies find it necessary to hire personnel based in the United States to edit and overcome some of the communication and cultural differences in projects developed elsewhere.

A recent study rated outsourcing countries based on cost competitiveness, resources and skills, and business and economic environment. The results are listed in Figure 10.7.

Before the era of corporate downsizing and offshoring, IT workers could remain with a firm for many years, perhaps until retirement. Workers with business savvy and good communication skills could move into management. If employees needed to acquire additional skills, the employer might arrange and pay for additional training.

Today, with technology changing daily, IT professionals must always be on the cutting edge of technology to compete with new college graduates and foreign labor. This means that continuing education is part of the job. However, before investigating how individuals already in the field stay up to date, let's look first at the components and foundations of a traditional IT career.

Education for Traditional IT Careers

Reflecting the long-standing split in computing between science and business, education for traditional IT careers has been divided between four very different majors: computer science, management information systems, systems and software engineering, and electrical engineering (Figure 10.8).

Computer Science The study of the storage, change, and transfer of information, **computer science (CS)**, includes both the theoretical study of algorithms and the practical problems to which they can be applied. For students, the emphasis is typically on learning a programming language and understanding how the programs they develop and the logic those programs employ affect the overall performance of the system. In general, CS programs focus on cutting-edge technologies, fundamental principles, and theories. Computer science is a very broad discipline with applications in almost every other discipline imaginable. Computer scientists use their honed analytical and technical skills to develop solutions to problems and determine how to best use computing resources. CS typically involves various high-level programming languages and a considerable amount of mathematical ability. At most colleges and universities, CS programs grew out of mathematics programs and are often housed in the engineering school.

Qualified CS graduates find that their theoretical and analytical skills make them good candidates for jobs in cutting-edge software development and engineering firms; as researchers for government-funded programs with computer simulators; and in IS departments that are working with advanced technologies or developing software in-house.

Management Information Systems

Generally located in business schools, management information systems (MIS) departments are often the flip side of CS departments. Some schools may still refer to this program as computer information systems (CIS), but MIS is becoming more commonplace and helps to clearly differentiate the program from CS. **Management information systems (MIS)** focuses on the practical application of information systems and technology to provide the skills businesses need right now to successfully compete in the marketplace. In addition to work in programming and systems analysis, MIS departments strongly emphasize important business topics such as finance and marketing, communication

FIGURE 10.8 Information Technology-Related College Degrees

Degree Field	Description	Course Focus
Computer Science	Theoretical study of algorithms and the problems they can be applied to	Programming languages and mathematics
Management Information Systems	Combines information technology with business skills	Programming languages, application software, and business processes
System and Software Engineering	Reviews the whole IT picture, including the people and the organization as well as the technologies	Analysis and problem solving using engineering and math applications, business processes, and project management skills
Electrical Engineering	Focuses on digital circuit design and cutting-edge communication technologies	Engineering concepts and mathematics

skills, and interpersonal skills required for effective teamwork and leadership. With their business savvy and communication skills, MIS graduates can find jobs in almost any department of a corporation. All departments need people with IT skills to interface with other employees, subcontractors, and outsourcing firms; MIS graduates fill this demand very well.

Systems and Software Engineering The engineering discipline called **systems engineering** applies an interdisciplinary approach to creating and maintaining quality systems. Unlike other engineering disciplines, systems engineering looks at the whole picture, including the people and the organization as well as the technologies. The principles of systems engineering are useful for software development, systems analysis, and program development. Systems engineering students learn strong project management skills, and graduates are, and will continue to be, in high demand.

Computer software engineering is projected to be one of the fastest-growing occupations over the next five to eight years, especially in the computer and data-processing services industry. **Software engineering** involves upgrading, managing, and modify-

FIGURE 10.9 Training seminars are offered by hardware or software developers or by established IT training companies and usually focus on new products or programs.

ing computer programs. Software engineers will continue to develop applications for the Internet, the new age of cloud computing, and highly popular portable devices. Software engineers with strong programming, systems analysis, interpersonal, and business skills are those most likely to succeed. Of course, the future will bring with it many new problems for software engineers to solve—problems we can't even think of because they don't exist yet.

Electrical Engineering The engineering discipline called **electrical engineering (EE)** offers a strong focus on digital circuit design as well as cutting-edge communication technologies. It's the primary choice for those whose interests lean more toward

hardware design, including computer chips, integrated circuits, robotics, and devices that include solid-state, mobile, and embedded technology.

Continuing Education for Traditional IT Careers

In traditional IT careers, professionals keep up with new technologies by attending seminars and continuing education courses, subscribing to computer-related periodicals, attending conferences and shows, and actively participating in professional associations.

Training Seminars or Conferences

Computer-related **training seminars** are typically presented by the developer of a new hardware or software product or by a company specializing in training IT professionals in a new technology (Figure 10.9). These seminars usually last from one day to a week and are often advertised in the local paper's technology or business section as well as in trade magazines such as *PC World* or *Wired*. Often they can be taken in person or as a Web conference, webinar, or online workshop. In a **Web conference** each individual usually sits at his or her own computer and is connected to and interacts with other participants via the Internet. Often the registered individual receives an e-mail link (a meeting invitation) that he or she uses to access the conference site and login. **Webinar** is a relatively new term and refers to a Web conference that is typically one-way—from speaker to audience, with limited attendee participation. There may be some polling and a question-and-answer segment at the end, but that is usually the extent of audience participation. An **online workshop** is usually a structured interactive session that is assisted by an electronic meeting system, a set of tools that enable discussion, brainstorming, voting, and categorization.

Due to the challenging financial times, many companies have slashed their training programs. One side effect of this cut in training is the decrease in employee job mobility. Today, employees may need to foot the bill to attend training seminars to bolster their own skill levels and improve their opportunities for advancement.

Computer Magazines, Newspapers, and Journals Computer-related trade journals are an indispensable resource for IT professionals. Some, such as *Computerworld*, *PC Magazine*, or *Wired*, cover a wide range of computer issues. Others are aimed at a specific section of the IT industry, such as networking (*Network World*), technology management (*InformationWeek*), or security (*SC Magazine*). More than 100 of these types of periodicals are in print. If you have a particular area of interest, you can probably find a periodical that reports late-breaking developments in your field. Most of these periodicals are also published on the Web. A quick search using the magazine's title in your favorite search engine should lead you to such sites as Techweb (**www.techweb.com**), IDG (**www.idg.net**), and Ziff Davis PCMag Network (**www.pcmagnetwork.com**).

Computer Career–Related Web Sites Besides online journals and magazines, there are Web sites dedicated to the computer professionals that provide training information, instructional guides, and forums to exchange information. The InformIT (**www.InformIT.com**) and SANS (**www.sans.org**) sites are two valuable sources of information. InformIT is a true learning site with courses, videos, and relevant articles, while the SANS site is a resource for security information and certification.

Conferences and Shows One way to keep in touch with others in your profession and learn about the latest trends is to attend conferences and trade shows. A **trade show** is typically an annual meeting at which computer product manufacturers, designers, and dealers showcase their products. Some shows are held nationally, whereas others are regional, and some include job fairs that offer on-the-spot interviews and provide incentives for job seekers.

Every year the International Consumer Electronics Show (CES), the world's largest technology trade show, sponsored by the Consumer Electronics Association, draws representatives from many facets of the technology industry. Exhibitors at the show include representatives from music, broadcasting, motion picture, cable, and engineering industries, in addition to well-known technology companies. Held yearly in January in Las Vegas, Nevada, the show attracts at least 140,000 attendees from more than 130 countries (Figure 10.10).

Many of the 2,700 exhibitors provide seminars on topics such as cutting-edge

FIGURE 10.10 The International Consumer Electronics Show in Las Vegas is the largest show of its kind. At this event each year, exhibitors unveil new technologies to the world.

audio developments, digital imaging, gaming, home theater and video, home networking, in-vehicle technology, wireless connectivity, mobile devices, and emerging technologies. Many of the latest technology innovations are launched at CES. The show is by invitation, not open to the general public, and is considered a must-see for those involved in the technology industry.

Professional Organizations Joining one of the many IT **professional organizations** or **professional associations** can help you keep up with your area of interest as well as provide valuable career contacts. Some associations have local chapters, and most offer publications, training seminars, and conferences for members. Figure 10.11 provides a listing of some of the most important IT organizations and related resources.

Two of the best resources on the Web for familiarizing yourself with the myriad issues and legislation related to technology are the Association for Computing Machinery (ACM, **www.acm.org**) and the Electronic Frontier Foundation (EFF, **www.eff.org**). One major goal of the ACM is to educate its members about important legal, technical, and ethical issues. Whether you're an IT professional or a

FIGURE 10.11 Professional Associations and IT Resources

Organization Name	Description
American Society for Information Science and Technology (ASIS&T) **www.asis.org**	This organization supports information professionals in the advancement of information sciences and related fields, uniting researchers, developers, and end users.
Association for Computing Machinery (ACM) **www.acm.org**	ACM is the oldest and largest scientific computing society, providing access to computing literature, publications, conferences, and special interest groups.
Association for Women in Computing (AWC) **www.awc-hq.org**	A nonprofit organization, the AWC promotes the advancement of women in the IT field.
Computer Professionals for Social Responsibility (CPSR) **http://cpsr.org**	This global organization promotes the responsible use of computer technology and seeks to educate the public and policy makers on technology-related issues.
Diversity/Careers in Engineering & Information Technology **www.diversitycareers.com**	Devoted to diversity issues in the IT field, this site is a resource for people with disabilities, women, and other minority groups who are traditionally underrepresented in the fields of engineering and information technology.
Gamasutra **www.gamasutra.com**	Gamasutra is a comprehensive resource for the game development community.
IEEE **www.ieee.org**	The IEEE, formerly known as the Institute of Electrical and Electronics Engineers, Inc., is a professional society dedicated to promoting the growth of technology.
International Game Developers Association (IGDA) **www.igda.org**	The largest nonprofit organization for game developers, IGDA promotes professional development and advocates for issues affecting the gaming community.
Project Management Institute **www.pmi.org**	This organization certifies project managers and provides project management standards and good practices.
Women in Technology International (WITI) **www.witi.com**	This global organization empowers women in business and technology by providing information, networking opportunities, and career development advice.
World Organization of Webmasters (WOW) **www.webprofessionals.org**	A professional association, WOW provides education and certification opportunities, as well as technical and employment services, to Web professionals.

FIGURE 10.12 The Electronic Frontier Foundation (EFF) Web site includes a large list of important ethical and legislative issues. You can find the link by clicking on the "Our Work" link at the top of the EFF home page.

savvy consumer, the ACM's computing and public policy page at **www.acm.org/public-policy** is a great place to start. You'll be able to research everything from the "legal regulation of technology" to copyright policy.

Although not a professional organization like ACM, the EFF shares some similar objectives, such as protecting fundamental rights regardless of technology; educating the media, policy makers, and the public about technology-related civil liberties issues; and defending those liberties. The EFF has done an excellent job of aggregating a large list of important ethical and legislative issues on a single page, which can be found by clicking on the "Our Work" link at the top of their home page (Figure 10.12).

Now that you're familiar with how to prepare for a more traditional IT career path, let's take a look at new career paths in IT.

Alternative Information Technology Career Paths

IT careers are changing, driven both by rapid technological change and by shifts in the nature of today's businesses. Increasingly, a four-year college degree sometimes isn't enough to convince prospective employers that would-be employees possess needed skills, because many of these skills aren't yet taught in many colleges and universities.

As you'll see in this section, good communication skills, business savvy, and technical skills are necessary for success in fast-emerging areas such as Web 2.0, virtualization, and mobile technology. For this reason, IT workers must learn how to manage their careers. You may change jobs often, or you may forsake the job market altogether, preferring—as do increasing numbers of IT professionals—to work as an independent contractor or consultant. Whichever path you choose, it's increasingly becoming the worker's responsibility to develop the skills needed to keep up with fast-changing technology and manage his or her career in an ever-changing job market. For information, including videos, about various IT careers go to **www.careertv.com**. For podcasts and blogs provided by employers describing their companies, job requirements, and ideal employee go to **http://jobsinpods.com**.

Sought-After Business Skills

Ten years ago, most IT jobs were internally focused: IT professionals worked inside companies. They created and supported computer services, such as payroll and inventory systems. But this picture is changing—and it's changing radically.

Today, driven by new network-based information systems, IT jobs increasingly combine both an internal and an external focus. IT professionals are expected to work with a company's external partners and customers. They'll work in teams that include people from different divisions of the enterprise. Rather than performing a specific function, IT professionals are much more likely to work on a series of projects on which they'll use different skills. For all of these reasons, today's businesses are looking for workers that possess "soft" business skills in addition to "hard" business skills or technical knowledge. **Soft business skills** are people-related skills. These are some of the soft skills that businesses are seeking in IT employees:

- **Communication.** Today, every employee needs communication skills, even those who formerly worked internally and seldom had contact with people outside their departments. Employers are looking for excellent

> " . . . it's increasingly becoming the **worker's responsibility** to **develop** the skills needed to **keep up with** fast-changing **technology** and manage his or her **career** in an ever-changing job market. "

written, verbal, and interpersonal skills. Good presentation skills and the ability to convey technical ideas to nontechnical audiences are also highly valued.

- **Analytical/Research Skills.** These skills deal with your ability to assess a situation, seek multiple perspectives, gather more information if necessary, and identify key issues that need to be addressed.

- **Teamwork.** Increasingly, IT personnel are working in teams with workers from finance, marketing, and other corporate divisions. IT professionals need to appreciate varying intellectual styles, work effectively in a team environment, and understand business perspectives.

- **Project management.** The need is increasing for skills such as the ability to plan and budget a project, itemize the resources needed for completion, and determine the availability and cost of those resources, especially with project management software, making project management not only a skill, but also a profession in today's job market.

- **Business acumen.** Information technology is now part of most companies' strategic planning, and IT employees are expected to possess some basic business knowledge. In the past, you could focus on technology and ignore business and communication skills, but that's no longer true. Older, experienced IT workers who suffer job losses due to downsizing may have difficulty finding employment if they don't possess these skills. As a result, the wise IT student also takes courses in general business subjects, including finance and marketing.

In addition to reviewing resumes for soft skills and basic qualifications a job applicant possesses, employers are using phone interviews, Web interviews, and virtual Web interviews to dig into the moral and ethical status of an applicant. These

STUDENT
VIDEO

are referred to as personal values, and in the IT field, with security and confidentiality as essential job components, they are considered non-negotiable. So what personal values and attributes are employers of IT professional looking for?

- **Honesty/Integrity/Morality.** With scandals like Enron, the recent antitrust violations against IBM, and Nokia's recent lawsuit against other mobile phone manufacturers over price fixing, personal integrity and honesty have moved to the top of the list.
- **Dedicated/Hard-Working/ Tenacious.** Companies are looking for the employee that is dedicated not only to his/her work but also to the company. In general, they are looking for the one that will stick with a project until it is completed.
- **Dependable/Reliable/Professional.** Employers respect an employee that arrives on time every day, is professional in their appearance, and takes responsibility for their actions.
- **Self-Confident/Self-Motivated.** An employee that believes in his/her skills and can bring them forward when needed is highly sought after. Additionally, employers look for applicants that can work independently, without constant supervision or guidance.

ETHICS

As an IT professional, you will often have access to the data residing on other people's computers. Although deliberate snooping is probably not part of your job description, it is possible that you could happen upon information of a sensitive or even illegal nature. Some companies have policies governing how such a situation should be handled, and the Electronic Communications Act of 1986 prohibits unlawful access and certain disclosures of communication content. But what would you do if your company didn't have a policy? What types of information would you report? Who would you report it to—someone within your company or an outside agency? Would you act differently depending on whose computer the information was discovered?

Hard business skills are more process related with emphasis on technological expertise in areas such as networking, Web development, and knowledge of UNIX, C++, and firewall administration. In addition, familiarity with the processes involved in content areas such as accounting, finance, and logistics are essential, depending on the professional's focus and concentration in the industry.

Sought-After Technical Skills

Businesses are also demanding new **technical skills**. Here's what's hot as of this writing:

- **Networking.** Skills related to the process of interconnecting computers are in high demand. Experience with Ethernet, TCP/IP (Internet protocols), and LAN administration are key qualifications.
- **Microsoft Product Skills.** Expertise in managing Microsoft Office applications, working with operating systems, and being able to handle the .NET environment continues to pay big rewards within organizations.
- **Linux.** There is a strong demand for IT workers skilled in Linux operating system configuration and maintenance, networking, and systems programming.
- **TCP/IP.** Knowledge of the protocols underlying the Internet, such as TCP/IP, are needed to manage both external Web servers and internal intranets.
- **Oracle.** Experience with products, especially relational database and client/server application tools are skills always sought by companies.
- **AJAX.** Knowledge of **AJAX**, a group of interrelated Web development techniques used on the client side that combine HTML/XHTML and JavaScript to provide interactive Web pages, and other Web 2.0 development techniques, is in high demand.
- **Enterprise Resource Planning systems (ERP systems).** Experience with company-wide computer software systems, such as SAP, that are used to manage and coordinate all the resources, information, and functions of a business from shared data stores is a real advantage. Today such ERP systems are used by most large corporations and many smaller ones.

Although a four-year degree in CS or MIS may fail to give you all of these desirable skills, the best preparation for a successful IT career still involves the invaluable theoretical background you get from a four-year college degree.

Now that you understand both traditional and alternative IT career paths along with the soft skills, values, and technical skills that employers are seeking, let's examine how IT professionals can adapt to further change.

Web Technologies, Related Jobs

New technology brings not just more jobs but new *types* of jobs. Many of these new jobs are inherently cross-disciplinary, involving artistic or communication skills as well as top-notch technical capabilities. Existing CS and MIS programs may produce graduates who lack creativity, marketing knowledge, graphic design experience, or communication skills. For this reason, many companies are hiring students who have taken many computer courses and also have a concentration in other fields, such as design, marketing, or English.

For example, Web design involves technical skills and knowledge in areas such as HTML/XHTML, XML, CSS, AJAX, Flash, JavaScript, and server configuration. But in many cases, that's not enough to keep a Web site up and running. Increasingly, companies are looking for Web administrators and content developers who understand marketing, advertising, and graphic design. These jobs (Figure 10.13) require not only technical skills and business smarts, but also artistic sensitivity, including some background in the aesthetics of design and color, coupled with a good deal of creativity.

A recently compiled study, done in 2008, surveyed 30,000 people working in the Web industry. The typical employee was a white male between the ages of 19 and 44 with a college degree, who works in the Western hemisphere and averages between 30 and 49 hours a week. The typical employee receives an annual salary of $80,000. When respondents asked for their job title, the results were interesting:

- 28 percent replied "Developer"
- 13 percent responded "Web Designer"
- 8 percent, simply "Designer"
- 26 percent marked "Other"

FIGURE 10.13 Jobs in Web Technologies

Job Title	Responsibilities
Interactive Digital Media Specialist	Uses multimedia software to create engaging presentations, including animation and video
Web Database Engineer	Designs and maintains databases deployed on the Web and their related database servers
Web Application Engineer	Designs, develops, tests, and documents new Web-based services for Web sites
Web Designer/Developer	Works with internal and external customers to create attractive and usable Web sites
Network/Internet Security Specialist	Installs and maintains firewalls, antivirus software, and other security software; maintains network security

- 25 percent included titles like Web Master, Web Producer, Information Architect, Usability Consultant, Marketer, Educator, and Accessibility Consultant.

The survey indicated that the title of the job is not as important as the responsibilities and the salary.

Some future jobs might seem to be somewhat removed from the CS or MIS fields; however, do not let an initial overview fool you. **Telemedicine**, for one, is on the rise and seems to be catching on. This field combines computers and medical expertise to create the equivalent of a long-distance house call. Through the use of computers and telecommunication devices, a physician can consult and diagnose a case literally from continents away. **Telehealth** is an expansion of telemedicine that extends services beyond the remedial level to the preventive side of medicine. Such services include the use of e-mail to communicate with patients and telecommunication links to pharmacies for fast and accurate processing of prescriptions.

The mandate made for an electronic (digital) health record for each person in the United States by 2014 was embedded within the $838 billion stimulus bill passed by the senate in 2009. This requirement for digital medical records is in large part the reason for the increase of IT positions in the medical/health care industry. The U.S. Bureau of Labor Statistics states that medical billing and coding is one of the top 10 growing health-related jobs, while another study by the American Hospital Association states that 18 percent of the current positions in this field remain vacant due to the lack of qualified candidates. Qualified individuals entering this field should have a promising job outlook.

Certification

Rapid changes in IT have created a demand for new ways to ensure that job applicants possess the skills they claim. Certification is increasingly seen as a way that employers can assure themselves that newly hired workers can do necessary tasks.

In brief, **certification** is a skills and knowledge assessment process organized by computer industry vendors and sometimes by professional associations (Figure 10.14). To obtain a certificate, you choose your preferred method of training. You can take courses at a college or at a private training center, or study on your own using vendor-approved books, CD/DVD materials, or the Web. When you're ready, you take a comprehensive examination. If you pass, you receive the certificate. But unlike a college degree, the certificate isn't good for life. To retain certification, you may need to take refresher courses and exams periodically, sometimes as often as every six months.

The Institute for Certification of Computing Professionals (ICCP) offers credentials for the highest level of computer professionals. The institute certifies competency for a variety of computer professionals, including computer scientists, system analysts, and computer programmers. Visit the ICCP Web site at **www.iccp.org/iccpnew/index.html**.

Benefits of Certification

How does certification pay off for job applicants? A certificate won't guarantee a job or even higher pay, but it does provide a

FIGURE 10.14 Selected Certification Programs

Certification Program	Description
Microsoft Certified Systems Administrator (MCSA)	Microsoft Windows Server 2003 implementation, management, and maintenance, as well as LAN-based client/server administration (Microsoft Corporation)
Microsoft Certified Systems Engineer (MCSE)	Microsoft Windows 2000 and Windows Server 2003; operating system and network planning, design, and implementation, as well as LAN-based client/server development (Microsoft Corporation)
Microsoft Certified Technology Specialist (MCTS)	New generation of Microsoft certification; indicates expertise within a specific technology (Microsoft Corporation)
Microsoft Certified IT Professional (MCITP)	New generation of Microsoft certification; builds on core technology expertise to demonstrate key IT professional job and role skills (Microsoft Corporation)
Systems Security Certified Practitioner (SSCP)	To demonstrate vendor-neutral skills and competency for information security practitioners [(ISC)2]
Red Hat Certified Engineer (RHCE)	Performance-based certification for Linux network design, deployment, and administration (Red Hat)
Novell Certified Linux Administrator (CLA)	Administration of installed SUSE Linux Enterprise Server networks (Novell)
Sun Certified Java Programmer (SCJP)	Programming in Java (Sun Microsystems)
Sun Certified Java Developer (SCJD)	Programming and application development in Java (Sun Microsystems)
A+	To validate vendor-neutral skills for entry-level computer technicians (Computing Technology Industry Association [CompTIA])
Network+	To validate vendor-neutral skills for network technicians (CompTIA)
Cisco Certified Network Associate/Cisco Certified Internetwork Expert (CCNA/CCIE)	Installation, configuration, and operation of LAN, WAN, and dial-up access services for small networks (Cisco Systems)

benchmark that enables prospective employers to assess an applicant's skills. In areas of high demand, certification can translate into salary offers that are 7.5 to 8 percent higher than the norm.

How does certification benefit employers? Although the effects of certification haven't been rigorously studied by independent investigators, vendors and trainers claim that employers who hire certified employees have less downtime and lower IT costs. This makes sense, because certification sets a standard that helps guarantee that new employees will have a certain skill set. When an employee's skill set is matched with the employer's job requirements, everyone wins (Figure 10.15).

Risks of Certification

Certification entails some risks for employees and employers alike. The reason lies in the nature of the certification process, which emphasizes a form of learning that is both narrow (focused on a specific technology) and deep (rigorous and thorough).

For employees, certification requires that they devote a great deal of time and effort to a specific vendor's technology. But changing technology may make vendor-specific skills less marketable. If you're

FIGURE 10.15 Many Web sites contain current information about technical certification programs.

certified as a Novell Linux administrator, for example, you won't impress a prospective employer who's running a Windows network. If you make a bad bet on which certificate to pursue, you could wind up with excellent skills in a technology or application that's losing market share.

For employers, hiring people with narrow training is a risk. People with narrow training may not be able to adjust to rapidly changing technologies. In addition, having just one skill isn't enough. Some companies expect employees to possess strong skills in as many as four or five areas. That's why it's a good idea to take as many CS and MIS courses as you can. With a solid theoretical foundation, you are better equipped for lifelong learning and the transfer of knowledge that enables the learning of new skills throughout your career. You'll prove most attractive to employers if you combine certification with a solid college transcript, communication skills, and business-related courses.

How To:

Use Technology to Find Your Dream Job!

1. **Assessment.** Assess your skills by using any of the free online career assessment tools. Two possible sites recommended in this chapter are located at Assessment.com (**www.assessment.com/**) and Career Explorer (**www.careerexplorer.net/aptitude.asp**).

   a. See whether your assessment and the career you had in mind match. If not, then work on obtaining the skills needed for the career you desire. If you need to locate an educational facility that provides courses or training, make use of the suggestions in this chapter or use your Web-searching skills to locate a training institute.

   b. Use the Internet, search engines, and job search sites to locate jobs in the career you are targeting. See whether the companies that are hiring in that field are ones that you would want to work for. Again, research their job requirements, and see whether you are on the right track with your education.

2. **Sell Yourself.** Once you have the skills for the career of your choice, you will need a resume and cover letter.

   a. Many application programs, like Microsoft Word, provide an incredible selection of templates for resumes and cover letters (Figure 10.16 and Figure 10.17). It is best to use these as a guide for what to include and as an example of possible layouts. These templates do not always transfer well or upload to employer sites correctly. Use them only as a reference or guide.

   b. Review suggestions at Web sites that specifically focus on resumes and cover letters. One such site, **www.resumark.com**, posts suggestions on what to and not to do. Go to **www.resumark.com/job-resources/resume-writing/a-dozen--things-we-recommend-you-to-leave-off-of-your-resume.html** to view a list of a things to leave off a resume.

   c. Remember to change your resume for each job application and include the keywords used in the job posting.

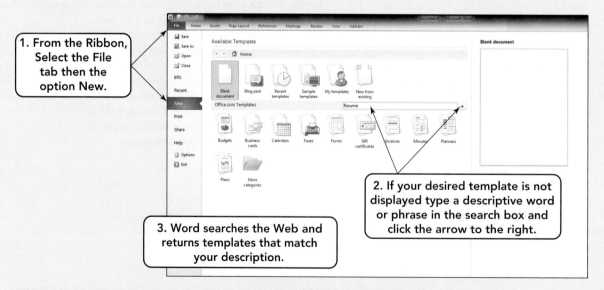

1. From the Ribbon, Select the File tab then the option New.

2. If your desired template is not displayed type a descriptive word or phrase in the search box and click the arrow to the right.

3. Word searches the Web and returns templates that match your description.

FIGURE 10.16 Word 2010 provides an easy-to-use template interface with a built-in search box.

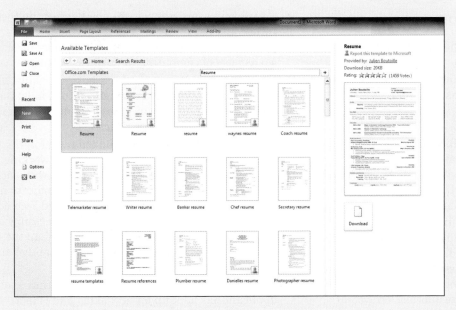

FIGURE 10.17 Microsoft's Web site provides many resume options.

3. **Prepare for the Interview.** For an employer, an interview is an opportunity to see if you are who you said you were in the resume. For the applicant, the interview is a chance to display personal attributes that a resume cannot exhibit, for example, honesty, communication skills, and self-confidence.

   a. Research the company thoroughly. Use your research skills and the Internet to find out as much about the company as possible. Your responses to questions on corporate goals and history should be quick, concise, and accurate.

   b. Use the job placement center at your school for information on interview techniques. See whether someone can run through a mock interview with you and, if possible, record it. Reviewing your responses, as well as your body language and mannerisms, will help you see yourself as others see you. Rehearse, rehearse, and rehearse!

   c. Again locate Web sites that are focused on interview skills. Visit **www.resumark.com/job-resources/interviewing/what-employers-want-to-hear-at-a-job-interview--tips-for-successful-job-interviews.html** for a list of what employers want to hear at interviews.

   d. Jobs interviews at companies like Microsoft and Apple can be very stressful and can last all day. Many applicants that have gone through the process are willing to share their experiences and suggestions. A simple search will lead to many hits.

4. **Congratulate Yourself.** Hopefully all of your work paid off and you received your dream job. Now go to work!!

Chapter Summary

Careers and Certification

- Computer literacy is the ability to understand how to use a computer effectively. Employers view computer literacy skills as "important" or "very important" in their hiring decisions.

- Enrollment in traditional information technology (IT) career paths that require a four-year college degree in computer science (CS), management information systems (MIS), software engineering, or electrical engineering (EE) are increasing. The two main fields of projected growth for 2018 are software engineering (34 percent) and networking systems and data communication analysis (53 percent).

- Projections though the year 2016 made by the U.S. Bureau of Labor Statistics indicate that the need for information technology professionals will continue to be in high demand. Two settings in which IT workers find employment are corporate information system departments and software development firms. Some common positions in these settings include: network engineer, system administrator, system analyst, programmer, software engineer, software developer, and customer service support technician.

- Training in computer science emphasizes the theoretical and cutting-edge aspects of computing, whereas training in MIS emphasizes more practical aspects of computing in business settings.

- IT professionals today need soft business skills, like good verbal and written communication skills, the ability to work on a team, project management experience, and business perspectives.

- Technical skills in high demand today and in the future for the IT professional include networking, database management and development with such high end systems as Oracle, Microsoft application use and development, Linux, Internet and Web development experience. In addition to possessing these skills, IT professionals need to keep up these skills, stay ahead of the times, and be adaptive and ready to pursue adjusted career paths.

- Certifications can prove to an employer that a job applicant has kept up on new skills and is motivated. They can also indicate a narrow focus of knowledge and limited skill set.

Key Terms and Concepts

Identification

Identify the job title described in this chapter that best fits each list of responsibilities.

1. _____ Job responsibilities
   - Works closely with users and application developers to prioritize goals and needs
   - Seeks and develops efficient and cost-effective solutions

- Evaluates system specifications against business development and goals

2. _____ Job responsibilities
   - Installs, supports, and maintains network services, systems, and devices

- Troubleshoots servers, workstations, and associated systems
- Monitors and supports computing and network infrastructure

3. _____ Job responsibilities
- Develops and designs an interface that will be attractive and promote interaction by customers viewing or using it on the Internet
- Has an understanding of both software functionality and graphic design
- Listens closely to a client's suggestions in order to create a design with an attractive Web presence that meets those conditions

4. _____ Job responsibilities
- Creates code that meets system standards and specifications
- Maintains existing applications
- Develops a new application from beginning to end

5. _____ Job responsibilities
- Creates a Web presence through the use of animation, video, podcasts, and other media methods
- Edits, organizes, and compresses audio and video content based on requirements and time constraints
- Designs an interface appropriate for the presentation of active media

6. _____ Job responsibilities
- Dictates design choices including the platforms, coding, and technical level while staying abreast with cutting-edge technologies
- Monitors the full cycle of software development including: research, review, and testing
- Reports on project status to senior management

Matching

Match each key term in the left column with the most accurate definition in the right column.

_____ 1. webinar

_____ 2. outsourcing

_____ 3. certification

_____ 4. trade show

_____ 5. offshoring

_____ 6. keywords

_____ 7. Web conference

_____ 8. white formatting

_____ 9. labor dumping

_____ 10. application tracking system

_____ 11. online workshop

_____ 12. computer literacy

_____ 13. computer science

_____ 14. training seminar

_____ 15. management information systems

a. A skill and knowledge assessment process

b. Training in a new technology, usually presented by the developer of the new hardware or software product or by a company specializing in training IT professionals.

c. The practical application of information systems and technology to provide the skills a business needs to compete successfully.

d. The practice of changing the font of certain text to white in order to evade notice by a human reviewer but still get detected by an automated review system

e. A computer program that scans documents for words that match a list specified by the user

f. A conference that uses the Internet and is typically one-way—from speaker to audience with limited attendee participation

g. The study of the theoretical foundations of information and computation

h. A working knowledge of the efficient use of a computer

i. A conference that uses the Internet to connect attendees in different geographical locations and enable them to interact with each other

j. Periodic meetings at which computer product manufacturers, designers, and dealers showcase their products

k. Used by employers when listing the minimum qualifications for a job

l. The flooding of a labor market with foreign workers

m. A structured interactive instructional session done over the Internet and assisted by an electronic meeting system that enables discussions, brainstorming, voting, and categorization

n. The transfer of labor from workers in one country to workers in other countries

o. One company contracting with another to provide services that might otherwise be performed by in-house employees

Multiple Choice

Circle the correct choice for each of the following.

1. Which statement about computer science is *not* true?
   a. Computer science majors study algorithms and their practical applications.
   b. Computer science majors have been on the increase since 2008.
   c. Computer science focuses on the technology needed to promote business success.
   d. Computer science majors learn to program in several high-level languages.

2. Which certification is needed for an entry-level computer technician position?
   a. Network +
   b. A+
   c. Microsoft Certified IT Professional
   d. Microsoft Certified Technology Specialist

3. Which of the following is *not* a soft business skill?
   a. Communication   b. Project management
   c. Programming skill   d. Teamwork

4. Which of the following statements about management information systems is true?
   a. The theoretical aspects of computing are emphasized.
   b. To drive business success, finance and marketing knowledge, along with communication and interpersonal skills, is essential.
   c. Training usually includes several semesters of higher math.
   d. Topics such as artificial intelligence and programming language structure are required.

5. Which of the following jobs in the Web technology industry designs, develops, tests, and documents new Web-based services for Web sites?
   a. Network/Internet Security Specialist
   b. Web Application Engineer
   c. Web Database Engineer
   d. Web Designer

6. Which of the following is a high-end relational database product whose use is considered to be a sought-after technical skill today?
   a. Oracle
   b. Linux
   c. Project management software
   d. AJAX

7. Which of the following is *not* an example of an Internet-based method of training discussed in this chapter?
   a. Webinar
   b. Web conference
   c. Trade show
   d. Online training

8. Which statement is true about an IT professional?
   a. Most IT professionals do not have four-year degrees.
   b. IT professionals continually have to learn new technologies.
   c. IT professionals rarely change jobs.
   d. IT professionals will not be in demand by the year 2016.

9. Who manages the details of a software development project?
   a. Software Engineer
   b. Programmer
   c. Network Engineer
   d. Chief Information Officer

10. Which of the following is a valid certification?
    a. Microsoft Certified Application Developer (MCAD)
    b. Microsoft Certified Application User (MCAU)
    c. Digital Media Specialist (DMS)
    d. Microsoft Certified IT Professional (MCITP)

Fill-In

In the blanks provided, write the correct answer for each of the following.

1. _____ business skills focus on technological expertise.

2. A _____ is an outside firm that manages the information technology for a company or institution.

3. The World Organization of Webmasters (WOW) and the IEEE are examples of _____.

4. A(n) _____ defines the IS department's mission, budget, and strategic plan.

5. The _____ is the oldest and largest scientific computing society.

6. _____ is the use of computers and medical expertise to provide the equivalent of a long-distance house call.

7. The International Consumer Electronics show held in Las Vegas annually is an example of a(n) _____.

8. _____ focuses on digital circuit design and cutting-edge communications technology.

9. _____ is a group of interrelated Web development techniques.

10. India and Malaysia are the two top _____ countries.

11. _____ is a business management skill that encompasses the ability to budget a project, itemize resources, and determine the availability and cost of those resources.

12. HTML, XHTML, CSS, Flash, and JavaScript are areas of knowledge in the field of _____.

13. The _____ department is the functional area responsible for managing information technology and systems at a business or university.

14. Communication and teamwork are known as nontechnical or _____ business skills

15. Information about job trends can be found in the Occupational Outlook Handbook located on the _____ Web site.

Short Answer

1. Describe the types of companies that compose the information technology industry and provide an example of each.

2. Define computer literacy and list four computer skills that employers are looking for in job applicants.

3. Define software engineering and explain why it is expected to grow by 34 percent by 2018.

4. Explain the difference between offshoring and outsourcing.

5. Define soft business skills and provide three examples that employers are looking for in an IT professional.

Teamwork

1. **Emerging Technology and Job Impact** As a team, identify five new emerging technologies. Provide a brief description of each. Come to a consensus on which of the five the team believes will lead to the greatest expansion of jobs in the IT job market. In a one-page, double-spaced paper, list the five chosen technologies and their descriptions. Then state the reasons the team believed the technology they choose will turn out to be the leader in job expansion. List the types of jobs the team believed the technology would foster or create.

2. **Evaluate IT Job Search Sites** In this exercise, divide your team into groups and explore the various IT job search sites listed in Figure 10.2. Assess them with respect to ease of use, search capabilities, content presentation, accuracy of job search results, and depth of information provided. Add any additional assessments that the team thinks are suitable for comparison. Regroup and, in a Word table or Excel spreadsheet, enter each site and its ranking for each assessment criteria. When finished, as a team, designate the one site that exceeds all the rest. Provide your justification for this ranking in a summary statement below your table or in a separate Word document.

3. **Online versus Personal Interviews** As a team set up a mock interview for an IT help desk position at your school. Generate five questions that an interviewer would ask a job candidate for the help desk position. Break into groups of two, with one team member being the interviewer and other the job applicant. Role-play a live interview session. Regroup and assess the feelings the applicant had during the interview process. Additionally have

the interviewer rate the applicant on such points as clarity of response, body language, eye contact, and any other points that the team establishes. Then select a few team members to simulate a virtual Web interview. Place the interview questions in a PowerPoint presentation, with one question per slide and the timing for each question set by the team. Set up a video recorder or Web cam to record the applicant's response to each question. When several team members have performed the virtual Web interview, note the feelings they had during the Web interview process. Again, have the interviewer rate the applicant on the same points as were used in the live interview. Compare the applicant's responses and interviewer ratings between the live versus Web interview. In a PowerPoint presentation of at least five slides, present your team's findings, including answers to such questions as these: Which method did the applicant find more comfortable? With which method did the applicant feel more connected to the potential employer? Which interview did the applicant think gave him or her more time and freedom to respond? How was the applicant rated by the interviewer? What did the interviewer find most different between an applicant's live and Web session?

4. **A Change in Course** As a team, come up with a list of at least 10 jobs that have changed over the past 15 years from manual or low-tech positions to computer-based jobs. In a one-page, double-spaced paper, describe each job, how it was previously performed, and how a computer is used to perform it today. Indicate whether the education requirements of the individual performing the job have also changed.

5. **Resume Examples** Break into smaller groups and research keyword resumes. Use the library at your school, the placement office, and any other resources you can locate. Regroup and as a team, come up with a list of the five top features a good keyword resume should contain. Locate examples or resume templates, and as a team, select the top two that you agree contain your five top features and have the professional look and feel that supports your team's research. Present your top five resume features and two examples in a PowerPoint presentation of at least five slides. Remember to cite your references.

On the Web

1. **The Ethics of White Formatting** Using online resources, locate several articles that promote white formatting on keyword resumes and several articles that oppose its use. Summarize the views of both sides in a one-page, double-spaced paper. At the conclusion of your summary, indicate whether your research has led you to believe that the practice of white formatting is ethical or unethical. Support your stance, and remember to cite your references.

2. **Local IT Jobs in Your Community** The U.S. Department of Labor's Bureau of Statistics Web site indicates that software engineers and network system and data communication analysts are the technology positions that will see the most growth between now and 2018. Research the current availability of these jobs in a 50-mile radius of your school. Use the job search Web sites listed in Figures 10.1 and 10.2 and any others that you might be familiar with or locate. In a Word table, keep track of each site and the number of technology-related jobs posted in your area and how many of those fall into the category of software engineer or network system analyst or data communication analyst. Use at least five to seven sites to get a true picture of the demand for these positions. How does your community measure up to the predicted rise in

these job categories? Do you see a correlation between your community and the predictions made by the Department of Labor? Place your answers to these questions and any other observations you've made below the table. Remember to cite your references.

3. **MIS versus CS** Using your school and other local educational institutions, compare the course requirements for a degree in computer science and a degree in management information systems. Determine the number of mathematic courses, technology courses, and soft skills courses (for example, public speaking and communications) that each require. Does either program offer an internship to provide practical experience? Are any certificates that focus on a subcategory of either department offered? Summarize your comparisons and answers to these questions in a one-page, double-spaced paper. Remember to cite your references.

4. **Ten Top IT Certificates** Visit **http://certification. about.com/od/entrylevelcertification1/tp/ topbeginner.htm**, a Web site that identifies the top 10 IT certificates. Then visit job search Web sites and locate job postings in your region that seek or recommend these certificates for employment. Use an Excel spreadsheet to keep track of

each certificate, the types of posted jobs that require or recommend them for employment, and, if possible, the salary associated with the job. Indicate which certificate seemed the most in demand and which seemed to attract the highest salary. Remember to cite your references.

5. **Web Tech Job Titles** As indicated in the chapter, Web positions have a variety of names. Using the Internet and job search sites, develop a list of 10 different IT jobs in your area that are Web related. In a Word table, list the name of the position, a description of expected job duties, the education or certificate required, the type of company advertising the position, and the salary range (if posted).

chapter 11

Programming Languages and Program Development

Chapter Objectives

1 Explain what a programming language is and how it works. (p. 474)

2 Explain the development of programming languages over the years and the benefits and drawbacks of high-level programming languages. (p. 477)

3 Explain how object-oriented languages attempt to remedy the shortcomings of earlier languages. (p. 481)

4 List several popular object-oriented languages and explain their advantage over older languages. (p. 488)

5 List the six phases of the program development life cycle (PDLC) and explain why the PDLC is needed. (p. 494)

6 Explain why defining the problem in a top-down design manner leads to programs that are easier to debug and maintain. (p. 495)

7 Differentiate between problems that can arise in the testing and debugging phase as syntax and logic errors. (p. 498)

Have you ever been on a rollercoaster, had the restraining bar come down, and raised your arms as you went down that first hill? I bet you never thought of the amount of time that went into the design, layout, engineering, testing, and final construction of the ride. In the same way, we turn on our computers, click on an app on our smartphones, or punch an address into our GPS units; and we never think twice about the time that went into the design, layout, engineering, testing, and final development of the programs that we take for granted. The whole process is more complicated than you think. Yet, it seems so instantaneous and automatic. How is it done?

Programmers and programming languages are behind the software we use today. A **programmer** is an individual, usually having four to six years of higher education, who works individually, or as part of a team, to design, write, and test software applications for everything from word processing programs to virus protection software. A **programming language** is an artificial language, one that is deliberately created to tell the computer what to do in a step-by-step manner. Even if you don't plan to study programming or want to become a programmer, this chapter will expose you to

- A variety of programming languages
- The development of these languages and the difference between the traditional procedural languages, functional languages, and the popular object-oriented languages
- The type of applications that each language supports
- The step-by-step program development life cycle (PDLC) that starts with defining the problem and ends with the implementation and maintenance of the program
- The difference between syntax errors and logic errors and the importance of maintaining programs ▪

Programming Languages and How They Work

Programming is the process used to create the software programs you use every day. These programs are the result of the efforts of programmers, individuals that use programming languages to create software. Unlike the natural languages that people speak, each programming language consists of a vocabulary and a set of rules. These rules are called **syntax**. It usually refers to the proper use of commas, parentheses, braces, semicolons, and other punctuation, symbols, or keywords that are used to accurately construct a segment of code. A programmer must learn these rules because they govern the structure of the instructions, commands, and statements of the language he or she uses to write a program. A typical technology user, if able to view the code, would probably not match the code to the finished product. The **interface**, the point of interaction between components, in this case the user's screen and code, which are seen when running a program, and the actual code used to create that program look nothing alike (Figure 11.1).

FIGURE 11.1 The actual home page of Amazon.com that a viewer sees and the HTML code, with embedded cascading style sheets and JavaScript, that provides the instructions to create it are very different.

Planning Precedes Writing

When a programmer begins a software project, the answers to five questions will guide him/her to determine the program's interface, options, and method of presentation and ultimately the programming language used to create it.

Who will be interested in the product? This involves getting a feel for the type of individuals that will use the program, any new technologies that relate to that group, and the languages that are used to develop those types of technologies.

What is the competition? To answer this question, there has to be an analysis of the features used in competitive programs—an investigation into what the market leaders are featuring and then determining whether these features can be included and whether they add value to your program is an important next step. Again, it is necessary to investigate the languages needed to create these features and to determine whether they can be used in your product.

Where will the program be used? The location in which the target audience will use the program and the type of device that the program will be used on or embedded within will affect the development of the program as much as the program's purpose. Small business, large corporations, home, education, automobiles, entertainment facilities, and smartphones are some of the possibilities.

When will the program be used? Most software purchasers spend money on the programs that they use the most or find the hardest to do without. Ease of use and an engaging interface can help make a program a must-buy, along with the use of a programming language that will allow settings to be changed by the user through an intuitive interface.

Why will they want to purchase your product? A purchaser will want to buy a program that does

what it is advertised to do, does it well, has a fast learning curve, and provides value for that user.

The answers to all five of these questions will help determine the language or languages that will be needed to create the program. Programming languages are not all alike. They differ in syntax, design capabilities, and the way they are converted into machine-understandable instructions. This conversion can either be done through a compiler or an interpreter. Let's take a closer look at each.

Compilers and Interpreters

In most cases, the language used by a programmer, **source code**, has to be translated from its original form into a form recognized by the internal hardware before a computer can actually run it. In general, the written computer instructions that programmers create are called **code** (Figure 11.2). The term *code* can be a noun or a verb. For example, a programmer might say, "I wrote most of the code for this project" or "I must code a new program." Code comes in many forms. We'll discuss another form of code, called *object code*, in subsequent sections.

FIGURE 11.2 Take a peek at the code of three languages: XHTML and Cascading Styles that create and format a Web page and the SQL that searches a database for matching information.

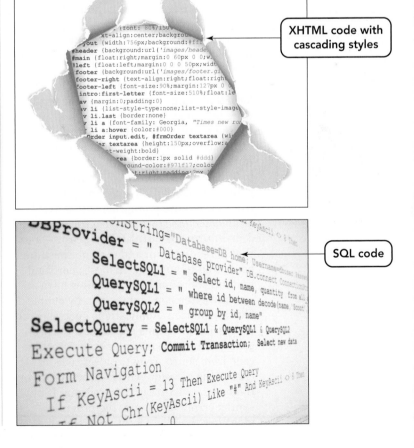

XHTML code with cascading styles

SQL code

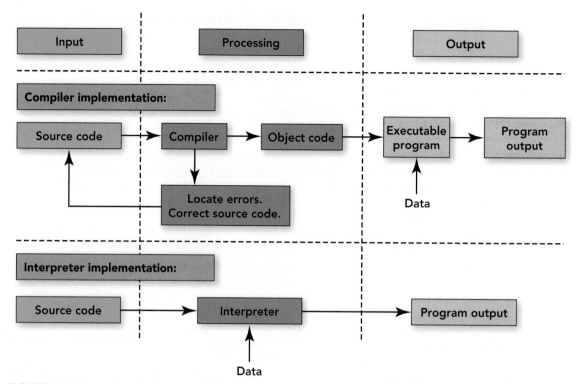

FIGURE 11.3 A compiler and an interpreter both translate source code, but a compiler makes use of an intermediate object file and produces an executable file.

STUDENT VIDEO

Programmers create source code in a **high-level language**, a language that mimics English and does not require the programmer to understand the intimate details of how hardware, especially the processor, handles data. For the source code to run on a specific type of computer system, it must be translated by a compiler or an interpreter, also referred to as a *language translator* (Figure 11.3), into a form that is understandable by the hardware in that system.

A **compiler** is a utility program that translates all of the source code into **object code**, which is a set of instructions in (or close to) a specific computer's machine language. With some compilers, it's necessary to use a program called a *linker* or an *assembler* to transform the object code into an **executable program**—one that is ready to run and does not need to be altered in any way. In most operating system environments, these files have an .exe file extension and are run by double-clicking an icon. Applications such as word processing programs are executable programs. When the compiler translates the code from source code to object code, it checks the code for syntax errors, flaws in the basic structure of the program. If any syntax errors are found, the program identifies the likely location of the error

(Figure 11.4). The errors must be corrected and the cycle of compile and correct continued until the source code is free of any syntax errors. Once no errors exist, the error-free executable file can be run.

Another translation program, an **interpreter**, doesn't produce object code. Instead, it translates one line of the source code at a time and executes the translated instruction. Interpreters are helpful tools for learning and locating program errors. Because the program executes line by line, the programmer can see exactly what each line does. When a line with an error is encountered, the interpreter either bypasses it or stops the program execution and the program is displayed up to the encountered error (Figure 11.5).

Every programming language has its advantages and disadvantages. What's the best programming language? If you ask 10 IT professionals, chances are you'll get 10 different answers. The truth is that there isn't any one language that's best for all programming purposes, which is the reason for the abundance of languages that exist today. The better question is, Which language is the right one for the job? A look at the history of the development of programming languages will help clarify the progression that led to the object-oriented, user-friendly interfaces in use today.

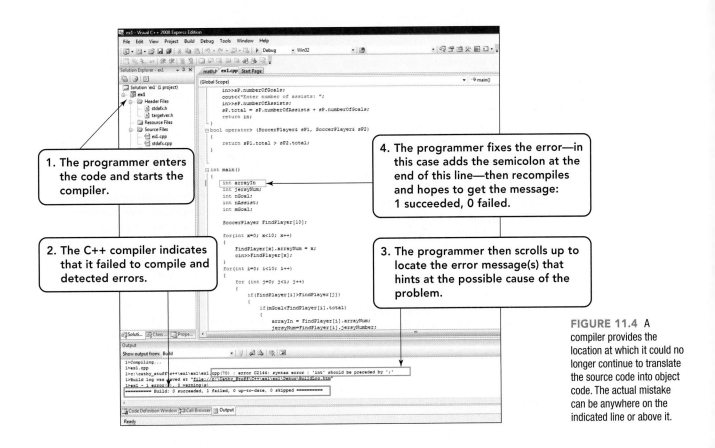

1. The programmer enters the code and starts the compiler.

2. The C++ compiler indicates that it failed to compile and detected errors.

3. The programmer then scrolls up to locate the error message(s) that hints at the possible cause of the problem.

4. The programmer fixes the error—in this case adds the semicolon at the end of this line—then recompiles and hopes to get the message: 1 succeeded, 0 failed.

FIGURE 11.4 A compiler provides the location at which it could no longer continue to translate the source code into object code. The actual mistake can be anywhere on the indicated line or above it.

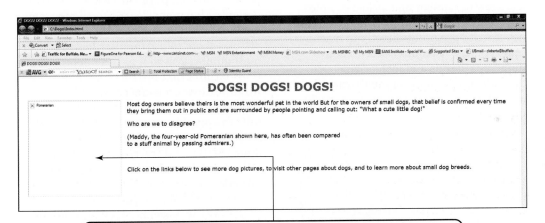

If an image is not located where indicated in the XHTML code, the interpreter (browser) usually just places an image placeholder and continues to display the rest of the page.

More serious errors will stop the page display at the error.

FIGURE 11.5 A browser acts as an interpreter of the XHTML code that creates Web pages.

Development of Programming Languages

Programming languages are classified by levels, or generations. Each generation is a step closer to the languages that humans use. These are the five generations of programming languages:

- Machine language
- Assembly language
- Procedural languages
- Nonprocedural languages
- Natural languages

This section discusses the development of these languages and how they've evolved to keep up with changing technology.

First-Generation Languages (1GL): 0S and 1S

Because the earliest computers predated programming languages, computers had to be programmed in the computer's language, also known as **machine language**. Machine language consists of binary numbers—0s and 1s—that directly correspond to the computer's electrical states. Though tedious for humans to work with, machine language is the only programming language that a computer can understand directly without translation. Each type or family of processor requires its own machine language with instructions that conform to the processor's special characteristics. For this reason, machine language is said to be **machine dependent** (or **hardware dependent**).

During the first generation of computing, programmers had to use machine language because no other option was available. Programmers had to know a great deal about the processor's design and how it functioned. As a result, programs were few in number and lacked complex functionality. Today, programmers almost never write programs directly in machine code, because it requires attention to numerous details and memorizing numerical codes for every instruction that is used. It also locks the code to a specific platform.

More recent programming languages, which resemble natural language, make it easier for programmers to write programs, but all of the code they write, no matter what language is used, must still be translated into machine language before the processor can execute the program on a system.

Second-Generation Languages (2GL): Using Mnemonics

The first programming language to break programmers' dependence on machine language was assembly language. In **assembly language**, each program statement corresponds to an instruction that the microprocessor can carry out. Assembly language closely resembles machine language in that it's processor dependent and closely tied to the hardware inside the system unit. For this reason, assembly and machine languages are called **low-level languages**. The word *low* refers to the small or nonexistent amount of difference between the language and machine language; because of this, low-level languages are sometimes described as being "close to the hardware."

To program in assembly language, programmers still need to know how the computer's internal hardware works. However, assembly language doesn't force programmers to program in binary. Instead, it enables them to use familiar base-10 (decimal) numbers as well as brief abbreviations for program instructions called **mnemonics** (pronounced "nih-MON-icks"). For example, the mnemonic MOV tells the processor to move a value, while ADD instructs it to add one value to another, SUB to subtract, MUL to multiply, DIV to divide, and JMP to jump to an instruction in the code. Notice the use of the mnemonic MOV in Figure 11.6.

Before an assembly language program can be run on a computer, it must be translated into machine language. The source code is translated into machine language by a utility program called an **assembler**.

Assembly language is still used occasionally to write short programs, such as a **device driver** (a program that controls a device attached to a computer), and in game console programming.

Third-Generation Languages (3GL): Programming Comes of Age

Because of the difficulties of writing code in machine and assembly languages,

```
Title           Hello World      (hello.asm)
                Program
; This program will display "Hello, World!"
dosseg
.model          Small
.stack          100h
.data
    hello_message db 'Hello, World!',0dh,0ah,'$'
.code
main            Proc
                Mov              ax,@data
                Mov              ds,ax
                Mov              ah,9
                Mov              dx, offset hello_message
                Int              21h
                Mov              ax,4C00h
                Int              21h
main            Endp
end             Main
```

FIGURE 11.6 Assembly language for the IBM-PC to output "Hello, World!"

third-generation languages were developed with the goal of making programming languages more user-friendly, modular, and reusable. Third-generation languages are considered high-level languages. Unlike machine and assembly languages, high-level languages eliminate the need for programmers to understand the intimate details of how the hardware handles data. The programmer can write an instruction using familiar English words such as PRINT or DISPLAY. Such an instruction sums up many lines of assembly or machine language code. As a result, third-generation languages are much easier to read, write, and maintain than machine and assembly languages.

Spaghetti Code and the Great Software Crisis

Early third-generation languages represented a major improvement over assembly and machine languages. However, these languages also used GOTO statements to enable programs to branch or jump to new locations if specified conditions were met. This wasn't a problem for simple, short programs, but for lengthier programs, the use of many GOTO statements resulted in code that was difficult to follow, messy in design, and prone to errors, earning it the label **spaghetti code**.

The attempt to create larger and more complex programs led to the software crisis of the 1960s. Programs were not ready on time, exceeded their budgets, contained too many errors, and didn't satisfy customers.

Structured Programming Languages

One response to spaghetti code problems focused on improving the management of software development. Another response focused on improving the languages themselves. The earliest product of such efforts (in the late 1960s) was the concept of structured programming and languages that reflected structured programming concepts. **Structured programming**, also referred to as top-down program design, is a set of quality standards that makes programs more verbose but more readable, reliable, and maintainable. With structured programming, GOTO statements are forbidden, resulting in code that is more logically developed. Examples of structured languages include Algol, Pascal, and Ada.

Modular Programming Languages

By the 1970s, it was clear that structured programming languages, although better than their predecessors, weren't able to solve the problems encountered in the even larger development projects underway. As a result, programmers developed the modular programming concept. With **modular programming**, larger programs are divided into separate modules, each of which takes care of a specific function that the program has to carry out. Each module requires a specified input and produces a specified output, so the programming job can be easily divided among members of the programming team. Modular languages include Fortran and C. As programs became more and more complex and the applications more sensitive in nature, the need for more modularity coupled with **information hiding** (or **encapsulation**) increased. This approach of hiding details and developing individual modules led to the creation of object-oriented programming languages like C++ and Java. These languages further encapsulate information and increase code security by defining objects, their components, and actions. Once an object is defined, it can be reused or become a subcomponent within another object definition. Each component of an object is assigned a certain level of accessibility by the programmer based on the purpose of the program. Components that are private cannot be directly used in the main section of code but must be accessed by other components of that object that are assigned public accessibility. These levels of accessibility increase information hiding and add an additional layer of security to the code (Figure 11.7). Object-oriented languages are discussed in detail later in this chapter.

```
class BankAccount {
    private:
        int accNo;
        double accBal;
        double interest;
    public:
        BankAccount(int, double, double);
        void enterAccountData();
        void computeInterest(int);
        void displayAccount();
};
```

FIGURE 11.7 This C++ Bank Account object is defined with three private components and four public components.

Fourth-Generation Languages (4GL): Getting Away from Procedure

Procedural languages provide detailed instructions that are designed to carry out a specific action, for example printing information in a tabular format. **Nonprocedural languages**, on the other hand, aren't tied down to step-by-step procedures that force the programmer to consider the procedure that must be followed to obtain the desired result. The 4GLs are designed to reduce programming effort, the time it takes to develop software, and the cost of software development—while generating the equivalent of very complicated 3GL instructions with fewer errors. In general, 3GL focused on software engineering, while 4GL and 5GL focus on problem solving and system engineering. Various types of programming languages have claimed to be "fourth-generation," including **report generators** (languages for printing database reports that provide a user-friendly interface and enable a user to design and generate high-quality reports and graphs) and **query languages** (languages with instructions designed to retrieve and edit information included in databases). FoxPro, Agile, ColdFusion, Mathematica, and SPSS are nonprocedural languages. A specialized query language known as **structured query language**, or **SQL** (pronounced "sequel"), enables users to phrase simple or complex requests for data. For example, in SQL you can ask the following question of the data in a database:

```
SELECT employee-name
FROM employee-salary-table
WHERE salary > 50000
AND position = 'Engineer'
```

In everyday terms, this request is to "Get the names of all engineers who make more than $50,000 from the employee-salary-table." Note that this question isn't totally nonprocedural; you still have to know quite a bit about how the database is structured. (For example, you have to specify which table the information should come from.)

Fifth-Generation Languages: Natural Language

The ultimate nonprocedural language would be **natural language**, the everyday language that people speak. Computers would be much easier to use if they could understand natural language, whether the input was spoken or typed. For example, instead of looking through folder after folder in search of a missing file, imagine asking the computer, "Where's that file I created a couple of days ago—the one I wrote about those two paintings we saw in my art history class?"

Despite years of effort to create natural language interfaces, computers are still not very good at understanding what they hear and acting on this understanding. Much of what passes for a natural language interface amounts to word matching; for example, you can navigate the folders on a Mac by speaking their names and giving a few simple commands, such as "Open" or "Close." Combined with software that can parse (decode) a sentence's grammatical structure, word-matching programs can work well in areas with highly specialized vocabularies of a few thousand words.

Attempts to create natural language systems with more general capabilities have run into profound problems. One such problem is the ambiguity of human language. The term *intelligence*, for instance, has at least four other meanings. In the military, for example, *intelligence* means knowledge about the enemy. A program capable of understanding the various contexts of a word would have to know a great deal about the world. For example, natural language software should be able to understand that "the day before Christmas" is December 24. The underlying problems presented by these ambiguities are exceedingly complex and will require many more years of research to solve.

This trend toward the use of natural language is currently a focal point of many software companies and is being assisted by major advances in speech recognition

> "Despite **years** of effort to **create** natural language interfaces, **computers** are still **not very good** at understanding what they **hear** and **acting** on this understanding."

Human: hi alice
ALICE: Hello there.
Human: Are you a computer?
ALICE: Would it matter to you if I were metal instead of flesh?
Human: No
ALICE: I am glad that you don't discriminate against robots.
You say:

FIGURE 11.8 The chat robot ALICE (Artificial Linguistic Internet Computer Entity) uses speech recognition and natural language programming to converse with visitors at **http://alice.pandorabots.com.**

software, programs that translate the spoken word into text. Previously, speech-recognition software worked only if the speaker paused between words or completed a brief (10-minute) tutorial provided with the software. Users would read out loud several designated sentences to help the computer adjust to their speaking style. However, that is changing. Using the speech recognition component of Windows 7 and the newest release of Dragon NaturallySpeaking, no voice training is required. In any instance, the user will encounter some errors in the application's interpretation of his or her spoken word initially; but the software continues to improve its accuracy with repeated use.

Continuous speech recognition is the first step toward a true natural language interface, because such an interface would require the computer to recognize anyone's natural speech. With reliable speech recognition technology developing rapidly, the day is approaching when you'll be able to control a computer solely by talking to it in ordinary speech (Figure 11.8).

In the next section, you'll learn how expanding a language to work with objects, brings programming closer to human thinking and natural language.

Object-Oriented Programming

Object-oriented programming (OOP) is a popular programming technique (Figure 11.9) based on data being conceptualized as objects. An object is defined by its features and behavior. Multiple objects can be assembled into one program, or one object can be nested (contained) within another to create a solution for a specific problem.

Objects An **object** in object-oriented programming (OOP) is a unit of computer information that defines a data element and is used to model real-world objects that you use every day. It contains **attributes** (members) that define the object's features and **methods** (actions or behaviors) that can process or manipulate the attributes. With object-oriented programming, information hiding (or encapsulation) becomes a reality by setting the access level of attributes and methods as private or public. Private attributes and methods cannot be directly used in the programming source code. They can only be manipulated though methods set with a public level of access. Thus, the private elements are not visible to the user (or other objects) and the specifics of how the object was implemented internally remains concealed. The object is simply acted on by its public components, which provide the information requested or perform the programmed behavior on the objects private members.

Suppose you're running a bike shop and you have a specific type of racing bike in stock called the DASHER. Dasher is an object in your shop, and your books or records on DASHER contain all of the data attributes about a Dasher bicycle (including inventory ID number, unit price, and quantity in stock). You can also perform actions (methods) on the DASHER's data. For example, you can increase or decrease its price, update the quantity, and calculate the total inventory value of the DASHER bikes in your shop.

Classes An important feature of object-oriented programming is the concept of a **class**, a blueprint or prototype from which objects are made. In the DASHER example, the DASHER object is part of a broader, more abstract category of objects called BIKES. In other words, BIKES is

FIGURE 11.9 Popularity of Object-Oriented Languages

Category	Respondents' Preferences as of June 2010
Object-oriented languages	55.5%
Procedural languages	39.9%
Functional languages	3.2%
Logical languages	1.5%

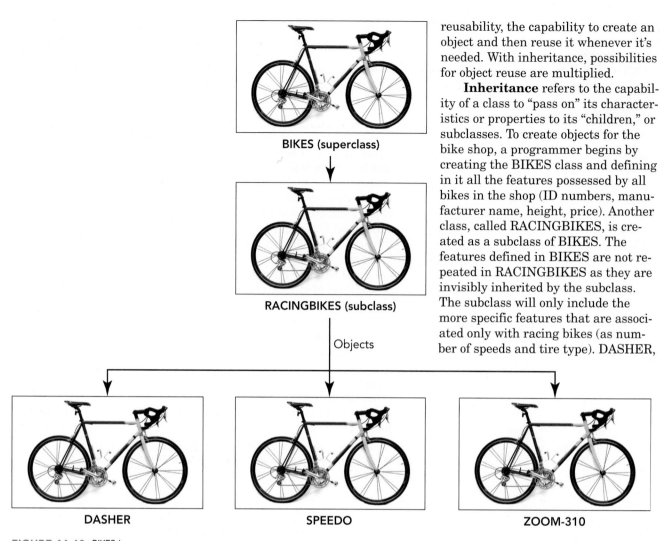

BIKES (superclass)

RACINGBIKES (subclass)

Objects

DASHER

SPEEDO

ZOOM-310

FIGURE 11.10 BIKES is a superclass, RACINGBIKES is a subclass of BIKES, and DASHER, SPEEDO, and ZOOM-310 are objects of the RACINGBIKES subclass.

reusability, the capability to create an object and then reuse it whenever it's needed. With inheritance, possibilities for object reuse are multiplied.

Inheritance refers to the capability of a class to "pass on" its characteristics or properties to its "children," or subclasses. To create objects for the bike shop, a programmer begins by creating the BIKES class and defining in it all the features possessed by all bikes in the shop (ID numbers, manufacturer name, height, price). Another class, called RACINGBIKES, is created as a subclass of BIKES. The features defined in BIKES are not repeated in RACINGBIKES as they are invisibly inherited by the subclass. The subclass will only include the more specific features that are associated only with racing bikes (as number of speeds and tire type). DASHER,

the blueprint, general design, or class of which DASHER is an object. Suppose, however, that you carry several racing bikes besides DASHER, like the SPEEDO and ZOOM-310. It would make sense to group these three bikes and create a RACING-BIKES **subclass**, a more specialized class of the BIKES class but with additional features just for RACINGBIKES. BIKES then becomes the base class, superclass, or parent of RACINGBIKES because it is the more abstract blueprint and generic category. RACINGBIKES is referred to as the subclass or child of BIKES. DASHER, SPEEDO, and ZOOM-310 are then objects of the RACINGBIKES subclass of the BIKES base class (Figure 11.10).

The benefit of creating this structure of subclasses, which might seem complex at the moment, is the feature of inheritance and the invisible passing of features from a parent class to a child class.

Inheritance One of the major objectives of object-oriented programming is

SPEEDO, and ZOOM-310, objects of this RACINGBIKES subclass, each possess all of the features of the RACINGBIKES class plus the inherited features of the more general BIKE superclass (Figure 11.11).

This gives RACINGBIKES all the same fields and methods as BIKES, yet allows for the addition of new features that make it unique.

Program Development Because objects can be easily reused, object-oriented programming enables a fast method of

```
class RACINGBIKES extends BIKES {
   // new fields and methods
   defining a racing bike would
   go here
}
```

FIGURE 11.11 The Java programming language syntax for creating a subclass uses the keyword *extends* followed by the name of the parent or superclass.

program development called **rapid application development (RAD)**. With RAD, which was developed to respond to the need to deliver systems very quickly, a programmer works with a library of prebuilt objects that have been created for a huge variety of applications. For instance, a text box is considered to be an object that contains a label and the contents of a field object. Using RAD, a programmer does not have to write code that describes the object each time the object is used, but instead simply inserts the prebuilt text box object and then modifies it to suit the program's needs. Project scope, size, and circumstances all determine the success of a RAD approach.

Joint application development (JAD) is another program development method, which uses a team approach and involves end users throughout the planning and development stages. The objective is to better design objects that suit end user needs. **Agile software development**, a term coined in 2001, refers to a group of software development techniques with which solutions are created through collaboration between teams. Agile methods follow a project management process that aligns development with customer needs and company goals. It encourages frequent inspection and adaptation as well as teamwork, self-organization, and accountability; and it uses a set of engineering practices that allow for rapid delivery of high-quality software that was developed by following a business approach to solution development.

Middleware (Accessing Objects across Networks)

Stimulated by the growth of network-based applications, middleware technologies are becoming more important. Suppose you have hundreds, or even thousands, of objects with processes being performed on them accessible on a network. To access these objects, you need middleware. **Middleware** is software that does what its name implies: It sits "in the middle" and mediates the interaction between applications working on multiple networks being supported by different operating systems. It has been referred to as the glue between software components or between software and the network that integrates dissimilar systems. Middleware is especially integral to modern information technology based on XML, Web services, and service-oriented architecture, where software applications

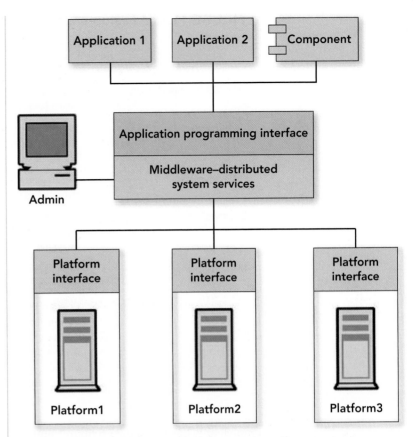

FIGURE 11.12 Middleware, sometimes referred to as the slash in client/server, allows applications to communicate across a network, regardless of the operating system used.

need to exchange data between different types of facilities like networks and database managers (Figure 11.12).

Middleware services are provided by IBM and Oracle, Microsoft with its .NET standard, and the OW2 Consortium (**www.ow2.org**) through the open source middleware that it developed and distributes.

Other Advantages of Object-Oriented Programming

In traditional programming, the program and data are kept separate. If the data must change—because, for example, a company needs to start tracking the exact time of orders as well as the date—all programs that access that data also must be changed to accommodate that new piece of information or feature. That's an expensive, time-consuming process.

With object-oriented programming, however, the object's attributes or features and the methods used to access those attributes are stored as part of the object's definition. If another program accesses the object, it accesses it as a total package and

FIGURE 11.13 Features/Benefits of Object-Oriented Programming

Feature/Benefit	Reason
Testability/increased quality	An object is a self-contained entity and can be designed and tested before being embedded within a larger program.
Code reusability	Objects can be modified to create new objects possessing similar attributes and methods, thus reducing development cost by enabling reusability.
Code extensibility	The attributes and methods of a superclass are extended to (inherited by) the subclass.
Maintainability	It is easy to include additional attributes and methods by simply changing the object's definition and not having to change every piece of programming code that uses that object.
Manageability	Object-oriented programming reduces large problems to smaller ones by dealing with individual objects first and then the larger program.
Fits the way the real world works	Object-oriented programming encourages the programmer to start thinking from the beginning about the real-world environment in which the program will function, because each object contains not only the data and attributes but also the methods for manipulating the data.

immediately has use of the attributes and methods of that object, including any additional new ones. Because a change to an object occurs in the object's definition and the object is accessed as a total package, it eliminates the need to change individual programs just because of a minor change in the object's attributes, thus saving both time and money. Refer to Figure 11.13 for additional benefits of object-oriented programming.

Now that you understand how programming methods have developed over time, let's take a look at some of the specific languages that programmers use today.

Just think, in the future, a programmer may learn only one language, write all programs in that language, and rely on visualization tools, like ViLLE, to transfer that program into other languages that are more appropriate for an application.

A Guide to Programming Languages: One Size Doesn't Fit All

This section provides a guide to programming languages found in the various generations, with emphasis on the five most popular languages today: Java, C, C++, PHP, and Visual Basic (Figure 11.14). As you'll see, each program has its pros and cons. Successful programming involves choosing the right language for the job.

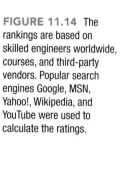

FIGURE 11.14 The rankings are based on skilled engineers worldwide, courses, and third-party vendors. Popular search engines Google, MSN, Yahoo!, Wikipedia, and YouTube were used to calculate the ratings.

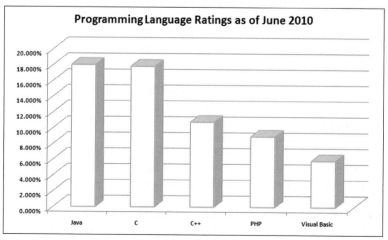

Programming Language Ratings as of June 2010

With the constant demand for new and more engaging applications and the development of new programming languages to meet this demand, how do programmers keep ahead of the game? In one posted article on the Web, a programmer stated that he has a goal of learning one new language a month; another programmer set the goal of learning a new language every six months. Is there an easier way?

Programming visualization tools like ViLLE, developed at the University of Turku, are attempting to facilitate the learning of new programming languages by providing an interface that allows the user to view the events taking place as the program executes (Figure 11.15). Additionally, ViLLE has a programming language independence paradigm built into its development so that a program written in one language can be viewed and executed in another (Figure 11.16). This language independence feature enables the learner to focus on program similarities and not on the specific syntax differences. The focus is on how programming concepts work and not on the specific language used

to develop those concepts. Instructors can customize and create learning examples that can be viewed during lectures or over the Web.

Currently this tool is primarily for educational purposes and is not suitable for some intense real world problems. Once this process is perfected, probably with help from the advancements in artificial intelligence, human programmers might find themselves replaced by the very computers that they programmed and the languages that they developed.

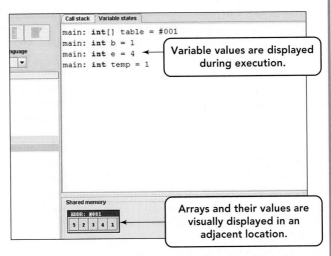

FIGURE 11.15 ViLLE provides a view of the activity taking place in RAM while the program executes.

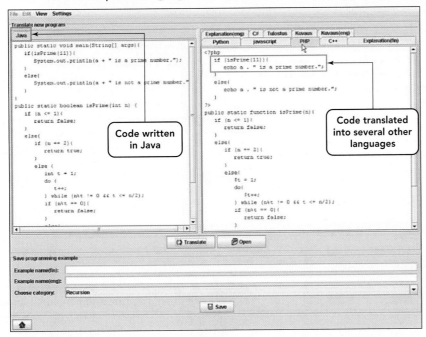

FIGURE 11.16 Code written in one program can be converted into other languages and viewed in a side-by-side display.

COBOL and Fortran: Historically Important

Imagine it's 1959. Cars have big fins. Dwight Eisenhower is president of the United States. Hawaii becomes a state. And computer programmers are using COBOL and Fortran. Thanks goes to these early languages for being the springboard of user-friendly language development.

COBOL One of the earliest high-level programming languages, **COBOL**, short for Common Business-Oriented Language, was the most widely used 3GL business programming language for decades. COBOL's success was due to the simple fact that it was a proven way to handle a large organization's accounting information, including inventory control, billing, and payroll. Today it is not a popular language, and its current use is attributed to the survival of legacy (obsolete) mainframe computer systems, where COBOL programming had dominated. Employment opportunities for programmers with COBOL skills usually focus on editing and fixing aged code.

Fortran Fortran, short for "formula translator," is a 3GL language well suited for scientific, mathematical, and engineering applications. In its time, if you needed to solve a complex engineering equation, no other programming language came close to Fortran's simplicity, economy, and ease of use (Figure 11.17).

```
! Hello World in Fortran 90 and 95

PROGRAM HelloWorld
  WRITE(*,*)"Hello World!"
END PROGRAM
```

FIGURE 11.17 Example of a Fortran 90 or 95 program that will display Hello World! on the screen.

Currently, it is being replaced by more object-oriented programming languages like C++ and Java, or by formula-solving programs such as Wolfram Research's Mathematica, which can transform equations into complex (and often beautiful) graphics that reveal underlying mathematical patterns (Figure 11.18).

Mathematica is a single system that can handle all the various aspects of technical computing in a coherent and unified way. The key to this system was the invention of a new kind of symbolic computer language that could, for the first time, manipulate the very wide range of objects, using only a fairly small number of basic elements.

FIGURE 11.18
Mathematica's 2D and 3D capabilities provide visual displays of complex mathematical formulas.

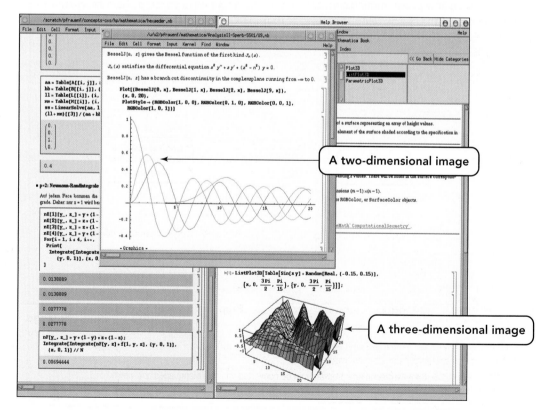

A two-dimensional image

A three-dimensional image

Structured and Modular Languages

COBOL and Fortran may still be used with some legacy systems, but large-scale program development requires structured and modular languages. The following languages are in widespread use among professional developers and software firms.

Ada Ada, a programming language (Figure 11.19) that incorporates modular programming principles, is named after Augusta Ada Byron (1815–1852), who helped 19th-century inventor Charles Babbage conceptualize what may have been the world's first digital computer. Part of this language's popularity lies in the fact that it was the required language for most U.S. Department of Defense projects until 1996. Major advantages of Ada include its suitability for the reliable control of real-time systems (such as missiles). For example, the U.S. Navy's Seawolf submarine uses more than 5 million lines of Ada code running on more than 100 Motorola processors.

BASIC Short for Beginner's All-Purpose Symbolic Instruction Code, **BASIC** is an easy-to-use, high-level programming language that was available on many older personal computers. Developed at Dartmouth College in the mid-1960s to teach programming basics to beginners, BASIC has been used by many hobbyists to create simple programs. Some high schools and colleges still teach BASIC in beginning

```
– Hello World in Ada

with Text_IO;
procedure Hello_World is

begin
   Text_IO.Put_Line("Hello World!");
end Hello_World;
```

FIGURE 11.19 Example of an Ada program that will display Hello World! on the screen.

programming courses. Many educators, however, believe that the original versions of BASIC taught flawed programming skills because of BASIC's reliance on GOTO statements. More recent versions of BASIC incorporate the principles of structured, modular, and object-oriented programming.

Visual Basic Developed in the early 1990s and based on the BASIC programming language, Microsoft's **Visual Basic (VB)** is an event-driven programming language. With an **event-driven programming language**, the program's code (Figure 11.20) is not written to execute in any specific sequence. Instead, the code executes in response to user actions, such as the clicking of a mouse button. The newest version of VB enables a programmer to develop an application quickly by designing the graphical user interface on the screen as the *first* step in program development (Figure 11.21). When the program is actually running, it can be compared to a suspended standby mode, waiting for an event, like a mouse click, from the user. When the event occurs, the program performs the associated instructions in response. This cycle of waiting for an event to occur and then responding is called an *event loop*.

Each on-screen control, such as a text box or a radio button, is linked to a segment of BASIC programming code that performs an action. The programmer doesn't have to worry about any of the code that generates the user interface, the

FIGURE 11.20
Comparison of the Original BASIC Language and the Visual Basic in Use.

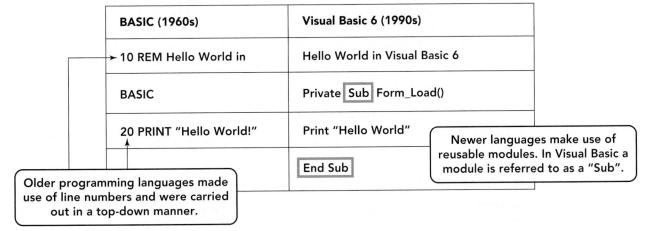

BASIC (1960s)	Visual Basic 6 (1990s)
10 REM Hello World in	Hello World in Visual Basic 6
BASIC	Private Sub Form_Load()
20 PRINT "Hello World!"	Print "Hello World"
	End Sub

Older programming languages made use of line numbers and were carried out in a top-down manner.

Newer languages make use of reusable modules. In Visual Basic a module is referred to as a "Sub".

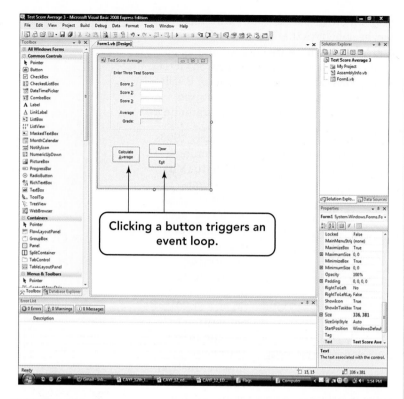

FIGURE 11.21 The Visual Basic 2008 graphical user interface greatly simplifies program development.

Clicking a button triggers an event loop.

of software development, but the honor of being cutting edge goes to object-oriented (OO) languages.

C++ A more recent version of C, **C++**, was developed at Bell Labs in the 1980s and incorporates object-oriented features—but doesn't force a programmer to adhere to the object-oriented model (Figure 11.22). Thanks to this flexibility and the fast execution speed of compiled C++ programs, the language is in widespread use for professional program development. For more specific information on C and C++, examples of source code, virtual courses, and tutorials go to **www.cprogramming.com/ tutorial.html**.

```
// Hello World in C++

#include <iostream>

int main()
{
    std::cout << "Hello World!\n";
}
```

FIGURE 11.22 This simple C++ program displays "Hello World!" on the screen.

Java Developed by a consortium led by Sun Microsystems in 1995 for consumer electronic devices, **Java** is an object-oriented, high-level programming language (Figure 11.23). According to Java backers, it's the world's first truly **cross-platform programming language**, a programming language capable of running on many different types of computers, including those using the Windows, Mac OS, or Linux operating systems. Java enables programmers to create programs that "write once, run anywhere."

How is it possible to write one program and run it on any computer? The secret to this remarkable capability is the Java Virtual Machine, which must be installed on

text boxes or radio buttons, because it's all handled automatically by the VB compiler, which creates an executable program capable of running on its own. Using VB, even a novice programmer can develop an impressive application in short order.

Although VB was a widely used program development package, it has been replaced by Visual Basic. NET an object-oriented language. Microsoft ended support for VB in 2008.

C A high-level programming language developed by AT&T's Bell Labs in the 1970s, **C** combines the virtues of high-level programming languages with the efficiency of an assembly language. Using C, programmers can directly manipulate bits of data inside the processing unit. As a result, wellwritten C programs run significantly faster than programs written in other high-level programming languages. However, C is difficult to learn, and programming in C is a time-consuming activity.

Object-Oriented Languages

Structured and modular languages are the workhorses

```
// Hello World in Java

class HelloWorld {
  public static void main(String[] args) {
    System.out.println("Hello World!");
  }
}
```

FIGURE 11.23 Java has gained acceptance faster than any programming language in computing history. Here is an example of Java code.

any computer that runs Java. The **Java Virtual Machine (VM)** is a Java interpreter and runtime environment for Java applets and applications that provides a "home away from home" for Java, no matter what type of computer it's running on. It is called a "virtual machine" because it creates a simulated computer that provides the correct platform for executing Java programs.

Javabeans are the programming specifications that are created in Java and used to create reusable, platform-independent Java components. You can combine these components into **applets** (miniprograms embedded in a Web document), applications, or composite components (Figure 11.24). Javabean

languages, such as Ruby on Rails, PHP, and AJAX, when it comes to developing rich Internet applications. For this reason, it is often recommended that Java programmers learn these additional languages.

Ruby Ruby is an open-source (free-of-charge) object-oriented programming language. It was released in 1995 and described by its developer, Yukihiro "Matz" Matsumoto, as simple in appearance (see Figure 11.25) but very complex inside, just like the human body. The TIOBE index, which measures the growth of programming languages, ranks Ruby as tenth among programming languages worldwide. Much of the growth is attributed to

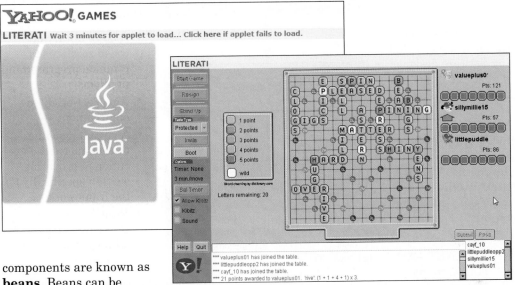

FIGURE 11.24 Some Web-based games need to download a Java applet before they will run.

components are known as **beans**. Beans can be changed or customized. For more information on this powerful platform-independent language, visit **http://java.sun.com**. For tutorials and specific applets, use the Java Boutique at **www.javaboutique.internet.com**.

Java is ranked by many as the number one programming language today. Many believe Java is one of the best RAD tools available. However, despite Java's considerable advantages, the language has many of the weaknesses of a programming language that's still evolving. For example, downloaded applets pose a security risk, so they're limited to actions that don't involve storage devices. Another concern involves speed. Java programs aren't as slow as those that use an interpreter, but they're considerably slower than those that use a compiler.

An article in *InfoWorld* cites Java's competition as formidable. It suggests that Java may be losing ground to newer

the popularity of software written in Ruby, particularly Ruby on Rails, a Web framework that allows applications that took months to create to be developed in days. Ruby is a pure object-oriented approach in which even primitive data types like numbers are treated as objects.

Visual Basic .NET In 2001, Microsoft introduced **Visual Basic .NET (VB .NET)** as the next evolution of VB, moving from an object-based language to an object-oriented language. This news was greeted with a great deal of controversy. Many programmers felt the changes to VB

```
# Hello World in Ruby
puts "Hello World!"
```

FIGURE 11.25 Hello World! Program Written in Ruby

.NET were so significant that it was essentially a different language. Microsoft's refusal to continue supporting VB—at one time considered the world's most popular programming language—disappointed many developers. VB .NET is used for building powerful applications for Microsoft Windows and for the Web. It competes with Java but has been unable to attain the same market share that VB once held.

Some major trends in program usage are changing the languages of choice and might make some of those languages cited here obsolete in the future. One critical trend is the exploding use of the Internet, where the browser becomes the interface of choice. A second trend is the continuing migration to packaged software starting with the Office Suites, but extending into every corner of work, including software designed for document management and accounting.

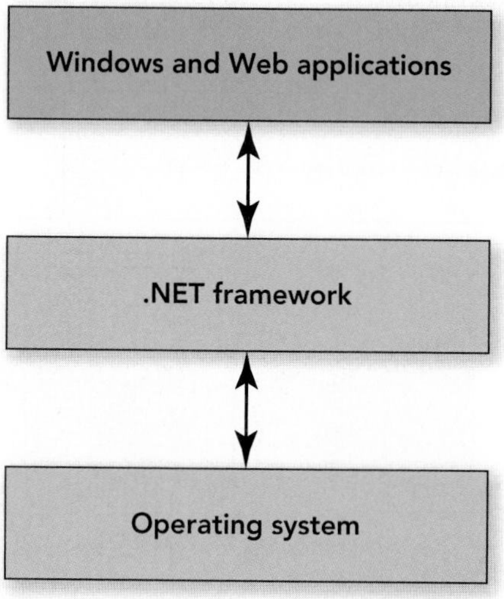

Visual Studio .NET Microsoft's answer to Java and JavaScript, **Visual Studio .NET**, is a suite of products that contains

- Visual Basic.NET—A programming language that enables programmers to work with complex objects.
- Visual C++—A powerful and flexible development environment for creating Microsoft Windows-based and Microsoft .NET-based applications. It can be used as an integrated development system, or as a set of individual tools, and includes debugging tools, support for large projects, and solutions for smart-client mobile devices.
- Visual C# (pronounced "C sharp")—A .NET-aware language for .NET development. C# allows C and C++ coders to use their existing knowledge of C to create .NET applications and services quickly. Innovations in Visual C# enable rapid application development while retaining the features of C-styled languages.
- F# (pronounced "F sharp")—An efficient programming language for .NET

that combines object-oriented features with the assets of a **functional language**. A functional language reflects the way people think mathematically. It is useful in mathematical programs or programs that can express findings in mathematical form.

The .NET Framework (NET in all caps) is a Microsoft-developed software framework, actually middleware, that supports both Windows and Web applications. It can be installed on computers running Microsoft Windows operating systems and sits between application programs and the operating system (Figure 11.26). Applications developed for .NET run inside .NET and are controlled by .NET. The following features are included in .NET:

- A large library of coded solutions to common programming problems
- An object-oriented environment
- A virtual machine that manages the execution of programs written specifically for the framework
- Runtime validation that checks for errors while an application is running

FIGURE 11.26 The .NET Framework acts as an intermediate, middle layer that supports and runs .NET applications.

This sharing of solutions and integration of development tools as programs used for building graphical user interfaces, editors to facilitate inserting and changing of code, and debuggers that make possible the detection and correction of errors is referred to as an **integrated development environment (IDE)**. The .NET Framework is a key Microsoft offering and is intended to be used in creating new applications for the Windows platform that are reusable and customizable.

Web-Based Languages

Strictly speaking, Web-based languages are not considered programming languages. Whereas programming languages tell the computer what to do and how to do it, **Web-based languages** tell a browser how to interpret text and objects. Web-based languages include markup languages and scripting languages.

Markup Languages A markup language is composed of a set of codes, or **elements**, used to define the structure of text, such as a title, a heading, or a bulleted list, that a Web browser reads. These elements are identified by markers, known as **tags**, which usually come in pairs. The actual text to be displayed, known as **content**, is enclosed by an opening and closing tag. By using this method, a browser interprets the tags and renders the content between them on the screen the way the tag indicates. The following are some of today's most commonly used markup languages.

To create a Web page, programmers use a markup language called **HTML (Hypertext Markup Language)**. HTML supports links to other documents as well as graphics, audio, and video files. This means that you can jump from one document to another simply by clicking a link. Through the use of element tags, HTML enables hypertext and describes the structure of Web pages. For example, using the b tag (which stands for bold) as follows,

This text is bold.,

will cause this line, when viewed with a Web browser, to produce the following sentence:

This text is bold.

The following illustrates HTML tags for a level 1 (major) heading, a paragraph of text, and an ordered list, a list whose elements are preceded by numbers as opposed to bullets:

```
<h1>This is the text of a
major heading.</h1>
<p>This is a paragraph of
text. Most browsers display
paragraph text with a blank
line before the paragraph and
flush left alignment.</p>
<ol>This is the line above
the start of the list items.
It will not be numbered.
<li>first item labelled as
1</li>
<li>second item labelled as
2</li>
<li>third item labelled as
3</li></ol>
```

You do not need special tools to create a simple marked-up document. Most word processors today include an option to save a document as a Web page using the "Save as type" feature. Use your Web browser to open the saved file, then right-click the Web page and choose View Source (for Internet Explorer) or View Page Source (for Firefox) to view the tags that have been added by the word processor for you. A word of warning: A Web document created in this manner may contain more tags, including ones of a higher complexity than would be included if the document were written in a program designed to create Web pages like Adobe Dreamweaver or if it were manually coded in a text program like Notepad.

> "HTML's simplicity is an important reason for the Web's popularity—nearly anyone can learn how to create a simple Web page using HTML."

HTML's simplicity is an important reason for the Web's popularity—nearly anyone can learn how to create a simple Web page using HTML. As a result, it's possible for millions of people to contribute content to the Web.

XML (Extensible Markup Language) is a markup language that enables programmers to capture specific types of data by creating their own elements. XML is to data what HTML is to text. XML elements do not *do* anything. It was developed to structure, store, and transport information by wrapping it in user-created tags. Someone must write a piece of software to send, receive, or display it. XML is not a replacement for HTML. HTML is used to display data, whereas XML is used to store and transport it. Because XML tags have no universal meaning, they can be used to transport data and make it viewable on many different devices, such as PDAs, notebooks, and desktops. How it will be displayed on that device is up to the software written to interpret it.

XHTML (eXtensible Hypertext Markup Language) is a newer version of HTML that uses XML to produce Web pages that are easily accessible by these portable, newer devices. Regular documents created with Microsoft Office 2007 are saved in a file format based on XML standards. Files saved in this new XML format may be up to 75 percent smaller than files saved in the old format.

Here's an example of XML that can be used to define part of a bibliographic citation:

```
<citation><last>Smith</last>
<first>Janet</first><pubdate>
2002</pubdate>
<booktitle>Easy Guide to
XML</booktitle>
<publisher>Xdirections
</publisher><place>
Charlottesville, VA</place>
</citation>
```

All tags in this segment of code are XML tags. An XML-savvy browser doesn't know anything about what these tags mean, but it does know that <last> and <place> (and the other tags) go within the <citation> element. An XML-capable browser, such as Microsoft Internet Explorer (versions 5 and later) and Mozilla Firefox (versions 0.9 and later), can detect the nested structure of XML tags and can display the structure in a navigation panel. These browsers also relate the sub tags as components of the main citation tag.

What's so great about a browser being able to detect the structure of XML tags? Simple: It means that it's possible for Web authors to invent all the tags they want and still have them displayed in a meaningful fashion. Suddenly, the information presented on a Web page becomes more *meaningful*. To understand why this is an advantage, suppose you're running an online art gallery and you're exhibiting and selling works by Tom Smith—a great artist, but one with a very common name. Entering "Tom Smith" in a popular search engine might result in millions of Web pages, however on your Web page, the artist's name is coded with XML as follows: <artist>Smith, Tom (1956–)</artist>. Thanks to an XML-created artist tag, people can now search effectively for the very few Tom Smiths who are artists.

Although XML enables anyone to create new tags, efforts are going on in virtually every type of business and profession to develop common XML vocabularies, which are sets of elements and tags for a particular field or discipline. For example, architectural associations are developing XML coding schemes for special architectural documents.

XML will be a big part of your computing future as more documents are encoded and placed online. Wireless devices use a specialized form of XML called **WML (Wireless Markup Language)**. This language enables developers to create pages specifically designed for wireless devices.

Standardizing HTML and XHTML for the layout of a Web page and imposing the use of **cascading style sheets (CSS)** to define the look and formatting of a Web page is the responsibility of **World Wide Web Consortium (W3C)**. The W3C is an international consortium in which member organizations, a full-time staff, and the public work together to develop Web standards. W3C's mission is to lead the World Wide Web to its full potential by developing protocols and guidelines that ensure long-term growth for the Web. Part of their standards is the separation of the design of a Web page from the formatting. Recently the organization has developed an Education Alliance Incubator Group to promote the inclusion of high standards and "best" coding practices in the education of future generations of Web professionals. You can learn more about the W3C at the organization's Web site (**www.w3.org**).

```
<html>
<body>
<script language="JavaScript"
type="text/javascript">
// Hello World in JavaScript
document.write('Hello World');
</script>
</body>
</html>
```

FIGURE 11.27 The code for the JavaScript Hello World! program is embedded within HTML tags.

Scripting Languages
Scripting languages enable users to quickly create useful **scripts**, simple programs that control action or user feedback on a Web page. You probably have seen a script in action when you rolled your mouse over an image on a Web page and the image changed, or when you filled in an online form and were reminded that you forgot a required field. A script, like mark-up languages, isn't compiled; it's interpreted by the Web browser, line by line. **VBScript** and JavaScript are examples of client-side scripting languages; their scripts run on a user's computer (Figure 11.27). Other scripting languages, like PHP, are server-side scripting languages that manipulate

the data, usually within a database, located on the server.

ActiveX controls are miniprograms (mainly written in VB) that can be downloaded from Web pages and used to add functionality to Web browsers. However, VBScript and ActiveX controls require users to be running Microsoft Windows and Microsoft Internet Explorer.

Like VBScript, **JavaScript** is a simple, easy-to-learn scripting language designed for writing scripts on Web pages. Despite including "Java" in its name, JavaScript isn't based on Java. Rather, JavaScript was created by Netscape Communications. Although still called JavaScript, it was recently standardized by the European Computer Manufacturers Association (ECMA), and is now properly known as **ECMAScript**.

AJAX, shorthand for asynchronous JavaScript and XML (sometimes written as Ajax), is a group of client-side, interrelated Web development techniques used to create interactive Web applications. AJAX is not a technology in itself, but a term that refers to the use of a group of technologies including HTML, CSS, JavaScript, XML, and JSON. The use of AJAX has led to an increase in interactive animation on Web pages and better quality of Web services.

JSON (short for JavaScript Object Notation), is a text-based, human-readable technique for representing simple data structures and objects. The JSON format is often used for **serialization**, transmitting structured data over a network connection. Its main application is in AJAX Web application programming, where it serves as an alternative to the use of the XML format. Although JSON was based on a subset of the JavaScript programming language and is commonly used with that language, it is considered to be a language-independent data format.

Another very popular scripting language is PHP. **PHP** is a general purpose, server-side, open source, cross-platform scripting language used primarily to make dynamic Web sites. So what is PHP really? PHP is a language located on the server, unlike JavaScript, which is a component of the user's browser; it is open source, unlike ASP or ColdFusion (its competitors), which means it is a free download over the Internet; it will run on any server running any operating system, and thus it is cross-platform and similar to coding C or C++; and its coding makes pages interactive so

the user can manipulate the page content, thus making it dynamic.

Let's take a Web page created with HTML, JavaScript, and PHP and see how it works. When a user opens the page, the HTML and any embedded JavaScript are interpreted by the browser and displayed for the user to see. If PHP is within the page, for example as a form that allows you to select a product being sold (like a ski jacket in size medium), those instructions are sent to the computer that is hosting the Web page (the server). The server, with the help of SQL embedded within the PHP, processes the form requests by searching the database of products, and the results (a list of all ski jackets in size medium) are sent back over the Internet, again with the help of PHP, and are displayed on the user's computer screen. Sound complicated? Well, if you have ever had a Web page display a pop-up box and ask you for data, or filled in a form online and received a Web page back with a personalized thank-you after you submitted it, or had a cookie (a small string of text that holds information about the user) placed on your computer, or had a password authenticated, or made an online purchase in which the products were

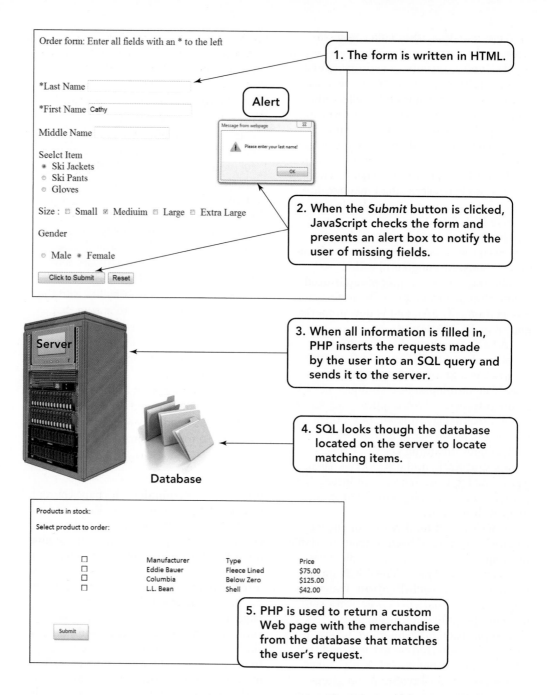

1. The form is written in HTML.

2. When the *Submit* button is clicked, JavaScript checks the form and presents an alert box to notify the user of missing fields.

3. When all information is filled in, PHP inserts the requests made by the user into an SQL query and sends it to the server.

4. SQL looks though the database located on the server to locate matching items.

5. PHP is used to return a custom Web page with the merchandise from the database that matches the user's request.

FIGURE 11.28 A Web Page, Its Activity, and Associated Languages

located in an inventory database, then you have encountered several of these languages (Figure 11.28).

You now know enough about programming methods and languages to appreciate the next section, which covers program development.

The Program Development Life Cycle

At the dawn of the modern computer era, no one thought about managing the software development process. Programs were written for specific, well-defined purposes such as calculating missile trajectories. If a program didn't work, the programmer corrected it. As a result, this approach came to be known as code-and-fix (or "cut-and-run").

When businesses began using computers for more complex purposes, problems arose. Often, programmers didn't really understand what managers wanted a program to do, and correcting problems became expensive and time-consuming. In addition, programmers didn't document their programs well (if at all), and some developed idiosyncratic programming styles that assured their continued employment because no one else could figure out what their code did! These early programs were almost impossible to maintain (especially if the original programmer left the company).

To address these problems, the program development life cycle was introduced in the 1970s, and it is still in widespread use today. The **program development life cycle (PDLC)** is a component of the system development life cycle (SDLC), a project management technique that divides projects into smaller more manageable segments. The PDLC component focuses on program development and provides an organized plan for breaking down this task into manageable chunks, each of which must be successfully completed before programmers move on to the next phase (Figure 11.29). Let's look at each of these six phases in detail.

Phase 1: Defining the Problem

The first step in developing a program is to define the problem that the program is to solve. This is the job of systems analysts who, after considerable interaction with end users, provide the results of their work to programmers in the form of a program specification. The **program specification**, or spec, precisely defines the input data, the processing that should occur, what the output should look like, and how the user interface should appear. All of this information is a combination of user involvement and the analyst's knowledge of system capabilities. Depending on the size of the job, program development might be handled by an individual or by a team of analysts.

Phase 2: Designing the Program

After an analyst has determined the program's specs, the next step is for programmers to create a **program design**—a plan drawn on paper that can be reviewed and discussed until everything's right. The program design specifies the components that make the program work.

Top-Down Program Design Program design begins by focusing on the main goal that the program is trying to achieve and then breaking up the program into manageable components. This approach is called **top-down program design**. The first step involves identifying the main routine. A **routine** (also referred to as a procedure, function, or subroutine) is a

section of code that executes a specific task in a program. Multiple routines grouped together are called **modules**; modules grouped together make up programs. After identifying the main routine, programmers try to break down the various components of the main routine into smaller subroutines until each subroutine is highly focused and accomplishes only one major task. Experience shows that this is the best way to ensure program quality. For example, if an error appears in a program designed in this way, it's relatively easy to identify the module causing the error.

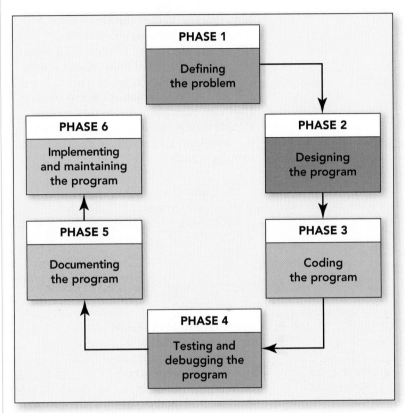

FIGURE 11.29 The program development life cycle has six phases.

Structured Design Within each subroutine, the programmer draws on control structures to envision how the subroutine will do its job. **Control structures** are logical elements grouped in a block with an END statement that specify how the instructions in a program are to be executed. This section discusses the three basic control structures.

In a **sequence control structure**, instructions to the computer are executed, or performed, by the computer in the order, or sequence, in which they appear. Sequence control structures provide the basic building blocks for computer programs. If you can imagine yourself as a computer, here's an example of a sequence of instructions you'd follow to obtain a pizza:

```
Go to the phone.
Dial the pizza place.
Order the pizza.
Hang up.
```

In a **selection control structure** (also called a conditional, or branch, control structure), the program branches to different instructions depending on whether a condition is met. A condition is an expression that compares instructions. Most conditions are based on IF . . . THEN . . . ELSE logic. If a condition is true, one set of instructions is executed. If the condition is not true, a different set of instructions is executed. Here's an example of a selection control structure that includes a *very* important test—making sure you have enough money to order a pizza.

```
Open your wallet.
IF you have enough money,
THEN Go to the phone.
Dial the pizza place.
Order the pizza.
Hang up.
ELSE Forget the whole thing.
```

A variant of the selection control structure is the case control structure. In a **case control structure**, the condition is fundamental, and each branch leads to its own lengthy series of instructions. For example, the IRS processes tax returns differently depending on five categories of marital status. A coded field indicates whether the taxpayer is married filing a joint return, married filing separately, single, head of household, or widowed. A case control structure can be used so that the computer can determine which of those five categories a taxpayer belongs to and then use the correct set of instructions to process the return.

In a **repetition control structure** (also called a looping, or iteration, control structure), the program repeats the same instructions over and over. The set of instructions that is repeated is called a loop. The two types of repetition structures are DO-WHILE and DO-UNTIL. In a DO-WHILE structure, the program tests a condition at the beginning of the loop and executes the specified instructions only if the condition is true. The following example illustrates a DO-WHILE structure:

```
DO gobble down pizza,
WHILE there is still more pizza.
```

Note that a DO-WHILE structure doesn't guarantee that the action will be performed even once. If the initial test condition is false, the action doesn't occur. In a DO-UNTIL structure, the program executes the instructions and then tests to see whether a specified condition is true. If not, the loop repeats. Here's a DO-UNTIL structure:

```
DO gobble down pizza,
UNTIL none remains.
```

Developing an Algorithm Control structures are combined to create an algorithm. An **algorithm** is a step-by-step description of how to arrive at a solution. You can think of an algorithm as a recipe or as a how-to sheet. But algorithms aren't restricted to computers. In fact, we use them every day. Figure 11.30 illustrates the algorithm for ordering pizza. Most people follow an algorithm to perform long division. Here's another example: Suppose that you want to determine your car's gas mileage. You probably do this by filling the tank and noting your mileage. The next time you get gas, you note the mileage again, determine the number of miles you drove, and then divide the miles driven by the amount of gas you put in. The result tells you your car's gas mileage, which you generated by using a simple algorithm.

> "Coming up with an **algorithm** involves figuring out **how** to get the desired result by assembling **control structures**."

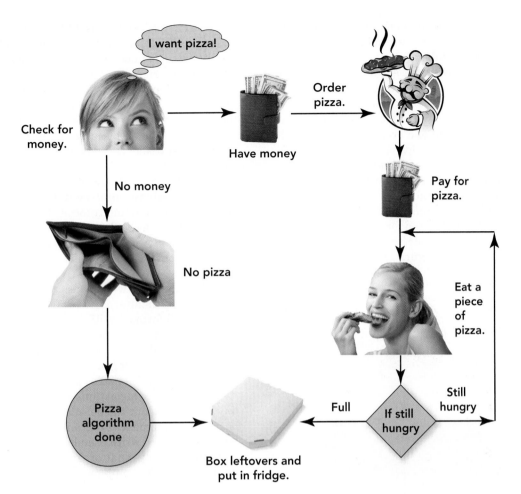

FIGURE 11.30 This flowchart is a visual representation of the algorithm of the process to follow when making a decision to purchase and eat pizza.

In programming, coming up with an algorithm involves figuring out how to get the desired result by assembling control structures. To get programs to do useful things, programmers use **nesting**, a process of embedding control structures within one another. Here's an example that remedies some of the unhealthy implications of the examples in the previous section:

```
DO check to see whether
  you're still hungry,
IF you are still hungry,
THEN gobble down a piece of
  pizza
ELSE Put the rest in the
  fridge.
WHILE there is still more
  pizza, repeat the loop,
  starting with the DO
  statement.
```

Program Design Tools A variety of design tools are available to help programmers develop well-structured programs.

Structure charts (also called **hierarchy charts**) show the top-down design of a program. Each box, or module, in the chart indicates a task that the program must accomplish (Figure 11.31). The

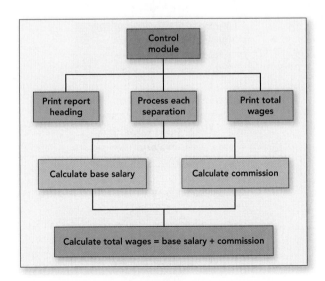

FIGURE 11.31 Each box, or module, in a structure chart indicates a task that the program must accomplish.

top module, called the **control module**, oversees the transfer of control to the other modules.

A **flowchart** is a diagram that shows the logic of a program. Programmers create flowcharts either by hand, using a flowcharting template; or on the computer with the aid of a program like Visio, which supplies a catalog of data-driven shapes; or with the drawing tools located in several programs like Word and Excel. Each flowchart symbol has a meaning. A diamond, for example, indicates a condition; a rectangle is used for a process; and a parallelogram indicates an input or output procedure (Figure 11.32). A variation on flowcharting is the **Unified Modeling Language (UML)**, an open method used to illustrate and document the components of an object-oriented software system under development. UML offers a standard way to visualize conceptual components such as business processes, system components and activities, programming language statements, and database schemas.

Visit the SmartDraw Web site at **www.smartdraw.com/specials/ flowchart.asp** to find tutorials for drawing flowcharts as well as examples of professional flowcharts and flowcharting templates that can be downloaded for free.

Pseudocode, which was created in the 1970s as an alternative to flowcharts, is a stylized form of writing used to describe the logic of a program. Pseudocode can't be compiled or executed—it doesn't follow any formatting or syntax rules. Instead, pseudocode enables programmers to focus on basic algorithms without having to worry about the details of a programming language. Programmers are even able to write pseudocode without knowing what programming language they're going to use upon implementation.

Phase 3: Coding the Program

Creating the code involves translating the algorithm into specific programming language instructions. The programming team must choose an appropriate programming language and then create the program by writing the code. The programmers must carefully follow the language's rules of syntax, which specify precisely how to express certain operations. For example, different programming languages specify basic arithmetic operations in different ways. Program development tools can check for **syntax errors**, or flaws in the structure of commands, while the program is being written. Syntax errors must be eliminated before the program will run.

Phase 4: Testing and Debugging the Program

The fourth step in a programming project is to eliminate all errors. After the syntax errors are eliminated, the program will

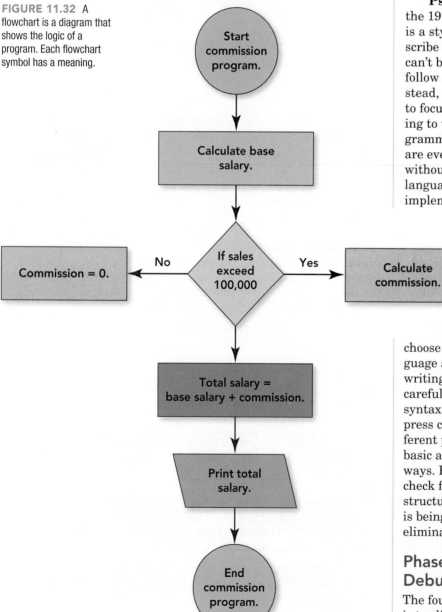

FIGURE 11.32 A flowchart is a diagram that shows the logic of a program. Each flowchart symbol has a meaning.

execute. The output may still not be correct, however, because the language translator can't detect logic errors. A **logic error** is a mistake the programmer made in designing the solution to the problem, for example, telling the computer to calculate net pay by adding deductions to gross pay instead of subtracting them. The programmer must find and correct logic errors by carefully examining the program output. Syntax errors and logic errors are collectively known as **bugs**. The process of eliminating these errors is known as **debugging**.

After the visible logic errors have been eliminated, the programming team must test the program to find hidden errors. However, it's not always possible to examine every outcome for each program condition. Inevitably, some errors will surface only when the program is put into use.

After suffering from a 22-hour outage in 1999, eBay is an example of a company that changed its way of thinking and has established one of the most thorough methods of testing and debugging its software. After the outage, eBay switched from one server and one massive database to a series of 2,500 servers (plus 2,500 backup servers) and 20 databases (plus 6 backups). Any new software feature is tested on one server; if successful, it is expanded to 25 percent of the servers, tested again, and then expanded to all 5,000 servers. As a result, eBay counts only 325 bugs among its 5 million lines of code, a tremendous improvement over the 3,000 bugs it had in 2003.

Phase 5: Documenting the Program

The job isn't finished until the program is thoroughly documented. This requires writing a manual that provides an overview of the program's functionality, tutorials for beginning users, in-depth explanations of major program features, reference documentation of all program commands, and a thorough description of the error messages generated by the program. These manuals, along with the program design work, are known as **documentation**.

For example, the structure chart and pseudocode or flowchart developed during the design phase become documentation for others who will modify the program in the future. In addition, other documentation should have been created as the program was coded: lists of variable names and definitions, descriptions of files that the program needs to work with, and layouts of output that the program produces. All of this documentation must be gathered and saved for future reference.

Phase 6: Implementing and Maintaining the Program

All that is left is the sixth and final step: implementation and maintenance. Even if the program has been developed by in-house programmers, the program will still need to be tested by end users. Even the best-written program is useless if the user

> " The **job isn't finished** until the **program** is **thoroughly documented.** "

GREEN tech tips

You may be wondering how programmers can help the environment. One way is by creating online documentation materials rather than printed materials. It is estimated that the energy used to create the average software manual creates approximately 6.5 pounds of CO_2 emissions. Another way to be more eco-friendly is to develop well-designed Web sites. Poorly designed sites often generate more network traffic due to frequent requests to the server—each request requires additional power. Creating more efficient Web pages can help reduce power consumption. Taken individually, these may seem like small steps, but they do add up! ●

does not understand how to work with it, if it does not fulfill the intended purpose, or if it contains disruptive errors. What's more, no matter how exhaustively the program was tested, users will still discover program errors as the program is implemented and used on a daily basis.

As a result, even after a program is complete, it needs to be maintained and evaluated. Maintenance is by far the most expensive part of the software development process, so good design and documentation are crucial to keep costs in check. During **program maintenance**, the programming team fixes program errors discovered by users. The team conducts periodic evaluations asking users whether the program is fulfilling its objectives. The evaluation may lead to modifications to update the program or to add features for the users. It may even lead to a decision to abandon the current program and develop a new one, and so the program development life cycle begins anew.

Create a Simple Web Page
Using Notepad

All you will need for this exercise is a text program like Notepad and the knowledge of HTML presented in this chapter.

1. Open Notepad.

2. Enter the lines of HTML code in the order displayed in Figure 11.33. These lines are the essential components of any Web page. Refer to Figure 11.34 for an explanation of each tag.

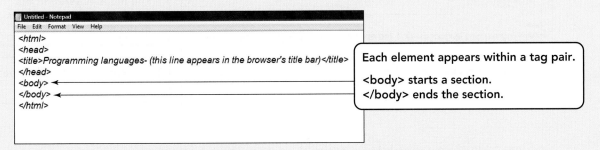

FIGURE 11.33 Elements between the head tags are preloaded, sent to the client's computer before the rest of the page. Elements in the body tag appear in the Web page itself.

FIGURE 11.34 Essential Elements of a Web Page

Essential Element Tags	Purpose
`<html> </html>`	Indicates the beginning and end of the Web page.
`<head> </head>`	Indicates the beginning and end of the section to preload.
`<title> </title>`	Surrounds the text that will appear on the title bar, or tab, of the browser that displays the page.
`<body> </body>`	Indicates the beginning and end of the content to appear in the body of the Web page when it opens in the browser window.

3. Save this notepad file as a Web page.

   a. From the Menu in Notepad, select *File > Save As*

   b. In the Save As dialog box, set the location in which you want this Web page to be saved, and then enter the filename, **FirstWebPage.html**, into the File Name input box. Then click the *Save* button.

   c. Notice that the new name appears on the title bar of the Notepad window. The file extension (.html) might also appear, depending on your settings.

4. Your Web page actually has no content yet. Let's start with a title and subtitle. Note that the content between the tags in this example can be edited to create a Web page on a different topic that your instructor approves.

a. Between the body tags, enter the code below, replacing the text "Your Name" with your own name (Figure 11.35):

```
Programming Languages</h1>
Web Page designed by: Your Name</h2>
```

b. Save your file.

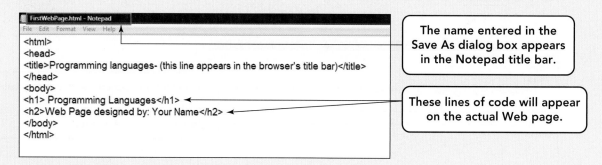

FIGURE 11.35 Tags that indicate headers, like h1 and h2, are displayed in bold font and left aligned.

5. View the Web Page, created up to this point, in a browser window.

a. Minimize the Notepad document.

b. Using the Computer window or file management program on your system, locate the file that you named *FirstWebPage.html*.

c. Once you have located the file, just double-click the file icon and the default browser that you have set on your system will open the file and display the content placed between the body tags (Figure 11.36).

FIGURE 11.36 The Web Page Displayed in Internet Explorer

6. Add additional content to the page using a paragraph tag and an unordered list. Use Figure 11.37 as a guide on how and where to enter the tags and content. The table in Figure 11.38 provides an explanation.

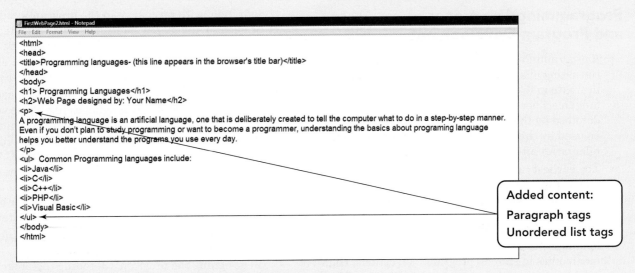

FIGURE 11.37 Use tag elements to create a paragraph and an unordered list.

FIGURE 11.38 Additional Tag Elements and Their Purpose

Element Tags	Purpose
`<p> </p>`	Surrounds text that is to be treated as a paragraph. Paragraphs in HTML are followed by a segment of white space.
`<ul> </ul>`	Indicates the beginning and end of an unordered list, a list whose list elements are preceded by a bullet.
`<li> </li>`	Surrounds each item to be incuded in the unordered list and receive a bullet.

7. Resave the file.

8. View the page with the added code (follow step 5 above). It should look similar to Figure 11.39.

9. Congratulations! You have just completed your first Web page.

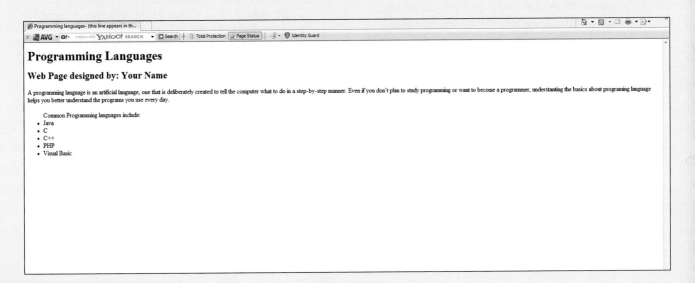

FIGURE 11.39 The Complete Web Page as Displayed in Internet Explorer

Chapter Summary

Programming Languages and Program Development

- A programming language is an artificial language consisting of a vocabulary and a set of rules used to create instructions for a computer to follow. All languages need to be converted into a language understood by the respective hardware before it can be used by the sytem. This can be done by a compiler or an interpreter.

- The earliest (and lowest-level) programming language, first-generation, is machine language, which consists of instructions using binary numbers—0s and 1s. Assembly language, the second generation, is easier to use than machine language because the programmer can use mnemonics to sum up program instructions. High-level languages, third-generation, eliminated the need to understand the details of the processor in use, but these languages still required the programmer to specify the procedure to be followed to solve the problem. Fourth-generation languages freed programmers from having to worry about the problem-solving procedure, but most of these languages, like SQL, are restricted to accessing databases. Fifth-generation languages are focused on the use of natural language to make programming and the use of programs easier.

- Object-oriented programming is a popular programming technique based on data being conceptualized as objects and defined by their features (attributes) and behavior (methods). Multiple objects can be assembled into one program or one object can be nested, contained within another. In traditional programming, any change in data meant that all programs using that data needed to be changed. With object-oriented programming, the object's attributes and methods are stored as part of the object's definition, and that definition is passed from program to program as a total package. Any change in the definition is automatically available to any program using that object's definition, with no change in the program's code. Besides saving money and time, object-oriented programming increases testability, reusability, extensibility, and maintainability of the objects and their associated programs.

- Languages can be categorized by the design used within their code. Early languages like Basic were called structured and were followed by Fortran and Pascal, which were modular in design. Object-oriented, 3GL programming languages, like C++, Java, Ruby, and the .NET suite, work with pre-built objects and focus more on encapsulating and hiding data. They also allow for easy transfer of features though the use of classes and inheritance.

- The six phases of the program development life cycle (PDLC) are (1) defining the problem, (2) designing the program, (3) coding the program, (4) testing and debugging the program, (5) documenting the program, and (6) implementing and maintaining the program. The PDLC is needed because earlier ad hoc programming techniques produced software that was riddled with errors and virtually impossible to debug or maintain.

- When using top-down design, program design begins by focusing on the main goal that the program is trying to achieve and then breaking up the program into manageable components. The PDLC focuses on breaking a program into manageable chunks, each of which must be successfully completed before programmers move on to the next phase. This breakdown into subsections makes the program easier to debug and maintain in the future.

- When debugging and testing a program, syntax and logic errors can be detected. Syntax errors are flaws in the way a command was written and must be eliminated before a program will run. A logic error is a mistake the programmer made in designing the solution to the problem. Both types of errors are known as bugs, and the process of eliminating them is called debugging.

Key Terms and Concepts

Identification

Indicate whether each program segment or error description below is a syntax or logic error.

1. A program used the segment of code below to calculate the average of four numbers entered by the user.

   Average = number1 + number2 + number 3 + number 4/4

   _____

2. When typing a line of code the programmer incorrectly spells *print* as "pint."

   _____

3. A program uses the segment of code to check whether a number is between 0 and 100.

   If (number < 0) and (number > 100)

   _____

4. A segment of C++ code is used to print the words *Hello World*.

   std::cout<<"Hello World;

   _____

5. A segment of code is used to define a subclass in Java.

   ```
   class NFL subclass HOCKEY {

   // new fields and methods defining NFL
   would go here

   }
   ```

   _____

6. A Basic program uses the following segment of code to calculate the amount of interest on a deposit and prints the amount of interest.

   Interest = Deposit + InterestRate

   Print Interest

   _____

Matching

Match each key term in the left column with the most accurate definition in the right column.

_____ 1. object

_____ 2. bug

_____ 3. mnemonic

_____ 4. beans

_____ 5. middleware

_____ 6. inheritance

_____ 7. algorithm

_____ 8. subclass

_____ 9. object code

_____ 10. pseudocode

_____ 11. class

_____ 12. machine language

_____ 13. query language

_____ 14. functional language

_____ 15. tag

a. A blueprint to construct an object

b. Software that creates a connection between applications and a network

c. A specialized unit of a larger category

d. Consists of binary numbers—0s and 1s

e. Code markers that come in pairs and identify elements in a markup language like HTML

f. Customized components created in Java and used to create reusable, platform-independent Java components

g. A step-by-step description for solving a problem

h. A unit of computer information that defines real-world data and provides such options as data hiding or encapsulation

i. Reflects the way people think mathematically

j. A language independent method of developing an algorithm

k. An abbreviation

l. Used to obtain information from a database

m. An error in syntax or logic

n. The capacity of an object to pass on characteristics or properties to a subclass

o. Code generated by a compiler that is combined with other components to create a final program

Multiple Choice

Circle the correct choice for each of the following.

1. Which is an example of a scripting language?
   a. C++
   b. HTML
   c. JavaScript
   d. Visual Basic .NET

2. Which software development methodology is based on an iterative project management process that aligns development with customer needs?
   a. RAD
   b. JAD
   c. Agile
   d. ActiveX

3. Which language is compiled?
   a. HTML
   b. JavaScript
   c. XHTML
   d. C++

4. Developing an algorithm for a program occurs during which phase of the PDLC?
   a. Designing the program phase
   b. Testing and debugging phase
   c. Implementation phase
   d. Problem definition phase

5. Which is the most popular programming language today?
   a. C++
   b. C
   c. Java
   d. PHP

6. Which is *not* an example a markup language?
   a. HTML
   d. PHP
   a. XML
   d. XHTML

7. Which markup language is concerned more with the structure and transporting of information than with displaying it?
   a. HTML
   b. XML
   c. XHTML
   d. PHP

8. Which language is used to produce Web pages that can be read on many different types of devices, including mobile devices?
   a. XHTML
   b. Visual Studio .NET
   c. C++
   d. ECMAScript

9. Which is a program, written in assembly language, that controls a device attached to a computer?
   a. Script
   b. Device driver
   c. Bean
   d. Applet

10. Using the Bike class example in this chapter, if DIRTBIKES were added to the structure, which element in the class would it be?
    a. Superclass
    b. Subclass
    c. Object
    d. Nested class

Fill-In

In the blanks provided, write the correct answer for each of the following.

1. _____ is the only language a computer understands without having to be translated.

2. ECMAScript is the proper name for _____.

3. The .NET platform is an example of _____.

4. _____ is a fourth-generation language used to obtain data from a database.

5. _____ errors will cause a program to fail to compile.

6. _____ is the collection of all recorded design, development, and production information pertinent to a programming project's completion.

7. _____ is a cross-platform programming language capable of running on many different types of computers with different operating systems.

8. A(n) _____ is a Java miniprogram made available over a network.

9. _____ is a process of embedding control structures within one another.

10. A simple program interpreted by a Web browser that controls an action or provides form feedback on a Web page is known as a(n) _____.

11. _____ is a program development method that involves the end user in the planning stage.

12. _____ is a language that enables developers to create Web pages for wireless devices.

13. _____ is a method used to illustrate and document the components of an object-oriented software system under development.

14. This sharing of solutions and integration of development tools such as programs used for building graphical user interfaces, editors to facilitate inserting and changing of code, and debuggers that make possible the detection and correction of errors is referred to as a(n) _____.

15. The development of a program through the use of a library of prebuilt objects is called a(n) _____.

Short Answer

1. Explain the difference between a compiled language and an interpreted language and give an example of each.

2. List the five questions that can help guide a programmer in the initial stages of developing a program and in choosing the appropriate programming languages for that project.

3. List and explain the six phases of the PDLC.

4. List three benefits of object-oriented programming.

5. Clarify the difference between a class and an object. Provide an example, other than the one in this chapter, to support your explanation.

Teamwork

1. **Plan before Programming** As a team, come up with an idea for a program that might facilitate some academic activity. Identify the academic activity that you want to enhance, and develop an outline of a program that will make the activity easier to do with the aid of a computer. You are not to write any code. Just provide an outline of your program. Use the five planning questions described in this chapter to help you define the scope of your project. Research the languages used to write similar programs. In a PowerPoint presentation of five slides or more, present your idea, the answers your team came up with to the five planning questions, and the programming languages that best suit your project. Remember to cite your research references.

2. **Programming Course Guide** Break into smaller groups and research the programming courses offered by the computer science (CS), computer information systems (CIS), management information systems (MIS) department, and any other departments on your campus. Regroup, and as a team, using an Excel spreadsheet, combine your lists into one complete course guide. Decide on a method of categorizing the courses, perhaps alphabetically or by department. Provide a brief explanation, indicate the associated credits, and list the department that is responsible for each course. Turn in your completed guide. Remember to cite your references. You might inquire whether the college would like to post your completed guide on its Web site!

3. **Classes and Inheritance Example** Use a word processor or any familiar drawing program, and as a team, develop an example of a superclass that contains at least two subclasses. You can use clothing, sporting events, or any other topic approved by your instructor. Name the superclass and list at least three attributes and two methods of the superclass. Remember that the attributes and methods of the superclass are fully inherited by the subclasses. Name at least two subclasses and list two additional attributes and one method for each. Finally, list two specific objects of each subclass. You do not have to define the subclasses in actual programming code. You can use natural language and a word processor or drawings (as was done in the chapter). Submit either your natural language description or the diagrams of your class structure.

4. **Web Site Languages** Break into smaller groups and interview the individuals on campus that are familiar with the development of the college's Web site. This could be an individual in the IT department, the Web master, or an instructor in the computer science or management information department. Inquire about the programming languages and/or the Web-based languages used to create the Web site. Identify the pages in the site each language was instrumental in creating. Regroup and combine your findings. Come up with a comprehensive list of the languages and the pages created by them in the college's Web site. Use either a Word table or an Excel spreadsheet to present your list.

5. **Solve the Problem** You downloaded and installed a free copy of Visual C++ Express Edition from the official Microsoft Web site. The version of Microsoft C++ that you use on the computers in the school labs have tutorials that help guide you through the syntax of basic structures such as loops and IF statements. You cannot locate these tutorials on the Express edition that you installed on your home computer. As a team, come up with a few possibilities that could cause this problem.

On the Web

1. **Programmers' Code of Ethics** Using your favorite search engines, locate sources that list the ethics or ethical behavior that is sought in programmers, especially those seeking security clearances. Create one list of 7 to 10 ethical behaviors that, in your opinion, a programmer should exhibit. Rank your choices, with the first one being the most important. Present your list in a PowerPoint presentation of 7 to 10 slides. Justify your lists and their ranking. Remember to cite your references.

2. **Flowcharting** Using a search engine, locate Web sites that show the symbols used in flow charts. Make a list of these symbols and explain their purpose in algorithm design. Then, using the appropriate symbols, create a flowchart of an algorithm to follow when your car has a flat tire. You can use Visio or Word to create the flowchart symbols and insert the appropriate labels. Present your completed visual algorithm. Remember to cite your references.

3. **Documentation** Using the Internet and your browser of choice, identify the two groups for which documentation is written. For each group, develop a list of what the documentation should contain. Prioritize the lists if possible.

4. **Game Engines** Game engines are software systems designed for the creation and development of video games. Using the Internet and your favorite browser, locate information on at least four game engines; list the games they were used to create; and, if possible, locate the programming languages behind these engines. An example is the Unreal game engine, first illustrated in 1998, developed by Epic Games and written in C++ and UnrealScript.

Present your findings in a one-page, double-spaced paper. Remember to cite your references.

5. **Programming Smartphones** Using your favorite browser, research the background or recommended education for programmers and the languages they use to program smartphones. Focus your research on a few of the popular models like the iPhone and Droid. In a Word table, list the phone model, the recommended education, courses, or experience, and the language used to create the applications for each model. Try to locate any job advertisements that are posted for portable application developers and, below the Word table, provide the job description and requirements that each list.

12

Databases and Information Systems

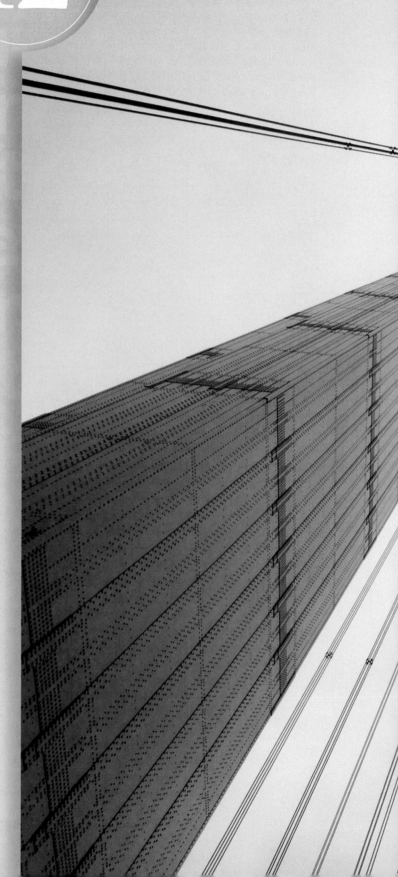

Chapter Objectives

How often, in one day, have you checked the contact list in your smartphone to locate a phone number, used a login and password to access a computer system, paid for food with a meal card or credit card, or played a song from the playlist on your iPod? Without thinking about it, every time you access such a list or use something that is recorded in one, you are probably making use of some type of database. Just thinking about all of the databases that contain information about you can be a little scary. Have you ever wondered about how information in a database is stored and accessed? Who has the right to access it? Is it secured from outside hackers? Can the information about you in a database be sold or distributed to other sources without your consent?

Recall that data refers to unorganized text, graphics, sound, or video, whereas information is data that has been processed and organized in a way that people find meaningful and useful. But information isn't useful if it is overwhelming, difficult to sift through, or tedious to interpret. Databases and database management programs are used to cut the amount of information down to a more manageable size and provide methods of viewing and extracting target information so that people can cope with it more efficiently. This chapter will focus on several aspects of databases:

- Organizing data in a database into tables, records, and fields to enable accessibility in an informative and efficient manner
- Identifying and explaining the qualities of a good database
- Distinguishing among the various types of databases and the programs that create them
- Understanding such database trends as data warehouses, data marts, data mining, Web mining, and the method of locating specific data elements through the use of drill-down techniques
- Familiarizing you with the functional divisions of an organization and the way each makes use of databases and their extracted information
- Relating the business sector's use of databases to accomplishing its goal of increasing sales and gaining a competitive edge ■

Check out **f Facebook** for our latest updates

The Levels of Data in a Database

A **database** is a collection of related data that is organized in a manner that makes it easy to access, manage, update, group, and summarize. Prior to actually creating any database, it is essential to map out the logical arrangement of the data that you plan to insert into the database (Figure 12.1). The following are six steps to use when starting to design a database:

1. Define the reason for the database and identify the type of information you expect to extract from it.

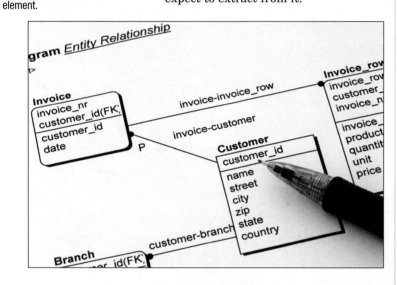

FIGURE 12.1 In this database design, the data has been organized into a Customer and Invoice group. These two groups are connected through the common customer_id data element.

2. Interview the individuals that will be using the database to gather information and clarify their needs.
3. Develop a list of the data that will be part of the database.
4. Organize the related data into logical groups or tables.
5. Create a relationship between the groups or tables by connecting them to one another through common data elements.
6. Test, refine, and improve the design, as needed, throughout the development process.

In most databases, data is constructed from the bottom up, like the layers of a cake (Figure 12.2). At the lowest level, or layer, is the **bit**, a 1 or a 0, which is the smallest unit of data that the computer can store and understand. The next level up, the smallest unit of data that an individual can work with, is made up of bytes that represent

FIGURE 12.2 The Levels, or Layers, of Data in a Database

Database	One or more data files
Data file (or table)	A collection of records
Record	All the combined fields about a person, place, thing, or event
Field	A unit of relative information of a specific data type
Character	8 bits (the letter M = 01001101)
Bit	0 or 1

characters, including letters, numbers, and special symbols produced by keyboard keys or key combinations. When you enter characters, the computer translates them into bits. For example, the letter M or the number 4 represents the character level of the database. (M in a particular binary code is represented by the bit string 01001101; 4 is represented by 00110100.)

The next layer in this development is a field. In a database, a **field** is a single unit of relative information; it is often identified as a column in the data table. When you create a field, you must make its content a specific defined **data type**. In a computerized database, data types are defined by the overall purpose of the database coupled with the specific data being entered. Common data types include AutoNumber, Text, Number, Currency, Date/Time, and Hyperlink (Figure 12.3). One data type called **Yes/No**, **Logical**, or **Boolean**, depending on the program, allows a yes or no, true or false, or 1 or 0 value. The **Memo data type** is used for large units of text, whereas the **OLE Object data type** is used for nontextual data. Examples of objects include pictures, sounds, and videos. Modern databases include a data type for very large objects up to several gigabytes in size, such as an entire spreadsheet file or a picture file, called a **BLOB**, or **binary large object**.

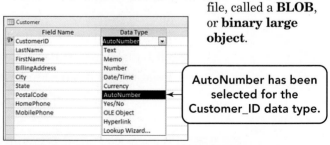

AutoNumber has been selected for the Customer_ID data type.

FIGURE 12.3 The AutoNumber data type allows the database program, instead of the user, to automatically assign the next available integer to the data being entered.

Except for fields containing Memo and Object data types, each field has a specified field size. For example, a field for U.S. states (such as Minnesota) would have a text data type and a field size of two characters to hold the state's abbreviation, such as MN. Field size along with format, input mask, caption, default value, and validation rule are the field properties. These properties are set and changed by the database creator or user and vary based on the data type selected for a field (Figure 12.4)

Each field has a name, called a **field name**, a descriptive label that helps identify the type of content to be entered into a field. Fields contain items that are all of the same type. For example, in a database of customers, a field named "Credit Limit" could be defined for each customer and contain data of the Currency data type, with a range set for the lower and upper acceptable limits. Some fields have a **default value** specified in their properties, which is an automatic entry placed into a field when no other value is provided. For a credit limit field, that default value might be $100.00. So if no other value were entered for the credit limit of a customer, then $100.00 would be entered by default. Of course $100.00 would have to be within the range set for acceptable limits.

The next level up from a field is a **record**, which contains a group of one or more related fields. In a database of customer information, a record would be the group of all fields containing information on one customer. Usually a record is identified as a row in the data table. A typical customer record might include a customer ID number, the last name of the customer, the first name of the customer, billing address, city, state, zip code, home phone, and mobile phone (Figure 12.5).

Within a record, one of the fields is identified as the **primary key** (also called the **key field**). This field contains a code, a number, a name, or some other piece of information that uniquely identifies the record. In other words, no two records can have the same value or information in the primary key. In your school record, for example, chances are you're identified by your student identification number. When you register for courses or request transcripts, you must supply this number so that the registrar's computer system can find your data. Your student identification number would be the unique value and the primary key field in your school record. In the customer example, the Customer ID is the unique value and thus the primary key field for each customer's record. Remember, fields that have been designated as primary keys are an integral part of a relational database. If you redesign a database structure, do not delete a field unless you are certain that it is not a primary or foreign key and that the deleted data is never going to be needed again.

Near the top of the layers in a database is the data file. A database consists of one or more related data files. A **data file**, also called a **table**, is a collection of related records. In the customer database, in order

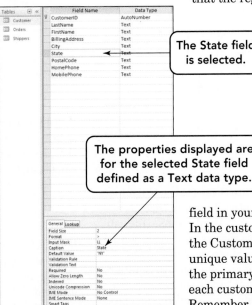

FIGURE 12.4 Some of the properties for the State field, defined as a text data type, include field size, format, input mask, caption, and default value.

The State field is selected.

The properties displayed are for the selected State field defined as a Text data type.

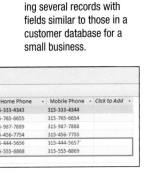

FIGURE 12.5 This is an example of a table containing several records with fields similar to those in a customer database for a small business.

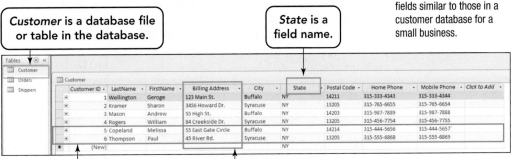

Customer is a database file or table in the database.

State is a field name.

A record is a row containing all the information on one customer.

A field is a column in a data table.

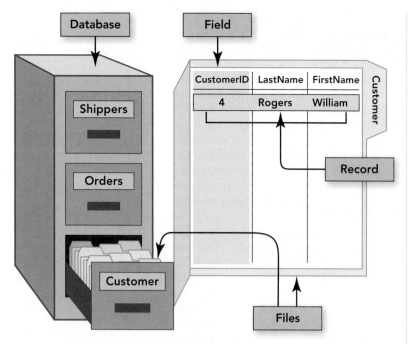

FIGURE 12.6 The structural relationship between database files, records, and fields is vital to the accuracy of the information extracted from the database.

Database

Field

Shippers

Orders

Customer

CustomerID | LastName | FirstName

4 | Rogers | William

Record

Files

Customer

Customer

FIGURE 12.7 The Five Characteristics of a Good Database

Characteristic	Result
Data integrity	Validity of data is ensured.
Data independence	Input data is kept separate from program data.
Avoiding data redundancy	Data is only entered one time.
Data security	Data is not accessible to unauthorized users.
Data maintenance	Procedures for adding, updating, deleting, and backing up records are in place.

to keep the information grouped in a meaningful way, there are three tables: Customer, Orders, and Shippers. To summarize, as shown in Figure 12.6, the database (file cabinet) contains data files or tables (individual drawers) made up of records (customers) organized into fields (CompanyID, CompanyName, LastName, and so on).

Now that you understand the levels that make up a database, let's look at some of the programs that can be used to create them.

Advantages of Database Management Systems

A database management system (DBMS) helps people work with all aspects of data in a database. But a database wouldn't be of much use if it contained errors or made confidential data available to people who weren't authorized to access it. In this section, you'll learn the advantages of DBMSs and five characteristics of quality databases (Figure 12.7).

Data Integrity

Data integrity refers to the validity of the data contained in a database. Data integrity can be compromised in many ways, including typing errors during input, hardware malfunctions, and data transmission errors. To avoid data integrity errors (such as typing mistakes), database programs use **data**

validation procedures, which define acceptable input ranges for each field in a record. If the user tries to input data that is out of this range, an error message is displayed.

Database programs use several different types of data validation (Figure 12.8). An **alphabetic check** ensures that only alphabetic data (the letters of the alphabet) are entered into a field, for instance, state abbreviations. Similarly, a **numeric check**, ensures that only numbers are entered. A **range check** verifies that the entered data falls within an acceptable range. For example, a U.S. ZIP code must not exceed 99999 (or 99999-9999). A **consistency check** examines the data typed into two different fields to determine identical entries. For example, a Web page that asks you to create a user name and a password for yourself typically asks you to type your password twice. If there is a discrepancy between the two typed passwords, you will be asked to type them again. This ensures that you've typed the password correctly. A **completeness check** determines whether a required field has been left empty. If it has, the database program prompts the user to fill in the needed data.

Data Independence

Data independence means that the data is separate from the applications, and changes in data do not require changes in the structure of forms, reports, or programs accessing the database. If a user changes data in an Access database, data independence makes further changes to any other applications within the program unnecessary. In older database programs, the

FIGURE 12.8 Data Validation Techniques

Technique	Result
Alphabetic check	Ensures that a field contains only letters of the alphabet
Numeric check	Ensures that a field contains only numbers
Range check	Verifies that entered data falls within a certain range
Consistency check	Determines whether incorrect data has been entered
Completeness check	Determines whether a required field has been left empty

database and the applications that access the database were closely connected, so any changes to data in the database required changing the program's code. DBMSs with data independence are much more flexible, allow other programs to access data, and make it easier to modify the database.

Avoiding Data Redundancy

Data should be entered once—and only once. **Data redundancy** (repetition of data) is a characteristic of poorly designed systems and can cause peculiar query and report results. For example, in many companies customer names and addresses may appear in two different, unrelated databases. This not only doubles the amount of work needed to update the customer's records if the customer moves, it increases the chance of an error and adds to the overall size of the database. Will the data be typed the same way twice? If the data is entered differently, some of it will be unavailable upon retrieval. Data redundancy can be avoided by proper database design.

Data Security

Data security means that the data stored in a database shouldn't be accessible to people who might misuse it, particularly when the collected data is sensitive. Sensitive data includes personal data such as medical records and data about an organization's finances. Protection can be as simple as a password locking the database or setting permissions for users on a network to prohibit access by unauthorized individuals. Creating an audit trail,

a report of who accesses what data on a system, is an additional security measure. Audit trails help with maintaining security and recovering lost transactions. Most accounting systems and database management systems include an audit trail component. Besides monitoring who accesses the database, it is equally important to protect against the loss of data due to equipment failure or power outages. Regular backup procedures are needed so that data can be restored after an equipment failure.

Data Maintenance

A user controls the design of a database by using the six steps mentioned earlier to develop the database and set the correct field types and properties for each field. Once the design is complete and the database is created, the next step is **data maintenance**—the procedures for adding, modifying, and deleting records for the purpose of keeping the database in optimal shape. The first rule of maintenance is to always create a backup copy of the database before performing any maintenance actions. It is also important to be particularly careful when deleting records or fields. Each maintenance activity is explained in more detail below:

- **Add records**—This task is often called populating the database. The user enters the information for each field of a record. If a database has been created correctly, then each field should have a value.

- **Modify records**—This is the action of changing information already in the database. The task is undertaken either when a change has been requested or the data was inaccurately entered in the first place. Inaccurate data entry can be reduced by the database developer through the inclusion of data validation.

- **Delete records**—This task involves the removal of all the fields of a record that is no longer needed. Depending on the database, the record can be removed from the database file immediately—an action that cannot be reversed—or it can be marked or flagged and removed with another instruction later. When a record is removed immediately, an alert box should warn the user that the action is permanent and ask whether he or she wants to continue. When deleted data is flagged, the user can continue to use the database to obtain information; however, the flagged records are treated as nonexistent and do not appear in any reports. The user should delete all flagged records frequently to make sure that the database is updated and optimized.

Visit **www.geekgirls.com/menu_databases.htm** and explore the step-by-step guides and tutorials on creating and using databases. The site displays eight steps with easy-to-follow instructions and directions. Screen captures act as visual aids.

Types of Database Programs

Database programs are software applications that are used to create databases or to work with the data in existing databases. Two types of database programs enable you to create or work with database files: file management programs and database management systems.

File Management Programs

A **file management program** enables users to create, edit, and manage databases in which files or tables are independent of each other, with no link between the data stored in each. A **flat file** refers to the type of file generated by a file management program. Flat files, sometimes called lists, are independent structures. That means that there is no relation between fields in one flat file and fields in another. Examples of flat files include a list of addresses, appointments, or items, such as favorite music CDs or books. Flat-file databases can be accessed randomly to retrieve a specific record or sorted so that the records can be accessed sequentially in a different order. You can create a flat-file database with Microsoft Excel or any other spreadsheet program.

File management programs come in handy when an individual or small business needs to set up a simple computerized information storage and retrieval system. The owner of a baseball card store, for example, could create a flat-file database of available baseball cards for inventory purposes. This simple database would consist of one file, or table, containing all of the information related to the available baseball cards. The file would contain a record for each baseball card, including fields for the player's name, team jersey, quantity of that card in stock, and its retail price.

Because file management programs are less complex than database management systems, they're also less expensive

and easier to use. The ease of use comes at a price, though. The data stored in a flat-file database cannot be joined with or related to data in another flat file. For example, if that same baseball card store owner had another flat-file database that contained information on customers, the data in the baseball card file and the data in the customer file would be independent data with no relation or connection. The store owner could not locate a player's name in the baseball card file and then find the customers in the customer file that recently purchased it. There would be no connection between any of the data in the two flat files.

Database Management Systems

In contrast to file management programs, which manage only a single flat file at a time, a **database management system (DBMS)** is a database program that can join or connect several files or tables to manage, access, store, and edit data in a structured, cross-referenced manner. DBMSs come in many types and sizes, from smaller programs for PCs to very large programs for mainframes. DBMSs aren't usually platform specific, but some are. For example, popular DBMSs for PCs include Microsoft Access and MySQL. A popular DBMS for Macs is FileMaker Pro, which also runs on Microsoft Windows. See the list of popular database management systems in Figure 12.9.

FIGURE 12.9 Popular Database Management System Software

Software	Company
Access 2010	Microsoft
DB2	IBM
FileMaker Pro	FileMaker, Inc.
MySQL	Open source
Oracle Database 11g	Oracle, Inc.
Paradox	Corel
R:BASE 7.6	R:BASE Technologies, Inc.
SQL Server 2008	Microsoft
Sybase	Sybase Inc.
Teradata Database	Teradata
Visual FoxPro	Microsoft

View a video on Alpha Five, Version 10, designed by Alpha Software at **http://wiki. alphasoftware.com/Read+ me+first+V10.** This is an easy-to-use relational database management system with an enhanced ability to develop Web and desktop applications.

Information from a database can be presented in many different formats, including reports, graphs, or charts. DBMSs enable a user to create these items, with little effort, through the use of built-in components, referred to as wizards. A wizard acts like an assistant guiding a user each step of the way toward the final creation (Figure 12.10). DBMSs are categorized as flat, relational, object-oriented, and multidimensional based on the way they organize information internally. Using a DBMS to organize data in a database in flat form, with disconnected and unlinked files, is treating the management system like a file management program and not using it to its true capacity. The most widely used type of DBMS is called a relational database management system (RDBMS). Microsoft Access is a popular RDBMS for casual users, whereas Oracle has the largest market share for business database applications.

In a **relational database management system (RDBMS)**, data in several files is related by a common primary key. The RDBMS uses the primary key field as an index to locate records without having to read through all the records in the files and to make connections between files. This connection is often made between a primary and a foreign key. As mentioned earlier, in the customer example the CustomerID is the unique value in the primary key field for each record in the Customers table. The Orders table also contains a CustomerID; however, in the Orders table it is a **foreign key** field, a field that is a primary key in another file.

A relational database is best envisioned as a collection of two-dimensional tables, where each table corresponds to a data file. Each row in the table corresponds to a record, and each column corresponds to a field. A relational database structure can link a Customer table and an Orders table, for example, by a common field, such as CustomerID (Figure 12.11). This connectivity between tables permits the user, through the use of the popular

language, **Structured Query Language (SQL)**, to manage, update, and retrieve data across multiple tables at the same time. To keep track of the tables that make up the database, the DBMS uses a data dictionary. The **data dictionary** is essentially a table of tables. It contains a list of all the tables in the database along with details concerning the structure of each table, including field names, field lengths, data types, and validation settings. In many databases the user can get familiar with the overall database environment by investigating the data dictionary.

An RDBMS is usually more expensive and more difficult to learn than a file management program. However the advantages of a RDBMS far exceed its drawbacks and include these:

- The ability to manipulate data through the creation of relations between tables and to make use of those relations to accumulate data from several tables and generate information in response to a single inquiry
- The elimination of most data duplication by removing the need to repeat data in multiple tables
- The use of a data dictionary to provide an overall map of the database design and relationships between fields

Object-oriented database management systems (ODBMS) are a type of database structure that suits multimedia applications in which data is represented as objects. In an object-oriented database,

Wizards act as a guide through the development process.

FIGURE 12.11 In this Microsoft Access window, the relationship between fields located in different tables is indicated by the line drawn between them.

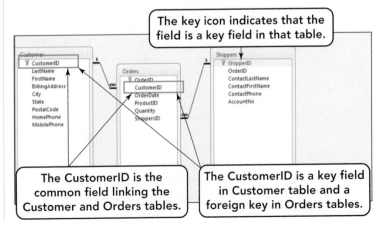

The key icon indicates that the field is a key field in that table.

The CustomerID is the common field linking the Customer and Orders tables.

The CustomerID is a key field in Customer table and a foreign key in Orders tables.

the result of a retrieval operation is an object of some kind, such as a document. Within this object are miniprograms that enable the object to perform tasks, such as display a graphic. Object-oriented databases can incorporate sound, video, text, and graphics into a single database record, making them suitable for supporting such applications as financial portfolio risk analysis, design and manufacturing systems, and hospital patient record systems. This type of database works well with object-oriented programming languages, such as C++, C#, Java, Ruby, and Visual Basic.NET. The Federal Aviation Bureau uses an object-oriented database to simulate passenger and baggage traffic, and the French National Center for Space Studies uses one as a multimedia database to model complex and integrated aircraft systems.

Multidimensional databases store data in more than the two dimensions used by relational databases. Conceptually, multidimensional databases are depicted as a data cube to represent the dimensions of data available to the user that provide simultaneous alternative views of datasets. Dimensions are typically categories like time, products, sales, customers, budget, and markets. These dimensions can be further broken down into subcategories. For example, markets can be broken into regions, states, and then cities. Each added dimension increases the size of the cube geometrically, making the model more complex (Figure 12.12). Multidimensional databases are becoming the choice for **online analytical processing (OLAP)**, a popular process for business analysis that involves manipulation and analysis of data from multiple perspectives.

Multidimensional database attributes include those listed here:

- The ability to extract and integrate a variety of data from a variety of sources
- Dynamic data rotation that assists in the creation and analysis of output from several perspectives to meet an end user's expectation

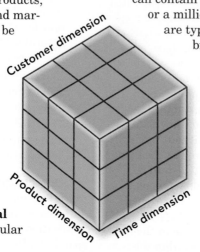

FIGURE 12.12 The multidimensional database structure allows an inquiry to be made across three or more dimensions. In this example, an inquiry could be made on a product like a Ford Focus to display all customers that purchased this vehicle in 2009.

- Concurrent users and diverse views of the same data models, facilitating decision making

Unlike relational databases that use SQL for database maintenance and information requests, no such language exists for multidimensional databases. In 1997, Microsoft introduced the **MDX query language**, a language similar to SQL but with the added ability to access multiple dimensions. MDX has since become the de facto query standard for multidimensional databases.

Now that you know about the basic types of database programs and management systems, let's look more closely at some advanced database programs and applications.

Data Warehouses and Data Mining

In large corporations, a trend has emerged toward ever-larger databases called **data warehouses**, a central location capable of storing all the information that a corporation possesses and making this data available for analysis. These data warehouses can contain more than 1 petabyte, or a million gigabytes, of data and are typically the result of combining several smaller databases from different areas within an organization. Today, data warehouses are typically multidimensional databases.

The collection of data in data warehouses helps managers make decisions by representing what business conditions look like at a particular point in time. Using a technique called **drill down**, managers are able to view information in a data warehouse and focus their attention on a specific data element. They accomplish this by starting at the summary level of information and narrowing their search at each progressive level of data (department, region, office, individual employee). Smaller-scale data warehouse projects that support one division rather than the entire organization are called **data marts**.

Could relational databases soon be a thing of the past? Over the last 30 years, relational databases have dominated the database industry. There have been several attempts by newcomers to overthrow the powerful relational database, but none have succeeded. The constraints and relationships between the tables that compose the database, along with the queries created in SQL, have provided a simple, flexible, and dependable standard that the competition could not match.

The one limitation that a relational database seems to have is its scalability, the power to take full advantage when a change occurs in size or volume. The need for scalability is being driven by the increase in cloud computing and the fact that more and more applications are being hosted in environments with high-end workloads, such as Web services like Google Docs. These applications have the ability to change rapidly and grow very large very quickly. Relational databases for Web services are not meeting the challenge. They work and scale well when the database is on a single server node. However, when the database becomes so large that it needs to be distributed across several server nodes, the scalability of relational databases declines.

So, what is replacing the relational database for applications like Web services? A new kind of database management system, commonly called key/value, is moving to the forefront. Key/value databases are item oriented. Each item contains all the relevant data for an object. The structure used by key/value databases is called a domain and can be compared to a bucket that contains the information about an object (Figure 12.13). The reason for making the comparison of a domain to a bucket instead of a table is that a table usually indicates some sort of structure or schema. A domain has no schema, can vary in content from object to object, and contains all related data for an object. This reduces the need to create relationships between tables to access related data, and provides the positive consequence of quicker inquiry results. The downside of a key/value database is that data is duplicated in items and increases the size of the database. This duplication also increases the possibility of errors and thus decreases data integrity. Key/value databases have been used in the past, but only when a relational database was not suitable. With the rise of cloud computing and an increase in Web-based services, watch out for an increase in the use of key/value databases.

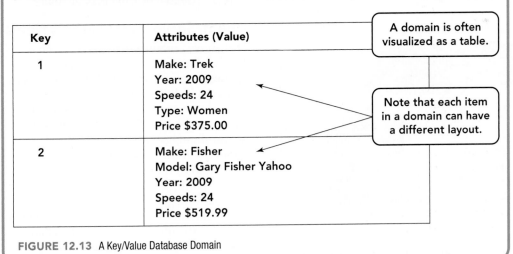

Key	Attributes (Value)
1	Make: Trek Year: 2009 Speeds: 24 Type: Women Price $375.00
2	Make: Fisher Model: Gary Fisher Yahoo Year: 2009 Speeds: 24 Price $519.99

A domain is often visualized as a table.

Note that each item in a domain can have a different layout.

FIGURE 12.13 A Key/Value Database Domain

The payoff from data warehouses can be huge. Fraudulent returns cost retailers an estimated $16 billion annually. The Canadian retailer Hudson's Bay Company (Hbc) stores more than 10 terabytes of data in its data warehouse. This allows Hbc to update sales, returns, voids, and exchanges almost instantaneously, making it almost impossible for someone to return merchandise illegally. Hbc saved $26,000 in the first week this fraud control system was implemented and more than $2 million in the first year.

For more information on data warehousing, including articles and new developments, see The Data Warehousing Institute (TDWI) Web site at **www.tdwi.org.** You can read articles on such topics as data mining and business intelligence in *Information Management*, an online magazine, at **www.information-management.com/**.

Using a data exploration and analysis technique called **data mining**, managers can explore data in an attempt to discover previously unknown patterns. The resulting information can be used to increase revenue, cut costs, or both. Data mining uncovers information through statistical analysis and modeling, and its results help managers better understand their customers and market and predict future trends (Figure 12.14). A variation of data mining is **Web mining**—a new term that refers to the integration of traditional data mining methods with information gathered over the Web. The collection of information on or entered on the Web is facilitated by a **Web crawler**, a simple automated program that scans the Web for specific data and inserts it into a designated database. Retail leader Wal-Mart takes full advantage of data and Web mining. Its 136,000 point-of-sale (POS)

terminals worldwide and its Web site send the data warehouse precise records of what each day's 200 million customers have searched for, purchased, at what price, where, and when. Wal-Mart then slices and dices the data to turn up nuggets of information. Wal-Mart's data warehouse was designed with no particular purpose in mind, but that's the point: Data warehouses are intended to support data mining's exploration and discovery of data patterns that aren't obvious even to experienced managers and executives.

Another company that uses data mining is Delta Air Lines. In the past, Delta had difficulty making sense of all the data it had collected. Because Delta's old data was not housed in one central database, it used to take days or weeks for users to get answers to information requests. Now, with the help of technologies and solutions supplied by Teradata, a hardware and software vendor specializing in data warehousing and analytic applications, businesses and organizations can get more specific and accurate results in just minutes.

Data mining can be used in other sectors besides the business world. The Pentagon's Total Information Awareness program was a massive data mining project designed to identify terrorists and protect against terrorist acts. Developed as a surveillance system that would link a number of different databases storing public and private information, it met with high levels of opposition because of privacy issues and was deactivated by Congress in 2003.

Client/Server Database Systems

Database server software runs on a LAN and responds to remote users' requests for information. Database server software is difficult to use because users never interact with the database server software directly. To access the data in the server database, users run a database client program, a user-friendly program that enables them to add data to the database, maintain existing records, perform queries, and generate reports. Because these database systems draw a distinction between the database server and client, they are often called **client/server database systems**. Many users—hundreds or even thousands—can access the database simultaneously. The front end of the database server software consists of the part of the program that the user manipulates. The back end of the software refers to the server and program

FIGURE 12.14 The CRISP-DM (Cross Industry Standard Process for Data Mining) diagram provides an overview of the life cycle of a data mining project.

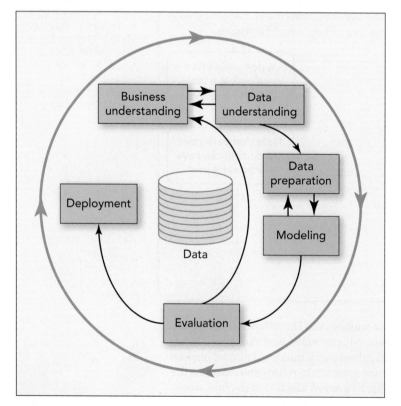

Business understanding

Data understanding

Data preparation

Modeling

Data

Deployment

Evaluation

code (Figure 12.15). You probably work with the front end of database server software fairly often, for example, whenever you use an ATM or use a computer for online banking. Examples of database server software include the market-leading Oracle from Oracle Corporation, DB2 from IBM, and SQL Server from Microsoft. A Web site that focuses on server software is **www.serverfiles.com**. The site is a hardware directory for network administrators and IT professionals and does not focus on single-user software.

To request information from a client/server database, remote users formulate the request as a query. A **query** is a specially phrased question used to locate data in a database. A college administrator using a client program might query your school's database to provide the names and addresses of students with junior standing who have a GPA greater than 3.5. A query language uses distinct rules to build a query.

Many DBMSs rely on the query language SQL (Structured Query Language) to request data in a way that the server can understand. SQL isn't difficult to learn. However, most users prefer to use client software that provides more user-friendly tools for constructing SQL queries. One such

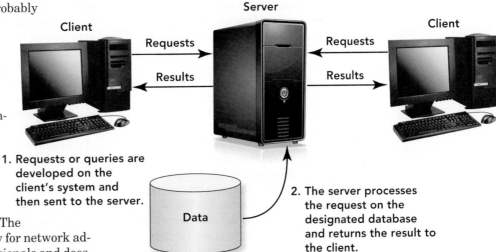

Server

Client

Requests

Results

Client

Requests

Results

1. Requests or queries are developed on the client's system and then sent to the server.

Data

2. The server processes the request on the designated database and returns the result to the client.

FIGURE 12.15
Client/server database systems minimize network traffic by dividing the processes between the client and server.

client is Microsoft Access. With Access, you can build queries by inserting fields and conditions into a table, which are transformed into SQL queries (never actually seen by the user) that are then sent to a database server and applied to the database.

The Internet Connection: Going Public with Data

The latest trend in database software is **Web–database integration**, a name for techniques that make information stored in databases available through Internet connections. Web–database integration enables USPS customers to access shipping information through the USPS Web site (Figure 12.16). You don't have to learn SQL or any other query language to use this or similar sites. The Web server uses a form to accept your input and translates it into a query that is then sent to the database. The database responds with the

STUDENT VIDEO

FIGURE 12.16 The USPS Web site's tracking system uses Web–database integration to track a shipment from pickup to delivery. All the customer has to do is enter the label/receipt tracking number and click *Go*.

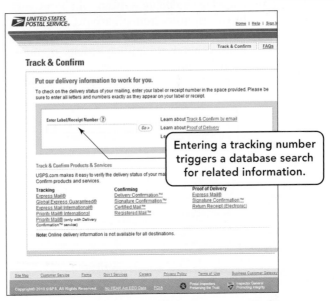

Entering a tracking number triggers a database search for related information.

requested information, and the server generates a new Web page on the fly that contains the information you've requested.

Web databases are everywhere—and whether you know it or not, you use them every day. Search engines such as Google and Yahoo! use large database systems to store all of the information they collect about the Web. When you search the Web, you are actually making use of Web-based integration software to search the huge database of information that has been collected and stored by the company providing the Web-searching service. If a Web page has not been cataloged in a search engine's database, it will not appear in your search results. Search engines are reluctant to reveal the exact number of sites they index, but experts estimate at least 30 billion Web pages are available on the Internet. Even though Google's database does not contain every page on the Web, the company catalogs more Web pages than any other search engine.

You can use many online databases to explore topics ranging from obscure computer terminology to pop culture. If you love movies, you may already know about the Internet Movie Database (IMDB) at **www.imdb.com**. Do you want to know all of the movies and television appearances that your favorite star has made? Will there be more *Star Wars* movies? Who did the special effects for *The Matrix*? The IMDB has more information about television shows and movies than you can imagine, including cast and crew listings, plot summaries, ratings, dates, interesting tidbits, and user comments.

If movies aren't your thing, take a look at **www.wikipedia.org** (Figure 12.17). Wikipedia claims to be "a free content encyclopedia being written collaboratively by contributors from all around the world." As of this writing, Wikipedia contains approximately 15 million articles in more than 255 languages. You can use Wikipedia as you would any traditional encyclopedia,

with the exception that you can add new articles as well as correct inaccuracies in articles you find during your research. The site allows any Web user to edit articles by clicking the "Edit this page" link that appears at the top of each page. In the constantly evolving Wikipedia, you won't find old articles exploring how humans may someday walk on the moon. The downside of this constant updating by multiple sources is that Wikipedia should not be used as an authoritative source for academic research and may contain false information and self-serving content. A search for Wikipedia inaccuracies will provide you with some interesting examples.

With the use of cloud computing to support Web services like Google Docs, it is not surprising that a number of Web service vendors are offering database models for use. With cloud computing and its related services expected to continue to grow, reviewing a few of these Web-supported databases seems appropriate.

Cloud Computing Database Contenders

Web–database integration is a key factor in the success of online retailers such as Amazon. Amazon's catalog includes millions of new and used products that are made available to customers through Web servers linked to Amazon's databases. Amazon's Web–database integration capabilities have become so successful that they now offer database storage and solutions, such as Amazon SimpleDB, to a number of companies, including photo-sharing site SmugMug, blog-hosting site WordPress, and social networking site Facebook.

Amazon SimpleDB This database is founded on the attribute-oriented key/value model. SimpleDB is still in public beta form, so it is a free download, with some limits on file size. Its limitations include an upper bound of 5 seconds for execution of a query;

FIGURE 12.17 The Web has many databases, such as Wikipedia, that you can use to explore topics ranging from technical terminology to pop culture.

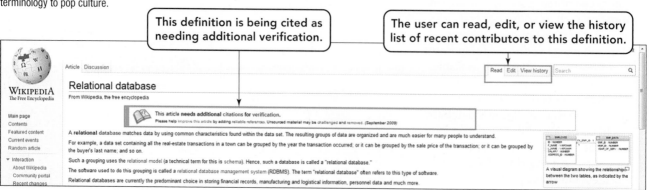

the conversion of all data to strings in order to be stored, retrieved, and compared; and the string limit of 1024 bytes, which places constraints on the size of an entered description.

Google AppEngine Datastore This database system is based on Google's internal storage system for structured data, referred to as the "Bigtable." This model stores richer data types than SimpleDB; but, at the moment the Bigtable cannot be accessed by an application outside of Google's Web service platform.

Microsoft: SQL Data Services This Microsoft product, still in beta, is part of the Azure Web Service platform. It is actually an application that sits on top of an SQL server and supports a key/value database.

Employees with knowledge of Web–database integration skills are and will continue to be in high demand. Such skills include knowing how to configure and maintain a Web server such as Apache (the market leader) or Microsoft's Internet Information Services (IIS); knowing how to write scripts that tell the server how to interact with the database software; and knowing how to design and maintain the database.

If you would like to learn more about databases, you may want to download and explore some of the free open source DBMSs such as MySQL (**www.mysql.com**) or PostgreSQL (**www.postgresql.org/download/**). Both Web sites provide you with the necessary information to get started. Books on both of these database management systems are also available at most bookstores. You can also find details about getting certified as a database administrator (DBA) in either Oracle or Microsoft SQL Server by visiting their respective Web sites at **www.oracle.com/education/chooser/selectcountry_new.html** and **www.microsoft.com/learning/mcp**.

You're now familiar with database programs and applications that you might encounter in the real world. Let's take a look at the benefits of using DBMSs and the qualities of a well-built database.

Information Systems: Tools for Global Competitiveness

An **information system** is a purposefully designed system that includes the collection of people, hardware, software, data records, and activities that process the data and information in an organization. Information systems, which include both the organization's manual and automated processes, are constantly changing and evolving as the business changes, grows, and alters its mission (Figure 12.18).

An information system's main functions include accepting input in the form of mission-critical data, processing this data to produce information, storing the data,

FIGURE 12.18 The Components of an Information System

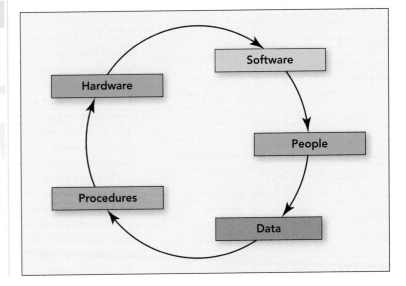

and disseminating information throughout the organization. Information systems help organizations achieve their goals by providing essential information services, including recording and keeping track of transactions, assisting decision makers by providing them with needed facts and figures, and providing documentation needed by customers and suppliers.

Smart businesses know that information systems aren't merely a cost to the business. Viewed properly, an information system adds more value than its cost and can be considered a wealth-producing asset that enables a firm to compete more effectively on a global scale.

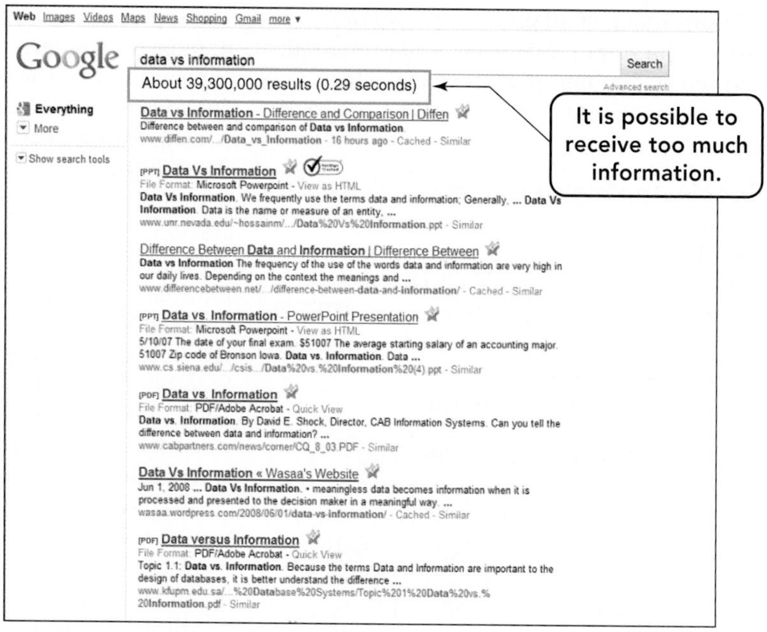

Even with all of these benefits, a company needs to be aware that information systems create a deluge of information, sometimes more than employees and managers can handle. The next section discusses how to combat this problem.

It is possible to receive too much information.

FIGURE 12.20 Not all information is valuable. All too often, people are overwhelmed with more information than they can use.

Computers are indispensable, but they also pose the threat of **information overload**, providing too much information, which makes processing, absorbing, and validating it difficult (Figure 12.20). It's important to control information to keep it from overwhelming people and reducing productivity in an organization. With an information system, the following control methods are possible:

- Route information only to those people who really need to see it.
- Summarize information so that decision makers do not drown in the details.
- Enable selectivity so that people with specific information needs can get that information (and ignore the rest).
- Eliminate unnecessary information (exclusion) so that it doesn't take up time and resources.

Now that you understand what makes information valuable and why organizations need to control the flow of information, let's examine how information systems fit into existing organizational structures.

Functional Divisions of an Organization

An organization is composed of **functional divisions** (also referred to as **functional areas** or **functional units**) that handle business processes of an organization

Techniques for Reducing Information Overload

It's important that you understand a few things about information in general. For one, not all information is valuable, a fact you'll appreciate after doing some research on the Internet. Figure 12.19 describes the characteristics of valuable information.

FIGURE 12.19 The Characteristics of Valuable Information

Characteristic	Result
Accessible	It can be found quickly and easily.
Accurate	It doesn't contain errors.
Complete	It doesn't omit anything important.
Economical	The benefit exceeds the cost of producing the information.
Relevant	It is related to the task you're trying to perform.
Reliable	It is available every time you need it.
Secure	Unauthorized people can't access the information.
Simple	It doesn't overwhelm you.
Timely	It is up to date.
Verifiable	It can be confirmed or double-checked.

(Figure 12.21). No matter which functional unit an information system supports, it still includes hardware, software, data, people, and procedures. Let's look at each of the functional units typically found in an organization and the information systems that support them.

Accounting The accounting function is responsible for accounts payable, accounts receivable, cost accounting, sales information, and accounting reports for management and government audits. This division makes use of spreadsheet software usually installed on PCs connected in a client/server network.

Finance The finance function is responsible for forecasting, budgeting, cash management, budget analysis, and financial reports. Both accounting and finance use spreadsheet software, such as Peachtree Accounting (Figure 12.22), or may purchase proprietary software. The finance division, like accounting, mainly uses PCs in a client/server networked environment.

Marketing and Sales The marketing function is responsible for maintaining the company's public image and for generating sales. Marketing professionals use database, spreadsheet, and proprietary software packages to manage sales figures and customers.

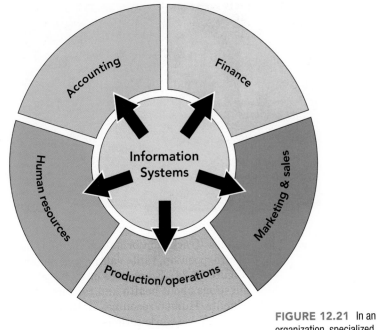

FIGURE 12.21 In an organization, specialized divisions handle each of the organization's core functions.

Salespeople rely heavily on computers and technology to do their jobs (Figure 12.23). In addition to desktop computers, they often use mobile devices, such as notebooks, tablet PCs, and smartphones, to interact with mainframes and client/server networks.

Human Resources The human resources function uses technology to keep track of employees and to service employee

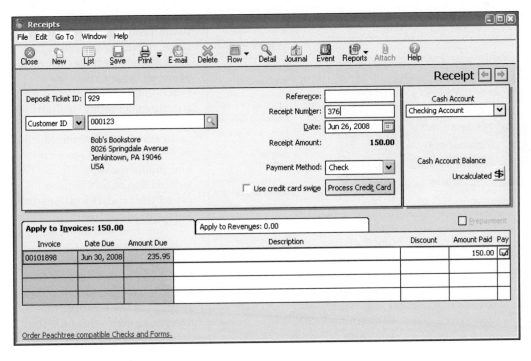

FIGURE 12.22 Software packages such as Peachtree enable companies to manage their customer and vendor accounts as well as make financial forecasts with more accuracy and efficiency.

FIGURE 12.23
Salespeople often use mobile technology in support of their work.

FIGURE 12.24 In addition to company sponsored human resource Web sites, many employees seek information from government sponsored sites.

queries. Tracked information includes date of hire, position, rank, salary, and benefits (Figure 12.24). Employees often have questions about health and retirement benefits. Human resources (HR) managers and staff use workstations to interact with mainframes, and PCs to interact with client/server networks. The HR function often uses spreadsheets, databases, and in the case of a large organization, an employee relationship management system. Such a system can help an employee gather information regarding his or her retirement account. Most employee relationship management software applications include a Web interface.

At Charles Schwab & Co., employees use a client/server network to access detailed information about benefits, training, technical support, and other company information. Instead of contacting the company's HR department, employees obtain information about themselves, their responsibilities, and the company itself.

Production/Operation The production/operation function plans and controls processes that produce goods and services (Figure 12.25). Information systems in this function help monitor and maintain inventories and purchases, and track the flow of goods and services. Transportation companies, wholesalers, retailers, banks and brokerage firms, and utility companies use production/operations information systems to plan and control their overall operations, with the same logistics required to actually manufacture a physical product. In the production/manufacturing setting, the control systems usually exist on mainframe computers that are accessed by highly specialized control stations.

Information Systems Information systems (ISs) refer to the systems of people, data records, hardware, and software that process the data and information in an organization, including the organization's manual and automated processes. Besides managing existing systems in an organization, information systems can include the planning and purchasing of new systems, establishing the level of user training required to stay current, and dealing with day-to-day operational problems. All organizations, including nonprofit organizations and government agencies, tend to develop a functionally differentiated structure, a method of distributing the core functions of an organization into divisions such as finance, human resources, and production/operations. This subdivision of functions is called the **traditional organizational structure**.

Now that you understand an organization's functional divisions and how they are serviced by the IS division, let's move on to the importance of information systems in the business units of an organization, the units that actually make money.

Business Units of an Organization

Where the functional divisions of an organization handle the business processes, business units are more concerned with developing and sustaining a competitive advantage for the goods and services the company or organization produces. Succinctly, the business units are concerned with making profit. A typical **business unit** is a division of a company, product line, or special focus group whose actions can be planned independently of other business units of the company.

At the business unit level, information systems services are utilized for these purposes:

- Analyzing the market and competition in order to keep a competitive advantage
- Providing an analysis and summary of market information that will allow the business unit to readjust and postively position itself against its competitors
- Reviewing and adjusting strategies to coincide with changes in demand and technologies
- Influencing the nature of competition through the analysis of such actions as a change in management control and political actions like lobbying

Information systems are as critical to the business units of an organization as they are to the functional divisions. Their interactions with business units are more analytical, and success is determined by increased market share and profit.

Information Systems in Organizations: A Survey

Many different systems have been developed to meet the information needs of an organization's employees. In a very small business, a single computer might meet all of the business's information needs. Larger organizations supplement single-user systems with desktop, notebook, and handheld computers; mainframe computers; LANs; and WANs. Some of these larger systems are used by teams of two or more people working on the same project; others are available throughout an organization, including all of the organization's branch offices.

Transaction Processing Systems

A **transaction processing system (TPS**; also called an **operational system** or a **data processing system**) handles an organization's day-to-day accounting needs. It keeps a verifiable record of every transaction involving money, including purchases, sales, and payroll payments. In businesses that sell products, a TPS is often linked with production and inventory control systems so that sales personnel will know whether an item is in stock. TPSs date to the earliest years of business computing, and the cost savings they introduced created a huge market for business computers. A TPS saves money by automating routine, labor-intensive recordkeeping.

Early TPSs used **batch processing**, whereby the data was gathered and processed at periodic intervals, such as once a week. Batch processing uses computer resources efficiently but is less convenient than **online** or **interactive processing**, in which you see the results of your commands on-screen so that you can correct errors and make necessary adjustments before completing the operation. In the 1970s, TPSs began to use online processing to enter transaction data and see totals and other results immediately.

TPSs provide useful tools for employees, such as sales and human resources personnel, but they're useful for managers too. Operational managers focus on supervision and control, and they make **operational decisions** concerning localized issues (such as an inventory shortage) that need immediate action. A well-designed TPS can produce periodic **summary reports** that provide managers with a quick overview of the organization's performance. They also can provide **exception reports** that alert managers to unexpected developments (such as high demand for a new product).

TPSs are only as good as the integrity of the data they contain and only as useful as the information they provide to users. Using the example of an inventory control system, you can imagine the problems that would be caused by a TPS that didn't accurately reflect the volume of inventory on hand. Likewise, managers need reports that will help them make good decisions—inaccurate data or unsophisticated reports are not valued.

Management Information Systems

TPSs work with management information systems (Figure 12.26). A **management information system (MIS)** is a computer-based system that supports the information needs of various levels of management. This type of system helps management make informed decisions. Middle managers must make **tactical decisions** about how to best organize resources to achieve their division's goals. MISs can produce reports that display resource usage of all or selected resources, where they were allocated, and the percentage of the assigned project completed. In short, the reports can tell middle managers whether they are meeting their goals

Although MISs continue to play an important role in organizations, they do have drawbacks. They generate predefined reports that may not contain the information a manager wants. The information may not be available when it's needed, and it might be buried within reams of printouts.

Decision Support Systems

A **decision support system (DSS)** is a computer-based system that addresses the deficiencies of MISs by enabling managers to retrieve information that cannot be supplied by fixed, predefined MIS reports. For example, a retail chain manager can find information on how an advertising campaign affected sales of advertised versus nonadvertised items. Many DSS applications enable managers to create simulations that begin with real data and ask *what if* questions, such as "What would happen to profits if we used a shipper who could cut our packaging costs by 2 percent, but who would sometimes cause slight delivery delays?"

Some DSSs include online analytical processing (OLAP) applications, which provide decision support by enabling managers to import rich, up-to-the-minute data from transaction databases. For example, managers at Pizzeria Uno, a chain of more than 100 pizza stores, obtain and analyze all of the sales information from each of the firm's stores every morning, using OLAP. As a result, they can quickly spot trends that may be emerging in customer preferences and

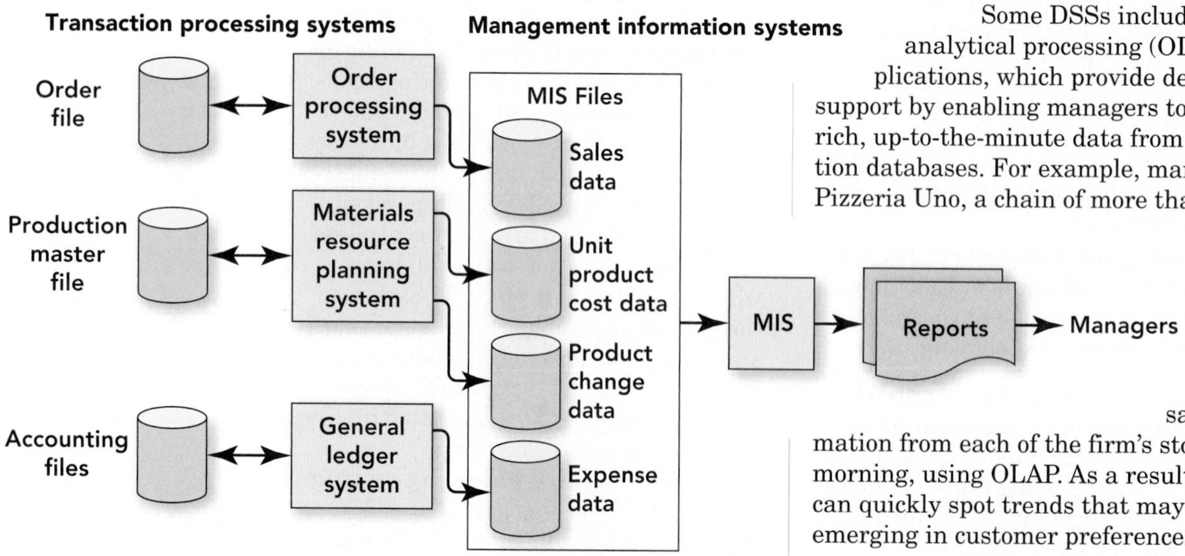

FIGURE 12.26 A management information system (MIS) produces easy-to-read reports that provide a valuable snapshot of information to facilitate decisions.

Transaction processing systems

Management information systems

Order file → Order processing system

Production master file → Materials resource planning system

Accounting files → General ledger system

MIS Files: Sales data, Unit product cost data, Product change data, Expense data

→ MIS → Reports → Managers

employee performance. Visit Decision Support Systems Resources at **www .dssresources.com** for information, articles, and case studies on various types of decision support systems.

Executive Information Systems

An **executive information system (EIS)**, also known as an **executive support system (ESS)**, supports management's strategic-planning function. Executives in senior management (including the CEO) are concerned with high-level planning and leadership. They make **strategic decisions** concerning the organization's overall goals and direction. Though similar to a DSS, an EIS supports decisions made by top-level management that will affect the entire company.

An EIS filters critical information (including information about the firm's external environment) so that overall trends are apparent and presents this information in an easy-to-use graphical interface. For instance, an executive might create a report that compares the company's inventory levels with the industry average. Little training is required to use these systems.

An executive information system that is gaining in popularity is referred to as the **dashboard**. This system has a user interface, similar to an automobile's dashboard, that is designed to be easy to read. The information provided to the dashboard units might be obtained from the local operating system in a computer, from one or more applications that may be running, and from one or more remote sites on the Web. Nonetheless, it appears as though it all came from the same source. A dashboard provides decision makers with the input necessary to "drive" the business and make effective up-to-the-minute decisions. Thus, a graphical user interface on a dashboard may be designed to display summaries, graphics (e.g., bar charts, pie charts, bullet graphs, and so on), and gauges (with colors similar to traffic lights) in a portal-like framework to highlight

important information on a designated component of an organization, like sales or production, or the organization as a whole (Figure 12.27).

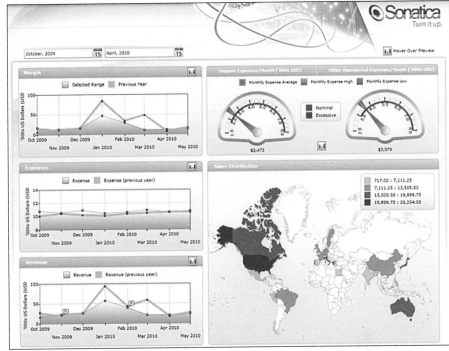

FIGURE 12.27 A digital dashboard can be custom designed to provide current, up-to-the-minute information required to make sound decisions.

Knowledge Management Systems

Organizations are increasingly aware not only that information is crucial but also that knowledge is a valuable asset. As you've already learned, information is data that is organized in a way that has meaning. But knowledge is more than just information found in documents, reports, and spreadsheets stored on computers. Knowledge is information in context, including the processes, procedures, best practices, and other information employees create. How can organizations capture the knowledge employees create? A variety of information technologies are being used to create **knowledge management systems (KMSs)**, which capture knowledge from books and experienced individuals and make it available where it is needed. This process doesn't have to be high tech. Organizations can document successful business processes, also known as best practices, by meeting with employees and recording useful procedures; by engaging a consulting firm specializing in standardizing best practices procedures; or by investing in a KMS. The resulting information is then made available to others within the organization.

Expert Systems

An **expert system (ES)** is an information system that deals with detailed and in-depth knowledge in a specific area supplied by experts in that field. An expert system formulates a decision in the way that a human expert in the field might. Research in expert systems attempts to formulate the knowledge of human experts (such as doctors) according to *if-then* rules ("If you have a temperature, then you might have an infection"). These rules formally express the knowledge used by human experts as they reason their way to a conclusion. The process of eliciting these rules from human experts is called *knowledge representation*. When elicited, the rules are programmed into expert systems. Expert systems use these rules to reach a conclusion the same way that a human expert does.

An expert system relies on a **knowledge base**, a database of knowledge designed to meet the complex storage and retrieval needs of computerized expert systems. To use an expert system, the user supplies information to the program. On the basis of the information supplied, the program consults its knowledge base and draws a conclusion, if possible.

> " **Expert systems** work **best** where they are **limited** to **sharply defined subjects**, such as engine maintenance, **planning** and **scheduling**, **diagnosis** and **troubleshooting** of a specific device, or financial decision making. "

Expert systems work best when they are limited to sharply defined subjects, such as engine maintenance, planning and scheduling, diagnosis and troubleshooting of a specific device, or financial decision making. However, expert system technology is making its appearance in application software too. Microsoft Word uses rule-based reasoning to check documents for grammatical errors. Similarly, spam filtering software often uses a combination of preset and user-defined rules to determine whether an e-mail should be sent to the junk mail folder or to your Inbox.

Expert systems are improving service in one area in which organizations sometimes perform an unsatisfactory job: providing technical support for customers. Expert systems also can provide expert knowledge in areas outside the business arena, such as medicine and health care. To better understand the various types of decisions made by the various stages of management and the information systems they use to make them, see Figure 12.28.

Computers and Databases in the Retail Sector

In the retail sector, computers are indispensable for traditional applications, such

FIGURE 12.28 Types of Decisions and Information Systems for Managers

Managers	Decisions	Type	Information System
Senior managers	Strategic	Determining the organization's goals and direction	Executive information systems (EISs) and expert systems
Middle managers	Management/Tactical	Deciding how to organize resources to achieve their division's goals	Management information systems (MISs) and decision support systems (DSSs)
Operational managers	Operational	Deciding how to handle localized issues involving elementary activities and transactions requiring immediate action	Knowledge management systems (KMSs) and transaction processing systems (TPSs)

as automating the checkout process. But some companies have also figured out how to use computers and databases for strategic purposes, enabling them to get an edge on their competitors. Such companies have grown rapidly and have made fortunes for their shareholders.

At the Checkout Stand Today's cash registers are really computers—referred to as POS terminals (Figure 12.29). Clerks check out items by passing them over an optical scanner, which reads the universal product code (UPC) encoded on the item's label or tag. The UPC code is located in a database of product codes. When the matching code is located in the database, the associated price is displayed and charged to the customer. The first live use of the UPC was in a Marsh Supermarkets Store in Troy, Ohio, June 26, 1974. The product: a pack of Wrigley's gum. The use of POS terminals and UPCs has resulted in faster checkout times and fewer price errors.

The latest POS terminals are fully integrated with credit card authorization systems that automatically send calls to call centers. A **call center** is a centralized computer-based routing system used for the purpose of receiving and transmitting a large volume of requests by telephone.

Because POS terminals produce digitized data, they're useful for more purposes than just determining the customer's bill. POS terminals also are linked to the store's inventory database. When a customer buys an item, the database is automatically updated to reflect the lowered stock level. When the inventory gets too low, a reorder is auto-generated.

POS terminals also are used as marketing devices. If a customer buys a particular brand of coffee, the terminal may produce a coupon for a discount on a competing brand. Another POS feature is to list the total of the discounts a customer received on his or her purchase. Marketers

FIGURE 12.29 The latest POS terminals are fully integrated with credit card authorization systems.

believe that creating a sense of well-being at the point of sale will subliminally influence the customer to associate the store with good feelings, causing the customer to come back in the future.

Chain stores such as Wal-Mart link their POS terminals to central computer systems using public data networks (PDNs). Disney, however, is taking POS data to the airwaves. At Walt Disney World, POS terminals at hundreds of retail carts supply data to company computers using wireless communications. As a result, the Lion King cart never runs out of those cute stuffed animals, which means bigger profits for Disney.

POS terminals also can reduce losses due to bad checks and credit card fraud. According to one estimate, banks and retailers lose a staggering $58 billion annually because of bounced checks and check fraud. A **check-screening system** reads a check's account number, accesses a database containing delinquent accounts, and compares the account numbers. Such systems allow vendors to catch problem transactions before they become losses. Check-screening systems have reduced bad check losses by as much as 25 percent, translating into big savings for retail firms.

Databases and Information Systems **531**

Stores can use **signature capture systems** to capture a customer's digital signature by having the customer sign the receipt on a pressure-sensitive pad, using a special stylus. What's the point? The system cuts down on credit card disputes. With a receipt signed by the customer, the store can prove that the purchase was made. This system isn't popular with consumers, however, because of fears that a dishonest employee could use the captured signatures for fraudulent purposes. **Photo checkout systems** access a database of customer photos and display the customer's picture when a credit card is used. In a New York test, this system cut credit card fraud by 94 percent.

The Future of Shopping

Imagine that you're standing in the supermarket, deciding which type of candy to buy. Would you want to know whether one of the sweets had just been recalled or whether the parent company of another candy had recently paid a big fine to settle charges of unethical behavior? In the not-so-distant future, you may be able to research nearly anything and everything about a product before you buy it—without leaving your shopping cart.

In such a scenario, shoppers would use a wireless Internet connection to send a product's bar code to an online database and retrieve information about the product and its manufacturer. You could use the Internet to obtain other details too. You might find that a product contains an ingredient you're trying to avoid because of allergy or diet. Or you might learn that a manufacturer has just been honored for its environmentally friendly practices. Digging deeper, you might examine a company's product safety record or trace its global operations. Of course, such research takes time, so you probably wouldn't investigate every product on every shopping trip. But if you did a quick scan before buying at least some items, you would still be a better-informed consumer.

The MediaCart computerized shopping cart is putting some of these concepts into action (**www.mediacart. com**). It uses Microsoft technologies, including SQL Server, and has already been piloted at selected ShopRite supermarkets (Figure 12.30). Shoppers slide their store loyalty card through a scanner. Once identified, shoppers receive ads and special promotions on the basis of their

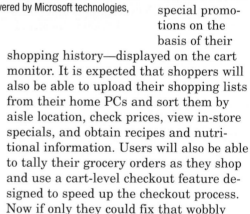

FIGURE 12.30 The MediaCart, powered by Microsoft technologies, may change the way you shop.

shopping history—displayed on the cart monitor. It is expected that shoppers will also be able to upload their shopping lists from their home PCs and sort them by aisle location, check prices, view in-store specials, and obtain recipes and nutritional information. Users will also be able to tally their grocery orders as they shop and use a cart-level checkout feature designed to speed up the checkout process. Now if only they could fix that wobbly wheel!

Create and Edit an Access Database Query

In this How to exercise, the Query wizard will be used to create the query, and the Design view will be used to insert the specific criteria the query is to locate within the database records. The customer database, whose screen captures were used in this chapter, will be used for this example

1. Open Access 2010.
2. Open the database on which the query is to be applied, in this example, the customer database.
3. On the Ribbon, select the *Create* tab and in the Queries group, select *Query Wizard* (Figure 12.31).

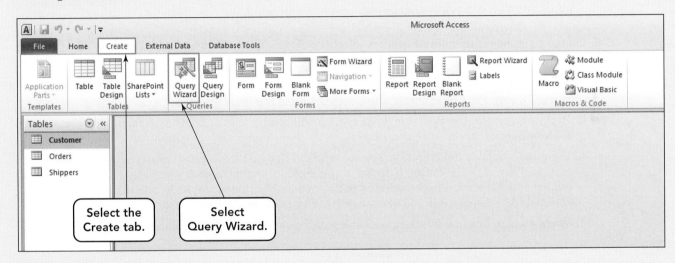

FIGURE 12.31 Accessing the Query Wizard

4. The New Query Wizard will start, and the screen displayed in Figure 12.32 will appear within the Access Window.

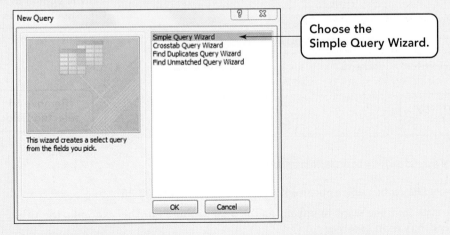

FIGURE 12.32 The Query Wizard has four separate wizards. The one selected depends on the user's desired outcome.

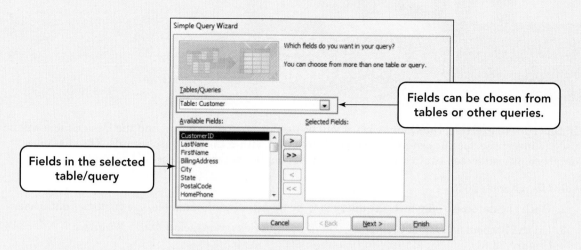

FIGURE 12.33 This query will only use the fields from the Customer table.

5. On the right side of this initial window select the *Simple Query Wizard*. Then click *OK*.

6. The Simple Query Wizard dialog box will appear (Figure 12.33).

a. From the drop-down list in the Tables/Queries section, choose the table on which you want to run the query. For this example, the Customer table has been selected.

b. In this dialog box, the available fields section will display all the fields associated with the selected table or query.

c. From the available fields section, select each field that you want to be displayed in the query results. Then click the button with the single right arrow to transfer your selected field from the available fields section to the selected fields section. For this example, four fields have been selected to be displayed in the query results (Figure 12.34).

d. When you are finished selecting the tables/queries and their related fields, click *Next*.

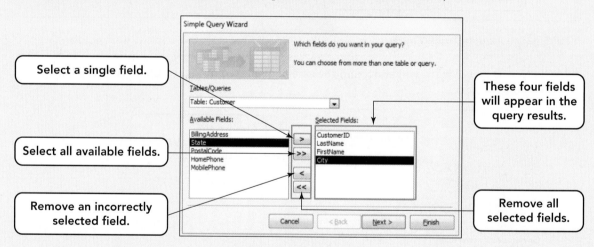

FIGURE 12.34 Only the selected fields will be displayed in the query results.

7. Another Simple Query Dialog box will appear with two options. (Figure 12.35)

a. You can enter the title that you want to appear as the query name. For this example, the title "Buffalo Customers" has been entered.

b. You can view the query results or make modifications to the query design. For this example, choose the option to view the query results.

c. Click *Finish*.

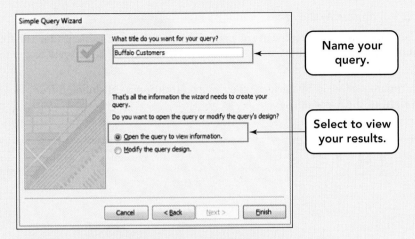

FIGURE 12.35 This is the final step of the Simple Query Wizard.

8. The results for the created query appear in the Access window, with the four selected fields displayed for all six customers that were in the original customer table (Figure 12.36).

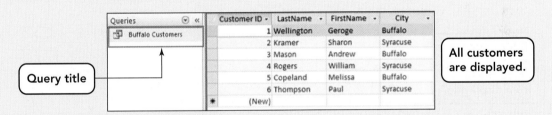

FIGURE 12.36 The query results are displayed in the access main window, directly below the ribbon.

9. This exercise titled the query "Buffalo Customers," but customers in all cities were displayed in the query results. Query results can be filtered by setting criteria in the Design view of the query.

   a. With the query results still displayed, on the Ribbon, click the *Home* tab, if necessary.

   b. Click the arrow below the word View at the top left. From the drop-down menu select *Design View* (Figure 12.37).

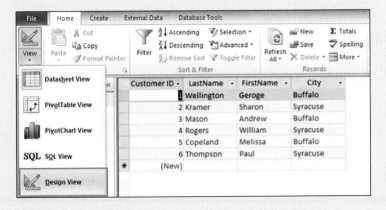

FIGURE 12.37 Selecting the Design View will change the display to the query design screen.

10. The Query design screen will appear in the Access window (Figure 12.38).

    a. In this window, you can enter specific criteria in the criteria row of the edit table under the field name that the criterion is limiting. For this exercise, enter = **"Buffalo"** in the criteria row under the City field.

    b. Rerun the query with the new criteria by clicking the red exclamation point labeled *Run*, located on the File tab to the right of the View option.

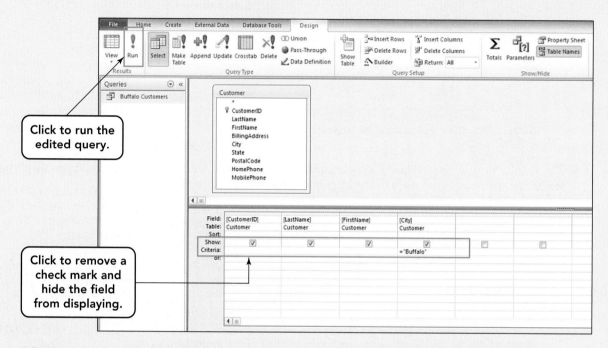

FIGURE 12.38 To remove a field from displaying in the results, simply click the checkmark in the Show row under the field you want to hide.

11. The results of the edited query, displaying only customers in the city of Buffalo, will appear in the Access window (Figure 12.39).

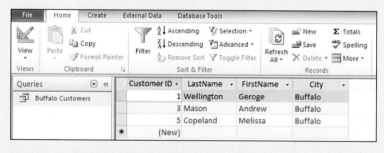

FIGURE 12.39 The edited query will only display records from the Customer table that match the criteria set in the Design view.

Chapter Summary

Databases and Information Systems

- A database is a collection of data stored in an organized way. A data file, or table, is made up of records, which are units of information about a person, place, thing, or event. Each of these units of information is called a field. Each field is assigned a specific data type and has properties associated with that data type that can be set by the database developer. The content entered into each field is characters that are, in turn, translated by the computer system into bits, the smallest unit of data that a computer can understand.

- A good database ensures data integrity (validity of the data), promotes data independence (separation of data from applications), avoids data redundancy (entry of the same data in two or more places), ensures data security (protection from loss of confidentiality), and provides procedures for data maintenance (adding, updating, and deleting records).

- File management programs work with only one data file, called a flat file, at a time. Database management systems (DBMSs) work with two or more data files, called tables, at a time. The data in the various tables can be related by common fields. The different types of database management systems are flat, relational, object oriented, and multidimensional.

- Data warehouses bring data together from many smaller databases in different areas of an organization into a massive database that managers can use to make decisions. Data mining and Web mining use several techniques to explore data in an attempt to discover previously unknown patterns. Client/server database systems enable many users to access the database simultaneously, usually over a local area network. Web–database integration refers to techniques that make information stored in databases available through Internet connections.

- An information system includes data, hardware, software, people, and procedures. An information system's main functions are accepting input in the form of mission-critical data, processing this data to produce information, storing the data, and disseminating information throughout functional divisions of an organization.

- Functional divisions of an organization handle the business processes and typically include accounting, finance, marketing and sales, human resources, production/operations, and information systems. Business units are more concerned with developing and sustaining a competitive advantage for the goods and service the company or organization produces. Succinctly, the business units are concerned with making profit. A typical business unit is a division of a company, product line, or special focus group whose actions can be planned independently of other business units of the company.

- Information systems used in organizations today include transaction processing systems (TPSs), management information systems (MISs), decision support system (DSSs), executive information system (EISs), knowledge management systems (KMSs), and expert systems. These systems help managers at different levels make operations, tactical, procedural, and strategic decisions for the organization.

- Today retailers use databases linked to POS terminals for fast checkout and inventory control. These terminals can also be fully integrated with credit card authorization and check-screening systems that either approve or disapprove a purchase. The use of a database in this manner reduces fraudulent changes or purchases that exceed a customer's credit limit. Linked to these systems are also marketing features like printing coupons for related products and listing the total amount of savings for that shopping trip.

Key Terms and Concepts

Identification

Identify the elements of a database.

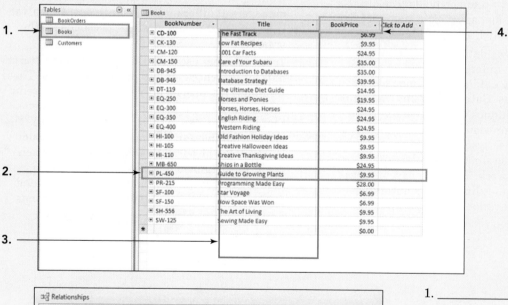

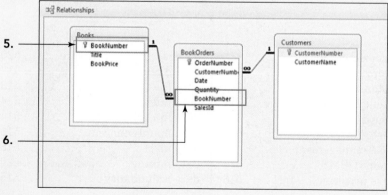

1. _____
2. _____
3. _____
4. _____
5. _____
6. _____

Matching

Match each key term in the left column with the most accurate definition in the right column.

_____ 1. primary key

_____ 2. data warehouse

_____ 3. query

_____ 4. data type

_____ 5. data dictionary

_____ 6. data mart

_____ 7. field

_____ 8. record

_____ 9. data file

_____ 10. data mining

_____ 11. data integrity

_____ 12. drill down

_____ 13. data validation

_____ 14. data maintenance

_____ 15. default value

a. A specifically phrased question used to locate data in a database

b. A location that stores the information of a single division of a corporation

c. A collection of records

d. The processes used to define acceptable input in a database

e. A single unit of relative information, usually identified as a column of information.

f. A technique used to zero in on specific data elements

g. Field containing information that uniquely identifies a record

h. The adding, updating, and deleting of data

i. An analysis technique that explores data in an attempt to discover previously unknown patterns

j. A setting that is automatically selected unless another is provided

k. A central location for the storage of all the information a corporation possesses

l. The accuracy of data in a database

m. A list of all the tables in a database along with a description of their structure

n. All the information about an individual, inventory product, or other database element, usually identified as a row of information

o. The specification that defines the kind of data a field will contain

Multiple Choice

Circle the correct choice for each of the following:

1. Which TPS report alerts managers to unexpected developments?
   a. Summary report   b. Tactical report
   c. Exception report   d. Operational report

2. Which system allows vendors to detect insufficient funds for a purchase by accessing a database of delinquent accounts?
   a. Executive information system
   b. Management information system
   c. Expert system
   d. Check-screening system

3. Which language is commonly used to create queries in relational databases?
   a. MDX query language   b. SQL
   c. Visual Basic   d. OLAP

4. Which database is usually visualized as a cube?
   a. Flat   b. Relational
   c. Object-oriented   d. Multidimensional

5. Which type of management decision focuses on localized issues that need immediate attention?
   a. Strategic   b. Tactical
   c. Operational   d. Exception

6. Which technique makes information stored in databases available via Internet?
   a. Web–database integration
   b. Web mining
   c. Data warehousing
   d. Online analytical processing

7. Which of the following is an example of a file management program?
   a. Microsoft Access   b. Microsoft Excel
   c. Microsoft Word   d. MySQL

8. Which is a check that verifies a required field has not been left empty?
   a. Range   b. Consistency
   c. Completeness   d. Numeric

9. Which is a functional division of an organization?
   a. Investment   b. Engineering
   c. Shipping & Receiving d. Marketing & Sales

10. Which of the following is *not* an acceptable data type?
   a. Text   b. Memo
   c. Number   d. Character

Fill-In

In the blanks provided, write the correct answer for each of the following.

1. _____ is the repetition of data in a database.

2. _____ is the providing of too much information, which makes processing, absorbing, and validating it difficult.

3. An expert system consults its _____ to draw a conclusion or provide a possible solution.

4. A(n) _____ system captures information from books and/or experienced individuals.

5. _____ is a query language created by Microsoft and used with multidimensional databases.

6. A(n) _____ is a field in one table of a relational database that is a primary key in another.

7. A(n) _____ is a TPS report that provides information on the overall performance of an organization.

8. A(n) _____ system deals with detailed and in-depth knowledge in a specific area.

9. A manager makes a(n) _____ decision when it concerns the organization's overall goals and direction.

10. The _____ data type allows only a "yes" or "no" value.

11. A(n) _____ is used to determine whether a field has been left empty.

12. _____ is the combining of traditional methods of analyzing data with additional information gathered from the Web to discover previously unknown patterns.

13. A(n) _____ system enables managers to create simulations beginning with real data and simulate what-if question scenarios.

14. A(n) _____ is the collection of people, hardware, software, data records, and activities that process the data and information in an organization.

15. _____ is an information system whose user-friendly desktop interface is the key to the collection and consolidation of information from multiple sources.

Short Answer

1. List the six steps to follow when designing a database.

2. Explain the statement: Repetition of data cannot be totally eliminated from a database.

3. Explain the difference between data security and data maintenance in a relational database.

4. List three advantages of a relational database system over a file management program?

5. Explain the difference between a knowledge management system and an expert system.

Teamwork

1. **Erroneous Data**   Preventing erroneous data from being entered into a database is extremely important. As a team, work together to explain the validation rules in the table at the right, which are being defined from an Access database. Brainstorm and discuss at least five consequences of entering erroneous data into a database. Write a group report that answers these questions and that summarizes your brainstorming.

Validation Rule Setting	Meaning
>=0	
"Yes" Or "No"	
Like "Wh*"	
Like "B?ll"	
>=#1/1/2009# And <#1/1/2010#	
<=Date( )	
> 0 And <10000	

2. **Database Manager versus Database Architect** As a team, investigate the job requirements for the positions of database manager and database architect. Locate several ads for these positions through online job searches. Compare the list of required skills and educational requirements. As a team, piece the ads together and create the ultimate job description for each position. Include a list of required skills, educational requirements, specific programming languages, and security clearances desired. If possible, interview the database manager and architect at your school. See whether he or she has any additions or deletions to make to your job description. Using a word processor, submit your finalized job descriptions written as a real job advertisement. Include a listing of the sources of the original ads that the team reviewed.

3. **How Many Databases Are You In?** Come up with a list of 10 to 15 databases that members of your team might be a part of. For each of these databases, list at least three tables that might compose the database and at least five fields within each table. Try to determine what might be the primary key field of each table. Using PowerPoint, create an organized presentation of your results.

4. **Design a Dashboard** As team, assume that you own an online business that places items on eBay for others to purchase. Indicate the type of products that you will sell (keep it simple—like baseball hats or school jerseys). As a team, come up with 5 to 10 dashboard features that you would like to see displayed on your monitor in order to monitor online interest in your product, levels of inventory, number of bids or items purchased through buy-now options, and any other information that the team finds essential to monitor. Describe the dashboard features and how they will display the information (graphically or in table form), or actually draw a sample of the way the dashboard might look. Submit your descriptions in a word-processed document or submit your dashboard drawing.

5. **A Database for This Course** As a team, create a database outline on paper or with a database program like Access that will describe the components of this course. Start by determining the tables that you will need (students, grades, assignments, and so on). Then list all the fields that each table will contain and their corresponding data type. Identify key fields and any fields that will be shared among tables. Submit your final outline or completed database file to your instructor as directed.

On the Web

1. **Null Values in a Database** Use a search engine to locate articles and information on the use of the Null value in a database. In a one-page, double-spaced paper, define what the Null value stands for and provide examples of where it might be used. After reading articles in support of its use and those against its use, take a side in this debate and defend it in your paper. Remember to cite your references.

2. **Compare SQL and MDX** Using a search engine, locate articles and information on both the SQL and MDX query languages. List the similarities and differences of each. Create or locate at least two examples of queries in each language. Explain the purpose of the query and how it works. Use a PowerPoint presentation to report your research and examples. Remember to cite your references.

3. **Investigate a Graph Database** Using Web resources, locate information on an open source graph-database named *Neo4j*. Explain the data model used by this database and the programming languages that work with it. If possible, locate a few examples of databases using this model. Investigate the applications that best suit this model's logic, and list the assets and weaknesses of such a databases. Attempt to locate other graph databases. Provide a brief explanation of each and a link to their Web site.

Summarize your findings and provide answers to the questions posed in a one-page, double-spaced paper. Remember to cite your references.

4. **Normalizing Databases** The purpose of normalizing a database is to avoid data redundancy and make the data more accessible through queries. Using the Web and any other research sources, investigate the three levels of recommended database normalization. Explain what each level is trying to achieve in the database and provide an example. Present your findings and examples in a one-page, double-spaced report. Remember to cite your references.

5. **Data Disasters** Data disasters can occur at all levels of business and personal computer usage. For some humorous, and not so humorous, episodes of lost data in 2009 go to **www.ontrackdatarecovery. com/data-recovery-press/index.aspx?getPress Release=61397** or **www.ontrackdatarecovery. com/data-disaster-2008/** for the 2008 list. After reading the crazy, humorous disasters from this site or any others that a search might target, locate five that relate to business. In a one-page, double-spaced report or a PowerPoint presentation, describe each of the five disasters, the year it occurred, and what action could have prevented its occurrence.

chapter 13

Systems Analysis and Design

Chapter Objectives

1 Define system analysis. (p. 544)

2 Explain the goals and activities of a systems analyst. (p. 544)

3 Understand the concept of a system and its life cycle. (p. 546)

4 Discuss why the systems development life cycle (SDLC) is so widely used. (p. 546)

5 List the five phases of the SDLC. (p. 546)

6 Describe the classic mistakes of failed information systems development projects and how systems analysts can avoid them. (p. 547)

7 Discuss the activities in each of the five phases of the SDLC. (p. 551)

8 Name the deliverables of each of the five phases of the SDLC. (p. 551)

9 Recognize the importance of security in each of the five phases of the SDLC. (p. 558)

Have you recently visited your physician, pharmacist, or school registrar and had to confirm your personal data so that the computerized information system being implemented could be updated? If the system is already up and running, does it feel that more time is being spent entering data than listening to your problems or concerns? Do you get a similar feeling every time you attempt to get some type of customer service? What is happening? Is the need to maintain information and the system designed to access it becoming more important than servicing the individual? How is an information system developed, implemented, maintained and secured? Can a more personal interface be considered in the development stage of the system?

You may be wondering what systems analysis and design has to do with computers. Well, actually, quite a bit. You see, it's through the analysis and design of information systems that we can create new, innovative ways of doing things. An information system encompasses the people, hardware, software, data records, and activities that process an organization's data and information into a usable form. Accessing information and the systems designed to provide that access are important in today's information-based society. Because we constantly interact with information systems, understanding the capabilities of information systems and their structure will better prepare you to capitalize on the systematic management of information.

Creating the computerized component of an information system isn't something to take lightly. The benefits are great, but so are the risks. This chapter will explore proven strategies used to analyze and design information systems. These topics are covered:

- A review of the meaning of systems analysis
- The basic proficiencies and communication skills needed by a systems analyst
- An in-depth breakdown of the five steps of the systems development life cycle (SDLC)
- An overview of the classic mistakes that permeate the development of information systems and suggestions on how to avoid them
- Details of the activities and deliverables expected from each of the five phases of the systems development life cycle (SDLC) ■

Systems Analysis: Communication Counts

Is it too much to ask that computerized information systems be finished on time and within budget and that they perform their intended job? Admittedly, information systems development is a difficult challenge, and the unique requirements of many businesses don't make it any easier. Whether it's how they track customers and sales, or inventory and expenses, most businesses need something a little different. (For example, a pizza delivery company needs a different type of information system than a pharmaceutical firm or an automaker.) In addition, users and clients may have difficulty communicating their needs clearly, leading to the development of systems that don't satisfy them, or systems that need costly changes. Another frustrating component of system development is that the time estimated for development is usually overly optimistic, typically by as much as 20 to 30 percent. Just like any construction project, such as building a new home, building an information system takes longer than most people care to admit. An example of this delay and underestimation of cost is the paperless case management system designed for the Federal Bureau of Investigation (FBI). This system was originally to be completed by September 2010, but release has been pushed back to 2011. Along with the time delay, the cost of the project seems to have been underestimated by $30 billion.

In the face of such chaos, it makes good sense to be organized and communicate your goals clearly. **Systems analysis** is the field concerned with the planning, development, and implementation of artificial systems, including information systems. The systems analysis discipline learns from previous development efforts and formulates strategies for improved planning, organization, control, and execution of information systems development projects. Modern information systems are all about managing data to provide information, entertainment, and systems to support society's many activities. The one underlying key, fundamental to the development of a system that is functional, meets the specific needs of the company, and is positively received by its users, is communication.

With that said, let's now turn our attention to the individuals whose communication skills are essential in the development of these information systems.

The Human Component

The human component of an information system includes representatives of the company, including management, users, and professionals trained in the development of such systems.

Systems analysts The computer professional who works with users and management as a guide during the development of an organization's information system is the **systems analyst** (Figure 13.1). An analyst is responsible for determining the requirements needed to modify an existing system or to develop a new one. They don't ordinarily do the development; the development is reserved for other trained computer professionals such as computer programmers or systems developers. Rather, systems analysts do the following:

- Collect information, identify, and evaluate existing systems and proposed solutions.
- Prepare flowcharts and diagrams outlining a system's capabilities.
- Research and recommend hardware and software development.

FIGURE 13.1
Systems analysts must communicate with a variety of individuals during the development of a system.

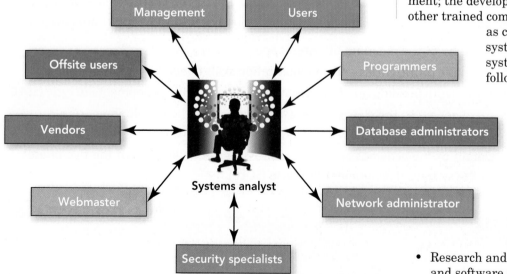

- Work as part of a team with technical staff to ensure connectivity and compatibility.
- Maintain confidentiality with information processed or accessed by the system.
- Assist in guiding the development of the system after a strategy has been chosen.

Much of a systems analyst's job involves communication, including listening skills. Analysts must listen to users, understand their needs, and involve them in the project so that they feel some element of ownership. They keep in close contact with project team members and the project manager so that they know how the project is progressing. They must write ample documentation that explains, at every step, what was performed, why and how it was performed, and who did it. They must know who (the user, the project manager, or the vendor) is supposed to do what during the systems development process. To stay organized and keep track of these various tasks, systems analysts follow an organized procedure for planning and building information systems called the systems development life cycle.

Information technology steering committee

Generally representatives from senior management, information systems personnel, and middle managers are chosen to compose the **information technology steering committee**. This is the committee that provides guidance on key issues that affect the information division of a company such as policy and objectives, budgetary review, marketing strategy, resource allocation, and most decisions involving large expenditures. It reviews requests and, depending on the overall state of the company and the request's alignment with the company's long-term plan, determines which ones to approve for action.

Project team Once a project request is approved by the steering committee a **project team** is appointed to act as a liaison between the systems analyst and others involved in the project's design and implementation and the client's organization. Some of the responsibilities of this committee are listed here:

- Being actively involved in the development and review of the system design
- Assisting in the customizing of the design and providing direction on the system as it is being developed so that it best suits the needs of the organization
- Monitoring progress against the projected time line
- Sustaining momentum and company enthusiasm for the project
- Answering questions for the system analyst and development team

Members of the project team are recruited from various divisions of the organization and provide a broad yet in-depth range of skills and experience that make the team's input into the system development essential.

"... systems analysts follow an organized procedure for planning and building information systems call the systems development life cycle."

Project manager The **project manager** is responsible for managing the project according to the project plan and making formal presentations to management or an appointed committee on strategies for the development and implementation of a system. Together, the project manager, systems analyst, and project team create a positive environment, communicate frequently, and make adjustments as needed to bring a project to completion and successfully implement an information system. The project manager's responsibilities include the following:

- Disseminating information to all having an active role in the system development
- Identifying and managing project risk
- Ensuring that what was agreed to is delivered
- Keeping a pulse on the progress of the project and determining whether the deliverables are acceptable

The project manager may not do all this alone, but the responsibility for these activities is within the scope of that position. A project manager must be well organized, have great follow-up skills and good analytical ability, be able to budget and make estimations, and possess self-discipline.

The Systems Development Life Cycle: A Problem-Solving Approach

In the early years of business computing, information systems development was a disorganized, ad hoc process that frequently produced discouraging results. Systems typically were delivered late, went over their budgets, and didn't provide the services users expected. As hardware and software systems became more complex and users more dissatisfied with systems riddled with errors, it became more apparent that a successful system needed to employ a method that combined ideas and reviews of both users and developers. In order to manage this diverse group and maintain an overall grasp on the progress of a project, a model or approach was developed for system development. The **systems development life cycle (SDLC)** provides a structure or logical guide to system development with the goal of improving the development process, itself, as well as the quality of the final system created. The SDLC is better understood if it's broken down into digestible pieces. Let's begin with what the "systems" part means.

A **system** is a collection of components purposefully organized into a functioning whole to accomplish a goal. Systems occur in nature, but what we're talking about here are **artificial systems**, systems deliberately constructed by people to serve some purpose. Artificial systems, like natural systems, are all around us. The commercial airline transportation system, is an example of a complex artificial system that does a remarkably good job of safely delivering millions of people to their destinations every day.

At the core of the systems concept lies the recognition that various parts of a system need to be modified or adapted to function together smoothly. (After all, you wouldn't want to fly on an airplane that

had the wrong type of wing installed.) A second important concept about systems is that they have a **life cycle**: They are born, go through a process of maturation, live an adult life, and become obsolete to the point that they have to be modified or abandoned. This sequence of life is also referred to as "cradle to grave." Figure 13.2 displays the key tasks associated with each phase of a system's life cycle. If you think about yesterday's transportation systems, such as canals or covered wagons, you'll see it's obvious that systems outlive their usefulness.

FIGURE 13.2 The Systems Development Life Cycle

Life Cycle Phase	Key Tasks
Planning Phase	Identifying systems development goals
Analysis Phase	Designing specific components
Design Phase	Putting it all together
Implementation Phase	Using and testing the system
Maintenance Phase	Maintaining and eventually terminating and retiring the system

At this point, we could be talking about any kind of system, including a manufacturing system such as an assembly line, the public switched telephone network, or the highway toll collection system. No organization, not even a small one, can function without an information system of some kind, even if it doesn't have a computer-based component. But developing the right information system for the right purpose takes communication, patience, time, review, and a development plan. That's exactly the function of the SDLC and its steps, or phases.

The Phases of the SDLC

At the core of the SDLC model is a simple idea: You shouldn't go on to the next step until you're certain that the current one has been performed properly. Several models of the SDLC exist. Interestingly, they vary in depth from 5 to 14 steps. The five basic phases (steps or stages) of the SDLC are (1) planning or investigation, (2) analysis, (3) design or development,

(4) implementation and testing, and (5) maintenance or support. Each phase is intended to address key issues and to produce **deliverables**, which are outcomes or tangible output such as reports or other documents. Figure 13.3 displays each of the five basic phases with the deliverable each phase produces. The deliverables from one phase often are the input for the next phase.

Note that different organizations and systems development teams may use modified or slightly different versions of the SDLC; some versions identify more phases than others, and some use different names for the individual phases. The five-part process described here represents what is common practice. Visit the Startvbdotnet Web site at **www.startvbdotnet.com/ sdlc/sdlc.aspx** to see a basic explanation of how the waterfall model of the system development life cycle works.

Avoiding Mistakes

Systems analysts have learned, often through bitter experience, to avoid the classic mistakes of failed projects. Consequently, the information systems development process looks at an organization's overall goals and objectives and identifies the various systems and subsystems that the organization uses to achieve its goals and objectives. The following essentials of systems development wisdom are built into the SDLC:

- User involvement is crucial. Users include any person for whom the system is built, and that may include customers. Users are the ultimate judges of the system's usability, although they may not know how to express their needs clearly. Without user involvement, the system may not meet users' needs, and they may then resist or even sabotage efforts to use the new system.

- A problem-solving approach works best. To create an effective system, you must identify the problem, place the problem in context, define the solution, examine alternative solutions, and choose the best one. Without this approach, the new system may not fully address the underlying shortcomings of the existing system.

- Good project management skills are needed. Many failed systems development projects are characterized by unrealistic expectations, overly optimistic schedules, lack of solid backing from management, people's inability to make

decisions and stick with them, lack of control over insertion of new but unnecessary features, and interference from problem personnel. A poorly managed project may become so chaotic that it must be cancelled.

- Documentation is required. The term **documentation** refers to the recording of all information pertinent to the project, for instance, manuals, tutorials, start-up procedures, and installation instructions. A **project notebook**, which is frequently a digital file that is maintained online, is often used to store the documentation for a project. The documentation enables everyone connected with the project to understand all the decisions that have been made. Documentation should be an ongoing process; it shouldn't be put off until the end of the project, at which time important information or key personnel might not be available. Tools like Microsoft Project and Sharepoint assist with this portion of the SDLC by providing monitoring tools like calendars and Gantt charts and an overall environment in which project documents can be managed, viewed by

FIGURE 13.3 The Five Basic Phases of the Systems Development Life Cycle

Systems Development Life Cycle

Phase 1: Planning:

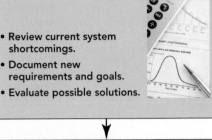

- Review and prioritize requests.
- Set the budget.
- Create the project proposal.
- Create the project team.

Phase 2: Analysis

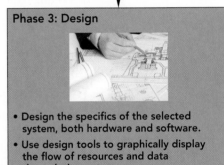

- Review current system shortcomings.
- Document new requirements and goals.
- Evaluate possible solutions.

Phase 3: Design

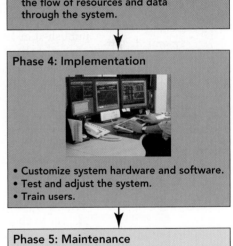

- Design the specifics of the selected system, both hardware and software.
- Use design tools to graphically display the flow of resources and data through the system.

Phase 4: Implementation

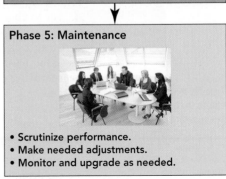

- Customize system hardware and software.
- Test and adjust the system.
- Train users.

Phase 5: Maintenance

- Scrutinize performance.
- Make needed adjustments.
- Monitor and upgrade as needed.

project participants, and connected to generate meaningful reports. Without documentation, the system can't be properly supported or modified (especially after key development personnel have left).

- Checkpoints or milestones should be used to make sure the project is on track. At the end of each phase, the project must be critically and independently evaluated to make sure that it's on track. An organization shouldn't be afraid to cancel the project (or repeat a phase) if results aren't satisfactory. Some of the worst development disasters occur when the project team conceals the fact that the system couldn't possibly work.

- Systems should be designed for growth and change. A system should be designed so that it won't break down or require a major redesign in the event of change (including unanticipated increases in usage). Failure to anticipate change and growth could make the entire system useless in short order.

Avoiding mistakes doesn't guarantee success. On the other hand, making mistakes may very well guarantee failure!

The Waterfall Model

The SDLC outlines a step-by-step process that is the base for many system development models. The **waterfall model** is a linear and sequential framework for system development that was originally published in 1970 and follows the basic phases of the SDLC (Figure 13.4). An important aspect of the waterfall model is that each phase is an individual entity and must be completed before the next phase can begin. Once a phase begins, there is no turning back. Feedback loops exist between phases so that when evaluation takes place at the completion of each phase, the decision to continue, return to the previous phase to make appropriate modifications, or to abort the project can be made. Phases do not overlap, inhibiting feedback on exposed problems and presenting great difficulty in incorporating changes requested by the customer.

With that said, however, the waterfall method does have some advantages, including these:

- Simple and easy to use because of its linear design and clear project objectives

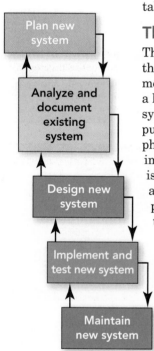

FIGURE 13.4 The waterfall model demonstrates the two-way flow of progress through the SDLC. Progress can advance to the next stage or return to the previous one if results do not measure up.

- Easy to manage due to each phase being self-contained and having to produce defined deliverables
- Best used with small projects in which requirements are clearly stated and changes are not likely to occur

Some disadvantages of the waterfall method are listed:

- Difficult to adjust scope during the process
- Working software not produced till late in the cycle and, if faulty, might require terminating the process and starting a new process
- Not suitable for long, complex, or object-oriented projects
- Not suitable for projects where there is a moderate to high risk of change

The waterfall method is just one implementation of the SDLC.

Modern Approaches to Software Development

Although the traditional waterfall model is still used by many organizations, the fast pace of change in information technology today sometimes requires more responsive techniques. The waterfall approach, which requires sequentially progressing from phase to phase, has been criticized as time-consuming and lacking in flexibility. To address these issues, new methods and processes have developed.

Prototyping is a process used in several system development methodologies in which a developer creates a small scale mock-up of the system and presents it to the customer. The customer in turn provides feedback to the developer, and based on that feedback the developer makes adjustments. Although prototyping increases user involvement, the approach has several drawbacks, including the following:

1. **Incomplete analysis of the problem and solution:** Developers can get distracted while developing prototypes and neglect to fully analyze the problem and develop comprehensive solutions.
2. **User confusion:** Users may begin to think of the prototype as the finished system. This can lead to resentment if revisions to later prototypes change

the functionality of the original prototype.

3. **Too much time spent on developing prototypes:** If not properly managed, prototype development can take up too much time, leaving insufficient time for development of the final system.

Prototyping is an integral part of the **rapid application development** methodology **(RAD)**, which focuses on building systems in a short amount of time, often compromising usability, features, and/or execution speed. Two of its features include application prototyping and iterative development, the process of repeating a cycle of an operation. The focus of RAD is to increase development speed and decrease time to delivery. Features of RAD include these:

- Active user involvement through the use of workshops and focus groups to gather information
- Prototyping early and repeated testing
- Re-using software components
- Less formality in documentation and team communication

To combat some of the issues surrounding RAD and the traditional waterfall model of software development, **joint application development (JAD)** was born. This process attempts to speed up the overall development process by collecting the requirements of the new (or modified) system while the new system is being developed. This means that the first four phases of the traditional SDLC are conducted simultaneously. Emphasis is placed on the critical tasks of identifying the problem and developing solutions.

Sound impossible? It isn't, if it is properly coordinated by a skilled project leader. The leader develops workshops for participants and regularly brings them together to identify problems, develop solutions, create prototypes, and test and evaluate solutions. JAD is a complex process and requires an intense amount of face-to-face interaction among all team members (Figure 13.5). However, this level of interaction tends to increase communication and the likelihood of a positive project outcome. It also tends to significantly speed up the development process because problems and solutions tend to be more accurately identified and mapped out. JAD still uses the phases of

the SDLC but conducts the first four simultaneously. Again, several arrangements and combinations of the SDLC phases exist, but the basic steps are still usually embedded somewhere within each variation.

A type of RAD geared toward fully involving users at all points of the SDLC is a development methodology called **Agile**. The goal of the Agile method is to enable an organization to deliver systems quickly, change them quickly, and change them often. Agile involves iterative development, interaction, communication, and the reduction of resources that do not add value. Some advantages of the Agile method are listed:

- Quick adaptability to changing requirements because of its iterative development style
- Faster decisions and associated actions due to team members working in close proximity and communicating daily
- By reallocating valuable time and personnel from an activity that has no value to one having a priority, the project may be completed sooner

These methodologies, or some variation or combination of them, are used today in the development of systems. The method used depends on the organization, project, timetable, and cost, along with many other factors.

Let's look at phase 1 of the traditional SDLC.

FIGURE 13.5 JAD development requires superior project management skills and more face-to-face interaction than other strategies to communicate and interweave four steps of the SDLC into one smoothly.

One of the newest methodologies for system development is Extreme Programming (XP). This method takes the best processes used in all the other methodologies and turns them up to extreme levels. Extreme Programming uses a unique approach to system development in that it stresses customer satisfaction, delivering software as needed and not on a schedule that does not meet the customer's needs.

This process of system development uses several critical practices (Figure 13.6).

- The first is the "planning game" in which business representatives, referred to as customers, come up with desired features for the system to be developed and present them as a "user story." The user story is actually just a broad description of the feature with an associated name. Estimates are made as to how long each story will take to develop, and decisions are made as to which stories will be implemented.

- The "metaphor" is a description of how the system will work. It is developed by the XP team and incorporates the accepted stories.

- An "acceptance test" is a level of functionality, set by the customer, that software must reach before being released or developed further. Software and other system components in the XP process are produced as a series of small integrated releases, making functionality testing easier and customer-desired changes less of a challenge to the team.

- Communication is an essential practice among XP team members. The team codes segments of software together, troubleshoots a poor acceptance score, or redesigns a segment based on the new insight provided by the customer.

Simple design and continuous integration are practices that are a constant throughout the entire Extreme Programming process. In this programming process, changes can be suggested and the design altered at any time throughout the development.

Extreme Programming is an approach that focuses on simplicity, communication, and feedback. It is a methodology that is catching on and, in the future, may be recognized with the same reverence as the other methodologies discussed in this chapter. The practices of the XP method of system development seem to be flexible and encompassing enough to keep up with the technological changes we see daily.

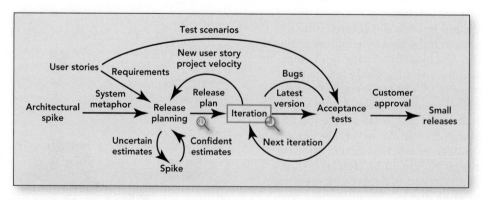

FIGURE 13.6 This process diagram illustrates how the practices of Extreme Programming (XP) work together to create a final product that the customer will accept.

Phase 1: Planning the System

Phase 1 is the planning or investigation phase. In phase 1 of the SDLC, an organization recognizes the need for an information system, defines the problem, examines alternative solutions, develops a plan, and determines the project's feasibility. The result is a project proposal submitted to senior management. If this phase is performed well, it can assure the foundation for the appropriate information system to be built, and just as important, it can assure that the wrong system won't be built.

Recognizing the Need for the System

New information systems (or modified ones) result from recognition of deficiencies in performance, information quality, economics, security, efficiency, or service (Figure 13.7). If the current system

FIGURE 13.7 Recognizing the Need for a New or Modified System

Deficiency	Example
Performance	Slow response time
Information quality	Out-of-date or inaccurate information
Economics	High operating costs
Security	Vulnerability to break-ins
Efficiency	Wasting resources (employee time, printer paper, toner, etc.)
Service	Difficult, awkward to use

demonstrates poor response time, users might experience delays when they attempt to process data or transfer files. If the existing system lacks information quality, a sales or customer service representative may give a customer an incorrect stock number on an item being ordered or report that an item is out of stock when there are actually plenty in stock. Economic deficiencies need to be addressed if the existing system generates high bills

from ISPs or other vendors. If the existing system lacks security, hackers or competitors can steal or destroy valuable company data, creating anxiety among users and eventually leading to the loss of customers and revenue. An inefficient system might automatically print customer statements even when their account balance is zero, wasting employee time, paper, toner, and other resources. A system demonstrates deficient service when employees must go through unnecessary or repetitive steps to perform a task.

Even if the current system doesn't have obvious deficiencies, it might still be worthwhile to replace it if a redesigned system could generate new business opportunities. For example, a new or redesigned airline reservation system could generate better customer profiles that would identify the need for additional services, such as providing more first-class seats, arranging car rentals, making hotel reservations, and so on, thus creating increased revenue and customer satisfaction by offering related services.

To get the project going, someone makes a formal project request to the organization's information technology steering committee, which generally includes representatives from senior management, information systems personnel, users, and middle managers. The steering committee reviews requests and decides which ones to address. If a project request is approved, the steering committee appoints a project team and phase 1 continues.

Defining the Problem

To solve a problem, you must first understand it. But that's not always as easy as it might seem. Problems are often confused with symptoms. A **symptom** is an unacceptable or undesirable result, whereas a **problem** is the underlying cause of the symptom. Another way to differentiate a symptom from a problem is that a symptom is an indication or a sign of something, whereas a problem is a state of difficulty that has to be resolved. For example, someone might say that a headache is a symptom of the wrong eyeglass prescription. Although the headache may seem like the problem, the incorrect prescription is actually the problem. In an information system, users might complain about a symptom, such as slow response time when entering a transaction into their computers. Users may think the solution is to demand more powerful computers, because they think the problem is with the computers. But the slow response time is just a symptom. The problem could be any number of different things, such as the slow speed of network transmissions. If this is the case, then it's a waste of money to buy faster computers! If a symptom is confused with a problem, the wrong solution might be implemented.

Determining the exact problem often is a difficult task. Ideally, the problem definition stage identifies the features that need to be added to or built into the information system to make it acceptable to users. Although users must be involved in defining the problem, they're not accustomed to looking at information systems in a structured, unbiased way. The systems analyst talks to as many users as possible, and slowly a picture emerges of what these people do, when they do it, how they do it, and why they do it (Figure 13.8). From these facts, the analyst then derives recommendations for new system features (if an existing system will be modified) or proposes that a new system be built from scratch.

Examining Alternative Solutions

After the problem has been identified, system requirements need to be specified. A process called **requirements analysis** determines the requirements of the system by analyzing how the system will meet the needs of end users. The requirements analysis is extremely important because errors or omissions could lead to expensive missteps or modifications later in the development process or after users express dissatisfaction with the new or modified system. It also is important for the project team to focus the requirements analysis primarily on user needs and not get caught up in the technical details.

After system requirements have been determined, the project team then looks at a range of possible solutions. The range of solutions that the project team examines often includes internally developed systems, off-the-shelf software, and outsourcing. The project team should consider the advantages and disadvantages of each potential solution, along with the security features that each proposed solution requires. For example, an internally developed system offers the project team control over each phase of development. However, this control has a price—internally developed systems are usually the most expensive to build and maintain. Purchasing off-the-shelf software would obviously save the project team the hassle of creating its own software or hiring programmers if none exist in-house. However, some companies require specialized software features that aren't available in off-the-shelf software packages. Outsourcing the development of the system offers a range of additional options: A project team may outsource one part of the project for which there is no in-house expertise (such as programming software or providing security solutions) or choose to outsource the entire project. Obviously, as more portions of the project are outsourced, the expense of the potential solution increases. When the project team agrees on a solution, the project proceeds.

One business adept at solving organizational problems is a company called EDS, a Hewlett-Packard Enterprise Service. Visit the EDS Web site at **www.eds.com** to view examples of their successes.

Developing a Plan

When an appropriate solution has been identified, the project manager participates in the development of a project plan and sees that project budgets and schedules are maintained. The **project plan**

FIGURE 13.8 The systems analyst interacts with a variety of users to understand their roles and how they work with the system. Armed with this knowledge, the analyst can make better, more accurate recommendations for new system features or a complete overhaul.

identifies the project's goal and specifies all of the activities that must be completed for the project to succeed. For each activity, the plan specifies the estimated time that the project will require, as well as the estimated costs. The plan also identifies activities that must be completed before new ones can begin and indicates which activities can occur simultaneously.

Before developing a system, it is imperative that system specifications be created. Think of system specifications in the same vein as blueprints for a building or a house. These specifications act as benchmarks to evaluate as well as implement the system while it is being developed. System specifications also assist in answering tough questions, such as whether the correct system solution is being implemented, whether it meets user requirements, and whether it matches the project plan.

Project plans are often graphically summarized with a **Gantt chart**, a type of bar chart that indicates task due dates and project milestones (Figure 13.9).

speech, they do make errors. If the error rate is unacceptable, the project isn't technically feasible until speech recognition technology improves.

Operational feasibility refers to a project that can be accomplished with the organization's available resources. If some of the project's goals include changes beyond the organization's control (such as regulations in a foreign country), the project isn't operationally feasible.

When a project demonstrates **economic feasibility**, it can be accomplished with available financial resources. The question of whether a project is economically feasible is usually answered by a **cost-benefit analysis**, an examination of the losses and gains related to a project. The costs are the expected costs to develop and run the new system.

A cost-benefit analysis examines both tangible and intangible benefits. You can easily measure **tangible benefits**, such as increased sales, faster response time, and decreased complaints. **Intangible benefits**, such as improved employee

ID	Task Name	Duration	Jan	Feb	Mar	Apr	May	Jun	Jul	Aug
1	Planning	3w	1/26 ▩ 2/13							
2	Analysis	10w		2/9 ▩▩▩ 4/17						
3	Design	11w			3/23 ▩▩▩▩▩ 6/5					
4	Implementation	4w						6/5 ▩ 7/3		

FIGURE 13.9 A Gantt chart is a graphical summary of project plans that indicates activities performed over a period of time.

Project management software, such as Microsoft Office Project, provides an excellent means of developing and modifying project plans.

Determining Feasibility

A feasible project is one that can be successfully completed. To determine whether a project is feasible, three types of feasibility must be examined: technical, operational, and economic.

Technical feasibility means that a project can be accomplished with existing, proven technology. For example, consider a project that requires speech recognition. Although computers are getting much better at recognizing and transcribing human

morale and customer satisfaction, may be difficult or impossible to measure. Bank managers, for example, may decide to install an ATM because they believe that many people won't deal with a bank that doesn't have one. The improved customer satisfaction that would occur as a result of installing the new system is an intangible benefit.

In many companies, managers will request a study of the proposed system's **return on investment (ROI)**, its overall financial yield at the end of its lifetime. The money invested in the system should produce a return that is greater than alternative investments, such as putting the money in the bank.

Preparing the Project Proposal

At the conclusion of phase 1, the project leader writes a **project proposal**, a document that introduces the nature of the existing system's problem, explains the proposed solution and its benefits, details the proposed project plan, and concludes with a recommendation. A good project proposal will include the **scope**, the sum total of all project elements and features, as well as some funds to cover **scope creep**, the small, continuous changes to the project not in the original plan or documentation that lead to increased costs and a longer development schedule. In response, management decides whether to continue the project. The project proposal is the deliverable from phase 1.

Phase 2: Analyzing and Documenting the Existing Information System

In phase 2 of the SDLC, the systems analyst or the systems development team determines precisely what the new system should accomplish. Here, the emphasis is placed on what the system should do, not how. (That comes next, in phase 3.) This phase includes two steps: analyzing the existing system and determining the needs of the new system. Phase 2 is often referred to as the systems analysis (or just analysis) phase.

Analyzing the Existing System

A study of the existing system (whether computerized or manual) determines which activities currently being performed should be continued in the new system. This step can be simple if the current system is well documented. Unfortunately, most systems are not well documented, and that's especially true of updates to an original system. Thus, a major part of the analysis of the existing system is to document it. If the existing system is computerized, the current hardware needs to be examined to see whether it's adequate to do the job.

An unexpected but valuable benefit of the systems analysis phase is that it often points out problems that weren't fully identified in phase 1. This analysis may be the first time a group of people sits down in the same room and talks about the existing system. The discussion can result in new insights, and problems that were not uncovered in the preliminary investigation can be brought to light and resolved.

Determining the New System's Requirements

After the existing system has been exhaustively documented, the new system's requirements are precisely stated. This listing of the new system's requirements is the deliverable for phase 2. The requirements state the innovations that need to occur for the system to be acceptable to users. Again, user involvement is crucial, because systems analysts often obtain information about system requirements through interviews, surveys, and observations of how the system is currently used.

Phase 3: Designing the System

Phase 3, the design phase of the SDLC, is concerned with how the new information system will work. This phase isn't concerned with the nitty-gritty details of how the software will be coded. Instead, this phase's deliverable is a logical design that provides an overall picture of how the new system will work. The goal of this phase of the project is to specify in exact terms the type of data that flows into the system, where the data goes, how the data is processed, who uses the data, how the data is stored, what data entry forms are involved, and what procedures people follow. To do this, the project team can use graphical tools, such as entity-relationship diagrams, data flow diagrams, project dictionaries, and data dictionaries.

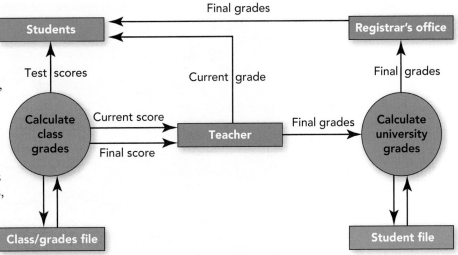

FIGURE 13.11 A data flow diagram shows how data moves through the existing system.

Design Tools

To describe the new information system, analysts use methods of graphical analysis to convey their findings to managers, programmers, and users. An **entity-relationship diagram (ERD)** shows all of the entities (organizations, departments, users, programs, and data) that play a role in the system as well as the relationships among those entities (Figure 13.10).

Team members create a **project dictionary**, which explains all the terminology relevant to the project; they also develop a data dictionary, which defines the types of data that are inputted into the system.

Two recent approaches, prototyping and computer-aided software engineering, are helping to improve the design phase.

The first approach is prototyping, an integral part of rapid application development (RAD), in which a small-scale mock-up, or prototype, of the system is developed and shown to users (Figure 13.12). The prototype is developed at an early stage and isn't intended to be fully functional. It provides just enough functionality so that users can give feedback. Some of the

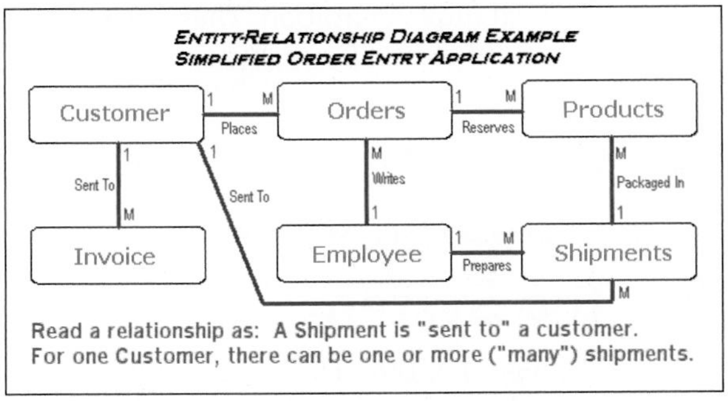

FIGURE 13.10 An entity-relationship diagram depicts all of the entities that play a role in the system.

A **data flow diagram (DFD)** uses a set of graphical symbols to show how data moves through the existing system (Figure 13.11). The DFD also specifies the details of how the data is processed.

ERD and DFD software are available from several sources. Visit **www.smartdraw.com/tutorials/software/dfd/tutorial_01.htm**, **http://office.microsoft.com/en-us/visio/default.aspx**, and **www.conceptdraw.com/en/products/cd5/ap_data_flow.php** to learn about several different products.

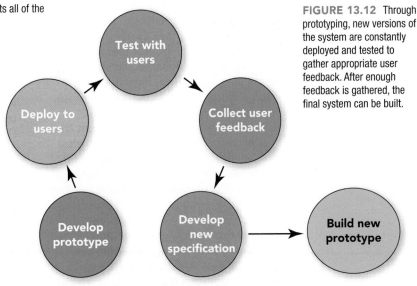

FIGURE 13.12 Through prototyping, new versions of the system are constantly deployed and tested to gather appropriate user feedback. After enough feedback is gathered, the final system can be built.

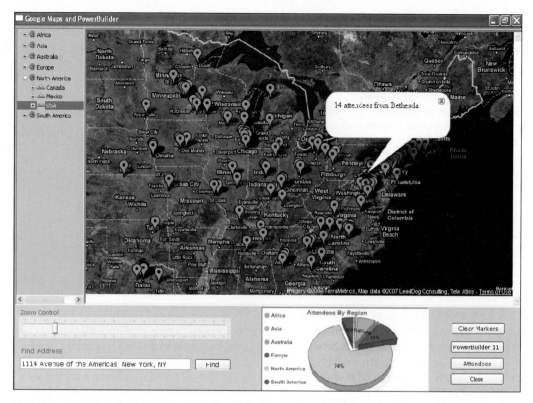

FIGURE 13.13 PowerBuilder is an example of a CASE tool that can be used to build powerful Web applications such as Google Maps.

disadvantages of prototyping were discussed earlier in this chapter; however prototyping can be very beneficial. The main advantage is that users don't have to imagine what the system specifications mean in terms of a working system. They can experience the system and thus find problems or enhancements that they may not have considered otherwise.

The second approach, **computer-aided software engineering (CASE)**, automates the often tedious task of documenting entity relationships and data flows in a complex new system. Most CASE tools include project management features, data dictionaries, documentation support, and graphical output support; some even automatically generate prototype code (Figure 13.13).

During this phase, it's important that analysts think about the system's logical requirements and not think about what can be accomplished (and what can't) with existing information systems and software. Such thinking might prevent them from realizing that they may need to create an entirely new type of system, one that's never been developed before. This is the reason phase 3 is clearly separated from phase 4, in which attention turns to the system's

physical implementation. These two phases must be rigorously kept separate.

Phase 4: Implementing the System

In phase 4 of the SDLC, the system implementation phase, the project team and management decide whether to create the physical system using internal expertise or to purchase it from outside vendors. If the project team decides to build the system in-house, hardware must be purchased and installed, and programs must be written. The system must be exhaustively tested, and users must be trained. When the team is confident that the new system is ready for use, the conversion to the new system takes place.

Deciding Whether to Build or Buy

After the new system's requirements and logical design have been specified, the project team faces the **build-or-buy decision**: Should the new system be developed in-house or purchased from an outside vendor?

In-house development provides the opportunity for detailed customization, but it often carries with it the high costs of programmer salaries, testing, and time. Most organizations cannot afford to have programmers on staff and don't have the time that is required to properly develop an application. For these reasons, an organization will often purchase an off-the-shelf product and then customize it for its specific needs. Another option is to outsource the project to a company that specializes in creating systems applications.

If the decision is made to outsource the project, the project team sends out either a request for quotation or a request for proposal. A **request for quotation (RFQ)** is a request for a vendor to quote a price for specific components of the information system. A **request for proposal (RFP)** is a request for a vendor to write a proposal for the design, installation, and configuration of the information

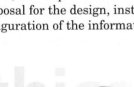
“It's **essential** that **errors or problems** be detected **before** the **system** is released for **use** in the **organization.**”

system. RFQs and RFPs are often sent to vendors called **value-added resellers (VARs)**, independent companies that combine and install equipment and software from several sources.

Developing the Software

Developing the software can be considered a separate subset of the information systems development process. However, in most cases, developing the software amounts to less than 15 percent of the time involved in the entire project. To develop the software required for the new system, programmers use the program development life cycle (PDLC). Recall that the PDLC separates the task of software program development into six manageable phases. Programmers must define the problem, design the program, code the program, and then test and debug, document, and implement it.

Software development can affect an organization's cost-benefit analysis according to whether the new software will be used as a replacement for a manual procedure or simply to enhance an already automated process.

Testing

Thorough testing is essential. The two basic types of testing are application testing and acceptance testing. With **application testing**, programs are tested individually and then tested together. With **acceptance testing**, users evaluate the system to see whether it meets their needs and whether it functions correctly. It's essential that errors or problems be detected before the system is released for use in the organization.

Training

A computerized information system includes not only computer hardware and software but also knowledgeable users and procedures. A successful conclusion to the project requires training the users of the new system. The best training methods involve sitting users down with the new system in one-on-one training sessions. Users also will need manuals that include tutorials as well as reference information.

Converting Systems

After the new system has been tested and the users have been trained, conversion to the new system occurs. System conversion can be performed in any of the following ways:

- A **parallel conversion** involves running both the new and the old systems for a while to check that the new system produces answers at least as good as those of the old system. This type of conversion is the safest; the old system can carry the load until any problems with the new system are cleared up. This conversion is also the most expensive, however, because the work is duplicated.

- With a **pilot conversion**, one part of the organization converts to the new system while the rest of the organization continues to run the old system. When the pilot group is satisfied with the new system, the rest of the organization can start using it.

- A **phased conversion** occurs when the new system is implemented over different time periods, one part at a time. After one part of the new system is running, another piece is implemented.

- A **direct conversion**, sometimes called a **crash conversion** or **plunge**, requires stopping the old system and then starting the new system. A direct conversion is the most risky type of conversion, but it may be necessary in some situations.

Phase 5: Maintaining the System

In the final phase of the SDLC, the new system is evaluated to ensure that it has met its intended needs and works correctly. A **postimplementation system review** is a process of ongoing evaluation that determines whether the system has met its goals. After conversion, widespread use may reveal errors that were not detected during testing that must be corrected. In addition, changes will be needed as the business environment changes. For example, changes may be needed in data entry forms to deal with an expanded product line.

In addition to the postimplementation review, the system must be maintained. Maintenance includes such tasks as making adjustments to the system as the organization changes; adding, deleting, and adjusting records; making backup copies of files; and providing security for the system. Most organizations spend much more time and money on maintenance than any other component of the SDLC.

In time, the system may be found to be so deficient that a new round of systems development must take place—and the systems development life cycle begins anew.

> "Most **organizations spend** much more time and money on **maintenance** than any **other component** of the SDLC."

Security and the SDLC

The SDLC provides the structure to develop systems and products that are technology related. This development system has withstood the test of time because, besides providing a sequential structured process, it also possesses the flexibility to adjust for each new system developed. A rising concern in system development is the inclusion of security and the recognition that it is an aspect that cannot be added on in the final phase or after the development process is complete. Instead, security is being viewed as a feature that needs to be integrated in every step of development (Figure 13.14).

The Software Engineering Process Group provided a security track at their 2007 conference, with the idea that this segment of the conference would act as a forum and collect ideas on how to improve

FIGURE 13.14 Security Activities and Deliverables for Each Phase of the SDLC

Planning Phase	
Activities	**Deliverables**
Categorize information and the security needs of each category. Establish privacy requirements for each category based on the confidentiality, availability, and integrity of the data each contains.	Prepare security proposal.

Analysis Phase	
Activities	**Deliverables**
Identify appropriate security controls and their associated requirements.	Provide a security risk assessment.

Design Phase	
Activities	**Deliverables**
Develop the specifics of the security system. Plan and initiate documents for certification and accreditation.	Design security architecture and simulate its behavior.

Implementation Phase	
Activities	**Deliverables**
Validate security checks. Perform system certification and accreditation requirements.	Integrate the security features into the operational environment.

Maintenance Phase	
Activities	**Deliverables**
Monitor security controls. Perform re-certification and re-accreditation activities as required.	Update security features to secure against new threats.

the relationship between process development and security. The forum provided two areas of comments (Figure 13.15). The first was how security is currently viewed in the SDLC, and the second was how and why it should be integrated into the entire SDLC process.

The ideas gathered at this forum have led to the continual promotion of the strengthening of the ties between security and the SDLC, resulting in a number of initiatives at both the government and industrial level, including these:

- The National Defense Industrial Association developed The Engineering for System Assurance guidebook to provide guidelines to ensure that control,

FIGURE 13.15 SDLC and Security

Current Relationship between Security and SDLC	Security Integrated into the SDLC
There is the awareness that security must be addressed in the development process but no set direction on how to go about embedding it.	Security must be an integrated part of the development process and not an add-on if it is to be effective and efficient.
Current security standards and regulations are not implemented correctly or consistently during the process.	Security should not just be recognized as important but should, instead, be emphasized as being critical at all levels of the organization. This change in attitude will facilitate the acceptance of security into the organization's overall plan and the development process.
Security effectiveness has to be continually assessed to ensure that it meets the challenges in today's environments.	Security may be a separate entity, but it has to work in partnership with each phase of the SDLC.

communication, and weapon systems cannot be compromised.

- The National Institute of Standards and Technology publication on security considerations in the SDLC draws attention to the need to integrate security milestones into the SDLC for all U.S. federal agencies.

- Security touchpoints in the SDLC were identified to highlight focal points of security concern.

- The Institute for Infrastructure and Information Assurance published "Toward an Organization for Software System Security Principles and Guidelines" to provide a base for teaching and learning about security issues.

Security development can be viewed as a process paralleling the system development life cycle. The security development process uses the same five phases: planning, analysis, design, implementation, and maintenance; and it requires the creation of deliverables relative to security in each phase. Security can no longer be on the back or even side burner. It must be up front and addressed from the onset of system development, starting with the initial information gathering in the planning phase. Addressing the level of desired security and the mechanisms needed to obtain that desired level in the initial phases of planning guarantees that security will be an integral part of the big plan.

Create a Data Flow Diagram
with Word 2010

1. Open Microsoft Office Word 2010. You will use the shapes in Word 2010 to create a data flow diagram for a businessman who designs and sells T-shirts and gives a receipt to each customer.

2. In a new blank document window, on the Ribbon, click the *Insert* tab.

3. From the Illustrations group, click the *Shapes* button (Figure 13.16).

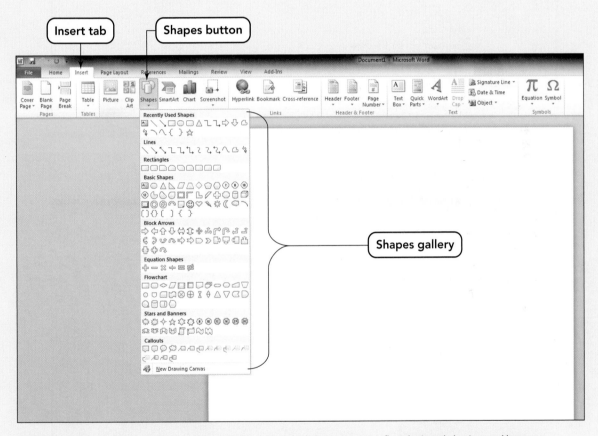

FIGURE 13.16 The Shapes button provides a list of such readymade items as arrows, flow chart symbols, stars, and banners.

4. From the Basic Shapes section, select the *Double Bracket* shape (Figure 13.17).

   a. When you position your mouse on the document, it will have the shape of a black plus sign (+). Click and drag the mouse to establish the size of the shape.

   b. Once the Double Bracket shape is the desired size, release the mouse button.

   c. With the shape still selected, use the keyboard to type the label **T-Shirt Inventory** (Figure 13.18). What you type should appear in the middle of the shape.

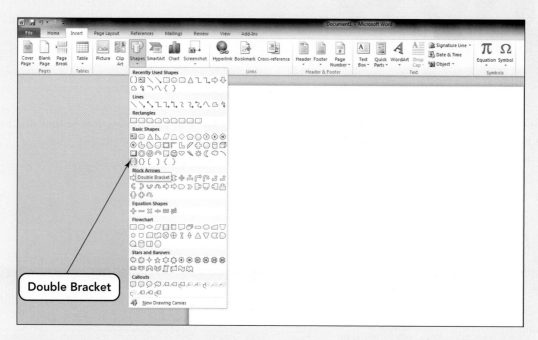

FIGURE 13.17 An open rectangle in many drawing programs is often used to represent a data store in data flow diagrams.

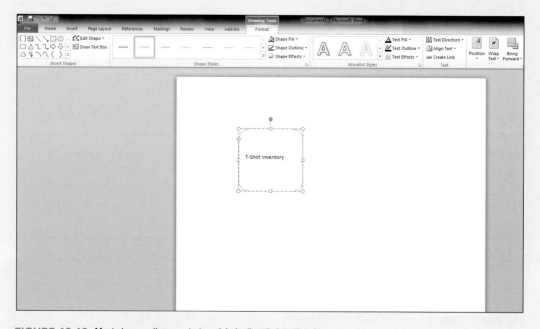

FIGURE 13.18 Most shapes allow you to type labels directly into the shape.

5. Repeat the instructions in step 4, positioning the second double bracket shape to the right of the first one. Label it **Client Data** (Figure 13.19).

6. Use the Shapes gallery to create two more shapes: a circle and a rectangle. Position and label both as displayed in Figure 13.20.

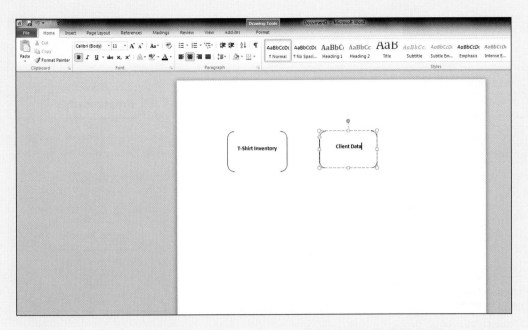

FIGURE 13.19 T-Shirt Inventory and Client Data are referred to as data stores but are actually databases containing information on inventory and client accounts.

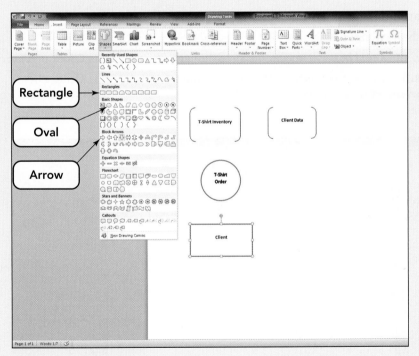

FIGURE 13.20 In data flow diagrams, each shape symbolizes a different action or item. A circle represents a process, and a rectangle represents an external interactor, in this case the client.

7. The next step is to insert arrow shapes to indicate the flow of information between the items in the data flow diagram.

   a. Use the Block Arrows located in the Shapes gallery to create and position five arrows as displayed in Figure 13.21. You will change the color of the arrows in step 9 of this section.

   b. You can rotate the arrow, or any shape, by clicking on the green circle, located near the shape, with the mouse and dragging the mouse. The shape will rotate in the direction of the mouse movement.

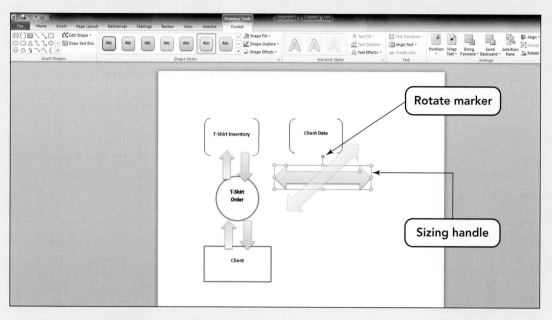

FIGURE 13.21 All shapes can be resized and rotated.

8. Position a label next to each arrow to indicate the activity each arrow represents.

   a. Make sure that no shape is selected.

   b. On the Insert tab, in the Text group, click the *Text Box* button.

   c. Select *Simple Text Box,* and a text box will appear on the document. Type the label **Check Inventory**.

   d. Use your mouse to position the text box next to the arrow going from the T-Shirt Order circle shape to the T-Shirt Inventory data store (Figure 13.22).

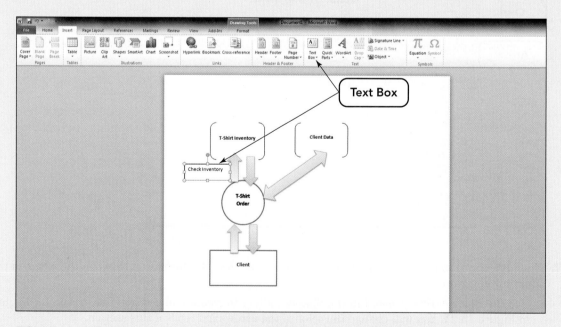

FIGURE 13.22 The text typed into a text box can be formatted in the same manner as text in any Word document.

e. Repeat the steps in this section, creating a text box and labeling every arrow in the diagram. Use Figure 13.23 as a guide.

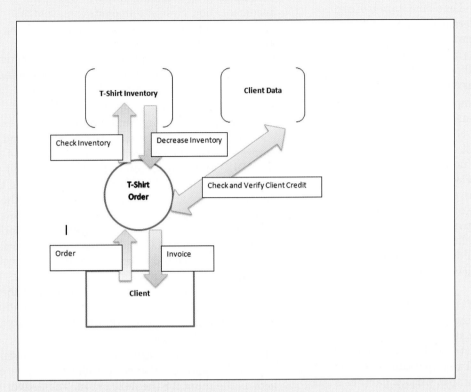

FIGURE 13.23 Labels identify the action that each arrow represents. Notice the arrow between the client data store and the T-Shirt Order represents the two-way process of checking entered data and returning a validation notice so the order can continue to be processed.

9. You can format shapes in a data flow diagram by selecting the shape. A format tab becomes available. The options on the Format tab provide choices to change Shape Fill, Shape Outline, and Shape Effects, including shadow effects, 3D effects, and many other shape properties.

10. The data flow diagram is now complete.

Chapter Summary

Systems Analysis and Design

- Systems analysis is the field concerned with the planning, development, and implementation of artificial systems, including information systems. The systems analysis discipline learns from previous development efforts and formulates strategies for improved planning, organization, control, and execution of information systems development projects.

- A systems analyst is a computer professional who works with users and management to guide them through the development of an organization's information system. An analyst is responsible for determining the requirements needed to modify an existing system or to develop a new one. An essential skill for a system analyst is the ability to communicate with both users and management. To stay organized and keep track of these various tasks, systems analysts follow an organized procedure for planning and building information systems called the systems development life cycle (SDLC).

- A system is a collection of components purposefully organized into a functioning whole to accomplish a goal. Systems occur in nature, but artificial systems are deliberately constructed by people to serve a specific purpose. Two important concepts about systems are the fact that various parts of a system have to be modified or adapted to function together smoothly and that all systems have a life cycle: They are born, go through a process of maturation, live an adult life, and become obsolete to the point that they have to be modified or abandoned.

- To impose order on earlier, haphazard development processes and to improve the quality of information systems the SDLC was developed.

- Although many models of the SDLC exist, the five traditional phases are (1) planning or investigation, (2) analysis, (3) design, (4) implementation, and (5) maintenance or support.

- The three classic mistakes of failed information systems development projects are lack of user involvement, poor project management, and lack of documentation. Systems analysts can avoid mistakes by involving users, using a problem-solving approach, applying project management skills, keeping thorough documentation, using checkpoints to make sure the project is on track, and designing the system with room for growth and change.

- In phase 1 of the SDLC, the organization recognizes the need for an information system, defines the problem, examines alternative solutions, and determines the project's feasibility. In phase 2 of the SDLC, the systems analyst determines what the new system should accomplish by analyzing the existing system and determining the needs of the new system. In phase 3 of the SDLC, the systems analyst determines how the new system will work. In phase 4 of the SDLC, the management team decides whether to build or buy a new system, develops the software, tests the system, trains users, and converts to the new system. In phase 5 of the SDLC, the new system receives ongoing evaluation and maintenance to ensure that it meets the organization's needs and works properly.

- The output of each phase of the SDLC is referred to as its deliverable. The deliverable of one phase acts as the input for the next phase. The deliverable for the planning phase is the project proposal; for the analysis phase, it is the list of new system requirements; for the design phase, the deliverable is the logical design that provides the overall picture of how the system will work. The implementation phase deliverable is the conversion to the new system, and the postimplementation system review is the deliverable of the final phase: the system maintenance and support phase.

- Security is no longer being considered an afterthought to the SDLC but is an interwoven element that has to be addressed at each phase of development.

Key Terms and Concepts

Identification

Identify the item or activity and the phase of the system development life cycle for which each is best associated.

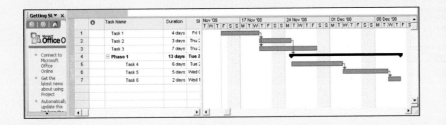

1. _____

Request
For
Proposal

2. _____

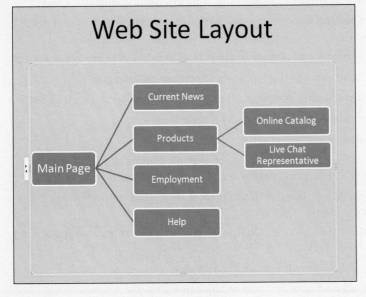

3. _____

4. _____

AutoCAD MEP

System Requirements

For 32-bit AutoCAD MEP

- Microsoft® Windows® XP Professional or Home edition (SP2 or later) or Microsoft® Windows Vista® (SP1), including Enterprise, Business, Ultimate, or Home edition (compare Windows Vista versions)
- Intel® Pentium® 4 or AMD Athlon® dual-core processor, 3 GHz or greater with SSE2 technology
- 2 GB RAM, 3 GB recommended
- 4 GB free disk space for default install, 4.2 GB for full install
- 1,024 x 768 display with true color, 1,280 x 1,024 true color recommended
- 128 MB graphics card; 256 MB or greater, Direct3D®-capable workstation-class 3D graphics card recommended (currently supported graphics cards)
- Microsoft® Internet Explorer® 7.0 or later
- Microsoft Mouse-compliant pointing device
- DVD drive (for installation only)

For 64-bit AutoCAD MEP

- Microsoft Windows XP Professional or Home edition (SP2 or later) or Microsoft Windows Vista (SP1), including Enterprise, Business, Ultimate, or Home edition (compare Windows Vista versions)
- AMD Athlon 64 with SSE2 technology, AMD Opteron® with SSE2 technology, Intel® Xeon® with Intel EM64T support and SSE2 technology, or Intel Pentium 4 with Intel EM64T support and SSE2 technology
- 2 GB RAM, 4 GB recommended
- 4.3 GB free disk space for default install, 4.7 GB for full install
- 1,024 x 768 display with true color, 1,280 x 1,024 true color recommended
- 128 MB graphics card; 256 MB or greater, Direct3D-capable workstation-class 3D graphics card recommended (currently supported graphics cards)
- Microsoft Internet Explorer 7.0 or later
- Microsoft Mouse-compliant pointing device
- DVD drive (for installation only)

5. _____

Matching

Match each key term in the left column with the most accurate definition in the right column.

_____ 1. data flow diagram

_____ 2. Gantt chart

_____ 3. joint application development

_____ 4. deliverable

_____ 5. prototyping

_____ 6. entity relationship diagram

_____ 7. parallel conversion

_____ 8. application testing

_____ 9. scope creep

_____ 10. acceptance testing

_____ 11. pilot conversion

_____ 12. phased conversion

_____ 13. direct conversion

_____ 14. project notebook

_____ 15. project dictionary

a. A process in which the first four phases of the traditional SDLC are conducted simultaneously

b. Occurs when a new system is implemented one part at a time, until the complete system is functional

c. Users evaluate a system to see whether it meets their needs and goals

d. The process of testing applications individually and then in connection with other components

e. Makes use of symbols and shapes to show how data moves through a system

f. Contains explanations of all terminology relevant to the project

g. Usually a digital file that contains all ongoing documentation on a project

h. An outcome or tangible output such as a report

i. Stopping an old system and starting a new system

j. Occurs when one part of an organization begins using a new system, while the rest of the organization continues to use the old system

k. The small, continuous changes to the project that were not in the original plan or documentation

l. Displays all units that have a role in a system and the relationships among them

m. Indicates task due dates and project milestones

n. Running both old and new systems at the same time for a while

o. A process in which a small scale mock-up of the system is developed

Multiple Choice

Circle the correct choice for each of the following:

1. What identifies the project's goals and specifies all activities that must be completed for the project to succeed?
   a. Project proposal
   b. Project dictionary
   c. Project plan
   d. Project notebook

2. What examines the losses and gains related to a project?
   a. Gantt chart
   b. Cost-benefit analysis
   c. Operational feasibility
   d. Technical feasibility

3. What automates the tedious activity of documenting entity relationships and data flow?
   a. Entity-relationship diagram
   b. Gantt Chart
   c. Computer-aided software engineering
   d. Data flow diagram

4. Which type of conversion method is the safest?
   a. Direct   b. Phased
   c. Parallel   d. Pilot

5. What phase of the SDLC involves ongoing evaluation, referred to as postimplementation system review?
   a. Analysis
   b. Implementation
   c. Design
   d. Maintenance

6. What is the deliverable for phase 3 of the SDLC?
   a. The decision to buy or build a new system
   b. The project proposal
   c. A logical design providing an overall picture of how the system will work
   d. A listing of the new system's requirements

7. What linear and sequential model for system development requires one step to be fully completed before the next can start?
   a. Computer-aided software engineering
   b. Joint application development
   c. Waterfall
   d. Rapid application development

8. Application and acceptance testing take place in which phase of the SDLC?
   a. Planning
   b. Design
   c. Implementation
   d. Maintenance

9. Which is an example of a tangible benefit?
   a. Increased sales
   b. Better employee morale
   c. Increased customer satisfaction
   d. Better vendor relationships

10. What is the decision to develop a system in-house or purchase one from an outside vendor?
    a. Request for quotation
    b. Request for proposal
    c. Build-or-buy
    d. Value-added reseller

Fill-In

In the blanks provided, write the correct answer for each of the following:

1. A list of the new system requirements is a deliverable for phase _____ of the SDLC.

2. _____ conversion is the most expensive type of conversion but presents the least risk.

3. _____ is a system development methodology that features application prototyping and iterative development to build systems in a short amount of time, often with compromises.

4. _____ refers to a project that can be accomplished with the organization's available resources.

5. The project proposal is the deliverable from the first phase, the _____ phase of the SDLC.

6. Crash conversion and plunge are alternate terms for a _____ conversion.

7. Improved employee morale and increased customer satisfaction are examples of _____ benefits.

8. A _____ is a state of difficulty that has to be resolved.

9. _____ is a process that determines the needs of a system by analyzing how the system will meet the needs of the end user.

10. The _____ is the process from birth, through maturation, into adulthood, obsolescence, and abandonment.

11. A request for _____ is sent to a vendor to obtain pricing for information system components.

12. The _____ of the project is the sum total of all project elements and features.

13. _____ is the overall financial yield of a system over its lifetime.

14. A(n) _____ works with both users and management to determine a project's requirements.

15. A(n) _____ is an unacceptable or undesirable result.

Short Answer

1. Explain the role of a system analyst in the development of an information system.

2. Differentiate between an information technology steering committee and the project team.

3. List the five phases of the SDLC and the activities that occur in each phase.

4. Identify and provide a brief description of the four ways to implement a system conversion.

5. List three drawbacks of prototyping a system under development.

Teamwork

1. **Artificial Systems** In this chapter several examples of artificial systems are cited. As a team, research artificial systems and come up with a list of five to seven artificial systems that team members have interacted with. In a one-page, double-spaced paper, provide a description of each system and the stage of the systems life cycle that the team believes the system is currently in. Explain your reasoning for the placement of the system in that stage.

2. **Prototyping** This chapter listed some of the drawbacks of prototyping. As a team, come up with a list of three to five industries where prototyping a system or product makes sense. In a PowerPoint presentation of 5 to 10 slides, name the industries or products the team selected and provide the reasons the team felt prototyping made sense.

3. **SmartDraw 2010** Go to **www.smartdraw.com** and download a free trial copy of SmartDraw 2010. Use this software to create a data flow diagram of a process that the team has agreed on and has been approved by your instructor. Use the "How-to" section of this chapter for diagram shapes and their associated purpose. As a team, in a one-page, double-spaced essay, evaluate the SmartDraw program with respect to its interface, ease of use, and help feature. Submit your team's evaluation of the SmartDraw program and the data flow diagram you developed.

4. **Security and the SDLC** As a team, investigate strategies for embedding security into the systems development life cycle. Research this topic and locate at least two models that exist and interconnect security with the SDLC. In a one-page, double-spaced paper, describe both models. Select the model that the team feels is the better one, and provide reasons for the selection. Remember to cite your references.

5. **Using the SDLC to Plan a Consignment Business System** As a team, make plans to start a consignment business that will take used computer game systems and game cartridges or CDs on consignment. Your business will sell those systems and games and return a percentage of the sale to the individual who placed the item on consignment. The business can be a brick-and-mortar set up, sell through e-Bay, or use both means for sales. Using the SDLC, create a chart of the problems, opportunities, business design, hardware requirements, and employee and customer components to be considered in each phase of the development process for your business. Keep in mind the information-processing component of the business and such questions as these: How will you track inventory and its consignor? How will you keep track of customers? How will you keep track of expenses, income, and payments to consignors? Remember, this does not have to be complete, but you do need to demonstrate that you can use the phases of the SDLC to develop your business. Present your detailed chart and answers to the questions in a one- to two-page, double-spaced paper.

1. **Investigate the Spiral Model of Software Development** This model is a combination of the waterfall model and prototyping model. It is used with large, expensive, and complicated projects. Using the Internet and a search engine of your choice, research the spiral-shaped model of software development. Locate a diagram that displays the relationship among the phases of this model. In a PowerPoint presentation of five to seven slides, summarize the model and state its advantages and disadvantages over other models; include the diagram, and cite your references.

2. **Project Proposal Templates** Using the Internet and a search engine of your choosing, research project proposal templates. Locate sites that offer free templates and a few that require payment. In a one-page, double-spaced report, list the URL of at least five sites, the categories of project templates available, the cost of registering or purchasing the product, and a sample of a proposal template (if possible).

3. **Systems Analyst Job Description** Using your college placement center, other employment references, and the Internet, locate systems analyst job descriptions. Notice the requirements that are similar among these postings. Using this information and a word processor, develop your own comprehensive job description for a systems analyst. Include a list of the responsibilities, required level of education and/or certificates, and the knowledge and skill level required. Cite your references at the bottom of your document.

4. **FBI Case Management Information System** Using the Internet and any other research sources, locate information on the FBI's case management information system currently under development. Find out the year the project commenced, the original completion date and projected cost, the company that the project was awarded to, some of the problems with the development of the system, and the new increased projected cost of the system. Add any other information you can locate on the design of the system and what is causing the holdup and increased cost. Use a PowerPoint presentation of 7 to 10 slides to present your information. Remember to include your references.

5. **Dream Green Jobs** Use the Internet and a search engine of your choice to locate employment sites that focus on green information technology jobs, specifically positions that require knowledge of the systems development life cycle (SDLC). Create a list of the job titles you find, along with their category (analyst, management, supervisory, educational, or assistant) and job description, the required level of education, pay rate (if posted), and location. Make sure to include the part of the job description that substantiates these posted jobs as "green" jobs that require knowledge of the SDLC. Present your list and the related information either in a Word table or an Excel spreadsheet. Remember to cite your references.

Enterprise Computing

Chapter Objectives

You are confident in your ability to use a computer for personal activities, but are you ready to make the move to a college system or a business setting? Are you familiar with cloud computing, blade servers, Web portals, and RAID? Do you know how to use a virtual private network to access files stored on the school's network storage device from off campus? Did you know that you can make network files available offline, edit them locally, and then have them sync to the originals when you reconnect to the network?

Until now, our focus has been on personal computing. **Personal computing** refers to any situation or setup where one person controls and uses a computer or handheld device for personal or business activities. You've learned about what goes on inside a computer with system and application software as well as the various input/output and storage devices. Along with these basic computing concepts, you've also been introduced to how networks, the Internet, wireless applications, and databases work and are used. Now that you have a solid foundation in the hardware and software associated with personal computing, let's turn our attention to computing within an enterprise.

An **enterprise** is simply a business or organization, for example a university, government agency, or not-for-profit group or charity. **Enterprise computing** is information technology on a large scale, encompassing all aspects of technology and information resources needed to connect and facilitate communication within an organization or business (Figure 14.1). Here are some of the topics covered in this chapter:

- Examining the use of computers in the networks that span an organization
- Explaining the business processes involved in daily business operations
- Exploring various enterprise computing solutions
- Reviewing the technology used to manage the flow and storage of data and information within an enterprise ■

Check out **f Facebook** for our latest updates

www.facebook.com

Components of Enterprise Computing

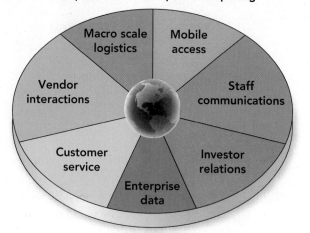

FIGURE 14.1 Enterprise computing encompasses all aspects of technology and information necessary to communicate and share data in an organization.

Business Processes and Activities

Companies use information systems, the collection of people, hardware, software, data records, and activities that process the data and information, to support business processes for internal operations such as manufacturing, order processing, and human resources management. A **business process** is an activity that has an identifiable output and value to the organization's customers. A business process begins with a customer's need and ends with that need being fulfilled. The activities that compose this progression from need to fulfillment can be viewed as a series of links in a chain

along which information flows within the organization. At each link, value is added in the form of the work performed by people associated with that process, and new, useful information is generated. Information begins to accumulate at the point of entry (for example, a customer sends an order to the company) and flows through the various links, or processes, within the organization. New, useful information is added every step of the way (Figure 14.2).

Information systems can be used to support or streamline business activities for a competitive advantage. A **competitive advantage** is a condition that gives an organization a superior position over the companies it competes with. For example, an enterprise might use an information system to support a billing process that reduces the use of paper and, more important, the handling of paper, thus reducing material and labor costs. This same system can help managers keep track of the billing process more effectively because they will have more accurate, up-to-date information about it, enabling them to make smart, timely business decisions.

Information systems can support either internally or externally focused business processes. Internally focused systems work to smooth communication among the functional areas (such as

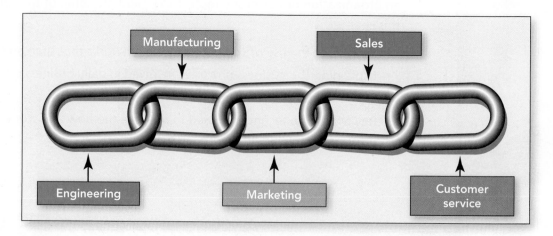

FIGURE 14.2 At each link in a business process, value is added to products to make them more desirable to the consumer.

accounting, finance, human resources, and so on) or activities within the organization. For instance, Visa International's accounting system automatically compares outgoing payments with invoices and sends e-mail requests to managers to review any discrepancies.

Externally focused systems coordinate business activities with customers, suppliers, business partners, and others who operate outside the organization's boundaries. The Nordstrom retail chain is noted for its exceptional customer service, including its easy-return policy and soft touches such as thank-you notes from employees. In 2008, in response to customer requests, it began offering a "buy online, pick up in store" option. Other companies have been doing this for some time but often face complaints about long waits and poor customer service. To avoid similar problems, Nordstrom implemented policies to ensure customers receive the same level of customer service they've come to expect. The initial program was limited to specific departments on a trial basis; transactions are confirmed via e-mail within one hour, and additional gift services are available at the time of pickup.

Businesses have used information systems to support business processes for decades, beginning with the installation of applications for specific business tasks such as issuing paychecks. Often these systems were built on different computing platforms. Each platform often operated in a unique hardware and software environment. Applications running on different computing platforms are difficult to integrate because customized interfaces are required for one system to communicate with another.

When systems get too complex and productivity suffers, businesses reevaluate the way departments and individuals interact and reassess their roles and positions in the overall business life cycle. Two methods of reevaluation are business process reengineering and business process management.

Business Process Reengineering

Business process reengineering (BPR) refers to the use of information technology to bring about major organizational changes and cost savings. At the core of BPR are the two most important aspects of an organization: the processes and the people. Supporters of BPR espouse the position that information technology doesn't bring big payoffs if you simply automate existing business processes; success results when information technology is used to redesign the process by which work is done, taking into account the ideas and proposals of the people that are part of that process. BPR is the key to changing how people work, leading to results like improved employee morale and customer service, and hopefully, reduced overall cost.

Each area of an organization has its own information systems and business processes. In BPR, designers ignore an organization's functional divisions and focus instead on business processes. The focus on the process often leads to the inclusion of components from several functional divisions and often results in the complete redesign of the process from the ground up. For example, in a traditional organization, the product development process involves many functional divisions, each of which works on the product's development separately before passing it on to the next division. BPR attempts to improve efficiency by restructuring how, where, and when activities are performed. After reengineering, cross-functional teams work together as a unit on a single activity, rather than working on it separately at different stages.

BPR can lead to big payoffs, but a high proportion of early BPR projects failed. Many companies came to see BPR as a means of downsizing, and employees learned to fear and resist these efforts. Figure 14.3 presents a list of critical factors, provided by New Generation Consulting & Associates, which can improve the chances of a successful BPR implementation.

FIGURE 14.3 Critical Success Factors for BPR

Development Considerations	Implementation Considerations
Visible active leadership	Ensure cross-functional participation
Clear vision of the enterprise	Choose the best people to be on the team
Sense of urgency	Leverage technology and human potential
Process focus	Provide some early positive results
Customer focus	Continual communication
Focus on components of the business system	

Business Process Management

Business process management (BPM) evolved from BPR. BPM's goal is to improve existing processes and optimize assets by effectively and efficiently managing the entire life cycle of these business processes.

BPM also uses a cross-functional approach and information technology. However, BPM examines the person-to-person interactions within a process, as well as the communications that take place among various systems. By doing so, BPM can enhance the effectiveness and integration of these processes while increasing their flexibility and providing opportunities for innovation. BPM is often applied to discrete parts of an organization rather than to the entire enterprise.

The BPM philosophy encourages employees to suggest and implement changes within their areas of expertise. Continuous improvement of processes and communication is a critical factor of success in any BPM solution. Various BPM systems have been developed to technologically manage this ongoing development. Typically, a business analyst or process architect from the business area with a strong IT background is selected to lead the BPM initiative and manage the underlying technology used to continually assess, design, model, execute, monitor, and optimize various business processes. To view industry resources and examples of successful BPM implementations, visit the bpm site at **www.bpm.com** (Figure 14.4).

During business process reengineering and business process management, the overall connectivity and efficiency of systems within the enterprise is evaluated. The next section will look at some of these systems, their purpose, and effectiveness in detail.

Enterprise Systems

Enterprise systems are information systems that integrate an organization's information and applications across all of the organization's functional divisions. Rather than storing information in separate places throughout the organization, enterprise systems provide an **enterprise data center**, a secure common repository, for **enterprise data**, the centralized data shared throughout an organization, and a common user interface to all corporate users. Enterprise systems enable personnel to share data, **enterprise software** (software designed to solve problems at the enterprise level of an organization rather that at the departmental level), and departmental level applications seamlessly, no matter where they originated, the platform they originated from, or who is using the application.

With the launching of its **e-business (electronic business)** campaign in 1997, IBM began to use the Internet to buy, sell, provide customer service, and collaborate with business partners. To continue to compete in global markets, competitors realized that they also had to provide quality customer service, buy materials more economically, and develop products faster and more efficiently. The emergence of the Internet and the World Wide Web resulted in the globalization of supplier networks, opening up new opportunities and methods of conducting business. **Globalization** refers to conducting business internationally or the process of making this happen. Due to the Web and telecommunication methods, the global marketplace is totally interconnected with no consideration for time zones or national boundaries. The abundance of McDonald's restaurants around the world is an example of globalization where the goods and services of a business or organization are identical (or nearly identical) in all locations. However, the adapting of a menu, slogan, or logo to match local taste or trends is called **internationalization**, or **glocalization**, the combination of globalization and localization. This means that a McDonald's in Singapore is almost the same as a McDonald's in Chicago except for some

FIGURE 14.4 Many Web sites are an excellent source of BPM information, examples, and some even provide links to current BPM software applications.

With data centers growing in size and operating 24/7, the cost to run and cool these facilities is constantly increasing. The growing concern about the consumption of electricity and the environmental footprint that these centers are creating has caused the Environmental Protection Agency (EPA) to issue a set of scenarios that define more efficient centers.

The efficiency of data centers can be measured by the power usage effectiveness (PUE) metric, which is the ratio of the total power consumed by a data center to the power consumed by the IT equipment that populates the facility. For example, a PUE of 2.0 indicates that for every watt of IT power used, an additional watt is used to cool the facility and perform other functions. An ideal PUE of 1.0 means that for every watt of IT power, no additional power is used to cool the facility and perform other functions. In 2006, the typical data center had a PUE of 2.0 or higher. In practice that translates into data centers consuming 61 billion kilowatt hours of power in 2006, at a cost of $4.5 billion. The EPA guidelines for 2011 are calling for all data centers to run at a PUE of 1.9, which can be obtained by just improving equipment efficiency. Adding better operational practices could lower the PUE to 1.7, and implementing advanced efficiency solutions could drop it to 1.3. Finally, implementing high-end power and cooling strategies could result in a state of the art data center with a 1.2 PUE.

Google recently announced that the average PUE for all of its Google-designed data centers is 1.18. This figure makes Google data centers performance exceed the EPA level for a state-of-the-art center. The PUE of a data center is not static and can change with server behavior and environmental conditions. However, with an average PUE of 1.18, without using the high-end power and cooling strategies recommended by the EPA, Google maintains one of the most efficient data centers in the world. If one organization can make these changes, hopefully others will follow. ●

FIGURE 14.5
McDonald's recently opened Quarter Pounder stores in Tokyo using the globally identifiable image of their product as the brand identifier but localizing it by eliminating the golden arches.

local twists or changes to mesh with the cultural differences (Figure 14.5).

Customers have increasing numbers of options available to them, and they are demanding products that are more sophisticated and customized to their unique needs. Enterprise systems can help companies find innovative ways to increase accurate and on-time shipments, minimize costs, and ultimately increase customer satisfaction and the overall profitability of the company.

Enterprise systems come in many shapes and sizes, each providing a unique set of features and functionality. Remember that an enterprise system is an information system; therefore, it is composed of data, hardware, software, people, and procedures. It can include network servers, database management systems, desktop and notebook computers, and handheld devices. When deciding whether to implement enterprise solutions, managers have to consider a number of different issues. One of the most important is selecting and implementing applications that meet the requirements of the business as well as its customers and suppliers. Let's start by examining how enterprise systems are categorized and managed.

Centralized Versus Distributed Structures

Enterprise networking, the technology infrastructure within an enterprise, requires an enormous amount of planning, integration, managing, and flexibility to continually adapt to the new interfaces, technology, and market demands that

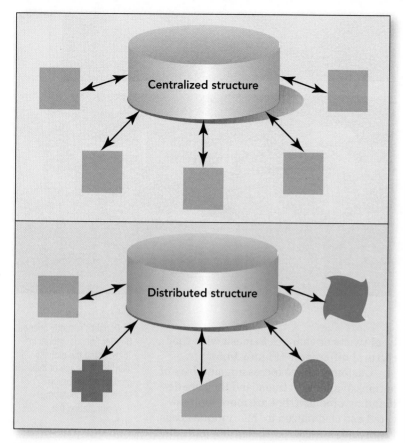

FIGURE 14.6 An enterprise has two options for managing its technology infrastructure: centralized structure or distributed structure.

a company chooses depends on a variety of factors including cost, applications being used, security, and objectives.

Now that you know how information systems can be structured within an enterprise, let's take a closer look at the ongoing process involved in maintaining and upgrading enterprise technology.

Applying Technology in the Enterprise

In this section, you'll learn about the day-to-day concerns an enterprise encounters as it manages its technology assets. The process is ongoing and active because technology changes every day. The enterprise must respond by staying current with both its internal and external constituents.

Keeping Current At any given moment, all of the technology used by an organization is more or less current with the marketplace. As time moves on, one would expect that administrators and end users would become more comfortable with the existing technology in the organization because they have used it for a period of time. However, as technology improves and programs update, a tension eventually develops between the current status of the system and the most current technology available. Keeping current has the benefit of having the latest tools, but it carries with it the risks of a reduced comfort level among users and a temporary reduction in employee productivity during the adjustment period.

Upgrading When an organization decides to **upgrade** its technology, installing current hardware or software, it should consider several things. First and foremost is the impact on the users. How difficult will it be for the users to adapt to the new hardware and applications? How much training will they need? What influence will the upgrade have on the organization's business constituents? Is the organization leading with this change or responding to market pressures?

The second consideration is whether hardware upgrades are required. Software applications upgrades may require minimum or no changes in hardware, or they might necessitate major hardware changes to accommodate new applications. Additionally, changes in the structure of the network or changes in communication pathways may be costly when new hardware must be purchased for these changes to be implemented.

constantly change the ground rules. Enterprise networks are managed in one of two ways: They are either centralized or distributed (Figure 14.6). In a **centralized structure**, technology management is centered in the IT department, and everyone within the organization works with standardized technology solutions in their everyday work. In a **distributed structure**, users are able to customize their technology tools to suit their individual needs and wants. Typically, an enterprise will start with one structure; but rarely does it use that structure exclusively.

For example, the computer labs at your school are most likely managed in a centralized way. Each time a student begins a work session, the computer operating environment, desktop, and applications are always the same. It doesn't matter which computer in the lab you use—they all look and function the same way. Conversely, your instructor's computer is most likely managed in a distributed way. Some things, such as applications, are the same on all faculty computers, but by and large, your instructor is able to customize the operating environment, desktop, and application configurations to suit his or her individual needs and wants. The structure

The third consideration is the cost of the upgrade. Obviously, there are costs to changes in hardware. But even if no new hardware will be required, upgrades can be costly. Not only does the organization need to purchase the requisite number of licenses for the software, but it needs to account for the time necessary to install and customize the software. This is where centralized versus distributed management structures are important. In a centralized structure, upgrading may be relatively easy and less expensive, because all of the computers are managed from one location. As a result, an IT staff member can install and release new software from one location. In a distributed environment, upgrading might involve sending IT personnel to many different locations to install the upgrade on user-managed machines.

Additional expenses might be incurred for user training during the transition from one version to another. File compatibility issues also may arise. For example, if external users are not using Office 2010, they may not be able to read documents created using the Office 2010 suite unless those documents are saved in a compatible format.

It appears that most business and IT executives put off upgrading as long as possible. According to Forrester research, a low percentage of enterprise customers, 5 to 10 percent, move to the latest release; approximately 50 percent stay on the release prior to the latest one; and approximately 40 percent remain on older releases. Upgrading is often referred to as a wild card, with its actual cost an unknown.

Maintenance Maintenance is another important consideration in managing technology within an organization. It too depends on whether IT structures are centralized or distributed. As with upgrading, maintenance may be easier and less expensive in a centralized environment. With a distributed infrastructure, maintenance and training might require IT personnel to travel to multiple sites for scheduled visits and training sessions.

Scalability Another important consideration is **scalability**, a hardware or software system's ability to continue functioning effectively as demands and use increase (Figure 14.7). For example, a network is scalable if an organization can easily expand it from a few nodes to hundreds or thousands of nodes. Scalability ensures that an organization's systems won't

FIGURE 14.7 A computer infrastructure is scalable when technicians can easily add new users to the system—even if there are hundreds of new users.

become obsolete as user needs and demands grow. Scalability does not depend on whether the system is centralized or distributed, although adding nodes to a centralized system is somewhat easier because the software installation is centralized and standardized.

Interoperability The ability to connect and exchange data with another computer, even one that is a different brand or model, is known as **interoperability**. Most enterprise systems have computers that run a variety of different platforms. For example, the enterprise may use Macs, Windows PCs, Linux machines, servers, and mainframes. Interoperability enables all of these computers to interact seamlessly on a network, regardless of whether the technology structure is centralized or distributed (Figure 14.8).

Adding Workstations and Applications What do enterprises do when new employees are hired and need a computer for their work? What if they want to implement a new application on a network? Adding a new user's workstation or installing a new application on a network increases the number of locations where problems can occur. One common problem is a single point of failure. A **single point of failure (SPOF)** refers to any system component, such as hardware or software, that causes the entire system to malfunction when it fails.

SPOF problems can be minimized by using a centralized technology management structure because it gives network administrators more control over the

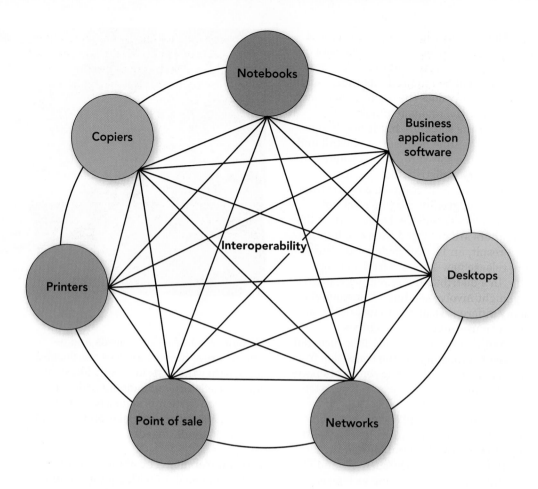

FIGURE 14.8 Total interoperability allows every user to pick up a device and use products that meet their needs and work with others that are equipped differently.

software that is installed and managed on the computers throughout the enterprise.

Adding a Network How can enterprises create networks on the fly, such as those that connect devices in a conference or at a meeting? **Zero configuration (Zeroconf)** is a method for networking devices via an Ethernet cable that does not require configuration and administration. Zeroconf is best used in small networking situations where the need for security is low. It also can be used to form a functional network in a home or a small business.

Disaster Recovery ≠ Business Continuity Two additional applications of technology in large enterprises are business continuity and disaster planning. These two titles are often used interchangeably when referring to practices that enable the operations to continue in the wake of unforeseen disasters. Actually they have very different focuses. A **disaster recovery plan** is a written plan with detailed instructions specifying alternative computing facilities to be used for emergency processing until nonoperational computers can be repaired or replaced after

a national disaster or national emergency. Such plans include restoring servers and mainframes with backups and reestablishing local networks to continue business needs. A **business continuity plan (BCP)** is a more comprehensive plan that focuses on long-term or continual problems that might impede success. Some of the continuity issues addressed by a BCP include the departure of a key team member, a malware infection, or a disastrous system failure. In short, a disaster recovery plan is reactive, whereas a business continuity plan is proactive. It is important to remember that there is no single approach to disaster recovery or business continuity and no one way to protect your business operations or guarantee continual uneventful operations. Strategies and procedures established by one company may be inappropriate for another.

Disaster recovery plans have some common features, but all start with a sound design. Listed here are some important essentials in that plan:

• For backup protection, be sure to place a copy of your backup in a different physical location.

- To recover the business from the backup, there must be enough data in a protected location backup to continue normal business operations.
- The recovery process must be completed in the time specified in the backup plan. If the physical building has been compromised, a secondary location for setup and providing business continuity should be established.
- A constant and ongoing evaluation of the process by supervisors and recovery personnel is required so that no disruption is perceived by customers or business associates.

Once a plan is developed, business leaders must take additional steps to ensure it will function appropriately when it is called into action.

- Test the backup system regularly.
- Update backup software when needed.
- Protect backup servers from accidental or deliberate damage.
- Check regularly for security breaches.
- Distribute the disaster recovery and/or business continuity plan to essential personnel.

Disasters can be created by humans, such as the Gulf of Mexico oil spill in 2010, or may be due to natural forces like Hurricane Katrina in the Gulf Coast states, and they can have far-reaching consequences. However, smaller-scale disasters, such as a fire, theft, or security breach, can also be detrimental to a company. A distributed technology structure is extremely important in disaster recovery plans. Enterprises have begun to see the importance of a backup system in a different geographical region. In the aftermath of September 11, many enterprises are moving their backup centers to suburban areas with independent utility and transportation systems.

Some backup centers are dedicated to functioning during emergencies and serve only as backup facilities, complete with their own electrical generators and telecommunications grids. These sites can be either hot disaster recovery sites or cold disaster recovery sites. A **hot site** is the more expensive as it is kept in a state of readiness at all times. A **cold site** only becomes operational once a disaster has occurred. Other backup centers have a dual purpose. They are fully functioning business facilities that act as satellite offices with the additional duty of duplicating all enterprise data. The backup portion of these dual-purpose sites can function as either a hot or cold site. Because such "mirroring" of data has to be performed in an organized fashion, professional backup and security companies can be hired to ensure that the job is done efficiently, effectively, and without compromising data integrity. The National Security Agency provides some guidelines and assistance with respect to information security (Figure 14.9).

The Disaster Recovery World Web site (**www.disasterrecoveryworld.com**) is an excellent location that provides a continuity and recovery directory along with software to help with business analysis and risk impact.

Now that you understand the issues that enterprises must consider when applying technology solutions, let's look at some of the specific software tools that enterprises use.

FIGURE 14.9 The National Security Agency (**www.nsa.gov**) provides information, programs, products, and guidelines to help businesses and other organizations keep their information systems secure.

Tools for Enterprise Computing

Enterprises have many opportunities to apply technology to different situations, whether to improve internal business processes or external interactions with customers and vendors. Software tools help the various areas of the enterprise manage their responsibilities.

Enterprise Resource Planning

Enterprise resource planning (ERP) software brings together various enterprise functions, such as manufacturing, sales, marketing, and finance, into a single

FIGURE 14.10 SAP is a leading ERP software company, providing solutions for companies of all sizes.

computer system. Managers implement ERP applications from vendors such as SAP, Oracle, and Sage to support activities in functional areas such as finance and human resources, as well as business processes such as order tracking and inventory, accounts payable, accounts receivable, and customer support (Figure 14.10).

Let's take a closer look at the order-tracking process in an enterprise that does not use ERP software. When a customer places an order with the sales division or customer service, the order travels to the individuals and departments that have to handle it. Errors and delays can be introduced along the way, or the order could be misplaced or lost. At any given time, few people in the enterprise can pinpoint the order's status should the customer inquire about it. For example, a salesperson may not have access to the manufacturing department's computer system to see whether manufacturing has even begun to fulfill the order.

With ERP software, one software program with separate modules for each functional unit replaces the separate, independent systems that sales and marketing, manu-

facturing, and other divisions use. The ERP software modules are linked so that a salesperson can access manufacturing's module to see whether an order has been processed. ERP improves the order process; provides customers with up-to-date, accurate information on the status of an order; and, in the end, accomplishes order fulfillment faster and with fewer errors.

Organizations undertake ERP projects to integrate financial, human resources, customer, and order information; speed up manufacturing processes; and reduce inventory. ERP systems have been implemented in many Fortune 500 companies but have been slower to catch on with small and mid-size companies (Figure 14.11). Although ERP sounds like an ideal solution, it does have some drawbacks. With ERP, customer service representatives' job duties are no longer confined to merely keying in orders. With ERP, their duties are associated with every department in the organization. They must make decisions and respond to situations that they never had to before, such as whether customers pay on time or whether the warehouse can ship orders in a timely manner.

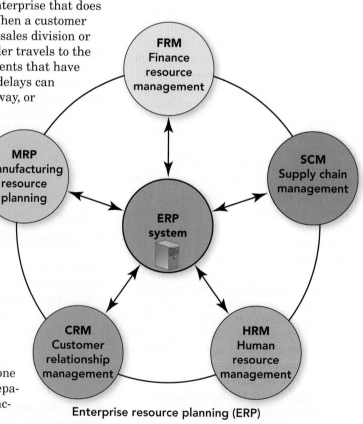

Enterprise resource planning (ERP)

FIGURE 14.11 Integration is important in an ERP system, where a wide range of functions are united into a single database.

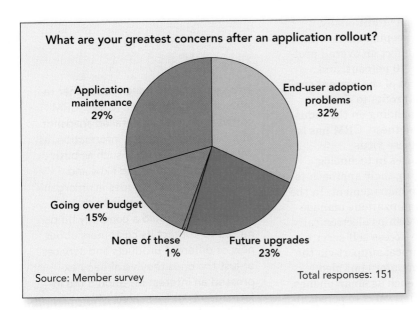

FIGURE 14.12 This survey indicates that the primary problem in ERP software rollout is related to end-users.

Some ERP projects fail because employees are resistant to change. If an organization simply installs ERP software without providing sufficient staff training and transition time to change processes, it won't experience the benefits of ERP. In fact, it may cause a chain reaction of negative effects. Replacing old software that everyone knows how to use with new software that no one knows how to use can slow business processes, causing delays in production, shipping, and billing. This concern over the end-user effects on ERP success is visible in Figure 14.12. However, when done properly with planning and training, an organization that switches to ERP software improves its order fulfillment, manufacturing, shipping, and billing processes.

Finally, the cost and time involved with ERP implementation sometimes blindsides organizations. For a large organization, the total cost of implementing ERP, including hardware, software, retraining, service, and support costs, might be $15 million and can easily exceed $100 million. Hidden costs for implementing an ERP system include integration and testing, customization, and data analysis and conversion. ERP vendors often estimate an implementation time of three to six months. More realistic time lines are usually between one and three years. It may take companies up to eight months before they begin to see any benefits from the new system. However, companies do see as much as $1.6 million in average annual savings from a new ERP system. Multi-million-dollar ERP projects can fail when the software chosen or developed does not support an organization's most important business process. When this occurs, organizations can either change business processes to fit the software or change the software to fit the processes. Both of these options have serious disadvantages and the potential to truly cripple an organization.

Customer Relationship Management

Customer relationship management (CRM) software keeps track of an organization's interactions with its customers and focuses on retaining those customers. Salespeople can use CRM software to match company resources with customer wants and needs (Figure 14.13). A recent survey found that it can cost five to seven times more to replace a current customer

FIGURE 14.13 CRM software enables organizations to track and communicate with customers from the original lead development phase through the established relationship phase.

- Locate leads, track prospects and proposals, achieve initial sale

  Customer acquisition

- Monitor customer satisfaction, gain repeat business

  Customer retention

- Continued customer contact, expand sales to new or extended products or services

  Customer enhancement

than it does to keep one. Additionally, a 2 percent increase in keeping current customers has the same effect on overall profits as cutting costs by 10 percent, and retaining just 5 percent of the current customer base can cause profits to rise by 25 to 125 percent, depending on the industry. With statistics like these, CRM has become a leading enterprise focus.

Due to new advances in technology, companies are changing their approach to customer relationship management. In the 21st century, most organizations manage their customer relationships electronically. Today, consumers can access self-service applications and technical support via the Web with not only computers but also Web-enabled devices such as smartphones. Organizations must find ways to personalize customers' online experiences, using tools such as help-desk software, e-mail organizers, and Web development applications. A current CRM trend in e-commerce is the use of an invisible timer that tracks when the user last viewed or placed an item in an online shopping cart. If a customer exceeds a specific amount of time, an instant message pops up and asks whether the user needs the help of a sales representative. A live chat can follow, and the shopper's questions can be answered. Hesitation is removed, and the cart can progress to check out.

Just as with ERP, an organization must consider its business processes along with its existing IT infrastructure before considering CRM solutions. CRM vendors include FrontRange Solutions, Oracle, SAP, and Salesforce.com Inc.

ETHICS

Privacy can be an issue in customer relationship management (CRM). CRM software provides a detailed snapshot of a customer's contact information, as well as personal details such as birth date, marital status, and likes and dislikes. Which employees in an organization should have access to this information? Should a company be permitted to contact its customers about new or different products and services or just the ones they've already expressed an interest in? Should the information ever be shared with another company?

Sales Force Automation

Often used interchangeably with CRM, **sales force automation (SFA) software** automates many of the business processes involved with sales, including processing and tracking orders, managing customers and other contacts, monitoring and controlling inventory, and analyzing sales forecasts (Figure 14.14).

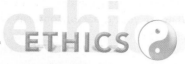

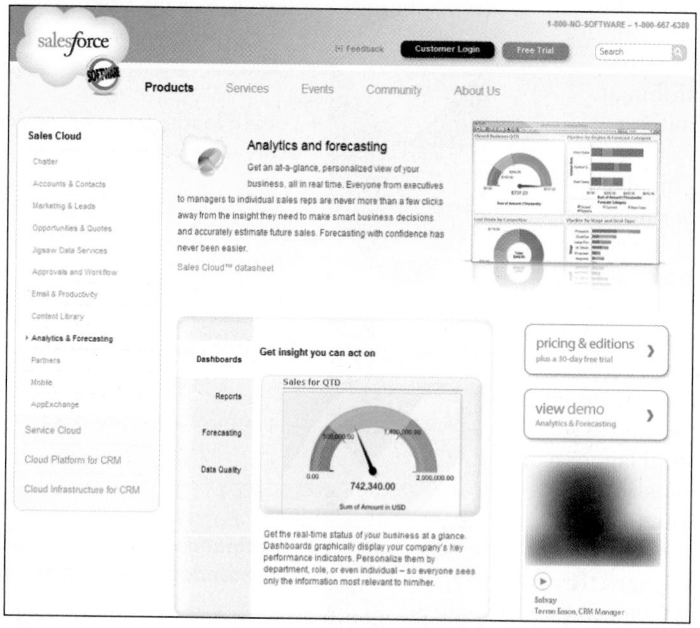

FIGURE 14.14 Relatively large enterprises sometimes use sales force automation software and services such as those provided by Salesforce.com (**www.salesforce.com**).

Extensible Business Reporting Language

Public and private enterprises use **Extensible Business Reporting Language (XBRL)** to publish and share financial information with each other and industry analysts across all computer platforms and the Internet. XBRL makes use of XML syntax and related technologies to standardize formatting to present various types of financial information, including net revenue, annual and quarterly reports, and

U.S. Securities and Exchange Commission (SEC) filings. XBRL is a Web protocol developed and promoted by an international not-for-profit consortium. It is free, but has some regulatory guidelines that the user must adhere to. Because of XBRL's broad usage and financial implications, the consortium that guides its use consists of more than 480 major international companies, organizations, and government agencies. Current users of XBRL include the Tokyo Stock Exchange; the U.S. Federal Financial Institutions Examination Council (FFIEC), including the Federal Reserve System and Federal Deposit Insurance Corporation (FDIC); Microsoft; IBM; and EDGAR Online. For more information on the language, its users, and current developments, visit **www.xbrl.org**.

Software-as-a-Service

Software-as-a-Service (SaaS) provides software-based services and solutions to companies that want to outsource some of their information technology needs. Rather than purchasing and installing software, businesses can access software that is hosted on the provider's site, or on the site of a third party known as an **application service provider (ASP)**, and deployed over the Internet to the provider's customers. Unlike an ERP solution, which takes time and often considerable amounts of money to implement, SaaS customers typically pay an initial fee based on the number of users and a monthly service fee. Because the software is Web based, companies can begin using the software with little or no setup time. The lower start-up costs and faster deployment times for SaaS have made it attractive to small and medium-size companies, where it is most often used in CRM, HR, and procurement. A recent report by Gartner research indicated that SaaS revenue totaled $8 billion in 2009, indicating a worldwide growth of 22 percent over figures for 2008. Gartner predicts that this figure will grow to $16 billion by 2013. These figures may seem high, but SaaS revenue accounts for only 3 percent of the total enterprise software sales.

Operational Support Systems

An **operational support system (OSS)** is a suite of programs that support an enterprise's network operations. OSS originally referred to a system that controlled telephone and computer networks for telecommunications service providers. The Telecommunications forum is working on a newer, more current model. Today, OSS enables an enterprise to monitor, analyze, and manage its network system. Functions of an OSS solution for a business or organization may include the following:

- *Creating a network inventory*—the process of surveying all computers on a network and reporting on the Operating system in use, service pack installed, and the hardware, software, and running processes.
- *Providing network discovery and reconciliation*—the process of monitoring a network's relationship to other operations and IT systems to reconcile information, provide fault and capacity management, and reduce integration costs.
- *Tracking network assets and maintenance*—the use of software to maintain an equipment maintenance schedule, automatically schedule service, and issue automatic purchase orders based on a service report.

Enterprise Application Integration

Enterprise application integration (EAI) is a combination of processes,

software, standards, and hardware that results in the integration of two or more enterprise systems. This integration enables multiple systems to operate as one and share data and business processes throughout an organization. In the past, enterprises used custom-built, proprietary software and systems for such functions as inventory control, human resources, sales automation, and database management that ran independently and didn't interact with each other. Enterprises now recognize the need to share information and applications among systems, so many companies are investing in EAI.

Organizations can choose from a range of EAI categories, from database and application linking to data warehousing. When enterprises want all aspects of their computing integrated into one application, it is referred to as a *common virtual system.*

As wonderful as EAI sounds, it is very complex, and a high percentage of such projects fail due to management issues. EAI incorporates every level of the enterprise system: architecture, hardware, software, and processes. EAI vendors include IBM, Microsoft, and Oracle.

Now that you are familiar with various enterprise computing software solutions, let's examine storage systems commonly used in an enterprise.

Enterprise Storage Systems

According to the Digital Universe study conducted by International Digital Corporation (IDC), digital information reached 0.8 zettabytes in 2009 (one zettabyte equals a trillion gigabytes), with a long-term prediction of 35 zettabytes by 2020. Add to that volume the increased demand created by employees, managers, executives, and customers expecting this information to be readily available when and where it's needed— and to be kept safe from prying eyes if it's confidential. It is not surprising that corporate demand for fast, secure, and reliable storage systems is skyrocketing.

New technologies are being developed to meet the unique needs of large organizations. To cope with their information storage needs, many corporations are developing enterprise storage systems. Enterprises invest in enterprise storage systems not necessarily to gain a competitive advantage or to meet government regulations but to protect and back up their mission-critical data. In a recent survey of 436 global datacenter professionals, approximately 77 percent cited business growth and meeting the demands of that growth for their increase of storage, whereas only 8 percent cited government regulations. Eighty-three percent of those surveyed were in the United States, and 10 percent oversaw a budget of $10 million or more.

RAID

A group of two or more hard drives that contain the same data is called **RAID (redundant array of independent disks)**. It is actually a technology that increases performance and reliability of data storage. The key word in this phrase is *redundant*, which means "extra copy." Everything that is recorded on the original drive is instantaneously recorded on the second disk. No matter how many disks a RAID 1 (or mirrored) device contains, they all work in parallel. The computer "thinks" it's dealing with just one disk. All of the disks contain an exact copy of all the data. If one of the disks fails, service is not interrupted. This helps to ensure against data loss if something happens to the original, or working, drive (Figure 14.15). If the original disk fails,

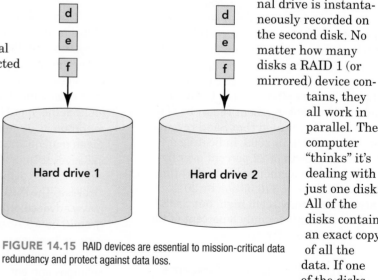

FIGURE 14.15 RAID devices are essential to mission-critical data redundancy and protect against data loss.

one of the other disks kicks in and delivers the requested data.

There are several types of RAID devices, such as RAID 0 and RAID 5. The process of using the array of disks differs in each RAID system, but the goal of each is the same: to improve storage speed and protect against data loss.

RAID devices offer a high degree of **fault tolerance**; that is, they keep working even if one or more components fail. For this reason, RAID devices are widely used wherever a service interruption could prove costly, hazardous, or inconvenient to customers. Most of the major Web sites use RAID devices to ensure that their Web pages are always available.

RAID is used primarily in medium to large enterprises. Most personal computer users don't need (and couldn't afford) RAID devices. RAID disk drives can be purchased from most computer manufacturers and are installed and maintained by network management personnel. RAID devices run constantly—24 hours a day, 7 days a week, 365 days a year.

CD and DVD Jukeboxes and Blu-Ray Optical Libraries

Digital content can be one of an enterprise's most valuable assets. But an enterprise loses time and money if employees are constantly searching for, repurchasing, or re-creating files. Enterprise storage systems should allow for quick and simple access, management, and organization of data. Jukeboxes and libraries are enterprise storage devices used to store or backup an enterprise's digital content and give users network access to it. The terms *jukebox* and *library* are sometimes used interchangeably—incorrectly. A **jukebox** is an enterprise storage unit that uses DVD and CD discs as the storage medium. A **library** is an enterprise storage unit that uses Blu-ray

optical media for storage. A double-sided, dual-layer DVD can hold approximately 17 GB per disc, whereas Blu-ray, the newest type of optical disc, supports up to 50 GB per disc.

Storage Area Networks

Another type of storage device available to all servers on a LAN or WAN is a **storage area network (SAN)**. A SAN is a network of high-capacity storage devices that link all of the organization's servers. In this way, any of the storage devices is accessible from any of the servers. In a SAN, servers provide only pathways between end users and stored data, keeping servers available for processing activities. A SAN contains nothing but disks that store data. SANs often

> "Enterprise storage systems should allow for **quick** **and simple** access, **management,** and **organization** of data."

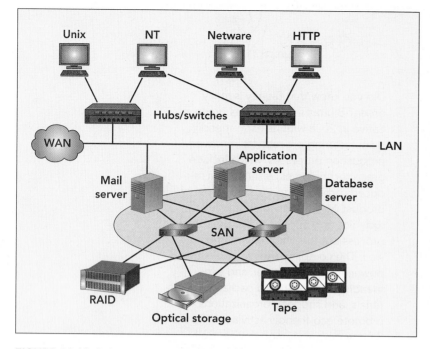

We've now examined the software and hardware solutions often employed in enterprise systems. Let's turn our attention to some of the technologies that pull both of these areas together within an enterprise.

Enterprise-Wide Technologies

Enterprise computing solutions don't exist in a vacuum. If an organization has no overall strategy for implementing CRM, RAID, or any of the other software and hardware solutions previously discussed, there's not much sense in spending hundreds of thousands or millions of dollars to install them. In this section, we will examine many of the enterprise-wide technologies being used for competitive advantage.

FIGURE 14.16 A storage area network (SAN) is an enterprise network that transfers data among servers and multiple storage devices.

make use of network-attached storage (Figure 14.16).

Network Attached Storage

Network attached storage (NAS) refers to high-performance devices that offer little more than data and file sharing to clients and other servers on a network. Unlike a file server in a client/server network, which typically handles all processing activities, such as e-mail, authentication, and file management, NAS merely supplies data to users. NAS can be installed anywhere in a LAN, not just within or near a server. When a network uses NAS, more hard disk storage space can be added to the network without shutting down the file servers for upgrading or maintenance. Storage capacities range from 1 terabyte (TB) to as much as 12 petabytes (PB).

Grid Computing

Grid computing is applying the abilities of many computers, referred to as executors, in a network to a single problem at the same time (Figure 14.17). This amount of concentrated power is usually directed at scientific or technical problems that require a high level of processing power and access to large amounts of data. Grids can make use of a central node, referred to as a grid manager, a combination of hardware and software that breaks the project into smaller tasks and assigns each task to an individual user or executor. A well-known example of grid computing in the public domain is the ongoing SETI (Search for Extraterrestrial Intelligence) @Home project in which thousands of people are sharing the

FIGURE 14.17 In a grid, the surplus power of many systems, regardless of location, are made available by their owners and are directed to a central node, where they are put to use performing calculations or researching information that otherwise would require extensive and expensive equipment.

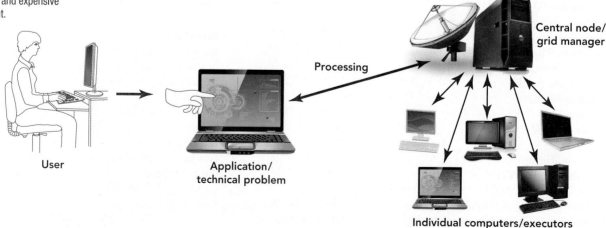

unused processor cycles of their PCs in the vast search for signs of "rational" signals from outer space. If you are interested in joining the search for ET, go to **www.seti.org** (Figure 14.18).

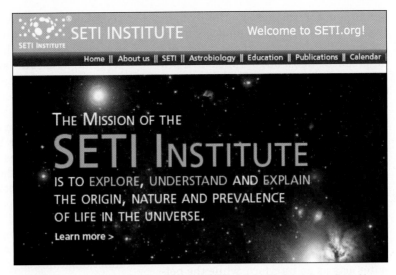

FIGURE 14.18 The search for extraterrestrials is global, with data being collected by thousands of people constantly. Grid computing provides the network infrastructure for this massive connectivity.

Cloud Computing

Cloud computing is a subscription-based or pay-per-use service that provides scalable resources and IT services over the Internet. The name comes from the use of the cloud symbol to represent the Internet in flowcharts and diagrams. A cloud service can be public, and sell its services to anyone on the Internet, or private and sell only to a limited number of users. Software-as-a-service (SaaS) is an example of a service that makes use of cloud technology to connect businesses partners. Recall that SaaS provides software-based services, usually Web-enabled, and solutions to companies that want to outsource some of their information technology. Cloud computing is one means by which some SaaS providers connect to their client accessing their data and returning their reports and other critical information. The power of cloud computing is the admission of users to a shared data center containing multi-tenancy applications. What does this actually mean? **Multi-tenancy** means that the application is installed only once in the cloud, on the cloud's server, but can be shared and customized with individual options for each user. So, instead of running your applications on your own system, using your own resources, you access the cloud, log into the application, customize it, and start using it. That's the power of cloud computing. You can view a video that clearly explains the power of cloud computing and its benefits for enterprise users at **www.salesforce.com/ cloudcomputing**.

Again as with any new development, there are negative aspects of cloud computing, security issues being the most prominent. Before subscribing to a cloud service, obtain detailed information on the security aspects and safeguards the service has in place. Ask questions related to the qualifications and integrity of the employees of the service and the testing that has been done to verify security and response to unanticipated intrusions.

Blade Servers

With data centers growing and becoming more complex, **blade servers**, stripped-down, energy-efficient, low-cost modular computers with server software installed, seem to be a solution (Figure 14.19). These space-saving units provide a powerful platform to fulfill the requirements of data centers and enterprise demands, enabling the reduction of power consumption without compromising performance. In general, blade servers simplify cabling, storage, and maintenance while consolidating related resources as network equipment. Some disadvantages of blade servers include the labor intensive and expensive initial configuration, the need to fill all blade slots in the blade chassis to

FIGURE 14.19 Blade servers are designed to get the most out of your power and space-constrained data center with a potential 90 percent reduction in energy costs.

Blade chassis

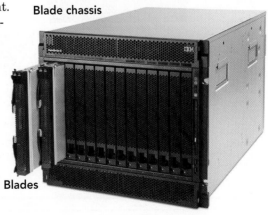

Blades

optimize usage, the incompatibility between chassis and blades made by different manufacturers, and the fact that not all products, like a large transaction processing application, run more efficiently on a blade server. The purpose of the system and applications that need to be accessed from it are key factors in determining the technology an enterprise selects.

Thin Clients

A **thin client** can refer to either a software program or to an actual computer that relies heavily on another computer to do most of its work. It is usually part of a network, and the client software or computer acts as an interface, while the network server computer does all the real work. In the case of a computer, a thin client is unable to perform many functions on its own. It is usually designed only for online use, sending and receiving e-mail, and surfing the net.

Web Portals

Web portals (or **portals**) are Web sites that provide multiple online services. A portal is a jumping-off place—a place that provides an organized way to go to other places on the Web. AOL, MSN, Yahoo! and Google are all examples of sites that have become Web portals to draw more traffic and dedicated users to their sites (Figure 14.20).

Organizations implement portals for different reasons. Merrill Lynch created an enterprise-wide portal to cut expenses and consolidate all of the Web sites and portal sites that had been built throughout the company. To avoid the expense of training its retail associates and partners on how to use many of its standard applications, Guess Jeans installed a portal that provides access to Web-based training materials. When Chevron acquired Texaco, merging the various Web applications from both companies would have been time-consuming and expensive. Instead, the newly merged company implemented a portal. Business portals offer centralized knowledge and content management, helping to ensure consistent business processes across different functional units.

Electronic Data Interchange

Electronic data interchange (EDI) is a set of standards that specifies how to transfer data and documents among enterprises using the Internet and other networks without human intervention. EDI is emerging as a popular way for companies to exchange information and to conduct business transactions. For instance, if two companies have compatible systems, they can establish a connection through EDI transmissions that enable purchase orders, shipping notices, and invoices to be sent from computer to computer. The entire operation occurs without any paper changing hands. EDI can make many business processes more efficient. For example, buyers can use EDI to order parts from suppliers that will be delivered just in time to be used. This capability reduces inventory costs and the time between the buying of the parts and the sale of the finished product.

To get an idea of the widespread use of EDI standards, view the list of companies that use EDI standards in their business transactions at **www.covalentworks.com/companies-and-edi.asp** Statistics indicate that there are 160,000 EDI partners in North America constituting 99% of companies in the United States, Canada, and Mexico (Figure 14.21).

Business-to-business e-commerce enterprises sometimes lease network capacity from a value-added network. A **value-added network (VAN)** is a public data communication network offered by a service provider that an enterprise uses for EDI or other services. Such a network offers end-to-end dedicated lines with guaranteed security. Enterprises can electronically exchange documents and

FIGURE 14.20 Visitors to portals such as Yahoo!'s can check their e-mail, get the latest news and weather forecasts, and shop all in one place.

data over a VAN, including shipping orders, tracking requests, and invoices as well as e-mail, management reports, and payments.

But those services come with a hefty per-byte fee for handling an enterprise's data and transactions. To compete with Internet based systems, like virtual private networks, many VANs offer additional services such as EDI translation, encryption, and other security measures.

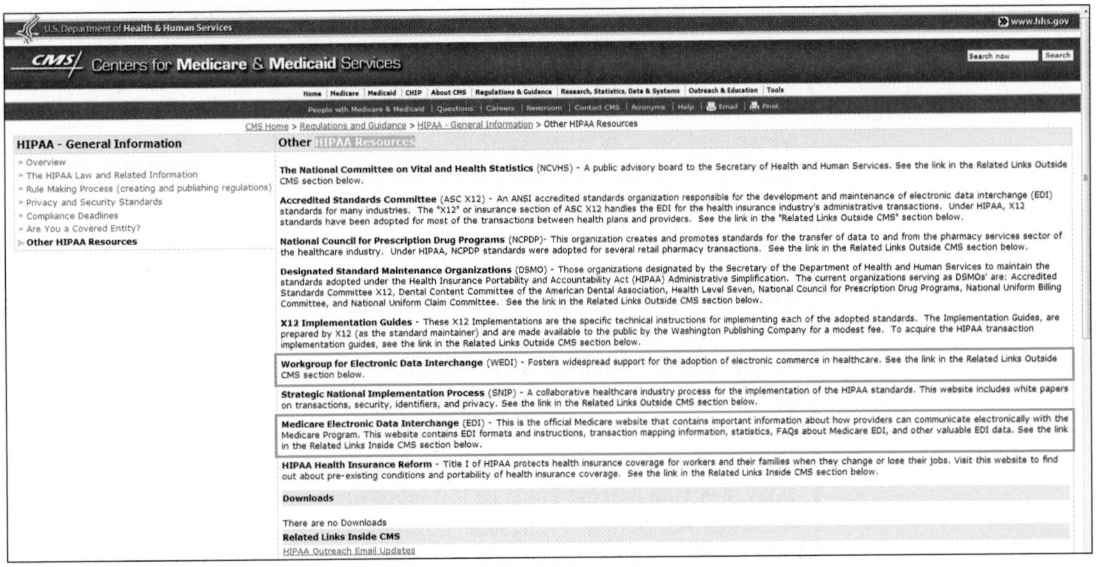

Virtual Private Networks

Enterprises use virtual private networks to connect distributed LANs over the Internet. A **virtual private network (VPN)**, an extension of an existing network, makes use of the Internet and leased lines to ensure excellent transmission and security. VPNs offer encryption and additional security measures to guarantee that only authorized external users have access to the network and its data (Figure 14.22).

Potomac Hospital in Virginia has more than 1,200 employees and medical professionals. The hospital uses a VPN to provide safe, secure access to hospital records and patient data for more than 250 medical professionals and vendors who frequently work off-site, including an Australian vendor who reads X-rays over the VPN.

Intranets and Extranets

Many companies are building internal networks, known as intranets, which are based on TCP/IP protocols. An **intranet** is a network that belongs to an enterprise and is accessible only by that enterprise's employees or authorized users. Intranets offer users the same familiar tools, such as browsers, that they use on the Internet. However, intranets are intended only for internal use and aren't accessible from the external Internet unless the user has a registered user name and password.

FIGURE 14.21 The use of EDI standards is becoming the way to conduct secure online business transactions within and among companies.

FIGURE 14.22 A virtual private network (VPN) allows authorized individuals to access a company's network using a secure connection.

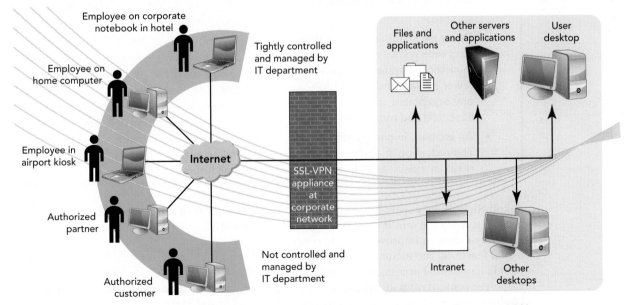

Employee on corporate notebook in hotel

Employee on home computer

Employee in airport kiosk

Authorized partner

Authorized customer

Tightly controlled and managed by IT department

Internet

Not controlled and managed by IT department

SSL-VPN appliance at corporate network

Files and applications

Other servers and applications

User desktop

Intranet

Other desktops

Corporate LAN

Virtualization is a process that has been gaining in popularity with business and corporate IT centers and is just making its appearance in the enterprise data center. It is viewed as a process that can improve efficiency and control cost. Before discussing the process of virtualization, let's review the definition of a virtual machine. A **virtual machine** is a software-created section of a hard disk that has its own operating system and applications. Essentially, a virtual machine acts as if it were an isolated independent physical computer, neither the operating system nor the applications can tell the difference. So what is virtualization? **Virtualization** is the process of running multiple virtual machines on one physical machine, a feature that makes a virtual machine different from a traditional partition (only one partition can be running at a time). The use of virtualization makes one computer behave as if it were several independent machines that could run simultaneously sharing the RAM and CPU power of a single computer without interfering with one another. Benefits of virtualization include these:

- *Reduction in complexity.* Fewer computers in a system, as one can actually be several virtual machines, will result in a simpler network design.
- *Reduction in cost.* Less equipment means less maintenance and repair.
- *Decrease in administration time.* Less time will be needed to administer the system because fewer servers and less peripheral equipment will have to be allocated and monitored.
- *An increase in energy efficiency.* The reduction in equipment will result in a decreased use of energy to both run and cool the data center.

The software that creates a virtual machine bundles all of its components together, as if in a container, making the virtual system reliable, isolated from other virtual machines created on the same hard drive, and independent from other virtual machines on the same hard drive. This makes it easy to delete if not needed or to transport to a different location if the virtual design is being reconfigured.

A study done by Forrester Research, Inc., in May 2009, interviewed individuals responsible for the IT infrastructure of 29 large enterprises about the benefits of virtualization to their organization. Key findings from this study include those listed here:

- A consensus that IT became more efficient not only in the savings on hardware, but also on the increased savings of being able to postpone expansion and regain space, power, and cooling costs.
- Virtualization decreased deployment time and simplified application development and testing.
- Virtualization provided better business continuity and disaster recovery.
- A plan to virtualize 50 percent of the IT services of an enterprise can significantly increase savings.

Of the 29 firms that participated in the study, 27 were happy with their move to virtualization and plan to continue its implementation. This is not a powerful testimonial to virtualization, but it does indicate a satisfaction with a process that, for some enterprises, may be part of their overall future plan.

Jakob Nielsen, an expert in Web site usability, rates the quality of Intranets annually based on improvements to traditional features, the inclusion of new trends like mobile access, allowance for employee content, and an effective business continuity plan. The following is his list of the ten best Intranet sites for 2010:

- Enbridge, Inc., Canada
- General Electric, United States
- Howard Hughes Medical Institute, United States

- Huron Consulting Group, United States
- Jet Propulsion Laboratory, a NASA center, United States
- The MITRE Corporation, United States
- SCANA Corporation, United States
- Trend Micro, Inc., Japan
- URS Corporation, United States
- Wal-Mart Stores, Inc., United States

Intranets are transforming the way organizations produce and share information with employees, vendors, and other select outside partners. Web sites on an intranet are similar to Internet Web sites, except that firewalls protect the enterprise content from unauthorized access. Because it's so easy to create a Web page, companies can distribute Web publishing duties throughout the enterprise. Every department can maintain its own internal Web page, making its resources available to everyone. By moving expensive print-based publications, such as employee manuals and telephone directories, to the intranet, companies can realize enormous savings and significantly reduce the amount of trash that goes to local landfills.

Some companies allow authorized outsiders, such as research labs, suppliers, or key customers, to access their intranets. Called **extranets**, these networks are connected over the Internet, and data traverses the Internet in encrypted form, safe from prying eyes. Access to an extranet is limited to those provided with valid user names and passwords. These security measures determine the extranet content that outsiders are allowed to view. Extranets have become a viable conduit for sharing information among business partners.

Intranets continue to be one of the fastest-growing enterprise applications in IT. They cost much less to build and maintain than public and private data networks such as VANs and virtual private networks.

Computer-Based and Web-Based Training

Computer-based training (CBT) is a form of education that uses multimedia, animation, and programmed learning to teach new skills with a computer. CBT has typically been used to train people how to use computer applications, because it enables students to learn by actually using the application. The tutorials included with many software applications are a form of CBT.

When new software is deployed within an enterprise, employee training is critical to its success. Traditional classroom-style training can be expensive and often requires employees to go off-site. CBT programs can be more convenient and affordable because they are typically not time or place dependent. Training is available whenever an employee has the time to access the tutorials.

Web-based training (WBT) is basically CBT implemented via the Internet or an intranet. Web-based training methods often include instant messaging, discussion forums, and chat tools, in addition to more advanced applications, such as live Web broadcasts with streaming audio or video and videoconferencing.

Enterprises often use Web-based training to educate employees about a new application, program, or system. WBT is often run by a facilitator or trainer; however, it can also be self-paced and involve only the trainee.

Teleconferencing

Teleconferencing is when two or more people, separated by distance, use telecommunications and computer equipment to conduct business activities. Enterprises use teleconferencing to gain a competitive advantage by cutting costs and facilitating enterprise-wide communications.

Large enterprises or small office–home office (SOHO) businesses seeking to employ teleconferencing should consider professional-grade or PC-based teleconferencing systems. Professional-grade teleconferencing requires enterprises to own, purchase, or rent dedicated conferencing equipment or to contract with a company or service provider that offers these

> "Intranets are transforming the way organizations produce and share information with employees, vendors, and other select outside partners."

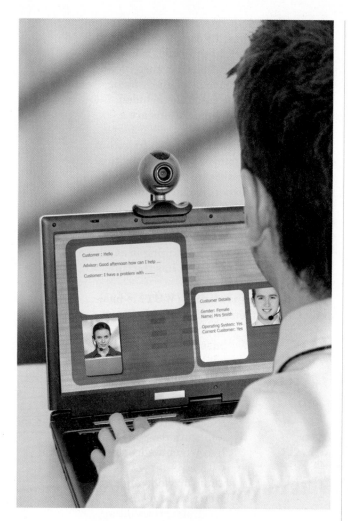

FIGURE 14.23
Teleconferencing allows many people in many locations to share the convenience of a common connection.

of teleconferencing is that the video portion requires lots of bandwidth. Other concerns include poor video quality, real-time transmission delays, lack of access to facilities or equipment, and potential threats to privacy.

Telecommuting

Because of the burgeoning home network market, many large and small enterprises are giving their employees the option of telecommuting. **Telecommuting**, sometimes referred to as **teleworking**, refers to using telecommunications and computer equipment to work from home while still being connected to the office (Figure 14.24). The home system must be able to connect to the company computer system to communicate with and transfer data to and from other employees.

A recent study of chief information officers confirmed that the IT workforce is telecommuting at a rate that is the same or higher than five years ago. Of those interviewed, only 3 percent said that there was a decrease in telecommuting over the last five years. Not all jobs lend themselves to telecommuting. Enterprises whose employees must serve or greet the public (bank tellers, wait staff, office receptionists, and so on) are not candidates for telecommuting.

Studies have shown that enterprises experience various benefits by allowing employees to telecommute, including productivity gains, lower employee turnover, and reduced costs for office space. One major disadvantage of telecommuting is the enterprise's lack of direct supervision over a telecommuting employee's workload.

services (Figure 14.23). One type of teleconferencing service is when each caller dials the teleconference number, provides a pass code, and is then connected with the other callers. Teleconferencing isn't limited to just voice communications, however.

PC-based solutions offer a number of benefits over professional-grade systems, such as lower cost and easier installation and maintenance. Many enterprises find it well worth the time and money to implement PC-based systems. Most companies immediately begin to reap the rewards of lower long-distance phone bills and higher productivity. They also can cut travel budgets because participants don't need to be physically present at meetings. The biggest drawback to the successful implementation

FIGURE 14.24 Enterprises experience numerous benefits by allowing employees to telecommute.

Teleworkers experience a variety of benefits, including little or no commuting, flexible hours, more family time, and savings on car expenses (gas, tolls, parking, and so on) and work clothes. Disadvantages include the lack of social interaction and the difficulties of keeping the work and home environments separate. Societal benefits from telecommuting include fuel conservation and less air pollution.

A vital technology for enterprises with telecommuters is teleconferencing. Thanks to inexpensive software and Webcams, telecommuters can attend important meetings they may otherwise have missed. Programs such as Office Live Meeting enable teleworkers to communicate, interact, and share applications with coworkers. Skype and iVisit are Web-based services that provide simultaneous audio chats among multiple users and two-way video chat capabilities (Figure 14.25). To use these services, you must first download and install their software. Many videoconferencing services also offer additional functions, such as file transfer, application sharing, or online whiteboards.

Telecommuting would be nearly impossible without broadband Internet service. With a high-speed Internet connection, telecommuters can talk with others in real time or record video messages to attach to e-mails.

Workgroup Computing

Another technology that enterprises are using for competitive advantage is workgroup computing. **Workgroup computing** occurs when all of the members of a *workgroup*—a collection of individuals working together on a task—have specific hardware, software, and networking equipment that enables them to connect, communicate, and collaborate. **Groupware**, also known as **teamware**, is software that provides computerized support for the information needs of these workgroups. Most groupware applications include e-mail, videoconferencing tools, group-scheduling systems, customizable electronic forms, real-time shared applications, and shared information databases.

The first successful groupware product, Lotus Notes, was designed to run on client/server systems. Newer groupware products, such as Microsoft Exchange Server and new versions of Lotus Notes, run on intranets and extranets. These groupware applications enable collaboration among geographically separated workgroups and even among group members who work for other organizations, such as affiliated research labs.

A groupware application such as Microsoft Exchange Server 2010 can quickly determine the optimum time for a meeting, locate an open room, send a notice asking for the meeting, and then coordinate responses to show who has confirmed that they will be at the meeting This new version also provides greater reliability, simplifies administration, prevents information loss, and addresses the increasing demands for business mobility.

STUDENT VIDEO

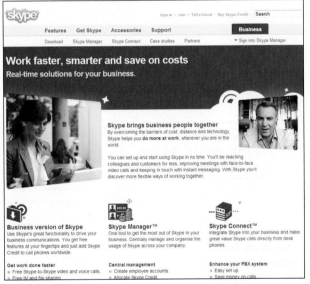

FIGURE 14.25 Web-based services such as Skype can provide telecommuters with simultaneous chat and video capabilities.

Groupware also facilitates workflow automation. **Workflow automation** is the process of sending documents and data to the next person who needs to see them. For example, a master document may be shared among a group, and then all of the group's comments can be collectively edited by the author of the document. Consider the case of an engineer at a firm who prepares a proposal for an external contract. The proposal goes to the engineer's supervisor for review and approval. The document may have to be seen by several other people before it's finally approved and sent.

Work with Network Files
Offline in Windows 7

If working on files stored in a network folder, as in most enterprise IT environments, you can make the folder available offline. That means you can work on the files when the network is not functioning or from a remote site where the network cannot be accessed. Making a network folder available offline copies the network files to your local computer. It is the copied files that are usable offline and allow you to continue working when the network is interrupted or not available. When you reconnect to the network folder, Windows will automatically sync the files on your computer with the files on the network folder.

1. Locate the network folder that you want to access offline.

2. Right-click the file or folder to be accessed offline and from the menu that appears, select *Always Available Offline* (Figure 14.26). A check mark appears to the left of the option. This step copies the folder or files to your local computer's hard drive.

   Note: To remove offline availability, right-click the file or folder and click *Always Available Offline* to clear the check mark to the left of the option.

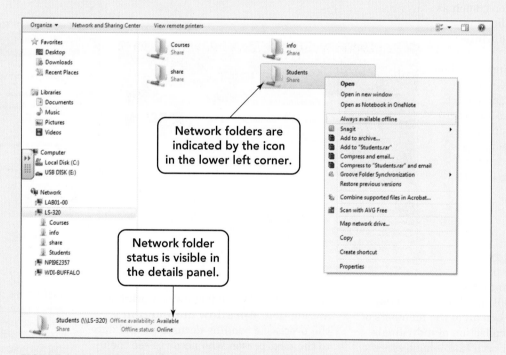

FIGURE 14.26 Windows 7 offline files feature will handle the file transfer and synchronizing for you.

3. Next, you need to access the sync center to enable the folders or files you just made available offline.

   a. Click the *Start* button on your system.

   b. In the search box type **sync center**.

   c. When the search options appear, select *Sync Center* (Figure 14.27)

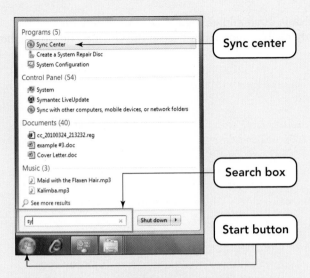

FIGURE 14.27 The Sync Center can also be opened by clicking the *Start* button, clicking *All Programs*, clicking *Accessories*, and then clicking *Sync Center*.

4. The Sync Center dialog box will open with sync options.

5. From the options on the left side of the dialog box, select *Manage offline files* (Figure 14.28).

6. The Offline Files dialog box will open. Click on the *General tab*.

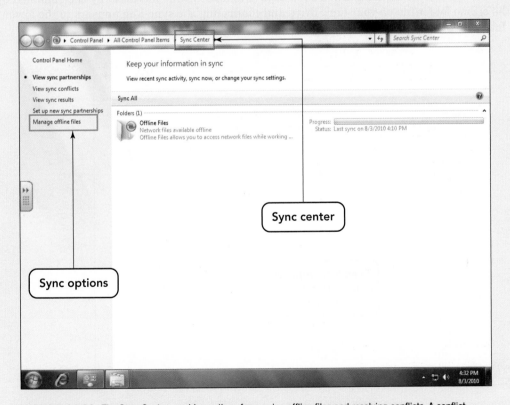

FIGURE 14.28 The Sync Center provides options for syncing offline files and resolving conflicts. A conflict usually occurs when both files, the local copy and network version, have been edited since the last sync.

7. If a button to *Enable offline files* is visible, click it. It should change to *Disable offline files* (Figure 14.29). If *Disable offline files* is already visible, then simply close the Offline Files dialog box.

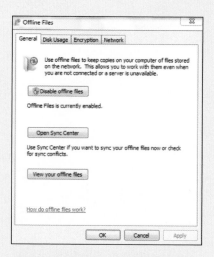

FIGURE 14.29 The Enable offline file option must be activated in the Offline Files dialog box to completely initiate the sync process.

8. Click the *Apply* button and then the *OK* button. Then close the Sync Center.

9. You can confirm that the folder/file marked as Always Available Offline has actually been enabled by checking the offline folder/file on your hard drive and confirming the sync icon appears to the lower left of the folder/file icon (Figure 14.30)

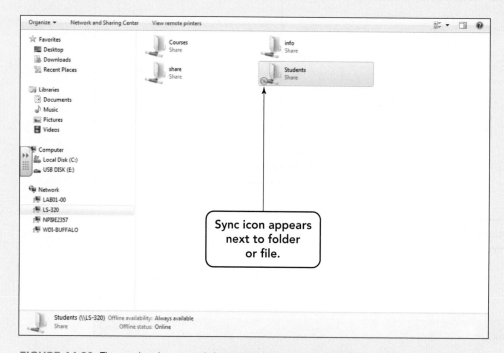

FIGURE 14.30 The sync icon is a green circle containing a set of curved arrows.

10. Windows syncs your offline files automatically, but not continuously. Sometimes you might need to sync your offline files manually. To do this right-click the folder/file that has been designated as an offline file on your local hard drive and from the context menu that appears, click *Sync* (Figure 14.31).

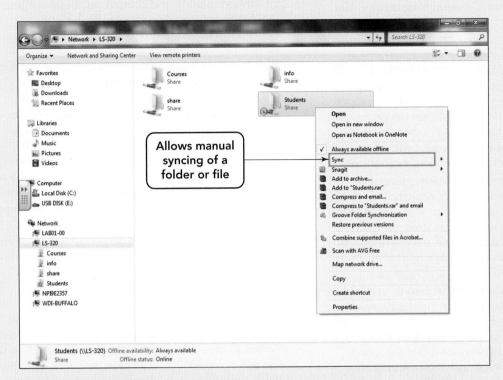

FIGURE 14.31 Manual syncing can be helpful if a network connection is inconsistent or a connection was disabled during an automatic sync.

Chapter Summary

Enterprise Computing

- Enterprise computing is the use of technology, information systems, and computers within an organization or business. Personal computing is the use of technology by an individual for business or personal activities.

- A business process begins with a customer's need and ends with the fulfillment of that need. The activities that compose this progression from need to fulfillment can be viewed as a series of links in a chain along which information flows within the organization. At each link, value is added in the form of the work performed by people associated with that process, and new, useful information is generated.

- In a centralized structure, the management of technology is centered in the IT department, and everyone within the organization works with standardized technology solutions in their everyday work. In a distributed structure, users are able to customize their technology tools to suit their individual needs and wants.

- Tools commonly used in enterprise computing include enterprise resource planning (ERP), customer relationship management (CRM), sales force automation (SFA), Extensible Business Reporting Language (XBRL), Software-as-a-Service (SaaS), operational support systems (OSSs), and enterprise application integration (EAI).

- Enterprise storage systems include RAID, CD and DVD jukeboxes, Blu-ray optical libraries, storage area networks (SAN), and network-attached storage (NAS). Enterprise-wide technologies that provide a competitive edge in today's business environment include grid computing, cloud computing, blade servers, thin clients, Web portals, electronic data interchange, intranets, extranets, virtual private networks, computer-based and Web-based training, teleconferencing, telecommuting, and workgroup computing.

- Electronic data interchange (EDI) is a set of standards that specifies how to transfer data and documents among enterprises using the Internet and other networks without human intervention. EDI makes business processes more efficient, reduces errors, allows for remote submissions, and avoids paper from being physically misplaced and changing hands.

- Teleconferencing is when two or more people, separated by distance, use telecommunications and computer equipment to conduct business activities. Businesses use teleconferencing to gain a competitive edge by cutting costs and facilitating enterprise-wide communications.

- Telecommuting, sometimes referred to as teleworking, is the use of telecommunications and computer equipment to work from home while still being connected to the office. Workgroup computing refers to the use of compatible hardware, software, and network equipment to enable individuals collaborating on a project to connect and communicate within the same building or remotely.

Key Terms and Concepts

Identification

Identify each technology.

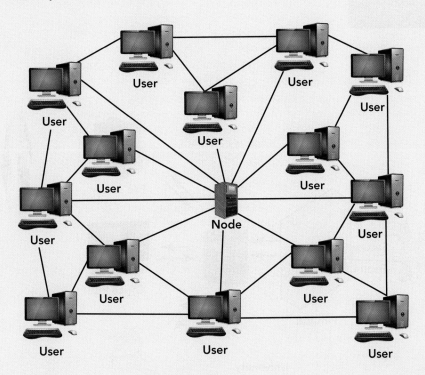

1. _____

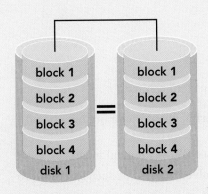

2. _____

3. _____

4. _____

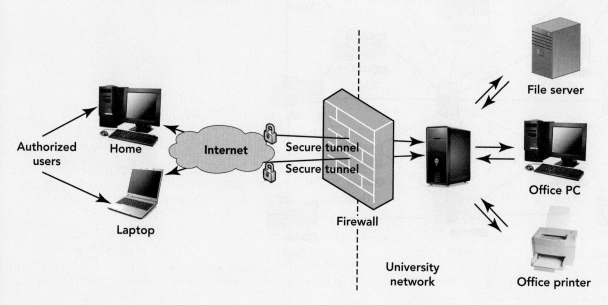

5. _____

Matching

Match each key term in the left column with the most accurate definition in the right column.

_____ 1. jukebox

_____ 2. intranet

_____ 3. customer relationship management software

_____ 4. business process reengineering

a. Use of information technology to bring about major organizational changes and cost savings

b. An enterprise storage unit that uses Blu-ray optical media

c. Automates business processes involved with sales such as order processing and tracking

d. Hardware, software, processes, and standards that integrate two or more enterprise systems

_____ 5. intranet

_____ 6. sales force automation software

_____ 7. blade server

_____ 8. library

_____ 9. Web portal

_____ 10. electronic data interchange

_____ 11. grid computing

_____ 12. extranet

_____ 13. enterprise application integration

_____ 14. Software-as-a-Service

_____ 15. value-added network

e. A public data network used by an enterprise that is offered by a service provider

f. Enterprise storage that uses DVDs and CDs

g. Applies the abilities of many computers in a network to a single problem

h. An enterprise network accessible only by authorized users

i. Standards that specify how to transfer data and documents among enterprises, using the Internet and other networks, without human intervention

j. Stripped down, energy-efficient, low-cost modular computers with server software installed

k. Tracks an organization's interaction with its customers

l. The providing of businesses with software solutions and services enabling the management of some of their information technology needs without having to actually purchase costly hardware and software

m. A Web site that provides links to multiple online services

n. Provides secure access to an organization's data for authorized outsiders

o. Provides secure access to an organization's data for employees of that organization

Multiple Choice

Circle the correct choice for each of the following:

1. Which network uses high-capacity storage devices to link all of an organization's servers?
   a. SAN
   b. VPN
   c. VAN
   d. NAS

2. Which is a feature of a virtual private network?
   a. Transports data only over private networks
   b. Provides encryption
   c. Allows use by both authorized and unauthorized users
   d. Cannot be used to transfer sensitive or confidential information

3. Which of the following statements about enterprise application integration (EAI) is true?
   a. EAI is a simple integration process.
   b. Management issues have caused a high EAI failure rate.
   c. EAI enables custom-built proprietary software to run independently from other programs.
   d. EAI is available for only a few categories of data management.

4. Which enterprise technology is associated with multi-tenancy?
   a. Grid computing
   b. Library
   c. Web portal
   d. Cloud computing

5. Which device provides a high degree of fault tolerance and is used when an interruption of service could be costly, hazardous, or inconvenient?
   a. Blade server
   b. Jukebox
   c. RAID
   d. Thin client

6. What term refers to the use of specific hardware, software, and network equipment to enable individuals collaborating on a project to connect and communicate regardless of location?
   a. Workgroup computing
   b. Workflow automation
   c. Grid computing
   d. Electronic data interchange

7. What is the term given to a system component that causes the entire system to malfunction when it stops working properly?
   a. Zero configuration
   b. Fault tolerant
   c. Scalability
   d. Single point of failure

8. What is used by enterprises to share financial information across all computer platforms and over the Internet?
   a. Enterprise data center
   b. Web portal
   c. XBRL
   d. CBT

9. Which activity has identifiable output and provides value to the customers of an organization?
   a. A business process
   b. Workgroup computing
   c. Teleconferencing
   d. Telecommuting

10. _____ is the ability to connect and exchange data with another computer even if it is of a different brand or model.
   a. Scalability
   b. Interoperability
   c. Keeping current
   d. Zero configuration

Fill-In

In the blanks provided, write the correct answer for each of the following:

1. _____ is a condition that gives one company a superior position over a competing company.

2. _____ is a subscription-based or pay-per-use service that provides scalable services and IT services over the Internet.

3. A(n) _____ is a backup center that becomes operational only when a disaster has occurred.

4. A(n) _____ is a common location used to house computer systems and centralize data, telecommunication devices, and storage systems.

5. _____ is the conducting of business internationally where goods and services are identical (or nearly identical) in all locations.

6. _____ is a method for networking devices via an Ethernet cable that does not require configuration and administration.

7. _____ is the sending of documents, without request, to individuals that need them.

8. The tradeoff for _____ is that using the latest tools may result in a low comfort level for users.

9. E-mail, videoconferencing, and calendar tools that enable individuals to work together collaboratively are called _____ applications.

10. _____ is the use of telecommunications and computer equipment to conduct business activities and promote interactivity among individuals in different physical locations.

11. _____ is an education style that uses multimedia, animation, and programmed learning to teach new skills with a computer.

12. A(n) _____ is a backup center that is always kept in a state of readiness.

13. _____ is the use of the Internet to buy, sell, provide customer service, and collaborate with business partners.

14. _____ is the changing of a product's menu, slogan, or logo to mesh with the local culture.

15. A(n) _____ is a detailed plan shared throughout an enterprise that is followed when a system or component of a system becomes nonfunctional due to a human or natural catastrophe.

Short Answer

1. Differentiate between e-business and globalization.

2. List three business processes automated by sales force automation (SFA) software.

3. List three steps that a business leader must take to ensure that a backup plan will function correctly when needed.

4. Describe the two types of disaster recovery centers that are usually part of a disaster recovery plan.

5. List three benefits of telecommuting.

Teamwork

1. **Web-based Training Survey** As a team, create a survey on taking Web-based classes. Include questions getting at whether or not the respondents felt that taking a Web-based class was as good as taking a face-to-face class. Ask for the positive and negative aspects of an online class and whether the respondents would take another online class. Include other questions that the team considers

appropriate and informational. Distribute the survey to at least 30 students. Accumulate the data obtained from the survey, analyze it, and present your results in a one-page, double-spaced report. You can use an Excel spreadsheet to display the accumulated statistics and graphs to provide your findings in a more visual style.

2. **Popular Web Portals** Have team members research popular Web portals. Visit each portal that a team member suggests. In an Excel spreadsheet list each Web portal and the team members' evaluation of it. Consider whether it was easy to navigate, had links relative to today's events, and was visually appealing. After evaluating all of the portals presented by group members, as a team, develop a list of the features that the team preferred in the portals visited and the features that the team disliked. Submit your Excel spreadsheet with your portal evaluations and list of features.

3. **Grid Computing Projects** As a team, research grid computing. Locate and investigate at least three grid computing projects. Using a word processing program, present the results of your research in a table that allows for an easy comparison of the projects. Include such items as a project description, registration process, security procedures, and other issues that the team considered important.

4. **E-Business Web Sites** Many companies conduct e-business through digital storefronts. As a team, list the online e-business companies that you or one of your family members have used. Provide the name of the company; what products were purchased; how the product was distributed; whether the company has brick-and-mortar stores as well as a digital presence; what the payment options were; how your payment was made; and how shipping was handled. Indicate whether team members would consider purchasing more products from this company? Why or why not? Accumulate your findings in a one-page, double-spaced report. Try to draw some summary conclusions on the success of the experience, the types of products purchased, and prevailing methods of payment.

5. **Disaster Recovery Plan** As a team, investigate the disaster recovery plan that the IT department at your school has in place. Does the school make use of a hot site, cold site, or both? What procedures are in place to back up and restore important data? How often are backups created? Is there a different plan for critical information, such as tuition payments and grades, versus student work files? Present a summary of the team's finding in a PowerPoint presentation of 7 to 10 slides.

On the Web

1. **Wal-Mart and CRM** Wal-Mart is currently one of the largest retail chains in the world. Its use of technology and the Internet to service customers and suppliers has set industry benchmarks. Using the Internet and your choice of search engines, locate statistics and information on the enterprise systems and customer relationship management strategies (CRM) employed by Wal-Mart. Present your research, citing references, in a one-page, double-spaced paper.

2. **Cloud Computing Career Options** Using the Internet, a search engine of your choice, and job listing Web sites, locate at least three careers that relate to cloud computing. List the job title, state the job description, describe the required qualifications, and if possible, provide a salary range. Interview faculty members at your school and come up with a list of courses that might prepare an individual for each job listed. Be sure to include the department that offers the course. Present your results in a table.

3. **Failed Government IT Projects** Use the Internet and your favorite search engine to research failed government IT projects. Select three projects and, in a two-page, double-spaced paper, describe each project, what each was suppose to accomplish, and what

each ended up accomplishing. How much over budget was each project? Did the projects get scrapped or did they go to completion? What branch of the government was involved in project development and implementation? Remember to cite your references.

4. **Data Disasters** Use the Internet and search engine of your choice to locate at least three data disasters due to equipment failure, technological malfunction, or environmental interference. Briefly describe each disaster and its effects on the business involved. Continue your research to locate articles or other journals on avoiding data disasters or data center disasters. From your research, compose a list of the five steps to take to avoid data disasters. Present your disaster descriptions, their effects on the business or government, and your list of five steps to take to avoid such disasters in either a one-page, double-spaced paper or a PowerPoint presentation.

5. **Enterprise 2.0** Using the Internet or other research options, define Enterprise 2.0. In a two-page, double-spaced paper, describe the technology and tools that facilitate this enterprise system. Identify what features make it different from other enterprise systems and how social networking fits into this strategy.

1G first generation

1GL first-generation languages

2G second generation

2GL second-generation languages

3D three-dimensional

3G third-generation

3GL third generation languages

4G fourth generation

4GL fourth-generation languages

AC alternating current

ACCS Alternative Computer Control System

ACM Association for Computing Machinery

ADC analog-to-digital converter

ADSL asymmetric digital subscriber line

AES Advanced Encryption Standard

AFIS Automated Fingerprint Identification System

AGP accelerated graphics port

AIM AOL Instant Messenger

AJAX asynchronous JavaScript and XML

ALU arithmetic logic unit

ARPANET Advanced Research Projects Agency Network

ASCII American Standard Code for Information Interchange

ASIMO Advance Step in Innovative Mobility

ASIS&T American Society for Information Science and Technology

ASP application service provider

ATM asynchronous transfer mode

ATS application tracking system

AUP acceptable use policies

AVI Audio Video Interleave

AWC Association for Women in Computing

B2B business-to-business

B2C business-to-consumer

BCP business continuity plan

BD Blu-ray disc

BDA Blu-ray Disc Association

BD-R Blu-Ray disc-recordable

BD-RE Blu-Ray disc rewritable

BD-ROM Blu-Ray disc ROM

BIOS basic input/output system

BLOB binary large object

BMP Windows Bitmap

BMS Bristol-Myers Squibb

BOINC Berkeley Open Infrastructure for Network Computing

BPM business process management

BPR business process reengineering

Bps bits per second

BRB be right back

BSA Business Software Alliance

BVA Bionic Vision Australia

C2C consumer-to-consumer

CAD computer-aided design

CAN campus area network

CASE computer-aided software engineering

cat-5 category 5

cat-5e category 5 enhanced

cat-6 category 6

CAVE Cave Automated Virtual Environment

CBE computer-based education

CBT computer-based training

CCD charge-coupled device

CCIE Cisco Certified Internetwork Expert

CCNA Cisco Certified Network Associate

CCRC Crimes Against Children Research Center

CDMA code division multiple access

CD-R compact disc-recordable

CD-ROM compact disc ROM

CD-RW compact disc-rewritable

CES Consumer Electronics Show

CIO chief information officer

CIPA Children's Internet Protection Act

CIS computer information systems

CLA Novell Certified Linux Administrator

CMOS complementary metaloxide semiconductor

CO central office

CPSR Computer Professionals for Social Responsibility

CPU central processing unit

CRISP-DM CRoss Industry Standard Process for Data Mining

CRM customer relationship management

CRT cathode ray tube

CS computer science

CSO chief security officers

CSS cascading style sheets

DAC digital-to-analog converter

DARPA Defense Advance Projects Research Agency

DBMS database management system

DBS direct broadcast satellite

DC direct current

DDOS disturbed denial of service attack

DFD data flow diagram

DHS U.S. Department of Homeland Security

DIMM dual inline memory module

DLCI data link control/connection identifier

DLP digital light processing

DMA Direct Marketing Association

DNS domain name service

DoS denial of service attack

DSL digital subscriber line

DSS decision support system

DVD digital video disc

DVD-R digital video disc-recordable

DVD-ROM digital video disc-ROM

DVD-RW digital video disc-rewritable

DVI digital video interface port

DVR digital video recorder

EAI enterprise application integration

EB exabyte

EBCDIC Extended Binary Coded Decimal Interchange Code

ECMA European Computer Manufacturers Association

EDI electronic data exchange

EE electrical engineering

EEPROM electrically erasable programmable ROM

EFF Electronic Frontier Foundation

EIS executive information system

EMPT electromagnetic pulse transformer

EPA Environmental Protection Agency

EPROM electrically programmable ROM

EPS Encapsulated PostScript

ERD entity-relationship diagram

ERP enterprise resource planning

ES expert system

ESS executive support system

EU European Union

f2f face-to-face

FAQ frequently asked questions

FAT file allocation table

FBI Federal Bureau of Investigation

FCC Federal Communications Commission

FCRA Fair Credit Reporting Act

FDIC Federal Reserve System and Federal Deposit Insurance Corporation

FED field-emission display

FERPA Family Educational Rights and Privacy Act

FFIEC U.S. Federal Financial Institutions Examination Council

FiOS fiber-optic service

FOLED flexible OLED displays

fps frames per second

FPU floating point unit

FTC Federal Trade Commission

FTP File Transfer Protocol

FTTH fiber-to-the-home

GB gigabyte

Gbps gigabits per second

GHz gigahertz

GIF Graphics Interchange Format

gigaPOP gigabits per second point of presence

GMSC gateway mobile switching center

gMUD graphical MUD

GPL General Public License

GPS Global Positioning System

GUI graphical user interface

GUID global unique identifier

HAN home area network

HaaS Hardware-as-a-Service

HD high-definition video

HDMI high-definition multimedia interface

HDR high dynamic range

HDSL high bit-rate DSL

HDTV high-definition TV

HERF high-energy radio frequency

HHD hybrid hard drive

HIPAA Health Insurance Portability and Privacy Act

HMD head-mounted display

HP Hewlett-Packard

HTML Hypertext Markup Language

HTTP Hypertext Transfer Protocol

HTTPS Hypertext Transfer Protocol Secure

Hz hertz

IaaS Infrastructure-as-a-Service

IC integrated circuit

IC3 Internet Crime Complaint Center

ICANN Internet Corporation for Assigned Names and Numbers

ICC integrated circuit card

ICCP Institute for Certification of Computing Professionals

ICE Intercity Express

IDC International Data Corporation

IDE integrated development environment

IE Internet Explorer

IEEE Institute of Electrical and Electronics Engineers

IGDA International Game Developers Association

IIS Microsoft's Internet Information Services

IM instant messaging

IMDB Internet Movie Database

I/O input/output

IP Internet Protocol

IPI Institution for Policy Innovation

IR infrared

IRC Internet relay chat

IrDA infrared data association

IRQ interrupt request

IRS Internal Revenue Service

IRU indoor receive unit

IS information systems

ISA Industry standard architecture

ISDN Integrated Services Digital Network

ISO International Organization for Standardization

ISP Internet service provider

IT information technology

ITU indoor transmit unit

JAD joint application development

JPEG Joint Photographic Experts Group

JSON JavaScript Object Notation

KB kilobyte

Kbps kilobits per second or thousand bits per second

KMS knowledge management system

LAN local area network

LCD liquid crystal display

LED light-emitting diode

LOL laughing out loud

MAC media access control

MAN metropolitan area network

MB megabyte

Mbps megabits per second or million bits per second

MCITP Microsoft Certified IT Professional

MCSA Microsoft Certified Systems Administrator

MCSE Microsoft Certified Systems Engineer

MCTS Microsoft Certified Technology Specialist

MIDI Musical Instrument Digital Interface

MIS management information system

MMDS multichannel multipoint distribution service, sometimes called multipoint microwave distribution system

MMPORG massively multiplayer online role-playing game

MMS multimedia messaging service

MPEG Moving Picture Experts Group

MSC mobile switching center

MUD multiuser dungeon

N.O.C. Network Operations Centre

NAP network access point

NAS network attached storage

NET No Electronic Theft Act

NIC network interface card

NOS Network operating system

NSA National Security Agency

NSP network service provider

NTFS new technology file system

OCR optical character recognition

ODBMS object-oriented database management systems

ODC Open Database Connectivity

OLAP online analytical processing

OLPC One Laptop per Child initiative

OMR optical mark reader

OO object-oriented

OOP object-oriented programming

OS operating system

OSI open system interconnection

OSP online service provider

OSS operational support system

P2P peer-to-peer network

PaaS Platform-as-a-Service

PAN personal area network

PARC Xerox Palo Alto Research Center

PB petabyte

PBX private branch exchange

PC personal computer

PCI peripheral component interconnect

PCMCIA Personal Computer Memory Card International Association

PCS personal communication service

PDA personal digital assistant

PDL page-description language

PDLC program development life cycle

PDN public data network

PGP Pretty Good Privacy

PIM personal information manager

PIN personal identification number

PKI public key infrastructure

PNG portable network graphics

PnP plug-and-play

PoP point of presence

POP Post Office Protocol

POS point-of-sale

POST power-on self-test

POTS plain old telephone service

ppm pages per minute

Pro-IP Prioritizing Resources and Organization for Intellectual Property Act

PROM programmable ROM

PSTN public switched telephone network

PUE power usage effectiveness

RAD rapid application development

RAID redundant array of independent disks

RAM random access memory

RDBMS relational database management system

RF radio frequency

RFIC Radio Frequency Integrated Circuit

RFID radio frequency identification device

RFP request for proposal

RFQ request for quotation

RHCE Red Hat Certified Engineer

ROI region of interest or return on investment

RSI repetitive strain injuries

ROM read-only memory

RSS Really Simple Syndication (or Rich Site Summary)

RUN Responsible Use of the Network Working Group

SaaS Software-as-a-Service

SAN storage area network

SATA serial advance technology attachment

SATAIO Serial ATA International Organization

SCJD Sun Certified Java Developer

SCJP Sun Certified Java Programmer

SCSI small computer system interface ports

SD standard definition

SDH synchronous digital hierarchy

SDLC systems development life cycle

SDMC Standard Duplicating Machines Corporation

SDSL symmetrical digital subscriber line

SEC Securities and Exchange Commission

SET secure electronic transfer

SETI Search for Extraterrestrial Intelligence

SFA sales force automation

SIIA Software & Information Industry Association

SIMM single inline memory module

SLC subscriber loop carrier

SLR single-lens reflex digital camera

SMDS switched multimegabit data service

SMIL Synchronized Multimedia Integration Language

SMS short messaging service, better known as text messaging

SOHO small office–home office

SONET synchronous optical network

SOX Sarbanes-Oxley

SPOF single point of failure

SQL structured query language

SSCP Systems Security Certified Practitioner

SSD solid-state drive

STOP SOMA Terror Organization Portal

SVGA super video graphics array

SXGA super extended graphics array

SYN synchronization

TB terabyte

TCO total cost of ownership

TCP Transmission Control Protocol

TCP/IP Transmission Control Protocol/Internet Protocol

TDWI The Data Warehousing Institute

TFT active matrix (thin film transistor)

TLD top-level domain

TPS transaction processing system

UM exchange unified messaging

UML Unified Modeling Language

UPC Universal Product Code

UPS uninterruptable power supply

URL Uniform Resource Locator

USB universal serial bus

US-CERT United States Computer Emergency Readiness Team

USDA Department of Agriculture

UXGA ultra extended graphics array

UV ultraviolet

VAN value-added network

VAR value-added reseller

VB Visual Basic

VDSL very high bit-rate DSL

VGA video graphics array

VM Java virtual machine

VOD video-on-demand

VoIP Voice over Internet Protocol

VPN virtual private network

VR virtual reality

VRML Virtual Reality Modeling Language

W3C World Wide Web Consortium

WAN wide area network

WAP Wireless Application Protocol

WBT Web-based training

WEP Wired Equivalent Privacy

WiMAX worldwide interoperability for microwave access

WITI Women in Technology International

WMA Windows Media Audio

WML Wireless Markup Language

WOW World Organization of Webmasters

WPA WiFi Protected Access

WSXGA+ Widescreen Super Extended Graphics Array Plus

WUXGA Widescreen Ultra Extended Language

WXGA+ Widescreen Extended Graphics Array plus

WWW World Wide Web

XBRL Extensible Business Reporting Language

XGA Extended Graphics Array

XHTML Extensible Hypertext Markup Language

XML Extensible Markup Language

XP Extreme Programming

YB yottabyte

ZB zettabyte

Glossary

1394 port An interface that offers high-speed connections for peripherals. It is ideal for real-time devices like digital video cameras. In an Apple computer, the 1394 port is called the FireWire port.

1G First generation of cellular technology, which used analog signals and allowed callers to make their own calls without operator assistance as they move seamlessly from cell to cell.

2G Second-generation cellular technology that quickly replaced most analog cellular services due to its use of digital signaling. Features of this generation were decreased signal interference, increased reception, better protection from eavesdropping, and increased security features that decreased cell phone fraud.

3G Third-generation cellular technology that offers faster data transmission; greater network capacity; more advanced network services; and transmission of voice, text, images, and video data.

4G Fourth-generation cellular technology, which is currently being rolled out, promises higher data transfer rates, as well as providing voice, data, and high-quality multimedia in real-time (streamed) format all the time from anywhere.

A

Accelerated Graphics Port (AGP) An interface, currently being phased out that is used to transfer graphics from the video card to the motherboard.

acceptable use policy A code of conduct created by colleges or employers that provides guidance for students and employees when dealing with ethical and legal dilemmas.

acceptance testing Testing in which users evaluate a system to see whether it meets their needs and functions correctly.

access time In secondary storage devices, the amount of time it takes a device to access information, from the request for the information to the delivery of that information.

account A record on multiuser systems that consists of a user's name, password, and storage space location, which is called the user's folder or user's directory. Accounts are usually set up and managed by a server/computer administrator.

active badge A small device, worn by an individual, that transmits a unique infrared signal every 5 to 10 seconds. Networked sensors detect these transmissions and the location of the badge—and hence the location of its wearer—allowing e-mail, phone calls, or messages to be forwarded.

active-matrix (thin film transistor [TFT]) A form of LCD display in which electric current drives the display by charging each pixel individually as needed.

ActiveX control A miniprogram that can be downloaded from a Web page and used to add functionality to a Web browser. ActiveX controls require Microsoft Windows and Microsoft Internet Explorer and are written in Visual Basic (VB).

Ada A programming language, named after Augusta Ada Byron, that incorporates modular programming principles. It was the required language for most U.S. Department of Defense projects until 1996 because of its suitability for the reliable control of real-time systems (such as missiles).

address bar (breadcrumb bar) Used for navigation, the address bar displays the route you've taken to get to the current location. It may or may not correspond with a file's path name.

ADSL (asymmetrical digital subscriber line) A transmission technology that separates an ordinary copper telephone line into three separate data channels with different capacities and speeds. The lowest capacity transmits analog voice for telephones; the second, medium capacity, uploads data to the network; and the third, highest capacity, downloads data from the network. This means that ADSL connections upload more slowly than they download.

adware Software similar to spyware, which is usually installed on your computer through the Internet without your knowledge or consent. Adware is created specifically by an advertising agency to collect information about Internet habits or encourage the purchase of a product. It is usually considered a nuisance rather than malicious.

aggregator A Web site that interacts with RSS feeds. It remembers your subscription list, checks each site on a regular basis, alerts you if new information has been published, and organizes the results for you. Many RSS aggregators are available through your browser and are either updated manually, such as the Drudge Report, or through the use of algorithms, as is the case with Google News.

Agile Refers to a group of software development methodologies based on an iterative project management process that aligns development with customer needs and company goals. It describes the development of solutions through collaboration between functional teams.

Agile software development See Agile.

AJAX Sometimes written as Ajax (shorthand for asynchronous JavaScript and XML). A group of interrelated Web development techniques used on the client-side to create interactive Web applications. AJAX is not a technology in itself, but a term that refers to the use of a group of technologies.

algorithm A series of steps that results in the solution to a problem.

all-in-one computer A compact version of a desktop computer, designed for individual use that combines the system unit and monitor into one component. Its smaller size suits cubicle layouts and apartments.

alphabetic check A data validation procedure that ensures that only alphabetic data (the letters of the alphabet) are entered into a database field.

analog signal Real-world signals, like sound and light, sent via continuous waves that vary in frequency and amplitude. It is the signal sent and received over phone lines.

analog-to-digital converter (ADC) A microchip that contains the circuitry to convert an analog signal into a digital signal.

Android An operating system developed by Google for mobile devices.

animation The technique involved in tricking the eye into seeing continuous motion, which makes static images appear to move.

anonymity The ability to convey a message without disclosing your name or identity.

anonymous FTP An Internet service that enables you to contact a distant computer system to which you have access rights, log on to its public directories, and transfer files from that computer to your own. These sites lack security and should never be used to send sensitive data.

antivirus software Software that protects a computer from computer viruses by using a pattern-matching technique that examines all of the files on a disk, looking for virus code signatures.

applet In Java, a miniprogram embedded in a Web document that, when downloaded, is executed by the browser. Most major browsers can execute Java applets.

application service provider (ASP) Provides software-based services and solutions to companies that want to outsource some or almost all of their information technology needs.

application software A set of integrated programs that can be thought of as sitting on top of the operating system and that direct the computer's hardware to perform a task for the user.

application testing One of two basic testing methodologies in which programs are tested individually and then together.

application tracking system (ATS) A computer program used as the first level of a job application screening to verify that a job applicant possesses the minimum criteria for a position. The program scans a submitted resume and is set to locate keywords. If a certain percentage of keywords in the resume match the preset scanned list of keywords, the application makes it to the next level.

application window The area on-screen that encloses and displays a launched application and work in progress.

application workspace The on-screen area that displays the document you are currently working on.

archive A single file that contains two or more files stored in a compressed format. An archive is handy for storage as well as file-exchange purposes because as many as several hundred separate files can be stored in a single, easily handled unit.

argument set In spreadsheet programs, such as Microsoft Excel, the part of a mathematical function that contains the parameters or variables that the function needs in order to perform the calculation. Usually the argument set is placed between parentheses.

arithmetic logic unit (ALU) The portion of the central processing unit that performs arithmetic operations, which return numeric values, and logical operations, which return a value of true or false.

arithmetic operation One of two groups of operations performed by the arithmetic logic unit (ALU). The arithmetic operations are addition, subtraction, multiplication, and division. An arithmetic operation returns the value of the operation.

artificial intelligence A computer science field that tries to improve computers by endowing them with some of the characteristics associated with human intelligence, such as the capability to understand natural language and to reason under conditions of uncertainty.

artificial system A system deliberately constructed by people to serve some purpose.

ASCII (American Standard Code for Information Interchange) A standard and widely used computer character set that makes use of seven bits and can represent 128 different characters. It is used on minicomputers, personal computers, and computers that make information available on the Internet.

aspect ratio A value that determines a monitor's quality and resolution; it is calculated by dividing a monitor's width by its height.

assembler A utility program that transforms source code written in assembly language into machine language, which is readable by a microprocessor.

assembly language A low-level, processor-dependent programming language, one level up from machine language, in which each program statement uses mnemonics and decimal values to create instructions that the microprocessor can carry out.

asynchronous communication Communication in which both parties are not necessarily online at the same time, for example, e-mail and text messaging.

attribute An element of an object's definition that describes that object's features.

Audio Video Interleave (AVI) A Microsoft-created specification for packaging audio and video data into a file. AVI makes no guarantee on the content of the package or the codec used to compress it.

authentication (login) The process that requests a user to enter a user name and password into a dialog box to verify that the user is indeed a person authorized to use the computer; also called login.

automation The replacement of human workers by machines and computer-guided robots.

AutoSave (AutoRecover) A software feature that backs up open documents at a default or user-specified interval; also called AutoRecover.

avatar A virtual representation of a player in a game or a person on a social networking site.

B

backbone In a wide area network (WAN), such as the Internet, a high-speed, high-capacity medium that transfers data over hundreds or thousands of miles. A variety of physical media are used for backbone services, including microwave relay, satellites, and dedicated telephone lines.

backdoor A method of bypassing normal authentication to secure access to a computer.

background application From the user's perspective, the application that appears inactive, as indicated by its appearance behind an active application on the desktop, when more than one application is running.

backup A copy of programs, data, and information created in one secondary storage medium that is duplicated to another.

backup procedure Procedures that protect against loss, change, or damage of an organization's data from natural or other disasters. This process usually involves making copies of data files and storing them in secure location.

backup software Programs that copy data from the computer's hard disk to backup devices, such as CDs or DVDs, an external hard drive, or an online storage location.

bad sector Areas of a hard disk that have become damaged and can no longer reliably hold data.

bandwidth The theoretical maximum amount of data that can be transmitted through a given communications channel, like a network, at one time (usually per second).

banner ad On a Web page, an ad that is not actually part of the Web page itself, but is supplied separately by an ad network based on analysis of cookies.

bar code reader A handheld or desktop-mounted device that scans bar codes and, with special software, converts the bar code into readable data.

BASIC An easy-to-use high-level programming language developed in the mid-1960s for instruction and still used in beginning programming classes and by many hobbyists to create simple programs.

batch processing An early transaction processing system whereby data was gathered and processed at periodic intervals, such as once a week.

baud The number of signaling elements per second. At slower rates, bauds and bps may be equal, but on higher speed transmissions, more than one bit can be encoded in each signaling element; thus a 4,800 baud may have a transmission rate of 9,600 bps.

BD-R An optical storage media that that can record high-definition video or PC data storage.

BD-RE An optical storage medium that can record and erase high-definition video or PC data storage.

BD-ROM A standard for storing read-only high-definition computer data on optical discs. It is a format used for video or data distribution.

beans The components of Javabean programming specifications.

beta version In software testing, a preliminary version of a program that is widely distributed before commercial release to users who test the program by operating it under realistic conditions.

binary digit The digits 0 and 1, which are used to represent the Off/On state of a computer switch, the smallest piece of data that a computer can process. In the Off state, current is not flowing through the switch and is represented by the digit 0. In the On state, current is flowing through the switch and is represented by the digit 1.

binary number Strings of binary digits, 0 and 1, which represent the pattern of Off/On current flowing through switches.

biometric authentication A method of authentication that requires a biological scan of some sort, such as a fingerprint, retinal scan, or voice recognition.

biometric input device A device that uses physical or chemical features of an individual's body to provide a unique method of identification.

BIOS (basic input/output system) A set of programs that are part of the system software, permanently encoded on the computer's ROM memory and executed when the system is powered on. They check and initialize such devices as the keyboard, display screens, and disk drives. Many modern systems have flash BIOS, which is a type of BIOS that makes use of flash memory chips that can be updated by the user if needed.

bit Short for binary digit, a single circuit that either contains a current (represented by the digit 1) or does not contain current (represented by the digit 0). The digits 0 and 1 are the base unit of information in the binary number system. The lowest level of data in a database, the smallest unit of data a computer can store and understand.

bitmapped graphic (raster graphic) An image formed by a pattern of tiny dots, each of which corresponds to a pixel on the computer's display; also called raster graphic.

bitmapped image A representation of an image as a matrix of dots called picture elements (pixels).

blade server Stripped-down, energy-efficient, low-cost modular computers with server software installed.

BLOB (binary large object) A data type for very large objects up to several gigabytes in size, such as an entire spreadsheet file or a picture file.

block A unit of memory on a flash drive.

blog (Web log) Short for Web log. A Web site that contains an online personal journal with reflections, images, comments, and often hyperlinks provided by the writer.

Bluetooth A trademarked personal area network (PAN) technology, conceived by cell phone giant Ericsson and named after a 10th-century Viking. It uses short-range radio transmission technology to provide automatic and wireless communication among computers, mobile phones, printers, PDAs, and other devices located within 30 feet of each other.

Blu-ray Disc (BD) One of the newest forms of optical storage, Blu-ray technology was developed for the management of high-definition video and for storing large amounts of data.

Boolean data type A data type that, depending on the program, allows a yes or no, true or false, or 1 or 0 value.

Boolean search A database or Web search that uses the logical operators AND, OR, and NOT to specify the logical relationship among search words or phrases.

boot disk (emergency disk) A storage device, like a USB drive, CD, DVD, or network device that, in case of an emergency or boot failure, can load a reduced version of the operating system that can be used for troubleshooting purposes; also called an emergency disk.

booting The process of loading the operating system into RAM memory.

boot sector virus A computer virus that copies itself to the beginning tracks of a hard drive where code is stored that automatically executes every time you start the computer. Unlike file infectors, boot sector viruses don't require you to start a specific program to infect your

computer; starting your system is sufficient.

Bootstrap Loader A program that locates and loads the operating system into RAM.

bot In a distributed denial of service (DDoS) attack, an automated program that connects the individual computers to the controller, usually a server with some type of real-time activity like Internet Relay Chat, that is under the power of a botnet controller; an abbreviation for robot.

bot herder An individual that controls a botnet.

botnet A set of computers infected with a malicious program that places the computers under the control of a bot herder. Such computers are typically used during a distributed denial of service (DDoS) attack.

bps rate The rate used to measure the exchange of data.

branch prediction A technique used by the central processing unit (CPU) to prevent a pipeline stall. The processor tries to predict what will happen with surprising accuracy.

broadband Refers to any transmission medium that carries several channels at once and thus transports high volumes of data at high speeds, typically greater than 1 Mbps.

browser cache A section of your hard drive in which Web pages visited for the first time are stored. If the user attempts to retrieve the page again, the browser does not go out on the Internet, but instead retrieves the page from the browser's cache. This eliminates excessive roundtrips to the server, brings the page up more quickly on the user's system, and greatly reduces Internet traffic.

buffer An area of RAM memory that temporarily holds data and instruction to make the processing of instructions more fluid.

bug Syntax and logical errors located in a computer program that can cause the program to perform erratically, produce incorrect results, or crash.

build-or-buy decision A decision project teams face when they must determine whether a new system should be developed in-house or purchased from an outside vendor.

business continuity plan (BCP) A comprehensive plan that focuses on long-term or continual problems that might impede success.

business process An activity that has an identifiable output and value to an organization's customers.

business process management (BPM) Evolved from BPR, BPM's goal is to improve existing processes and optimize assets by effectively and efficiently managing the entire life cycle of these business processes.

business process reengineering (BPR) The use of information technology

to bring about major organizational changes and cost savings.

business services Services sold to enterprise and business organizations, usually on a subscription basis.

business unit A division of a company, product line, or special focus group whose actions can be planned independently of other business units of the company.

business-to-business e-commerce (B2B) The online exchange or trade of goods, services, or information in which one business provides another business with the materials, services, and/or supplies it needs to conduct its operations.

business-to-consumer e-commerce (B2C) The same experience as shopping at a physical store except the business supplies consumers with services, information, or products online.

bus topology The physical layout of a local area network in which the network cable is a single conduit that forms a bus, or line; every node, whether it is a computer or peripheral device, is attached to that bus. At the ends of the bus, connectors called terminators signify the end of the circuit.

byte A group of eight bits that represents a single character such as the essential numbers (0–9), the basic letters of the alphabet (uppercase and lowercase), and the most common punctuation symbols. Also a unit of capacity for storage devices.

C

C A high-level programming language developed by Bell Labs in the 1970s. C combines the virtues of high-level programming with the efficiency of assembly language but is somewhat difficult to learn.

C++ A flexible high-level programming language derived from C that supports object-oriented programming but does not require programmers to adhere to the object-oriented model.

cable modem A device that enables a computer to access the Internet by means of a cable TV connection. Cable modems enable two-way communications through the cable system and do not require a phone line. Cable modems enable Internet access speeds from 1.5 Mbps to 6 Mbps, although most users typically experience slower speeds due to network congestion.

cache memory A small unit of ultrafast memory built into or near the processor that stores frequently or recently accessed program instructions and data, increasing the computer's overall performance.

call center A centralized computer-based routing system used for the purpose of receiving and transmitting a large volume of requests by telephone.

campus area network (CAN) A network that includes several LANs housed in various locations on a college or business campus. Usually smaller than a WAN, CANs use devices such as switches, hubs, and routers to interconnect.

carpal tunnel syndrome A painful injury caused by repeated motions (such as mouse movements or keystrokes) that damage sensitive nerves in the hands, wrists, and arms. These injuries can become so serious that they may require surgery.

cascading style sheets (CSS) A language embedded within HTML and XHTML that defines the look and formatting of a Web page.

case control structure In structured programming, a variant of the selection control structure, such as an if statement, in which the condition is fundamental. Each branch leads to its own lengthy series of instructions.

Cat-5 (Category 5) Short for Category 5, it's the fifth generation of twisted-pair data communication cable. Cat-5 cable contains four pairs of copper wire and supports speeds up to 100 Mbps over a maximum distance of 100 m (328 feet).

Cat-5e (Category 5 enhanced) Short for Category 5 enhanced, it uses all four wire pairs, enabling speeds up to 1,000 Mbps (1 Gbps) over a short distance. This enhanced medium is backward compatible with ordinary Cat-5.

Cat-6 (Category 6) Short for Category 6, it is the sixth generation of twisted-pair cable and is backward compatible with Cat-5 and Cat-5e. It contains four pairs of copper wire like that of the previous generation, utilizes all four pairs, supports speeds up to 1 gigabit per second (Gbps), expands available bandwidth from 100 MHz for Cat-5e to 200MHz, and has superior immunity from external noise.

Cave Automated Virtual Environment (CAVE) A virtual reality environment, used primarily by gamers, that replaces headsets with 3D glasses and uses the walls, ceiling, and floor to display projected three-dimensional images.

CD drive A read-only storage device that reads data encoded on CD-ROM media discs and transfers the data to the computer's internal memory.

CD-R (compact disc–recordable) Optical storage media that is a "write-once" technology. The data cannot be erased or written over once it has been saved; they're relatively inexpensive.

CD-ROM (compact disc read-only memory) A standard for storing read-only computer data (it cannot be changed or erased) on optical compact discs (CDs), which can be read by CD-ROM drives and DVD-ROM drives. CD-ROM discs can hold up to 700 MB of data.

CD-RW (compact disc–rewritable) An optical storage media that allows data that has been saved to be erased or written over.

CD-RW drive (burner or CD burner) A compact disc–rewritable storage device that provides full read/write capabilities using erasable CD-RWs.

cell 1. In a spreadsheet, the intersection of a column and row. 2. In telecommunications, a limited geographical area in which a signal can be broadcast.

cell address The column letter and row number that identifies a cell usually in a table or spreadsheet.

cell site In a cellular telephone network, an area in which a transmitting station repeats the system's broadcast signals so that the signal remains strong even though the user may move from one cell site to another.

cellular telephone A radio-based wireless computing device that provides widespread coverage through the use of repeating transmitters placed in zones (called cells). The zones are close enough so that signal strength is maintained throughout the calling area.

centralized structure An infrastructure where technology management is centered in the IT department and everyone within the organization works with standardized technology solutions in their everyday work.

central processing unit (CPU; microprocessor or processor) A chip, located on the motherboard within the system unit, that is composed of the control unit and the arithmetic logic unit (ALU). It applies directions received from software to the input data and converts it into information.

certification A skills and knowledge assessment process organized by computer industry vendors (and sometimes by professional associations).

channel In Internet Relay Chat (IRC), a chat group in which as many as several dozen people carry on a text-based conversation on a specific topic. This is dated technology that has been replaced by instant messaging, blogging, wikis, and tweeting.

character The smallest unit of data that an individual can work with, made up of bytes that represent the letters, numbers, and symbols on keyboard keys or key combinations.

character code An algorithm that translates the numerical language of the computer into keyboard characters readable by humans.

character map A comparison chart or lookup table located in a computer's read-only memory (ROM) on the motherboard. The system uses this table to locate the key that was struck on the keyboard and then notifies the processor of the character corresponding to that matrix location.

charged-coupled device (CCD) A photosensitive computer chip that transforms light patterns into pixels (individual dots). A CCD consists of a grid made up of light-sensitive elements. Each element converts the incoming light into a voltage that is proportional to the light's brightness. The digital camera's picture quality is determined by how many elements the CCD has.

chart A graphical representation of numbers that makes it easier to interpret data.

check-screening system A system that reads a check's account number, accesses a database containing delinquent accounts, and compares the account numbers,

allowing vendors to catch problematic transactions before they become losses.

chipset A collection of chips, located on the motherboard, that act like a traffic controller and work together to provide the switching circuitry needed by the microprocessor to move data throughout the computer via the microprocessor's system bus.

ciphertext The coded message that results from applying an encryption key to a message.

circuit switching One of two fundamental architectures for a wide area network (WAN), in which high-speed electronic switches create a direct connection between two communicating devices. The telephone system is a circuit-switching network.

class Blueprint or prototype from which objects are made.

clickstream The trail of Web links that you have followed to get to a particular site.

click wheel A variation of the touchpad that looks like a circle and uses a circular motion to move through song lists, movie lists, or photos. The click wheel is the method of navigation on the iPod and the iTouch.

client A desktop, notebook, workstation, terminal, or handheld device that is connected to a network and contains the software that enables it to send requests to a server.

client/server database system A system that incorporates a database server that is accessed through queries input through a user-friendly client program.

client/server network A network system in which individual users, called clients, are connected to each other through a central computer, called a server, which runs special software to enable the network connectivity.

clock speed The speed of the internal clock of a microprocessor that synchronizes and sets the pace of the computer's internal activities, including the movement from one stage of the machine cycle to another.

cloud computing A relatively new subscription-based or pay-per-use service that provides scalable resources and IT services over the Internet. Its power lies in the admission of users to a shared data center containing multi-tenancy applications.

cloud operating system A specially designed operating system created to run on a cloud provider's datacenter. The OS is delivered to subscribers over the Internet or other network. Windows Azure is a cloud operating system.

cluster On a magnetic disk, a storage unit that consists of two or more sectors.

CMOS (complementary metal-oxide semiconductor) Instructions located in read-only-memory (ROM) that control a variety of actions including starting the power-on self test and verifying that other components of the system are functioning correctly. The CMOS configuration should only be altered by an experienced user.

coaxial cable A broadband transmission medium that consists of a center copper wire surrounded by insulation, which is then surrounded by a layer of braided wire. Data travels through the center wire, and the braided wire provides a shield against electrical interference.

COBOL An early, high-level programming language primarily used for business applications.

code The written computer instructions that programmers create.

codec Short for compression/decompression standard. A standard for compressing and decompressing video information to reduce the size of digitized multimedia files. Popular codecs include MPEG (an acronym for Motion Picture Experts Group), Apple's QuickTime, and Microsoft's AVI.

code of conduct A set of ethical principles often developed by a professional organization, such as the Association for Computing Machinery (ACM).

cold boot Starting a computer that is not already on.

cold site A disaster recovery site that becomes operational once a disaster has occurred. It is typically less expensive than a hot site.

collaboration software A collection of programs that help people share ideas, create documents, and conduct meetings, regardless of location or time zone, through the use of proprietary networks or the Internet.

collaboration tools Applications that help you work in partnership with team members online.

collision The corruption of network data that results when two or more computers transmit to the same network cable at exactly the same time. Networks have means of detecting and preventing collisions.

column In Microsoft Excel and Word, a block of data presented vertically on the screen.

command-line user interface A method of interacting with an operating system that requires the user to type, one line at a time, commands using keywords and specific syntax (rules for entering commands) that tell the OS what to do (such as *format* or *copy*).

commerce The selling of goods and services with the expectation of making a reasonable profit.

commercial software Copyrighted software that must be purchased. The current trend is to make such software available as an online download or to give the potential customer a trial period. Once the trial period is over, the user can pay for the program directly on the Web site and download their official copy.

communications The high-speed electronic transfer of data or information within and between computers.

communications channel (link) The transmission media on which the message is sent from one location to the next; also referred to as the link).

communication device A hardware device that is capable of converting data into signals that can travel over a physical (wired) or wireless medium, and moving those signals into or out of the computer. These devices, which include modems, routers, switches, hubs, wireless access points, network interface cards, and other computers, also determine efficient data transfer pathways, boost signal strength, and facilitate overall digital communication.

communications device See communication device.

community cloud An extension of a private cloud in which organizations with similar missions share the infrastructure to reduce cost. This variation of the private cloud disperses cost while providing a high level of conformity and security by allowing access only to trusted users. Google's Gov Cloud is an example of a community cloud.

CompactFlash A popular flash memory storage device that can store up to 128 MB of digital camera images.

competitive advantage A condition that gives an organization a superior position over the companies it competes with.

compiler A program that translates source code in a third-generation programming language into instructions in (or close to) a specific computer's machine language

completeness check A data validation procedure that determines whether a required field has been left empty and, if so, prompts the user to fill in the needed data.

composite cloud Evolves when a primary cloud provider offers services that are distributed through another cloud provider.

computer An electronic device that receives data as input, processes that data based on a set of instructions, outputs the results of the processing for the user to review, and stores those results for later use.

computer-aided software engineering (CASE) Software that automates the often tedious task of documenting entity relationships and data flows in a complex new system. Such software includes project management features, data dictionaries, documentation support, and graphical output support; some even automatically generate prototype code.

computer-based training (CBT) A form of education that uses multimedia, animation, and programmed learning to teach new skills with a computer.

computer crime A computer-based activity that violates state, federal, or international laws.

computer ethics A branch of philosophy that deals with computer-related moral dilemmas and defines ethical principles, helping a user to make the morally correct decision in daily computer use.

computer forensics A branch of forensic science that deals with legal evidence found on computers. It is used to find and apprehend criminals.

computer literacy The ability to understand how to use a computer effectively.

computer science (CS) The study of storage, change, and transfer of information. It includes both the theoretical study of algorithms and the practical problems to which they can be applied.

computer security risk Any event, action, or situation—intentional or not—that could lead to the loss or destruction of computer systems or the data they contain.

computer system A collection of related computer components that have been designed to work together smoothly.

computer virus Hidden code that replicates itself by attaching to other programs, files, or e-mail messages, referred to as hosts, and usually carries out unwanted and sometimes dangerous operations.

congestion In a packet-switching network, a performance interruption that occurs when a segment of the network experiences an overload, too much traffic flooding the same network path.

connectivity The ability to link various media and devices, thereby enhancing communication and improving access to information.

connector A physical receptacle located on the system unit or an expansion card that is visible on the outside of the system unit and enables the connection of a cable to the computer's unit. A male connector contains extended pins or plugs that fit into the corresponding female connector.

consistency check A data validation procedure that examines the data typed into two different fields to determine whether they are identical entries.

consumer-oriented services One of two major categories of Software-as-a-Service (SaaS) that offers features like those supplied by Google Apps and Google Docs to the public, either on a subscription basis or, if supported by advertisement, for no cost.

consumer-to-consumer e-commerce (C2C) The online exchange or trade of goods, services, or information between individual consumers. Often C2C e-commerce involves the use of an intermediate site, such as the popular online auction destination eBay.

content The actual text, located between the tags of a markup language, that is to be displayed on a Web page.

content pane (file list) Displayed in the right pane of a Windows Explorer window. It shows the subfolders and files located within the selected folder

contention In a computer network, a problem that arises when two or more computers try to access the network at the same time. Contention can result in collisions, which can destroy data or require frequent and costly retransmissions.

contention management In a computer network, the use of one of several techniques for managing contention and preventing collisions. A common contention-management technique is to abandon any data that could have been corrupted by a collision.

contextual tab In Microsoft Office applications, a tab that is displayed and provides additional options for editing a selected feature, for example, an image.

continuous backup Programs that automatically create a backup, or duplicate, when a change in a system or a data file occurs.

control module In a program design tool called a structure chart, the top module or box that oversees the transfer of control to the other modules.

control structure In structured programming, logical elements that are grouped in a block with an END statement and that specify how the instructions in a program are to be executed.

control unit The portion of the central processing unit (CPU) that, under the direction of an embedded program, switches from one stage of the machine cycle to the next and performs the action of that stage.

convergence The merging of disparate objects or ideas (and even people) into new combinations and efficiencies. Within the IT industry, convergence means two things: the combination of various industries (computers, consumer electronics, and telecommunications) and the coming together of products such as PCs and telephones.

cookie A text file that is deposited by a Web site on a Web user's computer system, without the user's knowledge or consent. Mostly used for legitimate purposes, such as implementing "shopping carts," they can also be used to gather data on Web users' browsing and shopping habits.

cooling fan A fan designed to keep the system unit cool. The fan often is part of the power supply, although many systems include auxiliary fans to provide additional cooling.

copy-protected software Computer programs that include some mechanism to prevent users from making or running unauthorized copies.

copyright infringement The act of plagiarizing, using material from a copyrighted source without permission.

copyright protection scheme A method software manufacturers are working to develop to thwart the illegal use of their programs.

corporate espionage The unauthorized accessing of corporate information, usually to the benefit of one of the corporation's competitors.

cost-benefit analysis An examination of the losses and gains related to a project.

cracker (black hat) A computer user obsessed with gaining entry into highly secure computer systems; also called a black hat.

cross-platform programming language A programming language that can create programs capable of running on many different types of computers supported by different operating systems.

cryptographer An individual who specializes in encoding information.

cryptography The study of transforming information into an encoded or scrambled format.

cursor (insertion point) A blinking vertical bar, a horizontal underline character, or a highlighted box located on the monitor that indicates the location in which keystrokes will appear when typed.

cursor-movement keys (arrow keys) A set of four keys clustered together to the left of the number pad that move the cursor up, down, left, or right. The numeric keypad can also move the cursor when in the appropriate mode.

customer relationship management (CRM) software Keeps track of an organization's interactions with its customers and focuses on recording and tracking efforts to retain those customers.

custom software Application software designed by a professional programmer or programming team to meet the specific needs of a company or organization. Custom software is usually very expensive.

cyberbullying A cybercrime that involves situations in which one or more individuals harass or threaten another individual who is less capable of defending himself or herself, using the Internet or other forms of digital technology. Cyberbullying can include sending threatening e-mail or text messages or assuming someone else's online identity for the purpose of humiliating or misrepresenting him or her.

cybercrime Crime carried out by means of the Internet.

cybergang A group of computer users obsessed with gaining entry into highly secure computer systems.

cyberlaw A new legal field designed to track developments in cybercrime and combat occurrences of such abuses.

cyberspace The reference to the intangible, nonphysical territory that the Internet encompasses.

cyberstalker A person engaging in a form of harassment in which an individual uses the Internet, social networking sites, e-mail, or other electronic communications to repeatedly harass or threaten and disrupt a victim's real life.

cyberstalking A form of harassment in which an individual uses the Internet, social networking sites, e-mail, or other electronic communications to repeatedly harass or threaten a person. Cyberstalking, like real-world stalking, is a repeated, unwanted, and disruptive break into the life-world of the victim.

D

dashboard An executive information system with a user interface, similar to an automobile's dashboard, that highlights important information through the use of graphics and gauges, providing decision makers with the input necessary to "drive" the business and make effective up-to-the-minute decisions.

data Raw facts, which can be made up of words, numbers, images, sounds, or a combination of these. The data from the input phase of the information processing cycle is passed to the processing phase.

database A collection of related data that is organized in a manner that makes the data easy to access, manage, update, group, and summarize.

database management system (DBMS) A database program that can join or connect several files or tables to manage, access, store, and edit data in a structured manner.

database program A software application that is used to create databases or to work with the data in existing databases.

database server software Software that runs on a network and responds to information requests from remote users.

data bus A set of parallel wires that acts as an electronic highway on which data travels between computer components. It is the medium by which the entire system communicates with the CPU.

data dependency A microprocessor performance problem in which the CPU is slowed in its functioning by the need to wait for the results of one set of instructions before moving on to process another set of instructions.

data dictionary A list of the tables the database contains along with details concerning each table, including field names, field lengths, data types, and validation settings.

data diddling A computer crime in which data is modified in accounts or databases to conceal theft or embezzlement.

data file (table) A collection of related records; also called a table.

data flow diagram (DFD) A diagram that uses a set of graphical symbols to show how data moves through the existing system.

data independence The separation of data in a database from an application so that changes in data do not require changes in the structure of forms, reports, or programs accessing the database.

data integrity The validity of the data contained in a database.

data maintenance Procedures for adding, updating, and deleting records for the purpose of keeping the database in optimal shape.

data mart A smaller-scale data warehouse project that supports one division rather than the entire organization.

data mining A data exploration and analysis technique that uncovers information through statistical analysis and modeling in an attempt to discover previously unknown patterns.

data redundancy Repetition of data characteristic of poorly designed systems, which can cause peculiar query and report results.

data security Ensures that the data stored in a database is not accessible to people who might misuse it, particularly when the collected data is sensitive.

data set The contents of a table in Access.

data transfer rate 1. In secondary storage devices, the maximum number of bits per second that can be sent from the hard disk to the computer. The rate is determined by the drive interface. 2. The speed, expressed in bits per second (bps), at which a modem can transfer, or is transferring, data over a telephone line.

data type In a computerized database, a data type is defined by the overall purpose of the database coupled with the specific data being entered.

data validation Procedures that define acceptable input ranges for each field in a record.

data warehouse A central location capable of storing all the information that a corporation possesses and making this data available for analysis.

dead link (broken link) On the World Wide Web, a hyperlink that refers to a resource (such as a sound or a Web page) that has been moved or deleted; also called a broken link.

debugging In programming, the process of finding and correcting errors, or bugs, in the source code of a computer program.

decision support system (DSS) A computer-based system that addresses the deficiencies of management information systems (MIS) by enabling managers to retrieve information that cannot be supplied by fixed, predefined MIS reports.

default In a computer program, the settings that are in effect unless a user deliberately overrides them.

default value An automatic entry placed into a field when no other value is provided.

deliverable An outcome or tangible output such as a report or another document.

denial of service attack (DoS) A form of network vandalism that attempts to make a service unavailable to other users, generally by flooding the service with meaningless data.

design template A professionally created slide design that can be applied to a presentation and provides coordinated background color, font type, and bullet style.

desktop The screen image that appears after an operating system finishes loading into memory (RAM) and displays pictures (icons) representing files, folders, and windows in the file system. The desktop image can change with the operating system and version, or can be customized by the user.

desktop computer A computer that consists of a system unit, an independent monitor, and a keyboard designed for an individual's use at a desk or fixed location.

details pane Displayed along the bottom of the right pane of a Windows Explorer window. It provides a thumbnail view and information about the selected file or folder; the details vary depending on the object that has been selected.

device driver A program written in assembly language that controls a device attached to a computer.

digital camera A camera that uses digital technology, instead of film, to take and store images in digital format and can input those images directly into your system through a USB or FireWire port.

digital cash system A method for using smart cards and prepaid amounts of electronically stored money to pay for small charges such as parking and tolls.

digital certificate A form of digital identification enabled by public key encryption that serves as a method of validating a user, server, or Web site. For a user, a digital certificate validates identity in a manner similar to showing a driver's license. For a server or Web site, a digital certificate validates that a Web server or Web site is authentic so that the user can feel secure in his or her interaction.

digital divide The age, race, and/or income disparity in computer ownership and Internet access.

digital piracy The unauthorized reproduction and distribution of computer-based media.

digital signal A signal used by digital equipment, like computers, sent via discontinuous pulses, in which the presence or absence of electronic pulses is represented by 1s and 0s.

digital signature A technique enabled by public key encryption that is used to guarantee that a message is authentic, not sent by a hacker, and has not been tampered with.

digital telephony Telephone systems using all-digital protocols and transmission, offering the advantage over analog telephony of noise-free transmission and high-quality audio.

digital video camera (camcorder) A camera that takes and stores videos in digital format, instead of analog, and can input those images directly into your system through a USB or FireWire port.

digital-to-analog converter (DAC) A microchip that contains the circuitry to convert a digital signal to analog.

digitization The transformation of data such as voice, text, graphics, audio, and video into digital form, thereby allowing various technologies to transmit computer data through telephone lines, cables, or air and space. Digitization also allows the data to be shared as files enabling convergence, something difficult to do with analog technologies.

direct broadcast satellite (DBS) A consumer satellite technology that uses an 18- or 21-inch reception dish to receive digital TV signals at microwave frequencies directly from geostationary satellites broadcast at a bandwidth of 12 Mbps. Increasingly, DBS operators offer Internet access as well as digital TV service, but at much lower bandwidth.

direct conversion (crash conversion or plunge) Stopping an old system and then starting the new system; sometimes called a crash conversion or plunge.

disaster recovery plan A written plan with detailed instructions specifying alternative computing facilities to be used for emergency processing until nonoperational computers can be repaired or replaced after a national disaster or national emergency.

disk cache A type of RAM, usually incorporated on the circuit board within the hard drive case, that stores some of the program instructions and data you are working with. When the CPU needs to get information, it looks in the disk cache first. If it doesn't find the information it needs, it retrieves the information from the hard disk.

disk cleanup utility A program that improves system performance and increases storage space by removing files that you no longer need.

disk defragmentation program A utility program used to reorganize data on the disk so that file pieces are reassembled as one chunk of disk space (decreasing disk search time); storage is made more efficient by clustering files into structures more efficiently searched; and the time needed to access files is decreased.

disk scanning program An error-checking program that can detect and resolve a number of physical and logical problems that may occur when your computer stores files on a disk.

distributed denial of service (DDoS) attack A computer attack on multiple systems by a hacker who bombards an Internet server with a huge number of requests so that the server becomes overloaded and unable to respond to requests from valid users.

distributed hypermedia system A network-based content development system in which individuals connected to the network can each make a small contribution by developing content related to their area of expertise. The Web is a distributed hypermedia system.

distributed structure A technology infrastructure where users are able to customize their technology tools to suit their individual needs and wants.

DLP projector (digital light-processing projector) An output device that projects a computer's display on a screen by projecting light into a chip made of millions of microscopic mirrors to produce a brilliant, sharp image.

document A file created with an application program, such as a word processing or spreadsheet program.

documentation 1. Tutorials, Read Me files, help files, and printed manuals that contain information the software manufacturer believes the user will find helpful. 2. The output of the fifth phase of the Program Development Life Cycle in which in-depth explanations of major program features, reference documentation of all program commands, and a thorough description of the error messages generated by the program are detailed.

domain name On the Internet, a readable computer address, **http://www.microsoft.com**, that gets translated into an IP address and identifies a computer on the network.

domain name registration On the Internet, a process by which individuals and companies can obtain a domain name (such as **www.c34.org**) and link this name to a specific Internet address (IP address).

Domain Name System (DNS) A system used by the Internet to link domain names with their numeric IP address. It functions like a telephone directory for the Internet.

dot-matrix printer (impact printer) Once the most popular type of printer, the dot-matrix printer creates characters by striking pins against an ink ribbon. Each pin makes a dot, and combinations of dots form characters and illustrations.

dot pitch (aperture grill) The distance between the dots (pixels) on a CRT monitor. The lower the dot pitch, the closer the dots are to each other and the sharper the image.

downloading The process of transferring a file from another computer to your computer by means of a computer network.

drill down A technique that enables managers to view information in a data warehouse and focus their attention on a specific data element by starting at the summary level of information and narrowing their search at each progressive level of data.

drive A storage device in which files and folders reside. Drives can be internal (located within the system unit, such as a hard drive) or external (attached to the system unit via a port).

drive activity light The light on the front panel of most computers that signals when the hard drive is accessing data.

drive bay A receptacle or opening into which a hard disk drive, CD or DVD drive, or portable drive can be installed. An internal bay is within the system unit and an external bay is accessed from outside the system unit.

drive imaging software Software that creates a mirror image of the entire hard disk, including the operating system and applications, as well as all files and data. In the event of a hard disk or computer system failure, the drive image can be used to restore the system.

drive letter A letter of the alphabet followed by a colon and a backslash character that identifies the storage devices active on a system.

driver A utility program that contains instructions to make a peripheral device addressable or usable by an operating system.

DSL (digital subscriber line or xDSL) A general term for several technologies that enable high-speed Internet access through twisted-pair telephone lines. Also called xDSL.

DSL modem Similar to a traditional telephone modem in that it modulates and demodulates analog and digital signals for transmission over communications channels, but it does so using signaling methods based on broadband technology for much higher transfer speeds.

dual inline memory module (DIMM) A RAM memory module that fits into special slots on the motherboard that has a 168-pin connector and a 64-bit data transfer rate.

dumpster diving A technique to obtain passwords in which intruders go through an organization's trash hoping to find documents that contain lists of user IDs and passwords.

DVD drive A read-only storage device that reads the data encoded on a DVD-ROM disc and transfers this data to a computer.

DVD+R A recordable format that enables the disc to be written to one time and read many times.

DVD+RW A recordable format that enables the disc to be rewritten to many times.

DVD-R Digital video disc, a recordable optical storage medium that, like CD-R discs, cannot be erased or written over once data has been saved; the disk can be written to only once but read from many times.

DVD-ROM (digital video [or versatile] disc read-only memory) A digital video optical disc format capable of storing up to 17 GB on a single disc, enough for a feature-length movie.

DVD-RW Digital video disc, a recordable optical storage medium on which you can write, erase, and read from many times.

DVI (digital visual interface) port An interface that allows LCD monitors to use digital signals instead of analog signals.

dye sublimation printer A type of thermal-wax transfer printer that uses a heat process to transfer an impression onto paper. Although thermal-transfer printers are the best color printers currently available, they are slow and very expensive.

dynamic A term used to describe Windows Explorer searches that are automatically updated every time you open up a saved search. New files that meet the search criteria are added and ones that no longer meet the criteria are removed.

E

EBCDIC (Extended Binary Coded Decimal Interchange Code) An eight-bit character code used by IBM mainframe computers and some midrange systems that uses a low-to-high code sequence for punctuation, lowercase letters, uppercase letters, and then numbers.

e-book Short for electronic book. A book-sized device that displays e-books. E-book readers may be devices that are built solely for reading e-books or they may be PDAs, handheld devices, or other computing devices that have a processor and display screen. The newest e-book readers are available in a larger size, increasing the ease of reading. Some even boast an auto-rotating screen with a text-to-speech mode.

e-book reader A dedicated reading device dedicated to downloading, displaying, and reading books obtained through an e-bookstore (an electronic book store accessed via the Internet).

e-business (electronic business) Use of the Internet to buy, sell, provide customer service, and collaborate with business partners.

ECMAScript A vendor-neutral standard created by the European Computer Manufacturers Association (ECMA) for what was originally Netscape's JavaScript. It is a client-side scripting language for Web publishing.

e-commerce (electronic commerce) The use of networks or the Internet to carry out business of any type.

economic feasibility The capability of a project being accomplished with available financial resources.

e-discovery (electronic discovery) The obligation of parties to a lawsuit to exchange documents that exist only in electronic form, including e-mails, voicemails, instant messages, e-calendars, audio files, data on handheld devices, graphics, photographs, spreadsheets, Web sites, drawings, and other types of digital data.

EEPROM Electrically erasable programmable read-only memory that can be rewritten many times while the chip is in the computer. EEPROM is erased one byte at a time, using an electric field instead of a UV light source, eliminating the need for an erasing window.

e-learning The use of computers and computer programs to replace teachers and the time–place specificity of learning.

electrical engineering (EE) An engineering discipline that has a strong focus on digital circuit design as well as cutting-edge communication technologies.

electronic data interchange (EDI) A set of standards that specifies how to transfer data and documents between enterprises using the Internet and other networks without human intervention.

electronic mailing list Lists of e-mail addresses that automatically broadcast messages to all individuals on the list.

Because the messages are transmitted as e-mail, only individuals who are subscribers to the mailing list receive and view the messages.

element In HTML, a distinctive component of a document's structure, such as a title, heading, or list. HTML divides elements into two categories: head elements (such as the document's title) and body elements (headings, paragraphs, links, and text).

e-mail (electronic mail) An Internet service requiring a software application that enables you to send and receive messages though the use of computer networks.

e-mail address A series of characters that provides a unique cyberspace identity for a particular recipient that follows the form myname@somedomain.com and precisely identifies the location of a person's electronic mailbox. On the Internet, e-mail addresses consist of a mailbox name (such as jsmith) followed by an "at" sign (@) and the computer's domain name (as in jsmith@fictitiousschool.edu).

e-mail attachment Any type of computer file—document, photo, audio, or video—that is included with an e-mail message.

embedded operating system Operating systems that are found on ROM chips in the portable or dedicated devices that we use today. They are usually compact and efficient. Embedded operating systems go without some of the features found in nonembedded operating systems.

embedded processor A processor designed and programmed to perform only the tasks intended to be done by the device the processor is implanted within.

emergency disk A storage device, like a USB drive, CD, DVD, or network device that, in case of an emergency or boot failure, can load a reduced version of the operating system that can be used for troubleshooting purposes; also called a boot disk.

employee monitoring When large employers routinely engage in observing employees' phone calls, e-mails, Web browsing habits, and computer files.

encryption A coding or scrambling process that renders a message unreadable by anyone except the intended recipient.

encryption key A formula that is used to make a plaintext message unreadable.

enhanced keyboard A keyboard containing additional keys, usually positioned above the row of function keys, that consist of media control buttons that adjust speaker volume and access the optical disc drive, and Internet controls that open e-mail, a browser, or a search window, with a single keystroke.

enterprise A business or organization, which can include universities, government agencies, and not-for-profit groups or charities.

enterprise application integration (EAI) A combination of processes, software, standards, and hardware that results in the integration of two or more

enterprise systems, thus enabling multiple systems to operate as one and share data and business processes throughout an organization.

enterprise computing Information technology on a large scale, encompassing all aspects of technology and information resources, including problems or malfunctions, within an organization or a business. It also includes understanding the use of computers in the networks that span the organization as well as the software needed to processes and monitor activities involved in daily business operations.

enterprise data The centralized data shared throughout an organization

enterprise data center A secure common repository for enterprise data.

enterprise networking The technology infrastructure within an enterprise.

enterprise resource planning (ERP) software Software that brings together various enterprise functions, such as manufacturing, sales, marketing, and finance, into a single computer system.

enterprise server Powerful servers that are part of a networked system designed to connect hundreds of thousands of users at the same time. They are usually used in large corporations or government agencies, handle a high volume of data, can fill an entire wall of an average room, and cost from several thousand to millions of dollars.

enterprise software Software designed to solve problems at the enterprise level of an organization rather that at the departmental level.

enterprise system An information system that integrates an organization's information and applications across all of the organization's functional divisions.

entity-relationship diagram (ERD) A graphic that shows all of the organizations, departments, users, programs, and data that play a role in the system as well as the relationships among those entities.

EPROM Electrically programmable read-only memory is erasable PROM that can be reused many times. Erasure is accomplished using a UV (ultraviolet) light source that shines through a quartz erasing window in the EPROM package. It is used primarily by programmers in the program development process so that errors can be corrected.

ergonomics The field of study that is concerned with the fit between people, their equipment, and their work. It takes into account worker limitations and capabilities in attempting to ensure that the tasks, equipment, and overall environment suit each worker.

e-tailer A Web-based retailer.

Ethernet The most popular LAN standard for large and small businesses. According to International Data Corporation (IDC), approximately 85 percent of all installed networks use various versions of Ethernet.

ethical hacker (white hat) Hackers and crackers who have turned pro, offering their services to companies hoping to use hacker expertise to shore up their computer systems' defenses; also called a white hat.

ethical principle The standards that promote trust, fairness, good behavior, and kindness and are used to justify an act as morally right or morally wrong.

event-driven programming language A program design method in which the programming code is not written to execute in any specific sequence. Instead, it executes in response to user actions such as the clicking of the mouse.

evil twin A phony WiFi hot spot whose name makes users believe it is a legitimate spot. Typically situated in hotels and airports, an evil twin is usually connected to a fraudulent network.

e-waste Obsolete computer equipment.

exabyte A unit of measurement approximately equal to1 quintillion bytes.

exception report A report that alerts managers to unexpected developments (such as high demand for a new product).

exclusion operator In database and Internet searching, a symbol or a word that tells the software to exclude records or documents containing a certain word or phrase. It is usually denoted as a minus sign (–) in the search statement.

executable program A program that is ready to run and does not need to be altered in any way.

execution cycle (execute, store) In a machine cycle, a phase consisting of the execute and write-back (or store) operations.

executive information system (EIS, or executive support system [ESS]) A system that supports management's strategic-planning function; also known as an executive support system (ESS).

exiting Quitting or closing down an application or program.

expansion card (expansion board, adapter card, or adapter) A circuit board that fits into slots on the motherboard and is used to connect computers with various peripherals.

expansion slot Receptacles, usually located on the motherboard, that accept additional circuit boards or expansion cards.

expert system An information system that deals with detailed and in-depth knowledge in a specific area supplied by experts in that field and formulates a decision in the way that a human expert in the field might.

ExpressCard Also referred to as a PC card, a device approximately the size of a credit card that is usually used with notebook computers and that can be inserted or removed from PC card slots while the computer is running. ExpressCards can serve as modems, network adapters, or additional memory.

Extended ASCII A character coding system that uses eight bits and allows representation of 256 characters.

Extended Graphics Array (XGA) The resolution standard for most of today's monitors (1024 × 768).

Extensible Business Reporting Language (XBRL) A language used by businesses to publish and share financial information with each other and industry analysts across all computer platforms and the Internet.

Extensible Hypertext Markup Language (XHTML) A language that combines the flexibility of HTML with the extensibility of XML by allowing the user to define a tag for clarity across different browsers or create a new markup tag by simply defining it in an XHTML module and using it in a Web page as you would any other HTML tag. This feature makes a page truly compatible with all browsers.

Extensible Markup Language (XML) A language designed to reduce the complexity of HTML.

extension The second part of a file name added after the dot. It is supplied by an application to indicate that the file was created by that application and thus should be reopened with it.

extranets A network connected over the Internet in such a way that data traverses the Internet in encrypted form, safe from prying eyes.

F

Facebook Currently, the largest social networking site, allowing anyone over the age of 13, with a valid e-mail account and residing in a country where it has not been banned, to become a user. Facebook users often join groups set up by region, job, interest, or school and communicate with group members.

facsimile transmission (fax) The sending and receiving of printed pages between two locations using a telephone line and fax devices that digitize the page's image.

fair use An exception to copyright laws that justifies limited uses of copyrighted material without payment to or permission from the copyright holder. This exception limits the selection to no more than 5 percent of the original copyrighted work and only for the purposes of commentary, parody, news reporting, research, and education.

fat client A device that enables a user to connect to a network server but does most data processing in its own system, not on the server.

fault tolerance The ability of a device to keep working even if one or more components fail.

fax modem A modem that also functions as a fax machine, but unlike a traditional stand-alone fax machine, does everything in a digital way, providing the computer user with the capability of sending word-processing documents and other files as faxes.

fiber-optic cable A broadband transmission medium that consists of thin strands of glass or plastic that carry data by means of pulses of light. Fiber-optic cable carries data at transfer rates of 10 Gbps (gigabits per second) or more, without loss of signal strength and for longer distances than twisted-pair or coaxial cable.

fiber-optic service Fiber-optic lines that run directly to the home and provide users with incredibly fast Internet access, easily surpassing other methods.

field A single unit of relative information in a database. Each field has a specific, defined data type.

field name A descriptive label that helps to identify the type of content to be entered into a field.

file A named unit of related data stored in a computer system.

file compression utility A program that can reduce the size of a file by as much as 80 percent without harming the data, by substituting short codes for lengthy data patterns. The resulting smaller files can be shared more efficiently, particularly over the Internet. Prior to use, compressed files need to be decompressed and converted back to their lengthy form.

file infector A computer virus that attaches to a program file and, when that program is executed, spreads to other program files.

file management program A program that enables users to create, edit, and manage databases in which files or tables are independent of each other, with no link between the data stored in each.

file manager A program that helps you to organize and manage the data stored on your disk.

file name The name that the storage device uses to identify each unique file.

file server In client/server computing, a high-capacity, high-speed computer with a large hard disk set aside (dedicated) to make program and data files available to users on a network.

File Transfer Protocol (FTP) An Internet standard for the exchange of files between two computers connected to the Internet that is especially useful when the files are too large to send by e-mail. Although you can use special FTP client software, such as WS_FTP Home, you can also transfer files to and from an FTP server simply by using your browser or Windows Explorer.

filter In Microsoft Access, a simplified method of locating records that match criteria specified by the user.

firewall A program or device that permits an organization's internal computer users to access the Internet but places severe limits on the ability of outsiders to access internal data.

FireWire (1394 port) FireWire is Apple Computer's name for a 1394 input/output port, an interface that offers high-speed connections for peripherals. It is ideal for real-time devices like digital video cameras.

flame Messages sent through e-mail, chat rooms, instant messaging, and message boards that express an opinion without holding back any emotion and are frequently seen as being confrontational and argumentative.

flash drive A type of storage device that uses solid-state circuitry and has no moving parts, making it a solid-state drive. It retains the data stored in it even if disconnected from its source.

flash EPROM A type of PROM similar to EEPROM except that flash EPROMs are erased in blocks, whereas regular EEPROMs can be erased one byte at a time.

flash memory Nonvolatile memory found on flash drives and memory cards that can be electronically erased and reprogrammed.

flash memory card A wafer-thin, highly portable solid-state storage system that is capable of storing as much as 64 GB of data. Flash memory cards are used with smartphones, MP3 players, digital video cameras, and other portable digital devices.

flash memory reader A slot or compartment into which the flash memory card is inserted.

flat file The type of file generated by a file management program. Often called lists, they are independent structures having no relation between the fields in one flat file and another.

flexible OLED display (FOLED display) An extremely thin, flexible, and lightweight output display that produces outstanding color, contrast, brightness, and viewing angles. OLED displays are emissive devices, meaning they emit light rather than modulate transmitted or reflected light.

floating point standard A notation standard, created by the Institute of Electrical and Electronics Engineers (IEEE) and used to represent numbers with fractional parts. There is no fixed number of digits before or after the decimal point, so the computer can work with very large and very small numbers.

flowchart In structured programming, a diagram that shows the logic of a program.

folder (directory) An organizational tool for grouping files that have something in common.

folder structure (directory structure) An organized set of folders in which to save your files.

footprint The amount of physical space used by a device.

foreground application From the user's perspective, the application that is active (in use), as indicated by its appearance as the topmost image seen on the desktop, when more than one application is running.

foreign key A field that is a primary key in another file.

forgery The making of Internet data appear to come from one place when it's really coming from another.

form In the Microsoft Access database management system, a template used to enter data into the database in place of the Table entry method.

form factor The specifications for mounting internal components such as the motherboard into the system unit.

formula A combination of numeric constants, cell references, arithmetic operators, and functions that are used to calculate a result.

Fortran Short for formula translator. An early third-generation language that enabled scientists and engineers to write simple programs for solving complex mathematical equations in an easy-to-use environment.

fragmented A disk that has been used to the point that it becomes a patchwork of files, with portions of files scattered here and there. This placement of sectors slows disk access because the system must look in several locations to find all of a file's segments.

frame In a video or animation, single still images that are flashed on-screen at a rapid rate.

frame rate In a video or animation, a measurement of the number of still images shown per second.

freeware Copyrighted software that can be freely copied but not sold for profit.

full backup The duplicating of all files and data on the entire hard disk as a precaution should the hard disk drive fail.

function In spreadsheet programs such as Microsoft Excel, one of the two basic types of formulas (along with mathematical expressions). A function begins with an equal sign but is then followed by a descriptive name that is predefined in the software (such as SUM to calculate the total of a set of values) and an argument set, which is placed within parentheses and designates the locations of the values that the function needs to utilize in its calculations.

function key A row of keys positioned along the top of the keyboard, labeled F1 through F12. The action performed by each key varies with the program in use.

functional division (functional area, functional unit) Parts of an organization that handle each of the organization's core functions, for example, accounting and finance, marketing and sales, human resources, and management.

functional language A language that reflects the way people think mathematically. It is useful in mathematical programs or programs that can express findings in mathematical form.

G

gadget An application that appears as an active icon in the Windows sidebar.

Gadgets are selected or downloaded by the user and display photos and current weather conditions, control a multimedia player, or monitor the CPU's performance.

Gantt chart A type of bar chart that facilitates project management by indicating task due dates and project milestones.

General Public License (GPL) A free software license, devised by the Open Software Foundation (OSF), stipulating that anyone may freely copy, use, and modify the software. The modifications must be made available for all users, but no one can sell the software for profit.

general-purpose application A software program used by many people to accomplish frequently performed tasks such as writing (word processing), working with numbers (spreadsheets), and keeping track of information (databases).

gigabits per second (Gbps) A data transfer measurement equivalent to 1 billion bits per second.

gigabyte (GB) A unit of measurement approximately equal to 1 billion bits.

gigahertz (GHz) A unit used to measure a processor's speed in billions of cycles per second.

gigaPOP (gigabits per second point of presence) A point of presence (POP) that provides access to a backbone service capable of data transfer rates exceeding 1 Gbps (1 billion bits per second).

globalization Conducting business internationally or the process of making this happen.

globally unique identifier (GUID) An identification number that is generated by a hardware component or a program. The GUIDs can be read by Web servers or embedded in various documents, detecting which computer is accessing a site and inadvertently making it more difficult to use the Internet anonymously.

Google Docs A free Web-based service that allows project members to share and edit documents and spreadsheets online.

Google Groups A free service provided by Google to help users connect, share information, and communicate effectively over the Internet. Its current version allows group members to collaborate on shared Web pages; set group pictures, colors, and styles; upload and share individually created work; and learn more about other members in the group.

GPS (Global Positioning System) A satellite-based system consisting of a cluster of 27 Earth-orbiting satellites that enables portable GPS receivers to determine their location with an accuracy of 109 yards or less.

graphical MUD (gMUD) A multiuser dungeon (MUD) that uses 3D graphics instead of text to represent the interaction of characters and bring the virtual environment to life.

graphical user interface (GUI) The most popular method of interacting with a

computer system. It uses graphics and the point-and-click technology of the mouse to make the operating system and programs easier to use.

grid A combination of several computers or virtual machines that are connected over a network to make them appear and function as one single computer.

grid computing Applying the abilities of many computers in a network to a single problem at the same time. This amount of concentrated power is usually directed at scientific or technical problems that require a high level of processing power and access to large amounts of data.

grounding bracelet A device that is worn around the wrist with the other end attached to a grounded object. It is worn to avoid discharging static electricity into a system under repair.

grounding strap See grounding bracelet.

group In Microsoft Office, a collection of buttons and commands that appear on tabs within the Ribbon.

groupware (teamware) Software that provides computerized support for the information needs of workgroups. Most groupware applications include e-mail, videoconferencing tools, group-scheduling systems, customizable electronic forms, real-time shared applications, and shared information databases. Also called teamware.

H

hacker Traditionally a computer hobbyist who enjoys pushing his or her computer capabilities to the limit, especially by using clever or novel approaches to solving problems.

hacker ethic An unwritten code of conduct subscribed to by hackers that forbids the destruction of data.

handheld computer A computer designed for individual use and portability, it usually fits in the palm of your hand or pocket of your jeans and makes use of a stylus or virtual keyboard.

hard business skill A process-related skill. In the IT world, this type of skill refers to the knowledge and technological expertise in such areas as networking, Web development, knowledge of UNIX and C++, and firewall administration.

hard copy Output viewed in printed form.

hard disk controller An electronic circuit board that provides an interface between the CPU and the hard disk's electronics. The controller may be located on the computer's motherboard, on an expansion card, or within the hard disk.

hard disk drive (hard drive) A secondary storage, random access, high-capacity, high-speed device, usually housed in the system unit, that consists of several rapidly rotating disks called platters on which programs, data, and processed results are stored. In almost all modern computers, the hard disk is by far the easiest storage device to access and the most important storage medium.

hardware All the physical components that make up a computer system, including such items as circuit boards, disk drives, printers, and monitors.

Hardware-as-a-Service (HaaS) See Infrastructure-as-a-Service (IaaS).

HDSL (high bit-rate digital subscriber line) The most mature DSL technology, it is a form of SDSL that provides T1 connections over two or three twisted-pair copper lines. Unlike most other forms of DSL, HDSL is not a typical consumer service.

headset (head-mounted display) A wearable output device with twin LCD panels for creating the illusion that an individual is experiencing a three-dimensional, simulated environment.

heat sink A heat-dissipating component that drains heat from a chip. Heat sinks are usually used in combination with cooling fans.

hexadecimal (hex) number A number system, referred to as base-16, that uses the numbers 0 through 9 and the letters A through F to represent a binary string in a shorter, more compact form.

Hibernate mode Used primarily in notebooks to conserve battery life, this mode puts the documents and programs you have opened on your hard disk and then actually turns off your computer. When you restart your system, it is returned to the state prior to hibernation. All windows and programs that were open are restored automatically.

high-definition television (HDTV) A digital television standard found in such televisions as direct-view, plasma, rear screen, and front screen projection that have higher resolutions, typically (1920 × 1080) or better. HDTVs provide extremely high-quality video and audio, enabling the use of your HDTV as a computer monitor.

high-level language A programming language that eliminates the need for programmers to understand the intimate details of how the hardware, specifically the microprocessor, handles data.

History list In a Web browser, a window or list that shows all the Web sites that the browser has accessed during a given period, such as the last 30 days.

holographic storage A type of storage that uses two laser beams to create a pattern on photosensitive media, resulting in a three-dimensional image similar to the holograms you can buy in a novelty shop. This 3D approach will enable much higher-density storage capacities and is being promoted for its archiving capabilities.

home and educational program A general-purpose software program for personal finance, home design and landscaping, encyclopedias and other computerized reference information, and games.

home network (home area network or HAN) A personal and specific use of network technology that provides connectivity among users and devices located in or near one residence.

home page (index page) The start page that is automatically displayed when you enter a Web site through its top level; also called an index page.

honeypot A computer baited with fake data and purposely left vulnerable so as to study how intruders operate in order to prepare stronger defenses to thwart attacks.

host A networked computer that has two-way access to other computers; it can receive requests and reply to those requests.

host name The name of the group or institution operating a Web site. It is the first part of the domain portion of a URL. In the URL **www.microsoft.com/ windows/default.aspx** the host portion is Microsoft.

hot site A disaster recovery site that is kept in a state of readiness at all times. For this reason, it is very expensive.

hot spot Usually a public location like an airport, college campus, or coffee shop that provides Internet access for devices fitted with wireless technology.

hot swapping Connecting and disconnecting peripheral devices while your computer is running.

HTML (Hypertext Markup Language) A markup language used for marking Web pages. It divides elements (or tags) into two categories: head elements (such as the documents title) and body elements (headings, paragraphs, links, and text). The agency responsible for standardizing HTML is the World Wide Web Consortium (W3C).

hub A simple, inexpensive broadcast device that joins multiple computers together in a single network but does not manage the traffic between the connections, which usually results in frequent collisions. It is used as the central wiring mechanism in a star topology network layout

hybrid cloud The combination of two or more clouds (private, community, or public) that are unique but are connected by common, standard technology that enables the sharing of applications and data. Its infrastructure can be located both on-site and off the premises, and it can be managed by both the organization and a cloud provider. Users can be trusted and untrusted.

hybrid hard drive (HHD) A hard drive that incorporates flash technology in its design to speed up the boot process.

hybrid network A network that is a combination of both wired and wireless technology.

Hybrid sleep This mode, a combination of Sleep and Hibernate mode, puts open documents and programs in both RAM and on your hard disk, and then places the system in a low-power state so you can quickly resume your work. If power is suddenly terminated, the Hibernate portion of this mode guarantees that your work can be restored. Hybrid sleep is usually turned on by default on most desktops.

hyperlink (link) In a hypertext system, an element in an electronic document that acts as the connector to another place in the same document or to an entirely different document. Typically, you click on the hyperlink to get to the related object. Hyperlinks are the most essential ingredient of the World Wide Web.

hyptertext A system in which objects (text, pictures, music, programs, and so on) can be creatively linked to each other.

Hypertext Markup Language (HTML) A language that uses a tag system of code to create Web pages. This language is interpreted by browsers, which display the page according to the directions specified by the HTML language. HTML includes capabilities that enable authors to insert hyperlinks, which, when clicked, display another HTML document. The agency responsible for standardizing HTML is the World Wide Web Consortium (W3C).

Hypertext Transfer Protocol (HTTP) The Internet standard that supports the exchange of information on the Web by the use of uniform resource locators (URLs).

icon A small image that represents a computer resource (such as a program, data file, or network connection).

identity theft A form of fraud in which a thief obtains someone's personal information and then uses this information to impersonate the owner and fraudulently obtain and use the owner's credit.

image editor A sophisticated version of a paint program that is used to edit and transform—but not create—complex bitmapped images, such as photographs. Free programs like Picasa and GIMP, designed for personal and home use, incorporate automated image-processing algorithms to add a variety of special effects, remove blemishes, crop portions, and adjust coloring to photographic images.

inclusion operator In database or Web searching, a symbol or keyword that instructs the search software to make sure that any retrieved records or documents contain a certain word or phrase; it usually is a plus sign (+) in the search statement.

incremental backup Backing up only those files that have been created or changed since the last backup occurred.

information Data that has been converted into a meaningful form.

information hiding (encapsulation) A modular programming approach that refers to the ability of a programmer to write the code of one module without knowing or having to be concerned with the details of another module.

information kiosk An automated presentation system used for public information or employee training.

information overload A feeling of anxiety and incapacity experienced when people are presented with more information than they can handle.

information processing cycle A sequence of four operations: input, processing, output, and storage. These operations receive data, process it into information, allow it to be outputted for viewing, and save it for future use.

information system A purposefully designed system that includes the collection of people, hardware, software, data records, and activities that process the data and information in an organization.

information systems (IS) department The functional area within companies or universities responsible for managing information technology and systems.

information technology (IT) professional An individual who works with information technology in all its various forms (hardware, software, networks) and functions (management, development, maintenance).

information technology steering committee An organizational group, generally including representatives from senior management, information systems personnel, users, and middle managers, that reviews new project requests and decides which ones to address.

information warfare A military-like strategy that makes use of information technologies to corrupt or destroy an enemy's information and industrial infrastructure.

infrared A wireless data transmission medium, used in TV remote controls, that carries data via beams of light through the air. Transmitting and receiving devices must be in line of sight or the signal is lost.

Infrastructure-as-a-Service (IaaS) The category of cloud services that refers to the outsourcing of hardware, the equipment used to sustain the operations of a company or enterprise; also known as Hardware-as-a-Service (HaaS).

inheritance In object-oriented programming (OOP), the capacity of an object to pass its characteristics to a subclass or child.

inkjet printer A nonimpact printer, popular for home use, which sprays ionized ink from a series of small jets onto a sheet of paper, creating the desired character shapes. A typical inkjet printer provides a resolution of 300 dots per inch.

input The action of receiving data (raw facts) like a user's login ID number.

input device A hardware component that enables a user to enter data into a computer for processing. The most common input devices are the keyboard and mouse, but other devices include microphones, scanners, digital cameras, and camcorders.

input/output (I/O) bus An electrical pathway that connects the microprocessor to input and output devices via expansion slots.

installing To load and set up a program so that it is ready to function on a given computer system. The installation process may involve creating additional directories, making changes to system files, and other technical tasks. For this reason, most programs come with setup programs that handle the installation process automatically.

instant messaging (IM) A free, real-time method of interaction between computers that enables two or more parties to connect through the use of a buddy list that identifies and restricts the users a person wishes to communicate with.

instruction cycle (fetch, decode) In a machine cycle, a phase consisting of the fetch (retrieve) and decode (determine the action required) operations.

instruction set A list of instructions specific to a given brand and model of processor.

intangible benefit A benefit that is difficult or impossible to measure, such as improved employee morale and customer satisfaction.

integrated circuit (IC or chip) A circuit that carries an electrical current and contains millions of transistors.

integrated development environment (IDE) The sharing of solutions and integration of development tools used for building graphical user interfaces, editors to facilitate inserting and changing of code, and debuggers that make possible the detection and correction of errors.

integrated peripheral A device embedded within the system unit case, generally the power supply, cooling fans, memory, CD drive, DVD drive, and internal hard drive.

integrated program A single program that manages an entire business or set of related tasks. It combines the most commonly used functions of many productivity software programs, like word processing, database management, spreadsheet, accounting, and customer service into one application.

intelligent keyboard An onscreen keyboard to which software has been added that provides the user with such features as suggestions for misspelled words and grammar mistakes; magnification of the on-screen text being entered or modified; displaying an enlarged image of each key on the screen, providing visual confirmation of the keystroke; and allowing such features as cut, copy, and paste with the touch of the screen.

interface In programming, the means of exchanging messages between objects.

internal speaker One of the components inside a computer's system unit, typically useful for emitting beeps and other low-fidelity sounds.

internationalization (glocalization) The combination of globalization and localization. This means that a McDonald's in Singapore is almost the same as a McDonald's in Chicago except for some twists or changes to mesh with cultural differences.

Internet (Net) Thousands of privately and publicly owned computers and networks that grew and interlinked, over time, into one giant network. In short, the Internet is a network of networks.

Internet access provider Companies or businesses that provide access to the Internet free, for a fixed monthly charge, or an itemized per-use fee.

Internet address (IP address) A unique, 32-bit address assigned to every computer that is connected to the Internet. It is represented in four parts, which are separated by periods (such as 128.254.108.7).

Internet backbone The main high-speed routes for Internet data travel.

Internet hard drive Refers to storage space that a computer user pays a subscription fee to access on a remote server via the Internet for a specific period of time; also called remote storage.

Internet Protocol (IP) The lower layer of the TCP/IP suite of protocols that handles the address part of each packet so that it gets to the right recipient.

Internet Protocol address (IP address) A numerical identification and logical address that is assigned to devices participating in a computer network. The IP address consists of four groups of numbers, separated by periods. The value in each group ranges from 0 to 255. As an example, 64.12.245.203 is the IP address for the AOL Web site.

Internet relay chat (IRC) A real-time, Internet, text-based chat service, in which one can find "live" participants from the world over. Today it is mostly the province of specialized communities, such as gamers or programmers.

Internet service A set of standards (protocols) that define how two types of programs—a client, such as a Web browser that runs on the user's computer, and a server—can communicate with each other through the Internet. Examples of Internet services are e-mail, instant messaging, FTP, Usenet, IRC, and VoIP.

Internet service provider (ISP) A company that traditionally provided access to the Internet and no additional services. Today these providers have added features to make them a one-stop source for Internet services. There are both local and national ISPs, each having varied services and pricing, providing Internet access via telephone lines, cable, satellite, or fiber-optic technologies.

Internet telephony The use of the Internet (or of nonpublic networks based on Internet technology) for the transmission of real-time voice communication.

Internet TV The ability to view television shows, videos, and movies over the Internet, for no additional cost via download or streaming video. The benefit of this type of viewing over YouTube is that the content is provided by the original source, so copyright is not an issue; there is no limit on length; the user has a variety of selections from which to choose; and there is no time restriction on when the production needs to be watched.

interoperability The ability of the Internet to exchange data between computers regardless of the brand, model, or operating system the computers are running.

interpreter In programming, a translator program that converts one line of source code at a time into machine-readable code and executes the translated instruction. Interpreters are often used for learning and debugging.

interrupt A signal that informs the operating system that an event has occurred and is in need of immediate attention. For hardware, this can be the user pressing a key, the mouse moving to a new position, or a notice that a document is waiting to be printing.

interrupt handler (interrupt service routine) A miniprogram that immediately responds when an interrupt occurs; also called interrupt service routine

interrupt request (IRQ) The interrupting of an event by an interrupt signal.

interrupt vector table The location that holds the responses to multiple interrupts. The interrupts are processed by the operating system, starting with the ones in the table having the highest priority rating, to the one with the lowest.

intranet A password-protected network controlled by an enterprise and accessed only by employees or authorized users.

IP spoofing The sending of a message with an IP address disguised as an incoming message from a trusted source to a computer. It is an activity usually associated with hackers.

iPad A new, pad-sized portable handheld device for personal use that can download and read e-books, surf the Internet, play movies, view TV shows, make calls, instant/text message, take still photos or video, edit photos and videos, run off battery power for a full day, connect to a TV and play media, and sync its media with a computer.

iPhone OS An operating system developed by Apple for use in mobile devices, specifically the iPhone.

IrDA port A wireless communication device that uses infrared technology to transfer data from your PDA to your desktop or notebook computer or another PDA. The transmitting device must be in line of sight (usually within a few feet) of the port on the receiving device. IrDA ports offer data transfer rates of 4 Mbps.

ISDN (integrated services digital network) A standard for the delivery of digital telephone and data services to homes, schools, and offices using ordinary existing twisted-pair wiring, connections ranging from 56 to 128 Kbps (basic rate ISDN) or 1.5 Mbps (primary rate ISDN).

ISDN adapter (digital modem) An internal or external accessory that enables a computer to connect to remote computer networks or the Internet by means of ISDN lines. (Inaccurately called an ISDN modem.)

IT industry The industry that consists of organizations focused on the development and implementation of technology and applications.

J

Java A cross-platform programming language created by a consortium led by Sun Microsystems that enables programmers to write a program that will execute on any computer capable of running a Java interpreter. Java is an object-oriented programming (OOP) language similar to C++, except that it eliminates some features of C++ that programmers find tedious and time-consuming.

Java Virtual Machine (VM) A Java interpreter and runtime environment for Java applets and Java applications. This environment is called a virtual machine because, no matter what kind of computer it is running on, it creates a simulated computer that provides the correct platform for executing Java programs.

Javabeans Programming specifications created in Java that are used to create reusable, platform-independent Java components.

JavaScript Now known as ECMAScript. A client-side scripting language designed for writing scripts on Web pages.

joint application development (JAD) A program development method that uses a team approach and involves end users throughout the planning and development stages. The goal is to better design objects that suit end user needs.

joystick A pointing device used to move objects easily in any direction on-screen. It employs a vertical rod mounted on a base with one or two buttons. An input device commonly used for games.

JSON Short for JavaScript Object Notation, a text-based, human-readable technique for representing simple data structures and objects.

jukebox Enterprise storage units that use DVD and CD discs as the storage medium.

jump drive Another name for a USB flash drive.

K

kernel The central part of the operating system that controls the actions that the OS uses most frequently, for example starting applications and managing hardware devices and memory. When the system is booted (started) the computer copies the kernel along with other essential portions of the OS from the hard disk into the computer's RAM memory, where it remains the entire time the computer is powered on and functioning.

keyboard An input device that uses switches and circuits to translate keystrokes into a signal a computer can understand. It makes use of alphabetic, numeric, punctuation, function, arrow, and control keys.

key interception The act of stealing an encryption key.

keylogger Spyware that can record all the keystrokes you type—such as passwords, account numbers, or conversations—and relay them to others.

key matrix A grid of circuits located under the keys of a keypad. When a key is pressed, it completes a circuit on the matrix that provides the identity of the associated character to the system.

keypad A smaller and more compact keyboard, popular on smartphones, on which each key represents multiple letters. The user has to strike a key one to four times to get the desired character entered as input.

keyword Descriptive words matching the qualifications that an employer listed in a job posting. A potential employer will compare applicant skills with these keywords when reviewing resumes.

kilobits per second (Kbps) A data transfer rate of approximately a thousand bits of computer data per second.

kilobyte (KB) A unit of measurement for computer memory and disk capacity, equal to 1,024 bytes or characters.

Kindle 2 A portable reading device that allows the user to scroll though pages of a book, enlarge text size, purchase materials through an e-book store, and use the text-to-speech function.

Kindle DX The newest version of the Kindle portable reading device that boasts a larger display than the Kindle 2, better contrast, and a no-glare screen.

know-and-have authentication A type of computer security that requires using tokens, which are handheld electronic devices that generate a logon code.

knowledge base A database of knowledge designed to meet the complex storage and retrieval needs of computerized expert systems.

knowledge management system (KMS) A system that captures knowledge from books and experienced individuals and makes it available where it is needed.

L

label In Microsoft Excel, a text entry used to identify or group numeric entries.

labor dumping The flooding of a labor market with foreign workers.

land A flat reflective area on an optical disc that bounces the light back to a light-sensing device, corresponding to a 1 in the computer's binary number system.

laser printer A high-resolution nonimpact printer that uses an electrostatic reproductive technology similar to that used by copiers.

last-mile problem The problems associated with the inability of local area networks that support homes or businesses to access high bandwidth multimedia communications that can accommodate the information superhighway, along with the bottleneck of data on the last mile of twisted-pair phone lines connecting those homes and businesses.

last-mile technologies Digital telecommunications services and standards, such as coaxial cable and ISDN, that serve as interim solutions to the limitations associated with the twisted-pair analog phone wiring still common in many homes and businesses.

latency In a packet-switching network, the delay caused by the examining of a given packet by many routers.

launching Starting an application program.

LCD projector An output device that projects a computer's monitor display on a screen by passing light through three colored panels—red, green, and blue. LCD projectors produce sharp, accurate color images; however, they are subject to pixilation and low contrast.

leased line Sometimes called a dedicated line, leased lines are a connection set up by a telecommunication carrier and are usually a permanent fiber-optic or telephone connection that enables continuous, end-to-end communication between two points.

legacy technology Devices that were once used but are now viewed as obsolete.

Level 1 cache (primary cache) A unit of 4 KB to 16 KB of ultrafast memory included in the microprocessor chip that runs at approximately 10 nanoseconds (one-billionth of a second). This is the fastest memory and is used to store frequently accessed data and improve overall system performance.

Level 2 cache (secondary cache) A unit of up to 512 KB of ultrafast memory that can be located within the microprocessor, but further from the registers than Level 1 cache, or on a separate cache chip located on the motherboard very close to the microprocessor. It runs at 20 to 30 nanoseconds.

Level 3 cache A unit of memory found on some systems with newer microprocessors, like Intel's Xeon processor, that are embedded in some servers and workstations.It is located outside of the processor on a separate cache chip on the motherboard but positioned very close to the microprocessor.

libel The publication of a false statement, in written or faxed form, that injures someone's business or personal reputation.

library Enterprise storage units that use Blu-ray optical media for storage.

life cycle The stages through which systems pass: They are born, go through a process of maturation, live an adult life, and become obsolete to the point that they have to be modified or abandoned.

link rot The "out-of-datedness" that occurs in a search due to the amount of time it takes for spiders to accumulate data from the Web.

Linux A freeware operating system introduced by Linus Torvalds that is based on UNIX but is designed for personal computers. Linux is developed and maintained by volunteer programmers who have willingly donated their time to make sure that Linux's open source code is edited and revised to provide PC users with features similar to those found in commercial versions of UNIX.

liquid crystal display (LCD; flat-panel display) A flat-screen display that uses electrical current that controls the positioning of tiny crystals to either block or allow the current to pass through and form the viewable on-screen images and colors.

load To transfer something from a storage device, such as the hard disk, to RAM memory.

local area network (LAN) A network that uses cables, radio waves, or infrared signals to link computers or peripherals, such as printers, within a small geographic area, such as a building or a group of buildings. LANs are typically owned and managed by a single person or organization.

local exchange switch A telephone system device, based on digital technology and capable of handling thousands of calls, located in the local telephone company's central office.

local loop In the public switched telephone network (PSTN), the region serviced by a subscriber loop carrier (SLC) where analog connections from neighborhood distribution points are converted to digital signals.

location awareness (position awareness) A technology that uses GPS-enabled chips to pinpoint the location of a cell phone (and its user).

logic bomb Hidden computer code that sits dormant on a system until a certain event or set of circumstances triggers it into action. That action, or payload, is usually malicious and devastating to the individual or company under attack.

logic error In programming, a mistake made by the programmer in designing the program. Logic errors will not surface by themselves during program execution because they are not errors in the structure of the statements and commands. Such errors must located by the programmer through careful examination of the program output.

logical address A unique identifier assigned to a network node by the software in use.

Logical data type See Boolean data type.

logical operation One of two groups of operations performed by the arithmetic logic unit (ALU). An example of a logical operation is the comparison of data items to determine whether the first number is greater than the second. Logical operations return a value of true or false.

lossless compression In data compression, a method used to reduce the size of a file so it can be decompressed and restored to its original size without any flaws. Most lossless compression techniques reduce file size by replacing lengthy but frequently occurring data sequences with short codes. To decompress the file, the compression software reverses this process and restores the lengthy data sequences to their original form.

lossy compression In data compression, a method of reducing the size of multimedia files by eliminating information that is not normally perceived by human beings.

low-level language A language, like assembly or machine language, that is processor dependent and has a small or nonexistent amount of difference between the language and machine language; because of this, low-level languages are sometimes described as being "close to the hardware."

M

Mac OS An operating system released for the Apple Mac in 1984. It was the first OS to successful implement the GUI (graphical user interface).

Mac OS X Snow Leopard The current version of Mac OS X released in August 2009. It has a smaller footprint (taking up to 50 percent less storage space than the previous version) and includes a variety of useful features.

machine dependent (hardware dependent) The ability of a computer program to run only on a specific type or brand of computer equipment. With new antitheft features, it also refers to the link created between the program and system ID during the installation process. This link prevents the program from functioning on any other system.

machine language The native binary language consisting of 0s and 1s that is recognized and executed by a computer's central processing unit.

macro In a word processing or spreadsheet program, a saved sequence of commands or keyboard strokes that get recalled later with a single command or keyboard stroke.

macro virus A computer virus that uses the automatic execution capabilities of macros stored within productivity software, like word processing or spreadsheet programs, to spread itself to other files and, in many cases, cause harm to computer data.

magnetic storage device In computer storage systems, any storage device that retains data using a magnetically sensitive material, such as the magnetic coating found on floppy and hard disks.

magnetic stripe card reader A device that can detect and read information stored on magnetic strips that are usually located on the back of credit cards, gift cards, and other cards of similar use.

mainframe (enterprise server) Powerful servers that are part of a networked system designed to handle hundreds of thousands of clients. They are usually used in large corporations or government agencies that handle a high volume of data and can fill an entire wall of an average room.

maintenance release A minor revision to a software program that corrects bugs or adds minor features. Indicated by a decimal in the version number.

malicious network A network, sometimes referred to as an "evil twin" and designed to gather sensitive data such as passwords and credit card numbers, set up by a hacker within the operating area of a legitimate hot spot.

malware Short for malicious software, it describes software designed to damage or infiltrate a computer system without the owner's consent or knowledge. This type of software can wreak havoc on a user's system by deleting files and directory entries; it can also act as spyware, gathering data from a user's system without the user knowing it.

management information system (MIS) A computer-based system that supports the information needs of various levels of management. See also management information systems (MIS).

management information systems (MIS) A program of study that emphasizes the practical application of information systems and technology to provide the skills businesses need to compete successfully. See also management information system (MIS).

markup language A set of codes, or elements, used to define the structure of text, such as a title, heading, or bulleted list, that a Web browser reads and interprets. HTML is a markup language.

mashup Two or more applications combined into one application, a trend helping in the development of Web 3.0.

massively multiplayer online role-playing game (MMORPG) An online game that permits increasingly larger numbers of players to interact with one another in virtual worlds. These virtual worlds are often hosted and maintained by the software publisher and encourage team building in order to progress to higher levels and continue to progress even when you are not actively playing the game.

Mathematica A single system that can handle all the various aspects of technical computing in a coherent and unified way. The key to this system was the invention of a new kind of symbolic computer language that could, for the first time, manipulate the very wide range of objects, using only a fairly small number of basic elements.

mathematical formula In spreadsheet programs such as Microsoft Excel, one of the two basic types of formulas (along with functions) that makes use of numeric constants, cell references, arithmetic operators, or functions and calculates a result by following the mathematical order of operations.

maximize To enlarge a window so that it fits the entire screen.

MDX query language A query language introduced by Microsoft in 1997, similar to SQL but with the added ability to access multiple dimensions. MDX has since become the de facto query standard for multidimensional databases.

media Technology used to present information including pictures, sound, and video.

media center PC An all-in-one entertainment device that provides easy access to photos, TV, movies, and the latest in online media, all from the comfort of the couch by using a remote control.

megabits per second (Mbps) A data transfer measurement equivalent to 1 million bits per second.

megabyte (MB) A unit of measurement approximately equal to 1 million bytes.

Memo data type A data type used for large units of text.

memory Chips or circuitry, located on the motherboard or within the CPU, that retain instructions and data to be accessed by the central processing unit (CPU).

memory address A number that enables memory locations to be found and accessed in random order.

memory footprint The amount of RAM a program uses while it operates.

memory module (memory card) A small circuit board that holds several memory chips and fits into special slots on the motherboard.

memory shaving A type of computer crime in which knowledgeable thieves remove some of a computer's RAM chips but leave enough to start the computer.

memory stick Another name for a USB flash drive.

menu-driven user interface A user interface that enables the user to avoid memorizing keywords (such as *copy* and *paste*) and syntax (a set of rules for entering commands) by displaying on-screen, text-based menus that show all the options available at a given point.

message board A method of communicating over the Internet that is similar to a newsgroup but is easier to use and does not require a newsreader. Many colleges and universities have switched to message boards for this reason.

method An element of an object's definition that describes that object's actions or behavior.

metropolitan area network (MAN) A network designed for a city or town. It is usually larger than a LAN but smaller than a WAN. Typically, a MAN is owned by a single government or organization.

MICR reader A device that reduces human data entry by scanning and automatically inputting characters printed with special magnetic ink. Such characters are often located on the bottom of checks and some billing statements so that when they are returned to the creator, the numbers are simply scanned by a MICR reader and inputted into the company's data system; short for magnetic-ink character recognition.

microbrowser A special Web browser that has all of the features of computer-based browsers but is simplified to meet handheld device limitations.

microcomputer Another word for personal computer.

microprocessor (processor) Another name for the central processing unit.

Microsoft Windows The most popular operating system, available in several iterations, and installed on almost all of the personal computers made today.

Microsoft Windows 7 The newest version of the Windows operating system released in 2009. It is more efficient than its predecessor, often performing better on the same hardware, and has resolved the compatibility issues that existed between applications. There are six versions and many new features, including jump list, snap, pin, and Windows Search.

Microsoft Windows Mobile The version of Windows operating system designed for smartphones and PDAs. It includes a simplified user interface and quicker synchronization of mobile devices with corresponding programs on the user's desktop computer.

Microsoft Windows Server 2008 A sophisticated operating system specifically designed to support client/server computing systems in a corporate environment.

Microsoft Windows Vista The version of Windows operating system released in 2007. Its main improvements included a slick new interface, mobile support, increased security features, improved search features and networking tools, integrated speech recognition capabilities, and new multimedia tools such as gadgets.

microwave An electromagnetic radio wave with a very short frequency that travels at speeds of 1 to 10 Mbps and is used to transmit data from a source to a receiving site.

middleware Software that does what its name implies: It sits "in the middle," making the connections among varied applications working on multiple networks being supported by different operating systems. Middleware is essential for scalability as well as interoperability in the cloud.

minicomputer (midrange server) Midsized servers approximately the size of one or several four-drawer file cabinets with the hardware and software to handle computing needs of 4 to 200 client computers in a smaller corporation or organization.

mini-keyboard A keyboard option available on many smartphones and portable devices that has a key for each letter of the alphabet. It is usually is hidden when the phone is held in a vertical position but slides out when the phone is turned horizontally.

minimize To reduce the size of a window so that it appears only as an icon or an item on the taskbar.

minitower case A smaller version of the tower case, used for less complex systems, with a smaller amount of internal room for components.

mnemonics In programming, an abbreviation or short word for an instruction.

mobile switching center (MSC) The part of a cellular network that handles communications within a group of cells. Each cell tower reports signal strength to the MSC, which then switches the signal to whatever cell tower will provide the clearest connection for the conversation.

modeling (what-if analysis) A method by which spreadsheet programs are able to predict future outcomes; also called what-if analysis.

modem Short for modulator/demodulator, a communications device that converts (modulates) data from one form into another, transmits the modulated data, and on the receiving end converts (demodulates) the data for use. It is hardware that enables the computer, a digital device, to access data through nondigital media, such as telephone lines, cable, satellite, and cellular connections.

modifier key A key, like Shift, Alt, or Ctrl, that is pressed to modify the meaning of the next key that is pressed.

modular programming A programming style that breaks down programs into independent modules, each of which accomplishes one function.

modulation protocol In modems, the communications standard or rules that govern how the modem translates between the computer's digital signals and the analog tones used to convey computer data over the Internet so that the message is received and understood by the destination modem regardless of the manufacturer.

module A collection of routines in a program; independently developed modules are combined to create the final program.

monitor (display) A screen that displays data and processed information. This type of output is not permanent.

motherboard The circuit board, located within the system unit, that contains the central processing unit, support chips, random access memory, and expansion slots. It provides the circuitry to connect the central processing unit(s) anchored on the motherboard and other system components.

mouse A palm-sized pointing device designed to move about on a clean, flat surface. As you move the mouse, its movements are mirrored by the on-screen

pointer. Actions are initiated by using the mouse buttons.

MUD (multiuser dungeons or dimension) The early name for a genre of role-playing games in which multiple players could use their imaginations to construct a persona and build their environment. Players interacted in a text-based environment through text chatting.

multidimensional database A database structure that stores data in more than the two dimensions used by popular relational databases. Conceptually, multidimensional databases are depicted as a data cube to represent the dimensions of data available to the user. Multidimensional databases are becoming the choice for online analytical processing.

multifunction device A device that combines printing, scanning, faxing, and copying.

multimedia An application that involves two or more media, such as audio, graphics, or video. Multisensory stimulators that stimulate our senses of sight, sound, touch, smell, or taste.

multimedia and graphics software A general category of software programs for professional desktop publishing, image editing, three-dimensional rendering, and audio and video editing

multiplexing A technique that enables more than one signal to be conveyed on a physical transmission medium.

multitasking A process by which the CPU gives the user the illusion of performing instructions from multiple programs at once when in reality the CPU is rapidly switching between the programs and instructions.

multitasking operating system A descriptive phrase applied to personal computer operating systems that enable multiple applications to run at the same time.

multi-tenancy Refers to the ability of an application to be installed only once in a cloud, on the cloud's server, but to be shared and customized with individual options for each user.

N

name The first part of a file name.

nanosecond One-billionth of a second.

native application A program that is compatible with a given processor and therefore capable of running on that processor.

natural language In programming, a language that would provide instruction to a computer in normal human language, such as English or Japanese.

navigation pane The pane that appears on the left side of a Windows Explorer window. It allows a user to navigate directly to a specific folder listed in the content pane (file list), access a prior search that was saved by clicking on a desired folder, and add a shortcut to a frequently used folder by dragging the folder into the Favorite Links area of the navigation pane.

nesting A process of embedding control structures within one another.

netbook A handheld computing device with a relatively small hard drive that is used primarily for Web browsing, e-mail, and cloud computing.

netiquette A lengthy series of specific behavior guidelines, developed by Internet and computer users, that provide specific pointers on how to show respect for others—and for yourself—while you're online.

network A group of two or more computer systems linked together to exchange data and share resources, including expensive peripherals such as high-performance laser printers.

network access point (NAP) A special communications device that sends and receives data between computers that contain wireless adapters. 2. The location where equipment from one network service provider connects with equipment from another provider.

network administrator Computer professionals who install, maintain, and support computer networks, interact with users, handle security, and troubleshoot problems. Also called a network engineer.

network architecture The collection of protocol suites that specify how the network functions.

network attached storage (NAS) High-performance devices that offer little more than data and file sharing to clients and other servers on a network. An NAS is comprised primarily of hard drives or other media used for data storage and is attached directly to a network.

network interface card (NIC) An expansion board that fits into a computer's expansion slots, or an adapter built into the motherboard, that provides the electronic components to make the connection between a computer and a network. This can be either wired or wireless.

network layers Separate divisions within the network architecture with specific functions and protocols. Each layer's protocol precisely defines how that layer passes data to another layer. Because of this distinction between layers, it's possible to make changes within one layer without having to rebuild the entire network.

network operating system (NOS) An operating system designed to enable data transfer and application usage among computers and other devices connected to a local area network.

network service provider (NSP) A company or organization that maintains the Internet backbone.

network topology The physical layout of a network, which provides a solution to the problem of contention. Typical topologies include bus, star, and ring.

newsgroup In Usenet, a discussion group devoted to a single topic that typically requires participants to use a program called a news reader. Those reading the

discussion send reply messages to the author individually or post replies that can be read by the group as a whole.

node Any device connected to a network. A node can be any computer, peripheral (such as a printer or scanner), or communication device (such as a modem).

nonprocedural language A language not tied down to step-by-step procedures. In programming, a nonprocedural programming language does not force the programmer to consider the procedure that must be followed to obtain the desired result.

nonvolatile memory Memory, like ROM, that is not easily edited and keeps its content even when the system powers off. It's used primarily to hold programs essential to system start up.

notebook computer A computer, designed for individual use, approximately the size of a spiral bound notebook and popular with individuals that travel and students.

NTFS (new technology file system) A file allocation table that contains the name of each file and the file's exact location on the disk for Windows NT, 2000, XP, Vista, and Windows 7. It provides improved security and encryption ability.

numeric check A data validation procedure that ensures that only numbers are entered into a field.

O

object In object-oriented programming (OOP), a unit of computer information that defines a data element and is used to model real-world objects that you use every day. It consists of attributes and methods.

object code In programming, the instructions in (or close to) a specific computer's machine language that are created by a compiler from source code.

object-oriented database management system (ODBMS) The type of database structure, which suits multimedia applications, in which the retrieved object incorporates miniprograms that enable the object to perform tasks, such as display a graphic.

object-oriented programming (OOP) A programming technique based on defining data as objects. The user then assembles different sets of objects as needed to solve specific problems.

offshoring The transfer of labor from workers in one country to workers in other countries.

OLE Object data type A data type used for nontextual data like pictures, sounds, and videos.

OLED (organic light-emitting diode) display An emissive output device that displays images by emitting light rather than modulating transmitted or reflected light. These displays are extremely thin and lightweight, and produce outstanding color, contrast, brightness, and viewing angles.

onboard video Video circuitry that is built into the motherboard.

online analytical processing (OLAP) An application included in some decision support systems that provides decision support by enabling managers to import rich, up-to-the-minute data from transaction databases.

online (interactive) processing A transaction processing system in which you see the results of your commands on-screen so that you can correct errors and make necessary adjustments immediately, before completing an operation; also called interactive processing.

online service provider A for-profit firm that provides a proprietary network offering special services that are available only to subscribers. Members may participate in chat rooms and discussions and take advantage of fee-based content, such as magazines and newspapers.

online workshop A structured, interactive Web-based session that is assisted by an electronic meeting system, a set of tools that enable discussion, brainstorming, voting, and categorization.

Open Cloud Manifesto A document published in March 2009 to provided some guides and business practices for cloud providers in an attempt to guarantee subscribers the freedom of choice, flexibility, and openness they need in order to take full advantage of the benefits of cloud computing.

open source software Software whose source code (the code of the program itself) is available for all to see and use. Users of open source software are invited to scrutinize the source code for errors and to share their discoveries with the software's publisher. Linux is an open source operating system.

operating system (OS) The most important type of system software. It integrates and controls the computer's internal functions and provides the connectivity for the user to interact with the computer's hardware. Common operating systems include Microsoft Windows 7, Microsoft Vista, Microsoft Windows XP, Linux, and Mac OS X Snow Leopard.

operational decision A decision on a localized issue, such as inventory level, that requires immediate attention.

operational feasibility A project's capability of being accomplished with the organization's available resources.

operational support system (OSS) A suite of programs that supports an enterprise's network operations.

optical character recognition (OCR) Software that automatically decodes imaged content into text. Most scanners come with OCR software.

optical mark reader (OMR) A device that scans the magnetized marks from a no. 2 pencil, or other device that produces such marks, to determine which responses were made. The response is compared against a provided key with the correct

answers. OMR devices facilitate the tabulation of responses to large surveys.

optical mouse A palm-sized pointing device that makes use of an LED (light-emitting diode) light, located on the underside of the mouse, and a small camera that takes continuous images of the changes in the surface under the mouse as it is moved. The differences are compared and the direction and speed of the mouse movement are recognized and the on-screen pointer shifted accordingly.

optical storage device A computer storage device that retains data in microscopic patterns, pits and lands, which are encoded on the surface of plastic discs and detected by a laser beam.

option Choices made by a user to specify how that user wants the program to operate.

output The display of the results (information) of the processing operation.

output device A monitor, printer, speaker, or other device that enables people to see, hear, and—with some newer inventions—feel the results of processing operations.

outsourcing The subcontracting of portions of a job to a third party to reduce cost, time, and energy consumption.

P

packaged software Aimed at a mass market that includes both home and business users, packaged software can be customized, but its appeal lies in the fact that is ready to use off the shelf. Synonymous with commercial off-the-shelf software (COTS) and shrink-wrapped software.

packet In a packet-switching network, a unit of data of a fixed size—not exceeding the network's maximum transmission unit (MTU) size—that has been prepared for network transmission. Each packet contains a header that indicates its origin and its destination.

packet switching One of two fundamental architectures for a wide area network (WAN); the other is a circuit-switching network. In a packet-switching network, such as the Internet, no effort is made to establish a single electrical circuit between two computing devices; instead, the sending computer divides a message into packets, each of which contains the address of the destination computer, and dumps them onto the network. They are intercepted by devices called routers, which send the packets in the appropriate direction. The receiving computer assembles the packets, puts them in order, and delivers the received message to the appropriate application. Packet-switching networks are highly reliable and efficient, but they are not suited to the delivery of real-time voice and video.

page In virtual memory, a unit of fixed size into which program instructions and data are divided.

paging Transferring of files from the hard disk to RAM and back, as needed.

Palm OS A mobile operating system initially developed in 1996 by Palm Inc. for personal digital assistants (PDAs). It's designed for use with a touch screen, uses graphical user interfaces and natural gestures, and comes with a suite of personal information management applications.

parallel conversion Running both the new and the old systems for a while to check that the new system produces answers at least as good as those of the old system.

parallel port Considered legacy technology, these ports were commonly used to connect a printer to a PC but have been replaced by USB and Ethernet ports.

parallel processing The use of more than one processor to run two or more portions of a program at the same time.

partition A section of a hard disk set aside as if it were a physically separate disk. Partitions are required if a system is going to give the user an option of running more than one operating system.

passive-matrix (dual scan) Technology that creates the content of a display or monitor by charging groups of pixels, either in a row or column, at once. The screen brightens and fades as the current moves from group to group. Appliances, toys, remote controls, and home medical products use this type of display.

path The sequence of directories that the user must follow to locate a file.

payload The actions, most often malicious and devastating, performed by rogue programs like spyware and viruses to the individual or company under attack.

PC card (PCMCIA card) A credit card–sized accessory, typically used to enhance the abilities of notebook computers, designed to fit into a compatible PC card slot located on or within the computer's case. Some PC cards are modems, others are network adapters, and still others provide additional memory or storage capacity.

PCI (peripheral component interconnect) bus An input/output bus that connects devices like hard drives and sound cards to the faster microprocessor system bus usually through expansion slots.

PCI Express An interface currently in use that transfers graphics from the video card to the motherboard. Most current video cards from manufacturers like ATI and NVIDIA use PCI Express.

PCI Express Base 2.1 The most current version of the PCI express interface.

PCS (personal communication service) A group of related digital cellular technologies that are rapidly replacing analog cellular services.

peer-to-peer (P2P) network A computer network design in which all the computers on the network are equals or peers. There is no file server. File sharing is decided by each computer user. A user may choose to share a few files, an entire directory, or even an entire disk. They also can choose to share peripherals, such as printers and scanners. P2P is best used for home networks or small businesses connecting fewer than ten computers and does not require a network operating system (NOS).

peripheral device Computer components located outside the system unit housing that are connected physically or wirelessly to the system unit and motherboard, such as keyboards, monitors, speakers, and external storage devices.

personal area network (PAN) A network created among an individual's own personal devices, usually within a range of 32 feet. Such networks involve wireless technology.

personal computer (PC or microcomputer) A computer designed to meet the computing needs of an individual or, when connected to a network, to be used by a contributor in a collaborative project. The two most commonly used types of personal computers are Apple's Macintosh, referred to as a Mac, and the more numerous IBM-compatible systems referred to as PCs.

personal computing Any situation or setup where one person controls and uses a computer or handheld device for personal or business activities.

personal digital assistant (PDA) A small handheld personal computing device that usually uses a stylus or virtual keyboard to interface with built-in software to manage contacts, use e-mail, and schedule appointments.

petabyte A unit of measurement approximately equal to 1 quadrillion bytes.

petaflop A unit of measurement for computer processing speed that is the equivalent of one quadrillion calculations per second, approximately 150,000 calculations for every human being on the planet per second.

phased conversion Implementing a new system over different time periods, one part at a time.

phishing Posing as a legitimate company in an e-mail or on a Web site in an attempt to learn personal information such as Social Security numbers, user names, passwords, and account numbers.

photo checkout system A system that accesses a database of customer photos and displays the customer's picture when a credit card is used.

photo-editing program A program that enables a person to enhance, edit, crop, or resize the images.

photo printer An inkjet or laser printer that makes use of special inks and good-quality photo paper to produce pictures that are as good as those generated by commercial photo processors. Many permit bypassing a computer and printing directly from a digital camera or memory card.

PHP A general purpose, server-side, open source, cross-platform scripting language used primarily to make dynamic Web sites.

phrase searching In database and Web searching, the placing of a phrase between quotation marks so the search retrieves only documents that contain the entire phrase.

physical address Also called the data link control address, data link control/connection identifier (DLCI), or media access control (MAC) address; a unique numeric identifier built into the hardware of a network node and used to identify the node.

picture messaging (MMS) A mobile service that allows you to send full-color pictures, backgrounds, and even picture caller IDs on your cell phone.

piggybacking The use of a network without permission.

pilot conversion One part of the organization converts to a new system while the rest of the organization continues to run the old system.

pipelining A processing technique used in CPUs built with superscalar architecture. It feeds a new instruction into the processor at every step of the processing cycle so that four or more instructions are worked on simultaneously, increasing the speed at which instructions are performed.

pit A microscopic indentation in the surface of an optical disc that scatters the laser's light so that the drive's light-sensing device receives no light from these areas and sends a signal to the computer that corresponds to a 0 in the computer's binary numbering system.

plagiarism The use of someone else's intellectual property, ideas, or written work, as one's own or without permission.

plaintext A readable message before it is encrypted.

platform The combination of microprocessor chip and operating system used by a distinct type of computer, such as a Mac or a PC.

Platform-as-a-Service (PaaS) The category of cloud services that permits subscribers to have remote access to application development, interface development, database development, storage, and testing to facilitate the creation and testing of subscriber-developed programs and interfaces, using a cloud provider's hardware and development environment.

platter The fixed, high-capacity, rapidly rotating, storage medium in a hard drive that is coated with a magnetically sensitive material. High-capacity hard drives typically have two or more platters.

plotter An output device that produces high-quality images by moving ink pens over the surface of the paper.

plug-and-play (PnP) Refers to a set of standards, jointly developed by Intel Corporation and Microsoft, which enable a computer to automatically detect the brand, model, and characteristics of a device when you plug it in and configure the system accordingly.

plug-in An additional software program, located on the user's computer, that is activated by a Web page to enhance the ability of the browser, usually to enable multimedia features such as sound or video.

podcast A blend of the words *iPod* and *broadcast*. It has come to mean a program (of music or talk) that is made available in digital format for automatic download over the Internet. Such files contain audio, images, and videos and are released periodically by means of Web syndication.

podcatcher Applications, such as Apple Inc.'s iTunes or Nullsoft's Winamp, that can automatically identify and retrieve new files in a given series and make them available through a centrally maintained Web site.

pod slurping An activity in which employees use USB drives, iPods, or other removable storage media to create an unauthorized copy of confidential data.

point-and-shoot digital camera A camera that includes automatic focus, automatic exposure, built-in automatic electronic flash with red-eye reduction, and optical zoom lenses with digital enhancement. Sometimes called a compact camera.

pointer An on-screen symbol, usually an arrow, that shows the current location of on-the-screen activity.

pointing device An input device that allows you to control the movements of the on-screen pointer.

pointing stick A pointing device that looks like a pencil eraser located between the G, H, and B keys. It is pressure sensitive and is pressed and moved in various directions with the forefinger.

point of presence (POP) A wired or wireless access connection point in a wide area network. ISPs that provide connectivity to the largest WAN, the Internet, are likely to have POPs in many cities and towns; however, rural areas may not be so lucky.

pop-up A small window that suddenly appears ("pops up") in the foreground of the current window.

port An electronically defined pathway or interface for getting information into and out of the computer.

portable storage (removable storage) A popular, removable, compact storage device that is easy to carry around, simple to use, and can be quickly plugged into any computer with the correct connector. Examples are USB flash drives, also known as memory sticks, thumb drives, or jump drives.

portal A Web page that acts as a gateway to a lot of diverse sources and presents those sources in an organized way and enables a user to locate fast-breaking news, local weather, stock quotes, sports scores, and e-mail with the click of a mouse. Portal sites usually use indexes and lists of links to provide a jumping-off point for your search. Sites such as MSNBC, AOL, iGoogle, and Yahoo! are examples of portals.

positioning performance A measure of how much time elapses from the initiation of drive activity until the hard disk has

positioned the read/write head so that it can begin transferring data.

POST (power-on self test) A program, stored in ROM memory, that conducts a series of tests during system startup after the BIOS instructions are loaded into memory. It checks the circuitry, making sure that the computer and circuitry are working correctly, and marks any RAM locations that are defective so that they do not get used.

postimplementation system review A process of ongoing evaluation that determines whether a system has met its goals.

power-on light The light, located on the front panel of most computers, that signals whether the power is on.

power-on self-test (POST) A series of tests conducted during a system boot, after the BIOS instructions are loaded into memory, to make sure that the computer and associated peripherals are operating correctly.

preemptive multitasking An environment in which programs that are running receive a recurring slice of time from the CPU. Depending on the operating system, the time slice may be the same for all programs or it may be adjustable to meet the various program and user demands. This method of multitasking ensures that all applications have fair access to the CPU and prevents one program from monopolizing it at the expense of the others.

primary key (key field) A field that contains a code, a number, a name, or some other piece of information that uniquely identifies a record; also called the key field.

printer An output device that produces a permanent version, or hard copy, of the contents on a computer's display screen.

privacy An individual's ability to restrict or eliminate the collection, use, and sale of confidential personal information.

private cloud Operated for a single organization and its authorized users. The infrastructure can exist on-site or off-site and is controlled by either the organization or a contracted third party.

private key A decryption key associated with a public key in a public key encryption scheme.

problem The underlying cause of a symptom.

procedural language A programming language that directs the computer to perform an action by grouping together instructions in a very specific step-by-step manner.

processing The actions performed on data (input) to convert it into information.

processing cycle (machine cycle) A four-step process performed in the central processing unit (CPU) that involves the fetch, decode, execute, and store operations.

productivity program A program that helps individuals work more efficiently

and effectively on both personal and business-related documents. The value of a productivity program is that it performs its functions regardless of the subject matter. Productivity software includes word processors, spreadsheets, databases, presentation, project management, and a personal information management programs.

product registration key An alphanumeric code that is unique and specific to a particular copy of a program. It is necessary to enter this key after installation in order to validate authenticity and activate the program. The key may be necessary later to download upgrades, patches, or templates.

professional organization (professional association) An IT organization that can help you keep up with your area of interest as well as provide valuable career contacts.

professional workstation High-end desktop computers with system units equipped with more powerful CPUs, extra RAM, additional graphics power, and multitasking capabilities for handling technical or scientific applications that require exceptionally powerful processing and output capabilities.

profile A record of a specific user's preferences for the desktop theme, icons, and menu styles.

program A set of instructions that tells the hardware how to perform an operation on the inputted data.

program design The result of phase 2 of the program development life cycle (PDLC) in which a written plan that specifies the components that make the program work is created, reviewed, and discussed.

program development life cycle (PDLC) A six-phase, organized plan for breaking down the task of program development into manageable chunks, each of which must be successfully completed before programmers move on to the next phase.

program maintenance In phase 6 of the program development life cycle (PDLC), the process in which the programming team fixes program errors discovered by users.

program specification Part of the first phase of the program development life cycle (PDLC) in which the systems analyst precisely defines the input data, the processing that should occur, the output format, and the user interface.

programmer A trained expert who works individually or in a group to design, write, and test software applications for everything from word processing to virus protection.

programming The process used to create the software applications you use every day.

programming language An artificial language composed of a fixed vocabulary and a set of rules used to create instructions, commands, or statements for a computer to follow.

project dictionary A document that explains all the terminology relevant to a project.

project manager The individual responsible for guiding the project so it progresses according to plan. The project manager's responsibilities include disseminating information to all having an active role in the system development, identifying and managing project risk, ensuring that what was agreed to is delivered, keeping a pulse on the progress of the project, and determining whether the deliverables are acceptable.

project notebook A digital file maintained online, it is often used to store the documentation for a project, thus enabling everyone connected with the project to understand all the decisions that have been made.

project plan Identifies the project's goal and specifies all the activities that must be completed for the project to succeed.

project proposal A document that introduces the nature of the existing system's problem, explains the proposed solution and its benefits, details the proposed project plan, and concludes with a recommendation.

project team The liaison between the systems analyst and others involved in the project's design and implementation and the client's organization. The responsibilities of the project team include being actively involved in the development and review of the system design, assisting in the customizing of the design and providing direction on the system as it is being developed so that it best suits the needs of the organization, monitoring progress against the projected time line, sustaining momentum and company enthusiasm for the project, and answering questions for the system analyst and development team.

PROM Programmable read-only memory that can be written on only once, but requires a special writing device.

property A setting that provides information on a file such as its date of creation, size, and the date it was last modified.

proprietary file A file whose format is patented or copyright protected and controlled by a single company. The extent of restriction depends on the company and its policies.

protocol In data communications and networking, the standard or set of rules that enable network-connected devices to communicate with each other.

protocol stack In a computer network, a means of conceptualizing network architecture as vertical layers, connected by protocols that move the data down the stack from its initial level, or transmitting node, to the lowest, physical hardware level that sends it over the network. When the data arrives at its destination, it moves back up the stack through the layers in reverse order, eventually arriving at the receiving node.

protocol suite In a computer network, the collection of network protocols, or rules, that defines the network's functionality.

prototyping A process used in several systems development methodologies in which a developer creates a small scale mock-up of the system and presents it to the customer; also called rapid application development (RAD).

PS/2 port Considered legacy technology, these ports were typically used for mice and keyboards, but were not interchangeable. Today most mice and keyboards connect via USB connectors.

pseudocode In structured programming, a stylized form of writing used as an alternative to flowcharts to describe the logic of a program.

public cloud Available to the general public, large organizations, or a group of organizations, the public cloud offers the most risk because it is accessed by users that have not been authenticated or established as trusted. The infrastructure is owned and operated by a cloud provider and is located off site.

public domain software Noncopyrighted, free programs that can be used, copied, modified, or sold without restriction or acknowledging the source.

public key In public key cryptography, the encoding key, which you make public so that others can send you encrypted messages. The message can be encoded with the public key, but it cannot be decoded without the private key, which you alone possess.

public key encryption (asymmetric key encryption) A computer security process in which an encryption (or public) key and a decryption (or private) key are used to safeguard data and thus provide confidentiality. This system allows a digital signature to be verified by anyone who has access to the sender's public key, thereby proving that the sender is authentic and has access to the private key; also called asymmetric key encryption.

public key infrastructure (PKI) A uniform set of encryption standards that specifies how public key encryption, digital signatures, and digital certificates should be implemented in computer systems and on the Internet.

public switched telephone network (PSTN) The global telephone system, a massive network used for data as well as voice communications, comprising various transmission media ranging from twisted-pair wire to fiber-optic cable.

Q

query A specially phrased question used to locate data in a database. It can specify multiple criteria and designate the fields to be displayed.

query language A language, like SQL, designed to extract and edit information in a database.

Quick Access Toolbar Located above the Ribbon in the Windows environment. This customizable toolbar displays a series of buttons used to perform common tasks, such as saving a document and undoing or redoing the last action performed.

R

racetrack memory A type of memory under development that uses the spin of electrons to store information. This technology will greatly increase the speeds for transferring and retrieving data.

radio frequency identification (RFID) A tracking device, replacing bar codes, which does not require direct contact or line-of-sight scanning. Instead, an antenna using radio frequency waves transmits a signal that activates the transponder, or tag. When activated, the tag transmits data back to the antenna.

radio transmission Data in a variety of forms (music, voice conversations, and photos) travels through the air as radio frequency (RF) signals or radio waves via a transmitting device and a receiving device.

RAID (redundant array of independent disks) A group of two or more hard drives that contain the same data.

random access memory (RAM) Memory chips, located on the motherboard, which temporarily store the programs and data being used and accessed by the central processing unit through a high-speed data bus. RAM is also referred to as primary memory or temporary memory. The designation of temporary comes from the fact that the information located in this memory in not permanent and is lost when the computer is turned off.

random access storage device A storage device that can begin reading data without having to go through a lengthy linear search.

range In Microsoft Excel, a range consists of two or more contiguous cells and is identified by the addresses of first cell (the top left) and last cell (bottom right) separated by a colon. For example, the range from cell A1 to cell D5 would be represented as A1:D5.

range check A data validation procedure that verifies that the entered data fall within an acceptable range.

rapid application development (RAD) A program development method that is able to deliver systems very quickly. A programmer works with a library of prebuilt objects that have been created for a huge variety of applications.

ray tracing A 3D rendering technique in which color intensity on a graphic object is varied to simulate light falling on the object from multiple directions.

read/write head An electromagnet located within magnetic storage devices, such as a hard disk drive, that moves across the surface of a disk and records information by transforming electrical impulses into a varying magnetic field. When reading, the read/write head senses the recorded pattern and transforms this pattern into electrical impulses that are decoded into text characters.

read-only memory (ROM) Nonvolatile memory that does not lose its content when power is shut off. It contains essential prerecorded computer start up instructions that cannot be erased or changed by the computer without user initiation.

Really Simple Syndication (RSS) A way to keep abreast of updates on news, weather, and sports in our fast-moving and informative world. Once a user sets up a connection to a Web site that has an RSS feed, he or she will receive constant updates over the Internet from that site without any further involvement.

receiving device A component of communication that accepts a transmission and responds.

record A group of one or more related fields.

register Temporary memory located in the microprocessor that is used to store values and external memory addresses while the processor performs arithmetic and logical operations on them.

registration fee The amount of money paid to an author of a piece of software to continue to use it beyond the duration of the evaluation period.

registry In Microsoft Windows, the name of the database in which configuration information about installed peripherals and software is stored.

relational database management system (RDBMS) A database system in which data in several tables is related by a common primary key, allowing the user to make connections between the tables.

remote storage Sometimes referred to as an Internet hard drive, this is a type of storage space on a server, accessible from the Internet, and usually requires the user to pay a subscription free.

repetition control structure In structured programming, a control structure that repeats the same instructions over and over. Two examples of repetition structures are DO-WHILE and DO-UNTIL; also called a looping or iteration control structure.

report A database feature that displays information from tables, queries, or a combination of both in a professionally styled manner.

report generator In programming, a programming language for printing database reports. It provides a user-friendly interface enabling a user to design and generate high-quality reports and graphs.

request for proposal (RFP) A request for a vendor to write a proposal for the design, installation, and configuration of an information system.

request for quotation (RFQ) A request for a vendor to quote a price for specific components of the information system.

requirements analysis A process to determine the requirements of a system by analyzing how the system will meet the needs of end users.

resolution Refers to the sharpness of an image and is controlled by the number of pixels on the screen. The higher the resolution number, the sharper the image.

restore down A mode that, if the window is full screen, will cause the window to revert to a smaller size.

return on investment (ROI) A system's overall financial yield at the end of its lifetime.

RFID reader A device used to detect radio signals being emitted from a radio frequency identification tag placed on an item.

Ribbon A band located across the top of the application window and below the title bar in Office 2007 and Office 2010 applications. It consists of tabs with icons assembled into groups based on their function. Each application has a Ribbon with tab options that match the activities performed by that application.

ring topology The physical layout of a local network in which all nodes are attached in a circle, without a central host computer. This topology, which is no longer used frequently, employs a unit of data called a *token* that travels around the ring. A node can transmit only when it possesses the token, thus avoiding collisions.

risk management The process of analyzing exposure to risk and determining how to best handle it within the tolerance level set by the enterprise.

ROM (read-only memory) The part of a computer's primary storage that contains essential computer start-up instructions and doesn't lose its contents when the power is turned off. Information in read-only memory cannot be erased by the computer without initiation by the user.

rootkit A malicious program that is disguised as a useful program that enables the attacker to gain administrator level access to a computer or network. The primary purpose of a rootkit is to allow an attacker repeated and undetected access to a compromised system.

router A complex device, or in some cases software, used to connect two or more networks. Routers have the capability to determine the best path to route data and locate alternative pathways so that the data reaches its destination.

routine A section of code that executes a specific task in a program; also referred to as a procedure, function, or subroutine.

row In Microsoft Excel and Word, a block of data presented horizontally across the screen.

RSS (Really Simple Syndication or Rich Site Summary) A technology that publishes content to you and lets you know when Web content has been updated or news events are taking place.

Ruby An open-source (free-of-charge), object-oriented programming language released in 1995 that is simple in appearance but complex inside. Its growth is attributed to the popularity of its software, a Web framework that allows applications that took months to create to be developed in days.

S

Safe Mode An operating mode in which Windows loads a minimal set of drivers that are known to function correctly. Within Safe Mode, the user can use the Control Panel to determine which devices are causing a configuration problem that may occur after adding a new peripheral device such as an external hard drive or new printer to the system.

salami shaving A computer crime in which a program is altered so that it transfers a small amount of money from a large number of accounts to make a large profit.

sales force automation (SFA) software Software that automates many of the business processes involved with sales, including processing and tracking orders, managing customers and other contacts, monitoring and controlling inventory, and analyzing sales forecasts.

Sarbanes-Oxley (SOX) An act administered by the Securities and Exchange Commission (SEC) that specifies the type of business records that need to be stored and how long they must be kept, but leaves the method of storage up to the business.

SATA (serial advance technology attachment) An interface developed by the Serial ATA International Organization (SATA IO) as a replacement for legacy ports that greatly increases the data transfer rate between the motherboard and storage devices like hard drives and optical drives. The user benefits from greater speed, simpler upgradable storage devices, and easier configuration.

satellite In data communications, a communication device placed in a geosynchronous (stationary) orbit that transmits data by sending and receiving microwave signals to and from Earth-based stations.

satellite radio A type of communications technology that broadcasts radio signals back and forth between satellites orbiting more than 22,000 miles above the Earth and radio receivers on Earth.

saving The process of transferring a file from the computer's temporary memory, or RAM, to a permanent storage device, such as a hard disk.

scalability The ability of a hardware or software system to continue functioning effectively as demands and use increase.

scanner A device that copies anything that is printed on a sheet of paper, including artwork, handwriting, and typed or printed documents, and converts the input into a graphical image for the computer. The scanner does not recognize or differentiate the type of material it is scanning and converts everything into a graphic bitmapped image.

scope The sum total of all project elements and features.

scope creep The uncontrolled changes or bumps that arise during a project that lead to increased costs and a longer development schedule.

script A program, written in a scripting language like VBScript or JavaScript, that controls any action or feedback on a Web page.

scripting language A language that enables users to create useful programs, called scripts, to control actions or feedback on a Web page. VBScript and JavaScript are examples of client-side scripting languages; their scripts run on a user's computer. Other scripting languages are server-side scripting languages that manipulate the data, usually in a database, on the server.

scroll arrows An arrow appearing within the scroll bar that enables the user to scroll up or down (or, in a horizontal scroll bar, left and right) by small increments.

scroll bar A vertical or horizontal bar that contains scroll arrows and a scroll box. The scroll bar enables the user to navigate though content, revealing hidden portions of a document in the application workspace.

SCSI (small computer system interface) port Considered legacy technology, a type of parallel interface that enabled users to connect up to 15 SCSI-compatible devices, such as printers, scanners, and digital cameras, in a daisy-chain series.

SDSL (symmetrical digital subscriber line) A transmission technology that splits the copper telephone line channels into three channels: telephone, upload, and download. The bandwidth is distributed equally among the channels. On SDSL connections, uploads and downloads occur at the same rate.

Search box A Windows Explorer input box that allows the user to locate files. Select one of the main folders and begin typing a search term in the search input box. As you are typing, Windows Explorer searches the contents of the folders and subfolders of your selected main folder and immediately filters the view to display any files that match your search input.

search engine Any program that locates needed information in a database, or on an Internet-accessible search service (such as Google or Ask) that enables you to search for information on the Internet.

search operator In a database or a Web search engine, a word or a symbol that enables you to specify your search with precision.

search utility A program that enables you to search an entire hard disk and any indexed network storage device for a file by querying single or multiple specifics about the file such as the name, date, and/or size.

secondary cache An additional location for memory storage located on the processor's architecture or very close to it, allowing for quick access; also known as L2 cache.

secondary storage (fixed storage) Hardware that retains the programs and data even when power is disrupted or turned off. Examples include hard disks, USB flash drives, CDs, and DVDs.

sector A pie-shaped wedge of the concentric tracks encoded on a disk during formatting (set up). Two or more sectors combine to form a cluster.

secure electronic transaction (SET) An online shopping security standard for merchants and customers that uses digital certificates.

seek time In a secondary storage device, the time it takes for the read/write head to locate the data on the disk before reading begins.

selection control structure In structured programming, a control structure that branches in different directions, depending on whether a condition is met. An efficient selection control statement is an IF-THEN-ELSE structure. This control is also called a conditional or branch control structure.

semiconductor The material that transistors are made out of that conducts electrical current or blocks the current's passage through the circuit.

sending device A component of communication that initiates a transmission.

sequence control structure In structured programming, a control structure in which instructions are executed in the order, or sequence, in which they appear.

serial port Considered legacy technology, it is an interface that was used with dial-up modems to achieve two-way communication. Although they are still in use on servers, many new computers no longer include serial ports, opting to use USB ports instead.

serialization The transmission of structured data over a network connection.

server A computer that ranges in size from a two-drawer file cabinet to a four-drawer file cabinet and is equipped with the hardware and software to manage network resources like files, e-mail, printers, and databases, and that makes the programs and data it manages available to people who are connected via a network.

server operating system An operating system used in client/server network environments.

setup program A program located in the computer system's BIOS that contains settings that control the computer's hardware.

sexting A combination of sex and texting. Sending sexually explicit messages or photos electronically, primarily between cell phones.

shareware Copyrighted programs that may be used or copied, without cost, during the specified trial period. Once the trial period has expired, a registration fee must be paid or the software must be deleted from your computer.

shill In an auction, an accomplice of the seller who drives up prices by bidding for an item that the accomplice has no intention of buying.

shoulder surfing The attempt by an individual to obtain information from your computer screen by looking over your shoulder.

sidebar An invisible vertical strip located on the right side of the desktop in a graphical user interface where the user can place and arrange applications referred to as gadgets.

signature capture system A system that captures a customer's digital signature by having the customer sign the receipt on a pressure-sensitive pad, using a special stylus.

single inline memory module (SIMM) A RAM memory module that fits into special slots on the motherboard; it preceded the dual inline memory modules in use today, used a 72-pin connector, and had a 32-bit data transfer rate.

single-lens reflex (SLR) digital camera A digital camera that uses a mechanical mirror system to direct light from the lens to an optical viewfinder on the back of the camera. Such cameras offer the features that professional photographers demand, such as interchangeable lenses, through-the-lens image previewing, and the ability to override the automatic focus and exposure settings.

single point of failure (SPOF) Any system component, such as hardware or software, that causes the entire system to malfunction when it fails.

single-tasking operating system An operating system that could run only one application at a time, which was often inconvenient. To switch between applications, you had to quit one application before you could start the second.

site license A contract with the software publisher that allows an organization to install copies of a program on a specified number of computers at a reduced price per unit.

Sleep mode A power-saving feature that transfers the current state of your computer to RAM, turns off all unneeded functions, and places the system in a low-power state. Returning from Sleep mode is faster than returning from Hibernate due to the state of the computer being held in RAM not stored on the hard drive.

slide In a presentation graphics program, the equivalent of a canvas, sized in proportion to a 35 mm slide, on which the user organizes text boxes and graphics to represent ideas or points.

smart card (chip card, integrated circuit card [ICC]) A credit card–sized device that combines flash memory with a tiny microprocessor, enabling the card to process as well as store information. It is viewed as a replacement for magnetic stripe cards, from which data is eventually lost.

smartphone Mobile devices that fit in the palm of your hand or pocket of your jeans. Designed primarily for use as a mobile phone but can be enabled with Web access. The added features and downloadable applications for these devices are making the line between the smartphones and handheld computers more difficult to distinguish.

social network site Web sites like Facebook, MySpace, LinkedIn, or Twitter, where users join groups set up by region, job, school, or family and communicate through postings, instant messaging, and e-mail.

social networking A method of creating and expanding online communities. For example, sites such as Facebook, MySpace, and LinkedIn allow users to create online profiles, post images, and invite friends and acquaintances to join their network. Many view it as a substitute for e-mail.

soft business skill A people-related skill that in business is associated with human resources, communication, research skills, teamwork, project management, learning, personal development, and ethics.

soft copy Output displayed on a monitor or played through speakers.

soft keyboard (virtual keyboard, on-screen keyboard) Also known as a virtual or on-screen keyboard. A keyboard that appears on a touch-sensitive screen. Tapping the key on the screen with a stylus or finger is the same as pressing a key on a traditional keyboard.

software One of two basic components of a computer system (the other is hardware). It is a collection of programs, and associated documentation, that directs the operation of the computer to complete a desired end result. There are two categories of software: system software and application software.

software engineering An occupation that involves upgrading, managing, and modifying of computer programs.

software license An agreement included with most commercial software that defines what the user may and may not do with the software.

software piracy The unauthorized copying or distribution of copyrighted software, an act that is a federal offense in the United States.

software suite (office suite) A collection of individual, full-featured, stand-alone programs, usually possessing a similar interface and sharing a common command structure, that are bundled and sold together; sometimes called an office suite.

software upgrading The process of keeping a version of an application current with the marketplace, whether through patches, service releases, or new versions.

Software-as-a-Service (SaaS) 1. The most widely used and widely known form of cloud computing, it enables software to be deployed from a cloud provider, delivered over the Internet, and accessed by a subscriber through a browser.

2. Provides software-based services and solutions to companies that want to outsource some of their information technology needs.

solid-state drive (SSD) A drive with no moving parts; another name for a flash drive.

solid-state storage device A device that consists of nonvolatile memory chips, which retain the data stored in them even if disconnected from their source. Solid-state storage devices are small, lightweight, highly reliable, and portable. See flash drives.

SONET (synchronous optical network) A standard for high-performance networks using optical fiber with data transfer rates of 52 Mbps to higher levels of approximately 20 Gbps.

sound file A file containing digitized data in the form of digital audio waveforms (recorded live sounds or music), which are saved in one of several standardized sound formats. These formats specify how sounds should be digitally represented and generally include some type of data compression that reduces the size of the file. The file can be played back if a computer is equipped with multimedia.

source code Program instructions in their original form as written by the programmer. A source program is translated into machine instructions that the computer can execute.

spaghetti code In programming, source code that contains numerous GOTO statements and is consequently difficult to follow, messy in design, and prone to errors.

spam Unsolicited e-mail or newsgroup advertising.

sparklines In an Excel spreadsheet, tiny charts embedded into the background of a cell that help users visualize and detect trends in their data more easily.

spear phishing Behavior similar to phishing, in that it uses fake e-mails and social engineering to trick recipients into providing personal information to enable identity theft. Rather than being sent randomly, spear phishing attempts are targeted to specific people, such as senior executives or members of a particular organization.

specialized search engines Web location programs, like Infoplease, that index particular types of information, such as job advertisements, newspaper articles, or quotations.

speculative execution A technique used by advanced CPUs to prevent a pipeline stall. The processor executes and temporarily stores the next instruction in case it proves useful.

speech recognition (voice recognition) The conversion of spoken words into computer text. The spoken word is first digitized and then matched against a dictionary of coded voice waves. The matches are converted into text as if the words were typed on the keyboard.

spider A computer program used by search engines to roam the World Wide Web via the Internet, visit sites and databases, and keep the search engine's database of Web pages up to date. They obtain new pages, update known pages, and delete obsolete ones. Their findings are then integrated into the search engine's database.

spim A spam text message.

spimming Sending unsolicited messages (spam) as an instant message.

spyware Internet software that is installed on your computer without your knowledge or consent. It may monitor your computer or online activity, relay information about you to the spyware's source, or allow others to take control of your computer. Spyware usually enters your system through the Internet.

stand-alone operating system An operating system designed to be used by a single user on a desktop computer, notebook, or any portable computing device. The name *stand-alone* comes from the fact that it does not need to be connected to any other system or computer in order to run.

stand-alone program An application sold individually.

star topology The physical layout of a local network in which a central wiring device, which can be a hub, switch, or computer, manages the network. A new user is added by simply running a cable to the hub or switch and plugging the new user into a vacant connector.

status bar An area within a typical application's window that displays information about the application and the document.

storage (mass storage, auxiliary storage, secondary storage) The operation in which information generated during processing is stored for later use.

storage area network (SAN) A network of high-capacity storage devices that link all of the organization's servers so that any of the storage devices are accessible from any of the servers.

storage device A general term for hardware that holds programs and data.

strategic decision A decision by management concerning an organization's overall goals and direction.

streaming A transmission method that enables the ability to hear or see content while it is being downloaded from a Web site instead of waiting till the download is complete.

strong password A strong password should be difficult to guess; be at least 14 characters or more in length; include uppercase letters, lowercase letters, numbers, and special characters; not be a recognizable word or phrase; not be the name of anything or anyone close to you; and not be a recognizable string of numbers such as a Social Security number or birth date.

structural unemployment Unemployment caused by advancing technology that makes an entire job category obsolete.

structure chart (hierarchy chart) In structured programming, a program planning chart that shows the top-down design of the program and the relationship between program modules.

structured programming A set of quality standards that makes programs more verbose but more readable, reliable, and maintainable. GOTO statements are forbidden, resulting in more logically developed code; also referred to as top-down program design.

structured query language (SQL) A language used to phrase simple or complex requests for data from a database.

stylus A device that looks like an ordinary pen except that the tip is dry and semi-blunt. It is commonly used as an alternative to fingers on touch-screen devices.

subclass In programming, a more specialized class than its parent or superclass.

subfolder A folder positioned within another folder that enables you to organize your files even further.

subject guide On the World Wide Web, a search site that contains hyperlinks classified by subjects in broad categories like business, news, or travel, and multiple levels of subcategories.

subnotebook A portable computer that omits some components, such as a DVD drive, and usually has a smaller screen and weighs less than a notebook. It is used by individuals that like full application features but not all the peripheral devices.

subscriber loop carrier (SLC) A small, waist-high, curbside installation of the public switched telephone network that transforms local home and business analog calls into digital signals and routes them through high-capacity cables to the local exchange switch.

summary report A report that provides managers with a quick overview of an organization's performance.

Super Extended Graphics Array (SXGA) A resolution of 1280 × 1024, typically found on standard 17- and 19-inch monitors.

supercomputer An ultrafast system, stored in a special secure room that has a controlled climate. It processes a few sets of instructions as fast as possible and is used primarily to handle large amounts of scientific data, often to search for underlying patterns. A supercomputer can be a single computer or a series of computers working in parallel as a single computer.

superscalar architecture The design of the fastest CPUs today that enables them to execute more than one instruction per clock cycle.

swap file A hard disk file that serves as a temporary storage space for pages, the bits and bytes that the operating system will access as the user works.

swindler An individual that perpetrates bogus work-at-home opportunities, illegal pyramid schemes, chain letters, risky business opportunities, bogus franchises, phony goods that won't be delivered, overpriced scholarship searches, and get-rich-quick scams.

switch A device that filters and forwards data between computers, printers, and other nodes on the same network, enabling them to talk to each other. It is more intelligent than a hub and actually inspects the source and destination of a data packet to facilitate its delivery, an activity that condenses bandwidth and improves network performance.

Symbian OS An open industry standard operating system for data-enabled mobile phones that powers devices at the lower end of the smartphone price spectrum.

symmetric key encryption An encryption technique that uses the same key for encryption and decryption.

symptom An unacceptable or undesirable result.

syn flooding A form of denial of service attack in which a hostile client repeatedly sends SYN (synchronization) packets to every port on the server, using fake IP addresses, which uses up all the available network connections and locks them up until they time out. This results in a denial of service.

Synchronized Multimedia Integration Language (SMIL) A simple multimedia scripting language designed for Web pages. SMIL enables Internet users to view multimedia without having to download plug-ins.

synchronous communication Communication in which both parties are online at the time and have a coherent conversation, as in instant messaging.

syntax The set of rules governing the structure of instructions, commands, and statements of a programming language.

syntax error In programming, a flaw in the structure of instructions, commands, and statements. Syntax errors must be eliminated before the program will run.

system A collection of components purposefully organized into a functioning whole to accomplish a goal.

system clock An electronic circuit in the computer that emits pulses at regular intervals, enabling the computer's internal components to operate in synchrony.

system requirements The minimum level of equipment that a program needs to run.

system software The collection of programs written and configured to provide the infrastructure, basic services, and hardware control that enables other programs to function smoothly. It includes the operating system and utility programs.

system unit The base unit of the computer made up of the plastic or metal enclosure, the motherboard, and the integrated peripherals. It provides a sturdy frame for mounting and protecting internal devices, connectors, and drives.

system utilities (utility programs) Programs that work in tandem with the operating system and are considered essential to the effective management of a computer system. They perform such functions as system backup, antivirus protection, file search and management, system scans, disk and file defragmentation, and file compression; also called utility programs.

systems analysis The field concerned with the planning, development, and implementation of artificial systems, including information systems.

systems analyst A problem-solving computer professional who works with users and management to determine an organization's information system needs.

systems development life cycle (SDLC) An approach or model used in the development of information systems. Its intent is to provide a structure or systematic guide to development with the goal of improving system quality.

systems engineering An interdisciplinary approach to creating and maintaining quality systems. Unlike other engineering disciplines that focus on technology, systems engineering looks at the whole picture, including the people and the organization.

T

T1 line A high-bandwidth telephone trunk line made of fiber-optic (or specially conditioned copper) cables that can handle 24 digitized voice channels or transferring computer data at a rate of up to 1.544 megabits per second (Mbps).

T2 line A high-bandwidth telephone trunk line made of fiber-optic cable that can handle up to 44.7 Mbps of computer data.

T3 line A high-bandwidth telephone trunk line made of fiber-optic cable that can handle up to 44.7 Mbps of computer data. T3 lines can cost approximately $3,000 per month. Internet service providers, financial institutions, and large corporations that move a large amount of data find these lines critical to their operations. One T3 line is equivalent to having 28 T1 lines.

tab A segment of the Ribbon that contains category titles of tasks you can accomplish within an application. Several advanced tabs, such as Add-Ins and Developer, which are not visible by default, can be turned on.

tabbed browsing A feature on most Internet browsers today that makes use of tabs located at the top of the browsers window, allowing the user to have several Web pages open at once and switch quickly between them. You can customize your home page by adding tabs for sites that you frequently access.

table A series of columns (fields) and rows (records) that compose the content of a data set.

tablet PC A type of notebook computer whose LCD screen swivels and can be made to lie flat over the keyboard, allowing the user to input data in handwritten form with a stylus. Recognition software converts it to digital text.

tactical decision A middle management decision about how to best organize resources to achieve a division's goals.

tag A marker that identifies various elements within markup language codes. Tags usually come in pairs. The actual text to be displayed is enclosed by an opening tag and a closing tag.

tailgating The entry of someone into a restricted area that requires authorization, by simply sticking close behind the approved individual. Tailgating was once associated only with the physical entry into a restricted zone, but it can also be extended to electronic entry and occurs when a user does not log out of a system and another user sits down and begins to work under the guise of the authorized user instead of logging out and re-logging in as his- or herself.

tailor-made application A piece of software designed for specialized fields or the consumer market, such as a program to handle the billing needs of medical offices, manage restaurants, and track occupational injuries.

tangible benefit A material benefit, such as increased sales, faster response time, and decreased complaints, that can be easily assessed.

TCP/IP (Transmission Control Protocol/Internet Protocol) The standard suite of methods used to package and transmit information on the Internet. TCP/IP employs a two-layer communication design. The TCP layer, Transmission Control Protocol, manages the assembling of a message or file into smaller packets that are transmitted over the Internet and received by a TCP layer on the destination computer that reassembles the packets into the original message. The lower layer, the Internet Protocol, handles the address part of each packet so that it gets to the right destination.

technical feasibility A project's capability of being accomplished with existing, proven technology.

technical skill A practice in businesses that is about working with specific tools. In the IT field, technical skills include such skills as knowledge and experience in networking, Microsoft Windows products, UNIX, C++, and Internet-related technologies.

telecommuting (teleworking) Using telecommunications and computer equipment to work from home while still being connected to the office; also called teleworking.

teleconferencing When two or more people, separated by distance, use telecommunications and computer equipment to conduct business activities.

telehealth An expansion of telemedicine that extends services beyond the remedial level to the preventive side of medicine. Such services include the use of e-mail to communicate with patients and telecommunication links to pharmacies for fast and accurate processing of prescriptions.

telemedicine The use of computers and medical expertise to provide the equivalent of the long-distance house call.

terabyte (TB) A unit of measurement approximately equal to 1 trillion bytes.

terminal An input/output device made up of a keyboard and video display, used as an inexpensive means to connect to a server.

terminator A special connector that signifies the end of a circuit in the bus topology.

text messaging (SMS) A mobile service, similar to using your phone for instant messaging or as a receiver and transmitter for brief e-mail messages.

texting A quick communication that might include text, images, video, and/or sound content that is generally delivered using a cell phone.

thermal-transfer printer A printer that uses a heat process to transfer colored dyes or inks to the paper's surface. Although thermal-transfer printers are the best color printers currently available, they are very expensive.

thin client A device that enables a user to connect to a network server and relies on that server for most of its processing ability.

thrashing The excessive transfer of files from the hard disk to RAM and back (paging).

thread In Usenet, a series of articles that offer a continuing commentary on the same specific subject.

throughput The actual amount of data that can be sent through a specific transmission medium at one time (usually per second). Throughput is almost always lower than bandwidth, especially with wireless communications.

thumb drive Another name for a USB flash drive.

thumbscrew Small screws that are usually attached to the plug and are used to secure the plug to the system unit or expansion card extender to prevent an accidental disconnect.

time bomb A hidden piece of computer code set to go off on some date and time in the future, usually causing a malicious act to occur to the system. Time bombs are less sophisticated than logic bombs, because they are not programmed to be activated by a specific trigger.

time-limited trial version A commercial program offered over the Internet that can be used on a trial basis for a period of time, after which the software is unusable.

title bar In a graphical user interface (GUI), the top bar of an application window. The title bar typically contains the name of the application, the name of the document, and window controls.

toggle key A key on a keyboard that has two states: on and off. When pressed, the function is turned on, and when pressed again, the function is turned off. The Caps Lock key is an example of a toggle key.

token A special unit of data that travels around the ring in a ring topology layout of a network. A node can transmit only when it possesses the token, thus preventing collisions.

top-down program design Sometimes used to describe structured programming. A design strategy that starts by focusing on the main goal that the program is trying to achieve and then breaks up the program into manageable components.

top-level domain (TLD) name The last part of the domain portion of a URL. For computers located in the United States, it indicates the type of organization in which the computer is located, such as commercial businesses (.com), educational institutions (.edu), and government agencies (.gov).

top-level folder The folder at the beginning of the folder structure; in a path, it is directly after the drive letter indicator. It is the starting point of an organization strategy to place files with common or related content in the same location.

touch screen A touch-sensitive display that enables users to input choices by touching a region of the screen.

touchpad (trackpad) A stationary, pressure-sensitive, pointing device that provides a small, flat surface on which you slide your finger, using the same movements as you would with a mouse. An area is set aside along the right and bottom edges of the pad to accommodate vertical or horizontal scroll operations. Commands are issued through one of the touchpad keys located near the edge of the pad or by tapping on the pad's surface.

tower case A tall and deep vertical system unit container designed to sit on the floor next to a desk and to easily accommodate add-on components.

track One of several concentric circular bands on computer disks where data is recorded. Tracks are created during formatting (set up) and are divided into sectors.

trackball A stationary pointing device that contains a movable ball held in a cradle. The on-screen cursor is moved by rotating the ball with the fingers or palm. From one to three keys can be located in various positions, depending on the unit, to perform the equivalent of mouse actions like a click and right-click.

trade show Typically, an annual meeting in which computer product manufacturers, designers, and dealers display their products.

traditional organizational structure The subdivision of the functions of an organization into units such as finance, human resources, and production/operations.

training seminar A computer-related training session, typically presented by the developer of a new hardware or software product or by a company specializing in training IT professionals in a new technology.

transaction processing system (TPS or operational system or data processing system) A system for handling an organization's day-to-day accounting needs by keeping a verifiable record of every transaction involving money, including purchases, sales, and payroll payments; also called an operational system or a data processing system.

transfer performance A measure of how quickly read/write heads are able to transfer data from a hard disk to RAM.

transistor An electronic switch (or gate) that controls the flow of electrical signals through the circuit. Due to their small size, reduced power consumption, and lower heat output, transistors replaced vacuum tubes in the second generation of computers.

transition In a presentation graphics program, it is the visual movement and effects that appear as one slide exits the presentation and another enters.

Transmission Control Protocol (TCP) Part of the TCP/IP suite of protocols that regulate packaging and transmitting information over the Internet. TCP is the higher layer of the standard of transmission that permits two Internet-connected computers to establish a reliable connection. It is responsible for managing the assembling of a message or file into smaller packets that are transmitted over the Internet and received by a TCP layer on the destination computer that reassembles the packets into the original message.

trap door In computer security, a security hole created on purpose that can be exploited at a later time.

travel mouse A pointing device half the size of a normal mouse, but with all the same capabilities.

Trojan horse A rogue program that contains instructions to perform a malicious task that is disguised as a useful program.

truncation In using a search engine, the action of inserting wildcard symbols such as ? and *, also called truncation symbols, to search for various word endings and spellings simultaneously.

tweet A posting on a Twitter account that cannot exceed 140 characters.

twisted-pair An inexpensive copper cable used for telephone and data communications. The term *twisted-pair* refers to the interweaving of the paired wires, a practice that reduces interference from electrical fields.

Twitter A free, real-time social messaging utility that allows postings of up to 140 characters.

U

ubiquitous computing A scenario for future computing that foresees an emerging trend in which individuals no longer interact with one computer at a time but instead interact with multiple devices connected through an omnipresent network, enabling technology to become virtually embedded and invisible in every aspect of our lives.

Unicode A character coding system that uses 16 bits and can represent over 65,000 characters and symbolize all the world's written languages. The first 128 codes in the Unicode system represent the same characters as the first 128 in the ASCII system.

Unified Modeling Language (UML) An open method used to illustrate and document the components of an object-oriented software system under development.

uninstalling The act of removing a program from a computer system by using a special utility.

uninterruptible power supply (UPS) A device that provides power to a computer system for a short time if electrical power is lost.

UNIX An operating system developed by Bell Laboratories in 1969. It was the first operating system written in the C language. It is a free OS installed primarily on workstations and features preemptive multitasking.

upgrade The process of keeping current with the latest tools. Upgrading carries with it the risks of a reduced comfort level among users and a temporary reduction in employee productivity during the adjustment period.

uploading Transferring a file from your computer to another computer by means of a computer network.

URL (Uniform Resource Locator) On the World Wide Web, a string of characters that precisely identifies an Internet resource's type and location. For example, the fictitious URL http://www.wolverine. virginia.edu/~toros/winerefs/merlot. html identifies a World Wide Web document (http://), indicates the domain name of the computer on which it is stored (www.wolverine.virginia.edu), fully describes the document's location in the directory structure (~toros/winerefs/), and includes the document's name and extension (merlot.html).

USB dongle A device that is inserted into a USB port and adds additional features to the base system, such as enabling network connectivity, increasing RAM memory, and permitting Bluetooth communication.

USB flash drive An average user's choice of portable storage that is about the size of an adult's thumb and can hold up to 64 GB of data; also referred to as a flash drive or solid-state drive.

USB hub A device that plugs into an existing USB port and contains four or more additional ports.

USB (universal serial bus) port An external bus architecture designed to replace older parallel and serial ports that became popular in 1998 with the release of the iMac. It connects keyboards, mice, digital cameras, and many other peripheral devices. A single USB port can connect up to 127 peripheral devices, eliminating the need for special ports that work only with specific devices.

USB wireless network adapter A communication device that plugs into a USB port and usually provides an intuitive graphical user interface (GUI) for easy configuration. It supports data encryption for secure wireless communication and is perfect for the traveler and notebook user.

Usenet A worldwide computer-based discussion system that uses the Internet and other networks for transmission media. Discussion is channeled into thousands of topically named newsgroups, which contain original contributions called articles, as well as commentaries on these articles called follow-up posts. As follow-up posts continue to appear on a given subject, a thread of discussion emerges.

user interface The part of the operating system that the user sees, interacts with, and uses to communicate with programs.

utility programs Programs that work in tandem with the operating system and are considered essential to the effective management of a computer system. They perform such functions as system backup, antivirus protection, file search and management, system scans, disk and file defragmentation, and file compression; also called system utilities.

V

vacation hacking Usually occurs in hotels and airports, where an unsuspected traveler accesses a rogue WiFi access point, called an evil twin, on a fraudulent network. The information the traveler enters is not reaching the desired destination but is being captured by criminals running the fraudulent network.

validate After purchasing a software program, it is the process of providing a special code or product key before you can use it. Validation proves that you are using a legal copy, not a pirated version.

value-added network (VAN) A public data network offered by a service provider that an enterprise uses for EDI or other services.

value-added reseller (VAR) An independent company that combines and installs equipment and software from several sources.

variant A copy of a self-modifying virus. Each new copy is slightly different from the previous one, making it difficult to protect your computer.

VBScript A client-side scripting language used to write short programs (scripts) that can be embedded in Web pages.

VDSL (very high bit-rate digital subscriber line) The next generation of DSL transmission technology providing super-accelerated rates of 52 Mbps for downloads and 12 Mbps for uploads. It will provide services like HDTV and Video-on-Demand along with Internet access.

vector graphic An image composed of distinct objects, such as lines, shapes, or any element created by a mathematical equation. Thus, the final image is described by a complex mathematical formula that can be edited quite easily to accommodate a change in size, location, or shape.

vendor A company that sells goods or services. In this context, it refers to a company that develops software and sells it to other firms.

VGA (video graphics array) connector A 15-pin male connector that works with standard monitor cables. VGA connectors transmit analog video signals and are used for legacy technology cathode ray tube (CRT) monitors.

video card Video circuitry that fits into an expansion bus and determines the quality of the display and resolution of your monitor.

video editor A program that enables you to modify digitized videos by cutting segments, resequencing frames, adding transitions, and compressing a file, as well as determining a video's frame rate and saving the digitized video file in several video file formats.

Video Graphics Array (VGA) The lowest resolution standard for color graphics displays (640 × 480).

videoconferencing (Web conferencing) The use of digital video technology to transmit sound and video images to facilitate online, virtual meetings through which two or more people can have a face-to-face meeting even though they're geographically separated; also called Web conferencing.

virtualization The process of running multiple virtual machines on one physical machine, which means that the applications and infrastructure are separate, a feature critical to the category of cloud service referred to as Infrastructure-as-a-Service (IaaS).

virtual laser keyboard A keyboard image generated by a device about the size of a small cellular phone that displays a light projection of a full-sized computer keyboard on almost any surface. Its adaptable technology studies the user's finger movements to interpret and record keystrokes.

virtual machine Not an actual physical machine, but a software-created segment of a hard drive that contains its own operating system and applications, which makes it behave as a separate physical machine in the eyes of the user.

virtual memory A term used to refer to a portion of the hard drive that the operating system treats as a portion of RAM when RAM is full.

virtual private network (VPN) A network that operates as a private network over a public network, usually the Internet, using exclusive leased lines, that makes data accessible to authorized users in remote locations through the use of secure, encrypted connections and special software.

Visual Basic (VB) An event-driven programming language that responds to user actions, like the click of a mouse. It was developed by Microsoft and based on the BASIC programming language. Visual Basic, which was one of the world's most widely used program development packages, has been largely replaced by Visual Basic.NET.

Visual Basic .NET (VB .NET) Microsoft's next evolution of Visual Basic (VB), released in 2001, which uses an object-oriented language.

VISUAL STUDIO .NET A suite of products that contains Visual Basic .NET, which enables programmers to work with complex objects; Visual C++, which is based upon C++; and Visual C# (pronounced "C sharp").

vlog (video log) Short for video log. A series of personal reflective videos that are usually created simply by talking to a webcam and uploading the video. Many vloggers post their vlogs on YouTube.

vodcast (video podcast) Short for video podcast. A term used for the online delivery of video clips on demand.

VoIP (Voice over Internet Protocol) A type of Internet telephony that uses the Internet for real-time voice communication.

volatile memory Storage that is very fast but that is erased when the power goes off. RAM is volatile memory.

W

WAP (Wireless Application Protocol) A standard that specifies how users can access the Web securely using pagers, smartphones, PDAs, and other wireless handheld devices.

wardriving A process in which an individual drives around with a wireless device, such as a notebook or smartphone, to look for wireless networks to break into.

warm boot (restart) Restarting a computer that is already on.

waterfall model A systems development method that builds correction pathways into the process so that analysts can return to a previous phase.

Web 1.0 A set of techniques that were used in the early years of the Web for developing static Web pages that included no interactivity other than hyperlinks.

Web 2.0 A set of techniques currently in use that collectively provides an upgraded presentation and usefulness for the World Wide Web. It provides even more opportunities for individuals to collaborate, interact with one another, and create new content by using applications such as blogs, wikis, and podcasts.

Web 3.0 The future generation of the Web. Many experts believe that the Web 3.0 browser will act like a personal assistant, learning what you are interested in as you browse.

Web-based language A language that tells a browser how to interpret text and objects, as compared to a programming language that tells a computer (specifically the microprocessor) what to do and how to do it. Markup and scripting languages are examples.

Web-based training (WBT) Computer-based training implemented over the Internet.

Web beacon A transparent graphic image, usually no larger than 1 pixel × 1 pixel, that is placed on a Web site or in an e-mail and used to monitor the behavior of the user visiting the Web site or sending the e-mail. One common use is to alert a sender when a message has been opened.

Web browser A program on the user's computer that displays a Web document by interpreting the HTML or XHTML format, enabling the user to view Web pages and activate hyperlinks embedded within those pages.

webcam An inexpensive camera attached to the computer, can be used to hold live chat sessions and make video phone calls. In most newer systems, a Webcam is standard equipment.

Web conference A conference format in which an individual usually sits at his or her own computer and is connected to and interacts with other participants via the Internet.

Web crawler A simple automated program that scans the Web for specific data and inserts it into a designated database.

Web–database integration A name for techniques that make information stored in databases available through Internet connections.

Web-enabled device Any device that can connect to the Internet and display and respond to the codes in markup languages, such as HTML (Hypertext Markup Language) or XML (Extensible Markup Language). Web-enabled devices include PDAs, smartphones, and notebook PCs.

Web-hosted technology A new wave of office suites that, for application software, provides the capability to upload files to an online site so the documents can be viewed and edited from another location. This technology makes file sharing and collaboration easier. Windows Office Live and Google Docs are two examples of online services that offer these capabilities.

webinar Refers to a Web conference that is typically one-way—from speaker to audience, with limited attendee participation. There may be some attendee polling and a question-and-answer segment at the end, but that is usually the extent of audience participation.

Web interview An interview conducted through the use of a webcam and the Internet.

Web mining The integration of traditional data mining methods with information gathered over the Web.

Web page A document or resource on a Web site, transported over the Internet, created using the established standards, and made viewable to a user through a program called a browser.

Web portal (portal) Web sites that provide multiple online services.

Web server A computer on the Web running server software that accepts inputted information and makes that information available to an Internet user when requested.

Web site A collection of related Web pages.

WEP (Wired Equivalent Privacy) One of the earliest security methods for wireless networks, WEP has several well-known weaknesses, but it may be the only option for some devices or older equipment.

wheel mouse A type of mouse that has a rotating wheel that is used to scroll text vertically within a document or on a Web page.

white formatting The typing of keywords in the footer or margin of a resume and then changing the font color to white. This makes the words invisible to the human eye, but the application tracking system will detect them, not reject the resume, and will successfully move the resume to the next level of screening.

whiteboard A separate area of a videoconferencing screen that enables participants to create a shared workspace. Participants can write or draw in this space as if they were using a chalkboard in a meeting.

wide area network (WAN) A network that uses long-distance transmission media, including microwave relay, satellites, and phone lines, to link computers separated by a few miles or several thousand miles. A WAN is a geographically dispersed collection of LANs. The Internet is the largest WAN. A WAN is not owned by a single organization; it has a collective ownership or management, like the Internet.

Widescreen Extended Graphics Array plus (WXGA+) A resolution of 1440 × 900, typically found in 19-inch monitors.

Widescreen Super Extended Graphics Array plus (WSXGA+) A resolution of 1680 × 1050, typically found in 20-inch monitors.

Widescreen Ultra Extended Graphics Array (WUXGA) A resolution of 1920 × 1200, typically found in 24-inch monitors.

WiFi A wireless LAN standard used for home networks that offers Ethernet speeds through the use of radio signals instead of wires.

wiki A collection of Web pages designed to let anyone with access contribute or modify content. Wikis are often used to create collaborative or community Web sites.

wildcard (truncation symbol) A symbol that stands for any character or any group of characters. Common wildcards are the ? for a single character and * for multiple characters; also called a truncation symbol.

WiMAX A wireless up-and-coming digital communication system designed to deliver high-speed access over long distances, either point to point (both sender and receiver are stationary) or through mobile access (sender or receiver is moving).

window border A thick line that encloses the window and can be manipulated to resize the window larger or smaller.

window control buttons In a graphical user interface (GUI), a group of window management tools, located on the right side of the title bar, that enable the user to minimize, maximize, restore, or close the window.

Windows CE One of the early embedded operating systems, first introduced in 1996, with upgrades made available in 1997. It is used by consumer electronic devices like handheld PCs, video game players, and digital cameras, and by industrial products like barcode readers. Its primary features include a low overhead device driver and a built-in power manager.

Windows Update A free operating system update service designed to keep your Windows operating system up to date with fixes (service patches) or protections against external environment changes.

wireless access point (AP or WAP) A node on a network that acts as a receiver and transmitter of wireless radio signals between other nodes on a network. A WAP can also act as a bridge connecting wireless clients to a wired network.

wireless Internet service provider An Internet access provider that can be a local or national company that provides wireless Internet access to computers and other mobile devices, such as notebooks and smartphones. Some familiar providers are AT&T, T-Mobile, and Verizon Wireless.

wireless keyboard A keyboard that connects to the computer through infrared (IR), radio frequency (RF), or Bluetooth connections instead of a cable.

wireless LAN A local area network that connects its nodes though the use of radio signals spread over a seemingly random series of frequencies for greater security.

wireless memory card A card that has all the storage features of a regular flash memory card and combines it with wireless circuitry. It can connect with your PC via a wireless network or send pictures directly from your digital camera to your favorite online photo site.

wireless mouse (cordless mouse) A mouse with no cord that transmits infrared or radio signals (RF) to a base station receiver. Wireless mice eliminate the cord tangling associated with the corded variety. The infrared type requires line of sight to the receiver, whereas the RF variety uses radio waves that transmit in a wider pattern.

wireless PC card adapter A device, approximately the size of a credit card, that is inserted into a slot on the side of most notebooks and netbooks. It has a built-in WiFi antenna that provides wireless capability and LED lights that indicate whether the computer is connected.

wiring closet A central location that extends through all floors of the building in which the appropriate wiring is housed to support most types of data transfer that the individuals or companies that occupy the building might want to access.

WML (Wireless Markup Language) A specialized form of XML that enables developers to create pages specifically for wireless devices.

word size The maximum number of bits the central processing unit (CPU) can work with at once.

workbook In a spreadsheet program such as Microsoft Excel, a file that can contain two or more spreadsheets, each of which has its own tab in the workbook.

workflow automation The process of sending documents and data to the next person who needs to see them.

workgroup computing A situation in which all of the members of a *workgroup*—a collection of individuals working together on a task—have specific hardware, software, and networking equipment that enables them to connect, communicate, and collaborate.

worksheet In a spreadsheet program such as Microsoft Excel, a single tab of a workbook.

World Wide Web (Web or WWW) The portion of the Internet that contains billions of documents. The Web uses the Internet as its transport mechanism but is a separate entity. The Web is an information resource that enables millions of Internet users to research products, get medical advice, read about current events, and much more.

World Wide Web Consortium (W3C) An international consortium in which member organizations, a full-time staff, and the public work together to develop Web standards. W3C's mission is to lead the World Wide Web to its full potential by developing protocols and guidelines that ensure long-term growth for the Web.

worm A program resembling a computer virus that can spread over networks without the user executing an infected file.

WPA (WiFi Protected Access) A security method for wireless networks that was developed to provide stronger security than WEP.

WPA2 A security method for wireless networks that improves on WPA's abilities. WPA2 provides confidentiality and data integrity and is far superior to WEP, because it uses AES (Advanced Encryption Standard) to provide government-grade security.

X

X.25 A packet-switching network protocol optimized for use on noisy analog telephone lines.

xD Picture Card A type of flash memory card used in digital cameras. It is available in capacities of 64 MB to 32 GB of digital data.

XHTML (eXtensible Hypertext Markup Language) A newer version of HTML, it uses XML to produce Web pages that are easily accessible by PDAs, notebooks, and desktops. See Extensible Hypertext Markup Language.

XML (eXtensible Markup Language) A set of rules for creating markup languages that enables programmers to capture specific types of data by creating their own elements. It is used for sharing data and complex forms and objects in a Web-based environment. See Extensible Markup Language.

Y

Yes/No data type See Boolean data type.

yottabyte A unit of measurement approximately equal to 1 septillion bytes.

Z

Zero configuration (Zeroconf) A method for networking devices via an Ethernet cable that does not require configuration and administration.

zettabyte A unit of measurement approximately equal to 1 sextillion bytes.

zombie A single computer commandeered during a denial of service (DoS) attack.

Illustration Credits

Chapter 1

Fig. 00-01 JGI/Tom Grill/Blend Images/ Corbis Fig. 01-02 iStockphoto Fig. 01-03 U.P.images_ photo/Shutterstock Fig. 01-04 Studio 37/Shutterstock Fig. 01-04c Courtesy of Apple Fig. 01-04d Courtesy of Research In Motion (RIM). Research In Motion, the RIM logo, BlackBerry, the BlackBerry logo and SureType are registered with the U.S. Patent and Trademark Office and may be pending or registered in other countries - these and other marks of Research In Motion Limited are used under license. Fig. 01-05 Jason Stitt/Shutterstock Fig. 01-06 jcwait/Shutterstock Fig. 01-06a © Dell, Inc. All Rights Reserved. The Dell logo is a trademark of Dell Inc. Fig. 01-06b Michael Jarrett/Gateway Inc. Fig. 01-06j Susan Van Etten/PhotoEdit Inc. Fig. 01-06k Motorola, Inc. Fig. 01-06l © Greg Nicholas/ Courtesy of www.istockphoto.com Fig. 01-06m Courtesy of Cisco Fig. 01-07 Photographer's Choice/Superstock Royalty Free Fig. 01-07a Courtesy of Apple Fig. 01-08a Shutterstock Fig. 01-08b iStock-photo Fig. 01-09 Shutterstock Fig. 01-10 Microsoft product screen shot(s) reprinted with permission from Microsoft Corporation. Fig. 01-11 Shutterstock Fig. 01-12a Eyewire, Inc./Getty Images Fig. 01-12b Alan Klehr/Churchill & Klehr Photography Fig. 01-12c Shutterstock Fig. 01-13a Zefa Collection/CORBIS- NY Fig. 01-13b Courtesy of Intel Corporation Fig. 01-13c jossnat/Shutterstock Fig. 01-13d Nick Koudis/Getty Images, Inc.- Photodisc./ Royalty Free Fig. 01-14a Shutterstock Fig. 01-14b iStockphoto Fig. 01-14c Apple Computer, Inc. Fig. 01-14d Realimage/ Alamy Images Fig. 01-14e Shutterstock Fig. 01-15a francesco riccard iacomino/ Shutterstock Fig. 01-15b Apple Computer, Inc. Fig. 01-15c Anatoliy Samara/ Shutterstock Fig. 01-15d Henrik Andersen/ Shutterstock Fig. 01-16 iStockphoto Fig. 01-17 iStockphoto Fig. 01-18 Shutterstock Fig. 01-19 Shutterstock Fig. 01-20 iStockphoto Fig. 01-25 iStockphoto Fig. 01-27 Photodisc/Getty Images Fig. 01-29 iStockphoto Fig. 01-30 iStockphoto Fig. 01-32 Shutterstock Fig. 01-33 Gravitonus, Inc. Fig. 01-34 iStockphoto Fig. 01-35 Alan Howden/Alamy Images Fig. 01-36 michael ledray/Shutterstock Fig. 01-aa A1Stock/Shutterstock Fig. 01-bb Pedro Tavares/Shutterstock Fig. 01-cc Lomaney/Shutterstock Fig. 01-dd juliengrondin/Shutterstock Fig. 01-ee Shutterstock Fig. 01-ff Shutterstock Fig. 01-gg Shutterstock Fig. 01-hh Shutterstock

Spotlight 1

Fig. SP01-CO iStockphoto Fig. SP01-A Shutterstock Fig. SP01-B Reprinted with permission. Fig. SP01-C Mikael Damkier/Shutterstock Fig. SP01-E AmyWalters/Shutterstock Fig. SP01-F beerkoff/Shutterstock Fig. SP01-G Reprinted with permission. Fig. SP01-H

The Software & Information Industry Association Fig. SP01-I Source: Rhapsody

Chapter 2

Fig. 02-13a Lenovo, Inc. Fig. 02-13b Lenovo, Inc. Fig. 02-14 Alan Evans/ Diane M. Coyle Fig. 02-16a Kingston Technology Co., Inc. Fig. 02-16b © Creative Technology Ltd. Fig. 02-16c © US Robotics Fig. 02-16d Replace on Revision Fig. 02-16e Manic Photos/Alamy Images Fig. 02-17a thumb/iStockphoto.com Fig. 02-17b ranplett/iStockphoto.com Fig. 02-17c gdpozzi/iStockphoto.com Fig. 02-17d Zocha_K/iStockphoto.com Fig. 02-17e zoomstudio/iStockphoto.com Fig. 02-17f maelms/iStockphoto.com Fig. 02-17g Pannonia/iStockphoto.com Fig. 02-17h Norman Chan/Shutterstock Fig. 02-24 Courtesy of Intel Corporation Fig. 02-27 Fotosearch.com, LLC Fig. 02-28 © Carolina K. Smith, M.D. / Courtesy of www.istockphoto.com Fig. 02-29 David A. Tietz Fig. 02-30 Phil Burton/Alamy Images Fig. 02-31 Lewis - Global Public Relations Fig. 02-32 Goodshot/Corbis RF

Chapter 3

Fig. 03-01a Shutterstock Fig. 03-01b Shutterstock Fig. 03-01c Shutterstock Fig. 03-01d iStockphoto Fig. 03-01e Shutterstock Fig. 03-01f Shutterstock Fig. 03-01g Shutterstock Fig. 03-01h iStockphoto Fig. 03-01i iStockphoto Fig. 03-02 Alexander Selektor/iStockphoto.com Fig. 03-05 Shutterstock Fig. 03-06a Apple Computer, Inc. Fig. 03-06b Shutterstock Fig. 03-06c iStockphoto Fig. 03-07 Steve Marcus/ CORBIS - NY Fig. 03-08 ilian studio/Alamy Images Royalty Free Fig. 03-11 © 2008 Logitech. All rights reserved. Used with permission from Logitech. Fig. 03-12a Reprinted with permission from Microsoft Corporation. Fig. 03-12b Logitech Inc. Fig. 03-12c Courtesy of IBM Archives. Unauthorized use not permitted. Fig. 03-12d EyeWire Collection/Getty Images - Photodisc-Royalty Free Fig. 03-12e Courtesy of IBM Archives. Unauthorized use not permitted. Fig. 03-12f © Kim Kulish/ CORBIS All Rights Reserved Fig. 03-12g © Hank Drew/Stock this Way/CORBIS All Rights Reserved Fig. 03-13 Logitech Inc. Fig. 03-14 Alamy Fig. 03-15 Microsoft Fig. 03-18 Nuance Communications, Inc Fig. 03-19b Visioneer Inc. Fig. 03-20 iStockphoto. com Fig. 03-21a Shutterstock Fig. 03-21b iStockphoto Fig. 03-23a Courtesy of IBM Archives. Unauthorized use not permitted. Fig. 03-23b AP Wide World Photos Fig. 03-23c iStockphoto Fig. 03-29 Brother Inter-national Corporation Fig. 03-30 Alamy Fig. 03-31 Shutterstock Fig. 03-32 Photo cour-tesy of XEROX Corporate Public Relations. Fig. 03-33 ViewSonic Corporation Fig. 03-34 Epson America, Inc. Fig. 03-35 Alamy Fig. 03-39 Alamy Fig. 03-41 Alamy Fig. 03-42 PhotoDisc/Getty Images, Inc.-Photodisc./Royalty Free Fig. 03-44 ExpressCard - PCMCIA Fig. 03-45a

SanDisk Corporation Fig. 03-45b SanDisk Corporation Fig. 03-45c Lexar Media Fig. 03-46 SanDisk Corporation Fig. 03-47 © William Whitehurst/CORBIS All Rights Reserved Fig. 03-ID01 Alamy Fig. 03-ID02 Alamy Fig. 03-ID03 Alamy Fig. 03-ID04 Alamy Fig. 03-ID05 Shutterstock Fig. 03-ID06 Shutterstock Fig. 03-ID07 AFP Photo/Sony Corporation/HO Fig. 03-ID08 Alamy

Spotlight 2

Fig. SP02-CO iStockphoto

Chapter 4

Fig. 04-11b Thomas Brummett/Getty Images Inc. - PhotoDisc Figs. 04-14–04-16 Source: Google Fig. 04-19 Aurora Photos/ Alamy Fig. 04-24 Source: Ubuntu Fig. 04-25 One Laptop per Child Fig. 04-27a robophobic/Shutterstock Fig. 04-27b Alex Segre/Alamy Images Fig. 04-27c Wave Royalty Free/Alamy Images Royalty Free Fig. 04-28 Newscom Fig. 04-29 HTCAmerica Fig. 04-30 PRNewsFoto/ VerizonWireless Fig. 04-31 Courtesy of Apple Fig. 04-40 Computers Are Your Future is an independent publication and has not been authorized, sponsored, or otherwise approved by Apple Inc.

Spotlight 3

Fig. SP03-A1 jossnat/Shutterstock Fig. SP03-A2 goory/Shutterstock Fig. SP03-A3 Dmitry Melnikov/Shutterstock Fig. SP03-Ba Xebeche/Shutterstock Fig. SP03-Bb iStockphoto.com Fig. SP03-Bc iStockphoto.com Fig. SP03-C Shutterstock Fig. SP03-D Reprinted with permission. Fig. SP03-E Pioneer Electronics (USA) Inc. Fig. SP03-F Advanced Micro Devices Fig. SP03-G1 Ximagination/Shutterstock Fig. SP03-G2 Reprinted with permission from Microsoft Corporation. Fig. SP03-H American Power Conversion Corporation Fig. SP03-I Targus, Inc. Fig. SP03-J Peter Cade/Image Bank/Getty Images Fig. SP03-L Falk Kienas/Shutterstock Fig. SP03-M Natalia Siverina/Shutterstock

Chapter 5

Fig. 05-16 cloki/Shutterstock Fig. 05-17 iStockphoto.com Fig. 05-19 © 2010 Microsoft Corporation. Used with permission from Microsoft Corporation. http://blogs.msdn. com/visio/archive/2009/08/25/organizing-diagrams-with-containers.aspx Fig. 05-20 Gilles Tran/Wikipedia, The Free Encyclopedia Fig. 05-21a Alamy Fig. 05-21b YAK0BCHUK VASYL/Shutterstock Fig. 05-22 Nirun Dowlath/Getty Images, Inc. - Liaison Fig. 05-23 Shutterstock Fig. 05-24a David A.Tietz/ iStockphoto.com Fig. 05-24b David A. Tietz/ iStockphoto.com Fig. 05-34 Reprinted with permission by Home Designer. Fig. 05-36 Newscom Fig. 05-37 Reprinted with permission from the author. Fig. 05-41 Reprinted with permission by Tucows.

Index

bad sectors, 101, 154
Bag-Claim, 355
bandwidth, 348–350
banner ads, 404
bar code readers, 92
Bargainist, 280
BASIC, 487
batch processing, 527–528
baud, 351
BD-R, 105
BD-RE, 105
BD-ROM, 105
beans, 489
benchmarking, 171–172
beta versions, 216
binary digits, 50
binary large object (BLOB), 512
binary numbers, 50
biometric authentication devices,
    54–55, 82, 431–432
biometric input devices, 93
bionic eyes, 149
BIOS (basic input/output system), 67,
    131–133
bitmapped graphics, 199
bitmapped image, 92
bits, 50–51, 512
BitTorrent, 316, 421
biz newsgroups, 277
black hats. *See* crackers
Blackberry devices, 363, 368
Blackboard, 4, 241
blade servers, 589–599
BLOB, 512
blocks, 102
blogger.com, 231
BlogPulse, 266
blogs, 231–232, 264
Blu-ray Disc (BD), 104–105,
    173–174, 587
Bluetooth, 355, 356
Boolean searches, 268–269
boot disk, 157
boot sector viruses, 417
booting, 131
bootstrap leader, 67
bot herder, 275
botnets, 275, 418–419
bots, 418
Boucher, Sebastian, 435
BPM. *See* business process
    management (BPM)
BPR. *See* business process
    reengineering (BPR)
bps rate, 351
branch prediction, 61
Brandeis, Louis, 400
breadcrumb bar. *See* address bar
broadband, 349–350
broken links. *See* dead links
Brooks, Mark, 20
browser cache, 259–260
bsecure, 285
buffer, 135–136
bugs, 24, 41–42, 216, 493, 499
build-or-buy decisions,
    556–557
burners, 104
bus topology, 319–320

business continuity plans (BCPs),
    580–581
business process management
    (BPM), 576
business process reengineering
    (BPR), 575
business processes, 574–576
business services, 297
business skills, 459–460
Business Software Alliance (BSA), 45
business-to-business (B2B)
    e-commerce, 279
business-to-consumer (B2C)
    e-commerce, 279–280
business units, 527
buying a computer, 72, 169–181
    choosing the right hardware,
        171–176
    expensive v. inexpensive, 176
    Mac or PC?, 170–171
    name-brand v. generic, 177–179
    notebook, netbook or desktop?,
        169–170
    shopping comparison worksheet, 178
    used or refurbished?, 177
    where to buy, 177
Byron, Augusta Ada, 487
bytes, 50–51

C

C++, 479, 488
C (programming language), 479, 488
cable Internet access, 253, 360–361
cable modems, 9, 12, 361
cache memory, 66, 101–102, 173
CAD. *See* computer aided design (CAD)
call centers, 531
camcorders. *See* digital camcorders
camera phones, 376
campus area networks. *See* CANs
    (campus area networks)
CAN-SPAM Act, 275, 408–409
CANs (campus area networks),
    308, 310
careerbuilder.com, 242
CareerExplorer, 450
careers and employment
    alternative career paths, 458–461
    automation, 27
    certification, 462–463
    computer literacy, 448
    continuing education, 455–458
    demand for IT professionals,
        450–451
    education for, 454–455
    effect of computers on, 26–28
    employee monitoring, 412–413
    green jobs, 453
    importance of computer skills, 5–6
    job market sites, 6
    job titles and responsibilities, 452
    jobs in Web technologies, 461–462
    labor dumping, 451
    outsourcing, 27–28, 451, 452–454
    professional organizations, 457–458
    salaries, 6
    sought after business skills, 459–460
    sought after technical skills,
        460–461

structural unemployment, 28
    using the Internet in job search,
        448–450, 456, 464–465
caring for computers, 180–181
carpal tunnel syndrome, 23–24
cascading style sheets (CSS), 492
CASE. *See* computer aided software
    engineering (CASE)
case control structures, 496
Cat-5 cables, 352
Cat-6 cables, 352–353
Cave Automated Virtual Environment
    (CAVE), 393–394
CBT. *See* computer-based
    training (CBT)
CD (compact disc) technologies
    CD burners, 104
    CD drives, 9, 11, 56, 103–104, 173
    CD-R, 104
    CD-ROMs, 103
    CD-RW, 104
    jukeboxes, 587
    protection of, 105
cell address, 191
cell phones, 4, 363, 364–368, 375–376.
    See also smartphones
cell sites, 364
cells (cell phone areas), 364
cells (in Excel), 191
central processing units (CPUs), 10, 55,
    58–64
    arithmetic logic unit (ALU), 58–59
    choice of, 63, 171–173
    control unit, 58–59
    embedded processors, 58
    instruction set, 58
    multi-core processing, 61–62
    performance, 59–62
    popular microprocessors, 62–63
    slots and sockets, 58
centralized structure, 578
certification, 462–463
channels, 276
character code, 53–54
character map, 83
characters, 512
charge-coupled device (CCD), 389
Charles Schwab & Co, 526
charts, 192
chat rooms. *See* online discussion
    forums
CheapTickets, 282
check-screening system, 531
checkout stands, 531–532
Chevron, 590
children
    and cell phones, 376
    and the Internet, 284–285, 410,
        425–426
Children's Internet Protection Act
    (CIPA), 409–410
China, 429
chip cards. *See* smart cards
chips, 57
chipset, 63
Chrome, 258
ciphertext, 433
circuit switching, 327
Cisco Systems, 313

Microsoft (*continued*)
  Visio, 201
  Works, 214
  Xbox 360, 393
microwave transmission, 355–357
middleware, 300, 483
MIDI. *See* Musical Instrument Digital
    Interface (MIDI)
midrange servers. *See* minicomputers
mini keyboards, 85
minicomputers, 17
minimize, 188–189
minitower case, 54
mission-critical systems, 24–25
MMDS (multichannel multipoint
    distribution service), 362
MMORPGs. *See* massive multi-player
    online role-playing games
    (MMORPGs)
MMS. *See* picture messaging
mnemonics, 478
mobile phones. *See* cell phones
mobile switching centers (MSCs),
    364–365
modeling, 191
modem cards, 56, 57
modems, 350–351
  cable, 9, 12, 361
  DSL, 9, 12, 351, 359–360, 361
  fax, 372
  modulation protocols, 320
  satellite, 12
modifier keys, 84
modular programming, 479, 487–488
modules, 214, 495
monitors, 9, 10, 94–96
  choosing, 174
  CRT, 94, 174
  FOLED (flexible OLED), 96
  LCD, 94–95, 174
  OLED (organic light emitting
    diode), 96
  resolution, 95
  screen size, 95
  televisions as, 95–96
  touch screen, 82
Mosaic, 258
motherboards, 7, 55, 56–64
Moving Picture Experts Group
    (MPEG), 206
Mozilla Firefox, 258, 272
  Bookmarks feature, 263
  pop-up blocker, 415, 416
MP3, 205
MP3 players, 387–388. *See also* iPod
mp3.com, 387
MSN, 590
MSNBC, 265
MUDs. *See* multiuser
    dungeons/dimensions (MUDs)
multi-core processing, 61–62
multi-tenancy, 589
multidimensional databases, 518
multifunction devices, 98
multimedia authoring systems,
    207, 208
multimedia devices, 386–395
  audio, 387–388
  computer gaming, 393–394

digital camcorders, 9, 93
digital cameras, 9, 93
digital video recorders (DVRs), 393
headsets, 393–394
smartphones. *See* smartphones
visual, 388–391
multimedia software, 196–208
multiplexing, 358
multitasking, 61
multitasking operating systems, 135
multiuser dungeons/dimensions
    (MUDs), 212
music file sharing, 45, 316, 387, 421
Music Maker, 204
Musical Instrument Digital Interface
    (MIDI), 98, 206
MySpace, 19, 237, 242, 277, 408
MySQL, 516, 523

N

nanoseconds, 66
Napster, 316
NAS. *See* network-attached storage
    (NAS)
National Defense Industrial
    Association, 559
National Institute of Standards and
    Technology, 560
National Security Agency, 581
native application, 58
natural languages, 480–481
Navajo Nation, 374–375
navigation pane, 119, 120
NEC Japan, 421
Negroponte, Nicholas, 146
Nessus, 430
nesting, 269, 497
Net. *See* Internet
Net Nanny, 285
netbooks, 7, 13, 15, 84, 169–170
netiquette, 38–39, 242, 283, 366
Netscape Navigator, 258
Netware, 148
network access points (NAPs), 249,
    332, 357
network administrators, 313
network architecture, 320–321
network-attached storage (NAS),
    102, 588
network connector (Ethernet/RJ-45), 70
network files, offline, 596–599
network interface cards (NICs), 9, 12,
    56, 57, 175, 308, 331
network layers, 321
network operating system (NOS), 312
network service providers (NSPs), 249
Network World, 456
networks, 11–12
  adding, 580
  advantages and disadvantages of, 314
  CANs, 308, 310
  client/server, 16, 316–318, 332
  communication devices, 308–313
  defined, 308
  employment in, 460
  Ethernet, 322
  fundamentals, 308–313
  home, 329–338

  LANs, 308, 309, 314–324
  MANs, 308, 310
  PANs, 308
  peer-to-peer (P2P), 315–316, 332
  protocols, 320–324
  security issues and, 314
  topologies, 319–320
  virtual private networks (VPNs),
    319, 591
  WANs, 308, 309, 324–329
  Wi-Fi, 322–324, 331–333
newsgroups, 277–278
NexTag, 280
NICs. *See* network interface cards (NICs)
Nielsen, Jakob, 592
9/11, 434–435
Ning, 237–238, 277
Nintendo Wii, 393
No Electronic Theft (NET) Act, 421
nodes, 308
nonprocedural languages, 480
nonvolatile memory, 133
Nook, 15, 389
Nordstrom, 575
Norton, Richard, 403
notebook computers, 7, 13, 14, 54, 56,
    169–170
  bags for, 169
  connectors on, 69
  cooling pads for, 176
  keyboard, 84
Notepad, 501–503
Novell SUSE, 312
NTFS (new technology file system), 101
numeric check, 514, 515

O

object code, 476
Object data type, 512
object-oriented database management
    system (ODBMS),
    517–518
object-oriented programming (OOP),
    481–484, 518
objects, 481
Occupational Outlook Handbook, 450
office suites. *See* software suites
offshoring. *See* outsourcing
Ogg Vorbis, 206
OLE Object data type, 512
OLED (organic light emitting diode)
    displays, 96
on-screen keyboards. *See* virtual
    keyboards
onboard video, 70
One Laptop per Child (OLPC), 146
1394 port, 70
OnGuard Online, 413
online analytical processing
    (OLAP), 518
online banking, 4, 282
online bill paying, 523
online business, building an,
    280–282
online career assessment
    tools, 450
online classes, 4
online dating, 426

RFID. *See* radio frequency
identification (RFID)
Ribbon, 189
ring topology, 320
risk management, 301–302
RJ-45 connectors, 70
RJ-11 telephone connector, 70
robots, 27
Rollyo, 242
ROM. *See* read-only memory (ROM)
rootkit, 419
Rosedale, Philip, 235
routers, 249, 311
routines, 495
rows, 191
RSS aggregator, 263–264
RSS feeds, 238, 263–264
Ruby, 489
Ruby on Rails, 489

S

SaaS. *See* Software-as-a-Service (SaaS)
Safari, 258, 272
Safe Mode, 157
safety-critical systems, 24–25,
41–42, 430
safety issues. *See also* security issues
carpal tunnel syndrome, 23–24
cell phone usage, 366
ergonomics, 23–24
grounding bracelets, 55, 180
hardware organization, 22–23
safety-critical systems, 24–25,
41–42, 430
static electricity, 55, 180
surge protectors, 19, 431
terrorism prevention, 430–431
Sage, 582
salami shaving, 422
sales force automation (SFA)
software, 584
sales functional unit, 525
Samsung Galaxy X, 392
Samsung Intercept, 392
SAN. *See* storage area networks
(SANs)
SANS, 456
SAP, 582
Sarbanes-Oxley (SOX), 301
Sasser, 418
SATA (serial advance technology
attachment), 71
satellite, 357. *See also* GPS (Global
Positioning System)
Internet access, 253–254, 357,
374–375
modems, 12
radio, 373
save as, 124–125
saving files, 124–125
SC Magazine, 456
scalability, 579
scams, 422–423, 432
scanners, 9, 92
scope, 554
scope creep, 554
screen size, 95
scripting languages, 492–494
scripts, 492

scroll arrows, 189
scroll bars, 189
Scrolling Multi-Touch pad, 89
Scrolling TrackPad, 89
SCSI (small computer system
interface), 71
SDLC. *See* systems development life
cycle (SDLC)
SDSL (symmetrical digital subscriber
line), 359, 360
search box, 121
search engines, 266–267, 522
search operators, 267–268
search utility, 154
Second Life, 235–236
secondary cache, 66, 173
secondary storage. *See* storage devices
sectors, 100, 101
Secure Electronic Transaction
(SET), 434
security clearances for
programmers, 475
security issues. *See also* computer
crime and cybercrime; privacy;
safety issues
avoiding e-commerce hazards, 285
blogs and, 232
children and the Internet, 284–285,
410, 425–426
cloud computing and, 301
corporate espionage, 428–429
databases and, 515
encryption, 433–436
information warfare, 429–430
Internet, 6
location awareness, 356, 376
malware. *See* malware
networks and, 314
personal information, 40–41,
401–413
P2P networks and, 316
protection tips, 411, 414, 431–432
RSS feeds and, 238
security loophole detection
programs, 430
social networking and, 234–235, 236,
242–243, 277
systems analysis and, 558–560
texting and, 240
USB flash drives, 103
wireless networks, 323–324, 377, 427
security loophole detection
programs, 430
seek time, 101
selection control structures, 496
semiconductors, 57
sending devices, 348
sequence control structures, 495–496
serial ports, 71
serialization, 493
server operating systems, 141, 148
servers, 16, 312
SETI, 588–589
setup program, 133
sexting, 239–240
shareware, 44, 218, 219
shills, 422
Shockwave, 207
Shopzilla, 280

shoulder surfing, 412
shutdown procedure, 68, 157
sidebars, 138
signature capture systems, 532
SIMM. *See* single inline memory
modules (SIMM)
single inline memory modules
(SIMM), 65
single-lens reflex (SLR) digital
cameras, 390–391
single point of failure (SPOF),
579–580
single-tasking operating
systems, 135
Sirius XM Radio, 373
site licenses, 44, 217
Skinput, 90
Skype, 239, 316, 369–370,
378–379, 595
Slammer, 418
sleep mode, 132, 160–161
slides, 193
Slingbox, 394
Sliwa, Curtis, 284
small computer system interface ports.
See SCSI (small computer
system interface)
smart cards, 106, 431
smart homes, 322, 394–395
smartphones, 7, 13, 15, 16, 54, 88, 93,
148–150, 243, 363–364,
366–368, 392–393
SMIL. *See* Synchronized Multimedia
Integration Language (SMIL)
Smith, David L., 424
SMS. *See* texting
Snopes.com, 418
social isolation, 29
social networking, 19–20, 234–238
for businesses, 20
Digg, 238
ethics, 6
Facebook, 19–20, 234–235, 236,
249, 277
Flickr, 236–237
job searches and, 242
LinkedIn, 19, 237
MySpace, 19, 237, 277
Ning, 237–238, 277
RSS feeds, 238
Second Life, 235–236
security issues and, 234–235, 236,
242–243, 277
Twitter, 19, 20, 236, 241
soft business skills, 459–460
soft copy, 94
soft keyboards. *See* virtual keyboards
Soft Walls, 213
software. *See also* application
software
bugs, 24, 41–42, 216
development, 494–500
free, 44, 218
open source software, 144–145,
150–151
public domain software, 44, 218
shareware, 44
system software, 8
upgrades for, 29